Java™ SE 8
FOR PROGRAMMERS
THIRD EDITION
DEITEL® DEVELOPER SERIES

Many of the designations used by manufacturers and sellers to distinguish their products are claimed as trademarks. Where those designations appear in this book, and the publisher was aware of a trademark claim, the designations have been printed with initial capital letters or in all capitals.

The authors and publisher have taken care in the preparation of this book, but make no expressed or implied warranty of any kind and assume no responsibility for errors or omissions. No liability is assumed for incidental or consequential damages in connection with or arising out of the use of the information or programs contained herein.

For information about buying this title in bulk quantities, or for special sales opportunities (which may include electronic versions; custom cover designs; and content particular to your business, training goals, marketing focus, or branding interests), please contact our corporate sales department at corpsales@pearsoned.com or (800) 382-3419.

For government sales inquiries, please contact governmentsales@pearsoned.com.

For questions about sales outside the U.S., please contact international@pearsoned.com.

Visit us on the web: informit.com/ph

Library of Congress Cataloging-in-Publication Data

On file

© 2014 Pearson Education, Inc.

Portions of the cover are modifications based on work created and shared by Google (http://code.google.com/policies.html) and used according to terms described in the Creative Commons 3.0 Attribution License (http://creativecommons.org/licenses/by/3.0/).

ISBN-13: 978-0-13389138-6
ISBN-10: 0-13-389138-0

Text printed in the United States at Edwards Brothers Malloy in Ann Arbor, Michigan.
First printing, March 2014

Java™ SE 8
FOR PROGRAMMERS
THIRD EDITION
DEITEL® DEVELOPER SERIES

Paul Deitel • Harvey Deitel
Deitel & Associates, Inc.

DEITEL®

PRENTICE
HALL

Upper Saddle River, NJ • Boston • Indianapolis • San Francisco
New York • Toronto • Montreal • London • Munich • Paris • Madrid
Capetown • Sydney • Tokyo • Singapore • Mexico City

Deitel® Series Page

Deitel® Developer Series

Android for Programmers: An App-Driven
    Approach, 2/E, Volume 1
C for Programmers with an Introduction to C11
C++11 for Programmers
C# 2012 for Programmers
Dive Into® iOS 6 for Programmers: An App-Driven
    Approach
Java™ for Programmers, 3/E
JavaScript for Programmers

How To Program Series

Android How to Program, 2/E
C++ How to Program, 9/E
C How to Program, 7/E
Java™ How to Program, 10/E
Java™ How to Program, Late Objects Version, 10/E
Internet & World Wide Web How to Program, 5/E
Visual C++® 2008 How to Program, 2/E
Visual Basic® 2012 How to Program, 6/E
Visual C#® 2012 How to Program, 5/E

Simply Series

Simply C++: An App-Driven Tutorial Approach
Simply Java™ Programming: An App-Driven
    Tutorial Approach

(continued from previous column)
Simply C#: An App-Driven Tutorial Approach
Simply Visual Basic® 2010: An App-Driven
    Approach, 4/E

CourseSmart Web Books

www.deitel.com/books/CourseSmart/

C++ How to Program, 8/E and 9/E
Simply C++: An App-Driven Tutorial Approach
Java™ How to Program, 9/E and 10/E
Simply Visual Basic® 2010: An App-Driven
    Approach, 4/E
Visual Basic® 2012 How to Program, 6/E
Visual Basic® 2010 How to Program, 5/E
Visual C#® 2012 How to Program, 5/E
Visual C#® 2010 How to Program, 4/E

LiveLessons Video Learning Products

www.deitel.com/books/LiveLessons/

Android App Development Fundamentals
C++ Fundamentals
Java™ Fundamentals
C# 2012 Fundamentals
C# 2010 Fundamentals
iOS® 6 App Development Fundamentals
JavaScript Fundamentals
Visual Basic® Fundamentals

To receive updates on Deitel publications, Resource Centers, training courses, partner offers and more, please join the Deitel communities on

- Facebook®—facebook.com/DeitelFan
- Twitter®—@deitel
- Google+™—google.com/+DeitelFan
- YouTube™—youtube.com/DeitelTV
- LinkedIn®—linkedin.com/company/deitel-&-associates

and register for the free *Deitel® Buzz Online* e-mail newsletter at:

    www.deitel.com/newsletter/subscribe.html

To communicate with the authors, send e-mail to:

    deitel@deitel.com

For information on *Dive-Into® Series* on-site seminars offered by Deitel & Associates, Inc. worldwide, write to us at deitel@deitel.com or visit:

    www.deitel.com/training/

For continuing updates on Pearson/Deitel publications visit:

    www.deitel.com
    www.pearsonhighered.com/deitel/

Visit the Deitel Resource Centers that will help you master programming languages, software development, Android and iOS app development, and Internet- and web-related topics:

    www.deitel.com/ResourceCenters.html

To Brian Goetz,
   Oracle's Java Language Architect and
   Specification Lead for Java SE 8's Project Lambda:

Your mentorship helped us make a better book.
Thank you for insisting that we get it right.

Paul and Harvey Deitel

Trademarks

DEITEL, the double-thumbs-up bug and DIVE-INTO are registered trademarks of Deitel & Associates, Inc.

Java is a registered trademark of Oracle and/or its affiliates. Other names may be trademarks of their respective owners.

Google, Android, Google Play, Google Maps, Google Wallet, Nexus, YouTube, AdSense and AdMob are trademarks of Google, Inc.

Microsoft and/or its respective suppliers make no representations about the suitability of the information contained in the documents and related graphics published as part of the services for any purpose. All such documents and related graphics are provided "as is" without warranty of any kind. Microsoft and/or its respective suppliers hereby disclaim all warranties and conditions with regard to this information, including all warranties and conditions of merchantability, whether express, implied or statutory, fitness for a particular purpose, title and non-infringement. In no event shall Microsoft and/or its respective suppliers be liable for any special, indirect or consequential damages or any damages whatsoever resulting from loss of use, data or profits, whether in an action of contract, negligence or other tortious action, arising out of or in connection with the use or performance of information available from the services.

The documents and related graphics contained herein could include technical inaccuracies or typographical errors. Changes are periodically added to the information herein. Microsoft and/or its respective suppliers may make improvements and/or changes in the product(s) and/or the program(s) described herein at any time. Partial screen shots may be viewed in full within the software version specified.

Microsoft® and Windows® are registered trademarks of the Microsoft Corporation in the U.S.A. and other countries. Screen shots and icons reprinted with permission from the Microsoft Corporation. This book is not sponsored or endorsed by or affiliated with the Microsoft Corporation.

Throughout this book, trademarks are used. Rather than put a trademark symbol in every occurrence of a trademarked name, we state that we are using the names in an editorial fashion only and to the benefit of the trademark owner, with no intention of infringement of the trademark.

Contents

3   Introduction to Classes, Objects, Methods and Strings   38

4   Control Statements: Part 1; Assignment, ++ and −− Operators   59

8 Classes and Objects: A Deeper Look 193

9 Object-Oriented Programming: Inheritance 234

10 Object-Oriented Programming: Polymorphism and Interfaces

11 Exception Handling: A Deeper Look

12 Swing GUI Components: Part 1   332

13 Graphics and Java 2D   402

20 Concurrency   653

21 Accessing Databases with JDBC   732

Foreword

I've been enamored with Java even prior to its 1.0 release in 1995, and have subsequently been a Java developer, author, speaker, teacher and Oracle Java Technology Ambassador. In this journey, it has been my privilege to call Paul Deitel a colleague, and to often leverage and recommend his Java books. In their many editions, these books have proven to be great texts for college and professional courses that I and others have developed to teach the Java programming language.

One of the qualities that makes *Java SE 8 for Programmers, 3/e*, a great resource is its thorough and insightful coverage of Java concepts. Another useful quality is its treatment of concepts and practices essential to effective software development.

I'd like to point out some of the features of this new edition about which I'm most excited:

- An ambitious new chapter on Java lambda expressions and streams. This chapter starts out with a primer on functional programming, and introduces Java lambda expressions and how to use streams to perform functional programming tasks on collections.

- Although concurrency has been addressed since the first edition of the book, it is increasingly important because of multi-core architectures. There are timing examples—using the new Date/Time API classes introduced in Java SE 8—in the concurrency chapter that show the performance improvements with multi-core over single-core.

- JavaFX is Java's GUI/graphics/multimedia technology moving forward, so it is nice to see JavaFX introduced in the Deitel live-code pedagogic style.

Please join me in congratulating Paul and Harvey Deitel on their latest edition of a wonderful resource for software developers!

James L. Weaver
Java Technology Ambassador
Oracle Corporation

Preface

Welcome to Java and *Java SE 8 for Programmers, Third Edition*! This book presents leading-edge computing technologies for software developers.

We focus on software engineering best practices. At the heart of the book is the Deitel signature "live-code approach"—rather than using code snippets, we present concepts in the context of complete working programs that run on recent versions of Windows®, Linux® and OS X®. Each complete code example is accompanied by live sample executions. All the source code is available at

        http://www.deitel.com/books/javafp3/

Keeping in Touch with the Authors
As you read the book, if you have questions, send an e-mail to us at

        deitel@deitel.com

and we'll respond promptly. For updates on this book, visit

        http://www.deitel.com/books/jfp3

subscribe to the *Deitel® Buzz Online* newsletter at

        http://www.deitel.com/newsletter/subscribe.html

and join the Deitel social networking communities on

- Facebook® (http://www.deitel.com/deitelfan)
- Twitter® (@deitel)
- Google+™ (http://google.com/+DeitelFan)
- YouTube® (http://youtube.com/DeitelTV)
- LinkedIn® (http://linkedin.com/company/deitel-&-associates)

Modular Organization

Java SE 8 for Programmers, 3/e, is appropriate for programmers with a background in high-level language programming. It features a modular organization:

Introduction
- Chapter 1, Introduction to Java and Test-Driving a Java Application
- Chapter 2, Introduction to Java Applications; Input/Output and Operators
- Chapter 3, Introduction to Classes, Objects, Methods and Strings

Additional Programming Fundamentals

- Chapter 4, Control Statements: Part 1; Assignment, ++ and -- Operators
- Chapter 5, Control Statements: Part 2; Logical Operators
- Chapter 6, Methods: A Deeper Look
- Chapter 7, Arrays and ArrayLists
- Chapter 14, Strings, Characters and Regular Expressions
- Chapter 15, Files, Streams and Object Serialization

Object-Oriented Programming

- Chapter 8, Classes and Objects: A Deeper Look
- Chapter 9, Object-Oriented Programming: Inheritance
- Chapter 10, Object-Oriented Programming: Polymorphism and Interfaces
- Chapter 11, Exception Handling: A Deeper Look

Swing and JavaFX Graphical User Interfaces; Java 2D Graphics

- Chapter 12, Swing GUI Components: Part 1
- Chapter 13, Graphics and Java 2D
- Chapter 19, Swing GUI Components: Part 2
- Chapter 22, JavaFX GUI

Generic Collections, Lambdas and Streams

- Chapter 16, Generic Collections
- Chapter 17, Java SE 8 Lambdas and Streams
- Chapter 18, Generic Classes and Methods

Concurrency/Database

- Chapter 20, Concurrency
- Chapter 21, Accessing Databases with JDBC

Object-Oriented Design

- Chapter 23, ATM Case Study, Part 1: Object-Oriented Design with the UML
- Chapter 24, ATM Case Study Part 2: Implementing an Object-Oriented Design

New and Updated Features

Here are the updates we've made for *Java SE 8 for Programmers, 3/e*:

- ***Easy to use with Java SE 7 or Java SE 8.*** This book was published coincident with the release of Java SE 8. To meet the needs of our diverse audiences, we designed the book for professionals interested in Java SE 7, Java SE 8 or a mixture of both. The Java SE 8 features (Fig. 4.1) are covered in Chapter 17 and in easy-to-include-or-omit sections book wide.

Java SE 8 features
Lambda expressions
Type-inference improvements
`@FunctionalInterface` annotation
Parallel array sorting
Bulk data operations for Java Collections—`filter`, `map` and `reduce`
Library enhancements to support lambdas (e.g., `java.util.stream`, `java.util.function`)
Date & Time API (`java.time`)
Java concurrency API improvements
`static` and `default` methods in interfaces
Functional interfaces—interfaces that define only one `abstract` method and can include `static` and `default` methods
JavaFX enhancements

Fig. 4.1 | Java SE 8 features we discuss.

- *Java SE 8 lambdas, streams, and interfaces with **default** and **static** methods.* The most significant new features in Java SE 8 are lambdas and complementary technologies. In Chapter 17, you'll see that functional programming with lambdas and streams can help you write programs faster, more concisely, more simply, with fewer bugs and that are easier to parallelize (to get performance improvements on multi-core systems) than programs written with previous techniques (Fig. 4.2). You'll see that functional programming complements object-oriented programming.

Pre-Java-SE-8 topics	Corresponding Java SE 8 discussions and examples
Chapter 7, Arrays and ArrayLists	Sections 17.3–17.4 introduce basic lambda and streams capabilities that process one-dimensional arrays.
Chapter 10, Object-Oriented Programming: Polymorphism and Interfaces	Section 10.10 introduces the new Java SE 8 interface features (`default` methods, `static` methods and the concept of functional interfaces) that support functional programming with lambdas and streams.
Chapters 12 and 19, Swing GUI Components: Parts 1 and 2	Section 17.9 shows how to use a lambda to implement a Swing event-listener functional interface.
Chapter 14, Strings, Characters and Regular Expressions	Section 17.5 shows how to use lambdas and streams to process collections of `String` objects.

Fig. 4.2 | Java SE 8 lambdas and streams discussions and examples. (Part 1 of 2.)

Pre-Java-SE-8 topics	Corresponding Java SE 8 discussions and examples
Chapter 15, Files, Streams and Object Serialization	Section 17.7 shows how to use lambdas and streams to process lines of text from a file.
Chapter 20, Concurrency	Shows that functional programs are easier to parallelize so that they can take advantage of multi-core architectures to enhance performance. Demonstrates parallel stream processing. Shows that Arrays method parallelSort improves performance on multi-core architectures when sorting large arrays.
Chapter 22, JavaFX GUI	Section 22.5.5 shows how to use a lambda to implement a JavaFX event-listener functional interface.

Fig. 4.2 | Java SE 8 lambdas and streams discussions and examples. (Part 2 of 2.)

- *Java SE 7's **try-with-resources statement and the AutoClosable interface.*** AutoClosable objects reduce the likelihood of resource leaks when you use them with the try-with-resources statement, which automatically closes the AutoClosable objects. In this edition, we use try-with-resources and AutoClosable objects as appropriate starting in Chapter 15, Files, Streams and Object Serialization.

- *Java security.* We audited our book against the CERT Oracle Secure Coding Standard for Java:

      http://bit.ly/CERTOracleSecureJava

  See this Preface's Secure Java Programming section for more about CERT.

- *Java NIO API.* We updated the file-processing examples in Chapter 15 to use features from the Java NIO (new IO) API.

- *Java Documentation.* Throughout the book, we provide links to Java documentation where you can learn more about various topics that we present. For Java SE 7 documentation, the links begin with

      http://docs.oracle.com/javase/7/

  and for Java SE 8 documentation, the links begin with

      http://download.java.net/jdk8/

  These links could change when Oracle releases Java SE 8—*possibly* to links beginning with

      http://docs.oracle.com/javase/8/

  For any links that change after publication, we'll post updates at

      http://www.deitel.com/books/jfp3

Swing and JavaFX GUI; Java 2D Graphics

- *Swing GUI and Java 2D graphics.* Java's Swing GUI is discussed in Chapters 12 and 19. Swing is now in maintenance mode—Oracle has stopped development and will provide only bug fixes going forward, however it will remain part of Java and is still widely used. Most of GUI-based legacy code in industry uses Swing GUI. Chapter 13 discusses Java 2D graphics.

- *JavaFX GUI.* Java's GUI, graphics and multimedia technology going forward is JavaFX. In Chapter 22, we use JavaFX 2.2 with Java SE 7. We use Scene Builder—a drag-and-drop tool for creating JavaFX GUIs quickly and conveniently. It's a standalone tool that you can use separately or with Java IDEs.

Concurrency

- *Concurrency for optimal multi-core performance.* In this edition, we were privileged to have as a reviewer Brian Goetz, co-author of *Java Concurrency in Practice* (Addison-Wesley). We updated Chapter 20, Concurrency, with Java SE 8 technology and idiom. We added a parallelSort vs. sort example that uses the Java SE 8 Date/Time API to time each operation and demonstrate parallelSort's better performance on a multi-core system. We include a Java SE 8 parallel vs. sequential stream processing example, again using the Date/Time API to show performance improvements. Finally, we added a Java SE 8 CompletableFuture example that compares the relative performance of sequential and parallel execution of long-running calculations.

- *SwingWorker class.* We use class SwingWorker to create multithreaded user interfaces.

- *Concurrency is challenging.* There's a great variety of concurrency features. We point out the ones that most developers should use and mention those that should be left to the experts.

Getting Monetary Amounts Right

- *Monetary amounts.* In the early chapters, for convenience, we use type double to represent monetary amounts. Due to the potential for incorrect monetary calculations with type double, class BigDecimal (which is a bit more complex) should be used to represent monetary amounts. We demonstrate BigDecimal in Chapters 8 and 22.

Object Technology

- *Object-oriented programming.* We use an *early objects* approach, reviewing the basic concepts and terminology of object technology in Chapter 1. Readers develop their first customized classes and objects in Chapter 3.

- *Early objects real-world case studies.* The early classes and objects presentation features Account, Student, AutoPolicy, Time, Employee, GradeBook and Card shuffling-and-dealing case studies, gradually introducing deeper OO concepts.

- *Inheritance, Interfaces, Polymorphism and Composition.* We use a series of real-world case studies to illustrate each of these OO concepts and explain situations in which each is preferred in building industrial-strength applications. We discuss Java SE 8's improvements to the interface concept.

- *Exception handling.* We integrate basic exception handling early in the book then present a deeper treatment in Chapter 11. Exception handling is important for building "mission-critical" and "business-critical" applications. Programmers need to be concerned with, "What happens when the component I call on to do a job experiences difficulty? How will that component signal that it had a problem?" To use a Java component, you need to know not only how that component behaves when "things go well," but also what exceptions that component "throws" when "things go poorly."

- *Class `Arrays` and `ArrayList`.* Chapter 7 covers class `Arrays`—which contains methods for performing common array manipulations—and class `ArrayList`—which implements a dynamically resizable array-like data structure. This follows our philosophy of getting lots of practice using existing classes while learning how to define your own classes.

- *Case Study: Developing an Object-Oriented Design and Java Implementation of an ATM.* Chapters 23–24 include a case study on object-oriented design with the UML (Unified Modeling Language™)—the industry-standard graphical language for modeling object-oriented systems. We design and implement the software for a simple automated teller machine (ATM). We analyze a typical requirements document that specifies the system to be built. We determine the classes needed to implement that system, the attributes the classes need to have, the behaviors the classes need to exhibit and specify how the classes must interact with one another to meet the system requirements. From the design we produce a completely coded Java implementation. Participants in our professional Java courses often report having a "light-bulb moment"—the case study helps them "tie it all together" and really understand Java-based object-oriented programming.

Generic Collections

- *Generic collections presentation.* We begin with generic class `ArrayList` in Chapter 7. Chapters 16–18 provide a deeper treatment of generic collections—showing how to use the built-in collections of the Java API. We show how to implement generic methods and classes. Lambdas and streams (introduced in Chapter 17) are especially useful for working with generic collections.

Database

- *JDBC.* Chapter 21 covers JDBC and uses the Java DB database management system. The chapter introduces Structured Query Language (SQL) and features an OO case study on developing a database-driven address book that demonstrates prepared statements.

Secure Java Programming

It's difficult to build industrial-strength systems that stand up to attacks from viruses, worms, and other forms of "malware." Today, via the Internet, such attacks can be instantaneous and global in scope. Building security into software from the beginning of the development cycle can greatly reduce vulnerabilities. We incorporate various secure Java coding practices into our discussions and code examples.

The CERT® Coordination Center (www.cert.org) was created to analyze and respond promptly to attacks. CERT—the Computer Emergency Response Team—is a government-funded organization within the Carnegie Mellon University Software Engineering Institute™. CERT publishes and promotes secure coding standards for various popular programming languages to help software developers implement industrial-strength systems that avoid the programming practices which leave systems open to attack.

We'd like to thank Robert C. Seacord, Secure Coding Manager at CERT and an adjunct professor in the Carnegie Mellon University School of Computer Science. Mr. Seacord was a technical reviewer for our book, *C11 for Programmers*, where he scrutinized our C programs from a security standpoint, recommending that we adhere to the *CERT C Secure Coding Standard*. This experience influenced our coding practices in *C++11 for Programmers* and *Java SE 8 for Programmers, 3/e* as well.

Teaching Approach

Java SE 8 for Programmers, 3/e, contains hundreds of complete working examples. We stress program clarity and concentrate on building well-engineered software.

Syntax Shading. For readability, we syntax shade the code, similar to the way most integrated-development environments and code editors syntax color the code. Our syntax-shading conventions are:

```
comments appear like this
keywords appear like this
constants and literal values appear like this
all other code appears in black
```

Code Highlighting. We place gray rectangles around each program's key code.

Using Fonts for Emphasis. We place the key terms and the index's page reference for each defining occurrence in **bold** text for easier reference. On-screen components are emphasized in the **bold Helvetica** font (e.g., the **File** menu) and Java program text in the Lucida font (e.g., int x = 5;).

Web Access. All of the source-code examples can be downloaded from:

```
http://www.deitel.com/books/javafp3
http://www.pearsonhighered.com/deitel
```

Objectives. The opening quotations are followed by a list of chapter objectives.

Illustrations/Figures. Abundant tables, line drawings, UML diagrams, programs and program outputs are included.

Programming Tips. We include programming tips to help you focus on important aspects of program development. These tips and practices represent the best we've gleaned from a combined seven decades of programming and teaching experience.

Good Programming Practice

The Good Programming Practices *call attention to techniques that will help you produce programs that are clearer, more understandable and more maintainable.*

Common Programming Error

Pointing out these Common Programming Errors *reduces the likelihood that you'll make them.*

Error-Prevention Tip

These tips contain suggestions for exposing and removing bugs from your programs; many of the tips describe aspects of Java that prevent bugs from getting into programs.

Performance Tip 4.1

These tips highlight opportunities for making your programs run faster or minimizing the amount of memory that they occupy.

Portability Tip

The Portability Tips *help you write code that will run on a variety of platforms.*

Software Engineering Observation

The Software Engineering Observations *highlight architectural and design issues that affect the construction of software systems, especially large-scale systems.*

Look-and-Feel Observation

The Look-and-Feel Observations *highlight graphical-user-interface conventions. These observations help you design attractive, user-friendly graphical user interfaces that conform to industry norms.*

Index. We've included an extensive index. Defining occurrences of key terms are highlighted with a **bold** page number.

Software Used in *Java SE 8 for Programmers, 3/e*

All the software you'll need for this book is available free for download from the Internet. See the Before You Begin section that follows this Preface for links to each download.

We wrote most of the examples in *Java SE 8 for Programmers, 3/e*, using the free Java Standard Edition Development Kit (JDK) 7. For the Java SE 8 modules, we used the OpenJDK's early access version of JDK 8. In Chapter 22, we also used the Netbeans IDE. See the Before You Begin section that follows this Preface for more information.

Java Fundamentals: Parts I, II, III and IV LiveLessons, Second Edition, Video Training Product

Our *Java Fundamentals: Parts I, II, III and IV* LiveLessons,2/e (summer 2014), video training product shows you what you need to know to start building robust, powerful software with Java. It includes 30+ hours of expert training synchronized with *Java SE 8 for Programmers, Third Edition*. Visit

```
http://www.deitel.com/livelessons
```

for information on purchasing Deitel LiveLessons video products online from Informit and Udemy. You may also access our LiveLessons videos if you have a subscription to Safari Books Online (http://www.safaribooksonline.com).

Acknowledgments

We'd like to thank Abbey Deitel and Barbara Deitel of Deitel & Associates, Inc. for long hours devoted to this project. Abbey co-authored Chapter 1 and this Preface, and she and Barbara painstakingly researched the new capabilities of Java SE 8.

We're fortunate to have worked on this project with the dedicated publishing professionals at Prentice Hall/Pearson. We appreciate the extraordinary efforts and 19-year mentorship of our friend and professional colleague Mark L. Taub, Editor-in-Chief of Pearson Technology Group. Carole Snyder recruited distinguished members of the Java community to review the manuscript and managed the review process. Chuti Prasertsith designed the cover. John Fuller managed the book's publication.

Reviewers

We wish to acknowledge the efforts of our recent editions reviewers—a distinguished group of Oracle Java team members, Oracle Java Champions, other industry professionals and academics. They scrutinized the text and the programs and provided countless suggestions for improving the presentation.

Third Edition reviewers: Lance Andersen (Oracle Corporation), Dr. Danny Coward (Oracle Corporation), Brian Goetz (Oracle Corporation), Evan Golub (University of Maryland), Dr. Huiwei Guan (Professor, Department of Computer & Information Science, North Shore Community College), Manfred Riem (Java Champion), Simon Ritter (Oracle Corporation), Robert C. Seacord (CERT, Software Engineering Institute, Carnegie Mellon University), Khallai Taylor (Assistant Professor, Triton College and Adjunct Professor, Lonestar College—Kingwood), Jorge Vargas (Yumbling and a Java Champion), Johan Vos (LodgON and Oracle Java Champion) and James L. Weaver (Oracle Corporation and author of *Pro JavaFX 2*).

Other recent editions reviewers: Soundararajan Angusamy (Sun Microsystems), Joseph Bowbeer (Consultant), William E. Duncan (Louisiana State University), Diana Franklin (University of California, Santa Barbara), Edward F. Gehringer (North Carolina State University), Ric Heishman (George Mason University), Dr. Heinz Kabutz (JavaSpecialists.eu), Patty Kraft (San Diego State University), Lawrence Premkumar (Sun Microsystems), Tim Margush (University of Akron), Sue McFarland Metzger (Villanova University), Shyamal Mitra (The University of Texas at Austin), Peter Pilgrim (Consultant), Manjeet Rege, Ph.D. (Rochester Institute of Technology), Susan Rodger (Duke University), Amr Sabry (Indiana University), José Antonio González Seco (Parliament of Andalusia), Sang Shin (Sun Microsystems), S. Sivakumar (Astra Infotech Private Limited), Raghavan "Rags" Srinivas (Intuit), Monica Sweat (Georgia Tech), Vinod Varma (Astra Infotech Private Limited) and Alexander Zuev (Sun Microsystems).

A Special Thank You to Brian Goetz

We were privileged to have Brian Goetz, Oracle's Java Language Architect and Specification Lead for Java SE 8's Project Lambda, and co-author of *Java Concurrency in Practice*, do a detailed full-book review. He thoroughly scrutinized every chapter, providing extremely helpful insights and constructive comments. Any remaining faults in the book are our own.

Well, there you have it! As you read the book, we'd appreciate your comments, criticisms, corrections and suggestions for improvement. Please address all correspondence to:

```
deitel@deitel.com
```

We'll respond promptly. We hope you enjoy working with *Java SE 8 for Programmers, 3/e*, as much as we enjoyed writing it!

Paul and Harvey Deitel

About the Authors

Paul Deitel, CEO and Chief Technical Officer of Deitel & Associates, Inc., is a graduate of MIT, where he studied Information Technology. He holds the Java Certified Programmer and Java Certified Developer designations, and is an Oracle Java Champion. Through Deitel & Associates, Inc., he has delivered hundreds of programming courses worldwide to clients, including Cisco, IBM, Siemens, Sun Microsystems, Dell, Fidelity, NASA at the Kennedy Space Center, the National Severe Storm Laboratory, White Sands Missile Range, Rogue Wave Software, Boeing, SunGard Higher Education, Nortel Networks, Puma, iRobot, Invensys and many more. He and his co-author, Dr. Harvey M. Deitel, are the world's best-selling programming-language textbook/professional book/video authors.

Dr. Harvey Deitel, Chairman and Chief Strategy Officer of Deitel & Associates, Inc., has over 50 years of experience in the computer field. Dr. Deitel earned B.S. and M.S. degrees in Electrical Engineering from MIT and a Ph.D. in Mathematics from Boston University. He has extensive college teaching experience, including earning tenure and serving as the Chairman of the Computer Science Department at Boston College before founding Deitel & Associates, Inc., in 1991 with his son, Paul. The Deitels' publications have earned international recognition, with translations published in Japanese, German, Russian, Spanish, French, Polish, Italian, Simplified Chinese, Traditional Chinese, Korean, Portuguese, Greek, Urdu and Turkish. Dr. Deitel has delivered hundreds of programming courses to corporate, academic, government and military clients.

About Deitel® & Associates, Inc.

Deitel & Associates, Inc., founded by Paul Deitel and Harvey Deitel, is an internationally recognized authoring and corporate training organization, specializing in computer programming languages, object technology, mobile app development and Internet and web software technology. The company's training clients include many of the world's largest companies, government agencies, branches of the military, and academic institutions. The company offers instructor-led training courses delivered at client sites worldwide on major programming languages and platforms, including Java™, Android app development, Objective-C and iOS app development, C++, C, Visual C#®, Visual Basic®, Visual C++®, Python®, object technology, Internet and web programming and a growing list of additional programming and software development courses.

Through its 39-year publishing partnership with Pearson/Prentice Hall, Deitel & Associates, Inc., publishes leading-edge programming textbooks and professional books in print and a wide range of e-book formats, and *LiveLessons* video courses. Deitel & Associates, Inc. and the authors can be reached at:

```
deitel@deitel.com
```

To learn more about Deitel's *Dive-Into*® *Series* Corporate Training curriculum, visit:

```
http://www.deitel.com/training
```

To request a proposal for worldwide on-site, instructor-led training at your organization, e-mail deitel@deitel.com.

Individuals wishing to purchase Deitel books and *LiveLessons* video training can do so through www.deitel.com. Bulk orders by corporations, the government, the military and academic institutions should be placed directly with Pearson. For more information, visit

```
http://www.informit.com/store/sales.aspx
```

Before You Begin

This section contains information you should review before using this book. Any updates to the information presented here will be posted at:

```
http://www.deitel.com/books/javafp3
```

In addition, we provide Dive-Into® videos (which will be available in time for Fall 2014 classes) that demonstrate the instructions in this Before You Begin section.

Font and Naming Conventions

We use fonts to distinguish between on-screen components (such as menu names and menu items) and Java code or commands. Our convention is to emphasize on-screen components in a sans-serif bold **Helvetica** font (for example, **File** menu) and to emphasize Java code and commands in a sans-serif Lucida font (for example, System.out.println()).

Software Used in the Book

All the software you'll need for this book is available free for download from the web. With the exception of the examples that are specific to Java SE 8, all of the examples were tested with the Java SE 7 and Java SE 8 Java Standard Edition Development Kits (JDKs).

Java Standard Edition Development Kit 7 (JDK 7)
JDK 7 for Windows, OS X and Linux platforms is available from:

```
http://www.oracle.com/technetwork/java/javase/downloads/index.html
```

Java Standard Edition Development Kit (JDK) 8
At the time of this publication, the near-final version of JDK 8 for Windows, OS X and Linux platforms was available from:

```
https://jdk8.java.net/download.html
```

Once JDK 8 is released as final, it will be available from:

```
http://www.oracle.com/technetwork/java/javase/downloads/index.html
```

JDK Installation Instructions

After downloading the JDK installer, be sure to carefully follow the JDK installation instructions for your platform at:

```
http://docs.oracle.com/javase/7/docs/webnotes/install/index.html
```

Though these instructions are for JDK 7, they also apply to JDK 8—you'll need to update the JDK version number in any version-specific instructions.

Setting the PATH Environment Variable

The PATH environment variable on your computer designates which directories the computer searches when looking for applications, such as the applications that enable you to compile and run your Java applications (called javac and java, respectively). *Carefully follow the installation instructions for Java on your platform to ensure that you set the PATH environment variable correctly.* The steps for setting environment variables differ by operating system and sometimes by operating system version (e.g., Windows 7 vs. Windows 8). Instructions for various platforms are listed at:

```
http://www.java.com/en/download/help/path.xml
```

If you do not set the PATH variable correctly on Windows and some Linux installations, when you use the JDK's tools, you'll receive a message like:

```
'java' is not recognized as an internal or external command,
operable program or batch file.
```

In this case, go back to the installation instructions for setting the PATH and recheck your steps. If you've downloaded a newer version of the JDK, you may need to change the name of the JDK's installation directory in the PATH variable.

JDK Installation Directory and the bin Subdirectory

The JDK's installation directory varies by platform. The directories listed below are for Oracle's JDK 7 update 51:

- 32-bit JDK on Windows:
  `C:\Program Files (x86)\Java\jdk1.7.0_51`

- 64-bit JDK on Windows:
  `C:\Program Files\Java\jdk1.7.0_51`

- Mac OS X:
  `/Library/Java/JavaVirtualMachines/jdk1.7.0_51.jdk/Contents/Home`

- Ubuntu Linux:
  `/usr/lib/jvm/java-7-oracle`

Depending on your platform, the JDK installation folder's name might differ if you're using a different update of JDK 7 or using JDK 8. For Linux, the install location depends on the installer you use and possibly the version of Linux that you use. We used Ubuntu Linux. The PATH environment variable must point to the JDK installation directory's bin subdirectory.

When setting the PATH, be sure to use the proper JDK-installation-directory name for the specific version of the JDK you installed—as newer JDK releases become available, the JDK-installation-directory name changes to include an *update version number*. For example, at the time of this writing, the most recent JDK 7 release was update 51. For this version, the JDK-installation-directory name ends with "_51".

Setting the CLASSPATH Environment Variable

If you attempt to run a Java program and receive a message like

```
Exception in thread "main" java.lang.NoClassDefFoundError: YourClass
```

then your system has a CLASSPATH environment variable that must be modified. To fix the preceding error, follow the steps in setting the PATH environment variable to locate the CLASSPATH variable, then edit the variable's value to include the local directory—typically represented as a dot (.). On Windows add

```
.;
```

at the beginning of the CLASSPATH's value (with no spaces before or after these characters). On other platforms, replace the semicolon with the appropriate path separator characters—typically a colon (:).

Setting the JAVA_HOME Environment Variable

The Java DB database software that you'll use in Chapter 21 requires you to set the JAVA_HOME environment variable to your JDK's installation directory. The same steps you used to set the PATH may also be used to set other environment variables, such as JAVA_HOME.

Java Integrated Development Environments (IDEs)

There are many Java integrated development environments that you can use for Java programming. For this reason, we used only the JDK command-line tools for most of the book's examples. We provide Dive-Into® videos (which will be available in time for Fall 2014 classes) that show how to download, install and use three popular IDEs—NetBeans, Eclipse and IntelliJ IDEA. We use NetBeans in Chapter 22.

NetBeans Downloads
You can download the JDK/NetBeans bundle from:

```
http://www.oracle.com/technetwork/java/javase/downloads/index.html
```

The NetBeans version that's bundled with the JDK is for Java SE development. The online JavaServer Faces (JSF) chapters and web services chapter use the Java Enterprise Edition (Java EE) version of NetBeans, which you can download from:

```
https://netbeans.org/downloads/
```

This version supports both Java SE and Java EE development.

Eclipse Downloads
You can download the Eclipse IDE from:

```
https://www.eclipse.org/downloads/
```

For Java SE development choose the Eclipse IDE for Java Developers. For Java Enterprise Edition (Java EE) development (such as JSF and web services), choose the Eclipse IDE for Java EE Developers—this version supports both Java SE and Java EE development.

IntelliJ IDEA Community Edition Downloads
You can download the free IntelliJ IDEA Community Edition from:

```
http://www.jetbrains.com/idea/download/index.html
```

The free version supports only Java SE development.

Obtaining the Code Examples

The examples for *Java SE 8 for Programmers, 3/e* are available for download at

```
http://www.deitel.com/books/javafp3
```

under the heading **Download Code Examples and Other Premium Content**. The examples are also available from

```
http://www.pearsonhighered.com/deitel
```

When you download the ZIP archive file, write down the location where you choose to save it on your computer.

Extract the contents of examples.zip using a ZIP extraction tool such as 7-Zip (www.7-zip.org), WinZip (www.winzip.com) or the built-in capabilities of your operating system. Instructions throughout the book assume that the examples are located at:

- C:\examples on Windows

- your user account home folder's examples subfolder on Linux

- your Documents folders examples subfolder on Mac OS X

Java's Nimbus Look-and-Feel

Java comes bundled with a cross-platform look-and-feel known as Nimbus. For programs with Swing graphical user interfaces (e.g., Chapters 12 and 19), we configured our test computers to use Nimbus as the default look-and-feel.

To set Nimbus as the default for all Java applications, you must create a text file named swing.properties in the lib folder of both your JDK installation folder and your JRE installation folder. Place the following line of code in the file:

```
swing.defaultlaf=com.sun.java.swing.plaf.nimbus.NimbusLookAndFeel
```

For more information on locating these folders visit http://docs.oracle.com/javase/7/docs/webnotes/install/index.html. [*Note:* In addition to the standalone JRE, there's a JRE nested in your JDK's installation folder. If you're using an IDE that depends on the JDK (e.g., NetBeans), you may also need to place the swing.properties file in the nested jre folder's lib folder.]

You're now ready to begin your Java studies with *Java SE 8 for Programmers, 3/e*. We hope you enjoy the book!

Introduction to Java and Test-Driving a Java Application

Objectives

In this chapter you'll:

- Understand object-oriented programming basics.

- Learn a typical Java program-development environment.

- Test-drive a Java application.

- Learn about various software technologies.

- Learn about various websites for keeping up-to-date with information technologies.

1.1 Introduction

Welcome to Java—one of the world's most widely used computer programming languages. You'll learn *object-oriented programming*—today's key programming methodology. You'll create and work with many *software objects*.

For many organizations, the preferred language for meeting their enterprise programming needs is Java. Java is also widely used for implementing Internet-based applications and software for devices that communicate over a network.

Forrester Research predicts more than two billion PCs will be in use by 2015.[1] According to Oracle, 97% of enterprise desktops, 89% of PC desktops, three billion devices (Fig. 1.1) and 100% of all Blu-ray Disc™ players run Java, and there are over 9 million Java developers.[2]

Devices		
Airplane systems	ATMs	Automobile infotainment systems
Blu-ray Disc™ players	Cable boxes	Copiers
Credit cards	CT scanners	Desktop computers
e-Readers	Game consoles	GPS navigation systems
Home appliances	Home security systems	Light switches
Lottery terminals	Medical devices	Mobile phones
MRIs	Parking payment stations	Printers

Fig. 1.1 | Some devices that use Java. (Part 1 of 2.)

1. http://www.worldometers.info/computers.
2. http://www.oracle.com/technetwork/articles/java/javaone12review-1863742.html.

Devices		
Transportation passes	Robots	Routers
Smart cards	Smart meters	Smartpens
Smartphones	Tablets	Televisions
TV set-top boxes	Thermostats	Vehicle diagnostic systems

Fig. 1.1 | Some devices that use Java. (Part 2 of 2.)

According to a study by Gartner, mobile devices will continue to outpace PCs as users' primary computing devices; an estimated 1.96 billion smartphones and 388 million tablets will be shipped in 2015—8.7 times the number of PCs.[3] By 2018, the mobile applications (apps) market is expected to reach $92 billion.[4] This is creating significant career opportunities for people who program mobile applications, many of which are programmed in Java (see Section 1.3).

Java Standard Edition

This book is based on **Java Standard Edition 7 (Java SE 7)** and **Java Standard Edition 8 (Java SE 8)**. Java Standard Edition contains the capabilities needed to develop desktop and server applications. The book can be used with *either* Java SE 7 *or* Java SE 8 (released as this book was published). All of the Java SE 8 features are discussed in modular, easy-to-include-or-omit sections throughout the book.

Prior to Java SE 8, Java supported three programming paradigms—*procedural programming, object-oriented programming* and *generic programming*. Java SE 8 adds *functional programming*. In Chapter 17, we'll show how to use functional programming to write programs faster, more concisely, with fewer bugs and that are easier to *parallelize* (i.e., perform multiple calculations simultaneously) to take advantage of today's multi-core hardware architectures to enhance application performance.

Java Enterprise Edition

Java is used in such a broad spectrum of applications that it has two other editions. The **Java Enterprise Edition (Java EE)** is geared toward developing large-scale, distributed networking applications and web-based applications. In the past, most computer applications ran on "standalone" computers (computers that were not networked together). Today's applications can be written with the aim of communicating among the world's computers via the Internet and the web.

Java Micro Edition

The **Java Micro Edition (Java ME)**—a subset of Java SE—is geared toward developing applications for resource-constrained embedded devices, such as smartwatches, MP3 players, television set-top boxes, smart meters (for monitoring electric energy usage) and more.

---

3. http://www.gartner.com/newsroom/id/2645115.
4. https://www.abiresearch.com/press/tablets-will-generate-35-of-this-years-25-billion-.

1.2 Object Technology Concepts

Today, as demands for new and more powerful software are soaring, building software quickly, correctly and economically remains an elusive goal. *Objects*, or more precisely, the *classes* objects come from, are essentially *reusable* software components. There are date objects, time objects, audio objects, video objects, automobile objects, people objects, etc. Almost any *noun* can be reasonably represented as a software object in terms of *attributes* (e.g., name, color and size) and *behaviors* (e.g., calculating, moving and communicating). Software-development groups can use a modular, object-oriented design-and-implementation approach to be much more productive than with earlier popular techniques like "structured programming"—object-oriented programs are often easier to understand, correct and modify.

1.2.1 The Automobile as an Object

To help you understand objects and their contents, let's begin with a simple analogy. Suppose you want to *drive a car and make it go faster by pressing its accelerator pedal*. What must happen before you can do this? Well, before you can drive a car, someone has to *design* it. A car typically begins as engineering drawings, similar to the *blueprints* that describe the design of a house. These drawings include the design for an accelerator pedal. The pedal *hides* from the driver the complex mechanisms that actually make the car go faster, just as the brake pedal "hides" the mechanisms that slow the car, and the steering wheel "hides" the mechanisms that turn the car. This enables people with little or no knowledge of how engines, braking and steering mechanisms work to drive a car easily.

Just as you cannot cook meals in the kitchen of a blueprint, you cannot drive a car's engineering drawings. Before you can drive a car, it must be *built* from the engineering drawings that describe it. A completed car has an *actual* accelerator pedal to make it go faster, but even that's not enough—the car won't accelerate on its own (hopefully!), so the driver must *press* the pedal to accelerate the car.

1.2.2 Methods and Classes

Let's use our car example to introduce some key object-oriented programming concepts. Performing a task in a program requires a **method**. The method houses the program statements that actually perform its tasks. The method hides these statements from its user, just as the accelerator pedal of a car hides from the driver the mechanisms of making the car go faster. In Java, we create a program unit called a **class** to house the set of methods that perform the class's tasks. For example, a class that represents a bank account might contain one method to *deposit* money to an account, another to *withdraw* money from an account and a third to *inquire* what the account's current balance is. A class is similar in concept to a car's engineering drawings, which house the design of an accelerator pedal, steering wheel, and so on.

1.2.3 Instantiation

Just as someone has to *build a car* from its engineering drawings before you can actually drive a car, you must *build an object* of a class before a program can perform the tasks that the class's methods define. The process of doing this is called *instantiation*. An object is then referred to as an **instance** of its class.

1.2.4 Reuse

Just as a car's engineering drawings can be *reused* many times to build many cars, you can *reuse* a class many times to build many objects. Reuse of existing classes when building new classes and programs saves time and effort. Reuse also helps you build more reliable and effective systems, because existing classes and components often have undergone extensive *testing*, *debugging* and *performance* tuning. Just as the notion of *interchangeable parts* was crucial to the Industrial Revolution, reusable classes are crucial to the software revolution that has been spurred by object technology.

 Software Engineering Observation 1.1
Use a building-block approach to creating your programs. Avoid reinventing the wheel—use existing high-quality pieces wherever possible. This software reuse is a key benefit of object-oriented programming.

1.2.5 Messages and Method Calls

When you drive a car, pressing its gas pedal sends a *message* to the car to perform a task—that is, to go faster. Similarly, you *send messages to an object*. Each message is implemented as a **method call** that tells a method of the object to perform its task. For example, a program might call a bank-account object's *deposit* method to increase the account's balance.

1.2.6 Attributes and Instance Variables

A car, besides having capabilities to accomplish tasks, also has *attributes*, such as its color, its number of doors, the amount of gas in its tank, its current speed and its record of total miles driven (i.e., its odometer reading). Like its capabilities, the car's attributes are represented as part of its design in its engineering diagrams (which, for example, include an odometer and a fuel gauge). As you drive an actual car, these attributes are carried along with the car. Every car maintains its *own* attributes. For example, each car knows how much gas is in its own gas tank, but *not* how much is in the tanks of *other* cars.

An object, similarly, has attributes that it carries along as it's used in a program. These attributes are specified as part of the object's class. For example, a bank-account object has a *balance attribute* that represents the amount of money in the account. Each bank-account object knows the balance in the account it represents, but *not* the balances of the *other* accounts in the bank. Attributes are specified by the class's **instance variables**.

1.2.7 Encapsulation and Information Hiding

Classes (and their objects) **encapsulate**, i.e., encase, their attributes and methods. A class's (and its object's) attributes and methods are intimately related. Objects may communicate with one another, but they're normally not allowed to know how other objects are implemented—implementation details are *hidden* within the objects themselves. This **information hiding**, as we'll see, is crucial to good software engineering.

1.2.8 Inheritance

A new class of objects can be created conveniently by **inheritance**—the new class (called the **subclass**) starts with the characteristics of an existing class (called the **superclass**), possibly customizing them and adding unique characteristics of its own. In our car analogy, an object of class "convertible" certainly *is an* object of the more *general* class "automobile," but more *specifically*, the roof can be raised or lowered.

1.2.9 Interfaces

Java also supports **interfaces**—collections of related methods that typically enable you to tell objects *what* to do, but not *how* to do it (we'll see an exception to this in Java SE 8). In the car analogy, a "basic-driving-capabilities" interface consisting of a steering wheel, an accelerator pedal and a brake pedal would enable a driver to tell the car *what* to do. Once you know how to use this interface for turning, accelerating and braking, you can drive many types of cars, even though manufacturers may *implement* these systems *differently*.

A class **implements** zero or more interfaces, each of which can have one or more methods, just as a car implements separate interfaces for basic driving functions, controlling the radio, controlling the heating and air conditioning systems, and the like. Just as car manufacturers implement capabilities *differently*, classes may implement an interface's methods *differently*. For example a software system may include a "backup" interface that offers the methods *save* and *restore*. Classes may implement those methods differently, depending on the types of things being backed up, such as programs, text, audios, videos, etc., and the types of devices where these items will be stored.

1.2.10 Object-Oriented Analysis and Design (OOAD)

Soon you'll be writing programs in Java. How will you create the **code** (i.e., the program instructions) for your programs? Perhaps, like many programmers, you'll simply turn on your computer and start typing. This approach may work for small programs (like the ones we present in the early chapters of the book), but what if you were asked to create a software system to control thousands of automated teller machines for a major bank? Or suppose you were asked to work on a team of 1,000 software developers building the next generation of the U.S. air traffic control system? For projects so large and complex, you should not simply sit down and start writing programs.

To create the best solutions, you should follow a detailed **analysis** process for determining your project's **requirements** (i.e., defining *what* the system is supposed to do) and developing a **design** that satisfies them (i.e., specifying *how* the system should do it). Ideally, you'd go through this process and carefully review the design (and have your design reviewed by other software professionals) before writing any code. If this process involves analyzing and designing your system from an object-oriented point of view, it's called an **object-oriented analysis-and-design (OOAD) process**. Languages like Java are object oriented. Programming in such a language, called **object-oriented programming (OOP)**, allows you to implement an object-oriented design as a working system.

1.2.11 The UML (Unified Modeling Language)

Although many different OOAD processes exist, a single graphical language for communicating the results of *any* OOAD process has come into wide use. The Unified Modeling Language (UML) is now the most widely used graphical scheme for modeling object-oriented systems. We present our first UML diagrams in Chapters 3 and 4, then use them in our deeper treatment of object-oriented programming through Chapter 11. In our ATM Software Engineering Case Study in Chapters 23–24 we present a simple subset of the UML's features as we guide you through an object-oriented design experience.

1.3 Open Source Software

The **Linux** operating system—which is popular in servers, personal computers and embedded systems—is perhaps the greatest success of the *open-source* movement. The **open-source software** development style departs from the *proprietary* style (used, for example, with Microsoft's Windows and Apple's Mac OS X). With open-source development, individuals and companies—often worldwide—contribute their efforts in developing, maintaining and evolving software. Anyone can use and customize it for their own purposes, typically at no charge. The Java Development Kit and many related Java technologies are now open source.

Some organizations in the open-source community are the *Eclipse Foundation* (the *Eclipse Integrated Development Environment* helps Java programmers conveniently develop software), the *Mozilla Foundation* (creators of the *Firefox web browser*), the *Apache Software Foundation* (creators of the *Apache web server* that *delivers web pages over the Internet* in response to web-browser requests) and *GitHub* and *SourceForge* (which provide the *tools for managing open-source projects*).

Rapid improvements to computing and communications, decreasing costs and open-source software have made it easier and more economical to create software-based businesses now than just a few decades ago. Facebook, which was launched from a college dorm room, was built with open-source software.[5]

A variety of issues—such as Microsoft's market power, the relatively small number of user-friendly Linux applications and the diversity of Linux distributions (Red Hat Linux, Ubuntu Linux and many others)—have prevented widespread Linux use on desktop computers. But Linux has become extremely popular on servers and in embedded systems, such as Google's Android-based smartphones.

Android
Android—the fastest-growing mobile and smartphone operating system—is based on the Linux kernel and uses Java. Experienced Java programmers can quickly dive into Android development. One benefit of developing Android apps is the openness of the platform. The operating system is open source and free.

The Android operating system was developed by Android, Inc., which was acquired by Google in 2005. In 2007, the Open Handset Alliance™—which now has 87 company members worldwide (`http://www.openhandsetalliance.com/oha_members.html`)—was formed to develop, maintain and evolve Android, driving innovation in mobile technology and improving the user experience while reducing costs. As of April 2013, more than 1.5 million Android devices (smartphones, tablets, etc.) were being activated *daily*.[6] By October 2013, a Strategy Analytics report showed that Android had 81.3% of the global *smartphone* market share, compared to 13.4% for Apple, 4.1% for Microsoft and 1% for Blackberry.[7] Android devices now include smartphones, tablets, e-readers, robots, jet engines, NASA satellites, game consoles, refrigerators, televisions, cameras, health-care

---

5. `http://developers.facebook.com/opensource`.
6. `http://www.technobuffalo.com/2013/04/16/google-daily-android-activations-1-5-million/`.
7. `http://blogs.strategyanalytics.com/WSS/post/2013/10/31/Android-Captures-Record-81-Percent-Share-of-Global-Smartphone-Shipments-in-Q3-2013.aspx`.

devices, smartwatches, automobile in-vehicle infotainment systems (for controlling the radio, GPS, phone calls, thermostat, etc.) and more.[8]

Android smartphones include the functionality of a mobile phone, Internet client (for web browsing and Internet communication), MP3 player, gaming console, digital camera and more. These handheld devices feature full-color *multitouch screens* which allow you to control the device with *gestures* involving one touch or multiple simultaneous touches. You can download apps directly onto your Android device through Google Play and other app marketplaces. At the time of this writing, there were over one million apps in **Google Play**, and the number is growing quickly.[9]

We present an introduction to Android app development in our textbook, *Android How to Program, Second Edition,* and in our professional book, *Android for Programmers: An App-Driven Approach, Second Edition, Volume 1.* After you learn Java, you'll find it straightforward to begin developing and running Android apps. You can place your apps on Google Play (http://play.google.com), and if they're successful, you may even be able to launch a business. Just remember—Facebook, Microsoft and Dell were all launched from college dorm rooms.

1.4 Java

The microprocessor revolution's most important contribution to date is that it enabled the development of personal computers. Microprocessors have had a profound impact in intelligent consumer-electronic devices. Recognizing this, Sun Microsystems in 1991 funded an internal corporate research project led by James Gosling, which resulted in a C++-based object-oriented programming language that Sun called Java.

A key goal of Java is to be able to write programs that will run on a great variety of computer systems and computer-controlled devices. This is sometimes called "write once, run anywhere."

The web exploded in popularity in 1993, and Sun saw the potential of using Java to add *dynamic content,* such as interactivity and animations, to web pages. Java drew the attention of the business community because of the phenomenal interest in the web. Java is now used to develop large-scale enterprise applications, to enhance the functionality of web servers (the computers that provide the content we see in our web browsers), to provide applications for consumer devices (cell phones, smartphones, television set-top boxes and more) and for many other purposes. Java is also the key language for developing Android smartphone and tablet apps. Sun Microsystems was acquired by Oracle in 2010.

Java Class Libraries
You can create each class and method you need to form your Java programs. However, most Java programmers take advantage of the rich collections of existing classes and methods in the **Java class libraries**, also known as the **Java APIs** (**Application Programming Interfaces**).

---

8. http://www.businessweek.com/articles/2013-05-29/behind-the-internet-of-things-is-android-and-its-everywhere.
9. http://en.wikipedia.org/wiki/Google_Play.

> **Performance Tip 1.1**
> *Using Java API classes and methods instead of writing your own versions can improve program performance, because they're carefully written to perform efficiently. This also shortens program development time.*

1.5 A Typical Java Development Environment

We now explain the steps to create and execute a Java application. Normally there are five phases—edit, compile, load, verify and execute. We discuss them in the context of the Java SE 8 Development Kit (JDK). See the *Before You Begin* section *for information on downloading and installing the JDK on Windows, Linux and OS X.*

Phase 1: Creating a Program

Phase 1 consists of editing a file with an *editor program*, normally known simply as an *editor* (Fig. 1.2). Using the editor, you type a Java program (typically referred to as **source code**), make any necessary corrections and save it on a secondary storage device, such as your hard drive. Java source code files are given a name ending with the **.java extension**, indicating that the file contains Java source code.

Two editors widely used on Linux systems are vi and emacs. Windows provides **Notepad**. OS X provides **TextEdit**. Many freeware and shareware editors are also available online, including Notepad++ (notepad-plus-plus.org), EditPlus (www.editplus.com), TextPad (www.textpad.com) and jEdit (www.jedit.org).

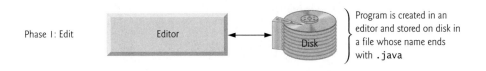

Fig. 1.2 | Typical Java development environment—editing phase.

Integrated development environments (IDEs) provide tools that support the software development process, such as editors, debuggers for locating **logic errors** (errors that cause programs to execute incorrectly) and more. There are many popular Java IDEs, including:

- Eclipse (www.eclipse.org)
- NetBeans (www.netbeans.org)
- IntelliJ IDEA (www.jetbrains.com)

On the book's website at

www.deitel.com/books/javafp3

we provide Dive-Into® videos that show you how to executes this book's Java applications and how to develop new Java applications with Eclipse, NetBeans and IntelliJ IDEA.

Phase 2: Compiling a Java Program into Bytecodes
In Phase 2, you use the command **javac** (the **Java compiler**) to **compile** a program (Fig. 1.3). For example, to compile a program called Welcome.java, you'd type

```
javac Welcome.java
```

in your system's command window (i.e., the **Command Prompt** in Windows, the **Terminal** application in OS X) or a Linux shell (also called **Terminal** in some versions of Linux). If the program compiles, the compiler produces a **.class** file called Welcome.class that contains the compiled version. IDEs typically provide a menu item, such as **Build** or **Make**, that invokes the javac command for you. If the compiler detects errors, you'll need to go back to Phase 1 and correct them. In Chapter 2, we'll say more about the kinds of errors the compiler can detect.

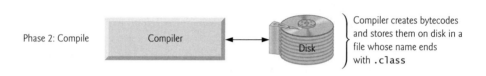

Fig. 1.3 | Typical Java development environment—compilation phase.

The Java compiler translates Java source code into **bytecodes** that represent the tasks to execute in the execution phase (Phase 5). The **Java Virtual Machine (JVM)**—a part of the JDK and the foundation of the Java platform—executes bytecodes. A **virtual machine (VM)** is a software application that simulates a computer but hides the underlying operating system and hardware from the programs that interact with it. If the same VM is implemented on many computer platforms, applications written for that type of VM can be used on all those platforms. The JVM is one of the most widely used virtual machines. Microsoft's .NET uses a similar virtual-machine architecture.

Unlike machine-language instructions, which are *platform dependent* (that is, dependent on specific computer hardware), bytecode instructions are *platform independent*. So, Java's bytecodes are **portable**—without recompiling the source code, the same bytecode instructions can execute on any platform containing a JVM that understands the version of Java in which the bytecodes were compiled. The JVM is invoked by the **java** command. For example, to execute a Java application called Welcome, you'd type the command

```
java Welcome
```

in a command window to invoke the JVM, which would then initiate the steps necessary to execute the application. This begins Phase 3. IDEs typically provide a menu item, such as **Run**, that invokes the java command for you.

Phase 3: Loading a Program into Memory
In Phase 3, the JVM places the program in memory to execute it—this is known as **loading** (Fig. 1.4).The JVM's **class loader** takes the .class files containing the program's byte-codes and transfers them to primary memory. It also loads any of the .class files provided by Java that your program uses. The .class files can be loaded from a disk on your system or over a network (e.g., your local college or company network, or the Internet).

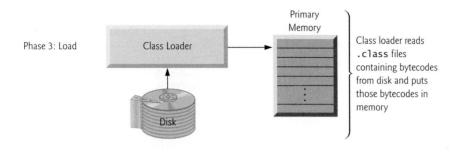

Fig. 1.4 | Typical Java development environment—loading phase.

Phase 4: Bytecode Verification

In Phase 4, as the classes are loaded, the **bytecode verifier** examines their bytecodes to ensure that they're valid and do not violate Java's security restrictions (Fig. 1.5). Java enforces strong security to make sure that Java programs arriving over the network do not damage your files or your system (as computer viruses and worms might).

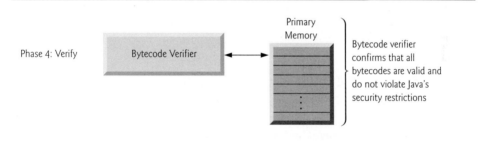

Fig. 1.5 | Typical Java development environment—verification phase.

Phase 5: Execution

In Phase 5, the JVM **executes** the program's bytecodes, thus performing the actions specified by the program (Fig. 1.6). In early Java versions, the JVM was simply an *interpreter* for Java bytecodes. Most Java programs would execute slowly, because the JVM would interpret and execute one bytecode at a time. Some modern computer architectures can execute several instructions in parallel. Today's JVMs typically execute bytecodes using a combination of interpretation and so-called **just-in-time (JIT) compilation**. In this process, the JVM analyzes the bytecodes as they're interpreted, searching for *hot spots*—parts of the bytecodes that execute frequently. For these parts, a **just-in-time (JIT) compiler**, such as Oracle's **Java HotSpot™ compiler**, translates the bytecodes into the underlying computer's machine language. When the JVM encounters these compiled parts again, the faster machine-language code executes. Thus Java programs actually go through *two* compilation phases—one in which source code is translated into bytecodes (for portability across JVMs on different computer platforms) and a second in which, during execution, the *bytecodes* are translated into *machine language* for the actual computer on which the program executes.

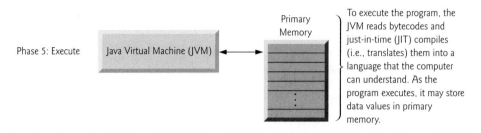

Fig. 1.6 | Typical Java development environment—execution phase.

Problems That May Occur at Execution Time

Programs might not work on the first try. Each of the preceding phases can fail because of errors that we'll discuss throughout this book. For example, an executing program might try to divide by zero (illegal for whole-number arithmetic in Java). This would cause the program to display an error message.

Common Programming Error 1.1

*Errors such as division by zero occur as a program runs, so they're called **runtime errors** or **execution-time errors**. Fatal runtime errors cause programs to terminate immediately without having successfully performed their jobs. **Nonfatal runtime errors** allow programs to run to completion, often producing incorrect results.*

1.6 Test-Driving a Java Application

In this section, you'll run and interact with your first Java application. The **Painter** application, which you can build after studying through Chapter 13, allows you to drag the mouse to "paint." The elements and functionality you see here are typical of what you'll learn to program in this book. Using the **Painter**'s graphical user interface (GUI), you can control the drawing color, the shape to draw (line, rectangle or oval) and whether the shape is filled with the drawing color. You can also undo the last shape you added to the drawing or clear the entire drawing. [*Note:* We use fonts to distinguish between features. Our convention is to emphasize screen features like titles and menus (e.g., the **File** menu) in a semibold **sans-serif Helvetica** font and to emphasize nonscreen elements, such as file names, program code or input (e.g., `ProgramName.java`), in a `sans-serif Lucida` font.]

The steps in this section show you how to execute the **Painter** app from a **Command Prompt** (Windows), **Terminal** (OS X) or shell (Linux) window on your system. Throughout the book, we'll refer to these windows simply as *command windows*. Perform the following steps to use the **Painter** application to draw a smiley face:

1. *Checking your setup.* Read the Before You Begin section to confirm that you've set up Java properly on your computer, that you've copied the book's examples to your hard drive and that you know how to open a command window on your system.

2. *Changing to the completed application's directory.* Open a command window and use the `cd` command to change to the directory (also called a *folder*) for the **Painter** application. We assume that the book's examples are located in `C:\examples` on Windows or in your user account's `Documents/examples` folder on Linux/OS X.

On Windows type cd C:\examples\ch01\painter, then press *Enter*. On Linux/ OS X, type cd ~/Documents/examples/ch01/painter, then press *Enter*.

3. ***Running the Painter application.*** Recall that the java command, followed by the name of the application's .class file (in this case, Painter), executes the application. Type java Painter and press *Enter* to execute the app. Figure 1.7 shows the app running on Windows, Linux and OS X, respectively. [*Note:* Java commands are *case sensitive*—that is, uppercase letters are different from lowercase letters. It's important to type the name of this application as Painter with a capital P. Otherwise, the application will *not* execute. Specifying the .class extension when using the java command results in an error. Also, if you receive the error message, "Exception in thread "main" java.lang.NoClassDefFoundError: Painter," your system has a CLASSPATH problem. Please refer to the Before You Begin section for instructions to help you fix this problem.]

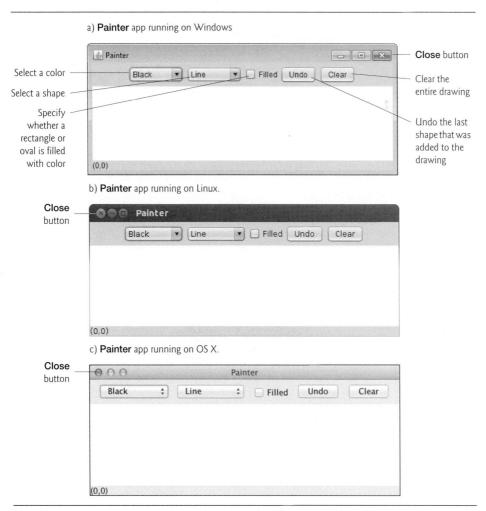

Fig. 1.7 | **Painter** app executing in Windows 7, Linux and OS X.

4. *Drawing a filled yellow oval for the face.* Select **Yellow** as the drawing color, **Oval** as the shape and check the **Filled** checkbox, then drag the mouse to draw a large oval (Fig. 1.8).

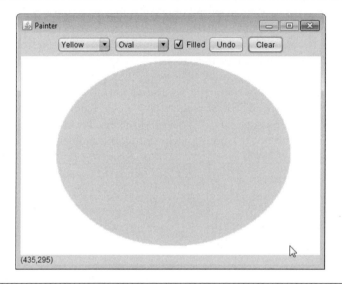

Fig. 1.8 | Drawing a filled yellow oval for the face.

5. *Drawing blue eyes.* Select **Blue** as the drawing color, then draw two small ovals as the eyes (Fig. 1.9).

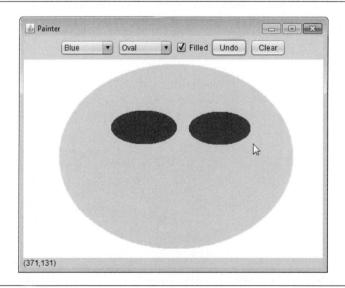

Fig. 1.9 | Drawing blue eyes.

6. *Drawing black eyebrows and a nose.* Select **Black** as the drawing color and **Line** as the shape, then draw eyebrows and a nose (Fig. 1.10). Lines do not have fill, so leaving the **Filled** checkbox checked has no effect when drawing lines.

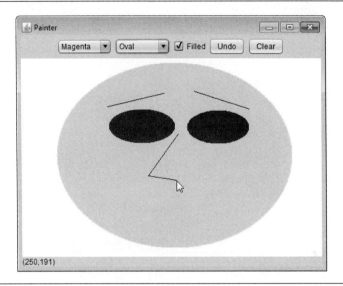

Fig. 1.10 | Drawing black eyebrows and a nose.

7. *Drawing a magenta mouth.* Select **Magenta** as the drawing color and **Oval** as the shape, then draw a mouth (Fig. 1.11).

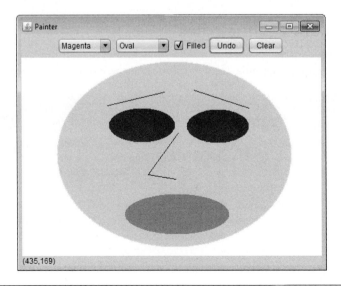

Fig. 1.11 | Drawing a magenta mouth.

8. *Drawing a yellow oval on the mouth to make a smile.* Select **Yellow** as the drawing color, then draw an oval to change the magenta oval into a smile (Fig. 1.12).

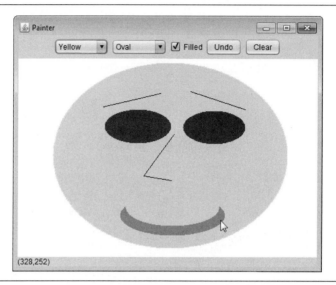

Fig. 1.12 | Drawing a yellow oval on the mouth to make a smile.

9. *Exiting the Painter application.* To exit the **Painter** application, click the **Close** button (in the window's upper-right corner on Windows and the upper-left corner on Linux and OS X). Closing the window causes the **Painter** application to terminate.

1.7 Software Technologies

Figure 1.13 lists a number of buzzwords that you'll hear in the software development community. We've created Resource Centers on most of these topics, with more on the way.

Technology	Description
Agile software development	**Agile software development** is a set of methodologies that try to get software implemented faster and using fewer resources. Check out the Agile Alliance (www.agilealliance.org) and the Agile Manifesto (www.agilemanifesto.org).
Refactoring	**Refactoring** involves reworking programs to make them clearer and easier to maintain while preserving their correctness and functionality. It's widely employed with agile development methodologies. Many IDEs contain built-in *refactoring tools* to do major portions of the reworking automatically.

Fig. 1.13 | Software technologies. (Part 1 of 2.)

Technology	Description
Design patterns	**Design patterns** are proven architectures for constructing flexible and maintainable object-oriented software. The field of design patterns tries to enumerate those recurring patterns, encouraging software designers to *reuse* them to develop better-quality software using less time, money and effort. We discuss Java design patterns in Appendix N.
LAMP	**LAMP** is an acronym for the open-source technologies that many developers use to build web applications—it stands for *Linux, Apache, MySQL* and *PHP* (or *Perl* or *Python*—two other scripting languages). MySQL is an open-source database management system. PHP is the most popular open-source server-side "scripting" language for developing web applications. Apache is the most popular web server software. The equivalent for Windows development is WAMP—*Windows*, Apache, MySQL and PHP.
Software as a Service (SaaS)	Software has generally been viewed as a product; most software still is offered this way. If you want to run an application, you buy a software package from a software vendor—often a CD, DVD or web download. You then install that software on your computer and run it as needed. As new versions appear, you upgrade your software, often at considerable cost in time and money. This process can become cumbersome for organizations that must maintain tens of thousands of systems on a diverse array of computer equipment. With **Software as a Service (SaaS)**, the software runs on servers elsewhere on the Internet. When that server is updated, all clients worldwide see the new capabilities—no local installation is needed. You access the service through a browser. Browsers are quite portable, so you can run the same applications on a wide variety of computers from anywhere in the world. Salesforce.com, Google, and Microsoft's Office Live and Windows Live all offer SaaS.
Platform as a Service (PaaS)	**Platform as a Service (PaaS)** provides a computing platform for developing and running applications as a service over the web, rather than installing the tools on your computer. Some PaaS providers are Google App Engine, Amazon EC2 and Windows Azure™.
Cloud computing	SaaS and PaaS are examples of **cloud computing**. You can use software and data stored in the "cloud"—i.e., accessed on remote computers (or servers) via the Internet and available on demand—rather than having it stored on your desktop, notebook computer or mobile device. This allows you to increase or decrease computing resources to meet your needs at any given time, which is more cost effective than purchasing hardware to provide enough storage and processing power to meet occasional peak demands. Cloud computing also saves money by shifting the burden of managing these apps to the service provider.
Software Development Kit (SDK)	**Software Development Kits (SDKs)** include the tools and documentation developers use to program applications. For example, you'll use the Java Development Kit (JDK) to build and run Java applications.

Fig. 1.13 | Software technologies. (Part 2 of 2.)

Software is complex. Large, real-world software applications can take many months or even years to design and implement. When large software products are under development, they typically are made available to the user communities as a series of releases, each more complete and polished than the last (Fig. 1.14).

Version	Description
Alpha	*Alpha* software is the earliest release of a software product that's still under active development. Alpha versions are often buggy, incomplete and unstable and are released to a relatively small number of developers for testing new features, getting early feedback, etc.
Beta	*Beta* versions are released to a larger number of developers later in the development process after most major bugs have been fixed and new features are nearly complete. Beta software is more stable, but still subject to change.
Release candidates	*Release candidates* are generally *feature complete*, (mostly) bug free and ready for use by the community, which provides a diverse testing environment—the software is used on different systems, with varying constraints and for a variety of purposes.
Final release	Any bugs that appear in the release candidate are corrected, and eventually the final product is released to the general public. Software companies often distribute incremental updates over the Internet.
Continuous beta	Software that's developed using this approach (for example, Google search or Gmail) generally does not have version numbers. It's hosted in the *cloud* (not installed on your computer) and is constantly evolving so that users always have the latest version.

Fig. 1.14 | Software product-release terminology.

1.8 Keeping Up-to-Date with Information Technologies

Figure 1.15 lists key technical and business publications that will help you stay up-to-date with the latest news and trends and technology. You can also find a growing list of Internet- and web-related Resource Centers at `www.deitel.com/ResourceCenters.html`.

Publication	URL
AllThingsD	`allthingsd.com`
Bloomberg BusinessWeek	`www.businessweek.com`
CNET	`news.cnet.com`
Communications of the ACM	`cacm.acm.org`
Computerworld	`www.computerworld.com`
Engadget	`www.engadget.com`

Fig. 1.15 | Technical and business publications. (Part 1 of 2.)

Publication	URL
eWeek	www.eweek.com
Fast Company	www.fastcompany.com/
Fortune	money.cnn.com/magazines/fortune
GigaOM	gigaom.com
Hacker News	news.ycombinator.com
IEEE Computer Magazine	www.computer.org/portal/web/computingnow/computer
InfoWorld	www.infoworld.com
Mashable	mashable.com
PCWorld	www.pcworld.com
SD Times	www.sdtimes.com
Slashdot	slashdot.org/
Technology Review	technologyreview.com
Techcrunch	techcrunch.com
The Next Web	thenextweb.com
The Verge	www.theverge.com
Wired	www.wired.com

Fig. 1.15 | Technical and business publications. (Part 2 of 2.)

2

Introduction to Java Applications; Input/Output and Operators

Objectives

In this chapter you'll:

- Write simple Java applications.
- Use input and output statements.
- Learn about Java's primitive types.
- Use arithmetic operators.
- Learn the precedence of arithmetic operators.
- Write decision-making statements.
- Use relational and equality operators.

2.1 Introduction

This chapter introduces Java application programming. We begin with examples of programs that display (output) messages on the screen. We then present a program that obtains (inputs) two numbers from a user, calculates their sum and displays the result. You'll perform arithmetic calculations and save their results for later use. The last example demonstrates how to make decisions. The application compares two numbers, then displays messages that show the comparison results. You'll use the JDK command-line tools to compile and run programs. If you prefer to use an integrated development environment (IDE), we've also posted Dive Into® videos at http://www.deitel.com/books/jfp3/ for Eclipse, NetBeans and IntelliJ IDEA.

2.2 Your First Program in Java: Printing a Line of Text

A Java **application** executes when you use the **java command** to launch the Java Virtual Machine (JVM). We'll discuss how to compile and run a Java application. First we consider a simple application that displays a line of text. Figure 2.1 shows the program followed by a box that displays its output.

```
1   // Fig. 2.1: Welcome1.java
2   // Text-printing program.
3
4   public class Welcome1
5   {
6      // main method begins execution of Java application
7      public static void main(String[] args)
8      {
9         System.out.println("Welcome to Java Programming!");
10     } // end method main
11  } // end class Welcome1
```

```
Welcome to Java Programming!
```

Fig. 2.1 | Text-printing program.

The program includes line numbers—they're *not* part of a Java program. Line 9 does the work—displaying the phrase Welcome to Java Programming! on the screen.

Commenting Your Programs

The Java compiler *ignores* comments. By convention, we begin every program with a comment indicating the figure number and filename. The comment in line 1 begins with //, indicating that it's an **end-of-line comment**—it terminates at the end of the line on which the // appears. An end-of-line comment need not begin a line; it also can begin in the middle of a line and continue until the end (as in lines 6, 10 and 11). Line 2, by our convention, is a comment that describes the purpose of the program.

Java also has **traditional comments**, which can be spread over several lines as in

```
/* This is a traditional comment. It
   can be split over multiple lines */
```

These begin and end with delimiters, /* and */. The compiler ignores all text between the delimiters. Java incorporated traditional comments and end-of-line comments from the C and C++ programming languages, respectively. We prefer using // comments.

Java provides comments of a third type—**Javadoc comments**. These are delimited by /** and */. The compiler ignores all text between the delimiters. Javadoc comments enable you to embed program documentation directly in your programs. Such comments are the preferred Java documenting format in industry. The **javadoc utility program** (part of the JDK) reads Javadoc comments and uses them to prepare program documentation in HTML format. We demonstrate Javadoc comments and the javadoc utility in Appendix G, Creating Documentation with javadoc.

 Common Programming Error 2.1
Forgetting one of the delimiters of a traditional or Javadoc comment is a syntax error.

Using Blank Lines

Line 3 is a blank line. Blank lines, space characters and tabs make programs easier to read. Together, they're known as **white space** (or whitespace). The compiler ignores white space.

Declaring a Class

Line 4 begins a **class declaration** for class Welcome1. Every Java program consists of at least one class that you (the programmer) define. The **class keyword** introduces a class declaration and is immediately followed by the **class name** (Welcome1). **Keywords** (sometimes called **reserved words**) are reserved for use by Java and are always spelled with all lowercase letters. The complete list of keywords is shown in Appendix C.

In Chapters 2–7, every class we define begins with the **public** keyword. For now, we simply require public. You'll learn more about public and non-public classes in Chapter 8.

*Filename for a **public** Class*

A public class *must* be placed in a file that has a filename of the form *ClassName*.java, so class Welcome1 is stored in the file Welcome1.java.

 Common Programming Error 2.2
A compilation error occurs if a public class's filename is not exactly same name as the class (in terms of both spelling and capitalization) followed by the .java extension.

Class Names and Identifiers

By convention, class names begin with a capital letter and capitalize the first letter of each word they include (e.g., SampleClassName). A class name is an **identifier**—a series of characters consisting of letters, digits, underscores (_) and dollar signs ($) that does *not* begin with a digit and does *not* contain spaces. Some valid identifiers are Welcome1, $value, _value, m_inputField1 and button7. The name 7button is *not* a valid identifier because it begins with a digit, and the name input field is *not* a valid identifier because it contains a space. Normally, an identifier that does not begin with a capital letter is not a class name. Java is **case sensitive**—uppercase and lowercase letters are distinct—so value and Value are different (but both valid) identifiers.

Class Body

A **left brace** (as in line 5), {, begins the **body** of every class declaration. A corresponding **right brace** (at line 11), }, must end each class declaration. Lines 6–10 are indented.

Good Programming Practice 2.1

Indent the entire body of each class declaration one "level" between the left brace and the right brace that delimit the body of the class. This format emphasizes the class declaration's structure and makes it easier to read. We use three spaces to form a level of indent—many programmers prefer two or four spaces. Whatever you choose, use it consistently.

Error-Prevention Tip 2.1

When you type an opening left brace, {, immediately type the closing right brace, }, then reposition the cursor between the braces and indent to begin typing the body. This practice helps prevent errors due to missing braces. Many IDEs insert the closing right brace for you when you type the opening left brace.

Good Programming Practice 2.2

IDEs typically indent code for you. The Tab key may also be used to indent code. You can configure each IDE to specify the number of spaces inserted when you press Tab.

Declaring a Method

Line 6 is an end-of-line comment indicating the purpose of lines 7–10 of the program. Line 7 is the starting point of every Java application. The **parentheses** after the identifier main indicate that it's a **method**. For a Java application, one of the methods *must* be called main and must be defined as shown in line 7; otherwise, the Java Virtual Machine (JVM) will not execute the application. We'll explain the purpose of keyword **static** in Section 3.2.5. Keyword **void** indicates that this method will *not* return any information. In line 7, the String[] args in parentheses is a required part of the method main's declaration—we discuss this in Chapter 7.

The left brace in line 8 begins the **body of the method declaration**. A corresponding right brace must end it (line 10). Line 9 in the method body is indented between the braces.

Good Programming Practice 2.3

Indent the entire body of each method declaration one "level" between the braces that define the body of the method.

*Performing Output with **System.out.println***
Line 9 displays the characters contained between the double quotation marks (the quotation marks themselves are *not* displayed). Together, the quotation marks and the characters between them are a **string**—also known as a **character string** or a **string literal**. Whitespace characters in strings are *not* ignored by the compiler. Strings *cannot* span multiple lines of code.

The **System.out** object—which is predefined for you—is known as the **standard output object**. It allows a Java application to display information in the **command window** from which it executes. In recent versions of Microsoft Windows, the command window is the **Command Prompt**. In UNIX/Linux/Mac OS X, the command window is called a **terminal window**, a **shell**. Many programmers call it simply the **command line**.

Method **System.out.println** displays (or prints) a line of text in the command window. The string in the parentheses in line 9 is the argument to the method. When System.out.println completes its task, it positions the output cursor (the location where the next character will be displayed) at the beginning of the next line in the command window. This is similar to what happens when you press the *Enter* key while typing in a text editor—the cursor appears at the beginning of the next line in the document.

The entire line 9, including System.out.println, the argument "Welcome to Java Programming!" in the parentheses and the semicolon (;), is called a **statement**. A method typically contains one or more statements that perform its task. Most statements end with a semicolon. When the statement in line 9 executes, it displays Welcome to Java Programming! in the command window.

> **Error-Prevention Tip 2.2**
> *When the compiler reports a syntax error, it may not be on the line that the error message indicates. First, check the line for which the error was reported. If you don't find an error on that line, check several preceding lines.*

Compiling Your First Java Application
We assume you're using the Java Development Kit's command-line tools, not an IDE. To help you compile and run your programs in an IDE, we provide online Dive Into® videos for the popular IDEs Eclipse, NetBeans and IntelliJ IDEA. These are located on the book's website:

```
http://www.deitel.com/books/jfp3
```

Open a command window and change to the directory where the program is stored. Many operating systems use the command cd to change directories. On Windows, for example,

```
cd c:\examples\ch02\fig02_01
```

changes to the fig02_01 directory. On UNIX/Linux/Max OS X, the command

```
cd ~/examples/ch02/fig02_01
```

changes to the fig02_01 directory. To compile the program, type

```
javac Welcome1.java
```

If the program contains no compilation errors, this command creates a new file called Welcome1.class (known as the **class file** for Welcome1) containing the platform-independent Java bytecodes that represent our application. When we use the java command to execute the application on a given platform, the JVM will translate these bytecodes into instructions that are understood by the underlying operating system and hardware.

Common Programming Error 2.3

When using java c, *if you receive a message such as "bad command or* filename," "javac: command not found" *or* "'javac' is not recognized as an internal or external command, operable program or batch file," *then your Java software installation was not completed properly. This indicates that the system's* PATH *environment variable was not set properly. Review the installation instructions in the Before You Begin section of this book. On some systems, after correcting the* PATH, *you may need to reboot your computer or open a new command window for these settings to take effect.*

Each syntax-error message contains the filename and line number where the error occurred. For example, Welcome1.java:6 indicates that an error occurred at line 6 in Welcome1.java. The rest of the message provides information about the syntax error.

Common Programming Error 2.4

*The compiler error message "*class Welcome1 is public, should be declared in a file named Welcome1.java*" indicates that the filename does not match the name of the public class in the file or that you typed the class name incorrectly when compiling the class.*

Executing the Welcome1 Application

The following instructions assume that the book's examples are located in C:\examples on Windows or in your user account's Documents/examples folder on Linux/OS X. To execute this program in a command window, change to the directory containing Welcome1.java—C:\examples\ch02\fig02_01 on Microsoft Windows or ~/Documents/examples/ch02/fig02_01 on Linux/OS X. Next, type

```
java Welcome1
```

and press *Enter*. This command launches the JVM, which loads the Welcome1.class file. The command *omits* the .class file-name extension; otherwise, the JVM will *not* execute the program. The JVM calls class Welcome1's main method. Next, the statement at line 9 of main displays "Welcome to Java Programming!". Figure 2.2 shows the program executing in a Microsoft Windows **Command Prompt** window. [*Note:* Many environments show command windows with black backgrounds and white text. We adjusted these settings to make our screen captures more readable.]

Error-Prevention Tip 2.3

When attempting to run a Java program, if you receive a message such as "Exception in thread "main" java.lang.NoClassDefFoundError: Welcome1," your CLASSPATH environment variable has not been set properly. Please carefully review the installation instructions in the Before You Begin section of this book. On some systems, you may need to reboot your computer or open a new command window after configuring the CLASSPATH.

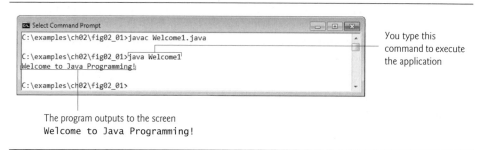

The program outputs to the screen
`Welcome to Java Programming!`

Fig. 2.2 | Executing `Welcome1` from the **Command Prompt**.

2.3 Modifying Your First Java Program

Let's modify the example in Fig. 2.1 to print text on one line by using multiple statements and print text on several lines by using a single statement.

Displaying a Single Line of Text with Multiple Statements

`Welcome to Java Programming!` can be displayed several ways. Class `Welcome2`, shown in Fig. 2.3, uses two statements (lines 9–10) to produce the output shown in Fig. 2.1. [*Note:* From this point forward, we highlight with a gray background the new and key features in each code listing, as we've done for lines 9–10.]

```
1   // Fig. 2.3: Welcome2.java
2   // Printing a line of text with multiple statements.
3
4   public class Welcome2
5   {
6      // main method begins execution of Java application
7      public static void main(String[] args)
8      {
9         System.out.print("Welcome to ");
10        System.out.println("Java Programming!");
11     } // end method main
12  } // end class Welcome2
```

```
Welcome to Java Programming!
```

Fig. 2.3 | Printing a line of text with multiple statements.

The program is similar to Fig. 2.1, so we discuss only the changes here. Line 4 begins the `Welcome2` class declaration. Lines 9–10 of method `main` display one line of text. The first statement uses `System.out`'s method `print` to display a string. Each `print` or `println` statement resumes displaying characters from where the last `print` or `println` statement stopped displaying characters. Unlike `println`, after displaying its argument, `print` does *not* position the output cursor at the beginning of the next line in the command window—

the next character the program displays will appear *immediately after* the last character that print displays. So, line 10 positions the first character in its argument (the letter "J") immediately after the last character that line 9 displays (the *space character* before the string's closing double-quote character).

Displaying Multiple Lines of Text with a Single Statement

A single statement can display multiple lines by using **newline characters**, which indicate to System.out's print and println methods when to position the output cursor at the beginning of the next line in the command window. Like blank lines, space characters and tab characters, newline characters are whitespace characters. The program in Fig. 2.4 outputs four lines of text, using newline characters to determine when to begin each new line. Most of the program is identical to those in Figs. 2.1 and 2.3.

```java
 1   // Fig. 2.4: Welcome3.java
 2   // Printing multiple lines of text with a single statement.
 3
 4   public class Welcome3
 5   {
 6      // main method begins execution of Java application
 7      public static void main(String[] args)
 8      {
 9         System.out.println("Welcome\nto\nJava\nProgramming!");
10      } // end method main
11   } // end class Welcome3
```

```
Welcome
to
Java
Programming!
```

Fig. 2.4 | Printing multiple lines of text with a single statement.

Line 9 displays four lines of text in the command window. Normally, the characters in a string are displayed *exactly* as they appear in the double quotes. However, the paired characters \ and n (repeated three times in the statement) do *not* appear on the screen. The **backslash** (\) is an **escape character**, which has special meaning to System.out's print and println methods. When a backslash appears in a string, Java combines it with the next character to form an **escape sequence**—\n represents the newline character. When a newline character appears in a string being output with System.out, the newline character causes the screen's output cursor to move to the beginning of the next line in the command window.

Figure 2.5 lists several common escape sequences and describes how they affect the display of characters in the command window. For the complete list of escape sequences, visit

```
http://docs.oracle.com/javase/specs/jls/se7/html/
    jls-3.html#jls-3.10.6
```

Escape sequence	Description
\n	Newline. Position the screen cursor at the beginning of the *next* line.
\t	Horizontal tab. Move the screen cursor to the next tab stop.
\r	Carriage return. Position the screen cursor at the beginning of the *current* line—do *not* advance to the next line. Any characters output after the carriage return *overwrite* the characters previously output on that line.
\\	Backslash. Used to print a backslash character.
\"	Double quote. Used to print a double-quote character. For example, `System.out.println("\"in quotes\"");` displays "in quotes".

Fig. 2.5 | Some common escape sequences.

2.4 Displaying Text with `printf`

The `System.out.printf` method (f means "formatted") displays *formatted* data. Figure 2.6 uses this method to output on two lines the strings `"Welcome to"` and `"Java Programming!"`.

```
1   // Fig. 2.6: Welcome4.java
2   // Displaying multiple lines with method System.out.printf.
3
4   public class Welcome4
5   {
6      // main method begins execution of Java application
7      public static void main(String[] args)
8      {
9         System.out.printf("%s%n%s%n",
10           "Welcome to", "Java Programming!");
11     } // end method main
12  } // end class Welcome4
```

```
Welcome to
Java Programming!
```

Fig. 2.6 | Displaying multiple lines with method `System.out.printf`.

Lines 9–10 call method `System.out.printf` to display the program's output. The method call specifies three arguments.

Lines 9–10 represent only *one* statement. Java allows large statements to be split over many lines. We indent line 10 to indicate that it's a *continuation* of line 9.

Method `printf`'s first argument is a **format string** that may consist of **fixed text** and **format specifiers**. Fixed text is output by `printf` just as it would be by `print` or `println`. Each format specifier is a *placeholder* for a value and specifies the *type of data* to output. Format specifiers also may include optional formatting information.

Format specifiers begin with a percent sign (%) followed by a character that represents the *data type*. For example, the format specifier **%s** is a placeholder for a string. The format string in line 9 specifies that printf should output two strings, each followed by a newline character. At the first format specifier's position, printf substitutes the value of the first argument after the format string. At each subsequent format specifier's position, printf substitutes the value of the next argument. So this example substitutes "Welcome to" for the first %s and "Java Programming!" for the second %s. The output shows that two lines of text are displayed on two lines.

Notice that instead of using the escape sequence \n, we used the **%n** format specifier, which is a line separator that's *portable* across operating systems. You cannot use %n in the argument to System.out.print or System.out.println; however, the line separator output by System.out.println *after* it displays its argument *is* portable across operating systems. Appendix I presents more details of formatting output with printf.

2.5 Another Application: Adding Integers

Our next application (Fig. 2.7) reads (or inputs) two integers typed by a user at the keyboard, computes their sum and displays it. In the sample output, we use bold text to identify the user's input (i.e., **45** and **72**).

```java
 1   // Fig. 2.7: Addition.java
 2   // Addition program that inputs two numbers then displays their sum.
 3   import java.util.Scanner; // program uses class Scanner
 4
 5   public class Addition
 6   {
 7      // main method begins execution of Java application
 8      public static void main(String[] args)
 9      {
10         // create a Scanner to obtain input from the command window
11         Scanner input = new Scanner(System.in);
12
13         int number1; // first number to add
14         int number2; // second number to add
15         int sum; // sum of number1 and number2
16
17         System.out.print("Enter first integer: "); // prompt
18         number1 = input.nextInt(); // read first number from user
19
20         System.out.print("Enter second integer: "); // prompt
21         number2 = input.nextInt(); // read second number from user
22
23         sum = number1 + number2; // add numbers, then store total in sum
24
25         System.out.printf("Sum is %d%n", sum); // display sum
26      } // end method main
27   } // end class Addition
```

Fig. 2.7 | Addition program that inputs two numbers then displays their sum. (Part 1 of 2.)

```
Enter first integer: 45
Enter second integer: 72
Sum is 117
```

Fig. 2.7 | Addition program that inputs two numbers then displays their sum. (Part 2 of 2.)

import Declarations

A great strength of Java is its rich set of predefined classes that you can *reuse* rather than "reinventing the wheel." These classes are grouped into **packages**—*named groups of related classes*—and are collectively referred to as the **Java class library**, or the **Java Application Programming Interface (Java API)**. Line 3 is an **import declaration** that helps the compiler locate a class that's used in this program. It indicates that the program uses the predefined Scanner class (discussed shortly) from the package named **java.util**. The compiler then ensures that you use the class correctly.

Common Programming Error 2.5

All import declarations must appear before the first class declaration in the file. Placing an import declaration inside or after a class declaration is a syntax error.

Common Programming Error 2.6

Forgetting to include an import declaration for a class that must be imported results in a compilation error containing a message such as "cannot find symbol."

Software Engineering Observation 2.1

*In each new Java version, the APIs typically contain new capabilities that fix bugs, improve performance or offer better means for accomplishing tasks. The corresponding older versions are no longer needed and should not be used. Such APIs are said to be **deprecated** and might be removed from later Java versions.*

You'll often encounter deprecated APIs when browsing the online API documentation. The compiler will warn you when you compile code that uses deprecated APIs. If you compile your code with javac using the command-line argument -deprecation, the compiler will tell you which deprecated features you're using. For each one, the online documentation (http://docs.oracle.com/javase/7/docs/api/) indicates and typically links to the new feature that replaces the deprecated one.

Declaring Class Addition

Line 5 begins the declaration of class Addition. The filename for this public class must be Addition.java. Remember that the body of each class declaration starts with an opening left brace (line 6) and ends with a closing right brace (line 27).

The application begins execution with the main method (lines 8–26). The left brace (line 9) marks the beginning of method main's body, and the corresponding right brace (line 26) marks its end. Method main is indented one level in the body of class Addition, and the code in the body of main is indented another level for readability.

*Declaring and Creating a **Scanner** to Obtain User Input from the Keyboard*
All Java variables *must* be declared with a name and a type *before* they can be used. A variable's name can be any valid identifier. Like other statements, declaration statements end with a semicolon (;).

Line 11 is a **variable declaration statement** that specifies the *name* (input) and *type* (Scanner) of a variable that's used in this program. A **Scanner** enables a program to read data (e.g., numbers and strings) for use in a program. The data can come from many sources, such as the user at the keyboard or a file on disk. Before using a Scanner, you must create it and specify the *source* of the data.

The = in line 11 indicates that Scanner variable input should be initialized in its declaration with the result of the expression to the right of the equals sign— new Scanner(System.in). This expression uses the **new** keyword to create a Scanner object that reads characters typed by the user at the keyboard. The **standard input object**, **System.in**, enables applications to read *bytes* of data typed by the user. The Scanner translates these bytes into types (like ints) that can be used in a program.

Declaring Variables to Store Integers
The variable declaration statements in lines 13–15 declare that variables number1, number2 and sum hold data of type **int**—they can hold *integer* values. These variables are *not* yet initialized. The range of values for an int is –2,147,483,648 to +2,147,483,647.

Some other types of data are **float** and **double**, for holding real numbers, and **char**, for holding character data. Real numbers contain decimal points, such as in 3.4, 0.0 and –11.19. Variables of type char represent individual characters, such as an uppercase letter (e.g., A), a digit (e.g., 7), a special character (e.g., * or %) or an escape sequence (e.g., the tab character, \t). The types int, float, double and char are called **primitive types**. Primitive-type names are keywords and must appear in all lowercase letters. Appendix D summarizes the characteristics of the eight primitive types (boolean, byte, char, short, int, long, float and double).

Several variables of the same type may be declared in a single declaration with the variable names separated by commas. For example, lines 13–15 can also be written as:

```
int number1, // first number to add
    number2, // second number to add
    sum; // sum of number1 and number2
```

Good Programming Practice 2.4
*By convention, variable-name identifiers begin with a lowercase letter, and every word in the name after the first word begins with a capital letter. For example, variable-name identifier firstNumber starts its second word, Number, with a capital N. This naming convention is known as **camel case**, because the uppercase letters stand out like a camel's humps.*

Prompting the User for Input
Line 17 uses System.out.print to display the message "Enter first integer: ". We use method print here rather than println so that the user's input appears on the same line as the prompt. Class System is part of package **java.lang**. Notice that class System is *not* imported with an import declaration at the beginning of the program.

Software Engineering Observation 2.2

By default, package java.lang *is imported in every Java program; thus, classes in* java.lang *are the only ones in the Java API that do not require an* import *declaration.*

Obtaining ints as Input from the User

Line 18 uses Scanner object input's nextInt method to obtain an integer from the user at the keyboard. At this point the program *waits* for the user to type the number and press the *Enter* key to submit the number to the program.

Our program assumes that the user enters a valid integer value. If not, a runtime logic error will occur and the program will terminate. Chapter 11, Exception Handling: A Deeper Look, discusses how to make your programs more robust by enabling them to handle such errors.

In line 18, we place the result of the call to method nextInt (an int value) in variable number1 by using the **assignment operator**, =. The statement is read as "number1 *gets* the value of input.nextInt()." Operator = is a **binary operator**). Everything to the *right* of the assignment operator, =, is always evaluated *before* the assignment is performed.

Line 20 prompts the user to enter the second integer. Line 21 reads the second integer and assigns it to variable number2.

Using Variables in a Calculation

Line 23 calculates the sum of the variables number1 and number2 then assigns the result to variable sum by using the assignment operator, =. The addition operator is a binary operator. Portions of statements that contain calculations are called **expressions**. An expression is any portion of a statement that has a value associated with it. The value of the expression number1 + number2 is the sum of the numbers. The value of the expression input.nextInt() is the integer typed by the user.

Displaying the Result of the Calculation

After the calculation has been performed, line 25 uses method System.out.printf to display the sum. The format specifier **%d** is a *placeholder* for an int value (in this case the value of sum)—the letter d stands for "decimal integer." The remaining characters in the format string are all fixed text. So, method printf displays "Sum is ", followed by the value of sum (in the position of the %d format specifier) and a newline. We could have combined the statements at lines 23 and 25 into the statement

```
System.out.printf("Sum is %d%n", (number1 + number2));
```

The parentheses around the expression number1 + number2 are optional.

Java API Documentation

For each new Java API class we use, we indicate the package in which it's located. This information helps you locate descriptions of each package and class in the Java API documentation. A web-based version of this documentation can be found at

```
http://docs.oracle.com/javase/7/docs/api/index.html
```

You can download it from the Additional Resources section at

```
http://www.oracle.com/technetwork/java/javase/downloads/index.html
```

Appendix F shows how to use this documentation.

2.6 Arithmetic

The **arithmetic operators** are summarized in Fig. 2.8. The **asterisk** (*) indicates multiplication, and the percent sign (%) is the remainder operator, which we'll discuss shortly. The arithmetic operators in Fig. 2.8 are binary operators.

Integer division yields an integer quotient. For example, the expression 7 / 4 evaluates to 1, and the expression 17 / 5 evaluates to 3. Any fractional part in integer division is simply *truncated*—no *rounding* occurs. Java provides the remainder operator, %, which yields the remainder after division. The expression x % y yields the remainder after x is divided by y. Thus, 7 % 4 yields 3, and 17 % 5 yields 2. This operator is most commonly used with integer operands but it can also be used with other arithmetic types. One interesting application of the remainder operator is determining whether one number is a multiple of another—in this case, the remainder is 0.

Java operation	Operator	Algebraic expression	Java expression
Addition	+	$f + 7$	f + 7
Subtraction	–	$p - c$	p – c
Multiplication	*	bm	b * m
Division	/	x / y or $\frac{x}{y}$ or $x \div y$	x / y
Remainder	%	$r \bmod s$	r % s

Fig. 2.8 | Arithmetic operators.

Rules of Operator Precedence

Java applies the operators in arithmetic expressions in a precise sequence determined by the **rules of operator precedence**, which are generally the same as those followed in algebra:

1. Multiplication, division and remainder operations are applied first. If an expression contains several such operations, they're applied from left to right. Multiplication, division and remainder operators have the same level of precedence.

2. Addition and subtraction operations are applied next. If an expression contains several such operations, the operators are applied from left to right. Addition and subtraction operators have the same level of precedence.

These rules enable Java to apply operators in the correct order.[1] When we say that operators are applied from left to right, we're referring to their **associativity**. Some operators associate from right to left. Figure 2.9 summarizes these rules of operator precedence. A complete precedence chart is included in Appendix A.

---

1. We use simple examples to explain the *order of evaluation* of expressions. Subtle issues occur in the more complex expressions you'll encounter later in the book. For more information on order of evaluation, see Chapter 15 of *The Java™ Language Specification* (http://docs.oracle.com/javase/specs/jls/se7/html/index.html).

Operator(s)	Operation(s)	Order of evaluation (precedence)
* / %	Multiplication Division Remainder	Evaluated first. If there are several operators of this type, they're evaluated from *left to right*.
+ –	Addition Subtraction	Evaluated next. If there are several operators of this type, they're evaluated from *left to right*.
=	Assignment	Evaluated last.

Fig. 2.9 | Precedence of arithmetic operators.

2.7 Decision Making: Equality and Relational Operators

A **condition** is an expression that can be **true** or **false**. This section introduces Java's **if selection statement**, which allows a program to make a **decision** based on a condition's value. If the condition in an if statement is *true*, the body of the if statement executes. If the condition is *false*, the body does not execute.

Conditions in if statements can be formed by using the **equality operators** (== and !=) and **relational operators** (>, <, >= and <=) summarized in Fig. 2.10. Both equality operators have the same level of precedence, which is lower than that of the relational operators. The equality operators associate from left to right. The relational operators all have the same level of precedence and also associate from left to right.

Algebraic operator	Java equality or relational operator	Sample Java condition	Meaning of Java condition
Equality operators			
=	==	x == y	x is equal to y
≠	!=	x != y	x is not equal to y
Relational operators			
>	>	x > y	x is greater than y
<	<	x < y	x is less than y
≥	>=	x >= y	x is greater than or equal to y
≤	<=	x <= y	x is less than or equal to y

Fig. 2.10 | Equality and relational operators.

Figure 2.11 uses six if statements to compare two integers input by the user. If the condition in any of these if statements is *true*, the statement associated with that if statement executes; otherwise, the statement is skipped. We use a Scanner to input the integers from the user and store them in variables number1 and number2. The program *compares* the numbers and displays the results of the comparisons that are true.

```
 1   // Fig. 2.11: Comparison.java
 2   // Compare integers using if statements, relational operators
 3   // and equality operators.
 4   import java.util.Scanner; // program uses class Scanner
 5
 6   public class Comparison
 7   {
 8      // main method begins execution of Java application
 9      public static void main(String[] args)
10      {
11         // create Scanner to obtain input from command line
12         Scanner input = new Scanner(System.in);
13
14         int number1; // first number to compare
15         int number2; // second number to compare
16
17         System.out.print("Enter first integer: "); // prompt
18         number1 = input.nextInt(); // read first number from user
19
20         System.out.print("Enter second integer: "); // prompt
21         number2 = input.nextInt(); // read second number from user
22
23         if (number1 == number2)
24            System.out.printf("%d == %d%n", number1, number2);
25
26         if (number1 != number2)
27            System.out.printf("%d != %d%n", number1, number2);
28
29         if (number1 < number2)
30            System.out.printf("%d < %d%n", number1, number2);
31
32         if (number1 > number2)
33            System.out.printf("%d > %d%n", number1, number2);
34
35         if (number1 <= number2)
36            System.out.printf("%d <= %d%n", number1, number2);
37
38         if (number1 >= number2)
39            System.out.printf("%d >= %d%n", number1, number2);
40      } // end method main
41   } // end class Comparison
```

```
Enter first integer: 777
Enter second integer: 777
777 == 777
777 <= 777
777 >= 777
```

Fig. 2.11 | Compare integers using if statements, relational operators and equality operators.
(Part 1 of 2.)

```
Enter first integer: 1000
Enter second integer: 2000
1000 != 2000
1000 < 2000
1000 <= 2000
```

```
Enter first integer: 2000
Enter second integer: 1000
2000 != 1000
2000 > 1000
2000 >= 1000
```

Fig. 2.11 | Compare integers using if statements, relational operators and equality operators. (Part 2 of 2.)

The declaration of class Comparison begins at line 6. The class's main method (lines 9–40) begins the execution of the program. Line 12 declares Scanner variable input and assigns it a Scanner that inputs data from the standard input (i.e., the keyboard).

Lines 14–15 declare the int variables used to store the values input from the user. Lines 17–18 prompt the user to enter the first integer and input the value, respectively. The value is stored in variable number1.

Lines 20–21 prompt the user to enter the second integer and input the value, respectively. The value is stored in variable number2.

Lines 23–24 compare the values of number1 and number2 to determine whether they're equal. An if statement always begins with keyword if, followed by a condition in parentheses. An if statement expects one statement in its body, but may contain multiple statements if they're enclosed in a set of braces ({}). The indentation of the body statement shown here is not required, but it improves the program's readability by emphasizing that the statement in line 24 *is part of* the if statement that begins at line 23. Line 24 executes only if the numbers stored in variables number1 and number2 are equal (i.e., the condition is *true*). The if statements in lines 26–27, 29–30, 32–33, 35–36 and 38–39 compare number1 and number2 using the operators !=, <, >, <= and >=, respectively. If the condition in one or more of the if statements is *true*, the corresponding body statement executes.

Common Programming Error 2.7

Confusing the equality operator, ==, with the assignment operator, =, can cause a logic error or a compilation error.

There's no semicolon (;) at the end of the first line of each if statement. Such a semicolon would result in a logic error at execution time. For example,

```
if (number1 == number2); // logic error
    System.out.printf("%d == %d%n", number1, number2);
```

would actually be interpreted by Java as

```
if (number1 == number2)
    ; // empty statement

System.out.printf("%d == %d%n", number1, number2);
```

where the semicolon on the line by itself—called the **empty statement**—is the statement to execute if the condition in the if statement is *true*. When the empty statement executes, no task is performed. The program then continues with the output statement, which *always* executes, regardless of whether the condition is true or false, because the output statement is *not* part of the if statement.

Operators Discussed So Far

Figure 2.12 shows the operators discussed so far in decreasing order of precedence. All but the assignment operator, =, associate from *left to right*. The assignment operator, =, associates from *right to left*. An assignment expression's value is whatever was assigned to the variable on the = operator's left side—for example, the value of the expression x = 7 is 7. So an expression like x = y = 0 is evaluated as if it had been written as x = (y = 0), which first assigns the value 0 to variable y, then assigns the result of that assignment, 0, to x.

Operators				Associativity	Type
*	/	%		left to right	multiplicative
+	–			left to right	additive
<	<=	>	>=	left to right	relational
==	!=			left to right	equality
=				right to left	assignment

Fig. 2.12 | Precedence and associativity of operators discussed.

2.8 Wrap-Up

In this chapter, you learned many important features of Java, including displaying data on the screen in a **Command Prompt**, inputting data from the keyboard, performing calculations and making decisions. As you'll see in Chapter 3, Java applications typically contain just a few lines of code in method main—these statements normally create the objects that perform the work of the application. In Chapter 3, you'll learn how to implement your own classes and use objects of those classes in applications.

3

Introduction to Classes, Objects, Methods and Strings

Objectives

In this chapter you'll:

- Declare a class and use it to create an object.

- Implement a class's behaviors as methods.

- Implement a class's attributes as instance variables.

- Call an object's methods to make them perform their tasks.

- Understand how local variables of a method differ from instance variables.

- Understand what primitive types and reference types are.

- Use a constructor to initialize an object's data.

3.1 Introduction

[*Note:* This chapter depends on the terminology and concepts discussed in Section 1.2, Object Technology Concepts.]

In Chapter 2, you worked with existing classes, objects and methods. You used the predefined standard output object System.out, invoking its methods print, println and printf to display information on the screen. You used the existing Scanner class to create an object that reads into memory integer data typed by the user at the keyboard. Throughout the book, you'll use many more preexisting classes and objects.

In this chapter, you'll create your own classes and methods. Each new class you create becomes a new type that can be used to declare variables and create objects. You can declare new classes as needed; this is one reason why Java is known as an *extensible* language.

We present a case study on creating and using a simple, real-world bank account class—Account. Such a class should maintain as *instance variables* attributes such as its name and balance, and provide *methods* for tasks such as querying the balance (get-Balance), making deposits that increase the balance (deposit) and making withdrawals that decrease the balance (withdraw). We'll build the getBalance and deposit methods into the class in the chapter's examples.

In Chapter 2 we used the data type int to represent integers. In this chapter, we introduce data type double to represent an account balance as a number that can contain a decimal *point*—such numbers are called floating-point numbers. [In Chapter 8, when we get a bit deeper into object technology, we'll begin representing monetary amounts precisely with class BigDecimal (package java.math) as you should do when writing industrial-strength monetary applications.]

3.2 Instance Variables, *set* Methods and *get* Methods

In this section, you'll create two classes—Account (Fig. 3.1) and AccountTest (Fig. 3.2). Class AccountTest is an *application class* in which the main method will create and use an Account object to demonstrate class Account's capabilities.

3.2.1 Account Class with an Instance Variable, a *set* Method and a *get* Method

Different accounts typically have different names. For this reason, class Account (Fig. 3.1) contains a name *instance variable*. A class's instance variables maintain data for each object (that is, each instance) of the class. Later in the chapter we'll add an instance variable named balance so we can keep track of how much money is in the account. Class Account contains two methods—method setName stores a name in an Account object and method getName obtains a name from an Account object.

```java
1   // Fig. 3.1: Account.java
2   // Account class that contains a name instance variable
3   // and methods to set and get its value.
4
5   public class Account
6   {
7      private String name; // instance variable
8
9      // method to set the name in the object
10     public void setName(String name)
11     {
12        this.name = name; // store the name
13     }
14
15     // method to retrieve the name from the object
16     public String getName()
17     {
18        return name; // return value of name to caller
19     }
20  } // end class Account
```

Fig. 3.1 | Account class that contains a name instance variable and methods to *set* and *get* its value.

Class Declaration

The *class declaration* begins in line 5. The keyword public (which Chapter 8 explains in detail) is an **access modifier**. For now, we'll simply declare every class public. Each public class declaration must be stored in a file having the *same* name as the class and ending with the .java filename extension; otherwise, a compilation error will occur. Thus, public classes Account and AccountTest (Fig. 3.2) *must* be declared in the *separate* files Account.java and AccountTest.java, respectively.

Every class declaration contains the keyword class followed immediately by the class's name—in this case, Account. Every class's body is enclosed in a pair of left and right braces as in lines 6 and 20 of Fig. 3.1.

Identifiers and Camel Case Naming

Class names, method names and variable names are all *identifiers* and by convention all use the same *camel case* naming scheme we discussed in Chapter 2. Also by convention, class names begin with an initial *uppercase* letter, and method names and variable names begin with an initial *lowercase* letter.

Instance Variable **name**

Recall that an object has attributes, implemented as instance variables and carried with it throughout its lifetime. Instance variables exist before methods are called on an object, while the methods are executing and after the methods complete execution. Each object (instance) of the class has its *own* copy of the class's instance variables. A class normally contains one or more methods that manipulate the instance variables belonging to particular objects of the class.

Instance variables are declared *inside* a class declaration but *outside* the bodies of the class's methods. Line 7

```
private String name; // instance variable
```

declares instance variable name of type String *outside* the bodies of methods setName (lines 10–13) and getName (lines 16–19). String variables can hold character string values such as "Jane Green". If there are many Account objects, each has its own name. Because name is an instance variable, it can be manipulated by each of the class's methods.

Good Programming Practice 3.1

We prefer to list a class's instance variables first in the class's body, so that you see the names and types of the variables before they're used in the class's methods. You can list the class's instance variables anywhere in the class outside its method declarations, but scattering the instance variables can lead to hard-to-read code.

Access Modifiers **public** and **private**

Most instance-variable declarations are preceded with the keyword private (as in line 7). Like public, **private** is an *access modifier*. Variables or methods declared with access modifier private are accessible only to methods of the class in which they're declared. So, the variable name can be used only in each Account object's methods (setName and getName in this case). You'll soon see that this presents powerful software engineering opportunities.

setName *Method of Class* **Account**

Let's walk through the code of setName's method declaration (lines 10–13):

```
public void setName(String name) ── This line is the method header
{
    this.name = name; // store the name
}
```

We refer to the first line of each method declaration (line 10 in this case) as the *method header*. The method's return type (which appears before the method name) specifies the type of data the method returns to its caller after performing its task. The return type void (line 10) indicates that setName will perform a task but will not return (i.e., give back) any information to its caller. In Chapter 2, you used methods that return information—for example, you used Scanner method nextInt to input an integer typed by the user at the keyboard. When nextInt reads a value from the user, it returns that value for use in the program. As you'll soon see, Account method getName returns a value.

Method `setName` receives parameter `name` of type `String`. Parameters are declared in the parameter list, which is located inside the parentheses that follow the method name in the method header. When there are multiple parameters, each is separated from the next by a comma. Each parameter must specify a type (in this case, `String`) followed by a variable name (in this case, `name`).

Parameters Are Local Variables

In Chapter 2, we declared all of an app's variables in the `main` method. Variables declared in a particular method's body (such as `main`) are local variables which can be used only in that method. Each method can access only its own local variables, not those of other methods. When a method terminates, the values of its local variables are lost. A method's parameters also are local variables of the method.

setName Method Body

Every method body is delimited by a pair of braces (as in lines 11 and 13 of Fig. 3.1) containing one or more statements that perform the method's task(s). In this case, the method body contains a single statement (line 12) that assigns the value of the `name` parameter (a `String`) to the class's `name` instance variable, thus storing the account name in the object.

If a method contains a local variable with the same name as an instance variable (as in lines 10 and 7, respectively), that method's body will refer to the local variable rather than the instance variable. In this case, the local variable is said to *shadow* the instance variable in the method's body. The method's body can use the keyword **this** to refer to the shadowed instance variable explicitly, as shown on the left side of the assignment in line 12.

Good Programming Practice 3.2
We could have avoided the need for keyword `this` here by choosing a different name for the parameter in line 10, but using the `this` keyword as shown in line 12 is a widely accepted practice to minimize the proliferation of identifier names.

After line 12 executes, the method has completed its task, so it returns to its *caller*. As you'll soon see, the statement in line 21 of `main` (Fig. 3.2) calls method `setName`.

getName Method of Class Account

Method getName (lines 16–19 of Fig. 3.1)

```
public String getName()                Keyword return passes the String name back to
{                                        the method's caller
    return name; // return value of name to caller
}
```

returns a particular `Account` object's name to the caller. The method has an empty parameter list, so it does not require additional information to perform its task. The method returns a `String`. When a method that specifies a return type other than `void` is called and completes its task, it must return a result to its caller. A statement that calls method get-Name on an `Account` object (such as the ones in lines 16 and 26 of Fig. 3.2) expects to receive the `Account`'s name—a `String`, as specified in the method declaration's return type.

The return statement in line 18 of Fig. 3.1 passes the `String` value of instance variable name back to the caller. For example, when the value is returned to the statement in lines 25–26 of Fig. 3.2, the statement uses that value to output the name.

3.2.2 AccountTest Class That Creates and Uses an Object of Class Account

Next, we'd like to use class Account in an app and *call* each of its methods. A class that contains a main method begins the execution of a Java app. Class Account cannot execute by itself because it does not contain a main method—if you type java Account in the command window, you'll get an error indicating "Main method not found in class Account." To fix this problem, you must either declare a separate class that contains a main method or place a main method in class Account.

Driver Class AccountTest

We use a separate class AccountTest (Fig. 3.2) containing method main to test class Account. Once main begins executing, it may call other methods in this and other classes; those may, in turn, call other methods, and so on. Class AccountTest's main method creates one Account object and calls its getName and setName methods. Such a class is sometimes called a *driver class*—just as a Person object drives a Car object by telling it what to do (go faster, go slower, turn left, turn right, etc.), class AccountTest drives an Account object, telling it what to do by calling its methods.

```java
1   // Fig. 3.2: AccountTest.java
2   // Creating and manipulating an Account object.
3   import java.util.Scanner;
4
5   public class AccountTest
6   {
7      public static void main(String[] args)
8      {
9         // create a Scanner object to obtain input from the command window
10        Scanner input = new Scanner(System.in);
11
12        // create an Account object and assign it to myAccount
13        Account myAccount = new Account();
14
15        // display initial value of name (null)
16        System.out.printf("Initial name is: %s%n%n", myAccount.getName());
17
18        // prompt for and read name
19        System.out.println("Please enter the name:");
20        String theName = input.nextLine(); // read a line of text
21        myAccount.setName(theName); // put theName in myAccount
22        System.out.println(); // outputs a blank line
23
24        // display the name stored in object myAccount
25        System.out.printf("Name in object myAccount is:%n%s%n",
26           myAccount.getName());
27     }
28  } // end class AccountTest
```

Fig. 3.2 | Creating and manipulating an Account object. (Part 1 of 2.)

```
Initial name is: null

Please enter the name:
Jane Green

Name in object myAccount is:
Jane Green
```

Fig. 3.2 | Creating and manipulating an Account object. (Part 2 of 2.)

Scanner *Object for Receiving Input from the User*

Line 10 creates a Scanner object named input for inputting the name from the user. Line 19 prompts the user to enter a name. Line 20 uses the Scanner object's **nextLine** method to read the name from the user and assign it to the local variable theName. You type the name and press *Enter* to submit it to the program. Pressing *Enter* inserts a newline character after the characters you typed. Method nextLine reads characters (including whitespace characters, such as the blank in "Jane Green") until it encounters the newline, then returns a String containing the characters up to, but *not* including, the newline, which is discarded.

Class Scanner provides various other input methods, as you'll see throughout the book. A method similar to nextLine—named **next**—reads the next word. When you press *Enter* after typing some text, method next reads characters until it encounters a white-space character (such as a space, tab or newline), then returns a String containing the characters up to, but *not* including, the white-space character, which is discarded. All information after the first white-space character is not lost—it can be read by subsequent statements that call the Scanner's methods later in the program.

Instantiating an Object—Keyword **new** *and Constructors*

Line 13 creates an Account object and assigns it to variable myAccount of type Account. Variable myAccount is initialized with the result of the **class instance creation expression** new Account(). Keyword **new** creates a new object of the specified class—in this case, Account. The parentheses to the right of Account are required. As you'll learn in Section 3.4, those parentheses in combination with a class name represent a call to a **constructor**, which is similar to a method but is called implicitly by the new operator to initialize an object's instance variables when the object is created. In Section 3.4, you'll see how to place an argument in the parentheses to specify an initial value for an Account object's name instance variable—you'll enhance class Account to enable this. For now, we simply leave the parentheses empty. Line 10 contains a class instance creation expression for a Scanner object—the expression initializes the Scanner with System.in, which tells the Scanner where to read the input from (i.e., the keyboard).

Calling Class **Account's** **getName** *Method*

Line 16 displays the initial name, which is obtained by calling the object's getName method. Just as we can use object System.out to call its methods print, printf and println, we can use object myAccount to call its methods getName and setName. Line 16 calls getName using the myAccount object created in line 13, followed by a **dot separator** (.), then the method name getName and an empty set of parentheses because no arguments are being passed. When getName is called:

1. The app transfers program execution from the call (line 16 in main) to method get-Name's declaration (lines 16–19 of Fig. 3.1). Because getName was called via the my-Account object, getName "knows" which object's instance variable to manipulate.

2. Next, method getName performs its task—that is, it returns the name (line 18 of Fig. 3.1). When the return statement executes, program execution continues where getName was called (line 16 in Fig. 3.2).

3. System.out.printf displays the String returned by method getName, then the program continues executing at line 19 in main.

Error-Prevention Tip 3.1

Never use as a format-control a string that was input from the user. When method System.out.printf evaluates the format-control string in its first argument, the method performs tasks based on the conversion specifier(s) in that string. If the format-control string were obtained from the user, a malicious user could supply conversion specifiers that would be executed by System.out.printf, possibly causing a security breach.

null—the Default Initial Value for *String* Variables

The first line of the output shows the name "null." Unlike local variables, which are *not* automatically initialized, every instance variable has a **default initial value**—a value provided by Java when you do not specify the instance variable's initial value. Thus, instance variables are not required to be explicitly initialized before they're used in a program—unless they must be initialized to values other than their default values. The default value for an instance variable of type String (like name in this example) is null, which we discuss further in Section 3.3 when we consider reference types.

Calling Class *Account*'s *setName* Method

Line 21 calls myAccounts's setName method. A method call can supply arguments whose values are assigned to the corresponding method parameters. In this case, the value of main's local variable theName in parentheses is the argument that's passed to setName so that the method can perform its task. When setName is called:

1. The app transfers program execution from line 21 in main to setName method's declaration (lines 10–13 of Fig. 3.1), and the argument value in the call's parentheses (theName) is assigned to the corresponding parameter (name) in the method header (line 10 of Fig. 3.1). Because setName was called via the myAccount object, setName "knows" which object's instance variable to manipulate.

2. Next, method setName performs its task—that is, it assigns the name parameter's value to instance variable name (line 12 of Fig. 3.1).

3. When program execution reaches setName's closing right brace, it returns to where setName was called (line 21 of Fig. 3.2), then continues at line 22.

The number of arguments in a method call must match the number of parameters in the method declaration's parameter list. Also, the argument types in the method call must be consistent with the types of the corresponding parameters in the method's declaration. (As you'll see in Chapter 6, an argument's type and its corresponding parameter's type are *not* required to be identical.) In our example, the method call passes one argument of type String (theName)—and the method declaration specifies one parameter of type String (name, declared in line 10 of Fig. 3.1). So in this example, the type of the argument in the method call exactly matches the type of the parameter in the method header.

Displaying the Name That Was Entered by the User
Line 22 of Fig. 3.2 outputs a blank line. When the second call to method getName (line 26) executes, the name entered by the user in line 20 is displayed. When the statement at lines 25–26 completes execution, the end of method main is reached, so the program terminates.

3.2.3 Compiling and Executing an App with Multiple Classes

You must compile the classes in Figs. 3.1 and 3.2 before you can execute the app. This is the first time you've created an app with multiple classes. Class AccountTest has a main method; class Account does not. To compile this app, first change to the directory that contains the app's source-code files. Next, type the command

```
javac Account.java AccountTest.java
```

to compile both classes at once. If the directory containing the app includes *only* this app's files, you can compile both classes with the command

```
javac *.java
```

The asterisk (*) in *.java indicates that all files in the current directory ending with the filename extension ".java" should be compiled. If both classes compile correctly—that is, no compilation errors are displayed—you can then run the app with the command

```
java AccountTest
```

3.2.4 Account UML Class Diagram with an Instance Variable and *set* and *get* Methods

We'll often use UML class diagrams to summarize a class's attributes and operations. In industry, UML diagrams help systems designers specify a system in a concise, graphical, programming-language-independent manner, before programmers implement the system in a specific programming language. Figure 3.3 presents a **UML class diagram** for class Account of Fig. 3.1.

Top Compartment
In the UML, each class is modeled in a class diagram as a rectangle with three compartments. In this diagram the top compartment contains the class name Account centered horizontally in boldface type.

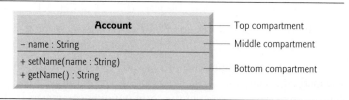

Fig. 3.3 | UML class diagram for class Account of Fig. 3.1.

Middle Compartment

The middle compartment contains the class's attribute name, which corresponds to the instance variable of the same name in Java. Instance variable name is private in Java, so the UML class diagram lists a minus sign (–) access modifier before the attribute name. Following the attribute name are a colon and the attribute type, in this case String.

Bottom Compartment

The bottom compartment contains the class's **operations**, setName and getName, which correspond to the methods of the same names in Java. The UML models operations by listing the operation name preceded by an access modifier, in this case + getName. This plus sign (+) indicates that getName is a public operation in the UML (because it's a public method in Java). Operation getName does not have any parameters, so the parentheses following the operation name in the class diagram are empty, just as they are in the method's declaration in line 16 of Fig. 3.1. Operation setName, also a public operation, has a String parameter called name.

Return Types

The UML indicates the return type of an operation by placing a colon and the return type after the parentheses following the operation name. Account method getName (Fig. 3.1) has a String return type. Method setName does not return a value (because it returns void in Java), so the UML class diagram does not specify a return type after the parentheses of this operation.

Parameters

The UML models a parameter a bit differently from Java by listing the parameter name, followed by a colon and the parameter type in the parentheses after the operation name. The UML has its own data types similar to those of Java, but for simplicity, we'll use the Java data types. Account method setName (Fig. 3.1) has a String parameter named name, so Fig. 3.3 lists name : String between the parentheses following the method name.

3.2.5 Additional Notes on Class AccountTest

static Method main

In Chapter 2, each class we declared had one method named main. Recall that main is a special method that's always called automatically by the Java Virtual Machine (JVM) when you execute an app. You must call most other methods explicitly to tell them to perform their tasks.

Lines 7–27 of Fig. 3.2 declare method main. A key part of enabling the JVM to locate and call method main to begin the app's execution is the static keyword (line 7), which indicates that main is a static method. A static method is special, because you can call it *without first creating an object of the class in which the method is declared*—in this case class AccountTest. We discuss static methods in detail in Chapter 6.

Notes on import Declarations

Notice the import declaration in Fig. 3.2 (line 3), which indicates to the compiler that the program uses class Scanner. As mentioned in Chapter 2, classes System and String are in package java.lang, which is *implicitly* imported into every Java program, so all programs can use that package's classes without explicitly importing them. Most other classes you'll use in Java programs must be imported explicitly.

There's a special relationship between classes that are compiled in the same directory, like classes Account and AccountTest. By default, such classes are considered to be in the same package—known as the **default package**. Classes in the same package are implicitly imported into the source-code files of other classes in that package. Thus, an import declaration is not required when one class in a package uses another in the same package— such as when class AccountTest uses class Account.

The import declaration in line 3 is *not* required if we refer to class Scanner throughout this file as java.util.Scanner, which includes the full package name and class name. This is known as the class's **fully qualified class name**. For example, line 10 of Fig. 3.2 also could be written as

```
java.util.Scanner input = new java.util.Scanner(System.in);
```

Software Engineering Observation 3.1

The Java compiler does not require import declarations in a Java source-code file if the fully qualified class name is specified every time a class name is used. Most Java programmers prefer the more concise programming style enabled by import declarations.

3.2.6 Software Engineering with private Instance Variables and public *set* and *get* Methods

As you'll see, through the use of *set* and *get* methods, you can *validate* attempted modifications to private data and control how that data is presented to the caller—these are compelling software engineering benefits. We'll discuss this in more detail in Section 3.5.

If the instance variable were public, any **client** of the class—that is, any other class that calls the class's methods—could see the data and do whatever it wanted with it, including setting it to an invalid value.

You might think that even though a client of the class cannot directly access a private instance variable, the client can do whatever it wants with the variable through public *set* and *get* methods. You would think that you could peek at the private data any time with the public *get* method and that you could modify the private data at will through the public *set* method. But *set* methods can be programmed to validate their arguments and reject any attempts to *set* the data to bad values, such as a negative body temperature, a day in March out of the range 1 through 31, a product code not in the company's product catalog, etc. And a *get* method can present the data in a different form. For example, a Grade class might store a grade as an int between 0 and 100, but a getGrade method might return a letter grade as a String, such as "A" for grades between 90 and 100, "B" for grades between 80 and 89, etc. Tightly controlling the access to and presentation of private data can greatly reduce errors, while increasing the robustness and security of your programs.

Declaring instance variables with access modifier private is known as *data hiding* or *information hiding*. When a program creates (instantiates) an object of class Account, variable name is *encapsulated* (hidden) in the object and can be accessed only by methods of the object's class.

Software Engineering Observation 3.2

Precede each instance variable and method declaration with an access modifier. Generally, instance variables should be declared `private` *and methods* `public`. *Later in the book, we'll discuss why you might want to declare a method* `private`.

*Conceptual View of an **Account** Object with Encapsulated Data*
You can think of an `Account` object as shown in Fig. 3.4. The `private` instance variable name is *hidden* inside the object (represented by the inner circle containing name) and *protected* by an outer layer of `public` methods (represented by the outer circle containing get-Name and setName). Any client code that needs to interact with the `Account` object can do so *only* by calling the `public` methods of the protective outer layer.

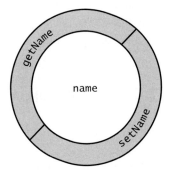

Fig. 3.4 | Conceptual view of an `Account` object with its encapsulated `private` instance variable name and protective layer of `public` methods.

3.3 Primitive Types vs. Reference Types

Java's types are divided into primitive types and **reference types**. In Chapter 2, you worked with variables of type `int`—one of the primitive types. The other primitive types are `boolean`, `byte`, `char`, `short`, `long`, `float` and `double`, each of which we discuss in this book—these are summarized in Appendix D. All nonprimitive types are reference types, so classes, which specify the types of objects, are reference types.

A primitive-type variable can hold exactly *one* value of its declared type at a time. For example, an `int` variable can store one integer at a time. When another value is assigned to that variable, the new value replaces the previous one—which is *lost*.

Recall that local variables are *not* initialized by default. Primitive-type instance variables *are* initialized by default—instance variables of types `byte`, `char`, `short`, `int`, `long`, `float` and `double` are initialized to 0, and variables of type `boolean` are initialized to `false`. You can specify your own initial value for a primitive-type variable by assigning the variable a value in its declaration, as in

```
private int numberOfStudents = 10;
```

Programs use variables of reference types (normally called **references**) to store the *addresses* of objects in the computer's memory. Such a variable is said to **refer to an object** in the program. *Objects* that are referenced may each contain *many* instance variables. Line 10 of Fig. 3.2:

```
Scanner input = new Scanner(System.in);
```

creates an object of class `Scanner`, then assigns to the variable `input` a *reference* to that Scanner object. Line 13 of Fig. 3.2:

```
Account myAccount = new Account();
```

creates an object of class `Account`, then assigns to the variable `myAccount` a *reference* to that Account object. *Reference-type instance variables, if not explicitly initialized, are initialized by default to the value `null`*—which represents a "reference to nothing." That's why the first call to `getName` in line 16 of Fig. 3.2 returns `null`—the value of name has *not* yet been set, so the *default initial value* `null` is returned.

To call methods on an object, you need a reference to the object. In Fig. 3.2, the statements in method `main` use the variable `myAccount` to call methods `getName` (lines 16 and 26) and `setName` (line 21) to interact with the `Account` object. Primitive-type variables do *not* refer to objects, so such variables *cannot* be used to call methods.

3.4 Account Class: Initializing Objects with Constructors

As mentioned in Section 3.2, when an object of class `Account` (Fig. 3.1) is created, its `String` instance variable name is initialized to `null` by *default*. But what if you want to provide a name when you *create* an `Account` object?

Each class you declare can optionally provide a *constructor* with parameters that can be used to initialize an object of a class when the object is created. Java *requires* a constructor call for *every* object that's created, so this is the ideal point to initialize an object's instance variables. The next example enhances class `Account` (Fig. 3.5) with a constructor that can receive a name and use it to initialize instance variable `name` when an `Account` object is created (Fig. 3.6).

3.4.1 Declaring an Account Constructor for Custom Object Initialization

When you declare a class, you can provide your own constructor to specify *custom initialization* for objects of your class. For example, you might want to specify a name for an Account object when the object is created, as in line 10 of Fig. 3.6:

```
Account account1 = new Account("Jane Green");
```

In this case, the `String` argument `"Jane Green"` is passed to the `Account` object's constructor and used to initialize the name instance variable. The preceding statement requires that the class provide a constructor that takes only a `String` parameter. Figure 3.5 contains a modified `Account` class with such a constructor.

```
1   // Fig. 3.5: Account.java
2   // Account class with a constructor that initializes the name.
3
```

Fig. 3.5 | Account class with a constructor that initializes the name. (Part 1 of 2.)

```
 4   public class Account
 5   {
 6      private String name; // instance variable
 7
 8      // constructor initializes name with parameter name
 9      public Account(String name) // constructor name is class name
10      {
11         this.name = name;
12      }
13
14      // method to set the name
15      public void setName(String name)
16      {
17         this.name = name;
18      }
19
20      // method to retrieve the name
21      public String getName()
22      {
23         return name;
24      }
25   } // end class Account
```

Fig. 3.5 | Account class with a constructor that initializes the name. (Part 2 of 2.)

Account Constructor Declaration

Lines 9–12 of Fig. 3.5 declare Account's constructor. A constructor *must* have the *same name* as the class. A constructor's *parameter list* specifies that the constructor requires one or more pieces of data to perform its task. Line 9 indicates that the constructor has a String parameter called name. When you create a new Account object (as you'll see in Fig. 3.6), you'll pass a person's name to the constructor, which will receive that name in the parameter name. The constructor will then assign name to *instance variable* name in line 11.

Error-Prevention Tip 3.2

Even though it's possible to do so, do not call methods from constructors. We'll explain this in Chapter 10, Object-Oriented Programming: Polymorphism and Interfaces.

Parameter name of Class Account's Constructor and Method setName

Recall from Section 3.2.1 that method parameters are local variables. In Fig. 3.5, the constructor and method setName both have a parameter called name. Although these parameters have the same identifier (name), the parameter in line 9 is a local variable of the constructor that's *not* visible to method setName, and the one in line 15 is a local variable of setName that's *not* visible to the constructor.

3.4.2 Class AccountTest: Initializing Account Objects When They're Created

The AccountTest program (Fig. 3.6) initializes two Account objects using the constructor. Line 10 creates and initializes the Account object account1. Keyword new requests memory from the system to store the Account object, then implicitly calls the class's constructor to *initialize* the object. The call is indicated by the parentheses after the class name, which contain the *argument* "Jane Green" that's used to initialize the new object's name. The class instance creation expression in line 10 returns a *reference* to the new object, which is assigned to the variable account1. Line 11 repeats this process, passing the argument "John Blue" to initialize the name for account2. Lines 14–15 use each object's getName method to obtain the names and show that they were indeed initialized when the objects were *created*. The output shows *different* names, confirming that each Account maintains its *own copy* of instance variable name.

```
 1   // Fig. 3.6: AccountTest.java
 2   // Using the Account constructor to initialize the name instance
 3   // variable at the time each Account object is created.
 4
 5   public class AccountTest
 6   {
 7      public static void main(String[] args)
 8      {
 9         // create two Account objects
10         Account account1 = new Account("Jane Green");
11         Account account2 = new Account("John Blue");
12
13         // display initial value of name for each Account
14         System.out.printf("account1 name is: %s%n", account1.getName());
15         System.out.printf("account2 name is: %s%n", account2.getName());
16      }
17   } // end class AccountTest
```

```
account1 name is: Jane Green
account2 name is: John Blue
```

Fig. 3.6 | Using the Account constructor to initialize the name instance variable at the time each Account object is created.

Constructors Cannot Return Values

An important difference between constructors and methods is that *constructors cannot return values*, so they *cannot* specify a return type (not even void). Normally, constructors are declared public—later in the book we'll explain when to use private constructors.

Default Constructor

Recall that line 13 of Fig. 3.2

```
      Account myAccount = new Account();
```

used new to create an Account object. The *empty* parentheses after "new Account" indicate a call to the class's **default constructor**—in any class that does *not* explicitly declare a constructor, the compiler provides a default constructor (which always has no parameters). When a class has only the default constructor, the class's instance variables are initialized to their *default values*. In Section 8.5, you'll learn that classes can have multiple constructors.

There's No Default Constructor in a Class That Declares a Constructor
If you declare a constructor for a class, the compiler will *not* create a *default constructor* for that class. In that case, you will not be able to create an Account object with the class instance creation expression new Account() as we did in Fig. 3.2—unless the custom constructor you declare takes *no* parameters.

> **Software Engineering Observation 3.3**
>
> *Unless default initialization of your class's instance variables is acceptable, provide a custom constructor to ensure that your instance variables are properly initialized with meaningful values when each new object of your class is created.*

*Adding the Constructor to Class **Account**'s UML Class Diagram*
The UML class diagram of Fig. 3.7 models class Account of Fig. 3.5, which has a constructor with a String name parameter. Like operations, the UML models constructors in the *third* compartment of a class diagram. To distinguish a constructor from the class's operations, the UML requires that the word "constructor" be enclosed in **guillemets (« and »)** and placed before the constructor's name. It's customary to list constructors *before* other operations in the third compartment.

Account
– name : String
«constructor» Account(name: String) + setName(name: String) + getName() : String

Fig. 3.7 | UML class diagram for Account class of Fig. 3.5.

3.5 Account Class with a Balance; Floating-Point Numbers

We now declare an Account class that maintains the *balance* of a bank account in addition to the name. Most account balances are not integers. So, class Account represents the account balance as a **floating-point number**—a number with a *decimal point*, such as 43.95, 0.0, –129.8873. [In Chapter 8, we'll begin representing monetary amounts precisely with class BigDecimal as you should do when writing industrial-strength monetary applications.]

Java provides two primitive types for storing floating-point numbers in memory—float and double. Variables of type **float** represent **single-precision floating-point numbers** and can hold up to *seven significant digits*. Variables of type **double** represent **double-precision floating-point numbers**. These require *twice* as much memory as float variables and can hold up to *15 significant digits*—about *double* the precision of float variables.

Most programmers represent floating-point numbers with type double. In fact, Java treats all floating-point numbers you type in a program's source code (such as 7.33 and 0.0975) as double values by default. Such values in the source code are known as **floating-point literals**. See Appendix D, Primitive Types, for the precise ranges of values for floats and doubles.

3.5.1 Account Class with a balance Instance Variable of Type double

Our next app contains a version of class Account (Fig. 3.8) that maintains as instance variables the name *and* the balance of a bank account. A typical bank services *many* accounts, each with its *own* balance, so line 8 declares an instance variable balance of type double. Every instance (i.e., object) of class Account contains its *own* copies of *both* the name and the balance.

```java
1   // Fig. 3.8: Account.java
2   // Account class with a double instance variable balance and a constructor
3   // and deposit method that perform validation.
4
5   public class Account
6   {
7      private String name; // instance variable
8      private double balance; // instance variable
9
10     // Account constructor that receives two parameters
11     public Account(String name, double balance)
12     {
13        this.name = name; // assign name to instance variable name
14
15        // validate that the balance is greater than 0.0; if it's not,
16        // instance variable balance keeps its default initial value of 0.0
17        if (balance > 0.0) // if the balance is valid
18           this.balance = balance; // assign it to instance variable balance
19     }
20
21     // method that deposits (adds) only a valid amount to the balance
22     public void deposit(double depositAmount)
23     {
24        if (depositAmount > 0.0) // if the depositAmount is valid
25           balance = balance + depositAmount; // add it to the balance
26     }
27
28     // method returns the account balance
29     public double getBalance()
30     {
31        return balance;
32     }
33
34     // method that sets the name
35     public void setName(String name)
36     {
37        this.name = name;
38     }
39
40     // method that returns the name
41     public String getName()
42     {
```

Fig. 3.8 | Account class with a double instance variable balance and a constructor and deposit method that perform validation. (Part 1 of 2.)

```
43          return name; // give value of name back to caller
44      } // end method getName
45  } // end class Account
```

Fig. 3.8 | Account class with a `double` instance variable `balance` and a constructor and `deposit` method that perform validation. (Part 2 of 2.)

Account Class Two-Parameter Constructor

The class has a *constructor* and four *methods*. It's common for someone opening an account to deposit money immediately, so the constructor (lines 11–19) now receives a second parameter—`initialBalance` of type `double` that represents the *starting balance*. Lines 17–18 ensure that `initialBalance` is greater than 0.0. If so, `initialBalance`'s value is assigned to instance variable `balance`. Otherwise, `balance` remains at 0.0—its *default initial value*.

Account Class `deposit` Method

Method `deposit` (lines 22–26) does *not* return any data when it completes its task, so its return type is `void`. The method receives one parameter named `depositAmount`—a `double` value that's *added* to the `balance` *only* if the parameter value is *valid* (i.e., greater than zero). Line 25 first adds the current `balance` and `depositAmount`, forming a *temporary* sum which is *then* assigned to `balance`, *replacing* its prior value (recall that addition has a *higher* precedence than assignment). It's important to understand that the calculation on the right side of the assignment operator in line 25 does *not* modify the `balance`—that's why the assignment is necessary.

Account Class `getBalance` Method

Method `getBalance` (lines 29–32) allows *clients* of the class (i.e., other classes whose methods call the methods of this class) to obtain the value of a particular `Account` object's `balance`. The method specifies return type `double` and an *empty* parameter list.

Account's Methods Can All Use `balance`

Once again, the statements in lines 18, 25 and 31 use the variable `balance` even though it was *not* declared in *any* of the methods. We can use `balance` in these methods because it's an *instance variable* of the class.

3.5.2 AccountTest Class to Use Class Account

Class `AccountTest` (Fig. 3.9) creates two `Account` objects (lines 9–10) and initializes them with a *valid* balance of 50.00 and an *invalid* balance of -7.53, respectively—for the purpose of our examples, we assume that balances must be greater than or equal to zero. The calls to method `System.out.printf` in lines 13–16 output the account names and balances, which are obtained by calling each `Account`'s `getName` and `getBalance` methods.

```
1   // Fig. 3.9: AccountTest.java
2   // Inputting and outputting floating-point numbers with Account objects.
3   import java.util.Scanner;
```

Fig. 3.9 | Inputting and outputting floating-point numbers with `Account` objects. (Part 1 of 3.)

```
 4
 5   public class AccountTest
 6   {
 7      public static void main(String[] args)
 8      {
 9         Account account1 = new Account("Jane Green", 50.00);
10         Account account2 = new Account("John Blue", -7.53);
11
12         // display initial balance of each object
13         System.out.printf("%s balance: $%.2f%n",
14            account1.getName(), account1.getBalance());
15         System.out.printf("%s balance: $%.2f%n%n",
16            account2.getName(), account2.getBalance());
17
18         // create a Scanner to obtain input from the command window
19         Scanner input = new Scanner(System.in);
20
21         System.out.print("Enter deposit amount for account1: "); // prompt
22         double depositAmount = input.nextDouble(); // obtain user input
23         System.out.printf("%nadding %.2f to account1 balance%n%n",
24            depositAmount);
25         account1.deposit(depositAmount); // add to account1's balance
26
27         // display balances
28         System.out.printf("%s balance: $%.2f%n",
29            account1.getName(), account1.getBalance());
30         System.out.printf("%s balance: $%.2f%n%n",
31            account2.getName(), account2.getBalance());
32
33         System.out.print("Enter deposit amount for account2: "); // prompt
34         depositAmount = input.nextDouble(); // obtain user input
35         System.out.printf("%nadding %.2f to account2 balance%n%n",
36            depositAmount);
37         account2.deposit(depositAmount); // add to account2 balance
38
39         // display balances
40         System.out.printf("%s balance: $%.2f%n",
41            account1.getName(), account1.getBalance());
42         System.out.printf("%s balance: $%.2f%n%n",
43            account2.getName(), account2.getBalance());
44      } // end main
45   } // end class AccountTest
```

```
Jane Green balance: $50.00
John Blue balance: $0.00

Enter deposit amount for account1: 25.53

adding 25.53 to account1 balance

Jane Green balance: $75.53
John Blue balance: $0.00
```

Fig. 3.9 | Inputting and outputting floating-point numbers with Account objects. (Part 2 of 3.)

```
Enter deposit amount for account2: 123.45

adding 123.45 to account2 balance

Jane Green balance: $75.53
John Blue balance: $123.45
```

Fig. 3.9 | Inputting and outputting floating-point numbers with Account objects. (Part 3 of 3.)

Displaying the Account Objects' Initial Balances

When method getBalance is called for account1 from line 14, the value of account1's balance is returned from line 31 of Fig. 3.8 and displayed by the System.out.printf statement (Fig. 3.9, lines 13–14). Similarly, when method getBalance is called for account2 from line 16, the value of the account2's balance is returned from line 31 of Fig. 3.8 and displayed by the System.out.printf statement (Fig. 3.9, lines 15–16). The balance of account2 is initially 0.00, because the constructor rejected the attempt to start account2 with a *negative* balance, so the balance retains its default initial value.

Formatting Floating-Point Numbers for Display

Each of the balances is output by printf with the format specifier %.2f. The **%f format specifier** is used to output values of type float or double. The .2 between % and f represents the number of decimal places (2) that should be output to the right of the decimal point in the floating-point number—also known as the number's **precision**. Any floating-point value output with %.2f will be rounded to the hundredths *position*—for example, 123.457 would be rounded to 123.46 and 27.33379 would be rounded to 27.33.

Reading a Floating-Point Value from the User and Making a Deposit

Line 21 (Fig. 3.9) prompts the user to enter a deposit amount for account1. Line 22 declares local variable depositAmount to store each deposit amount entered by the user. Unlike instance variables (such as name and balance in class Account), local variables (like depositAmount in main) are not initialized by default, so they normally must be initialized explicitly. As you'll learn momentarily, variable depositAmount's initial value will be determined by the user's input.

Common Programming Error 3.1

The Java compiler will issue a compilation error if you attempt to use the value of an uninitialized local variable. This helps you avoid dangerous execution-time logic errors. It's always better to get the errors out of your programs at compilation time rather than execution time.

Line 22 obtains the input from the user by calling Scanner object input's **nextDouble** method, which returns a double value entered by the user. Lines 23–24 display the depositAmount. Line 25 calls object account1's deposit method with the depositAmount as the method's argument. When the method is called, the argument's value is assigned to the parameter depositAmount of method deposit (line 22 of Fig. 3.8); then method deposit adds that value to the balance. Lines 28–31 (Fig. 3.9) output the names and balances of both Accounts again to show that *only* account1's balance has changed.

Line 33 prompts the user to enter a deposit amount for account2. Line 34 obtains the input from the user by calling Scanner object input's nextDouble method. Lines 35–36 display the depositAmount. Line 37 calls object account2's deposit method with depositAmount as the method's argument; then method deposit adds that value to the balance. Finally, lines 40–43 output the names and balances of both Accounts again to show that only account2's balance has changed.

UML Class Diagram for Class **Account**

The UML class diagram in Fig. 3.10 concisely models class Account of Fig. 3.8. The diagram models in its second compartment the private attributes name of type String and balance of type double.

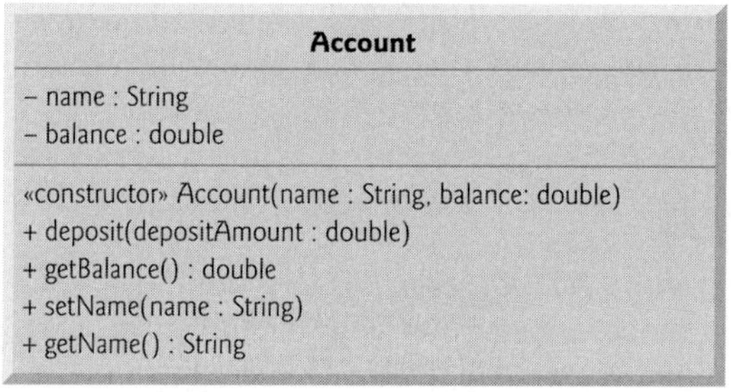

Fig. 3.10 | UML class diagram for Account class of Fig. 3.8.

Class Account's constructor is modeled in the third compartment with parameters name of type String and initialBalance of type double. The class's four public methods also are modeled in the *third* compartment—operation deposit with a depositAmount parameter of type double, operation getBalance with a return type of double, operation setName with a name parameter of type String and operation getName with a return type of String.

3.6 Wrap-Up

In this chapter, you learned how to create your own Java classes and methods, create objects of those classes and call methods of those objects to perform useful actions. You declared instance variables of a class to maintain data for each object of the class, and you declared your own methods to operate on that data. You called methods and passed information to them as arguments whose values are assigned to the method's parameters. You learned the difference between a local variable of a method and an instance variable of a class, and that only instance variables are initialized automatically. You also learned how to use a class's constructor to specify the initial values for an object's instance variables. You saw how to create UML class diagrams that model the methods, attributes and constructors of classes. Finally, you learned about floating-point numbers (numbers with decimal points)—how to store them with variables of primitive type double, how to input them with a Scanner object and how to format them with printf and format specifier %f for display purposes. [In Chapter 8, we'll begin representing monetary amounts precisely with class BigDecimal.] In the next chapter we discuss control statements, which specify the order in which a program's actions are performed.

4

Control Statements: Part 1; Assignment, ++ and -- Operators

Objectives

In this chapter you'll:

- Use the `if` and `if...else` selection statements to choose between alternative actions.

- Use nested `if...else` selection statements.

- Use the `while` repetition statement to execute statements in a program repeatedly.

- Use counter-controlled repetition and sentinel-controlled repetition.

- Use the compound assignment operators, and the increment and decrement operators.

- Learn about the portability of primitive data types.

4.1 Introduction

In this chapter, we discuss Java's if statement in additional detail, and introduce the if...else and while statements—all of these building blocks help you to specify the logic required for methods to perform their tasks. We stack and nest these building blocks. We examine counter-controlled repetition and sentinel-controlled repetition. We introduce the compound assignment operators and the increment and decrement operators. Finally, we consider the portability of Java's primitive types.

4.2 Control Structures

During the 1960s, it became clear that the indiscriminate use of transfers of control was the root of much difficulty experienced by software development groups. The blame was pointed at the **goto statement** (used in most programming languages of the time), which allows you to specify a transfer of control to one of a wide range of destinations in a program. The term **structured programming** became almost synonymous with "goto elimination." [*Note:* Java does *not* have a goto statement; however, the word goto is *reserved* by Java and should *not* be used as an identifier in programs.]

Bohm and Jacopini's work demonstrated that all programs could be written in terms of only three control structures—the **sequence structure**, the **selection structure** and the **repetition structure**.[1] When we introduce Java's control-structure implementations, we'll refer to them in the terminology of the *Java Language Specification* as "control statements."

Sequence Structure in Java
The sequence structure is built into Java. Unless directed otherwise, the computer executes Java statements one after the other in the order in which they're written—that is, in sequence. The **activity diagram** in Fig. 4.1 illustrates a typical sequence structure in which two calculations are performed in order. Java lets you have as many actions as you want in a sequence structure. As we'll soon see, anywhere a single action may be placed, we may place several actions in sequence.

A UML activity diagram models the **workflow** (also called the **activity**) of a portion of a software system. Such workflows may include a portion of an algorithm, like the

---

1.   C. Bohm, and G. Jacopini, "Flow Diagrams, Turing Machines, and Languages with Only Two Formation Rules," *Communications of the ACM*, Vol. 9, No. 5, May 1966, pp. 336–371.

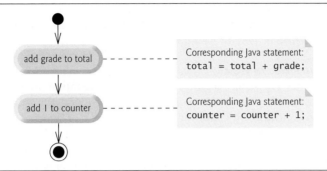

Fig. 4.1 │ Sequence-structure activity diagram.

sequence structure in Fig. 4.1. Activity diagrams are composed of symbols, such as **action-state symbols** (rectangles with their left and right sides replaced with outward arcs), **diamonds** and **small circles**. These symbols are connected by **transition arrows**, which represent the *flow of the activity*—that is, the *order* in which the actions should occur.

Activity diagrams help you develop and represent algorithms—they clearly show how control structures operate. We use the UML in this chapter and Chapter 5 to show control flow in control statements. Chapters 23–24 use the UML in a real-world automated-teller-machine object-oriented design case study.

Consider the sequence-structure activity diagram in Fig. 4.1. It contains two **action states**, each containing an **action expression**—for example, "add grade to total" or "add 1 to counter"—that specifies a particular action to perform. Other actions might include calculations or input/output operations. The arrows in the activity diagram represent **transitions**, which indicate the *order* in which the actions represented by the action states occur. The program that implements the activities illustrated by the diagram in Fig. 4.1 first adds `grade` to `total`, then adds `1` to `counter`.

The **solid circle** at the top of the activity diagram represents the **initial state**—the beginning of the workflow before the program performs the modeled actions. The **solid circle surrounded by a hollow circle** at the bottom of the diagram represents the **final state**—the *end* of the workflow *after* the program performs its actions.

Figure 4.1 also includes rectangles with the upper-right corners folded over. These are UML **notes** (like comments in Java)—explanatory remarks that describe the purpose of symbols in the diagram. Figure 4.1 uses UML notes to show the Java code associated with each action state. A **dotted line** connects each note with the element it describes. Activity diagrams normally do *not* show the Java code that implements the activity. We do this here to illustrate how the diagram relates to Java code.

Selection Statements in Java

Java has three types of **selection statements** (discussed in this chapter and Chapter 5). The `if` *statement* either performs (selects) an action, if a condition is *true*, or skips it, if the condition is *false*. The `if...else` *statement* performs an action if a condition is *true* and performs a different action if the condition is *false*. The `switch` *statement* (Chapter 5) performs one of *many* different actions, depending on the value of an expression.

The `if` statement is a **single-selection statement** because it selects or ignores a *single* action (or, as we'll soon see, a *single group of actions*). The `if...else` statement is called a

double-selection statement because it selects between *two different actions* (or *groups of actions*). The switch statement is called a **multiple-selection statement** because it selects among *many different actions* (or *groups of actions*).

Repetition Statements in Java
Java provides three **repetition statements** (also called **iteration statements** or **looping statements**) that enable programs to perform statements repeatedly as long as a condition (called the **loop-continuation condition**) remains *true*. The repetition statements are the while, do...while and for statements (and a variation called enhanced for). Chapter 5 presents the do...while and for statements and Chapter 7 presents the enhanced for statement. The while and for statements perform the action (or group of actions) in their bodies zero or more times—if the loop-continuation condition is initially *false*, the action (or group of actions) will *not* execute. The do...while statement performs the action (or group of actions) in its body *one or more* times. The words if, else, switch, while, do and for are Java keywords. A complete list of Java keywords appears in Appendix C.

Summary of Control Statements in Java
Java has only three kinds of control statements: the *sequence statement*, *selection statements* (three types) and *repetition statements* (three types). Every program is formed by combining as many of these statements as is appropriate for the algorithm the program implements. We can model each control statement as an activity diagram. Like Fig. 4.1, each diagram contains an initial state and a final state that represent a control statement's entry point and exit point, respectively. **Single-entry/single-exit control statements** make it easy to build programs—we simply connect the exit point of one to the entry point of the next. We call this **control-statement stacking**. The only other way in which control statements may be connected is **control-statement nesting**—which occurs when one control statement appears inside another. Thus, algorithms in Java programs are constructed from only three kinds of control statements, combined in only two ways. This is the essence of simplicity.

4.3 if Single-Selection Statement

Programs use selection statements to choose among alternative courses of action. For example, suppose that the passing grade on an exam is 60. The statement

```
if (studentGrade >= 60)
    System.out.println("Passed");
```

determines whether the condition studentGrade >= 60 is true. If so, "Passed" is printed, and the next statement in order is performed. If the condition is false, the printing statement is ignored, and the next statement in order is performed. The indentation of the second line of this selection statement is optional, but recommended, because it emphasizes the inherent structure of structured programs.

UML Activity Diagram for an if Statement
Figure 4.2 illustrates the single-selection if statement. This figure contains the most important symbol in an activity diagram—the *diamond*, or **decision symbol**, which indicates that a *decision* is to be made. The workflow continues along a path determined by the symbol's associated **guard conditions**, which can be true or false. Each transition arrow emerg-

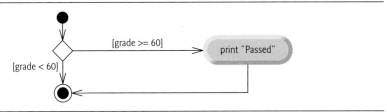

Fig. 4.2 | if single-selection statement UML activity diagram.

ing from a decision symbol has a guard condition specified in square brackets next to the arrow. If a guard condition is true, the workflow enters the action state to which the transition arrow points. In Fig. 4.2, if the grade is greater than or equal to 60, the program prints "Passed," then transitions to the activity's final state. If the grade is less than 60, the program immediately transitions to the final state without displaying a message.

The if statement is a single-entry/single-exit control statement. We'll see that the activity diagrams for the remaining control statements also contain initial states, transition arrows, action states that indicate actions to perform, decision symbols (with associated guard conditions) that indicate decisions to be made, and final states.

4.4 if...else Double-Selection Statement

The if single-selection statement performs an indicated action only when the condition is true; otherwise, the action is skipped. The **if...else double-selection statement** allows you to specify an action to perform when the condition is true and another action when the condition is false. For example, the statement

```
if (grade >= 60)
    System.out.println("Passed");
else
    System.out.println("Failed");
```

prints "Passed" if the student's grade is greater than or equal to 60, but prints "Failed" if it's less than 60. In either case, after printing occurs, the next statement in sequence is performed. The body of the else is also indented. Whatever indentation convention you choose should be applied consistently throughout your programs.

Good Programming Practice 4.1
Indent both body statements of an if...else statement. Many IDEs do this for you.

Good Programming Practice 4.2
If there are several levels of indentation, indent each level the same amount of space.

UML Activity Diagram for an **if...else** *Statement*
Figure 4.3 illustrates the flow of control in the if...else statement. Once again, the symbols in the UML activity diagram (besides the initial state, transition arrows and final state) represent action states and decisions.

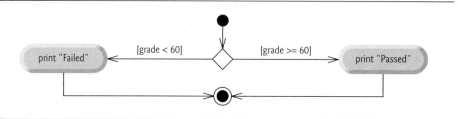

Fig. 4.3 | if...else double-selection statement UML activity diagram.

Nested *if...else Statements*

A program can test multiple cases by placing if...else statements inside other if...else statements to create **nested if...else statements**. For example, the following if...else statement prints A for exam grades greater than or equal to 90, B for grades 80 to 89, C for grades 70 to 79, D for grades 60 to 69 and F for all other grades:

```
if (studentGrade >= 90)
    System.out.println("A");
else
    if (studentGrade >= 80)
        System.out.println("B");
    else
        if (studentGrade >= 70)
            System.out.println("C");
        else
            if (studentGrade >= 60)
                System.out.println("D");
            else
                System.out.println("F");
```

 Error-Prevention Tip 4.1

In a nested if...else statement, ensure that you test for all possible cases.

If variable studentGrade is greater than or equal to 90, the first four conditions in the nested if...else statement will be true, but only the statement in the if part of the first if...else statement will execute. After that statement executes, the else part of the "outermost" if...else statement is skipped. Many programmers prefer to write the preceding nested if...else statement as

```
if (studentGrade >= 90)
    System.out.println("A");
else if (studentGrade >= 80)
    System.out.println("B");
else if (studentGrade >= 70)
    System.out.println("C");
else if (studentGrade >= 60)
    System.out.println("D");
else
    System.out.println("F");
```

The two forms are identical except for the spacing and indentation, which the compiler ignores. The latter form avoids deep indentation of the code to the right. Such indentation often leaves little room on a line of source code, forcing lines to be split.

Dangling-else Problem

The Java compiler always associates an else with the immediately preceding if unless told to do otherwise by the placement of braces ({ and }). This behavior can lead to what is referred to as the **dangling-else problem**. For example,

```
if (x > 5)
    if (y > 5)
        System.out.println("x and y are > 5");
else
    System.out.println("x is <= 5");
```

appears to indicate that if x is greater than 5, the nested if statement determines whether y is also greater than 5. If so, the string "x and y are > 5" is output. Otherwise, it appears that if x is not greater than 5, the else part of the if...else outputs the string "x is <= 5". Beware! This nested if...else statement does *not* execute as it appears. The compiler actually interprets the statement as

```
if (x > 5)
    if (y > 5)
        System.out.println("x and y are > 5");
    else
        System.out.println("x is <= 5");
```

in which the body of the first if is a *nested* if...else. The outer if statement tests whether x is greater than 5. If so, execution continues by testing whether y is also greater than 5. If the second condition is *true*, the proper string—"x and y are > 5"—is displayed. However, if the second condition is *false*, the string "x is <= 5" is displayed, even though we know that x is greater than 5. Equally bad, if the outer if statement's condition is false, the inner if...else is skipped and nothing is displayed.

To force the nested if...else statement to execute as it was originally intended, we must write it as follows:

```
if (x > 5)
{
    if (y > 5)
        System.out.println("x and y are > 5");
}
else
    System.out.println("x is <= 5");
```

The braces indicate that the second if is in the body of the first and that the else is associated with the *first* if.

Blocks

The if statement normally expects only one statement in its body. To include several statements in the body of an if (or the body of an else for an if...else statement), enclose the statements in braces. Statements contained in a pair of braces (such as the body of a method) form a **block**. A block can be placed anywhere in a method that a single statement can be placed.

The following example includes a block in the `else` part of an `if...else` statement:

```
if (grade >= 60)
    System.out.println("Passed");
else
{
    System.out.println("Failed");
    System.out.println("You must take this course again.");
}
```

In this case, if `grade` is less than 60, the program executes *both* statements in the body of the `else` and prints

```
Failed
You must take this course again.
```

Note the braces surrounding the two statements in the `else` clause. These braces are important. Without the braces, the statement

```
System.out.println("You must take this course again.");
```

would be outside the body of the `else` part of the `if...else` statement and would execute *regardless* of whether the grade was less than 60.

Just as a block can be placed anywhere a single statement can be placed, it's also possible to have an empty statement. Recall from Section 2.7 that the empty statement is represented by placing a semicolon (;) where a statement would normally be.

Common Programming Error 4.1

Placing a semicolon after the condition in an `if` or `if...else` statement leads to a logic error in single-selection `if` statements and a syntax error in double-selection `if...else` statements (when the `if`-part contains an actual body statement).

Conditional Operator (?:)

Java provides the **conditional operator (?:)** that can be used in place of an `if...else` statement. This can make your code shorter and clearer. The conditional operator is Java's only **ternary operator** (i.e., an operator that takes *three* operands). Together, the operands and the `?:` symbol form a **conditional expression**. The first operand (to the left of the `?`) is a **boolean expression** (i.e., a *condition* that evaluates to a `boolean` value—**true** or **false**), the second operand (between the `?` and `:`) is the value of the conditional expression if the `boolean` expression is `true` and the third operand (to the right of the `:`) is the value of the conditional expression if the `boolean` expression evaluates to `false`. For example, the statement

```
System.out.println(studentGrade >= 60 ? "Passed" : "Failed");
```

prints the value of `println`'s conditional-expression argument. The conditional expression in this statement evaluates to the string `"Passed"` if the `boolean` expression `student-Grade >= 60` is true and to the string `"Failed"` if it's false. Thus, this statement with the conditional operator performs essentially the same function as the `if...else` statement shown earlier in this section. The precedence of the conditional operator is low, so the entire conditional expression is normally placed in parentheses. We'll see that conditional expressions can be used in some situations where `if...else` statements cannot.

Error-Prevention Tip 4.2

Use expressions of the same type for the second and third operands of the ?: operator to avoid subtle errors.

4.5 Student Class: Nested if...else Statements

The example of Figs. 4.4–4.5 demonstrates a nested if...else statement that determines a student's letter grade based on the student's average in a course.

Class Student

Class Student (Fig. 4.4) has features similar to those of class Account (discussed in Chapter 3). Class Student stores a student's name and average and provides methods for manipulating these values. The class contains:

- instance variable name of type String (line 5) to store a Student's name

- instance variable average of type double (line 6) to store a Student's average in a course

- a constructor (lines 9–18) that initializes the name and average—in Section 5.9, you'll express lines 15–16 and 37–38 more concisely with logical operators that can test multiple conditions

- methods setName and getName (lines 21–30) to *set* and *get* the Student's name

- methods setAverage and getAverage (lines 33–46) to *set* and *get* the Student's average

- method getLetterGrade (lines 49–65), which uses *nested if...else statements* to determine the Student's *letter grade* based on the Student's average

The constructor and method setAverage each use *nested if statements* (lines 15–17 and 37–39) to *validate* the value used to set the average—these statements ensure that the value is greater than 0.0 *and* less than or equal to 100.0; otherwise, average's value is left *unchanged*. Each if statement contains a *simple* condition. If the condition in line 15 is *true*, only then will the condition in line 16 be tested, and *only* if the conditions in both line 15 *and* line 16 are *true* will the statement in line 17 execute.

Software Engineering Observation 4.1

Recall from Chapter 3 that you should not call methods from constructors (we'll explain why in Chapter 10, Object-Oriented Programming: Polymorphism and Interfaces). For this reason, there is duplicated validation code in lines 15–17 and 37–39 of Fig. 4.4 and in subsequent examples.

```
1   // Fig. 4.4: Student.java
2   // Student class that stores a student name and average.
3   public class Student
4   {
5      private String name;
6      private double average;
```

Fig. 4.4 | Student class that stores a student name and average. (Part 1 of 3.)

```
7
8      // constructor initializes instance variables
9      public Student(String name, double average)
10     {
11        this.name = name;
12
13        // validate that average is > 0.0 and <= 100.0; otherwise,
14        // keep instance variable average's default value (0.0)
15        if (average > 0.0)
16           if (average <= 100.0)
17              this.average = average; // assign to instance variable
18     }
19
20     // sets the Student's name
21     public void setName(String name)
22     {
23        this.name = name;
24     }
25
26     // retrieves the Student's name
27     public String getName()
28     {
29        return name;
30     }
31
32     // sets the Student's average
33     public void setAverage(double studentAverage)
34     {
35        // validate that average is > 0.0 and <= 100.0; otherwise,
36        // keep instance variable average's current value
37        if (average > 0.0)
38           if (average <= 100.0)
39              this.average = average; // assign to instance variable
40     }
41
42     // retrieves the Student's average
43     public double getAverage()
44     {
45        return average;
46     }
47
48     // determines and returns the Student's letter grade
49     public String getLetterGrade()
50     {
51        String letterGrade = ""; // initialized to empty String
52
53        if (average >= 90.0)
54           letterGrade = "A";
55        else if (average >= 80.0)
56           letterGrade = "B";
57        else if (average >= 70.0)
58           letterGrade = "C";
```

Fig. 4.4 | Student class that stores a student name and average. (Part 2 of 3.)

```
59              else if (average >= 60.0)
60                  letterGrade = "D";
61              else
62                  letterGrade = "F";
63
64              return letterGrade;
65          }
66      } // end class Student
```

Fig. 4.4 | Student class that stores a student name and average. (Part 3 of 3.)

Class StudentTest
To demonstrate the nested if...else statements in class Student's getLetterGrade method, class StudentTest's main method (Fig. 4.5) creates two Student objects (lines 7–8). Next, lines 10–13 display each Student's name and letter grade by calling the objects' getName and getLetterGrade methods, respectively.

```
 1      // Fig. 4.5: StudentTest.java
 2      // Create and test Student objects.
 3      public class StudentTest
 4      {
 5          public static void main(String[] args)
 6          {
 7              Student account1 = new Student("Jane Green", 93.5);
 8              Student account2 = new Student("John Blue", 72.75);
 9
10              System.out.printf("%s's letter grade is: %s%n",
11                  account1.getName(), account1.getLetterGrade());
12              System.out.printf("%s's letter grade is: %s%n",
13                  account2.getName(), account2.getLetterGrade());
14          }
15      } // end class StudentTest
```

```
Jane Green's letter grade is: A
John Blue's letter grade is: C
```

Fig. 4.5 | Create and test Student objects.

4.6 while Repetition Statement

A repetition statement allows you to specify that a program should repeat an action while some condition remains *true*. As an example of Java's **while repetition statement**, consider a program segment that finds the first power of 3 larger than 100. Suppose that the int variable product is initialized to 3. After the following while statement executes, product contains the result:

```
while (product <= 100)
    product = 3 * product;
```

Each iteration of the while statement multiplies product by 3, so product takes on the values 9, 27, 81 and 243 successively. When product becomes 243, product <= 100 becomes false. This terminates the repetition, so the final value of product is 243. At this point, program execution continues with the next statement after the while statement.

> **Common Programming Error 4.2**
>
> *Not providing in the body of a while statement an action that eventually causes the con-dition in the while to become false normally results in an infinite loop.*

UML Activity Diagram for a *while* Statement

The UML activity diagram in Fig. 4.6 illustrates the flow of control in the preceding while statement. Once again, the symbols in the diagram (besides the initial state, transition arrows, a final state and three notes) represent an action state and a decision. This diagram introduces the UML's **merge symbol**. The UML represents both the merge symbol and the decision symbol as diamonds. The merge symbol joins two flows of activity into one. In this diagram, the merge symbol joins the transitions from the initial state and from the action state, so they both flow into the decision that determines whether the loop should begin (or continue) executing.

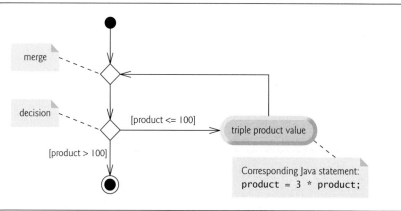

Fig. 4.6 | while repetition statement UML activity diagram.

The decision and merge symbols can be distinguished by the number of "incoming" and "outgoing" transition arrows. A decision symbol has one transition arrow pointing to the diamond and two or more pointing out from it to indicate possible transitions from that point. In addition, each transition arrow pointing out of a decision symbol has a guard condition next to it. A merge symbol has two or more transition arrows pointing to the diamond and only one pointing from the diamond, to indicate multiple activity flows merging to continue the activity. *None* of the transition arrows associated with a merge symbol has a guard condition.

Figure 4.6 clearly shows the repetition of the while statement discussed earlier in this section. The transition arrow emerging from the action state points back to the merge, from which program flow transitions back to the decision that's tested at the beginning of each iteration of the loop. The loop continues to execute until the guard condition product > 100 becomes true. Then the while statement exits (reaches its final state), and control passes to the next statement in sequence in the program.

4.7 Counter-Controlled Repetition

Consider the following problem statement:

> *A class of ten students took a quiz. The grades (integers in the range 0–100) for this quiz are available to you. Determine the class average on the quiz.*

The class average is equal to the sum of the grades divided by the number of students. The program for solving this problem must input each grade, keep track of the total of all the grades that are entered, perform the averaging calculation and print the result.

Program with Counter-Controlled Repetition

We use **counter-controlled repetition** to input the grades one at a time. This technique uses a variable called a **counter** (or **control variable**) to control the number of times a set of statements executes. In this example, repetition terminates when the counter exceeds 10.

Implementing Counter-Controlled Repetition

ClassAverage's main method (Fig. 4.7, lines 7–31) implements counter-controlled class-averaging—it allows the user to enter 10 grades, then calculates and displays the average.

```java
 1   // Fig. 4.7: ClassAverage.java
 2   // Solving the class-average problem using counter-controlled repetition.
 3   import java.util.Scanner; // program uses class Scanner
 4
 5   public class ClassAverage
 6   {
 7      public static void main(String[] args)
 8      {
 9         // create Scanner to obtain input from command window
10         Scanner input = new Scanner(System.in);
11
12         // initialization phase
13         int total = 0;   // initialize sum of grades entered by the user
14         int gradeCounter = 1; // initialize # of grade to be entered next
15
16         // processing phase uses counter-controlled repetition
17         while (gradeCounter <= 10) // loop 10 times
18         {
19            System.out.print("Enter grade: "); // prompt
20            int grade = input.nextInt(); // input next grade
21            total = total + grade; // add grade to total
22            gradeCounter = gradeCounter + 1; // increment counter by 1
23         }
24
25         // termination phase
26         int average = total / 10; // integer division yields integer result
27
28         // display total and average of grades
29         System.out.printf("%nTotal of all 10 grades is %d%n", total);
30         System.out.printf("Class average is %d%n", average);
31      }
32   } // end class ClassAverage
```

Fig. 4.7 | Solving the class-average problem using counter-controlled repetition. (Part 1 of 2.)

```
Enter grade: 67
Enter grade: 78
Enter grade: 89
Enter grade: 67
Enter grade: 87
Enter grade: 98
Enter grade: 93
Enter grade: 85
Enter grade: 82
Enter grade: 100

Total of all 10 grades is 846
Class average is 84
```

Fig. 4.7 | Solving the class-average problem using counter-controlled repetition. (Part 2 of 2.)

Local Variables in Method `main`

Line 10 declares and initializes Scanner variable `input`, which is used to read values entered by the user. Lines 13, 14, 20 and 26 declare local variables `total`, `gradeCounter`, `grade` and `average`, respectively, to be of type int. Variable `grade` stores the user input.

These declarations appear in the body of method `main`. Recall that variables declared in a method body are local variables and can be used only from the line of their declaration to the closing right brace of the method declaration. A local variable's declaration must appear before the variable is used in that method. A local variable cannot be accessed outside the method in which it's declared. Variable `grade`, declared in the body of the `while` loop, can be used only in that block.

Initialization Phase: Initializing Variables `total` and `gradeCounter`

The assignments (in lines 13–14) initialize `total` to 0 and `gradeCounter` to 1. These initializations occur before the variables are used in calculations.

Common Programming Error 4.3

Using the value of a local variable before it's initialized results in a compilation error. All local variables must be initialized before their values are used in expressions.

Error-Prevention Tip 4.3

Initialize each total and counter, either in its declaration or in an assignment statement. Totals are normally initialized to 0. Counters are normally initialized to 0 or 1, depending on how they're used (we'll show examples of when to use 0 and when to use 1).

Processing Phase: Reading 10 Grades from the User

Line 17 indicates that the `while` statement should continue looping (also called **iterating**) as long as `gradeCounter`'s value is less than or equal to 10. While this condition remains *true*, the `while` statement repeatedly executes the statements between the braces that delimit its body (lines 18–23).

Line 19 displays the prompt "Enter grade: ". Line 20 reads the grade entered by the user and assigns it to variable `grade`. Then line 21 adds the new `grade` entered by the user to the `total` and assigns the result to `total`.

Line 22 adds 1 to gradeCounter to indicate that the program has processed a grade and is ready to input the next grade from the user. Incrementing gradeCounter eventually causes it to exceed 10. Then the loop terminates, because its condition (line 17) becomes *false*.

Termination Phase: Calculating and Displaying the Class Average
When the loop terminates, line 26 performs the averaging calculation and assigns its result to the variable average. Line 29 uses System.out's printf method to display the text "Total of all 10 grades is " followed by variable total's value. Line 30 then uses printf to display the text "Class average is " followed by variable average's value. When execution reaches line 31, the program terminates.

Notice that this example contains only one class, with method main performing all the work. In this chapter and in Chapter 3, you've seen examples consisting of two classes—one containing instance variables and methods that perform tasks using those variables and one containing method main, which creates an object of the other class and calls its methods. Occasionally, when it does not make sense to try to create a reusable class to demonstrate a concept, we'll place the program's statements entirely within a single class's main method.

Notes on Integer Division and Truncation
The averaging calculation performed by method main produces an integer result. The program's output indicates that the sum of the grade values in the sample execution is 846, which, when divided by 10, should yield the floating-point number 84.6. However, the result of the calculation total / 10 (line 26 of Fig. 4.7) is the integer 84, because total and 10 are both integers. Dividing two integers results in **integer division**—any fractional part of the calculation is **truncated** (i.e., *lost*); no rounding occurs. In the next section we'll see how to obtain a floating-point result from the averaging calculation.

Common Programming Error 4.4

Assuming that integer division rounds (rather than truncates) can lead to incorrect results. For example, 7 ÷ 4, which yields 1.75 in conventional arithmetic, truncates to 1 in integer arithmetic, rather than rounding to 2.

A Note About Arithmetic Overflow
In Fig. 4.7, line 21

```
total = total + grade; // add grade to total
```

added each grade entered by the user to the total. Even this simple statement has a *potential* problem—adding the integers could result in a value that's *too large* to store in an int variable. This is known as **arithmetic overflow** and causes *undefined behavior*, which can lead to unintended results (http://en.wikipedia.org/wiki/Integer_overflow#Security_ramifications). Figure 2.7's Addition program had the same issue in line 23, which calculated the sum of two int values entered by the user:

```
sum = number1 + number2; // add numbers, then store total in sum
```

The maximum and minimum values that can be stored in an int variable are represented by the constants MIN_VALUE and MAX_VALUE, respectively, which are defined in class Integer. There are similar constants for the other integral types and for floating-point types.

Each primitive type has a corresponding class type in package java.lang. You can see the values of these constants in each class's online documentation. The documentation for class Integer is at:

```
http://docs.oracle.com/javase/7/docs/api/java/lang/Integer.html
```

It's considered a good practice to ensure, *before* you perform arithmetic calculations like those in line 21 of Fig. 4.7 and line 23 of Fig. 2.7, that they will *not* overflow. The code for doing this is shown on the CERT website www.securecoding.cert.org—just search for guideline "NUM00-J." The code uses the && (logical AND) and || (logical OR) operators, which are introduced in Chapter 5. In industrial-strength code, you should perform checks like these for *all* calculations.

A Deeper Look at Receiving User Input

Any time a program receives input from the user, various problems might occur. For example, in line 20 of Fig. 4.7

```
int grade = input.nextInt(); // input next grade
```

we assume that the user will enter an integer grade in the range 0 to 100. However, the person entering a grade could enter an integer less than 0, an integer greater than 100, an integer outside the range of values that can be stored in an int variable, a number containing a decimal point or a value containing letters or special symbols that's not even an integer.

To ensure that inputs are valid, industrial-strength programs must test for all possible erroneous cases. A program that inputs grades should **validate** the grades by using **range checking** to ensure that they are values from 0 to 100. You can then ask the user to reenter any value that's out of range. If a program requires inputs from a specific set of values (e.g., nonsequential product codes), you can ensure that each input matches a value in the set.

4.8 Sentinel-Controlled Repetition

Let's generalize Section 4.7's class-average problem. Consider the following problem:

> *Develop a class-averaging program that processes grades for an arbitrary number of students each time it's run.*

In the previous class-average example, the problem statement specified the number of students, so the number of grades (10) was known in advance. In this example, no indication is given of how many grades the user will enter during the program's execution. The program must process an arbitrary number of grades.

One way to solve this problem is to use a special value called a *sentinel* value (also called a *signal value*, a *dummy value* or a *flag value*) to indicate "end of data entry." The user enters grades until all legitimate grades have been entered. The user then types the sentinel value to indicate that no more grades will be entered. Sentinel-controlled repetition is often called indefinite repetition because the number of repetitions is not known before the loop begins executing.

Clearly, a sentinel value must be chosen that cannot be confused with an acceptable input value. Grades on a quiz are nonnegative integers, so –1 is an acceptable sentinel value for this problem. Thus, a run of the class-average program might process a stream of inputs such as 95, 96, 75, 74, 89 and –1. The program would then compute and print the class average for the grades 95, 96, 75, 74 and 89; since −1 is the sentinel value, it should *not* enter into the averaging calculation.

Implementing Sentinel-Controlled Repetition

The program of Fig. 4.8 implements sentinel-controlled class averaging. Although each grade is an integer, the averaging calculation is likely to produce a number with a *decimal point*—in other words, a real (floating-point) number. The type int cannot represent such a number, so this class uses type double to do so. You'll also see that control statements may be *stacked* on top of one another (in sequence). The while statement (lines 22–30) is followed in sequence by an if...else statement (lines 34–45). Much of the code in this program is identical to that in Fig. 4.7, so we concentrate on the new concepts.

```java
1   // Fig. 4.8: ClassAverage.java
2   // Solving the class-average problem using sentinel-controlled repetition.
3   import java.util.Scanner; // program uses class Scanner
4
5   public class ClassAverage
6   {
7      public static void main(String[] args)
8      {
9         // create Scanner to obtain input from command window
10        Scanner input = new Scanner(System.in);
11
12        // initialization phase
13        int total = 0; // initialize sum of grades
14        int gradeCounter = 0; // initialize # of grades entered so far
15
16        // processing phase
17        // prompt for input and read grade from user
18        System.out.print("Enter grade or -1 to quit: ");
19        int grade = input.nextInt();
20
21        // loop until sentinel value read from user
22        while (grade != -1)
23        {
24           total = total + grade; // add grade to total
25           gradeCounter = gradeCounter + 1; // increment counter
26
27           // prompt for input and read next grade from user
28           System.out.print("Enter grade or -1 to quit: ");
29           grade = input.nextInt();
30        }
31
32        // termination phase
33        // if user entered at least one grade...
34        if (gradeCounter != 0)
35        {
36           // use number with decimal point to calculate average of grades
37           double average = (double) total / gradeCounter;
38
```

Fig. 4.8 | Solving the class-average problem using sentinel-controlled repetition. (Part 1 of 2.)

```
39              // display total and average (with two digits of precision)
40              System.out.printf("%nTotal of the %d grades entered is %d%n",
41                 gradeCounter, total);
42              System.out.printf("Class average is %.2f%n", average);
43           }
44           else // no grades were entered, so output appropriate message
45              System.out.println("No grades were entered");
46        }
47     } // end class ClassAverage
```

```
Enter grade or -1 to quit: 97
Enter grade or -1 to quit: 88
Enter grade or -1 to quit: 72
Enter grade or -1 to quit: -1

Total of the 3 grades entered is 257
Class average is 85.67
```

Fig. 4.8 | Solving the class-average problem using sentinel-controlled repetition. (Part 2 of 2.)

Program Logic for Sentinel-Controlled Repetition vs. Counter-Controlled Repetition
Line 37 declares double variable average, which allows us to store the class average as a floating-point number. Line 14 initializes gradeCounter to 0, because no grades have been entered yet. Remember that this program uses *sentinel-controlled repetition* to input the grades. To keep an accurate record of the number of grades entered, the program increments gradeCounter only when the user enters a valid grade.

Compare the program logic for sentinel-controlled repetition in this application with that for counter-controlled repetition in Fig. 4.7. In counter-controlled repetition, each iteration of the while statement (lines 17–23 of Fig. 4.7) reads a value from the user, for the specified number of iterations. In sentinel-controlled repetition, the program reads the first value (lines 18–19 of Fig. 4.8) before reaching the while. This value determines whether the program's flow of control should enter the body of the while. If the condition of the while is false, the user entered the sentinel value, so the body of the while does not execute (i.e., no grades were entered). If, on the other hand, the condition is *true*, the body begins execution, and the loop adds the grade value to the total and increments the gradeCounter (lines 24–25). Then lines 28–29 in the loop body input the next value from the user. Next, program control reaches the closing right brace of the loop body at line 30, so execution continues with the test of the while's condition (line 22). The condition uses the most recent grade input by the user to determine whether the loop body should execute again. The value of variable grade is always input from the user immediately before the program tests the while condition. This allows the program to determine whether the value just input is the sentinel value *before* the program processes that value (i.e., adds it to the total). If the sentinel value is input, the loop terminates, and the program does not add −1 to the total.

Good Programming Practice 4.3
In a sentinel-controlled loop, prompts should remind the user of the sentinel.

After the loop terminates, the if...else statement at lines 34–45 executes. The condition at line 34 determines whether any grades were input. If none were input, the else part (lines 44–45) of the `if...else` statement executes and displays the message "No grades were entered" and the method returns control to the calling method.

Braces in a `while` statement

Notice the `while` statement's *block* in Fig. 4.8 (lines 23–30). Without the braces, the loop would consider its body to be only the first statement, which adds the `grade` to the `total`. The last three statements in the block would fall outside the loop body, causing the computer to interpret the code incorrectly as follows:

```java
while (grade != -1)
    total = total + grade; // add grade to total
gradeCounter = gradeCounter + 1; // increment counter

// prompt for input and read next grade from user
System.out.print("Enter grade or -1 to quit: ");
grade = input.nextInt();
```

The preceding code would cause an *infinite loop* in the program if the user did not input the sentinel -1 at line 19 (before the `while` statement).

Common Programming Error 4.5

Omitting the braces that delimit a block can lead to logic errors, such as infinite loops. To prevent this problem, some programmers enclose the body of every control statement in braces, even if the body contains only a single statement.

Explicitly and Implicitly Converting Between Primitive Types

If at least one grade was entered, line 37 of Fig. 4.8 calculates the average of the grades. Recall from Fig. 4.7 that integer division yields an integer result. Even though variable `average` is declared as a `double`, if we had written the averaging calculation as

```java
double average = total / gradeCounter;
```

it would lose the fractional part of the quotient *before* the result of the division is assigned to `average`. This occurs because `total` and `gradeCounter` are *both* integers, and integer division yields an integer result.

Most averages are not whole numbers (e.g., 0, –22 and 1024). For this reason, we calculate the class average in this example as a floating-point number. To perform a floating-point calculation with integer values, we must *temporarily* treat these values as floating-point numbers for use in the calculation. Java provides the **unary cast operator** to accomplish this task. Line 37 of Fig. 4.8 uses the **(double)** cast operator—a unary operator—to create a *temporary* floating-point copy of its operand `total` (which appears to the right of the operator). Using a cast operator in this manner is called **explicit conversion** or **type casting**. The value stored in `total` is still an integer.

The calculation now consists of a floating-point value (the temporary `double` copy of `total`) divided by the integer `gradeCounter`. Java can evaluate only arithmetic expressions in which the operands' types are *identical*. To ensure this, Java performs an operation called **promotion** (or **implicit conversion**) on selected operands. For example, in an expression containing `int` and `double` values, the `int` values are promoted to `double` values for use in the expression. In this example, the value of `gradeCounter` is promoted to type `double`, then floating-point division is performed and the result of the calculation is assigned to `average`. As long as the (double) cast operator is applied to *any* variable in the calculation, the calculation will yield a `double` result. Later in this chapter, we discuss all the primitive types. You'll learn more about the promotion rules in Section 6.6.

Common Programming Error 4.6

A cast operator can be used to convert between primitive numeric types, such as int and double, and between related reference types (as we discuss in Chapter 10, Object-Oriented Programming: Polymorphism and Interfaces). Casting to the wrong type may cause compilation errors or runtime errors.

A cast operator is formed by placing parentheses around any type's name. The operator is a **unary operator** (i.e., an operator that takes only one operand). Java also supports unary versions of the plus (+) and minus (–) operators, enabling you to write expressions like -7 or +5. Cast operators associate from *right to left* and have the same precedence as other unary operators, such as unary + and unary -. This precedence is one level higher than that of the **multiplicative operators** *, / and %. (See the operator precedence chart in Appendix A.) We indicate the cast operator with the notation (*type*) in our precedence charts, to indicate that any type name can be used to form a cast operator.

Line 42 displays the class average. In this example, we display the class average *rounded* to the nearest hundredth. The format specifier %.2f in `printf`'s format control string indicates that variable `average`'s value should be displayed with two digits of precision to the right of the decimal point—indicated by .2 in the format specifier. The three grades entered during the sample execution (Fig. 4.8) total 257, which yields the average 85.666666…. Method `printf` uses the precision in the format specifier to round the value to the specified number of digits. In this program, the average is rounded to the hundredths position and is displayed as 85.67.

Floating-Point Number Precision

Floating-point numbers are not always 100% precise, but they have numerous applications. For example, when we speak of a "normal" body temperature of 98.6, we do not need to be precise to a large number of digits. When we read the temperature on a thermometer as 98.6, it may actually be 98.5999473210643. Calling this number simply 98.6 is fine for most applications involving body temperatures.

Floating-point numbers often arise as a result of division, such as in this example's class-average calculation. In conventional arithmetic, when we divide 10 by 3, the result is 3.3333333…, with the sequence of 3s repeating infinitely. The computer allocates only a fixed amount of space to hold such a value, so clearly the stored floating-point value can be only an approximation.

Owing to the imprecise nature of floating-point numbers, type `double` is preferred over type `float`, because `double` variables can represent floating-point numbers more accurately. For this reason, we primarily use type `double` throughout the book. In some applications, the precision of `float` and `double` variables will be inadequate. For precise floating-point numbers (such as those required by monetary calculations), Java provides class `BigDecimal` (package `java.math`), which we'll discuss in Chapter 8.

Common Programming Error 4.7

Using floating-point numbers in a manner that assumes they're represented precisely can lead to incorrect results.

4.9 Nested Control Statements

We've seen that control statements can be stacked on top of one another (in sequence). In this case study, we examine the only other structured way control statements can be connected—namely, by **nesting** one control statement within another.

Consider the following problem statement:

> *A college offers a course that prepares students for the state licensing exam for real-estate brokers. Last year, ten of the students who completed this course took the exam. The college wants to know how well its students did on the exam. You've been asked to write a program to summarize the results. You've been given a list of these 10 students. Next to each name is written a 1 if the student passed the exam or a 2 if the student failed.*
>
> *Your program should analyze the results of the exam as follows:*
>
> 1. *Input each test result (i.e., a 1 or a 2). Display the message "Enter result" on the screen each time the program requests another test result.*
>
> 2. *Count the number of test results of each type.*
>
> 3. *Display a summary of the test results, indicating the number of students who passed and the number who failed.*
>
> 4. *If more than eight students passed the exam, print "Bonus to instructor!"*

The Java class that solves this problem is shown in Fig. 4.9. Lines 13, 14, 15 and 22 of main declare the variables that are used to process the examination results.

Error-Prevention Tip 4.4

Initializing local variables when they're declared helps you avoid any compilation errors that might arise from attempts to use uninitialized variables. While Java does not require that local-variable initializations be incorporated into declarations, it does require that local variables be initialized before their values are used in an expression.

```java
1   // Fig. 4.9: Analysis.java
2   // Analysis of examination results using nested control statements.
3   import java.util.Scanner; // class uses class Scanner
4
5   public class Analysis
6   {
7      public static void main(String[] args)
8      {
9         // create Scanner to obtain input from command window
10        Scanner input = new Scanner(System.in);
11
12        // initializing variables in declarations
13        int passes = 0;
14        int failures = 0;
15        int studentCounter = 1;
16
17        // process 10 students using counter-controlled loop
18        while (studentCounter <= 10)
19        {
```

Fig. 4.9 | Analysis of examination results using nested control statements. (Part 1 of 2.)

```
20            // prompt user for input and obtain value from user
21            System.out.print("Enter result (1 = pass, 2 = fail): ");
22            int result = input.nextInt();
23
24            // if...else is nested in the while statement
25            if (result == 1)
26               passes = passes + 1;
27            else
28               failures = failures + 1;
29
30            // increment studentCounter so loop eventually terminates
31            studentCounter = studentCounter + 1;
32         }
33
34         // termination phase; prepare and display results
35         System.out.printf("Passed: %d%nFailed: %d%n", passes, failures);
36
37         // determine whether more than 8 students passed
38         if (passes > 8)
39            System.out.println("Bonus to instructor!");
40      }
41   } // end class Analysis
```

```
Enter result (1 = pass, 2 = fail): 1
Enter result (1 = pass, 2 = fail): 2
Enter result (1 = pass, 2 = fail): 1
Enter result (1 = pass, 2 = fail): 1
Enter result (1 = pass, 2 = fail): 1
Enter result (1 = pass, 2 = fail): 1
Enter result (1 = pass, 2 = fail): 1
Enter result (1 = pass, 2 = fail): 1
Enter result (1 = pass, 2 = fail): 1
Enter result (1 = pass, 2 = fail): 1
Passed: 9
Failed: 1
Bonus to instructor!
```

```
Enter result (1 = pass, 2 = fail): 1
Enter result (1 = pass, 2 = fail): 2
Enter result (1 = pass, 2 = fail): 1
Enter result (1 = pass, 2 = fail): 2
Enter result (1 = pass, 2 = fail): 1
Enter result (1 = pass, 2 = fail): 2
Enter result (1 = pass, 2 = fail): 2
Enter result (1 = pass, 2 = fail): 1
Enter result (1 = pass, 2 = fail): 1
Enter result (1 = pass, 2 = fail): 1
Passed: 6
Failed: 4
```

Fig. 4.9 | Analysis of examination results using nested control statements. (Part 2 of 2.)

The `while` statement (lines 18–32) loops 10 times. During each iteration, the loop inputs and processes one exam result. Notice that the `if...else` statement (lines 25–28) for processing each result is *nested* in the `while` statement. If the `result` is 1, the `if...else` statement increments `passes`; otherwise, it assumes the `result` is 2 and increments `failures`. Line 31 increments `studentCounter` before the loop condition is tested again at line 18. After 10 values have been input, the loop terminates and line 35 displays the number of `passes` and `failures`. The `if` statement at lines 38–39 determines whether more than eight students passed the exam and, if so, outputs the message `"Bonus to instructor!"`.

Figure 4.9 shows the input and output from two sample excutions of the program. During the first, the condition at line 38 of method `main` is `true`—more than eight students passed the exam, so the program outputs a message to bonus the instructor.

4.10 Compound Assignment Operators

The **compound assignment operators** abbreviate assignment expressions. Statements like

> *variable = variable   operator   expression*;

where *operator* is one of the binary operators +, -, *, / or % (or others we discuss later in the text) can be written in the form

> *variable   operator=   expression*;

For example, you can abbreviate the statement

> `c = c + 3;`

with the **addition compound assignment operator, +=,** as

> `c += 3;`

The += operator adds the value of the expression on its right to the value of the variable on its left and stores the result in the variable on the left of the operator. Thus, the assignment expression c += 3 adds 3 to c. Figure 4.10 shows the arithmetic compound assignment operators, sample expressions using the operators and explanations of what the operators do.

Assignment operator	Sample expression	Explanation	Assigns
Assume: `int c = 3, d = 5, e = 4, f = 6, g = 12;`			
+=	c += 7	c = c + 7	10 to c
-=	d -= 4	d = d - 4	1 to d
*=	e *= 5	e = e * 5	20 to e
/=	f /= 3	f = f / 3	2 to f
%=	g %= 9	g = g % 9	3 to g

Fig. 4.10 | Arithmetic compound assignment operators.

4.11 Increment and Decrement Operators

Java provides two unary operators (summarized in Fig. 4.11) for adding 1 to or subtracting 1 from the value of a numeric variable. These are the unary **increment operator, ++,** and the unary **decrement operator**, --. A program can increment by 1 the value of a variable called c using the increment operator, ++, rather than the expression c = c + 1 or c += 1. An increment or decrement operator that's prefixed to (placed before) a variable is referred to as the **prefix increment** or **prefix decrement operator**, respectively. An increment or decrement operator that's postfixed to (placed after) a variable is referred to as the **postfix increment** or **postfix decrement operator**, respectively.

Operator	Operator name	Sample expression	Explanation
++	prefix increment	++a	Increment a by 1, then use the new value of a in the expression in which a resides.
++	postfix increment	a++	Use the current value of a in the expression in which a resides, then increment a by 1.
--	prefix decrement	--b	Decrement b by 1, then use the new value of b in the expression in which b resides.
--	postfix decrement	b--	Use the current value of b in the expression in which b resides, then decrement b by 1.

Fig. 4.11 | Increment and decrement operators.

Using the prefix increment (or decrement) operator to add 1 to (or subtract 1 from) a variable is known as **preincrementing** (or **predecrementing**). This causes the variable to be incremented (decremented) by 1; then the new value of the variable is used in the expression in which it appears. Using the postfix increment (or decrement) operator to add 1 to (or subtract 1 from) a variable is known as **postincrementing** (or **postdecrementing**). This causes the current value of the variable to be used in the expression in which it appears; then the variable's value is incremented (decremented) by 1.

Good Programming Practice 4.4

Unlike binary operators, the unary increment and decrement operators should be placed next to their operands, with no intervening spaces.

Difference Between Prefix Increment and Postfix Increment Operators
Figure 4.12 demonstrates the difference between the prefix increment and postfix increment versions of the ++ increment operator. The decrement operator (--) works similarly.

```
1   // Fig. 4.12: Increment.java
2   // Prefix increment and postfix increment operators.
3
4   public class Increment
5   {
6      public static void main(String[] args)
7      {
```

Fig. 4.12 | Prefix increment and postfix increment operators. (Part 1 of 2.)

```
 8            // demonstrate postfix increment operator
 9            int c = 5;
10            System.out.printf("c before postincrement: %d%n", c); // prints 5
11            System.out.printf("    postincrementing c: %d%n", c++); // prints 5
12            System.out.printf(" c after postincrement: %d%n", c); // prints 6
13
14            System.out.println(); // skip a line
15
16            // demonstrate prefix increment operator
17            c = 5;
18            System.out.printf(" c before preincrement: %d%n", c); // prints 5
19            System.out.printf("     preincrementing c: %d%n", ++c); // prints 6
20            System.out.printf("  c after preincrement: %d%n", c); // prints 6
21        }
22   } // end class Increment
```

```
c before postincrement: 5
    postincrementing c: 5
 c after postincrement: 6

c before preincrement: 5
    preincrementing c: 6
  c after preincrement: 6
```

Fig. 4.12 | Prefix increment and postfix increment operators. (Part 2 of 2.)

Line 9 initializes the variable c to 5, and line 10 outputs c's initial value. Line 11 outputs the value of the expression c++. This expression postincrements the variable c, so c's *original* value (5) is output, then c's value is incremented (to 6). Thus, line 11 outputs c's initial value (5) again. Line 12 outputs c's new value (6) to prove that the variable's value was indeed incremented in line 11.

Line 17 resets c's value to 5, and line 18 outputs c's value. Line 19 outputs the value of the expression ++c. This expression preincrements c, so its value is incremented; then the *new* value (6) is output. Line 20 outputs c's value again to show that the value of c is still 6 after line 19 executes.

Simplifying Statements with the Arithmetic Compound Assignment, Increment and Decrement Operators

The arithmetic compound assignment operators and the increment and decrement operators can be used to simplify program statements. For example, the three assignment statements in Fig. 4.9 (lines 26, 28 and 31)

```
passes = passes + 1;
failures = failures + 1;
studentCounter = studentCounter + 1;
```

can be written more concisely with compound assignment operators as

```
passes += 1;
failures += 1;
studentCounter += 1;
```

with prefix increment operators as

```
++passes;
++failures;
++studentCounter;
```

or with postfix increment operators as

```
passes++;
failures++;
studentCounter++;
```

When incrementing or decrementing a variable in a statement by itself, the prefix increment and postfix increment forms have the *same* effect, and the prefix decrement and postfix decrement forms have the *same* effect. It's only when a variable appears in the context of a larger expression that preincrementing and postincrementing the variable have different effects (and similarly for predecrementing and postdecrementing).

Common Programming Error 4.8

Attempting to use the increment or decrement operator on an expression other than one to which a value can be assigned is a syntax error. For example, writing ++(x + 1) is a syntax error, because (x + 1) is not a variable.

Operator Precedence and Associativity
Figure 4.13 shows the precedence and associativity of the operators we've introduced. They're shown from top to bottom in decreasing order of precedence. The second column describes the associativity of the operators at each level of precedence.

Operators					Associativity	Type
++	--				right to left	unary postfix
++	--	+	-	(*type*)	right to left	unary prefix
*	/	%			left to right	multiplicative
+	-				left to right	additive
<	<=	>	>=		left to right	relational
==	!=				left to right	equality
?:					right to left	conditional
=	+=	-=	*=	/= %=	right to left	assignment

Fig. 4.13 | Precedence and associativity of the operators discussed so far.

4.12 Primitive Types

The table in Appendix D lists the eight primitive types in Java. Like its predecessor languages C and C++, Java requires all variables to have a type. For this reason, Java is referred to as a **strongly typed language**.

In C and C++, programmers frequently have to write separate versions of programs to support different computer platforms, because the primitive types are not guaranteed to be identical from computer to computer. For example, an `int` on one machine might be represented by 16 bits (2 bytes) of memory, on a second machine by 32 bits (4 bytes), and on another machine by 64 bits (8 bytes). In Java, `int` values are always 32 bits (4 bytes).

Portability Tip 4.1

The primitive types in Java are portable across all computer platforms that support Java.

Each type in Appendix D is listed with its size in bits (there are eight bits to a byte) and its range of values. Because the designers of Java want to ensure portability, they use internationally recognized standards for character formats (Unicode; for more information, visit `www.unicode.org`) and floating-point numbers (IEEE 754; for more information, visit `grouper.ieee.org/groups/754/`).

Recall from Section 3.2 that variables of primitive types declared outside of a method as instance variables of a class are *automatically assigned default values unless explicitly initialized*. Instance variables of types `char`, `byte`, `short`, `int`, `long`, `float` and `double` are all given the value 0 by default. Instance variables of type `boolean` are given the value `false` by default. Reference-type instance variables are initialized by default to the value `null`.

4.13 Wrap-Up

In this chapter we began our discussion of control statements. Only three types of control statements—sequence, selection and repetition—are needed to develop any program. This chapter demonstrated the `if` single-selection statement, the `if...else` double-selection statement and the `while` repetition statement. We used control-statement stacking to total and compute the average of a set of student grades with counter- and sentinel-controlled repetition, and we used control-statement nesting to analyze and make decisions based on a set of exam results. We introduced Java's compound assignment operators and its increment and decrement operators. Finally, we discussed Java's primitive types. In Chapter 5, we continue our discussion of control statements, introducing the `for`, `do...while` and `switch` statements.

5

Control Statements: Part 2;
Logical Operators

Objectives

In this chapter you'll:

- Review the essentials of counter-controlled repetition.

- Use the `for` and `do...while` repetition statements to execute statements in a program repeatedly.

- Perform multiple selection using the `switch` selection statement.

- Use the `break` and `continue` program control statements to alter the flow of control.

- Use the logical operators to form complex conditional expressions in control statements.

5.1 Introduction

This chapter continues our presentation of structured programming theory and principles by introducing all but one of Java's remaining control statements. We demonstrate Java's for, do...while and switch statements. Through a series of short examples using while and for, we explore the essentials of counter-controlled repetition. We use a switch statement to count the number of A, B, C, D and F grade equivalents in a set of numeric grades entered by the user. We introduce the break and continue program-control statements. Finally, we discuss Java's logical operators, which enable you to use more complex conditional expressions in control statements.

5.2 Essentials of Counter-Controlled Repetition

This section uses the while repetition statement introduced in Chapter 4 to formalize the elements required to perform counter-controlled repetition, which requires

1. a **control variable** (or loop counter)

2. the **initial value** of the control variable

3. the **increment** by which the control variable is modified each time through the loop (also known as each **iteration** of the loop)

4. the **loop-continuation condition** that determines if looping should continue.

To see these elements of counter-controlled repetition, consider the application of Fig. 5.1, which uses a loop to display the numbers from 1 through 10.

In Fig. 5.1, the elements of counter-controlled repetition are defined in lines 8, 10 and 13. Line 8 *declares* the control variable (counter) as an int, *reserves space* for it in memory and sets its *initial value* to 1. Variable counter also could have been declared and initialized with the following local-variable declaration and assignment statements:

```
int counter; // declare counter
counter = 1; // initialize counter to 1
```

Line 12 displays control variable counter's value during each iteration of the loop. Line 13 *increments* the control variable for each iteration of the loop. The loop-continuation condition in the while (line 10) tests whether the value of the control variable is less than or equal to 10 (the final value for which the condition is true). The program performs the body of this while even when the control variable is 10. The loop terminates when the control variable exceeds 10 (i.e., counter becomes 11).

```
 1  // Fig. 5.1: WhileCounter.java
 2  // Counter-controlled repetition with the while repetition statement.
 3
 4  public class WhileCounter
 5  {
 6     public static void main(String[] args)
 7     {
 8        int counter = 1; // declare and initialize control variable
 9
10        while (counter <= 10) // loop-continuation condition
11        {
12           System.out.printf("%d  ", counter);
13           ++counter; // increment control variable
14        }
15
16        System.out.println();
17     }
18  } // end class WhileCounter
```

```
1  2  3  4  5  6  7  8  9  10
```

Fig. 5.1 │ Counter-controlled repetition with the `while` repetition statement.

Common Programming Error 5.1
Because floating-point values may be approximate, controlling loops with floating-point variables may result in imprecise counter values and inaccurate termination tests.

Error-Prevention Tip 5.1
Use integers to control counting loops.

The program in Fig. 5.1 can be made more concise by initializing counter to 0 in line 8 and *preincrementing* counter in the `while` condition as follows:

```
while (++counter <= 10) // loop-continuation condition
   System.out.printf("%d  ", counter);
```

This code saves a statement, because the `while` condition performs the increment before testing the condition. (Recall from Section 4.11 that the precedence of ++ is higher than that of <=.) Coding in such a condensed fashion takes practice, might make code more difficult to read, debug, modify and maintain, and typically should be avoided.

Software Engineering Observation 5.1
"Keep it simple" is good advice for most of the code you'll write.

5.3 for Repetition Statement

Section 5.2 presented the essentials of counter-controlled repetition. The `while` statement can be used to implement any counter-controlled loop. Java also provides the **for repeti-**

tion statement, which specifies the counter-controlled-repetition details in a single line of code. Figure 5.2 reimplements the application of Fig. 5.1 using `for`.

```java
1   // Fig. 5.2: ForCounter.java
2   // Counter-controlled repetition with the for repetition statement.
3
4   public class ForCounter
5   {
6      public static void main(String[] args)
7      {
8         // for statement header includes initialization,
9         // loop-continuation condition and increment
10        for (int counter = 1; counter <= 10; counter++)
11           System.out.printf("%d  ", counter);
12
13        System.out.println();
14     }
15  } // end class ForCounter
```

```
1  2  3  4  5  6  7  8  9  10
```

Fig. 5.2 | Counter-controlled repetition with the `for` repetition statement.

When the `for` statement (lines 10–11) begins executing, the control variable `counter` is *declared* and *initialized* to 1. (Recall from Section 5.2 that the first two elements of counter-controlled repetition are the *control variable* and its *initial value*.) Next, the program checks the *loop-continuation condition*, `counter <= 10`, which is between the two required semicolons. Because the initial value of `counter` is 1, the condition initially is true. Therefore, the body statement (line 11) displays control variable `counter`'s value, namely 1. After executing the loop's body, the program increments `counter` in the expression `counter++`, which appears to the right of the second semicolon. Then the loop-continuation test is performed again to determine whether the program should continue with the next iteration of the loop. At this point, the control variable's value is 2, so the condition is still true (the *final value* is not exceeded)—thus, the program performs the body statement again (i.e., the next iteration of the loop). This process continues until the numbers 1 through 10 have been displayed and the `counter`'s value becomes 11, causing the loop-continuation test to fail and repetition to terminate (after 10 repetitions of the loop body). Then the program performs the first statement after the `for`—in this case, line 13.

Figure 5.2 uses (in line 10) the loop-continuation condition `counter <= 10`. If you incorrectly specified `counter < 10` as the condition, the loop would iterate only nine times—an **off-by-one error**.

Error-Prevention Tip 5.2

As Chapter 4 mentioned, integers can overflow, causing logic errors. A loop's control variable also could overflow. Write your loop conditions carefully to prevent this.

*A Closer Look at the **for** Statement's Header*

Figure 5.3 takes a closer look at the `for` statement in Fig. 5.2. The first line—including the keyword `for` and everything in parentheses after `for` (line 10 in Fig. 5.2)—is sometimes called the **for statement header**. The for header "does it all"—it specifies each item needed for counter-controlled repetition with a control variable. If there's more than one statement in the body of the for, braces are required to define the body of the loop.

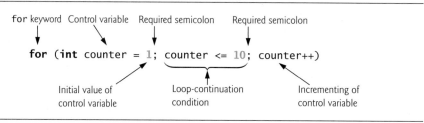

Fig. 5.3 | for statement header components.

*General Format of a **for** Statement*

The general format of the for statement is

> **for** (*initialization*; *loopContinuationCondition*; *increment*)
>   *statement*

where the *initialization* expression names the loop's control variable and *optionally* provides its initial value, *loopContinuationCondition* determines whether the loop should continue executing and *increment* modifies the control variable's value, so that the loop-continuation condition eventually becomes false. The two semicolons in the for header are required. If the loop-continuation condition is initially false, the program does *not* execute the for statement's body. Instead, execution proceeds with the statement following the for.

*Representing a **for** Statement with an Equivalent **while** Statement*

The for statement often can be represented with an equivalent while statement as follows:

> *initialization*;
> **while** (*loopContinuationCondition*)
> {
>   *statement*
>   *increment*;
> }

In Section 5.8, we show a case in which a for statement cannot be represented with an equivalent while statement. Typically, for statements are used for counter-controlled repetition and while statements for sentinel-controlled repetition. However, while and for can each be used for either repetition type.

*Scope of a **for** Statement's Control Variable*

If the *initialization* expression in the for header declares the control variable (i.e., the control variable's type is specified before the variable name, as in Fig. 5.2), the control variable can be used *only* in that for statement—it will not exist outside it. This restricted use is known as the variable's **scope**. The scope of a variable defines where it can be used in a program. For example, a *local variable* can be used *only* in the method that declares it and *only* from the point of declaration through the end of the method. Scope is discussed in detail in Chapter 6, Methods: A Deeper Look.

Common Programming Error 5.2

When a for *statement's control variable is declared in the initialization section of the* for*'s header, using the control variable after the* for*'s body is a compilation error.*

Expressions in a *for* Statement's Header Are Optional

All three expressions in a for header are optional. If the *loopContinuationCondition* is omitted, Java assumes that the loop-continuation condition is *always true*, thus creating an *infinite loop*. You might omit the *initialization* expression if the program initializes the control variable before the loop. You might omit the *increment* expression if the program calculates the increment with statements in the loop's body or if no increment is needed. The increment expression in a for acts as if it were a standalone statement at the end of the for's body. Therefore, the expressions

```
counter = counter + 1
counter += 1
++counter
counter++
```

are equivalent increment expressions in a for statement. Many programmers prefer counter++ because it's concise and because a for loop evaluates its increment expression *after* its body executes, so the postfix increment form seems more natural. In this case, the variable being incremented does not appear in a larger expression, so preincrementing and postincrementing actually have the *same* effect.

Common Programming Error 5.3

Placing a semicolon immediately to the right of the right parenthesis of a for *header makes that* for*'s body an empty statement. This is normally a logic error.*

Error-Prevention Tip 5.3

Infinite loops occur when the loop-continuation condition in a repetition statement never becomes false. *To prevent this situation in a counter-controlled loop, ensure that the control variable is modified during each iteration of the loop so that the loop-continuation condition will eventually become* false. *In a sentinel-controlled loop, ensure that the sentinel value is able to be input.*

Placing Arithmetic Expressions in a *for* Statement's Header

The initialization, loop-continuation condition and increment portions of a for statement can contain arithmetic expressions. For example, assume that x = 2 and y = 10. If x and y are not modified in the body of the loop, the statement

```
for (int j = x; j <= 4 * x * y; j += y / x)
```

is equivalent to the statement

```
for (int j = 2; j <= 80; j += 5)
```

The increment of a for statement may also be *negative*, in which case it's a **decrement**, and the loop counts *downward*.

*Using a **for** Statement's Control Variable in the Statement's Body*

Programs frequently display the control-variable value or use it in calculations in the loop body, but this use is *not* required. The control variable is commonly used to control repetition *without* being mentioned in the body of the for.

> **Error-Prevention Tip 5.4**
>
> *Although the value of the control variable can be changed in the body of a for loop, avoid doing so, because this can lead to subtle errors.*

*UML Activity Diagram for the **for** Statement*

The for statement's UML activity diagram is similar to that of the while statement (Fig. 4.6). Figure 5.4 shows the activity diagram of the for statement in Fig. 5.2. The diagram makes it clear that initialization occurs *once before* the loop-continuation test is evaluated the first time, and that incrementing occurs *each* time through the loop *after* the body statement executes.

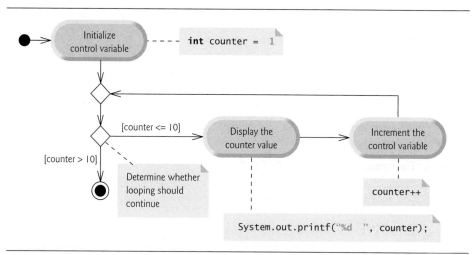

Fig. 5.4 | UML activity diagram for the for statement in Fig. 5.2.

5.4 Examples Using the **for** Statement

The following examples show techniques for varying the control variable in a for statement. In each case, we write *only* the appropriate for header. Note the change in the relational operator for the loops that *decrement* the control variable.

a) Vary the control variable from 1 to 100 in increments of 1.

```
for (int i = 1; i <= 100; i++)
```

b) Vary the control variable from 100 to 1 in *decrements* of 1.

```
for (int i = 100; i >= 1; i--)
```

c) Vary the control variable from 7 to 77 in increments of 7.

```
for (int i = 7; i <= 77; i += 7)
```

d) Vary the control variable from 20 to 2 in *decrements* of 2.

```
for (int i = 20; i >= 2; i -= 2)
```

e) Vary the control variable over the values 2, 5, 8, 11, 14, 17, 20.

```
for (int i = 2; i <= 20; i += 3)
```

f) Vary the control variable over the values 99, 88, 77, 66, 55, 44, 33, 22, 11, 0.

```
for (int i = 99; i >= 0; i -= 11)
```

 Common Programming Error 5.4

Using an incorrect relational operator in the loop-continuation condition of a loop that counts downward (e.g., using i <= 1 instead of i >= 1 in a loop counting down to 1) is usually a logic error.

 Common Programming Error 5.5

Do not use equality operators (!= or ==) in a loop-continuation condition if the loop's control variable increments or decrements by more than 1. For example, consider the for *statement header* for (int counter = 1; counter != 10; counter += 2). *The loop-continuation test* counter != 10 *never becomes false (resulting in an* infinite loop*) because* counter *increments by 2 after each iteration.*

Application: Summing the Even Integers from 2 to 20

We now consider two sample applications that demonstrate simple uses of for. The application in Fig. 5.5 uses a for statement to sum the even integers from 2 to 20 and store the result in an int variable called total.

```java
1   // Fig. 5.5: Sum.java
2   // Summing integers with the for statement.
3
4   public class Sum
5   {
6      public static void main(String[] args)
7      {
8         int total = 0;
9
10        // total even integers from 2 through 20
11        for (int number = 2; number <= 20; number += 2)
12           total += number;
13
14        System.out.printf("Sum is %d%n", total);
15     }
16  } // end class Sum
```

```
Sum is 110
```

Fig. 5.5 | Summing integers with the for statement.

The *initialization* and *increment* expressions can be comma-separated lists of multiple initialization expressions or multiple increment expressions. For example, although this is discouraged, you could merge the body of the for statement in lines 11–12 of Fig. 5.5 into the increment portion of the for header by using a comma as follows:

```
for (int number = 2; number <= 20; total += number, number += 2)
   ; // empty statement
```

Application: Compound-Interest Calculations

Let's use the for statement to compute compound interest. Consider the following problem:

> A person invests $1,000 in a savings account yielding 5% interest. Assuming that all the interest is left on deposit, calculate and print the amount of money in the account at the end of each year for 10 years. Use the following formula to determine the amounts:
>
> $$a = p\,(1 + r)^n$$
>
> where
>
> p is the original amount invested (i.e., the principal)
> r is the annual interest rate (e.g., use 0.05 for 5%)
> n is the number of years
> a is the amount on deposit at the end of the nth year.

The solution to this problem (Fig. 5.6) involves a loop that performs the indicated calculation for each of the 10 years the money remains on deposit. Lines 8–10 in method main declare double variables amount, principal and rate, and initialize principal to 1000.0 and rate to 0.05. Java treats floating-point constants like 1000.0 and 0.05 as type double. Similarly, Java treats whole-number constants like 7 and -22 as type int.

```
 1   // Fig. 5.6: Interest.java
 2   // Compound-interest calculations with for.
 3
 4   public class Interest
 5   {
 6      public static void main(String[] args)
 7      {
 8         double amount; // amount on deposit at end of each year
 9         double principal = 1000.0; // initial amount before interest
10         double rate = 0.05; // interest rate
11
12         // display headers
13         System.out.printf("%s%20s%n", "Year", "Amount on deposit");
14
15         // calculate amount on deposit for each of ten years
16         for (int year = 1; year <= 10; ++year)
17         {
18            // calculate new amount for specified year
19            amount = principal * Math.pow(1.0 + rate, year);
20
21            // display the year and the amount
22            System.out.printf("%4d%,20.2f%n", year, amount);
23         }
24      }
25   } // end class Interest
```

Fig. 5.6 | Compound-interest calculations with for. (Part 1 of 2.)

```
Year    Amount on deposit
   1            1,050.00
   2            1,102.50
   3            1,157.63
   4            1,215.51
   5            1,276.28
   6            1,340.10
   7            1,407.10
   8            1,477.46
   9            1,551.33
  10            1,628.89
```

Fig. 5.6 | Compound-interest calculations with for. (Part 2 of 2.)

Formatting Strings with Field Widths and Justification

Line 13 outputs the headers for two columns of output. The first column displays the year and the second column the amount on deposit at the end of that year. We use the format specifier %20s to output the String "Amount on Deposit". The integer 20 between the % and the conversion character s indicates that the value should be displayed with a **field width** of 20—that is, printf displays the value with at least 20 character positions. If the value to be output is less than 20 character positions wide (17 characters in this example), the value is **right justified** in the field by default. If the year value to be output were more than four character positions wide, the field width would be extended to the right to accommodate the entire value—this would push the amount field to the right, upsetting the neat columns of our tabular output. To output values **left justified**, simply precede the field width with the **minus sign (–) formatting flag** (e.g., %-20s).

Performing the Interest Calculations with **static** *Method* **pow** *of Class* **Math**

The for statement (lines 16–23) executes its body 10 times, varying control variable year from 1 to 10 in increments of 1. This loop terminates when year becomes 11. (Variable year represents *n* in the problem statement.)

Classes provide methods that perform common tasks on objects. In fact, most methods must be called on a specific object. For example, to output text in Fig. 5.6, line 13 calls method printf on the System.out object. Some classes also provide methods that perform common tasks and do *not* require you to first create objects of those classes. These are called static methods. For example, Java does not include an exponentiation operator, so the designers of Java's Math class defined static method pow for raising a value to a power. You can call a static method by specifying the *class name* followed by a dot (.) and the method name, as in

> *ClassName.methodName(arguments)*

In Chapter 6, you'll learn how to implement static methods in your own classes.

We use static method **pow** of class **Math** to perform the compound-interest calculation in Fig. 5.6. Math.pow(*x*, *y*) calculates the value of *x* raised to the *y*th power. The method receives two double arguments and returns a double value. Line 19 performs the calculation $a = p(1 + r)^n$, where a is amount, p is principal, r is rate and n is year. Class Math is defined in package java.lang, so you do *not* need to import class Math to use it.

The body of the for statement contains the calculation 1.0 + rate, which appears as an argument to the Math.pow method. In fact, this calculation produces the *same* result each time through the loop, so repeating it in every iteration of the loop is wasteful.

Performance Tip 5.1

In loops, avoid calculations for which the result never changes—such calculations should typically be placed before the loop. Optimizing compilers will typically do this for you.

Formatting Floating-Point Numbers

After each calculation, line 22 outputs the year and the amount on deposit at the end of that year. The year is output in a field width of four characters (as specified by %4d). The amount is output as a floating-point number with the format specifier %,20.2f. The **comma (,) formatting flag** indicates that the floating-point value should be output with a **grouping separator**. The actual separator used is specific to the user's locale (i.e., country). For example, in the United States, the number will be output using commas to separate every three digits and a decimal point to separate the fractional part of the number, as in 1,234.45. The number 20 in the format specification indicates that the value should be output right justified in a *field width* of 20 characters. The .2 specifies the formatted number's *precision*—in this case, the number is *rounded* to the nearest hundredth and output with two digits to the right of the decimal point.

A Warning about Displaying Rounded Vhalues

We declared variables amount, principal and rate to be of type double in this example. We're dealing with fractional parts of dollars and thus need a type that allows decimal points in its values. Unfortunately, floating-point numbers can cause trouble. Here's a simple explanation of what can go wrong when using double (or float) to represent dollar amounts (assuming that dollar amounts are displayed with two digits to the right of the decimal point): Two double dollar amounts stored in the machine could be 14.234 (which would normally be rounded to 14.23 for display purposes) and 18.673 (which would normally be rounded to 18.67 for display purposes). When these amounts are added, they produce the internal sum 32.907, which would normally be rounded to 32.91 for display purposes. Thus, your output could appear as

```
   14.23
+ 18.67
-------
   32.91
```

but a person adding the individual numbers as displayed would expect the sum to be 32.90. You've been warned!

Error-Prevention Tip 5.5

Do not use variables of type double (or float) to perform precise monetary calculations. The imprecision of floating-point numbers can lead to errors. Java provides class java.math.BigDecimal for this purpose, which we demonstrate in Fig. 8.18.

5.5 do...while Repetition Statement

The **do...while repetition statement** is similar to the while statement. In the while, the program tests the loop-continuation condition at the *beginning* of the loop, *before* executing the loop's body; if the condition is *false*, the body *never* executes. The do...while statement tests the loop-continuation condition *after* executing the loop's body; therefore, *the body always executes at least once*. When a do...while statement terminates, execution continues with the next statement in sequence. Figure 5.7 uses a do...while to output the numbers 1–10. Line 8 declares and initializes control variable counter. Upon entering the do...while statement, line 12 outputs counter's value and line 13 increments counter. Then the program evaluates the loop-continuation test at the *bottom* of the loop (line 14). If the condition is *true*, the loop continues at the first body statement (line 12). If the condition is *false*, the loop terminates and the program continues at the next statement after the loop.

```java
1   // Fig. 5.7: DoWhileTest.java
2   // do...while repetition statement.
3
4   public class DoWhileTest
5   {
6      public static void main(String[] args)
7      {
8         int counter = 1;
9
10        do
11        {
12           System.out.printf("%d  ", counter);
13           ++counter;
14        } while (counter <= 10); // end do...while
15
16        System.out.println();
17     }
18  } // end class DoWhileTest
```

```
1 2 3 4 5 6 7 8 9 10
```

Fig. 5.7 | do...while repetition statement.

Braces in a *do...while Repetition Statement*
It isn't necessary to use braces in the do...while repetition statement if there's only one statement in the body. However, many programmers include the braces, to avoid confusion between the while and do...while statements. For example,

```
while (condition)
```

is normally the first line of a while statement. A do...while statement with no braces around a single-statement body appears as:

```
do
    statement
while (condition);
```

which can be confusing. A reader may misinterpret the last line—while(*condition*);—as a while statement containing an empty statement (the semicolon by itself). Thus, the do...while statement with one body statement is usually written with braces as follows:

```
do
{
    statement
} while (condition);
```

Good Programming Practice 5.1

Always include braces in a do...while statement. This helps eliminate ambiguity between the while statement and a do...while statement containing only one statement.

*UML Activity Diagram for the **do...while** Repetition Statement*
Figure 5.8 contains the UML activity diagram for the do...while statement. This diagram makes it clear that the loop-continuation condition is not evaluated until *after* the loop performs the action state *at least once*. Compare this activity diagram with that of the while statement (Fig. 4.6).

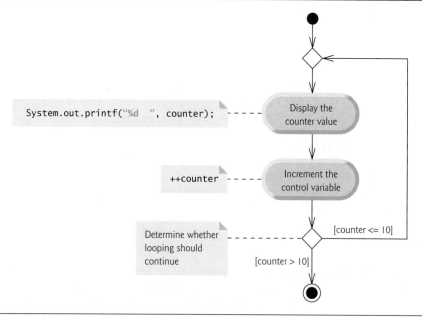

Fig. 5.8 | do...while repetition statement UML activity diagram.

5.6 switch Multiple-Selection Statement

Chapter 4 discussed the if single-selection statement and the if...else double-selection statement. The **switch multiple-selection statement** performs different actions based on the possible values of a **constant integral expression** of type byte, short, int or char. As of Java SE 7, the expression may also be a String, which we discuss in Section 5.7.

*Using a **switch** Statement to Count A, B, C, D and F Grades*

Figure 5.9 calculates the class average of a set of numeric grades entered by the user, and uses a switch statement to determine whether each grade is the equivalent of an A, B, C, D or F and to increment the appropriate grade counter. The program also displays a summary of the number of students who received each grade.

Like earlier versions of the class-average program, the main method of class Letter-Grades (Fig. 5.9) declares local variables total (line 9) and gradeCounter (line 10) to keep track of the sum of the grades entered by the user and the number of grades entered, respectively. Lines 11–15 declare counter variables for each grade category. Note that the variables in lines 9–15 are explicitly initialized to 0.

Method main has two key parts. Lines 26–56 read an arbitrary number of integer grades from the user using sentinel-controlled repetition, update instance variables total and gradeCounter, and increment an appropriate letter-grade counter for each grade entered. Lines 59–80 output a report containing the total of all grades entered, the average of the grades and the number of students who received each letter grade. Let's examine these parts in more detail.

```java
1   // Fig. 5.9: LetterGrades.java
2   // LetterGrades class uses the switch statement to count letter grades.
3   import java.util.Scanner;
4
5   public class LetterGrades
6   {
7      public static void main(String[] args)
8      {
9         int total = 0; // sum of grades
10        int gradeCounter = 0; // number of grades entered
11        int aCount = 0; // count of A grades
12        int bCount = 0; // count of B grades
13        int cCount = 0; // count of C grades
14        int dCount = 0; // count of D grades
15        int fCount = 0; // count of F grades
16
17        Scanner input = new Scanner(System.in);
18
19        System.out.printf("%s%n%s%n   %s%n   %s%n",
20           "Enter the integer grades in the range 0-100.",
21           "Type the end-of-file indicator to terminate input:",
22           "On UNIX/Linux/Mac OS X type <Ctrl> d then press Enter",
23           "On Windows type <Ctrl> z then press Enter");
24
25        // loop until user enters the end-of-file indicator
26        while (input.hasNext())
27        {
28           int grade = input.nextInt(); // read grade
29           total += grade; // add grade to total
30           ++gradeCounter; // increment number of grades
31
```

Fig. 5.9 | LetterGrades class uses the switch statement to count letter grades. (Part 1 of 3.)

```
32            // increment appropriate letter-grade counter
33            switch (grade / 10)
34            {
35               case 9:  // grade was between 90
36               case 10: // and 100, inclusive
37                  ++aCount;
38                  break; // exits switch
39
40               case 8: // grade was between 80 and 89
41                  ++bCount;
42                  break; // exits switch
43
44               case 7: // grade was between 70 and 79
45                  ++cCount;
46                  break; // exits switch
47
48               case 6: // grade was between 60 and 69
49                  ++dCount;
50                  break; // exits switch
51
52               default: // grade was less than 60
53                  ++fCount;
54                  break; // optional; exits switch anyway
55            } // end switch
56         } // end while
57
58         // display grade report
59         System.out.printf("%nGrade Report:%n");
60
61         // if user entered at least one grade...
62         if (gradeCounter != 0)
63         {
64            // calculate average of all grades entered
65            double average = (double) total / gradeCounter;
66
67            // output summary of results
68            System.out.printf("Total of the %d grades entered is %d%n",
69               gradeCounter, total);
70            System.out.printf("Class average is %.2f%n", average);
71            System.out.printf("%n%s%n%s%d%n%s%d%n%s%d%n%s%d%n%s%d%n",
72               "Number of students who received each grade:",
73               "A: ", aCount,   // display number of A grades
74               "B: ", bCount,   // display number of B grades
75               "C: ", cCount,   // display number of C grades
76               "D: ", dCount,   // display number of D grades
77               "F: ", fCount); // display number of F grades
78         } // end if
79         else // no grades were entered, so output appropriate message
80            System.out.println("No grades were entered");
81      } // end main
82   } // end class LetterGrades
```

Fig. 5.9 | LetterGrades class uses the switch statement to count letter grades. (Part 2 of 3.)

```
Enter the integer grades in the range 0-100.
Type the end-of-file indicator to terminate input:
   On UNIX/Linux/Mac OS X type <Ctrl> d then press Enter
   On Windows type <Ctrl> z then press Enter
99
92
45
57
63
71
76
85
90
100
^Z

Grade Report:
Total of the 10 grades entered is 778
Class average is 77.80

Number of students who received each grade:
A: 4
B: 1
C: 2
D: 1
F: 2
```

Fig. 5.9 | LetterGrades class uses the switch statement to count letter grades. (Part 3 of 3.)

Reading Grades from the User

Lines 19–23 prompt the user to enter integer grades and to type the end-of-file indicator to terminate the input. The **end-of-file indicator** is a system-dependent keystroke combination which the user enters to indicate that there's *no more data to input*. In Chapter 15, Files, Streams and Object Serialization, you'll see how the end-of-file indicator is used when a program reads its input from a file.

On UNIX/Linux/Mac OS X systems, end-of-file is entered by typing the sequence

    <Ctrl> d

on a line by itself. This notation means to simultaneously press both the *Ctrl* key and the *d* key. On Windows systems, end-of-file can be entered by typing

    <Ctrl> z

[*Note:* On some systems, you must press *Enter* after typing the end-of-file key sequence. Also, Windows typically displays the characters ^Z on the screen when the end-of-file indicator is typed, as shown in the output of Fig. 5.9.]

Portability Tip 5.1

The keystroke combinations for entering end-of-file are system dependent.

The while statement (lines 26–56) obtains the user input. The condition at line 26 calls Scanner method **hasNext** to determine whether there's more data to input. This method returns the boolean value true if there's more data; otherwise, it returns false. The returned value is then used as the value of the condition in the while statement. Method hasNext returns false once the user types the end-of-file indicator.

Line 28 inputs a grade value from the user. Line 29 adds grade to total. Line 30 increments gradeCounter. These variables are used to compute the average of the grades. Lines 33–55 use a switch statement to increment the appropriate letter-grade counter based on the numeric grade entered.

Processing the Grades

The switch statement (lines 33–55) determines which counter to increment. We assume that the user enters a valid grade in the range 0–100. A grade in the range 90–100 represents A, 80–89 represents B, 70–79 represents C, 60–69 represents D and 0–59 represents F. The switch statement consists of a block that contains a sequence of **case labels** and an optional **default case**. These are used in this example to determine which counter to increment based on the grade.

When the flow of control reaches the switch, the program evaluates the expression in the parentheses (grade / 10) following keyword switch. This is the switch's **controlling expression**. The program compares this expression's value (which must evaluate to an integral value of type byte, char, short or int, or to a String) with each case label. The controlling expression in line 33 performs integer division, which *truncates the fractional part* of the result. Thus, when we divide a value from 0 to 100 by 10, the result is always a value from 0 to 10. We use several of these values in our case labels. For example, if the user enters the integer 85, the controlling expression evaluates to 8. The switch compares 8 with each case label. If a match occurs (case 8: at line 40), the program executes that case's statements. For the integer 8, line 41 increments bCount, because a grade in the 80s is a B. The **break statement** (line 42) causes program control to proceed with the first statement after the switch—in this program, we reach the end of the while loop, so control returns to the loop-continuation condition in line 26 to determine whether the loop should continue executing.

The cases in our switch explicitly test for the values 10, 9, 8, 7 and 6. Note the cases at lines 35–36 that test for the values 9 and 10 (both of which represent the grade A). Listing cases consecutively in this manner with no statements between them enables the cases to perform the same set of statements—when the controlling expression evaluates to 9 or 10, the statements in lines 37–38 will execute. The switch statement does *not* provide a mechanism for testing *ranges* of values, so *every* value you need to test must be listed in a separate case label. Each case can have multiple statements. The switch statement differs from other control statements in that it does *not* require braces around multiple statements in a case.

case without a break Statement

Without break statements, each time a match occurs, the statements for that case and subsequent cases execute until a break statement or the end of the switch is encountered. This is often referred to as "falling through" to the statements in subsequent cases.

Common Programming Error 5.6

Forgetting a break statement when one is needed in a switch is a logic error.

The default Case

If no match occurs between the controlling expression's value and a case label, the default case (lines 52–54) executes. We use the default case in this example to process all controlling-expression values that are less than 6—that is, all failing grades. If no match occurs and the switch does not contain a default case, program control simply continues with the first statement after the switch.

Error-Prevention Tip 5.6

In a switch statement, ensure that you test all possible values of the controlling expression.

Displaying the Grade Report

Lines 59–80 output a report based on the grades entered (as shown in the input/output window in Fig. 5.9). Line 62 determines whether the user entered at least one grade—this helps us avoid dividing by zero. If so, line 65 calculates the average of the grades. Lines 68–77 then output the total of all the grades, the class average and the number of students who received each letter grade. If no grades were entered, line 80 outputs an appropriate message. The output in Fig. 5.9 shows a sample grade report based on 10 grades.

switch Statement UML Activity Diagram

Figure 5.10 shows the UML activity diagram for the general switch statement. Most switch statements use a break in each case to terminate the switch statement after processing the case. Figure 5.10 emphasizes this by including break statements in the activity diagram. The diagram makes it clear that the break statement at the end of a case causes control to exit the switch statement immediately.

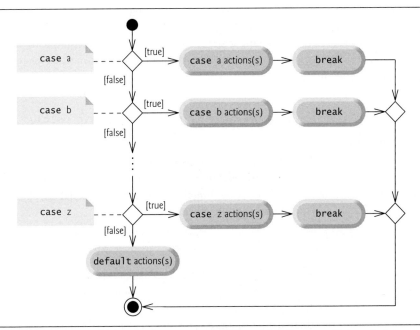

Fig. 5.10 | switch multiple-selection statement UML activity diagram with break statements.

The break statement is *not* required for the switch's last case (or the optional default case, when it appears last), because execution continues with the next statement after the switch.

Error-Prevention Tip 5.7

Provide a default case in switch statements. This focuses you on the need to process exceptional conditions.

Good Programming Practice 5.2

Although each case and the default case in a switch can occur in any order, place the default case last. When the default case is listed last, the break for that case is not required.

Notes on the Expression in Each case of a switch

When using the switch statement, remember that each case must contain a constant integral expression—that is, any combination of integer constants that evaluates to a constant integer value (e.g., –7, 0 or 221)—or a String. An integer constant is simply an integer value. In addition, you can use **character constants**—specific characters in single quotes, such as 'A', '7' or '$'—which represent the integer values of characters and enum constants (introduced in Section 6.9). (Appendix B shows the integer values of the characters in the ASCII character set, which is a subset of the Unicode® character set used by Java.)

The expression in each case can also be a **constant variable**—a variable containing a value which does not change for the entire program. Such a variable is declared with keyword final (discussed in Chapter 6). Java has a feature called enum types, which we also present in Chapter 6—enum type constants can also be used in case labels.

In Chapter 10, Object-Oriented Programming: Polymorphism and Interfaces, we present a more elegant way to implement switch logic—we use the technique of polymorphism to create programs that are often clearer, easier to maintain and easier to extend than programs using switch logic.

5.7 Class AutoPolicy Case Study: Strings in switch Statements

Strings can be used as controlling expressions in switch statements, and String literals can be used in case labels. To demonstrate that Strings can be used as controlling expressions in switch statements and that String literals can be used in case labels, we'll implement an app that meets the following requirements:

> *You've been hired by an auto insurance company that serves these northeast states—Connecticut, Maine, Massachusetts, New Hampshire, New Jersey, New York, Pennsylvania, Rhode Island and Vermont. The company would like you to create a program that produces a report indicating for each of their auto insurance policies whether the policy is held in a state with "no-fault" auto insurance—Massachusetts, New Jersey, New York and Pennsylvania.*

The Java app that meets these requirements contains two classes—AutoPolicy (Fig. 5.11) and AutoPolicyTest (Fig. 5.12).

Class *AutoPolicy*

Class AutoPolicy (Fig. 5.11) represents an auto insurance policy. The class contains:

- int instance variable accountNumber (line 5) to store the policy's account number

- String instance variable makeAndModel (line 6) to store the car's make and model (such as a "Toyota Camry")

- String instance variable state (line 7) to store a two-character state abbreviation representing the state in which the policy is held (e.g., "MA" for Massachusetts)

- a constructor (lines 10–15) that initializes the class's instance variables

- methods setAccountNumber and getAccountNumber (lines 18–27) to *set* and *get* an AutoPolicy's accountNumber instance variable

- methods setMakeAndModel and getMakeAndModel (lines 30–39) to *set* and *get* an AutoPolicy's makeAndModel instance variable

- methods setState and getState (lines 42–51) to *set* and *get* an AutoPolicy's state instance variable

- method isNoFaultState (lines 54–70) to return a boolean value indicating whether the policy is held in a no-fault auto insurance state; note the method name—the naming convention for a *get* method that returns a boolean value is to begin the name with "is" rather than "get" (such a method is commonly called a *predicate method*).

In method isNoFaultState, the switch statement's controlling expression (line 59) is the String returned by AutoPolicy method getState. The switch statement compares the controlling expression's value with the case labels (line 61) to determine whether the policy is held in Massachusetts, New Jersey, New York or Pennsylvania (the no-fault states). If there's a match, then line 62 sets local variable noFaultState to true and the switch statement terminates; otherwise, the default case sets noFaultState to false (line 65). Then method isNoFaultState returns local variable noFaultState's value.

For simplicity, we did not validate an AutoPolicy's data in the constructor or *set* methods, and we assume that state abbreviations are always two uppercase letters. In addition, a real AutoPolicy class would likely contain many other instance variables and methods for data such as the account holder's name, address, etc.

```java
1   // Fig. 5.11: AutoPolicy.java
2   // Class that represents an auto insurance policy.
3   public class AutoPolicy
4   {
5      private int accountNumber; // policy account number
6      private String makeAndModel; // car that the policy applies to
7      private String state; // two-letter state abbreviation
8
9      // constructor
10     public AutoPolicy(int accountNumber, String makeAndModel, String state)
11     {
```

Fig. 5.11 | Class that represents an auto insurance policy. (Part 1 of 3.)

```
12          this.accountNumber = accountNumber;
13          this.makeAndModel = makeAndModel;
14          this.state = state;
15      }
16
17      // sets the accountNumber
18      public void setAccountNumber(int accountNumber)
19      {
20          this.accountNumber = accountNumber;
21      }
22
23      // returns the accountNumber
24      public int getAccountNumber()
25      {
26          return accountNumber;
27      }
28
29      // sets the makeAndModel
30      public void setMakeAndModel(String makeAndModel)
31      {
32          this.makeAndModel = makeAndModel;
33      }
34
35      // returns the makeAndModel
36      public String getMakeAndModel()
37      {
38          return makeAndModel;
39      }
40
41      // sets the state
42      public void setState(String state)
43      {
44          this.state = state;
45      }
46
47      // returns the state
48      public String getState()
49      {
50          return state;
51      }
52
53      // predicate method returns whether the state has no-fault insurance
54      public boolean isNoFaultState()
55      {
56          boolean noFaultState;
57
58          // determine whether state has no-fault auto insurance
59          switch (getState()) // get AutoPolicy object's state abbreviation
60          {
61              case "MA": case "NJ": case "NY": case "PA":
62                  noFaultState = true;
63                  break;
```

Fig. 5.11 | Class that represents an auto insurance policy. (Part 2 of 3.)

```
64              default:
65                  noFaultState = false;
66                  break;
67          }
68
69          return noFaultState;
70      }
71  } // end class AutoPolicy
```

Fig. 5.11 | Class that represents an auto insurance policy. (Part 3 of 3.)

Class *AutoPolicyTest*

Class AutoPolicyTest (Fig. 5.12) creates two AutoPolicy objects (lines 8–11 in main). Lines 14–15 pass each object to static method policyInNoFaultState (lines 20–28), which uses AutoPolicy methods to determine and display whether the object it receives represents a policy in a no-fault auto insurance state.

```
1   // Fig. 5.12: AutoPolicyTest.java
2   // Demonstrating Strings in switch.
3   public class AutoPolicyTest
4   {
5       public static void main(String[] args)
6       {
7           // create two AutoPolicy objects
8           AutoPolicy policy1 =
9               new AutoPolicy(11111111, "Toyota Camry", "NJ");
10          AutoPolicy policy2 =
11              new AutoPolicy(22222222, "Ford Fusion", "ME");
12
13          // display whether each policy is in a no-fault state
14          policyInNoFaultState(policy1);
15          policyInNoFaultState(policy2);
16      }
17
18      // method that displays whether an AutoPolicy
19      // is in a state with no-fault auto insurance
20      public static void policyInNoFaultState(AutoPolicy policy)
21      {
22          System.out.println("The auto policy:");
23          System.out.printf(
24              "Account #: %d; Car: %s; State %s %s a no-fault state%n%n",
25              policy.getAccountNumber(), policy.getMakeAndModel(),
26              policy.getState(),
27              (policy.isNoFaultState() ? "is": "is not"));
28      }
29  } // end class AutoPolicyTest
```

```
The auto policy:
Account #: 11111111; Car: Toyota Camry;
State NJ is a no-fault state
```

Fig. 5.12 | Demonstrating Strings in switch. (Part 1 of 2.)

```
The auto policy:
Account #: 22222222; Car: Ford Fusion;
State ME is not a no-fault state
```

Fig. 5.12 | Demonstrating Strings in switch. (Part 2 of 2.)

5.8 break and continue Statements

In addition to selection and repetition statements, Java provides statements break (which we discussed in the context of the switch statement)and **continue** (presented in this section and Appendix L) to alter the flow of control. The preceding section showed how break can be used to terminate a switch statement's execution. This section discusses how to use break in repetition statements.

break *Statement*

The break statement, when executed in a while, for, do...while or switch, causes *immediate* exit from that statement. Execution continues with the first statement after the control statement. Common uses of the break statement are to escape early from a loop or to skip the remainder of a switch (as in Fig. 5.9). Figure 5.13 demonstrates a break statement exiting a for. When the if statement nested at lines 11–12 in the for statement (lines 9–15) detects that count is 5, the break statement at line 12 executes. This terminates the for statement, and the program proceeds to line 17 (immediately after the for statement), which displays a message indicating the value of the control variable when the loop terminated. The loop fully executes its body only four times instead of 10.

```
 1   // Fig. 5.13: BreakTest.java
 2   // break statement exiting a for statement.
 3   public class BreakTest
 4   {
 5      public static void main(String[] args)
 6      {
 7         int count; // control variable also used after loop terminates
 8
 9         for (count = 1; count <= 10; count++) // loop 10 times
10         {
11            if (count == 5)
12               break; // terminates loop if count is 5
13
14            System.out.printf("%d ", count);
15         }
16
17         System.out.printf("%nBroke out of loop at count = %d%n", count);
18      }
19   } // end class BreakTest
```

```
1 2 3 4
Broke out of loop at count = 5
```

Fig. 5.13 | break statement exiting a for statement.

continue *Statement*

The continue statement, when executed in a while, for or do...while, skips the remaining statements in the loop body and proceeds with the next iteration of the loop. In while and do...while statements, the program evaluates the loop-continuation test immediately after the continue statement executes. In a for statement, the increment expression executes, then the program evaluates the loop-continuation test.

```java
1   // Fig. 5.14: ContinueTest.java
2   // continue statement terminating an iteration of a for statement.
3   public class ContinueTest
4   {
5      public static void main(String[] args)
6      {
7         for (int count = 1; count <= 10; count++) // loop 10 times
8         {
9            if (count == 5)
10              continue; // skip remaining code in loop body if count is 5
11
12           System.out.printf("%d ", count);
13        }
14
15        System.out.printf("%nUsed continue to skip printing 5%n");
16     }
17  } // end class ContinueTest
```

```
1 2 3 4 6 7 8 9 10
Used continue to skip printing 5
```

Fig. 5.14 | continue statement terminating an iteration of a for statement.

Figure 5.14 uses continue (line 10) to skip the statement at line 12 when the nested if determines that count's value is 5. When the continue statement executes, program control continues with the increment of the control variable in the for statement (line 7).

In Section 5.3, we stated that while could be used in most cases in place of for. This is not true when the increment expression in the while follows a continue statement. In this case, the increment does *not* execute before the program evaluates the repetition-continuation condition, so the while does not execute in the same manner as the for.

Software Engineering Observation 5.2

Some programmers feel that break and continue violate structured programming. Since the same effects are achievable with structured programming techniques, these programmers do not use break or continue.

Software Engineering Observation 5.3

There's a tension between achieving quality software engineering and achieving the best-performing software. Sometimes one of these goals is achieved at the expense of the other. For all but the most performance-intensive situations, apply the following rule: First, make your code simple and correct; then make it fast and small, but only if necessary.

5.9 Logical Operators

The if, if...else, while, do...while and for statements each require a *condition* to determine how to continue a program's flow of control. So far, we've studied only simple conditions, such as count <= 10, number != sentinelValue and total > 1000. Simple conditions are expressed in terms of the relational operators >, <, >= and <= and the equality operators == and !=, and each expression tests only one condition. To test *multiple* conditions in the process of making a decision, we performed these tests in separate statements or in nested if or if...else statements. Sometimes control statements require more complex conditions to determine a program's flow of control.

Java's **logical operators** enable you to form more complex conditions by combining simple conditions. The logical operators are && (conditional AND), || (conditional OR), & (boolean logical AND), | (boolean logical inclusive OR), ∧ (boolean logical exclusive OR) and ! (logical NOT). [*Note:* The &, | and ∧ operators are also bitwise operators when they're applied to integral operands. We discuss the bitwise operators in Appendix K.]

Conditional AND (&&) Operator

Suppose we wish to ensure at some point in a program that two conditions are *both* true before we choose a certain path of execution. In this case, we can use the **&&** (**conditional AND**) operator, as follows:

```
if (gender == FEMALE && age >= 65)
    ++seniorFemales;
```

This if statement contains two simple conditions. The condition gender == FEMALE compares variable gender to the constant FEMALE to determine whether a person is female. The condition age >= 65 might be evaluated to determine whether a person is a senior citizen. The if statement considers the combined condition

```
gender == FEMALE && age >= 65
```

which is true if and only if *both* simple conditions are true. In this case, the if statement's body increments seniorFemales by 1. If either or both of the simple conditions are false, the program skips the increment. Some programmers find that the preceding combined condition is more readable when *redundant* parentheses are added, as in:

```
(gender == FEMALE) && (age >= 65)
```

The table in Fig. 5.15 summarizes the && operator. The table shows all four possible combinations of false and true values for *expression1* and *expression2*. Such tables are called **truth tables**. Java evaluates to false or true all expressions that include relational operators, equality operators or logical operators.

expression1	expression2	expression1 && expression2
false	false	false
false	true	false
true	false	false
true	true	true

Fig. 5.15 | && (conditional AND) operator truth table.

Conditional OR (||) Operator

Now suppose we wish to ensure that *either or both* of two conditions are true before we choose a certain path of execution. In this case, we use the || (**conditional OR**) operator, as in the following program segment:

```
if ((semesterAverage >= 90) || (finalExam >= 90))
    System.out.println ("Student grade is A");
```

This statement also contains two simple conditions. The condition semesterAverage >= 90 evaluates to determine whether the student deserves an A in the course because of a solid performance throughout the semester. The condition finalExam >= 90 evaluates to determine whether the student deserves an A in the course because of an outstanding performance on the final exam. The if statement then considers the combined condition

```
(semesterAverage >= 90) || (finalExam >= 90)
```

and awards the student an A if *either or both* of the simple conditions are true. The only time the message "Student grade is A" is *not* printed is when *both* of the simple conditions are *false*. Figure 5.16 is a truth table for operator conditional OR (||). Operator && has a higher precedence than operator ||. Both operators associate from left to right.

expression1	expression2	expression1 || expression2
false	false	false
false	true	true
true	false	true
true	true	true

Fig. 5.16 | || (conditional OR) operator truth table.

Short-Circuit Evaluation of Complex Conditions

The parts of an expression containing && or || operators are evaluated *only* until it's known whether the condition is true or false. Thus, evaluation of the expression

```
(gender == FEMALE) && (age >= 65)
```

stops immediately if gender *is not* equal to FEMALE (i.e., the entire expression is false) and continues if gender *is* equal to FEMALE (i.e., the entire expression could still be true if the condition age >= 65 is true). This feature of conditional AND and conditional OR expressions is called **short-circuit evaluation**.

Common Programming Error 5.7

In expressions using operator &&, a condition—we'll call this the dependent condition—*may require another condition to be true for the evaluation of the dependent condition to be meaningful. In this case, the dependent condition should be placed after the && operator to prevent errors. Consider the expression (i != 0) && (10 / i == 2). The dependent condition (10 / i == 2) must appear after the && operator to prevent the possibility of division by zero.*

Boolean Logical AND (&) and Boolean Logical Inclusive OR (|) Operators
The **boolean logical AND (&)** and **boolean logical inclusive OR (|)** operators are identical
to the && and || operators, except that the & and | operators *always* evaluate *both* of their
operands (i.e., they do *not* perform short-circuit evaluation). So, the expression

```
(gender == 1) & (age >= 65)
```

evaluates age >= 65 *regardless* of whether gender is 1. This is useful if the right operand has
a required **side effect**—a modification of a variable's value. For example, the expression

```
(birthday == true) | (++age >= 65)
```

guarantees that the condition ++age >= 65 will be evaluated. Thus, the variable age is incremented, regardless of whether the overall expression is true or false.

Error-Prevention Tip 5.8

*For clarity, avoid expressions with side effects (such as assignments) in conditions. They
can make code harder to understand and can lead to subtle logic errors.*

Error-Prevention Tip 5.9

Assignment (=) expressions generally should not *be used in conditions. Every condition
must* result in a boolean value; otherwise, a compilation error occurs. In a condition, an
assignment will compile *only if a boolean expression is assigned to a* boolean *variable.*

Boolean Logical Exclusive OR (^)
A simple condition containing the **boolean logical exclusive OR (^)** operator is true *if and
only if one of its operands is* true *and the other is* false. If both are true or both are false,
the entire condition is false. Figure 5.17 is a truth table for the boolean logical exclusive
OR operator (^). This operator is guaranteed to evaluate *both* of its operands.

expression1	expression2	expression1 ^ expression2
false	false	false
false	true	true
true	false	true
true	true	false

Fig. 5.17 | ^ (boolean logical exclusive OR) operator truth table.

Logical Negation (!) Operator
The ! (**logical NOT**, also called **logical negation** or **logical complement**) operator "revers-
es" the meaning of a condition. Unlike the logical operators &&, ||, &, | and ^, which are
binary operators that combine two conditions, the logical negation operator is a *unary* operator that has only one condition as an operand. The operator is placed *before* a condition
to choose a path of execution if the original condition (without the logical negation operator) is false, as in the program segment

```
if (! (grade == sentinelValue))
    System.out.printf("The next grade is %d%n", grade);
```

which executes the printf call only if grade is *not* equal to sentinelValue. The parentheses around the condition grade == sentinelValue are needed because the logical negation operator has a *higher* precedence than the equality operator.

In most cases, you can avoid using logical negation by expressing the condition differently with an appropriate relational or equality operator. For example, the previous statement may also be written as follows:

```
if (grade != sentinelValue)
    System.out.printf("The next grade is %d%n", grade);
```

This flexibility can help you express a condition in a more convenient manner. Figure 5.18 is a truth table for the logical negation operator.

expression	!expression
false	true
true	false

Fig. 5.18 | ! (logical NOT) operator truth table.

Logical Operators Example
Figure 5.19 uses logical operators to produce the truth tables discussed in this section. The output shows the boolean expression that was evaluated and its result. We used the **%b format specifier** to display the word "true" or the word "false" based on a boolean expression's value. Lines 9–13 produce the truth table for &&. Lines 16–20 produce the truth table for ||. Lines 23–27 produce the truth table for &. Lines 30–35 produce the truth table for |. Lines 38–43 produce the truth table for ^. Lines 46–47 produce the truth table for !.

```
 1  // Fig. 5.19: LogicalOperators.java
 2  // Logical operators.
 3
 4  public class LogicalOperators
 5  {
 6     public static void main(String[] args)
 7     {
 8        // create truth table for && (conditional AND) operator
 9        System.out.printf("%s%n%s: %b%n%s: %b%n%s: %b%n%s: %b%n%n",
10           "Conditional AND (&&)", "false && false", (false && false) ,
11           "false && true", (false && true) ,
12           "true && false", (true && false) ,
13           "true && true", (true && true) );
14
15        // create truth table for || (conditional OR) operator
16        System.out.printf("%s%n%s: %b%n%s: %b%n%s: %b%n%s: %b%n%n",
17           "Conditional OR (||)", "false || false", (false || false) ,
18           "false || true", (false || true) ,
19           "true || false", (true || false) ,
20           "true || true", (true || true) );
```

Fig. 5.19 | Logical operators. (Part 1 of 3.)

```
21
22          // create truth table for & (boolean logical AND) operator
23          System.out.printf("%s%n%s: %b%n%s: %b%n%s: %b%n%s: %b%n%n",
24             "Boolean logical AND (&)", "false & false", (false & false)  ,
25             "false & true", (false & true)  ,
26             "true & false", (true & false)  ,
27             "true & true", (true & true)  );
28
29          // create truth table for | (boolean logical inclusive OR) operator
30          System.out.printf("%s%n%s: %b%n%s: %b%n%s: %b%n%s: %b%n%n",
31             "Boolean logical inclusive OR (|)",
32             "false | false", (false | false)  ,
33             "false | true", (false | true)  ,
34             "true | false", (true | false)  ,
35             "true | true", (true | true)  );
36
37          // create truth table for ^ (boolean logical exclusive OR) operator
38          System.out.printf("%s%n%s: %b%n%s: %b%n%s: %b%n%s: %b%n%n",
39             "Boolean logical exclusive OR (^)",
40             "false ^ false", (false ^ false)  ,
41             "false ^ true", (false ^ true)  ,
42             "true ^ false", (true ^ false)  ,
43             "true ^ true", (true ^ true)  );
44
45          // create truth table for ! (logical negation) operator
46          System.out.printf("%s%n%s: %b%n%s: %b%n", "Logical NOT (!)",
47             "!false", (!false)  , "!true", (!true)  );
48       }
49    } // end class LogicalOperators
```

```
Conditional AND (&&)
false && false: false
false && true: false
true && false: false
true && true: true

Conditional OR (||)
false || false: false
false || true: true
true || false: true
true || true: true

Boolean logical AND (&)
false & false: false
false & true: false
true & false: false
true & true: true

Boolean logical inclusive OR (|)
false | false: false
false | true: true
true | false: true
true | true: true
```

Fig. 5.19 | Logical operators. (Part 2 of 3.)

```
Boolean logical exclusive OR (^)
false ^ false: false
false ^ true: true
true ^ false: true
true ^ true: false

Logical NOT (!)
!false: true
!true: false
```

Fig. 5.19 | Logical operators. (Part 3 of 3.)

Precedence and Associativity of the Operators Presented So Far
Figure 5.20 shows the precedence and associativity of the Java operators introduced so far.
The operators are shown from top to bottom in decreasing order of precedence.

Operators						Associativity	Type
++	--					right to left	unary postfix
++	--	+	-	!	(*type*)	right to left	unary prefix
*	/	%				left to right	multiplicative
+	-					left to right	additive
<	<=	>	>=			left to right	relational
==	!=					left to right	equality
&						left to right	boolean logical AND
^						left to right	boolean logical exclusive OR
|						left to right	boolean logical inclusive OR
&&						left to right	conditional AND
||						left to right	conditional OR
?:						right to left	conditional
=	+=	-=	*=	/=	%=	right to left	assignment

Fig. 5.20 | Precedence/associativity of the operators discussed so far.

5.10 Wrap-Up

In this chapter, we completed our introduction to control statements, which enable you
to control the flow of execution in methods. Chapter 4 discussed if, if...else and while.
This chapter demonstrated for, do...while and switch. We showed that any program can
be developed using combinations of sequence, the three types of selection statements—if,
if...else and switch—and the three types of repetition statements—while, do...while
and for. In this chapter and Chapter 4, we discussed how you can combine these building
blocks to utilize proven program-construction techniques. You used the break statement

to exit a `switch` statement and to immediately terminate a loop, and used a `continue` statement to terminate a loop's current iteration and proceed with the loop's next iteration. This chapter also introduced the logical operators, which enable you to use more complex conditional expressions in control statements. In Chapter 6, we examine methods in greater depth.

Methods: A Deeper Look

6.1 Introduction

In this chapter, we study methods in more depth. You'll learn more about `static` methods, which can be called without the need for an object of the class to exist. We'll discuss Java's promotion rules for converting implicitly between primitive types and how to perform explicit conversions with cast operators.

We'll take a brief diversion into simulation techniques with random-number generation and develop a version of the dice game called craps that uses most of the programming techniques you've used to this point in the book. You'll learn how to declare constants in your programs. You'll also learn about the scope of fields and local variables in a class.

Many of the classes you'll use or create while developing applications will have more than one method of the same name. This technique, called *overloading*, is used to implement methods that perform similar tasks for arguments of different types or for different numbers of arguments.

6.2 Program Modules in Java

You write Java programs by combining new methods and classes with predefined ones available in the **Java Application Programming Interface** (also referred to as the **Java API** or **Java class library**) and in various other class libraries. Related classes are typically grouped into packages so that they can be imported into programs and reused. You'll learn how to group your own classes into packages in Section 8.14. The Java API provides a rich collection of predefined classes that contain methods for performing common mathematical calculations, string manipulations, character manipulations, input/output operations, database operations, networking operations, file processing, error checking and more.

Software Engineering Observation 6.1

Familiarize yourself with the rich collection of classes and methods provided by the Java API (http://docs.oracle.com/javase/7/docs/api/). Section 6.7 overviews several common packages. Appendix F explains how to navigate the API documentation. Don't reinvent the wheel. When possible, reuse Java API classes and methods. This reduces program development time and avoids introducing programming errors.

Error-Prevention Tip 6.1

When you call a method that returns a value indicating whether the method performed its task successfully, be sure to check the return value of that method and, if that method was unsuccessful, deal with the issue appropriately.

6.3 static Methods, static Fields and Class Math

Although most methods execute in response to method calls *on specific objects*, this is not always the case. Sometimes a method performs a task that does not depend on an object. Such a method applies to the class in which it's declared as a whole and is known as a static method or a **class method**.

It's common for classes to contain convenient static methods to perform common tasks. For example, recall that we used static method pow of class Math to raise a value to a power in Fig. 5.6. To declare a method as static, place the keyword static before the return type in the method's declaration. For any class imported into your program, you can call the class's static methods by specifying the name of the class in which the method is declared, followed by a dot (.) and the method name, as in

> *ClassName.methodName(arguments)*

Math *Class Methods*

We use Math class methods here to present the static methods concept. Class Math provides a collection of methods that enable you to perform common mathematical calculations. For example, you can calculate the square root of 900.0 with the static method call

```
Math.sqrt(900.0)
```

This expression evaluates to 30.0. Method sqrt takes an argument of type double and returns a result of type double. To output the value of the preceding method call in the command window, you might write the statement

```
System.out.println(Math.sqrt(900.0));
```

In this statement, the value that sqrt returns becomes the argument to method println. There was no need to create a Math object before calling method sqrt. Also *all* Math class methods are static—therefore, each is called by preceding its name with the class name Math and the dot (.) separator.

> **Software Engineering Observation 6.2**
>
> *Class Math is part of the java.lang package, which is implicitly imported by the compiler, so it's not necessary to import class Math to use its methods.*

Method arguments may be constants, variables or expressions. If c = 13.0, d = 3.0 and f = 4.0, then the statement

```
System.out.println(Math.sqrt(c + d * f));
```

calculates and prints the square root of 13.0 + 3.0 * 4.0 = 25.0—namely, 5.0. Figure 6.1 summarizes several Math class methods. In the figure, *x* and *y* are of type double.

Method	Description	Example
abs(*x*)	absolute value of *x*	abs(23.7) is 23.7 abs(0.0) is 0.0 abs(-23.7) is 23.7

Fig. 6.1 | Math class methods. (Part 1 of 2.)

Method	Description	Example
ceil(x)	rounds x to the smallest integer not less than x	ceil(9.2) is 10.0 ceil(-9.8) is -9.0
cos(x)	trigonometric cosine of x (x in radians)	cos(0.0) is 1.0
exp(x)	exponential method e^x	exp(1.0) is 2.71828 exp(2.0) is 7.38906
floor(x)	rounds x to the largest integer not greater than x	floor(9.2) is 9.0 floor(-9.8) is -10.0
log(x)	natural logarithm of x (base e)	log(Math.E) is 1.0 log(Math.E * Math.E) is 2.0
max(x, y)	larger value of x and y	max(2.3, 12.7) is 12.7 max(-2.3, -12.7) is -2.3
min(x, y)	smaller value of x and y	min(2.3, 12.7) is 2.3 min(-2.3, -12.7) is -12.7
pow(x, y)	x raised to the power y (i.e., x^y)	pow(2.0, 7.0) is 128.0 pow(9.0, 0.5) is 3.0
sin(x)	trigonometric sine of x (x in radians)	sin(0.0) is 0.0
sqrt(x)	square root of x	sqrt(900.0) is 30.0
tan(x)	trigonometric tangent of x (x in radians)	tan(0.0) is 0.0

Fig. 6.1 | Math class methods. (Part 2 of 2.)

static *Variables*

Recall from Section 3.2 that each object of a class maintains its *own* copy of every instance variable of the class. There are variables for which each object of a class does *not* need its own separate copy (as you'll see momentarily). Such variables are declared static and are also known as **class variables**. When objects of a class containing static variables are created, all the objects of that class share *one* copy of those variables. Together a class's static variables and instance variables are known as its **fields**. You'll learn more about static fields in Section 8.11.

Math Class static *Constants* PI *and* E

Class Math declares constants **Math.PI** and **Math.E** that represent *high-precision approximations* to commonly used mathematical constants. Math.PI (3.141592653589793) is the ratio of a circle's circumference to its diameter. Math.E (2.718281828459045) is the base value for natural logarithms (calculated with static Math method log). These Math constants are declared with the modifiers public, final and static. Making them public allows you to use them in your own classes. Any field declared with keyword **final** is *constant*—its value cannot change after the field is initialized. Making these fields static allows them to be accessed via the class name Math and a dot (.) separator, just as class Math's methods are.

Why Is Method main *Declared* static?

When you execute the Java Virtual Machine (JVM) with the java command, the JVM attempts to invoke the main method of the class you specify—at this point no objects of the class have been created. Declaring main as static allows the JVM to invoke main without creating an instance of the class. When you execute your application, you specify its class name as an argument to the java command, as in

>   java *ClassName argument1 argument2 ...*

The JVM loads the class specified by *ClassName* and uses that class name to invoke method main. In the preceding command, *ClassName* is a **command-line argument** to the JVM that tells it which class to execute. Following the *ClassName*, you can also specify a list of Strings (separated by spaces) as command-line arguments that the JVM will pass to your application. Such arguments might be used to specify options (e.g., a filename) to run the application. As you'll learn in Chapter 7, Arrays and ArrayLists, your application can access those command-line arguments and use them to customize the application.

6.4 Declaring Methods with Multiple Parameters

Methods often require more than one piece of information to perform their tasks. We now consider how to write your own methods with *multiple* parameters. Figure 6.2 uses a method called maximum to determine and return the largest of three double values. In main, lines 14–18 prompt the user to enter three double values, then read them from the user. Line 21 calls method maximum (declared in lines 28–41) to determine the largest of the three values it receives as arguments. When method maximum returns the result to line 21, the program assigns maximum's return value to local variable result. Then line 24 outputs the maximum value. At the end of this section, we'll discuss the use of operator + in line 24.

```
1    // Fig. 6.2: MaximumFinder.java
2    // Programmer-declared method maximum with three double parameters.
3    import java.util.Scanner;
4
5    public class MaximumFinder
6    {
7       // obtain three floating-point values and locate the maximum value
8       public static void main(String[] args)
9       {
10          // create Scanner for input from command window
11          Scanner input = new Scanner(System.in);
12
13          // prompt for and input three floating-point values
14          System.out.print(
15             "Enter three floating-point values separated by spaces: ");
16          double number1 = input.nextDouble(); // read first double
17          double number2 = input.nextDouble(); // read second double
18          double number3 = input.nextDouble(); // read third double
19
20          // determine the maximum value
21          double result = maximum(number1, number2, number3);
22
23          // display maximum value
24          System.out.println("Maximum is: " + result);
25       }
```

Fig. 6.2 | Programmer-declared method maximum with three double parameters. (Part 1 of 2.)

```
26
27     // returns the maximum of its three double parameters
28     public static double maximum(double x, double y, double z)
29     {
30        double maximumValue = x; // assume x is the largest to start
31
32        // determine whether y is greater than maximumValue
33        if (y > maximumValue)
34           maximumValue = y;
35
36        // determine whether z is greater than maximumValue
37        if (z > maximumValue)
38           maximumValue = z;
39
40        return maximumValue;
41     }
42  } // end class MaximumFinder
```

```
Enter three floating-point values separated by spaces: 9.35 2.74 5.1
Maximum is: 9.35
```

```
Enter three floating-point values separated by spaces: 5.8 12.45 8.32
Maximum is: 12.45
```

```
Enter three floating-point values separated by spaces: 6.46 4.12 10.54
Maximum is: 10.54
```

Fig. 6.2 | Programmer-declared method maximum with three double parameters. (Part 2 of 2.)

Keywords *public* and *static*

Method maximum's declaration begins with keyword public to indicate that the method is "available to the public"—it can be called from methods of other classes. The keyword static enables the main method (another static method) to call maximum as shown in line 21 without qualifying the method name with the class name MaximumFinder—static methods in the same class can call each other directly. Any other class that uses maximum must fully qualify the method name with the class name.

Method *maximum*

Consider maximum's declaration (lines 28–41). Line 28 indicates that it returns a double value, that the method's name is maximum and that the method requires three double parameters (x, y and z) to accomplish its task. Multiple parameters are specified as a comma-separated list. When maximum is called from line 21, the parameters x, y and z are initialized with copies of the values of arguments number1, number2 and number3, respectively. There must be one argument in the method call for each parameter in the method declaration. Also, each argument must be *consistent* with the type of the corresponding parameter. For example, a parameter of type double can receive values like 7.35, 22 or –0.03456, but not `Strings` like `"hello"` nor the `boolean` values `true` or `false`. Section 6.6 discusses the argument types that can be provided in a method call for each parameter of a primitive type.

To determine the maximum value, we begin with the assumption that parameter x contains the largest value, so line 30 declares local variable `maximumValue` and initializes it with the value of parameter x. Of course, it's possible that parameter y or z contains the actual largest value, so we must compare each of these values with `maximumValue`. The `if` statement at lines 33–34 determines whether y is greater than `maximumValue`. If so, line 34 assigns y to `maximumValue`. The `if` statement at lines 37–38 determines whether z is greater than `maximumValue`. If so, line 38 assigns z to `maximumValue`. At this point the largest of the three values resides in `maximumValue`, so line 40 returns that value to line 21. When program control returns to the point in the program where `maximum` was called, `maximum`'s parameters x, y and z no longer exist in memory.

Software Engineering Observation 6.3
Methods can return at most one value, but the returned value could be a reference to an object that contains many values.

Software Engineering Observation 6.4
Variables should be declared as fields only if they're required for use in more than one method of the class or if the program should save their values between calls to the class's methods.

Common Programming Error 6.1
Declaring method parameters of the same type as `float x, y` instead of `float x, float y` is a syntax error—a type is required for each parameter in the parameter list.

Implementing Method `maximum` by Reusing Method `Math.max`
The entire body of our maximum method could also be implemented with two calls to `Math.max`, as follows:

```
return Math.max(x, Math.max(y, z));
```

The first call to `Math.max` specifies arguments x and `Math.max(y, z)`. Before any method can be called, its arguments must be evaluated to determine their values. If an argument is a method call, the method call must be performed to determine its return value. So, in the preceding statement, `Math.max(y, z)` is evaluated to determine the maximum of y and z. Then the result is passed as the second argument to the other call to `Math.max`, which returns the larger of its two arguments. This is a good example of software reuse—we find the largest of three values by reusing `Math.max`, which finds the larger of two values. Note how concise this code is compared to lines 30–38 of Fig. 6.2.

Assembling Strings with String Concatenation
Java allows you to assemble `String` objects into larger strings by using operators + or +=. This is known as **string concatenation**. When both operands of operator + are `String` objects, operator + creates a new `String` object in which the characters of the right operand are placed at the end of those in the left operand—e.g., the expression `"hello " + "there"` creates the `String` `"hello there"`.

In line 24 of Fig. 6.2, the expression "Maximum is: " + result uses operator + with operands of types String and double. *Every primitive value and object in Java can be represented as a String.* When one of the + operator's operands is a String, the other is converted to a String, then the two are concatenated. In line 24, the double value is converted to its String representation and placed at the end of the String "Maximum is: ". If there are any trailing zeros in a double value, these will be discarded when the number is converted to a String—for example 9.3500 would be represented as 9.35.

Primitive values used in String concatenation are converted to Strings. A boolean concatenated with a String is converted to the String "true" or "false". *All objects have a toString method that returns a String representation of the object.* (We discuss toString in more detail in subsequent chapters.) When an object is concatenated with a String, the object's toString method is implicitly called to obtain the String representation of the object. Method toString also can be called explicitly.

You can break large String literals into several smaller Strings and place them on multiple lines of code for readability. In this case, the Strings can be reassembled using concatenation. We discuss the details of Strings in Chapter 14.

Common Programming Error 6.2

It's a syntax error to break a String literal across lines. If necessary, you can split a String into several smaller Strings and use concatenation to form the desired String.

Common Programming Error 6.3

Confusing the + operator used for string concatenation with the + operator used for addition can lead to strange results. Java evaluates the operands of an operator from left to right. For example, if integer variable y has the value 5, the expression "y + 2 = " + y + 2 results in the string "y + 2 = 52", not "y + 2 = 7", because first the value of y (5) is concatenated to the string "y + 2 = ", then the value 2 is concatenated to the new larger string "y + 2 = 5". The expression "y + 2 = " + (y + 2) produces the desired result "y + 2 = 7".

6.5 Notes on Declaring and Using Methods

There are three ways to call a method:

1. Using a method name by itself to call another method of the *same* class—such as maximum(number1, number2, number3) in line 21 of Fig. 6.2.

2. Using a variable that contains a reference to an object, followed by a dot (.) and the method name to call a non-static method of the referenced object—such as the method call in line 16 of Fig. 3.2, myAccount.getName(), which calls a method of class Account from the main method of AccountTest. Non-static methods are typically called **instance methods**.

3. Using the class name and a dot (.) to call a static method of a class—such as Math.sqrt(900.0) in Section 6.3.

A static method can call other static methods of the same class directly (i.e., using the method name by itself) and can manipulate static variables in the same class directly. To access the class's instance variables and instance methods, a static method must use a reference to an object of the class. Instance methods can access all fields (static variables and instance variables) and methods of the class.

Recall that `static` methods relate to a class as a whole, whereas instance methods are associated with a specific instance (object) of the class and may manipulate the instance variables of that object. Many objects of a class, each with its *own* copies of the instance variables, may exist at the same time. Suppose a `static` method were to invoke an instance method directly. How would the `static` method know which object's instance variables to manipulate? What would happen if *no* objects of the class existed at the time the instance method was invoked? Thus, Java does *not* allow a `static` method to directly access instance variables and instance methods of the same class.

There are three ways to return control to the statement that calls a method. If the method does not return a result, control returns when the program flow reaches the method-ending right brace or when the statement

```
return;
```

is executed. If the method returns a result, the statement

```
return expression;
```

evaluates the *expression*, then returns the result to the caller.

Common Programming Error 6.4
Declaring a method outside the body of a class declaration or inside the body of another method is a syntax error.

Common Programming Error 6.5
Redeclaring a parameter as a local variable in the method's body is a compilation error.

Common Programming Error 6.6
Forgetting to return a value from a method that should return a value is a compilation error. If a return type other than `void` *is specified, the method* must *contain a* `return` *statement that returns a value consistent with the method's return type. Returning a value from a method whose return type has been declared* `void` *is a compilation error.*

6.6 Argument Promotion and Casting

Another important feature of method calls is **argument promotion**—converting an *argument's value*, if possible, to the type that the method expects to receive in its corresponding *parameter*. For example, a program can call `Math` method `sqrt` with an `int` argument even though a `double` argument is expected. The statement

```
System.out.println(Math.sqrt(4));
```

correctly evaluates `Math.sqrt(4)` and prints the value `2.0`. The method declaration's parameter list causes Java to convert the `int` value `4` to the `double` value `4.0` *before* passing the value to method `sqrt`. Such conversions may lead to compilation errors if Java's **promotion rules** are not satisfied. These rules specify which conversions are allowed—that is, which ones can be performed *without losing data*. In the `sqrt` example above, an `int` is converted to a `double` without changing its value. However, converting a `double` to an `int` *truncates* the fractional part of the `double` value—thus, part of the value is lost. Converting large integer types to small integer types (e.g., long to int, or int to short) may also result in changed values.

The promotion rules apply to expressions containing values of two or more primitive types and to primitive-type values passed as arguments to methods. Each value is promoted to the "highest" type in the expression. Actually, the expression uses a *temporary copy* of each value—the types of the original values remain unchanged. Figure 6.3 lists the primitive types and the types to which each can be promoted. The valid promotions for a given type are always to a type higher in the table. For example, an int can be promoted to the higher types long, float and double.

Converting values to types lower in the table of Fig. 6.3 will result in different values if the lower type cannot represent the value of the higher type (e.g., the int value 2000000 cannot be represented as a short, and any floating-point number with digits after its decimal point cannot be represented in an integer type such as long, int or short). Therefore, in cases where information may be lost due to conversion, the Java compiler requires you to use a *cast operator* (introduced in Section 4.8) to explicitly force the conversion to occur—otherwise a compilation error occurs. This enables you to "take control" from the compiler. You essentially say, "I know this conversion might cause loss of information, but for my purposes here, that's fine." Suppose method square calculates the square of an integer and thus requires an int argument. To call square with a double argument named doubleValue, we would be required to write the method call as

```
square((int) doubleValue)
```

This method call explicitly casts (converts) doubleValue's value to a a temporary integer for use in method square. Thus, if doubleValue's value is 4.5, the method receives the value 4 and returns 16, not 20.25.

 Common Programming Error 6.7

Casting a primitive-type value to another primitive type may change the value if the new type is not a valid promotion. For example, casting a floating-point value to an integer value may introduce truncation errors (loss of the fractional part) into the result.

Type	Valid promotions
double	None
float	double
long	float or double
int	long, float or double
char	int, long, float or double
short	int, long, float or double (but not char)
byte	short, int, long, float or double (but not char)
boolean	None (boolean values are not considered to be numbers in Java)

Fig. 6.3 | Promotions allowed for primitive types.

6.7 Java API Packages

As you've seen, Java contains many *predefined* classes that are grouped into categories of related classes called *packages*. Together, these are known as the Java Application Programming Interface (Java API), or the Java class library. A great strength of Java is the Java API's thousands of classes. Some key Java API packages that we use in this book are described in Fig. 6.4, which represents only a small portion of the *reusable components* in the Java API.

Package	Description
java.awt.event	The **Java Abstract Window Toolkit Event Package** contains classes and interfaces that enable event handling for GUI components in both the java.awt and javax.swing packages. (See Chapter 12, Swing GUI Components: Part 1, and Chapter 19, Swing GUI Components: Part 2.)
java.awt.geom	The **Java 2D Shapes Package** contains classes and interfaces for working with Java's advanced two-dimensional graphics capabilities. (See Chapter 13, Graphics and Java 2D.)
java.io	The **Java Input/Output Package** contains classes and interfaces that enable programs to input and output data. (See Chapter 15, Files, Streams and Object Serialization.)
java.lang	The **Java Language Package** contains classes and interfaces (discussed throughout the book) that are required by many Java programs. This package is imported by the compiler into all programs.
java.security	The **Java Security Package** contains classes and interfaces for enhancing application security.
java.sql	The **JDBC Package** contains classes and interfaces for working with databases. (See Chapter 21, Accessing Databases with JDBC.)
java.util	The **Java Utilities Package** contains utility classes and interfaces that enable storing and processing of large amounts of data. Many of these classes and interfaces have been updated to support Java SE 8's new lambda capabilities. (See Chapter 16, Generic Collections.)
java.util.concurrent	The **Java Concurrency Package** contains utility classes and interfaces for implementing programs that can perform multiple tasks in parallel. (See Chapter 20, Concurrency.)
javax.swing	The **Java Swing GUI Components Package** contains classes and interfaces for Java's Swing GUI components that provide support for portable GUIs. This package still uses some elements of the older java.awt package. (See Chapter 12, Swing GUI Components: Part 1, and Chapter 19, Swing GUI Components: Part 2.)
javax.swing.event	The **Java Swing Event Package** contains classes and interfaces that enable event handling (e.g., responding to button clicks) for GUI components in package javax.swing. (See Chapter 12, Swing GUI Components: Part 1, and Chapter 19, Swing GUI Components: Part 2.)

Fig. 6.4 | Java API packages (a subset). (Part 1 of 2.)

Package	Description
javafx packages	JavaFX is the preferred GUI technology for the future. We discuss these packages in Chapter 22, JavaFX GUI.
Some Java SE 8 Packages Used in This Book	
java.time	The new Java SE 8 **Date/Time API Package** contains classes and interfaces for working with dates and times. These features are designed to replace the older date and time capabilities of package java.util. (See Chapter 20, Concurrency.)
java.util.function and java.util.stream	These packages contain classes and interfaces for working with Java SE 8's functional programming capabilities. (See Chapter 17, Java SE 8 Lambdas and Streams.)

Fig. 6.4 | Java API packages (a subset). (Part 2 of 2.)

The set of packages available in Java is quite large. In addition to those summarized in Fig. 6.4, Java includes packages for complex graphics, advanced graphical user interfaces, printing, advanced networking, security, multimedia, accessibility (for people with disabilities), cryptography, XML processing and many other capabilities. For an overview of the packages in Java, visit

```
http://docs.oracle.com/javase/7/docs/api/overview-summary.html
http://download.java.net/jdk8/docs/api/overview-summary.html
```

You can locate additional information about a predefined Java class's methods in the Java API documentation at

```
http://docs.oracle.com/javase/7/docs/api/
```

When you visit this site, click the **Index** link to see an alphabetical listing of all the classes and methods in the Java API. Locate the class name and click its link to see the online description of the class. Click the **METHOD** link to see a table of the class's methods. Each static method will be listed with the word "static" preceding its return type.

6.8 Case Study: Secure Random-Number Generation

We now take a brief diversion into a popular type of programming application—simulation and game playing. In this and the next section, we develop a game-playing program with multiple methods. The program uses most of the control statements presented thus far in the book and introduces several new programming concepts.

The **element of chance** can be introduced in a program via an object of class **Secure-Random** (package java.security). Such objects can produce random boolean, byte, float, double, int, long and Gaussian values. In the next several examples, we use objects of class SecureRandom to produce random values.

Moving to Secure Random Numbers
Previous editions of this book used Java's Random class to obtain "random" values. This class produced *deterministic* values that could be *predicted* by malicious programmers. SecureRandom objects produce **nondeterministic random numbers** that *cannot* be predicted.

Deterministic random numbers have been the source of many software security breaches. Most programming languages now have library features similar to Java's Secure-Random class for producing nondeterministic random numbers to help prevent such problems. From this point forward in the text, when we refer to "random numbers" we mean "secure random numbers."

A Note About Performance
Using SecureRandom instead of Random to achieve higher levels of security incurs a significant performance penalty. For "casual" applications, you might want to use class Random from package java.util—simply replace SecureRandom with Random.

Creating a *SecureRandom* Object
A new secure random-number generator object can be created as follows:

```
SecureRandom randomNumbers = new SecureRandom();
```

It can then be used to generate random values—we discuss only random int values here. For more information on the SecureRandom class, see docs.oracle.com/javase/7/docs/api/java/security/SecureRandom.html.

Obtaining a Random *int* Value
Consider the following statement:

```
int randomValue = randomNumbers.nextInt();
```

SecureRandom method **nextInt** generates a random int value. If it truly produces values *at random*, then every value in the range should have an *equal chance* (or probability) of being chosen each time nextInt is called.

Changing the Range of Values Produced By *nextInt*
The range of values produced by method nextInt generally differs from the range of values required in a particular Java application. For example, a program that simulates coin tossing might require only 0 for "heads" and 1 for "tails." A program that simulates the rolling of a six-sided die might require random integers in the range 1–6. A program that randomly predicts the next type of spaceship (out of four possibilities) that will fly across the horizon in a video game might require random integers in the range 1–4. For cases like these, class SecureRandom provides another version of method nextInt that receives an int argument and returns a value from 0 up to, but not including, the argument's value. For example, for coin tossing, the following statement returns 0 or 1.

```
int randomValue = randomNumbers.nextInt(2);
```

Rolling a Six-Sided Die
To demonstrate random numbers, let's develop a program that simulates 20 rolls of a six-sided die and displays the value of each roll. We begin by using nextInt to produce random values in the range 0–5, as follows:

```
int face = randomNumbers.nextInt(6);
```

The argument 6—called the **scaling factor**—represents the number of unique values that nextInt should produce (in this case six—0, 1, 2, 3, 4 and 5). This manipulation is called **scaling** the range of values produced by SecureRandom method nextInt.

A six-sided die has the numbers 1–6 on its faces, not 0–5. So we **shift** the range of numbers produced by adding a **shifting value**—in this case 1—to our previous result, as in

```
int face = 1 + randomNumbers.nextInt(6);
```

The shifting value (1) specifies the *first* value in the desired range of random integers. The preceding statement assigns face a random integer in the range 1–6.

Rolling a Six-Sided Die 20 Times

Figure 6.5 shows two sample outputs which confirm that the results of the preceding calculation are integers in the range 1–6, and that each run of the program can produce a *different* sequence of random numbers. Line 3 imports class SecureRandom from the java.security package. Line 10 creates the SecureRandom object randomNumbers to produce random values. Line 16 executes 20 times in a loop to roll the die. The if statement (lines 21–22) in the loop starts a new line of output after every five numbers to create a neat, five-column format.

```java
 1   // Fig. 6.5: RandomIntegers.java
 2   // Shifted and scaled random integers.
 3   import java.security.SecureRandom; // program uses class SecureRandom
 4
 5   public class RandomIntegers
 6   {
 7      public static void main(String[] args)
 8      {
 9         // randomNumbers object will produce secure random numbers
10         SecureRandom randomNumbers = new SecureRandom();
11
12         // loop 20 times
13         for (int counter = 1; counter <= 20; counter++)
14         {
15            // pick random integer from 1 to 6
16            int face = 1 + randomNumbers.nextInt(6);
17
18            System.out.printf("%d  ", face); // display generated value
19
20            // if counter is divisible by 5, start a new line of output
21            if (counter % 5 == 0)
22               System.out.println();
23         }
24      }
25   } // end class RandomIntegers
```

```
1  5  3  6  2
5  2  6  5  2
4  4  4  2  6
3  1  6  2  2
```

Fig. 6.5 | Shifted and scaled random integers. (Part 1 of 2.)

```
6   5   4   2   6
1   2   5   1   3
6   3   2   2   1
6   4   2   6   4
```

Fig. 6.5 | Shifted and scaled random integers. (Part 2 of 2.)

Rolling a Six-Sided Die 6,000,000 Times

To show that the numbers produced by nextInt occur with approximately equal likelihood, let's simulate 6,000,000 rolls of a die with the application in Fig. 6.6. Each integer from 1 to 6 should appear approximately 1,000,000 times.

```java
 1  // Fig. 6.6: RollDie.java
 2  // Roll a six-sided die 6,000,000 times.
 3  import java.security.SecureRandom;
 4
 5  public class RollDie
 6  {
 7     public static void main(String[] args)
 8     {
 9        // randomNumbers object will produce secure random numbers
10        SecureRandom randomNumbers = new SecureRandom();
11
12        int frequency1 = 0; // count of 1s rolled
13        int frequency2 = 0; // count of 2s rolled
14        int frequency3 = 0; // count of 3s rolled
15        int frequency4 = 0; // count of 4s rolled
16        int frequency5 = 0; // count of 5s rolled
17        int frequency6 = 0; // count of 6s rolled
18
19        // tally counts for 6,000,000 rolls of a die
20        for (int roll = 1; roll <= 6000000; roll++)
21        {
22           int face = 1 + randomNumbers.nextInt(6); // number from 1 to 6
23
24           // use face value 1-6 to determine which counter to increment
25           switch (face)
26           {
27              case 1:
28                 ++frequency1; // increment the 1s counter
29                 break;
30              case 2:
31                 ++frequency2; // increment the 2s counter
32                 break;
33              case 3:
34                 ++frequency3; // increment the 3s counter
35                 break;
36              case 4:
37                 ++frequency4; // increment the 4s counter
38                 break;
```

Fig. 6.6 | Roll a six-sided die 6,000,000 times. (Part 1 of 2.)

```
39                    case 5:
40                        ++frequency5; // increment the 5s counter
41                        break;
42                    case 6:
43                        ++frequency6; // increment the 6s counter
44                        break;
45                }
46            }
47
48            System.out.println("Face\tFrequency"); // output headers
49            System.out.printf("1\t%d%n2\t%d%n3\t%d%n4\t%d%n5\t%d%n6\t%d%n",
50                frequency1, frequency2, frequency3, frequency4,
51                frequency5, frequency6);
52        }
53    } // end class RollDie
```

```
Face      Frequency
1         999501
2         1000412
3         998262
4         1000820
5         1002245
6         998760
```

```
Face      Frequency
1         999647
2         999557
3         999571
4         1000376
5         1000701
6         1000148
```

Fig. 6.6 | Roll a six-sided die 6,000,000 times. (Part 2 of 2.)

As the sample outputs show, scaling and shifting the values produced by nextInt enables the program to simulate rolling a six-sided die. The application uses nested control statements (the switch is nested inside the for) to determine the number of times each side of the die appears. The for statement (lines 20–46) iterates 6,000,000 times. During each iteration, line 22 produces a random value from 1 to 6. That value is then used as the controlling expression (line 25) of the switch statement (lines 25–45). Based on the face value, the switch statement increments one of the six counter variables during each iteration of the loop. This switch statement has no default case, because we have a case for every possible die value that the expression in line 22 could produce. Run the program, and observe the results. As you'll see, every time you run this program, it produces *different* results.

When we study arrays in Chapter 7, we'll show an elegant way to replace the entire switch statement in this program with a *single* statement. Then, when we study Java SE 8's new functional programming capabilities in Chapter 17, we'll show how to replace the loop that rolls the dice, the switch statement *and* the statement that displays the results with a *single* statement!

Generalized Scaling and Shifting of Random Numbers
Previously, we simulated the rolling of a six-sided die with the statement

```
int face = 1 + randomNumbers.nextInt(6);
```

This statement always assigns to variable face an integer in the range $1 \leq face \leq 6$. The *width* of this range (i.e., the number of consecutive integers in the range) is 6, and the *starting number* in the range is 1. In the preceding statement, the width of the range is determined by the number 6 that's passed as an argument to SecureRandom method nextInt, and the starting number of the range is the number 1 that's added to randomNumbers.nextInt(6). We can generalize this result as

```
int number = shiftingValue + randomNumbers.nextInt(scalingFactor);
```

where *shiftingValue* specifies the *first number* in the desired range of consecutive integers and *scalingFactor* specifies *how many numbers* are in the range.

It's also possible to choose integers at random from sets of values other than ranges of consecutive integers. For example, to obtain a random value from the sequence 2, 5, 8, 11 and 14, you could use the statement

```
int number = 2 + 3 * randomNumbers.nextInt(5);
```

In this case, randomNumbers.nextInt(5) produces values in the range 0–4. Each value produced is multiplied by 3 to produce a number in the sequence 0, 3, 6, 9 and 12. We add 2 to that value to *shift* the range of values and obtain a value from the sequence 2, 5, 8, 11 and 14. We can generalize this result as

```
int number = shiftingValue +
    differenceBetweenValues * randomNumbers.nextInt(scalingFactor);
```

where *shiftingValue* specifies the first number in the desired range of values, *differenceBetweenValues* represents the *constant difference* between consecutive numbers in the sequence and *scalingFactor* specifies how many numbers are in the range.

6.9 Case Study: A Game of Chance; Introducing enum Types

A popular game of chance is a dice game known as craps, which is played in casinos and back alleys throughout the world. The rules of the game are straightforward:

> *You roll two dice. Each die has six faces, which contain one, two, three, four, five and six spots, respectively. After the dice have come to rest, the sum of the spots on the two upward faces is calculated. If the sum is 7 or 11 on the first throw, you win. If the sum is 2, 3 or 12 on the first throw (called "craps"), you lose (i.e., the "house" wins). If the sum is 4, 5, 6, 8, 9 or 10 on the first throw, that sum becomes your "point." To win, you must continue rolling the dice until you "make your point" (i.e., roll that same point value). You lose by rolling a 7 before making your point.*

Figure 6.7 simulates the game of craps, using methods to implement the game's logic. The main method (lines 21–65) calls the rollDice method (lines 68–81) as necessary to roll the dice and compute their sum. The sample outputs show winning and losing on the first roll, and winning and losing on a subsequent roll.

```java
 1   // Fig. 6.7: Craps.java
 2   // Craps class simulates the dice game craps.
 3   import java.security.SecureRandom;
 4
 5   public class Craps
 6   {
 7      // create secure random number generator for use in method rollDice
 8      private static final SecureRandom randomNumbers = new SecureRandom();
 9
10      // enum type with constants that represent the game status
11      private enum Status { CONTINUE, WON, LOST };
12
13      // constants that represent common rolls of the dice
14      private static final int SNAKE_EYES = 2;
15      private static final int TREY = 3;
16      private static final int SEVEN = 7;
17      private static final int YO_LEVEN = 11;
18      private static final int BOX_CARS = 12;
19
20      // plays one game of craps
21      public static void main(String[] args)
22      {
23         int myPoint = 0; // point if no win or loss on first roll
24         Status gameStatus; // can contain CONTINUE, WON or LOST
25
26         int sumOfDice = rollDice(); // first roll of the dice
27
28         // determine game status and point based on first roll
29         switch (sumOfDice)
30         {
31            case SEVEN: // win with 7 on first roll
32            case YO_LEVEN: // win with 11 on first roll
33               gameStatus = Status.WON;
34               break;
35            case SNAKE_EYES: // lose with 2 on first roll
36            case TREY: // lose with 3 on first roll
37            case BOX_CARS: // lose with 12 on first roll
38               gameStatus = Status.LOST;
39               break;
40            default: // did not win or lose, so remember point
41               gameStatus = Status.CONTINUE; // game is not over
42               myPoint = sumOfDice; // remember the point
43               System.out.printf("Point is %d%n", myPoint);
44               break;
45         }
46
47         // while game is not complete
48         while (gameStatus == Status.CONTINUE) // not WON or LOST
49         {
50            sumOfDice = rollDice(); // roll dice again
51
```

Fig. 6.7 | Craps class simulates the dice game craps. (Part 1 of 2.)

```
52              // determine game status
53              if (sumOfDice == myPoint) // win by making point
54                  gameStatus = Status.WON;
55              else
56                  if (sumOfDice == SEVEN) // lose by rolling 7 before point
57                      gameStatus = Status.LOST;
58          }
59
60          // display won or lost message
61          if (gameStatus == Status.WON)
62              System.out.println("Player wins");
63          else
64              System.out.println("Player loses");
65      }
66
67      // roll dice, calculate sum and display results
68      public static int rollDice()
69      {
70          // pick random die values
71          int die1 = 1 + randomNumbers.nextInt(6); // first die roll
72          int die2 = 1 + randomNumbers.nextInt(6); // second die roll
73
74          int sum = die1 + die2; // sum of die values
75
76          // display results of this roll
77          System.out.printf("Player rolled %d + %d = %d%n",
78              die1, die2, sum);
79
80          return sum;
81      }
82  } // end class Craps
```

```
Player rolled 5 + 6 = 11
Player wins
```

```
Player rolled 5 + 4 = 9
Point is 9
Player rolled 4 + 2 = 6
Player rolled 3 + 6 = 9
Player wins
```

```
Player rolled 1 + 2 = 3
Player loses
```

```
Player rolled 2 + 6 = 8
Point is 8
Player rolled 5 + 1 = 6
Player rolled 2 + 1 = 3
Player rolled 1 + 6 = 7
Player loses
```

Fig. 6.7 | Craps class simulates the dice game craps. (Part 2 of 2.)

Method *rollDice*

In the rules of the game, the player must roll *two* dice on the first and all subsequent rolls. We declare method rollDice (lines 68–81) to roll the dice and compute and print their sum. Method rollDice is declared once, but it's called from two places (lines 26 and 50) in main, which contains the logic for one complete game of craps. Method rollDice takes no arguments, so it has an empty parameter list. Each time it's called, rollDice returns the sum of the dice, so the return type int is indicated in the method header (line 68). Although lines 71 and 72 look the same (except for the die names), they do not necessarily produce the same result. Each of these statements produces a *random* value in the range 1–6. Variable randomNumbers (used in lines 71–72) is *not* declared in the method. Instead it's declared as a private static final variable of the class and initialized in line 8. This enables us to create one SecureRandom object that's reused in each call to rollDice. If there were a program that contained multiple instances of class Craps, they'd all share this one SecureRandom object.

Method *main*'s Local Variables

The game is reasonably involved. The player may win or lose on the first roll, or may win or lose on any subsequent roll. Method main (lines 21–65) uses local variable myPoint (line 23) to store the "point" if the player doesn't win or lose on the first roll, local variable gameStatus (line 24) to keep track of the overall game status and local variable sumOfDice (line 26) to hold the sum of the dice for the most recent roll. Variable myPoint is initialized to 0 to ensure that the application will compile. If you do not initialize myPoint, the compiler issues an error, because myPoint is not assigned a value in *every* case of the switch statement, and thus the program could try to use myPoint before it's assigned a value. By contrast, gameStatus *is* assigned a value in *every* case of the switch statement (including the default case)—thus, it's guaranteed to be initialized before it's used, so we do not need to initialize it in line 24.

enum *Type* Status

Local variable gameStatus (line 24) is declared to be of a new type called Status (declared at line 11). Type Status is a private member of class Craps, because Status will be used only in that class. Status is a type called an **enum type**, which, in its simplest form, declares a set of constants represented by identifiers. An enum type is a special kind of class that's introduced by the keyword enum and a type name (in this case, Status). As with classes, braces delimit an enum declaration's body. Inside the braces is a comma-separated list of **enum constants**, each representing a unique value. The identifiers in an enum must be *unique*. You'll learn more about enum types in Chapter 8.

Good Programming Practice 6.1

Use only uppercase letters in the names of enum constants to make them stand out and remind you that they're not variables.

Variables of type Status can be assigned only the three constants declared in the enum (line 11) or a compilation error will occur. When the game is won, the program sets local variable gameStatus to Status.WON (lines 33 and 54). When the game is lost, the program sets local variable gameStatus to Status.LOST (lines 38 and 57). Otherwise, the program sets local variable gameStatus to Status.CONTINUE (line 41) to indicate that the game is not over and the dice must be rolled again.

Good Programming Practice 6.2

Using enum constants (like Status.WON, Status.LOST and Status.CONTINUE) rather than literal values (such as 0, 1 and 2) makes programs easier to read and maintain.

Logic of the main Method

Line 26 in main calls rollDice, which picks two random values from 1 to 6, displays the values of the first die, the second die and their sum, and returns the sum. Method main next enters the switch statement (lines 29–45), which uses the sumOfDice value from line 26 to determine whether the game has been won or lost, or should continue with another roll. The values that result in a win or loss on the first roll are declared as private static final int constants in lines 14–18. The identifier names use casino parlance for these sums. These constants, like enum constants, are declared by convention with all capital letters, to make them stand out in the program. Lines 31–34 determine whether the player won on the first roll with SEVEN (7) or YO_LEVEN (11). Lines 35–39 determine whether the player lost on the first roll with SNAKE_EYES (2), TREY (3), or BOX_CARS (12). After the first roll, if the game is not over, the default case (lines 40–44) sets gameStatus to Status.CONTINUE, saves sumOfDice in myPoint and displays the point.

If we're still trying to "make our point" (i.e., the game is continuing from a prior roll), lines 48–58 execute. Line 50 rolls the dice again. If sumOfDice matches myPoint (line 53), line 54 sets gameStatus to Status.WON, then the loop terminates because the game is complete. If sumOfDice is SEVEN (line 56), line 57 sets gameStatus to Status.LOST, and the loop terminates because the game is complete. When the game completes, lines 61–64 display a message indicating whether the player won or lost, and the program terminates.

The program uses the various program-control mechanisms we've discussed. The Craps class uses two methods—main and rollDice (called twice from main)—and the switch, while, if...else and nested if control statements. Note also the use of multiple case labels in the switch statement to execute the same statements for sums of SEVEN and YO_LEVEN (lines 31–32) and for sums of SNAKE_EYES, TREY and BOX_CARS (lines 35–37).

Why Some Constants Are Not Defined as enum Constants

You might be wondering why we declared the sums of the dice as private static final int constants rather than as enum constants. The reason is that the program must compare the int variable sumOfDice (line 26) to these constants to determine the outcome of each roll. Suppose we declared enum Sum containing constants (e.g., Sum.SNAKE_EYES) representing the five sums used in the game, then used these constants in the switch statement (lines 29–45). Doing so would prevent us from using sumOfDice as the switch statement's controlling expression, because Java does *not* allow an int to be compared to an enum constant. To achieve the same functionality as the current program, we would have to use a variable currentSum of type Sum as the switch's controlling expression. Unfortunately, Java does not provide an easy way to convert an int value to a particular enum constant. This could be done with a separate switch statement. This would be cumbersome and would not improve the program's readability (thus defeating the purpose of using an enum).

6.10 Scope of Declarations

You've seen declarations of various Java entities, such as classes, methods, variables and parameters. Declarations introduce names that can be used to refer to such Java entities. The **scope** of a declaration is the portion of the program that can refer to the declared entity by its name. Such an entity is said to be "in scope" for that portion of the program. This section introduces several important scope issues.

The basic scope rules are as follows:

1. The scope of a parameter declaration is the body of the method in which the declaration appears.

2. The scope of a local-variable declaration is from the point at which the declaration appears to the end of that block.

3. The scope of a local-variable declaration that appears in the initialization section of a `for` statement's header is the body of the `for` statement and the other expressions in the header.

4. A method or field's scope is the entire body of the class. This enables a class's instance methods to use the fields and other methods of the class.

Any block may contain variable declarations. If a local variable or parameter in a method has the same name as a field of the class, the field is *hidden* until the block terminates execution—this is called **shadowing**. To access a shadowed field in a block:

- If the field is an instance variable, precede its name with the `this` keyword and a dot (.), as in `this.x`.

- If the field is a `static` class variable, precede its name with the class's name and a dot (.), as in *ClassName*.`x`.

Figure 6.8 demonstrates scoping issues with fields and local variables. Line 7 declares and initializes the field x to 1. This field is *shadowed* in any block (or method) that declares a local variable named x. Method `main` (lines 11–23) declares a local variable x (line 13) and initializes it to 5. This local variable's value is output to show that the field x (whose value is 1) is *shadowed* in `main`. The program declares two other methods—`useLocalVariable` (lines 26–35) and `useField` (lines 38–45)—that each take no arguments and return no results. Method `main` calls each method twice (lines 17–20). Method `useLocalVariable` declares local variable x (line 28). When `useLocalVariable` is first called (line 17), it creates local variable x and initializes it to 25 (line 28), outputs the value of x (lines 30–31), increments x (line 32) and outputs the value of x again (lines 33–34). When `useLocalVariable` is called a second time (line 19), it *recreates* local variable x and *reinitializes* it to 25, so the output of each `useLocalVariable` call is identical.

```
1   // Fig. 6.8: Scope.java
2   // Scope class demonstrates field and local variable scopes.
3
4   public class Scope
5   {
```

Fig. 6.8 | Scope class demonstrates field and local-variable scopes. (Part 1 of 3.)

```
6      // field that is accessible to all methods of this class
7      private static int x = 1;
8
9      // method main creates and initializes local variable x
10     // and calls methods useLocalVariable and useField
11     public static void main(String[] args)
12     {
13        int x = 5; // method's local variable x shadows field x
14
15        System.out.printf("local x in main is %d%n", x);
16
17        useLocalVariable(); // useLocalVariable has local x
18        useField(); // useField uses class Scope's field x
19        useLocalVariable(); // useLocalVariable reinitializes local x
20        useField(); // class Scope's field x retains its value
21
22        System.out.printf("%nlocal x in main is %d%n", x);
23     }
24
25     // create and initialize local variable x during each call
26     public static void useLocalVariable()
27     {
28        int x = 25; // initialized each time useLocalVariable is called
29
30        System.out.printf(
31           "%nlocal x on entering method useLocalVariable is %d%n", x);
32        ++x; // modifies this method's local variable x
33        System.out.printf(
34           "local x before exiting method useLocalVariable is %d%n", x);
35     }
36
37     // modify class Scope's field x during each call
38     public static void useField()
39     {
40        System.out.printf(
41           "%nfield x on entering method useField is %d%n", x);
42        x *= 10; // modifies class Scope's field x
43        System.out.printf(
44           "field x before exiting method useField is %d%n", x);
45     }
46  } // end class Scope
```

```
local x in main is 5

local x on entering method useLocalVariable is 25
local x before exiting method useLocalVariable is 26

field x on entering method useField is 1
field x before exiting method useField is 10

local x on entering method useLocalVariable is 25
local x before exiting method useLocalVariable is 26
```

Fig. 6.8 | Scope class demonstrates field and local-variable scopes. (Part 2 of 3.)

```
field x on entering method useField is 10
field x before exiting method useField is 100

local x in main is 5
```

Fig. 6.8 | Scope class demonstrates field and local-variable scopes. (Part 3 of 3.)

Method useField does not declare any local variables. Therefore, when it refers to x, field x (line 7) of the class is used. When method useField is first called (line 18), it outputs the value (1) of field x (lines 40–41), multiplies the field x by 10 (line 42) and outputs the value (10) of field x again (lines 43–44) before returning. The next time method useField is called (line 20), the field has its modified value (10), so the method outputs 10, then 100. Finally, in method main, the program outputs the value of local variable x again (line 22) to show that none of the method calls modified main's local variable x, because the methods all referred to variables named x in other scopes.

Principle of Least Privilege
In a general sense, "things" should have the capabilities they need to get their job done, but no more. An example is the scope of a variable. A variable should not be visible when it's not needed.

 Good Programming Practice 6.3
Declare variables as close to where they're first used as possible.

6.11 Method Overloading

Methods of the *same* name can be declared in the same class, as long as they have *different* sets of parameters (determined by the number, types and order of the parameters)—this is called **method overloading**. When an overloaded method is called, the compiler selects the appropriate method by examining the number, types and order of the arguments in the call. Method overloading is commonly used to create several methods with the *same* name that perform the *same* or *similar* tasks, but on *different* types or *different* numbers of arguments. For example, Math methods abs, min and max (summarized in Section 6.3) are overloaded with four versions each:

1. One with two double parameters.
2. One with two float parameters.
3. One with two int parameters.
4. One with two long parameters.

Our next example demonstrates declaring and invoking overloaded methods. We demonstrate overloaded constructors in Chapter 8.

Declaring Overloaded Methods
Class MethodOverload (Fig. 6.9) includes two overloaded versions of method square—one that calculates the square of an int (and returns an int) and one that calculates the

square of a double (and returns a double). Although these methods have the same name and similar parameter lists and bodies, think of them simply as *different* methods. It may help to think of the method names as "square of int" and "square of double," respectively.

```
1   // Fig. 6.9: MethodOverload.java
2   // Overloaded method declarations.
3
4   public class MethodOverload
5   {
6      // test overloaded square methods
7      public static void main(String[] args)
8      {
9         System.out.printf("Square of integer 7 is %d%n", square(7));
10        System.out.printf("Square of double 7.5 is %f%n", square(7.5));
11     }
12
13     // square method with int argument
14     public static int square(int intValue)
15     {
16        System.out.printf("%nCalled square with int argument: %d%n",
17           intValue);
18        return intValue * intValue;
19     }
20
21     // square method with double argument
22     public static double square(double doubleValue)
23     {
24        System.out.printf("%nCalled square with double argument: %f%n",
25           doubleValue);
26        return doubleValue * doubleValue;
27     }
28  } // end class MethodOverload
```

```
Called square with int argument: 7
Square of integer 7 is 49

Called square with double argument: 7.500000
Square of double 7.5 is 56.250000
```

Fig. 6.9 | Overloaded method declarations.

Line 9 invokes method square with the argument 7. Literal integer values are treated as type int, so the method call in line 9 invokes the version of square at lines 14–19 that specifies an int parameter. Similarly, line 10 invokes method square with the argument 7.5. Literal floating-point values are treated as type double, so the method call in line 10 invokes the version of square at lines 22–27 that specifies a double parameter. Each method first outputs a line of text to prove that the proper method was called in each case. The values in lines 10 and 24 are displayed with the format specifier %f. We did not specify a precision in either case. By default, floating-point values are displayed with six digits of precision if the precision is *not* specified in the format specifier.

Distinguishing Between Overloaded Methods

The compiler distinguishes overloaded methods by their **signatures**—a combination of the method's *name* and the *number*, *types* and *order* of its parameters, but *not* its return type. If the compiler looked only at method names during compilation, the code in Fig. 6.9 would be ambiguous—the compiler would not know how to distinguish between the two `square` methods (lines 14–19 and 22–27). Internally, the compiler uses longer method names that include the original method name, the types of each parameter and the exact order of the parameters to determine whether the methods in a class are *unique* in that class.

For example, in Fig. 6.9, the compiler might (internally) use the logical name "`square` of `int`" for the `square` method that specifies an `int` parameter and "`square` of `double`" for the `square` method that specifies a `double` parameter (the actual names the compiler uses are messier). If `method1`'s declaration begins as

```
void method1(int a, float b)
```

then the compiler might use the logical name "`method1` of `int` and `float`." If the parameters are specified as

```
void method1(float a, int b)
```

then the compiler might use the logical name "`method1` of `float` and `int`." The *order* of the parameter types is important—the compiler considers the preceding two `method1` headers to be *distinct*.

Return Types of Overloaded Methods

In discussing the logical names of methods used by the compiler, we did not mention the return types of the methods. *Method calls cannot be distinguished only by return type.* If you had overloaded methods that differed *only* by their return types and you called one of the methods in a standalone statement as in:

```
square(2);
```

the compiler would not be able to determine the version of the method to call, because the return value is ignored. When two methods have the same signature and different return types, the compiler issues an error message indicating that the method is already defined in the class. Overloaded methods can have different return types if the methods have different parameter lists. Also, overloaded methods need *not* have the same number of parameters.

Common Programming Error 6.8

Declaring overloaded methods with identical parameter lists is a compilation error regardless of whether the return types are different.

6.12 Wrap-Up

In this chapter, you learned more about method declarations. You learned the difference between instance methods and `static` methods and how to call `static` methods by preceding the method name with the name of the class in which it appears and the dot (.) separator. You used operators + and += to perform string concatenations. We also discussed Java's promotion rules for converting implicitly between primitive types and how to perform explicit conversions with cast operators. Next, you learned about some of the commonly used packages in the Java API.

You saw how to declare named constants using both enum types and `private static final` variables. You used class `SecureRandom` to generate random numbers for simulations. You also learned about the scope of fields and local variables in a class. Finally, you learned that multiple methods in one class can be overloaded by providing methods with the same name and different signatures. Such methods can be used to perform the same or similar tasks using different types or different numbers of parameters.

In Chapter 7, you'll learn how to maintain lists and tables of data in arrays. You'll see a more elegant implementation of the application that rolls a die 6,000,000 times. We'll present two versions of a `GradeBook` case study that stores sets of student grades in a `GradeBook` object. You'll also learn how to access an application's command-line arguments that are passed to method `main` when an application begins execution.

7

Arrays and ArrayLists

Objectives

In this chapter you'll:

- Use arrays to store data in and retrieve data from lists and tables of values.

- Declare arrays, initialize arrays and refer to individual elements of arrays.

- Iterate through arrays with the enhanced **for** statement.

- Pass arrays to methods.

- Declare and manipulate multidimensional arrays.

- Use variable-length argument lists.

- Read command-line arguments into a program.

- Build single-array and double array versions of an instructor gradebook class.

- Perform common array manipulations with the methods of class **Arrays**.

- Use class **ArrayList** to manipulate a dynamically resizable arraylike data structure.

7.1 **Introduction**

This chapter introduces **data structures**—collections of related data items. **Array** objects are data structures consisting of related data items of the same type. Arrays make it convenient to process related groups of values. Arrays remain the same length once they're created.

After discussing how arrays are declared, created and initialized, we present practical examples that demonstrate common array manipulations. We introduce Java's *exception-handling* mechanism and use it to allow a program to continue executing when it attempts to access an array element that does not exist. We also present a case study that examines how arrays can help simulate the shuffling and dealing of playing cards in a card-game application. We introduce Java's *enhanced for statement*, which allows a program to access the data in an array more easily than does the counter-controlled `for` statement presented in Section 5.3. We build two versions of an instructor `GradeBook` class that use arrays to maintain sets of student grades *in memory* and analyze student grades. We show how to use *variable-length argument lists* to create methods that can be called with varying numbers of arguments, and we demonstrate how to process *command-line arguments* in method `main`. Next, we present some common array manipulations with `static` methods of class `Arrays` from the `java.util` package.

Although commonly used, arrays have limited capabilities. For instance, you must specify an array's size, and if at execution time you wish to modify it, you must do so by creating a new array. At the end of this chapter, we introduce one of Java's prebuilt data structures from the Java API's *collection classes*. These offer greater capabilities than traditional arrays. They're reusable, reliable, powerful and efficient. We focus on the `ArrayList` collection. `ArrayList`s are similar to arrays but provide additional functionality, such as *dynamic resizing* as necessary to accommodate more or fewer elements at execution time.

Java SE 8
After reading Chapter 17, Java SE 8 Lambdas and Streams, you'll be able to reimplement many of this chapter's examples in a more concise and elegant manner, and in a way that makes them easier to parallelize to improve performance on today's multi-core systems.

7.2 Arrays

An array is a group of variables (called **elements** or **components**) containing values that all have the *same* type. Arrays are objects, so they're considered *reference types*. As you'll soon see, what we typically think of as an array is actually a *reference* to an array object in memory. The *elements* of an array can be either *primitive types* or *reference types* (including arrays, as we'll see in Section 7.11). To refer to a particular element in an array, we specify the *name* of the reference to the array and the *position number* of the element in the array. The position number of the element is called the element's **index** or **subscript**.

Logical Array Representation
Figure 7.1 shows a logical representation of an integer array called c. This array contains 12 elements. A program refers to any one of these elements with an **array-access expression** that includes the *name* of the array followed by the *index* of the particular element in **square brackets** (**[]**). The first element in every array has **index zero** and is sometimes called the **zeroth element**. Thus, the elements of array c are c[0], c[1], c[2] and so on. The highest index in array c is 11, which is 1 less than 12—the number of elements in the array. Array names follow the same conventions as other variable names.

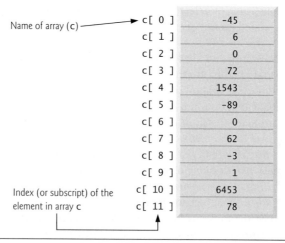

Name of array (c) ⟶ c[0]   -45
c[1]   6
c[2]   0
c[3]   72
c[4]   1543
c[5]   -89
c[6]   0
c[7]   62
c[8]   -3
c[9]   1
Index (or subscript) of the   c[10]   6453
element in array c   c[11]   78

Fig. 7.1 | A 12-element array.

An index must be a nonnegative integer. A program can use an expression as an index. For example, if we assume that variable a is 5 and variable b is 6, then the statement

```
c[a + b] += 2;
```

adds 2 to array element c[11]. An indexed array name is an *array-access expression*, which can be used on the left side of an assignment to place a new value into an array element.

Common Programming Error 7.1

An index must be an int value or a value of a type that can be promoted to int—namely, byte, short or char, but not long; otherwise, a compilation error occurs.

Let's examine array c in Fig. 7.1 more closely. The **name** of the array is c. Every array object knows its own length and stores it in a **length instance variable**. The expression c.length returns array c's length. Even though the length instance variable of an array is public, it cannot be changed because it's a final variable. This array's 12 elements are referred to as c[0], c[1], c[2], ..., c[11]. The value of c[0] is -45, the value of c[1] is 6, the value of c[2] is 0, the value of c[7] is 62 and the value of c[11] is 78. To calculate the sum of the values contained in the first three elements of array c and store the result in variable sum, we would write

```
sum = c[0] + c[1] + c[2];
```

To divide the value of c[6] by 2 and assign the result to the variable x, we would write

```
x = c[6] / 2;
```

7.3 Declaring and Creating Arrays

Array objects occupy space in memory. Like other objects, arrays are created with keyword new. To create an array object, you specify the type of the array elements and the number of elements as part of an **array-creation expression** that uses keyword new. Such an expression returns a reference that can be stored in an array variable. The following declaration and array-creation expression create an array object containing 12 int elements and store the array's reference in the array variable named c:

```
int[] c = new int[12];
```

This expression can be used to create the array in Fig. 7.1. When an array is created, each of its elements receives a default value—zero for the numeric primitive-type elements, false for boolean elements and null for references. As you'll soon see, you can provide nondefault element values when you create an array.

Creating the array in Fig. 7.1 can also be performed in two steps as follows:

```
int[] c; // declare the array variable
c = new int[12]; // create the array; assign to array variable
```

In the declaration, the square brackets following the type indicate that c is a variable that will refer to an array (i.e., the variable will store an array reference). In the assignment statement, the array variable c receives the reference to a new array of 12 int elements.

Common Programming Error 7.2

In an array declaration, specifying the number of elements in the square brackets of the declaration (e.g., int[12] c;) is a syntax error.

A program can create several arrays in a single declaration. The following declaration reserves 100 elements for b and 27 elements for x:

```
String[] b = new String[100], x = new String[27];
```

When the type of the array and the square brackets are combined at the beginning of the declaration, all the identifiers in the declaration are array variables. In this case, variables b and x refer to String arrays. For readability, we prefer to declare only *one* variable per declaration. The preceding declaration is equivalent to:

```
String[] b = new String[100]; // create array b
String[] x = new String[27]; // create array x
```

Good Programming Practice 7.1

For readability, declare only one variable per declaration. Keep each declaration on a separate line, and include a comment describing the variable being declared.

When only one variable is declared in each declaration, the square brackets can be placed either after the type or after the array variable name, as in:

```
String b[] = new String[100]; // create array b
String x[] = new String[27]; // create array x
```

but placing the square brackets after the type is preferred.

Common Programming Error 7.3

Declaring multiple array variables in a single declaration can lead to subtle errors. Consider the declaration int[] a, b, c;. If a, b and c should be declared as array variables, then this declaration is correct—placing square brackets directly following the type indicates that all the identifiers in the declaration are array variables. However, if only a is intended to be an array variable, and b and c are intended to be individual int variables, then this declaration is incorrect—the declaration int a[], b, c; would achieve the desired result.

A program can declare arrays of any type. Every element of a primitive-type array contains a value of the array's declared element type. Similarly, in an array of a reference type, every element is a reference to an object of the array's declared element type. For example, every element of an int array is an int value, and every element of a String array is a reference to a String object.

7.4 Examples Using Arrays

This section presents several examples that demonstrate declaring arrays, creating arrays, initializing arrays and manipulating array elements.

7.4.1 Creating and Initializing an Array

The application of Fig. 7.2 uses keyword new to create an array of 10 int elements, which are initially zero (the default initial value for int variables). Line 9 declares array—a reference capable of referring to an array of int elements—then initializes the variable with a reference to an array object containing 10 int elements. Line 11 outputs the column headings. The first column contains the index (0–9) of each array element, and the second column contains the default initial value (0) of each array element. The for statement (lines 14–15) outputs the index (represented by counter) and value of each array element (represented by array[counter]). Control variable counter is initially 0—index values start at 0, so using **zero-based counting** allows the loop to access every element of the array. The for's loop-continuation condition uses the expression array.length (line 14) to determine the length of the array. In this example, the length of the array is 10, so the loop continues executing as long as the value of control variable counter is less than 10. The highest index value of a 10-element array is 9, so using the less-than operator in the loop-continuation condition guarantees that the loop does not attempt to access an element *beyond* the end of the array (i.e., during the final iteration of the loop, counter is 9). We'll soon see what Java does when it encounters such an *out-of-range index* at execution time.

```
 1   // Fig. 7.2: InitArray.java
 2   // Initializing the elements of an array to default values of zero.
 3
 4   public class InitArray
 5   {
 6      public static void main(String[] args)
 7      {
 8         // declare variable array and initialize it with an array object
 9         int[] array = new int[10]; // create the array object
10
11         System.out.printf("%s%8s%n", "Index", "Value"); // column headings
12
13         // output each array element's value
14         for (int counter = 0; counter < array.length; counter++)
15            System.out.printf("%5d%8d%n", counter, array[counter]);
16      }
17   } // end class InitArray
```

```
Index   Value
    0       0
    1       0
    2       0
    3       0
    4       0
    5       0
    6       0
    7       0
    8       0
    9       0
```

Fig. 7.2 | Initializing the elements of an array to default values of zero.

7.4.2 Using an Array Initializer

You can create an array and initialize its elements with an **array initializer**—a comma-separated list of expressions (called an **initializer list**) enclosed in braces. In this case, the array length is determined by the number of elements in the initializer list. For example,

```
int[] n = { 10, 20, 30, 40, 50 };
```

creates a five-element array with index values 0–4. Element n[0] is initialized to 10, n[1] is initialized to 20, and so on. When the compiler encounters an array declaration that includes an initializer list, it counts the number of initializers in the list to determine the size of the array, then sets up the appropriate new operation "behind the scenes."

The application in Fig. 7.3 initializes an integer array with 10 values (line 9) and displays the array in tabular format. The code for displaying the array elements (lines 14–15) is identical to that in Fig. 7.2 (lines 15–16).

```
1    // Fig. 7.3: InitArray.java
2    // Initializing the elements of an array with an array initializer.
3
4    public class InitArray
5    {
6       public static void main(String[] args)
7       {
8          // initializer list specifies the initial value for each element
9          int[] array = { 32, 27, 64, 18, 95, 14, 90, 70, 60, 37 };
10
11         System.out.printf("%s%8s%n", "Index", "Value"); // column headings
12
13         // output each array element's value
14         for (int counter = 0; counter < array.length; counter++)
15            System.out.printf("%5d%8d%n", counter, array[counter]);
16
17    } // end class InitArray
```

```
Index  Value
    0     32
    1     27
    2     64
    3     18
    4     95
    5     14
    6     90
    7     70
    8     60
    9     37
```

Fig. 7.3 | Initializing the elements of an array with an array initializer.

7.4.3 Calculating the Values to Store in an Array

The application in Fig. 7.4 creates a 10-element array and assigns to each element one of the even integers from 2 to 20 (2, 4, 6, …, 20). Then the application displays the array in tabular format. The for statement at lines 12–13 calculates an array element's value by multiplying the current value of the control variable counter by 2, then adding 2.

```
1    // Fig. 7.4: InitArray.java
2    // Calculating the values to be placed into the elements of an array.
3
4    public class InitArray
5    {
6       public static void main(String[] args)
7       {
```

Fig. 7.4 | Calculating the values to be placed into the elements of an array. (Part 1 of 2.)

```
8            final int ARRAY_LENGTH = 10; // declare constant
9            int[] array = new int[ARRAY_LENGTH]; // create array
10
11           // calculate value for each array element
12           for (int counter = 0; counter < array.length; counter++)
13               array[counter] = 2 + 2 * counter;
14
15           System.out.printf("%s%8s%n", "Index", "Value"); // column headings
16
17           // output each array element's value
18           for (int counter = 0; counter < array.length; counter++)
19               System.out.printf("%5d%8d%n", counter, array[counter]);
20       }
21  } // end class InitArray
```

```
Index   Value
    0       2
    1       4
    2       6
    3       8
    4      10
    5      12
    6      14
    7      16
    8      18
    9      20
```

Fig. 7.4 | Calculating the values to be placed into the elements of an array. (Part 2 of 2.)

Line 8 uses the modifier final to declare the constant variable ARRAY_LENGTH with the value 10. Constant variables must be initialized before they're used and cannot be modified thereafter. If you attempt to modify a final variable after it's initialized in its declaration, the compiler issues an error message like

```
cannot assign a value to final variable variableName
```

Good Programming Practice 7.2

*Constant variables also are called **named constants**. They often make programs more readable than programs that use literal values (e.g., 10)—a named constant such as ARRAY_LENGTH clearly indicates its purpose, whereas a literal value could have different meanings based on its context.*

Good Programming Practice 7.3

Multiword named constants should have each word separated from the next with an underscore (_) as in ARRAY_LENGTH.

Common Programming Error 7.4

Assigning a value to a final variable after it has been initialized is a compilation error. Similarly, attempting to access the value of a final variable before it's initialized results in a compilation error like "variable variableName might not have been initialized."

7.4.4 Summing the Elements of an Array

Often, the elements of an array represent a series of values to be used in a calculation. If, for example, they represent exam grades, a professor may wish to total the elements of the array and use that sum to calculate the class average for the exam. The GradeBook examples in Figs. 7.14 and 7.18 use this technique.

Figure 7.5 sums the values contained in a 10-element integer array. The program declares, creates and initializes the array at line 8. The for statement performs the calculations. [*Note:* The values supplied as array initializers are often read into a program rather than specified in an initializer list. For example, an application could input the values from a user or from a file on disk (as discussed in Chapter 15, Files, Streams and Object Serialization).]

```java
 1   // Fig. 7.5: SumArray.java
 2   // Computing the sum of the elements of an array.
 3
 4   public class SumArray
 5   {
 6      public static void main(String[] args)
 7      {
 8         int[] array = { 87, 68, 94, 100, 83, 78, 85, 91, 76, 87 };
 9         int total = 0;
10
11         // add each element's value to total
12         for (int counter = 0; counter < array.length; counter++)
13            total += array[counter];
14
15         System.out.printf("Total of array elements: %d%n", total);
16      }
17   } // end class SumArray
```

```
Total of array elements: 849
```

Fig. 7.5 | Computing the sum of the elements of an array.

7.4.5 Using Bar Charts to Display Array Data Graphically

Many programs present data to users in a graphical manner. For example, numeric values are often displayed as bars in a bar chart. In such a chart, longer bars represent proportionally larger numeric values. One simple way to display numeric data graphically is with a bar chart that shows each numeric value as a bar of asterisks (*).

Professors often like to examine the distribution of grades on an exam. A professor might graph the number of grades in each of several categories to visualize the grade distribution. Suppose the grades on an exam were 87, 68, 94, 100, 83, 78, 85, 91, 76 and 87. They include one grade of 100, two grades in the 90s, four grades in the 80s, two grades in the 70s, one grade in the 60s and no grades below 60. Our next application (Fig. 7.6) stores this grade distribution data in an array of 11 elements, each corresponding to a category of grades. For example, array[0] indicates the number of grades in the range 0–9, array[7] the number of grades in the range 70–79 and array[10] the number of 100 grades. The GradeBook classes later in the chapter (Figs. 7.14 and 7.18) contain code that calculates these grade frequencies based on a set of grades. For now, we manually create the array with the given grade frequencies.

```java
1   // Fig. 7.6: BarChart.java
2   // Bar chart printing program.
3
4   public class BarChart
5   {
6      public static void main(String[] args)
7      {
8         int[] array = { 0, 0, 0, 0, 0, 0, 1, 2, 4, 2, 1 };
9
10        System.out.println("Grade distribution:");
11
12        // for each array element, output a bar of the chart
13        for (int counter = 0; counter < array.length; counter++)
14        {
15           // output bar label ("00-09: ", ..., "90-99: ", "100: ")
16           if (counter == 10)
17              System.out.printf("%5d: ", 100);
18           else
19              System.out.printf("%02d-%02d: ",
20                 counter * 10, counter * 10 + 9);
21
22           // print bar of asterisks
23           for (int stars = 0; stars < array[counter]; stars++)
24              System.out.print("*");
25
26           System.out.println();
27        }
28     }
29  } // end class BarChart
```

```
Grade distribution:
00-09:
10-19:
20-29:
30-39:
40-49:
50-59:
60-69: *
70-79: **
80-89: ****
90-99: **
  100: *
```

Fig. 7.6 | Bar chart printing program.

The application reads the numbers from the array and graphs the information as a bar chart. It displays each grade range followed by a bar of asterisks indicating the number of grades in that range. To label each bar, lines 16–20 output a grade range (e.g., "70-79: ") based on the current value of counter. When counter is 10, line 17 outputs 100 with a field width of 5, followed by a colon and a space, to align the label "100: " with the other bar labels. The nested `for` statement (lines 23–24) outputs the bars. Note the loop-continuation condition at line 23 (`stars < array[counter]`). Each time the program reaches the inner `for`, the loop counts from 0 up to `array[counter]`, thus using a value in `array` to determine the number of asterisks to display. In this example, *no* students received a grade below 60, so `array[0]`–`array[5]` contain zeroes, and *no* asterisks are displayed next to the first six grade ranges. In line 19, the format specifier `%02d` indicates that an `int` value should be formatted as a field of two digits. The **0 flag** in the format specifier displays a leading 0 for values with fewer digits than the field width (2).

7.4.6 Using the Elements of an Array as Counters

Sometimes, programs use counter variables to summarize data, such as the results of a survey. In Fig. 6.6, we used separate counters in our die-rolling program to track the number of occurrences of each side of a six-sided die as the program rolled the die 6,000,000 times. An array version of this application is shown in Fig. 7.7.

```java
 1   // Fig. 7.7: RollDie.java
 2   // Die-rolling program using arrays instead of switch.
 3   import java.security.SecureRandom;
 4
 5   public class RollDie
 6   {
 7      public static void main(String[] args)
 8      {
 9         SecureRandom randomNumbers = new SecureRandom();
10         int[] frequency = new int[7]; // array of frequency counters
11
12         // roll die 6,000,000 times; use die value as frequency index
13         for (int roll = 1; roll <= 6000000; roll++)
14            ++frequency[1 + randomNumbers.nextInt(6)];
15
16         System.out.printf("%s%10s%n", "Face", "Frequency");
17
18         // output each array element's value
19         for (int face = 1; face < frequency.length; face++)
20            System.out.printf("%4d%10d%n", face, frequency[face]);
21      }
22   } // end class RollDie
```

```
Face Frequency
   1    999690
   2    999512
   3   1000575
   4    999815
   5    999781
   6   1000627
```

Fig. 7.7 | Die-rolling program using arrays instead of `switch`.

Figure 7.7 uses the array `frequency` (line 10) to count the occurrences of each side of the die. The *single* statement in line 14 of this program replaces lines 22–45 of Fig. 6.6.

Line 14 uses the random value to determine which frequency element to increment during each iteration of the loop. The calculation in line 14 produces random numbers from 1 to 6, so the array frequency must be large enough to store six counters. However, we use a seven-element array in which we ignore frequency[0]—it's more logical to have the face value 1 increment frequency[1] than frequency[0]. Thus, each face value is used as an index for array frequency. In line 14, the calculation inside the square brackets evaluates first to determine which element of the array to increment, then the ++ operator adds one to that element. We also replaced lines 49–51 from Fig. 6.6 by looping through array frequency to output the results (lines 19–20). When we study Java SE 8's new functional programming capabilities in Chapter 17, we'll show how to replace lines 13–14 and 19–20 with a *single* statement!

7.4.7 Using Arrays to Analyze Survey Results

Our next example uses arrays to summarize data collected in a survey. Consider the following problem statement:

> *Twenty students were asked to rate on a scale of 1 to 5 the quality of the food in the student cafeteria, with 1 being "awful" and 5 being "excellent." Place the 20 responses in an integer array and determine the frequency of each rating.*

This is a typical array-processing application (Fig. 7.8). We wish to summarize the number of responses of each type (that is, 1–5). Array responses (lines 9–10) is a 20-element integer array containing the students' survey responses. The last value in the array *is intentionally* an incorrect response (14). When a Java program executes, array element indices are checked for validity—all indices must be greater than or equal to 0 and less than the length of the array. Any attempt to access an element outside that range of indices results in a runtime error that's known as an ArrayIndexOutOfBoundsException. At the end of this section, we'll discuss the invalid response value, demonstrate array **bounds checking** and introduce Java's *exception-handling* mechanism, which can be used to detect and handle an ArrayIndexOutOfBoundsException.

```
1   // Fig. 7.8: StudentPoll.java
2   // Poll analysis program.
3
4   public class StudentPoll
5   {
6      public static void main(String[] args)
7      {
8         // student response array (more typically, input at runtime)
9         int[] responses = { 1, 2, 5, 4, 3, 5, 2, 1, 3, 3, 1, 4, 3, 3, 3,
10           2, 3, 3, 2, 14 };
11        int[] frequency = new int[6]; // array of frequency counters
12
13        // for each answer, select responses element and use that value
14        // as frequency index to determine element to increment
15        for (int answer = 0; answer < responses.length; answer++)
16        {
```

Fig. 7.8 | Poll analysis program. (Part 1 of 2.)

```
17          try
18          {
19              ++frequency[responses[answer]];
20          }
21          catch (ArrayIndexOutOfBoundsException e)
22          {
23              System.out.println(e); // invokes toString method
24              System.out.printf("    responses[%d] = %d%n%n",
25                  answer, responses[answer]);
26          }
27      }
28
29      System.out.printf("%s%10s%n", "Rating", "Frequency");
30
31      // output each array element's value
32      for (int rating = 1; rating < frequency.length; rating++)
33          System.out.printf("%6d%10d%n", rating, frequency[rating]);
34  }
35 } // end class StudentPoll
```

```
java.lang.ArrayIndexOutOfBoundsException: 14
    responses[19] = 14

Rating Frequency
     1       3
     2       4
     3       8
     4       2
     5       2
```

Fig. 7.8 | Poll analysis program. (Part 2 of 2.)

The frequency Array

We use the six-element array frequency (line 11) to count the number of occurrences of each response. Each element is used as a counter for one of the possible types of survey responses—frequency[1] counts the number of students who rated the food as 1, frequency[2] counts the number of students who rated the food as 2, and so on.

Summarizing the Results

The for statement (lines 15–27) reads the responses from the array responses one at a time and increments one of the counters frequency[1] to frequency[5]; we ignore frequency[0] because the survey responses are limited to the range 1–5. The key statement in the loop appears in line 19. This statement increments the appropriate frequency counter as determined by the value of responses[answer].

Let's step through the first few iterations of the for statement:

- When the counter answer is 0, responses[answer] is the value of responses[0] (that is, 1—see line 9). In this case, frequency[responses[answer]] is interpreted as frequency[1], and the counter frequency[1] is incremented by one. To evaluate the expression, we begin with the value in the *innermost* set of brackets (answer, currently 0). The value of answer is plugged into the expression, and the next set of brackets (responses[answer]) is evaluated. That value is used as the index for the frequency array to determine which counter to increment (in this case, frequency[1]).

- The next time through the loop answer is 1, responses[answer] is the value of responses[1] (that is, 2—see line 9), so frequency[responses[answer]] is interpreted as frequency[2], causing frequency[2] to be incremented.

- When answer is 2, responses[answer] is the value of responses[2] (that is, 5—see line 9), so frequency[responses[answer]] is interpreted as frequency[5], causing frequency[5] to be incremented, and so on.

Regardless of the number of responses processed, only a six-element array (in which we ignore element zero) is required to summarize the results, because all the correct response values are values from 1 to 5, and the index values for a six-element array are 0–5. In the program's output, the Frequency column summarizes only 19 of the 20 values in the responses array—the last element of the array responses contains an (intentionally) incorrect response that was not counted. Section 7.5 discusses what happens when the program in Fig. 7.8 encounters the invalid response (14) in the last element of array responses.

7.5 Exception Handling: Processing the Incorrect Response

An **exception** indicates a problem that occurs while a program executes. The name "exception" suggests that the problem occurs infrequently—if the "rule" is that a statement normally executes correctly, then the problem represents the "exception to the rule." **Exception handling** helps you create **fault-tolerant programs** that can resolve (or handle) exceptions. In many cases, this allows a program to continue executing as if no problems were encountered. For example, the StudentPoll application still displays results (Fig. 7.8), even though one of the responses was out of range. More severe problems might prevent a program from continuing normal execution, instead requiring the program to notify the user of the problem, then terminate. When the JVM or a method detects a problem, such as an invalid array index or an invalid method argument, it **throws** an exception—that is, an exception occurs. Methods in your own classes can also throw exceptions, as you'll learn in Chapter 8.

7.5.1 The try Statement

To handle an exception, place any code that might throw an exception in a **try statement** (lines 17–26). The **try block** (lines 17–20) contains the code that might throw an exception, and the **catch block** (lines 21–26) contains the code that handles the exception if one occurs. You can have many catch blocks to handle different types of exceptions that might be thrown in the corresponding try block. When line 19 correctly increments an element of the frequency array, lines 21–26 are ignored. The braces that delimit the bodies of the try and catch blocks are required.

7.5.2 Executing the catch Block

When the program encounters the invalid value 14 in the responses array, it attempts to add 1 to frequency[14], which is outside the bounds of the array—the frequency array has only six elements (with indexes 0–5). Because array bounds checking is performed at execution time, the JVM generates an exception—specifically line 19 throws an `ArrayIndexOutOfBoundsException` to notify the program of this problem. At this point the `try` block terminates and the `catch` block begins executing—if you declared any local variables in the `try` block, they're now out of scope (and no longer exist), so they're not accessible in the `catch` block.

The `catch` block declares an exception parameter (`e`) of type (`IndexOutOfRangeException`). The `catch` block can handle exceptions of the specified type. Inside the `catch` block, you can use the parameter's identifier to interact with a caught exception object.

Error-Prevention Tip 7.1

When writing code to access an array element, ensure that the array index remains greater than or equal to 0 and less than the length of the array. This would prevent `ArrayIndexOutOfBoundsExceptions` if your program is correct.

Software Engineering Observation 7.1

Systems in industry that have undergone extensive testing are still likely to contain bugs. Our preference for industrial-strength systems is to catch and deal with runtime exceptions, such as `ArrayIndexOutOfBoundsExceptions`, to ensure that a system either stays up and running or degrades gracefully, and to inform the system's developers of the problem.

7.5.3 `toString` Method of the Exception Parameter

When lines 21–26 catch the exception, the program displays a message indicating the problem that occurred. Line 23 implicitly calls the exception object's `toString` method to get the error message that's implicitly stored in the exception object and display it. Once the message is displayed in this example, the exception is considered *handled* and the program continues with the next statement after the `catch` block's closing brace. In this example, the end of the for statement is reached (line 27), so the program continues with the increment of the control variable in line 15. We discuss exception handling again in Chapter 8, and more deeply in Chapter 11.

7.6 Case Study: Card Shuffling and Dealing Simulation

The examples in the chapter thus far have used arrays containing elements of primitive types. Recall from Section 7.2 that the elements of an array can be either primitive types or reference types. This section uses random-number generation and an array of reference-type elements, namely objects representing playing cards, to develop a class that simulates card shuffling and dealing. This class can then be used to implement applications that play specific card games. You can use the classes developed here to implement various card-playing applications.

We first develop class `Card` (Fig. 7.9), which represents a playing card that has a face (e.g., `"Ace"`, `"Deuce"`, `"Three"`, ..., `"Jack"`, `"Queen"`, `"King"`) and a suit (e.g., `"Hearts"`, `"Diamonds"`, `"Clubs"`, `"Spades"`). Next, we develop the `DeckOfCards` class (Fig. 7.10), which creates a deck of 52 playing cards in which each element is a `Card` object. We then build a test application (Fig. 7.11) that demonstrates class `DeckOfCards`'s card shuffling and dealing capabilities.

Class *Card*

Class Card (Fig. 7.9) contains two String instance variables—face and suit—that are used to store references to the face name and suit name for a specific Card. The constructor for the class (lines 10–14) receives two Strings that it uses to initialize face and suit. Method toString (lines 17–20) creates a String consisting of the face of the card, the String " of " and the suit of the card. Card's toString method can be invoked *explicitly* to obtain a string representation of a Card object (e.g., "Ace of Spades"). The toString method of an object is called *implicitly* when the object is used where a String is expected (e.g., when printf outputs the object as a String using the %s format specifier or when the object is concatenated to a String using the + operator). For this behavior to occur, toString must be declared with the header shown in Fig. 7.9.

```java
1   // Fig. 7.9: Card.java
2   // Card class represents a playing card.
3
4   public class Card
5   {
6      private final String face; // face of card ("Ace", "Deuce", ...)
7      private final String suit; // suit of card ("Hearts", "Diamonds", ...)
8
9      // two-argument constructor initializes card's face and suit
10     public Card(String cardFace, String cardSuit)
11     {
12        this.face = cardFace; // initialize face of card
13        this.suit = cardSuit; // initialize suit of card
14     }
15
16     // return String representation of Card
17     public String toString()
18     {
19        return face + " of " + suit;
20     }
21  } // end class Card
```

Fig. 7.9 | Card class represents a playing card.

Class *DeckOfCards*

Class DeckOfCards (Fig. 7.10) declares as an instance variable a Card array named deck (line 7). An array of a reference type is declared like any other array. Class DeckOfCards also declares an integer instance variable currentCard (line 8) representing the sequence number (0–51) of the next Card to be dealt from the deck array, and a named constant NUMBER_OF_CARDS (line 9) indicating the number of Cards in the deck (52).

```java
1   // Fig. 7.10: DeckOfCards.java
2   // DeckOfCards class represents a deck of playing cards.
3   import java.security.SecureRandom;
4
```

Fig. 7.10 | DeckOfCards class represents a deck of playing cards. (Part 1 of 2.)

```
 5   public class DeckOfCards
 6   {
 7      private Card[] deck; // array of Card objects
 8      private int currentCard; // index of next Card to be dealt (0-51)
 9      private static final int NUMBER_OF_CARDS = 52; // constant # of Cards
10      // random number generator
11      private static final SecureRandom randomNumbers = new SecureRandom();
12
13      // constructor fills deck of Cards
14      public DeckOfCards()
15      {
16         String[] faces = { "Ace", "Deuce", "Three", "Four", "Five", "Six",
17            "Seven", "Eight", "Nine", "Ten", "Jack", "Queen", "King" };
18         String[] suits = { "Hearts", "Diamonds", "Clubs", "Spades" };
19
20         deck = new Card[NUMBER_OF_CARDS]; // create array of Card objects
21         currentCard = 0; // first Card dealt will be deck[0]
22
23         // populate deck with Card objects
24         for (int count = 0; count < deck.length; count++)
25            deck[count] =
26               new Card(faces[count % 13], suits[count / 13]);
27      }
28
29      // shuffle deck of Cards with one-pass algorithm
30      public void shuffle()
31      {
32         // next call to method dealCard should start at deck[0] again
33         currentCard = 0;
34
35         // for each Card, pick another random Card (0-51) and swap them
36         for (int first = 0; first < deck.length; first++)
37         {
38            // select a random number between 0 and 51
39            int second = randomNumbers.nextInt(NUMBER_OF_CARDS);
40
41            // swap current Card with randomly selected Card
42            Card temp = deck[first];
43            deck[first] = deck[second];
44            deck[second] = temp;
45         }
46      }
47
48      // deal one Card
49      public Card dealCard()
50      {
51         // determine whether Cards remain to be dealt
52         if (currentCard < deck.length)
53            return deck[currentCard++]; // return current Card in array
54         else
55            return null; // return null to indicate that all Cards were dealt
56      }
57   } // end class DeckOfCards
```

Fig. 7.10 | DeckOfCards class represents a deck of playing cards. (Part 2 of 2.)

DeckOfCards Constructor

The class's constructor instantiates the deck array (line 20) with NUMBER_OF_CARDS (52) elements. The elements of deck are null by default, so the constructor uses a for statement (lines 24–26) to fill the deck with Cards. The loop initializes control variable count to 0 and loops while count is less than deck.length, causing count to take on each integer value from 0 to 51 (the indices of the deck array). Each Card is instantiated and initialized with two Strings—one from the faces array (which contains the Strings "Ace" through "King") and one from the suits array (which contains the Strings "Hearts", "Diamonds", "Clubs" and "Spades"). The calculation count % 13 always results in a value from 0 to 12 (the 13 indices of the faces array in lines 16–17), and the calculation count / 13 always results in a value from 0 to 3 (the four indices of the suits array in line 18). When the deck array is initialized, it contains the Cards with faces "Ace" through "King" in order for each suit (all 13 "Hearts", then all the "Diamonds", then the "Clubs", then the "Spades"). We use arrays of Strings to represent the faces and suits in this example. Alternatively, you might want to modify this example to use arrays of enum constants to represent the faces and suits.

DeckOfCards Method **shuffle**

Method shuffle (lines 30–46) shuffles the Cards in the deck. The method loops through all 52 Cards (array indices 0 to 51). For each Card, a number between 0 and 51 is picked randomly to select another Card. Next, the current Card object and the randomly selected Card object are swapped in the array. This exchange is performed by the three assignments in lines 42–44. The extra variable temp temporarily stores one of the two Card objects being swapped. The swap cannot be performed with only the two statements

```
deck[first] = deck[second];
deck[second] = deck[first];
```

If deck[first] is the "Ace" of "Spades" and deck[second] is the "Queen" of "Hearts", after the first assignment, both array elements contain the "Queen" of "Hearts" and the "Ace" of "Spades" is lost—so, the extra variable temp is needed. After the for loop terminates, the Card objects are randomly ordered. A total of only 52 swaps are made in a single pass of the entire array, and the array of Card objects is shuffled!

[*Note:* It's recommended that you use a so-called *unbiased* shuffling algorithm for real card games. Such an algorithm ensures that all possible shuffled card sequences are equally likely to occur. You may want to research the popular unbiased Fisher-Yates shuffling algorithm and use it to reimplement the DeckOfCards method shuffle.]

DeckOfCards Method **dealCard**

Method dealCard (lines 49–56) deals one Card in the array. Recall that currentCard indicates the index of the next Card to be dealt (i.e., the Card at the *top* of the deck). Thus, line 52 compares currentCard to the length of the deck array. If the deck is not empty (i.e., currentCard is less than 52), line 53 returns the "top" Card and postincrements currentCard to prepare for the next call to dealCard—otherwise, null is returned. Recall from Chapter 3 that null represents a "reference to nothing."

Shuffling and Dealing Cards

Figure 7.11 demonstrates class DeckOfCards. Line 9 creates a DeckOfCards object named myDeckOfCards. The DeckOfCards constructor creates the deck with the 52 Card objects in order by suit and face. Line 10 invokes myDeckOfCards's shuffle method to rearrange the Card objects. Lines 13–20 deal all 52 Cards and print them in four columns of 13 Cards each. Line 16 deals one Card object by invoking myDeckOfCards's dealCard method, then displays the Card left justified in a field of 19 characters. When a Card is output as a String, the Card's toString method (lines 17–20 of Fig. 7.9) is implicitly invoked. Lines 18–19 start a new line after every four Cards.

```
1   // Fig. 7.11: DeckOfCardsTest.java
2   // Card shuffling and dealing.
3
4   public class DeckOfCardsTest
5   {
6      // execute application
7      public static void main(String[] args)
8      {
9         DeckOfCards myDeckOfCards = new DeckOfCards();
10        myDeckOfCards.shuffle(); // place Cards in random order
11
12        // print all 52 Cards in the order in which they are dealt
13        for (int i = 1; i <= 52; i++)
14        {
15           // deal and display a Card
16           System.out.printf("%-19s", myDeckOfCards.dealCard());
17
18           if (i % 4 == 0) // output a newline after every fourth card
19              System.out.println();
20        }
21     }
22  } // end class DeckOfCardsTest
```

```
Six of Spades      Eight of Spades    Six of Clubs       Nine of Hearts
Queen of Hearts    Seven of Clubs     Nine of Spades     King of Hearts
Three of Diamonds  Deuce of Clubs     Ace of Hearts      Ten of Spades
Four of Spades     Ace of Clubs       Seven of Diamonds  Four of Hearts
Three of Clubs     Deuce of Hearts    Five of Spades     Jack of Diamonds
King of Clubs      Ten of Hearts      Three of Hearts    Six of Diamonds
Queen of Clubs     Eight of Diamonds  Deuce of Diamonds  Ten of Diamonds
Three of Spades    King of Diamonds   Nine of Clubs      Six of Hearts
Ace of Spades      Four of Diamonds   Seven of Hearts    Eight of Clubs
Deuce of Spades    Eight of Hearts    Five of Hearts     Queen of Spades
Jack of Hearts     Seven of Spades    Four of Clubs      Nine of Diamonds
Ace of Diamonds    Queen of Diamonds  Five of Clubs      King of Spades
Five of Diamonds   Ten of Clubs       Jack of Spades     Jack of Clubs
```

Fig. 7.11 | Card shuffling and dealing.

Preventing *NullPointerExceptions*

In Fig. 7.10, we created a deck array of 52 Card references—each element of every reference-type array created with new is default initialized to null. Reference-type variables which are fields of a class are also initialized to null by default. A NullPointerException occurs when you try to call a method on a null reference. In industrial-strength code, ensuring that references are not `null` before you use them to call methods prevents `Null-PointerExceptions`.

7.7 Enhanced for Statement

The **enhanced for statement** iterates through the elements of an array without using a counter, thus avoiding the possibility of "stepping outside" the array. We show how to use the enhanced for statement with the Java API's prebuilt data structures (called collections) in Section 7.16. The syntax of an enhanced for statement is:

> **for** (*parameter* : *arrayName*)
>   *statement*

where *parameter* has a type and an identifier (e.g., `int number`), and *arrayName* is the array through which to iterate. The type of the parameter must be *consistent* with the type of the elements in the array. As the next example illustrates, the identifier represents successive element values in the array on successive iterations of the loop.

Figure 7.12 uses the enhanced for statement (lines 12–13) to sum the integers in an array of student grades. The enhanced for's parameter is of type `int`, because `array` contains `int` values—the loop selects one `int` value from the array during each iteration. The enhanced for statement iterates through successive values in the array one by one. The statement's header can be read as "for each iteration, assign the next element of `array` to `int` variable `number`, then execute the following statement." Thus, for each iteration, identifier `number` represents an `int` value in `array`. Lines 12–13 are equivalent to the following counter-controlled repetition used in lines 12–13 of Fig. 7.5 to total the integers in `array`, except that `counter` cannot be accessed in the enhanced for statement:

> **for** (**int** counter = 0; counter < array.length; counter++)
>   total += array[counter];

```java
1   // Fig. 7.12: EnhancedForTest.java
2   // Using the enhanced for statement to total integers in an array.
3
4   public class EnhancedForTest
5   {
6      public static void main(String[] args)
7      {
8         int[] array = { 87, 68, 94, 100, 83, 78, 85, 91, 76, 87 };
9         int total = 0;
10
11         // add each element's value to total
12         for (int number : array)
13            total += number;
14
15         System.out.printf("Total of array elements: %d%n", total);
16      }
17   } // end class EnhancedForTest
```

```
Total of array elements: 849
```

Fig. 7.12 | Using the enhanced for statement to total integers in an array.

The enhanced for statement can be used only to obtain array elements—it cannot be used to modify elements. If your program needs to modify elements, use the traditional counter-controlled for statement.

The enhanced for statement can be used in place of the counter-controlled for statement whenever code looping through an array does not require access to the counter indicating the index of the current array element. For example, totaling the integers in an array requires access only to the element values—the index of each element is irrelevant. However, if a program must use a counter for some reason other than simply to loop through an array (e.g., to print an index number next to each array element value, as in the examples earlier in this chapter), use the counter-controlled for statement.

Error-Prevention Tip 7.2

The enhanced for statement simplifies the code for iterating through an array making the code more readable and eliminating several error possibilities, such as improperly specifying the control variable's initial value, the loop-continuation test and the increment expression.

Java SE 8

The for statement and the enhanced for statement each iterate sequentially from a starting value to an ending value. In Chapter 17, Java SE 8 Lambdas and Streams, you'll learn about class Stream and its forEach method. Working together, these provide an elegant, more concise and less error prone means for iterating through collections so that some of the iterations may occur in parallel with others to achieve better multi-core system performance.

7.8 Passing Arrays to Methods

This section demonstrates how to pass arrays and individual array elements as arguments to methods. To pass an array argument to a method, specify the name of the array without any brackets. For example, if array hourlyTemperatures is declared as

```
double[] hourlyTemperatures = new double[24];
```

then the method call

```
modifyArray(hourlyTemperatures);
```

passes the reference of array hourlyTemperatures to method modifyArray. Every array object "knows" its own length. Thus, when we pass an array object's reference into a method, we need not pass the array length as an additional argument.

For a method to receive an array reference through a method call, the method's parameter list must specify an array parameter. For example, the method header for method modifyArray might be written as

```
void modifyArray(double[] b)
```

indicating that modifyArray receives the reference of a double array in parameter b. The method call passes array hourlyTemperature's reference, so when the called method uses the array variable b, it refers to the same array object as hourlyTemperatures in the caller.

When an argument to a method is an entire array or an individual array element of a reference type, the called method receives a copy of the reference. However, when an argument to a method is an individual array element of a primitive type, the called method receives a copy of the element's value. Such primitive values are called **scalars** or **scalar quantities**. To pass an individual array element to a method, use the indexed name of the array element as an argument in the method call.

Figure 7.13 demonstrates the difference between passing an entire array and passing a primitive-type array element to a method. Notice that main invokes static methods modifyArray (line 19) and modifyElement (line 30) directly. Recall from Section 6.4 that a static method of a class can invoke other static methods of the same class directly.

The enhanced for statement at lines 16–17 outputs the elements of array. Line 19 invokes method modifyArray, passing array as an argument. The method (lines 36–40) receives a copy of array's reference and uses it to multiply each of array's elements by 2. To prove that array's elements were modified, lines 23–24 output array's elements again. As the output shows, method modifyArray doubled the value of each element. We could *not* use the enhanced for statement in lines 38–39 because we're modifying the array's elements.

```java
1   // Fig. 7.13: PassArray.java
2   // Passing arrays and individual array elements to methods.
3
4   public class PassArray
5   {
6      // main creates array and calls modifyArray and modifyElement
7      public static void main(String[] args)
8      {
9         int[] array = { 1, 2, 3, 4, 5 };
10
11        System.out.printf(
12           "Effects of passing reference to entire array:%n" +
13           "The values of the original array are:%n");
14
15        // output original array elements
16        for (int value : array)
17           System.out.printf("   %d", value);
18
19        modifyArray(array); // pass array reference
20        System.out.printf("%n%nThe values of the modified array are:%n");
21
22        // output modified array elements
23        for (int value : array)
24           System.out.printf("   %d", value);
25
26        System.out.printf(
27           "%n%nEffects of passing array element value:%n" +
28           "array[3] before modifyElement: %d%n", array[3]);
29
30        modifyElement(array[3]); // attempt to modify array[3]
31        System.out.printf(
32           "array[3] after modifyElement: %d%n", array[3]);
33     }
34
```

Fig. 7.13 | Passing arrays and individual array elements to methods. (Part 1 of 2.)

```
35    // multiply each element of an array by 2
36    public static void modifyArray(int[] array2)
37    {
38       for (int counter = 0; counter < array2.length; counter++)
39          array2[counter] *= 2;
40    }
41
42    // multiply argument by 2
43    public static void modifyElement(int element)
44    {
45       element *= 2;
46       System.out.printf(
47          "Value of element in modifyElement: %d%n", element);
48    }
49 } // end class PassArray
```

```
Effects of passing reference to entire array:
The values of the original array are:
   1   2   3   4   5

The values of the modified array are:
   2   4   6   8   10

Effects of passing array element value:
array[3] before modifyElement: 8
Value of element in modifyElement: 16
array[3] after modifyElement: 8
```

Fig. 7.13 | Passing arrays and individual array elements to methods. (Part 2 of 2.)

Figure 7.13 next demonstrates that when a copy of an individual primitive-type array element is passed to a method, modifying the *copy* in the called method does *not* affect the original value of that element in the calling method's array. Lines 26–28 output the value of array[3] before invoking method modifyElement. Remember that the value of this element is now 8 after it was modified in the call to modifyArray. Line 30 calls method modifyElement and passes array[3] as an argument. Remember that array[3] is actually one int value (8) in array. Therefore, the program passes a copy of the value of array[3]. Method modifyElement (lines 43–48) multiplies the value received as an argument by 2, stores the result in its parameter element, then outputs the value of element (16). Since method parameters, like local variables, cease to exist when the method in which they're declared completes execution, the method parameter element is destroyed when method modifyElement terminates. When the program returns control to main, lines 31–32 output the *unmodified* value of array[3] (i.e., 8).

7.9 Pass-By-Value vs. Pass-By-Reference

The preceding example demonstrated how arrays and primitive-type array elements are passed as arguments to methods. We now take a closer look at how arguments in general are passed to methods. Two ways to pass arguments in method calls in many programming languages are **pass-by-value** and **pass-by-reference** (sometimes called **call-by-value** and **call-by-reference**). When an argument is passed by value, a copy of the argument's value is passed to the called method. The called method works exclusively with the copy. Changes to the called method's copy do not affect the original variable's value in the caller.

When an argument is passed by reference, the called method can access the argument's value in the caller directly and modify that data, if necessary. Pass-by-reference improves performance by eliminating the need to copy possibly large amounts of data.

Unlike some other languages, Java does not allow you to choose pass-by-value or pass-by-reference—*all arguments are passed by value*. A method call can pass two types of values to a method—copies of primitive values (e.g., values of type `int` and `double`) and copies of references to objects. Objects themselves cannot be passed to methods. When a method modifies a primitive-type parameter, changes to the parameter have no effect on the original argument value in the calling method. For example, when line 30 in `main` of Fig. 7.13 passes `array[3]` to method `modifyElement`, the statement in line 45 that doubles the value of parameter `element` has no effect on the value of `array[3]` in `main`. This is also true for reference-type parameters. If you modify a reference-type parameter so that it refers to another object, only the parameter refers to the new object—the reference stored in the caller's variable still refers to the original object.

Although an object's reference is passed by value, a method can still interact with the referenced object by calling its `public` methods using the copy of the object's reference. Since the reference stored in the parameter is a copy of the reference that was passed as an argument, the parameter in the called method and the argument in the calling method refer to the *same* object in memory. For example, in Fig. 7.13, both parameter `array2` in method `modifyArray` and variable `array` in `main` refer to the *same* array object in memory. Any changes made using the parameter `array2` are carried out on the object that `array` references in the calling method. In Fig. 7.13, the changes made in `modifyArray` using `array2` affect the contents of the array object referenced by `array` in `main`. Thus, with a reference to an object, the called method *can* manipulate the caller's object directly.

Performance Tip 7.1

Passing references to arrays, instead of the array objects themselves, makes sense for performance reasons. Because everything in Java is passed by value, if array objects were passed, a copy of each element would be passed. For large arrays, this would waste time and consume considerable storage for the copies of the elements.

7.10 Case Study: Class GradeBook Using an Array to Store Grades

We now present the first part of our case study on developing a `GradeBook` class that instructors can use to maintain students' grades on an exam and display a grade report that includes the grades, class average, lowest grade, highest grade and a grade distribution bar chart. The version of class `GradeBook` presented in this section stores the grades for one exam in a one-dimensional array. In Section 7.12, we present a version of class `GradeBook` that uses a two-dimensional array to store students' grades for *several* exams.

Storing Student Grades in an Array in Class *GradeBook*

Class `GradeBook` (Fig. 7.14) uses an array of `int`s to store several students' grades on a single exam. Array `grades` is declared as an instance variable (line 7), so each `GradeBook` object maintains its *own* set of grades. The constructor (lines 10–14) has two parameters—the name of the course and an array of grades. When an application (e.g., class GradeBookTest in Fig. 7.15) creates a GradeBook object, the application passes an existing int array to the constructor, which assigns the array's reference to instance variable grades (line 13). The grades array's *size* is determined by the length instance variable of the constructor's array parameter. Thus, a GradeBook object can process a variable number of grades. The grade values in the argument could have been input from a user, read from a file on disk (as discussed in Chapter 15) or come from a variety of other sources. In class GradeBookTest, we initialize an array with grade values (Fig. 7.15, line 10). Once the grades are stored in instance variable grades of class GradeBook, all the class's methods can access the elements of grades.

```java
1   // Fig. 7.14: GradeBook.java
2   // GradeBook class using an array to store test grades.
3
4   public class GradeBook
5   {
6      private String courseName; // name of course this GradeBook represents
7      private int[] grades; // array of student grades
8
9      // constructor
10     public GradeBook(String courseName, int[] grades)
11     {
12        this.courseName = courseName;
13        this.grades = grades;
14     }
15
16     // method to set the course name
17     public void setCourseName(String courseName)
18     {
19        this.courseName = courseName;
20     }
21
22     // method to retrieve the course name
23     public String getCourseName()
24     {
25        return courseName;
26     }
27
28     // perform various operations on the data
29     public void processGrades()
30     {
31        // output grades array
32        outputGrades();
33
34        // call method getAverage to calculate the average grade
35        System.out.printf("%nClass average is %.2f%n", getAverage());
36
37        // call methods getMinimum and getMaximum
38        System.out.printf("Lowest grade is %d%nHighest grade is %d%n%n",
39           getMinimum(), getMaximum());
40
```

Fig. 7.14 | GradeBook class using an array to store test grades. (Part 1 of 3.)

```
41         // call outputBarChart to print grade distribution chart
42         outputBarChart();
43      }
44
45      // find minimum grade
46      public int getMinimum()
47      {
48         int lowGrade = grades[0]; // assume grades[0] is smallest
49
50         // loop through grades array
51         for (int grade : grades)
52         {
53            // if grade lower than lowGrade, assign it to lowGrade
54            if (grade < lowGrade)
55               lowGrade = grade; // new lowest grade
56         }
57
58         return lowGrade;
59      }
60
61      // find maximum grade
62      public int getMaximum()
63      {
64         int highGrade = grades[0]; // assume grades[0] is largest
65
66         // loop through grades array
67         for (int grade : grades)
68         {
69            // if grade greater than highGrade, assign it to highGrade
70            if (grade > highGrade)
71               highGrade = grade; // new highest grade
72         }
73
74         return highGrade;
75      }
76
77      // determine average grade for test
78      public double getAverage()
79      {
80         int total = 0;
81
82         // sum grades for one student
83         for (int grade : grades)
84            total += grade;
85
86         // return average of grades
87         return (double) total / grades.length;
88      }
89
90      // output bar chart displaying grade distribution
91      public void outputBarChart()
92      {
93         System.out.println("Grade distribution:");
```

Fig. 7.14 | GradeBook class using an array to store test grades. (Part 2 of 3.)

```
 94
 95     // stores frequency of grades in each range of 10 grades
 96     int[] frequency = new int[11];
 97
 98     // for each grade, increment the appropriate frequency
 99     for (int grade : grades)
100        ++frequency[grade / 10];
101
102     // for each grade frequency, print bar in chart
103     for (int count = 0; count < frequency.length; count++)
104     {
105        // output bar label ("00-09: ", ..., "90-99: ", "100: ")
106        if (count == 10)
107           System.out.printf("%5d: ", 100);
108        else
109           System.out.printf("%02d-%02d: ",
110              count * 10, count * 10 + 9);
111
112        // print bar of asterisks
113        for (int stars = 0; stars < frequency[count]; stars++)
114           System.out.print("*");
115
116        System.out.println();
117     }
118  }
119
120  // output the contents of the grades array
121  public void outputGrades()
122  {
123     System.out.printf("The grades are:%n%n");
124
125     // output each student's grade
126     for (int student = 0; student < grades.length; student++)
127        System.out.printf("Student %2d: %3d%n",
128           student + 1, grades[student]);
129  }
130 } // end class GradeBook
```

Fig. 7.14 | GradeBook class using an array to store test grades. (Part 3 of 3.)

Method processGrades (lines 29–43) contains a series of method calls that output a report summarizing the grades. Line 32 calls method outputGrades to print the contents of the array grades. Lines 126–128 in method outputGrades output the students' grades. A counter-controlled for statement must be used in this case, because lines 127–128 use counter variable student's value to output each grade next to a particular student number (see the output in Fig. 7.15). Although array indices start at 0, a professor might typically number students starting at 1. Thus, lines 127–128 output student + 1 as the student number to produce grade labels "Student 1: ", "Student 2: ", and so on.

Method processGrades next calls method getAverage (line 35) to obtain the average of the grades in the array. Method getAverage (lines 78–88) uses an enhanced for statement to total the values in array grades before calculating the average. The parameter in the enhanced for's header (e.g., int grade) indicates that for each iteration, the int variable grade takes on a value in the array grades. The averaging calculation in line 87 uses grades.length to determine the number of grades being averaged.

Lines 38–39 in method processGrades call methods getMinimum and getMaximum to determine the lowest and highest grades of any student on the exam, respectively. Each of these methods uses an enhanced for statement to loop through array grades. Lines 51–56 in method getMinimum loop through the array. Lines 54–55 compare each grade to lowGrade; if a grade is less than lowGrade, lowGrade is set to that grade. When line 58 executes, lowGrade contains the lowest grade in the array. Method getMaximum (lines 62–75) works similarly to method getMinimum.

Finally, line 42 in method processGrades calls outputBarChart to print a grade distribution chart using a technique similar to that in Fig. 7.6. In that example, we manually calculated the number of grades in each category (i.e., 0–9, 10–19, …, 90–99 and 100) by simply looking at a set of grades. Here, lines 99–100 use a technique similar to that in Figs. 7.7–7.8 to calculate the frequency of grades in each category. Line 96 declares and creates array frequency of 11 ints to store the frequency of grades in each category. For each grade in array grades, lines 99–100 increment the appropriate frequency array element. To determine which one to increment, line 100 divides the current grade by 10 using *integer division*—e.g., if grade is 85, line 100 increments frequency[8] to update the count of grades in the range 80–89. Lines 103–117 print the bar chart (as shown in Fig. 7.15) based on the values in array frequency. Like lines 23–24 of Fig. 7.6, lines 113–116 of Fig. 7.14 use a value in array frequency to determine the number of asterisks to display in each bar.

Class *GradeBookTest* That Demonstrates Class *GradeBook*
The application of Fig. 7.15 creates an object of class GradeBook (Fig. 7.14) using the int array gradesArray (declared and initialized in line 10). Lines 12–13 pass a course name and gradesArray to the GradeBook constructor. Lines 14–15 display a welcome message that includes the course name stored in the GradeBook object. Line 16 invokes the GradeBook object's processGrades method. The output summarizes the 10 grades in myGradeBook.

> ### Software Engineering Observation 7.2
> *A test harness (or test application) is responsible for creating an object of the class being tested and providing it with data. This data could come from any of several sources. Test data can be placed directly into an array with an array initializer, it can come from the user at the keyboard, from a file (as you'll see in Chapter 15), from a database (as you'll see in Chapter 21) or from a network. After passing this data to the class's constructor to instantiate the object, the test harness should call upon the object to test its methods and manipulate its data. Gathering data in the test harness like this allows the class to be more reusable, able to manipulate data from several sources.*

```
1   // Fig. 7.15: GradeBookTest.java
2   // GradeBookTest creates a GradeBook object using an array of grades,
3   // then invokes method processGrades to analyze them.
4   public class GradeBookTest
5   {
```

Fig. 7.15 | GradeBookTest creates a GradeBook object using an array of grades, then invokes method processGrades to analyze them. (Part 1 of 2.)

```
 6      // main method begins program execution
 7      public static void main(String[] args)
 8      {
 9          // array of student grades
10          int[] gradesArray = { 87, 68, 94, 100, 83, 78, 85, 91, 76, 87 };
11
12          GradeBook myGradeBook = new GradeBook(
13              "CS101 Introduction to Java Programming", gradesArray);
14          System.out.printf("Welcome to the grade book for%n%s%n%n",
15              myGradeBook.getCourseName());
16          myGradeBook.processGrades();
17      }
18  } // end class GradeBookTest
```

```
Welcome to the grade book for
CS101 Introduction to Java Programming

The grades are:

Student  1:  87
Student  2:  68
Student  3:  94
Student  4: 100
Student  5:  83
Student  6:  78
Student  7:  85
Student  8:  91
Student  9:  76
Student 10:  87

Class average is 84.90
Lowest grade is 68
Highest grade is 100

Grade distribution:
00-09:
10-19:
20-29:
30-39:
40-49:
50-59:
60-69: *
70-79: **
80-89: ****
90-99: **
  100: *
```

Fig. 7.15 | GradeBookTest creates a GradeBook object using an array of grades, then invokes method processGrades to analyze them. (Part 2 of 2.)

Java SE 8

In Chapter 17, Java SE 8 Lambdas and Streams, the example of Fig. 17.5 uses stream methods min, max, count and average to process the elements of an int array elegantly and concisely without having to write repetition statements. In Chapter 20, Concurrency, the example of Fig. 20.29 uses stream method summaryStatistics to perform all of these operations in *one* method call.

7.11 Multidimensional Arrays

Multidimensional arrays with two dimensions are often used to represent *tables* of values with data arranged in *rows* and *columns*. To identify a particular table element, you specify *two* indices. By convention, the first identifies the element's row and the second its column. Arrays that require two indices to identify each element are called **two-dimensional arrays**. (Multidimensional arrays can have more than two dimensions.) Java does not support multidimensional arrays directly, but it allows you to specify one-dimensional arrays whose elements are also one-dimensional arrays, thus achieving the same effect. Figure 7.16 illustrates a two-dimensional array named a with three rows and four columns (i.e., a three-by-four array). In general, an array with m rows and n columns is called an **m-by-n array**.

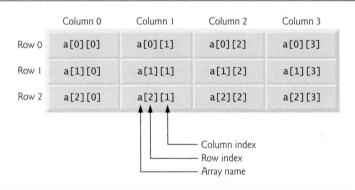

Fig. 7.16 | Two-dimensional array with three rows and four columns.

Every element in array a is identified in Fig. 7.16 by an array-access expression of the form a[*row*][*column*]; a is the name of the array, and *row* and *column* are the indices that uniquely identify each element by row and column index. The names of the elements in *row* 0 all have a *first* index of 0, and the names of the elements in *column* 3 all have a *second* index of 3.

Arrays of One-Dimensional Arrays

Like one-dimensional arrays, multidimensional arrays can be initialized with array initializers in declarations. A two-dimensional array b with two rows and two columns could be declared and initialized with **nested array initializers** as follows:

```
int[][] b = {{1, 2}, {3, 4}};
```

The initial values are grouped by row in braces. So 1 and 2 initialize b[0][0] and b[0][1], respectively, and 3 and 4 initialize b[1][0] and b[1][1], respectively. The compiler counts the number of nested array initializers (represented by sets of braces within the outer braces) to determine the number of *rows* in array b. The compiler counts the initializer values in the nested array initializer for a row to determine the number of *columns* in that row. As we'll see momentarily, this means that rows can have *different* lengths.

Multidimensional arrays are maintained as *arrays of one-dimensional arrays*. Therefore array b in the preceding declaration is actually composed of two separate one-dimensional arrays—one containing the values in the first nested initializer list {1, 2} and one containing the values in the second nested initializer list {3, 4}. Thus, array b itself is an array of two elements, each a one-dimensional array of int values.

Two-Dimensional Arrays with Rows of Different Lengths

The manner in which multidimensional arrays are represented makes them quite flexible. In fact, the lengths of the rows in array b are *not* required to be the same. For example,

```java
int[][] b = {{1, 2}, {3, 4, 5}};
```

creates integer array b with two elements (determined by the number of nested array initializers) that represent the rows of the two-dimensional array. Each element of b is a *reference* to a one-dimensional array of int variables. The int array for row 0 is a one-dimensional array with *two* elements (1 and 2), and the int array for row 1 is a one-dimensional array with *three* elements (3, 4 and 5).

Creating Two-Dimensional Arrays with Array-Creation Expressions

A multidimensional array with the *same* number of columns in every row can be created with an array-creation expression. For example, the following line declares array b and assign it a reference to a three-by-four array:

```java
int[][] b = new int[3][4];
```

In this case, we use the literal values 3 and 4 to specify the number of rows and number of columns, respectively, but this is *not* required. Programs can also use variables to specify array dimensions, because new creates arrays at *execution* time—not at compile time. The elements of a multidimensional array are initialized when the array object is created.

A multidimensional array in which each row has a *different* number of columns can be created as follows:

```java
int[][] b = new int[2][];   // create 2 rows
b[0] = new int[5]; // create 5 columns for row 0
b[1] = new int[3]; // create 3 columns for row 1
```

The preceding statements create a two-dimensional array with two rows. Row 0 has five columns, and row 1 has three columns.

Two-Dimensional Array Example: Displaying Element Values

Figure 7.17 demonstrates initializing two-dimensional arrays with array initializers, and using nested for loops to **traverse** the arrays (i.e., manipulate *every* element of each array). Class InitArray's main declares two arrays. The declaration of array1 (line 9) uses nested array initializers of the *same* length to initialize the first row to the values 1, 2 and 3, and the second row to the values 4, 5 and 6. The declaration of array2 (line 10) uses nested initializers of *different* lengths. In this case, the first row is initialized to two elements with the values 1 and 2, respectively. The second row is initialized to one element with the value 3. The third row is initialized to three elements with the values 4, 5 and 6, respectively.

```java
1   // Fig. 7.17: InitArray.java
2   // Initializing two-dimensional arrays.
3
```

Fig. 7.17 | Initializing two-dimensional arrays. (Part 1 of 2.)

```
4    public class InitArray
5    {
6       // create and output two-dimensional arrays
7       public static void main(String[] args)
8       {
9          int[][] array1 = {{1, 2, 3}, {4, 5, 6}};
10         int[][] array2 = {{1, 2}, {3}, {4, 5, 6}};
11
12         System.out.println("Values in array1 by row are");
13         outputArray(array1); // displays array1 by row
14
15         System.out.printf("%nValues in array2 by row are%n");
16         outputArray(array2); // displays array2 by row
17      }
18
19      // output rows and columns of a two-dimensional array
20      public static void outputArray(int[][] array)
21      {
22         // loop through array's rows
23         for (int row = 0; row < array.length; row++)
24         {
25            // loop through columns of current row
26            for (int column = 0; column < array[row].length; column++)
27               System.out.printf("%d  ", array[row][column]);
28
29            System.out.println();
30         }
31      }
32   } // end class InitArray
```

```
Values in array1 by row are
1   2   3
4   5   6

Values in array2 by row are
1   2
3
4   5   6
```

Fig. 7.17 | Initializing two-dimensional arrays. (Part 2 of 2.)

Lines 13 and 16 call method outputArray (lines 20–31) to output the elements of array1 and array2, respectively. Method outputArray's parameter—int[][] array— indicates that the method receives a two-dimensional array. The nested for statement (lines 23–30) outputs the rows of a two-dimensional array. In the loop-continuation condition of the outer for statement, the expression array.length determines the number of rows in the array. In the inner for statement, the expression array[row].length determines the number of columns in the current row of the array. The inner for statement's condition enables the loop to determine the exact number of columns in each row. We demonstrate nested enhanced for statements in Fig. 7.18.

*Common Multidimensional-Array Manipulations Performed with **for** Statements*
Many common array manipulations use for statements. As an example, the following for statement sets all the elements in row 2 of array a in Fig. 7.16 to zero:

```
for (int column = 0; column < a[2].length; column++)
    a[2][column] = 0;
```

We specified row 2; therefore, we know that the *first* index is always 2 (0 is the first row, and 1 is the second row). This for loop varies only the *second* index (i.e., the column index). If row 2 of array a contains four elements, then the preceding for statement is equivalent to the assignment statements

```
a[2][0] = 0;
a[2][1] = 0;
a[2][2] = 0;
a[2][3] = 0;
```

The following nested for statement totals the values of all the elements in array a:

```
int total = 0;

for (int row = 0; row < a.length; row++)
{
    for (int column = 0; column < a[row].length; column++)
        total += a[row][column];
}
```

These nested for statements total the array elements *one row at a time.* The outer for statement begins by setting the row index to 0 so that the first row's elements can be totaled by the inner for statement. The outer for then increments row to 1 so that the second row can be totaled. Then, the outer for increments row to 2 so that the third row can be totaled. The variable total can be displayed when the outer for statement terminates. In the next example, we show how to process a two-dimensional array in a similar manner using nested enhanced for statements.

7.12 Case Study: Class GradeBook Using a Two-Dimensional Array

In Section 7.10, we presented class GradeBook (Fig. 7.14), which used a one-dimensional array to store student grades on a single exam. In most semesters, students take several exams. Professors are likely to want to analyze grades across the entire semester, both for a single student and for the class as a whole.

*Storing Student Grades in a Two-Dimensional Array in Class **GradeBook***
Figure 7.18 contains a GradeBook class that uses a two-dimensional array grades to store the grades of *several* students on *multiple* exams. Each *row* of the array represents a single student's grades for the entire course, and each *column* represents the grades of all the students who took a particular exam. Class GradeBookTest (Fig. 7.19) passes the array as an argument to the GradeBook constructor. In this example, we use a ten-by-three array for ten students' grades on three exams. Five methods perform array manipulations to process the grades. Each method is similar to its counterpart in the earlier one-dimensional array version of GradeBook (Fig. 7.14). Method getMinimum (lines 46–62) determines the lowest grade of

any student for the semester. Method getMaximum (lines 65–83) determines the highest grade of any student for the semester. Method getAverage (lines 86–96) determines a particular student's semester average. Method outputBarChart (lines 99–129) outputs a grade bar chart for the entire semester's student grades. Method outputGrades (lines 132–156) outputs the array in a tabular format, along with each student's semester average.

```java
1   // Fig. 7.18: GradeBook.java
2   // GradeBook class using a two-dimensional array to store grades.
3
4   public class GradeBook
5   {
6      private String courseName; // name of course this grade book represents
7      private int[][] grades; // two-dimensional array of student grades
8
9      // two-argument constructor initializes courseName and grades array
10     public GradeBook(String courseName, int[][] grades)
11     {
12        this.courseName = courseName;
13        this.grades = grades;
14     }
15
16     // method to set the course name
17     public void setCourseName(String courseName)
18     {
19        this.courseName = courseName;
20     }
21
22     // method to retrieve the course name
23     public String getCourseName()
24     {
25        return courseName;
26     }
27
28     // perform various operations on the data
29     public void processGrades()
30     {
31        // output grades array
32        outputGrades();
33
34        // call methods getMinimum and getMaximum
35        System.out.printf("%n%s %d%n%s %d%n%n",
36           "Lowest grade in the grade book is", getMinimum(),
37           "Highest grade in the grade book is", getMaximum());
38
39        // output grade distribution chart of all grades on all tests
40        outputBarChart();
41     }
42
43     // find minimum grade
44     public int getMinimum()
45     {
```

Fig. 7.18 | GradeBook class using a two-dimensional array to store grades. (Part 1 of 4.)

```
46          // assume first element of grades array is smallest
47          int lowGrade = grades[0][0];
48
49          // loop through rows of grades array
50          for (int[] studentGrades : grades)
51          {
52             // loop through columns of current row
53             for (int grade : studentGrades)
54             {
55                // if grade less than lowGrade, assign it to lowGrade
56                if (grade < lowGrade)
57                   lowGrade = grade;
58             }
59          }
60
61          return lowGrade;
62       }
63
64       // find maximum grade
65       public int getMaximum()
66       {
67          // assume first element of grades array is largest
68          int highGrade = grades[0][0];
69
70          // loop through rows of grades array
71          for (int[] studentGrades : grades)
72          {
73             // loop through columns of current row
74             for (int grade : studentGrades)
75             {
76                // if grade greater than highGrade, assign it to highGrade
77                if (grade > highGrade)
78                   highGrade = grade;
79             }
80          }
81
82          return highGrade;
83       }
84
85       // determine average grade for particular set of grades
86       public double getAverage(int[] setOfGrades)
87       {
88          int total = 0;
89
90          // sum grades for one student
91          for (int grade : setOfGrades)
92             total += grade;
93
94          // return average of grades
95          return (double) total / setOfGrades.length;
96       }
97
```

Fig. 7.18 | GradeBook class using a two-dimensional array to store grades. (Part 2 of 4.)

```
 98        // output bar chart displaying overall grade distribution
 99        public void outputBarChart()
100        {
101           System.out.println("Overall grade distribution:");
102
103           // stores frequency of grades in each range of 10 grades
104           int[] frequency = new int[11];
105
106           // for each grade in GradeBook, increment the appropriate frequency
107           for (int[] studentGrades : grades)
108           {
109              for (int grade : studentGrades)
110                 ++frequency[grade / 10];
111           }
112
113           // for each grade frequency, print bar in chart
114           for (int count = 0; count < frequency.length; count++)
115           {
116              // output bar label ("00-09: ", ..., "90-99: ", "100: ")
117              if (count == 10)
118                 System.out.printf("%5d: ", 100);
119              else
120                 System.out.printf("%02d-%02d: ",
121                    count * 10, count * 10 + 9);
122
123              // print bar of asterisks
124              for (int stars = 0; stars < frequency[count]; stars++)
125                 System.out.print("*");
126
127              System.out.println();
128           }
129        }
130
131        // output the contents of the grades array
132        public void outputGrades()
133        {
134           System.out.printf("The grades are:%n%n");
135           System.out.print("            "); // align column heads
136
137           // create a column heading for each of the tests
138           for (int test = 0; test < grades[0].length; test++)
139              System.out.printf("Test %d  ", test + 1);
140
141           System.out.println("Average"); // student average column heading
142
143           // create rows/columns of text representing array grades
144           for (int student = 0; student < grades.length; student++)
145           {
146              System.out.printf("Student %2d", student + 1);
147
148              for (int test : grades[student]) // output student's grades
149                 System.out.printf("%8d", test);
150
```

Fig. 7.18 | GradeBook class using a two-dimensional array to store grades. (Part 3 of 4.)

```
151                 // call method getAverage to calculate student's average grade;
152                 // pass row of grades as the argument to getAverage
153                 double average = getAverage(grades[student]);
154                 System.out.printf("%9.2f%n", average);
155             }
156         }
157     } // end class GradeBook
```

Fig. 7.18 | GradeBook class using a two-dimensional array to store grades. (Part 4 of 4.)

Methods getMinimum and getMaximum

Methods getMinimum, getMaximum, outputBarChart and outputGrades each loop through array grades by using nested for statements—for example, the nested enhanced for statement (lines 50–59) from the declaration of method getMinimum. The outer enhanced for statement iterates through the two-dimensional array grades, assigning successive rows to parameter studentGrades on successive iterations. The square brackets following the parameter name indicate that studentGrades refers to a one-dimensional int array—namely, a row in array grades containing one student's grades. To find the lowest overall grade, the inner for statement compares the elements of the current one-dimensional array studentGrades to variable lowGrade. For example, on the first iteration of the outer for, row 0 of grades is assigned to parameter studentGrades. The inner enhanced for statement then loops through studentGrades and compares each grade value with lowGrade. If a grade is less than lowGrade, lowGrade is set to that grade. On the second iteration of the outer enhanced for statement, row 1 of grades is assigned to studentGrades, and the elements of this row are compared with variable lowGrade. This repeats until all rows of grades have been traversed. When execution of the nested statement is complete, lowGrade contains the lowest grade in the two-dimensional array. Method getMaximum works similarly to method getMinimum.

Method outputBarChart

Method outputBarChart in Fig. 7.18 is nearly identical to the one in Fig. 7.14. However, to output the overall grade distribution for a whole semester, the method here uses nested enhanced for statements (lines 107–111) to create the one-dimensional array frequency based on all the grades in the two-dimensional array. The rest of the code in each of the two outputBarChart methods that displays the chart is identical.

Method outputGrades

Method outputGrades (lines 132–156) uses nested for statements to output values of the array grades and each student's semester average. The output (Fig. 7.19) shows the result, which resembles the tabular format of a professor's physical grade book. Lines 138–139 print the column headings for each test. We use a counter-controlled for statement here so that we can identify each test with a number. Similarly, the for statement in lines 144–155 first outputs a row label using a counter variable to identify each student (line 146). Although array indices start at 0, lines 139 and 146 output test + 1 and student + 1, respectively, to produce test and student numbers starting at 1 (see the output in Fig. 7.19). The inner for statement (lines 148–149) uses the outer for statement's counter variable student to loop through a specific row of array grades and output each student's test grade. An enhanced for statement can be nested in a counter-controlled for statement, and vice versa. Finally, line 153 obtains each student's semester average by passing the current row of grades (i.e., grades[student]) to method getAverage.

Method getAverage

Method getAverage (lines 86–96) takes one argument—a one-dimensional array of test results for a particular student. When line 153 calls getAverage, the argument is grades[student], which specifies that a particular row of the two-dimensional array grades should be passed to getAverage. For example, based on the array created in Fig. 7.19, the argument grades[1] represents the three values (a one-dimensional array of grades) stored in row 1 of the two-dimensional array grades. Recall that a two-dimensional array is one whose elements are one-dimensional arrays. Method getAverage calculates the sum of the array elements, divides the total by the number of test results and returns the floating-point result as a double value (line 95).

Class GradeBookTest That Demonstrates Class GradeBook

Figure 7.19 creates an object of class GradeBook (Fig. 7.18) using the two-dimensional array of ints named gradesArray (declared and initialized in lines 10–19). Lines 21–22 pass a course name and gradesArray to the GradeBook constructor. Lines 23–24 display a welcome message containing the course name, then line 25 invokes myGradeBook's processGrades method to display a report summarizing the students' grades for the semester.

```java
1   // Fig. 7.19: GradeBookTest.java
2   // GradeBookTest creates GradeBook object using a two-dimensional array
3   // of grades, then invokes method processGrades to analyze them.
4   public class GradeBookTest
5   {
6      // main method begins program execution
7      public static void main(String[] args)
8      {
9         // two-dimensional array of student grades
10        int[][] gradesArray = {{87, 96, 70},
11                               {68, 87, 90},
12                               {94, 100, 90},
13                               {100, 81, 82},
14                               {83, 65, 85},
15                               {78, 87, 65},
16                               {85, 75, 83},
17                               {91, 94, 100},
18                               {76, 72, 84},
19                               {87, 93, 73}};
20
21        GradeBook myGradeBook = new GradeBook(
22           "CS101 Introduction to Java Programming", gradesArray);
23        System.out.printf("Welcome to the grade book for%n%s%n%n",
24           myGradeBook.getCourseName());
25        myGradeBook.processGrades();
26     }
27  } // end class GradeBookTest
```

Fig. 7.19 | GradeBookTest creates GradeBook object using a two-dimensional array of grades, then invokes method processGrades to analyze them. (Part 1 of 2.)

```
Welcome to the grade book for
CS101 Introduction to Java Programming

The grades are:

          Test 1  Test 2  Test 3  Average
Student  1    87      96      70    84.33
Student  2    68      87      90    81.67
Student  3    94     100      90    94.67
Student  4   100      81      82    87.67
Student  5    83      65      85    77.67
Student  6    78      87      65    76.67
Student  7    85      75      83    81.00
Student  8    91      94     100    95.00
Student  9    76      72      84    77.33
Student 10    87      93      73    84.33

Lowest grade in the grade book is 65
Highest grade in the grade book is 100

Overall grade distribution:
00-09:
10-19:
20-29:
30-39:
40-49:
50-59:
60-69: ***
70-79: ******
80-89: ***********
90-99: *******
  100: ***
```

Fig. 7.19 | GradeBookTest creates GradeBook object using a two-dimensional array of grades, then invokes method processGrades to analyze them. (Part 2 of 2.)

7.13 Variable-Length Argument Lists

With **variable-length argument lists**, you can create methods that receive an unspecified number of arguments. A type followed by an **ellipsis (...)** in a method's parameter list indicates that the method receives a variable number of arguments of that particular type. This use of the ellipsis can occur only *once* in a parameter list, and the ellipsis, together with its type and the parameter name, must be placed at the *end* of the parameter list. While you can use method overloading and array passing to accomplish much of what is accomplished with variable-length argument lists, using an ellipsis in a method's parameter list is more concise.

Figure 7.20 demonstrates method average (lines 7–16), which receives a variable-length sequence of doubles. Java treats the variable-length argument list as an array whose elements are all of the same type. So, the method body can manipulate the parameter numbers as an array of doubles. Lines 12–13 use the enhanced for loop to walk through the array and calculate the total of the doubles in the array. Line 15 accesses numbers.length to obtain the size of the numbers array for use in the averaging calculation. Lines 29, 31 and 33 in main call method average with two, three and four arguments, respectively. Method average has a variable-length argument list (line 7), so it can average as many double arguments as the caller passes. The output shows that each call to method average returns the correct value.

Common Programming Error 7.5
Placing the variable-length argument list ellipsis in the beginning or the middle of a pa-rameter list is a syntax error. An ellipsis can be placed only at the end of the parameter list.

```
1   // Fig. 7.20: VarargsTest.java
2   // Using variable-length argument lists.
3
4   public class VarargsTest
5   {
6      // calculate average
7      public static double average(double... numbers)
8      {
9         double total = 0.0;
10
11        // calculate total using the enhanced for statement
12        for (double d : numbers)
13           total += d;
14
15        return total / numbers.length;
16     }
17
18     public static void main(String[] args)
19     {
20        double d1 = 10.0;
21        double d2 = 20.0;
22        double d3 = 30.0;
23        double d4 = 40.0;
24
25        System.out.printf("d1 = %.1f%nd2 = %.1f%nd3 = %.1f%nd4 = %.1f%n%n",
26           d1, d2, d3, d4);
27
28        System.out.printf("Average of d1 and d2 is %.1f%n",
29           average(d1, d2)   );
30        System.out.printf("Average of d1, d2 and d3 is %.1f%n",
31           average(d1, d2, d3)   );
32        System.out.printf("Average of d1, d2, d3 and d4 is %.1f%n",
33           average(d1, d2, d3, d4)   );
34     }
35  } // end class VarargsTest
```

```
d1 = 10.0
d2 = 20.0
d3 = 30.0
d4 = 40.0

Average of d1 and d2 is 15.0
Average of d1, d2 and d3 is 20.0
Average of d1, d2, d3 and d4 is 25.0
```

Fig. 7.20 | Using variable-length argument lists.

7.14 Using Command-Line Arguments

It's possible to pass arguments from the command line to an application via method main's String[] parameter, which receives an array of Strings. By convention, this parameter is named args. When an application is executed using the java command, Java passes the **command-line arguments** that appear after the class name in the java command to the application's main method as Strings in the array args. The number of command-line arguments is obtained by accessing the array's length attribute. Common uses of command-line arguments include passing options and filenames to applications.

Our next example uses command-line arguments to determine the size of an array, the value of its first element and the increment used to calculate the values of the array's remaining elements. The command

```
java InitArray 5 0 4
```

passes three arguments, 5, 0 and 4, to the application InitArray. Command-line arguments are separated by white space, not commas. When this command executes, InitArray's main method receives the three-element array args (i.e., args.length is 3) in which args[0] contains the String "5", args[1] contains the String "0" and args[2] contains the String "4". The program determines how to use these arguments—in Fig. 7.21 we convert the three command-line arguments to int values and use them to initialize an array. When the program executes, if args.length is not 3, the program prints an error message and terminates (lines 9–12). Otherwise, lines 14–32 initialize and display the array based on the values of the command-line arguments.

Line 16 gets args[0]—a String that specifies the array size—and converts it to an int value that the program uses to create the array in line 17. The static method parseInt of class Integer converts its String argument to an int.

Lines 20–21 convert the args[1] and args[2] command-line arguments to int values and store them in initialValue and increment, respectively. Lines 24–25 calculate the value for each array element.

```
1   // Fig. 7.21: InitArray.java
2   // Initializing an array using command-line arguments.
3
4   public class InitArray
5   {
6      public static void main(String[] args)
7      {
8         // check number of command-line arguments
9         if (args.length != 3)
10            System.out.printf(
11               "Error: Please re-enter the entire command, including%n" +
12               "an array size, initial value and increment.%n");
13         else
14         {
15            // get array size from first command-line argument
16            int arrayLength = Integer.parseInt(args[0]);
17            int[] array = new int[arrayLength];
```

Fig. 7.21 | Initializing an array using command-line arguments. (Part 1 of 2.)

```
18
19          // get initial value and increment from command-line arguments
20          int initialValue = Integer.parseInt(args[1]);
21          int increment = Integer.parseInt(args[2]);
22
23          // calculate value for each array element
24          for (int counter = 0; counter < array.length; counter++)
25             array[counter] = initialValue + increment * counter;
26
27          System.out.printf("%s%8s%n", "Index", "Value");
28
29          // display array index and value
30          for (int counter = 0; counter < array.length; counter++)
31             System.out.printf("%5d%8d%n", counter, array[counter]);
32       }
33    }
34 } // end class InitArray
```

```
java InitArray
Error: Please re-enter the entire command, including
an array size, initial value and increment.
```

```
java InitArray 5 0 4
Index    Value
    0        0
    1        4
    2        8
    3       12
    4       16
```

```
java InitArray 8 1 2
Index    Value
    0        1
    1        3
    2        5
    3        7
    4        9
    5       11
    6       13
    7       15
```

Fig. 7.21 | Initializing an array using command-line arguments. (Part 2 of 2.)

The output of the first execution shows that the application received an insufficient number of command-line arguments. The second execution uses command-line arguments 5, 0 and 4 to specify the size of the array (5), the value of the first element (0) and the increment of each value in the array (4), respectively. The corresponding output shows that these values create an array containing the integers 0, 4, 8, 12 and 16. The output from the third execution shows that the command-line arguments 8, 1 and 2 produce an array whose 8 elements are the nonnegative odd integers from 1 to 15.

7.15 Class Arrays

Class **Arrays** helps you avoid reinventing the wheel by providing static methods for common array manipulations. These methods include **sort** for sorting an array, **binarySearch** for searching a *sorted* array, **equals** for comparing arrays and **fill** for placing values into an array. These methods are overloaded for primitive-type arrays and for arrays of objects. Our focus in this section is on using the built-in capabilities provided by the Java API.

Figure 7.22 uses Arrays methods sort, binarySearch, equals and fill, and shows how to copy arrays with class System's static **arraycopy method**. In main, line 11 sorts the elements of array doubleArray. The static method sort of class Arrays orders the array's elements in ascending order by default. We discuss how to sort in descending order later in the chapter. Overloaded versions of sort allow you to sort a specific range of elements within the array. Lines 12–15 output the sorted array.

```
 1    // Fig. 7.22: ArrayManipulations.java
 2    // Arrays class methods and System.arraycopy.
 3    import java.util.Arrays;
 4
 5    public class ArrayManipulations
 6    {
 7       public static void main(String[] args)
 8       {
 9          // sort doubleArray into ascending order
10          double[] doubleArray = { 8.4, 9.3, 0.2, 7.9, 3.4 };
11          Arrays.sort(doubleArray);
12          System.out.printf("%ndoubleArray: ");
13
14          for (double value : doubleArray)
15             System.out.printf("%.1f ", value);
16
17          // fill 10-element array with 7s
18          int[] filledIntArray = new int[10];
19          Arrays.fill(filledIntArray, 7);
20          displayArray(filledIntArray, "filledIntArray");
21
22          // copy array intArray into array intArrayCopy
23          int[] intArray = { 1, 2, 3, 4, 5, 6 };
24          int[] intArrayCopy = new int[intArray.length];
25          System.arraycopy(intArray, 0, intArrayCopy, 0, intArray.length);
26          displayArray(intArray, "intArray");
27          displayArray(intArrayCopy, "intArrayCopy");
28
29          // compare intArray and intArrayCopy for equality
30          boolean b = Arrays.equals(intArray, intArrayCopy);
31          System.out.printf("%n%nintArray %s intArrayCopy%n",
32             (b ? "==" : "!="));
33
34          // compare intArray and filledIntArray for equality
35          b = Arrays.equals(intArray, filledIntArray);
36          System.out.printf("intArray %s filledIntArray%n",
37             (b ? "==" : "!="));
```

Fig. 7.22 | Arrays class methods and System.arraycopy. (Part 1 of 2.)

```
38
39        // search intArray for the value 5
40        int location = Arrays.binarySearch(intArray, 5);
41
42        if (location >= 0)
43           System.out.printf(
44              "Found 5 at element %d in intArray%n", location);
45        else
46           System.out.println("5 not found in intArray");
47
48        // search intArray for the value 8763
49        location = Arrays.binarySearch(intArray, 8763);
50
51        if (location >= 0)
52           System.out.printf(
53              "Found 8763 at element %d in intArray%n", location);
54        else
55           System.out.println("8763 not found in intArray");
56     }
57
58     // output values in each array
59     public static void displayArray(int[] array, String description)
60     {
61        System.out.printf("%n%s: ", description);
62
63        for (int value : array)
64           System.out.printf("%d ", value);
65     }
66  } // end class ArrayManipulations
```

```
doubleArray: 0.2 3.4 7.9 8.4 9.3
filledIntArray: 7 7 7 7 7 7 7 7 7 7
intArray: 1 2 3 4 5 6
intArrayCopy: 1 2 3 4 5 6

intArray == intArrayCopy
intArray != filledIntArray
Found 5 at element 4 in intArray
8763 not found in intArray
```

Fig. 7.22 | Arrays class methods and System.arraycopy. (Part 2 of 2.)

Line 19 calls static method fill of class Arrays to populate all 10 elements of filledIntArray with 7s. Overloaded versions of fill allow you to populate a specific range of elements with the same value. Line 20 calls our class's displayArray method (declared at lines 59–65) to output the contents of filledIntArray.

Line 25 copies the elements of intArray into intArrayCopy. The first argument (intArray) passed to System method arraycopy is the array from which elements are to be copied. The second argument (0) is the index that specifies the *starting point* in the range of elements to copy from the array. This value can be any valid array index. The third argument (intArrayCopy) specifies the *destination array* that will store the copy. The fourth argument (0) specifies the index in the destination array *where the first copied element should be stored*. The last argument specifies the *number of elements to copy* from the array in the first argument. In this case, we copy all the elements in the array.

Lines 30 and 35 call `static` method `equals` of class `Arrays` to determine whether all the elements of two arrays are equivalent. If the arrays contain the same elements in the same order, the method returns `true`; otherwise, it returns `false`.

Error-Prevention Tip 7.3

When comparing array contents, always use `Arrays.equals(array1, array2)`, which compares the two arrays' contents, rather than `array1.equals(array2)`, which compares whether `array1` and `array2` refer to the same array object.

Lines 40 and 49 call `static` method `binarySearch` of class `Arrays` to perform a binary search on `intArray`, using the second argument (5 and 8763, respectively) as the key. If `value` is found, `binarySearch` returns the index of the element; otherwise, `binarySearch` returns a negative value. The negative value returned is based on the search key's *insertion point*—the index where the key would be inserted in the array if we were performing an insert operation. After `binarySearch` determines the insertion point, it changes its sign to negative and subtracts 1 to obtain the return value. For example, in Fig. 7.22, the insertion point for the value 8763 is the element with index 6 in the array. Method `binarySearch` changes the insertion point to –6, subtracts 1 from it and returns the value –7. Subtracting 1 from the insertion point guarantees that method `binarySearch` returns positive values (>= 0) if and only if the key is found. This return value is useful for inserting elements in a sorted array.

Common Programming Error 7.6

Passing an unsorted array to `binarySearch` is a logic error—the value returned is undefined.

*Java SE 8—Class **Arrays** Method `parallelSort`*
The `Arrays` class now has several new "parallel" methods that take advantage of multi-core hardware. `Arrays` method `parallelSort` can sort large arrays more efficiently on multi-core systems. In Section 20.12, we create a very large array and use features of the Java SE 8 Date/Time API to compare how long it takes to sort the array with methods `sort` and `parallelSort`.

7.16 Introduction to Collections and Class ArrayList

The Java API provides several predefined data structures, called **collections**, used to store groups of related objects in memory. These classes provide efficient methods that organize, store and retrieve your data without requiring knowledge of how the data is being stored. This can reduce application-development time and help you produce higher-quality, better-performing software.

You've used arrays to store sequences of objects. Arrays do not automatically change their size at execution time to accommodate additional elements. The collection class `ArrayList<T>` (package `java.util`) provides a convenient solution to this problem—it can *dynamically* change its size to accommodate more elements. The T (by convention) is a *placeholder*—when declaring a new `ArrayList`, replace it with the type of elements that you want the `ArrayList` to hold. For example,

```
ArrayList<String> list;
```

declares `list` as an `ArrayList` collection that can store only `String`s. Classes with this kind of placeholder that can be used with any type are called **generic classes.** *Only nonprimitive types can be used to declare variables and create objects of generic classes.* However, Java provides a mechanism—known as *boxing*—that allows primitive values to be wrapped as objects for use with generic classes. So, for example,

```
ArrayList<Integer> integers;
```

declares `integers` as an `ArrayList` that can store only `Integer`s. When you place an `int` value into an `ArrayList<Integer>`, the `int` value is *boxed* (wrapped) as an `Integer` object, and when you get an `Integer` object from an `ArrayList<Integer>`, then assign the object to an `int` variable, the `int` value inside the object is *unboxed* (unwrapped).

Additional generic collection classes and generics are discussed in Chapters 16 and 18, respectively. Figure 7.23 shows some common methods of class `ArrayList<T>`.

Method	Description
add	Adds an element to the *end* of the `ArrayList`.
clear	Removes all the elements from the `ArrayList`.
contains	Returns `true` if the `ArrayList` contains the specified element; otherwise, returns `false`.
get	Returns the element at the specified index.
indexOf	Returns the index of the first occurrence of the specified element in the `ArrayList`.
remove	Overloaded. Removes the first occurrence of the specified value or the element at the specified index.
size	Returns the number of elements stored in the `ArrayList`.
trimToSize	Trims the capacity of the `ArrayList` to the current number of elements.

Fig. 7.23 | Some methods and properties of class `ArrayList<T>`.

Demonstrating an *ArrayList<String>*

Figure 7.24 demonstrates some common `ArrayList` capabilities. Line 10 creates a new empty `ArrayList` of `String`s with a default initial capacity of 10 elements. The capacity indicates how many items the `ArrayList` can hold *without growing*. `ArrayList` is implemented using a conventional array behind the scenes. When the `ArrayList` grows, it must create a larger internal array and *copy* each element to the new array. This is a time-consuming operation. It would be inefficient for the `ArrayList` to grow each time an element is added. Instead, it grows only when an element is added *and* the number of elements is equal to the capacity—i.e., there's no space for the new element.

```
1   // Fig. 7.24: ArrayListCollection.java
2   // Generic ArrayList<T> collection demonstration.
3   import java.util.ArrayList;
4
5   public class ArrayListCollection
6   {
7      public static void main(String[] args)
8      {
9         // create a new ArrayList of Strings with an initial capacity of 10
10        ArrayList<String> items = new ArrayList<String>();
11
12        items.add("red"); // append an item to the list
13        items.add(0, "yellow"); // insert "yellow" at index 0
14
15        // header
16        System.out.print(
17           "Display list contents with counter-controlled loop:");
18
19        // display the colors in the list
20        for (int i = 0; i < items.size(); i++)
21           System.out.printf(" %s", items.get(i));
22
23        // display colors using enhanced for in the display method
24        display(items,
25           "%nDisplay list contents with enhanced for statement:");
26
27        items.add("green"); // add "green" to the end of the list
28        items.add("yellow"); // add "yellow" to the end of the list
29        display(items, "List with two new elements:");
30
31        items.remove("yellow"); // remove the first "yellow"
32        display(items, "Remove first instance of yellow:");
33
34        items.remove(1); // remove item at index 1
35        display(items, "Remove second list element (green):");
36
37        // check if a value is in the List
38        System.out.printf("\"red\" is %sin the list%n",
39           items.contains("red") ? "": "not ");
40
41        // display number of elements in the List
42        System.out.printf("Size: %s%n", items.size());
43     }
44
45     // display the ArrayList's elements on the console
46     public static void display(ArrayList<String> items, String header)
47     {
48        System.out.printf(header); // display header
49
50        // display each element in items
51        for (String item : items)
52           System.out.printf(" %s", item);
53
```

Fig. 7.24 | Generic ArrayList<T> collection demonstration. (Part 1 of 2.)

```
54              System.out.println();
55      }
56  } // end class ArrayListCollection
```

```
Display list contents with counter-controlled loop: yellow red
Display list contents with enhanced for statement: yellow red
List with two new elements: yellow red green yellow
Remove first instance of yellow: red green yellow
Remove second list element (green): red yellow
"red" is in the list
Size: 2
```

Fig. 7.24 | Generic `ArrayList<T>` collection demonstration. (Part 2 of 2.)

The **add** method adds elements to the `ArrayList` (lines 12–13). The add method with one argument *appends* its argument to the end of the `ArrayList`. The add method with two arguments *inserts* a new element at the specified position. The first argument is an index. As with arrays, collection indices start at zero. The second argument is the value to insert at that index. The indices of all subsequent elements are incremented by one. Inserting an element is usually slower than adding an element to the end of the `ArrayList`

Lines 20–21 display the items in the `ArrayList`. Method **size** returns the number of elements currently in the `ArrayList`. Method **get** (line 21) obtains the element at a specified index. Lines 24–25 display the elements again by invoking method `display` (defined at lines 46–55). Lines 27–28 add two more elements to the `ArrayList`, then line 29 displays the elements again to confirm that the two elements were added to the end of the collection.

The **remove** method is used to remove an element with a specific value (line 31). It removes only the first such element. If no such element is in the `ArrayList`, remove does nothing. An overloaded version of the method removes the element at the specified index (line 34). When an element is removed, the indices of any elements after the removed element decrease by one.

Line 39 uses the **contains** method to check if an item is in the `ArrayList`. The contains method returns true if the element is found in the `ArrayList`, and false otherwise. The method compares its argument to each element of the `ArrayList` in order, so using contains on a large `ArrayList` can be inefficient. Line 42 displays the `ArrayList`'s size.

Java SE 7—Diamond (<>) Notation for Creating an Object of a Generic Class
Consider line 10 of Fig. 7.24:

```
ArrayList<String> items = new ArrayList<String>();
```

Notice that `ArrayList<String>` appears in the variable declaration *and* in the class instance creation expression. Java SE 7 introduced the **diamond (<>) notation** to simplify statements like this. Using <> in a class instance creation expression for an object of a *generic* class tells the compiler to determine what belongs in the angle brackets. In Java SE 7 and higher, the preceding statement can be written as:

```
ArrayList<String> items = new ArrayList<>();
```

When the compiler encounters the diamond (<>) in the class instance creation expression, it uses the declaration of variable items to determine the ArrayList's element type (String)—this is known as *inferring the element type*.

7.17 Wrap-Up

This chapter began our introduction to data structures, exploring the use of arrays to store data in and retrieve data from lists and tables of values. The chapter examples demonstrated how to declare an array, initialize an array and refer to individual elements of an array. The chapter introduced the enhanced for statement to iterate through arrays. We used exception handling to test for ArrayIndexOutOfBoundsExceptions that occur when a program attempts to access an array element outside the bounds of an array. We illustrated how to pass arrays to methods and how to declare and manipulate multidimensional arrays. We showed how to write methods that use variable-length argument lists and how to read arguments passed to a program from the command line.

We introduced the ArrayList<T> generic collection, which provides all the functionality and performance of arrays, along with other useful capabilities such as dynamic resizing. We used the add methods to add new items to the end of an ArrayList and to insert items in an ArrayList. The remove method was used to remove the first occurrence of a specified item, and an overloaded version of remove was used to remove an item at a specified index. We used the size method to obtain number of items in the ArrayList.

We continue our coverage of data structures in Chapter 16, Generic Collections. Chapter 16 introduces the Java Collections Framework, which uses generics to allow you to specify the exact types of objects that a particular data structure will store. Chapter 16 also introduces Java's other predefined data structures and additional methods of class Arrays. You'll be able to use some of the Arrays methods discussed in Chapter 16 after reading Chapter 7, but some methods require knowledge of concepts presented later in the book. Chapter 18 discusses generics, which enable you to create general models of methods and classes that can be declared once, but used with many different data types.

We've now introduced the basic concepts of classes, objects, control statements, methods, arrays and collections. In Chapter 8, we take a deeper look at classes and objects.

8

Classes and Objects: A Deeper Look

Objectives

In this chapter you'll:

- Use the **throw** statement to indicate that a problem has occurred.

- Use keyword **this** in a constructor to call another constructor in the same class.

- Use **static** variables and methods.

- Import **static** members of a class.

- Use the **enum** type to create sets of constants with unique identifiers.

- Declare **enum** constants with parameters.

- Use **BigDecimal** for precise monetary calculations.

8.1 Introduction

We now take a deeper look at building classes, controlling access to members of a class and creating constructors. We show how to throw an exception to indicate that a problem has occurred (Section 7.5 discussed catching exceptions). We use the this keyword to enable one constructor to conveniently call another constructor of the same class. We discuss *composition*—a capability that allows a class to have references to objects of other classes as members. We reexamine the use of *set* and *get* methods. Recall that Section 6.9 introduced the basic enum type to declare a set of constants. In this chapter, we discuss the relationship between enum types and classes, demonstrating that an enum type, like a class, can be declared in its own file with constructors, methods and fields. The chapter also discusses static class members and final instance variables in detail. We show a special relationship between classes in the same package. Finally, we demonstrate how to use class Big-Decimal to perform precise monetary calculations. Two additional types of classes—nested classes and anonymous inner classes—are discussed in Chapter 12.

8.2 Time Class Case Study

Our first example consists of two classes—Time1 (Fig. 8.1) and Time1Test (Fig. 8.2). Class Time1 represents the time of day. Class Time1Test's main method creates one object of class Time1 and invokes its methods. The output of this program appears in Fig. 8.2.

Time1 Class Declaration
Class Time1's private int instance variables hour, minute and second (lines 6–8) represent the time in universal-time format (24-hour clock format in which hours are in the range 0–23, and minutes and seconds are each in the range 0–59). Time1 contains public methods setTime (lines 12–25), toUniversalString (lines 28–31) and toString (lines 34–39). These methods are also called the **public services** or the **public interface** that the class provides to its clients.

```
1   // Fig. 8.1: Time1.java
2   // Time1 class declaration maintains the time in 24-hour format.
3
4   public class Time1
5   {
6      private int hour; // 0 - 23
7      private int minute; // 0 - 59
8      private int second; // 0 - 59
9
10     // set a new time value using universal time; throw an
11     // exception if the hour, minute or second is invalid
12     public void setTime(int hour, int minute, int second)
13     {
14        // validate hour, minute and second
15        if (hour < 0 || hour >= 24 || minute < 0 || minute >= 60 ||
16           second < 0 || second >= 60)
17        {
18           throw new IllegalArgumentException(
19              "hour, minute and/or second was out of range");
20        }
21
22        this.hour = hour;
23        this.minute = minute;
24        this.second = second;
25     }
26
27     // convert to String in universal-time format (HH:MM:SS)
28     public String toUniversalString()
29     {
30        return String.format("%02d:%02d:%02d", hour, minute, second);
31     }
32
33     // convert to String in standard-time format (H:MM:SS AM or PM)
34     public String toString()
35     {
36        return String.format("%d:%02d:%02d %s",
37           ((hour == 0 || hour == 12) ? 12 : hour % 12),
38           minute, second, (hour < 12 ? "AM" : "PM"));
39     }
40  } // end class Time1
```

Fig. 8.1 | Time1 class declaration maintains the time in 24-hour format.

Default Constructor

In this example, class Time1 does *not* declare a constructor, so the compiler supplies a default constructor. Each instance variable implicitly receives the default int value. Instance variables also can be initialized when they're declared in the class body, using the same initialization syntax as with a local variable.

Method setTime and Throwing Exceptions

Method setTime (lines 12–25) is a public method that declares three int parameters and uses them to set the time. Lines 15–16 test each argument to determine whether the value is outside the proper range. The hour value must be greater than or equal to 0 and less than

24, because universal-time format represents hours as integers from 0 to 23 (e.g., 1 PM is hour 13 and 11 PM is hour 23; midnight is hour 0 and noon is hour 12). Similarly, both `minute` and `second` values must be greater than or equal to 0 and less than 60. For values outside these ranges, `setTime` **throws an exception** of type **`IllegalArgumentException`** (lines 18–19), which notifies the client code that an invalid argument was passed to the method. As you learned in Section 7.5, you can use `try...catch` to catch exceptions and attempt to recover from them, which we'll do in Fig. 8.2. The class instance creation expression in the **throw statement** (Fig. 8.1; line 18) creates a new object of type `Illegal-ArgumentException`. The parentheses following the class name indicate a call to the `IllegalArgumentException` constructor. In this case, we call the constructor that allows us to specify a custom error message. After the exception object is created, the `throw` statement immediately terminates method `setTime` and the exception is returned to the calling method that attempted to set the time. If the argument values are all valid, lines 22–24 assign them to the `hour`, `minute` and `second` instance variables.

 Software Engineering Observation 8.1

For a method like `setTime` in Fig. 8.1, validate all of the method's arguments before using them to set instance variable values to ensure that the object's data is modified only if all the arguments are valid.

Method `toUniversalString`

Method `toUniversalString` (lines 28–31) takes no arguments and returns a `String` in *universal-time format*, consisting of two digits each for the hour, minute and second—recall that you can use the 0 flag in a `printf` format specification (e.g., `"%02d"`) to display leading zeros for a value that doesn't use all the character positions in the specified field width. For example, if the time were 1:30:07 PM, the method would return `13:30:07`. Line 30 uses `static` method **`format`** of class `String` to return a `String` containing the formatted hour, minute and second values, each with two digits and possibly a leading 0 (specified with the 0 flag). Method `format` is similar to method `System.out.printf` except that `format` *returns* a formatted `String` rather than displaying it in a command window. The formatted `String` is returned by method `toUniversalString`.

Method `toString`

Method `toString` (lines 34–39) takes no arguments and returns a `String` in *standard-time format*, consisting of the `hour`, `minute` and `second` values separated by colons and followed by AM or PM (e.g., `11:30:17 AM` or `1:27:06 PM`). Like method `toUniversalString`, method `toString` uses `static` `String` method `format` to format the `minute` and `second` as two-digit values, with leading zeros if necessary. Line 37 uses a conditional operator (`?:`) to determine the value for hour in the `String`—if the hour is 0 or 12 (AM or PM), it appears as 12; otherwise, it appears as a value from 1 to 11. The conditional operator in line 30 determines whether AM or PM will be returned as part of the `String`.

Recall all objects in Java have a `toString` method that returns a `String` representation of the object. We chose to return a `String` containing the time in standard-time format. Method `toString` is called *implicitly* whenever a `Time1` object appears in the code where a `String` is needed, such as the value to output with a `%s` format specifier in a call to `System.out.printf`. You may also call `toString` *explicitly* to obtain a `String` representation of a `Time` object.

Using Class Time1

Class Time1Test (Fig. 8.2) uses class Time1. Line 9 declares and creates a Time1 object time. Operator **new** implicitly invokes class Time1's default constructor, because Time1 does not declare any constructors. To confirm that the Time1 object was initialized properly, line 12 calls the private method displayTime (lines 35–39), which, in turn, calls the Time1 object's toUniversalString and toString methods to output the time in universal-time format and standard-time format, respectively. Note that toString could have been called implicitly here rather than explicitly. Next, line 16 invokes method setTime of the time object to change the time. Then line 17 calls displayTime again to output the time in both formats to confirm that it was set correctly.

> **Software Engineering Observation 8.2**
>
> *Recall from Chapter 3 that methods declared with access modifier private can be called only by other methods of the class in which the private methods are declared. Such methods are commonly referred to as **utility methods** or **helper methods** because they're typically used to support the operation of the class's other methods.*

```java
 1   // Fig. 8.2: Time1Test.java
 2   // Time1 object used in an app.
 3
 4   public class Time1Test
 5   {
 6      public static void main(String[] args)
 7      {
 8         // create and initialize a Time1 object
 9         Time1 time = new Time1(); // invokes Time1 constructor
10
11         // output string representations of the time
12         displayTime("After time object is created", time);
13         System.out.println();
14
15         // change time and output updated time
16         time.setTime(13, 27, 6);
17         displayTime("After calling setTime", time);
18         System.out.println();
19
20         // attempt to set time with invalid values
21         try
22         {
23            time.setTime(99, 99, 99); // all values out of range
24         }
25         catch (IllegalArgumentException e)
26         {
27            System.out.printf("Exception: %s%n%n", e.getMessage());
28         }
29
30         // display time after attempt to set invalid values
31         displayTime("After calling setTime with invalid values", time);
32      }
```

Fig. 8.2 | Time1 object used in an app. (Part 1 of 2.)

```
33
34      // displays a Time1 object in 24-hour and 12-hour formats
35      private static void displayTime(String header, Time1 t)
36      {
37          System.out.printf("%s%nUniversal time: %s%nStandard time: %s%n",
38              header, t.toUniversalString(), t.toString());
39      }
40   } // end class Time1Test
```

```
After time object is created
Universal time: 00:00:00
Standard time: 12:00:00 AM

After calling setTime
Universal time: 13:27:06
Standard time: 1:27:06 PM

Exception: hour, minute and/or second was out of range

After calling setTime with invalid values
Universal time: 13:27:06
Standard time: 1:27:06 PM
```

Fig. 8.2 | Time1 object used in an app. (Part 2 of 2.)

Calling *Time1* Method *setTime* with Invalid Values

To illustrate that method setTime *validates* its arguments, line 23 calls method setTime with *invalid* arguments of 99 for the hour, minute and second. This statement is placed in a try block (lines 21–24) in case setTime throws an IllegalArgumentException, which it will do since the arguments are all invalid. When this occurs, the exception is caught at lines 25–28, and line 27 displays the exception's error message by calling its getMessage method. Line 31 outputs the time again in both formats to confirm that setTime did *not* change the time when invalid arguments were supplied.

Software Engineering of the *Time1* Class Declaration

Consider several issues of class design with respect to class Time1. The instance variables hour, minute and second are each declared private. The actual data representation used within the class is of no concern to the class's clients. For example, it would be perfectly reasonable for Time1 to represent the time internally as the number of seconds since midnight or the number of minutes and seconds since midnight. Clients could use the same public methods and get the same results without being aware of this.

Software Engineering Observation 8.3

Classes simplify programming, because the client can use only a class's public methods. Such methods are usually client oriented rather than implementation oriented. Clients are neither aware of, nor involved in, a class's implementation. Clients generally care about what the class does but not how the class does it.

Software Engineering Observation 8.4

Interfaces change less frequently than implementations. When an implementation changes, implementation-dependent code must change accordingly. Hiding the implementation reduces the possibility that other program parts will become dependent on class implementation details.

Java SE 8—Date/Time API

This section's example and several of this chapter's later examples demonstrate various class-implementation concepts in classes that represent dates and times. In professional Java development, rather than building your own date and time classes, you'll typically reuse the ones provided by the Java API. Though Java has always had classes for manipulating dates and times, Java SE 8 introduces a new **Date/Time API**—defined by the classes in the package **java.time**—applications built with Java SE 8 should use the Date/Time API's capabilities, rather than those in earlier Java versions. The new API fixes various issues with the older classes and provides more robust, easier-to-use capabilities for manipulating dates, times, time zones, calendars and more. We use some Date/Time API features in Chapter 20. You can learn more about the Date/Time API's classes at:

```
download.java.net/jdk8/docs/api/java/time/package-summary.html
```

8.3 Controlling Access to Members

The access modifiers public and private control access to a class's variables and methods. In Chapter 9, we'll introduce the additional access modifier protected. The primary purpose of public methods is to present to the class's clients a view of the services the class provides (i.e., the class's public interface). Clients need not be concerned with how the class accomplishes its tasks. For this reason, the class's private variables and private methods (i.e., its *implementation details*) are *not* accessible to its clients.

Figure 8.3 demonstrates that private class members are *not* accessible outside the class. Lines 9–11 attempt to access the private instance variables hour, minute and second of the Time1 object time. When this program is compiled, the compiler generates error messages that these private members are not accessible. This program assumes that the Time1 class from Fig. 8.1 is used.

```
 1   // Fig. 8.3: MemberAccessTest.java
 2   // Private members of class Time1 are not accessible.
 3   public class MemberAccessTest
 4   {
 5      public static void main(String[] args)
 6      {
 7         Time1 time = new Time1(); // create and initialize Time1 object
 8
 9         time.hour = 7; // error: hour has private access in Time1
10         time.minute = 15; // error: minute has private access in Time1
11         time.second = 30; // error: second has private access in Time1
12      }
13   } // end class MemberAccessTest
```

Fig. 8.3 | Private members of class Time1 are not accessible. (Part 1 of 2.)

```
MemberAccessTest.java:9: hour has private access in Time1
      time.hour = 7; // error: hour has private access in Time1
           ^
MemberAccessTest.java:10: minute has private access in Time1
      time.minute = 15; // error: minute has private access in Time1
           ^
MemberAccessTest.java:11: second has private access in Time1
      time.second = 30; // error: second has private access in Time1
           ^
3 errors
```

Fig. 8.3 | Private members of class Time1 are not accessible. (Part 2 of 2.)

Common Programming Error 8.1

An attempt by a method that's not a member of a class to access a private member of that class generates a compilation error.

8.4 Referring to the Current Object's Members with the this Reference

Every object can access a *reference to itself* with keyword **this** (sometimes called the **this reference**). When an instance method is called for a particular object, the method's body *implicitly* uses keyword this to refer to the object's instance variables and other methods. This enables the class's code to know which object should be manipulated. As you'll see in Fig. 8.4, you can also use keyword this *explicitly* in an instance method's body. Section 8.5 shows another interesting use of keyword this. Section 8.11 explains why keyword this cannot be used in a static method.

We now demonstrate implicit and explicit use of the this reference (Fig. 8.4). This example is the first in which we declare *two* classes in one file—class ThisTest is declared in lines 4–11, and class SimpleTime in lines 14–47. We do this to demonstrate that when you compile a .java file containing more than one class, the compiler produces a separate class file with the .class extension for every compiled class. In this case, two separate files are produced—SimpleTime.class and ThisTest.class. When one source-code (.java) file contains multiple class declarations, the compiler places both class files for those classes in the *same* directory. Note also in Fig. 8.4 that only class ThisTest is declared public. A source-code file can contain only *one* public class—otherwise, a compilation error occurs. *Non-public classes* can be used only by other classes in the *same package*. So, in this example, class SimpleTime can be used only by class ThisTest.

```
1   // Fig. 8.4: ThisTest.java
2   // this used implicitly and explicitly to refer to members of an object.
3
4   public class ThisTest
5   {
6      public static void main(String[] args)
7      {
```

Fig. 8.4 | this used implicitly and explicitly to refer to members of an object. (Part 1 of 2.)

```
 8          SimpleTime time = new SimpleTime(15, 30, 19);
 9          System.out.println(time.buildString());
10      }
11  } // end class ThisTest
12
13  // class SimpleTime demonstrates the "this" reference
14  class SimpleTime
15  {
16      private int hour;   // 0-23
17      private int minute; // 0-59
18      private int second; // 0-59
19
20      // if the constructor uses parameter names identical to
21      // instance variable names the "this" reference is
22      // required to distinguish between the names
23      public SimpleTime(int hour, int minute, int second)
24      {
25          this.hour = hour;   // set "this" object's hour
26          this.minute = minute; // set "this" object's minute
27          this.second = second; // set "this" object's second
28      }
29
30      // use explicit and implicit "this" to call toUniversalString
31      public String buildString()
32      {
33          return String.format("%24s: %s%n%24s: %s",
34              "this.toUniversalString()", this.toUniversalString(),
35              "toUniversalString()", toUniversalString());
36      }
37
38      // convert to String in universal-time format (HH:MM:SS)
39      public String toUniversalString()
40      {
41          // "this" is not required here to access instance variables,
42          // because method does not have local variables with same
43          // names as instance variables
44          return String.format("%02d:%02d:%02d",
45              this.hour, this.minute, this.second);
46      }
47  } // end class SimpleTime
```

```
this.toUniversalString(): 15:30:19
    toUniversalString(): 15:30:19
```

Fig. 8.4 | `this` used implicitly and explicitly to refer to members of an object. (Part 2 of 2.)

Class SimpleTime (lines 14–47) declares three private instance variables—hour, minute and second (lines 16–18). The class's constructor (lines 23–28) receives three int arguments to initialize a SimpleTime object. Once again, we used parameter names for the constructor (line 23) that are *identical* to the class's instance-variable names (lines 16–18), so we use the this reference to refer to the instance variables in lines 25–27.

Error-Prevention Tip 8.1
Most IDEs will issue a warning if you say x = x; *instead of* this.x = x;. *The statement* x = x; *is often called a no-op (no operation).*

Method buildString (lines 31–36) returns a String created by a statement that uses the this reference explicitly and implicitly. Line 34 uses it *explicitly* to call method toUniversalString. Line 35 uses it *implicitly* to call the same method. Both lines perform the same task. You typically will not use this explicitly to reference other methods within the current object. Also, line 45 in method toUniversalString explicitly uses the this reference to access each instance variable. This is *not* necessary here, because the method does *not* have any local variables that shadow the instance variables of the class.

Performance Tip 8.1
Java conserves storage by maintaining only one copy of each method per class—this method is invoked by every object of the class. Each object, on the other hand, has its own copy of the class's instance variables. Each method of the class implicitly uses this *to determine the specific object of the class to manipulate.*

Class ThisTest's main method (lines 6–10) demonstrates class SimpleTime. Line 8 creates an instance of class SimpleTime and invokes its constructor. Line 9 invokes the object's buildString method, then displays the results.

8.5 Time Class Case Study: Overloaded Constructors

As you know, you can declare your own constructor to specify how objects of a class should be initialized. Next, we demonstrate a class with several **overloaded constructors** that enable objects of that class to be initialized in different ways. To overload constructors, simply provide multiple constructor declarations with different signatures.

Class *Time2 with Overloaded Constructors*

The Time1 class's default constructor in Fig. 8.1 initialized hour, minute and second to their default 0 values (i.e., midnight in universal time). The default constructor does not enable the class's clients to initialize the time with nonzero values. Class Time2 (Fig. 8.5) contains five overloaded constructors that provide convenient ways to initialize objects. In this program, four of the constructors invoke a fifth, which in turn ensures that the value supplied for hour is in the range 0 to 23, and the values for minute and second are each in the range 0 to 59. The compiler invokes the appropriate constructor by matching the number, types and order of the types of the arguments specified in the constructor call with the number, types and order of the types of the parameters specified in each constructor declaration. Class Time2 also provides *set* and *get* methods for each instance variable.

```
1   // Fig. 8.5: Time2.java
2   // Time2 class declaration with overloaded constructors.
3
4   public class Time2
5   {
```

Fig. 8.5 | Time2 class with overloaded constructors. (Part 1 of 4.)

```
 6      private int hour; // 0 - 23
 7      private int minute; // 0 - 59
 8      private int second; // 0 - 59
 9
10      // Time2 no-argument constructor:
11      // initializes each instance variable to zero
12      public Time2()
13      {
14         this(0, 0, 0); // invoke constructor with three arguments
15      }
16
17      // Time2 constructor: hour supplied, minute and second defaulted to 0
18      public Time2(int hour)
19      {
20         this(hour, 0, 0); // invoke constructor with three arguments
21      }
22
23      // Time2 constructor: hour and minute supplied, second defaulted to 0
24      public Time2(int hour, int minute)
25      {
26         this(hour, minute, 0); // invoke constructor with three arguments
27      }
28
29      // Time2 constructor: hour, minute and second supplied
30      public Time2(int hour, int minute, int second)
31      {
32         if (hour < 0 || hour >= 24)
33            throw new IllegalArgumentException("hour must be 0-23");
34
35         if (minute < 0 || minute >= 60)
36            throw new IllegalArgumentException("minute must be 0-59");
37
38         if (second < 0 || second >= 60)
39            throw new IllegalArgumentException("second must be 0-59");
40
41         this.hour = hour;
42         this.minute = minute;
43         this.second = second;
44      }
45
46      // Time2 constructor: another Time2 object supplied
47      public Time2(Time2 time)
48      {
49         // invoke constructor with three arguments
50         this(time.getHour(), time.getMinute(), time.getSecond());
51      }
52
53      // Set Methods
54      // set a new time value using universal time;
55      // validate the data
56      public void setTime(int hour, int minute, int second)
57      {
```

Fig. 8.5 | Time2 class with overloaded constructors. (Part 2 of 4.)

```
58          if (hour < 0 || hour >= 24)
59             throw new IllegalArgumentException("hour must be 0-23");
60
61          if (minute < 0 || minute >= 60)
62             throw new IllegalArgumentException("minute must be 0-59");
63
64          if (second < 0 || second >= 60)
65             throw new IllegalArgumentException("second must be 0-59");
66
67          this.hour = hour;
68          this.minute = minute;
69          this.second = second;
70       }
71
72       // validate and set hour
73       public void setHour(int hour)
74       {
75          if (hour < 0 || hour >= 24)
76             throw new IllegalArgumentException("hour must be 0-23");
77
78          this.hour = hour;
79       }
80
81       // validate and set minute
82       public void setMinute(int minute)
83       {
84          if (minute < 0 && minute >= 60)
85             throw new IllegalArgumentException("minute must be 0-59");
86
87          this.minute = minute;
88       }
89
90       // validate and set second
91       public void setSecond(int second)
92       {
93          if (second >= 0 && second < 60)
94             throw new IllegalArgumentException("second must be 0-59");
95
96          this.second = second;
97       }
98
99       // Get Methods
100      // get hour value
101      public int getHour()
102      {
103         return hour;
104      }
105
106      // get minute value
107      public int getMinute()
108      {
109         return minute;
110      }
```

Fig. 8.5 | Time2 class with overloaded constructors. (Part 3 of 4.)

```
111
112     // get second value
113     public int getSecond()
114     {
115        return second;
116     }
117
118     // convert to String in universal-time format (HH:MM:SS)
119     public String toUniversalString()
120     {
121        return String.format(
122           "%02d:%02d:%02d", getHour(), getMinute(), getSecond());
123     }
124
125     // convert to String in standard-time format (H:MM:SS AM or PM)
126     public String toString()
127     {
128        return String.format("%d:%02d:%02d %s",
129           ((getHour() == 0 || getHour() == 12) ? 12 : getHour() % 12),
130           getMinute(), getSecond(), (getHour() < 12 ? "AM" : "PM"));
131     }
132  } // end class Time2
```

Fig. 8.5 | Time2 class with overloaded constructors. (Part 4 of 4.)

Class *Time2's* Constructors—Calling One Constructor from Another via **this**

Lines 12–15 declare a so-called **no-argument constructor** that's invoked without arguments. Once you declare any constructors in a class, the compiler will *not* provide a *default constructor*. This no-argument constructor ensures that class Time2's clients can create Time2 objects with default values. Such a constructor simply initializes the object as specified in the constructor's body. In the body, we introduce a use of this that's allowed only as the *first* statement in a constructor's body. Line 14 uses this in method-call syntax to invoke the Time2 constructor that takes three parameters (lines 30–44) with values of 0 for the hour, minute and second. Using this as shown here is a popular way to *reuse* initialization code provided by another of the class's constructors rather than defining similar code in the no-argument constructor's body. We use this syntax in four of the five Time2 constructors to make the class easier to maintain and modify. If we need to change how objects of class Time2 are initialized, only the constructor that the class's other constructors call will need to be modified.

Common Programming Error 8.2

It's a compilation error when this is used in a constructor's body to call another of the class's constructors if that call is not the first statement in the constructor. It's also a compilation error when a method attempts to invoke a constructor directly via this.

Lines 18–21 declare a Time2 constructor with a single int parameter representing the hour, which is passed with 0 for the minute and second to the constructor at lines 30–44. Lines 24–27 declare a Time2 constructor that receives two int parameters representing the hour and minute, which are passed with 0 for the second to the constructor at lines 30–44. Like the no-argument constructor, each of these constructors invokes the constructor at lines 30–44 to minimize code duplication. Lines 30–44 declare the Time2 constructor that receives three int parameters representing the hour, minute and second. This constructor validates and initializes the instance variables.

Lines 47–51 declare a Time2 constructor that receives a reference to another Time2 object. The values from the Time2 argument are passed to the three-argument constructor at lines 30–44 to initialize the hour, minute and second. Line 50 could have directly accessed the hour, minute and second values of the argument time with the expressions time.hour, time.minute and time.second—even though hour, minute and second are declared as private variables of class Time2. This is due to a special relationship between objects of the same class. We'll see in a moment why it's preferable to use the *get* methods.

Software Engineering Observation 8.5

When one object of a class has a reference to another object of the same class, the first object can access all the second object's data and methods (including those that are private).

Class *Time2's* setTime *Method*

Method setTime (lines 56–70) throws an IllegalArgumentException (lines 59, 62 and 65) if any the method's arguments is out of range. Otherwise, it sets Time2's instance variables to the argument values (lines 67–69).

Notes Regarding Class *Time2's* set *and* get *Methods and Constructors*

Time2's *get* methods are called throughout the class. In particular, methods toUniversal-String and toString call methods getHour, getMinute and getSecond in line 122 and lines 129–130, respectively. In each case, these methods could have accessed the class's private data directly without calling the *get* methods. However, consider changing the representation of the time from three int values (requiring 12 bytes of memory) to a single int value representing the total number of seconds that have elapsed since midnight (requiring only four bytes of memory). If we made such a change, only the bodies of the methods that access the private data directly would need to change—in particular, the three-argument constructor, the setTime method and the individual *set* and *get* methods for the hour, minute and second. There would be no need to modify the bodies of methods toUniversalString or toString because they do *not* access the data directly. Designing the class in this manner reduces the likelihood of programming errors when altering the class's implementation.

Similarly, each Time2 constructor could include a copy of the appropriate statements from the three-argument constructor. Doing so may be slightly more efficient, because the extra constructor calls are eliminated. But, *duplicating* statements makes changing the class's internal data representation more difficult. Having the Time2 constructors call the constructor with three arguments requires that any changes to the implementation of the three-argument constructor be made only once. Also, the compiler can optimize programs by removing calls to simple methods and replacing them with the expanded code of their declarations—a technique known as **inlining the code**, which improves program performance.

Using Class *Time2's Overloaded Constructors*

Class Time2Test (Fig. 8.6) invokes the overloaded Time2 constructors (lines 8–12 and 24). Line 8 invokes the Time2 no-argument constructor. Lines 9–12 demonstrate passing arguments to the other Time2 constructors. Line 9 invokes the single-argument constructor that receives an int at lines 18–21 of Fig. 8.5. Line 10 invokes the two-argument constructor at lines 24–27 of Fig. 8.5. Line 11 invokes the three-argument constructor at lines 30–44 of

Fig. 8.5. Line 12 invokes the single-argument constructor that takes a Time2 at lines 47–51 of Fig. 8.5. Next, the app displays the String representations of each Time2 object to confirm that it was initialized properly (lines 15–19). Line 24 attempts to initialize t6 by creating a new Time2 object and passing three *invalid* values to the constructor. When the constructor attempts to use the invalid hour value to initialize the object's hour, an IllegalArgumentException occurs. We catch this exception at line 26 and display its error message, which results in the last line of the output.

```java
 1   // Fig. 8.6: Time2Test.java
 2   // Overloaded constructors used to initialize Time2 objects.
 3
 4   public class Time2Test
 5   {
 6      public static void main(String[] args)
 7      {
 8         Time2 t1 = new Time2(); // 00:00:00
 9         Time2 t2 = new Time2(2); // 02:00:00
10         Time2 t3 = new Time2(21, 34); // 21:34:00
11         Time2 t4 = new Time2(12, 25, 42); // 12:25:42
12         Time2 t5 = new Time2(t4); // 12:25:42
13
14         System.out.println("Constructed with:");
15         displayTime("t1: all default arguments", t1);
16         displayTime("t2: hour specified; default minute and second", t2);
17         displayTime("t3: hour and minute specified; default second", t3);
18         displayTime("t4: hour, minute and second specified", t4);
19         displayTime("t5: Time2 object t4 specified", t5);
20
21         // attempt to initialize t6 with invalid values
22         try
23         {
24            Time2 t6 = new Time2(27, 74, 99); // invalid values
25         }
26         catch (IllegalArgumentException e)
27         {
28            System.out.printf("%nException while initializing t6: %s%n",
29               e.getMessage());
30         }
31      }
32
33      // displays a Time2 object in 24-hour and 12-hour formats
34      private static void displayTime(String header, Time2 t)
35      {
36         System.out.printf("%s%n    %s%n    %s%n",
37            header, t.toUniversalString(), t.toString());
38      }
39   } // end class Time2Test
```

```
Constructed with:
t1: all default arguments
   00:00:00
   12:00:00 AM
```

Fig. 8.6 | Overloaded constructors used to initialize Time2 objects. (Part 1 of 2.)

```
t2: hour specified; default minute and second
   02:00:00
   2:00:00 AM
t3: hour and minute specified; default second
   21:34:00
   9:34:00 PM
t4: hour, minute and second specified
   12:25:42
   12:25:42 PM
t5: Time2 object t4 specified
   12:25:42
   12:25:42 PM
Exception while initializing t6: hour must be 0-23
```

Fig. 8.6 | Overloaded constructors used to initialize `Time2` objects. (Part 2 of 2.)

8.6 Default and No-Argument Constructors

Every class *must* have at least *one* constructor. If you do not provide any in a class's declaration, the compiler creates a *default constructor* that takes *no* arguments when it's invoked. The default constructor initializes the instance variables to the initial values specified in their declarations or to their default values (zero for primitive numeric types, `false` for `boolean` values and `null` for references). In Section 9.4.1, you'll learn that the default constructor also performs another task.

Recall that if your class declares constructors, the compiler will *not* create a default constructor. In this case, you must declare a no-argument constructor if default initialization is required. Like a default constructor, a no-argument constructor is invoked with empty parentheses. The `Time2` no-argument constructor (lines 12–15 of Fig. 8.5) explicitly initializes a `Time2` object by passing to the three-argument constructor 0 for each parameter. Since 0 is the default value for `int` instance variables, the no-argument constructor in this example could actually be declared with an empty body. In this case, each instance variable would receive its default value when the no-argument constructor is called. If we omit the no-argument constructor, clients of this class would not be able to create a `Time2` object with the expression `new Time2()`.

Error-Prevention Tip 8.2

Ensure that you do not include a return type in a constructor definition. Java allows other methods of the class besides its constructors to have the same name as the class and to specify return types. Such methods are not constructors and will not be called when an object of the class is instantiated.

Common Programming Error 8.3

A compilation error occurs if a program attempts to initialize an object of a class by passing the wrong number or types of arguments to the class's constructor.

8.7 Notes on *Set* and *Get* Methods

As you know, a class's `private` fields can be manipulated *only* by its methods. A typical manipulation might be the adjustment of a customer's bank balance (e.g., a `private` instance variable of a class BankAccount) by a method computeInterest. *Set* methods are also commonly called **mutator methods**, because they typically *change* an object's state—i.e., *modify* the values of instance variables. *Get* methods are also commonly called **accessor methods** or **query methods**.

Set *and* Get *Methods vs.* public *Data*

It would seem that providing *set* and *get* capabilities is essentially the same as making a class's instance variables public. This is one of the subtleties that makes Java so desirable for software engineering. A public instance variable can be read or written by any method that has a reference to an object containing that variable. If an instance variable is declared private, a public *get* method certainly allows other methods to access it, but the *get* method can *control* how the client can access it. For example, a *get* method might control the format of the data it returns, shielding the client code from the actual data representation. A public *set* method can—and should—carefully scrutinize attempts to modify the variable's value and throw an exception if necessary. For example, attempts to *set* the day of the month to 37 or a person's weight to a negative value should be rejected. Thus, although *set* and *get* methods provide access to private data, the access is restricted by the implementation of the methods. This helps promote good software engineering.

Software Engineering Observation 8.6

Classes should never have public *nonconstant data, but declaring data* public static final *enables you to make constants available to clients of your class. For example, class* Math *offers* public static final *constants* Math.E *and* Math.PI.

Error-Prevention Tip 8.3

Do not provide public static final *constants if the constants' values are likely to change in future versions of your software.*

Validity Checking in Set *Methods*

The benefits of data integrity do not follow automatically simply because instance variables are declared private—you must provide validity checking. A class's *set* methods could determine that attempts were made to assign invalid data to objects of the class. Typically *set* methods have void return type and use exception handling to indicate attempts to assign invalid data. We discuss exception handling in detail in Chapter 11.

Software Engineering Observation 8.7

When appropriate, provide public *methods to change and retrieve the values of* private *instance variables. This architecture helps hide the implementation of a class from its clients, which improves program modifiability.*

Error-Prevention Tip 8.4

Using set *and* get *methods helps you create classes that are easier to debug and maintain. If only one method performs a particular task, such as setting an instance variable in an object, it's easier to debug and maintain the class. If the instance variable is not being set properly, the code that actually modifies instance variable is localized to one* set *method. Your debugging efforts can be focused on that one method.*

Predicate Methods

Another common use for accessor methods is to test whether a condition is *true* or *false*—such methods are often called **predicate methods**. An example would be class ArrayList's isEmpty method, which returns true if the ArrayList is empty and false otherwise. A program might test isEmpty before attempting to read another item from an ArrayList.

8.8 Composition

A class can have references to objects of other classes as members. This is called **composition** and is sometimes referred to as a *has-a* relationship. For example, an AlarmClock object needs to know the current time *and* the time when it's supposed to sound its alarm, so it's reasonable to include *two* references to Time objects in an AlarmClock object. A car *has-a* steering wheel, a break pedal and an accelerator pedal.

Class **Date**

This composition example contains classes Date (Fig. 8.7), Employee (Fig. 8.8) and EmployeeTest (Fig. 8.9). Class Date (Fig. 8.7) declares instance variables month, day and year (lines 6–8) to represent a date. The constructor receives three int parameters. Lines 17–19 validate the month—if it's out-of-range, lines 18–19 throw an exception. Lines 22–25 validate the day. If the day is incorrect based on the number of days in the particular month (except February 29th which requires special testing for leap years), lines 24–25 throw an exception. Lines 28–31 perform the leap year testing for February. If the month is February and the day is 29 and the year is not a leap year, lines 30–31 throw an exception. If no exceptions are thrown, then lines 33–35 initialize the Date's instance variables and lines 38–38 output the this reference as a String. Since this is a reference to the current Date object, the object's toString method (lines 42–45) is called *implicitly* to obtain the object's String representation. In this example, we assume that the value for year is correct—an industrial-strength Date class should also validate the year.

```
 1   // Fig. 8.7: Date.java
 2   // Date class declaration.
 3
 4   public class Date
 5   {
 6      private int month; // 1-12
 7      private int day; // 1-31 based on month
 8      private int year; // any year
 9
10      private static final int[] daysPerMonth =
11         { 0, 31, 28, 31, 30, 31, 30, 31, 31, 30, 31, 30, 31 };
12
13      // constructor: confirm proper value for month and day given the year
14      public Date(int month, int day, int year)
15      {
16         // check if month in range
17         if (month <= 0 || month > 12)
18            throw new IllegalArgumentException(
19               "month (" + month + ") must be 1-12");
```

Fig. 8.7 | Date class declaration. (Part 1 of 2.)

```
20
21          // check if day in range for month
22          if (day <= 0 ||
23              (day > daysPerMonth[month] && !(month == 2 && day == 29)))
24              throw new IllegalArgumentException("day (" + day +
25                  ") out-of-range for the specified month and year");
26
27          // check for leap year if month is 2 and day is 29
28          if (month == 2 && day == 29 && !(year % 400 == 0 ||
29              (year % 4 == 0 && year % 100 != 0)))
30              throw new IllegalArgumentException("day (" + day +
31                  ") out-of-range for the specified month and year");
32
33          this.month = month;
34          this.day = day;
35          this.year = year;
36
37          System.out.printf(
38              "Date object constructor for date %s%n", this);
39      }
40
41      // return a String of the form month/day/year
42      public String toString()
43      {
44          return String.format("%d/%d/%d", month, day, year);
45      }
46  } // end class Date
```

Fig. 8.7 | Date class declaration. (Part 2 of 2.)

Class *Employee*

Class Employee (Fig. 8.8) has instance variables firstName, lastName, birthDate and hireDate. Members firstName and lastName are references to String objects. Members birthDate and hireDate are references to Date objects. This demonstrates that a class can have as instance variables references to objects of other classes. The Employee constructor (lines 12–19) takes four parameters representing the first name, last name, birth date and hire date. The objects referenced by the parameters are assigned to the Employee object's instance variables. When class Employee's toString method is called, it returns a String containing the employee's name and the String representations of the two Date objects. Each of these Strings is obtained with an *implicit* call to the Date class's toString method.

```
1   // Fig. 8.8: Employee.java
2   // Employee class with references to other objects.
3
4   public class Employee
5   {
6       private String firstName;
7       private String lastName;
8       private Date birthDate;
9       private Date hireDate;
```

Fig. 8.8 | Employee class with references to other objects. (Part 1 of 2.)

```
10
11      // constructor to initialize name, birth date and hire date
12      public Employee(String firstName, String lastName, Date birthDate,
13         Date hireDate)
14      {
15         this.firstName = firstName;
16         this.lastName = lastName;
17         this.birthDate = birthDate;
18         this.hireDate = hireDate;
19      }
20
21      // convert Employee to String format
22      public String toString()
23      {
24         return String.format("%s, %s  Hired: %s  Birthday: %s",
25            lastName, firstName, hireDate, birthDate);
26      }
27   } // end class Employee
```

Fig. 8.8 | Employee class with references to other objects. (Part 2 of 2.)

Class EmployeeTest

Class EmployeeTest (Fig. 8.9) creates two Date objects to represent an Employee's birthday and hire date, respectively. Line 10 creates an Employee and initializes its instance variables by passing to the constructor two Strings (representing the Employee's first and last names) and two Date objects (representing the birthday and hire date). Line 12 *implicitly* invokes the Employee's toString method to display the values of its instance variables and demonstrate that the object was initialized properly.

```
1    // Fig. 8.9: EmployeeTest.java
2    // Composition demonstration.
3
4    public class EmployeeTest
5    {
6       public static void main(String[] args)
7       {
8          Date birth = new Date(7, 24, 1949);
9          Date hire = new Date(3, 12, 1988);
10         Employee employee = new Employee("Bob", "Blue", birth, hire);
11
12         System.out.println(employee);
13      }
14   } // end class EmployeeTest
```

```
Date object constructor for date 7/24/1949
Date object constructor for date 3/12/1988
Blue, Bob  Hired: 3/12/1988  Birthday: 7/24/1949
```

Fig. 8.9 | Composition demonstration.

8.9 enum Types

In Fig. 6.7, we introduced the basic enum type, which defines a set of constants represented as unique identifiers. In that program the enum constants represented the game's status. In this section we discuss the relationship between enum types and classes. Like classes, all enum types are *reference* types. An enum type is declared with an **enum declaration**, which is a comma-separated list of *enum constants*—the declaration may optionally include other components of traditional classes, such as constructors, fields and methods (as you'll see momentarily). Each enum declaration declares an enum class with the following restrictions:

1. enum constants are *implicitly* final.

2. enum constants are *implicitly* static.

3. Any attempt to create an object of an enum type with operator new results in a compilation error.

The enum constants can be used anywhere constants can be used, such as in the case labels of switch statements and to control enhanced for statements.

Declaring Instance Variables, a Constructor and Methods in an **enum** *Type*

Figure 8.10 demonstrates instance variables, a constructor and methods in an enum type. The enum declaration (lines 5–37) contains two parts—the enum constants and the other members of the enum type. The first part (lines 8–13) declares six constants. Each is optionally followed by arguments that are passed to the **enum constructor** (lines 20–24). Like the constructors you've seen in classes, an enum constructor can specify any number of parameters and can be overloaded. In this example, the enum constructor requires two String parameters. To properly initialize each enum constant, we follow it with parentheses containing two String arguments. The second part (lines 16–36) declares the other members of the enum type—two instance variables (lines 16–17), a constructor (lines 20–24) and two methods (lines 27–30 and 33–36).

Lines 16–17 declare the instance variables title and copyrightYear. Each enum constant in enum type Book is actually an object of enum type Book that has its own copy of instance variables title and copyrightYear. The constructor (lines 20–24) takes two String parameters, one that specifies the book's title and one that specifies its copyright year. Lines 22–23 assign these parameters to the instance variables. Lines 27–36 declare methods, which return the book title and copyright year, respectively.

```
1   // Fig. 8.10: Book.java
2   // Declaring an enum type with a constructor and explicit instance fields
3   // and accessors for these fields
4
5   public enum Book
6   {
7      // declare constants of enum type
8      JHTP("Java How to Program", "2015"),
9      CHTP("C How to Program", "2013"),
10     IW3HTP("Internet & World Wide Web How to Program", "2012"),
```

Fig. 8.10 | Declaring an enum type with a constructor and explicit instance fields and accessors for these fields. (Part 1 of 2.)

```
11        CPPHTP("C++ How to Program", "2014"),
12        VBHTP("Visual Basic How to Program", "2014"),
13        CSHARPHTP("Visual C# How to Program", "2014");
14
15        // instance fields
16        private final String title; // book title
17        private final String copyrightYear; // copyright year
18
19        // enum constructor
20        Book(String title, String copyrightYear)
21        {
22           this.title = title;
23           this.copyrightYear = copyrightYear;
24        }
25
26        // accessor for field title
27        public String getTitle()
28        {
29           return title;
30        }
31
32        // accessor for field copyrightYear
33        public String getCopyrightYear()
34        {
35           return copyrightYear;
36        }
37     } // end enum Book
```

Fig. 8.10 | Declaring an enum type with a constructor and explicit instance fields and accessors for these fields. (Part 2 of 2.)

Using enum type Book

Figure 8.11 tests the enum type Book and illustrates how to iterate through a range of enum constants. For every enum, the compiler generates the static method **values** (called in line 12) that returns an array of the enum's constants in the order they were declared. Lines 12–14 use the enhanced for statement to display all the constants declared in the enum Book. Line 14 invokes the enum Book's getTitle and getCopyrightYear methods to get the title and copyright year associated with the constant. When an enum constant is converted to a String (e.g., book in line 13), the constant's identifier is used as the String representation (e.g., JHTP for the first enum constant).

```
1     // Fig. 8.11: EnumTest.java
2     // Testing enum type Book.
3     import java.util.EnumSet;
4
5     public class EnumTest
6     {
7        public static void main(String[] args)
8        {
```

Fig. 8.11 | Testing enum type Book. (Part 1 of 2.)

```
9        System.out.println("All books:");
10
11       // print all books in enum Book
12       for (Book book : Book.values())
13          System.out.printf("%-10s%-45s%s%n", book,
14             book.getTitle(), book.getCopyrightYear());
15
16       System.out.printf("%nDisplay a range of enum constants:%n");
17
18       // print first four books
19       for (Book book : EnumSet.range(Book.JHTP, Book.CPPHTP))
20          System.out.printf("%-10s%-45s%s%n", book,
21             book.getTitle(), book.getCopyrightYear());
22    }
23 } // end class EnumTest
```

```
All books:
JHTP       Java How to Program                          2015
CHTP       C How to Program                             2013
IW3HTP     Internet & World Wide Web How to Program     2012
CPPHTP     C++ How to Program                           2014
VBHTP      Visual Basic How to Program                  2014
CSHARPHTP  Visual C# How to Program                     2014

Display a range of enum constants:
JHTP       Java How to Program                          2015
CHTP       C How to Program                             2013
IW3HTP     Internet & World Wide Web How to Program     2012
CPPHTP     C++ How to Program                           2014
```

Fig. 8.11 | Testing enum type Book. (Part 2 of 2.)

Lines 19–21 use the static method **range** of class **EnumSet** (declared in package java.util) to display a range of the enum Book's constants. Method range takes two parameters—the first and the last enum constants in the range—and returns an EnumSet that contains all the constants between these two constants, inclusive. For example, the expression EnumSet.range(Book.JHTP, Book.CPPHTP) returns an EnumSet containing Book.JHTP, Book.CHTP, Book.IW3HTP and Book.CPPHTP. The enhanced for statement can be used with an EnumSet just as it can with an array, so lines 12–14 use it to display the title and copyright year of every book in the EnumSet. Class EnumSet provides several other static methods for creating sets of enum constants from the same enum type.

Common Programming Error 8.4

In an enum declaration, it's a syntax error to declare enum constants after the enum type's constructors, fields and methods.

8.10 Garbage Collection

Every object uses system resources, such as memory. We need a disciplined way to give resources back to the system when they're no longer needed; otherwise, "resource leaks" might occur that would prevent resources from being reused by your program or possibly by other programs. The JVM performs automatic **garbage collection** to reclaim the *memory* occupied by objects that are no longer used. When there are *no more references* to an object, the object is *eligible* to be collected. Collection typically occurs when the JVM executes its **garbage collector**, which may not happen for a while, or even at all before a program terminates. So, memory leaks that are common in other languages like C and C++ (because memory is *not* automatically reclaimed in those languages) are *less* likely in Java, but some can still happen in subtle ways. Resource leaks other than memory leaks can also occur. For example, an app may open a file on disk to modify its contents—if the app does not close the file, it must terminate before any other app can use the file.

A Note about Class `Object`'s `finalize` Method

Every class in Java has the methods of class `Object` (package `java.lang`), one of which is method **`finalize`**. (You'll learn more about class `Object` in Chapter 9.) You should *never* use method `finalize`, because it can cause many problems and there's uncertainty as to whether it will *ever* get called before a program terminates.

The original intent of `finalize` was to allow the garbage collector to perform **termination housekeeping** on an object just before reclaiming the object's memory. Now, it's considered better practice for any class that uses system resources—such as files on disk— to provide a method that programmers can call to release resources when they're no longer needed in a program. `AutoClosable` objects reduce the likelihood of resource leaks when you use them with the `try`-with-resources statement. As its name implies, an `AutoClosable` object is closed automatically, once a `try`-with-resources statement finishes using the object. We discuss this in more detail in Section 11.12.

 Software Engineering Observation 8.8

Many Java API classes (e.g., class `Scanner` and classes that read files from or write files to disk) provide `close` or `dispose` methods that programmers can call to release resources when they're no longer needed in a program.

8.11 `static` Class Members

Every object has its own copy of all the instance variables of the class. In certain cases, only one copy of a particular variable should be *shared* by all objects of a class. A **`static` field**— called a **class variable**—is used in such cases. A `static` variable represents **classwide information**—all objects of the class share the *same* piece of data. The declaration of a `static` variable begins with the keyword `static`.

Motivating `static`

Let's motivate `static` data with an example. Suppose that we have a video game with Martians and other space creatures. Each Martian tends to be brave and willing to attack other space creatures when the Martian is aware that at least four other Martians are present. If fewer than five Martians are present, each of them becomes cowardly. Thus, each Martian needs to know the `martianCount`. We could endow class Martian with `martianCount` as an *instance variable*. If we do this, then every Martian will have *a separate copy* of the instance variable, and every time we create a new Martian, we'll have to update the instance variable `martianCount` in every Martian object. This wastes space with the redundant copies, wastes time in updating the separate copies and is error prone. Instead, we declare martianCount to be static, making martianCount classwide data. Every Martian can see the martianCount as if it were an instance variable of class Martian, but only *one* copy of the static martianCount is maintained. This saves space. We save time by having the Martian constructor increment the static martianCount—there's only one copy, so we do not have to increment separate copies for each Martian object.

Software Engineering Observation 8.9
Use a static variable when all objects of a class must use the same copy of the variable.

Class Scope

Static variables have *class scope*—they can be used in all of the class's methods. We can access a class's public static members through a reference to any object of the class, or by qualifying the member name with the class name and a dot (.), as in Math.random(). A class's private static class members can be accessed by client code only through methods of the class. Actually, *static class members exist even when no objects of the class exist—* they're available as soon as the class is loaded into memory at execution time. To access a public static member when no objects of the class exist (and even when they do), prefix the class name and a dot (.) to the static member, as in Math.PI. To access a private static member when no objects of the class exist, provide a public static method and call it by qualifying its name with the class name and a dot.

Software Engineering Observation 8.10
Static class variables and methods exist, and can be used, even if no objects of that class have been instantiated.

static *Methods Cannot Directly Access Instance Variables and Instance Methods*

A static method *cannot* access a class's instance variables and instance methods, because a static method can be called even when no objects of the class have been instantiated. For the same reason, the this reference *cannot* be used in a static method. The this reference must refer to a specific object of the class, and when a static method is called, there might not be any objects of its class in memory.

Common Programming Error 8.5
A compilation error occurs if a static method calls an instance method in the same class by using only the method name. Similarly, a compilation error occurs if a static method attempts to access an instance variable in the same class by using only the variable name.

Common Programming Error 8.6
Referring to this in a static method is a compilation error.

Tracking the Number of Employee Objects That Have Been Created

Our next program declares two classes—Employee (Fig. 8.12) and EmployeeTest (Fig. 8.13). Class Employee declares private static variable count (Fig. 8.12, line 7) and public static method getCount (lines 36–39). The static variable count maintains a count of the number of objects of class Employee that have been created so far. This class variable is initialized to zero in line 7. If a `static` variable is *not* initialized, the compiler assigns it a default value—in this case 0, the default value for type `int`.

```java
 1   // Fig. 8.12: Employee.java
 2   // static variable used to maintain a count of the number of
 3   // Employee objects in memory.
 4
 5   public class Employee
 6   {
 7      private static int count = 0; // number of Employees created
 8      private String firstName;
 9      private String lastName;
10
11      // initialize Employee, add 1 to static count and
12      // output String indicating that constructor was called
13      public Employee(String firstName, String lastName)
14      {
15         this.firstName = firstName;
16         this.lastName = lastName;
17
18         ++count;  // increment static count of employees
19         System.out.printf("Employee constructor: %s %s; count = %d%n",
20            firstName, lastName, count);
21      }
22
23      // get first name
24      public String getFirstName()
25      {
26         return firstName;
27      }
28
29      // get last name
30      public String getLastName()
31      {
32         return lastName;
33      }
34
35      // static method to get static count value
36      public static int getCount()
37      {
38         return count;
39      }
40   } // end class Employee
```

Fig. 8.12 | `static` variable used to maintain a count of the number of `Employee` objects in memory.

When `Employee` objects exist, variable `count` can be used in any method of an `Employee` object—this example increments `count` in the constructor (line 18). The `public` `static` method `getCount` (lines 36–39) returns the number of `Employee` objects that have been created so far. When no objects of class `Employee` exist, client code can access variable `count` by calling method `getCount` via the class name, as in `Employee.getCount()`. When objects exist, method `getCount` can also be called via any reference to an `Employee` object.

Good Programming Practice 8.1

Invoke every static *method by using the class name and a dot (.) to emphasize that the method being called is a* static *method.*

Class EmployeeTest

EmployeeTest method main (Fig. 8.13) instantiates two Employee objects (lines 13–14). When each Employee object's constructor is invoked, lines 15–16 of Fig. 8.12 assign the Employee's first name and last name to instance variables firstName and lastName. These two statements do *not* make copies of the original String arguments. Actually, String objects in Java are **immutable**—they cannot be modified after they're created. Therefore, it's safe to have *many* references to one String object. This is not normally the case for objects of most other classes in Java. If String objects are immutable, you might wonder why we're able to use operators + and += to concatenate String objects. String-concatenation actually results in a *new* String object containing the concatenated values. The original String objects are *not* modified.

```java
 1   // Fig. 8.13: EmployeeTest.java
 2   // static member demonstration.
 3
 4   public class EmployeeTest
 5   {
 6      public static void main(String[] args)
 7      {
 8         // show that count is 0 before creating Employees
 9         System.out.printf("Employees before instantiation: %d%n",
10            Employee.getCount());
11
12         // create two Employees; count should be 2
13         Employee e1 = new Employee("Susan", "Baker");
14         Employee e2 = new Employee("Bob", "Blue");
15
16         // show that count is 2 after creating two Employees
17         System.out.printf("%nEmployees after instantiation:%n");
18         System.out.printf("via e1.getCount(): %d%n", e1.getCount());
19         System.out.printf("via e2.getCount(): %d%n", e2.getCount());
20         System.out.printf("via Employee.getCount(): %d%n",
21            Employee.getCount());
22
23         // get names of Employees
24         System.out.printf("%nEmployee 1: %s %s%nEmployee 2: %s %s%n",
25            e1.getFirstName(), e1.getLastName(),
26            e2.getFirstName(), e2.getLastName());
27      }
28   } // end class EmployeeTest
```

```
Employees before instantiation: 0
Employee constructor: Susan Baker; count = 1
Employee constructor: Bob Blue; count = 2
```

Fig. 8.13 | static member demonstration. (Part 1 of 2.)

```
Employees after instantiation:
via e1.getCount(): 2
via e2.getCount(): 2
via Employee.getCount(): 2

Employee 1: Susan Baker
Employee 2: Bob Blue
```

Fig. 8.13 | static member demonstration. (Part 2 of 2.)

When main terminates, local variables e1 and e2 are discarded—remember that a local variable exists *only* until the block in which it's declared completes execution. Because e1 and e2 were the only references to the Employee objects created in lines 13–14 (Fig. 8.13), these objects become "eligible for garbage collection" as main terminates.

In a typical app, the garbage collector *might* eventually reclaim the memory for any objects that are eligible for collection. If any objects are not reclaimed before the program terminates, the operating system will reclaim the memory used by the program. The JVM does *not* guarantee when, or even whether, the garbage collector will execute. When it does, it's possible that no objects or only a subset of the eligible objects will be collected.

8.12 static Import

In Section 6.3, you learned about the static fields and methods of class Math. We access class Math's static fields and *methods* by preceding each with the class name Math and a dot (.). A **static import** declaration enables you to import the static members of a class or interface so you can access them via their *unqualified names* in your class—that is, the class name and a dot (.) are *not* required when using an imported static member.

static *Import Forms*
A static import declaration has two forms—one that imports a particular static member (which is known as **single static import**) and one that imports *all* static members of a class (known as **static import on demand**). The following syntax imports a particular static member:

> import static *packageName.ClassName.staticMemberName*;

where *packageName* is the package of the class (e.g., java.lang), *ClassName* is the name of the class (e.g., Math) and *staticMemberName* is the name of the static field or method (e.g., PI or abs). The following syntax imports *all* static members of a class:

> import static *packageName.ClassName.**;

The asterisk (*) indicates that *all* static members of the specified class should be available for use in the file. static import declarations import *only* static class members. Regular import statements should be used to specify the classes used in a program.

Demonstrating static *Import*
Figure 8.14 demonstrates a static import. Line 3 is a static import declaration, which imports *all* static fields and methods of class Math from package java.lang. Lines 9–12 access the Math class's static fields E (line 11) and PI (line 12) and the static methods

sqrt (line 9) and ceil (line 10) *without* preceding the field names or method names with class name Math and a dot.

> **Common Programming Error 8.7**
>
> *A compilation error occurs if a program attempts to import two or more classes' static methods that have the same signature or static fields that have the same name.*

```
1   // Fig. 8.14: StaticImportTest.java
2   // Static import of Math class methods.
3   import static java.lang.Math.*;
4
5   public class StaticImportTest
6   {
7      public static void main(String[] args)
8      {
9         System.out.printf("sqrt(900.0) = %.1f%n", sqrt(900.0));
10        System.out.printf("ceil(-9.8) = %.1f%n", ceil(-9.8));
11        System.out.printf("E = %f%n", E);
12        System.out.printf("PI = %f%n", PI);
13     }
14  } // end class StaticImportTest
```

```
sqrt(900.0) = 30.0
ceil(-9.8) = -9.0
E = 2.718282
PI = 3.141593
```

Fig. 8.14 | static import of Math class methods.

8.13 **final** Instance Variables

The **principle of least privilege** is fundamental to good software engineering. In the context of an app's code, it states that code should be granted only the amount of privilege and access that it needs to accomplish its designated task, but no more. This makes your programs more robust by preventing code from accidentally (or maliciously) modifying variable values and calling methods that should *not* be accessible.

Let's see how this principle applies to instance variables. Some of them need to be *modifiable* and some do not. You can use the keyword final to specify that a variable is *not* modifiable (i.e., it's a *constant*) and that any attempt to modify it is an error. For example,

```
private final int INCREMENT;
```

declares a final (constant) instance variable INCREMENT of type int. Such variables can be initialized when they're declared. If they're not, they *must* be initialized in every constructor of the class. Initializing constants in constructors enables each object of the class to have a different value for the constant. If a final variable is *not* initialized in its declaration or in every constructor, a compilation error occurs.

Software Engineering Observation 8.11

Declaring an instance variable as final *helps enforce the principle of least privilege. If an instance variable should not be modified, declare it to be* final *to prevent modification. For example, in Fig. 8.8, the instance variables* firstName, lastName, birthDate *and* hireDate *are never modified after they're initialized, so they should be declared* final. *We'll enforce this practice in all programs going forward. You'll see additional benefits of* final *in Chapter 20, Concurrency.*

Common Programming Error 8.8

Attempting to modify a final *instance variable after it's initialized is a compilation error.*

Error-Prevention Tip 8.5

Attempts to modify a final *instance variable are caught at compilation time rather than causing execution-time errors. It's always preferable to get bugs out at compilation time, if possible, rather than allow them to slip through to execution time (where experience has found that repair is often many times more expensive).*

Software Engineering Observation 8.12

A final *field should also be declared* static *if it's initialized in its declaration to a value that's the same for all objects of the class. After this initialization, its value can never change. Therefore, we don't need a separate copy of the field for every object of the class. Making the field* static *enables all objects of the class to share the* final *field.*

8.14 Time Class Case Study: Creating Packages

As you know, the Java API types (classes, interfaces and enums) are organized in *packages* that group related types. Packages facilitate software reuse by enabling programs to import existing classes, rather than *copying* them into the folders of each program that uses them. Programmers use packages to organize program components, especially in large programs. For example, you might have one package containing the types that make up your program's graphical user interface, another for the types that manage your application's data and another for the types that communicate with servers over a network. In addition, packages help you specify unique names for every type you declare, which (as we'll discuss) helps prevent class-name conflicts. This section introduces how to create and use your own packages. Much of what we discuss here is handled for you by IDEs such as NetBeans, Eclipse and IntelliJ IDEA. We focus on creating and using packages with the JDK's command-line tools.

Steps for Declaring a Reusable Class

Before a class can be imported into multiple programs, it must be placed in a package to make it reusable. The steps for creating a reusable class are:

1. Declare one or more public types (classes, interfaces and enums). Only public types can be reused outside the package in which they're declared.

2. Choose a unique package name and add a **package declaration** to the source-code file for each reusable type that should be part of the package.

3. Compile the types so that they're placed in the appropriate package directory.

4. Import the reusable types into a program and use them.

We'll now discuss each of these steps in more detail.

Steps 1 and 2: Creating a **public** Class and Adding the **package** Statement

For *Step 1*, you declare the types that will be placed in the package, including both the reusable types and any supporting types. For demonstration purposes, we reused public class Time1 from Fig. 8.1. The new version is shown in Fig. 8.15. No modifications have been made to the class's implementation, so we do not discuss it again here.

```
1   // Fig. 8.15: Time1.java
2   // Time1 class declaration maintains the time in 24-hour format.
3   package com.deitel.javafp.ch08;
4
5   public class Time1
6   {
7      private int hour; // 0 - 23
8      private int minute; // 0 - 59
9      private int second; // 0 - 59
10
11     // set a new time value using universal time; throw an
12     // exception if the hour, minute or second is invalid
13     public void setTime(int hour, int minute, int second)
14     {
15        // validate hour, minute and second
16        if (hour < 0 || hour >= 24 || minute < 0 || minute >= 60 ||
17           second < 0 || second >= 60)
18        {
19           throw new IllegalArgumentException(
20              "hour, minute and/or second was out of range");
21        }
22
23        this.hour = hour;
24        this.minute = minute;
25        this.second = second;
26     }
27
28     // convert to String in universal-time format (HH:MM:SS)
29     public String toUniversalString()
30     {
31        return String.format("%02d:%02d:%02d", hour, minute, second);
32     }
33
34     // convert to String in standard-time format (H:MM:SS AM or PM)
35     public String toString()
36     {
37        return String.format("%d:%02d:%02d %s",
38           ((hour == 0 || hour == 12) ? 12 : hour % 12),
39           minute, second, (hour < 12 ? "AM" : "PM"));
40     }
41  } // end class Time1
```

Fig. 8.15 | Packaging class Time1 for reuse.

For *Step 2*, we add a package declaration (line 3) containing the package's name. All source-code files containing types that should be part of the same package must contain the *same* package declaration. The declaration

```
package com.deitel.javafp.ch08;
```

indicates that all the types declared in the file (and any other files that contain the same package declaration) are part of the com.deitel.javafp.ch08 package.

Each Java source-code file may contain only *one* package declaration, and it must *precede* all other declarations and statements. If no package statement is provided in a Java source-code file, the types declared in that file are placed in the so-called *default package* and are accessible only to other classes in the default package that are located in the *same directory*. All prior programs in this book have used this default package.

Package Naming Conventions

A package name's parts are separated by dots (.), and there typically are two or more parts. To ensure *unique* package names, you typically begin the name with your institution's or company's Internet domain name in reverse order—e.g., our domain name is deitel.com, so we begin our package names with com.deitel. For the domain name *yourcollege*.edu, you'd begin the package name with edu.*yourcollege*.

After the reversed domain name, you can specify additional parts in a package name. If you're part of a university with many schools or company with many divisions, you might use the school or division name as the next part of the package name. Similarly, if the types are for a specific project, you might include the project name as part of the package name. We chose javafp.ch08 as the next parts in our package name to indicate that class Time1 is from the book *Java SE 8 for Programmers* (javafp) and in Chapter 8 (ch08) of the book.

Fully Qualified Names

The package name is part of the **fully qualified type name**, so the name of class Time1 is actually com.deitel.javafp.ch08.Time1. You can use this fully qualified name in your programs, or you can import the class and use its **simple name** (the class name by itself—Time1) in the program. If another package also contains a Time1 class, the fully qualified class names can be used to distinguish between the classes in the program and prevent a **name conflict** (also called a **name collision**).

Step 3: Compiling the Packaged Class

Step 3 is to compile the class so that it's stored in the appropriate package. When a Java file containing a package declaration is compiled, the resulting class file is placed in the directory specified by the declaration. Classes in the package com.deitel.javafp.ch08 are placed in the directory

```
com
   deitel
      javafp
         ch08
```

The names in the package declaration specify the exact location of the package's classes.

The javac command-line option **-d** causes the compiler to create the directories based on the package declaration. The option also specifies where the top-level directory in the package name should be placed on your system—you may specify a relative or complete path to this location. For example, the command

```
javac -d . Time1.java
```

specifies that the first directory in our package name (com) should be placed in the current directory. The period (.) after -d in the preceding command represents the *current directory* on the Windows, UNIX, Linux and Mac OS X operating systems (and several others as well). Similarly, the command

```
javac -d .. Time1.java
```

specifies that the first directory in our package name (com) should be placed in the *parent* directory. Once you compile with the -d option, the package's ch08 directory contains the file Time1.class.

Step 4: Importing Types from Your Package

Once types are compiled into a package, they can be imported (*Step 4*). Class Time1PackageTest (Fig. 8.16) is in the *default package* because its .java file does not contain a package declaration. Because class Time1PackageTest is in a *different* package from Time1, you must either import Time1 so that class Time1PackageTest can use it (line 3 of Fig. 8.16) or you must *fully qualify* the name Time1 everywhere they're used throughout class Time1PackageTest. For example, line 10 of Fig. 8.16 could have been written as:

```
com.deitel.javafp.ch08.Time1 time =
    new com.deitel.javafp.ch08.Time1();
```

```
1   // Fig. 8.16: Time1PackageTest.java
2   // Time1 object used in an app.
3   import com.deitel.javafp.ch08.Time1; // import class Time1
4
5   public class Time1PackageTest
6   {
7       public static void main(String[] args)
8       {
9           // create and initialize a Time1 object
10          Time1 time = new Time1(); // invokes Time1 constructor
11
12          // output string representations of the time
13          displayTime("After time object is created", time);
14          System.out.println();
15
16          // change time and output updated time
17          time.setTime(13, 27, 6);
18          displayTime("After calling setTime", time);
19          System.out.println();
20
21          // attempt to set time with invalid values
22          try
23          {
24              time.setTime(99, 99, 99); // all values out of range
25          }
```

Fig. 8.16 | Time1 object used in an application. (Part 1 of 2.)

```
26            catch (IllegalArgumentException e)
27            {
28               System.out.printf("Exception: %s%n%n", e.getMessage());
29            }
30
31            // display time after attempt to set invalid values
32            displayTime("After calling setTime with invalid values", time);
33         }
34
35         // displays a Time1 object in 24-hour and 12-hour formats
36         private static void displayTime(String header, Time1 t)
37         {
38            System.out.printf("%s%nUniversal time: %s%nStandard time: %s%n",
39               header, t.toUniversalString(), t.toString());
40         }
41      } // end class Time1PackageTest
```

```
After time object is created
Universal time: 00:00:00
Standard time: 12:00:00 AM

After calling setTime
Universal time: 13:27:06
Standard time: 1:27:06 PM

Exception: hour, minute and/or second was out of range

After calling setTime with invalid values
Universal time: 13:27:06
Standard time: 1:27:06 PM
```

Fig. 8.16 | Time1 object used in an application. (Part 2 of 2.)

Single-Type-Import vs. Type-Import-On-Demand Declarations

Line 3 is a **single-type-import declaration**—it specifies *one* class to import. When a source-code file uses *multiple* classes from a package, you can import those classes with a a **type-import-on-demand declaration** of the form

> **import** *packagename*.*;

which uses an asterisk (*) at its end to inform the compiler that *all* public classes from the *packagename* package can be used in the file containing the import. Only those classes that are *used* are loaded at execution time. The preceding import allows you to use the simple name of any type from the *packagename* package. Throughout this book, we provide single-type-import declarations as a form of documentation to show you specifically which types are used in each program.

 Common Programming Error 8.9

Using the import declaration import java.; causes a compilation error. You must spec-ify the full package name from which you want to import classes.*

Error-Prevention Tip 8.6

Using single-type-import declarations helps avoid naming conflicts by importing only the types you actually use in your code.

Specifying the Classpath When Compiling a Program

When compiling `Time1PackageTest`, `javac` must locate the `.class` files for class `Time1` to ensure that class `Time1PackageTest` uses `Time1` correctly. The compiler uses a special object called a **class loader** to locate the classes it needs. The class loader begins by searching the standard Java classes that are bundled with the JDK. Then it searches for **optional packages**. Java provides an **extension mechanism** that enables new (optional) packages to be added to Java for development and execution purposes. If the class is not found in the standard Java classes or in the extension classes, the class loader searches the **classpath**—a list of directories or **archive files** containing reusable types. Each directory or archive file is separated from the next by a **directory separator**—a semicolon (;) on Windows or a colon (:) on UNIX/Linux/Mac OS X. Archive files are individual files that contain directories of other files, typically in a compressed format. For example, the standard classes used by your programs are contained in the archive file `rt.jar`, which is installed with the JDK. Archive files normally end with the `.jar` or `.zip` file-name extensions.

By default, the classpath consists only of the current directory. However, the classpath can be modified by

1. providing the **-classpath** *listOfDirectories* option to the `javac` compiler or

2. setting the **CLASSPATH environment variable** (a special variable that you define and the operating system maintains so that programs can search for classes in the specified locations).

If you compile `Time1PackageTest.java` without specifying the `-classpath` option, as in

```
javac Time1PackageTest.java
```

the class loader assumes that the additional package(s) used by the `Time1PackageTest` program are in the *current directory*. If the package is in the *parent* directory, you'd use the command

```
javac -classpath .;.. Time1PackageTest.java
```

on Windows or the command

```
javac -classpath .:.. Time1PackageTest.java
```

on UNIX/Linux/Mac OS X. The `.` in the classpath enables the class loader to locate `Time1PackageTest` in the current directry. The `..` enables the class loader to locate the contents of package `com.deitel.javafp.ch08` in the parent directory.

Common Programming Error 8.10

Specifying an explicit classpath eliminates the current directory from the classpath. This prevents classes in the current directory (including packages in the current directory) from loading properly. If classes must be loaded from the current directory, include a dot (.) in the classpath to specify the current directory.

Software Engineering Observation 8.13

In general, it's a better practice to use the -classpath option of the compiler, rather than the CLASSPATH environment variable, to specify the classpath for a program. This enables each program to have its own classpath.

Error-Prevention Tip 8.7

Specifying the classpath with the CLASSPATH environment variable can cause subtle and difficult-to-locate errors in programs that use different versions of the same package.

Specifying the Classpath When Executing a Program
When you execute a program, the JVM must be able to locate the .class files for the program's classes. Like the compiler, the java command uses a *class loader* that searches the standard classes and extension classes first, then searches the classpath (the current directory by default). The classpath can be specified explicitly by using the same techniques discussed for the compiler. As with the compiler, it's better to specify an individual program's classpath via command-line JVM options. You can specify the classpath in the java command via the **-classpath** or **-cp** command-line options, followed by a list of directories or archive files. Again, if classes must be loaded from the current directory, be sure to include a dot (.) in the classpath to specify the current directory. To execute the Time1PackageTest, use the following command:

```
java -classpath .:.. Time1PackageTest
```

For more information on the classpath, visit http://docs.oracle.com/javase/7/docs/technotes/tools/index.html#general.

8.15 Package Access

If no access modifier (public, protected or private—we discuss protected in Chapter 9) is specified for a method or variable when it's declared in a class, the method or variable is considered to have **package access**. In a program that consists of one class declaration, this has no specific effect. However, if a program uses *multiple* classes from the *same* package (i.e., a group of related classes), these classes can access each other's package-access members directly through references to objects of the appropriate classes, or in the case of static members through the class name. Package access is rarely used.

Figure 8.17 demonstrates package access. The app contains two classes in one source-code file—the PackageDataTest class containing main (lines 5–21) and the PackageData class (lines 24–41). Classes in the same source file are part of the same package. Consequently, class PackageDataTest is allowed to modify the package-access data of PackageData objects. When you compile this program, the compiler produces two separate .class files—PackageDataTest.class and PackageData.class. The compiler places the two .class files in the same directory. You can also place class PackageData (lines 24–41) in a separate source-code file.

In the PackageData class declaration, lines 26–27 declare the instance variables number and string with no access modifiers—therefore, these are package-access instance variables. Class PackageDataTest's main method creates an instance of the PackageData class (line 9) to demonstrate the ability to modify the PackageData instance variables directly (as shown in lines 15–16). The results of the modification can be seen in the output window.

```
 1   // Fig. 8.17: PackageDataTest.java
 2   // Package-access members of a class are accessible by other classes
 3   // in the same package.
 4
 5   public class PackageDataTest
 6   {
 7      public static void main(String[] args)
 8      {
 9         PackageData packageData = new PackageData();
10
11         // output String representation of packageData
12         System.out.printf("After instantiation:%n%s%n", packageData);
13
14         // change package access data in packageData object
15         packageData.number = 77;
16         packageData.string = "Goodbye";
17
18         // output String representation of packageData
19         System.out.printf("%nAfter changing values:%n%s%n", packageData);
20      }
21   } // end class PackageDataTest
22
23   // class with package access instance variables
24   class PackageData
25   {
26      int number; // package-access instance variable
27      String string; // package-access instance variable
28
29      // constructor
30      public PackageData()
31      {
32         number = 0;
33         string = "Hello";
34      }
35
36      // return PackageData object String representation
37      public String toString()
38      {
39         return String.format("number: %d; string: %s", number, string);
40      }
41   } // end class PackageData
```

```
After instantiation:
number: 0; string: Hello

After changing values:
number: 77; string: Goodbye
```

Fig. 8.17 | Package-access members of a class are accessible by other classes in the same package.

8.16 Using BigDecimal for Precise Monetary Calculations

In earlier chapters, we demonstrated monetary calculations using values of type double. In Chapter 5, we discussed the fact that some double values are represented *approximately*. Any application that requires precise floating-point calculations—such as those in financial applications—should instead use class **BigDecimal** (from package **java.math**).

Interest Calculations Using BigDecimal
Figure 8.18 reimplements the interest calculation example of Fig. 5.6 using objects of class BigDecimal to perform the calculations. We also introduce class **NumberFormat** (package **java.text**) for formatting numeric values as *locale-specific* Strings—for example, in the U.S. locale, the value 1234.56, would be formatted as "1,234.56", whereas in many European locales it would be formatted as "1.234,56".

Creating BigDecimal Objects
Lines 11–12 declare and initialize BigDecimal variables principal and rate using the BigDecimal static method **valueOf** that receives a double argument and returns a BigDecimal object that represents the *exact* value specified.

```java
1   // Interest.java
2   // Compound-interest calculations with BigDecimal.
3   import java.math.BigDecimal;
4   import java.text.NumberFormat;
5
6   public class Interest
7   {
8      public static void main(String args[])
9      {
10         // initial principal amount before interest
11         BigDecimal principal = BigDecimal.valueOf(1000.0);
12         BigDecimal rate = BigDecimal.valueOf(0.05); // interest rate
13
14         // display headers
15         System.out.printf("%s%20s%n", "Year", "Amount on deposit");
16
17         // calculate amount on deposit for each of ten years
18         for (int year = 1; year <= 10; year++)
19         {
20            // calculate new amount for specified year
21            BigDecimal amount =
22               principal.multiply(rate.add(BigDecimal.ONE).pow(year));
23
24            // display the year and the amount
25            System.out.printf("%4d%20s%n", year,
26               NumberFormat.getCurrencyInstance().format(amount));
27         }
28      }
29   } // end class Interest
```

Fig. 8.18 | Compound-interest calculations with BigDecimal. (Part 1 of 2.)

```
Year   Amount on deposit
  1          $1,050.00
  2          $1,102.50
  3          $1,157.62
  4          $1,215.51
  5          $1,276.28
  6          $1,340.10
  7          $1,407.10
  8          $1,477.46
  9          $1,551.33
 10          $1,628.89
```

Fig. 8.18 | Compound-interest calculations with `BigDecimal`. (Part 2 of 2.)

*Performing the Interest Calculations with **BigDecimal***
Lines 21–22 perform the interest calculation using BigDecimal methods **multiply**, **add** and **pow**. The expression in line 22 evaluates as follows:

1. First, the expression `rate.add(BigDecimal.ONE)` adds 1 to the `rate` to produce a BigDecimal containing 1.05—this is equivalent to 1.0 + rate in line 19 of Fig. 5.6. The BigDecimal constant **ONE** represents the value 1. Class BigDecimal also provides the commonly used constants **ZERO** (0) and **TEN** (10).

2. Next, BigDecimal method pow is called on the preceding result to raise 1.05 to the power year—this is equivalent to passing 1.0 + rate and year to method Math.pow in line 19 of Fig. 5.6.

3. Finally, we call BigDecimal method `multiply` on the principal object, passing the preceding result as the argument. This returns a BigDecimal representing the amount on deposit at the end of the specified year.

Since the expression `rate.add(BigDecimal.ONE)` produces the same value in each iteration of the loop, we could have simply initialized rate to 1.05 in line 12; however, we chose to mimic the precise calculations we used in line 19 of Fig. 5.6.

*Formatting Currency Values with **NumberFormat***
During each iteration of the loop, line 26

```
NumberFormat.getCurrencyInstance().format(amount)
```

evaluates as follows:

1. First, the expression uses NumberFormat's static method **getCurrencyInstance** to get a NumberFormat that's pre-configured to format numeric values as locale-specific currency Strings—for example, in the U.S. locale, the numeric value 1628.89 is formatted as $1,628.89. Locale-specific formatting is an important part of **internationalization**—the process of customizing your applications for users' various locales and spoken languages.

2. Next, the expression invokes method NumberFormat method **format** (on the object returned by getCurrencyInstance) to perform the formatting of the amount value. Method format then returns the locale-specific String representation, rounded to two-digits to the right of the decimal point.

Rounding *BigDecimal* Values

In addition to precise calculations, BigDecimal also gives you control over how values are rounded—by default all calculations are exact and *no* rounding occurs. If you do not specify how to round BigDecimal values and a given value cannot be represented exactly—such as the result of 1 divided by 3, which is 0.3333333…—an ArithmeticException occurs.

Though we do not do so in this example, you can specify the *rounding mode* for BigDecimal by supplying a MathContext object (package java.math) to class BigDecimal's constructor when you create a BigDecimal. You may also provide a MathContext to various BigDecimal methods that perform calculations. Class MathContext contains several pre-configured MathContext objects that you can learn about at

```
http://docs.oracle.com/javase/7/docs/api/java/math/MathContext.html
```

By default, each pre-configured MathContext uses so called "bankers rounding" as explained for the RoundingMode constant HALF_EVEN at:

```
http://docs.oracle.com/javase/7/docs/api/java/math/
    RoundingMode.html#HALF_EVEN
```

Scaling *BigDecimal* Values

A BigDecimal's scale is the number of digits to the right of its decimal point. If you need a BigDecimal rounded to a specific digit, you can call BigDecimal method setScale. For example, the following expression returns a BigDecimal with two digits to the right of the decimal point and using bankers rounding:

```
amount.setScale(2, RoundingMode.HALF_EVEN)
```

8.17 Wrap-Up

In this chapter, we presented additional class concepts. The Time class case study showed a complete class declaration consisting of private data, overloaded public constructors for initialization flexibility, *set* and *get* methods for manipulating the class's data, and methods that returned String representations of a Time object in two different formats. You also learned that every class can declare a toString method that returns a String representation of an object of the class and that method toString can be called implicitly whenever an object of a class appears in the code where a String is expected. We showed how to throw an exception to indicate that a problem has occurred.

You learned that the this reference is used implicitly in a class's instance methods to access the class's instance variables and other instance methods. You also saw explicit uses of the this reference to access the class's members (including shadowed fields) and how to use keyword this in a constructor to call another constructor of the class.

We discussed the differences between default constructors provided by the compiler and no-argument constructors provided by the programmer. You learned that a class can have references to objects of other classes as members—a concept known as composition. You learned more about enum types and how they can be used to create a set of constants for use in a program. You learned about Java's garbage-collection capability and how it (unpredictably) reclaims the memory of objects that are no longer used. The chapter explained the motivation for static fields in a class and demonstrated how to declare and use static fields and methods in your own classes. You also learned how to declare and initialize final variables.

You learned that fields declared without an access modifier are given package access by default. You saw the relationship between classes in the same package that allows each class in a package to access the package-access members of other classes in the package. Finally, we demonstrated how to use class BigDecimal to perform precise monetary calculations.

In the next chapter, we continue our discussion of object-oriented programming by introducing inheritance, in which new classes can be created by basing them on existing proven and debugged high-quality classes. You'll see how the inheritance relationships among classes can help you build better software faster.

9

Object-Oriented Programming: Inheritance

Objectives

In this chapter you'll:

- Understand inheritance and how to use it to develop new classes based on existing classes.

- Learn the notions of superclasses and subclasses and the relationship between them.

- Use keyword **extends** to create a class that inherits attributes and behaviors from another class.

- Use access modifier **protected** in a superclass to give subclass methods access to these superclass members.

- Access superclass members with **super** from a subclass.

- Learn how constructors are used in inheritance hierarchies.

- Learn about the methods of class **Object**, the direct or indirect superclass of all classes.

- Use class **ArrayList** to manipulate a dynamically resizable arraylike data structure.

9.1 Introduction

This chapter continues our discussion of object-oriented programming (OOP) by introducing **inheritance**, in which a new class is created by acquiring an existing class's members and possibly embellishing them with new or modified capabilities. With inheritance, you can save time during program development by basing new classes on existing proven and debugged high-quality software. This also increases the likelihood that a system will be implemented and maintained effectively.

When creating a class, rather than declaring completely new members, you can designate that the new class should *inherit* the members of an existing class. The existing class is called the **superclass**, and the new class is the **subclass**. (The C++ programming language refers to the superclass as the **base class** and the subclass as the **derived class**.) A subclass can become a superclass for future subclasses.

A subclass can add its own fields and methods. Therefore, a subclass is *more specific* than its superclass and represents a more specialized group of objects. The subclass exhibits the behaviors of its superclass and can modify those behaviors so that they operate appropriately for the subclass. This is why inheritance is sometimes referred to as **specialization**.

The **direct superclass** is the superclass from which the subclass explicitly inherits. An **indirect superclass** is any class above the direct superclass in the **class hierarchy**, which defines the inheritance relationships among classes—as you'll see in Section 9.2, diagrams help you understand these relationships. In Java, the class hierarchy begins with class Object (in package java.lang), which *every* class in Java directly or indirectly **extends** (or "inherits from"). Section 9.6 lists the methods of class Object that are inherited by all other Java classes. Java supports only **single inheritance**, in which each class is derived from exactly *one* direct superclass. Unlike C++, Java does *not* support multiple inheritance (which occurs when a class is derived from more than one direct superclass). Chapter 10, Object-Oriented Programming: Polymorphism and Interfaces, explains how to use Java *interfaces* to realize many of the benefits of multiple inheritance while avoiding the associated problems.

We distinguish between the *is-a* **relationship** and the *has-a* **relationship**. *Is-a* represents inheritance. In an *is-a* relationship, *an object of a subclass can also be treated as an object of its superclass*—e.g., a car *is a* vehicle. By contrast, *has-a* represents composition (see Chapter 8). In a *has-a* relationship, *an object contains as members references to other objects*—e.g., a car *has a* steering wheel (and a car object has a reference to a steering-wheel object).

New classes can inherit from classes in **class libraries**. Organizations develop their own class libraries and can take advantage of others available worldwide. Some day, most new software likely will be constructed from **standardized reusable components**, just as automobiles and most computer hardware are constructed today. This will facilitate the rapid development of more powerful, abundant and economical software.

9.2 Superclasses and Subclasses

Often, an object of one class *is an* object of another class as well. For example, a `CarLoan` *is a* `Loan` as are `HomeImprovementLoans` and `MortgageLoans`. Thus, in Java, class `CarLoan` can be said to inherit from class `Loan`. In this context, class `Loan` is a superclass and class `CarLoan` is a subclass. A `CarLoan` *is a* specific type of `Loan`, but it's incorrect to claim that every `Loan` *is a* `CarLoan`—the `Loan` could be any type of loan. Figure 9.1 lists several simple examples of superclasses and subclasses—superclasses tend to be "more general" and subclasses "more specific."

Superclass	Subclasses
Student	GraduateStudent, UndergraduateStudent
Shape	Circle, Triangle, Rectangle, Sphere, Cube
Loan	CarLoan, HomeImprovementLoan, MortgageLoan
Employee	Faculty, Staff
BankAccount	CheckingAccount, SavingsAccount

Fig. 9.1 | Inheritance examples.

Because every subclass object *is an* object of its superclass, and one superclass can have many subclasses, the set of objects represented by a superclass is often larger than the set of objects represented by any of its subclasses. For example, the superclass `Vehicle` represents *all* vehicles, including cars, trucks, boats, bicycles and so on. By contrast, subclass `Car` represents a smaller, more specific subset of vehicles.

University Community Member Hierarchy
Inheritance relationships form treelike *hierarchical* structures. A superclass exists in a hierarchical relationship with its subclasses. Let's develop a sample class hierarchy (Fig. 9.2), also called an **inheritance hierarchy**. A university community has thousands of members, including employees, students and alumni. Employees are either faculty or staff members. Faculty members are either administrators (e.g., deans and department chairpersons) or teachers. The hierarchy could contain many other classes. For example, students can be graduate or undergraduate students. Undergraduate students can be freshmen, sophomores, juniors or seniors.

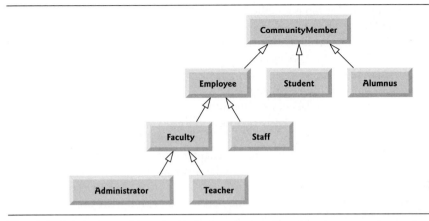

Fig. 9.2 | Inheritance hierarchy UML class diagram for university CommunityMembers.

Each arrow in the hierarchy represents an *is-a* relationship. As we follow the arrows upward in this class hierarchy, we can state, for example, that "an Employee *is a* CommunityMember" and "a Teacher *is a* Faculty member." CommunityMember is the direct superclass of Employee, Student and Alumnus and is an indirect superclass of all the other classes in the diagram. Starting from the bottom, you can follow the arrows and apply the *is-a* relationship up to the topmost superclass. For example, an Administrator *is a* Faculty member, *is an* Employee, *is a* CommunityMember and, of course, *is an* Object.

Shape Hierarchy

Now consider the Shape inheritance hierarchy in Fig. 9.3. This hierarchy begins with superclass Shape, which is extended by subclasses TwoDimensionalShape and ThreeDimensionalShape—Shapes are either TwoDimensionalShapes or ThreeDimensionalShapes. The third level of this hierarchy contains *specific* types of TwoDimensionalShapes and ThreeDimensionalShapes. As in Fig. 9.2, we can follow the arrows from the bottom of the diagram to the topmost superclass in this class hierarchy to identify several *is-a* relationships. For example, a Triangle *is a* TwoDimensionalShape and *is a* Shape, while a Sphere *is a* ThreeDimensionalShape and *is a* Shape. This hierarchy could contain many other classes. For example, ellipses and trapezoids also are TwoDimensionalShapes.

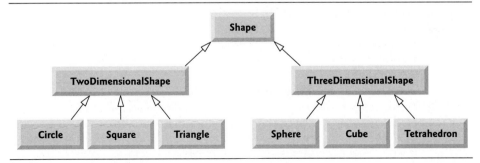

Fig. 9.3 | Inheritance hierarchy UML class diagram for Shapes.

Not every class relationship is an inheritance relationship. In Chapter 8, we discussed the *has-a* relationship, in which classes have members that are references to objects of other classes. Such relationships create classes by *composition* of existing classes. For example, given the classes Employee, BirthDate and TelephoneNumber, it's improper to say that an Employee *is a* BirthDate or that an Employee *is a* TelephoneNumber. However, an Employee *has a* BirthDate, and an Employee *has a* TelephoneNumber.

It's possible to treat superclass objects and subclass objects similarly—their commonalities are expressed in the superclass's members. Objects of all classes that extend a common superclass can be treated as objects of that superclass—such objects have an *is-a* relationship with the superclass. Later in this chapter and in Chapter 10, we consider many examples that take advantage of the *is-a* relationship.

A subclass can customize methods that it inherits from its superclass. To do this, the subclass **overrides** (*redefines*) the superclass method with an appropriate implementation, as we'll see in the chapter's code examples.

9.3 protected Members

Chapter 8 discussed access modifiers public and private. A class's public members are accessible wherever the program has a *reference* to an *object* of that class or one of its *subclasses*. A class's private members are accessible only within the class itself. In this section, we introduce the access modifier **protected**. Using protected access offers an intermediate level of access between public and private. A superclass's protected members can be accessed by members of that superclass, by members of its subclasses and by members of other classes in the *same package*—protected members also have *package access*.

All public and protected superclass members retain their original access modifier when they become members of the subclass—public members of the superclass become public members of the subclass, and protected members of the superclass become protected members of the subclass. A superclass's private members are *not* accessible outside the class itself. Rather, they're *hidden* from its subclasses and can be accessed only through the public or protected methods inherited from the superclass.

Subclass methods can refer to public and protected members inherited from the superclass simply by using the member names. When a subclass method *overrides* an inherited superclass method, the *superclass* version of the method can be accessed from the *subclass* by preceding the superclass method name with keyword **super** and a dot (.) separator. We discuss accessing overridden members of the superclass in Section 9.4.

Software Engineering Observation 9.1

Methods of a subclass cannot directly access private members of their superclass. A subclass can change the state of private superclass instance variables only through non-private methods provided in the superclass and inherited by the subclass.

Software Engineering Observation 9.2

Declaring private instance variables helps you test, debug and correctly modify systems. If a subclass could access its superclass's private instance variables, classes that inherit from that subclass could access the instance variables as well. This would propagate access to what should be private instance variables, and the benefits of information hiding would be lost.

9.4 Relationship Between Superclasses and Subclasses

We now use an inheritance hierarchy containing types of *employees* in a company's payroll application to discuss the relationship between a superclass and its subclass. In this company, *commission employees* (who will be represented as objects of a superclass) are paid a percentage of their sales, while *base-salaried commission employees* (who will be represented as objects of a subclass) receive a base salary *plus* a percentage of their sales.

We divide our discussion of the relationship between these classes into five examples. The first declares class CommissionEmployee, which directly inherits from class Object and declares as private instance variables a first name, last name, social security number, commission rate and gross (i.e., total) sales amount.

The second example declares class BasePlusCommissionEmployee, which also directly inherits from class Object and declares as private instance variables a first name, last name, social security number, commission rate, gross sales amount *and* base salary. We create this class by *writing every line of code* the class requires—we'll soon see that it's much more efficient to create it by inheriting from class CommissionEmployee.

The third example declares a new BasePlusCommissionEmployee class that *extends* class CommissionEmployee (i.e., a BasePlusCommissionEmployee *is a* CommissionEmployee who also has a base salary). This *software reuse lets us write much less code* when developing the new subclass. In this example, class BasePlusCommissionEmployee attempts to access class CommissionEmployee's private members—this results in compilation errors, because the subclass *cannot* access the superclass's private instance variables.

The fourth example shows that if CommissionEmployee's instance variables are declared as protected, the BasePlusCommissionEmployee subclass *can* access that data directly. Both BasePlusCommissionEmployee classes contain identical functionality, but we show how the inherited version is easier to create and manage.

After we discuss the convenience of using protected instance variables, we create the fifth example, which sets the CommissionEmployee instance variables back to private to enforce good software engineering. Then we show how the BasePlusCommissionEmployee subclass can use CommissionEmployee's public methods to manipulate (in a controlled manner) the private instance variables inherited from CommissionEmployee.

9.4.1 Creating and Using a CommissionEmployee Class

We begin by declaring class CommissionEmployee (Fig. 9.4). Line 4 begins the class declaration and indicates that class CommissionEmployee **extends** (i.e., *inherits from*) class **Object** (from package java.lang). This causes class CommissionEmployee to inherit the class Object's methods—class Object does not have any fields. If you don't explicitly specify which class a new class extends, the class extends Object implicitly. For this reason, you typically will not include "extends Object" in your code—we do so in this one example only for demonstration purposes.

Overview of Class CommissionEmployee's Methods and Instance Variables

Class CommissionEmployee's public services include a constructor (lines 13–34) and methods earnings (lines 87–90) and toString (lines 93–101). Lines 37–52 declare public *get* methods for the class's final instance variables (declared in lines 6–8) firstName, lastName and socialSecurityNumber. These three instance variables are declared final because they do not need to be modified after they're initialized—this is also why we do not provide corresponding *set* methods. Lines 55–84 declare public *set* and *get* methods for the class's grossSales and commissionRate instance variables (declared in lines 9–10). The class declares its instance variables as private, so objects of other classes cannot directly access these variables.

```java
1   // Fig. 9.4: CommissionEmployee.java
2   // CommissionEmployee class represents an employee paid a
3   // percentage of gross sales.
4   public class CommissionEmployee extends Object
5   {
6      private final String firstName;
7      private final String lastName;
8      private final String socialSecurityNumber;
9      private double grossSales; // gross weekly sales
10     private double commissionRate; // commission percentage
11
12     // five-argument constructor
13     public CommissionEmployee(String firstName, String lastName,
14        String socialSecurityNumber, double grossSales,
15        double commissionRate)
16     {
17        // implicit call to Object's default constructor occurs here
18
19        // if grossSales is invalid throw exception
20        if (grossSales < 0.0)
21           throw new IllegalArgumentException(
22              "Gross sales must be >= 0.0");
23
24        // if commissionRate is invalid throw exception
25        if (commissionRate <= 0.0 || commissionRate >= 1.0)
26           throw new IllegalArgumentException(
27              "Commission rate must be > 0.0 and < 1.0");
28
29        this.firstName = firstName;
30        this.lastName = lastName;
31        this.socialSecurityNumber = socialSecurityNumber;
32        this.grossSales = grossSales;
33        this.commissionRate = commissionRate;
34     } // end constructor
35
36     // return first name
37     public String getFirstName()
38     {
39        return firstName;
40     }
41
42     // return last name
43     public String getLastName()
44     {
45        return lastName;
46     }
```

Fig. 9.4 | CommissionEmployee class represents an employee paid a percentage of gross sales. (Part 1 of 3.)

```
47
48      // return social security number
49      public String getSocialSecurityNumber()
50      {
51         return socialSecurityNumber;
52      }
53
54      // set gross sales amount
55      public void setGrossSales(double grossSales)
56      {
57         if (grossSales < 0.0)
58            throw new IllegalArgumentException(
59               "Gross sales must be >= 0.0");
60
61         this.grossSales = grossSales;
62      }
63
64      // return gross sales amount
65      public double getGrossSales()
66      {
67         return grossSales;
68      }
69
70      // set commission rate
71      public void setCommissionRate(double commissionRate)
72      {
73         if (commissionRate <= 0.0 || commissionRate >= 1.0)
74            throw new IllegalArgumentException(
75               "Commission rate must be > 0.0 and < 1.0");
76
77         this.commissionRate = commissionRate;
78      }
79
80      // return commission rate
81      public double getCommissionRate()
82      {
83         return commissionRate;
84      }
85
86      // calculate earnings
87      public double earnings()
88      {
89         return commissionRate * grossSales;
90      }
91
92      // return String representation of CommissionEmployee object
93      @Override // indicates that this method overrides a superclass method
94      public String toString()
95      {
96         return String.format("%s: %s %s%n%s: %s%n%s: %.2f%n%s: %.2f",
97            "commission employee", firstName, lastName,
98            "social security number", socialSecurityNumber,
```

Fig. 9.4 | CommissionEmployee class represents an employee paid a percentage of gross sales. (Part 2 of 3.)

```
 99              "gross sales", grossSales,
100              "commission rate", commissionRate);
101      }
102   } // end class CommissionEmployee
```

Fig. 9.4 | CommissionEmployee class represents an employee paid a percentage of gross sales. (Part 3 of 3.)

Class *CommissionEmployee's Constructor*

Constructors are *not* inherited, so class CommissionEmployee does not inherit class Object's constructor. However, a superclass's constructors are still available to be called by subclasses. In fact, Java requires that *the first task of any subclass constructor is to call its direct superclass's constructor*, either explicitly or implicitly (if no constructor call is specified), to ensure that the instance variables inherited from the superclass are initialized properly. The syntax for calling a superclass constructor explicitly is discussed in Section 9.4.3. In this example, class CommissionEmployee's constructor calls class Object's constructor implicitly. If the code does not include an explicit call to the superclass constructor, Java *implicitly* calls the superclass's default or *no-argument* constructor. The comment in line 17 of Fig. 9.4 indicates where the implicit call to the superclass Object's default constructor is made (you do *not* write the code for this call). Object's default constructor does nothing. Even if a class does not have constructors, the default constructor that the compiler implicitly declares for the class will call the superclass's default or no-argument constructor.

After the implicit call to Object's constructor, lines 20–22 and 25–27 validate the grossSales and commissionRate arguments. If these are valid (that is, the constructor does not throw an IllegalArgumentException), lines 29–33 assign the constructor's arguments to the class's instance variables.

We did not validate the values of arguments firstName, lastName and socialSecurityNumber before assigning them to the corresponding instance variables. We could validate the first and last names—perhaps to ensure that they're of a reasonable length. Similarly, a social security number could be validated using regular expressions (Section 14.7) to ensure that it contains nine digits, with or without dashes (e.g., 123-45-6789 or 123456789).

Class *CommissionEmployee's* **earnings** *Method*

Method earnings (lines 87–90) calculates a CommissionEmployee's earnings. Line 89 multiplies the commissionRate by the grossSales and returns the result.

Class *CommissionEmployee's* **toString** *Method and the* **@Override** *Annotation*

Method toString (lines 93–101) is special—it's one of the methods that *every* class inherits directly or indirectly from class Object (summarized in Section 9.6). Method toString returns a String representing an object. It's called implicitly whenever an object must be converted to a String representation, such as when an object is output by printf or output by String method format via the %s format specifier. Class Object's toString method returns a String that includes the name of the object's class. It's primarily a placeholder that can be *overridden* by a subclass to specify an appropriate String representation of the data in a subclass object. Method toString of class CommissionEmployee overrides (redefines) class Object's toString method. When invoked, CommissionEmployee's toString method uses String method format to return a String containing information about the CommissionEmployee. To override a superclass method, a subclass must declare a method with the *same signature* (method name, number of parameters, parameter types and order of parameter types) as the superclass method—Object's toString method takes no parameters, so CommissionEmployee declares toString with no parameters.

Line 93 uses the optional **@Override annotation** to indicate that the following method declaration (i.e., toString) should *override* an *existing* superclass method. This annotation helps the compiler catch a few common errors. For example, in this case, you intend to override superclass method toString, which is spelled with a lowercase "t" and an uppercase "S." If you inadvertently use a lowercase "s," the compiler will flag this as an error because the superclass does not contain a method named toString. If you didn't use the @Override annotation, toString would be an entirely different method that would *not* be called if a CommissionEmployee were used where a String was needed.

Another common overriding error is declaring the wrong number or types of parameters in the parameter list. This creates an *unintentional overload* of the superclass method, rather than overriding the existing method. If you then attempt to call the method (with the correct number and types of parameters) on a subclass object, the superclass's version is invoked—potentially leading to subtle logic errors. When the compiler encounters a method declared with @Override, it compares the method's signature with the superclass's method signatures. If there isn't an exact match, the compiler issues an error message, such as "method does not override or implement a method from a supertype." You would then correct your method's signature so that it matches one in the superclass.

Error-Prevention Tip 9.1

Though the @Override annotation is optional, declare overridden methods with it to ensure at compilation time that you defined their signatures correctly. It's always better to find errors at compile time rather than at runtime. For this reason, the toString methods in Fig. 7.9 and in Chapter 8's examples should have been declared with @Override.

Common Programming Error 9.1

It's a compilation error to override a method with a more restricted access modifier—a public superclass method cannot become a protected or private subclass method; a protected superclass method cannot become a private subclass method. Doing so would break the is-a relationship, which requires that all subclass objects be able to respond to method calls made to public methods declared in the superclass. If a public method, could be overridden as a protected or private method, the subclass objects would not be able to respond to the same method calls as superclass objects. Once a method is declared public in a superclass, the method remains public for all that class's direct and indirect subclasses.

Class *CommissionEmployeeTest*

Figure 9.5 tests class CommissionEmployee. Lines 9–10 instantiate a CommissionEmployee object and invoke CommissionEmployee's constructor (lines 13–34 of Fig. 9.4) to initialize it with "Sue" as the first name, "Jones" as the last name, "222-22-2222" as the social security number, 10000 as the gross sales amount ($10,000) and .06 as the commission rate (i.e., 6%). Lines 15–24 use CommissionEmployee's *get* methods to retrieve the object's instance-variable values for output. Lines 26–27 invoke the object's setGrossSales and setCommissionRate methods to change the values of instance variables grossSales and commission-

Rate. Lines 29–30 output the String representation of the updated CommissionEmployee. When an object is output using the %s format specifier, the object's toString method is invoked *implicitly* to obtain the object's String representation. [*Note:* In this chapter, we do not use the earnings method in each class, but it's used extensively in Chapter 10.]

```java
1   // Fig. 9.5: CommissionEmployeeTest.java
2   // CommissionEmployee class test program.
3
4   public class CommissionEmployeeTest
5   {
6      public static void main(String[] args)
7      {
8         // instantiate CommissionEmployee object
9         CommissionEmployee employee = new CommissionEmployee(
10           "Sue", "Jones", "222-22-2222", 10000, .06);
11
12        // get commission employee data
13        System.out.println(
14           "Employee information obtained by get methods:");
15        System.out.printf("%n%s %s%n", "First name is",
16           employee.getFirstName());
17        System.out.printf("%s %s%n", "Last name is",
18           employee.getLastName());
19        System.out.printf("%s %s%n", "Social security number is",
20           employee.getSocialSecurityNumber());
21        System.out.printf("%s %.2f%n", "Gross sales is",
22           employee.getGrossSales());
23        System.out.printf("%s %.2f%n", "Commission rate is",
24           employee.getCommissionRate());
25
26        employee.setGrossSales(5000);
27        employee.setCommissionRate(.1);
28
29        System.out.printf("%n%s:%n%n%s%n",
30           "Updated employee information obtained by toString", employee);
31     } // end main
32  } // end class CommissionEmployeeTest
```

```
Employee information obtained by get methods:

First name is Sue
Last name is Jones
Social security number is 222-22-2222
Gross sales is 10000.00
Commission rate is 0.06

Updated employee information obtained by toString:

commission employee: Sue Jones
social security number: 222-22-2222
gross sales: 5000.00
commission rate: 0.10
```

Fig. 9.5 | CommissionEmployee class test program.

9.4.2 Creating and Using a BasePlusCommissionEmployee Class

We now discuss the second part of our introduction to inheritance by declaring and testing (a completely new and independent) class BasePlusCommissionEmployee (Fig. 9.6), which contains a first name, last name, social security number, gross sales amount, commission rate *and* base salary. Class BasePlusCommissionEmployee's public services include a BasePlusCommissionEmployee constructor (lines 15–42) and methods earnings (lines 111–114) and toString (lines 117–126). Lines 45–108 declare public *get* and *set* methods for the class's private instance variables (declared in lines 7–12) firstName, lastName, socialSecurityNumber, grossSales, commissionRate and baseSalary. These variables and methods encapsulate all the necessary features of a base-salaried commission employee. Note the *similarity* between this class and class CommissionEmployee (Fig. 9.4)—in this example, we'll not yet exploit that similarity.

```java
1   // Fig. 9.6: BasePlusCommissionEmployee.java
2   // BasePlusCommissionEmployee class represents an employee who receives
3   // a base salary in addition to commission.
4
5   public class BasePlusCommissionEmployee
6   {
7      private final String firstName;
8      private final String lastName;
9      private final String socialSecurityNumber;
10     private double grossSales; // gross weekly sales
11     private double commissionRate; // commission percentage
12     private double baseSalary; // base salary per week
13
14     // six-argument constructor
15     public BasePlusCommissionEmployee(String firstName, String lastName,
16        String socialSecurityNumber, double grossSales,
17        double commissionRate, double baseSalary)
18     {
19        // implicit call to Object's default constructor occurs here
20
21        // if grossSales is invalid throw exception
22        if (grossSales < 0.0)
23           throw new IllegalArgumentException(
24              "Gross sales must be >= 0.0");
25
26        // if commissionRate is invalid throw exception
27        if (commissionRate <= 0.0 || commissionRate >= 1.0)
28           throw new IllegalArgumentException(
29              "Commission rate must be > 0.0 and < 1.0");
30
31        // if baseSalary is invalid throw exception
32        if (baseSalary < 0.0)
33           throw new IllegalArgumentException(
34              "Base salary must be >= 0.0");
35
```

Fig. 9.6 | BasePlusCommissionEmployee class represents an employee who receives a base salary in addition to a commission. (Part 1 of 3.)

```
36          this.firstName = firstName;
37          this.lastName = lastName;
38          this.socialSecurityNumber = socialSecurityNumber;
39          this.grossSales = grossSales;
40          this.commissionRate = commissionRate;
41          this.baseSalary = baseSalary;
42       } // end constructor
43
44       // return first name
45       public String getFirstName()
46       {
47          return firstName;
48       }
49
50       // return last name
51       public String getLastName()
52       {
53          return lastName;
54       }
55
56       // return social security number
57       public String getSocialSecurityNumber()
58       {
59          return socialSecurityNumber;
60       }
61
62       // set gross sales amount
63       public void setGrossSales(double grossSales)
64       {
65          if (grossSales < 0.0)
66             throw new IllegalArgumentException(
67                "Gross sales must be >= 0.0");
68
69          this.grossSales = grossSales;
70       }
71
72       // return gross sales amount
73       public double getGrossSales()
74       {
75          return grossSales;
76       }
77
78       // set commission rate
79       public void setCommissionRate(double commissionRate)
80       {
81          if (commissionRate <= 0.0 || commissionRate >= 1.0)
82             throw new IllegalArgumentException(
83                "Commission rate must be > 0.0 and < 1.0");
84
85          this.commissionRate = commissionRate;
86       }
87
```

Fig. 9.6 | BasePlusCommissionEmployee class represents an employee who receives a base salary in addition to a commission. (Part 2 of 3.)

```
88      // return commission rate
89      public double getCommissionRate()
90      {
91          return commissionRate;
92      }
93
94      // set base salary
95      public void setBaseSalary(double baseSalary)
96      {
97          if (baseSalary < 0.0)
98              throw new IllegalArgumentException(
99                  "Base salary must be >= 0.0");
100
101         this.baseSalary = baseSalary;
102     }
103
104     // return base salary
105     public double getBaseSalary()
106     {
107         return baseSalary;
108     }
109
110     // calculate earnings
111     public double earnings()
112     {
113         return baseSalary + (commissionRate * grossSales);
114     }
115
116     // return String representation of BasePlusCommissionEmployee
117     @Override
118     public String toString()
119     {
120         return String.format(
121             "%s: %s %s%n%s: %s%n%s: %.2f%n%s: %.2f%n%s: %.2f",
122             "base-salaried commission employee", firstName, lastName,
123             "social security number", socialSecurityNumber,
124             "gross sales", grossSales, "commission rate", commissionRate,
125             "base salary", baseSalary);
126     }
127 } // end class BasePlusCommissionEmployee
```

Fig. 9.6 | BasePlusCommissionEmployee class represents an employee who receives a base salary in addition to a commission. (Part 3 of 3.)

Class BasePlusCommissionEmployee does *not* specify "extends Object" in line 5, so the class *implicitly* extends Object. Also, like class CommissionEmployee's constructor (lines 13–34 of Fig. 9.4), class BasePlusCommissionEmployee's constructor invokes class Object's default constructor *implicitly*, as noted in the comment in line 19.

Class BasePlusCommissionEmployee's earnings method (lines 111–114) returns the result of adding the BasePlusCommissionEmployee's base salary to the product of the commission rate and the employee's gross sales.

Class BasePlusCommissionEmployee overrides Object method toString to return a String containing the BasePlusCommissionEmployee's information. Once again, we use format specifier %.2f to format the gross sales, commission rate and base salary with two digits of precision to the right of the decimal point (line 121).

Testing Class *BasePlusCommissionEmployee*

Figure 9.7 tests class BasePlusCommissionEmployee. Lines 9–11 create a BasePlusCommissionEmployee object and pass "Bob", "Lewis", "333-33-3333", 5000, .04 and 300 to the constructor as the first name, last name, social security number, gross sales, commission rate and base salary, respectively. Lines 16–27 use BasePlusCommissionEmployee's *get* methods to retrieve the values of the object's instance variables for output. Line 29 invokes the object's setBaseSalary method to change the base salary. Method setBaseSalary (Fig. 9.6, lines 95–102) ensures that instance variable baseSalary is not assigned a negative value. Line 33 of Fig. 9.7 invokes method toString *explicitly* to get the object's String representation.

```java
1   // Fig. 9.7: BasePlusCommissionEmployeeTest.java
2   // BasePlusCommissionEmployee test program.
3
4   public class BasePlusCommissionEmployeeTest
5   {
6      public static void main(String[] args)
7      {
8         // instantiate BasePlusCommissionEmployee object
9         BasePlusCommissionEmployee employee =
10           new BasePlusCommissionEmployee(
11           "Bob", "Lewis", "333-33-3333", 5000, .04, 300);
12
13        // get base-salaried commission employee data
14        System.out.println(
15           "Employee information obtained by get methods:%n");
16        System.out.printf("%s %s%n", "First name is",
17           employee.getFirstName());
18        System.out.printf("%s %s%n", "Last name is",
19           employee.getLastName());
20        System.out.printf("%s %s%n", "Social security number is",
21           employee.getSocialSecurityNumber());
22        System.out.printf("%s %.2f%n", "Gross sales is",
23           employee.getGrossSales());
24        System.out.printf("%s %.2f%n", "Commission rate is",
25           employee.getCommissionRate());
26        System.out.printf("%s %.2f%n", "Base salary is",
27           employee.getBaseSalary());
28
29        employee.setBaseSalary(1000);
30
31        System.out.printf("%n%s:%n%n%s%n",
32           "Updated employee information obtained by toString",
33           employee.toString());
34     } // end main
35  } // end class BasePlusCommissionEmployeeTest
```

Fig. 9.7 | BasePlusCommissionEmployee test program. (Part 1 of 2.)

```
Employee information obtained by get methods:

First name is Bob
Last name is Lewis
Social security number is 333-33-3333
Gross sales is 5000.00
Commission rate is 0.04
Base salary is 300.00

Updated employee information obtained by toString:

base-salaried commission employee: Bob Lewis
social security number: 333-33-3333
gross sales: 5000.00
commission rate: 0.04
base salary: 1000.00
```

Fig. 9.7 | BasePlusCommissionEmployee test program. (Part 2 of 2.)

Notes on Class *BasePlusCommissionEmployee*

Much of class BasePlusCommissionEmployee's code (Fig. 9.6) is *similar*, or *identical*, to that of class CommissionEmployee (Fig. 9.4). For example, private instance variables firstName and lastName and methods setFirstName, getFirstName, setLastName and getLastName are identical to those of class CommissionEmployee. The classes also both contain private instance variables socialSecurityNumber, commissionRate and gross-Sales, and corresponding *get* and *set* methods. In addition, the BasePlusCommissionEmployee constructor is *almost* identical to that of class CommissionEmployee, except that BasePlusCommissionEmployee's constructor also sets the baseSalary. The other additions to class BasePlusCommissionEmployee are private instance variable baseSalary and methods setBaseSalary and getBaseSalary. Class BasePlusCommissionEmployee's toString method is *almost* identical to that of class CommissionEmployee except that it also outputs instance variable baseSalary with two digits of precision to the right of the decimal point.

We literally *copied* code from class CommissionEmployee and *pasted* it into class Base-PlusCommissionEmployee, then modified class BasePlusCommissionEmployee to include a base salary and methods that manipulate the base salary. This *"copy-and-paste" approach* is often error prone and time consuming. Worse yet, it spreads copies of the same code throughout a system, creating code-maintenance problems—changes to the code would need to be made in multiple classes. Is there a way to "acquire" the instance variables and methods of one class in a way that makes them part of other classes *without duplicating code*? Next we answer this question, using a more elegant approach to building classes that emphasizes the benefits of inheritance.

Software Engineering Observation 9.3

With inheritance, the instance variables and methods that are the same for all the classes in the hierarchy are declared in a superclass. Changes made to these common features in the superclass are inherited by the subclass. Without inheritance, changes would need to be made to all the source-code files that contain a copy of the code in question.

9.4.3 Creating a CommissionEmployee–BasePlusCommissionEmployee Inheritance Hierarchy

Now we declare class BasePlusCommissionEmployee (Fig. 9.8) to *extend* class CommissionEmployee (Fig. 9.4). A BasePlusCommissionEmployee object *is a* CommissionEmployee, because inheritance passes on class CommissionEmployee's capabilities. Class BasePlusCommissionEmployee also has instance variable baseSalary (Fig. 9.8, line 6). Keyword extends (line 4) indicates inheritance. BasePlusCommissionEmployee *inherits* CommissionEmployee's instance variables and methods.

Software Engineering Observation 9.4

At the design stage in an object-oriented system, you'll often find that certain classes are closely related. You should "factor out" common instance variables and methods and place them in a superclass. Then use inheritance to develop subclasses, specializing them with capabilities beyond those inherited from the superclass.

Software Engineering Observation 9.5

Declaring a subclass does not affect its superclass's source code. Inheritance preserves the integrity of the superclass.

Only CommissionEmployee's public and protected members are directly accessible in the subclass. The CommissionEmployee constructor is *not* inherited. So, the public BasePlusCommissionEmployee services include its constructor (lines 9–23), public methods inherited from CommissionEmployee, and methods setBaseSalary (lines 26–33), getBaseSalary (lines 36–39), earnings (lines 42–47) and toString (lines 50–60). Methods earnings and toString *override* the corresponding methods in class CommissionEmployee because their superclass versions do not properly calculate a BasePlusCommissionEmployee's earnings or return an appropriate String representation, respectively.

```java
1   // Fig. 9.8: BasePlusCommissionEmployee.java
2   // private superclass members cannot be accessed in a subclass.
3
4   public class BasePlusCommissionEmployee extends CommissionEmployee
5   {
6      private double baseSalary; // base salary per week
7
8      // six-argument constructor
9      public BasePlusCommissionEmployee(String firstName, String lastName,
10        String socialSecurityNumber, double grossSales,
11        double commissionRate, double baseSalary)
12     {
13        // explicit call to superclass CommissionEmployee constructor
14        super(firstName, lastName, socialSecurityNumber,
15          grossSales, commissionRate);
16
17        // if baseSalary is invalid throw exception
18        if (baseSalary < 0.0)
19           throw new IllegalArgumentException(
20             "Base salary must be >= 0.0");
21
```

Fig. 9.8 | private superclass members cannot be accessed in a subclass. (Part 1 of 3.)

```
22          this.baseSalary = baseSalary;
23      }
24
25      // set base salary
26      public void setBaseSalary(double baseSalary)
27      {
28          if (baseSalary < 0.0)
29              throw new IllegalArgumentException(
30                  "Base salary must be >= 0.0");
31
32          this.baseSalary = baseSalary;
33      }
34
35      // return base salary
36      public double getBaseSalary()
37      {
38          return baseSalary;
39      }
40
41      // calculate earnings
42      @Override
43      public double earnings()
44      {
45          // not allowed: commissionRate and grossSales private in superclass
46          return baseSalary + (commissionRate * grossSales);
47      }
48
49      // return String representation of BasePlusCommissionEmployee
50      @Override
51      public String toString()
52      {
53          // not allowed: attempts to access private superclass members
54          return String.format(
55              "%s: %s %s%n%s: %s%n%s: %.2f%n%s: %.2f%n%s: %.2f",
56              "base-salaried commission employee", firstName, lastName,
57              "social security number", socialSecurityNumber,
58              "gross sales", grossSales, "commission rate", commissionRate,
59              "base salary", baseSalary);
60      }
61  } // end class BasePlusCommissionEmployee
```

```
BasePlusCommissionEmployee.java:46: error: commissionRate has private access
in CommissionEmployee
        return baseSalary + (commissionRate * grossSales);
                             ^
BasePlusCommissionEmployee.java:46: error: grossSales has private access in
CommissionEmployee
        return baseSalary + (commissionRate * grossSales);
                                              ^
BasePlusCommissionEmployee.java:56: error: firstName has private access in
CommissionEmployee
            "base-salaried commission employee", firstName, lastName,
                                                  ^
```

Fig. 9.8 | private superclass members cannot be accessed in a subclass. (Part 2 of 3.)

```
BasePlusCommissionEmployee.java:56: error: lastName has private access in
CommissionEmployee
        "base-salaried commission employee", firstName, lastName,
                                                                 ^
BasePlusCommissionEmployee.java:57: error: socialSecurityNumber has private
access in CommissionEmployee
        "social security number", socialSecurityNumber,
                                 ^
BasePlusCommissionEmployee.java:58: error: grossSales has private access in
CommissionEmployee
        "gross sales", grossSales, "commission rate", commissionRate,
                      ^
BasePlusCommissionEmployee.java:58: error: commissionRate has private access
inCommissionEmployee
        "gross sales", grossSales, "commission rate", commissionRate,
                                                                    ^
```

Fig. 9.8 | `private` superclass members cannot be accessed in a subclass. (Part 3 of 3.)

A Subclass's Constructor Must Call Its Superclass's Constructor

Each subclass constructor must implicitly or explicitly call one of its superclass's constructors to initialize the instance variables inherited from the superclass. Lines 14–15 in Base-PlusCommissionEmployee's six-argument constructor (lines 9–23) explicitly call class CommissionEmployee's five-argument constructor (declared at lines 13–34 of Fig. 9.4) to initialize the superclass portion of a BasePlusCommissionEmployee object (i.e., variables firstName, lastName, socialSecurityNumber, grossSales and commissionRate). We do this by using the **superclass constructor call syntax**—keyword super, followed by a set of parentheses containing the superclass constructor arguments, which are used to initialize the superclass instance variables firstName, lastName, socialSecurityNumber, grossSales and commissionRate, respectively. If BasePlusCommissionEmployee's constructor did not invoke the superclass's constructor explicitly, the compiler would attempt to insert a call to the superclass's default or no-argument constructor. Class Commission-Employee does not have such a constructor, so the compiler would issue an error. The explicit superclass constructor call in lines 14–15 of Fig. 9.8 must be the *first* statement in the constructor's body. When a superclass contains a no-argument constructor, you can use super() to call that constructor explicitly, but this is rarely done.

Software Engineering Observation 9.6

You learned previously that you should not call a class's instance methods from its constructors and that we'll say why in Chapter 10. Calling a superclass constructor from a subclass constructor does not contradict this advice.

BasePlusCommissionEmployee Methods Earnings and toString

The compiler generates errors for line 46 (Fig. 9.8) because CommissionEmployee's instance variables commissionRate and grossSales are private—subclass BasePlusCommissionEmployee's methods are *not* allowed to access superclass CommissionEmployee's private instance variables. We used **red text** in Fig. 9.8 to indicate erroneous code. The compiler issues additional errors at lines 56–58 of BasePlusCommissionEmployee's toString method for the same reason. The errors in BasePlusCommissionEmployee could have been prevented by using the *get* methods inherited from class CommissionEmployee.

For example, line 46 could have called `getCommissionRate` and `getGrossSales` to access `CommissionEmployee`'s private instance variables `commissionRate` and `grossSales`, respectively. Lines 56–58 also could have used appropriate *get* methods to retrieve the values of the superclass's instance variables.

9.4.4 CommissionEmployee–BasePlusCommissionEmployee Inheritance Hierarchy Using protected Instance Variables

To enable class `BasePlusCommissionEmployee` to directly access superclass instance variables `firstName`, `lastName`, `socialSecurityNumber`, `grossSales` and `commissionRate`, we can declare those members as protected in the superclass. As we discussed in Section 9.3, a superclass's protected members are accessible by all subclasses of that superclass. In the new `CommissionEmployee` class, we modified only lines 6–10 of Fig. 9.4 to declare the instance variables with the protected access modifier as follows:

```
protected final String firstName;
protected final String lastName;
protected final String socialSecurityNumber;
protected double grossSales; // gross weekly sales
protected double commissionRate; // commission percentage
```

The rest of the class declaration (which is not shown here) is identical to that of Fig. 9.4.

We could have declared `CommissionEmployee`'s instance variables public to enable subclass `BasePlusCommissionEmployee` to access them. However, declaring public instance variables is poor software engineering because it allows unrestricted access to the these variables from any class, greatly increasing the chance of errors. With protected instance variables, the subclass gets access to the instance variables, but classes that are not subclasses and classes that are not in the same package cannot access these variables directly—recall that protected class members are also visible to other classes in the same package.

Class BasePlusCommissionEmployee

Class `BasePlusCommissionEmployee` (Fig. 9.9) extends the new version of class `CommissionEmployee` with protected instance variables. `BasePlusCommissionEmployee` objects inherit `CommissionEmployee`'s protected instance variables `firstName`, `lastName`, `socialSecurityNumber`, `grossSales` and `commissionRate`—all these variables are now protected members of `BasePlusCommissionEmployee`. As a result, the compiler does not generate errors when compiling line 45 of method `earnings` and lines 54–56 of method `toString`. If another class extends this version of class `BasePlusCommissionEmployee`, the new subclass also can access the protected members.

```
1   // Fig. 9.9: BasePlusCommissionEmployee.java
2   // BasePlusCommissionEmployee inherits protected instance
3   // variables from CommissionEmployee.
4
5   public class BasePlusCommissionEmployee extends CommissionEmployee
6   {
7       private double baseSalary; // base salary per week
```

Fig. 9.9 | BasePlusCommissionEmployee inherits protected instance variables from CommissionEmployee. (Part 1 of 2.)

```java
 8
 9     // six-argument constructor
10     public BasePlusCommissionEmployee(String firstName, String lastName,
11        String socialSecurityNumber, double grossSales,
12        double commissionRate, double baseSalary)
13     {
14        super(firstName, lastName, socialSecurityNumber,
15           grossSales, commissionRate);
16
17        // if baseSalary is invalid throw exception
18        if (baseSalary < 0.0)
19           throw new IllegalArgumentException(
20              "Base salary must be >= 0.0");
21
22        this.baseSalary = baseSalary;
23     }
24
25     // set base salary
26     public void setBaseSalary(double baseSalary)
27     {
28        if (baseSalary < 0.0)
29           throw new IllegalArgumentException(
30              "Base salary must be >= 0.0");
31
32        this.baseSalary = baseSalary;
33     }
34
35     // return base salary
36     public double getBaseSalary()
37     {
38        return baseSalary;
39     }
40
41     // calculate earnings
42     @Override // indicates that this method overrides a superclass method
43     public double earnings()
44     {
45        return baseSalary + (commissionRate * grossSales);
46     }
47
48     // return String representation of BasePlusCommissionEmployee
49     @Override
50     public String toString()
51     {
52        return String.format(
53           "%s: %s %s%n%s: %s%n%s: %.2f%n%s: %.2f%n%s: %.2f",
54           "base-salaried commission employee", firstName, lastName,
55           "social security number", socialSecurityNumber,
56           "gross sales", grossSales, "commission rate", commissionRate,
57           "base salary", baseSalary);
58     }
59  } // end class BasePlusCommissionEmployee
```

Fig. 9.9 | BasePlusCommissionEmployee inherits protected instance variables from CommissionEmployee. (Part 2 of 2.)

A Subclass Object Contains the Instance Variables of All of Its Superclasses

When you create a `BasePlusCommissionEmployee` object, it contains all instance variables declared in the class hierarchy to that point—that is, those from classes `Object` (which does not have instance variables), `CommissionEmployee` and `BasePlusCommissionEmploy-ee`. Class `BasePlusCommissionEmployee` does *not* inherit `CommissionEmployee`'s five-argument constructor, but *explicitly invokes* it (lines 14–15) to initialize the instance variables that `BasePlusCommissionEmployee` inherited from `CommissionEmployee`. Similarly, `CommissionEmployee`'s constructor *implicitly* calls class `Object`'s constructor. `BasePlusCommissionEmployee`'s constructor must *explicitly* call `CommissionEmployee`'s constructor because `CommissionEmployee` does *not* have a no-argument constructor that could be invoked implicitly.

Testing Class `BasePlusCommissionEmployee`

The `BasePlusCommissionEmployeeTest` class for this example is identical to that of Fig. 9.7 and produces the same output, so we do not show it here. Although the version of class `BasePlusCommissionEmployee` in Fig. 9.6 does not use inheritance and the version in Fig. 9.9 does, both classes provide the *same* functionality. The source code in Fig. 9.9 (59 lines) is considerably shorter than that in Fig. 9.6 (127 lines), because most of the class's functionality is now inherited from `CommissionEmployee`—there's now only one copy of the `CommissionEmployee` functionality. This makes the code easier to maintain, modify and debug, because the code related to a `CommissionEmployee` exists only in that class.

Notes on Using `protected` Instance Variables

In this example, we declared superclass instance variables as `protected` so that subclasses could access them. Inheriting `protected` instance variables enables direct access to the variables by subclasses. In most cases, however, it's better to use `private` instance variables to encourage proper software engineering. Your code will be easier to maintain, modify and debug.

Using `protected` instance variables creates several potential problems. First, the subclass object can set an inherited variable's value directly without using a *set* method. Therefore, a subclass object can assign an invalid value to the variable, possibly leaving the object in an inconsistent state. For example, if we were to declare `CommissionEmployee`'s instance variable `grossSales` as `protected`, a subclass object (e.g., `BasePlusCommissionEmployee`) could then assign a negative value to `grossSales`. Another problem with using `protected` instance variables is that subclass methods are more likely to be written so that they depend on the superclass's data implementation. In practice, subclasses should depend only on the superclass services (i.e., non-`private` methods) and not on the superclass data implementation. With `protected` instance variables in the superclass, we may need to modify all the subclasses of the superclass if the superclass implementation changes. For example, if for some reason we were to change the names of instance variables `firstName` and `lastName` to `first` and `last`, then we would have to do so for all occurrences in which a subclass directly references superclass instance variables `firstName` and `lastName`. Such a class is said to be **fragile** or **brittle**, because a small change in the superclass can "break" subclass implementation. You should be able to change the superclass implementation while still providing the same services to the subclasses. Of course, if the superclass services change, we must reimplement our subclasses. A third problem is that a class's `protected` members are visible to all classes in the same package as the class containing the protected members—this is not always desirable.

Software Engineering Observation 9.7

Use the protected access modifier when a superclass should provide a method only to its subclasses and other classes in the same package, but not to other clients.

Software Engineering Observation 9.8

Declaring superclass instance variables private (as opposed to protected) enables the superclass implementation of these instance variables to change without affecting subclass implementations.

Error-Prevention Tip 9.2

When possible, do not include protected instance variables in a superclass. Instead, include non-private methods that access private instance variables. This will help ensure that objects of the class maintain consistent states.

9.4.5 CommissionEmployee–BasePlusCommissionEmployee Inheritance Hierarchy Using private Instance Variables

Let's reexamine our hierarchy once more, this time using good software engineering practices.

Class CommissionEmployee

Class CommissionEmployee (Fig. 9.10) declares instance variables firstName, lastName, socialSecurityNumber, grossSales and commissionRate as *private* (lines 6–10) and provides public methods getFirstName, getLastName, getSocialSecurityNumber, set-GrossSales, getGrossSales, setCommissionRate, getCommissionRate, earnings and toString for manipulating these values. Methods earnings (lines 87–90) and toString (lines 93–101) use the class's *get* methods to obtain the values of its instance variables. If we decide to change the names of the instance variables, the earnings and toString declarations will *not* require modification—only the bodies of the *get* and *set* methods that directly manipulate the instance variables will need to change. These changes occur solely within the superclass—no changes to the subclass are needed. *Localizing the effects of changes* like this is a good software engineering practice.

```
1   // Fig. 9.10: CommissionEmployee.java
2   // CommissionEmployee class uses methods to manipulate its
3   // private instance variables.
4   public class CommissionEmployee
5   {
6      private final String firstName;
7      private final String lastName;
8      private final String socialSecurityNumber;
9      private double grossSales; // gross weekly sales
10     private double commissionRate; // commission percentage
```

Fig. 9.10 | CommissionEmployee class uses methods to manipulate its private instance variables. (Part 1 of 3.)

```
11
12      // five-argument constructor
13      public CommissionEmployee(String firstName, String lastName,
14         String socialSecurityNumber, double grossSales,
15         double commissionRate)
16      {
17         // implicit call to Object constructor occurs here
18
19         // if grossSales is invalid throw exception
20         if (grossSales < 0.0)
21            throw new IllegalArgumentException(
22               "Gross sales must be >= 0.0");
23
24         // if commissionRate is invalid throw exception
25         if (commissionRate <= 0.0 || commissionRate >= 1.0)
26            throw new IllegalArgumentException(
27               "Commission rate must be > 0.0 and < 1.0");
28
29         this.firstName = firstName;
30         this.lastName = lastName;
31         this.socialSecurityNumber = socialSecurityNumber;
32         this.grossSales = grossSales;
33         this.commissionRate = commissionRate;
34      } // end constructor
35
36      // return first name
37      public String getFirstName()
38      {
39         return firstName;
40      }
41
42      // return last name
43      public String getLastName()
44      {
45         return lastName;
46      }
47
48      // return social security number
49      public String getSocialSecurityNumber()
50      {
51         return socialSecurityNumber;
52      }
53
54      // set gross sales amount
55      public void setGrossSales(double grossSales)
56      {
57         if (grossSales < 0.0)
58            throw new IllegalArgumentException(
59               "Gross sales must be >= 0.0");
60
61         this.grossSales = grossSales;
62      }
```

Fig. 9.10 | CommissionEmployee class uses methods to manipulate its private instance variables. (Part 2 of 3.)

```
63
64     // return gross sales amount
65     public double getGrossSales()
66     {
67        return grossSales;
68     }
69
70     // set commission rate
71     public void setCommissionRate(double commissionRate)
72     {
73        if (commissionRate <= 0.0 || commissionRate >= 1.0)
74           throw new IllegalArgumentException(
75              "Commission rate must be > 0.0 and < 1.0");
76
77        this.commissionRate = commissionRate;
78     }
79
80     // return commission rate
81     public double getCommissionRate()
82     {
83        return commissionRate;
84     }
85
86     // calculate earnings
87     public double earnings()
88     {
89        return getCommissionRate() * getGrossSales();
90     }
91
92     // return String representation of CommissionEmployee object
93     @Override
94     public String toString()
95     {
96        return String.format("%s: %s %s%n%s: %s%n%s: %.2f%n%s: %.2f",
97           "commission employee", getFirstName(), getLastName(),
98           "social security number", getSocialSecurityNumber(),
99           "gross sales", getGrossSales(),
100          "commission rate", getCommissionRate());
101    }
102 } // end class CommissionEmployee
```

Fig. 9.10 | CommissionEmployee class uses methods to manipulate its private instance variables. (Part 3 of 3.)

Class *BasePlusCommissionEmployee*

Subclass BasePlusCommissionEmployee (Fig. 9.11) inherits CommissionEmployee's non-private methods and can access (in a controlled way) the private superclass members via those methods. Class BasePlusCommissionEmployee has several changes that distinguish it from Fig. 9.9. Methods earnings (lines 43–47) and toString (lines 50–55) each invoke method getBaseSalary to obtain the base salary value, rather than accessing baseSalary directly. If we decide to rename instance variable baseSalary, only the bodies of method setBaseSalary and getBaseSalary will need to change.

```
1    // Fig. 9.11: BasePlusCommissionEmployee.java
2    // BasePlusCommissionEmployee class inherits from CommissionEmployee
3    // and accesses the superclass's private data via inherited
4    // public methods.
5
6    public class BasePlusCommissionEmployee extends CommissionEmployee
7    {
8       private double baseSalary; // base salary per week
9
10      // six-argument constructor
11      public BasePlusCommissionEmployee(String firstName, String lastName,
12         String socialSecurityNumber, double grossSales,
13         double commissionRate, double baseSalary)
14      {
15         super(firstName, lastName, socialSecurityNumber,
16            grossSales, commissionRate);
17
18         // if baseSalary is invalid throw exception
19         if (baseSalary < 0.0)
20            throw new IllegalArgumentException(
21               "Base salary must be >= 0.0");
22
23         this.baseSalary = baseSalary;
24      }
25
26      // set base salary
27      public void setBaseSalary(double baseSalary)
28      {
29         if (baseSalary < 0.0)
30            throw new IllegalArgumentException(
31               "Base salary must be >= 0.0");
32
33         this.baseSalary = baseSalary;
34      }
35
36      // return base salary
37      public double getBaseSalary()
38      {
39         return baseSalary;
40      }
41
42      // calculate earnings
43      @Override
44      public double earnings()
45      {
46         return getBaseSalary() + super.earnings();
47      }
48
49      // return String representation of BasePlusCommissionEmployee
50      @Override
51      public String toString()
52      {
```

Fig. 9.11 | BasePlusCommissionEmployee class inherits from CommissionEmployee and accesses the superclass's private data via inherited public methods. (Part 1 of 2.)

```
53          return String.format("%s %s%n%s: %.2f", "base-salaried",
54              super.toString(), "base salary", getBaseSalary());
55      }
56   } // end class BasePlusCommissionEmployee
```

Fig. 9.11 | BasePlusCommissionEmployee class inherits from CommissionEmployee and accesses the superclass's private data via inherited public methods. (Part 2 of 2.)

Class *BasePlusCommissionEmployee's* earnings *Method*

Method earnings (lines 43–47) overrides class CommissionEmployee's earnings method (Fig. 9.10, lines 87–90) to calculate a base-salaried commission employee's earnings. The new version obtains the portion of the earnings based on commission alone by calling CommissionEmployee's earnings method with super.earnings() (line 46), then adds the base salary to this value to calculate the total earnings. Note the syntax used to invoke an *overridden* superclass method from a subclass—place the keyword super and a dot (.) separator before the superclass method name. This method invocation is a good software engineering practice—if a method performs all or some of the actions needed by another method, call that method rather than duplicate its code. By having BasePlusCommissionEmployee's earnings method invoke CommissionEmployee's earnings method to calculate part of a BasePlusCommissionEmployee object's earnings, we *avoid duplicating the code* and *reduce code-maintenance problems*.

Common Programming Error 9.2

When a superclass method is overridden in a subclass, the subclass version often calls the superclass version to do a portion of the work. Failure to prefix the superclass method name with the keyword super and the dot (.) separator when calling the superclass's method causes the subclass method to call itself, potentially creating an error called infinite recursion, which would eventually cause the method-call stack to overflow—a fatal runtime error.

Class *BasePlusCommissionEmployee's* toString *Method*

Similarly, BasePlusCommissionEmployee's toString method (Fig. 9.11, lines 50–55) overrides CommissionEmployee's toString method (Fig. 9.10, lines 93–101) to return a String representation that's appropriate for a base-salaried commission employee. The new version creates part of a BasePlusCommissionEmployee object's String representation (i.e., the String "commission employee" and the values of class CommissionEmployee's private instance variables) by calling CommissionEmployee's toString method with the expression super.toString() (Fig. 9.11, line 54). BasePlusCommissionEmployee's toString method then completes the remainder of a BasePlusCommissionEmployee object's String representation (i.e., the value of class BasePlusCommissionEmployee's base salary).

Testing Class *BasePlusCommissionEmployee*

Class BasePlusCommissionEmployeeTest performs the same manipulations on a BasePlusCommissionEmployee object as in Fig. 9.7 and produces the same output, so we do not show it here. Although each BasePlusCommissionEmployee class you've seen behaves identically, the version in Fig. 9.11 is the best engineered. By using inheritance and by calling methods that hide the data and ensure consistency, we've efficiently and effectively constructed a well-engineered class.

9.5 Constructors in Subclasses

As we explained, instantiating a subclass object begins a chain of constructor calls in which the subclass constructor, before performing its own tasks, explicitly uses super to call one of the constructors in its direct superclass or implicitly calls the superclass's default or no-argument constructor. Similarly, if the superclass is derived from another class—true of every class except Object—the superclass constructor invokes the constructor of the next class up the hierarchy, and so on. The last constructor called in the chain is *always* Object's constructor. The original subclass constructor's body finishes executing *last*. Each super-class's constructor manipulates the superclass instance variables that the subclass object inherits. For example, consider again the CommissionEmployee–BasePlusCommission-Employee hierarchy from Figs. 9.10–9.11. When an app creates a BasePlusCommission-Employee object, its constructor is called. That constructor calls CommissionEmployee's constructor, which in turn calls Object's constructor. Class Object's constructor has an *empty body*, so it immediately returns control to CommissionEmployee's constructor, which then initializes the CommissionEmployee instance variables that are part of the BasePlusCommissionEmployee object. When CommissionEmployee's constructor completes execution, it returns control to BasePlusCommissionEmployee's constructor, which initializes the baseSalary.

> **Software Engineering Observation 9.9**
>
> *Java ensures that even if a constructor does not assign a value to an instance variable, the variable is still initialized to its default value (e.g., 0 for primitive numeric types,* false *for booleans,* null *for references).*

9.6 Class Object

As we discussed earlier in this chapter, all classes in Java inherit directly or indirectly from class Object (package java.lang), so its 11 methods (some are overloaded) are inherited by all other classes. Figure 9.12 summarizes Object's methods. We discuss several Object methods throughout this book (as indicated in Fig. 9.12).

Method	Description
equals	This method compares two objects for equality and returns true if they're equal and false otherwise. The method takes any Object as an argument. When objects of a particular class must be compared for equality, the class should override method equals to compare the *contents* of the two objects. For the requirements of implementing this method (which include also overriding method hashCode), refer to the method's documentation at docs.oracle.com/javase/7/docs/api/java/lang/Object.html#equals(java.lang.Object). The default equals implementation uses operator == to determine whether two references *refer to the same object* in memory. Section 14.3.3 demonstrates class String's equals method and differentiates between comparing String objects with == and with equals.

Fig. 9.12 | Object methods. (Part 1 of 2.)

Method	Description
hashCode	Hashcodes are int values used for high-speed storage and retrieval of information stored in a data structure that's known as a hashtable (see Section 16.11). This method is also called as part of Object's default toString method implementation.
toString	This method (introduced in Section 9.4.1) returns a String representation of an object. The default implementation of this method returns the package name and class name of the object's class typically followed by a hexadecimal representation of the value returned by the object's hashCode method.
wait, notify, notifyAll	Methods notify, notifyAll and the three overloaded versions of wait are related to multithreading, which is discussed in Chapter 20.
getClass	Every object in Java knows its own type at execution time. Method getClass (used in Sections 10.5– and 12.5) returns an object of class Class (package java.lang) that contains information about the object's type, such as its class name (returned by Class method getName).
finalize	This protected method is called by the garbage collector to perform termination housekeeping on an object just before the garbage collector reclaims the object's memory. Recall from Section 8.10 that it's unclear whether, or when, finalize will be called. For this reason, most programmers should avoid method finalize.
clone	This protected method, which takes no arguments and returns an Object reference, makes a copy of the object on which it's called. The default implementation performs a so-called **shallow copy**—instance-variable values in one object are copied into another object of the same type. For reference types, only the references are copied. A typical overridden clone method's implementation would perform a **deep copy** that creates a new object for each reference-type instance variable. *Implementing clone correctly is difficult. For this reason, its use is discouraged.* Some industry experts suggest that object serialization should be used instead. We discuss object serialization in Chapter 15. Recall from Chapter 7 that arrays are objects. As a result, like all other objects, arrays inherit the members of class Object. Every array has an overridden clone method that copies the array. However, if the array stores references to objects, the objects are not copied—a shallow copy is performed.

Fig. 9.12 | Object methods. (Part 2 of 2.)

9.7 Wrap-Up

This chapter introduced inheritance—the ability to create classes by acquiring an existing class's members (without copying and pasting the code) and having the ability to embellish them with new capabilities. You learned the notions of superclasses and subclasses and used keyword extends to create a subclass that inherits members from a superclass. We showed how to use the @Override annotation to prevent unintended overloading by indicating that a method overrides a superclass method. We introduced the access modifier protected; subclass methods can directly access protected superclass members. You learned how to use super to access overridden superclass members. You also saw how constructors are used in inheritance hierarchies. Finally, you learned about the methods of class Object, the direct or indirect superclass of all Java classes.

In Chapter 10, Object-Oriented Programming: Polymorphism and Interfaces, we build on our discussion of inheritance by introducing *polymorphism*—an object-oriented concept that enables us to write programs that conveniently handle, in a more general and convenient manner, objects of a wide variety of classes related by inheritance. After studying Chapter 10, you'll be familiar with classes, objects, encapsulation, inheritance and polymorphism—the key technologies of object-oriented programming.

10

Object-Oriented Programming: Polymorphism and Interfaces

Objectives

In this chapter you'll:

- Learn the concept of polymorphism.

- Use overridden methods to effect polymorphism.

- Distinguish between abstract and concrete classes.

- Declare abstract methods to create abstract classes.

- Learn how polymorphism makes systems extensible and maintainable.

- Determine an object's type at execution time.

- Declare and implement interfaces, and become familiar with the Java SE 8 interface enhancements.

Outline

10.1 Introduction

We continue our study of object-oriented programming by explaining and demonstrating **polymorphism** with inheritance hierarchies. Polymorphism enables you to "program in the *general*" rather than "program in the *specific*." In particular, polymorphism enables you to write programs that process objects that share the same superclass, either directly or indirectly, as if they were all objects of the superclass; this can simplify programming.

Consider the following example of polymorphism. Suppose we create a program that simulates the movement of several types of animals for a biological study. Classes Fish, Frog and Bird represent the types of animals under investigation. Imagine that each class extends superclass Animal, which contains a method move and maintains an animal's current location as *x-y* coordinates. Each subclass implements method move. Our program maintains an Animal array containing references to objects of the various Animal subclasses. To simulate the animals' movements, the program sends each object the *same* message once per second—namely, move. Each specific type of Animal responds to a move message in its own way—a Fish might swim three feet, a Frog might jump five feet and a Bird might fly ten feet. Each object knows how to modify its *x-y* coordinates appropriately for its *specific* type of movement. Relying on each object to know how to "do the right thing" (i.e., do what's appropriate for that type of object) in response to the *same* method call is the key concept of polymorphism. The *same* message (in this case, move) sent to a *variety* of objects has *many forms* of results—hence the term polymorphism.

Implementing for Extensibility

With polymorphism, we can design and implement systems that are easily *extensible*—new classes can be added with little or no modification to the general portions of the program, as long as the new classes are part of the inheritance hierarchy that the program processes generically. The new classes simply "plug right in." The only parts of a program that must be altered are those that require direct knowledge of the new classes that we add to the hierarchy. For example, if we extend class Animal to create class Tortoise (which might respond to a move message by crawling one inch), we need to write only the Tortoise class and the part of the simulation that instantiates a Tortoise object. The portions of the simulation that tell each Animal to move generically can remain the same.

Chapter Overview

First, we discuss common examples of polymorphism. We then provide a simple example demonstrating polymorphic behavior. We use superclass references to manipulate *both* superclass objects and subclass objects polymorphically.

We then present a case study that revisits the employee hierarchy of Section 9.4.5. We develop a simple payroll application that polymorphically calculates the weekly pay of several different types of employees using each employee's earnings method. Though the earnings of each type of employee are calculated in a *specific* way, polymorphism allows us to process the employees "in the *general*." In the case study, we enlarge the hierarchy to include two new classes—SalariedEmployee (for people paid a fixed weekly salary) and HourlyEmployee (for people paid an hourly salary and "time-and-a-half" for overtime). We declare a common set of functionality for all the classes in the updated hierarchy in an "abstract" class, Employee, from which "concrete" classes SalariedEmployee, HourlyEmployee and CommissionEmployee inherit directly and "concrete" class BasePlusCommissionEmployee inherits indirectly. As you'll soon see, *when we invoke each employee's earnings method off a superclass Employee reference (regardless of the employee's type), the correct earnings subclass calculation is performed,* due to Java's polymorphic capabilities.

Programming in the Specific

Occasionally, when performing polymorphic processing, we need to program "in the *specific*." Our Employee case study demonstrates that a program can determine the *type* of an object at *execution time* and act on that object accordingly. In the case study, we've decided that BasePlusCommissionEmployees should receive 10% raises on their base salaries. So, we use these capabilities to determine whether a particular employee object *is a* BasePlusCommissionEmployee. If so, we increase that employee's base salary by 10%.

Interfaces

The chapter continues with an introduction to Java *interfaces*, which are particularly useful for assigning *common* functionality to possibly *unrelated* classes. This allows objects of these classes to be processed polymorphically—objects of classes that **implement** the *same* interface can respond to all of the interface method calls. To demonstrate creating and using interfaces, we modify our payroll application to create a generalized accounts payable application that can calculate payments due for company employees *and* invoice amounts to be billed for purchased goods.

10.2 Polymorphism Examples

Let's consider several additional examples of polymorphism.

Quadrilaterals

If class Rectangle is derived from class Quadrilateral, then a Rectangle object *is a* more *specific* version of a Quadrilateral. Any operation (e.g., calculating the perimeter or the area) that can be performed on a Quadrilateral can also be performed on a Rectangle. These operations can also be performed on other Quadrilaterals, such as Squares, Parallelograms and Trapezoids. The polymorphism occurs when a program invokes a method through a superclass Quadrilateral variable—at execution time, the correct subclass version of the method is called, based on the type of the reference stored in the superclass variable. You'll see a simple code example that illustrates this process in Section 10.3.

Space Objects in a Video Game

Suppose we design a video game that manipulates objects of classes Martian, Venusian, Plutonian, SpaceShip and LaserBeam. Imagine that each class inherits from the superclass SpaceObject, which contains method draw. Each subclass implements this method. A screen manager maintains a collection (e.g., a SpaceObject array) of references to objects of the various classes. To refresh the screen, the screen manager periodically sends each object the *same* message—namely, draw. However, each object responds its *own* way, based on its class. For example, a Martian object might draw itself in red with green eyes and the appropriate number of antennae. A SpaceShip object might draw itself as a bright silver flying saucer. A LaserBeam object might draw itself as a bright red beam across the screen. Again, the *same* message (in this case, draw) sent to a *variety* of objects has "many forms" of results.

A screen manager might use polymorphism to facilitate adding new classes to a system with minimal modifications to the system's code. Suppose that we want to add Mercurian objects to our video game. To do so, we'd build a class Mercurian that extends SpaceObject and provides its own draw method implementation. When Mercurian objects appear in the SpaceObject collection, the screen-manager code *invokes method draw, exactly as it does for every other object in the collection, regardless of its type.* So the new Mercurian objects simply "plug right in" without any modification of the screen manager code by the programmer. Thus, without modifying the system (other than to build new classes and modify the code that creates new objects), you can use polymorphism to conveniently include additional types that were not even considered when the system was created.

Software Engineering Observation 10.1

Polymorphism enables you to deal in generalities and let the execution-time environment handle the specifics. You can tell objects to behave in manners appropriate to those objects, without knowing their specific types, as long as they belong to the same inheritance hierarchy.

Software Engineering Observation 10.2

Polymorphism promotes extensibility: Software that invokes polymorphic behavior is independent of the object types to which messages are sent. New object types that can respond to existing method calls can be incorporated into a system without modifying the base system. Only client code that instantiates new objects must be modified to accommodate new types.

10.3 Demonstrating Polymorphic Behavior

Section 9.4 created a class hierarchy, in which class BasePlusCommissionEmployee inherited from CommissionEmployee. The examples in that section manipulated CommissionEmployee and BasePlusCommissionEmployee objects by using references to them to invoke their methods—we aimed superclass variables at superclass objects and subclass variables at subclass objects. These assignments are natural and straightforward—superclass variables are *intended* to refer to superclass objects, and subclass variables are *intended* to refer to subclass objects. However, as you'll soon see, other assignments are possible.

In the next example, we aim a *superclass* reference at a *subclass* object. We then show how invoking a method on a subclass object via a superclass reference invokes the *subclass* functionality—the type of the *referenced object*, *not* the type of the *variable*, determines which method is called. This example demonstrates that *an object of a subclass can be treated as an object of its superclass,* enabling various interesting manipulations. A program can create an array of superclass variables that refer to objects of many subclass types. This is allowed because each subclass object *is an* object of its superclass. For instance, we can assign the reference of a BasePlusCommissionEmployee object to a superclass CommissionEmployee variable, because a BasePlusCommissionEmployee *is a* CommissionEmployee—so we can treat a BasePlusCommissionEmployee as a CommissionEmployee.

As you'll learn later in the chapter, you *cannot treat a superclass object as a subclass object,* because a superclass object is *not* an object of any of its subclasses. For example, we cannot assign the reference of a CommissionEmployee object to a subclass BasePlusCommissionEmployee variable, because a CommissionEmployee is *not* a BasePlusCommissionEmployee—a CommissionEmployee does *not* have a baseSalary instance variable and does *not* have methods setBaseSalary and getBaseSalary. The *is-a* relationship applies only *up the hierarchy* from a subclass to its direct (and indirect) superclasses, and *not* vice versa (i.e., not down the hierarchy from a superclass to its subclasses or indirect subclasses).

The Java compiler *does* allow the assignment of a superclass reference to a subclass variable if we explicitly *cast* the superclass reference to the subclass type. Why would we ever want to perform such an assignment? A superclass reference can be used to invoke *only* the methods declared in the superclass—attempting to invoke *subclass-only* methods through a superclass reference results in compilation errors. If a program needs to perform a subclass-specific operation on a subclass object referenced by a superclass variable, the program must first cast the superclass reference to a subclass reference through a technique known as **downcasting**. This enables the program to invoke subclass methods that are *not* in the superclass. We demonstrate the mechanics of downcasting in Section 10.5.

Software Engineering Observation 10.3
Although it's allowed, you should generally avoid downcasting.

The example in Fig. 10.1 demonstrates three ways to use superclass and subclass variables to store references to superclass and subclass objects. The first two are straightforward—as in Section 9.4, we assign a superclass reference to a superclass variable, and a subclass reference to a subclass variable. Then we demonstrate the relationship between subclasses and superclasses (i.e., the *is-a* relationship) by assigning a subclass reference to a superclass variable. This program uses classes CommissionEmployee and BasePlusCommissionEmployee from Fig. 9.10 and Fig. 9.11, respectively.

```
 1   // Fig. 10.1: PolymorphismTest.java
 2   // Assigning superclass and subclass references to superclass and
 3   // subclass variables.
 4
 5   public class PolymorphismTest
 6   {
 7      public static void main(String[] args)
 8      {
 9         // assign superclass reference to superclass variable
10         CommissionEmployee commissionEmployee = new CommissionEmployee(
11            "Sue", "Jones", "222-22-2222", 10000, .06);
12
13         // assign subclass reference to subclass variable
14         BasePlusCommissionEmployee basePlusCommissionEmployee =
15            new BasePlusCommissionEmployee(
16            "Bob", "Lewis", "333-33-3333", 5000, .04, 300);
17
18         // invoke toString on superclass object using superclass variable
19         System.out.printf("%s %s:%n%n%s%n%n",
20            "Call CommissionEmployee's toString with superclass reference ",
21            "to superclass object", commissionEmployee.toString());
22
23         // invoke toString on subclass object using subclass variable
24         System.out.printf("%s %s:%n%n%s%n%n",
25            "Call BasePlusCommissionEmployee's toString with subclass",
26            "reference to subclass object",
27            basePlusCommissionEmployee.toString());
28
29         // invoke toString on subclass object using superclass variable
30         CommissionEmployee commissionEmployee2 =
31            basePlusCommissionEmployee;
32         System.out.printf("%s %s:%n%n%s%n",
33            "Call BasePlusCommissionEmployee's toString with superclass",
34            "reference to subclass object", commissionEmployee2.toString());
35      } // end main
36   } // end class PolymorphismTest
```

```
Call CommissionEmployee's toString with superclass reference to superclass
object:

commission employee: Sue Jones
social security number: 222-22-2222
gross sales: 10000.00
commission rate: 0.06

Call BasePlusCommissionEmployee's toString with subclass reference to
subclass object:

base-salaried commission employee: Bob Lewis
social security number: 333-33-3333
gross sales: 5000.00
commission rate: 0.04
base salary: 300.00
```

Fig. 10.1 | Assigning superclass and subclass references to superclass and subclass variables. (Part 1 of 2.)

```
Call BasePlusCommissionEmployee's toString with superclass reference to
subclass object:

base-salaried commission employee: Bob Lewis
social security number: 333-33-3333
gross sales: 5000.00
commission rate: 0.04
base salary: 300.00
```

Fig. 10.1 | Assigning superclass and subclass references to superclass and subclass variables. (Part 2 of 2.)

In Fig. 10.1, lines 10–11 create a `CommissionEmployee` object and assign its reference to a `CommissionEmployee` variable. Lines 14–16 create a `BasePlusCommissionEmployee` object and assign its reference to a `BasePlusCommissionEmployee` variable. These assignments are natural—for example, a `CommissionEmployee` variable's primary purpose is to hold a reference to a `CommissionEmployee` object. Lines 19–21 use `commissionEmployee` to invoke `toString` *explicitly*. Because `commissionEmployee` refers to a `CommissionEmployee` object, superclass `CommissionEmployee`'s version of `toString` is called. Similarly, lines 24–27 use `basePlusCommissionEmployee` to invoke `toString` *explicitly* on the `BasePlusCommissionEmployee` object. This invokes subclass `BasePlusCommissionEmployee`'s version of `toString`.

Lines 30–31 then assign the reference of subclass object `basePlusCommissionEmployee` to a superclass `CommissionEmployee` variable, which lines 32–34 use to invoke method `toString`. *When a superclass variable contains a reference to a subclass object, and that reference is used to call a method, the subclass version of the method is called.* Hence, `commissionEmployee2.toString()` in line 34 actually calls class `BasePlusCommissionEmployee`'s `toString` method. The Java compiler allows this "crossover" because an object of a subclass *is an* object of its superclass (but *not* vice versa). When the compiler encounters a method call made through a variable, the compiler determines if the method can be called by checking the variable's class type. If that class contains the proper method declaration (or inherits one), the call is compiled. At execution time, the type of the object to which the variable refers determines the actual method to use. This process, called *dynamic binding*, is discussed in detail in Section 10.5.

10.4 Abstract Classes and Methods

When we think of a class, we assume that programs will create objects of that type. Sometimes it's useful to declare classes—called **abstract classes**—for which you *never* intend to create objects. Because they're used only as superclasses in inheritance hierarchies, we refer to them as **abstract superclasses**. These classes cannot be used to instantiate objects, because, as we'll soon see, abstract classes are *incomplete*. Subclasses must declare the "missing pieces" to become "concrete" classes, from which you can instantiate objects. Otherwise, these subclasses, too, will be abstract. We demonstrate abstract classes in Section 10.5.

Purpose of Abstract Classes
An abstract class's purpose is to provide an appropriate superclass from which other classes can inherit and thus share a common design. In the `Shape` hierarchy of Fig. 9.3, for exam-

ple, subclasses inherit the notion of what it means to be a Shape—perhaps common attributes such as location, color and borderThickness, and behaviors such as draw, move, resize and changeColor. Classes that can be used to instantiate objects are called **concrete classes**. Such classes provide implementations of *every* method they declare (some of the implementations can be inherited). For example, we could derive concrete classes Circle, Square and Triangle from abstract superclass TwoDimensionalShape. Similarly, we could derive concrete classes Sphere, Cube and Tetrahedron from abstract superclass ThreeDimensionalShape. Abstract superclasses are *too general* to create real objects—they specify only what is common among subclasses. We need to be more *specific* before we can create objects. For example, if you send the draw message to abstract class TwoDimensionalShape, the class knows that two-dimensional shapes should be *drawable*, but it does not know what *specific* shape to draw, so it cannot implement a real draw method. Concrete classes provide the specifics that make it reasonable to instantiate objects.

Not all hierarchies contain abstract classes. However, you'll often write client code that uses only abstract superclass types to reduce the client code's dependencies on a range of subclass types. For example, you can write a method with a parameter of an abstract superclass type. When called, such a method can receive an object of *any* concrete class that directly or indirectly extends the superclass specified as the parameter's type.

Abstract classes sometimes constitute several levels of a hierarchy. For example, the Shape hierarchy of Fig. 9.3 begins with abstract class Shape. On the next level of the hierarchy are *abstract* classes TwoDimensionalShape and ThreeDimensionalShape. The next level of the hierarchy declares *concrete* classes for TwoDimensionalShapes (Circle, Square and Triangle) and for ThreeDimensionalShapes (Sphere, Cube and Tetrahedron).

Declaring an Abstract Class and Abstract Methods

You make a class abstract by declaring it with keyword **abstract**. An abstract class normally contains one or more **abstract methods**. An abstract method is an *instance method* with keyword abstract in its declaration, as in

```
public abstract void draw(); // abstract method
```

Abstract methods do *not* provide implementations. A class that contains *any* abstract methods must be explicitly declared abstract even if that class contains some concrete (nonabstract) methods. Each concrete subclass of an abstract superclass also must provide concrete implementations of each of the superclass's abstract methods. Constructors and static methods cannot be declared abstract. Constructors are *not* inherited, so an abstract constructor could never be implemented. Though non-private static methods are inherited, they cannot be overridden. Since abstract methods are meant to be overridden so that they can process objects based on their types, it would not make sense to declare a static method as abstract.

Software Engineering Observation 10.4

An abstract class declares common attributes and behaviors (both abstract and concrete) of the various classes in a class hierarchy. An abstract class typically contains one or more abstract methods that subclasses must override if they are to be concrete. The instance variables and concrete methods of an abstract class are subject to the normal rules of inheritance.

Common Programming Error 10.1

Attempting to instantiate an object of an abstract class is a compilation error.

Common Programming Error 10.2

Failure to implement a superclass's abstract methods in a subclass is a compilation error unless the subclass is also declared abstract.

Using Abstract Classes to Declare Variables

Although we cannot instantiate objects of abstract superclasses, you'll soon see that we *can* use abstract superclasses to declare variables that can hold references to objects of *any* concrete class *derived from* those abstract superclasses. We'll use such variables to manipulate subclass objects *polymorphically*. You also can use abstract superclass names to invoke static methods declared in those abstract superclasses.

Consider another application of polymorphism. A drawing program needs to display many shapes, including types of new shapes that you'll *add* to the system *after* writing the drawing program. The drawing program might need to display shapes, such as Circles, Triangles, Rectangles or others, that derive from abstract class Shape. The drawing program uses Shape variables to manage the objects that are displayed. To draw any object in this inheritance hierarchy, the drawing program uses a superclass Shape variable containing a reference to the subclass object to invoke the object's draw method. This method is declared abstract in superclass Shape, so each concrete subclass *must* implement method draw in a manner specific to that shape—each object in the Shape inheritance hierarchy *knows how to draw itself*. The drawing program does not have to worry about the type of each object or whether the program has ever encountered objects of that type.

Layered Software Systems

Polymorphism is particularly effective for implementing so-called *layered software systems*. In operating systems, for example, each type of physical device could operate quite differently from the others. Even so, commands to read or write data from and to devices may have a certain uniformity. For each device, the operating system uses a piece of software called a *device driver* to control all communication between the system and the device. The write message sent to a device-driver object needs to be interpreted specifically in the context of that driver and how it manipulates devices of a specific type. However, the write call itself really is no different from the write to any other device in the system—place some number of bytes from memory onto that device. An object-oriented operating system might use an abstract superclass to provide an "interface" appropriate for all device drivers. Then, through inheritance from that abstract superclass, subclasses are formed that all behave similarly. The device-driver methods are declared as abstract methods in the abstract superclass. The implementations of these abstract methods are provided in the concrete subclasses that correspond to the specific types of device drivers. New devices are always being developed, often long after the operating system has been released. When you buy a new device, it comes with a device driver provided by the device vendor. The device is immediately operational after you connect it to your computer and install the driver. This is another elegant example of how polymorphism makes systems *extensible*.

10.5 Case Study: Payroll System Using Polymorphism

This section reexamines the CommissionEmployee-BasePlusCommissionEmployee hierarchy that we explored throughout Section 9.4. Now we use an abstract method and polymorphism to perform payroll calculations based on an enhanced employee inheritance hierarchy that meets the following requirements:

> *A company pays its employees on a weekly basis. The employees are of four types: Salaried employees are paid a fixed weekly salary regardless of the number of hours worked, hourly employees are paid by the hour and receive overtime pay (i.e., 1.5 times their hourly salary rate) for all hours worked in excess of 40 hours, commission employees are paid a percentage of their sales and base-salaried commission employees receive a base salary plus a percentage of their sales. For the current pay period, the company has decided to reward salaried-commission employees by adding 10% to their base salaries. The company wants you to write an application that performs its payroll calculations polymorphically.*

We use abstract class Employee to represent the general concept of an employee. The classes that extend Employee are SalariedEmployee, CommissionEmployee and HourlyEmployee. Class BasePlusCommissionEmployee—which extends CommissionEmployee—represents the last employee type. The UML class diagram in Fig. 10.2 shows the inheritance hierarchy for our polymorphic employee-payroll application. Abstract class name Employee is italicized—a convention of the UML.

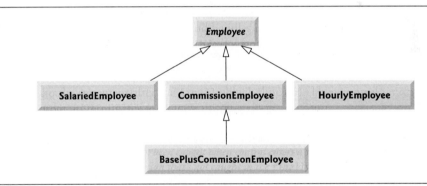

Fig. 10.2 | Employee hierarchy UML class diagram.

Abstract superclass Employee declares the "interface" to the hierarchy—that is, the set of methods that a program can invoke on all Employee objects. We use the term "interface" here in a *general* sense to refer to the various ways programs can communicate with objects of *any* Employee subclass. Be careful not to confuse the general notion of an "interface" with the formal notion of a Java interface, the subject of Section 10.9. Each employee, regardless of the way his or her earnings are calculated, has a first name, a last name and a social security number, so private instance variables firstName, lastName and social-SecurityNumber appear in abstract superclass Employee.

The diagram in Fig. 10.3 shows each of the five classes in the hierarchy down the left side and methods earnings and toString across the top. For each class, the diagram shows the desired results of each method. We do not list superclass Employee's *get* methods because they're *not* overridden in any of the subclasses—each of these methods is inherited and used "as is" by each subclass.

	earnings	toString
Employee	abstract	*firstName lastName* social security number: *SSN*
Salaried- Employee	weeklySalary	salaried employee: *firstName lastName* social security number: *SSN* weekly salary: *weeklySalary*

Hourly-
Employee
	if (hours <= 40)
	  wage * hours
	else if (hours > 40)
	{
	  40 * wage +
	  (hours - 40) *
	  wage * 1.5
	}
		hourly employee: *firstName lastName*
		social security number: *SSN*
		hourly wage: *wage*; hours worked: *hours*

Commission- Employee	commissionRate * grossSales	commission employee: *firstName lastName* social security number: *SSN* gross sales: *grossSales*; commission rate: *commissionRate*
BasePlus- Commission- Employee	(commissionRate * grossSales) + baseSalary	base salaried commission employee: *firstName lastName* social security number: *SSN* gross sales: *grossSales*; commission rate: *commissionRate*; base salary: *baseSalary*

Fig. 10.3 | Polymorphic interface for the Employee hierarchy classes.

The following sections implement the Employee class hierarchy of Fig. 10.2. The first section implements *abstract superclass* Employee. The next four sections each implement one of the *concrete* classes. The last section implements a test program that builds objects of all these classes and processes those objects polymorphically.

10.5.1 Abstract Superclass Employee

Class Employee (Fig. 10.4) provides methods earnings and toString, in addition to the *get* methods that return the values of Employee's instance variables. An earnings method certainly applies *generically* to all employees. But each earnings calculation depends on the employee's particular class. So we declare earnings as abstract in superclass Employee because a *specific* default implementation does not make sense for that method—there isn't enough information to determine what amount earnings should return.

Each subclass overrides earnings with an appropriate implementation. To calculate an employee's earnings, the program assigns to a superclass Employee variable a reference to the employee's object, then invokes the earnings method on that variable. We maintain an array of Employee variables, each holding a reference to an Employee object. You *cannot* use class Employee directly to create Employee *objects*, because Employee is an *abstract* class. Due to inheritance, however, all objects of all Employee subclasses may be thought of as Employee objects. The program will iterate through the array and call method `earnings` for each `Employee` object. Java processes these method calls *polymorphically*. Declaring `earnings` as an `abstract` method in `Employee` enables the calls to `earnings` through `Employee` variables to compile and forces every direct *concrete* subclass of `Employee` to *override* `earnings`.

Method `toString` in class `Employee` returns a `String` containing the first name, last name and social security number of the employee. As we'll see, each subclass of `Employee` *overrides* method `toString` to create a `String` representation of an object of that class that contains the employee's type (e.g., `"salaried employee:"`) followed by the rest of the employee's information.

Let's consider class `Employee`'s declaration (Fig. 10.4). The class includes a constructor that receives the first name, last name and social security number (lines 11–17); *get* methods that return the first name, last name and social security number (lines 20–23, 26–29 and 32–35, respectively); method `toString` (lines 38–43), which returns the `String` representation of an `Employee`; and abstract method `earnings` (line 46), which will be implemented by each of the *concrete* subclasses. The `Employee` constructor does *not* validate its parameters in this example; normally, such validation should be provided.

```java
1   // Fig. 10.4: Employee.java
2   // Employee abstract superclass.
3
4   public abstract class Employee
5   {
6      private final String firstName;
7      private final String lastName;
8      private final String socialSecurityNumber;
9
10     // constructor
11     public Employee(String firstName, String lastName,
12        String socialSecurityNumber)
13     {
14        this.firstName = firstName;
15        this.lastName = lastName;
16        this.socialSecurityNumber = socialSecurityNumber;
17     }
18
19     // return first name
20     public String getFirstName()
21     {
22        return firstName;
23     }
24
25     // return last name
26     public String getLastName()
27     {
28        return lastName;
29     }
30
31     // return social security number
32     public String getSocialSecurityNumber()
33     {
```

Fig. 10.4 | `Employee` abstract superclass. (Part 1 of 2.)

```
34          return socialSecurityNumber;
35       }
36
37       // return String representation of Employee object
38       @Override
39       public String toString()
40       {
41          return String.format("%s %s%nsocial security number: %s",
42             getFirstName(), getLastName(), getSocialSecurityNumber());
43       }
44
45       // abstract method must be overridden by concrete subclasses
46       public abstract double earnings(); // no implementation here
47    } // end abstract class Employee
```

Fig. 10.4 | Employee abstract superclass. (Part 2 of 2.)

Why did we decide to declare earnings as an abstract method? It simply does not make sense to provide a *specific* implementation of this method in class Employee. We cannot calculate the earnings for a *general* Employee—we first must know the *specific* type of Employee to determine the appropriate earnings calculation. By declaring this method abstract, we indicate that each concrete subclass *must* provide an appropriate earnings implementation and that a program will be able to use superclass Employee variables to invoke method earnings *polymorphically* for any type of Employee.

10.5.2 Concrete Subclass SalariedEmployee

Class SalariedEmployee (Fig. 10.5) extends class Employee (line 4) and overrides *abstract* method earnings (lines 38–42), which makes SalariedEmployee a *concrete* class. The class includes a constructor (lines 9–19) that receives a first name, a last name, a social security number and a weekly salary; a *set* method to assign a new *nonnegative* value to instance variable weeklySalary (lines 22–29); a *get* method to return weeklySalary's value (lines 32–35); a method earnings (lines 38–42) to calculate a SalariedEmployee's earnings; and a method toString (lines 45–50), which returns a String including "salaried employee: " followed by employee-specific information produced by superclass Employee's toString method and Salaried-Employee's getWeeklySalary method. Class SalariedEmployee's constructor passes the first name, last name and social security number to the Employee constructor (line 12) to initialize the private instance variables of the superclass. Once again, we've duplicated the weeklySalary validation code in the constructor and the setWeekly-Salary method. Recall that more complex validation could be placed in a static class method that's called from the constructor and the *set* method.

>
> **Error-Prevention Tip 10.1**
> *We've said that you should not call a class's instance methods from its constructors—you can call static class methods and make the required call to one of the superclass's constructors. If you follow this advice, you'll avoid the problem of calling the class's overridable methods either directly or indirectly, which can lead to runtime errors.*

Method earnings overrides Employee's *abstract* method earnings to provide a *concrete* implementation that returns the SalariedEmployee's weekly salary. If we do not

```
1    // Fig. 10.5: SalariedEmployee.java
2    // SalariedEmployee concrete class extends abstract class Employee.
3
4    public class SalariedEmployee extends Employee
5    {
6       private double weeklySalary;
7
8       // constructor
9       public SalariedEmployee(String firstName, String lastName,
10          String socialSecurityNumber, double weeklySalary)
11      {
12         super(firstName, lastName, socialSecurityNumber);
13
14         if (weeklySalary < 0.0)
15            throw new IllegalArgumentException(
16               "Weekly salary must be >= 0.0");
17
18         this.weeklySalary = weeklySalary;
19      }
20
21      // set salary
22      public void setWeeklySalary(double weeklySalary)
23      {
24         if (weeklySalary < 0.0)
25            throw new IllegalArgumentException(
26               "Weekly salary must be >= 0.0");
27
28         this.weeklySalary = weeklySalary;
29      }
30
31      // return salary
32      public double getWeeklySalary()
33      {
34         return weeklySalary;
35      }
36
37      // calculate earnings; override abstract method earnings in Employee
38      @Override
39      public double earnings()
40      {
41         return getWeeklySalary();
42      }
43
44      // return String representation of SalariedEmployee object
45      @Override
46      public String toString()
47      {
48         return String.format("salaried employee: %s%n%s: $%,.2f",
49            super.toString(), "weekly salary", getWeeklySalary());
50      }
51   } // end class SalariedEmployee
```

Fig. 10.5 | SalariedEmployee concrete class extends abstract class Employee.

implement earnings, class SalariedEmployee must be declared abstract—otherwise, class SalariedEmployee will not compile. Of course, we want SalariedEmployee to be a *concrete* class in this example.

Method toString (lines 45–50) overrides Employee method toString. If class SalariedEmployee did *not* override toString, SalariedEmployee would have inherited the Employee version of toString. In that case, SalariedEmployee's toString method would simply return the employee's full name and social security number, which does *not* adequately represent a SalariedEmployee. To produce a complete String representation of a SalariedEmployee, the subclass's toString method returns "salaried employee: " followed by the superclass Employee-specific information (i.e., first name, last name and social security number) obtained by invoking the *superclass's* toString method (line 49)—this is a nice example of *code reuse*. The String representation of a SalariedEmployee also contains the employee's weekly salary obtained by invoking the class's getWeeklySalary method.

10.5.3 Concrete Subclass HourlyEmployee

Class HourlyEmployee (Fig. 10.6) also extends Employee (line 4). The class includes a constructor (lines 10–25) that receives a first name, a last name, a social security number, an hourly wage and the number of hours worked. Lines 28–35 and 44–51 declare *set* methods that assign new values to instance variables wage and hours, respectively. Method setWage (lines 28–35) ensures that wage is *nonnegative*, and method setHours (lines 44–51) ensures that the value of hours is between 0 and 168 (the total number of hours in a week) inclusive. Class HourlyEmployee also includes *get* methods (lines 38–41 and 54–57) to return the values of wage and hours, respectively; a method earnings (lines 60–67) to calculate an HourlyEmployee's earnings; and a method toString (lines 70–76), which returns a String containing the employee's type ("hourly employee: ") and the employee-specific information. The HourlyEmployee constructor, like the SalariedEmployee constructor, passes the first name, last name and social security number to the superclass Employee constructor (line 13) to initialize the private instance variables. In addition, method toString calls *superclass* method toString (line 74) to obtain the Employee-specific information (i.e., first name, last name and social security number)—this is another nice example of *code reuse*.

```
1   // Fig. 10.6: HourlyEmployee.java
2   // HourlyEmployee class extends Employee.
3
4   public class HourlyEmployee extends Employee
5   {
6      private double wage; // wage per hour
7      private double hours; // hours worked for week
8
9      // constructor
10     public HourlyEmployee(String firstName, String lastName,
11        String socialSecurityNumber, double wage, double hours)
12     {
13        super(firstName, lastName, socialSecurityNumber);
14
```

Fig. 10.6 | HourlyEmployee class extends Employee. (Part 1 of 3.)

```
15          if (wage < 0.0) // validate wage
16              throw new IllegalArgumentException(
17                  "Hourly wage must be >= 0.0");
18
19          if ((hours < 0.0) || (hours > 168.0)) // validate hours
20              throw new IllegalArgumentException(
21                  "Hours worked must be >= 0.0 and <= 168.0");
22
23          this.wage = wage;
24          this.hours = hours;
25      }
26
27      // set wage
28      public void setWage(double wage)
29      {
30          if (wage < 0.0) // validate wage
31              throw new IllegalArgumentException(
32                  "Hourly wage must be >= 0.0");
33
34          this.wage = wage;
35      }
36
37      // return wage
38      public double getWage()
39      {
40          return wage;
41      }
42
43      // set hours worked
44      public void setHours(double hours)
45      {
46          if ((hours < 0.0) || (hours > 168.0)) // validate hours
47              throw new IllegalArgumentException(
48                  "Hours worked must be >= 0.0 and <= 168.0");
49
50          this.hours = hours;
51      }
52
53      // return hours worked
54      public double getHours()
55      {
56          return hours;
57      }
58
59      // calculate earnings; override abstract method earnings in Employee
60      @Override
61      public double earnings()
62      {
63          if (getHours() <= 40) // no overtime
64              return getWage() * getHours();
65          else
66              return 40 * getWage() + (getHours() - 40) * getWage() * 1.5;
67      }
```

Fig. 10.6 | HourlyEmployee class extends Employee. (Part 2 of 3.)

```
68
69     // return String representation of HourlyEmployee object
70     @Override
71     public String toString()
72     {
73        return String.format("hourly employee: %s%n%s: $%,.2f; %s: %,.2f",
74           super.toString(), "hourly wage", getWage(),
75           "hours worked", getHours());
76     }
77  } // end class HourlyEmployee
```

Fig. 10.6 | HourlyEmployee class extends Employee. (Part 3 of 3.)

10.5.4 Concrete Subclass CommissionEmployee

Class CommissionEmployee (Fig. 10.7) extends class Employee (line 4). The class includes a constructor (lines 10–25) that takes a first name, a last name, a social security number, a sales amount and a commission rate; *set* methods (lines 28–34 and 43–50) to assign valid new values to instance variables commissionRate and grossSales, respectively; *get* methods (lines 37–40 and 53–56) that retrieve the values of these instance variables; method earnings (lines 59–63) to calculate a CommissionEmployee's earnings; and method toString (lines 66–73), which returns the employee's type, namely, "commission employee: " and employee-specific information. The constructor also passes the first name, last name and social security number to *superclass* Employee's constructor (line 14) to initialize Employee's private instance variables. Method toString calls *superclass* method toString (line 70) to obtain the Employee-specific information (i.e., first name, last name and social security number).

```
1   // Fig. 10.7: CommissionEmployee.java
2   // CommissionEmployee class extends Employee.
3
4   public class CommissionEmployee extends Employee
5   {
6      private double grossSales; // gross weekly sales
7      private double commissionRate; // commission percentage
8
9      // constructor
10     public CommissionEmployee(String firstName, String lastName,
11        String socialSecurityNumber, double grossSales,
12        double commissionRate)
13     {
14        super(firstName, lastName, socialSecurityNumber);
15
16        if (commissionRate <= 0.0 || commissionRate >= 1.0) // validate
17           throw new IllegalArgumentException(
18              "Commission rate must be > 0.0 and < 1.0");
19
20        if (grossSales < 0.0) // validate
21           throw new IllegalArgumentException("Gross sales must be >= 0.0");
22
```

Fig. 10.7 | CommissionEmployee class extends Employee. (Part 1 of 2.)

```
23            this.grossSales = grossSales;
24            this.commissionRate = commissionRate;
25        }
26
27        // set gross sales amount
28        public void setGrossSales(double grossSales)
29        {
30            if (grossSales < 0.0) // validate
31                throw new IllegalArgumentException("Gross sales must be >= 0.0");
32
33            this.grossSales = grossSales;
34        }
35
36        // return gross sales amount
37        public double getGrossSales()
38        {
39            return grossSales;
40        }
41
42        // set commission rate
43        public void setCommissionRate(double commissionRate)
44        {
45            if (commissionRate <= 0.0 || commissionRate >= 1.0) // validate
46                throw new IllegalArgumentException(
47                    "Commission rate must be > 0.0 and < 1.0");
48
49            this.commissionRate = commissionRate;
50        }
51
52        // return commission rate
53        public double getCommissionRate()
54        {
55            return commissionRate;
56        }
57
58        // calculate earnings; override abstract method earnings in Employee
59        @Override
60        public double earnings()
61        {
62            return getCommissionRate() * getGrossSales();
63        }
64
65        // return String representation of CommissionEmployee object
66        @Override
67        public String toString()
68        {
69            return String.format("%s: %s%n%s: $%,.2f; %s: %.2f",
70                "commission employee", super.toString(),
71                "gross sales", getGrossSales(),
72                "commission rate", getCommissionRate());
73        }
74    } // end class CommissionEmployee
```

Fig. 10.7 | CommissionEmployee class extends Employee. (Part 2 of 2.)

10.5.5 Indirect Concrete Subclass BasePlusCommissionEmployee

Class BasePlusCommissionEmployee (Fig. 10.8) extends class CommissionEmployee (line 4) and therefore is an *indirect* subclass of class Employee. Class BasePlusCommission-Employee has a constructor (lines 9–20) that receives a first name, a last name, a social security number, a sales amount, a commission rate and a base salary. It then passes all of these except the base salary to the CommissionEmployee constructor (lines 13–14) to initialize the superclass instance variables. BasePlusCommissionEmployee also contains a *set* method (lines 23–29) to assign a new value to instance variable baseSalary and a *get* method (lines 32–35) to return baseSalary's value. Method earnings (lines 38–42) calculates a BasePlusCommissionEmployee's earnings. Line 41 in method earnings calls *superclass* CommissionEmployee's earnings method to calculate the commission-based portion of the employee's earnings—this is another nice example of *code reuse*. Base-PlusCommissionEmployee's toString method (lines 45–51) creates a String representation of a BasePlusCommissionEmployee that contains "base-salaried", followed by the String obtained by invoking *superclass* CommissionEmployee's toString method (line 49), then the base salary. The result is a String beginning with "base-salaried commission employee" followed by the rest of the BasePlusCommissionEmployee's information. Recall that CommissionEmployee's toString obtains the employee's first name, last name and social security number by invoking the toString method of its *superclass* (i.e., Employee)—yet another example of *code reuse*. BasePlusCommissionEmployee's toString initiates a *chain of method calls* that span all three levels of the Employee hierarchy.

```java
1   // Fig. 10.8: BasePlusCommissionEmployee.java
2   // BasePlusCommissionEmployee class extends CommissionEmployee.
3
4   public class BasePlusCommissionEmployee extends CommissionEmployee
5   {
6      private double baseSalary; // base salary per week
7
8      // constructor
9      public BasePlusCommissionEmployee(String firstName, String lastName,
10        String socialSecurityNumber, double grossSales,
11        double commissionRate, double baseSalary)
12     {
13        super(firstName, lastName, socialSecurityNumber,
14           grossSales, commissionRate);
15
16        if (baseSalary < 0.0) // validate baseSalary
17           throw new IllegalArgumentException("Base salary must be >= 0.0");
18
19        this.baseSalary = baseSalary;
20     }
21
22     // set base salary
23     public void setBaseSalary(double baseSalary)
24     {
25        if (baseSalary < 0.0) // validate baseSalary
26           throw new IllegalArgumentException("Base salary must be >= 0.0");
```

Fig. 10.8 | BasePlusCommissionEmployee class extends CommissionEmployee. (Part 1 of 2.)

```
27
28          this.baseSalary = baseSalary;
29      }
30
31      // return base salary
32      public double getBaseSalary()
33      {
34          return baseSalary;
35      }
36
37      // calculate earnings; override method earnings in CommissionEmployee
38      @Override
39      public double earnings()
40      {
41          return getBaseSalary() + super.earnings();
42      }
43
44      // return String representation of BasePlusCommissionEmployee object
45      @Override
46      public String toString()
47      {
48          return String.format("%s %s; %s: $%,.2f",
49              "base-salaried", super.toString(),
50              "base salary", getBaseSalary());
51      }
52  } // end class BasePlusCommissionEmployee
```

Fig. 10.8 | BasePlusCommissionEmployee class extends CommissionEmployee. (Part 2 of 2.)

10.5.6 Polymorphic Processing, Operator instanceof and Downcasting

To test our Employee hierarchy, the application in Fig. 10.9 creates an object of each of the four *concrete* classes SalariedEmployee, HourlyEmployee, CommissionEmployee and Base-PlusCommissionEmployee. The program manipulates these objects *nonpolymorphically*, via variables of each object's own type, then *polymorphically*, using an array of Employee variables. While processing the objects polymorphically, the program increases the base salary of each BasePlusCommissionEmployee by 10%—this requires *determining the object's type at execution time*. Finally, the program polymorphically determines and outputs the *type* of each object in the Employee array. Lines 9–18 create objects of each of the four concrete Employee subclasses. Lines 22–30 output the String representation and earnings of each of these objects *nonpolymorphically*. Each object's toString method is called *implicitly* by printf when the object is output as a String with the %s format specifier.

```
1   // Fig. 10.9: PayrollSystemTest.java
2   // Employee hierarchy test program.
3
4   public class PayrollSystemTest
5   {
```

Fig. 10.9 | Employee hierarchy test program. (Part 1 of 4.)

```
 6      public static void main(String[] args)
 7      {
 8         // create subclass objects
 9         SalariedEmployee salariedEmployee =
10            new SalariedEmployee("John", "Smith", "111-11-1111", 800.00);
11         HourlyEmployee hourlyEmployee =
12            new HourlyEmployee("Karen", "Price", "222-22-2222", 16.75, 40);
13         CommissionEmployee commissionEmployee =
14            new CommissionEmployee(
15               "Sue", "Jones", "333-33-3333", 10000, .06);
16         BasePlusCommissionEmployee basePlusCommissionEmployee =
17            new BasePlusCommissionEmployee(
18               "Bob", "Lewis", "444-44-4444", 5000, .04, 300);
19
20         System.out.println("Employees processed individually:");
21
22         System.out.printf("%n%s%n%s: $%,.2f%n%n",
23            salariedEmployee, "earned", salariedEmployee.earnings());
24         System.out.printf("%s%n%s: $%,.2f%n%n",
25            hourlyEmployee, "earned", hourlyEmployee.earnings());
26         System.out.printf("%s%n%s: $%,.2f%n%n",
27            commissionEmployee, "earned", commissionEmployee.earnings());
28         System.out.printf("%s%n%s: $%,.2f%n%n",
29            basePlusCommissionEmployee,
30            "earned", basePlusCommissionEmployee.earnings());
31
32         // create four-element Employee array
33         Employee[] employees = new Employee[4];
34
35         // initialize array with Employees
36         employees[0] = salariedEmployee;
37         employees[1] = hourlyEmployee;
38         employees[2] = commissionEmployee;
39         employees[3] = basePlusCommissionEmployee;
40
41         System.out.printf("Employees processed polymorphically:%n%n");
42
43         // generically process each element in array employees
44         for (Employee currentEmployee : employees)
45         {
46            System.out.println(currentEmployee); // invokes toString
47
48            // determine whether element is a BasePlusCommissionEmployee
49            if (currentEmployee instanceof BasePlusCommissionEmployee()
50            {
51               // downcast Employee reference to
52               // BasePlusCommissionEmployee reference
53               BasePlusCommissionEmployee employee =
54                  (BasePlusCommissionEmployee) currentEmployee  ;
55
56               employee.setBaseSalary(1.10 * employee.getBaseSalary());
57
```

Fig. 10.9 | Employee hierarchy test program. (Part 2 of 4.)

```
58                 System.out.printf(
59                     "new base salary with 10%% increase is: $%,.2f%n",
60                     employee.getBaseSalary());
61             } // end if
62
63             System.out.printf(
64                 "earned $%,.2f%n%n", currentEmployee.earnings());
65         } // end for
66
67         // get type name of each object in employees array
68         for (int j = 0; j < employees.length; j++)
69             System.out.printf("Employee %d is a %s%n", j,
70                 employees[j].getClass().getName());
71     } // end main
72 } // end class PayrollSystemTest
```

```
Employees processed individually:

salaried employee: John Smith
social security number: 111-11-1111
weekly salary: $800.00
earned: $800.00

hourly employee: Karen Price
social security number: 222-22-2222
hourly wage: $16.75; hours worked: 40.00
earned: $670.00

commission employee: Sue Jones
social security number: 333-33-3333
gross sales: $10,000.00; commission rate: 0.06
earned: $600.00

base-salaried commission employee: Bob Lewis
social security number: 444-44-4444
gross sales: $5,000.00; commission rate: 0.04; base salary: $300.00
earned: $500.00

Employees processed polymorphically:

salaried employee: John Smith
social security number: 111-11-1111
weekly salary: $800.00
earned $800.00

hourly employee: Karen Price
social security number: 222-22-2222
hourly wage: $16.75; hours worked: 40.00
earned $670.00

commission employee: Sue Jones
social security number: 333-33-3333
gross sales: $10,000.00; commission rate: 0.06
earned $600.00
```

Fig. 10.9 | Employee hierarchy test program. (Part 3 of 4.)

```
base-salaried commission employee: Bob Lewis
social security number: 444-44-4444
gross sales: $5,000.00; commission rate: 0.04; base salary: $300.00
new base salary with 10% increase is: $330.00
earned $530.00

Employee 0 is a SalariedEmployee
Employee 1 is a HourlyEmployee
Employee 2 is a CommissionEmployee
Employee 3 is a BasePlusCommissionEmployee
```

Fig. 10.9 | Employee hierarchy test program. (Part 4 of 4.)

Creating the Array of *Employees*

Line 33 declares employees and assigns it an array of four Employee variables. Line 36 assigns to employees[0] a reference to a SalariedEmployee object. Line 37 assigns to employees[1] a reference to an HourlyEmployee object. Line 38 assigns to employees[2] a reference to a CommissionEmployee object. Line 39 assigns to employee[3] a reference to a BasePlusCommissionEmployee object. These assignments are allowed, because a SalariedEmployee *is an* Employee, an HourlyEmployee *is an* Employee, a CommissionEmployee *is an* Employee and a BasePlusCommissionEmployee *is an* Employee. Therefore, we can assign the references of SalariedEmployee, HourlyEmployee, CommissionEmployee and BasePlusCommissionEmployee objects to *superclass* Employee variables, *even though Employee is an abstract class.*

Polymorphically Processing *Employees*

Lines 44–65 iterate through array employees and invoke methods toString and earnings with Employee variable currentEmployee, which is assigned the reference to a different Employee in the array on each iteration. The output illustrates that the specific methods for each class are indeed invoked. All calls to method toString and earnings are resolved at *execution* time, based on the *type* of the object to which currentEmployee refers. This process is known as **dynamic binding** or **late binding**. For example, line 46 *implicitly* invokes method toString of the object to which currentEmployee refers. As a result of *dynamic binding*, Java decides which class's toString method to call *at execution time rather than at compile time*. Only the methods of class Employee can be called via an Employee variable (and Employee, of course, includes the methods of class Object). A superclass reference can be used to invoke only methods of the *superclass*—the *subclass* method implementations are invoked *polymorphically.*

Performing Type-Specific Operations on *BasePlusCommissionEmployees*

We perform special processing on BasePlusCommissionEmployee objects—as we encounter these objects at execution time, we increase their base salary by 10%. When processing objects *polymorphically*, we typically do not need to worry about the *specifics*, but to adjust the base salary, we *do* have to determine the *specific* type of Employee object at *execution time*. Line 49 uses the **instanceof** operator to determine whether a particular Employee object's type is BasePlusCommissionEmployee. The condition in line 49 is *true* if the object referenced by currentEmployee *is a* BasePlusCommissionEmployee. This would also be *true* for any object of a BasePlusCommissionEmployee subclass because of the *is-a* relationship a subclass has with its superclass. Lines 53–54 *downcast* currentEmployee from type Employee to type BasePlusCommissionEmployee—this cast is allowed only if the object has an *is-a* relationship with BasePlusCommissionEmployee. The condition at line 49 ensures that this is the case. This cast is required if we're to invoke subclass BasePlusCommissionEmployee methods getBaseSalary and setBaseSalary on the current Employee object—as you'll see momentarily, *attempting to invoke a subclass-only method directly on a superclass reference is a compilation error.*

Common Programming Error 10.3
Assigning a superclass variable to a subclass variable is a compilation error.

Common Programming Error 10.4
When downcasting a reference, a ClassCastException *occurs if the referenced object at execution time does not have an* is-a *relationship with the type specified in the cast operator.*

If the instanceof expression in line 49 is true, lines 53–60 perform the special processing required for the BasePlusCommissionEmployee object. Using BasePlusCommissionEmployee variable employee, line 56 invokes subclass-only methods getBaseSalary and setBaseSalary to retrieve and update the employee's base salary with the 10% raise.

Calling **earnings** *Polymorphically*
Lines 63–64 invoke method earnings on currentEmployee, which polymorphically calls the appropriate subclass object's earnings method. Obtaining the earnings of the SalariedEmployee, HourlyEmployee and CommissionEmployee polymorphically in lines 63–64 produces the same results as obtaining these employees' earnings individually in lines 22–27. The earnings amount obtained for the BasePlusCommissionEmployee in lines 63–64 is higher than that obtained in lines 28–30, due to the 10% increase in its base salary.

Getting Each **Employee**'s *Class Name*
Lines 68–70 display each employee's type as a String. Every object *knows its own class* and can access this information through the **getClass** method, which all classes inherit from class Object. Method getClass returns an object of type **Class** (from package java.lang), which contains information about the object's type, including its class name. Line 70 invokes getClass on the current object to get its class. The result of the getClass call is used to invoke **getName** to get the object's class name.

Avoiding Compilation Errors with Downcasting
In the previous example, we avoided several compilation errors by *downcasting* an Employee variable to a BasePlusCommissionEmployee variable in lines 53–54. If you remove the cast operator (BasePlusCommissionEmployee) from line 54 and attempt to assign Employee variable currentEmployee directly to BasePlusCommissionEmployee variable employee, you'll receive an "incompatible types" compilation error. This error indicates that the attempt to assign the reference of superclass object currentEmployee to subclass variable employee is *not* allowed. The compiler prevents this assignment because a CommissionEmployee is *not* a BasePlusCommissionEmployee—*the* is-a *relationship applies only between the subclass and its superclasses, not vice versa.*

Similarly, if lines 56 and 60 used superclass variable currentEmployee to invoke subclass-only methods getBaseSalary and setBaseSalary, we'd receive "cannot find symbol" compilation errors at these lines. Attempting to invoke subclass-only methods via a superclass variable is *not* allowed—even though lines 56 and 60 execute only if instanceof in line 49 returns true to indicate that currentEmployee holds a reference to a BasePlusCommissionEmployee object. Using a superclass Employee variable, we can invoke only methods found in class Employee—earnings, toString and Employee's *get* and *set* methods.

Software Engineering Observation 10.5

Although the actual method that's called depends on the runtime type of the object to which a variable refers, a variable can be used to invoke only those methods that are members of that variable's type, which the compiler verifies.

10.6 Allowed Assignments Between Superclass and Subclass Variables

Now that you've seen a complete application that processes diverse subclass objects *polymorphically*, we summarize what you can and cannot do with superclass and subclass objects and variables. Although a subclass object also *is a* superclass object, the two classes are nevertheless different. As discussed previously, subclass objects can be treated as objects of their superclass. But because the subclass can have additional subclass-only members, assigning a superclass reference to a subclass variable is not allowed without an *explicit cast*—such an assignment would leave the subclass members undefined for the superclass object.

We've discussed three proper ways to assign superclass and subclass references to variables of superclass and subclass types:

1. Assigning a superclass reference to a superclass variable is straightforward.

2. Assigning a subclass reference to a subclass variable is straightforward.

3. Assigning a subclass reference to a superclass variable is safe, because the subclass object *is an* object of its superclass. However, the superclass variable can be used to refer *only* to superclass members. If this code refers to subclass-only members through the superclass variable, the compiler reports errors.

10.7 final Methods and Classes

We saw in Sections 6.3– and 6.9 that variables can be declared final to indicate that they cannot be modified *after* they're initialized—such variables represent constant values. It's also possible to declare methods, method parameters and classes with the final modifier.

Final Methods Cannot Be Overridden

A **final method** in a superclass *cannot* be overridden in a subclass—this guarantees that the final method implementation will be used by all direct and indirect subclasses in the hierarchy. Methods that are declared private are implicitly final, because it's not possible to override them in a subclass. Methods that are declared static are also implicitly final. A final method's declaration can never change, so all subclasses use the same method implementation, and calls to `final` methods are resolved at compile time—this is known as **static binding**.

Final Classes Cannot Be Superclasses

A **final class** cannot extended to create a subclass. All methods in a `final` class are implicitly `final`. Class `String` is an example of a `final` class. If you were allowed to create a subclass of `String`, objects of that subclass could be used wherever `String`s are expected. Since class `String` cannot be extended, programs that use `String`s can rely on the functionality of `String` objects as specified in the Java API. Making the class `final` also prevents programmers from creating subclasses that might bypass security restrictions.

We've now discussed declaring variables, methods and classes `final`, and we've emphasized that if something *can* be `final` it *should* be `final`. Compilers can perform various optimizations when they know something is `final`. When we study concurrency in Chapter 20, you'll see that `final` variables make it much easier to parallelize your programs for use on today's multi-core processors. For more insights on the use of `final`, visit

```
http://docs.oracle.com/javase/tutorial/java/IandI/final.html
```

Common Programming Error 10.5

Attempting to declare a subclass of a `final` class is a compilation error.

Software Engineering Observation 10.6

In the Java API, the vast majority of classes are not declared `final`. This enables inheritance and polymorphism. However, in some cases, it's important to declare classes `final`—typically for security reasons. Also, unless you carefully design a class for extension, you should declare the class as `final` to avoid (often subtle) errors.

10.8 A Deeper Explanation of Issues with Calling Methods from Constructors

Do not call overridable methods from constructors. When creating a *subclass* object, this could lead to an overridden method being called before the *subclass* object is fully initialized.

Recall that when you construct a *subclass* object, its constructor first calls one of the direct *superclass's* constructors. If the *superclass* constructor calls an overridable method, the *subclass's* version of that method will be called by the *superclass* constructor—before the *subclass* constructor's body has a chance to execute. This could lead to subtle, difficult-to-detect errors if the *subclass* method that was called depends on initialization that has not yet been performed in the *subclass* constructor's body.

It's acceptable to call a `static` method from a constructor. For example, a constructor and a *set* method often perform the same validation for a particular instance variable. If the validation code is brief, it's acceptable to duplicate it in the constructor and the *set* method. If lengthier validation is required, define a `static` validation method (typically a `private` helper method) then call it from the constructor and the *set* method. It's also acceptable for a constructor to call a `final` instance method, provided that the method does not directly or indirectly call an overridable instance method.

10.9 Creating and Using Interfaces

[Note: As written, this section and its code example apply through Java SE 7. Java SE 8's interface enhancements are introduced in Section 10.10 and discussed in more detail in Chapter 17.]

Our next example (Figs. 10.11–10.15) reexamines the payroll system of Section 10.5. Suppose that the company involved wishes to perform several accounting operations in a single accounts payable application—in addition to calculating the earnings that must be paid to each employee, the company must also calculate the payment due on each of several invoices (i.e., bills for goods purchased). Though applied to *unrelated* things (i.e., employees and invoices), both operations have to do with obtaining some kind of payment amount. For an employee, the payment refers to the employee's earnings. For an invoice, the payment refers to the total cost of the goods listed on the invoice. Can we calculate such *different* things as the payments due for employees and invoices in *a single* application *polymorphically*? Does Java offer a capability requiring that *unrelated* classes implement a set of *common* methods (e.g., a method that calculates a payment amount)? Java **interfaces** offer exactly this capability.

Standardizing Interactions

Interfaces define and standardize the ways in which things such as people and systems can interact with one another. For example, the controls on a radio serve as an interface between radio users and a radio's internal components. The controls allow users to perform only a limited set of operations (e.g., change the station, adjust the volume, choose between AM and FM), and different radios may implement the controls in different ways (e.g., using push buttons, dials, voice commands). The interface specifies *what* operations a radio must permit users to perform but does not specify *how* the operations are performed.

Software Objects Communicate Via Interfaces

Software objects also communicate via interfaces. A Java interface describes a set of methods that can be called on an object to tell it, for example, to perform some task or return some piece of information. The next example introduces an interface named `Payable` to describe the functionality of any object that must be "capable of being paid" and thus must offer a method to determine the proper payment amount due. An **interface declaration** begins with the keyword **interface** and contains *only* constants and `abstract` methods. Unlike classes, all interface members *must* be `public`, and *interfaces may not specify any implementation details*, such as concrete method declarations and instance variables. All methods declared in an interface are implicitly `public abstract` methods, and all fields are implicitly `public`, `static` and `final`.

Good Programming Practice 10.1

According to the Java Language Specification, *it's proper style to declare an interface's* `abstract` *methods without keywords* `public` *and* `abstract`, *because they're redundant in interface-method declarations. Similarly, an interface's constants should be declared without keywords* `public`, `static` *and* `final`, *because they, too, are redundant.*

Using an Interface

To use an interface, a concrete class must specify that it **implements** the interface and must declare each method in the interface with the signature specified in the interface declaration. To specify that a class implements an interface, add the `implements` keyword and the name of the interface to the end of your class declaration's first line. A class that does not implement *all* the methods of the interface is an *abstract* class and must be declared `abstract`. Implementing an interface is like signing a *contract* with the compiler that states, "I will declare all the methods specified by the interface or I will declare my class `abstract`."

> **Common Programming Error 10.6**
>
> *Failing to implement any method of an interface in a concrete class that `implements` the interface results in a compilation error indicating that the class must be declared `abstract`.*

Relating Disparate Types

An interface is often used when *disparate* classes—i.e., classes that are not related by a class hierarchy—need to share common methods and constants. This allows objects of *unrelated* classes to be processed *polymorphically*—objects of classes that implement the *same* interface can respond to the *same* method calls. You can create an interface that describes the desired functionality, then implement this interface in any classes that require that functionality. For example, in the accounts payable application developed in this section, we implement interface `Payable` in any class that must be able to calculate a payment amount (e.g., `Employee`, `Invoice`).

Interfaces vs. Abstract Classes

An interface is often used in place of an `abstract` class when there's no *default implementation to inherit*—that is, no fields and no default method implementations. Like `public abstract` classes, interfaces are typically `public` types. Like a `public` class, a `public` interface must be declared in a file with the same name as the interface and the `.java` filename extension.

> **Software Engineering Observation 10.7**
>
> *Many developers feel that interfaces are an even more important modeling technology than classes, especially with the new interface enhancements in Java SE 8 (see Section 10.10).*

Tagging Interfaces

We'll see in Chapter 15, Files, Streams and Object Serialization, the notion of *tagging interfaces* (also called *marker interfaces*)—empty interfaces that have *no* methods or constant values. They're used to add *is-a* relationships to classes. For example, in Chapter 15 we'll discuss a mechanism called *object serialization*, which can convert objects to byte representations and can convert those byte representations back to objects. To enable this mechanism to work with your objects, you simply have to mark them as `Serializable` by adding `implements Serializable` to the end of your class declaration's first line. Then, all the objects of your class have the *is-a* relationship with `Serializable`.

10.9.1 Developing a `Payable` Hierarchy

To build an application that can determine payments for employees and invoices alike, we first create interface `Payable`, which contains method `getPaymentAmount` that returns a `double` amount that must be paid for an object of any class that implements the interface. Method `getPaymentAmount` is a general-purpose version of method `earnings` of the `Employee` hierarchy—method `earnings` calculates a payment amount specifically for an `Employee`, while `getPaymentAmount` can be applied to a broad range of possibly unrelated objects. After declaring interface `Payable`, we introduce class `Invoice`, which `implements` interface `Payable`. We then modify class `Employee` such that it also implements interface `Payable`. Finally, we update `Employee` subclass `SalariedEmployee` to "fit" into the `Payable` hierarchy by renaming `SalariedEmployee` method `earnings` as `getPaymentAmount`.

> **Good Programming Practice 10.2**
>
> *When declaring a method in an interface, choose a method name that describes the method's purpose in a* general *manner, because the method may be implemented by many* unrelated *classes.*

Classes `Invoice` and `Employee` both represent things for which the company must be able to calculate a payment amount. Both classes implement the `Payable` interface, so a program can invoke method `getPaymentAmount` on `Invoice` objects and `Employee` objects alike. As we'll soon see, this enables the *polymorphic* processing of `Invoice`s and `Employee`s required for the company's accounts payable application.

The UML class diagram in Fig. 10.10 shows the interface and class hierarchy used in our accounts payable application. The hierarchy begins with interface `Payable`. The UML distinguishes an interface from other classes by placing the word "interface" in guillemets (« and ») above the interface name. The UML expresses the relationship between a class and an interface through a relationship known as **realization**. A class is said to *realize*, or *implement*, the methods of an interface. A class diagram models a realization as a dashed arrow with a hollow arrowhead pointing from the implementing class to the interface. The diagram in Fig. 10.10 indicates that classes `Invoice` and `Employee` each realize interface `Payable`. As in the class diagram of Fig. 10.2, class `Employee` appears in *italics*, indicating that it's an *abstract class. Concrete* class `SalariedEmployee` extends `Employee`, *inheriting its superclass's realization relationship* with interface `Payable`.

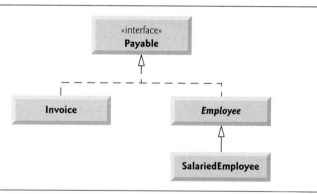

Fig. 10.10 | `Payable` hierarchy UML class diagram.

10.9.2 Interface Payable

The declaration of interface `Payable` begins in Fig. 10.11 at line 4. Interface `Payable` contains `public abstract` method `getPaymentAmount`. Interface methods are always `public` and `abstract`, so they do not need to be declared as such. Interface `Payable` has only one method, but interfaces can have *any* number of methods. In addition, method `getPaymentAmount` has no parameters, but interface methods *can* have parameters. Interfaces may also contain `final static` constants.

```
1   // Fig. 10.11: Payable.java
2   // Payable interface declaration.
3
4   public interface Payable
5   {
6      double getPaymentAmount(); // calculate payment; no implementation
7   }
```

Fig. 10.11 | Payable interface declaration.

10.9.3 Class Invoice

We now create class Invoice (Fig. 10.12) to represent a simple invoice that contains billing information for only one kind of part. The class declares private instance variables partNumber, partDescription, quantity and pricePerItem (in lines 6–9) that indicate the part number, a description of the part, the quantity of the part ordered and the price per item. Class Invoice also contains a constructor (lines 12–26), *get* and *set* methods (lines 29–69) that manipulate the class's instance variables and a toString method (lines 72–78) that returns a String representation of an Invoice object. Methods setQuantity (lines 41–47) and setPricePerItem (lines 56–63) ensure that quantity and pricePerItem obtain only nonnegative values.

```
1   // Fig. 10.12: Invoice.java
2   // Invoice class that implements Payable.
3
4   public class Invoice implements Payable
5   {
6      private final String partNumber;
7      private final String partDescription;
8      private int quantity;
9      private double pricePerItem;
10
11     // constructor
12     public Invoice(String partNumber, String partDescription, int quantity,
13        double pricePerItem)
14     {
15        if (quantity < 0) // validate quantity
16           throw new IllegalArgumentException("Quantity must be >= 0");
17
18        if (pricePerItem < 0.0) // validate pricePerItem
19           throw new IllegalArgumentException(
20              "Price per item must be >= 0");
21
22        this.quantity = quantity;
23        this.partNumber = partNumber;
24        this.partDescription = partDescription;
25        this.pricePerItem = pricePerItem;
26     } // end constructor
27
```

Fig. 10.12 | Invoice class that implements Payable. (Part 1 of 3.)

```java
28        // get part number
29        public String getPartNumber()
30        {
31           return partNumber; // should validate
32        }
33
34        // get description
35        public String getPartDescription()
36        {
37           return partDescription;
38        }
39
40        // set quantity
41        public void setQuantity(int quantity)
42        {
43           if (quantity < 0) // validate quantity
44              throw new IllegalArgumentException("Quantity must be >= 0");
45
46           this.quantity = quantity;
47        }
48
49        // get quantity
50        public int getQuantity()
51        {
52           return quantity;
53        }
54
55        // set price per item
56        public void setPricePerItem(double pricePerItem)
57        {
58           if (pricePerItem < 0.0) // validate pricePerItem
59              throw new IllegalArgumentException(
60                 "Price per item must be >= 0");
61
62           this.pricePerItem = pricePerItem;
63        }
64
65        // get price per item
66        public double getPricePerItem()
67        {
68           return pricePerItem;
69        }
70
71        // return String representation of Invoice object
72        @Override
73        public String toString()
74        {
75           return String.format("%s: %n%s: %s (%s) %n%s: %d %n%s: $%,.2f",
76              "invoice", "part number", getPartNumber(), getPartDescription(),
77              "quantity", getQuantity(), "price per item", getPricePerItem());
78        }
79
```

Fig. 10.12 | Invoice class that implements Payable. (Part 2 of 3.)

```
80        // method required to carry out contract with interface Payable
81        @Override
82        public double getPaymentAmount()
83        {
84            return getQuantity() * getPricePerItem(); // calculate total cost
85        }
86    } // end class Invoice
```

Fig. 10.12 | Invoice class that implements Payable. (Part 3 of 3.)

A Class Can Extend Only One Other Class But Can Implement Many Interfaces

Line 4 indicates that class Invoice implements interface Payable. Like all classes, class Invoice also *implicitly* extends Object. Java does not allow subclasses to inherit from more than one superclass, but it allows a class to *inherit* from one *superclass* and *implement* as many *interfaces* as it needs. To implement more than one interface, use a comma-separated list of interface names after keyword implements in the class declaration, as in:

> public class *ClassName* extends *SuperclassName* implements *FirstInterface*,
> *SecondInterface*, ...

Software Engineering Observation 10.8

All objects of a class that implements multiple interfaces have the is-a *relationship with each implemented interface type.*

Class Invoice implements the one abstract method in interface Payable—method getPaymentAmount is declared in lines 81–85. The method calculates the total payment required to pay the invoice. The method multiplies the values of quantity and pricePerItem (obtained through the appropriate *get* methods) and returns the result. This method satisfies the implementation requirement for this method in interface Payable—we've *fulfilled* the *interface contract* with the compiler.

10.9.4 Modifying Class Employee to Implement Interface Payable

We now modify class Employee such that it implements interface Payable. Figure 10.13 contains the modified class, which is identical to that of Fig. 10.4 with two exceptions. First, line 4 of Fig. 10.13 indicates that class Employee now implements interface Payable. For this example, we renamed method earnings to getPaymentAmount throughout the Employee hierarchy. As with method earnings in the version of class Employee in Fig. 10.4, however, it does not make sense to *implement* method getPaymentAmount in class Employee because we cannot calculate the earnings payment owed to a *general* Employee—we must first know the *specific* type of Employee. In Fig. 10.4, we declared method earnings as abstract for this reason, so class Employee had to be declared abstract. This forced each Employee *concrete* subclass to *override* earnings with an implementation.

```
1    // Fig. 10.13: Employee.java
2    // Employee abstract superclass that implements Payable.
3
```

Fig. 10.13 | Employee abstract superclass that implements Payable. (Part 1 of 2.)

```
4   public abstract class Employee implements Payable
5   {
6      private final String firstName;
7      private final String lastName;
8      private final String socialSecurityNumber;
9
10     // constructor
11     public Employee(String firstName, String lastName,
12        String socialSecurityNumber)
13     {
14        this.firstName = firstName;
15        this.lastName = lastName;
16        this.socialSecurityNumber = socialSecurityNumber;
17     }
18
19     // return first name
20     public String getFirstName()
21     {
22        return firstName;
23     }
24
25     // return last name
26     public String getLastName()
27     {
28        return lastName;
29     }
30
31     // return social security number
32     public String getSocialSecurityNumber()
33     {
34        return socialSecurityNumber;
35     }
36
37     // return String representation of Employee object
38     @Override
39     public String toString()
40     {
41        return String.format("%s %s%nsocial security number: %s",
42           getFirstName(), getLastName(), getSocialSecurityNumber());
43     }
44
45     // Note: We do not implement Payable method getPaymentAmount here so
46     // this class must be declared abstract to avoid a compilation error.
47  } // end abstract class Employee
```

Fig. 10.13 | Employee abstract superclass that implements Payable. (Part 2 of 2.)

In Fig. 10.13, we handle this situation differently. Recall that when a class implements an interface, it makes a *contract* with the compiler stating either that the class will implement *each* method in the interface or the class will be declared abstract. Because class Employee does not provide a getPaymentAmount method, the class must be declared abstract. Any concrete subclass of the abstract class *must* implement the interface methods to fulfill the superclass's contract with the compiler. If the subclass does *not* do so, it too *must* be declared abstract. As indicated by the comments in lines 45–46, class Employee of Fig. 10.13 does *not* implement method getPaymentAmount, so the class is declared abstract. Each direct Employee subclass *inherits the superclass's contract* to implement method getPaymentAmount and thus must implement this method to become a concrete class for which objects can be instantiated. A class that extends one of Employee's concrete subclasses will inherit an implementation of getPaymentAmount and thus will also be a concrete class.

10.9.5 Modifying Class `SalariedEmployee` for Use in the `Payable` Hierarchy

Figure 10.14 contains a modified SalariedEmployee class that extends Employee and fulfills superclass Employee's contract to implement Payable method getPaymentAmount. This version of SalariedEmployee is identical to that of Fig. 10.5, but it replaces method earnings with method getPaymentAmount (lines 39–43). Recall that the Payable version of the method has a more *general* name to be applicable to possibly *disparate* classes. (If we included the remaining Employee subclasses from Section 10.5—HourlyEmployee, CommissionEmployee and BasePlusCommissionEmployee—in this example, their earnings methods should also be renamed getPaymentAmount. We use only SalariedEmployee in our test program here. As an exercise, you can implement interface Payable in the entire Employee class hierarchy of Figs. 10.4–10.9 *without* modifying the Employee subclasses.)

```java
1   // Fig. 10.14: SalariedEmployee.java
2   // SalariedEmployee class that implements interface Payable.
3   // method getPaymentAmount.
4   public class SalariedEmployee extends Employee
5   {
6      private double weeklySalary;
7
8      // constructor
9      public SalariedEmployee(String firstName, String lastName,
10        String socialSecurityNumber, double weeklySalary)
11     {
12        super(firstName, lastName, socialSecurityNumber);
13
14        if (weeklySalary < 0.0)
15           throw new IllegalArgumentException(
16              "Weekly salary must be >= 0.0");
17
18        this.weeklySalary = weeklySalary;
19     }
20
21     // set salary
22     public void setWeeklySalary(double weeklySalary)
23     {
24        if (weeklySalary < 0.0)
25           throw new IllegalArgumentException(
26              "Weekly salary must be >= 0.0");
```

Fig. 10.14 | SalariedEmployee class that implements interface Payable method getPaymentAmount. (Part 1 of 2.)

```
27
28            this.weeklySalary = weeklySalary;
29      }
30
31      // return salary
32      public double getWeeklySalary()
33      {
34          return weeklySalary;
35      }
36
37      // calculate earnings; implement interface Payable method that was
38      // abstract in superclass Employee
39      @Override
40      public double getPaymentAmount()
41      {
42          return getWeeklySalary();
43      }
44
45      // return String representation of SalariedEmployee object
46      @Override
47      public String toString()
48      {
49          return String.format("salaried employee: %s%n%s: $%,.2f",
50              super.toString(), "weekly salary", getWeeklySalary());
51      }
52   } // end class SalariedEmployee
```

Fig. 10.14 | SalariedEmployee class that implements interface Payable method getPaymentAmount. (Part 2 of 2.)

When a class implements an interface, the same *is-a* relationship provided by inheritance applies. Class Employee implements Payable, so we can say that an Employee *is a* Payable. In fact, objects of any classes that extend Employee are also Payable objects. SalariedEmployee objects, for instance, are Payable objects. Objects of any subclasses of the class that implements the interface can also be thought of as objects of the interface type. Thus, just as we can assign the reference of a SalariedEmployee object to a superclass Employee variable, we can assign the reference of a SalariedEmployee object to an interface Payable variable. Invoice implements Payable, so an Invoice object also *is a* Payable object, and we can assign the reference of an Invoice object to a Payable variable.

Software Engineering Observation 10.9
When a method parameter is declared with a superclass or interface type, the method processes the object passed as an argument polymorphically.

Software Engineering Observation 10.10
Using a superclass reference, we can polymorphically invoke any method declared in the superclass and its superclasses (e.g., class Object). Using an interface reference, we can polymorphically invoke any method declared in the interface, its superinterfaces (one interface can extend another) and in class Object—a variable of an interface type must refer to an object to call methods, and all objects have the methods of class Object.

10.9.6 Using Interface Payable to Process Invoices and Employees Polymorphically

PayableInterfaceTest (Fig. 10.15) illustrates that interface Payable can be used to process a set of Invoices and Employees *polymorphically* in a single application. Line 9 declares payableObjects and assigns it an array of four Payable variables. Lines 12–13 assign the references of Invoice objects to the first two elements of payableObjects. Lines 14–17 then assign the references of SalariedEmployee objects to the remaining two elements of payableObjects. These assignments are allowed because an Invoice *is a* Payable, a SalariedEmployee *is an* Employee and an Employee *is a* Payable. Lines 23–29 use the enhanced for statement to *polymorphically* process each Payable object in payableObjects, printing the object as a String, along with the payment amount due. Line 27 invokes method toString via a Payable interface reference, even though toString is not declared in interface Payable—*all references (including those of interface types) refer to objects that extend Object and therefore have a toString method.* (Method toString also can be invoked *implicitly* here.) Line 28 invokes Payable method getPaymentAmount to obtain the payment amount for each object in payableObjects, *regardless* of the actual type of the object. The output reveals that each of the method calls in lines 27–28 invokes the appropriate class's implementation of methods toString and getPaymentAmount. For instance, when currentPayable refers to an Invoice during the first iteration of the for loop, class Invoice's toString and getPaymentAmount execute.

```
1   // Fig. 10.15: PayableInterfaceTest.java
2   // Payable interface test program processing Invoices and
3   // Employees polymorphically.
4   public class PayableInterfaceTest
5   {
6      public static void main(String[] args)
7      {
8         // create four-element Payable array
9         Payable[] payableObjects = new Payable[4];
10
11        // populate array with objects that implement Payable
12        payableObjects[0] = new Invoice("01234", "seat", 2, 375.00);
13        payableObjects[1] = new Invoice("56789", "tire", 4, 79.95);
14        payableObjects[2] =
15           new SalariedEmployee("John", "Smith", "111-11-1111", 800.00);
16        payableObjects[3] =
17           new SalariedEmployee("Lisa", "Barnes", "888-88-8888", 1200.00);
18
19        System.out.println(
20           "Invoices and Employees processed polymorphically:");
21
22        // generically process each element in array payableObjects
23        for (Payable currentPayable : payableObjects)
24        {
```

Fig. 10.15 | Payable interface test program processing Invoices and Employees polymorphically. (Part I of 2.)

```
25                // output currentPayable and its appropriate payment amount
26                System.out.printf("%n%s %n%s: $%,.2f%n",
27                  currentPayable.toString(), // could invoke implicitly
28                  "payment due", currentPayable.getPaymentAmount());
29              }
30        } // end main
31    } // end class PayableInterfaceTest
```

```
Invoices and Employees processed polymorphically:

invoice:
part number: 01234 (seat)
quantity: 2
price per item: $375.00
payment due: $750.00

invoice:
part number: 56789 (tire)
quantity: 4
price per item: $79.95
payment due: $319.80

salaried employee: John Smith
social security number: 111-11-1111
weekly salary: $800.00
payment due: $800.00

salaried employee: Lisa Barnes
social security number: 888-88-8888
weekly salary: $1,200.00
payment due: $1,200.00
```

Fig. 10.15 | Payable interface test program processing Invoices and Employees polymorphically. (Part 2 of 2.)

10.9.7 Some Common Interfaces of the Java API

You'll use interfaces extensively when developing Java applications. The Java API contains numerous interfaces, and many of the Java API methods take interface arguments and return interface values. Figure 10.16 overviews a few of the more popular interfaces of the Java API that we use in later chapters.

Interface	Description
Comparable	Java contains several comparison operators (e.g., <, <=, >, >=, ==, !=) that allow you to compare primitive values. However, these operators *cannot* be used to compare objects. Interface Comparable is used to allow objects of a class that implements the interface to be compared to one another. Interface Comparable is commonly used for ordering objects in a collection such as an array. We use Comparable in Chapter 16, Generic Collections, and Chapter 18, Generic Classes and Methods.

Fig. 10.16 | Common interfaces of the Java API. (Part 1 of 2.)

Interface	Description
`Serializable`	An interface used to identify classes whose objects can be written to (i.e., serialized) or read from (i.e., deserialized) some type of storage (e.g., file on disk, database field) or transmitted across a network. We use `Serializable` in Chapter 15, Files, Streams and Object Serialization.
`Runnable`	Implemented by any class that represents a task to perform. Objects of such as class are often executed in parallel using a technique called *multithreading* (discussed in Chapter 20, Concurrency). The interface contains one method, `run`, which specifies the behavior of an object when executed.
GUI event-listener interfaces	You work with graphical user interfaces (GUIs) every day. In your web browser, you might type the address of a website to visit, or you might click a button to return to a previous site. The browser responds to your interaction and performs the desired task. Your interaction is known as an *event*, and the code that the browser uses to respond to an event is known as an *event handler*. In Chapter 12, Swing GUI Components: Part 1, and Chapter 19, Swing GUI Components: Part 2, you'll learn how to build GUIs and event handlers that respond to user interactions. Event handlers are declared in classes that implement an appropriate *event-listener interface*. Each event-listener interface specifies one or more methods that must be implemented to respond to user interactions.
`AutoCloseable`	Implemented by classes that can be used with the try-with-resources statement (Chapter 11, Exception Handling: A Deeper Look) to help prevent resource leaks.

Fig. 10.16 | Common interfaces of the Java API. (Part 2 of 2.)

10.10 Java SE 8 Interface Enhancements

This section introduces Java SE 8's new interface features. We discuss these in more detail in later chapters.

10.10.1 default Interface Methods

Prior to Java SE 8, interface methods could be *only* `public abstract` methods. This meant that an interface specified *what* operations an implementing class must perform but not *how* the class should perform them.

In Java SE 8, interfaces also may contain `public` **default methods** with *concrete* default implementations that specify *how* operations are performed when an implementing class does not override the methods. If a class implements such an interface, the class also receives the interface's `default` implementations (if any). To declare a `default` method, place the keyword `default` before the method's return type and provide a concrete method implementation.

Adding Methods to Existing Interfaces
Prior to Java SE 8, adding methods to an interface would break any implementing classes that did not implement the new methods. Recall that if you didn't implement each of an interface's methods, you had to declare your class `abstract`.

Any class that implements the original interface will *not* break when a `default` method is added—the class simply receives the new `default` method. When a class implements a Java SE 8 interface, the class "signs a contract" with the compiler that says, "I will declare all the *abstract* methods specified by the interface or I will declare my class abstract"—the implementing class is not required to override the interface's default methods, but it can if necessary.

> **Software Engineering Observation 10.11**
>
> *Java SE 8 default methods enable you to evolve existing interfaces by adding new methods to those interfaces without breaking code that uses them.*

Interfaces vs. abstract Classes

Prior to Java SE 8, an interface was typically used (rather than an abstract class) when there were no implementation details to inherit—no fields and no method implementations. With default methods, you can instead declare common method implementations in interfaces, which gives you more flexibility in designing your classes.

10.10.2 static Interface Methods

Prior to Java SE 8, it was common to associate with an interface a class containing static helper methods for working with objects that implemented the interface. In Chapter 16, you'll learn about class Collections which contains many static helper methods for working with objects that implement interfaces Collection, List, Set and more. For example, Collections method sort can sort objects of *any* class that implements interface List. With static interface methods, such helper methods can now be declared directly in interfaces rather than in separate classes.

10.10.3 Functional Interfaces

As of Java SE 8, any interface containing only one abstract method is known as a **functional interface**. There are many such interfaces throughout the Java SE 7 APIs, and many new ones in Java SE 8. Some functional interfaces that you'll use in this book include:

- ActionListener (Chapter 12)—You'll implement this interface to define a method that's called when the user clicks a button.

- Comparator (Chapter 16)—You'll implement this interface to define a method that can compare two objects of a given type to determine whether the first object is less than, equal to or greater than the second.

- Runnable (Chapter 20)—You'll implement this interface to define a task that may be run in parallel with other parts of your program.

Functional interfaces are used extensively with Java SE 8's new lambda capabilities that we introduce in Chapter 17. In Chapter 12, you'll often implement an interface by creating a so-called anonymous inner class that implements the interface's method(s). In Java SE 8, lambdas provide a shorthand notation for creating *anonymous methods* that the compiler automatically translates into anonymous inner classes for you.

10.11 Wrap-Up

This chapter introduced polymorphism—the ability to process objects that share the same superclass in a class hierarchy as if they were all objects of the superclass. We discussed how polymorphism makes systems extensible and maintainable, then demonstrated how to use overridden methods to effect polymorphic behavior. We introduced abstract classes, which allow you to provide an appropriate superclass from which other classes can inherit. You learned that an abstract class can declare abstract methods that each subclass must implement to become a concrete class and that a program can use variables of an abstract class to invoke the subclasses' implementations of abstract methods polymorphically. You also learned how to determine an object's type at execution time. We explained the notions of `final` methods and classes. Finally, the chapter discussed declaring and implementing an interface as a way for possibly disparate classes to implement common functionality, enabling objects of those classes to be processed polymorphically.

You should now be familiar with classes, objects, encapsulation, inheritance, interfaces and polymorphism—the most essential aspects of object-oriented programming.

In the next chapter, you'll learn about exceptions, useful for handling errors during a program's execution. Exception handling provides for more robust programs.

Exception Handling:
A Deeper Look

Objectives

In this chapter you'll:

- Learn what exceptions are and how they're handled.
- Learn when to use exception handling.
- Use `try` blocks to delimit code in which exceptions might occur.
- Use `throw` to indicate a problem.
- Use `catch` blocks to specify exception handlers.
- Use the `finally` block to release resources.
- Understand the exception class hierarchy.
- Create user-defined exceptions.

11.1 Introduction

As you know from Chapter 7, an exception is an indication of a problem that occurs during a program's execution. Exception handling enables you to create applications that can resolve (or handle) exceptions. In many cases, handling an exception allows a program to continute executing as if no problem had been encountered. The features presented in this chapter help you write *robust* and *fault-tolerant* programs that can deal with problems and continue executing or *terminate gracefully*. Java exception handling is based in part on the work of Andrew Koenig and Bjarne Stroustrup.[1]

First, we demonstrate basic exception-handling techniques by handling an exception that occurs when a method attempts to divide an integer by zero. Next, we introduce several classes at the top of Java's exception-handling class hierarchy. As you'll see, only classes that extend `Throwable` (package `java.lang`) directly or indirectly can be used with exception handling. We then show how to use *chained exceptions*—when you invoke a method that indicates an exception, you can throw another exception and chain the original one to the new one. This enables you to add application-specific information to the orginal exception. Next, we introduce *preconditions* and *postconditions*, which must be true when your methods are called and when they return, respectively. We then present *assertions*, which you can use at development time to help debug your code. We also discuss two exception-handling features that were introduced in Java SE 7—catching multiple exceptions with one catch handler and the new `try`-with-resources statement that automatically releases a resource after it's used in the `try` block.

This chapter focuses on the exception-handling concepts and presents several mechanical examples that demonstrate various features. As you'll see in later chapters, many Java APIs methods throw exceptions that we handle in our code. Figure 11.1 shows some of the exception types you've already seen and others you'll learn about.

---

1. A. Koenig and B. Stroustrup, "Exception Handling for C++ (revised)," *Proceedings of the Usenix C++ Conference*, pp. 149–176, San Francisco, April 1990.

Chapter	Sample of exceptions used
Chapter 7	ArrayIndexOutOfBoundsException
Chapters 8–10	IllegalArgumentException
Chapter 11	ArithmeticException, InputMismatchException
Chapter 15	SecurityException, FileNotFoundException, IOException, ClassNotFoundException, IllegalStateException, FormatterClosedException, NoSuchElementException
Chapter 16	ClassCastException, UnsupportedOperationException, NullPointerException, custom exception types
Chapter 18	ClassCastException, custom exception types
Chapter 20	InterruptedException, IllegalMonitorStateException, ExecutionException, CancellationException
Chapter 21	SQLException, IllegalStateException, PatternSyntaxException

Fig. 11.1 | Various exception types that you'll see throughout this book

11.2 Example: Divide by Zero without Exception Handling

First we demonstrate what happens when errors arise in an application that does not use exception handling. Figure 11.2 prompts the user for two integers and passes them to method quotient, which calculates the integer quotient and returns an int result. In this example, you'll see that exceptions are **thrown** (i.e., the exception occurs) by a method when it detects a problem and is unable to handle it.

```
1   // Fig. 11.2: DivideByZeroNoExceptionHandling.java
2   // Integer division without exception handling.
3   import java.util.Scanner;
4
5   public class DivideByZeroNoExceptionHandling
6   {
7      // demonstrates throwing an exception when a divide-by-zero occurs
8      public static int quotient(int numerator, int denominator)
9      {
10        return numerator / denominator; // possible division by zero
11     }
12
13     public static void main(String[] args)
14     {
15        Scanner scanner = new Scanner(System.in);
```

Fig. 11.2 | Integer division without exception handling. (Part 1 of 2.)

```
16
17          System.out.print("Please enter an integer numerator: ");
18          int numerator = scanner.nextInt();
19          System.out.print("Please enter an integer denominator: ");
20          int denominator = scanner.nextInt();
21
22          int result = quotient(numerator, denominator);
23          System.out.printf(
24             "%nResult: %d / %d = %d%n", numerator, denominator, result);
25       }
26    } // end class DivideByZeroNoExceptionHandling
```

```
Please enter an integer numerator: 100
Please enter an integer denominator: 7

Result: 100 / 7 = 14
```

```
Please enter an integer numerator: 100
Please enter an integer denominator: 0
Exception in thread "main" java.lang.ArithmeticException: / by zero
        at DivideByZeroNoExceptionHandling.quotient(
           DivideByZeroNoExceptionHandling.java:10)
        at DivideByZeroNoExceptionHandling.main(
           DivideByZeroNoExceptionHandling.java:22)
```

```
Please enter an integer numerator: 100
Please enter an integer denominator: hello
Exception in thread "main" java.util.InputMismatchException
        at java.util.Scanner.throwFor(Unknown Source)
        at java.util.Scanner.next(Unknown Source)
        at java.util.Scanner.nextInt(Unknown Source)
        at java.util.Scanner.nextInt(Unknown Source)
        at DivideByZeroNoExceptionHandling.main(
           DivideByZeroNoExceptionHandling.java:20)
```

Fig. 11.2 | Integer division without exception handling. (Part 2 of 2.)

Stack Trace

The first sample execution in Fig. 11.2 shows a successful division. In the second execution, the user enters the value 0 as the denominator. Several lines of information are displayed in response to this invalid input. This information is known as a **stack trace**, which includes the name of the exception (java.lang.ArithmeticException) in a descriptive message that indicates the problem that occurred and the method-call stack (i.e., the call chain) at the time it occurred. The stack trace includes the path of execution that led to the exception method by method. This helps you debug the program.

*Stack Trace for an **ArithmeticException***

The first line specifies that an ArithmeticException has occurred. The text after the name of the exception ("/ by zero") indicates that this exception occurred as a result of an attempt to divide by zero. Java does not allow division by zero in integer arithmetic. When this occurs, Java throws an **ArithmeticException**. ArithmeticExceptions can arise from a number of different problems, so the extra data ("/ by zero") provides more specific information. Java *does* allow division by zero with floating-point values. Such a calculation results in the value positive or negative infinity, which is represented in Java as a floating-point value (but displays as the string Infinity or -Infinity). If 0.0 is divided by 0.0, the result is NaN (not a number), which is also represented in Java as a floating-point value (but displays as NaN). If you need to compare a floating-point value to NaN, use the method isNaN of class Float (for float values) or of class Double (for double values). Classes Float and Double are in package java.lang.

Starting from the last line of the stack trace, we see that the exception was detected in line 22 of method main. Each line of the stack trace contains the class name and method (e.g., DivideByZeroNoExceptionHandling.main) followed by the filename and line number (e.g., DivideByZeroNoExceptionHandling.java:22). Moving up the stack trace, we see that the exception occurs in line 10, in method quotient. The top row of the call chain indicates the **throw point**—the initial point at which the exception occurred. The throw point of this exception is in line 10 of method quotient.

Stack Trace for an *InputMismatchException*
In the third execution, the user enters the string "hello" as the denominator. Notice again that a stack trace is displayed. This informs us that an InputMismatchException has occurred (package java.util). Our prior examples that input numeric values assumed that the user would input a proper integer value. However, users sometimes make mistakes and input noninteger values. An **InputMismatchException** occurs when Scanner method nextInt receives a string that does not represent a valid integer. Starting from the end of the stack trace, we see that the exception was detected in line 20 of method main. Moving up the stack trace, we see that the exception occurred in method nextInt. Notice that in place of the filename and line number, we're provided with the text Unknown Source. This means that the so-called *debugging symbols* that provide the filename and line number information for that method's class were not available to the JVM—this is typically the case for the classes of the Java API. Many IDEs have access to the Java API source code and will display filenames and line numbers in stack traces.

Program Termination
In the sample executions of Fig. 11.2 when exceptions occur and stack traces are displayed, the program also *exits*. This does not always occur in Java. Sometimes a program may continue even though an exception has occurred and a stack trace has been printed. In such cases, the application may produce unexpected results. For example, a graphical user interface (GUI) application will often continue executing. In Fig. 11.2 both types of exceptions were detected in method main. In the next example, we'll see how to *handle* these exceptions so that you can enable the program to run to normal completion.

11.3 Example: Handling ArithmeticExceptions and InputMismatchExceptions
The application in Fig. 11.3, which is based on Fig. 11.2, uses *exception handling* to process any ArithmeticExceptions and InputMismatchExceptions that arise. The application still prompts the user for two integers and passes them to method quotient, which calculates the quotient and returns an int result. This version of the application uses ex-

ception handling so that if the user makes a mistake, the program catches and handles (i.e., deals with) the exception—in this case, allowing the user to re-enter the input.

```java
1   // Fig. 11.3: DivideByZeroWithExceptionHandling.java
2   // Handling ArithmeticExceptions and InputMismatchExceptions.
3   import java.util.InputMismatchException;
4   import java.util.Scanner;
5
6   public class DivideByZeroWithExceptionHandling
7   {
8      // demonstrates throwing an exception when a divide-by-zero occurs
9      public static int quotient(int numerator, int denominator)
10        throws ArithmeticException
11     {
12        return numerator / denominator; // possible division by zero
13     }
14
15     public static void main(String[] args)
16     {
17        Scanner scanner = new Scanner(System.in);
18        boolean continueLoop = true; // determines if more input is needed
19
20        do
21        {
22           try // read two numbers and calculate quotient
23           {
24              System.out.print("Please enter an integer numerator: ");
25              int numerator = scanner.nextInt();
26              System.out.print("Please enter an integer denominator: ");
27              int denominator = scanner.nextInt();
28
29              int result = quotient(numerator, denominator);
30              System.out.printf("%nResult: %d / %d = %d%n", numerator,
31                 denominator, result);
32              continueLoop = false; // input successful; end looping
33           }
34           catch (InputMismatchException inputMismatchException)
35           {
36              System.err.printf("%nException: %s%n",
37                 inputMismatchException);
38              scanner.nextLine(); // discard input so user can try again
39              System.out.printf(
40                 "You must enter integers. Please try again.%n%n");
41           }
42           catch (ArithmeticException arithmeticException)
43           {
44              System.err.printf("%nException: %s%n", arithmeticException);
45              System.out.printf(
46                 "Zero is an invalid denominator. Please try again.%n%n");
47           }
48        } while (continueLoop);
49     }
50  } // end class DivideByZeroWithExceptionHandling
```

Fig. 11.3 | Handling ArithmeticExceptions and InputMismatchExceptions. (Part 1 of 2.)

```
Please enter an integer numerator: 100
Please enter an integer denominator: 7

Result: 100 / 7 = 14
```

```
Please enter an integer numerator: 100
Please enter an integer denominator: 0

Exception: java.lang.ArithmeticException: / by zero
Zero is an invalid denominator. Please try again.

Please enter an integer numerator: 100
Please enter an integer denominator: 7

Result: 100 / 7 = 14
```

```
Please enter an integer numerator: 100
Please enter an integer denominator: hello

Exception: java.util.InputMismatchException
You must enter integers. Please try again.

Please enter an integer numerator: 100
Please enter an integer denominator: 7

Result: 100 / 7 = 14
```

Fig. 11.3 | Handling `ArithmeticException`s and `InputMismatchException`s. (Part 2 of 2.)

The first sample execution in Fig. 11.3 does *not* encounter any problems. In the second execution the user enters a *zero denominator*, and an `ArithmeticException` exception occurs. In the third execution the user enters the string `"hello"` as the denominator, and an `InputMismatchException` occurs. For each exception, the user is informed of the mistake and asked to try again, then is prompted for two new integers. In each sample execution, the program runs to completion successfully.

Class `InputMismatchException` is imported in line 3. Class `ArithmeticException` does not need to be imported because it's in package `java.lang`. Line 18 creates the `boolean` variable `continueLoop`, which is `true` if the user has *not* yet entered valid input. Lines 20–48 repeatedly ask users for input until a *valid* input is received.

Enclosing Code in a try Block

Lines 22–33 contain a **try block**, which encloses the code that *might* throw an exception and the code that should *not* execute if an exception occurs (i.e., if an exception occurs, the remaining code in the try block will be skipped). A try block consists of the keyword try followed by a block of code enclosed in curly braces. [*Note:* The term "try block" sometimes refers only to the block of code that follows the try keyword (not including the try keyword itself). For simplicity, we use the term "try block" to refer to the block of code that follows the try keyword, as well as the try keyword.] The statements that read the integers from the keyboard (lines 25 and 27) each use method nextInt to read an int value. Method nextInt throws an InputMismatchException if the value read in is *not* an integer.

The division that can cause an ArithmeticException is not performed in the try block. Rather, the call to method quotient (line 29) invokes the code that attempts the division (line 12); the JVM *throws* an ArithmeticException object when the denominator is zero.

Software Engineering Observation 11.1

Exceptions may surface through explicitly mentioned code in a try block, through deeply nested method calls initiated by code in a try block or from the Java Virtual Machine as it executes Java bytecodes.

Catching Exceptions

The try block in this example is followed by two catch blocks—one that handles an InputMismatchException (lines 34–41) and one that handles an ArithmeticException (lines 42–47). A **catch block** (also called a **catch clause** or **exception handler**) *catches* (i.e., receives) and *handles* an exception. A catch block begins with the keyword catch followed by a parameter in parentheses (called the *exception parameter*, discussed shortly) and a block of code enclosed in curly braces. [*Note:* The term "catch clause" is sometimes used to refer to the keyword catch followed by a block of code, whereas the term "catch block" refers to only the block of code following the catch keyword, but not including it. For simplicity, we use the term "catch block" to refer to the block of code following the catch keyword, as well as the keyword itself.]

At least one catch block or a **finally block** (discussed in Section 11.6) *must* immediately follow the try block. Each catch block specifies in parentheses an **exception parameter** that identifies the exception type the handler can process. When an exception occurs in a try block, the catch block that executes is the *first* one whose type matches the type of the exception that occurred (i.e., the type in the catch block matches the thrown exception type exactly or is a direct or indirect superclass of it). The exception parameter's name enables the catch block to interact with a caught exception object—e.g., to implicitly invoke the caught exception's toString method (as in lines 37 and 44), which displays basic information about the exception. Notice that we use the **System.err (standard error stream) object** to output error messages. By default, System.err's print methods, like those of System.out, display data to the *command prompt*.

Line 38 of the first catch block calls Scanner method nextLine. Because an InputMismatchException occurred, the call to method nextInt never successfully read in the user's data—so we read that input with a call to method nextLine. We do not do anything with the input at this point, because we know that it's *invalid*. Each catch block displays an error message and asks the user to try again. After either catch block terminates, the user is prompted for input. We'll soon take a deeper look at how this flow of control works in exception handling.

Common Programming Error 11.1

It's a syntax error to place code between a try block and its corresponding catch blocks.

Multi-catch

It's relatively common for a try block to be followed by several catch blocks to handle various types of exceptions. If the bodies of several catch blocks are identical, you can use the **multi-catch** feature (introduced in Java SE 7) to catch those exception types in a *single* catch handler and perform the same task. The syntax for a *multi-catch* is:

```
catch (Type1 | Type2 | Type3 e)
```

Each exception type is separated from the next with a vertical bar (|). The preceding line of code indicates that *any* of the types (or their subclasses) can be caught in the exception handler. Any number of Throwable types can be specified in a multi-catch.

Uncaught Exceptions

An **uncaught exception** is one for which there are no matching catch blocks. You saw uncaught exceptions in the second and third outputs of Fig. 11.2. Recall that when exceptions occurred in that example, the application terminated early (after displaying the exception's *stack trace*). This does not always occur as a result of uncaught exceptions. Java uses a "multithreaded" model of program execution—each **thread** is a *concurrent activity*. One program can have many threads. If a program has only *one* thread, an uncaught exception will cause the program to terminate. If a program has *multiple* threads, an uncaught exception will terminate *only* the thread in which the exception occurred. In such programs, however, certain threads may rely on others, and if one thread terminates due to an uncaught exception, there may be adverse effects on the rest of the program. Chapter 20, Concurrency, discusses these issues in depth.

Termination Model of Exception Handling

If an exception occurs in a try block (such as an InputMismatchException being thrown as a result of the code at line 25 of Fig. 11.3), the try block *terminates* immediately and program control transfers to the *first* of the following catch blocks in which the exception parameter's type matches the thrown exception's type. In Fig. 11.3, the first catch block catches InputMismatchExceptions (which occur if invalid input is entered) and the second catch block catches ArithmeticExceptions (which occur if an attempt is made to divide by zero). After the exception is handled, program control does *not* return to the throw point, because the try block has *expired* (and its *local variables* have been *lost*). Rather, control resumes after the last catch block. This is known as the **termination model of exception handling**. Some languages use the **resumption model of exception handling**, in which, after an exception is handled, control resumes just after the *throw point*.

Notice that we name our exception parameters (inputMismatchException and arithmeticException) based on their type. Java programmers often simply use the letter e as the name of their exception parameters.

After executing a catch block, this program's flow of control proceeds to the first statement after the last catch block (line 48 in this case). The condition in the do...while statement is true (variable continueLoop contains its initial value of true), so control returns to the beginning of the loop and the user is again prompted for input. This control statement will loop until *valid* input is entered. At that point, program control reaches line 32, which assigns false to variable continueLoop. The try block then *terminates*. If no exceptions are thrown in the try block, the catch blocks are *skipped* and control continues with the first statement after the catch blocks (we'll learn about another possibility when we discuss the finally block in Section 11.6). Now the condition for the do...while loop is false, and method main ends.

The try block and its corresponding catch and/or finally blocks form a **try statement**. Do not confuse the terms "try block" and "try statement"—the latter includes the try block as well as the following catch blocks and/or finally block.

As with any other block of code, when a try block terminates, *local variables* declared in the block *go out of scope* and are no longer accessible; thus, the local variables of a try block are not accessible in the corresponding catch blocks. When a catch block *terminates*, *local variables* declared within the catch block (including the exception parameter of that catch block) also *go out of scope* and are *destroyed*. Any remaining catch blocks in the try statement are *ignored*, and execution resumes at the first line of code after the try...catch sequence—this will be a finally block, if one is present.

Using the **throws** Clause

In method quotient (Fig. 11.3, lines 9–13), line 10 is known as a **throws clause**. It specifies the exceptions the method *might* throw if problems occur. This clause, which must appear after the method's parameter list and before the body, contains a comma-separated list of the exception types. Such exceptions may be thrown by statements in the method's body or by methods called from there. We've added the throws clause to this application to indicate that this method might throw an ArithmeticException. Method quotient's callers are thus informed that the method might throw an ArithmeticException. Some exception types, such as ArithmeticException, are not required to be listed in the throws clause. For those that are, the method can throw exceptions that have the *is-a* relationship with the classes listed in the throws clause. You'll learn more about this in Section 11.5.

> **Error-Prevention Tip 11.1**
>
> *Read the online API documentation for a method before using it in a program. The documentation specifies the exceptions thrown by the method (if any) and indicates reasons why such exceptions may occur. Next, read the online API documentation for the specified exception classes. The documentation for an exception class typically contains potential reasons that such exceptions occur. Finally, provide for handling those exceptions in your program.*

When line 12 executes, if the denominator is zero, the JVM throws an ArithmeticException object. This object will be caught by the catch block at lines 42–47, which displays basic information about the exception by *implicitly* invoking the exception's toString method, then asks the user to try again.

If the denominator is not zero, method quotient performs the division and returns the result to the point of invocation of method quotient in the try block (line 29). Lines 30–31 display the result of the calculation and line 32 sets continueLoop to false. In this case, the try block completes successfully, so the program skips the catch blocks and fails the condition at line 48, and method main completes execution normally.

When quotient throws an ArithmeticException, quotient *terminates* and does *not* return a value, and quotient's *local variables go out of scope* (and are destroyed). If quotient contained local variables that were references to objects and there were no other references to those objects, the objects would be marked for *garbage collection*. Also, when an exception occurs, the try block from which quotient was called *terminates* before lines 30–32 can execute. Here, too, if local variables were created in the try block prior to the exception's being thrown, these variables would go out of scope.

If an InputMismatchException is generated by lines 25 or 27, the try block *terminates* and execution *continues* with the catch block at lines 34–41. In this case, method quotient is not called. Then method main continues after the last catch block (line 48).

11.4 When to Use Exception Handling

Exception handling is designed to process **synchronous errors**, which occur when a statement executes. Common examples we'll see throughout the book are *out-of-range array indices*, *arithmetic overflow* (i.e., a value outside the representable range of values), *division by zero*, *invalid method parameters* and *thread interruption* (as we'll see in Chapter 20). Exception handling is not designed to process problems associated with **asynchronous events** (e.g., disk I/O completions, network message arrivals, mouse clicks and keystrokes), which occur in parallel with, and *independent of*, the program's flow of control.

Software Engineering Observation 11.2

Incorporate your exception-handling and error-recovery strategy into your system from the inception of the design process—including these after a system has been implemented can be difficult.

Software Engineering Observation 11.3

Exception handling provides a single, uniform technique for documenting, detecting and recovering from errors. This helps programmers working on large projects understand each other's error-processing code.

Software Engineering Observation 11.4

There's a great variety of situations that generate exceptions—some exceptions are easier to recover from than others.

11.5 Java Exception Hierarchy

All Java exception classes inherit directly or indirectly from class **Exception**, forming an *inheritance hierarchy*. You can extend this hierarchy with your own exception classes.

Figure 11.4 shows a small portion of the inheritance hierarchy for class **Throwable** (a subclass of Object), which is the superclass of class Exception. Only Throwable objects can be used with the exception-handling mechanism. Class Throwable has two direct subclasses: Exception and Error. Class Exception and its subclasses—for instance, Runtime-Exception (package java.lang) and IOException (package java.io)—represent exceptional situations that can occur in a Java program and that can be caught by the application. Class **Error** and its subclasses represent *abnormal situations* that happen in the JVM. Most *Errors happen infrequently and should not be caught by applications—it's usually not possible for applications to recover from Errors.*

The Java exception hierarchy contains hundreds of classes. Information about Java's exception classes can be found throughout the Java API. You can view Throwable's documentation at docs.oracle.com/javase/7/docs/api/java/lang/Throwable.html. From there, you can look at this class's subclasses to get more information about Java's Exceptions and Errors.

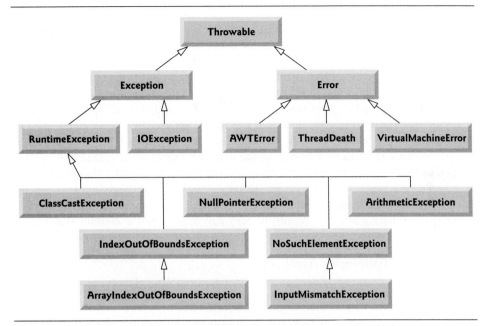

Fig. 11.4 | Portion of class Throwable's inheritance hierarchy.

Checked vs. Unchecked Exceptions

Java distinguishes between **checked exceptions** and **unchecked exceptions**. This distinction is important, because the Java compiler enforces special requirements for *checked* exceptions (discussed momentarily). An exception's type determines whether it's checked or unchecked.

RuntimeExceptions Are Unchecked Exceptions

All exception types that are direct or indirect subclasses of **RuntimeException** (package java.lang) are *unchecked* exceptions. These are typically caused by defects in your program's code. Examples of unchecked exceptions include:

- ArrayIndexOutOfBoundsExceptions (discussed in Chapter 7)—You can avoid these by ensuring that your array indices are always greater than or equal to 0 and less than the array's length.

- ArithmeticExceptions (shown in Fig. 11.3)—You can avoid the Arithmetic-Exception that occurs when you divide by zero by checking the denominator to determine whether it's 0 *before* performing the calculation.

Classes that inherit directly or indirectly from class Error (Fig. 11.4) are *unchecked*, because Errors are such serious problems that your program should not even attempt to deal with them.

Checked Exceptions

All classes that inherit from class Exception but *not* directly or indirectly from class RuntimeException are considered to be *checked* exceptions. Such exceptions are typically caused by conditions that are not under the control of the program—for example, in file processing, the program can't open a file if it does not exist.

The Compiler and Checked Exceptions

The compiler checks each method call and method declaration to determine whether the method throws a checked exception. If so, the compiler verifies that the checked exception is *caught* or is *declared* in a throws clause—this is known as the **catch-or-declare requirement**. We show how to catch or declare checked exceptions in the next several examples. Recall from Section 11.3 that the throws clause specifies the exceptions a method throws. Such exceptions are not caught in the method's body. To satisfy the *catch* part of the *catch-or-declare requirement*, the code that generates the exception must be wrapped in a try block and must provide a catch handler for the checked-exception type (or one of its superclasses). To satisfy the *declare* part of the catch-or-declare requirement, the method containing the code that generates the exception must provide a throws clause containing the checked-exception type after its parameter list and before its method body. If the catch-or-declare requirement is not satisfied, the compiler will issue an error message. This forces you to think about the problems that may occur when a method that throws checked exceptions is called.

Error-Prevention Tip 11.2

You must deal with checked exceptions. This results in more robust code than would be created if you were able to simply ignore them.

Common Programming Error 11.2

If a subclass method overrides a superclass method, it's an error for the subclass method to list more exceptions in its throws clause than the superclass method does. However, a subclass's throws clause can contain a subset of a superclass's throws clause.

Software Engineering Observation 11.5

If your method calls other methods that throw checked exceptions, those exceptions must be caught or declared. If an exception can be handled meaningfully in a method, the method should catch the exception rather than declare it.

The Compiler and Unchecked Exceptions

Unlike checked exceptions, the Java compiler does *not* examine the code to determine whether an unchecked exception is caught or declared. Unchecked exceptions typically can be *prevented* by proper coding. For example, the unchecked ArithmeticException thrown by method quotient (lines 9–13) in Fig. 11.3 can be avoided if the method ensures that the denominator is not zero *before* performing the division. Unchecked exceptions are *not* required to be listed in a method's throws clause—even if they are, it's *not* required that such exceptions be caught by an application.

Software Engineering Observation 11.6

Although the compiler does not enforce the catch-or-declare requirement for unchecked exceptions, provide appropriate exception-handling code when it's known that such exceptions might occur. For example, a program should process the NumberFormatException from Integer method parseInt, even though NumberFormatException is an indirect subclass of RuntimeException (and thus an unchecked exception). This makes your programs more robust.

Catching Subclass Exceptions
If a catch handler is written to catch *superclass* exception objects, it can also catch all objects of that class's *subclasses*. This enables catch to handle related exceptions *polymorphically*. You can catch each subclass individually if those exceptions require different processing.

Only the First Matching catch Executes
If *multiple* catch blocks match a particular exception type, only the *first* matching catch block executes when an exception of that type occurs. It's a compilation error to catch the *exact same type* in two different catch blocks associated with a particular try block. However, there can be several catch blocks that match an exception—i.e., several catch blocks whose types are the same as the exception type or a superclass of that type. For instance, we could follow a catch block for type ArithmeticException with a catch block for type Exception—both would match ArithmeticExceptions, but only the first matching catch block would execute.

> **Common Programming Error 11.3**
> *Placing a catch block for a superclass exception type before other catch blocks that catch subclass exception types would prevent those catch blocks from executing, so a compilation error occurs.*

> **Error-Prevention Tip 11.3**
> *Catching subclass types individually is subject to error if you forget to test for one or more of the subclass types explicitly; catching the superclass guarantees that objects of all subclasses will be caught. Positioning a catch block for the superclass type after all other subclass catch blocks ensures that all subclass exceptions are eventually caught.*

> **Software Engineering Observation 11.7**
> *In industry, throwing or catching type Exception is discouraged—we use it here simply to demonstrate exception-handling mechanics. In subsequent chapters, we generally throw and catch more specific exception types.*

11.6 finally Block

Programs that obtain certain resources must return them to the system to avoid so-called **resource leaks.** In programming languages such as C and C++, the most common resource leak is a *memory leak.* Java performs automatic *garbage collection* of memory no longer used by programs, thus avoiding most memory leaks. However, other types of resource leaks can occur. For example, files, database connections and network connections that are not closed properly after they're no longer needed might not be available for use in other programs.

> **Error-Prevention Tip 11.4**
> *A subtle issue is that Java does not entirely eliminate memory leaks. Java will not garbage-collect an object until there are no remaining references to it. Thus, if you erroneously keep references to unwanted objects, memory leaks can occur.*

The finally block (which consists of the finally keyword, followed by code enclosed in curly braces), sometimes referred to as the **finally clause,** is optional. If it's present, it's placed after the last catch block. If there are no catch blocks, the finally block, if present, immediately follows the try block.

When the *finally* Block Executes

The finally block will execute *whether or not* an exception is thrown in the corresponding try block. The finally block also will execute if a try block exits by using a return, break or continue statement or simply by reaching its closing right brace. The one case in which the finally block will *not* execute is if the application *exits early* from a try block by calling method **System.exit**. This method, which we demonstrate in Chapter 15, *immediately* terminates an application.

If an exception that occurs in a try block cannot be caught by one of that try block's catch handlers, the program skips the rest of the try block and control proceeds to the finally block. Then the program passes the exception to the next outer try block—normally in the calling method—where an associated catch block might catch it. This process can occur through many levels of try blocks. Also, the exception could go *uncaught* (as we discussed in Section 11.3).

If a catch block throws an exception, the finally block still executes. Then the exception is passed to the next outer try block—again, normally in the calling method.

Releasing Resources in a *finally* Block

Because a finally block always executes, it typically contains *resource-release code*. Suppose a resource is allocated in a try block. If no exception occurs, the catch blocks are *skipped* and control proceeds to the finally block, which frees the resource. Control then proceeds to the first statement after the finally block. If an exception occurs in the try block, the try block *terminates*. If the program catches the exception in one of the corresponding catch blocks, it processes the exception, then the finally block *releases the resource* and control proceeds to the first statement after the finally block. If the program doesn't catch the exception, the finally block *still* releases the resource and an attempt is made to catch the exception in a calling method.

Error-Prevention Tip 11.5

The finally block is an ideal place to release resources acquired in a try block (such as opened files), which helps eliminate resource leaks.

Performance Tip 11.1

Always release a resource explicitly and at the earliest possible moment at which it's no longer needed. This makes resources available for reuse as early as possible, thus improving resource utilization and program performance.

Demonstrating the *finally* Block

Figure 11.5 demonstrates that the finally block executes even if an exception is *not* thrown in the corresponding try block. The program contains static methods main (lines 6–18), throwException (lines 21–44) and doesNotThrowException (lines 47–64). Methods throwException and doesNotThrowException are declared static, so main can call them directly without instantiating a UsingExceptions object.

```
 1   // Fig. 11.5: UsingExceptions.java
 2   // try...catch...finally exception handling mechanism.
 3
 4   public class UsingExceptions
 5   {
 6      public static void main(String[] args)
 7      {
 8         try
 9         {
10            throwException();
11         }
12         catch (Exception exception) // exception thrown by throwException
13         {
14            System.err.println("Exception handled in main");
15         }
16
17         doesNotThrowException();
18      }
19
20      // demonstrate try...catch...finally
21      public static void throwException() throws Exception
22      {
23         try // throw an exception and immediately catch it
24         {
25            System.out.println("Method throwException");
26            throw new Exception(); // generate exception
27         }
28         catch (Exception exception) // catch exception thrown in try
29         {
30            System.err.println(
31               "Exception handled in method throwException");
32            throw exception; // rethrow for further processing
33
34            // code here would not be reached; would cause compilation errors
35
36         }
37         finally // executes regardless of what occurs in try...catch
38         {
39            System.err.println("Finally executed in throwException");
40         }
41
42         // code here would not be reached; would cause compilation errors
43
44      }
45
46      // demonstrate finally when no exception occurs
47      public static void doesNotThrowException()
48      {
49         try // try block does not throw an exception
50         {
51            System.out.println("Method doesNotThrowException");
52         }
```

Fig. 11.5 | try...catch...finally exception-handling mechanism. (Part 1 of 2.)

```
53        catch (Exception exception) // does not execute
54        {
55            System.err.println(exception);
56        }
57        finally // executes regardless of what occurs in try...catch
58        {
59            System.err.println(
60                "Finally executed in doesNotThrowException");
61        }
62
63        System.out.println("End of method doesNotThrowException");
64    }
65 } // end class UsingExceptions
```

```
Method throwException
Exception handled in method throwException
Finally executed in throwException
Exception handled in main
Method doesNotThrowException
Finally executed in doesNotThrowException
End of method doesNotThrowException
```

Fig. 11.5 | try...catch...finally exception-handling mechanism. (Part 2 of 2.)

System.out and System.err are **streams**—sequences of bytes. While System.out (known as the **standard output stream**) displays a program's output, System.err (known as the **standard error stream**) displays a program's errors. Output from these streams can be *redirected* (i.e., sent to somewhere other than the *command prompt*, such as to a *file*). Using two different streams enables you to easily *separate* error messages from other output. For instance, data output from System.err could be sent to a log file, while data output from System.out can be displayed on the screen. For simplicity, this chapter will *not* redirect output from System.err, but will display such messages to the *command prompt*. You'll learn more about streams in Chapter 15.

*Throwing Exceptions Using the **throw** Statement*
Method main (Fig. 11.5) begins executing, enters its try block and immediately calls method throwException (line 10). Method throwException throws an Exception. The statement at line 26 is known as a **throw statement**—it's executed to indicate that an exception has occurred. So far, you've caught only exceptions thrown by called methods. You can throw exceptions yourself by using the throw statement. Just as with exceptions thrown by the Java API's methods, this indicates to client applications that an error has occurred. A throw statement specifies an object to be thrown. The operand of a throw can be of any class derived from class Throwable.

Software Engineering Observation 11.8
When toString is invoked on any Throwable object, its resulting String includes the descriptive string that was supplied to the constructor, or simply the class name if no string was supplied.

Software Engineering Observation 11.9

An exception can be thrown without containing information about the problem that occurred. In this case, simply knowing that an exception of a particular type occurred may provide sufficient information for the handler to process the problem correctly.

Software Engineering Observation 11.10

Throw exceptions from constructors to indicate that the constructor parameters are not valid—this prevents an object from being created in an invalid state.

Rethrowing Exceptions

Line 32 of Fig. 11.5 **rethrows the exception**. Exceptions are rethrown when a catch block, upon receiving an exception, decides either that it cannot process that exception or that it can only partially process it. Rethrowing an exception defers the exception handling (or perhaps a portion of it) to another catch block associated with an outer try statement. An exception is rethrown by using the **throw keyword**, followed by a reference to the exception object that was just caught. Exceptions cannot be rethrown from a finally block, as the exception parameter (a local variable) from the catch block no longer exists.

When a rethrow occurs, the *next enclosing try block* detects the rethrown exception, and that try block's catch blocks attempt to handle it. In this case, the next enclosing try block is found at lines 8–11 in method main. Before the rethrown exception is handled, however, the finally block (lines 37–40) executes. Then method main detects the rethrown exception in the try block and handles it in the catch block (lines 12–15).

Next, main calls method doesNotThrowException (line 17). No exception is thrown in doesNotThrowException's try block (lines 49–52), so the program skips the catch block (lines 53–56), but the finally block (lines 57–61) nevertheless executes. Control proceeds to the statement after the finally block (line 63). Then control returns to main and the program terminates.

Common Programming Error 11.4

If an exception has not been caught when control enters a finally block and the finally block throws an exception that's not caught in the finally block, the first exception will be lost and the exception from the finally block will be returned to the calling method.

Error-Prevention Tip 11.6

Avoid placing in a finally block code that can throw an exception. If such code is required, enclose the code in a try...catch within the finally block.

Common Programming Error 11.5

Assuming that an exception thrown from a catch block will be processed by that catch block or any other catch block associated with the same try statement can lead to logic errors.

Good Programming Practice 11.1

Exception handling removes error-processing code from the main line of a program's code to improve program clarity. Do not place try...catch...finally around every statement that may throw an exception. This decreases readability. Rather, place one try block around a significant portion of your code, follow the try with catch blocks that handle each possible exception and follow the catch blocks with a single finally block (if one is required).

11.7 Stack Unwinding and Obtaining Information from an Exception Object

When an exception is thrown but *not caught* in a particular scope, the method-call stack is "unwound," and an attempt is made to catch the exception in the next outer try block. This process is called **stack unwinding**. Unwinding the method-call stack means that the method in which the exception was not caught *terminates*, all local variables in that method *go out of scope* and control returns to the statement that originally invoked that method. If a try block encloses that statement, an attempt is made to catch the exception. If a try block does not enclose that statement or if the exception is not caught, stack unwinding occurs again. Figure 11.6 demonstrates stack unwinding, and the exception handler in main shows how to access the data in an exception object.

Stack Unwinding

In main, the try block (lines 8–11) calls method1 (declared at lines 35–38), which in turn calls method2 (declared at lines 41–44), which in turn calls method3 (declared at lines 47–50). Line 49 of method3 throws an Exception object—this is the *throw point*. Because the throw statement at line 49 is *not* enclosed in a try block, *stack unwinding* occurs—method3 terminates at line 49, then returns control to the statement in method2 that invoked method3 (i.e., line 43). Because *no* try block encloses line 43, *stack unwinding* occurs again—method2 terminates at line 43 and returns control to the statement in method1 that invoked method2 (i.e., line 37). Because *no* try block encloses line 37, *stack unwinding* occurs one more time—method1 terminates at line 37 and returns control to the statement in main that invoked method1 (i.e., line 10). The try block at lines 8–11 encloses this statement. The exception has not been handled, so the try block terminates and the first matching catch block (lines 12–31) catches and processes the exception. If there were no matching catch blocks, and the exception is *not declared* in each method that throws it, a compilation error would occur. Remember that this is not always the case—for *unchecked* exceptions, the application will compile, but it will run with unexpected results.

```
1   // Fig. 11.6: UsingExceptions.java
2   // Stack unwinding and obtaining data from an exception object.
3
4   public class UsingExceptions
5   {
6      public static void main(String[] args)
7      {
8         try
9         {
10            method1();
11         }
12         catch (Exception exception) // catch exception thrown in method1
13         {
14            System.err.printf("%s%n%n", exception.getMessage());
15            exception.printStackTrace();
16
```

Fig. 11.6 | Stack unwinding and obtaining data from an exception object. (Part 1 of 2.)

```
17            // obtain the stack-trace information
18            StackTraceElement[] traceElements = exception.getStackTrace();
19
20            System.out.printf("%nStack trace from getStackTrace:%n");
21            System.out.println("Class\t\tFile\t\t\tLine\tMethod");
22
23            // loop through traceElements to get exception description
24            for (StackTraceElement element : traceElements)
25            {
26                System.out.printf("%s\t", element.getClassName());
27                System.out.printf("%s\t", element.getFileName());
28                System.out.printf("%s\t", element.getLineNumber());
29                System.out.printf("%s%n", element.getMethodName());
30            }
31        }
32    } // end main
33
34    // call method2; throw exceptions back to main
35    public static void method1() throws Exception
36    {
37        method2();
38    }
39
40    // call method3; throw exceptions back to method1
41    public static void method2() throws Exception
42    {
43        method3();
44    }
45
46    // throw Exception back to method2
47    public static void method3() throws Exception
48    {
49        throw new Exception("Exception thrown in method3");
50    }
51 } // end class UsingExceptions
```

```
Exception thrown in method3

java.lang.Exception: Exception thrown in method3
        at UsingExceptions.method3(UsingExceptions.java:49)
        at UsingExceptions.method2(UsingExceptions.java:43)
        at UsingExceptions.method1(UsingExceptions.java:37)
        at UsingExceptions.main(UsingExceptions.java:10)

Stack trace from getStackTrace:
Class              File                     Line    Method
UsingExceptions UsingExceptions.java        49      method3
UsingExceptions UsingExceptions.java        43      method2
UsingExceptions UsingExceptions.java        37      method1
UsingExceptions UsingExceptions.java        10      main
```

Fig. 11.6 | Stack unwinding and obtaining data from an exception object. (Part 2 of 2.)

Obtaining Data from an Exception Object

All exceptions derive from class Throwable, which has a **printStackTrace** method that outputs to the standard error stream the *stack trace* (discussed in Section 11.2). Often this is helpful in testing and debugging. Class Throwable also provides a **getStackTrace** method that retrieves the stack-trace information that might be printed by printStackTrace. Class Throwable's **getMessage** method returns the descriptive string stored in an exception.

Error-Prevention Tip 11.7
An exception that's not caught in an application causes Java's default exception handler to run. This displays the name of the exception, a descriptive message that indicates the problem that occurred and a complete execution stack trace. In an application with a single thread of execution, the application terminates. In an application with multiple threads, the thread that caused the exception terminates. We discuss multithreading in Chapter 20.

Error-Prevention Tip 11.8
Throwable method toString *(inherited by all* Throwable *subclasses) returns a* String *containing the name of the exception's class and a descriptive message.*

The catch handler in Fig. 11.6 (lines 12–31) demonstrates getMessage, print-StackTrace and getStackTrace. If we wanted to output the stack-trace information to streams other than the standard error stream, we could use the information returned from getStackTrace and output it to another stream or use one of the overloaded versions of method printStackTrace. Sending data to other streams is discussed in Chapter 15.

Line 14 invokes the exception's getMessage method to get the *exception description*. Line 15 invokes the exception's printStackTrace method to output the *stack trace* that indicates where the exception occurred. Line 18 invokes the exception's getStackTrace method to obtain the stack-trace information as an array of **StackTraceElement** objects. Lines 24–30 get each StackTraceElement in the array and invoke its methods **getClass-Name**, **getFileName**, **getLineNumber** and **getMethodName** to get the class name, filename, line number and method name, respectively, for that StackTraceElement. Each Stack-TraceElement represents *one* method call on the *method-call stack*.

The program's output shows that output of printStackTrace follows the pattern: *className.methodName(fileName:lineNumber)*, where *className*, *methodName* and *fileName* indicate the names of the class, method and file in which the exception occurred, respectively, and the *lineNumber* indicates where in the file the exception occurred. You saw this in the output for Fig. 11.2. Method getStackTrace enables custom processing of the exception information. Compare the output of printStackTrace with the output created from the StackTraceElements to see that both contain the same stack-trace information.

Software Engineering Observation 11.11
Occasionally, you might want to ignore an exception by writing a catch *handler with an empty body. Before doing so, ensure that the exception doesn't indicate a condition that code higher up the stack might want to know about or recover from.*

11.8 Chained Exceptions

Sometimes a method responds to an exception by throwing a different exception type that's specific to the current application. If a catch block throws a new exception, the original exception's information and stack trace are *lost*. Earlier Java versions provided no mechanism to wrap the original exception information with the new exception's information to provide a complete stack trace showing where the original problem occurred. This made debugging such problems particularly difficult. **Chained exceptions** enable an exception object to maintain the complete stack-trace information from the original exception. Figure 11.7 demonstrates chained exceptions.

```java
1   // Fig. 11.7: UsingChainedExceptions.java
2   // Chained exceptions.
3
4   public class UsingChainedExceptions
5   {
6      public static void main(String[] args)
7      {
8         try
9         {
10            method1();
11         }
12         catch (Exception exception) // exceptions thrown from method1
13         {
14            exception.printStackTrace();
15         }
16      }
17
18      // call method2; throw exceptions back to main
19      public static void method1() throws Exception
20      {
21         try
22         {
23            method2();
24         } // end try
25         catch (Exception exception) // exception thrown from method2
26         {
27            throw new Exception("Exception thrown in method1", exception);
28         }
29      }
30
31      // call method3; throw exceptions back to method1
32      public static void method2() throws Exception
33      {
34         try
35         {
36            method3();
37         }
38         catch (Exception exception) // exception thrown from method3
39         {
40            throw new Exception("Exception thrown in method2", exception);
41         }
42      }
43
```

Fig. 11.7 | Chained exceptions. (Part 1 of 2.)

```
44      // throw Exception back to method2
45      public static void method3() throws Exception
46      {
47          throw new Exception("Exception thrown in method3");
48      }
49  } // end class UsingChainedExceptions
```

```
java.lang.Exception: Exception thrown in method1
        at UsingChainedExceptions.method1(UsingChainedExceptions.java:27)
        at UsingChainedExceptions.main(UsingChainedExceptions.java:10)
Caused by: java.lang.Exception: Exception thrown in method2
        at UsingChainedExceptions.method2(UsingChainedExceptions.java:40)
        at UsingChainedExceptions.method1(UsingChainedExceptions.java:23)
        ... 1 more
Caused by: java.lang.Exception: Exception thrown in method3
        at UsingChainedExceptions.method3(UsingChainedExceptions.java:47)
        at UsingChainedExceptions.method2(UsingChainedExceptions.java:36)
        ... 2 more
```

Fig. 11.7 | Chained exceptions. (Part 2 of 2.)

Program Flow of Control

The program consists of four methods—main (lines 6–16), method1 (lines 19–29), method2 (lines 32–42) and method3 (lines 45–48). Line 10 in method main's try block calls method1. Line 23 in method1's try block calls method2. Line 36 in method2's try block calls method3. In method3, line 47 throws a new Exception. Because this statement is not in a try block, method3 terminates, and the exception is returned to the calling method (method2) at line 36. This statement *is* in a try block; therefore, the try block terminates and the exception is caught at lines 38–41. Line 40 in the catch block throws a new exception. In this case, the Exception constructor with *two* arguments is called. The second argument represents the exception that was the original cause of the problem. In this program, that exception occurred at line 47. Because an exception is thrown from the catch block, method2 terminates and returns the new exception to the calling method (method1) at line 23. Once again, this statement is in a try block, so the try block terminates and the exception is caught at lines 25–28. Line 27 in the catch block throws a new exception and uses the exception that was caught as the second argument to the Exception constructor. Because an exception is thrown from the catch block, method1 terminates and returns the new exception to the calling method (main) at line 10. The try block in main terminates, and the exception is caught at lines 12–15. Line 14 prints a stack trace.

Program Output

Notice in the program output that the first three lines show the most recent exception that was thrown (i.e., the one from method1 at line 27). The next four lines indicate the exception that was thrown from method2 at line 40. Finally, the last four lines represent the exception that was thrown from method3 at line 47. Also notice that, as you read the output in reverse, it shows how many more chained exceptions remain.

11.9 Declaring New Exception Types

Most Java programmers use *existing* classes from the Java API, third-party vendors and freely available class libraries (usually downloadable from the Internet) to build Java applications. The methods of those classes typically are declared to throw appropriate exceptions when problems occur. You write code that processes these existing exceptions to make your programs more robust.

If you build classes that other programmers will use, it's often appropriate to declare your own exception classes that are specific to the problems that can occur when another programmer uses your reusable classes.

A New Exception Type Must Extend an Existing One

A new exception class must extend an existing exception class to ensure that the class can be used with the exception-handling mechanism. An exception class is like any other class; however, a typical new exception class contains only four constructors:

- one that takes no arguments and passes a default error message String to the superclass constructor
- one that receives a customized error message as a String and passes it to the superclass constructor
- one that receives a customized error message as a String and a Throwable (for chaining exceptions) and passes both to the superclass constructor
- one that receives a Throwable (for chaining exceptions) and passes it to the superclass constructor.

Good Programming Practice 11.2

Associating each type of serious execution-time malfunction with an appropriately named Exception class improves program clarity.

Software Engineering Observation 11.12

When defining your own exception type, study the existing exception classes in the Java API and try to extend a related exception class. For example, if you're creating a new class to represent when a method attempts a division by zero, you might extend class ArithmeticException because division by zero occurs during arithmetic. If the existing classes are not appropriate superclasses for your new exception class, decide whether your new class should be a checked or an unchecked exception class. If clients should be required to handle the exception, the new exception class should be a checked exception (i.e., extend Exception but not RuntimeException). The client application should be able to reasonably recover from such an exception. If the client code should be able to ignore the exception (i.e., the exception is an unchecked one), the new exception class should extend RuntimeException.

11.10 Preconditions and Postconditions

Programmers spend significant amounts of time maintaining and debugging code. To facilitate these tasks and to improve the overall design, you can specify the expected states before and after a method's execution. These states are called preconditions and postconditions, respectively.

Preconditions

A **precondition** must be true when a method is *invoked*. Preconditions describe constraints on method parameters and any other expectations the method has about the current state of a program *just before it begins executing*. If the preconditions are *not* met, then the method's behavior is *undefined*—it may *throw an exception, proceed with an illegal value* or *attempt to recover* from the error. You should not expect consistent behavior if the preconditions are not satisfied.

Postconditions

A **postcondition** is true *after the method successfully returns*. Postconditions describe *constraints on the return value* and any other *side effects* the method may have. When defining a method, you should document all postconditions so that others know what to expect when they call your method, and you should make certain that your method honors all its postconditions if its preconditions are indeed met.

Throwing Exceptions When Preconditions or Postconditions Are Not Met

When their preconditions or postconditions are not met, methods typically throw exceptions. As an example, examine String method charAt, which has one int parameter—an index in the String. For a precondition, method charAt assumes that index is greater than or equal to zero and less than the length of the String. If the precondition is met, the postcondition states that the method will return the character at the position in the String specified by the parameter index. Otherwise, the method throws an IndexOutOfBounds-Exception. We trust that method charAt satisfies its postcondition, provided that we meet the precondition. We need not be concerned with the details of how the method actually retrieves the character at the index.

Typically, a method's preconditions and postconditions are described as part of its specification. When designing your own methods, you should state the preconditions and postconditions in a comment before the method declaration.

11.11 Assertions

When implementing and debugging a class, it's sometimes useful to state conditions that should be true at a particular point in a method. These conditions, called **assertions**, help ensure a program's validity by catching potential bugs and identifying possible logic errors during development. Preconditions and postconditions are two types of assertions. Preconditions are assertions about a program's state when a method is invoked, and postconditions are assertions about its state after a method finishes.

While assertions can be stated as comments to guide you during program development, Java includes two versions of the **assert** statement for validating assertions programatically. The assert statement evaluates a boolean expression and, if false, throws an **AssertionError** (a subclass of Error). The first form of the assert statement is

```
assert expression;
```

which throws an AssertionError if *expression* is false. The second form is

```
assert expression1 : expression2;
```

which evaluates *expression1* and throws an AssertionError with *expression2* as the error message if *expression1* is false.

You can use assertions to implement *preconditions* and *postconditions* programmatically or to verify any other *intermediate* states that help you ensure that your code is working correctly. Figure 11.8 demonstrates the assert statement. Line 11 prompts the user to enter a number between 0 and 10, then line 12 reads the number. Line 15 determines whether the user entered a number within the valid range. If the number is out of range, the assert statement reports an error; otherwise, the program proceeds normally.

```java
1   // Fig. 11.8: AssertTest.java
2   // Checking with assert that a value is within range
3   import java.util.Scanner;
4
5   public class AssertTest
6   {
7      public static void main(String[] args)
8      {
9         Scanner input = new Scanner(System.in);
10
11         System.out.print("Enter a number between 0 and 10: ");
12         int number = input.nextInt();
13
14         // assert that the value is >= 0 and <= 10
15         assert (number >= 0 && number <= 10) : "bad number: " + number;
16
17         System.out.printf("You entered %d%n", number);
18      }
19   } // end class AssertTest
```

```
Enter a number between 0 and 10: 5
You entered 5
```

```
Enter a number between 0 and 10: 50
Exception in thread "main" java.lang.AssertionError: bad number: 50
        at AssertTest.main(AssertTest.java:15)
```

Fig. 11.8 | Checking with assert that a value is within range.

You use assertions primarily for debugging and identifying logic errors in an application. You must explicitly enable assertions when executing a program, because they reduce performance and are unnecessary for the program's user. To do so, use the java command's -ea command-line option, as in

```
java -ea AssertTest
```

 Software Engineering Observation 11.13

Users shouldn't encounter AssertionErrors—these should be used only during program development. For this reason, you shouldn't catch AssertionErrors. Instead, allow the program to terminate, so you can see the error message, then locate and fix the source of the problem. You should not use assert to indicate runtime problems in production code (as we did in Fig. 11.8 for demonstration purposes)—use the exception mechanism for this purpose.

11.12 try-with-Resources: Automatic Resource Deallocation

Typically *resource-release code* should be placed in a `finally` block to ensure that a resource is released, regardless of whether there were exceptions when the resource was used in the corresponding `try` block. An alternative notation—the **try-with-resources** statement (introduced in Java SE 7)—simplifies writing code in which you obtain one or more resources, use them in a `try` block and release them in a corresponding `finally` block. For example, a file-processing application could process a file with a try-with-resources statement to ensure that the file is closed properly when it's no longer needed—we demonstrate this in Chapter 15. Each resource must be an object of a class that implements the **Auto-Closeable** interface, and thus provides a `close` method. The general form of a try-with-resources statement is

```
try (ClassName theObject = new ClassName())
{
    // use theObject here
}
catch (Exception e)
{
    // catch exceptions that occur while using the resource
}
```

where *ClassName* is a class that implements the `AutoCloseable` interface. This code creates an object of type *ClassName* and uses it in the `try` block, then calls its `close` method to release any resources used by the object. The try-with-resources statement *implicitly* calls the `theObject`'s `close` method *at the end of the try block*. You can allocate multiple resources in the parentheses following `try` by separating them with a semicolon (;). You'll see examples of the try-with-resources statement in Chapters 15 and 21.

11.13 Wrap-Up

In this chapter, you learned how to use exception handling to deal with errors. You learned that exception handling enables you to remove error-handling code from the "main line" of the program's execution. We showed how to use `try` blocks to enclose code that may throw an exception, and how to use `catch` blocks to deal with exceptions that may arise.

You learned about the termination model of exception handling, which dictates that after an exception is handled, program control does not return to the throw point. We discussed checked vs. unchecked exceptions, and how to specify with the `throws` clause the exceptions that a method might throw.

You learned how to use the `finally` block to release resources whether or not an exception occurs. You also learned how to throw and rethrow exceptions. We showed how to obtain information about an exception using methods `printStackTrace`, `getStackTrace` and `getMessage`. Next, we presented chained exceptions, which allow you to wrap original exception information with new exception information. Then, we showed how to create your own exception classes.

We introduced preconditions and postconditions to help programmers using your methods understand conditions that must be true when the method is called and when it returns, respectively. When preconditions and postconditions are not met, methods typically throw exceptions. We discussed the `assert` statement and how it can be used to help you debug your programs. In particular, `assert` can be used to ensure that preconditions and postconditions are met.

We also introduced multi-`catch` for processing several types of exceptions in the same `catch` handler and the try-with-resources statement for automatically deallocating a resource after it's used in the `try` block. In the next chapter, we take a deeper look at graphical user interfaces (GUIs).

12

Swing GUI Components: Part 1

Objectives

In this chapter you'll:

- Learn how to use the Nimbus look-and-feel.
- Build GUIs and handle events generated by user interactions with GUIs.
- Understand the packages containing GUI components, event-handling classes and interfaces.
- Create and manipulate buttons, labels, lists, text fields and panels.
- Handle mouse events and keyboard events.
- Use layout managers to arrange GUI components.

Outline

12.1 Introduction

A **graphical user interface** (**GUI**) presents a user-friendly mechanism for interacting with an application. A GUI (pronounced "GOO-ee") gives an application a distinctive "look-and-feel." GUIs are built from **GUI components**. These are sometimes called *controls* or *widgets*—short for window gadgets. A GUI component is an object with which the user *interacts* via the mouse, the keyboard or another form of input, such as voice recognition. In this chapter and Chapter 19, Swing GUI Components: Part 2, you'll learn about many of Java's so-called **Swing GUI components** from the `javax.swing` package. We cover other GUI components as they're needed throughout the book. In Chapter 22, you'll be introduced to JavaFX—Java's latest APIs for GUI, graphics and multimedia.

 Look-and-Feel Observation 12.1
Providing different applications with consistent, intuitive user-interface components gives users a sense of familiarity with a new application, so that they can learn it more quickly and use it more productively.

IDE Support for GUI Design
Many IDEs provide GUI design tools with which you can specify a component's *size, location* and other attributes in a visual manner by using the mouse, the keyboard and drag-and-drop. The IDEs generate the GUI code for you. This greatly simplifies creating GUIs, but each IDE generates this code differently. For this reason, we wrote the GUI code by hand, as you'll see in the source-code files for this chapter's examples. We encourage you to build each GUI visually using your preferred IDE(s).

*Sample GUI: The **SwingSet3** Demo Application*

As an example of a GUI, consider Fig. 12.1, which shows the **SwingSet3** demo application from the JDK demos and samples download at http://www.oracle.com/technetwork/ java/javase/downloads/index.html. This application is a nice way for you to browse through the various GUI components provided by Java's Swing GUI APIs. Simply click a component name (e.g., JFrame, JTabbedPane, etc.) in the **GUI Components** area at the left of the window to see a demonstration of the GUI component in the right side of the window. The source code for each demo is shown in the text area at the bottom of the window. We've labeled a few of the GUI components in the application. At the top of the window is a **title bar** that contains the window's title. Below that is a **menu bar** containing **menus** (**File** and **View**). In the top-right region of the window is a set of **buttons**—typically, users click buttons to perform tasks. In the **GUI Components** area of the window is a **combo box**; the user can click the down arrow at the right side of the box to select from a list of items. The menus, buttons and combo box are part of the application's GUI. They enable you to interact with the application.

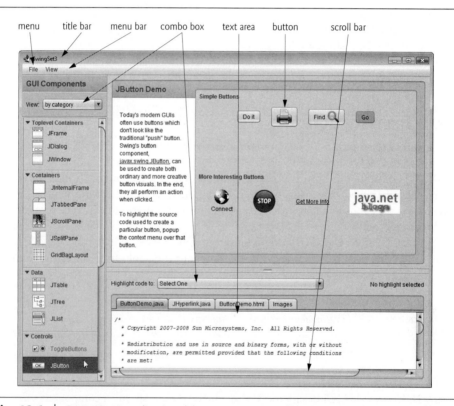

Fig. 12.1 | **SwingSet3** application demonstrates many of Java's Swing GUI components.

12.2 Java's Nimbus Look-and-Feel

A GUI's look consists of its visual aspects, such as its colors and fonts, and its feel consists of the components you use to interact with the GUI, such as buttons and menus. Together these are known as the GUI's look-and-feel. Swing has a cross-platform look-and-feel known as **Nimbus**. For GUI screen captures like Fig. 12.1, we've configured our systems to use Nimbus as the default look-and-feel. There are three ways that you can use Nimbus:

1. Set it as the default for all Java applications that run on your computer.

2. Set it as the look-and-feel at the time that you launch an application by passing a command-line argument to the java command.

3. Set it as the look-and-feel programatically in your application (see Section 19.6).

To set Nimbus as the default for all Java applications, you must create a text file named swing.properties in the lib folder of both your JDK installation folder and your JRE installation folder. Place the following line of code in the file:

```
swing.defaultlaf=com.sun.java.swing.plaf.nimbus.NimbusLookAndFeel
```

In addition to the standalone JRE, there is a JRE nested in your JDK's installation folder. If you're using an IDE that depends on the JDK, you may also need to place the swing.properties file in the nested jre folder's lib folder.

If you prefer to select Nimbus on an application-by-application basis, place the following command-line argument after the java command and before the application's name when you run the application:

```
-Dswing.defaultlaf=com.sun.java.swing.plaf.nimbus.NimbusLookAndFeel
```

12.3 Simple GUI-Based Input/Output with JOptionPane

The applications in Chapters 2–11 display text in the command window and obtain input from the command window. Most applications you use on a daily basis use windows or **dialog boxes** (also called **dialogs**) to interact with the user. For example, an e-mail program allows you to type and read messages in a window the program provides. Dialog boxes are windows in which programs display important messages to the user or obtain information from the user. Java's **JOptionPane** class (package javax.swing) provides prebuilt dialog boxes for both input and output. These are displayed by invoking static JOptionPane methods. Figure 12.2 presents a simple addition application that uses two **input dialogs** to obtain integers from the user and a **message dialog** to display the sum of the integers the user enters.

```
1   // Fig. 12.2: Addition.java
2   // Addition program that uses JOptionPane for input and output.
3   import javax.swing.JOptionPane;
4
5   public class Addition
6   {
7      public static void main(String[] args)
8      {
9         // obtain user input from JOptionPane input dialogs
10        String firstNumber =
11           JOptionPane.showInputDialog("Enter first integer");
```

Fig. 12.2 | Addition program that uses JOptionPane for input and output. (Part I of 2.)

```
12          String secondNumber =
13             JOptionPane.showInputDialog("Enter second integer");
14
15          // convert String inputs to int values for use in a calculation
16          int number1 = Integer.parseInt(firstNumber);
17          int number2 = Integer.parseInt(secondNumber);
18
19          int sum = number1 + number2;
20
21          // display result in a JOptionPane message dialog
22          JOptionPane.showMessageDialog(null, "The sum is " + sum,
23             "Sum of Two Integers", JOptionPane.PLAIN_MESSAGE);
24       }
25    } // end class Addition
```

(a) Input dialog displayed by lines 10–11

Prompt to the user

When the user clicks **OK**,
showInputDialog returns
to the program the 100 typed
by the user as a `String`; the
program must convert the
`String` to an `int`

Text field in which the
user types a value

Input
Enter first integer
100
OK   Cancel

(b) Input dialog displayed by lines 12–13

Input
Enter second integer
23
OK   Cancel

(c) Message dialog displayed by lines 22–23—When the user clicks
OK, the message dialog is dismissed (removed from the screen)

Sum of Two Integers
The sum is 123
OK

Fig. 12.2 | Addition program that uses JOptionPane for input and output. (Part 2 of 2.)

Input Dialogs

Line 3 imports class JOptionPane. Lines 10–11 declare the local String variable first-Number and assign it the result of the call to JOptionPane static method **showInputDialog**. This method displays an input dialog (see the screen capture in Fig. 12.2(a)), using the method's String argument ("Enter first integer") as a prompt.

Look-and-Feel Observation 12.2

*The prompt in an input dialog typically uses **sentence-style capitalization**—a style that capitalizes only the first letter of the first word in the text unless the word is a proper noun (for example, Jones).*

The user types characters in the text field, then clicks **OK** or presses the *Enter* key to submit the String to the program. Clicking **OK** also **dismisses (hides) the dialog**. [*Note:* If you type in the text field and nothing appears, activate the text field by clicking it with the mouse.] Unlike Scanner, which can be used to input values of *several* types from the user at the keyboard, *an input dialog can input only Strings*. This is typical of most GUI components. The user can type *any* characters in the input dialog's text field. Our program assumes that the user enters a *valid* integer. If the user clicks **Cancel**, showInputDialog returns null. If the user either types a noninteger value or clicks the **Cancel** button in the input dialog, an exception will occur and the program will not operate correctly. Lines 12–13 display another input dialog that prompts the user to enter the second integer. Each JOptionPane dialog that you display is a so called **modal dialog**—while the dialog is on the screen, the user *cannot* interact with the rest of the application.

Look-and-Feel Observation 12.3

Do not overuse modal dialogs, as they can reduce the usability of your applications. Use a modal dialog only when it's necessary to prevent users from interacting with the rest of an application until they dismiss the dialog.

Converting *Strings* to *int Values*

To perform the calculation, we convert the Strings that the user entered to int values. Recall that the Integer class's static method parseInt converts its String argument to an int value and might throw a NumberFormatException. Lines 16–17 assign the converted values to local variables number1 and number2, and line 19 sums these values.

Message Dialogs

Lines 22–23 use JOptionPane static method **showMessageDialog** to display a message dialog (the last screen of Fig. 12.2) containing the sum. The first argument helps the Java application determine where to *position* the dialog box. A dialog is typically displayed from a GUI application with its own window. The first argument refers to that window (known as the *parent window*) and causes the dialog to appear centered over the parent (as we'll do in Section 12.9). If the first argument is null, the dialog box is displayed at the *center* of your screen. The second argument is the *message* to display—in this case, the result of concatenating the String "The sum is " and the value of sum. The third argument—"Sum of Two Integers"—is the String that should appear in the *title bar* at the top of the dialog. The fourth argument—**JOptionPane.PLAIN_MESSAGE**—is the *type of message dialog to display*. A PLAIN_MESSAGE dialog does *not* display an *icon* to the left of the message. Class JOptionPane provides several overloaded versions of methods showInputDialog and showMessageDialog, as well as methods that display other dialog types. For complete information, visit http://docs.oracle.com/javase/7/docs/api/javax/swing/JOptionPane.html.

Look-and-Feel Observation 12.4

*The title bar of a window typically uses **book-title capitalization**—a style that capitalizes the first letter of each significant word in the text and does not end with any punctuation (for example, Capitalization in a Book Title).*

JOptionPane Message Dialog Constants

The constants that represent the message dialog types are shown in Fig. 12.3. All message dialog types except PLAIN_MESSAGE display an icon to the *left* of the message. These icons provide a visual indication of the message's importance to the user. A QUESTION_MESSAGE icon is the *default icon* for an input dialog box (see Fig. 12.2).

Message dialog type	Icon	Description
ERROR_MESSAGE		Indicates an error.
INFORMATION_MESSAGE		Indicates an informational message.
WARNING_MESSAGE		Warns of a potential problem.
QUESTION_MESSAGE		Poses a question. This dialog normally requires a response, such as clicking a **Yes** or a **No** button.
PLAIN_MESSAGE	no icon	A dialog that contains a message, but no icon.

Fig. 12.3 | JOptionPane static constants for message dialogs.

12.4 Overview of Swing Components

Though it's possible to perform input and output using the JOptionPane dialogs, most GUI applications require more elaborate user interfaces. The remainder of this chapter discusses many GUI components that enable application developers to create robust GUIs. Figure 12.4 lists several basic Swing GUI components that we discuss.

Component	Description
JLabel	Displays *uneditable text* and/or icons.
JTextField	Typically *receives input* from the user.
JButton	Triggers an event when clicked with the mouse.
JCheckBox	Specifies an option that can be *selected* or *not selected*.
JComboBox	A *drop-down list of items* from which the *user* can make a *selection*.
JList	A *list of items* from which the user can make a *selection* by *clicking* on *any one* of them. *Multiple* elements *can* be selected.
JPanel	An area in which *components* can be *placed* and *organized*.

Fig. 12.4 | Some basic Swing GUI components.

Swing vs. AWT

There are actually *two* sets of Java GUI components. In Java's early days, GUIs were built with components from the **Abstract Window Toolkit (AWT)** in package **java.awt**. These look like the native GUI components of the platform on which a Java program executes. For example, a Button object displayed in a Java program running on Microsoft Windows looks like those in other *Windows* applications. On Apple Mac OS X, the Button looks like those in other *Mac* applications. Sometimes, even the manner in which a user can interact with an AWT component *differs between platforms*. The component's appearance and the way in which the user interacts with it are known as its **look-and-feel**.

Look-and-Feel Observation 12.5

Swing GUI components allow you to specify a uniform look-and-feel for your application across all *platforms or to use each platform's custom look-and-feel. An application can even change the look-and-feel during execution to enable users to choose their own preferred look-and-feel.*

Lightweight vs. Heavyweight GUI Components

Most Swing components are **lightweight components**—they're written, manipulated and displayed completely in Java. AWT components are **heavyweight components**, because they rely on the local platform's **windowing system** to determine their functionality and their look-and-feel. Several Swing components are *heavyweight* components.

Superclasses of Swing's Lightweight GUI Components

The UML class diagram of Fig. 12.5 shows an *inheritance hierarchy* of classes from which lightweight Swing components inherit their common attributes and behaviors.

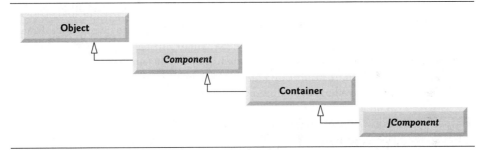

Fig. 12.5 | Common superclasses of the lightweight Swing components.

Class **Component** (package java.awt) is a superclass that declares the common features of GUI components in packages java.awt and javax.swing. Any object that *is a* **Container** (package java.awt) can be used to organize Components by *attaching* the Components to the Container. Containers can be placed in other Containers to organize a GUI.

Class **JComponent** (package javax.swing) is a subclass of Container. JComponent is the superclass of all *lightweight* Swing components and declares their common attributes and behaviors. Because JComponent is a subclass of Container, all lightweight Swing components are also Containers. Some common features supported by JComponent include:

1. A **pluggable look-and-feel** for *customizing* the appearance of components (e.g., for use on particular platforms). You'll see an example of this in Section 19.6.

2. Shortcut keys (called **mnemonics**) for direct access to GUI components through the keyboard. You'll see an example of this in Section 19.4.

3. Brief descriptions of a GUI component's purpose (called **tool tips**) that are displayed when the *mouse cursor is positioned over the component* for a short time. You'll see an example of this in the next section.

4. Support for *accessibility*, such as braille screen readers for the visually impaired.

5. Support for user-interface **localization**—that is, customizing the user interface to display in different languages and use local cultural conventions.

12.5 Displaying Text and Images in a Window

Our next example introduces a framework for building GUI applications. Several concepts in this framework will appear in many of our GUI applications. This is our first example in which the application appears in its own window. Most windows you'll create that can contain Swing GUI components are instances of class JFrame or a subclass of JFrame. JFrame is an *indirect* subclass of class java.awt.Window that provides the basic attributes and behaviors of a window—a *title bar* at the top, and *buttons* to *minimize, maximize* and *close* the window. Since an application's GUI is typically specific to the application, most of our examples will consist of *two* classes—a subclass of JFrame that helps us demonstrate new GUI concepts and an application class in which main creates and displays the application's primary window.

Labeling GUI Components
A typical GUI consists of many components. GUI designers often provide text stating the purpose of each. Such text is known as a **label** and is created with a **JLabel**—a subclass of JComponent. A JLabel displays read-only text, an image, or both text and an image. Applications rarely change a label's contents after creating it.

Look-and-Feel Observation 12.6
Text in a JLabel normally uses sentence-style capitalization.

The application of Figs. 12.6–12.7 demonstrates several JLabel features and presents the framework we use in most of our GUI examples. We did *not* highlight the code in this example, since most of it is new. [*Note:* There are many more features for each GUI component than we can cover in our examples. To learn the complete details of each GUI component, visit its page in the online documentation. For class JLabel, visit http://docs.oracle.com/javase/7/docs/api/javax/swing/JLabel.html.]

```
 1   // Fig. 12.6: LabelFrame.java
 2   // JLabels with text and icons.
 3   import java.awt.FlowLayout; // specifies how components are arranged
 4   import javax.swing.JFrame; // provides basic window features
 5   import javax.swing.JLabel; // displays text and images
 6   import javax.swing.SwingConstants; // common constants used with Swing
 7   import javax.swing.Icon; // interface used to manipulate images
 8   import javax.swing.ImageIcon; // loads images
 9
10   public class LabelFrame extends JFrame
11   {
12      private final JLabel label1; // JLabel with just text
13      private final JLabel label2; // JLabel constructed with text and icon
14      private final JLabel label3; // JLabel with added text and icon
15
16      // LabelFrame constructor adds JLabels to JFrame
17      public LabelFrame()
18      {
```

Fig. 12.6 | JLabels with text and icons. (Part 1 of 2.)

```
19        super("Testing JLabel");
20        setLayout(new FlowLayout()); // set frame layout
21
22        // JLabel constructor with a string argument
23        label1 = new JLabel("Label with text");
24        label1.setToolTipText("This is label1");
25        add(label1); // add label1 to JFrame
26
27        // JLabel constructor with string, Icon and alignment arguments
28        Icon bug = new ImageIcon(getClass().getResource( "bug1.png"));
29        label2 = new JLabel("Label with text and icon", bug,
30           SwingConstants.LEFT);
31        label2.setToolTipText("This is label2");
32        add(label2); // add label2 to JFrame
33
34        label3 = new JLabel(); // JLabel constructor no arguments
35        label3.setText("Label with icon and text at bottom");
36        label3.setIcon(bug); // add icon to JLabel
37        label3.setHorizontalTextPosition(SwingConstants.CENTER);
38        label3.setVerticalTextPosition(SwingConstants.BOTTOM);
39        label3.setToolTipText("This is label3");
40        add(label3); // add label3 to JFrame
41     }
42  } // end class LabelFrame
```

Fig. 12.6 | JLabels with text and icons. (Part 2 of 2.)

```
 1  // Fig. 12.7: LabelTest.java
 2  // Testing LabelFrame.
 3  import javax.swing.JFrame;
 4
 5  public class LabelTest
 6  {
 7     public static void main(String[] args)
 8     {
 9        LabelFrame labelFrame = new LabelFrame();
10        labelFrame.setDefaultCloseOperation(JFrame.EXIT_ON_CLOSE);
11        labelFrame.setSize(260, 180);
12        labelFrame.setVisible(true);
13     }
14  } // end class LabelTest
```

Fig. 12.7 | Testing LabelFrame.

Class `LabelFrame` (Fig. 12.6) extends `JFrame` to inherit the features of a window. We'll use an instance of class `LabelFrame` to display a window containing three `JLabels`. Lines 12–14 declare the three `JLabel` instance variables that are instantiated in the `Label-Frame` constructor (lines 17–41). Typically, the `JFrame` subclass's constructor builds the GUI that's displayed in the window when the application executes. Line 19 invokes super-class `JFrame`'s constructor with the argument `"Testing JLabel"`. `JFrame`'s constructor uses this `String` as the text in the window's title bar.

Specifying the Layout

When building a GUI, you must attach each GUI component to a container, such as a window created with a `JFrame`. Also, you typically must decide where to *position* each GUI component—known as *specifying the layout*. Java provides several **layout managers** that can help you position components, as you'll learn later in this chapter and in Chapter 19.

Many IDEs provide GUI design tools in which you can specify components' exact *sizes* and *locations* in a visual manner by using the mouse; then the IDE will generate the GUI code for you. Such IDEs can greatly simplify GUI creation.

To ensure that our GUIs can be used with *any* IDE, we did *not* use an IDE to create the GUI code. We use Java's layout managers to *size* and *position* components. With the **FlowLayout** layout manager, components are placed in a *container* from left to right in the order in which they're added. When no more components can fit on the current line, they continue to display left to right on the next line. If the container is *resized*, a `FlowLayout` *reflows* the components, possibly with fewer or more rows based on the new container width. Every container has a *default layout*, which we're changing for `LabelFrame` to a `FlowLayout` (line 20). Method **setLayout** is inherited into class `LabelFrame` indirectly from class `Container`. The argument to the method must be an object of a class that implements the `LayoutManager` interface (e.g., `FlowLayout`). Line 20 creates a new `FlowLayout` object and passes its reference as the argument to `setLayout`.

Creating and Attaching `label1`

Now that we've specified the window's layout, we can begin creating and attaching GUI components to the window. Line 23 creates a `JLabel` object and passes `"Label with text"` to the constructor. The `JLabel` displays this text on the screen. Line 24 uses method **set-ToolTipText** (inherited by `JLabel` from `JComponent`) to specify the tool tip that's displayed when the user positions the mouse cursor over the `JLabel` in the GUI. You can see a sample tool tip in the second screen capture of Fig. 12.7. When you execute this application, hover the mouse pointer over each `JLabel` to see its tool tip. Line 25 (Fig. 12.6) attaches `label1` to the `LabelFrame` by passing `label1` to the **add** method, which is inherited indirectly from class `Container`.

Common Programming Error 12.1

If you do not explicitly add a GUI component to a container, the GUI component will not be displayed when the container appears on the screen.

Look-and-Feel Observation 12.7

Use tool tips to add descriptive text to your GUI components. This text helps the user determine the GUI component's purpose in the user interface.

The *Icon Interface and Class* `ImageIcon`

Icons are a popular way to enhance the look-and-feel of an application and are also commonly used to indicate functionality. For example, the same icon is used to play most of today's media on devices like DVD players and MP3 players. Several Swing components can display images. An icon is normally specified with an `Icon` (package `javax.swing`) argument to a constructor or to the component's `setIcon` method. Class `ImageIcon` supports several image formats, including Graphics Interchange Format (GIF), Portable Network Graphics (PNG) and Joint Photographic Experts Group (JPEG).

Line 28 declares an `ImageIcon`. The file `bug1.png` contains the image to load and store in the `ImageIcon` object. This image is included in the directory for this example. The `ImageIcon` object is assigned to `Icon` reference bug.

Loading an Image Resource

In line 28, the expression `getClass().getResource("bug1.png")` invokes method **get-Class** (inherited indirectly from class `Object`) to retrieve a reference to the `Class` object that represents the `LabelFrame` class declaration. That reference is then used to invoke `Class` method **getResource**, which returns the location of the image as a URL. The `ImageIcon` constructor uses the URL to locate the image, then loads it into memory. As we discussed in Chapter 1, the JVM loads class declarations into memory, using a class loader. The class loader knows where each class it loads is located on disk. Method `getResource` uses the `Class` object's class loader to determine the *location* of a resource, such as an image file. In this example, the image file is stored in the same location as the `LabelFrame.class` file. The techniques described here enable an application to load image files from locations that are relative to the class file's location.

Creating and Attaching `label2`

Lines 29–30 use another `JLabel` constructor to create a `JLabel` that displays the text `"Label with text and icon"` and the `Icon` bug created in line 28. The last constructor argument indicates that the label's contents are left justified, or left aligned (i.e., the icon and text are at the left side of the label's area on the screen). Interface **SwingConstants** (package `javax.swing`) declares a set of common integer constants (such as `SwingConstants.LEFT`, `SwingConstants.CENTER` and `SwingConstants.RIGHT`) that are used with many Swing components. By default, the text appears to the right of the image when a label contains both text and an image. The horizontal and vertical alignments of a `JLabel` can be set with methods **setHorizontalAlignment** and **setVerticalAlignment**, respectively. Line 31 specifies the tool-tip text for `label2`, and line 32 adds `label2` to the `JFrame`.

Creating and Attaching `label3`

Class `JLabel` provides methods to change a `JLabel`'s appearance after it's been instantiated. Line 34 creates an empty `JLabel` with the no-argument constructor. Line 35 uses `JLabel` method **setText** to set the text displayed on the label. Method **getText** can be used to retrieve the `JLabel`'s current text. Line 36 uses `JLabel` method `setIcon` to specify the `Icon` to display. Method **getIcon** can be used to retrieve the current `Icon` displayed on a label. Lines 37–38 use `JLabel` methods **setHorizontalTextPosition** and **setVerticalTextPosition** to specify the text position in the label. In this case, the text will be centered *horizontally* and will appear at the *bottom* of the label. Thus, the `Icon` will appear *above* the text. The horizontal-position constants in `SwingConstants` are `LEFT`, `CENTER` and `RIGHT` (Fig. 12.8).

The vertical-position constants in SwingConstants are TOP, CENTER and BOTTOM (Fig. 12.8). Line 39 (Fig. 12.6) sets the tool-tip text for label3. Line 40 adds label3 to the JFrame.

Constant	Description	Constant	Description
Horizontal-position constants		*Vertical-position constants*	
LEFT	Place text on the left	TOP	Place text at the top
CENTER	Place text in the center	CENTER	Place text in the center
RIGHT	Place text on the right	BOTTOM	Place text at the bottom

Fig. 12.8 | Positioning constants (static members of interface SwingConstants).

*Creating and Displaying a **LabelFrame** Window*
Class LabelTest (Fig. 12.7) creates an object of class LabelFrame (line 9), then specifies the default close operation for the window. By default, closing a window simply *hides* the window. However, when the user closes the LabelFrame window, we would like the application to *terminate*. Line 10 invokes LabelFrame's **setDefaultCloseOperation** method (inherited from class JFrame) with constant **JFrame.EXIT_ON_CLOSE** as the argument to indicate that the program should *terminate* when the window is closed by the user. This line is important. Without it the application will *not* terminate when the user closes the window. Next, line 11 invokes LabelFrame's **setSize** method to specify the *width* and *height* of the window in *pixels*. Finally, line 12 invokes LabelFrame's **setVisible** method with the argument true to display the window on the screen. Try resizing the window to see how the FlowLayout changes the JLabel positions as the window width changes.

12.6 Text Fields and an Introduction to Event Handling with Nested Classes

Normally, a user interacts with an application's GUI to indicate the tasks that the application should perform. For example, when you write an e-mail in an e-mail application, clicking the **Send** button tells the application to send the e-mail to the specified e-mail addresses. GUIs are **event driven**. When the user interacts with a GUI component, the interaction—known as an **event**—drives the program to perform a task. Some common user interactions that cause an application to perform a task include *clicking* a button, *typing* in a text field, *selecting* an item from a menu, *closing* a window and *moving* the mouse. The code that performs a task in response to an event is called an **event handler**, and the process of responding to events is known as **event handling**.

Let's consider two other GUI components that can generate events—**JTextFields** and **JPasswordFields** (package javax.swing). Class JTextField extends class **JTextComponent** (package javax.swing.text), which provides many features common to Swing's text-based components. Class JPasswordField extends JTextField and adds methods that are specific to processing passwords. Each of these components is a single-line area in which the user can enter text via the keyboard. Applications can also display text in a JTextField (see the output of Fig. 12.10). A JPasswordField shows that characters are being typed as the user enters them, but hides the actual characters with an **echo character**, assuming that they represent a password that should remain known only to the user.

When the user types in a JTextField or a JPasswordField, then presses *Enter*, an *event* occurs. Our next example demonstrates how a program can perform a task *in response* to that event. The techniques shown here are applicable to all GUI components that generate events.

The application of Figs. 12.9–12.10 uses classes JTextField and JPasswordField to create and manipulate four text fields. When the user types in one of the text fields, then presses *Enter*, the application displays a message dialog box containing the text the user typed. You can type only in the text field that's "in **focus**." When you *click* a component, it *receives the focus*. This is important, because the text field with the focus is the one that generates an event when you press *Enter*. In this example, when you press *Enter* in the JPasswordField, the password is revealed. We begin by discussing the setup of the GUI, then discuss the event-handling code.

```java
 1  // Fig. 12.9: TextFieldFrame.java
 2  // JTextFields and JPasswordFields.
 3  import java.awt.FlowLayout;
 4  import java.awt.event.ActionListener;
 5  import java.awt.event.ActionEvent;
 6  import javax.swing.JFrame;
 7  import javax.swing.JTextField;
 8  import javax.swing.JPasswordField;
 9  import javax.swing.JOptionPane;
10
11  public class TextFieldFrame extends JFrame
12  {
13     private final JTextField textField1; // text field with set size
14     private final JTextField textField2; // text field with text
15     private final JTextField textField3; // text field with text and size
16     private final JPasswordField passwordField; // password field with text
17
18     // TextFieldFrame constructor adds JTextFields to JFrame
19     public TextFieldFrame()
20     {
21        super("Testing JTextField and JPasswordField");
22        setLayout(new FlowLayout());
23
24        // construct text field with 10 columns
25        textField1 = new JTextField(10);
26        add(textField1); // add textField1 to JFrame
27
28        // construct text field with default text
29        textField2 = new JTextField("Enter text here");
30        add(textField2); // add textField2 to JFrame
31
32        // construct text field with default text and 21 columns
33        textField3 = new JTextField("Uneditable text field", 21);
34        textField3.setEditable(false); // disable editing
35        add(textField3); // add textField3 to JFrame
```

Fig. 12.9 | JTextFields and JPasswordFields. (Part 1 of 2.)

```
36
37        // construct password field with default text
38        passwordField = new JPasswordField("Hidden text");
39        add(passwordField); // add passwordField to JFrame
40
41        // register event handlers
42        TextFieldHandler handler = new TextFieldHandler();
43        textField1.addActionListener(handler);
44        textField2.addActionListener(handler);
45        textField3.addActionListener(handler);
46        passwordField.addActionListener(handler);
47     }
48
49     // private inner class for event handling
50     private class TextFieldHandler implements ActionListener
51     {
52        // process text field events
53        @Override
54        public void actionPerformed(ActionEvent event)
55        {
56           String string = "";
57
58           // user pressed Enter in JTextField textField1
59           if (event.getSource() == textField1)
60              string = String.format("textField1: %s",
61                 event.getActionCommand());
62
63           // user pressed Enter in JTextField textField2
64           else if (event.getSource() == textField2)
65              string = String.format("textField2: %s",
66                 event.getActionCommand());
67
68           // user pressed Enter in JTextField textField3
69           else if (event.getSource() == textField3)
70              string = String.format("textField3: %s",
71                 event.getActionCommand());
72
73           // user pressed Enter in JTextField passwordField
74           else if (event.getSource() == passwordField)
75              string = String.format("passwordField: %s",
76                 event.getActionCommand());
77
78           // display JTextField content
79           JOptionPane.showMessageDialog(null, string);
80        }
81     } // end private inner class TextFieldHandler
82  } // end class TextFieldFrame
```

Fig. 12.9 | JTextFields and JPasswordFields. (Part 2 of 2.)

Class TextFieldFrame extends JFrame and declares three JTextField variables and a JPasswordField variable (lines 13–16). Each of the corresponding text fields is instantiated and attached to the TextFieldFrame in the constructor (lines 19–47).

Creating the GUI

Line 22 sets the TextFieldFrame's layout to FlowLayout. Line 25 creates textField1 with 10 columns of text. A text column's width in *pixels* is determined by the average width of a character in the text field's current font. When text is displayed in a text field and the text is wider than the field itself, a portion of the text at the right side is not visible. If you're typing in a text field and the cursor reaches the right edge, the text at the left edge is pushed off the left side of the field and is no longer visible. Users can use the left and right arrow keys to move through the complete text. Line 26 adds textField1 to the JFrame.

Line 29 creates textField2 with the initial text "Enter text here" to display in the text field. The width of the field is determined by the width of the default text specified in the constructor. Line 30 adds textField2 to the JFrame.

Line 33 creates textField3 and calls the JTextField constructor with two arguments—the default text "Uneditable text field" to display and the text field's width in columns (21). Line 34 uses method **setEditable** (inherited by JTextField from class JTextComponent) to make the text field *uneditable*—i.e., the user cannot modify the text in the field. Line 35 adds textField3 to the JFrame.

Line 38 creates passwordField with the text "Hidden text" to display in the text field. The width of the field is determined by the width of the default text. When you execute the application, notice that the text is displayed as a string of asterisks. Line 39 adds passwordField to the JFrame.

Steps Required to Set Up Event Handling for a GUI Component

This example should display a message dialog containing the text from a text field when the user presses *Enter* in that text field. Before an application can respond to an event for a particular GUI component, you must:

1. Create a class that represents the event handler and implements an appropriate interface—known as an **event-listener interface**.

2. Indicate that an object of the class from *Step 1* should be notified when the event occurs—known as **registering the event handler**.

Using a Nested Class to Implement an Event Handler

All the classes discussed so far were so-called **top-level classes**—that is, they *were* not declared *inside* another class. Java allows you to declare classes *inside* other classes—these are called **nested classes**. Nested classes can be static or non-static. Non-static nested classes are called **inner classes** and are frequently used to implement *event handlers*.

An inner-class object must be created by an object of the top-level class that contains the inner class. Each inner-class object *implicitly* has a reference to an object of its top-level class. The inner-class object is allowed to use this implicit reference to directly access all the variables and methods of the top-level class. A nested class that's static does not require an object of its top-level class and does not implicitly have a reference to an object of the top-level class. As you'll see in Chapter 13, Graphics and Java 2D, the Java 2D graphics API uses static nested classes extensively.

Inner Class TextFieldHandler

The event handling in this example is performed by an object of the private *inner class* TextFieldHandler (lines 50–81). This class is private because it will be used only to create event handlers for the text fields in top-level class TextFieldFrame. As with other class members, *inner classes* can be declared public, protected or private. Since event handlers tend to be specific to the application in which they're defined, they're often implemented as private inner classes or as *anonymous inner classes* (Section 12.11).

GUI components can generate many events in response to user interactions. Each event is represented by a class and can be processed only by the appropriate type of event handler. Normally, a component's supported events are described in the Java API documentation for that component's class and its superclasses. When the user presses *Enter* in a JTextField or JPasswordField, an **ActionEvent** (package java.awt.event) occurs. Such an event is processed by an object that implements the interface **ActionListener** (package java.awt.event). The information discussed here is available in the Java API documentation for classes JTextField and ActionEvent. Since JPasswordField is a subclass of JTextField, JPasswordField supports the same events.

To prepare to handle the events in this example, inner class TextFieldHandler implements interface ActionListener and declares the only method in that interface—actionPerformed (lines 53–80). This method specifies the tasks to perform when an ActionEvent occurs. So, inner class TextFieldHandler satisfies *Step 1* listed earlier in this section. We'll discuss the details of method actionPerformed shortly.

Registering the Event Handler for Each Text Field
In the TextFieldFrame constructor, line 42 creates a TextFieldHandler object and assigns it to variable handler. This object's actionPerformed method will be called automatically when the user presses *Enter* in any of the GUI's text fields. However, before this can occur, the program must register this object as the event handler for each text field. Lines 43–46 are the *event-registration* statements that specify handler as the event handler for the three JTextFields and the JPasswordField. The application calls JTextField method **addActionListener** to register the event handler for each component. This method receives as its argument an ActionListener object, which can be an object of any class that implements ActionListener. The object handler *is an* ActionListener, because class TextFieldHandler implements ActionListener. After lines 43–46 execute, the object handler **listens for events**. Now, when the user presses *Enter* in any of these four text fields, method actionPerformed (line 53–80) in class TextFieldHandler is called to handle the event. If an event handler is *not* registered for a particular text field, the event that occurs when the user presses *Enter* in that text field is **consumed**—i.e., it's simply *ignored* by the application.

Software Engineering Observation 12.1
The event listener for an event must implement the appropriate event-listener interface.

Common Programming Error 12.2
If you forget to register an event-handler object for a particular GUI component's event type, events of that type will be ignored.

Details of Class TextFieldHandler's actionPerformed Method
In this example, we use one event-handling object's actionPerformed method (lines 53–80) to handle the events generated by four text fields. Since we'd like to output the name of each text field's instance variable for demonstration purposes, we must determine *which* text field

generated the event each time actionPerformed is called. The **event source** is the component with which the user interacted. When the user presses *Enter* while a text field or the password field *has the focus*, the system creates a unique ActionEvent object that contains information about the event that just occurred, such as the event source and the text in the text field. The system passes this ActionEvent object to the event listener's actionPerformed method. Line 56 declares the String that will be displayed. The variable is initialized with the **empty string**—a String containing no characters. The compiler requires the variable to be initialized in case none of the branches of the nested if in lines 59–76 executes.

ActionEvent method getSource (called in lines 59, 64, 69 and 74) returns a reference to the event source. The condition in line 59 asks, "Is the event source textField1?" This condition compares references with the == operator to determine if they refer to the same object. If they *both* refer to textField1, the user pressed *Enter* in textField1. Then, lines 60–61 create a String containing the message that line 79 displays in a message dialog. Line 61 uses ActionEvent method **getActionCommand** to obtain the text the user typed in the text field that generated the event.

In this example, we display the text of the password in the JPasswordField when the user presses *Enter* in that field. Sometimes it's necessary to programatically process the characters in a password. Class JPasswordField method **getPassword** returns the password's characters as an array of type char.

Class *TextFieldTest*

Class TextFieldTest (Fig. 12.10) contains the main method that executes this application and displays an object of class TextFieldFrame. When you execute the application, even the uneditable JTextField (textField3) can generate an ActionEvent. To test this, click the text field to give it the focus, then press *Enter*. Also, the actual text of the password is displayed when you press *Enter* in the JPasswordField. Of course, you would normally not display the password!

```
1   // Fig. 12.10: TextFieldTest.java
2   // Testing TextFieldFrame.
3   import javax.swing.JFrame;
4
5   public class TextFieldTest
6   {
7      public static void main(String[] args)
8      {
9         TextFieldFrame textFieldFrame = new TextFieldFrame();
10        textFieldFrame.setDefaultCloseOperation(JFrame.EXIT_ON_CLOSE);
11        textFieldFrame.setSize(350, 100);
12        textFieldFrame.setVisible(true);
13     }
14  } // end class TextFieldTest
```

Fig. 12.10 | Testing TextFieldFrame. (Part 1 of 2.)

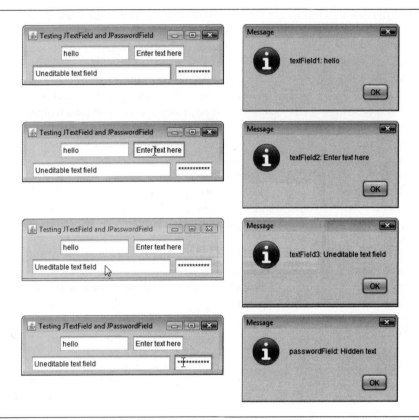

Fig. 12.10 | Testing `TextFieldFrame`. (Part 2 of 2.)

This application used a single object of class `TextFieldHandler` as the event listener for four text fields. Starting in Section 12.10, you'll see that it's possible to declare several event-listener objects of the same type and register each object for a separate GUI component's event. This technique enables us to eliminate the `if...else` logic used in this example's event handler by providing separate event handlers for each component's events.

Java SE 8: Implementing Event Listeners with Lambdas
Recall that interfaces like `ActionListener` that have only one `abstract` method are functional interfaces in Java SE 8. In Section 17.9, we show a more concise way to implement such event-listener interfaces with Java SE 8 lambdas.

12.7 Common GUI Event Types and Listener Interfaces

In Section 12.6, you learned that information about the event that occurs when the user presses *Enter* in a text field is stored in an `ActionEvent` object. Many different types of events can occur when the user interacts with a GUI. The event information is stored in an object of a class that extends `AWTEvent` (from package `java.awt`). Figure 12.11 illustrates a hierarchy containing many event classes from the package **java.awt.event**. Some of these are discussed in this chapter and Chapter 19. These event types are used with both

AWT and Swing components. Additional event types that are specific to Swing GUI components are declared in package **javax.swing.event**.

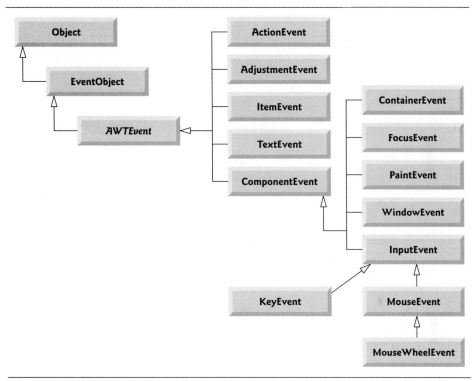

Fig. 12.11 | Some event classes of package java.awt.event.

Let's summarize the three parts to the event-handling mechanism that you saw in Section 12.6—the *event source*, the *event object* and the *event listener*. The event source is the GUI component with which the user interacts. The event object encapsulates information about the event that occurred, such as a reference to the event source and any event-specific information that may be required by the event listener for it to handle the event. The event listener is an object that's notified by the event source when an event occurs; in effect, it "listens" for an event, and one of its methods executes in response to the event. A method of the event listener receives an event object when the event listener is notified of the event. The event listener then uses the event object to respond to the event. This event-handling model is known as the **delegation event model**—an event's processing is delegated to an object (the event listener) in the application.

For each event-object type, there's typically a corresponding event-listener interface. An event listener for a GUI event is an object of a class that implements one or more of the event-listener interfaces from packages java.awt.event and javax.swing.event. Many of the event-listener types are common to both Swing and AWT components. Such types are declared in package java.awt.event, and some of them are shown in Fig. 12.12. Additional event-listener types that are specific to Swing components are declared in package javax.swing.event.

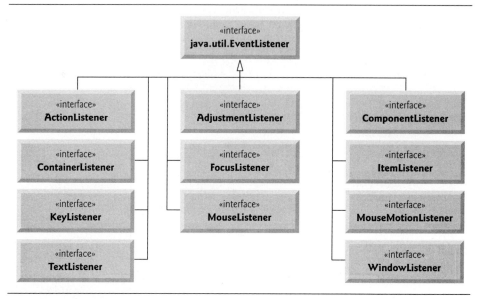

Fig. 12.12 | Some common event-listener interfaces of package `java.awt.event`.

Each event-listener interface specifies one or more event-handling methods that *must* be declared in the class that implements the interface. Recall from Section 10.9 that any class which implements an interface must declare *all* the `abstract` methods of that interface; otherwise, the class is an `abstract` class and cannot be used to create objects.

When an event occurs, the GUI component with which the user interacted notifies its *registered listeners* by calling each listener's appropriate *event-handling method*. For example, when the user presses the *Enter* key in a `JTextField`, the registered listener's `actionPerformed` method is called. In the next section, we complete our discussion of how the event handling works in the preceding example.

12.8 How Event Handling Works

Let's illustrate how the event-handling mechanism works, using `textField1` from the example of Fig. 12.9. We have two remaining open questions from Section 12.7:

1. How did the *event handler* get *registered*?
2. How does the GUI component know to call `actionPerformed` rather than some other event-handling method?

The first question is answered by the event registration performed in lines 43–46 of Fig. 12.9. Figure 12.13 diagrams `JTextField` variable `textField1`, `TextFieldHandler` variable `handler` and the objects to which they refer.

Registering Events

Every `JComponent` has an instance variable called `listenerList` that refers to an object of class **`EventListenerList`** (package `javax.swing.event`). Each object of a `JComponent` subclass maintains references to its *registered listeners* in the `listenerList`. For simplicity, we've diagramed `listenerList` as an array below the `JTextField` object in Fig. 12.13.

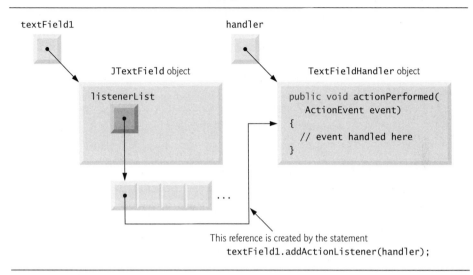

Fig. 12.13 | Event registration for `JTextField textField1`.

When the following statement (line 43 of Fig. 12.9) executes

```
textField1.addActionListener(handler);
```

a new entry containing a reference to the `TextFieldHandler` object is placed in `textField1`'s `listenerList`. Although not shown in the diagram, this new entry also includes the listener's type (`ActionListener`). Using this mechanism, each lightweight Swing component maintains its own list of *listeners* that were *registered* to *handle* the component's *events*.

Event-Handler Invocation
The event-listener type is important in answering the second question: How does the GUI component know to call `actionPerformed` rather than another method? Every GUI component supports several *event types*, including **mouse events**, **key events** and others. When an event occurs, the event is **dispatched** only to the *event listeners* of the appropriate type. Dispatching is simply the process by which the GUI component calls an event-handling method on each of its listeners that are registered for the event type that occurred.

Each *event type* has one or more corresponding *event-listener interfaces*. For example, `ActionEvents` are handled by `ActionListeners`, **MouseEvents** by **MouseListeners** and **MouseMotionListeners**, and **KeyEvents** by **KeyListeners**. When an event occurs, the GUI component receives (from the JVM) a unique *event ID* specifying the event type. The GUI component uses the event ID to decide the listener type to which the event should be dispatched and to decide which method to call on each listener object. For an `ActionEvent`, the event is dispatched to *every* registered `ActionListener`'s `actionPerformed` method (the only method in interface `ActionListener`). For a `MouseEvent`, the event is dispatched to *every* registered `MouseListener` or `MouseMotionListener`, depending on the mouse event that occurs. The MouseEvent's event ID determines which of the several mouse event-handling methods are called. All these decisions are handled for you by the GUI components. All you need to do is register an event handler for the particular event type that your application requires, and the GUI component will ensure that the event handler's appropriate method gets called when the event occurs. We discuss other event types and event-listener interfaces as they're needed with each new component we introduce.

Performance Tip 12.1

GUIs should always remain responsive to the user. Performing a long-running task in an event handler prevents the user from interacting with the GUI until that task completes. Section 20.11 demonstrates techniques prevent such problems.

12.9 JButton

A **button** is a component the user clicks to trigger a specific action. A Java application can use several types of buttons, including **command buttons**, **checkboxes**, **toggle buttons** and **radio buttons**. Figure 12.14 shows the inheritance hierarchy of the Swing buttons we cover in this chapter. As you can see, all the button types are subclasses of **AbstractButton** (package javax.swing), which declares the common features of Swing buttons. In this section, we concentrate on buttons that are typically used to initiate a command.

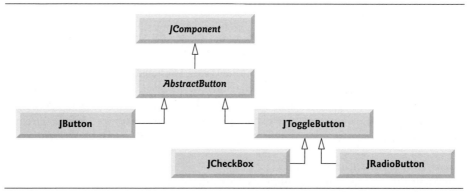

Fig. 12.14 | Swing button hierarchy.

A *command button* (see Fig. 12.16's output) generates an ActionEvent when the user clicks it. Command buttons are created with class **JButton**. The text on the face of a JButton is called a **button label**.

Look-and-Feel Observation 12.8

The text on buttons typically uses book-title capitalization.

Look-and-Feel Observation 12.9

A GUI can have many JButtons, but each button label should be unique in the portion of the GUI that's currently displayed. Having more than one JButton with the same label makes the JButtons ambiguous to the user.

The application of Figs. 12.15 and 12.16 creates two JButtons and demonstrates that JButtons can display Icons. Event handling for the buttons is performed by a single instance of *inner class* ButtonHandler (Fig. 12.15, lines 39–48).

```java
 1   // Fig. 12.15: ButtonFrame.java
 2   // Command buttons and action events.
 3   import java.awt.FlowLayout;
 4   import java.awt.event.ActionListener;
 5   import java.awt.event.ActionEvent;
 6   import javax.swing.JFrame;
 7   import javax.swing.JButton;
 8   import javax.swing.Icon;
 9   import javax.swing.ImageIcon;
10   import javax.swing.JOptionPane;
11
12   public class ButtonFrame extends JFrame
13   {
14      private final JButton plainJButton; // button with just text
15      private final JButton fancyJButton; // button with icons
16
17      // ButtonFrame adds JButtons to JFrame
18      public ButtonFrame()
19      {
20         super("Testing Buttons");
21         setLayout(new FlowLayout());
22
23         plainJButton = new JButton("Plain Button"); // button with text
24         add(plainJButton); // add plainJButton to JFrame
25
26         Icon bug1 = new ImageIcon(getClass().getResource("bug1.gif"));
27         Icon bug2 = new ImageIcon(getClass().getResource("bug2.gif"));
28         fancyJButton = new JButton("Fancy Button", bug1); // set image
29         fancyJButton.setRolloverIcon(bug2); // set rollover image
30         add(fancyJButton); // add fancyJButton to JFrame
31
32         // create new ButtonHandler for button event handling
33         ButtonHandler handler = new ButtonHandler();
34         fancyJButton.addActionListener(handler);
35         plainJButton.addActionListener(handler);
36      }
37
38      // inner class for button event handling
39      private class ButtonHandler implements ActionListener
40      {
41         // handle button event
42         @Override
43         public void actionPerformed(ActionEvent event)
44         {
45            JOptionPane.showMessageDialog(ButtonFrame.this, String.format(
46               "You pressed: %s", event.getActionCommand()));
47         }
48      }
49   } // end class ButtonFrame
```

Fig. 12.15 | Command buttons and action events.

```
1  // Fig. 12.16: ButtonTest.java
2  // Testing ButtonFrame.
3  import javax.swing.JFrame;
4
5  public class ButtonTest
6  {
7     public static void main(String[] args)
8     {
9        ButtonFrame buttonFrame = new ButtonFrame();
10       buttonFrame.setDefaultCloseOperation(JFrame.EXIT_ON_CLOSE);
11       buttonFrame.setSize(275, 110);
12       buttonFrame.setVisible(true);
13    }
14 } // end class ButtonTest
```

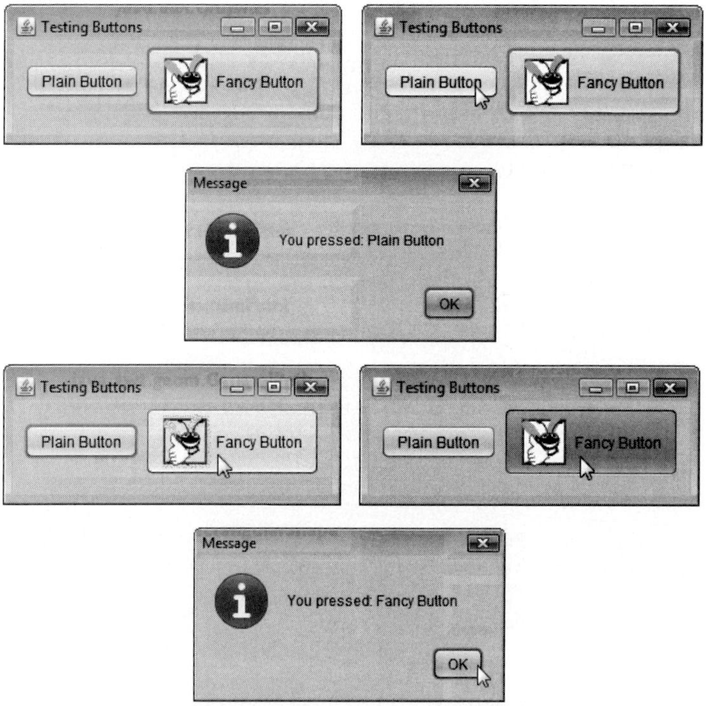

Fig. 12.16 | Testing ButtonFrame.

Lines 14–15 declare JButton variables plainJButton and fancyJButton. The corresponding objects are instantiated in the constructor. Line 23 creates plainJButton with the button label "Plain Button". Line 24 adds the JButton to the JFrame.

A JButton can display an Icon. To provide the user with an extra level of visual interaction with the GUI, a JButton can also have a **rollover Icon**—an Icon that's displayed when the user positions the mouse over the JButton. The icon on the JButton changes as the mouse moves in and out of the JButton's area on the screen. Lines 26–27 create two

ImageIcon objects that represent the default Icon and rollover Icon for the JButton created at line 28. Both statements assume that the image files are stored in the *same* directory as the application. Images are commonly placed in the *same* directory as the application or a subdirectory like images). These image files have been provided for you with the example.

Line 28 creates fancyButton with the text "Fancy Button" and the icon bug1. By default, the text is displayed to the *right* of the icon. Line 29 uses **setRolloverIcon** (inherited from class AbstractButton) to specify the image displayed on the JButton when the user positions the mouse over it. Line 30 adds the JButton to the JFrame.

Look-and-Feel Observation 12.10

Because class AbstractButton supports displaying text and images on a button, all subclasses of AbstractButton also support displaying text and images.

Look-and-Feel Observation 12.11

Rollover icons provide visual feedback indicating that an action will occur when when a JButton is clicked.

JButtons, like JTextFields, generate ActionEvents that can be processed by any ActionListener object. Lines 33–35 create an object of private *inner class* ButtonHandler and use addActionListener to *register* it as the *event handler* for each JButton. Class ButtonHandler (lines 39–48) declares actionPerformed to display a message dialog box containing the label for the button the user pressed. For a JButton event, ActionEvent method getActionCommand returns the label on the JButton.

*Accessing the **this** Reference in an Object of a Top-Level Class from an Inner Class*
When you execute this application and click one of its buttons, notice that the message dialog that appears is centered over the application's window. This occurs because the call to JOptionPane method showMessageDialog (lines 45–46) uses ButtonFrame.this rather than null as the first argument. When this argument is not null, it represents the so-called *parent GUI component* of the message dialog (in this case the application window is the parent component) and enables the dialog to be centered over that component when the dialog is displayed. ButtonFrame.this represents the this reference of the object of top-level class ButtonFrame.

Software Engineering Observation 12.2

When used in an inner class, keyword this refers to the current inner-class object being manipulated. An inner-class method can use its outer-class object's this by preceding this with the outer-class name and a dot (.) separator, as in ButtonFrame.this.

12.10 Buttons That Maintain State

The Swing GUI components contain three types of **state buttons**—**JToggleButton**, **JCheckBox** and **JRadioButton**—that have on/off or true/false values. Classes JCheckBox and JRadioButton are subclasses of JToggleButton (Fig. 12.14). A JRadioButton is different from a JCheckBox in that normally several JRadioButtons are grouped together and are *mutually exclusive*—only *one* in the group can be selected at any time, just like the buttons on a car radio. We first discuss class JCheckBox.

12.10.1 JCheckBox

The application of Figs. 12.17–12.18 uses two JCheckBoxes to select the desired font style of the text displayed in a JTextField. When selected, one applies a bold style and the other an italic style. If *both* are selected, the style is bold *and* italic. When the application initially executes, neither JCheckBox is checked (i.e., they're both false), so the font is plain. Class CheckBoxTest (Fig. 12.18) contains the main method that executes this application.

```
 1   // Fig. 12.17: CheckBoxFrame.java
 2   // JCheckBoxes and item events.
 3   import java.awt.FlowLayout;
 4   import java.awt.Font;
 5   import java.awt.event.ItemListener;
 6   import java.awt.event.ItemEvent;
 7   import javax.swing.JFrame;
 8   import javax.swing.JTextField;
 9   import javax.swing.JCheckBox;
10
11   public class CheckBoxFrame extends JFrame
12   {
13      private final JTextField textField; // displays text in changing fonts
14      private final JCheckBox boldJCheckBox; // to select/deselect bold
15      private final JCheckBox italicJCheckBox; // to select/deselect italic
16
17      // CheckBoxFrame constructor adds JCheckBoxes to JFrame
18      public CheckBoxFrame()
19      {
20         super("JCheckBox Test");
21         setLayout(new FlowLayout());
22
23         // set up JTextField and set its font
24         textField = new JTextField("Watch the font style change", 20);
25         textField.setFont(new Font("Serif", Font.PLAIN, 14));
26         add(textField); // add textField to JFrame
27
28         boldJCheckBox = new JCheckBox("Bold");
29         italicJCheckBox = new JCheckBox("Italic");
30         add(boldJCheckBox); // add bold checkbox to JFrame
31         add(italicJCheckBox); // add italic checkbox to JFrame
32
33         // register listeners for JCheckBoxes
34         CheckBoxHandler handler = new CheckBoxHandler();
35         boldJCheckBox.addItemListener(handler);
36         italicJCheckBox.addItemListener(handler);
37      }
38
39      // private inner class for ItemListener event handling
40      private class CheckBoxHandler implements ItemListener
41      {
```

Fig. 12.17 | JCheckBoxes and item events. (Part 1 of 2.)

```
42          // respond to checkbox events
43          @Override
44          public void itemStateChanged(ItemEvent event)
45          {
46              Font font = null; // stores the new Font
47
48              // determine which CheckBoxes are checked and create Font
49              if (boldJCheckBox.isSelected() && italicJCheckBox.isSelected())
50                  font = new Font("Serif", Font.BOLD + Font.ITALIC, 14);
51              else if (boldJCheckBox.isSelected())
52                  font = new Font("Serif", Font.BOLD, 14);
53              else if (italicJCheckBox.isSelected())
54                  font = new Font("Serif", Font.ITALIC, 14);
55              else
56                  font = new Font("Serif", Font.PLAIN, 14);
57
58              textField.setFont(font);
59          }
60      }
61  } // end class CheckBoxFrame
```

Fig. 12.17 | JCheckBoxes and item events. (Part 2 of 2.)

```
 1  // Fig. 12.18: CheckBoxTest.java
 2  // Testing CheckBoxFrame.
 3  import javax.swing.JFrame;
 4
 5  public class CheckBoxTest
 6  {
 7      public static void main(String[] args)
 8      {
 9          CheckBoxFrame checkBoxFrame = new CheckBoxFrame();
10          checkBoxFrame.setDefaultCloseOperation(JFrame.EXIT_ON_CLOSE);
11          checkBoxFrame.setSize(275, 100);
12          checkBoxFrame.setVisible(true);
13      }
14  } // end class CheckBoxTest
```

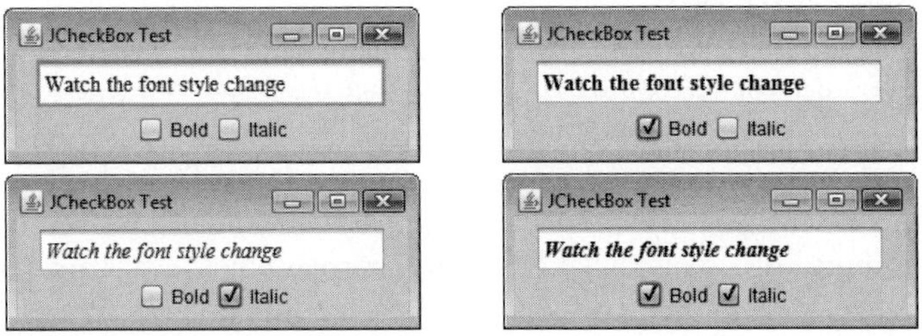

Fig. 12.18 | Testing CheckBoxFrame.

After the JTextField is created and initialized (Fig. 12.17, line 24), line 25 uses method **setFont** (inherited by JTextField indirectly from class Component) to set the font of the JTextField to a new object of class **Font** (package java.awt). The new Font is initialized with "Serif" (a generic font name that represents a font such as Times and is supported on all Java platforms), Font.PLAIN style and 14-point size. Next, lines 28–29 create two JCheckBox objects. The String passed to the JCheckBox constructor is the **checkbox label** that appears to the right of the JCheckBox by default.

When the user clicks a JCheckBox, an **ItemEvent** occurs. This event can be handled by an **ItemListener** object, which *must* implement method **itemStateChanged**. In this example, the event handling is performed by an instance of private *inner class* CheckBoxHandler (lines 40–60). Lines 34–36 create an instance of class CheckBoxHandler and register it with method **addItemListener** as the listener for both the JCheckBox objects.

CheckBoxHandler method itemStateChanged (lines 43–59) is called when the user clicks the either boldJCheckBox or italicJCheckBox. In this example, we do not determine which JCheckBox was clicked—we use both of their states to determine the font to display. Line 49 uses JCheckBox method **isSelected** to determine if both JCheckBoxes are selected. If so, line 50 creates a bold italic font by adding the Font constants Font.BOLD and Font.ITALIC for the font-style argument of the Font constructor. Line 51 determines whether the boldJCheckBox is selected, and if so line 52 creates a bold font. Line 53 determines whether the italicJCheckBox is selected, and if so line 54 creates an italic font. If none of the preceding conditions are true, line 56 creates a plain font using the Font constant Font.PLAIN. Finally, line 58 sets textField's new font, which changes the font in the JTextField on the screen.

Relationship Between an Inner Class and Its Top-Level Class

Class CheckBoxHandler used variables boldJCheckBox (lines 49 and 51), italicJCheckBox (lines 49 and 53) and textField (line 58) even though they are *not* declared in the inner class. Recall that an *inner class* has a special relationship with its *top-level class*—it's allowed to access *all* the variables and methods of the top-level class. CheckBoxHandler method itemStateChanged (line 43–59) uses this relationship to determine which JCheckBoxes are checked and to set the font on the JTextField. Notice that none of the code in inner class CheckBoxHandler requires an explicit reference to the top-level class object.

12.10.2 JRadioButton

Radio buttons (declared with class JRadioButton) are similar to checkboxes in that they have two states—*selected* and *not selected* (also called *deselected*). However, radio buttons normally appear as a **group** in which only *one* button can be selected at a time (see the output of Fig. 12.20). Radio buttons are used to represent **mutually exclusive options** (i.e., multiple options in the group *cannot* be selected at the same time). The logical relationship between radio buttons is maintained by a **ButtonGroup** object (package javax.swing), which itself is *not* a GUI component. A ButtonGroup object organizes a group of buttons and is *not* itself displayed in a user interface. Rather, the individual JRadioButton objects from the group are displayed in the GUI.

The application of Figs. 12.19–12.20 is similar to that of Figs. 12.17–12.18. The user can alter the font style of a JTextField's text. The application uses radio buttons that permit only a single font style in the group to be selected at a time. Class RadioButtonTest (Fig. 12.20) contains the main method that executes this application.

```
 I    // Fig. 12.19: RadioButtonFrame.java
 2    // Creating radio buttons using ButtonGroup and JRadioButton.
 3    import java.awt.FlowLayout;
 4    import java.awt.Font;
 5    import java.awt.event.ItemListener;
 6    import java.awt.event.ItemEvent;
 7    import javax.swing.JFrame;
 8    import javax.swing.JTextField;
 9    import javax.swing.JRadioButton;
10    import javax.swing.ButtonGroup;
11
12    public class RadioButtonFrame extends JFrame
13    {
14       private final JTextField textField; // used to display font changes
15       private final Font plainFont; // font for plain text
16       private final Font boldFont; // font for bold text
17       private final Font italicFont; // font for italic text
18       private final Font boldItalicFont; // font for bold and italic text
19       private final JRadioButton plainJRadioButton; // selects plain text
20       private final JRadioButton boldJRadioButton; // selects bold text
21       private final JRadioButton italicJRadioButton; // selects italic text
22       private final JRadioButton boldItalicJRadioButton; // bold and italic
23       private final ButtonGroup radioGroup; // holds radio buttons
24
25       // RadioButtonFrame constructor adds JRadioButtons to JFrame
26       public RadioButtonFrame()
27       {
28          super("RadioButton Test");
29          setLayout(new FlowLayout());
30
31          textField = new JTextField("Watch the font style change", 25);
32          add(textField); // add textField to JFrame
33
34          // create radio buttons
35          plainJRadioButton = new JRadioButton("Plain", true);
36          boldJRadioButton = new JRadioButton("Bold", false);
37          italicJRadioButton = new JRadioButton("Italic", false);
38          boldItalicJRadioButton = new JRadioButton("Bold/Italic", false);
39          add(plainJRadioButton); // add plain button to JFrame
40          add(boldJRadioButton); // add bold button to JFrame
41          add(italicJRadioButton); // add italic button to JFrame
42          add(boldItalicJRadioButton); // add bold and italic button
43
44          // create logical relationship between JRadioButtons
45          radioGroup = new ButtonGroup(); // create ButtonGroup
46          radioGroup.add(plainJRadioButton); // add plain to group
47          radioGroup.add(boldJRadioButton); // add bold to group
48          radioGroup.add(italicJRadioButton); // add italic to group
49          radioGroup.add(boldItalicJRadioButton); // add bold and italic
50
51          // create font objects
52          plainFont = new Font("Serif", Font.PLAIN, 14);
53          boldFont = new Font("Serif", Font.BOLD, 14);
```

Fig. 12.19 | Creating radio buttons using `ButtonGroup` and `JRadioButton`. (Part 1 of 2.)

```
54          italicFont = new Font("Serif", Font.ITALIC, 14);
55          boldItalicFont = new Font("Serif", Font.BOLD + Font.ITALIC, 14);
56          textField.setFont(plainFont);
57
58          // register events for JRadioButtons
59          plainJRadioButton.addItemListener(
60             new RadioButtonHandler(plainFont));
61          boldJRadioButton.addItemListener(
62             new RadioButtonHandler(boldFont));
63          italicJRadioButton.addItemListener(
64             new RadioButtonHandler(italicFont));
65          boldItalicJRadioButton.addItemListener(
66             new RadioButtonHandler(boldItalicFont));
67       }
68
69       // private inner class to handle radio button events
70       private class RadioButtonHandler implements ItemListener
71       {
72          private Font font; // font associated with this listener
73
74          public RadioButtonHandler(Font f)
75          {
76             font = f;
77          }
78
79          // handle radio button events
80          @Override
81          public void itemStateChanged(ItemEvent event)
82          {
83             textField.setFont(font);
84          }
85       }
86    } // end class RadioButtonFrame
```

Fig. 12.19 | Creating radio buttons using `ButtonGroup` and `JRadioButton`. (Part 2 of 2.)

```
1    // Fig. 12.20: RadioButtonTest.java
2    // Testing RadioButtonFrame.
3    import javax.swing.JFrame;
4
5    public class RadioButtonTest
6    {
7       public static void main(String[] args)
8       {
9          RadioButtonFrame radioButtonFrame = new RadioButtonFrame();
10         radioButtonFrame.setDefaultCloseOperation(JFrame.EXIT_ON_CLOSE);
11         radioButtonFrame.setSize(300, 100);
12         radioButtonFrame.setVisible(true);
13      }
14   } // end class RadioButtonTest
```

Fig. 12.20 | Testing `RadioButtonFrame`. (Part 1 of 2.)

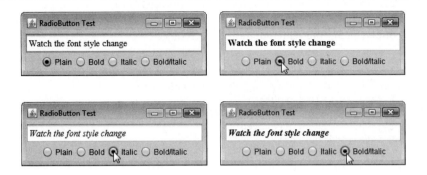

Fig. 12.20 | Testing RadioButtonFrame. (Part 2 of 2.)

Lines 35–42 (Fig. 12.19) in the constructor create four JRadioButton objects and add them to the JFrame. Each JRadioButton is created with a constructor call like that in line 35. This constructor specifies the label that appears to the right of the JRadioButton by default and the initial state of the JRadioButton. A true second argument indicates that the JRadioButton should appear *selected* when it's displayed.

Line 45 instantiates ButtonGroup object radioGroup. This object is the "glue" that forms the logical relationship between the four JRadioButton objects and allows only one of the four to be selected at a time. It's possible that no JRadioButtons in a ButtonGroup are selected, but this can occur *only* if *no* preselected JRadioButtons are added to the But-tonGroup and the user has *not* selected a JRadioButton yet. Lines 46–49 use ButtonGroup method **add** to associate each of the JRadioButtons with radioGroup. If more than one selected JRadioButton object is added to the group, the selected one that was added *first* will be selected when the GUI is displayed.

JRadioButtons, like JCheckBoxes, generate ItemEvents when they're *clicked*. Lines 59–66 create four instances of inner class RadioButtonHandler (declared at lines 70–85). In this example, each event-listener object is registered to handle the ItemEvent generated when the user clicks a particular JRadioButton. Notice that each RadioButtonHandler object is initialized with a particular Font object (created in lines 52–55).

Class RadioButtonHandler (line 70–85) implements interface ItemListener so it can handle ItemEvents generated by the JRadioButtons. The constructor stores the Font object it receives as an argument in the event-listener object's instance variable font (declared at line 72). When the user clicks a JRadioButton, radioGroup turns off the pre-viously selected JRadioButton, and method itemStateChanged (lines 80–84) sets the font in the JTextField to the Font stored in the JRadioButton's corresponding event-listener object. Notice that line 83 of inner class RadioButtonHandler uses the top-level class's textField instance variable to set the font.

12.11 JComboBox; Using an Anonymous Inner Class for Event Handling

A combo box (sometimes called a **drop-down list**) enables the user to select *one* item from a list (Fig. 12.22). Combo boxes are implemented with class **JComboBox**, which extends class JComponent. JComboBox is a generic class, like the class ArrayList (Chapter 7). When you create a JComboBox, you specify the type of the objects that it manages—the JCombo-Box then displays a String representation of each object.

```java
 1   // Fig. 12.21: ComboBoxFrame.java
 2   // JComboBox that displays a list of image names.
 3   import java.awt.FlowLayout;
 4   import java.awt.event.ItemListener;
 5   import java.awt.event.ItemEvent;
 6   import javax.swing.JFrame;
 7   import javax.swing.JLabel;
 8   import javax.swing.JComboBox;
 9   import javax.swing.Icon;
10   import javax.swing.ImageIcon;
11
12   public class ComboBoxFrame extends JFrame
13   {
14      private final JComboBox<String> imagesJComboBox; // holds icon names
15      private final JLabel label; // displays selected icon
16
17      private static final String[] names =
18         {"bug1.gif", "bug2.gif",  "travelbug.gif", "buganim.gif"};
19      private final Icon[] icons = {
20         new ImageIcon(getClass().getResource(names[0])),
21         new ImageIcon(getClass().getResource(names[1])),
22         new ImageIcon(getClass().getResource(names[2])),
23         new ImageIcon(getClass().getResource(names[3]))};
24
25      // ComboBoxFrame constructor adds JComboBox to JFrame
26      public ComboBoxFrame()
27      {
28         super("Testing JComboBox");
29         setLayout(new FlowLayout()); // set frame layout
30
31         imagesJComboBox = new JComboBox<String>(names); // set up JComboBox
32         imagesJComboBox.setMaximumRowCount(3); // display three rows
33
34         imagesJComboBox.addItemListener(
35            new ItemListener() // anonymous inner class
36            {
37               // handle JComboBox event
38               @Override
39               public void itemStateChanged(ItemEvent event)
40               {
41                  // determine whether item selected
42                  if (event.getStateChange() == ItemEvent.SELECTED)
43                     label.setIcon(icons[
44                        imagesJComboBox.getSelectedIndex()]);
45               }
46            } // end anonymous inner class
47         ); // end call to addItemListener
48
```

Fig. 12.21 | JComboBox that displays a list of image names. (Part 1 of 2.)

```
49            add(imagesJComboBox); // add combo box to JFrame
50            label = new JLabel(icons[0]); // display first icon
51            add(label); // add label to JFrame
52       }
53  } // end class ComboBoxFrame
```

Fig. 12.21 | JComboBox that displays a list of image names. (Part 2 of 2.)

```
 1   // Fig. 12.22: ComboBoxTest.java
 2   // Testing ComboBoxFrame.
 3   import javax.swing.JFrame;
 4
 5   public class ComboBoxTest
 6   {
 7       public static void main(String[] args)
 8       {
 9           ComboBoxFrame comboBoxFrame = new ComboBoxFrame();
10           comboBoxFrame.setDefaultCloseOperation(JFrame.EXIT_ON_CLOSE);
11           comboBoxFrame.setSize(350, 150);
12           comboBoxFrame.setVisible(true);
13       }
14   } // end class ComboBoxTest
```

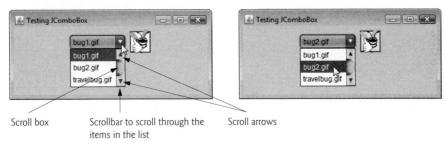

Scroll box   Scrollbar to scroll through the   Scroll arrows
              items in the list

Fig. 12.22 | Testing ComboBoxFrame.

JComboBoxes generate ItemEvents just as JCheckBoxes and JRadioButtons do. This example also demonstrates a special form of inner class that's used frequently in event handling. The application (Figs. 12.21–12.22) uses a JComboBox to provide a list of four image filenames from which the user can select one image to display. When the user selects a name, the application displays the corresponding image as an Icon on a JLabel. Class ComboBoxTest (Fig. 12.22) contains the main method that executes this application. The screen captures for this application show the JComboBox list after the selection was made to illustrate which image filename was selected.

Lines 19–23 (Fig. 12.21) declare and initialize array `icons` with four new `ImageIcon` objects. `String` array `names` (lines 17–18) contains the names of the four image files that are stored in the same directory as the application.

At line 31, the constructor initializes a `JComboBox` object with the `Strings` in array `names` as the elements in the list. Each item in the list has an **index**. The first item is added at index 0, the next at index 1 and so forth. The first item added to a `JComboBox` appears as the currently selected item when the `JComboBox` is displayed. Other items are selected by clicking the `JComboBox`, then selecting an item from the list that appears.

Line 32 uses `JComboBox` method **setMaximumRowCount** to set the maximum number of elements that are displayed when the user clicks the `JComboBox`. If there are additional items, the `JComboBox` provides a **scrollbar** (see the first screen) that allows the user to scroll through all the elements in the list. The user can click the **scroll arrows** at the top and bottom of the scrollbar to move up and down through the list one element at a time, or else drag the **scroll box** in the middle of the scrollbar up and down. To drag the scroll box, position the mouse cursor on it, hold the mouse button down and move the mouse. In this example, the drop-down list is too short to drag the scroll box, so you can click the up and down arrows or use your mouse's wheel to scroll through the four items in the list. Line 49 attaches the `JComboBox` to the `ComboBoxFrame`'s `FlowLayout` (set in line 29). Line 50 creates the `JLabel` that displays `ImageIcons` and initializes it with the first `ImageIcon` in array `icons`. Line 51 attaches the `JLabel` to the `ComboBoxFrame`'s `FlowLayout`.

Look-and-Feel Observation 12.12

Set the maximum row count for a `JComboBox` to a number of rows that prevents the list from expanding outside the bounds of the window in which it's used.

Using an Anonymous Inner Class for Event Handling

Lines 34–46 are one statement that declares the event listener's class, creates an object of that class and registers it as `imagesJComboBox`'s `ItemEvent` listener. This event-listener object is an instance of an **anonymous inner class**—a class that's declared without a name and typically appears inside a method declaration. *As with other inner classes, an anonymous inner class can access its top-level class's members.* However, an anonymous inner class has limited access to the local variables of the method in which it's declared. Since an anonymous inner class has no name, one object of the class must be created at the point where the class is declared (starting at line 35).

Software Engineering Observation 12.3

An anonymous inner class declared in a method can access the instance variables and methods of the top-level class object that declared it, as well as the method's `final` local variables, but cannot access the method's non-`final` local variables. As of Java SE 8, anonymous inner classes may also access a method's "effectively `final`" local variables—see Chapter 17 for more information.

Lines 34–47 are a call to `imagesJComboBox`'s `addItemListener` method. The argument to this method must be an object that *is an* `ItemListener` (i.e., any object of a class that implements `ItemListener`). Lines 35–46 are a class-instance creation expression that declares an anonymous inner class and creates one object of that class. A reference to that object is then passed as the argument to `addItemListener`. The syntax `ItemListener()`

after new begins the declaration of an anonymous inner class that implements interface ItemListener. This is similar to beginning a class declaration with

public class MyHandler **implements** ItemListener

The opening left brace at line 36 and the closing right brace at line 46 delimit the body of the anonymous inner class. Lines 38–45 declare the ItemListener's itemStateChanged method. When the user makes a selection from imagesJComboBox, this method sets label's Icon. The Icon is selected from array icons by determining the index of the selected item in the JComboBox with method **getSelectedIndex** in line 44. For each item selected from a JComboBox, another item is first deselected—so two ItemEvents occur when an item is selected. We wish to display only the icon for the item the user just selected. For this reason, line 42 determines whether ItemEvent method **getStateChange** returns ItemEvent.SELECTED. If so, lines 43–44 set label's icon.

Software Engineering Observation 12.4

Like any other class, when an anonymous inner class implements an interface, the class must implement every abstract method in the interface.

The syntax shown in lines 35–46 for creating an event handler with an anonymous inner class is similar to the code that would be generated by a Java integrated development environment (IDE). Typically, an IDE enables you to design a GUI visually, then it generates code that implements the GUI. You simply insert statements in the event-handling methods that declare how to handle each event.

Java SE 8: Implementing Anonymous Inner Classes with Lambdas
In Section 17.9, we show how to use Java SE 8 lambdas to create event handlers. As you'll learn, the compiler translates a lambda into an object of an anonymous inner class.

12.12 JList

A list displays a series of items from which the user may *select one or more items* (see the output of Fig. 12.24). Lists are created with class JList, which directly extends class JComponent. Class JList—which like JComboBox is a generic class—supports **single-selection lists** (which allow only one item to be selected at a time) and **multiple-selection lists** (which allow any number of items to be selected). In this section, we discuss single-selection lists.

The application of Figs. 12.23–12.24 creates a JList containing 13 color names. When a color name is clicked in the JList, a **ListSelectionEvent** occurs and the application changes the background color of the application window to the selected color. Class ListTest (Fig. 12.24) contains the main method that executes this application.

```
1   // Fig. 12.23: ListFrame.java
2   // JList that displays a list of colors.
3   import java.awt.FlowLayout;
4   import java.awt.Color;
5   import javax.swing.JFrame;
6   import javax.swing.JList;
```

Fig. 12.23 | JList that displays a list of colors. (Part 1 of 2.)

```
 7    import javax.swing.JScrollPane;
 8    import javax.swing.event.ListSelectionListener;
 9    import javax.swing.event.ListSelectionEvent;
10    import javax.swing.ListSelectionModel;
11
12    public class ListFrame extends JFrame
13    {
14       private final JList<String> colorJList; // list to display colors
15       private static final String[] colorNames = {"Black", "Blue", "Cyan",
16          "Dark Gray", "Gray", "Green", "Light Gray", "Magenta",
17          "Orange", "Pink", "Red", "White", "Yellow"};
18       private static final Color[] colors = {Color.BLACK, Color.BLUE,
19          Color.CYAN, Color.DARK_GRAY, Color.GRAY, Color.GREEN,
20          Color.LIGHT_GRAY, Color.MAGENTA, Color.ORANGE, Color.PINK,
21          Color.RED, Color.WHITE, Color.YELLOW};
22
23       // ListFrame constructor add JScrollPane containing JList to JFrame
24       public ListFrame()
25       {
26          super("List Test");
27          setLayout(new FlowLayout());
28
29          colorJList = new JList<String>(colorNames); // list of colorNames
30          colorJList.setVisibleRowCount(5); // display five rows at once
31
32          // do not allow multiple selections
33          colorJList.setSelectionMode(ListSelectionModel.SINGLE_SELECTION);
34
35          // add a JScrollPane containing JList to frame
36          add(new JScrollPane(colorJList));
37
38          colorJList.addListSelectionListener(
39             new ListSelectionListener() // anonymous inner class
40             {
41                // handle list selection events
42                @Override
43                public void valueChanged(ListSelectionEvent event)
44                {
45                   getContentPane().setBackground(
46                      colors[colorJList.getSelectedIndex()]);
47                }
48             }
49          );
50       }
51    } // end class ListFrame
```

Fig. 12.23 | JList that displays a list of colors. (Part 2 of 2.)

```
 1    // Fig. 12.24: ListTest.java
 2    // Selecting colors from a JList.
 3    import javax.swing.JFrame;
 4
```

Fig. 12.24 | Selecting colors from a JList. (Part 1 of 2.)

```
 5   public class ListTest
 6   {
 7      public static void main(String[] args)
 8      {
 9         ListFrame listFrame = new ListFrame(); // create ListFrame
10         listFrame.setDefaultCloseOperation(JFrame.EXIT_ON_CLOSE);
11         listFrame.setSize(350, 150);
12         listFrame.setVisible(true);
13      }
14   } // end class ListTest
```

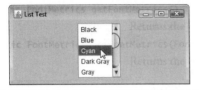 

Fig. 12.24 | Selecting colors from a JList. (Part 2 of 2.)

Line 29 (Fig. 12.23) creates JList object colorJList. The argument to the JList constructor is the array of Objects (in this case Strings) to display in the list. Line 30 uses JList method **setVisibleRowCount** to determine the number of items *visible* in the list.

Line 33 uses JList method **setSelectionMode** to specify the list's **selection mode**. Class **ListSelectionModel** (of package javax.swing) declares three constants that specify a JList's selection mode—**SINGLE_SELECTION** (which allows only one item to be selected at a time), **SINGLE_INTERVAL_SELECTION** (for a multiple-selection list that allows selection of several contiguous items) and **MULTIPLE_INTERVAL_SELECTION** (for a multiple-selection list that does not restrict the items that can be selected).

Unlike a JComboBox, a JList *does not provide a scrollbar* if there are more items in the list than the number of visible rows. In this case, a **JScrollPane** object is used to provide the scrolling capability. Line 36 adds a new instance of class JScrollPane to the JFrame. The JScrollPane constructor receives as its argument the JComponent that needs scrolling functionality (in this case, colorJList). Notice in the screen captures that a scrollbar created by the JScrollPane appears at the right side of the JList. By default, the scrollbar appears only when the number of items in the JList exceeds the number of visible items.

Lines 38–49 use JList method **addListSelectionListener** to register an object that implements **ListSelectionListener** (package javax.swing.event) as the listener for the JList's selection events. Once again, we use an instance of an anonymous inner class (lines 39–48) as the listener. In this example, when the user makes a selection from colorJList, method **valueChanged** (line 42–47) should change the background color of the List-Frame to the selected color. This is accomplished in lines 45–46. Note the use of JFrame method **getContentPane** in line 45. Each JFrame actually consists of *three layers*—the *background*, the *content pane* and the *glass pane*. The content pane appears in front of the background and is where the GUI components in the JFrame are displayed. The glass pane is used to display tool tips and other items that should appear in front of the GUI components on the screen. The content pane completely hides the background of the JFrame; thus, to change the background color behind the GUI components, you must change the content pane's background color. Method getContentPane returns a reference to the

JFrame's content pane (an object of class Container). In line 45, we then use that reference to call method **setBackground**, which sets the content pane's background color to an element in the colors array. The color is selected from the array by using the selected item's index. JList method **getSelectedIndex** returns the selected item's index. As with arrays and JComboBoxes, JList indexing is zero based.

12.13 Multiple-Selection Lists

A **multiple-selection list** enables the user to select many items from a JList (see the output of Fig. 12.26). A SINGLE_INTERVAL_SELECTION list allows selecting a contiguous range of items. To do so, click the first item, then press and hold the *Shift* key while clicking the last item in the range. A MULTIPLE_INTERVAL_SELECTION list (the default) allows continuous range selection as described for a SINGLE_INTERVAL_SELECTION list. Such a list also allows miscellaneous items to be selected by pressing and holding the *Ctrl* key while clicking each item to select. To *deselect* an item, press and hold the *Ctrl* key while clicking the item a second time.

The application of Figs. 12.25–12.26 uses multiple-selection lists to copy items from one JList to another. One list is a MULTIPLE_INTERVAL_SELECTION list and the other is a SINGLE_INTERVAL_SELECTION list. When you execute the application, try using the selection techniques described previously to select items in both lists.

```java
1   // Fig. 12.25: MultipleSelectionFrame.java
2   // JList that allows multiple selections.
3   import java.awt.FlowLayout;
4   import java.awt.event.ActionListener;
5   import java.awt.event.ActionEvent;
6   import javax.swing.JFrame;
7   import javax.swing.JList;
8   import javax.swing.JButton;
9   import javax.swing.JScrollPane;
10  import javax.swing.ListSelectionModel;
11
12  public class MultipleSelectionFrame extends JFrame
13  {
14     private final JList<String> colorJList; // list to hold color names
15     private final JList<String> copyJList; // list to hold copied names
16     private JButton copyJButton; // button to copy selected names
17     private static final String[] colorNames = {"Black", "Blue", "Cyan",
18        "Dark Gray", "Gray", "Green", "Light Gray", "Magenta", "Orange",
19        "Pink", "Red", "White", "Yellow"};
20
21     // MultipleSelectionFrame constructor
22     public MultipleSelectionFrame()
23     {
24        super("Multiple Selection Lists");
25        setLayout(new FlowLayout());
26
27        colorJList = new JList<String>(colorNames); // list of color names
28        colorJList.setVisibleRowCount(5); // show five rows
```

Fig. 12.25 | JList that allows multiple selections. (Part 1 of 2.)

```
29        colorJList.setSelectionMode(
30           ListSelectionModel.MULTIPLE_INTERVAL_SELECTION);
31        add(new JScrollPane(colorJList)); // add list with scrollpane
32
33        copyJButton = new JButton("Copy >>>");
34        copyJButton.addActionListener(
35           new ActionListener() // anonymous inner class
36           {
37              // handle button event
38              @Override
39              public void actionPerformed(ActionEvent event)
40              {
41                 // place selected values in copyJList
42                 copyJList.setListData(
43                    colorJList.getSelectedValuesList().toArray(
44                       new String[0]));
45              }
46           }
47        );
48
49        add(copyJButton); // add copy button to JFrame
50
51        copyJList = new JList<String>(); // list to hold copied color names
52        copyJList.setVisibleRowCount(5); // show 5 rows
53        copyJList.setFixedCellWidth(100); // set width
54        copyJList.setFixedCellHeight(15); // set height
55        copyJList.setSelectionMode(
56           ListSelectionModel.SINGLE_INTERVAL_SELECTION);
57        add(new JScrollPane(copyJList)); // add list with scrollpane
58     }
59  } // end class MultipleSelectionFrame
```

Fig. 12.25 | JList that allows multiple selections. (Part 2 of 2.)

```
1   // Fig. 12.26: MultipleSelectionTest.java
2   // Testing MultipleSelectionFrame.
3   import javax.swing.JFrame;
4
5   public class MultipleSelectionTest
6   {
7      public static void main(String[] args)
8      {
9         MultipleSelectionFrame multipleSelectionFrame =
10           new MultipleSelectionFrame();
11        multipleSelectionFrame.setDefaultCloseOperation(
12           JFrame.EXIT_ON_CLOSE);
13        multipleSelectionFrame.setSize(350, 150);
14        multipleSelectionFrame.setVisible(true);
15     }
16  } // end class MultipleSelectionTest
```

Fig. 12.26 | Testing MultipleSelectionFrame. (Part 1 of 2.)

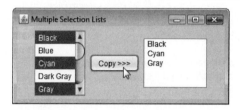

Fig. 12.26 | Testing `MultipleSelectionFrame`. (Part 2 of 2.)

Line 27 of Fig. 12.25 creates `JList colorJList` and initializes it with the `Strings` in the array `colorNames`. Line 28 sets the number of visible rows in `colorJList` to 5. Lines 29–30 specify that `colorJList` is a `MULTIPLE_INTERVAL_SELECTION` list. Line 31 adds a new `JScrollPane` containing `colorJList` to the `JFrame`. Lines 51–57 perform similar tasks for `copyJList`, which is declared as a `SINGLE_INTERVAL_SELECTION` list. If a `JList` does not contain items, it will not display in a `FlowLayout`. For this reason, lines 53–54 use `JList` methods **`setFixedCellWidth`** and **`setFixedCellHeight`** to set `copyJList`'s width to 100 pixels and the height of each item in the `JList` to 15 pixels, respectively.

Normally, an event generated by another GUI component (known as an **external event**) specifies when the multiple selections in a `JList` should be processed. In this example, the user clicks the `JButton` called `copyJButton` to trigger the event that copies the selected items in `colorJList` to `copyJList`.

Lines 34–47 declare, create and register an `ActionListener` for the `copyJButton`. When the user clicks `copyJButton`, method `actionPerformed` (lines 38–45) uses `JList` method **`setListData`** to set the items displayed in `copyJList`. Lines 43–44 call `color-JList`'s method **`getSelectedValuesList`**, which returns a `List<String>` (because the `JList` was created as a `JList<String>`) representing the selected items in `colorJList`. We call the `List<String>`'s toArray method to convert this into an array of `Strings` that can be passed as the argument to `copyJList`'s setListData method. `List` method `toArray` receives as its argument an array representing the type of array that the method will return. You'll learn more about `List` and `toArray` in Chapter 16.

You might be wondering why `copyJList` can be used in line 42 even though the application does not create the object to which it refers until line 49. Remember that method `actionPerformed` (lines 38–45) does not execute until the user presses the `copy-JButton`, which cannot occur until after the constructor completes execution and the application displays the GUI. At that point in the application's execution, `copyJList` is already initialized with a new `JList` object.

12.14 Mouse Event Handling

This section presents the **`MouseListener`** and **`MouseMotionListener`** event-listener interfaces for handling **mouse events**. Mouse events can be processed for any GUI component that derives from `java.awt.Component`. The methods of interfaces `MouseListener` and `MouseMotionListener` are summarized in Figure 12.27. Package `javax.swing.event` contains interface **`MouseInputListener`**, which extends interfaces `MouseListener` and `MouseMotionListener` to create a single interface containing all the `MouseListener` and

MouseMotionListener methods. The MouseListener and MouseMotionListener methods are called when the mouse interacts with a Component if appropriate event-listener objects are registered for that Component.

Each of the mouse event-handling methods receives as an argument a **MouseEvent** object that contains information about the mouse event that occurred, including the *x*- and *y*-coordinates of its location. These coordinates are measured from the *upper-left corner* of the GUI component on which the event occurred. The *x*-coordinates start at 0 and *increase from left to right*. The *y*-coordinates start at 0 and *increase from top to bottom*. The methods and constants of class **InputEvent** (MouseEvent's superclass) enable you to determine which mouse button the user clicked.

MouseListener and MouseMotionListener interface methods

Methods of interface MouseListener

public void mousePressed(MouseEvent event)

 Called when a mouse button is *pressed* while the mouse cursor is on a component.

public void mouseClicked(MouseEvent event)

 Called when a mouse button is *pressed and released* while the mouse cursor remains stationary on a component. Always preceded by a call to mousePressed and mouseReleased.

public void mouseReleased(MouseEvent event)

 Called when a mouse button is *released after being pressed*. Always preceded by a call to mousePressed and one or more calls to mouseDragged.

public void mouseEntered(MouseEvent event)

 Called when the mouse cursor *enters* the bounds of a component.

public void mouseExited(MouseEvent event)

 Called when the mouse cursor *leaves* the bounds of a component.

Methods of interface MouseMotionListener

public void mouseDragged(MouseEvent event)

 Called when the mouse button is *pressed* while the mouse cursor is on a component and the mouse is *moved* while the mouse button *remains pressed*. Always preceded by a call to mousePressed. All drag events are sent to the component on which the user began to drag the mouse.

public void mouseMoved(MouseEvent event)

 Called when the mouse is *moved* (with no mouse buttons pressed) when the mouse cursor is on a component. All move events are sent to the component over which the mouse is currently positioned.

Fig. 12.27 | MouseListener and MouseMotionListener interface methods.

Software Engineering Observation 12.5

Calls to mouseDragged are sent to the MouseMotionListener for the Component on which the drag started. Similarly, the mouseReleased call at the end of a drag operation is sent to the MouseListener for the Component on which the drag operation started.

Java also provides interface **MouseWheelListener** to enable applications to respond to the *rotation of a mouse wheel*. This interface declares method **mouseWheelMoved**, which receives a **MouseWheelEvent** as its argument. Class MouseWheelEvent (a subclass of Mouse-Event) contains methods that enable the event handler to obtain information about the amount of wheel rotation.

Tracking Mouse Events on a JPanel

The MouseTracker application (Figs. 12.28–12.29) demonstrates the MouseListener and MouseMotionListener interface methods. The event-handler class (lines 36–97 of Fig. 12.28) implements both interfaces. You *must* declare all seven methods from these two interfaces when your class implements them both. Each mouse event in this example displays a String in the JLabel called statusBar that is attached to the bottom of the window.

```
 1   // Fig. 12.28: MouseTrackerFrame.java
 2   // Mouse event handling.
 3   import java.awt.Color;
 4   import java.awt.BorderLayout;
 5   import java.awt.event.MouseListener;
 6   import java.awt.event.MouseMotionListener;
 7   import java.awt.event.MouseEvent;
 8   import javax.swing.JFrame;
 9   import javax.swing.JLabel;
10   import javax.swing.JPanel;
11
12   public class MouseTrackerFrame extends JFrame
13   {
14      private final JPanel mousePanel; // panel in which mouse events occur
15      private final JLabel statusBar; // displays event information
16
17      // MouseTrackerFrame constructor sets up GUI and
18      // registers mouse event handlers
19      public MouseTrackerFrame()
20      {
21         super("Demonstrating Mouse Events");
22
23         mousePanel = new JPanel();
24         mousePanel.setBackground(Color.WHITE);
25         add(mousePanel, BorderLayout.CENTER); // add panel to JFrame
26
27         statusBar = new JLabel("Mouse outside JPanel");
28         add(statusBar, BorderLayout.SOUTH); // add label to JFrame
29
30         // create and register listener for mouse and mouse motion events
31         MouseHandler handler = new MouseHandler();
32         mousePanel.addMouseListener(handler);
33         mousePanel.addMouseMotionListener(handler);
34      }
35
```

Fig. 12.28 | Mouse event handling. (Part 1 of 3.)

```
36    private class MouseHandler implements MouseListener,
37       MouseMotionListener
38    {
39       // MouseListener event handlers
40       // handle event when mouse released immediately after press
41       @Override
42       public void mouseClicked(MouseEvent event)'
43       {
44          statusBar.setText(String.format("Clicked at [%d, %d]",
45             event.getX(), event.getY()));
46       }
47
48       // handle event when mouse pressed
49       @Override
50       public void mousePressed(MouseEvent event)
51       {
52          statusBar.setText(String.format("Pressed at [%d, %d]",
53             event.getX(), event.getY()));
54       }
55
56       // handle event when mouse released
57       @Override
58       public void mouseReleased(MouseEvent event)
59       {
60          statusBar.setText(String.format("Released at [%d, %d]",
61             event.getX(), event.getY()));
62       }
63
64       // handle event when mouse enters area
65       @Override
66       public void mouseEntered(MouseEvent event)
67       {
68          statusBar.setText(String.format("Mouse entered at [%d, %d]",
69             event.getX(), event.getY()));
70          mousePanel.setBackground(Color.GREEN);
71       }
72
73       // handle event when mouse exits area
74       @Override
75       public void mouseExited(MouseEvent event)
76       {
77          statusBar.setText("Mouse outside JPanel");
78          mousePanel.setBackground(Color.WHITE);
79       }
80
81       // MouseMotionListener event handlers
82       // handle event when user drags mouse with button pressed
83       @Override
84       public void mouseDragged(MouseEvent event)
85       {
86          statusBar.setText(String.format("Dragged at [%d, %d]",
87             event.getX(), event.getY()));
88       }
```

Fig. 12.28 | Mouse event handling. (Part 2 of 3.)

```
89
90        // handle event when user moves mouse
91        @Override
92        public void mouseMoved(MouseEvent event)
93        {
94            statusBar.setText(String.format("Moved at [%d, %d]",
95                event.getX(), event.getY()));
96        }
97    } // end inner class MouseHandler
98  } // end class MouseTrackerFrame
```

Fig. 12.28 | Mouse event handling. (Part 3 of 3.)

```
1   // Fig. 12.29: MouseTrackerFrame.java
2   // Testing MouseTrackerFrame.
3   import javax.swing.JFrame;
4
5   public class MouseTracker
6   {
7       public static void main(String[] args)
8       {
9           MouseTrackerFrame mouseTrackerFrame = new MouseTrackerFrame();
10          mouseTrackerFrame.setDefaultCloseOperation(JFrame.EXIT_ON_CLOSE);
11          mouseTrackerFrame.setSize(300, 100);
12          mouseTrackerFrame.setVisible(true);
13      }
14  } // end class MouseTracker
```

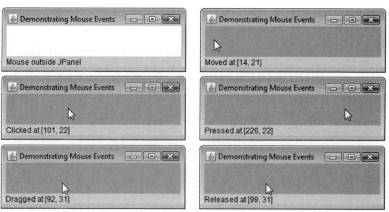

Fig. 12.29 | Testing MouseTrackerFrame.

Line 23 creates JPanel mousePanel. This JPanel's mouse events are tracked by the app. Line 24 sets mousePanel's background color to white. When the user moves the mouse into the mousePanel, the application will change mousePanel's background color to green. When the user moves the mouse out of the mousePanel, the application will change the background color back to white. Line 25 attaches mousePanel to the JFrame. As you've learned, you typically must specify the layout of the GUI components in a JFrame. In that section, we introduced the layout manager FlowLayout. Here we use the default layout of a JFrame's content pane—**BorderLayout**, which arranges component **NORTH**, **SOUTH**, **EAST**, **WEST** and **CENTER** regions. NORTH corresponds to the container's top. This example uses the CENTER and SOUTH regions. Line 25 uses a two-argument version of method add to place mousePanel in the CENTER region. The BorderLayout automatically sizes the component in the CENTER to use all the space in the JFrame that is not occupied by components in the other regions. Section 12.18.2 discusses BorderLayout in more detail.

Lines 27–28 in the constructor declare JLabel statusBar and attach it to the JFrame's SOUTH region. This JLabel occupies the width of the JFrame. The region's height is determined by the JLabel.

Line 31 creates an instance of inner class MouseHandler (lines 36–97) called handler that responds to mouse events. Lines 32–33 register handler as the listener for mouse-Panel's mouse events. Methods **addMouseListener** and **addMouseMotionListener** are inherited indirectly from class Component and can be used to register MouseListeners and MouseMotionListeners, respectively. A MouseHandler object *is a* MouseListener and *is a* MouseMotionListener because the class implements *both* interfaces. We chose to implement both interfaces here to demonstrate a class that implements more than one interface, but we could have implemented interface MouseInputListener instead.

When the mouse enters and exits mousePanel's area, methods mouseEntered (lines 65–71) and mouseExited (lines 74–79) are called, respectively. Method mouseEntered displays a message in the statusBar indicating that the mouse entered the JPanel and changes the background color to green. Method mouseExited displays a message in the statusBar indicating that the mouse is outside the JPanel (see the first sample output window) and changes the background color to white.

The other five events display a string in the statusBar that includes the event and the coordinates at which it occurred. MouseEvent methods **getX** and **getY** return the *x*- and *y*-coordinates, respectively, of the mouse at the time the event occurred.

12.15 Adapter Classes

Many event-listener interfaces, such as MouseListener and MouseMotionListener, contain multiple methods. It's not always desirable to declare every method in an event-listener interface. For instance, an application may need only the mouseClicked handler from MouseListener or the mouseDragged handler from MouseMotionListener. Interface WindowListener specifies seven window event-handling methods. For many of the listener interfaces that have multiple methods, packages java.awt.event and javax.swing.event provide event-listener adapter classes. An **adapter class** implements an interface and provides a default implementation (with an empty method body) of each method in the interface. Figure 12.30 shows several java.awt.event adapter classes and the interfaces they implement. You can extend an adapter class to inherit the default implementation of every method and subsequently override only the method(s) you need for event handling.

Software Engineering Observation 12.6

When a class implements an interface, the class has an is-a relationship with that interface. All direct and indirect subclasses of that class inherit this interface. Thus, an object of a class that extends an event-adapter class is an object of the corresponding event-listener type (e.g., an object of a subclass of MouseAdapter is a MouseListener).

Event-adapter class in `java.awt.event`	Implements interface
ComponentAdapter	ComponentListener
ContainerAdapter	ContainerListener
FocusAdapter	FocusListener
KeyAdapter	KeyListener
MouseAdapter	MouseListener
MouseMotionAdapter	MouseMotionListener
WindowAdapter	WindowListener

Fig. 12.30 | Event-adapter classes and the interfaces they implement.

Extending MouseAdapter

The application of Figs. 12.31–12.32 demonstrates how to determine the number of mouse clicks (i.e., the click count) and how to distinguish between the different mouse buttons. The event listener in this application is an object of inner class `MouseClickHandler` (Fig. 12.31, lines 25–46) that extends `MouseAdapter`, so we can declare just the `mouseClicked` method we need in this example.

```
1   // Fig. 12.31: MouseDetailsFrame.java
2   // Demonstrating mouse clicks and distinguishing between mouse buttons.
3   import java.awt.BorderLayout;
4   import java.awt.event.MouseAdapter;
5   import java.awt.event.MouseEvent;
6   import javax.swing.JFrame;
7   import javax.swing.JLabel;
8
9   public class MouseDetailsFrame extends JFrame
10  {
11     private String details; // String displayed in the statusBar
12     private final JLabel statusBar; // JLabel at bottom of window
13
14     // constructor sets title bar String and register mouse listener
15     public MouseDetailsFrame()
16     {
17        super("Mouse clicks and buttons");
18
19        statusBar = new JLabel("Click the mouse");
20        add(statusBar, BorderLayout.SOUTH);
21        addMouseListener(new MouseClickHandler()); // add handler
22     }
23
24     // inner class to handle mouse events
25     private class MouseClickHandler extends MouseAdapter
26     {
27        // handle mouse-click event and determine which button was pressed
28        @Override
29        public void mouseClicked(MouseEvent event)
30        {
```

Fig. 12.31 | Demonstrating mouse clicks and distinguishing between mouse buttons. (Part 1 of 2.)

```
31                  int xPos = event.getX(); // get x-position of mouse
32                  int yPos = event.getY(); // get y-position of mouse
33
34                  details = String.format("Clicked %d time(s)",
35                     event.getClickCount());
36
37                  if (event.isMetaDown()) // right mouse button
38                     details += " with right mouse button";
39                  else if (event.isAltDown()) // middle mouse button
40                     details += " with center mouse button";
41                  else // left mouse button
42                     details += " with left mouse button";
43
44                  statusBar.setText(details); // display message in statusBar
45            }
46      }
47 } // end class MouseDetailsFrame
```

Fig. 12.31 | Demonstrating mouse clicks and distinguishing between mouse buttons. (Part 2 of 2.)

```
 1  // Fig. 12.32: MouseDetails.java
 2  // Testing MouseDetailsFrame.
 3  import javax.swing.JFrame;
 4
 5  public class MouseDetails
 6  {
 7     public static void main(String[] args)
 8     {
 9        MouseDetailsFrame mouseDetailsFrame = new MouseDetailsFrame();
10        mouseDetailsFrame.setDefaultCloseOperation(JFrame.EXIT_ON_CLOSE);
11        mouseDetailsFrame.setSize(400, 150);
12        mouseDetailsFrame.setVisible(true);
13     }
14  } // end class MouseDetails
```

Fig. 12.32 | Testing MouseDetailsFrame.

Common Programming Error 12.3

If you extend an adapter class and misspell the name of the method you're overriding, and you do not declare the method with @Override, your method simply becomes another method in the class. This is a logic error that is difficult to detect, since the program will call the empty version of the method inherited from the adapter class.

A user of a Java application may be on a system with a one-, two- or three-button mouse. Class MouseEvent inherits several methods from class InputEvent that can distinguish among mouse buttons on a multibutton mouse or can mimic a multibutton mouse with a combined keystroke and mouse-button click. Figure 12.33 shows the InputEvent methods used to distinguish among mouse-button clicks. Java assumes that every mouse contains a left mouse button. Thus, it's simple to test for a left-mouse-button click. However, users with a one- or two-button mouse must use a combination of keystrokes and mouse-button clicks at the same time to simulate the missing buttons on the mouse. In the case of a one- or two-button mouse, a Java application assumes that the center mouse button is clicked if the user holds down the *Alt* key and clicks the left mouse button on a two-button mouse or the only mouse button on a one-button mouse. In the case of a one-button mouse, a Java application assumes that the right mouse button is clicked if the user holds down the *Meta* key (sometimes called the *Command* key or the "Apple" key on a Mac) and clicks the mouse button.

InputEvent method	Description
isMetaDown()	Returns true when the user clicks the *right mouse button* on a mouse with two or three buttons. To simulate a right-mouse-button click on a one-button mouse, the user can hold down the *Meta* key on the keyboard and click the mouse button.
isAltDown()	Returns true when the user clicks the *middle mouse button* on a mouse with three buttons. To simulate a middle-mouse-button click on a one- or two-button mouse, the user can press the *Alt* key and click the only or left mouse button, respectively.

Fig. 12.33 | InputEvent methods that help determine whether the right or center mouse button was clicked.

Line 21 of Fig. 12.31 registers a MouseListener for the MouseDetailsFrame. The event listener is an object of class MouseClickHandler, which extends MouseAdapter. This enables us to declare only method mouseClicked (lines 28–45). This method first captures the coordinates where the event occurred and stores them in local variables xPos and yPos (lines 31–32). Lines 34–35 create a String called details containing the number of consecutive mouse clicks, which is returned by MouseEvent method **getClickCount** at line 35. Lines 37–42 use methods **isMetaDown** and **isAltDown** to determine which mouse button the user clicked and append an appropriate String to details in each case. The resulting String is displayed in the statusBar. Class MouseDetails (Fig. 12.32) contains the main method that executes the application. Try clicking with each of your mouse's buttons repeatedly to see the click count increment.

12.16 JPanel Subclass for Drawing with the Mouse

Section 12.14 showed how to track mouse events in a JPanel. In this section, we use a JPanel as a **dedicated drawing area** in which the user can draw by dragging the mouse. In addition, this section demonstrates an event listener that extends an adapter class.

Method paintComponent
Lightweight Swing components that extend class JComponent (such as JPanel) contain method **paintComponent**, which is called when a lightweight Swing component is displayed. By overriding this method, you can specify how to draw shapes using Java's graphics capabilities. When customizing a JPanel for use as a dedicated drawing area, the subclass should override method paintComponent and call the superclass version of paintComponent as the first statement in the body of the overridden method to ensure that the component displays correctly. The reason is that subclasses of JComponent support **transparency**. To display a component correctly, the program must determine whether the component is transparent. The code that determines this is in superclass JComponent's paintComponent implementation. When a component is transparent, paintComponent will not clear its background when the program displays the component. When a component is **opaque**, paintComponent clears the component's background before the component is displayed. The transparency of a Swing lightweight component can be set with method **setOpaque** (a false argument indicates that the component is transparent).

> **Error-Prevention Tip 12.1**
>
> *In a JComponent subclass's paintComponent method, the first statement should always call the superclass's paintComponent method to ensure that an object of the subclass displays correctly.*

> **Common Programming Error 12.4**
>
> *If an overridden paintComponent method does not call the superclass's version, the subclass component may not display properly. If an overridden paintComponent method calls the superclass's version after other drawing is performed, the drawing will be erased.*

Defining the Custom Drawing Area
The Painter application of Figs. 12.34–12.35 demonstrates a customized subclass of JPanel that's used to create a dedicated drawing area. The application uses the mouseDragged event handler to create a simple drawing application. The user can draw pictures by dragging the mouse on the JPanel. This example does not use method mouseMoved, so our *event-listener class* (the *anonymous inner class* at lines 20–29 of Fig. 12.34) extends MouseMotionAdapter. Since this class already declares both mouseMoved and mouseDragged, we can simply override mouseDragged to provide the event handling this application requires.

```
1  // Fig. 12.34: PaintPanel.java
2  // Adapter class used to implement event handlers.
3  import java.awt.Point;
4  import java.awt.Graphics;
5  import java.awt.event.MouseEvent;
```

Fig. 12.34 | Adapter class used to implement event handlers. (Part 1 of 2.)

```
6   import java.awt.event.MouseMotionAdapter;
7   import java.util.ArrayList;
8   import javax.swing.JPanel;
9
10  public class PaintPanel extends JPanel
11  {
12     // list of Point references
13     private final ArrayList<Point> points = new ArrayList<>();
14
15     // set up GUI and register mouse event handler
16     public PaintPanel()
17     {
18        // handle frame mouse motion event
19        addMouseMotionListener(
20           new MouseMotionAdapter() // anonymous inner class
21           {
22              // store drag coordinates and repaint
23              @Override
24              public void mouseDragged(MouseEvent event)
25              {
26                 points.add(event.getPoint());
27                 repaint(); // repaint JFrame
28              }
29           }
30        );
31     }
32
33     // draw ovals in a 4-by-4 bounding box at specified locations on window
34     @Override
35     public void paintComponent(Graphics g)
36     {
37        super.paintComponent(g); // clears drawing area
38
39        // draw all points
40        for (Point point : points)
41           g.fillOval(point.x, point.y, 4, 4);
42     }
43  } // end class PaintPanel
```

Fig. 12.34 | Adapter class used to implement event handlers. (Part 2 of 2.)

Class PaintPanel (Fig. 12.34) extends JPanel to create the dedicated drawing area. Class **Point** (package java.awt) represents an *x-y* coordinate. We use objects of this class to store the coordinates of each mouse drag event. Class **Graphics** is used to draw. In this example, we use an ArrayList of Points (line 13) to store the location at which each mouse drag event occurs. As you'll see, method paintComponent uses these Points to draw.

Lines 19–30 register a MouseMotionListener to listen for the PaintPanel's mouse motion events. Lines 20–29 create an object of an anonymous inner class that extends the adapter class MouseMotionAdapter. Recall that MouseMotionAdapter implements Mouse-MotionListener, so the *anonymous inner class* object is a MouseMotionListener. The anonymous inner class inherits default mouseMoved and mouseDragged implementations, so it already implements all the interface's methods. However, the default implementations do nothing when they're called. So, we override method `mouseDragged` at lines 23–28 to capture the coordinates of a mouse drag event and store them as a `Point` object. Line 26 invokes the `MouseEvent`'s **getPoint** method to obtain the `Point` where the event occurred and stores it in the `ArrayList`. Line 27 calls method **repaint** (inherited indirectly from class `Component`) to indicate that the `PaintPanel` should be refreshed on the screen as soon as possible with a call to the `PaintPanel`'s `paintComponent` method.

Method `paintComponent` (lines 34–42), which receives a `Graphics` parameter, is called automatically any time the `PaintPanel` needs to be displayed on the screen—such as when the GUI is first displayed—or refreshed on the screen—such as when method `repaint` is called or when the GUI component has been *hidden* by another window on the screen and subsequently becomes visible again.

Look-and-Feel Observation 12.13

Calling repaint *for a Swing GUI component indicates that the component should be refreshed on the screen as soon as possible. The component's background is cleared only if the component is opaque.* JComponent *method* setOpaque *can be passed a boolean argument indicating whether the component is opaque (*true*) or transparent (*false*).*

Line 37 invokes the superclass version of `paintComponent` to clear the `PaintPanel`'s background (`JPanel`s are opaque by default). Lines 40–41 draw an oval at the location specified by each `Point` in the `ArrayList`. `Graphics` method **fillOval** draws a solid oval. The method's four parameters represent a rectangular area (called the *bounding box*) in which the oval is displayed. The first two parameters are the upper-left *x*-coordinate and the upper-left *y*-coordinate of the rectangular area. The last two coordinates represent the rectangular area's width and height. Method `fillOval` draws the oval so it touches the middle of each side of the rectangular area. In line 41, the first two arguments are specified by using class `Point`'s two `public` instance variables—`x` and `y`. You'll learn more `Graphics` features in Chapter 13.

Look-and-Feel Observation 12.14

Drawing on any GUI component is performed with coordinates that are measured from the upper-left corner (0, 0) of that GUI component, not the upper-left corner of the screen.

Using the Custom JPanel in an Application

Class `Painter` (Fig. 12.35) contains the `main` method that executes this application. Line 14 creates a `PaintPanel` object on which the user can drag the mouse to draw. Line 15 attaches the `PaintPanel` to the `JFrame`.

```
1   // Fig. 12.35: Painter.java
2   // Testing PaintPanel.
3   import java.awt.BorderLayout;
4   import javax.swing.JFrame;
5   import javax.swing.JLabel;
6
7   public class Painter
8   {
```

Fig. 12.35 | Testing `PaintPanel`. (Part 1 of 2.)

```
 9      public static void main(String[] args)
10      {
11         // create JFrame
12         JFrame application = new JFrame("A simple paint program");
13
14         PaintPanel paintPanel = new PaintPanel();
15         application.add(paintPanel, BorderLayout.CENTER);
16
17         // create a label and place it in SOUTH of BorderLayout
18         application.add(new JLabel("Drag the mouse to draw"),
19            BorderLayout.SOUTH);
20
21         application.setDefaultCloseOperation(JFrame.EXIT_ON_CLOSE);
22         application.setSize(400, 200);
23         application.setVisible(true);
24      }
25   } // end class Painter
```

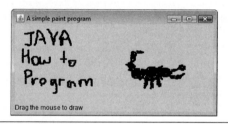

Fig. 12.35 | Testing `PaintPanel`. (Part 2 of 2.)

12.17 Key Event Handling

This section presents the `KeyListener` interface for handling **key events**. Key events are generated when keys on the keyboard are pressed and released. A class that implements `KeyListener` must provide declarations for methods **keyPressed**, **keyReleased** and **keyTyped**, each of which receives a KeyEvent as its argument. Class KeyEvent is a subclass of InputEvent. Method keyPressed is called in response to pressing any key. Method keyTyped is called in response to pressing any key that is not an **action key**. (The action keys are any arrow key, *Home*, *End*, *Page Up*, *Page Down*, any function key, etc.) Method keyReleased is called when the key is released after any keyPressed or keyTyped event.

The application of Figs. 12.36–12.37 demonstrates the `KeyListener` methods. Class KeyDemoFrame implements the `KeyListener` interface, so all three methods are declared in the application. The constructor (Fig. 12.36, lines 17–28) registers the application to handle its own key events by using method **addKeyListener** at line 27. Method addKeyListener is declared in class Component, so every subclass of Component can notify KeyListener objects of key events for that Component.

```
1   // Fig. 12.36: KeyDemoFrame.java
2   // Key event handling.
3   import java.awt.Color;
```

Fig. 12.36 | Key event handling. (Part 1 of 3.)

```java
 4   import java.awt.event.KeyListener;
 5   import java.awt.event.KeyEvent;
 6   import javax.swing.JFrame;
 7   import javax.swing.JTextArea;
 8
 9   public class KeyDemoFrame extends JFrame implements KeyListener
10   {
11      private final String line1 = ""; // first line of text area
12      private final String line2 = ""; // second line of text area
13      private final String line3 = ""; // third line of text area
14      private final JTextArea textArea; // text area to display output
15
16      // KeyDemoFrame constructor
17      public KeyDemoFrame()
18      {
19         super("Demonstrating Keystroke Events");
20
21         textArea = new JTextArea(10, 15); // set up JTextArea
22         textArea.setText("Press any key on the keyboard...");
23         textArea.setEnabled(false);
24         textArea.setDisabledTextColor(Color.BLACK);
25         add(textArea); // add text area to JFrame
26
27         addKeyListener(this); // allow frame to process key events
28      }
29
30      // handle press of any key
31      @Override
32      public void keyPressed(KeyEvent event)
33      {
34         line1 = String.format("Key pressed: %s",
35            KeyEvent.getKeyText(event.getKeyCode())); // show pressed key
36         setLines2and3(event); // set output lines two and three
37      }
38
39      // handle release of any key
40      @Override
41      public void keyReleased(KeyEvent event)
42      {
43         line1 = String.format("Key released: %s",
44            KeyEvent.getKeyText(event.getKeyCode())); // show released key
45         setLines2and3(event); // set output lines two and three
46      }
47
48      // handle press of an action key
49      @Override
50      public void keyTyped(KeyEvent event)
51      {
52         line1 = String.format("Key typed: %s", event.getKeyChar());
53         setLines2and3(event); // set output lines two and three
54      }
55
```

Fig. 12.36 | Key event handling. (Part 2 of 3.)

```
56      // set second and third lines of output
57      private void setLines2and3(KeyEvent event)
58      {
59         line2 = String.format("This key is %san action key",
60            (event.isActionKey() ? "" : "not "));
61
62         String temp = KeyEvent.getKeyModifiersText(event.getModifiers());
63
64         line3 = String.format("Modifier keys pressed: %s",
65            (temp.equals("") ? "none" : temp)); // output modifiers
66
67         textArea.setText(String.format("%s\n%s\n%s\n",
68            line1, line2, line3)); // output three lines of text
69      }
70   } // end class KeyDemoFrame
```

Fig. 12.36 | Key event handling. (Part 3 of 3.)

```
1    // Fig. 12.37: KeyDemo.java
2    // Testing KeyDemoFrame.
3    import javax.swing.JFrame;
4
5    public class KeyDemo
6    {
7       public static void main(String[] args)
8       {
9          KeyDemoFrame keyDemoFrame = new KeyDemoFrame();
10         keyDemoFrame.setDefaultCloseOperation(JFrame.EXIT_ON_CLOSE);
11         keyDemoFrame.setSize(350, 100);
12         keyDemoFrame.setVisible(true);
13      }
14   } // end class KeyDemo
```

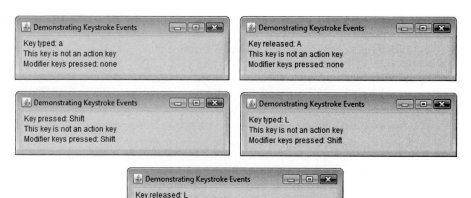

Fig. 12.37 | Testing KeyDemoFrame. (Part 1 of 2.)

Fig. 12.37 | Testing `KeyDemoFrame`. (Part 2 of 2.)

At line 25, the constructor adds the `JTextArea` `textArea` (where the application's output is displayed) to the `JFrame`. A `JTextArea` is a *multiline area* in which you can display text. (We discuss `JTextArea`s in more detail in Section 12.20.) Notice in the screen captures that `textArea` occupies the *entire window*. This is due to the `JFrame`'s default `BorderLayout` (discussed in Section 12.18.2 and demonstrated in Fig. 12.41). When a single `Component` is added to a `BorderLayout`, the `Component` occupies the *entire* Container. Line 23 disables the `JTextArea` so the user cannot type in it. This causes the text in the `JTextArea` to become gray. Line 24 uses method **setDisabledTextColor** to change the text color in the `JTextArea` to black for readability.

Methods `keyPressed` (lines 31–37) and `keyReleased` (lines 40–46) use KeyEvent method **getKeyCode** to get the **virtual key code** of the pressed key. Class KeyEvent contains virtual key-code constants that represent every key on the keyboard. These constants can be compared with getKeyCode's return value to test for individual keys on the keyboard. The value returned by getKeyCode is passed to static KeyEvent method **getKeyText**, which returns a string containing the name of the key that was pressed. For a complete list of virtual key constants, see the online documentation for class KeyEvent (package `java.awt.event`). Method `keyTyped` (lines 49–54) uses KeyEvent method **getKeyChar** (which returns a char) to get the Unicode value of the character typed.

All three event-handling methods finish by calling method `setLines2and3` (lines 57–69) and passing it the KeyEvent object. This method uses KeyEvent method **isActionKey** (line 60) to determine whether the key in the event was an action key. Also, InputEvent method **getModifiers** is called (line 62) to determine whether any modifier keys (such as *Shift*, *Alt* and *Ctrl*) were pressed when the key event occurred. The result of this method is passed to static KeyEvent method **getKeyModifiersText**, which produces a String containing the names of the pressed modifier keys.

[*Note:* If you need to test for a specific key on the keyboard, class KeyEvent provides a **key constant** for each one. These constants can be used from the key event handlers to determine whether a particular key was pressed. Also, to determine whether the *Alt*, *Ctrl*, *Meta* and *Shift* keys are pressed individually, InputEvent methods **isAltDown**, **isControlDown**, **isMetaDown** and **isShiftDown** each return a boolean indicating whether the particular key was pressed during the key event.]

12.18 Introduction to Layout Managers

Layout managers *arrange* GUI components in a container for presentation purposes. You can use the layout managers for basic layout capabilities instead of determining every GUI component's exact position and size. This functionality enables you to concentrate on the basic look-and-feel and lets the layout managers process most of the layout details. All layout managers implement the interface **LayoutManager** (in package `java.awt`). Class Container's setLayout method takes an object that implements the LayoutManager interface as an argument. There are basically three ways for you to arrange components in a GUI:

1. *Absolute positioning:* This provides the greatest level of control over a GUI's appearance. By setting a Container's layout to null, you can specify the *absolute position of each GUI component* with respect to the upper-left corner of the Container by using Component methods setSize and setLocation or setBounds. If you do this, you also must specify each GUI component's size. Programming a GUI with absolute positioning can be tedious, unless you have an integrated development environment (IDE) that can generate the code for you.

2. *Layout managers:* Using layout managers to position elements can be simpler and faster than creating a GUI with absolute positioning, and makes your GUIs more resizable, but you lose some control over the size and the precise positioning of each component.

3. *Visual programming in an IDE:* IDEs provide tools that make it easy to create GUIs. Each IDE typically provides a **GUI design tool** that allows you to drag and drop GUI components from a tool box onto a design area. You can then position, size and align GUI components as you like. The IDE generates the Java code that creates the GUI. In addition, you can typically add event-handling code for a particular component by double-clicking the component. Some design tools also allow you to use the layout managers described in this chapter and in Chapter 19.

Look-and-Feel Observation 12.15

Most Java IDEs provide GUI design tools for visually designing a GUI; the tools then write Java code that creates the GUI. Such tools often provide greater control over the size, position and alignment of GUI components than do the built-in layout managers.

Look-and-Feel Observation 12.16

It's possible to set a Container's layout to null, which indicates that no layout manager should be used. In a Container without a layout manager, you must position and size the components and take care that, on resize events, all components are repositioned as necessary. A component's resize events can be processed by a ComponentListener.

Figure 12.38 summarizes the layout managers presented in this chapter. A couple of additional layout managers are discussed in Chapter 19.

Layout manager	Description
FlowLayout	Default for javax.swing.JPanel. Places components *sequentially, left to right*, in the order they were added. It's also possible to specify the order of the components by using the Container method add, which takes a Component and an integer index position as arguments.
BorderLayout	Default for JFrames (and other windows). Arranges the components into five areas: NORTH, SOUTH, EAST, WEST and CENTER.
GridLayout	Arranges the components into rows and columns.

Fig. 12.38 | Layout managers.

12.18.1 FlowLayout

FlowLayout is the *simplest* layout manager. GUI components are placed in a container from left to right in the order in which they're added to the container. When the edge of the container is reached, components continue to display on the next line. Class FlowLayout allows GUI components to be *left aligned*, *centered* (the default) and *right aligned*.

The application of Figs. 12.39–12.40 creates three JButton objects and adds them to the application, using a FlowLayout. The components are center aligned by default. When the user clicks **Left**, the FlowLayout's alignment is changed to left aligned. When the user clicks **Right**, the FlowLayout's alignment is changed to right aligned. When the user clicks **Center**, the FlowLayout's alignment is changed to center aligned. The sample output windows show each alignment. The last sample output shows the centered alignment after the window has been resized to a smaller width so that the button **Right** flows onto a new line.

As seen previously, a container's layout is set with method setLayout of class Container. Line 25 (Fig. 12.39) sets the layout manager to the FlowLayout declared at line 23. Normally, the layout is set before any GUI components are added to a container.

Look-and-Feel Observation 12.17

Each individual container can have only one layout manager, but multiple containers in the same application can each use different layout managers.

```
1   // Fig. 12.39: FlowLayoutFrame.java
2   // FlowLayout allows components to flow over multiple lines.
3   import java.awt.FlowLayout;
4   import java.awt.Container;
5   import java.awt.event.ActionListener;
6   import java.awt.event.ActionEvent;
7   import javax.swing.JFrame;
8   import javax.swing.JButton;
9
10  public class FlowLayoutFrame extends JFrame
11  {
12     private final JButton leftJButton; // button to set alignment left
13     private final JButton centerJButton; // button to set alignment center
14     private final JButton rightJButton; // button to set alignment right
15     private final FlowLayout layout; // layout object
16     private final Container container; // container to set layout
17
18     // set up GUI and register button listeners
19     public FlowLayoutFrame()
20     {
21        super("FlowLayout Demo");
22
23        layout = new FlowLayout();
24        container = getContentPane(); // get container to layout
25        setLayout(layout);
26
27        // set up leftJButton and register listener
28        leftJButton = new JButton("Left");
29        add(leftJButton); // add Left button to frame
```

Fig. 12.39 | FlowLayout allows components to flow over multiple lines. (Part 1 of 2.)

```
30          leftJButton.addActionListener(
31              new ActionListener() // anonymous inner class
32              {
33                  // process leftJButton event
34                  @Override
35                  public void actionPerformed(ActionEvent event)
36                  {
37                      layout.setAlignment(FlowLayout.LEFT);
38
39                      // realign attached components
40                      layout.layoutContainer(container);
41                  }
42              }
43          );
44
45          // set up centerJButton and register listener
46          centerJButton = new JButton("Center");
47          add(centerJButton); // add Center button to frame
48          centerJButton.addActionListener(
49              new ActionListener() // anonymous inner class
50              {
51                  // process centerJButton event
52                  @Override
53                  public void actionPerformed(ActionEvent event)
54                  {
55                      layout.setAlignment(FlowLayout.CENTER);
56
57                      // realign attached components
58                      layout.layoutContainer(container);
59                  }
60              }
61          );
62
63          // set up rightJButton and register listener
64          rightJButton = new JButton("Right");
65          add(rightJButton); // add Right button to frame
66          rightJButton.addActionListener(
67              new ActionListener() // anonymous inner class
68              {
69                  // process rightJButton event
70                  @Override
71                  public void actionPerformed(ActionEvent event)
72                  {
73                      layout.setAlignment(FlowLayout.RIGHT);
74
75                      // realign attached components
76                      layout.layoutContainer(container);
77                  }
78              }
79          );
80      } // end FlowLayoutFrame constructor
81  } // end class FlowLayoutFrame
```

Fig. 12.39 | FlowLayout allows components to flow over multiple lines. (Part 2 of 2.)

```
1   // Fig. 12.40: FlowLayoutDemo.java
2   // Testing FlowLayoutFrame.
3   import javax.swing.JFrame;
4
5   public class FlowLayoutDemo
6   {
7      public static void main(String[] args)
8      {
9         FlowLayoutFrame flowLayoutFrame = new FlowLayoutFrame();
10        flowLayoutFrame.setDefaultCloseOperation(JFrame.EXIT_ON_CLOSE);
11        flowLayoutFrame.setSize(300, 75);
12        flowLayoutFrame.setVisible(true);
13     }
14  } // end class FlowLayoutDemo
```

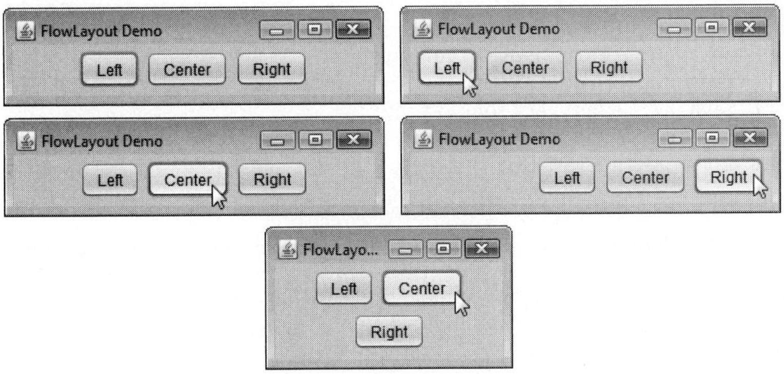

Fig. 12.40 | Testing FlowLayoutFrame.

Each button's event handler is specified with a separate anonymous inner-class object (lines 30–43, 48–61 and 66–79, respectively), and method actionPerformed in each case executes two statements. For example, line 37 in the event handler for leftJButton uses FlowLayout method **setAlignment** to change the alignment for the FlowLayout to a left-aligned (**FlowLayout.LEFT**) FlowLayout. Line 40 uses LayoutManager interface method **layoutContainer** (which is inherited by all layout managers) to specify that the JFrame should be rearranged based on the adjusted layout. According to which button was clicked, the actionPerformed method for each button sets the FlowLayout's alignment to Flow-Layout.LEFT (line 37), **FlowLayout.CENTER** (line 55) or **FlowLayout.RIGHT** (line 73).

12.18.2 BorderLayout

The BorderLayout layout manager (the default layout manager for a JFrame) arranges components into five regions: NORTH, SOUTH, EAST, WEST and CENTER. NORTH corresponds to the top of the container. Class BorderLayout extends Object and implements interface **LayoutManager2** (a subinterface of LayoutManager that adds several methods for enhanced layout processing).

A BorderLayout limits a Container to containing *at most five components*—one in each region. The component placed in each region can be a container to which other components are attached. The components placed in the NORTH and SOUTH regions extend horizontally to the sides of the container and are as tall as the components placed in those regions. The EAST and WEST regions expand vertically between the NORTH and SOUTH regions and are as wide as the components placed in those regions. The component placed in the CENTER region *expands to fill all remaining space in the layout* (which is the reason the JTextArea in Fig. 12.37 occupies the entire window). If all five regions are occupied, the entire container's space is covered by GUI components. If the NORTH or SOUTH region is not occupied, the GUI components in the EAST, CENTER and WEST regions expand vertically to fill the remaining space. If the EAST or WEST region is not occupied, the GUI component in the CENTER region *expands horizontally to fill the remaining space*. If the CENTER region is *not* occupied, the area is left *empty*—the other GUI components do *not* expand to fill the remaining space. The application of Figs. 12.41–12.42 demonstrates the BorderLayout layout manager by using five JButtons.

```java
1   // Fig. 12.41: BorderLayoutFrame.java
2   // BorderLayout containing five buttons.
3   import java.awt.BorderLayout;
4   import java.awt.event.ActionListener;
5   import java.awt.event.ActionEvent;
6   import javax.swing.JFrame;
7   import javax.swing.JButton;
8
9   public class BorderLayoutFrame extends JFrame implements ActionListener
10  {
11     private final JButton[] buttons; // array of buttons to hide portions
12     private static final String[] names = {"Hide North", "Hide South",
13        "Hide East", "Hide West", "Hide Center"};
14     private final BorderLayout layout;
15
16     // set up GUI and event handling
17     public BorderLayoutFrame()
18     {
19        super("BorderLayout Demo");
20
21        layout = new BorderLayout(5, 5); // 5 pixel gaps
22        setLayout(layout);
23        buttons = new JButton[names.length];
24
25        // create JButtons and register listeners for them
26        for (int count = 0; count < names.length; count++)
27        {
28           buttons[count] = new JButton(names[count]);
29           buttons[count].addActionListener(this);
30        }
31
32        add(buttons[0], BorderLayout.NORTH);
33        add(buttons[1], BorderLayout.SOUTH);
34        add(buttons[2], BorderLayout.EAST);
35        add(buttons[3], BorderLayout.WEST);
36        add(buttons[4], BorderLayout.CENTER);
37     }
```

Fig. 12.41 | BorderLayout containing five buttons. (Part 1 of 2.)

```
38
39       // handle button events
40       @Override
41       public void actionPerformed(ActionEvent event)
42       {
43          // check event source and lay out content pane correspondingly
44          for (JButton button : buttons)
45          {
46             if (event.getSource() == button)
47                button.setVisible(false); // hide the button that was clicked
48             else
49                button.setVisible(true); // show other buttons
50          }
51
52          layout.layoutContainer(getContentPane()); // lay out content pane
53       }
54    } // end class BorderLayoutFrame
```

Fig. 12.41 | BorderLayout containing five buttons. (Part 2 of 2.)

Line 21 of Fig. 12.41 creates a BorderLayout. The constructor arguments specify the number of pixels between components that are arranged horizontally (**horizontal gap space**) and between components that are arranged vertically (**vertical gap space**), respectively. The default is one pixel of gap space horizontally and vertically. Line 22 uses method setLayout to set the content pane's layout to layout.

We add Components to a BorderLayout with another version of Container method add that takes two arguments—the Component to add and the region in which the Component should appear. For example, line 32 specifies that buttons[0] should appear in the NORTH region. The components can be added in *any* order, but only *one* component should be added to each region.

Look-and-Feel Observation 12.18

If no region is specified when adding a Component to a BorderLayout, the layout manager assumes that the Component should be added to region BorderLayout.CENTER.

Common Programming Error 12.5

When more than one component is added to a region in a BorderLayout, only the last component added to that region will be displayed. There's no error that indicates this problem.

Class BorderLayoutFrame implements ActionListener directly in this example, so the BorderLayoutFrame will handle the events of the JButtons. For this reason, line 29 passes the this reference to the addActionListener method of each JButton. When the user clicks a particular JButton in the layout, method actionPerformed (lines 40–53) executes. The enhanced for statement at lines 44–50 uses an if...else to hide the particular JButton that generated the event. Method **setVisible** (inherited into JButton from class Component) is called with a false argument (line 47) to hide the JButton. If the current JButton in the array is not the one that generated the event, method setVisible is called with a true argument (line 49) to ensure that the JButton is displayed on the screen. Line 52 uses Layout-

Manager method layoutContainer to recalculate the layout of the content pane. Notice in the screen captures of Fig. 12.42 that certain regions in the BorderLayout change shape as JButtons are *hidden* and displayed in other regions. Try resizing the application window to see how the various regions resize based on the window's width and height. *For more complex layouts, group components in JPanels, each with a separate layout manager.* Place the JPanels on the JFrame using either the default BorderLayout or some other layout.

```java
 1   // Fig. 12.42: BorderLayoutDemo.java
 2   // Testing BorderLayoutFrame.
 3   import javax.swing.JFrame;
 4
 5   public class BorderLayoutDemo
 6   {
 7      public static void main(String[] args)
 8      {
 9         BorderLayoutFrame borderLayoutFrame = new BorderLayoutFrame();
10         borderLayoutFrame.setDefaultCloseOperation(JFrame.EXIT_ON_CLOSE);
11         borderLayoutFrame.setSize(300, 200);
12         borderLayoutFrame.setVisible(true);
13      }
14   } // end class BorderLayoutDemo
```

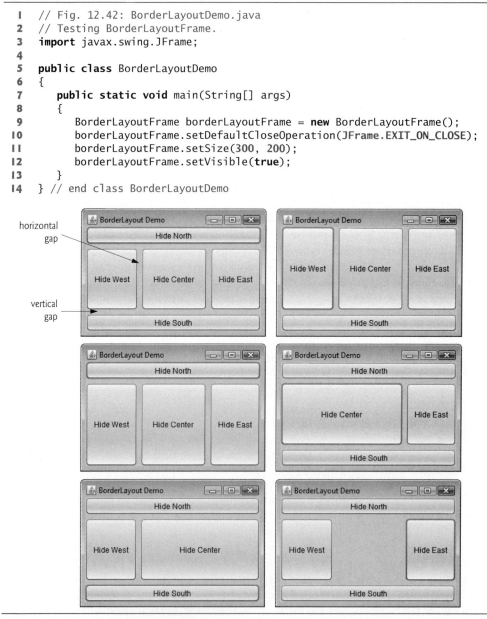

Fig. 12.42 | Testing BorderLayoutFrame.

12.18.3 GridLayout

The **GridLayout** layout manager divides the container into a *grid* so that components can be placed in *rows* and *columns*. Class GridLayout inherits directly from class Object and implements interface LayoutManager. Every Component in a GridLayout has the *same* width and height. Components are added to a GridLayout starting at the top-left cell of the grid and proceeding left to right until the row is full. Then the process continues left to right on the next row of the grid, and so on. The application of Figs. 12.43–12.44 demonstrates the GridLayout layout manager by using six JButtons.

```java
1  // Fig. 12.43: GridLayoutFrame.java
2  // GridLayout containing six buttons.
3  import java.awt.GridLayout;
4  import java.awt.Container;
5  import java.awt.event.ActionListener;
6  import java.awt.event.ActionEvent;
7  import javax.swing.JFrame;
8  import javax.swing.JButton;
9
10 public class GridLayoutFrame extends JFrame implements ActionListener
11 {
12    private final JButton[] buttons; // array of buttons
13    private static final String[] names =
14       { "one", "two", "three", "four", "five", "six" };
15    private boolean toggle = true; // toggle between two layouts
16    private final Container container; // frame container
17    private final GridLayout gridLayout1; // first gridlayout
18    private final GridLayout gridLayout2; // second gridlayout
19
20    // no-argument constructor
21    public GridLayoutFrame()
22    {
23       super("GridLayout Demo");
24       gridLayout1 = new GridLayout(2, 3, 5, 5); // 2 by 3; gaps of 5
25       gridLayout2 = new GridLayout(3, 2); // 3 by 2; no gaps
26       container = getContentPane();
27       setLayout(gridLayout1);
28       buttons = new JButton[names.length];
29
30       for (int count = 0; count < names.length; count++)
31       {
32          buttons[count] = new JButton(names[count]);
33          buttons[count].addActionListener(this); // register listener
34          add(buttons[count]); // add button to JFrame
35       }
36    }
37
38    // handle button events by toggling between layouts
39    @Override
40    public void actionPerformed(ActionEvent event)
41    {
```

Fig. 12.43 | GridLayout containing six buttons. (Part 1 of 2.)

```
42          if (toggle) // set layout based on toggle
43             container.setLayout(gridLayout2);
44          else
45             container.setLayout(gridLayout1);
46
47          toggle = !toggle;
48          container.validate(); // re-lay out container
49       }
50    } // end class GridLayoutFrame
```

Fig. 12.43 | GridLayout containing six buttons. (Part 2 of 2.)

```
1    // Fig. 12.44: GridLayoutDemo.java
2    // Testing GridLayoutFrame.
3    import javax.swing.JFrame;
4
5    public class GridLayoutDemo
6    {
7       public static void main(String[] args)
8       {
9          GridLayoutFrame gridLayoutFrame = new GridLayoutFrame();
10         gridLayoutFrame.setDefaultCloseOperation(JFrame.EXIT_ON_CLOSE);
11         gridLayoutFrame.setSize(300, 200);
12         gridLayoutFrame.setVisible(true);
13      }
14   } // end class GridLayoutDemo
```

Fig. 12.44 | Testing GridLayoutFrame.

Lines 24–25 (Fig. 12.43) create two GridLayout objects. The GridLayout constructor used at line 24 specifies a GridLayout with 2 rows, 3 columns, 5 pixels of horizontal-gap space between Components in the grid and 5 pixels of vertical-gap space between Components in the grid. The GridLayout constructor used at line 25 specifies a GridLayout with 3 rows and 2 columns that uses the default gap space (1 pixel).

The JButton objects in this example initially are arranged using gridLayout1 (set for the content pane at line 27 with method setLayout). The first component is added to the first column of the first row. The next component is added to the second column of the first row, and so on. When a JButton is pressed, method actionPerformed (lines 39–49) is called. Every call to actionPerformed toggles the layout between gridLayout2 and gridLayout1, using boolean variable toggle to determine the next layout to set.

Line 48 shows another way to reformat a container for which the layout has changed. Container method **validate** recomputes the container's layout based on the current layout manager for the Container and the current set of displayed GUI components.

12.19 Using Panels to Manage More Complex Layouts

Complex GUIs (like Fig. 12.1) often require that each component be placed in an exact location. They often consist of multiple panels, with each panel's components arranged in a specific layout. Class JPanel extends JComponent and JComponent extends class Container, so every JPanel is a Container. Thus, every JPanel may have components, including other panels, attached to it with Container method add. The application of Figs. 12.45–12.46 demonstrates how a JPanel can be used to create a more complex layout in which several JButtons are placed in the SOUTH region of a BorderLayout.

```java
 1   // Fig. 12.45: PanelFrame.java
 2   // Using a JPanel to help lay out components.
 3   import java.awt.GridLayout;
 4   import java.awt.BorderLayout;
 5   import javax.swing.JFrame;
 6   import javax.swing.JPanel;
 7   import javax.swing.JButton;
 8
 9   public class PanelFrame extends JFrame
10   {
11      private final JPanel buttonJPanel; // panel to hold buttons
12      private final JButton[] buttons;
13
14      // no-argument constructor
15      public PanelFrame()
16      {
17         super("Panel Demo");
18         buttons = new JButton[5];
19         buttonJPanel = new JPanel();
20         buttonJPanel.setLayout(new GridLayout(1, buttons.length));
21
22         // create and add buttons
23         for (int count = 0; count < buttons.length; count++)
24         {
25            buttons[count] = new JButton("Button " + (count + 1));
26            buttonJPanel.add(buttons[count]); // add button to panel
27         }
28
29         add(buttonJPanel, BorderLayout.SOUTH); // add panel to JFrame
30      }
31   } // end class PanelFrame
```

Fig. 12.45 | JPanel with five JButtons in a GridLayout attached to the SOUTH region of a BorderLayout.

```java
 1   // Fig. 12.46: PanelDemo.java
 2   // Testing PanelFrame.
 3   import javax.swing.JFrame;
 4
```

Fig. 12.46 | Testing PanelFrame. (Part 1 of 2.)

```
 5   public class PanelDemo extends JFrame
 6   {
 7      public static void main(String[] args)
 8      {
 9         PanelFrame panelFrame = new PanelFrame();
10         panelFrame.setDefaultCloseOperation(JFrame.EXIT_ON_CLOSE);
11         panelFrame.setSize(450, 200);
12         panelFrame.setVisible(true);
13      }
14   } // end class PanelDemo
```

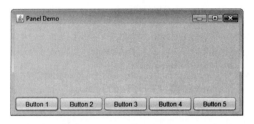

Fig. 12.46 | Testing `PanelFrame`. (Part 2 of 2.)

After `JPanel buttonJPanel` is declared (line 11 of Fig. 12.45) and created (line 19), line 20 sets `buttonJPanel`'s layout to a `GridLayout` of one row and five columns (there are five `JButton`s in array `buttons`). Lines 23–27 add the `JButton`s in the array to the `JPanel`. Line 26 adds the buttons directly to the `JPanel`—class `JPanel` does not have a content pane, unlike a `JFrame`. Line 29 uses the `JFrame`'s default `BorderLayout` to add `buttonJPanel` to the `SOUTH` region. The `SOUTH` region is as tall as the buttons on `buttonJPanel`. A `JPanel` is sized to the components it contains. As more components are added, the `JPanel` *grows* (according to the restrictions of its layout manager) to accommodate the components. Resize the window to see how the layout manager affects the size of the `JButton`s.

12.20 JTextArea

A **JTextArea** provides an area for *manipulating multiple lines of text*. Like class `JTextField`, `JTextArea` is a subclass of `JTextComponent`, which declares common methods for `JTextFields`, `JTextAreas` and several other text-based GUI components.

The application in Figs. 12.47–12.48 demonstrates `JTextArea`s. One `JTextArea` displays text that the user can select. The other is uneditable by the user and is used to display the text the user selected in the first `JTextArea`. Unlike `JTextFields`, `JTextAreas` do not have action events—when you press *Enter* while typing in a `JTextArea`, the cursor simply moves to the next line. As with multiple-selection `JLists` (Section 12.13), an external event from another GUI component indicates when to process the text in a `JTextArea`. For example, when typing an e-mail message, you normally click a **Send** button to send the text of the message to the recipient. Similarly, when editing a document in a word processor, you normally save the file by selecting a **Save** or **Save As...** menu item. In this program, the button **Copy >>>** generates the external event that copies the selected text in the left `JTextArea` and displays it in the right `JTextArea`.

```
 1   // Fig. 12.47: TextAreaFrame.java
 2   // Copying selected text from one JText area to another.
 3   import java.awt.event.ActionListener;
 4   import java.awt.event.ActionEvent;
 5   import javax.swing.Box;
 6   import javax.swing.JFrame;
 7   import javax.swing.JTextArea;
 8   import javax.swing.JButton;
 9   import javax.swing.JScrollPane;
10
11   public class TextAreaFrame extends JFrame
12   {
13      private final JTextArea textArea1; // displays demo string
14      private final JTextArea textArea2; // highlighted text is copied here
15      private final JButton copyJButton; // initiates copying of text
16
17      // no-argument constructor
18      public TextAreaFrame()
19      {
20         super("TextArea Demo");
21         Box box = Box.createHorizontalBox(); // create box
22         String demo = "This is a demo string to\n" +
23            "illustrate copying text\nfrom one textarea to \n" +
24            "another textarea using an\nexternal event\n";
25
26         textArea1 = new JTextArea(demo, 10, 15);
27         box.add(new JScrollPane(textArea1)); // add scrollpane
28
29         copyJButton = new JButton("Copy >>>"); // create copy button
30         box.add(copyJButton); // add copy button to box
31         copyJButton.addActionListener(
32            new ActionListener() // anonymous inner class
33            {
34               // set text in textArea2 to selected text from textArea1
35               @Override
36               public void actionPerformed(ActionEvent event)
37               {
38                  textArea2.setText(textArea1.getSelectedText());
39               }
40            }
41         );
42
43         textArea2 = new JTextArea(10, 15);
44         textArea2.setEditable(false);
45         box.add(new JScrollPane(textArea2)); // add scrollpane
46
47         add(box); // add box to frame
48      }
49   } // end class TextAreaFrame
```

Fig. 12.47 | Copying selected text from one JTextArea to another.

In the constructor (lines 18–48), line 21 creates a **Box** container (package javax.swing) to organize the GUI components. Box is a subclass of Container that uses

```
 1   // Fig. 12.48: TextAreaDemo.java
 2   // Testing TextAreaFrame.
 3   import javax.swing.JFrame;
 4
 5   public class TextAreaDemo
 6   {
 7      public static void main(String[] args)
 8      {
 9         TextAreaFrame textAreaFrame = new TextAreaFrame();
10         textAreaFrame.setDefaultCloseOperation(JFrame.EXIT_ON_CLOSE);
11         textAreaFrame.setSize(425, 200);
12         textAreaFrame.setVisible(true);
13      }
14   } // end class TextAreaDemo
```

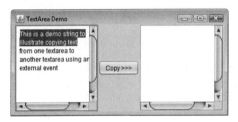
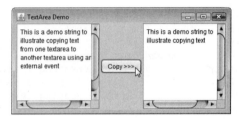

Fig. 12.48 | Testing `TextAreaFrame`.

a **BoxLayout** layout manager (discussed in detail in Section 19.9) to arrange the GUI components either horizontally or vertically. Box's `static` method **createHorizontalBox** creates a Box that arranges components from left to right in the order that they're attached.

Lines 26 and 43 create JTextAreas textArea1 and textArea2. Line 26 uses JTextArea's three-argument constructor, which takes a String representing the initial text and two ints specifying that the JTextArea has 10 rows and 15 columns. Line 43 uses JTextArea's two-argument constructor, specifying that the JTextArea has 10 rows and 15 columns. Line 26 specifies that demo should be displayed as the default JTextArea content. A JTextArea does not provide scrollbars if it cannot display its complete contents. So, line 27 creates a JScrollPane object, initializes it with textArea1 and attaches it to container box. By default, horizontal and vertical scrollbars appear as necessary in a JScrollPane.

Lines 29–41 create JButton object copyJButton with the label "Copy >>>", add copyJButton to container box and register the event handler for copyJButton's ActionEvent. This button provides the external event that determines when the program should copy the selected text in textArea1 to textArea2. When the user clicks copyJButton, line 38 in actionPerformed indicates that method **getSelectedText** (inherited into JTextArea from JTextComponent) should return the selected text from textArea1. The user selects text by dragging the mouse over the desired text to highlight it. Method setText changes the text in textArea2 to the string returned by getSelectedText.

Lines 43–45 create textArea2, set its editable property to false and add it to container box. Line 47 adds box to the JFrame. Recall from Section 12.18.2 that the default layout of a JFrame is a BorderLayout and that the add method by default attaches its argument to the CENTER of the BorderLayout.

When text reaches the right edge of a JTextArea the text can wrap to the next line. This is referred to as **line wrapping**. By default, JTextArea does *not* wrap lines.

> **Look-and-Feel Observation 12.19**
>
> *To provide line wrapping functionality for a JTextArea, invoke JTextArea method **set-LineWrap** with a true argument.*

JScrollPane *Scrollbar Policies*

This example uses a JScrollPane to provide scrolling for a JTextArea. By default, JScrollPane displays scrollbars *only* if they're required. You can set the horizontal and vertical **scrollbar policies** of a JScrollPane when it's constructed. If a program has a reference to a JScrollPane, the program can use JScrollPane methods **setHorizontal-ScrollBarPolicy** and **setVerticalScrollBarPolicy** to change the scrollbar policies at any time. Class JScrollPane declares the constants

```
JScrollPane.VERTICAL_SCROLLBAR_ALWAYS
JScrollPane.HORIZONTAL_SCROLLBAR_ALWAYS
```

to indicate that *a scrollbar should always appear*, constants

```
JScrollPane.VERTICAL_SCROLLBAR_AS_NEEDED
JScrollPane.HORIZONTAL_SCROLLBAR_AS_NEEDED
```

to indicate that *a scrollbar should appear only if necessary* (the defaults) and constants

```
JScrollPane.VERTICAL_SCROLLBAR_NEVER
JScrollPane.HORIZONTAL_SCROLLBAR_NEVER
```

to indicate that *a scrollbar should never appear*. If the horizontal scrollbar policy is set to JScrollPane.HORIZONTAL_SCROLLBAR_NEVER, a JTextArea attached to the JScrollPane will automatically wrap lines.

12.21 Wrap-Up

In this chapter, you learned many GUI components and how to handle their events. You also learned about nested classes, inner classes and anonymous inner classes. You saw the special relationship between an inner-class object and an object of its top-level class. You learned how to use JOptionPane dialogs to obtain text input from the user and how to display messages to the user. You also learned how to create applications that execute in their own windows. We discussed class JFrame and components that enable a user to interact with an application. We also showed you how to display text and images to the user. You learned how to customize JPanels to create custom drawing areas, which you'll use extensively in the next chapter. You saw how to organize components on a window using layout managers and how to creating more complex GUIs by using JPanels to organize components. Finally, you learned about the JTextArea component in which a user can enter text and an application can display text. In Chapter 19, you'll learn about more advanced GUI components, such as sliders, menus and more complex layout managers. In the next chapter, you'll learn how to add graphics to your GUI application. Graphics allow you to draw shapes and text with colors and styles.

13

Graphics and Java 2D

Objectives

In this chapter you'll:

- Understand graphics contexts and graphics objects.
- Manipulate colors and fonts.
- Use methods of class `Graphics` to draw various shapes.
- Use methods of class `Graphics2D` from the `Java` 2D API to draw various shapes.
- Specify `Paint` and `Stroke` characteristics of shapes displayed with `Graphics2D`.

13.1 Introduction

In this chapter, we overview several of Java's capabilities for drawing two-dimensional shapes, controlling colors and controlling fonts. Part of Java's initial appeal was its support for graphics that enabled programmers to visually enhance their applications. Java contains more sophisticated drawing capabilities as part of the Java 2D API (presented in this chapter) and its successor technology JavaFX (which we introduce in Chapter 22). This chapter begins by introducing many of Java's original drawing capabilities. Next we present several of the more powerful Java 2D capabilities, such as controlling the *style* of lines used to draw shapes and the way shapes are *filled* with *colors* and *patterns*. The classes that were part of Java's original graphics capabilities are now considered to be part of the Java 2D API.

Figure 13.1 shows a portion of the class hierarchy that includes various graphics classes and Java 2D API classes and interfaces covered in this chapter. Class **Color** contains methods and constants for manipulating colors. Class **JComponent** contains method **paintComponent**, which is used to draw graphics on a component. Class **Font** contains methods and constants for manipulating fonts. Class **FontMetrics** contains methods for obtaining *font* information. Class **Graphics** contains methods for drawing strings, lines, rectangles and other shapes. Class **Graphics2D**, which extends class **Graphics**, is used for drawing with the Java 2D API. Class **Polygon** contains methods for creating *polygons*. The bottom half of the figure lists several classes and interfaces from the Java 2D API. Class **BasicStroke** helps specify the drawing characteristics of *lines*. Classes **GradientPaint** and **TexturePaint** help specify the characteristics for filling *shapes* with *colors* or *patterns*. Classes **GeneralPath**, **Line2D**, **Arc2D**, **Ellipse2D**, **Rectangle2D** and **RoundRectangle2D** represent several Java 2D shapes.

To begin drawing in Java, we must first understand Java's **coordinate system** (Fig. 13.2), which is a scheme for identifying every *point* on the screen. By default, the *upper-left corner* of a GUI component (e.g., a window) has the coordinates (0, 0). A coordinate pair is composed of an *x*-**coordinate** (the **horizontal coordinate**) and a *y*-**coordinate** (the **vertical coordinate**). The *x*-coordinate is the horizontal distance moving *right* from the left edge of the screen. The *y*-coordinate is the vertical distance moving *down* from the *top* of the screen. The *x*-**axis** describes every horizontal coordinate, and the *y*-**axis** every vertical coordinate. The coordinates are used to indicate where graphics should be displayed on a screen. Coordinate units are measured in **pixels** (which stands for "picture elements"). A pixel is a display monitor's *smallest unit of resolution*.

Fig. 13.1 | Classes and interfaces used in this chapter from Java's original graphics capabilities and from the Java 2D API.

Portability Tip 13.1
Different display monitors have different resolutions (i.e., the density of the pixels varies). This can cause graphics to appear in different sizes on different monitors or on the same monitor with different settings.

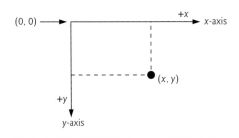

Fig. 13.2 | Java coordinate system. Units are measured in pixels.

13.2 Graphics Contexts and Graphics Objects

A **graphics context** enables drawing on the screen. A Graphics object manages a graphics context and draws pixels on the screen that represent *text* and other graphical objects (e.g., *lines, ellipses, rectangles* and other *polygons*). Graphics objects contain methods for *drawing, font manipulation, color manipulation* and the like.

Class Graphics is an abstract class (i.e., you cannot instantiate Graphics objects). This contributes to Java's portability. Because drawing is performed *differently* on every platform that supports Java, there cannot be only one implementation of the drawing capabilities across all systems. When Java is implemented on a particular platform, a subclass of Graphics is created that implements the drawing capabilities. This implementation is hidden by class Graphics, which supplies the interface that enables us to use graphics in a *platform-independent* manner.

Recall from Chapter 12 that class Component is the *superclass* for many of the classes in package java.awt. Class JComponent (package javax.swing), which inherits indirectly from class Component, contains a paintComponent method that can be used to draw graphics. Method paintComponent takes a Graphics object as an argument. This object is passed to the paintComponent method by the system when a lightweight Swing component needs to be repainted. The header for the paintComponent method is

```
public void paintComponent(Graphics g)
```

Parameter g receives a reference to an instance of the system-specific subclass of Graphics. The preceding method header should look familiar to you—it's the same one we used in some of the applications in Chapter 12. Actually, class JComponent is a *superclass* of JPanel. Many capabilities of class JPanel are inherited from class JComponent.

You seldom call method paintComponent directly, because drawing graphics is an *event-driven* process. As we mentioned in Chapter 11, Java uses a *multithreaded* model of program execution. Each thread is a *parallel* activity. Each program can have many threads. When you create a GUI-based application, one of those threads is known as the **event-dispatch thread (EDT)**—it's used to process all GUI events. All manipulation of the on-screen GUI components must be performed in that thread. When a GUI application executes, the application container calls method paintComponent (in the event-dispatch thread) for each lightweight component as the GUI is displayed. For paintComponent to be called again, an event must occur (such as *covering* and *uncovering* the component with another window).

If you need `paintComponent` to execute (i.e., if you want to update the graphics drawn on a Swing component), you can call method **repaint**, which returns void, takes no arguments and is inherited by all JComponents indirectly from class Component (package java.awt).

13.3 Color Control

Class Color declares methods and constants for manipulating colors in a Java program. The predeclared color constants are summarized in Fig. 13.3, and several color methods and constructors are summarized in Fig. 13.4. Two of the methods in Fig. 13.4 are Graphics methods that are specific to colors.

Color constant	RGB value
`public static final` Color RED	255, 0, 0
`public static final` Color GREEN	0, 255, 0
`public static final` Color BLUE	0, 0, 255
`public static final` Color ORANGE	255, 200, 0
`public static final` Color PINK	255, 175, 175
`public static final` Color CYAN	0, 255, 255
`public static final` Color MAGENTA	255, 0, 255
`public static final` Color YELLOW	255, 255, 0
`public static final` Color BLACK	0, 0, 0
`public static final` Color WHITE	255, 255, 255
`public static final` Color GRAY	128, 128, 128
`public static final` Color LIGHT_GRAY	192, 192, 192
`public static final` Color DARK_GRAY	64, 64, 64

Fig. 13.3 | Color constants and their RGB values.

Method	Description
Color constructors and methods	
`public` Color(`int r, int g, int b`)	Creates a color based on red, green and blue components expressed as integers from 0 to 255.
`public` Color(`float r, float g, float b`)	Creates a color based on red, green and blue components expressed as floating-point values from 0.0 to 1.0.
`public int` getRed()	Returns a value between 0 and 255 representing the red content.

Fig. 13.4 | Color methods and color-related Graphics methods. (Part I of 2.)

Method	Description
`public int getGreen()`	
	Returns a value between 0 and 255 representing the green content.
`public int getBlue()`	
	Returns a value between 0 and 255 representing the blue content.
Graphics methods for manipulating `Color`s	
`public Color getColor()`	
	Returns `Color` object representing current color for the graphics context.
`public void setColor(Color c)`	
	Sets the current color for drawing with the graphics context.

Fig. 13.4 | `Color` methods and color-related `Graphics` methods. (Part 2 of 2.)

Every color is created from a red, a green and a blue value. Together these are called **RGB values**. All three RGB components can be integers in the range from 0 to 255, or all three can be floating-point values in the range 0.0 to 1.0. The first RGB component specifies the amount of red, the second the amount of green and the third the amount of blue. The larger the value, the greater the amount of that particular color. Java enables you to choose from $256 \times 256 \times 256$ (approximately 16.7 million) colors. Not all computers are capable of displaying all these colors. The screen will display the closest color it can.

Two of class `Color`'s constructors are shown in Fig. 13.4—one that takes three `int` arguments and one that takes three `float` arguments, with each argument specifying the amount of red, green and blue. The `int` values must be in the range 0–255 and the `float` values in the range 0.0–1.0. The new `Color` object will have the specified amounts of red, green and blue. `Color` methods **getRed**, **getGreen** and **getBlue** return integer values from 0 to 255 representing the amounts of red, green and blue, respectively. `Graphics` method **getColor** returns a `Color` object representing the `Graphics` object's current drawing color. `Graphics` method **setColor** sets the current drawing color.

Drawing in Different Colors

Figures 13.5–13.6 demonstrate several methods from Fig. 13.4 by drawing *filled rectangles* and `String`s in several different colors. When the application begins execution, class `ColorJPanel`'s `paintComponent` method (lines 10–37 of Fig. 13.5) is called to paint the window. Line 17 uses `Graphics` method `setColor` to set the drawing color. Method `setColor` receives a `Color` object. The expression `new Color(255, 0, 0)` creates a new `Color` object that represents red (red value 255, and 0 for the green and blue values). Line 18 uses `Graphics` method **fillRect** to draw a *filled rectangle* in the current color. Method `fillRect` draws a rectangle based on its four arguments. The first two integer values represent the upper-left *x*-coordinate and upper-left *y*-coordinate, where the `Graphics` object begins drawing the rectangle. The third and fourth arguments are nonnegative integers that represent the width and the height of the rectangle in pixels, respectively. A rectangle drawn using method `fillRect` is filled by the current color of the `Graphics` object.

```
1   // Fig. 13.5: ColorJPanel.java
2   // Changing drawing colors.
3   import java.awt.Graphics;
4   import java.awt.Color;
5   import javax.swing.JPanel;
6
7   public class ColorJPanel extends JPanel
8   {
9      // draw rectangles and Strings in different colors
10     @Override
11     public void paintComponent(Graphics g)
12     {
13        super.paintComponent(g);
14        this.setBackground(Color.WHITE);
15
16        // set new drawing color using integers
17        g.setColor(new Color(255, 0, 0));
18        g.fillRect(15, 25, 100, 20);
19        g.drawString("Current RGB: " + g.getColor(), 130, 40);
20
21        // set new drawing color using floats
22        g.setColor(new Color(0.50f, 0.75f, 0.0f));
23        g.fillRect(15, 50, 100, 20);
24        g.drawString("Current RGB: " + g.getColor(), 130, 65);
25
26        // set new drawing color using static Color objects
27        g.setColor(Color.BLUE);
28        g.fillRect(15, 75, 100, 20);
29        g.drawString("Current RGB: " + g.getColor(), 130, 90);
30
31        // display individual RGB values
32        Color color = Color.MAGENTA;
33        g.setColor(color);
34        g.fillRect(15, 100, 100, 20);
35        g.drawString("RGB values: " + color.getRed() + ", " +
36           color.getGreen() + ", " + color.getBlue(), 130, 115);
37     }
38  } // end class ColorJPanel
```

Fig. 13.5 | Changing drawing colors.

```
1   // Fig. 13.6: ShowColors.java
2   // Demonstrating Colors.
3   import javax.swing.JFrame;
4
5   public class ShowColors
6   {
7      // execute application
8      public static void main(String[] args)
9      {
```

Fig. 13.6 | Demonstrating Colors. (Part 1 of 2.)

```
10          // create frame for ColorJPanel
11          JFrame frame = new JFrame("Using colors");
12          frame.setDefaultCloseOperation(JFrame.EXIT_ON_CLOSE);
13
14          ColorJPanel colorJPanel = new ColorJPanel();
15          frame.add(colorJPanel);
16          frame.setSize(400, 180);
17          frame.setVisible(true);
18      }
19  } // end class ShowColors
```

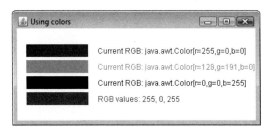

Fig. 13.6 | Demonstrating `Color`s. (Part 2 of 2.)

Line 19 uses `Graphics` method **`drawString`** to draw a `String` in the current color. The expression `g.getColor()` retrieves the current color from the `Graphics` object. We then concatenate the `Color` with string `"Current RGB: "`, resulting in an *implicit* call to class `Color`'s `toString` method. The `String` representation of a `Color` contains the class name and package (`java.awt.Color`) and the red, green and blue values.

> **Look-and-Feel Observation 13.1**
>
> *People perceive colors differently. Choose your colors carefully to ensure that your application is readable, both for people who can perceive color and for those who are color blind. Try to avoid using many different colors in close proximity.*

Lines 22–24 and 27–29 perform the same tasks again. Line 22 uses the `Color` constructor with three `float` arguments to create a dark green color (`0.50f` for red, `0.75f` for green and `0.0f` for blue). Note the syntax of the values. The letter `f` appended to a floating-point literal indicates that the literal should be treated as type `float`. Recall that by default, floating-point literals are treated as type `double`.

Line 27 sets the current drawing color to one of the predeclared `Color` constants (`Color.BLUE`). The `Color` constants are `static`, so they're created when class `Color` is loaded into memory at execution time.

The statement in lines 35–36 makes calls to `Color` methods `getRed`, `getGreen` and `getBlue` on the predeclared `Color.MAGENTA` constant. Method `main` of class `ShowColors` (lines 8–18 of Fig. 13.6) creates the `JFrame` that will contain a `ColorJPanel` object where the colors will be displayed.

> **Software Engineering Observation 13.1**
>
> *To change the color, you must create a new `Color` object (or use one of the predeclared `Color` constants). Like `String` objects, `Color` objects are immutable (not modifiable).*

The **JColorChooser** component (package javax.swing) enables application users to select colors. Figures 13.7–13.8 demonstrate a JColorChooser dialog. When you click the **Change Color** button, a JColorChooser dialog appears. When you select a color and press the dialog's **OK** button, the background color of the application window changes.

```java
1   // Fig. 13.7: ShowColors2JFrame.java
2   // Choosing colors with JColorChooser.
3   import java.awt.BorderLayout;
4   import java.awt.Color;
5   import java.awt.event.ActionEvent;
6   import java.awt.event.ActionListener;
7   import javax.swing.JButton;
8   import javax.swing.JFrame;
9   import javax.swing.JColorChooser;
10  import javax.swing.JPanel;
11
12  public class ShowColors2JFrame extends JFrame
13  {
14     private final JButton changeColorJButton;
15     private Color color = Color.LIGHT_GRAY;
16     private final JPanel colorJPanel;
17
18     // set up GUI
19     public ShowColors2JFrame()
20     {
21        super("Using JColorChooser");
22
23        // create JPanel for display color
24        colorJPanel = new JPanel();
25        colorJPanel.setBackground(color);
26
27        // set up changeColorJButton and register its event handler
28        changeColorJButton = new JButton("Change Color");
29        changeColorJButton.addActionListener(
30           new ActionListener() // anonymous inner class
31           {
32              // display JColorChooser when user clicks button
33              @Override
34              public void actionPerformed(ActionEvent event)
35              {
36                 color = JColorChooser.showDialog(
37                    ShowColors2JFrame.this, "Choose a color", color);
38
39                 // set default color, if no color is returned
40                 if (color == null)
41                    color = Color.LIGHT_GRAY;
42
43                 // change content pane's background color
44                 colorJPanel.setBackground(color);
45              } // end method actionPerformed
46           } // end anonymous inner class
47        ); // end call to addActionListener
```

Fig. 13.7 | Choosing colors with JColorChooser. (Part I of 2.)

```
48
49        add(colorJPanel, BorderLayout.CENTER);
50        add(changeColorJButton, BorderLayout.SOUTH);
51
52        setSize(400, 130);
53        setVisible(true);
54     } // end ShowColor2JFrame constructor
55  } // end class ShowColors2JFrame
```

Fig. 13.7 | Choosing colors with JColorChooser. (Part 2 of 2.)

```
 1   // Fig. 13.8: ShowColors2.java
 2   // Choosing colors with JColorChooser.
 3   import javax.swing.JFrame;
 4
 5   public class ShowColors2
 6   {
 7      // execute application
 8      public static void main(String[] args)
 9      {
10         ShowColors2JFrame application = new ShowColors2JFrame();
11         application.setDefaultCloseOperation(JFrame.EXIT_ON_CLOSE);
12      }
13   } // end class ShowColors2
```

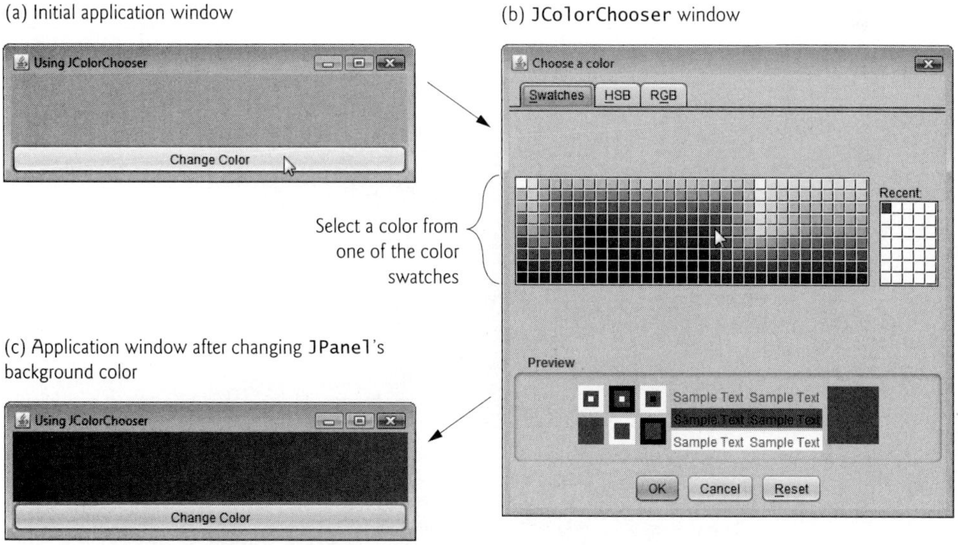

Fig. 13.8 | Choosing colors with JColorChooser.

Class JColorChooser provides static method **showDialog**, which creates a JColor-Chooser object, attaches it to a dialog box and displays the dialog. Lines 36–37 of Fig. 13.7

invoke this method to display the color-chooser dialog. Method `showDialog` returns the selected `Color` object, or `null` if the user presses **Cancel** or closes the dialog without pressing **OK**. The method takes three arguments—a reference to its parent `Component`, a `String` to display in the title bar of the dialog and the initial selected `Color` for the dialog. The parent component is a reference to the window from which the dialog is displayed (in this case the `JFrame`, with the reference name `frame`). The dialog will be centered on the parent. If the parent is `null`, the dialog is centered on the screen. While the color-chooser dialog is on the screen, the user cannot interact with the parent component until the dialog is dismissed. This type of dialog is called a modal dialog.

After the user selects a color, lines 40–41 determine whether `color` is `null`, and, if so, set `color` to `Color.LIGHT_GRAY`. Line 44 invokes method `setBackground` to change the background color of the `JPanel`. Method `setBackground` is one of the many `Component` methods that can be used on most GUI components. The user can continue to use the **Change Color** button to change the background color of the application. Figure 13.8 contains method `main`, which executes the program.

Figure 13.8(b) shows the default `JColorChooser` dialog that allows the user to select a color from a variety of **color swatches**. There are three tabs across the top of the dialog— **Swatches**, **HSB** and **RGB**. These represent three different ways to select a color. The **HSB** tab allows you to select a color based on **hue**, **saturation** and **brightness**—values that are used to define the amount of light in a color. Visit `http://en.wikipedia.org/wiki/HSL_and_HSV` for more information on HSB. The **RGB** tab allows you to select a color by using sliders to select the red, green and blue components. The **HSB** and **RGB** tabs are shown in Fig. 13.9.

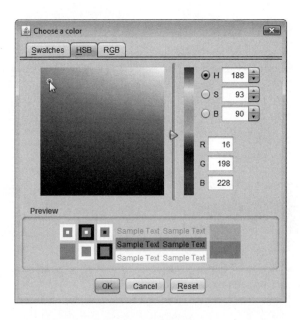

Fig. 13.9 | **HSB** and **RGB** tabs of the `JColorChooser` dialog. (Part 1 of 2.)

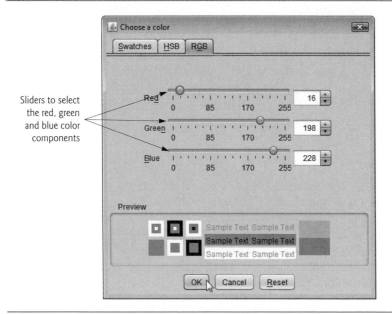

Sliders to select the red, green and blue color components

Fig. 13.9 | HSB and RGB tabs of the JColorChooser dialog. (Part 2 of 2.)

13.4 Manipulating Fonts

This section introduces methods and constants for manipulating fonts. Most font methods and font constants are part of class Font. Some constructors, methods and constants of class Font and class Graphics are summarized in Fig. 13.10.

Method or constant	Description
Font constants, constructors and methods	
public static final int PLAIN	A constant representing a plain font style.
public static final int BOLD	A constant representing a bold font style.
public static final int ITALIC	A constant representing an italic font style.
public Font(String name, **int** style, **int** size)	Creates a Font object with the specified font name, style and size.
public int getStyle()	Returns an int indicating the current font style.
public int getSize()	Returns an int indicating the current font size.
public String getName()	Returns the current font name as a string.
public String getFamily()	Returns the font's family name as a string.
public boolean isPlain()	Returns true if the font is plain, else false.
public boolean isBold()	Returns true if the font is bold, else false.
public boolean isItalic()	Returns true if the font is italic, else false.

Fig. 13.10 | Font-related methods and constants. (Part 1 of 2.)

Method or constant	Description
Graphics methods for manipulating Fonts	
public Font getFont()	Returns a Font object reference representing the current font.
public void setFont(Font f)	Sets the current font to the font, style and size specified by the Font object reference f.

Fig. 13.10 | Font-related methods and constants. (Part 2 of 2.)

Class Font's constructor takes three arguments—the **font name**, **font style** and **font size**. The font name is any font currently supported by the system on which the program is running, such as standard Java fonts Monospaced, SansSerif and Serif. The font style is **Font.PLAIN**, **Font.ITALIC** or **Font.BOLD** (each is a static field of class Font). Font styles can be used in combination (e.g., Font.ITALIC + Font.BOLD). The font size is measured in points. A **point** is 1/72 of an inch. Graphics method **setFont** sets the current drawing font—the font in which text will be displayed—to its Font argument.

Portability Tip 13.2

The number of fonts varies across systems. Java provides five font names—Serif, Mono-spaced, SansSerif, Dialog and DialogInput—that can be used on all Java platforms. The Java runtime environment (JRE) on each platform maps these logical font names to actual fonts installed on the platform. The actual fonts used may vary by platform.

The application of Figs. 13.11–13.12 displays text in four different fonts, with each font in a different size. Figure 13.11 uses the Font constructor to initialize Font objects (in lines 17, 21, 25 and 30) that are each passed to Graphics method setFont to change the drawing font. Each call to the Font constructor passes a font name (Serif, Monospaced or SansSerif) as a string, a font style (Font.PLAIN, Font.ITALIC or Font.BOLD) and a font size. Once Graphics method setFont is invoked, all text displayed following the call will appear in the new font until the font is changed. Each font's information is displayed in lines 18, 22, 26 and 31–32 using method drawString. The coordinates passed to drawString correspond to the lower-left corner of the baseline of the font. Line 29 changes the drawing color to red, so the next string displayed appears in red. Lines 31–32 display information about the final Font object. Method **getFont** of class Graphics returns a Font object representing the current font. Method **getName** returns the current font name as a string. Method **getSize** returns the font size in points.

Software Engineering Observation 13.2

To change the font, you must create a new Font object. Font objects are immutable—class Font has no set methods to change the characteristics of the current font.

Figure 13.12 contains the main method, which creates a JFrame to display a Font-JPanel. We add a FontJPanel object to this JFrame (line 15), which displays the graphics created in Fig. 13.11.

```
1   // Fig. 13.11: FontJPanel.java
2   // Display strings in different fonts and colors.
3   import java.awt.Font;
4   import java.awt.Color;
5   import java.awt.Graphics;
6   import javax.swing.JPanel;
7
8   public class FontJPanel extends JPanel
9   {
10     // display Strings in different fonts and colors
11     @Override
12     public void paintComponent(Graphics g)
13     {
14        super.paintComponent(g);
15
16        // set font to Serif (Times), bold, 12pt and draw a string
17        g.setFont(new Font("Serif", Font.BOLD, 12));
18        g.drawString("Serif 12 point bold.", 20, 30);
19
20        // set font to Monospaced (Courier), italic, 24pt and draw a string
21        g.setFont(new Font("Monospaced", Font.ITALIC, 24));
22        g.drawString("Monospaced 24 point italic.", 20, 50);
23
24        // set font to SansSerif (Helvetica), plain, 14pt and draw a string
25        g.setFont(new Font("SansSerif", Font.PLAIN, 14));
26        g.drawString("SansSerif 14 point plain.", 20, 70);
27
28        // set font to Serif (Times), bold/italic, 18pt and draw a string
29        g.setColor(Color.RED);
30        g.setFont(new Font("Serif", Font.BOLD + Font.ITALIC, 18));
31        g.drawString(g.getFont().getName() + " " + g.getFont().getSize() +
32           " point bold italic.", 20, 90);
33     }
34  } // end class FontJPanel
```

Fig. 13.11 | Display strings in different fonts and colors.

```
1   // Fig. 13.12: Fonts.java
2   // Using fonts.
3   import javax.swing.JFrame;
4
5   public class Fonts
6   {
7      // execute application
8      public static void main(String[] args)
9      {
10        // create frame for FontJPanel
11        JFrame frame = new JFrame("Using fonts");
12        frame.setDefaultCloseOperation(JFrame.EXIT_ON_CLOSE);
13
14        FontJPanel fontJPanel = new FontJPanel();
15        frame.add(fontJPanel);
```

Fig. 13.12 | Using fonts. (Part 1 of 2.)

```
16          frame.setSize(420, 150);
17          frame.setVisible(true);
18      }
19   } // end class Fonts
```

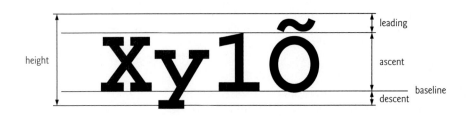

Fig. 13.12 | Using fonts. (Part 2 of 2.)

Font Metrics

Sometimes it's necessary to get information about the current drawing font, such as its name, style and size. Several Font methods used to get font information are summarized in Fig. 13.10. Method **getStyle** returns an integer value representing the current style. The integer value returned is either Font.PLAIN, Font.ITALIC, Font.BOLD or the combination of Font.ITALIC and Font.BOLD. Method **getFamily** returns the name of the font family to which the current font belongs. The name of the font family is platform specific. Font methods are also available to test the style of the current font, and these too are summarized in Fig. 13.10. Methods **isPlain**, **isBold** and **isItalic** return true if the current font style is plain, bold or italic, respectively.

Figure 13.13 illustrates some of the common **font metrics**, which provide precise information about a font, such as **height**, **descent** (the amount a character dips below the baseline), **ascent** (the amount a character rises above the baseline) and **leading** (the difference between the descent of one line of text and the ascent of the line of text below it—that is, the interline spacing).

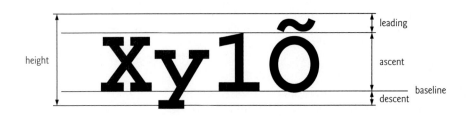

Fig. 13.13 | Font metrics.

Class **FontMetrics** declares several methods for obtaining font metrics. These methods and Graphics method **getFontMetrics** are summarized in Fig. 13.14. The application of Figs. 13.15–13.16 uses the methods of Fig. 13.14 to obtain font metric information for two fonts.

Method	Description
FontMetrics methods	
public int getAscent()	Returns the ascent of a font in points.
public int getDescent()	Returns the descent of a font in points.
public int getLeading()	Returns the leading of a font in points.
public int getHeight()	Returns the height of a font in points.
Graphics methods for getting a Font's FontMetrics	
public FontMetrics getFontMetrics()	
	Returns the FontMetrics object for the current drawing Font.
public FontMetrics getFontMetrics(Font f)	
	Returns the FontMetrics object for the specified Font argument.

Fig. 13.14 | FontMetrics and Graphics methods for obtaining font metrics.

```
1   // Fig. 13.15: MetricsJPanel.java
2   // FontMetrics and Graphics methods useful for obtaining font metrics.
3   import java.awt.Font;
4   import java.awt.FontMetrics;
5   import java.awt.Graphics;
6   import javax.swing.JPanel;
7
8   public class MetricsJPanel extends JPanel
9   {
10     // display font metrics
11     @Override
12     public void paintComponent(Graphics g)
13     {
14        super.paintComponent(g);
15
16        g.setFont(new Font("SansSerif", Font.BOLD, 12));
17        FontMetrics metrics = g.getFontMetrics();
18        g.drawString("Current font: " + g.getFont(), 10, 30);
19        g.drawString("Ascent: " + metrics.getAscent(), 10, 45);
20        g.drawString("Descent: " + metrics.getDescent(), 10, 60);
21        g.drawString("Height: " + metrics.getHeight(), 10, 75);
22        g.drawString("Leading: " + metrics.getLeading(), 10, 90);
23
24        Font font = new Font("Serif", Font.ITALIC, 14);
25        metrics = g.getFontMetrics(font);
26        g.setFont(font);
27        g.drawString("Current font: " + font, 10, 120);
28        g.drawString("Ascent: " + metrics.getAscent(), 10, 135);
29        g.drawString("Descent: " + metrics.getDescent(), 10, 150);
30        g.drawString("Height: " + metrics.getHeight(), 10, 165);
31        g.drawString("Leading: " + metrics.getLeading(), 10, 180);
32     }
33   } // end class MetricsJPanel
```

Fig. 13.15 | FontMetrics and Graphics methods useful for obtaining font metrics.

```
1   // Fig. 13.16: Metrics.java
2   // Displaying font metrics.
3   import javax.swing.JFrame;
4
5   public class Metrics
6   {
7      // execute application
8      public static void main(String[] args)
9      {
10        // create frame for MetricsJPanel
11        JFrame frame = new JFrame("Demonstrating FontMetrics");
12        frame.setDefaultCloseOperation(JFrame.EXIT_ON_CLOSE);
13
14        MetricsJPanel metricsJPanel = new MetricsJPanel();
15        frame.add(metricsJPanel);
16        frame.setSize(510, 240);
17        frame.setVisible(true);
18     }
19  } // end class Metrics
```

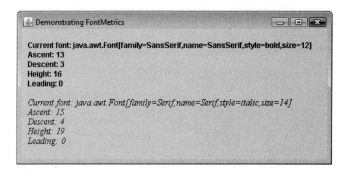

Fig. 13.16 | Displaying font metrics.

Line 16 of Fig. 13.15 creates and sets the current drawing font to a SansSerif, bold, 12-point font. Line 17 uses Graphics method getFontMetrics to obtain the FontMetrics object for the current font. Line 18 outputs the String representation of the Font returned by g.getFont(). Lines 19–22 use FontMetric methods to obtain the ascent, descent, height and leading for the font.

Line 24 creates a new Serif, italic, 14-point font. Line 25 uses a second version of Graphics method getFontMetrics, which accepts a Font argument and returns a corresponding FontMetrics object. Lines 28–31 obtain the ascent, descent, height and leading for the font. The font metrics are slightly different for the two fonts.

13.5 Drawing Lines, Rectangles and Ovals

This section presents Graphics methods for drawing lines, rectangles and ovals. The methods and their parameters are summarized in Fig. 13.17. For each drawing method that requires a width and height parameter, the width and height must be nonnegative values. Otherwise, the shape will not display.

Method	Description
public void drawLine(**int** x1, **int** y1, **int** x2, **int** y2)	
	Draws a line between the point (x1, y1) and the point (x2, y2).
public void drawRect(**int** x, **int** y, **int** width, **int** height)	
	Draws a rectangle of the specified width and height. The rectangle's top-left corner is located at (x, y). Only the outline of the rectangle is drawn using the Graphics object's color—the body of the rectangle is not filled with this color.
public void fillRect(**int** x, **int** y, **int** width, **int** height)	
	Draws a filled rectangle in the current color with the specified width and height. The rectangle's top-left corner is located at (x, y).
public void clearRect(**int** x, **int** y, **int** width, **int** height)	
	Draws a filled rectangle with the specified width and height in the current background color. The rectangle's *top-left* corner is located at (x, y). This method is useful if you want to remove a portion of an image.
public void drawRoundRect(**int** x, **int** y, **int** width, **int** height, **int** arcWidth, **int** arcHeight)	
	Draws a rectangle with rounded corners in the current color with the specified width and height. The arcWidth and arcHeight determine the rounding of the corners (see Fig. 13.20). Only the outline of the shape is drawn.
public void fillRoundRect(**int** x, **int** y, **int** width, **int** height, **int** arcWidth, **int** arcHeight)	
	Draws a filled rectangle in the current color with rounded corners with the specified width and height. The arcWidth and arcHeight determine the rounding of the corners (see Fig. 13.20).
public void draw3DRect(**int** x, **int** y, **int** width, **int** height, **boolean** b)	
	Draws a three-dimensional rectangle in the current color with the specified width and height. The rectangle's *top-left* corner is located at (x, y). The rectangle appears raised when b is true and lowered when b is false. Only the outline of the shape is drawn.
public void fill3DRect(**int** x, **int** y, **int** width, **int** height, **boolean** b)	
	Draws a filled three-dimensional rectangle in the current color with the specified width and height. The rectangle's *top-left* corner is located at (x, y). The rectangle appears raised when b is true and lowered when b is false.
public void drawOval(**int** x, **int** y, **int** width, **int** height)	
	Draws an oval in the current color with the specified width and height. The bounding rectangle's *top-left* corner is located at (x, y). The oval touches all four sides of the bounding rectangle at the center of each side (see Fig. 13.21). Only the outline of the shape is drawn.
public void fillOval(**int** x, **int** y, **int** width, **int** height)	
	Draws a filled oval in the current color with the specified width and height. The bounding rectangle's *top-left* corner is located at (x, y). The oval touches the center of all four sides of the bounding rectangle (see Fig. 13.21).

Fig. 13.17 | Graphics methods that draw lines, rectangles and ovals.

The application of Figs. 13.18–13.19 demonstrates drawing a variety of lines, rectangles, three-dimensional rectangles, rounded rectangles and ovals. In Fig. 13.18, line 17 draws a red line, line 20 draws an empty blue rectangle and line 21 draws a filled blue rectangle. Methods **fillRoundRect** (line 24) and **drawRoundRect** (line 25) draw rectangles with rounded corners. Their first two arguments specify the coordinates of the upper-left corner of the **bounding rectangle**—the area in which the rounded rectangle will be drawn. The upper-left corner coordinates are *not* the edge of the rounded rectangle, but the coordinates where the edge would be if the rectangle had square corners. The third and fourth arguments specify the width and height of the rectangle. The last two arguments determine the horizontal and vertical diameters of the arc (i.e., the arc width and arc height) used to represent the corners.

Figure 13.20 labels the arc width, arc height, width and height of a rounded rectangle. Using the same value for the arc width and arc height produces a quarter-circle at each

```
1   // Fig. 13.18: LinesRectsOvalsJPanel.java
2   // Drawing lines, rectangles and ovals.
3   import java.awt.Color;
4   import java.awt.Graphics;
5   import javax.swing.JPanel;
6
7   public class LinesRectsOvalsJPanel extends JPanel
8   {
9      // display various lines, rectangles and ovals
10     @Override
11     public void paintComponent(Graphics g)
12     {
13        super.paintComponent(g);
14        this.setBackground(Color.WHITE);
15
16        g.setColor(Color.RED);
17        g.drawLine(5, 30, 380, 30);
18
19        g.setColor(Color.BLUE);
20        g.drawRect(5, 40, 90, 55);
21        g.fillRect(100, 40, 90, 55);
22
23        g.setColor(Color.CYAN);
24        g.fillRoundRect(195, 40, 90, 55, 50, 50);
25        g.drawRoundRect(290, 40, 90, 55, 20, 20);
26
27        g.setColor(Color.GREEN);
28        g.draw3DRect(5, 100, 90, 55, true);
29        g.fill3DRect(100, 100, 90, 55, false);
30
31        g.setColor(Color.MAGENTA);
32        g.drawOval(195, 100, 90, 55);
33        g.fillOval(290, 100, 90, 55);
34     }
35  } // end class LinesRectsOvalsJPanel
```

Fig. 13.18 | Drawing lines, rectangles and ovals.

```
 I   // Fig. 13.19: LinesRectsOvals.java
 2   // Testing LinesRectsOvalsJPanel.
 3   import java.awt.Color;
 4   import javax.swing.JFrame;
 5
 6   public class LinesRectsOvals
 7   {
 8      // execute application
 9      public static void main(String[] args)
10      {
11         // create frame for LinesRectsOvalsJPanel
12         JFrame frame =
13            new JFrame("Drawing lines, rectangles and ovals");
14         frame.setDefaultCloseOperation(JFrame.EXIT_ON_CLOSE);
15
16         LinesRectsOvalsJPanel linesRectsOvalsJPanel =
17            new LinesRectsOvalsJPanel();
18         linesRectsOvalsJPanel.setBackground(Color.WHITE);
19         frame.add(linesRectsOvalsJPanel);
20         frame.setSize(400, 210);
21         frame.setVisible(true);
22      }
23   } // end class LinesRectsOvals
```

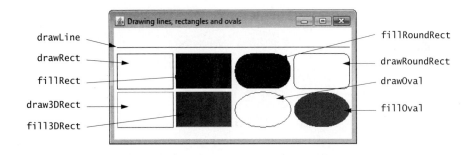

Fig. 13.19 | Testing LinesRectsOvalsJPanel.

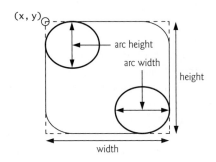

Fig. 13.20 | Arc width and arc height for rounded rectangles.

corner. When the arc width, arc height, width and height have the same values, the result is a circle. If the values for `width` and `height` are the same and the values of `arcWidth` and `arcHeight` are 0, the result is a square.

Methods **draw3DRect** (Fig. 13.18, line 28) and **fill3DRect** (line 29) take the same arguments. The first two specify the *top-left* corner of the rectangle. The next two arguments specify the width and height of the rectangle, respectively. The last argument determines whether the rectangle is **raised** (`true`) or **lowered** (`false`). The three-dimensional effect of `draw3DRect` appears as two edges of the rectangle in the original color and two edges in a slightly darker color. The three-dimensional effect of `fill3DRect` appears as two edges of the rectangle in the original drawing color and the fill and other two edges in a slightly darker color. Raised rectangles have the original drawing color edges at the top and left of the rectangle. Lowered rectangles have the original drawing color edges at the bottom and right of the rectangle. The three-dimensional effect is difficult to see in some colors.

Methods **drawOval** and **fillOval** (lines 32–33) take the same four arguments. The first two specify the top-left coordinate of the bounding rectangle that contains the oval. The last two specify the width and height of the bounding rectangle, respectively. Figure 13.21 shows an oval bounded by a rectangle. The oval touches the *center* of all four sides of the bounding rectangle. (The bounding rectangle is *not* displayed on the screen.)

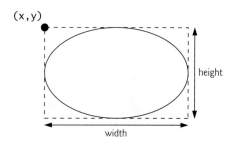

Fig. 13.21 | Oval bounded by a rectangle.

13.6 Drawing Arcs

An **arc** is drawn as a portion of an oval. Arc angles are measured in degrees. Arcs **sweep** (i.e., move along a curve) from a **starting angle** through the number of degrees specified by their **arc angle**. The starting angle indicates in degrees where the arc begins. The arc angle specifies the total number of degrees through which the arc sweeps. Figure 13.22 illustrates two arcs. The left set of axes shows an arc sweeping from zero degrees to approximately 110 degrees. Arcs that sweep in a *counterclockwise* direction are measured in **positive degrees**. The set of axes on the right shows an arc sweeping from zero degrees to approximately –110 degrees. Arcs that sweep in a *clockwise* direction are measured in **negative degrees**. Note the dashed boxes around the arcs in Fig. 13.22. When drawing an arc, we specify a bounding rectangle for an oval. The arc will sweep along part of the oval. Graphics methods **drawArc** and **fillArc** for drawing arcs are summarized in Fig. 13.23.

Fig. 13.22 | Positive and negative arc angles.

Method	Description
public void drawArc(**int** x, **int** y, **int** width, **int** height, **int** startAngle, **int** arcAngle)	
	Draws an arc relative to the bounding rectangle's top-left x- and y-coordinates with the specified width and height. The arc segment is drawn starting at startAngle and sweeps arcAngle degrees.
public void fillArc(**int** x, **int** y, **int** width, **int** height, **int** startAngle, **int** arcAngle)	
	Draws a filled arc (i.e., a sector) relative to the bounding rectangle's top-left x- and y-coordinates with the specified width and height. The arc segment is drawn starting at startAngle and sweeps arcAngle degrees.

Fig. 13.23 | Graphics methods for drawing arcs.

Figures 13.24–13.25 demonstrate the arc methods of Fig. 13.23. The application draws six arcs (three unfilled and three filled). To illustrate the bounding rectangle that helps determine where the arc appears, the first three arcs are displayed inside a red rectangle that has the same x, y, width and height arguments as the arcs.

```
 1   // Fig. 13.24: ArcsJPanel.java
 2   // Arcs displayed with drawArc and fillArc.
 3   import java.awt.Color;
 4   import java.awt.Graphics;
 5   import javax.swing.JPanel;
 6
 7   public class ArcsJPanel extends JPanel
 8   {
 9      // draw rectangles and arcs
10      @Override
11      public void paintComponent(Graphics g)
12      {
13         super.paintComponent(g);
14
```

Fig. 13.24 | Arcs displayed with drawArc and fillArc. (Part 1 of 2.)

```
15          // start at 0 and sweep 360 degrees
16          g.setColor(Color.RED);
17          g.drawRect(15, 35, 80, 80);
18          g.setColor(Color.BLACK);
19          g.drawArc(15, 35, 80, 80, 0, 360);
20
21          // start at 0 and sweep 110 degrees
22          g.setColor(Color.RED);
23          g.drawRect(100, 35, 80, 80);
24          g.setColor(Color.BLACK);
25          g.drawArc(100, 35, 80, 80, 0, 110);
26
27          // start at 0 and sweep -270 degrees
28          g.setColor(Color.RED);
29          g.drawRect(185, 35, 80, 80);
30          g.setColor(Color.BLACK);
31          g.drawArc(185, 35, 80, 80, 0, -270);
32
33          // start at 0 and sweep 360 degrees
34          g.fillArc(15, 120, 80, 40, 0, 360);
35
36          // start at 270 and sweep -90 degrees
37          g.fillArc(100, 120, 80, 40, 270, -90);
38
39          // start at 0 and sweep -270 degrees
40          g.fillArc(185, 120, 80, 40, 0, -270);
41      }
42  } // end class ArcsJPanel
```

Fig. 13.24 | Arcs displayed with drawArc and fillArc. (Part 2 of 2.)

```
 1   // Fig. 13.25: DrawArcs.java
 2   // Drawing arcs.
 3   import javax.swing.JFrame;
 4
 5   public class DrawArcs
 6   {
 7      // execute application
 8      public static void main(String[] args)
 9      {
10         // create frame for ArcsJPanel
11         JFrame frame = new JFrame("Drawing Arcs");
12         frame.setDefaultCloseOperation(JFrame.EXIT_ON_CLOSE);
13
14         ArcsJPanel arcsJPanel = new ArcsJPanel();
15         frame.add(arcsJPanel);
16         frame.setSize(300, 210);
17         frame.setVisible(true);
18      }
19   } // end class DrawArcs
```

Fig. 13.25 | Drawing arcs. (Part 1 of 2.)

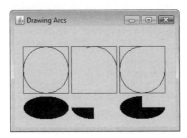

Fig. 13.25 | Drawing arcs. (Part 2 of 2.)

13.7 Drawing Polygons and Polylines

Polygons are *closed multisided shapes* composed of straight-line segments. **Polylines** are *sequences of connected points*. Figure 13.26 discusses methods for drawing polygons and polylines. Some methods require a **Polygon** object (package java.awt). Class Polygon's constructors are also described in Fig. 13.26. The application of Figs. 13.27–13.28 draws polygons and polylines.

Method	Description
Graphics methods for drawing polygons	
public void drawPolygon(**int**[] xPoints, **int**[] yPoints, **int** points)	
	Draws a polygon. The *x*-coordinate of each point is specified in the xPoints array and the *y*-coordinate of each point in the yPoints array. The last argument specifies the number of points. This method draws a *closed polygon*. If the last point is different from the first, the polygon is *closed* by a line that connects the last point to the first.
public void drawPolyline(**int**[] xPoints, **int**[] yPoints, **int** points)	
	Draws a sequence of connected lines. The *x*-coordinate of each point is specified in the xPoints array and the *y*-coordinate of each point in the yPoints array. The last argument specifies the number of points. If the last point is different from the first, the polyline is *not* closed.
public void drawPolygon(Polygon p)	
	Draws the specified polygon.
public void fillPolygon(**int**[] xPoints, **int**[] yPoints, **int** points)	
	Draws a *filled* polygon. The *x*-coordinate of each point is specified in the xPoints array and the *y*-coordinate of each point in the yPoints array. The last argument specifies the number of points. This method draws a *closed polygon*. If the last point is different from the first, the polygon is *closed* by a line that connects the last point to the first.
public void fillPolygon(Polygon p)	
	Draws the specified *filled* polygon. The polygon is *closed*.

Fig. 13.26 | Graphics methods for polygons and class Polygon methods. (Part 1 of 2.)

Method	Description
Polygon constructors and methods	
public Polygon()	
	Constructs a new polygon object. The polygon does not contain any points.
public Polygon(**int**[] xValues, **int**[] yValues, **int** numberOfPoints)	
	Constructs a new polygon object. The polygon has numberOfPoints sides, with each point consisting of an *x*-coordinate from xValues and a *y*-coordinate from yValues.
public void addPoint(**int** x, **int** y)	
	Adds pairs of *x*- and *y*-coordinates to the Polygon.

Fig. 13.26 | Graphics methods for polygons and class Polygon methods. (Part 2 of 2.)

```java
 1  // Fig. 13.27: PolygonsJPanel.java
 2  // Drawing polygons.
 3  import java.awt.Graphics;
 4  import java.awt.Polygon;
 5  import javax.swing.JPanel;
 6
 7  public class PolygonsJPanel extends JPanel
 8  {
 9     // draw polygons and polylines
10     @Override
11     public void paintComponent(Graphics g)
12     {
13        super.paintComponent(g);
14
15        // draw polygon with Polygon object
16        int[] xValues = {20, 40, 50, 30, 20, 15};
17        int[] yValues = {50, 50, 60, 80, 80, 60};
18        Polygon polygon1 = new Polygon(xValues, yValues, 6);
19        g.drawPolygon(polygon1);
20
21        // draw polylines with two arrays
22        int[] xValues2 = {70, 90, 100, 80, 70, 65, 60};
23        int[] yValues2 = {100, 100, 110, 110, 130, 110, 90};
24        g.drawPolyline(xValues2, yValues2, 7);
25
26        // fill polygon with two arrays
27        int[] xValues3 = {120, 140, 150, 190};
28        int[] yValues3 = {40, 70, 80, 60};
29        g.fillPolygon(xValues3, yValues3, 4);
30
31        // draw filled polygon with Polygon object
32        Polygon polygon2 = new Polygon();
33        polygon2.addPoint(165, 135);
34        polygon2.addPoint(175, 150);
35        polygon2.addPoint(270, 200);
```

Fig. 13.27 | Polygons displayed with drawPolygon and fillPolygon. (Part 1 of 2.)

```
36        polygon2.addPoint(200, 220);
37        polygon2.addPoint(130, 180);
38        g.fillPolygon(polygon2);
39     }
40  } // end class PolygonsJPanel
```

Fig. 13.27 | Polygons displayed with drawPolygon and fillPolygon. (Part 2 of 2.)

```
1   // Fig. 13.28: DrawPolygons.java
2   // Drawing polygons.
3   import javax.swing.JFrame;
4
5   public class DrawPolygons
6   {
7      // execute application
8      public static void main(String[] args)
9      {
10        // create frame for PolygonsJPanel
11        JFrame frame = new JFrame("Drawing Polygons");
12        frame.setDefaultCloseOperation(JFrame.EXIT_ON_CLOSE);
13
14        PolygonsJPanel polygonsJPanel = new PolygonsJPanel();
15        frame.add(polygonsJPanel);
16        frame.setSize(280, 270);
17        frame.setVisible(true);
18     }
19  } // end class DrawPolygons
```

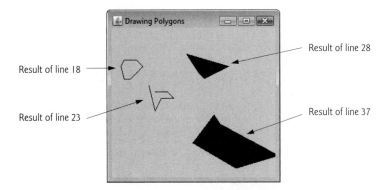

Fig. 13.28 | Drawing polygons.

Lines 16–17 of Fig. 13.27 create two int arrays and use them to specify the points for Polygon polygon1. The Polygon constructor call in line 18 receives array xValues, which contains the *x*-coordinate of each point; array yValues, which contains the *y*-coordinate of each point; and 6 (the number of points in the polygon). Line 19 displays polygon1 by passing it as an argument to Graphics method **drawPolygon**.

Lines 22–23 create two int arrays and use them to specify the points for a series of connected lines. Array xValues2 contains the *x*-coordinate of each point and array yValues2 the *y*-coordinate of each point. Line 24 uses Graphics method **drawPolyline** to display the series of connected lines specified with the arguments xValues2, yValues2 and 7 (the number of points).

Lines 27–28 create two int arrays and use them to specify the points of a polygon. Array xValues3 contains the *x*-coordinate of each point and array yValues3 the *y*-coordinate of each point. Line 29 displays a polygon by passing to Graphics method **fill-Polygon** the two arrays (xValues3 and yValues3) and the number of points to draw (4).

Common Programming Error 13.1
An ArrayIndexOutOfBoundsException is thrown if the number of points specified in the third argument to method drawPolygon or method fillPolygon is greater than the number of elements in the arrays of coordinates that specify the polygon to display.

Line 32 creates Polygon polygon2 with no points. Lines 33–37 use Polygon method **addPoint** to add pairs of *x*- and *y*-coordinates to the Polygon. Line 38 displays Polygon polygon2 by passing it to Graphics method fillPolygon.

13.8 Java 2D API

The **Java 2D API** provides advanced two-dimensional graphics capabilities for programmers who require detailed and complex graphical manipulations. The API includes features for processing line art, text and images in packages java.awt, java.awt.image, java.awt.color, java.awt.font, java.awt.geom, java.awt.print and java.awt.image.renderable. The capabilities of the API are far too broad to cover in this textbook. For an overview, visit http://docs.oracle.com/javase/7/docs/technotes/guides/2d/. In this section, we overview several Java 2D capabilities.

Drawing with the Java 2D API is accomplished with a **Graphics2D** reference (package java.awt). Graphics2D is an *abstract subclass* of class Graphics, so it has all the graphics capabilities demonstrated earlier in this chapter. In fact, the actual object used to draw in every paintComponent method is an instance of a *subclass* of Graphics2D that is passed to method paintComponent and accessed via the *superclass* Graphics. To access Graphics2D capabilities, we must cast the Graphics reference (g) passed to paintComponent into a Graphics2D reference with a statement such as

```
Graphics2D g2d = (Graphics2D) g;
```

The next two examples use this technique.

Lines, Rectangles, Round Rectangles, Arcs and Ellipses
This example demonstrates several Java 2D shapes from package java.awt.geom, including **Line2D.Double**, **Rectangle2D.Double**, **RoundRectangle2D.Double**, **Arc2D.Double** and **Ellipse2D.Double**. Note the syntax of each class name. Each class represents a shape with dimensions specified as double values. There's a *separate* version of each represented with float values (e.g., **Ellipse2D.Float**). In each case, Double is a public static nested class of the class specified to the left of the dot (e.g., Ellipse2D). To use the static nested class, we simply qualify its name with the outer-class name.

In Figs. 13.29–13.30, we draw Java 2D shapes and modify their drawing characteristics, such as changing line thickness, filling shapes with patterns and drawing dashed lines. These are just a few of the many capabilities provided by Java 2D.

Line 25 of Fig. 13.29 casts the `Graphics` reference received by `paintComponent` to a `Graphics2D` reference and assigns it to g2d to allow access to the Java 2D features.

```
1   // Fig. 13.29: ShapesJPanel.java
2   // Demonstrating some Java 2D shapes.
3   import java.awt.Color;
4   import java.awt.Graphics;
5   import java.awt.BasicStroke;
6   import java.awt.GradientPaint;
7   import java.awt.TexturePaint;
8   import java.awt.Rectangle;
9   import java.awt.Graphics2D;
10  import java.awt.geom.Ellipse2D;
11  import java.awt.geom.Rectangle2D;
12  import java.awt.geom.RoundRectangle2D;
13  import java.awt.geom.Arc2D;
14  import java.awt.geom.Line2D;
15  import java.awt.image.BufferedImage;
16  import javax.swing.JPanel;
17
18  public class ShapesJPanel extends JPanel
19  {
20     // draw shapes with Java 2D API
21     @Override
22     public void paintComponent(Graphics g)
23     {
24        super.paintComponent(g);
25        Graphics2D g2d = (Graphics2D) g; // cast g to Graphics2D
26
27        // draw 2D ellipse filled with a blue-yellow gradient
28        g2d.setPaint(new GradientPaint(5, 30, Color.BLUE, 35, 100,
29           Color.YELLOW, true));
30        g2d.fill(new Ellipse2D.Double(5, 30, 65, 100));
31
32        // draw 2D rectangle in red
33        g2d.setPaint(Color.RED);
34        g2d.setStroke(new BasicStroke(10.0f));
35        g2d.draw(new Rectangle2D.Double(80, 30, 65, 100));
36
37        // draw 2D rounded rectangle with a buffered background
38        BufferedImage buffImage = new BufferedImage(10, 10,
39           BufferedImage.TYPE_INT_RGB);
40
41        // obtain Graphics2D from buffImage and draw on it
42        Graphics2D gg = buffImage.createGraphics();
43        gg.setColor(Color.YELLOW);
44        gg.fillRect(0, 0, 10, 10);
45        gg.setColor(Color.BLACK);
46        gg.drawRect(1, 1, 6, 6);
47        gg.setColor(Color.BLUE);
48        gg.fillRect(1, 1, 3, 3);
49        gg.setColor(Color.RED);
```

Fig. 13.29 | Demonstrating some Java 2D shapes. (Part 1 of 2.)

```
50          gg.fillRect(4, 4, 3, 3); // draw a filled rectangle
51
52          // paint buffImage onto the JFrame
53          g2d.setPaint(new TexturePaint(buffImage,
54             new Rectangle(10, 10)));
55          g2d.fill(
56             new RoundRectangle2D.Double(155, 30, 75, 100, 50, 50));
57
58          // draw 2D pie-shaped arc in white
59          g2d.setPaint(Color.WHITE);
60          g2d.setStroke(new BasicStroke(6.0f));
61          g2d.draw(
62             new Arc2D.Double(240, 30, 75, 100, 0, 270, Arc2D.PIE));
63
64          // draw 2D lines in green and yellow
65          g2d.setPaint(Color.GREEN);
66          g2d.draw(new Line2D.Double(395, 30, 320, 150));
67
68          // draw 2D line using stroke
69          float[] dashes = {10}; // specify dash pattern
70          g2d.setPaint(Color.YELLOW);
71          g2d.setStroke(new BasicStroke(4, BasicStroke.CAP_ROUND,
72             BasicStroke.JOIN_ROUND, 10, dashes, 0));
73          g2d.draw(new Line2D.Double(320, 30, 395, 150));
74       }
75    } // end class ShapesJPanel
```

Fig. 13.29 | Demonstrating some Java 2D shapes. (Part 2 of 2.)

```
1    // Fig. 13.30: Shapes.java
2    // Testing ShapesJPanel.
3    import javax.swing.JFrame;
4
5    public class Shapes
6    {
7       // execute application
8       public static void main(String[] args)
9       {
10          // create frame for ShapesJPanel
11          JFrame frame = new JFrame("Drawing 2D shapes");
12          frame.setDefaultCloseOperation(JFrame.EXIT_ON_CLOSE);
13
14          // create ShapesJPanel
15          ShapesJPanel shapesJPanel = new ShapesJPanel();
16
17          frame.add(shapesJPanel);
18          frame.setSize(425, 200);
19          frame.setVisible(true);
20       }
21    } // end class Shapes
```

Fig. 13.30 | Testing ShapesJPanel. (Part 1 of 2.)

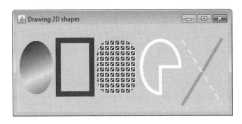

Fig. 13.30 | Testing ShapesJPanel. (Part 2 of 2.)

Ovals, Gradient Fills and **Paint** Objects

The first shape we draw is an *oval filled with gradually changing colors*. Lines 28–29 invoke Graphics2D method **setPaint** to set the **Paint** object that determines the color for the shape to display. A Paint object implements interface java.awt.Paint. It can be something as simple as one of the predeclared Color objects introduced in Section 13.3 (class Color implements Paint), or it can be an instance of the Java 2D API's GradientPaint, **SystemColor**, TexturePaint, LinearGradientPaint or RadialGradientPaint classes. In this case, we use a GradientPaint object.

Class GradientPaint helps draw a shape in *gradually changing colors*—called a **gradient**. The GradientPaint constructor used here requires seven arguments. The first two specify the starting coordinates for the gradient. The third specifies the starting Color for the gradient. The fourth and fifth specify the ending coordinates for the gradient. The sixth specifies the ending Color for the gradient. The last argument specifies whether the gradient is **cyclic** (true) or **acyclic** (false). The two sets of coordinates determine the direction of the gradient. Because the second coordinate (35, 100) is down and to the right of the first coordinate (5, 30), the gradient goes down and to the right at an angle. Because this gradient is cyclic (true), the color starts with blue, gradually becomes yellow, then gradually returns to blue. If the gradient is acyclic, the color transitions from the first color specified (e.g., blue) to the second color (e.g., yellow).

Line 30 uses Graphics2D method **fill** to draw a filled **Shape** object—an object that implements interface Shape (package java.awt). In this case, we display an Ellipse2D.Double object. The Ellipse2D.Double constructor receives four arguments specifying the *bounding rectangle* for the ellipse to display.

Rectangles, **Strokes**

Next we draw a red rectangle with a thick border. Line 33 invokes setPaint to set the Paint object to Color.RED. Line 34 uses Graphics2D method **setStroke** to set the characteristics of the rectangle's border (or the lines for any other shape). Method setStroke requires as its argument an object that implements interface **Stroke** (package java.awt). In this case, we use an instance of class BasicStroke. Class BasicStroke provides several constructors to specify the width of the line, how the line ends (called the **end caps**), how lines join together (called **line joins**) and the dash attributes of the line (if it's a dashed line). The constructor here specifies that the line should be 10 pixels wide.

Line 35 uses Graphics2D method **draw** to draw a Shape object—in this case, a Rectangle2D.Double. The Rectangle2D.Double constructor receives arguments specifying the rectangle's *upper-left x*-coordinate, upper-left *y*-coordinate, width and height.

Rounded Rectangles, **BufferedImage**s *and* **TexturePaint** *Objects*

Next we draw a rounded rectangle filled with a pattern created in a **BufferedImage** (package java.awt.image) object. Lines 38–39 create the BufferedImage object. Class BufferedImage can be used to produce images in color and grayscale. This particular BufferedImage is 10 pixels wide and 10 pixels tall (as specified by the first two arguments of the constructor). The third argument **BufferedImage.TYPE_INT_RGB** indicates that the image is stored in color using the RGB color scheme.

To create the rounded rectangle's fill pattern, we must first draw into the Buffered-Image. Line 42 creates a Graphics2D object (by calling BufferedImage method **createGraphics**) that can be used to draw into the BufferedImage. Lines 43–50 use methods setColor, fillRect and drawRect to create the pattern.

Lines 53–54 set the Paint object to a new TexturePaint (package java.awt) object. A TexturePaint object uses the image stored in its associated BufferedImage (the first constructor argument) as the fill texture for a filled-in shape. The second argument specifies the Rectangle area from the BufferedImage that will be replicated through the texture. In this case, the Rectangle is the same size as the BufferedImage. However, a smaller portion of the BufferedImage can be used.

Lines 55–56 use Graphics2D method fill to draw a filled Shape object—in this case, a RoundRectangle2D.Double. The constructor for class RoundRectangle2D.Double receives six arguments specifying the rectangle dimensions and the arc width and arc height used to determine the rounding of the corners.

Arcs

Next we draw a pie-shaped arc with a thick white line. Line 59 sets the Paint object to Color.WHITE. Line 60 sets the Stroke object to a new BasicStroke for a line 6 pixels wide. Lines 61–62 use Graphics2D method draw to draw a Shape object—in this case, an Arc2D.Double. The Arc2D.Double constructor's first four arguments specify the upper-left *x*-coordinate, upper-left *y*-coordinate, width and height of the bounding rectangle for the arc. The fifth argument specifies the start angle. The sixth argument specifies the arc angle. The last argument specifies how the arc is *closed*. Constant **Arc2D.PIE** indicates that the arc is *closed* by drawing two lines—one line from the arc's starting point to the center of the bounding rectangle and one line from the center of the bounding rectangle to the ending point. Class Arc2D provides two other static constants for specifying how the arc is *closed*. Constant **Arc2D.CHORD** draws a line from the starting point to the ending point. Constant **Arc2D.OPEN** specifies that the arc should *not* be *closed*.

Lines

Finally, we draw two lines using **Line2D** objects—one solid and one dashed. Line 65 sets the Paint object to Color.GREEN. Line 66 uses Graphics2D method draw to draw a Shape object—in this case, an instance of class Line2D.Double. The Line2D.Double constructor's arguments specify the starting coordinates and ending coordinates of the line.

Line 69 declares a one-element float array containing the value 10. This array describes the dashes in the dashed line. In this case, each dash will be 10 pixels long. To create dashes of different lengths in a pattern, simply provide the length of each dash as an element in the array. Line 70 sets the Paint object to Color.YELLOW. Lines 71–72 set the Stroke object to a new BasicStroke. The line will be 4 pixels wide and will have rounded ends (**BasicStroke.CAP_ROUND**). If lines join together (as in a rectangle at the corners), their joining will be rounded (**BasicStroke.JOIN_ROUND**). The dashes argument specifies the dash lengths for the line. The last argument indicates the starting index in the dashes array for the first dash in the pattern. Line 73 then draws a line with the current Stroke.

Creating Your Own Shapes with General Paths

Next we present a **general path**—a shape constructed from straight lines and complex curves. A general path is represented with an object of class **GeneralPath** (package java.awt.geom). The application of Figs. 13.31 and 13.32 demonstrates drawing a general path in the shape of a five-pointed star.

```
 1   // Fig. 13.31: Shapes2JPanel.java
 2   // Demonstrating a general path.
 3   import java.awt.Color;
 4   import java.awt.Graphics;
 5   import java.awt.Graphics2D;
 6   import java.awt.geom.GeneralPath;
 7   import java.security.SecureRandom;
 8   import javax.swing.JPanel;
 9
10   public class Shapes2JPanel extends JPanel
11   {
12      // draw general paths
13      @Override
14      public void paintComponent(Graphics g)
15      {
16         super.paintComponent(g);
17         SecureRandom random = new SecureRandom();
18
19         int[] xPoints = {55, 67, 109, 73, 83, 55, 27, 37, 1, 43};
20         int[] yPoints = {0, 36, 36, 54, 96, 72, 96, 54, 36, 36};
21
22         Graphics2D g2d = (Graphics2D) g;
23         GeneralPath star = new GeneralPath();
24
25         // set the initial coordinate of the General Path
26         star.moveTo(xPoints[0], yPoints[0]);
27
28         // create the star--this does not draw the star
29         for (int count = 1; count < xPoints.length; count++)
30            star.lineTo(xPoints[count], yPoints[count]);
31
32         star.closePath(); // close the shape
33
34         g2d.translate(150, 150); // translate the origin to (150, 150)
35
36         // rotate around origin and draw stars in random colors
37         for (int count = 1; count <= 20; count++)
38         {
39            g2d.rotate(Math.PI / 10.0); // rotate coordinate system
40
```

Fig. 13.31 | Java 2D general paths. (Part 1 of 2.)

```
41              // set random drawing color
42              g2d.setColor(new Color(random.nextInt(256),
43                 random.nextInt(256), random.nextInt(256)));
44
45              g2d.fill(star); // draw filled star
46          }
47      }
48  } // end class Shapes2JPanel
```

Fig. 13.31 | Java 2D general paths. (Part 2 of 2.)

```
1   // Fig. 13.32: Shapes2.java
2   // Demonstrating a general path.
3   import java.awt.Color;
4   import javax.swing.JFrame;
5
6   public class Shapes2
7   {
8      // execute application
9      public static void main(String[] args)
10     {
11        // create frame for Shapes2JPanel
12        JFrame frame = new JFrame("Drawing 2D Shapes");
13        frame.setDefaultCloseOperation(JFrame.EXIT_ON_CLOSE);
14
15        Shapes2JPanel shapes2JPanel = new Shapes2JPanel();
16        frame.add(shapes2JPanel);
17        frame.setBackground(Color.WHITE);
18        frame.setSize(315, 330);
19        frame.setVisible(true);
20     }
21  } // end class Shapes2
```

Fig. 13.32 | Demonstrating a general path.

Lines 19–20 (Fig. 13.31) declare two int arrays representing the *x*- and *y*-coordinates of the points in the star. Line 23 creates GeneralPath object star. Line 26 uses General-Path method **moveTo** to specify the first point in the star. The for statement in lines 29–

30 uses GeneralPath method **lineTo** to draw a line to the next point in the star. Each new call to lineTo draws a line from the previous point to the current point. Line 32 uses GeneralPath method **closePath** to draw a line from the last point to the point specified in the last call to moveTo. This completes the general path.

Line 34 uses Graphics2D method **translate** to move the drawing origin to location (150, 150). All drawing operations now use location (150, 150) as (0, 0).

The for statement in lines 37–46 draws the star 20 times by rotating it around the new origin point. Line 39 uses Graphics2D method **rotate** to rotate the next displayed shape. The argument specifies the rotation angle in radians (with 360° = 2π radians). Line 45 uses Graphics2D method fill to draw a filled version of the star.

13.9 Wrap-Up

In this chapter, you learned how to use Java's graphics capabilities to produce colorful drawings. You learned how to specify the location of an object using Java's coordinate system, and how to draw on a window using the paintComponent method. You were introduced to class Color, and you learned how to use this class to specify different colors using their RGB components. You used the JColorChooser dialog to allow users to select colors in a program. You then learned how to work with fonts when drawing text on a window. You learned how to create a Font object from a font name, style and size, as well as how to access the metrics of a font. From there, you learned how to draw various shapes on a window, such as rectangles (regular, rounded and 3D), ovals and polygons, as well as lines and arcs. You then used the Java 2D API to create more complex shapes and to fill them with gradients or patterns. The chapter concluded with a discussion of general paths, used to construct shapes from straight lines and complex curves. In the next chapter, we discuss class String and its methods. We introduce regular expressions for pattern matching in strings and demonstrate how to validate user input with regular expressions.

14

Strings, Characters and Regular Expressions

Objectives

In this chapter you'll:

- Create and manipulate immutable character-string objects of class `String`.

- Create and manipulate mutable character-string objects of class `StringBuilder`.

- Create and manipulate objects of class `Character`.

- Break a `String` object into tokens using `String` method `split`.

- Use regular expressions to validate `String` data entered into an application.

14.1 Introduction

This chapter introduces Java's string- and character-processing capabilities. The techniques discussed here are appropriate for validating program input, displaying information to users and other text-based manipulations. They're also appropriate for developing text editors, word processors, page-layout software, computerized typesetting systems and other kinds of text-processing software. We've presented several string-processing capabilities in earlier chapters. This chapter discusses in detail the capabilities of classes `String`, `StringBuilder` and `Character` from the `java.lang` package—these classes provide the foundation for string and character manipulation in Java.

The chapter also discusses regular expressions that provide applications with the capability to validate input. The functionality is located in the `String` class along with classes `Matcher` and `Pattern` located in the `java.util.regex` package.

14.2 Fundamentals of Characters and Strings

Characters are the fundamental building blocks of Java source programs. Every program is composed of a sequence of characters that—when grouped together meaningfully—are interpreted by the Java compiler as a series of instructions used to accomplish a task. A program may contain **character literals**. A character literal is an integer value represented as a character in single quotes. For example, `'z'` represents the integer value of z, and `'\t'` represents the integer value of a tab character. The value of a character literal is the integer value of the character in the **Unicode character set**. Appendix B presents the integer equivalents of the characters in the ASCII character set, which is a subset of Unicode (discussed in Appendix H).

Recall from Section 2.2 that a string is a sequence of characters treated as a single unit. A string may include letters, digits and various **special characters**, such as +, -, *, / and $. A string is an object of class `String`. **String literals** (stored in memory as `String` objects) are written as a sequence of characters in double quotation marks, as in:

"John Q. Doe"	(a name)
"9999 Main Street"	(a street address)
"Waltham, Massachusetts"	(a city and state)
"(201) 555-1212"	(a telephone number)

A string may be assigned to a String reference. The declaration

```
String color = "blue";
```

initializes String variable color to refer to a String object that contains the string "blue".

Performance Tip 14.1

To conserve memory, Java treats all string literals with the same contents as a single String object that has many references to it.

14.3 Class String

Class String is used to represent strings in Java. The next several subsections cover many of class String's capabilities.

14.3.1 String Constructors

Class String provides constructors for initializing String objects in a variety of ways. Four of the constructors are demonstrated in the main method of Fig. 14.1.

```
 1   // Fig. 14.1: StringConstructors.java
 2   // String class constructors.
 3
 4   public class StringConstructors
 5   {
 6      public static void main(String[] args)
 7      {
 8         char[] charArray = {'b', 'i', 'r', 't', 'h', ' ', 'd', 'a', 'y'};
 9         String s = new String("hello");
10
11         // use String constructors
12         String s1 = new String();
13         String s2 = new String(s);
14         String s3 = new String(charArray);
15         String s4 = new String(charArray, 6, 3);
16
17         System.out.printf(
18            "s1 = %s%ns2 = %s%ns3 = %s%ns4 = %s%n", s1, s2, s3, s4);
19      }
20   } // end class StringConstructors
```

```
s1 =
s2 = hello
s3 = birth day
s4 = day
```

Fig. 14.1 | String class constructors.

Line 12 instantiates a new String using class String's no-argument constructor and assigns its reference to s1. The new String object contains no characters (i.e., the **empty string**, which can also be represented as "") and has a length of 0. Line 13 instantiates a new String object using class String's constructor that takes a String object as an argument and assigns its reference to s2. The new String object contains the same sequence of characters as the String object s that's passed as an argument to the constructor.

Performance Tip 14.2

It's not necessary to copy an existing String object. String objects are immutable, because class String does not provide methods that allow the contents of a String object to be modified after it is created.

Line 14 instantiates a new String object and assigns its reference to s3 using class String's constructor that takes a char array as an argument. The new String object contains a copy of the characters in the array.

Line 15 instantiates a new String object and assigns its reference to s4 using class String's constructor that takes a char array and two integers as arguments. The second argument specifies the starting position (the *offset*) from which characters in the array are accessed. Remember that the first character is at position 0. The third argument specifies the number of characters (the count) to access in the array. The new String object is formed from the accessed characters. If the offset or the count specified as an argument results in accessing an element outside the bounds of the character array, a StringIndexOutOfBoundsException is thrown.

14.3.2 String Methods length, charAt and getChars

String methods **length**, **charAt** and **getChars** return the length of a String, obtain the character at a specific location in a String and retrieve a set of characters from a String as a char array, respectively. Figure 14.2 demonstrates each of these methods.

```
1   // Fig. 14.2: StringMiscellaneous.java
2   // This application demonstrates the length, charAt and getChars
3   // methods of the String class.
4
5   public class StringMiscellaneous
6   {
7      public static void main(String[] args)
8      {
9         String s1 = "hello there";
10        char[] charArray = new char[5];
11
12        System.out.printf("s1: %s", s1);
13
14        // test length method
15        System.out.printf("%nLength of s1: %d", s1.length());
16
17        // loop through characters in s1 with charAt and display reversed
18        System.out.printf("%nThe string reversed is: ");
```

Fig. 14.2 | String methods length, charAt and getChars. (Part 1 of 2.)

```
19
20          for (int count = s1.length() - 1; count >= 0; count--)
21              System.out.printf("%c ", s1.charAt(count));
22
23          // copy characters from string into charArray
24          s1.getChars(0, 5, charArray, 0);
25          System.out.printf("%nThe character array is: ");
26
27          for (char character : charArray)
28              System.out.print(character);
29
30          System.out.println();
31      }
32  } // end class StringMiscellaneous
```

```
s1: hello there
Length of s1: 11
The string reversed is: e r e h t   o l l e h
The character array is: hello
```

Fig. 14.2 | String methods `length`, `charAt` and `getChars`. (Part 2 of 2.)

Line 15 uses String method `length` to determine the number of characters in String s1. Like arrays, strings know their own length. However, unlike arrays, you access a String's length via class String's `length` method.

Lines 20–21 print the characters of the String s1 in reverse order (and separated by spaces). String method `charAt` (line 21) returns the character at a specific position in the String. Method `charAt` receives an integer argument that's used as the index and returns the character at that position. Like arrays, the first element of a String is at position 0.

Line 24 uses String method `getChars` to copy the characters of a String into a character array. The first argument is the starting index from which characters are to be copied. The second argument is the index that's one past the last character to be copied from the String. The third argument is the character array into which the characters are to be copied. The last argument is the starting index where the copied characters are placed in the target character array. Next, lines 27–28 print the char array contents one character at a time.

14.3.3 Comparing Strings

Frequently, the information being sorted or searched in arrays consists of Strings that must be compared to place them into order or to determine whether a string appears in an array (or other collection). Class String provides methods for *comparing* strings, as demonstrated in the next two examples.

To understand what it means for one string to be greater than or less than another, consider the process of alphabetizing a series of last names. No doubt, you'd place "Jones" before "Smith" because the first letter of "Jones" comes before the first letter of "Smith" in the alphabet. But the alphabet is more than just a list of 26 letters—it's an *ordered* list of characters. Each letter occurs in a specific position within the list. Z is more than just a letter of the alphabet—it's specifically the twenty-sixth letter of the alphabet.

How does the computer know that one letter "comes before" another? All characters are represented in the computer as numeric codes (see Appendix B). When the computer compares Strings, it actually compares the numeric codes of the characters in the Strings.

Figure 14.3 demonstrates String methods equals, equalsIgnoreCase, compareTo and **regionMatches** and using the equality operator == to compare String objects.

```java
1   // Fig. 14.3: StringCompare.java
2   // String methods equals, equalsIgnoreCase, compareTo and regionMatches.
3
4   public class StringCompare
5   {
6      public static void main(String[] args)
7      {
8         String s1 = new String("hello"); // s1 is a copy of "hello"
9         String s2 = "goodbye";
10        String s3 = "Happy Birthday";
11        String s4 = "happy birthday";
12
13        System.out.printf(
14           "s1 = %s%ns2 = %s%ns3 = %s%ns4 = %s%n%n", s1, s2, s3, s4);
15
16        // test for equality
17        if (s1.equals("hello"))  // true
18           System.out.println("s1 equals \"hello\"");
19        else
20           System.out.println("s1 does not equal \"hello\"");
21
22        // test for equality with ==
23        if (s1 == "hello")  // false; they are not the same object
24           System.out.println("s1 is the same object as \"hello\"");
25        else
26           System.out.println("s1 is not the same object as \"hello\"");
27
28        // test for equality (ignore case)
29        if (s3.equalsIgnoreCase(s4))  // true
30           System.out.printf("%s equals %s with case ignored%n", s3, s4);
31        else
32           System.out.println("s3 does not equal s4");
33
34        // test compareTo
35        System.out.printf(
36           "%ns1.compareTo(s2) is %d", s1.compareTo(s2));
37        System.out.printf(
38           "%ns2.compareTo(s1) is %d", s2.compareTo(s1));
39        System.out.printf(
40           "%ns1.compareTo(s1) is %d", s1.compareTo(s1));
41        System.out.printf(
42           "%ns3.compareTo(s4) is %d", s3.compareTo(s4));
43        System.out.printf(
44           "%ns4.compareTo(s3) is %d%n%n", s4.compareTo(s3));
```

Fig. 14.3 | String methods equals, equalsIgnoreCase, compareTo and regionMatches. (Part 1 of 2.)

```
45
46          // test regionMatches (case sensitive)
47          if (s3.regionMatches(0, s4, 0, 5))
48              System.out.println("First 5 characters of s3 and s4 match");
49          else
50              System.out.println(
51                  "First 5 characters of s3 and s4 do not match");
52
53          // test regionMatches (ignore case)
54          if (s3.regionMatches(true, 0, s4, 0, 5))
55              System.out.println(
56                  "First 5 characters of s3 and s4 match with case ignored");
57          else
58              System.out.println(
59                  "First 5 characters of s3 and s4 do not match");
60      }
61  } // end class StringCompare
```

```
s1 = hello
s2 = goodbye
s3 = Happy Birthday
s4 = happy birthday

s1 equals "hello"
s1 is not the same object as "hello"
Happy Birthday equals happy birthday with case ignored

s1.compareTo(s2) is 1
s2.compareTo(s1) is -1
s1.compareTo(s1) is 0
s3.compareTo(s4) is -32
s4.compareTo(s3) is 32

First 5 characters of s3 and s4 do not match
First 5 characters of s3 and s4 match with case ignored
```

Fig. 14.3 | String methods `equals`, `equalsIgnoreCase`, `compareTo` and `regionMatches`. (Part 2 of 2.)

String Method `equals`

The condition at line 17 uses method `equals` to compare `String` s1 and the `String` literal "hello" for equality. Method `equals` (a method of class `Object` overridden in `String`) tests any two objects for equality—the strings contained in the two objects are *identical*. The method returns `true` if the contents of the objects are equal, and `false` otherwise. The preceding condition is `true` because `String` s1 was initialized with the string literal "hello". Method `equals` uses a **lexicographical comparison**—it compares the integer Unicode values (see Appendix H for more information) that represent each character in each `String`. Thus, if the `String` "hello" is compared to the string "HELLO", the result is `false`, because the integer representation of a lowercase letter is *different* from that of the corresponding uppercase letter.

*Comparing **String**s with the == Operator*
The condition at line 23 uses the equality operator == to compare String s1 for equality with the String literal "hello". When primitive-type values are compared with ==, the result is true if *both values are identical.* When references are compared with ==, the result is true if *both references refer to the same object in memory.* To compare the actual contents (or state information) of objects for equality, a method must be invoked. In the case of Strings, that method is equals. The preceding condition evaluates to false at line 23 because the reference s1 was initialized with the statement

```
s1 = new String("hello");
```

which creates a new String object with a copy of string literal "hello" and assigns the new object to variable s1. If s1 had been initialized with the statement

```
s1 = "hello";
```

which directly assigns the string literal "hello" to variable s1, the condition would be true. Remember that Java treats all string literal objects with the same contents as one String object to which there can be many references. Thus, lines 8, 17 and 23 all refer to the same String object "hello" in memory.

> **Common Programming Error 14.1**
> *Comparing references with == can lead to logic errors, because == compares the references to determine whether they* refer *to the same object, not whether two objects have the* same contents. *When two separate objects that contain the same values are compared with ==, the result will be* false. *When comparing objects to determine whether they have the same contents, use method* equals.

*String Method **equalsIgnoreCase***
If you're sorting Strings, you may compare them for equality with method equals-IgnoreCase, which ignores whether the letters in each String are uppercase or lowercase when performing the comparison. Thus, "hello" and "HELLO" compare as equal. Line 29 uses String method equalsIgnoreCase to compare String s3—Happy Birthday—for equality with String s4—happy birthday. The result of this comparison is true because the comparison ignores case.

*String Method **compareTo***
Lines 35–44 use method compareTo to compare Strings. Method compareTo is declared in the Comparable interface and implemented in the String class. Line 36 compares String s1 to String s2. Method compareTo returns 0 if the Strings are equal, a negative number if the String that invokes compareTo is less than the String that's passed as an argument and a positive number if the String that invokes compareTo is greater than the String that's passed as an argument. Method compareTo uses a *lexicographical* comparison—it compares the numeric values of corresponding characters in each String.

*String Method **regionMatches***
The condition at line 47 uses a version of String method regionMatches to compare portions of two Strings for equality. The first argument to this version of the method is the starting index in the String that invokes the method. The second argument is a compar-

ison String. The third argument is the starting index in the comparison String. The last argument is the number of characters to compare between the two Strings. The method returns true only if the specified number of characters are lexicographically equal.

Finally, the condition at line 54 uses a five-argument version of String method regionMatches to compare portions of two Strings for equality. When the first argument is true, the method ignores the case of the characters being compared. The remaining arguments are identical to those described for the four-argument regionMatches method.

String Methods startsWith and endsWith

The next example (Fig. 14.4) demonstrates String methods **startsWith** and **endsWith**. Method main creates array strings containing "started", "starting", "ended" and "ending". The remainder of method main consists of three for statements that test the elements of the array to determine whether they start with or end with a particular set of characters.

```java
 1   // Fig. 14.4: StringStartEnd.java
 2   // String methods startsWith and endsWith.
 3
 4   public class StringStartEnd
 5   {
 6      public static void main(String[] args)
 7      {
 8         String[] strings = {"started", "starting", "ended", "ending"};
 9
10         // test method startsWith
11         for (String string : strings)
12         {
13            if (string.startsWith("st"))
14               System.out.printf("\"%s\" starts with \"st\"%n", string);
15         }
16
17         System.out.println();
18
19         // test method startsWith starting from position 2 of string
20         for (String string : strings)
21         {
22            if (string.startsWith("art", 2))
23               System.out.printf(
24                  "\"%s\" starts with \"art\" at position 2%n", string);
25         }
26
27         System.out.println();
28
29         // test method endsWith
30         for (String string : strings)
31         {
32            if (string.endsWith("ed"))
33               System.out.printf("\"%s\" ends with \"ed\"%n", string);
34         }
35      }
36   } // end class StringStartEnd
```

Fig. 14.4 | String methods startsWith and endsWith. (Part 1 of 2.)

```
"started" starts with "st"
"starting" starts with "st"

"started" starts with "art" at position 2
"starting" starts with "art" at position 2

"started" ends with "ed"
"ended" ends with "ed"
```

Fig. 14.4 | String methods startsWith and endsWith. (Part 2 of 2.)

Lines 11–15 use the version of method startsWith that takes a String argument. The condition in the if statement (line 13) determines whether each String in the array starts with the characters "st". If so, the method returns true and the application prints that String. Otherwise, the method returns false and nothing happens.

Lines 20–25 use the startsWith method that takes a String and an integer as arguments. The integer specifies the index at which the comparison should begin in the String. The condition in the if statement (line 22) determines whether each String in the array has the characters "art" beginning with the third character in each String. If so, the method returns true and the application prints the String.

The third for statement (lines 30–34) uses method endsWith, which takes a String argument. The condition at line 32 determines whether each String in the array ends with the characters "ed". If so, the method returns true and the application prints the String.

14.3.4 Locating Characters and Substrings in Strings

Often it's useful to search a string for a character or set of characters. For example, if you're creating your own word processor, you might want to provide a capability for searching through documents. Figure 14.5 demonstrates the many versions of String methods **indexOf** and **lastIndexOf** that search for a specified character or substring in a String.

```
 1   // Fig. 14.5: StringIndexMethods.java
 2   // String searching methods indexOf and lastIndexOf.
 3
 4   public class StringIndexMethods
 5   {
 6      public static void main(String[] args)
 7      {
 8         String letters = "abcdefghijklmabcdefghijklm";
 9
10         // test indexOf to locate a character in a string
11         System.out.printf(
12            "'c' is located at index %d%n", letters.indexOf('c'));
13         System.out.printf(
14            "'a' is located at index %d%n", letters.indexOf('a', 1));
15         System.out.printf(
16            "'$' is located at index %d%n%n", letters.indexOf('$'));
17
```

Fig. 14.5 | String-searching methods indexOf and lastIndexOf. (Part 1 of 2.)

```
18          // test lastIndexOf to find a character in a string
19          System.out.printf("Last 'c' is located at index %d%n",
20             letters.lastIndexOf('c'));
21          System.out.printf("Last 'a' is located at index %d%n",
22             letters.lastIndexOf('a', 25));
23          System.out.printf("Last '$' is located at index %d%n%n",
24             letters.lastIndexOf('$'));
25
26          // test indexOf to locate a substring in a string
27          System.out.printf("\"def\" is located at index %d%n",
28             letters.indexOf("def"));
29          System.out.printf("\"def\" is located at index %d%n",
30             letters.indexOf("def", 7));
31          System.out.printf("\"hello\" is located at index %d%n%n",
32             letters.indexOf("hello"));
33
34          // test lastIndexOf to find a substring in a string
35          System.out.printf("Last \"def\" is located at index %d%n",
36             letters.lastIndexOf("def"));
37          System.out.printf("Last \"def\" is located at index %d%n",
38             letters.lastIndexOf("def", 25));
39          System.out.printf("Last \"hello\" is located at index %d%n",
40             letters.lastIndexOf("hello"));
41       }
42    } // end class StringIndexMethods
```

```
'c' is located at index 2
'a' is located at index 13
'$' is located at index -1

Last 'c' is located at index 15
Last 'a' is located at index 13
Last '$' is located at index -1

"def" is located at index 3
"def" is located at index 16
"hello" is located at index -1

Last "def" is located at index 16
Last "def" is located at index 16
Last "hello" is located at index -1
```

Fig. 14.5 | String-searching methods `indexOf` and `lastIndexOf`. (Part 2 of 2.)

All the searches in this example are performed on the String `letters` (initialized with "abcdefghijklmabcdefghijklm"). Lines 11–16 use method `indexOf` to locate the first occurrence of a character in a String. If the method finds the character, it returns the character's index in the String—otherwise, it returns -1. There are two versions of `indexOf` that search for characters in a String. The expression in line 12 uses the version of method `indexOf` that takes an integer representation of the character to find. The expression at line 14 uses another version of method `indexOf`, which takes two integer arguments—the character and the starting index at which the search of the String should begin.

Lines 19–24 use method lastIndexOf to locate the last occurrence of a character in a String. The method searches from the end of the String toward the beginning. If it finds the character, it returns the character's index in the String—otherwise, it returns –1. There are two versions of lastIndexOf that search for characters in a String. The expression at line 20 uses the version that takes the integer representation of the character. The expression at line 22 uses the version that takes two integer arguments—the integer representation of the character and the index from which to begin searching *backward*.

Lines 27–40 demonstrate versions of methods indexOf and lastIndexOf that each take a String as the first argument. These versions perform identically to those described earlier except that they search for sequences of characters (or substrings) that are specified by their String arguments. If the substring is found, these methods return the index in the String of the first character in the substring.

14.3.5 Extracting Substrings from Strings

Class String provides two substring methods to enable a new String object to be created by copying part of an existing String object. Each method returns a new String object. Both methods are demonstrated in Fig. 14.6.

```
1   // Fig. 14.6: SubString.java
2   // String class substring methods.
3
4   public class SubString
5   {
6      public static void main(String[] args)
7      {
8         String letters = "abcdefghijklmabcdefghijklm";
9
10        // test substring methods
11        System.out.printf("Substring from index 20 to end is \"%s\"%n",
12           letters.substring(20));
13        System.out.printf("%s \"%s\"%n",
14           "Substring from index 3 up to, but not including 6 is",
15           letters.substring(3, 6));
16     }
17  } // end class SubString
```

```
Substring from index 20 to end is "hijklm"
Substring from index 3 up to, but not including 6 is "def"
```

Fig. 14.6 | String class substring methods.

The expression letters.substring(20) at line 12 uses the substring method that takes one integer argument. The argument specifies the starting index in the original String letters from which characters are to be copied. The substring returned contains a copy of the characters from the starting index to the end of the String. Specifying an index outside the bounds of the String causes a **StringIndexOutOfBoundsException**.

Line 15 uses the substring method that takes two integer arguments—the starting index from which to copy characters in the original String and the index one beyond the last character to copy (i.e., copy up to, but *not including*, that index in the String). The substring returned contains a copy of the specified characters from the original String. An index outside the bounds of the String causes a StringIndexOutOfBoundsException.

14.3.6 Concatenating Strings

String method **concat** (Fig. 14.7) concatenates two String objects (similar to using the + operator) and returns a new String object containing the characters from both original Strings. The expression s1.concat(s2) at line 13 forms a String by appending the characters in s2 to the those in s1. The original Strings to which s1 and s2 refer are *not modified*.

```
 1   // Fig. 14.7: StringConcatenation.java
 2   // String method concat.
 3
 4   public class StringConcatenation
 5   {
 6      public static void main(String[] args)
 7      {
 8         String s1 = "Happy ";
 9         String s2 = "Birthday";
10
11         System.out.printf("s1 = %s%ns2 = %s%n%n",s1, s2);
12         System.out.printf(
13            "Result of s1.concat(s2) = %s%n", s1.concat(s2));
14         System.out.printf("s1 after concatenation = %s%n", s1);
15      }
16   } // end class StringConcatenation
```

```
s1 = Happy
s2 = Birthday

Result of s1.concat(s2) = Happy Birthday
s1 after concatenation = Happy
```

Fig. 14.7 | String method concat.

14.3.7 Miscellaneous String Methods

Class String provides several methods that return Strings or character arrays containing copies of an original String's contents which are then modified. These methods—none of which modify the String on which they're called—are demonstrated in Fig. 14.8.

```
 1   // Fig. 14.8: StringMiscellaneous2.java
 2   // String methods replace, toLowerCase, toUpperCase, trim and toCharArray.
 3
 4   public class StringMiscellaneous2
 5   {
 6      public static void main(String[] args)
 7      {
```

Fig. 14.8 | String methods replace, toLowerCase, toUpperCase, trim and toCharArray. (Part 1 of 2.)

```
 8           String s1 = "hello";
 9           String s2 = "GOODBYE";
10           String s3 = "   spaces   ";
11
12           System.out.printf("s1 = %s%ns2 = %s%ns3 = %s%n%n", s1, s2, s3);
13
14           // test method replace
15           System.out.printf(
16              "Replace 'l' with 'L' in s1: %s%n%n", s1.replace('l', 'L'));
17
18           // test toLowerCase and toUpperCase
19           System.out.printf("s1.toUpperCase() = %s%n", s1.toUpperCase());
20           System.out.printf("s2.toLowerCase() = %s%n%n", s2.toLowerCase());
21
22           // test trim method
23           System.out.printf("s3 after trim = \"%s\"%n%n", s3.trim());
24
25           // test toCharArray method
26           char[] charArray = s1.toCharArray();
27           System.out.print("s1 as a character array = ");
28
29           for (char character : charArray)
30              System.out.print(character);
31
32           System.out.println();
33        }
34  } // end class StringMiscellaneous2
```

```
s1 = hello
s2 = GOODBYE
s3 =    spaces

Replace 'l' with 'L' in s1: heLLo

s1.toUpperCase() = HELLO
s2.toLowerCase() = goodbye

s3 after trim = "spaces"

s1 as a character array = hello
```

Fig. 14.8 | String methods replace, toLowerCase, toUpperCase, trim and toCharArray. (Part 2 of 2.)

Line 16 uses String method replace to return a new String object in which every occurrence in s1 of character 'l' (lowercase el) is replaced with character 'L'. Method replace leaves the original String unchanged. If there are no occurrences of the first argument in the String, method replace returns the original String. An overloaded version of method replace enables you to replace substrings rather than individual characters.

Line 19 uses String method **toUpperCase** to generate a new String with uppercase letters where corresponding lowercase letters exist in s1. The method returns a new String object containing the converted String and leaves the original String unchanged. If there are no characters to convert, method toUpperCase returns the original String.

Line 20 uses String method **toLowerCase** to return a new String object with lower-case letters where corresponding uppercase letters exist in s2. The original String remains unchanged. If there are no characters in the original String to convert, toLowerCase returns the original String.

Line 23 uses String method **trim** to generate a new String object that removes all white-space characters that appear at the beginning and/or end of the String on which trim operates. The method returns a new String object containing the String without leading or trailing white space. The original String remains unchanged. If there are no white-space characters at the beginning and/or end, trim returns the original String.

Line 26 uses String method **toCharArray** to create a new character array containing a copy of the characters in s1. Lines 29–30 output each char in the array.

14.3.8 String Method valueOf

As we've seen, every object in Java has a toString method that enables a program to obtain the object's *string representation*. Unfortunately, this technique cannot be used with primitive types because they do not have methods. Class String provides static methods that take an argument of any type and convert it to a String object. Figure 14.9 demonstrates the String class **valueOf** methods.

The expression String.valueOf(charArray) at line 18 uses the character array char-Array to create a new String object. The expression String.valueOf(charArray, 3, 3) at line 20 uses a portion of the character array charArray to create a new String object. The second argument specifies the starting index from which the characters are used. The third argument specifies the number of characters to be used.

```
1   // Fig. 14.9: StringValueOf.java
2   // String valueOf methods.
3
4   public class StringValueOf
5   {
6      public static void main(String[] args)
7      {
8         char[] charArray = {'a', 'b', 'c', 'd', 'e', 'f'};
9         boolean booleanValue = true;
10        char characterValue = 'Z';
11        int integerValue = 7;
12        long longValue = 10000000000L; // L suffix indicates long
13        float floatValue = 2.5f; // f indicates that 2.5 is a float
14        double doubleValue = 33.333; // no suffix, double is default
15        Object objectRef = "hello"; // assign string to an Object reference
16
17        System.out.printf(
18           "char array = %s%n", String.valueOf(charArray));
19        System.out.printf("part of char array = %s%n",
20           String.valueOf(charArray, 3, 3));
21        System.out.printf(
22           "boolean = %s%n", String.valueOf(booleanValue));
23        System.out.printf(
24           "char = %s%n", String.valueOf(characterValue));
```

Fig. 14.9 | String valueOf methods. (Part 1 of 2.)

```
25          System.out.printf("int = %s%n", String.valueOf(integerValue));
26          System.out.printf("long = %s%n", String.valueOf(longValue));
27          System.out.printf("float = %s%n", String.valueOf(floatValue));
28          System.out.printf(
29              "double = %s%n", String.valueOf(doubleValue));
30          System.out.printf("Object = %s", String.valueOf(objectRef));
31      }
32  } // end class StringValueOf
```

```
char array = abcdef
part of char array = def
boolean = true
char = Z
int = 7
long = 10000000000
float = 2.5
double = 33.333
Object = hello
```

Fig. 14.9 | String valueOf methods. (Part 2 of 2.)

There are seven other versions of method valueOf, which take arguments of type boolean, char, int, long, float, double and Object, respectively. These are demonstrated in lines 21–30. The version of valueOf that takes an Object as an argument can do so because all Objects can be converted to Strings with method toString.

[*Note:* Lines 12–13 use literal values 10000000000L and 2.5f as the initial values of long variable longValue and float variable floatValue, respectively. By default, Java treats integer literals as type int and floating-point literals as type double. Appending the letter L to the literal 10000000000 and appending letter f to the literal 2.5 indicates to the compiler that 10000000000 should be treated as a long and 2.5 as a float. An uppercase L or lowercase l can be used to denote a variable of type long and an uppercase F or lowercase f can be used to denote a variable of type float.]

14.4 Class StringBuilder

We now discuss the features of class **StringBuilder** for creating and manipulating *dynamic* string information—that is, *modifiable* strings. Every StringBuilder is capable of storing a number of characters specified by its *capacity*. If a StringBuilder's capacity is exceeded, the capacity expands to accommodate the additional characters.

Performance Tip 14.3

Java can perform certain optimizations involving String objects (such as referring to one String object from multiple variables) because it knows these objects will not change. Strings (not StringBuilders) should be used if the data will not change.

Performance Tip 14.4

In programs that frequently perform string concatenation, or other string modifications, it's often more efficient to implement the modifications with class StringBuilder.

Software Engineering Observation 14.1

StringBuilders are not thread safe. If multiple threads require access to the same dynamic string information, use class **StringBuffer** *in your code. Classes* StringBuilder *and* StringBuffer *provide identical capabilities, but class* StringBuffer *is thread safe. For more details on threading, see Chapter 20.*

14.4.1 StringBuilder Constructors

Class StringBuilder provides four constructors. We demonstrate three of these in Fig. 14.10. Line 8 uses the no-argument StringBuilder constructor to create a String-Builder with no characters in it and an initial capacity of 16 characters (the default for a StringBuilder). Line 9 uses the StringBuilder constructor that takes an integer argument to create a StringBuilder with no characters in it and the initial capacity specified by the integer argument (i.e., 10). Line 10 uses the StringBuilder constructor that takes a String argument to create a StringBuilder containing the characters in the String argument. The initial capacity is the number of characters in the String argument plus 16.

Lines 12–14 implicitly use the method toString of class StringBuilder to output the StringBuilders with the printf method. In Section 14.4.4, we discuss how Java uses StringBuilder objects to implement the + and += operators for string concatenation.

```
1   // Fig. 14.10: StringBuilderConstructors.java
2   // StringBuilder constructors.
3
4   public class StringBuilderConstructors
5   {
6      public static void main(String[] args)
7      {
8         StringBuilder buffer1 = new StringBuilder();
9         StringBuilder buffer2 = new StringBuilder(10);
10        StringBuilder buffer3 = new StringBuilder("hello");
11
12        System.out.printf("buffer1 = \"%s\"%n", buffer1);
13        System.out.printf("buffer2 = \"%s\"%n", buffer2);
14        System.out.printf("buffer3 = \"%s\"%n", buffer3);
15     }
16  } // end class StringBuilderConstructors
```

```
buffer1 = ""
buffer2 = ""
buffer3 = "hello"
```

Fig. 14.10 | StringBuilder constructors.

14.4.2 StringBuilder Methods length, capacity, setLength and ensureCapacity

Class StringBuilder provides methods **length** and **capacity** to return the number of characters currently in a StringBuilder and the number of characters that can be stored in a StringBuilder without allocating more memory, respectively. Method **ensure-Capacity** guarantees that a StringBuilder has at least the specified capacity. Method **setLength** increases or decreases the length of a StringBuilder. Figure 14.11 demonstrates these methods.

```java
1   // Fig. 14.11: StringBuilderCapLen.java
2   // StringBuilder length, setLength, capacity and ensureCapacity methods.
3
4   public class StringBuilderCapLen
5   {
6      public static void main(String[] args)
7      {
8         StringBuilder buffer = new StringBuilder("Hello, how are you?");
9
10        System.out.printf("buffer = %s%nlength = %d%ncapacity = %d%n%n",
11           buffer.toString(), buffer.length(), buffer.capacity());
12
13        buffer.ensureCapacity(75);
14        System.out.printf("New capacity = %d%n%n", buffer.capacity());
15
16        buffer.setLength(10));
17        System.out.printf("New length = %d%nbuffer = %s%n",
18           buffer.length(), buffer.toString());
19     }
20  } // end class StringBuilderCapLen
```

```
buffer = Hello, how are you?
length = 19
capacity = 35

New capacity = 75

New length = 10
buffer = Hello, how
```

Fig. 14.11 | StringBuilder length, setLength, capacity and ensureCapacity methods.

The application contains one StringBuilder called buffer. Line 8 uses the StringBuilder constructor that takes a String argument to initialize the StringBuilder with "Hello, how are you?". Lines 10–11 print the contents, length and capacity of the StringBuilder. Note in the output window that the capacity of the StringBuilder is initially 35. Recall that the StringBuilder constructor that takes a String argument initializes the capacity to the length of the string passed as an argument plus 16.

Line 13 uses method ensureCapacity to expand the capacity of the StringBuilder to a minimum of 75 characters. Actually, if the original capacity is less than the argument, the method ensures a capacity that's the greater of the number specified as an argument and twice the original capacity plus 2. The StringBuilder's current capacity remains unchanged if it's more than the specified capacity.

> **Performance Tip 14.5**
>
> *Dynamically increasing the capacity of a StringBuilder can take a relatively long time. Executing a large number of these operations can degrade the performance of an application. If a StringBuilder is going to increase greatly in size, possibly multiple times, setting its capacity high at the beginning will increase performance.*

Line 16 uses method setLength to set the length of the StringBuilder to 10. If the specified length is less than the current number of characters in the StringBuilder, its contents are truncated to the specified length (i.e., the characters in the StringBuilder after the specified length are discarded). If the specified length is greater than the number of characters currently in the StringBuilder, null characters (characters with the numeric representation 0) are appended until the total number of characters in the StringBuilder is equal to the specified length.

14.4.3 StringBuilder Methods charAt, setCharAt, getChars and reverse

Class StringBuilder provides methods **charAt**, **setCharAt**, **getChars** and **reverse** to manipulate the characters in a StringBuilder (Fig. 14.12). Method charAt (line 12) takes an integer argument and returns the character in the StringBuilder at that index. Method getChars (line 15) copies characters from a StringBuilder into the character array passed as an argument. This method takes four arguments—the starting index from which characters should be copied in the StringBuilder, the index one past the last character to be copied from the StringBuilder, the character array into which the characters are to be copied and the starting location in the character array where the first character should be placed. Method setCharAt (lines 21 and 22) takes an integer and a character argument and sets the character at the specified position in the StringBuilder to the character argument. Method reverse (line 25) reverses the contents of the StringBuilder. Attempting to access a character that's outside the bounds of a StringBuilder results in a StringIndexOutOfBoundsException.

```
1   // Fig. 14.12: StringBuilderChars.java
2   // StringBuilder methods charAt, setCharAt, getChars and reverse.
3
4   public class StringBuilderChars
5   {
6      public static void main(String[] args)
7      {
8         StringBuilder buffer = new StringBuilder("hello there");
9
10        System.out.printf("buffer = %s%n", buffer.toString());
11        System.out.printf("Character at 0: %s%nCharacter at 4: %s%n%n",
12           buffer.charAt(0), buffer.charAt(4));
13
14        char[] charArray = new char[buffer.length()];
15        buffer.getChars(0, buffer.length(), charArray, 0);
16        System.out.print("The characters are: ");
```

Fig. 14.12 | StringBuilder methods charAt, setCharAt, getChars and reverse. (Part 1 of 2.)

```
17
18          for (char character : charArray)
19              System.out.print(character);
20
21          buffer.setCharAt(0, 'H');
22          buffer.setCharAt(6, 'T');
23          System.out.printf("%n%nbuffer = %s", buffer.toString());
24
25          buffer.reverse();
26          System.out.printf("%n%nbuffer = %s%n", buffer.toString());
27      }
28  } // end class StringBuilderChars
```

```
buffer = hello there
Character at 0: h
Character at 4: o

The characters are: hello there

buffer = Hello There

buffer = erehT olleH
```

Fig. 14.12 | StringBuilder methods charAt, setCharAt, getChars and reverse. (Part 2 of 2.)

14.4.4 StringBuilder append Methods

Class StringBuilder provides *overloaded* **append** methods (Fig. 14.13) to allow values of various types to be appended to the end of a StringBuilder. Versions are provided for each of the primitive types and for character arrays, Strings, Objects, and more. (Remember that method toString produces a string representation of any Object.) Each method takes its argument, converts it to a string and appends it to the StringBuilder.

```
1   // Fig. 14.13: StringBuilderAppend.java
2   // StringBuilder append methods.
3
4   public class StringBuilderAppend
5   {
6       public static void main(String[] args)
7       {
8           Object objectRef = "hello";
9           String string = "goodbye";
10          char[] charArray = {'a', 'b', 'c', 'd', 'e', 'f'};
11          boolean booleanValue = true;
12          char characterValue = 'Z';
13          int integerValue = 7;
14          long longValue = 10000000000L;
15          float floatValue = 2.5f;
16          double doubleValue = 33.333;
```

Fig. 14.13 | StringBuilder append methods. (Part 1 of 2.)

```
17
18          StringBuilder lastBuffer = new StringBuilder("last buffer");
19          StringBuilder buffer = new StringBuilder();
20
21          buffer.append(objectRef)
22                .append("%n")
23                .append(string)
24                .append("%n")
25                .append(charArray)
26                .append("%n")
27                .append(charArray, 0, 3)
28                .append("%n")
29                .append(booleanValue)
30                .append("%n")
31                .append(characterValue);
32                .append("%n")
33                .append(integerValue)
34                .append("%n")
35                .append(longValue)
36                .append("%n")
37                .append(floatValue)
38                .append("%n")
39                .append(doubleValue)
40                .append("%n")
41                .append(lastBuffer);
42
43          System.out.printf("buffer contains%n%s%n", buffer.toString());
44       }
45    } // end StringBuilderAppend
```

```
buffer contains
hello
goodbye
abcdef
abc
true
Z
7
10000000000
2.5
33.333
last buffer
```

Fig. 14.13 | StringBuilder append methods. (Part 2 of 2.)

The compiler can use StringBuilder and the append methods to implement the + and += String concatenation operators. For example, assuming the declarations

```
String string1 = "hello";
String string2 = "BC";
int value = 22;
```

the statement

```
String s = string1 + string2 + value;
```

concatenates "hello", "BC" and 22. The concatenation can be performed as follows:

```
String s = new StringBuilder().append("hello").append("BC").
    append(22).toString();
```

First, the preceding statement creates an *empty* `StringBuilder`, then appends to it the strings "hello" and "BC" and the integer 22. Next, `StringBuilder`'s toString method converts the `StringBuilder` to a `String` object to be assigned to `String` s. The statement

```
s += "!";
```

can be performed as follows (this may differ by compiler):

```
s = new StringBuilder().append(s).append("!").toString();
```

This creates an empty `StringBuilder`, then appends to it the current contents of s followed by "!". Next, `StringBuilder`'s method toString (which must be called *explicitly* here) returns the `StringBuilder`'s contents as a `String`, and the result is assigned to s.

14.4.5 `StringBuilder` Insertion and Deletion Methods

`StringBuilder` provides overloaded **insert** methods to insert values of various types at any position in a `StringBuilder`. Versions are provided for the primitive types and for character arrays, `Strings`, `Objects` and `CharSequences`. Each method takes its second argument and inserts it at the index specified by the first argument. If the first argument is less than 0 or greater than the `StringBuilder`'s length, a `StringIndexOutOfBounds-Exception` occurs. Class `StringBuilder` also provides methods **delete** and **deleteCharAt** to delete characters at any position in a `StringBuilder`. Method delete takes two arguments—the starting index and the index one past the end of the characters to delete. All characters beginning at the starting index up to but *not* including the ending index are deleted. Method deleteCharAt takes one argument—the index of the character to delete. Invalid indices cause both methods to throw a `StringIndexOutOfBoundsException`. Figure 14.14 demonstrates methods insert, delete and deleteCharAt.

```
 1   // Fig. 14.14: StringBuilderInsertDelete.java
 2   // StringBuilder methods insert, delete and deleteCharAt.
 3
 4   public class StringBuilderInsertDelete
 5   {
 6      public static void main(String[] args)
 7      {
 8         Object objectRef = "hello";
 9         String string = "goodbye";
10         char[] charArray = {'a', 'b', 'c', 'd', 'e', 'f'};
11         boolean booleanValue = true;
12         char characterValue = 'K';
13         int integerValue = 7;
14         long longValue = 10000000;
15         float floatValue = 2.5f; // f suffix indicates that 2.5 is a float
16         double doubleValue = 33.333;
17
```

Fig. 14.14 | StringBuilder methods insert, delete and deleteCharAt. (Part 1 of 2.)

```
18          StringBuilder buffer = new StringBuilder();
19
20          buffer.insert(0, objectRef);
21          buffer.insert(0, "  "); // each of these contains two spaces
22          buffer.insert(0, string);
23          buffer.insert(0, "  ");
24          buffer.insert(0, charArray);
25          buffer.insert(0, "  ");
26          buffer.insert(0, charArray, 3, 3);
27          buffer.insert(0, "  ");
28          buffer.insert(0, booleanValue);
29          buffer.insert(0, "  ");
30          buffer.insert(0, characterValue);
31          buffer.insert(0, "  ");
32          buffer.insert(0, integerValue);
33          buffer.insert(0, "  ");
34          buffer.insert(0, longValue);
35          buffer.insert(0, "  ");
36          buffer.insert(0, floatValue);
37          buffer.insert(0, "  ");
38          buffer.insert(0, doubleValue);
39
40          System.out.printf(
41             "buffer after inserts:%n%s%n%n", buffer.toString());
42
43          buffer.deleteCharAt(10); // delete 5 in 2.5
44          buffer.delete(2, 6); // delete .333 in 33.333
45
46          System.out.printf(
47             "buffer after deletes:%n%s%n", buffer.toString());
48       }
49    } // end class StringBuilderInsertDelete
```

```
buffer after inserts:
33.333  2.5  10000000  7  K  true  def  abcdef  goodbye  hello

buffer after deletes:
33  2.  10000000  7  K  true  def  abcdef  goodbye  hello
```

Fig. 14.14 | StringBuilder methods insert, delete and deleteCharAt. (Part 2 of 2.)

14.5 Class Character

Java provides eight **type-wrapper classes**—Boolean, Character, Double, Float, Byte, Short, Integer and Long—that enable primitive-type values to be treated as objects. In this section, we present class Character—the type-wrapper class for primitive type char.

Most Character methods are static methods designed for convenience in processing individual char values. These methods take at least a character argument and perform either a test or a manipulation of the character. Class Character also contains a constructor that receives a char argument to initialize a Character object. Most of the methods of class Character are presented in the next three examples. For more information on class Character (and all the type-wrapper classes), see the java.lang package in the Java API documentation.

Figure 14.15 demonstrates static methods that test characters to determine whether they're a specific character type and the static methods that perform case conversions on characters. You can enter any character and apply the methods to the character.

```java
 1   // Fig. 14.15: StaticCharMethods.java
 2   // Character static methods for testing characters and converting case.
 3   import java.util.Scanner;
 4
 5   public class StaticCharMethods
 6   {
 7      public static void main(String[] args)
 8      {
 9         Scanner scanner = new Scanner(System.in); // create scanner
10         System.out.println("Enter a character and press Enter");
11         String input = scanner.next();
12         char c = input.charAt(0); // get input character
13
14         // display character info
15         System.out.printf("is defined: %b%n", Character.isDefined(c));
16         System.out.printf("is digit: %b%n", Character.isDigit(c));
17         System.out.printf("is first character in a Java identifier: %b%n",
18            Character.isJavaIdentifierStart(c));
19         System.out.printf("is part of a Java identifier: %b%n",
20            Character.isJavaIdentifierPart(c));
21         System.out.printf("is letter: %b%n", Character.isLetter(c));
22         System.out.printf(
23            "is letter or digit: %b%n", Character.isLetterOrDigit(c));
24         System.out.printf(
25            "is lower case: %b%n", Character.isLowerCase(c));
26         System.out.printf(
27            "is upper case: %b%n", Character.isUpperCase(c));
28         System.out.printf(
29            "to upper case: %s%n", Character.toUpperCase(c));
30         System.out.printf(
31            "to lower case: %s%n", Character.toLowerCase(c));
32      }
33   } // end class StaticCharMethods
```

```
Enter a character and press Enter
A
is defined: true
is digit: false
is first character in a Java identifier: true
is part of a Java identifier: true
is letter: true
is letter or digit: true
is lower case: false
is upper case: true
to upper case: A
to lower case: a
```

Fig. 14.15 | Character static methods for testing characters and converting case. (Part 1 of 2.)

```
Enter a character and press Enter
8
is defined: true
is digit: true
is first character in a Java identifier: false
is part of a Java identifier: true
is letter: false
is letter or digit: true
is lower case: false
is upper case: false
to upper case: 8
to lower case: 8
```

```
Enter a character and press Enter
$
is defined: true
is digit: false
is first character in a Java identifier: true
is part of a Java identifier: true
is letter: false
is letter or digit: false
is lower case: false
is upper case: false
to upper case: $
to lower case: $
```

Fig. 14.15 | Character static methods for testing characters and converting case. (Part 2 of 2.)

Line 15 uses Character method **isDefined** to determine whether character c is defined in the Unicode character set. If so, the method returns true; otherwise, it returns false. Line 16 uses Character method **isDigit** to determine whether character c is a defined Unicode digit. If so, the method returns true, and otherwise, false.

Line 18 uses Character method **isJavaIdentifierStart** to determine whether c is a character that can be the first character of an identifier in Java—that is, a letter, an underscore (_) or a dollar sign ($). If so, the method returns true, and otherwise, false. Line 20 uses Character method **isJavaIdentifierPart** to determine whether character c is a character that can be used in an identifier in Java—that is, a digit, a letter, an underscore (_) or a dollar sign ($). If so, the method returns true, and otherwise, false.

Line 21 uses Character method **isLetter** to determine whether character c is a letter. If so, the method returns true, and otherwise, false. Line 23 uses Character method **isLetterOrDigit** to determine whether character c is a letter or a digit. If so, the method returns true, and otherwise, false.

Line 25 uses Character method **isLowerCase** to determine whether character c is a lowercase letter. If so, the method returns true, and otherwise, false. Line 27 uses Character method **isUpperCase** to determine whether character c is an uppercase letter. If so, the method returns true, and otherwise, false.

Line 29 uses Character method **toUpperCase** to convert the character c to its uppercase equivalent. The method returns the converted character if the character has an uppercase equivalent, and otherwise, the method returns its original argument. Line 31 uses Character method **toLowerCase** to convert the character c to its lowercase equivalent. The method returns the converted character if the character has a lowercase equivalent, and otherwise, the method returns its original argument.

Figure 14.16 demonstrates static Character methods **digit** and **forDigit**, which convert characters to digits and digits to characters, respectively, in different number systems. Common number systems include decimal (base 10), octal (base 8), hexadecimal (base 16) and binary (base 2). The base of a number is also known as its **radix**. For more information on conversions between number systems, see Appendix J.

```
1   // Fig. 14.16: StaticCharMethods2.java
2   // Character class static conversion methods.
3   import java.util.Scanner;
4
5   public class StaticCharMethods2
6   {
7      // executes application
8      public static void main(String[] args)
9      {
10        Scanner scanner = new Scanner(System.in);
11
12        // get radix
13        System.out.println("Please enter a radix:");
14        int radix = scanner.nextInt();
15
16        // get user choice
17        System.out.printf("Please choose one:%n1 -- %s%n2 -- %s%n",
18           "Convert digit to character", "Convert character to digit");
19        int choice = scanner.nextInt();
20
21        // process request
22        switch (choice)
23        {
24           case 1: // convert digit to character
25              System.out.println("Enter a digit:");
26              int digit = scanner.nextInt();
27              System.out.printf("Convert digit to character: %s%n",
28                 Character.forDigit(digit, radix));
29              break;
30
31           case 2: // convert character to digit
32              System.out.println("Enter a character:");
33              char character = scanner.next().charAt(0);
34              System.out.printf("Convert character to digit: %s%n",
35                 Character.digit(character, radix));
36              break;
37        }
38     }
39  } // end class StaticCharMethods2
```

Fig. 14.16 | Character class static conversion methods. (Part 1 of 2.)

```
Please enter a radix:
16
Please choose one:
1 -- Convert digit to character
2 -- Convert character to digit
2
Enter a character:
A
Convert character to digit: 10
```

```
Please enter a radix:
16
Please choose one:
1 -- Convert digit to character
2 -- Convert character to digit
1
Enter a digit:
13
Convert digit to character: d
```

Fig. 14.16 | Character class static conversion methods. (Part 2 of 2.)

Line 28 uses method forDigit to convert the integer digit into a character in the number system specified by the integer radix (the base of the number). For example, the decimal integer 13 in base 16 (the radix) has the character value 'd'. Lowercase and uppercase letters represent the *same* value in number systems. Line 35 uses method digit to convert variable character into an integer in the number system specified by the integer radix (the base of the number). For example, the character 'A' is the base 16 (the radix) representation of the base 10 value 10. The radix must be between 2 and 36, inclusive.

Figure 14.17 demonstrates the constructor and several instance methods of class Character—**charValue**, toString and equals. Lines 7–8 instantiate two Character objects by assigning the character constants 'A' and 'a', respectively, to the Character variables. Java automatically converts these char literals into Character objects—a process known as *autoboxing* that we discuss in more detail in Section 16.4. Line 11 uses Character method charValue to return the char value stored in Character object c1. Line 11 returns a string representation of Character object c2 using method toString. The condition in line 13 uses method equals to determine whether the object c1 has the same contents as the object c2 (i.e., the characters inside each object are equal).

```
1   // Fig. 14.17: OtherCharMethods.java
2   // Character class instance methods.
3   public class OtherCharMethods
4   {
5      public static void main(String[] args)
6      {
7         Character c1 = 'A';
8         Character c2 = 'a';
```

Fig. 14.17 | Character class instance methods. (Part 1 of 2.)

```
 9
10          System.out.printf(
11              "c1 = %s%nc2 = %s%n%n", c1.charValue(), c2.toString());
12
13          if (c1.equals(c2))
14              System.out.println("c1 and c2 are equal%n");
15          else
16              System.out.println("c1 and c2 are not equal%n");
17      }
18  } // end class OtherCharMethods
```

```
c1 = A
c2 = a

c1 and c2 are not equal
```

Fig. 14.17 | Character class instance methods. (Part 2 of 2.)

14.6 Tokenizing Strings

When you read a sentence, your mind breaks it into **tokens**—individual words and punctuation marks that convey meaning to you. Compilers also perform tokenization. They break up statements into individual pieces like keywords, identifiers, operators and other programming-language elements. We now study class String's **split** method, which breaks a String into its component tokens. Tokens are separated from one another by **delimiters**, typically white-space characters such as space, tab, newline and carriage return. Other characters can also be used as delimiters to separate tokens. The application in Fig. 14.18 demonstrates String's split method.

When the user presses the *Enter* key, the input sentence is stored in variable sentence. Line 17 invokes String method split with the String argument " ", which returns an array of Strings. The space character in the argument String is the delimiter that method split uses to locate the tokens in the String. As you'll learn in the next section, the argument to method split can be a regular expression for more complex tokenizing. Line 19 displays the length of the array tokens—i.e., the number of tokens in sentence. Lines 21–22 output each token on a separate line.

```
 1  // Fig. 14.18: TokenTest.java
 2  // StringTokenizer object used to tokenize strings.
 3  import java.util.Scanner;
 4  import java.util.StringTokenizer;
 5
 6  public class TokenTest
 7  {
 8      // execute application
 9      public static void main(String[] args)
10      {
11          // get sentence
12          Scanner scanner = new Scanner(System.in);
```

Fig. 14.18 | StringTokenizer object used to tokenize strings. (Part 1 of 2.)

```
13          System.out.println("Enter a sentence and press Enter");
14          String sentence = scanner.nextLine();
15
16          // process user sentence
17          String[] tokens = sentence.split(" ");
18          System.out.printf("Number of elements: %d%nThe tokens are:%n",
19              tokens.length);
20
21          for (String token : tokens)
22              System.out.println(token);
23      }
24  } // end class TokenTest
```

```
Enter a sentence and press Enter
This is a sentence with seven tokens
Number of elements: 7
The tokens are:
This
is
a
sentence
with
seven
tokens
```

Fig. 14.18 | `StringTokenizer` object used to tokenize strings. (Part 2 of 2.)

14.7 Regular Expressions, Class Pattern and Class Matcher

A **regular expression** is a `String` that describes a *search pattern* for *matching* characters in other `String`s. Such expressions are useful for *validating input* and ensuring that data is in a particular format. For example, a ZIP code must consist of five digits, and a last name must contain only letters, spaces, apostrophes and hyphens. One application of regular expressions is to facilitate the construction of a compiler. Often, a large and complex regular expression is used to *validate the syntax of a program*. If the program code does *not* match the regular expression, the compiler knows that there's a syntax error in the code.

Class `String` provides several methods for performing regular-expression operations, the simplest of which is the matching operation. `String` method **matches** receives a `String` that specifies the regular expression and matches the contents of the `String` object on which it's called to the regular expression. The method returns a `boolean` indicating whether the match succeeded.

A regular expression consists of literal characters and special symbols. Figure 14.19 specifies some **predefined character classes** that can be used with regular expressions. A character class is an *escape sequence* that represents a group of characters. A digit is any numeric character. A **word character** is any letter (uppercase or lowercase), any digit or the underscore character. A white-space character is a space, a tab, a carriage return, a newline or a form feed. Each character class matches a single character in the `String` we're attempting to match with the regular expression.

Character	Matches	Character	Matches
\d	any digit	\D	any nondigit
\w	any word character	\W	any nonword character
\s	any white-space character	\S	any non-whitespace character

Fig. 14.19 | Predefined character classes.

Regular expressions are not limited to these predefined character classes. The expressions employ various operators and other forms of notation to match complex patterns. We examine several of these techniques in the application in Figs. 14.20 and 14.21, which *validates user input* via regular expressions. [*Note:* This application is not designed to match all possible valid user input.]

```java
1   // Fig. 14.20: ValidateInput.java
2   // Validating user information using regular expressions.
3
4   public class ValidateInput
5   {
6      // validate first name
7      public static boolean validateFirstName(String firstName)
8      {
9         return firstName.matches("[A-Z][a-zA-Z]*");
10     }
11
12     // validate last name
13     public static boolean validateLastName(String lastName)
14     {
15        return lastName.matches("[a-zA-z]+(['-][a-zA-Z]+)*");
16     }
17
18     // validate address
19     public static boolean validateAddress(String address)
20     {
21        return address.matches(
22           "\\d+\\s+([a-zA-Z]+|[a-zA-Z]+\\s[a-zA-Z]+)");
23     }
24
25     // validate city
26     public static boolean validateCity(String city)
27     {
28        return city.matches("([a-zA-Z]+|[a-zA-Z]+\\s[a-zA-Z]+)");
29     }
30
31     // validate state
32     public static boolean validateState(String state)
33     {
```

Fig. 14.20 | Validating user information using regular expressions. (Part 1 of 2.)

```
34            return state.matches("([a-zA-Z]+|[a-zA-Z]+\\s[a-zA-Z]+)");
35        }
36
37        // validate zip
38        public static boolean validateZip(String zip)
39        {
40            return zip.matches("\\d{5}");
41        }
42
43        // validate phone
44        public static boolean validatePhone(String phone)
45        {
46            return phone.matches("[1-9]\\d{2}-[1-9]\\d{2}-\\d{4}");
47        }
48    } // end class ValidateInput
```

Fig. 14.20 | Validating user information using regular expressions. (Part 2 of 2.)

```
1    // Fig. 14.21: Validate.java
2    // Input and validate data from user using the ValidateInput class.
3    import java.util.Scanner;
4
5    public class Validate
6    {
7        public static void main(String[] args)
8        {
9            // get user input
10           Scanner scanner = new Scanner(System.in);
11           System.out.println("Please enter first name:");
12           String firstName = scanner.nextLine();
13           System.out.println("Please enter last name:");
14           String lastName = scanner.nextLine();
15           System.out.println("Please enter address:");
16           String address = scanner.nextLine();
17           System.out.println("Please enter city:");
18           String city = scanner.nextLine();
19           System.out.println("Please enter state:");
20           String state = scanner.nextLine();
21           System.out.println("Please enter zip:");
22           String zip = scanner.nextLine();
23           System.out.println("Please enter phone:");
24           String phone = scanner.nextLine();
25
26           // validate user input and display error message
27           System.out.println("%nValidate Result:");
28
29           if (!ValidateInput.validateFirstName(firstName))
30               System.out.println("Invalid first name");
31           else if (!ValidateInput.validateLastName(lastName))
32               System.out.println("Invalid last name");
33           else if (!ValidateInput.validateAddress(address))
34               System.out.println("Invalid address");
```

Fig. 14.21 | Input and validate data from user using the ValidateInput class. (Part 1 of 2.)

```
35            else if (!ValidateInput.validateCity(city))
36                System.out.println("Invalid city");
37            else if (!ValidateInput.validateState(state))
38                System.out.println("Invalid state");
39            else if (!ValidateInput.validateZip(zip))
40                System.out.println("Invalid zip code");
41            else if (!ValidateInput.validatePhone(phone))
42                System.out.println("Invalid phone number");
43            else
44                System.out.println("Valid input.  Thank you.");
45        }
46   } // end class Validate
```

```
Please enter first name:
Jane
Please enter last name:
Doe
Please enter address:
123 Some Street
Please enter city:
Some City
Please enter state:
SS
Please enter zip:
123
Please enter phone:
123-456-7890

Validate Result:
Invalid zip code
```

```
Please enter first name:
Jane
Please enter last name:
Doe
Please enter address:
123 Some Street
Please enter city:
Some City
Please enter state:
SS
Please enter zip:
12345
Please enter phone:
123-456-7890

Validate Result:
Valid input.  Thank you.
```

Fig. 14.21 | Input and validate data from user using the ValidateInput class. (Part 2 of 2.)

Figure 14.20 validates user input. Line 9 validates the first name. To match a set of characters that does not have a predefined character class, use square brackets, []. For example, the pattern "[aeiou]" matches a single character that's a vowel. Character ranges are represented by placing a dash (-) between two characters. In the example, "[A-Z]" matches a single uppercase letter. If the first character in the brackets is "^", the expression accepts any character other than those indicated. However, "[^Z]" is not the same as "[A-Y]", which matches uppercase letters A–Y—"[^Z]" matches *any character other than* capital Z, including lowercase letters and nonletters such as the newline character. Ranges in character classes are determined by the letters' integer values. In this example, "[A-Za-z]" matches all uppercase and lowercase letters. The range "[A-z]" matches all letters and also matches those characters (such as [and \) with an integer value between uppercase Z and lowercase a (for more information on integer values of characters see Appendix B). Like predefined character classes, character classes delimited by square brackets match a single character in the search object.

In line 9, the asterisk after the second character class indicates that any number of letters can be matched. In general, when the regular-expression operator "*" appears in a regular expression, the application attempts to match zero or more occurrences of the subexpression immediately preceding the "*". Operator "+" attempts to match one or more occurrences of the subexpression immediately preceding "+". So both "A*" and "A+" will match "AAA" or "A", but only "A*" will match an empty string.

If method validateFirstName returns true (line 29 of Fig. 14.21), the application attempts to validate the last name (line 31) by calling validateLastName (lines 13–16 of Fig. 14.20). The regular expression to validate the last name matches any number of letters split by spaces, apostrophes or hyphens.

Line 33 of Fig. 14.21 calls method validateAddress (lines 19–23 of Fig. 14.20) to validate the address. The first character class matches any digit one or more times (\\d+). Two \ characters are used, because \ normally starts an escape sequence in a string. So \\d in a String represents the regular-expression pattern \d. Then we match one or more white-space characters (\\s+). The character "|" matches the expression to its left or to its right. For example, "Hi (John|Jane)" matches both "Hi John" and "Hi Jane". The parentheses are used to group parts of the regular expression. In this example, the left side of | matches a single word, and the right side matches two words separated by any amount of white space. So the address must contain a number followed by one or two words. Therefore, "10 Broadway" and "10 Main Street" are both valid addresses in this example. The city (lines 26–29 of Fig. 14.20) and state (lines 32–35 of Fig. 14.20) methods also match any word of at least one character or, alternatively, any two words of at least one character if the words are separated by a single space, so both Waltham and West Newton would match.

Quantifiers

The asterisk (*) and plus (+) are formally called **quantifiers**. Figure 14.22 lists all the quantifiers. We've already discussed how the asterisk (*) and plus (+) quantifiers work. All quantifiers affect only the subexpression immediately preceding the quantifier. Quantifier question mark (?) matches zero or one occurrences of the expression that it quantifies. A set of braces containing one number ({n}) matches exactly n occurrences of the expression it quantifies. We demonstrate this quantifier to validate the zip code in Fig. 14.20 at line 40. Including a comma after the number enclosed in braces matches at least n occurrences of the quantified expression. The set of braces containing two numbers ({n,m}), matches between n and m occurrences of the expression that it qualifies. Quantifiers may be applied to patterns enclosed in parentheses to create more complex regular expressions.

Quantifier	Matches
*	Matches zero or more occurrences of the pattern.
+	Matches one or more occurrences of the pattern.
?	Matches zero or one occurrences of the pattern.
$\{n\}$	Matches exactly n occurrences.
$\{n,\}$	Matches at least n occurrences.
$\{n,m\}$	Matches between n and m (inclusive) occurrences.

Fig. 14.22 | Quantifiers used in regular expressions.

All of the quantifiers are **greedy**. This means that they'll match as many occurrences as they can as long as the match is still successful. However, if any of these quantifiers is followed by a question mark (?), the quantifier becomes **reluctant** (sometimes called **lazy**). It then will match as few occurrences as possible as long as the match is still successful.

The zip code (line 40 in Fig. 14.20) matches a digit five times. This regular expression uses the digit character class and a quantifier with the digit 5 between braces. The phone number (line 46 in Fig. 14.20) matches three digits (the first one cannot be zero) followed by a dash followed by three more digits (again the first one cannot be zero) followed by four more digits.

`String` method `matches` checks whether an entire `String` conforms to a regular expression. For example, we want to accept `"Smith"` as a last name, but not `"9@Smith#"`. If only a substring matches the regular expression, method `matches` returns `false`.

Replacing Substrings and Splitting Strings

Sometimes it's useful to replace parts of a string or to split a string into pieces. For this purpose, class `String` provides methods **replaceAll**, **replaceFirst** and **split**. These methods are demonstrated in Fig. 14.23.

```
1   // Fig. 14.23: RegexSubstitution.java
2   // String methods replaceFirst, replaceAll and split.
3   import java.util.Arrays;
4
5   public class RegexSubstitution
6   {
7      public static void main(String[] args)
8      {
9         String firstString = "This sentence ends in 5 stars *****";
10        String secondString = "1, 2, 3, 4, 5, 6, 7, 8";
11
12        System.out.printf("Original String 1: %s%n", firstString);
13
14        // replace '*' with '^'
15        firstString = firstString.replaceAll("\\*", "^");
16
17        System.out.printf("^ substituted for *: %s%n", firstString);
```

Fig. 14.23 | String methods `replaceFirst`, `replaceAll` and `split`. (Part I of 2.)

```
18
19        // replace 'stars' with 'carets'
20        firstString = firstString.replaceAll("stars", "carets");
21
22        System.out.printf(
23           "\"carets\" substituted for \"stars\": %s%n", firstString);
24
25        // replace words with 'word'
26        System.out.printf("Every word replaced by \"word\": %s%n%n",
27           firstString.replaceAll("\\w+", "word"));
28
29        System.out.printf("Original String 2: %s%n", secondString);
30
31        // replace first three digits with 'digit'
32        for (int i = 0; i < 3; i++)
33           secondString = secondString.replaceFirst("\\d", "digit");
34
35        System.out.printf(
36           "First 3 digits replaced by \"digit\" : %s%n", secondString);
37
38        System.out.print("String split at commas: ");
39        String[] results = secondString.split(",\\s*"); // split on commas
40        System.out.println(Arrays.toString(results));
41     }
42  } // end class RegexSubstitution
```

```
Original String 1: This sentence ends in 5 stars *****
^ substituted for *: This sentence ends in 5 stars ^^^^^
"carets" substituted for "stars": This sentence ends in 5 carets ^^^^^
Every word replaced by "word": word word word word word word ^^^^^

Original String 2: 1, 2, 3, 4, 5, 6, 7, 8
First 3 digits replaced by "digit" : digit, digit, digit, 4, 5, 6, 7, 8
String split at commas: ["digit", "digit", "digit", "4", "5", "6", "7", "8"]
```

Fig. 14.23 | String methods `replaceFirst`, `replaceAll` and `split`. (Part 2 of 2.)

Method `replaceAll` replaces text in a `String` with new text (the second argument) wherever the original `String` matches a regular expression (the first argument). Line 15 replaces every instance of `"*"` in `firstString` with `"^"`. The regular expression (`"\\*"`) precedes character `*` with two backslashes. Normally, `*` is a quantifier indicating that a regular expression should match *any number of occurrences* of a preceding pattern. However, in line 15, we want to find all occurrences of the literal character `*`—to do this, we must escape character `*` with character `\`. Escaping a special regular-expression character with `\` instructs the matching engine to find the actual character. Since the expression is stored in a Java `String` and `\` is a special character in Java `Strings`, we must include an additional `\`. So the Java `String` `"\\*"` represents the regular-expression pattern `\*` which matches a single `*` character in the search string. In line 20, every match for the regular expression `"stars"` in `firstString` is replaced with `"carets"`. Line 27 uses `replaceAll` to replace all words in the string with `"word"`.

Method `replaceFirst` (line 33) replaces the first occurrence of a pattern match. Java `Strings` are immutable; therefore, method `replaceFirst` returns a new `String` in which the appropriate characters have been replaced. This line takes the original `String` and replaces it with the `String` returned by `replaceFirst`. By iterating three times we replace the first three instances of a digit (\d) in `secondString` with the text `"digit"`.

Method `split` divides a `String` into several substrings. The original is broken in any location that matches a specified regular expression. Method `split` returns an array of `Strings` containing the substrings between matches for the regular expression. In line 39, we use method `split` to tokenize a `String` of comma-separated integers. The argument is the regular expression that locates the delimiter. In this case, we use the regular expression `",\\s*"` to separate the substrings wherever a comma occurs. By matching any white-space characters, we eliminate extra spaces from the resulting substrings. The commas and white-space characters are not returned as part of the substrings. Again, the Java `String` `",\\s*"` represents the regular expression ,\s*. Line 40 uses `Arrays` method `toString` to display the contents of array `results` in square brackets and separated by commas.

Classes *Pattern and Matcher*

In addition to the regular-expression capabilities of class `String`, Java provides other classes in package `java.util.regex` that help developers manipulate regular expressions. Class **Pattern** represents a regular expression. Class **Matcher** contains both a regular-expression pattern and a `CharSequence` in which to search for the pattern.

CharSequence (package `java.lang`) is an *interface* that allows read access to a sequence of characters. The interface requires that the methods `charAt`, `length`, `subSequence` and `toString` be declared. Both `String` and `StringBuilder` implement interface `CharSequence`, so an instance of either of these classes can be used with class `Matcher`.

 Common Programming Error 14.2
A regular expression can be tested against an object of any class that implements interface `CharSequence`, *but the regular expression must be a* `String`. *Attempting to create a regular expression as a* `StringBuilder` *is an error.*

If a regular expression will be used only once, `static` `Pattern` method **matches** can be used. This method takes a `String` that specifies the regular expression and a `CharSequence` on which to perform the match. This method returns a `boolean` indicating whether the search object (the second argument) *matches* the regular expression.

If a regular expression will be used more than once (in a loop, for example), it's more efficient to use `static` `Pattern` method **compile** to create a specific `Pattern` object for that regular expression. This method receives a `String` representing the pattern and returns a new `Pattern` object, which can then be used to call method **matcher**. This method receives a `CharSequence` to search and returns a `Matcher` object.

`Matcher` provides method **matches**, which performs the same task as `Pattern` method `matches`, but receives no arguments—the search pattern and search object are encapsulated in the `Matcher` object. Class `Matcher` provides other methods, including **find**, **lookingAt**, **replaceFirst** and **replaceAll**.

Figure 14.24 presents a simple example that employs regular expressions. This program matches birthdays against a regular expression. The expression matches only birthdays that do not occur in April and that belong to people whose names begin with `"J"`.

```
 1   // Fig. 14.24: RegexMatches.java
 2   // Classes Pattern and Matcher.
 3   import java.util.regex.Matcher;
 4   import java.util.regex.Pattern;
 5
 6   public class RegexMatches
 7   {
 8      public static void main(String[] args)
 9      {
10         // create regular expression
11         Pattern expression =
12            Pattern.compile("J.*\\d[0-35-9]-\\d\\d-\\d\\d");
13
14         String string1 = "Jane's Birthday is 05-12-75\n" +
15            "Dave's Birthday is 11-04-68\n" +
16            "John's Birthday is 04-28-73\n" +
17            "Joe's Birthday is 12-17-77";
18
19         // match regular expression to string and print matches
20         Matcher matcher = expression.matcher(string1);
21
22         while (matcher.find())
23            System.out.println(matcher.group());
24      }
25   } // end class RegexMatches
```

```
Jane's Birthday is 05-12-75
Joe's Birthday is 12-17-77
```

Fig. 14.24 | Classes Pattern and Matcher.

Lines 11–12 create a Pattern by invoking static Pattern method compile. The *dot character "."* in the regular expression (line 12) matches any single character except a new-line character. Line 20 creates the Matcher object for the compiled regular expression and the matching sequence (string1). Lines 22–23 use a while loop to *iterate* through the String. Line 22 uses Matcher method find to attempt to match a piece of the search object to the search pattern. Each call to this method starts at the point where the last call ended, so multiple matches can be found. Matcher method lookingAt performs the same way, except that it always starts from the beginning of the search object and will always find the *first* match if there is one.

Common Programming Error 14.3

Method matches (from class String, Pattern or Matcher) will return true only if the entire search object matches the regular expression. Methods find and lookingAt (from class Matcher) will return true if a portion of the search object matches the regular expression.

Line 23 uses Matcher method **group**, which returns the String from the search object that matches the search pattern. The String that's returned is the one that was last matched by a call to find or lookingAt. The output in Fig. 14.24 shows the two matches that were found in string1.

Java SE 8

As you'll see in Section 17.7, you can combine regular-expression processing with Java SE 8 lambdas and streams to implement powerful String-and-file processing applications.

14.8 Wrap-Up

In this chapter, you learned about more String methods for selecting portions of Strings and manipulating Strings. You learned about the Character class and some of the methods it declares to handle chars. The chapter also discussed the capabilities of the String-Builder class for creating Strings. The end of the chapter discussed regular expressions, which provide a powerful capability to search and match portions of Strings that fit a particular pattern. In the next chapter, you'll learn about file processing, including how persistent data is stored and and retrieved.

15

Files, Streams and Object Serialization

Objectives

In this chapter you'll:

- Create, read, write and update files.

- Retrieve information about files and directories using features of the NIO.2 APIs.

- Learn the differences between text files and binary files.

- Use class **Formatter** to output text to a file.

- Use class **Scanner** to input text from a file.

- Write objects to and read objects from a file using object serialization, interface **Serializable** and classes **ObjectOutputStream** and **ObjectInputStream**.

- Use a **JFileChooser** dialog to allow users to select files or directories on disk.

15.1 Introduction

Data stored in variables and arrays is *temporary*—it's lost when a local variable goes out of scope or when the program terminates. For long-term retention of data, even after the programs that create the data terminate, computers use **files**. You use files every day for tasks such as writing a document or creating a spreadsheet. Computers store files on **secondary storage devices**, including hard disks, flash drives, DVDs and more. Data maintained in files is **persistent data**—it exists beyond the duration of program execution. In this chapter, we explain how Java programs create, update and process files.

We begin with a discussion of Java's architecture for handling files programmatically. Next we explain that data can be stored in *text files* and *binary files*—and we cover the differences between them. We demonstrate retrieving information about files and directories using classes `Paths` and `Files` and interfaces `Path` and `DirectoryStream` (all from package `java.nio.file`), then consider the mechanisms for writing data to and reading data from files. We show how to create and manipulate sequential-access text files. Working with text files allows you to quickly and easily start manipulating files. As you'll learn, however, it's difficult to read data from text files back into object form. Fortunately, many object-oriented languages (including Java) provide ways to write objects to and read objects from files (known as *object serialization* and *deserialization*). To demonstrate this, we recreate some of our sequential-access programs that used text files, this time by storing objects in and retrieving objects from binary files.

15.2 Files and Streams

Java views each file as a sequential **stream of bytes** (Fig. 15.1).[1] Every operating system provides a mechanism to determine the end of a file, such as an **end-of-file marker** or a count of the total bytes in the file that's recorded in a system-maintained administrative data structure. A Java program processing a stream of bytes simply receives an indication from the operating system when it reaches the end of the stream—the program does *not* need to know how the underlying platform represents files or streams. In some cases, the

---

1. Java's NIO APIs also include classes and interfaces that implement so-called channel-based architecture for high-performance I/O. These topics are beyond the scope of this book.

end-of-file indication occurs as an exception. In others, the indication is a return value from a method invoked on a stream-processing object.

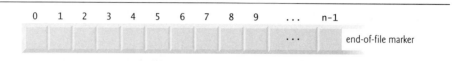

Fig. 15.1 | Java's view of a file of *n* bytes.

Byte-Based and Character-Based Streams
File streams can be used to input and output data as bytes or characters.

- **Byte-based streams** output and input data in its *binary* format—a char is two bytes, an int is four bytes, a double is eight bytes, etc.

- **Character-based streams** output and input data as a *sequence of characters* in which every character is two bytes—the number of bytes for a given value depends on the number of characters in that value. For example, the value 2000000000 requires 20 bytes (10 characters at two bytes per character) but the value 7 requires only two bytes (1 character at two bytes per character).

Files created using byte-based streams are referred to as **binary files**, while files created using character-based streams are referred to as **text files**. Text files can be read by text editors, while binary files are read by programs that understand the file's specific content and its ordering. A numeric value in a binary file can be used in calculations, whereas the character 5 is simply a character that can be used in a string of text, as in "Sarah Miller is 15 years old".

Standard Input, Standard Output and Standard Error Streams
A Java program **opens** a file by creating an object and associating a stream of bytes or characters with it. The object's constructor interacts with the operating system to *open* the file. Java can also associate streams with different devices. When a Java program begins executing, it creates three stream objects that are associated with devices—System.in, System.out and System.err. The System.in (standard input stream) object normally enables a program to input bytes from the keyboard. Object System.out (the standard output stream object) normally enables a program to output character data to the screen. Object System.err (the standard error stream object) normally enables a program to output character-based error messages to the screen. Each stream can be **redirected**. For System.in, this capability enables the program to read bytes from a different source. For System.out and System.err, it enables the output to be sent to a different location, such as a file on disk. Class System provides methods **setIn**, **setOut** and **setErr** to redirected the standard input, output and error streams, respectively.

The `java.io` and `java.nio` Packages
Java programs perform stream-based processing with classes and interfaces from package **java.io** and the subpackages of **java.nio**—Java's New I/O APIs that were first introduced in Java SE 6 and that have been enhanced since. There are also other packages throughout the Java APIs containing classes and interfaces based on those in the java.io and java.nio packages.

Character-based input and output can be performed with classes `Scanner` and **Formatter**, as you'll see in Section 15.4. You've used class `Scanner` extensively to input data from the keyboard. `Scanner` also can read data from a file. Class `Formatter` enables formatted data to be output to any text-based stream in a manner similar to method `System.out.printf`. Appendix I presents the details of formatted output with `printf`. All these features can be used to format text files as well.

Java SE 8 Adds Another Type of Stream
Chapter 17, Java SE 8 Lambdas and Streams, introduces a new type of stream that's used to process collections of elements (like arrays and `ArrayLists`), rather than the streams of bytes we discuss in this chapter's file-processing examples.

15.3 Using NIO Classes and Interfaces to Get File and Directory Information

Interfaces `Path` and `DirectoryStream` and classes `Paths` and `Files` (all from package java.nio.file) are useful for retrieving information about files and directories on disk:

- **Path** interface—Objects of classes that implement this interface represent the location of a file or directory. `Path` objects do not open files or provide any file-processing capabilities.

- **Paths** class—Provides `static` methods used to get a `Path` object representing a file or directory location.

- **Files** class—Provides `static` methods for common file and directory manipulations, such as copying files; creating and deleting files and directories; getting information about files and directories; reading the contents of files; getting objects that allow you to manipulate the contents of files and directories; and more

- **DirectoryStream** interface—Objects of classes that implement this interface enable a program to iterate through the contents of a directory.

Creating **Path** Objects
You'll use class `static` method **get** of class `Paths` to convert a `String` representing a file's or directory's location into a `Path` object. You can then use the methods of interface `Path` and class `Files` to determine information about the specified file or directory. We discuss several such methods momentarily. For complete lists of their methods, visit:

```
http://docs.oracle.com/javase/7/docs/api/java/nio/file/Path.html
http://docs.oracle.com/javase/7/docs/api/java/nio/file/Files.html
```

Absolute vs. Relative Paths
A file or directory's path specifies its location on disk. The path includes some or all of the directories leading to the file or directory. An **absolute path** contains *all* directories, starting with the **root directory**, that lead to a specific file or directory. Every file or directory on a particular disk drive has the *same* root directory in its path. A **relative path** is "relative" to another directory—for example, a path relative to the directory in which the application began executing.

*Getting **Path** Objects from URIs*
An overloaded version of Files static method get uses a URI object to locate the file or directory. A **Uniform Resource Identifier (URI)** is a more general form of the **Uniform Resource Locators (URLs)** that are used to locate websites. For example, the URL http:/ /www.deitel.com/ is the URL for the Deitel & Associates website. URIs for locating files vary across operating systems. On Windows platforms, the URI

```
file://C:/data.txt
```

identifies the file data.txt stored in the root directory of the C: drive. On UNIX/Linux platforms, the URI

```
file:/home/student/data.txt
```

identifies the file data.txt stored in the home directory of the user student.

Example: Getting File and Directory Information
Figure 15.2 prompts the user to enter a file or directory name, then uses classes Paths, Path, Files and DirectoryStream to output information about that file or directory. The program begins by prompting the user for a file or directory (line 16). Line 19 inputs the filename or directory name and passes it to Paths static method get, which converts the String to a Path. Line 21 invokes Files static method **exists**, which receives a Path and determines whether it exists (either as a file or as a directory) on disk. If the name does not exist, control proceeds to line 49, which displays a message containing the Path's String representation followed by "does not exist." Otherwise, lines 24–45 execute:

- Path method **getFileName** (line 24) gets the String name of the file or directory without any location information.

- Files static method **isDirectory** (line 26) receives a Path and returns a boolean indicating whether that Path represents a directory on disk.

- Path method **isAbsolute** (line 28) returns a boolean indicating whether that Path represents an absolute path to a file or directory.

- Files static method **getLastModifiedTime** (line 30) receives a Path and returns a FileTime (package java.nio.file.attribute) indicating when the file was last modified. The program outputs the FileTime's default String representation.

- Files static method **size** (line 31) receives a Path and returns a long representing the number of bytes in the file or directory. For directories, the value returned is platform specific.

- Path method **toString** (called implicitly at line 32) returns a String representing the Path.

- Path method **toAbsolutePath** (line 33) converts the Path on which it's called to an absolute path.

If the Path represents a directory (line 35), lines 40–41 use Files static method **newDirectoryStream** (lines 40–41) to get a DirectoryStream<Path> containing Path objects for the directory's contents. Lines 43–44 display the String representation of each Path in the DirectoryStream<Path>. Note that DirectoryStream is a generic type like ArrayList (Section 7.16).

The first output of this program demonstrates a Path for the folder containing this chapter's examples. The second output demonstrates a Path for this example's source code file. In both cases, we specified an absolute path.

```java
1   // Fig. 15.2: FileAndDirectoryInfo.java
2   // File class used to obtain file and directory information.
3   import java.io.IOException;
4   import java.nio.file.DirectoryStream;
5   import java.nio.file.Files;
6   import java.nio.file.Path;
7   import java.nio.file.Paths;
8   import java.util.Scanner;
9
10  public class FileAndDirectoryInfo
11  {
12     public static void main(String[] args) throws IOException
13     {
14        Scanner input = new Scanner(System.in);
15
16        System.out.println("Enter file or directory name:");
17
18        // create Path object based on user input
19        Path path = Paths.get(input.nextLine());
20
21        if (Files.exists(path)) // if path exists, output info about it
22        {
23           // display file (or directory) information
24           System.out.printf("%n%s exists%n", path.getFileName());
25           System.out.printf("%s a directory%n",
26              Files.isDirectory(path) ? "Is" : "Is not");
27           System.out.printf("%s an absolute path%n",
28              path.isAbsolute() ? "Is" : "Is not");
29           System.out.printf("Last modified: %s%n",
30              Files.getLastModifiedTime(path));
31           System.out.printf("Size: %s%n", Files.size(path));
32           System.out.printf("Path: %s%n", path);
33           System.out.printf("Absolute path: %s%n", path.toAbsolutePath());
34
35           if (Files.isDirectory(path)) // output directory listing
36           {
37              System.out.printf("%nDirectory contents:%n");
38
39              // object for iterating through a directory's contents
40              DirectoryStream<Path> directoryStream =
41                 Files.newDirectoryStream(path);
42
43              for (Path p : directoryStream)
44                 System.out.println(p);
45           }
46        }
47        else // not file or directory, output error message
48        {
```

Fig. 15.2 | File class used to obtain file and directory information. (Part I of 2.)

```
49              System.out.printf("%s does not exist%n", path);
50          }
51      } // end main
52  } // end class FileAndDirectoryInfo
```

```
Enter file or directory name:
c:\examples\ch15

ch15 exists
Is a directory
Is an absolute path
Last modified: 2013-11-08T19:50:00.838256Z
Size: 4096
Path: c:\examples\ch15
Absolute path: c:\examples\ch15

Directory contents:
C:\examples\ch15\fig15_02
C:\examples\ch15\fig15_12_13
C:\examples\ch15\SerializationApps
C:\examples\ch15\TextFileApps
```

```
Enter file or directory name:
C:\examples\ch15\fig15_02\FileAndDirectoryInfo.java

FileAndDirectoryInfo.java exists
Is not a directory
Is an absolute path
Last modified: 2013-11-08T19:59:01.848255Z
Size: 2952
Path: C:\examples\ch15\fig15_02\FileAndDirectoryInfo.java
Absolute path: C:\examples\ch15\fig15_02\FileAndDirectoryInfo.java
```

Fig. 15.2 | File class used to obtain file and directory information. (Part 2 of 2.)

Error-Prevention Tip 15.1

Once you've confirmed that a Path exists, it's still possible that the methods demonstrated in Fig. 15.2 will throw IOExceptions. For example, the file or directory represented by the Path could be deleted from the system after the call to Files method exists and before the other statements in lines 24–45 execute. Industrial strength file- and directory-processing programs require extensive exception handling to recover from such possibilities.

Separator Characters

A **separator character** is used to separate directories and files in a path. On a Windows computer, the *separator character* is a backslash (\). On a Linux or Mac OS X system, it's a forward slash (/). Java processes both characters identically in a path name. For example, if we were to use the path

```
c:\Program Files\Java\jdk1.6.0_11\demo/jfc
```

which employs each separator character, Java would still process the path properly.

Good Programming Practice 15.1

When building `Strings` *that represent path information, use* `File.separator` *to obtain the local computer's proper separator character rather than explicitly using* / *or* \. *This constant is a* `String` *consisting of one character—the proper separator for the system.*

Common Programming Error 15.1

Using \ *as a directory separator rather than* \\ *in a string literal is a logic error. A single* \ *indicates that the* \ *followed by the next character represents an escape sequence. Use* \\ *to insert a* \ *in a string literal.*

15.4 Sequential-Access Text Files

Next, we create and manipulate *sequential-access files* in which records are stored in order by the record-key field. We begin with *text files*, enabling the reader to quickly create and edit human-readable files. We discuss creating, writing data to, reading data from and updating sequential-access text files. We also include a credit-inquiry program that retrieves data from a file. The programs in Sections 15.4.1—15.4.3 are all in the chapter's `TextFileApps` directory so that they can manipulate the same text file, which is also stored in that directory.

15.4.1 Creating a Sequential-Access Text File

Java imposes no structure on a file—notions such as records do not exist as part of the Java language. Therefore, you must structure files to meet the requirements of your applications. In the following example, we see how to impose a *keyed* record structure on a file.

The program in this section creates a simple sequential-access file that might be used in an accounts receivable system to keep track of the amounts owed to a company by its credit clients. For each client, the program obtains from the user an account number and the client's name and balance (i.e., the amount the client owes the company for goods and services received). Each client's data constitutes a "record" for that client. This application uses the account number as the *record key*—the file's records will be created and maintained in account-number order. The program assumes that the user enters the records in account-number order. In a comprehensive accounts receivable system (based on sequential-access files), a *sorting* capability would be provided so that the user could enter the records in *any* order. The records would then be sorted and written to the file.

Class *CreateTextFile*

Class `CreateTextFile` (Fig. 15.3) uses a `Formatter` to output formatted `Strings`, using the same formatting capabilities as method `System.out.printf`. A `Formatter` object can output to various locations, such as to a command window or to a file, as we do in this example. The `Formatter` object is instantiated in line 26 in method `openFile` (lines 22–38). The constructor used in line 26 takes one argument—a `String` containing the name of the file, including its path. If a path is not specified, as is the case here, the JVM assumes that the file is in the directory from which the program was executed. For text files, we use the `.txt` file extension. If the file does *not* exist, it will be *created*. If an *existing* file is opened, its contents are **truncated**—all the data in the file is *discarded*. If no exception occurs, the file is open for writing and the resulting `Formatter` object can be used to write data to the file.

```
 1  // Fig. 15.3: CreateTextFile.java
 2  // Writing data to a sequential text file with class Formatter.
 3  import java.io.FileNotFoundException;
 4  import java.lang.SecurityException;
 5  import java.util.Formatter;
 6  import java.util.FormatterClosedException;
 7  import java.util.NoSuchElementException;
 8  import java.util.Scanner;
 9
10  public class CreateTextFile
11  {
12     private static Formatter output; // outputs text to a file
13
14     public static void main(String[] args)
15     {
16        openFile();
17        addRecords();
18        closeFile();
19     }
20
21     // open file clients.txt
22     public static void openFile()
23     {
24        try
25        {
26           output = new Formatter("clients.txt"); // open the file
27        }
28        catch (SecurityException securityException)
29        {
30           System.err.println("Write permission denied. Terminating.");
31           System.exit(1); // terminate the program
32        }
33        catch (FileNotFoundException fileNotFoundException)
34        {
35           System.err.println("Error opening file. Terminating.");
36           System.exit(1); // terminate the program
37        }
38     }
39
40     // add records to file
41     public static void addRecords()
42     {
43        Scanner input = new Scanner(System.in);
44        System.out.printf("%s%n%s%n? ",
45           "Enter account number, first name, last name and balance.",
46           "Enter end-of-file indicator to end input.");
47
48        while (input.hasNext()) // loop until end-of-file indicator
49        {
50           try
51           {
```

Fig. 15.3 | Writing data to a sequential text file with class Formatter. (Part 1 of 2.)

```
52                  // output new record to file; assumes valid input
53                  output.format("%d %s %s %.2f%n", input.nextInt(),
54                      input.next(), input.next(), input.nextDouble());
55              }
56              catch (FormatterClosedException formatterClosedException)
57              {
58                  System.err.println("Error writing to file. Terminating.");
59                  break;
60              }
61              catch (NoSuchElementException elementException)
62              {
63                  System.err.println("Invalid input. Please try again.");
64                  input.nextLine(); // discard input so user can try again
65              }
66
67              System.out.print("? ");
68          } // end while
69      } // end method addRecords
70
71      // close file
72      public static void closeFile()
73      {
74          if (output != null)
75              output.close();
76      }
77  } // end class CreateTextFile
```

```
Enter account number, first name, last name and balance.
Enter end-of-file indicator to end input.
? 100 Bob Blue 24.98
? 200 Steve Green -345.67
? 300 Pam White 0.00
? 400 Sam Red -42.16
? 500 Sue Yellow 224.62
? ^Z
```

Fig. 15.3 | Writing data to a sequential text file with class `Formatter`. (Part 2 of 2.)

Lines 28–32 handle the **SecurityException**, which occurs if the user does not have permission to write data to the file. Lines 33–37 handle the **FileNotFoundException**, which occurs if the file does not exist and a new file cannot be created. This exception may also occur if there's an error *opening* the file. In both exception handlers we call `static` method **System.exit** and pass the value 1. This method terminates the application. An argument of 0 to method `exit` indicates *successful* program termination. A nonzero value, such as 1 in this example, normally indicates that an error has occurred. This value is passed to the command window that executed the program. The argument is useful if the program is executed from a **batch file** on Windows systems or a **shell script** on UNIX/Linux/Mac OS X systems. Batch files and shell scripts offer a convenient way of executing several programs in sequence. When the first program ends, the next program begins execution. It's possible to use the argument to method `exit` in a batch file or shell script to determine whether other programs should execute. For more information on batch files or shell scripts, see your operating system's documentation.

Method addRecords (lines 41–69) prompts the user to enter the various fields for each record or the end-of-file key sequence when data entry is complete. Figure 15.4 lists the key combinations for entering end-of-file for various computer systems.

Operating system	Key combination
UNIX/Linux/Mac OS X	*<Enter> <Ctrl> d*
Windows	*<Ctrl> z*

Fig. 15.4 | End-of-file key combinations.

Lines 44–46 prompt the user for input. Line 48 uses Scanner method hasNext to determine whether the end-of-file key combination has been entered. The loop executes until hasNext encounters end-of-file.

Lines 53–54 use a Scanner to read data from the user, then output the data as a record using the Formatter. Each Scanner input method throws a **NoSuchElementException** (handled in lines 61–65) if the data is in the wrong format (e.g., a String when an int is expected) or if there's no more data to input. The record's information is output using method **format**, which can perform identical formatting to the System.out.printf method used extensively in earlier chapters. Method format outputs a formatted String to the output destination of the Formatter object—the file clients.txt. The format string "%d %s %s %.2f%n" indicates that the current record will be stored as an integer (the account number) followed by a String (the first name), another String (the last name) and a floating-point value (the balance). Each piece of information is separated from the next by a space, and the double value (the balance) is output with two digits to the right of the decimal point (as indicated by the .2 in %.2f). The data in the text file can be viewed with a text editor or retrieved later by a program designed to read the file (Section 15.4.2).

When lines 66–68 execute, if the Formatter object is closed, a **FormatterClosedException** will be thrown. This exception is handled in lines 76–80. [*Note:* You can also output data to a text file using class **java.io.PrintWriter**, which provides format and printf methods for outputting formatted data.]

Lines 93–97 declare method closeFile, which closes the Formatter and the underlying output file. Line 96 closes the object by simply calling method **close**. If method close is not called explicitly, the operating system normally will close the file when program execution terminates—this is an example of operating-system "housekeeping." However, you should always explicitly close a file when it's no longer needed.

Sample Output

The sample data for this application is shown in Fig. 15.5. In the sample output, the user enters information for five accounts, then enters end-of-file to signal that data entry is complete. The sample output does not show how the data records actually appear in the file. In the next section, to verify that the file was created successfully, we present a program that reads the file and prints its contents. Because this is a text file, you can also verify the information simply by opening the file in a text editor.

Sample data			
100	Bob	Blue	24.98
200	Steve	Green	-345.67
300	Pam	White	0.00
400	Sam	Red	-42.16
500	Sue	Yellow	224.62

Fig. 15.5 | Sample data for the program in Fig. 15.3.

15.4.2 Reading Data from a Sequential-Access Text File

Data is stored in files so that it may be retrieved for processing when needed. Section 15.4.1 demonstrated how to create a file for sequential access. This section shows how to read data sequentially from a text file. We demonstrate how class Scanner can be used to input data from a file rather than the keyboard. The application (Fig. 15.6) reads records from the file "clients.txt" created by the application of Section 15.4.1 and displays the record contents. Line 13 declares a Scanner that will be used to retrieve input from the file.

```java
1   // Fig. 15.6: ReadTextFile.java
2   // This program reads a text file and displays each record.
3   import java.io.IOException;
4   import java.lang.IllegalStateException;
5   import java.nio.file.Files;
6   import java.nio.file.Path;
7   import java.nio.file.Paths;
8   import java.util.NoSuchElementException;
9   import java.util.Scanner;
10
11  public class ReadTextFile
12  {
13     private static Scanner input;
14
15     public static void main(String[] args)
16     {
17        openFile();
18        readRecords();
19        closeFile();
20     }
21
22     // open file clients.txt
23     public static void openFile()
24     {
25        try
26        {
27           input = new Scanner(Paths.get("clients.txt"));
28        }
```

Fig. 15.6 | Sequential file reading using a Scanner. (Part 1 of 2.)

```
29          catch (IOException ioException)
30          {
31              System.err.println("Error opening file. Terminating.");
32              System.exit(1);
33          }
34      }
35
36      // read record from file
37      public static void readRecords()
38      {
39          System.out.printf("%-10s%-12s%-12s%10s%n", "Account",
40              "First Name", "Last Name", "Balance");
41
42          try
43          {
44              while (input.hasNext()) // while there is more to read
45              {
46                  // display record contents
47                  System.out.printf("%-10d%-12s%-12s%10.2f%n", input.nextInt(),
48                      input.next(), input.next(), input.nextDouble());
49              }
50          }
51          catch (NoSuchElementException elementException)
52          {
53              System.err.println("File improperly formed. Terminating.");
54          }
55          catch (IllegalStateException stateException)
56          {
57              System.err.println("Error reading from file. Terminating.");
58          }
59      } // end method readRecords
60
61      // close file and terminate application
62      public static void closeFile()
63      {
64          if (input != null)
65              input.close();
66      }
67  } // end class ReadTextFile
```

```
Account    First Name   Last Name    Balance
100        Bob          Blue           24.98
200        Steve        Green        -345.67
300        Pam          White          0.00
400        Sam          Red          -42.16
500        Sue          Yellow        224.62
```

Fig. 15.6 | Sequential file reading using a Scanner. (Part 2 of 2.)

Method openFile (lines 23–34) opens the file for reading by instantiating a Scanner object in line 27. We pass a Path object to the constructor, which specifies that the Scanner object will read from the file "clients.txt" located in the directory from which the application executes. If the file cannot be found, an IOException occurs. The exception is handled in lines 29–33.

Method `readRecords` (lines 37–59) reads and displays records from the file. Lines 39–40 display headers for the columns in the application's output. Lines 44–49 read and display data from the file until the *end-of-file marker* is reached (in which case, method `hasNext` will return `false` at line 44). Lines 47–48 use `Scanner` methods `nextInt`, `next` and `nextDouble` to input an `int` (the account number), two `String`s (the first and last names) and a `double` value (the balance). Each record is one line of data in the file. If the information in the file is not properly formed (e.g., there's a last name where there should be a balance), a `NoSuchElementException` occurs when the record is input. This exception is handled in lines 51–54. If the `Scanner` was closed before the data was input, an **IllegalStateException** occurs (handled in lines 55–58). Note in the format string in line 47 that the account number, first name and last name are left justified, while the balance is right justified and output with two digits of precision. Each iteration of the loop inputs one line of text from the text file, which represents one record. Lines 62–66 define method `closeFile`, which closes the `Scanner`.

15.4.3 Case Study: A Credit-Inquiry Program

To retrieve data sequentially from a file, programs start from the beginning of the file and read *all* the data consecutively until the desired information is found. It might be necessary to process the file sequentially several times (from the beginning of the file) during the execution of a program. Class `Scanner` does *not* allow repositioning to the beginning of the file. If it's necessary to read the file again, the program must *close* the file and *reopen* it.

The program in Figs. 15.7–15.8 allows a credit manager to obtain lists of customers with *zero balances* (i.e., customers who do not owe any money), customers with *credit balances* (i.e., customers to whom the company owes money) and customers with *debit balances* (i.e., customers who owe the company money for goods and services received). A credit balance is a *negative* amount, a debit balance a *positive* amount.

MenuOption enum

We begin by creating an `enum` type (Fig. 15.7) to define the different menu options the credit manager will have—this is required if you need to provide specific values for the `enum` constants. The options and their values are listed in lines 7–10.

```
1   // Fig. 15.7: MenuOption.java
2   // enum type for the credit-inquiry program's options.
3
4   public enum MenuOption
5   {
6      // declare contents of enum type
7      ZERO_BALANCE(1),
8      CREDIT_BALANCE(2),
9      DEBIT_BALANCE(3),
10     END(4);
11
12     private final int value; // current menu option
13
```

Fig. 15.7 | `enum` type for the credit-inquiry program's menu options. (Part 1 of 2.)

```
14      // constructor
15      private MenuOption(int value)
16      {
17          this.value = value;
18      }
19  } // end enum MenuOption
```

Fig. 15.7 | enum type for the credit-inquiry program's menu options. (Part 2 of 2.)

CreditInquiry Class

Figure 15.8 contains the functionality for the credit-inquiry program. The program displays a text menu and allows the credit manager to enter one of three options to obtain credit information:

- Option 1 (ZERO_BALANCE) displays accounts with zero balances.
- Option 2 (CREDIT_BALANCE) displays accounts with credit balances.
- Option 3 (DEBIT_BALANCE) displays accounts with debit balances.
- Option 4 (END) terminates program execution.

```
1   // Fig. 15.8: CreditInquiry.java
2   // This program reads a file sequentially and displays the
3   // contents based on the type of account the user requests
4   // (credit balance, debit balance or zero balance).
5   import java.io.IOException;
6   import java.lang.IllegalStateException;
7   import java.nio.file.Paths;
8   import java.util.NoSuchElementException;
9   import java.util.Scanner;
10
11  public class CreditInquiry
12  {
13      private final static MenuOption[] choices = MenuOption.values();
14
15      public static void main(String[] args)
16      {
17          // get user's request (e.g., zero, credit or debit balance)
18          MenuOption accountType = getRequest();
19
20          while (accountType != MenuOption.END)
21          {
22              switch (accountType)
23              {
24                  case ZERO_BALANCE:
25                      System.out.printf("%nAccounts with zero balances:%n");
26                      break;
27                  case CREDIT_BALANCE:
28                      System.out.printf("%nAccounts with credit balances:%n");
29                      break;
```

Fig. 15.8 | Credit-inquiry program. (Part 1 of 4.)

```
30                   case DEBIT_BALANCE:
31                      System.out.printf("%nAccounts with debit balances:%n");
32                      break;
33                }
34
35                readRecords(accountType);
36                accountType = getRequest(); // get user's request
37           }
38      }
39
40      // obtain request from user
41      private static MenuOption getRequest()
42      {
43         int request = 4;
44
45         // display request options
46         System.out.printf("%nEnter request%n%s%n%s%n%s%n%s%n",
47            " 1 - List accounts with zero balances",
48            " 2 - List accounts with credit balances",
49            " 3 - List accounts with debit balances",
50            " 4 - Terminate program");
51
52         try
53         {
54            Scanner input = new Scanner(System.in);
55
56            do // input user request
57            {
58               System.out.printf("%n? ");
59               request = input.nextInt();
60            } while ((request < 1) || (request > 4));
61         }
62         catch (NoSuchElementException noSuchElementException)
63         {
64            System.err.println("Invalid input. Terminating.");
65         }
66
67         return choices[request - 1]; // return enum value for option
68      }
69
70      // read records from file and display only records of appropriate type
71      private static void readRecords(MenuOption accountType)
72      {
73         // open file and process contents
74         try (Scanner input = new Scanner(Paths.get("clients.txt")))
75         {
76            while (input.hasNext()) // more data to read
77            {
78               int accountNumber = input.nextInt();
79               String firstName = input.next();
80               String lastName = input.next();
81               double balance = input.nextDouble();
82
```

Fig. 15.8 | Credit-inquiry program. (Part 2 of 4.)

```
83                 // if proper acount type, display record
84                 if (shouldDisplay(accountType, balance))
85                     System.out.printf("%-10d%-12s%-12s%10.2f%n", accountNumber,
86                         firstName, lastName, balance);
87                 else
88                     input.nextLine(); // discard the rest of the current record
89             }
90         }
91         catch (NoSuchElementException |
92             IllegalStateException | IOException e)
93         {
94             System.err.println("Error processing file. Terminating.");
95             System.exit(1);
96         }
97     } // end method readRecords
98
99     // use record type to determine if record should be displayed
100    private static boolean shouldDisplay(
101        MenuOption accountType, double balance)
102    {
103        if ((accountType == MenuOption.CREDIT_BALANCE) && (balance < 0))
104            return true;
105        else if ((accountType == MenuOption.DEBIT_BALANCE) && (balance > 0))
106            return true;
107        else if ((accountType == MenuOption.ZERO_BALANCE) && (balance == 0))
108            return true;
109
110        return false;
111    }
112 } // end class CreditInquiry
```

```
Enter request
 1 - List accounts with zero balances
 2 - List accounts with credit balances
 3 - List accounts with debit balances
 4 - Terminate program

? 1

Accounts with zero balances:
300        Pam          White              0.00

Enter request
 1 - List accounts with zero balances
 2 - List accounts with credit balances
 3 - List accounts with debit balances
 4 - Terminate program

? 2

Accounts with credit balances:
200        Steve        Green           -345.67
400        Sam          Red             -42.16
```

Fig. 15.8 | Credit-inquiry program. (Part 3 of 4.)

```
Enter request
 1 - List accounts with zero balances
 2 - List accounts with credit balances
 3 - List accounts with debit balances
 4 - Terminate program

? 3

Accounts with debit balances:
100        Bob        Blue              24.98
500        Sue        Yellow           224.62

Enter request
 1 - List accounts with zero balances
 2 - List accounts with credit balances
 3 - List accounts with debit balances
 4 - Terminate program

? 4
```

Fig. 15.8 | Credit-inquiry program. (Part 4 of 4.)

The record information is collected by reading through the file and determining if each record satisfies the criteria for the selected account type. Line 18 in main calls method getRequest (lines 41–68) to display the menu options, translates the number typed by the user into a MenuOption and stores the result in MenuOption variable accountType. Lines 20–37 loop until the user specifies that the program should terminate. Lines 22–33 display a header for the current set of records to be output to the screen. Line 35 calls method readRecords (lines 71–97), which loops through the file and reads every record.

Method readRecords uses a try-with-resources statement (introduced in Section 11.12) to create a Scanner that opens the file for reading (line 74)—recall that try-with-resources will close its resource(s) when the try block terminates successfully or due to an exception. The file will be opened for reading with a new Scanner object each time readRecords is called, so that we can again read from the beginning of the file. Lines 78–81 read a record. Line 84 calls method shouldDisplay (lines 100–111) to determine whether the current record satisfies the account type requested. If shouldDisplay returns true, the program displays the account information. When the *end-of-file marker* is reached, the loop terminates and the try-with-resources statement closes the Scanner and the file. Once all the records have been read, control returns to main and getRequest is again called (line 36) to retrieve the user's next menu option.

15.4.4 Updating Sequential-Access Files

The data in many sequential files cannot be modified without the risk of destroying other data in the file. For example, if the name "White" needs to be changed to "Worthington," the old name cannot simply be overwritten, because the new name requires more space. The record for White was written to the file as

```
300 Pam White 0.00
```

If the record is rewritten beginning at the same location in the file using the new name, the record will be

```
300 Pam Worthington 0.00
```

The new record is larger (has more characters) than the original record. "Worthington" would overwrite the "0.00" in the current record and the characters beyond the second "o" in "Worthington" will overwrite the beginning of the next sequential record in the file. The problem here is that fields in a text file—and hence records—can vary in size. For example, 7, 14, –117, 2074 and 27383 are all ints stored in the same number of bytes (4) internally, but they're different-sized fields when written to a file as text. Therefore, records in a sequential-access file are not usually updated in place—instead, the entire file is rewritten. To make the preceding name change, the records before 300 Pam White 0.00 would be copied to a new file, the new record (which can be of a different size than the one it replaces) would be written and the records after 300 Pam White 0.00 would be copied to the new file. Rewriting the entire file is uneconomical to update just one record, but reasonable if a substantial number of records need to be updated.

15.5 Object Serialization

In Section 15.4, we demonstrated how to write the individual fields of a record into a file as text, and how to read those fields from a file. When the data was output to disk, certain information was lost, such as the type of each value. For instance, if the value "3" is read from a file, there's no way to tell whether it came from an int, a String or a double. We have only data, not type information, on a disk.

Sometimes we want to read an object from or write an object to a file or over a network connection. Java provides **object serialization** for this purposes. A **serialized object** is an object represented as a sequence of bytes that includes the object's data as well as information about the object's type and the types of data stored in the object. After a serialized object has been written into a file, it can be read from the file and **deserialized**—that is, the type information and bytes that represent the object and its data can be used to recreate the object in memory.

Classes *ObjectInputStream* and *ObjectOutputStream*

Classes **ObjectInputStream** and **ObjectOutputStream** (package java.io), which respectively implement the **ObjectInput** and **ObjectOutput** interfaces, enable entire objects to be read from or written to a stream (possibly a file). To use serialization with files, we initialize ObjectInputStream and ObjectOutputStream objects with stream objects that read from and write to files. Initializing stream objects with other stream objects in this manner is sometimes called **wrapping**—the new stream object being created wraps the stream object specified as a constructor argument.

Classes ObjectInputStream and ObjectOutputStream simply read and write the byte-based representation of objects—they don't know where to read the bytes from or write them to. The stream object that you pass to the ObjectInputStream constructor supplies the bytes that the ObjectInputStream converts into objects. Similarly, the stream object that you pass to the ObjectOutputStream constructor takes the byte-based representation of the object that the ObjectOutputStream produces and writes the bytes to the specified destination (e.g., a file, a network connection, etc.).

Interfaces ObjectOutput and ObjectInput

The ObjectOutput interface contains method **writeObject**, which takes an Object as an argument and writes its information to an OutputStream. A class that implements interface ObjectOutput (such as ObjectOutputStream) declares this method and ensures that the object being output implements interface Serializable (discussed shortly). Similarly, the ObjectInput interface contains method **readObject**, which reads and returns a reference to an Object from an InputStream. After an object has been read, its reference can be cast to the object's actual type. Applications that communicate via a network, such as the Internet, can also transmit objects across the network.

15.5.1 Creating a Sequential-Access File Using Object Serialization

This section and Section 15.5.2 create and manipulate sequential-access files using object serialization. The object serialization we show here is performed with byte-based streams, so the sequential files created and manipulated will be *binary files*. Recall that binary files typically cannot be viewed in standard text editors. For this reason, we write a separate application that knows how to read and display serialized objects. We begin by creating and writing serialized objects to a sequential-access file. The example is similar to the one in Section 15.4, so we focus only on the new features.

Defining Class Account

We begin by defining class Account (Fig. 15.9), which encapsulates the client record information used by the serialization examples. These examples and class Account are all located in the SerializationApps directory with the chapter's examples. This allows class Account to be used by both examples, because their files are defined in the same default package. Class Account contains private instance variables account, firstName, lastName and balance (lines 7–10) and *set* and *get* methods for accessing these instance variables. Though the *set* methods do not validate the data in this example, they should do so in an "industrial-strength" system. Class Account implements interface **Serializable** (line 5), which allows objects of this class to be *serialized* and *deserialized* with ObjectOutputStreams and ObjectInputStreams, respectively. Interface Serializable is a **tagging interface**. Such an interface does *not* contain methods. A class that implements Serializable is *tagged* as being a Serializable object. This is important, because an ObjectOutputStream will *not* output an object unless it *is a* Serializable object, which is the case for any object of a class that implements Serializable.

```
 1   // Fig. 15.9: Account.java
 2   // Serializable Account class for storing records as objects.
 3   import java.io.Serializable;
 4
 5   public class Account implements Serializable
 6   {
 7      private int account;
 8      private String firstName;
 9      private String lastName;
10      private double balance;
11
```

Fig. 15.9 | Account class for serializable objects. (Part 1 of 3.)

```
12    // initializes an Account with default values
13    public Account()
14    {
15        this(0, "", "", 0.0); // call other constructor
16    }
17
18    // initializes an Account with provided values
19    public Account(int account, String firstName,
20        String lastName, double balance)
21    {
22        this.account = account;
23        this.firstName = firstName;
24        this.lastName = lastName;
25        this.balance = balance;
26    }
27
28    // set account number
29    public void setAccount(int acct)
30    {
31        this.account = account;
32    }
33
34    // get account number
35    public int getAccount()
36    {
37        return account;
38    }
39
40    // set first name
41    public void setFirstName(String firstName)
42    {
43        this.firstName = firstName;
44    }
45
46    // get first name
47    public String getFirstName()
48    {
49        return firstName;
50    }
51
52    // set last name
53    public void setLastName(String lastName)
54    {
55        this.lastName = lastName;
56    }
57
58    // get last name
59    public String getLastName()
60    {
61        return lastName;
62    }
63
```

Fig. 15.9 | Account class for serializable objects. (Part 2 of 3.)

```
64      // set balance
65      public void setBalance(double balance)
66      {
67          this.balance = balance;
68      }
69
70      // get balance
71      public double getBalance()
72      {
73          return balance;
74      }
75  } // end class Account
```

Fig. 15.9 | Account class for serializable objects. (Part 3 of 3.)

In a Serializable class, every instance variable must be Serializable. Non-Serializable instance variables must be declared **transient** to indicate that they should be ignored during the serialization process. *By default, all primitive-type variables are serializable.* For reference-type variables, you must check the class's documentation (and possibly its superclasses) to ensure that the type is Serializable. For example, Strings are Serializable. By default, arrays *are* serializable; however, in a reference-type array, the referenced objects might *not* be. Class Account contains private data members account, firstName, lastName and balance—all of which are Serializable. This class also provides public *get* and *set* methods for accessing the private fields.

Writing Serialized Objects to a Sequential-Access File
Now let's discuss the code that creates the sequential-access file (Fig. 15.10). We concentrate only on new concepts here. To open the file, line 27 calls Files static method **newOutputStream**, which receives a Path specifying the file to open and, if the file exists, returns an OutputStream that can be used to write to the file. Existing files that are opened for output in this manner are *truncated*. There is no standard filename extension for files that store serialized objects, so we chose the .ser.

```
1   // Fig. 15.10: CreateSequentialFile.java
2   // Writing objects sequentially to a file with class ObjectOutputStream.
3   import java.io.IOException;
4   import java.io.ObjectOutputStream;
5   import java.nio.file.Files;
6   import java.nio.file.Paths;
7   import java.util.NoSuchElementException;
8   import java.util.Scanner;
9
10  public class CreateSequentialFile
11  {
12      private static ObjectOutputStream output; // outputs data to file
13
```

Fig. 15.10 | Sequential file created using ObjectOutputStream. (Part 1 of 3.)

```
14      public static void main(String[] args)
15      {
16         openFile();
17         addRecords();
18         closeFile();
19      }
20
21      // open file clients.ser
22      public static void openFile()
23      {
24         try
25         {
26            output = new ObjectOutputStream(
27               Files.newOutputStream(Paths.get("clients.ser")));
28         }
29         catch (IOException ioException)
30         {
31            System.err.println("Error opening file. Terminating.");
32            System.exit(1); // terminate the program
33         }
34      }
35
36      // add records to file
37      public static void addRecords()
38      {
39         Scanner input = new Scanner(System.in);
40
41         System.out.printf("%s%n%s%n? ",
42            "Enter account number, first name, last name and balance.",
43            "Enter end-of-file indicator to end input.");
44
45         while (input.hasNext()) // loop until end-of-file indicator
46         {
47            try
48            {
49               // create new record; this example assumes valid input
50               Account record = new Account(input.nextInt(),
51                  input.next(), input.next(), input.nextDouble());
52
53               // serialize record object into file
54               output.writeObject(record);
55            }
56            catch (NoSuchElementException elementException)
57            {
58               System.err.println("Invalid input. Please try again.");
59               input.nextLine(); // discard input so user can try again
60            }
61            catch (IOException ioException)
62            {
63               System.err.println("Error writing to file. Terminating.");
64               break;
65            }
```

Fig. 15.10 | Sequential file created using `ObjectOutputStream`. (Part 2 of 3.)

```
66
67                 System.out.print("? ");
68         }
69     }
70
71     // close file and terminate application
72     public static void closeFile()
73     {
74         try
75         {
76             if (output != null)
77                 output.close();
78         }
79         catch (IOException ioException)
80         {
81             System.err.println("Error closing file. Terminating.");
82         }
83     }
84 } // end class CreateSequentialFile
```

```
Enter account number, first name, last name and balance.
Enter end-of-file indicator to end input.
? 100 Bob Blue 24.98
? 200 Steve Green -345.67
? 300 Pam White 0.00
? 400 Sam Red -42.16
? 500 Sue Yellow 224.62
? ^Z
```

Fig. 15.10 | Sequential file created using ObjectOutputStream. (Part 3 of 3.)

Class OutputStream provides methods for outputting byte arrays and individual bytes, but we wish to write *objects* to a file. For this reason, lines 26–27 pass the Input-Stream to class ObjectInputStream's constructor, which *wrap* the OutputStream in an ObjectOutputStream. The ObjectOutputStream object uses the OutputStream to write into the file the bytes that represent entire objects. Lines 26–27 might throw an **IOExcep-tion** if a problem occurs while opening the file (e.g., when a file is opened for writing on a drive with insufficient space or when a read-only file is opened for writing). If so, the program displays an error message (lines 29–33). If no exception occurs, the file is open, and variable output can be used to write objects to it.

This program assumes that data is input correctly and in the proper record-number order. Method addRecords (lines 37–69) performs the write operation. Lines 50–51 create an Account object from the data entered by the user. Line 54 calls ObjectOutput-Stream method writeObject to write the record object to the output file. Only one state-ment is required to write the *entire* object.

Method closeFile (lines 72–83) calls ObjectOutputStream method **close** on output to close both the ObjectOutputStream *and* its underlying OutputStream. The call to method close is contained in a try block, because close throws an IOException if the file cannot be closed properly. When using *wrapped* streams, closing the outermost stream *also* closes the wrapped stream as well.

In the sample execution for the program in Fig. 15.10, we entered information for five accounts—the same information shown in Fig. 15.5. The program does not show how the data records actually appear in the file. Remember that now we're using *binary files*, which are not humanly readable. To verify that the file has been created successfully, the next section presents a program to read the file's contents.

15.5.2 Reading and Deserializing Data from a Sequential-Access File

The preceding section showed how to create a file for sequential access using object serialization. In this section, we discuss how to *read serialized data* sequentially from a file.

The program in Fig. 15.11 reads records from a file created by the program in Section 15.5.1 and displays the contents. The program opens the file for input by calling `Files` static method **newInputStream**, which receives a `Path` specifying the file to open and, if the file exists, returns an `InputStream` that can be used to read from the file. In Fig. 15.10, we wrote objects to the file, using an `ObjectOutputStream` object. Data must be read from the file in the same format in which it was written. Therefore, we use an `ObjectInputStream` *wrapped* around an `InputStream` (lines 26–27). If no exceptions occur when opening the file, variable `input` can be used to read objects from the file.

```
 1   // Fig. 15.11: ReadSequentialFile.java
 2   // Reading a file of objects sequentially with ObjectInputStream
 3   // and displaying each record.
 4   import java.io.EOFException;
 5   import java.io.IOException;
 6   import java.io.ObjectInputStream;
 7   import java.nio.file.Files;
 8   import java.nio.file.Paths;
 9
10   public class ReadSequentialFile
11   {
12      private static ObjectInputStream input;
13
14      public static void main(String[] args)
15      {
16         openFile();
17         readRecords();
18         closeFile();
19      }
20
21      // enable user to select file to open
22      public static void openFile()
23      {
24         try // open file
25         {
26            input = new ObjectInputStream(
27               Files.newInputStream(Paths.get("clients.ser")));
28         }
29         catch (IOException ioException)
30         {
```

Fig. 15.11 | Reading a file of objects sequentially with `ObjectInputStream` and displaying each record. (Part 1 of 3.)

```
31              System.err.println("Error opening file.");
32              System.exit(1);
33          }
34      }
35
36      // read record from file
37      public static void readRecords()
38      {
39          System.out.printf("%-10s%-12s%-12s%10s%n", "Account",
40              "First Name", "Last Name", "Balance");
41
42          try
43          {
44              while (true) // loop until there is an EOFException
45              {
46                  Account record = (Account) input.readObject();
47
48                  // display record contents
49                  System.out.printf("%-10d%-12s%-12s%10.2f%n",
50                      record.getAccount(), record.getFirstName(),
51                      record.getLastName(), record.getBalance());
52              }
53          }
54          catch (EOFException endOfFileException)
55          {
56              System.out.printf("%No more records%n");
57          }
58          catch (ClassNotFoundException classNotFoundException)
59          {
60              System.err.println("Invalid object type. Terminating.");
61          }
62          catch (IOException ioException)
63          {
64              System.err.println("Error reading from file. Terminating.");
65          }
66      } // end method readRecords
67
68      // close file and terminate application
69      public static void closeFile()
70      {
71          try
72          {
73              if (input != null)
74                  input.close();
75          }
76          catch (IOException ioException)
77          {
78              System.err.println("Error closing file. Terminating.");
79              System.exit(1);
80          }
81      }
82  } // end class ReadSequentialFile
```

Fig. 15.11 | Reading a file of objects sequentially with `ObjectInputStream` and displaying each record. (Part 2 of 3.)

```
Account    First Name  Last Name       Balance
100        Bob         Blue              24.98
200        Steve       Green           -345.67
300        Pam         White             0.00
400        Sam         Red             -42.16
500        Sue         Yellow          224.62

No more records
```

Fig. 15.11 | Reading a file of objects sequentially with `ObjectInputStream` and displaying each record. (Part 3 of 3.)

The program reads records from the file in method `readRecords` (lines 37–66). Line 46 calls `ObjectInputStream` method `readObject` to read an `Object` from the file. To use `Account`-specific methods, we *downcast* the returned `Object` to type `Account`. Method `readObject` throws an **EOFException** (processed at lines 54–57) if an attempt is made to read beyond the end of the file. Method `readObject` throws a `ClassNotFoundException` if the class for the object being read cannot be located. This may occur if the file is accessed on a computer that does not have the class.

Software Engineering Observation 15.1

This section introduced object serialization and demonstrated basic serialization techniques. Serialization is a deep subject with many traps and pitfalls. Before implementing object serialization in industrial-strength applications, carefully read the online Java documentation for object serialization.

15.6 Opening Files with `JFileChooser`

Class `JFileChooser` displays a dialog that enables the user to easily select files or directories. To demonstrate `JFileChooser`, we enhance the example in Section 15.3, as shown in Figs. 15.12–15.13. The example now contains a graphical user interface, but still displays the same data as before. The constructor calls method `analyzePath` in line 24. This method then calls method `getFileOrDirectoryPath` in line 31 to retrieve a `Path` object representing the selected file or directory.

Method `getFileOrDirectoryPath` (lines 71–85 of Fig. 15.12) creates a `JFile-Chooser` (line 74). Lines 75–76 call method **setFileSelectionMode** to specify what the user can select from the `fileChooser`. For this program, we use `JFileChooser static` constant **FILES_AND_DIRECTORIES** to indicate that files and directories can be selected. Other `static` constants include **FILES_ONLY** (the default) and **DIRECTORIES_ONLY**.

Line 77 calls method **showOpenDialog** to display the `JFileChooser` dialog titled **Open**. Argument `this` specifies the `JFileChooser` dialog's parent window, which determines the position of the dialog on the screen. If `null` is passed, the dialog is displayed in the center of the screen—otherwise, the dialog is centered over the application window (specified by the argument `this`). A `JFileChooser` dialog is a *modal dialog* that does not allow the user to interact with any other window in the program until the dialog is closed. The user selects the drive, directory or filename, then clicks **Open**. Method `showOpenDialog` returns an integer specifying which button (**Open** or **Cancel**) the user clicked to close the dialog. Line

48 tests whether the user clicked **Cancel** by comparing the result with static constant **CANCEL_OPTION**. If they're equal, the program terminates. Line 84 calls JFileChooser method **getSelectedFile** to retrieve a File object (package java.io) representing the file or directory that the user selected, then calls File method **toPath** to return a Path object. The program then displays information about the selected file or directory.

```java
1   // Fig. 15.12: JFileChooserDemo.java
2   // Demonstrating JFileChooser.
3   import java.io.IOException;
4   import java.nio.file.DirectoryStream;
5   import java.nio.file.Files;
6   import java.nio.file.Path;
7   import java.nio.file.Paths;
8   import javax.swing.JFileChooser;
9   import javax.swing.JFrame;
10  import javax.swing.JOptionPane;
11  import javax.swing.JScrollPane;
12  import javax.swing.JTextArea;
13
14  public class JFileChooserDemo extends JFrame
15  {
16     private final JTextArea outputArea; // displays file contents
17
18     // set up GUI
19     public JFileChooserDemo() throws IOException
20     {
21        super("JFileChooser Demo");
22        outputArea = new JTextArea();
23        add(new JScrollPane(outputArea)); // outputArea is scrollable
24        analyzePath(); // get Path from user and display info
25     }
26
27     // display information about file or directory user specifies
28     public void analyzePath() throws IOException
29     {
30        // get Path to user-selected file or directory
31        Path path = getFileOrDirectoryPath();
32
33        if (path != null && Files.exists(path)) // if exists, display info
34        {
35           // gather file (or directory) information
36           StringBuilder builder = new StringBuilder();
37           builder.append(String.format("%s:%n", path.getFileName()));
38           builder.append(String.format("%s a directory%n",
39              Files.isDirectory(path) ? "Is" : "Is not"));
40           builder.append(String.format("%s an absolute path%n",
41              path.isAbsolute() ? "Is" : "Is not"));
42           builder.append(String.format("Last modified: %s%n",
43              Files.getLastModifiedTime(path)));
44           builder.append(String.format("Size: %s%n", Files.size(path)));
45           builder.append(String.format("Path: %s%n", path));
```

Fig. 15.12 | Demonstrating JFileChooser. (Part 1 of 2.)

```
46          builder.append(String.format("Absolute path: %s%n",
47              path.toAbsolutePath())));
48
49          if (Files.isDirectory(path)) // output directory listing
50          {
51              builder.append(String.format("%nDirectory contents:%n"));
52
53              // object for iterating through a directory's contents
54              DirectoryStream<Path> directoryStream =
55                  Files.newDirectoryStream(path);
56
57              for (Path p : directoryStream)
58                  builder.append(String.format("%s%n", p));
59          }
60
61          outputArea.setText(builder.toString()); // display String content
62      }
63      else // Path does not exist
64      {
65          JOptionPane.showMessageDialog(this, path.getFileName() +
66              " does not exist.", "ERROR", JOptionPane.ERROR_MESSAGE);
67      }
68  } // end method analyzePath
69
70  // allow user to specify file or directory name
71  private Path getFileOrDirectoryPath()
72  {
73      // configure dialog allowing selection of a file or directory
74      JFileChooser fileChooser = new JFileChooser();
75      fileChooser.setFileSelectionMode(
76          JFileChooser.FILES_AND_DIRECTORIES);
77      int result = fileChooser.showOpenDialog(this);
78
79      // if user clicked Cancel button on dialog, return
80      if (result == JFileChooser.CANCEL_OPTION)
81          System.exit(1);
82
83      // return Path representing the selected file
84      return fileChooser.getSelectedFile().toPath();
85  }
86 } // end class JFileChooserDemo
```

Fig. 15.12 | Demonstrating `JFileChooser`. (Part 2 of 2.)

```
1  // Fig. 15.13: JFileChooserTest.java
2  // Tests class JFileChooserDemo.
3  import java.io.IOException;
4  import javax.swing.JFrame;
5
6  public class JFileChooserTest
7  {
```

Fig. 15.13 | Testing class `FileDemonstration`. (Part 1 of 2.)

```
 8        public static void main(String[] args) throws IOException
 9        {
10            JFileChooserDemo application = new JFileChooserDemo();
11            application.setSize(400, 400);
12            application.setDefaultCloseOperation(JFrame.EXIT_ON_CLOSE);
13            application.setVisible(true);
14        }
15    } // end class JFileChooserTest
```

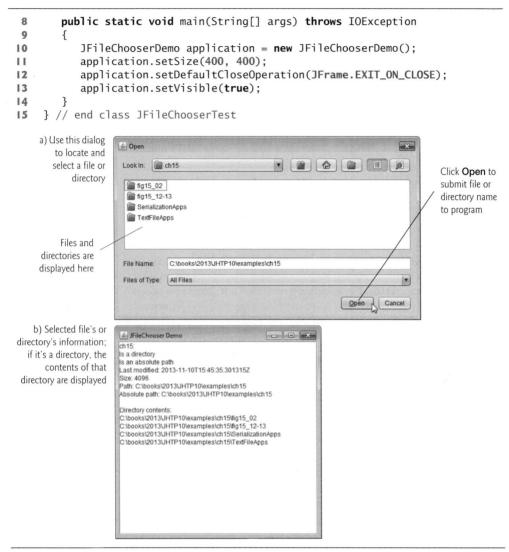

Fig. 15.13 | Testing class FileDemonstration. (Part 2 of 2.)

15.7 (Optional) Additional java.io Classes

This section overviews additional interfaces and classes (from package java.io).

15.7.1 Interfaces and Classes for Byte-Based Input and Output

InputStream and OutputStream are abstract classes that declare methods for performing byte-based input and output, respectively.

Pipe Streams

Pipes are synchronized communication channels between threads. We discuss threads in Chapter 20. Java provides **PipedOutputStream** (a subclass of OutputStream) and **Piped-**

InputStream (a subclass of InputStream) to establish pipes between two threads in a program. One thread sends data to another by writing to a PipedOutputStream. The target thread reads information from the pipe via a PipedInputStream.

Filter Streams

A **FilterInputStream** filters an InputStream, and a FilterOutputStream filters an OutputStream. **Filtering** means simply that the filter stream provides additional functionality, such as aggregating bytes into meaningful primitive-type units. FilterInputStream and FilterOutputStream are typically used as superclasses, so some of their filtering capabilities are provided by their subclasses.

A **PrintStream** (a subclass of FilterOutputStream) performs text output to the specified stream. Actually, we've been using PrintStream output throughout the text to this point—System.out and System.err are PrintStream objects.

Data Streams

Reading data as raw bytes is fast, but crude. Usually, programs read data as aggregates of bytes that form ints, floats, doubles and so on. Java programs can use several classes to input and output data in aggregate form.

Interface DataInput describes methods for reading primitive types from an input stream. Classes **DataInputStream** and RandomAccessFile each implement this interface to read sets of bytes and view them as primitive-type values. Interface DataInput includes methods such as readBoolean, readByte, readChar, readDouble, readFloat, readFully (for byte arrays), readInt, readLong, readShort, readUnsignedByte, readUnsignedShort, readUTF (for reading Unicode characters encoded by Java—we discuss UTF encoding in Appendix H) and skipBytes.

Interface DataOutput describes a set of methods for writing primitive types to an output stream. Classes **DataOutputStream** (a subclass of FilterOutputStream) and RandomAccessFile each implement this interface to write primitive-type values as bytes. Interface DataOutput includes overloaded versions of method write (for a byte or for a byte array) and methods writeBoolean, writeByte, writeBytes, writeChar, writeChars (for Unicode Strings), writeDouble, writeFloat, writeInt, writeLong, writeShort and writeUTF (to output text modified for Unicode).

Buffered Streams

Buffering is an I/O-performance-enhancement technique. With a **BufferedOutputStream** (a subclass of class FilterOutputStream), each output statement does *not* necessarily result in an actual physical transfer of data to the output device (which is a slow operation compared to processor and main memory speeds). Rather, each output operation is directed to a region in memory called a **buffer** that's large enough to hold the data of many output operations. Then, actual transfer to the output device is performed in one large **physical output operation** each time the buffer fills. The output operations directed to the output buffer in memory are often called **logical output operations**. With a BufferedOutputStream, a partially filled buffer can be forced out to the device at any time by invoking the stream object's **flush** method.

Using buffering can greatly increase the performance of an application. Typical I/O operations are extremely slow compared with the speed of accessing data in computer memory. Buffering reduces the number of I/O operations by first combining smaller outputs together in memory. The number of actual physical I/O operations is small compared with the number of I/O requests issued by the program. Thus, the program that's using buffering is more efficient.

> **Performance Tip 15.1**
> *Buffered I/O can yield significant performance improvements over unbuffered I/O.*

With a **BufferedInputStream** (a subclass of class FilterInputStream), many "logical" chunks of data from a file are read as one large **physical input operation** into a memory buffer. As a program requests each new chunk of data, it's taken from the buffer. (This procedure is sometimes referred to as a **logical input operation**.) When the buffer is empty, the next actual physical input operation from the input device is performed to read in the next group of "logical" chunks of data. Thus, the number of actual physical input operations is small compared with the number of read requests issued by the program.

Memory-Based **byte** Array Steams
Java stream I/O includes capabilities for inputting from byte arrays in memory and outputting to byte arrays in memory. A ByteArrayInputStream (a subclass of InputStream) reads from a byte array in memory. A ByteArrayOutputStream (a subclass of Output-Stream) outputs to a byte array in memory. One use of byte-array I/O is *data validation*. A program can input an entire line at a time from the input stream into a byte array. Then a validation routine can scrutinize the contents of the byte array and correct the data if necessary. Finally, the program can proceed to input from the byte array, "knowing" that the input data is in the proper format. Outputting to a byte array is a nice way to take advantage of the powerful output-formatting capabilities of Java streams. For example, data can be stored in a byte array, using the same formatting that will be displayed at a later time, and the byte array can then be output to a file to preserve the formatting.

Sequencing Input from Multiple Streams
A SequenceInputStream (a subclass of InputStream) logically concatenates several Input-Streams—the program sees the group as one continuous InputStream. When the program reaches the end of one input stream, that stream closes, and the next stream in the sequence opens.

15.7.2 Interfaces and Classes for Character-Based Input and Output
In addition to the byte-based streams, Java provides the **Reader** and **Writer** abstract classes, which are character-based streams like those you used for text-file processing in Section 15.4. Most of the byte-based streams have corresponding character-based concrete Reader or Writer classes.

Character-Based Buffering *Readers* and *Writers*
Classes **BufferedReader** (a subclass of abstract class Reader) and **BufferedWriter** (a subclass of abstract class Writer) enable buffering for character-based streams. Remember that character-based streams use Unicode characters—such streams can process data in any language that the Unicode character set represents.

*Memory-Based **char** Array **Readers** and **Writers***

Classes **CharArrayReader** and **CharArrayWriter** read and write, respectively, a stream of characters to a char array. A **LineNumberReader** (a subclass of BufferedReader) is a buffered character stream that keeps track of the number of lines read—newlines, returns and carriage-return–line-feed combinations increment the line count. Keeping track of line numbers can be useful if the program needs to inform the reader of an error on a specific line.

*Character-Based File, Pipe and String **Readers** and **Writers***

An InputStream can be converted to a Reader via class **InputStreamReader**. Similarly, an OutputStream can be converted to a Writer via class **OutputStreamWriter**. Class File-Reader (a subclass of InputStreamReader) and class FileWriter (a subclass of Output-StreamWriter) read characters from and write characters to a file, respectively. Class **PipedReader** and class **PipedWriter** implement piped-character streams for transferring data between threads. Class **StringReader** and **StringWriter** read characters from and write characters to Strings, respectively. A PrintWriter writes characters to a stream.

15.8 Wrap-Up

In this chapter, you learned how to manipulate persistent data. We compared byte-based and character-based streams, and introduced several classes from packages java.io and java.nio.file. You used classes Files and Paths and interfaces Path and Directory-Stream to retrieve information about files and directories. You used sequential-access file processing to manipulate records that are stored in order by the record-key field. You learned the differences between text-file processing and object serialization, and used serialization to store and retrieve entire objects. The chapter concluded with a small example of using a JFileChooser dialog to allow users to easily select files from a GUI. The next chapter discusses Java's classes for manipulating collections of data—such as class Array-List, which we introduced in Section 7.16.

16

Generic Collections

Objectives

In this chapter you'll:

- Learn what collections are.
- Use class **Arrays** for array manipulations.
- Learn the type-wrapper classes that enable programs to process primitive data values as objects.
- Use prebuilt generic data structures from the collections framework.
- Use iterators to "walk through" a collection.
- Use persistent hash tables manipulated with objects of class **Properties**.
- Learn about synchronization and modifiability wrappers.

16.1 Introduction

In Section 7.16, we introduced the generic ArrayList collection—a dynamically resizable array-like data structure that stores references to objects of a type that you specify when you create the ArrayList. In this chapter, we continue our discussion of the Java **collections framework**, which contains many other *prebuilt* generic data-structures.

Some examples of collections are your favorite songs stored on your smartphone or media player, your contacts list, the cards you hold in a card game, the members of your favorite sports team and the courses you take at once in school.

We discuss the collections-framework interfaces that declare the capabilities of each collection type, various classes that implement these interfaces, methods that process collection objects, and **iterators** that "walk through" collections.

Java SE 8
After reading Chapter 17, Java SE 8 Lambdas and Streams, you'll be able to reimplement many of Chapter 16's examples in a more concise and elegant manner, and in a way that makes them easier to parallelize to improve performance on today's multi-core systems. In Chapter 20, Concurrency, you'll learn how to improve performance on multi-core systems using Java's *concurrent collections* and *parallel stream* operations.

16.2 Collections Overview

A **collection** is a data structure—actually, an object—that can hold references to other objects. Usually, collections contain references to objects of any type that has the *is-a* relationship with the type stored in the collection. The collections-framework interfaces declare the operations to be performed generically on various types of collections. Figure 16.1 lists some of the collections framework interfaces. Several implementations of these interfaces are provided within the framework. You may also provide your own implementations.

Interface	Description
Collection	The root interface in the collections hierarchy from which interfaces Set, Queue and List are derived.
Set	A collection that does *not* contain duplicates.
List	An ordered collection that *can* contain duplicate elements.
Map	A collection that associates keys to values and *cannot* contain duplicate keys. Map does not derive from Collection.
Queue	Typically a *first-in, first-out* collection that models a *waiting line*; other orders can be specified.

Fig. 16.1 | Some collections-framework interfaces.

Object-Based Collections

The collections framework classes and interfaces are members of package java.util. In early Java versions, the collections framework classes stored and manipulated *only* Object references, enabling you to store *any* object in a collection, because all classes directly or indirectly derive from class Object. Programs normally need to process *specific* types of objects. As a result, the Object references obtained from a collection need to be *downcast* to an appropriate type to allow the program to process the objects correctly. As we discussed in Chapter 10, downcasting generally should be avoided.

Generic Collections

To elminate this problem, the collections framework was enhanced with the *generics* capabilities that we introduced with generic ArrayLists in Chapter 7 and that we discuss in more detail in Chapter 18, Generic Classes and Methods. Generics enable you to specify the *exact type* that will be stored in a collection and give you the benefits of *compile-time type checking*—the compiler issues error messages if you use inappropriate types in your collections. Once you specify the type stored in a generic collection, any reference you retrieve from the collection will have that type. This eliminates the need for explicit type casts that can throw ClassCastExceptions if the referenced object is *not* of the appropriate type. In addition, the generic collections are *backward compatible* with Java code that was written before generics were introduced.

Good Programming Practice 16.1

Avoid reinventing the wheel—rather than building your own data structures, use the interfaces and collections from the Java collections framework, which have been carefully tested and tuned to meet most application requirements.

Choosing a Collection

The documentation for each collection discusses its memory requirements and its methods' performance characteristics for operations such as adding and removing elements, searching for elements, sorting elements and more. Before choosing a collection, review the online documentation for the collection category you're considering (Set, List, Map, Queue, etc.), then choose the implementation that best meets your application's needs.

16.3 Type-Wrapper Classes

Each primitive type (listed in Appendix D) has a corresponding **type-wrapper class** (in package java.lang). These classes are called **Boolean**, **Byte**, **Character**, **Double**, **Float**, **Integer**, **Long** and **Short**. These enable you to manipulate primitive-type values as objects. This is important because Java's predefined data structures manipulate and share *objects*—they cannot manipulate variables of primitive types. However, they can manipulate objects of the type-wrapper classes, because every class ultimately derives from Object.

Each of the numeric type-wrapper classes—Byte, Short, Integer, Long, Float and Double—extends class Number. Also, the type-wrapper classes are final classes, so you cannot extend them. Primitive types do not have methods, so the methods related to a primitive type are located in the corresponding type-wrapper class (e.g., method parseInt, which converts a String to an int value, is located in class Integer).

16.4 Autoboxing and Auto-Unboxing

Java provides boxing and unboxing conversions that automatically convert between primitive-type values and type-wrapper objects. A **boxing conversion** converts a value of a primitive type to an object of the corresponding type-wrapper class. An **unboxing conversion** converts an object of a type-wrapper class to a value of the corresponding primitive type. These conversions are performed automatically—called **autoboxing** and **auto-unboxing**. Consider the following statements:

```
Integer[] integerArray = new Integer[5]; // create integerArray
integerArray[0] = 10; // assign Integer 10 to integerArray[0]
int value = integerArray[0]; // get int value of Integer
```

In this case, autoboxing occurs when assigning an int value (10) to integerArray[0], because integerArray stores references to Integer objects, not int values. Auto-unboxing occurs when assigning integerArray[0] to int variable value, because variable value stores an int value, not a reference to an Integer object. Boxing conversions also occur in conditions, which can evaluate to primitive boolean values or Boolean objects. Many of the examples in this chapter use these conversions to store primitive values in and retrieve them from data structures.

16.5 Interface Collection and Class Collections

Interface Collection contains **bulk operations** (i.e., operations performed on an *entire* collection) for operations such as *adding*, *clearing* and *comparing* objects (or elements) in a collection. A Collection can also be converted to an array. In addition, interface Collection provides a method that returns an **Iterator** object, which allows a program to walk through the collection and remove elements from it during the iteration. We discuss class Iterator in Section 16.6.1. Other methods of interface Collection enable a program to determine a collection's *size* and whether a collection is *empty*.

Software Engineering Observation 16.1

Collection is used commonly as a parameter type in methods to allow polymorphic processing of all objects that implement interface Collection.

Software Engineering Observation 16.2

Most collection implementations provide a constructor that takes a Collection argument, thereby allowing a new collection to be constructed containing the elements of the specified collection.

Class **Collections** provides static methods that *search*, *sort* and perform other operations on collections. Section 16.7 discusses more about Collections methods. We also cover Collections' **wrapper methods** that enable you to treat a collection as a *synchronized collection* (Section 16.13) or an *unmodifiable collection* (Section 16.14). Synchronized collections are for use with multithreading (discussed in Chapter 20), which enables programs to perform operations *in parallel*. When two or more threads of a program *share* a collection, problems might occur. As an analogy, consider a traffic intersection. If all cars were allowed to access the intersection at the same time, collisions might occur. For this reason, traffic lights are provided to control access to the intersection. Similarly, we can *synchronize* access to a collection to ensure that only *one* thread manipulates the collection at a time. The synchronization wrapper methods of class Collections return synchronized versions of collections that can be shared among threads in a program. Unmodifiable collections are useful when clients of a class need to *view* a collection's elements, but they should *not* be allowed to *modify* the collection by adding and removing elements.

16.6 Lists

A List (sometimes called a **sequence**) is an *ordered* Collection that can contain duplicate elements. Like array indices, List indices are zero based (i.e., the first element's index is zero). In addition to the methods inherited from Collection, List provides methods for manipulating elements via their indices, manipulating a specified range of elements, searching for elements and obtaining a **ListIterator** to access the elements.

Interface List is implemented by several classes, including **ArrayList**, **LinkedList** and **Vector**. Autoboxing occurs when you add primitive-type values to objects of these classes, because they store only references to objects. Classes ArrayList and Vector are resizable-array implementations of List. Inserting an element between existing elements of an ArrayList or Vector is an *inefficient* operation—all elements after the new one must be moved out of the way, which could be an expensive operation in a collection with a large number of elements. A LinkedList enables *efficient* insertion (or removal) of elements in the middle of a collection, but is much less efficient than an ArrayList for jumping to a specific element in the collection.

ArrayList and Vector have nearly identical behaviors. Operations on Vectors are *synchronized* by default, whereas those on ArrayLists are not. Also, class Vector is from Java 1.0, before the collections framework was added to Java. As such, Vector has some methods that are not part of interface List and are not implemented in class ArrayList. For example, Vector methods addElement and add both append an element to a Vector, but only method add is specified in interface List and implemented by ArrayList. *Unsynchronized collections provide better performance than synchronized ones.* For this reason, Array-

List is typically preferred over Vector in programs that do not share a collection among threads. Separately, the Java collections API provides *synchronization wrappers* (Section 16.13) that can be used to add synchronization to the unsynchronized collections, and several powerful synchronized collections are available in the Java concurrency APIs.

Performance Tip 16.1
ArrayLists behave like Vectors without synchronization and therefore execute faster than Vectors, because ArrayLists do not have the overhead of thread synchronization.

Software Engineering Observation 16.3
LinkedLists can be used to create stacks, queues and deques (double-ended queues, pronounced "decks"). The collections framework provides implementations of some of these data structures.

The following three subsections demonstrate the List and Collection capabilities. Section 16.6.1 removes elements from an ArrayList with an Iterator. Section 16.6.2 uses ListIterator and several List- and LinkedList-specific methods.

16.6.1 ArrayList and Iterator

Figure 16.2 uses an ArrayList (introduced in Section 7.16) to demonstrate several capabilities of interface Collection. The program places two Color arrays in ArrayLists and uses an Iterator to remove elements in the second ArrayList collection from the first.

```
1   // Fig. 16.2: CollectionTest.java
2   // Collection interface demonstrated via an ArrayList object.
3   import java.util.List;
4   import java.util.ArrayList;
5   import java.util.Collection;
6   import java.util.Iterator;
7
8   public class CollectionTest
9   {
10     public static void main(String[] args)
11     {
12        // add elements in colors array to list
13        String[] colors = {"MAGENTA", "RED", "WHITE", "BLUE", "CYAN"};
14        List<String> list = new ArrayList<String>();
15
16        for (String color : colors)
17           list.add(color); // adds color to end of list
18
19        // add elements in removeColors array to removeList
20        String[] removeColors = {"RED", "WHITE", "BLUE"};
21        List<String> removeList = new ArrayList<String>();
22
23        for (String color : removeColors)
24           removeList.add(color);
25
```

Fig. 16.2 | Collection interface demonstrated via an ArrayList object. (Part 1 of 2.)

```
26          // output list contents
27          System.out.println("ArrayList: ");
28
29          for (int count = 0; count < list.size(); count++)
30             System.out.printf("%s ", list.get(count));
31
32          // remove from list the colors contained in removeList
33          removeColors(list, removeList);
34
35          // output list contents
36          System.out.printf("%n%nArrayList after calling removeColors:%n");
37
38          for (String color : list)
39             System.out.printf("%s ", color);
40       }
41
42       // remove colors specified in collection2 from collection1
43       private static void removeColors(Collection<String> collection1,
44          Collection<String> collection2)
45       {
46          // get iterator
47          Iterator<String> iterator = collection1.iterator();
48
49          // loop while collection has items
50          while (iterator.hasNext())
51          {
52             if (collection2.contains(iterator.next()))
53                iterator.remove(); // remove current element
54          }
55       }
56    } // end class CollectionTest
```

```
ArrayList:
MAGENTA RED WHITE BLUE CYAN

ArrayList after calling removeColors:
MAGENTA CYAN
```

Fig. 16.2 | Collection interface demonstrated via an ArrayList object. (Part 2 of 2.)

Lines 13 and 20 declare and initialize String arrays colors and removeColors. Lines 14 and 21 create ArrayList<String> objects and assign their references to List<String> variables list and removeList, respectively. Recall that ArrayList is a *generic* class, so we can specify a *type argument* (String in this case) to indicate the type of the elements in each list. Because you specify the type to store in a collection at compile time, generic collections provide compile-time *type safety* that allows the compiler to catch attempts to use invalid types. For example, you cannot store Employees in a collection of Strings.

Lines 16–17 populate list with Strings stored in array colors, and lines 23–24 populate removeList with Strings stored in array removeColors using **List method add**. Lines 29–30 output each element of list. Line 29 calls **List method size** to get the number of elements in the ArrayList. Line 30 uses **List method get** to retrieve individual element values. Lines 29–30 also could have used the enhanced `for` statement (which we'll demonstrate with collections in other examples).

Line 33 calls method `removeColors` (lines 43–55), passing `list` and `removeList` as arguments. Method `removeColors` deletes the `Strings` in `removeList` from the `Strings` in `list`. Lines 38–39 print `list`'s elements after `removeColors` completes its task.

Method `removeColors` declares two `Collection<String>` parameters (lines 43–44)—any two `Collections` containing `Strings` can be passed as arguments. The method accesses the elements of the first `Collection` (`collection1`) via an `Iterator`. Line 47 calls **`Collection` method `iterator`** to get an `Iterator` for the `Collection`. Interfaces `Collection` and `Iterator` are generic types. The loop-continuation condition (line 50) calls **`Iterator` method `hasNext`** to determine whether there are more elements to iterate through. Method `hasNext` returns `true` if another element exists and `false` otherwise.

The `if` condition in line 52 calls **`Iterator` method `next`** to obtain a reference to the next element, then uses method **`contains`** of the second `Collection` (`collection2`) to determine whether `collection2` contains the element returned by `next`. If so, line 53 calls **`Iterator` method `remove`** to remove the element from the `Collection` `collection1`.

Common Programming Error 16.1

If a collection is modified by one of its methods after an iterator is created for that collection, the iterator immediately becomes invalid—any operation performed with the iterator fails immediate and throws a `ConcurrentModificationException`. For this reason, iterators are said to be "fail fast." Fail-fast iterators help ensure that a modifiable collection is not manipulated by two or more threads at the same time, which could corrupt the collection. In Chapter 20, Concurrency, you'll learn about concurrent collections (package `java.util.concurrent`) that can be safely manipulated by multiple concurrent threads.

Software Engineering Observation 16.4

We refer to the `ArrayLists` in this example via `List` variables. This makes our code more flexible and easier to modify—if we later determine that `LinkedLists` would be more appropriate, only the lines where we created the `ArrayList` objects (lines 14 and 21) need to be modified. In general, when you create a collection object, refer to that object with a variable of the corresponding collection interface type.

Type Inference with the <> Notation

Lines 14 and 21 specify the type stored in the `ArrayList` (that is, `String`) on the left and right sides of the initialization statements. Java SE 7 introduced *type inferencing* with the `<>` notation—known as the **diamond notation**—in statements that declare and create generic type variables and objects. For example, line 14 can be written as:

```
List<String> list = new ArrayList<>();
```

In this case, Java uses the type in angle brackets on the left of the declaration (that is, `String`) as the type stored in the `ArrayList` created on the right side of the declaration. We'll use this syntax for the remaining examples in this chapter.

16.6.2 LinkedList

Figure 16.3 demonstrates various operations on `LinkedLists`. The program creates two `LinkedLists` of `Strings`. The elements of one `List` are added to the other. Then all the `Strings` are converted to uppercase, and a range of elements is deleted.

```java
 1   // Fig. 16.3: ListTest.java
 2   // Lists, LinkedLists and ListIterators.
 3   import java.util.List;
 4   import java.util.LinkedList;
 5   import java.util.ListIterator;
 6
 7   public class ListTest
 8   {
 9      public static void main(String[] args)
10      {
11         // add colors elements to list1
12         String[] colors =
13            {"black", "yellow", "green", "blue", "violet", "silver"};
14         List<String> list1 = new LinkedList<>();
15
16         for (String color : colors)
17            list1.add(color);
18
19         // add colors2 elements to list2
20         String[] colors2 =
21            {"gold", "white", "brown", "blue", "gray", "silver"};
22         List<String> list2 = new LinkedList<>();
23
24         for (String color : colors2)
25            list2.add(color);
26
27         list1.addAll(list2); // concatenate lists
28         list2 = null; // release resources
29         printList(list1); // print list1 elements
30
31         convertToUppercaseStrings(list1); // convert to uppercase string
32         printList(list1); // print list1 elements
33
34         System.out.printf("%nDeleting elements 4 to 6...");
35         removeItems(list1, 4, 7); // remove items 4-6 from list
36         printList(list1); // print list1 elements
37         printReversedList(list1); // print list in reverse order
38      }
39
40      // output List contents
41      private static void printList(List<String> list)
42      {
43         System.out.printf("%nlist:%n");
44
45         for (String color : list)
46            System.out.printf("%s ", color);
47
48         System.out.println();
49      }
50
51      // locate String objects and convert to uppercase
52      private static void convertToUppercaseStrings(List<String> list)
53      {
```

Fig. 16.3 | Lists, LinkedLists and ListIterators. (Part 1 of 2.)

```
54          ListIterator<String> iterator = list.listIterator();
55
56          while (iterator.hasNext())
57          {
58              String color = iterator.next(); // get item
59              iterator.set(color.toUpperCase()); // convert to upper case
60          }
61      }
62
63      // obtain sublist and use clear method to delete sublist items
64      private static void removeItems(List<String> list,
65          int start, int end)
66      {
67          list.subList(start, end).clear(); // remove items
68      }
69
70      // print reversed list
71      private static void printReversedList(List<String> list)
72      {
73          ListIterator<String> iterator = list.listIterator(list.size());
74
75          System.out.printf("%nReversed List:%n");
76
77          // print list in reverse order
78          while (iterator.hasPrevious())
79              System.out.printf("%s ", iterator.previous());
80      }
81  } // end class ListTest
```

```
list:
black yellow green blue violet silver gold white brown blue gray silver

list:
BLACK YELLOW GREEN BLUE VIOLET SILVER GOLD WHITE BROWN BLUE GRAY SILVER

Deleting elements 4 to 6...
list:
BLACK YELLOW GREEN BLUE WHITE BROWN BLUE GRAY SILVER

Reversed List:
SILVER GRAY BLUE BROWN WHITE BLUE GREEN YELLOW BLACK
```

Fig. 16.3 | Lists, LinkedLists and ListIterators. (Part 2 of 2.)

Lines 14 and 22 create LinkedLists list1 and list2 of type String. LinkedList is a generic class that has one type parameter for which we specify the type argument String in this example. Lines 16–17 and 24–25 call List method add to *append* elements from arrays colors and colors2 to the *ends* of list1 and list2, respectively.

Line 27 calls **List method addAll** to *append all elements* of list2 to the end of list1. Line 28 sets list2 to null, because list2 is no longer needed. Line 29 calls method printList (lines 41–49) to output list1's contents. Line 31 calls method convertToUppercaseStrings (lines 52–61) to convert each String element to uppercase, then line 32 calls printList again to display the modified Strings. Line 35 calls method removeItems (lines 64–68) to remove the range of elements starting at index 4 up to, but not including, index 7 of the list. Line 37 calls method printReversedList (lines 71–80) to print the list in reverse order.

Method convertToUppercaseStrings

Method convertToUppercaseStrings (lines 52–61) changes lowercase String elements in its List argument to uppercase Strings. Line 54 calls **List method listIterator** to get the List's **bidirectional iterator** (i.e., one that can traverse a List *backward* or *forward*). ListIterator is also a generic class. In this example, the ListIterator references String objects, because method listIterator is called on a List of Strings. Line 56 calls method hasNext to determine whether the List *contains another element*. Line 58 gets the next String in the List. Line 59 calls **String method toUpperCase** to get an uppercase version of the String and calls **ListIterator method set** to replace the current String to which iterator refers with the String returned by method toUpperCase. Like method toUpperCase, **String method toLowerCase** returns a lowercase version of the String.

Method removeItems

Method removeItems (lines 64–68) *removes a range of items* from the list. Line 67 calls **List method subList** to obtain a portion of the List (called a **sublist**). This is called a **range-view method**, which enables the program to view a portion of the list. The sublist is simply a view into the List on which subList is called. Method subList takes as arguments the beginning and ending index for the sublist. The ending index is *not* part of the range of the sublist. In this example, line 35 passes 4 for the beginning index and 7 for the ending index to subList. The sublist returned is the set of elements with indices 4 through 6. Next, the program calls **List method clear** on the sublist to remove the elements of the sublist from the List. Any changes made to a sublist are also made to the original List.

Method printReversedList

Method printReversedList (lines 71–80) prints the list backward. Line 73 calls List method listIterator with the starting position as an argument (in our case, the last element in the list) to get a *bidirectional iterator* for the list. **List method size** returns the number of items in the List. The while condition (line 78) calls **ListIterator's hasPrevious method** to determine whether there are more elements while traversing the list *backward*. Line 79 calls **ListIterator's previous method** to get the previous element from the list and outputs it to the standard output stream.

Views into Collections and Arrays Method asList

Class Arrays provides static method **asList** to *view* an array (sometimes called the **backing array**) as a **List** collection. A List view allows you to manipulate the array as if it were a list. This is useful for adding the elements in an array to a collection and for sorting array elements. The next example demonstrates how to create a LinkedList with a List view of an array, because we cannot pass the array to a LinkedList constructor. Sorting array elements with a List view is demonstrated in Fig. 16.7. Any modifications made through the List view change the array, and any modifications made to the array change the List view. The only operation permitted on the view returned by asList is *set*, which changes the value of the view and the backing array. Any other attempts to change the view (such as adding or removing elements) result in an **UnsupportedOperationException**.

Viewing Arrays as Lists and Converting Lists to Arrays

Figure 16.4 uses Arrays method asList to view an array as a List and uses **List method toArray** to get an array from a LinkedList collection. The program calls method asList to create a List view of an array, which is used to initialize a LinkedList object, then adds a series of Strings to the LinkedList and calls method toArray to obtain an array containing references to the Strings.

```
 1   // Fig. 16.4: UsingToArray.java
 2   // Viewing arrays as Lists and converting Lists to arrays.
 3   import java.util.LinkedList;
 4   import java.util.Arrays;
 5
 6   public class UsingToArray
 7   {
 8      // creates a LinkedList, adds elements and converts to array
 9      public static void main(String[] args)
10      {
11         String[] colors = {"black", "blue", "yellow"};
12         LinkedList<String> links = new LinkedList<>(Arrays.asList(colors));
13
14         links.addLast("red"); // add as last item
15         links.add("pink"); // add to the end
16         links.add(3, "green"); // add at 3rd index
17         links.addFirst("cyan"); // add as first item
18
19         // get LinkedList elements as an array
20         colors = links.toArray(new String[links.size()]);
21
22         System.out.println("colors: ");
23
24         for (String color : colors)
25            System.out.println(color);
26      }
27   } // end class UsingToArray
```

```
colors:
cyan
black
blue
yellow
green
red
pink
```

Fig. 16.4 | Viewing arrays as Lists and converting Lists to arrays.

Line 12 constructs a LinkedList of Strings containing the elements of array colors. Arrays method asList returns a List view of the array, then uses that to initialize the LinkedList with its constructor that receives a Collection as an argument (a List *is a* Collection). Line 14 calls **LinkedList method addLast** to add "red" to the end of links. Lines 15–16 call **LinkedList method add** to add "pink" as the last element and "green" as the element at index 3 (i.e., the fourth element). Method addLast (line 14) functions identically to method add (line 15). Line 17 calls **LinkedList method addFirst** to add "cyan" as the new first item in the LinkedList. The add operations are permitted because they operate on the LinkedList object, not the view returned by asList. [*Note:* When "cyan" is added as the first element, "green" becomes the fifth element in the LinkedList.]

Line 20 calls the List interface's toArray method to get a String array from links. The array is a copy of the list's elements—modifying the array's contents does *not* modify the list. The array passed to method toArray is of the same type that you'd like method toArray to return. If the number of elements in that array is greater than or equal to the number of elements in the LinkedList, toArray copies the list's elements into its array argument and returns that array. If the LinkedList has more elements than the number of elements in the array passed to toArray, toArray *allocates a new array* of the same type it receives as an argument, *copies* the list's elements into the new array and returns the new array.

Common Programming Error 16.2

Passing an array that contains data to toArray can cause logic errors. If the number of elements in the array is smaller than the number of elements in the list on which toArray is called, a new array is allocated to store the list's elements—without preserving the array argument's elements. If the number of elements in the array is greater than the number of elements in the list, the elements of the array (starting at index zero) are overwritten with the list's elements. Array elements that are not overwritten retain their values.

16.7 Collections Methods

Class Collections provides several high-performance algorithms for manipulating collection elements. The algorithms (Fig. 16.5) are implemented as static methods. The methods sort, binarySearch, reverse, shuffle, fill and copy operate on Lists. Methods min, max, addAll, frequency and disjoint operate on Collections.

Method	Description
sort	Sorts the elements of a List.
binarySearch	Locates an object in a List, using the high-performance binary search algorithm which we introduced in Section 7.15.
reverse	Reverses the elements of a List.
shuffle	Randomly orders a List's elements.
fill	Sets every List element to refer to a specified object.
copy	Copies references from one List into another.
min	Returns the smallest element in a Collection.
max	Returns the largest element in a Collection.
addAll	Appends all elements in an array to a Collection.
frequency	Calculates how many collection elements are equal to the specified element.
disjoint	Determines whether two collections have no elements in common.

Fig. 16.5 | Collections methods.

Software Engineering Observation 16.5

The collections framework methods are polymorphic. That is, each can operate on objects that implement specific interfaces, regardless of the underlying implementations.

16.7.1 Method sort

Method **sort** sorts the elements of a List, which must implement the **Comparable** interface. The order is determined by the natural order of the elements' type as implemented by a compareTo method. For example, the natural order for numeric values is ascending order, and the natural order for Strings is based on their lexicographical ordering (Section 14.3). Method compareTo is declared in interface Comparable and is sometimes called the **natural comparison method**. The sort call may specify as a second argument a **Comparator** object that determines an alternative ordering of the elements.

Sorting in Ascending Order

Figure 16.6 uses Collections method sort to order the elements of a List in *ascending* order (line 17). Method sort performs an iterative merge sort. Line 14 creates list as a List of Strings. Lines 15 and 18 each use an *implicit* call to the list's toString method to output the list contents in the format shown in the output.

```java
1   // Fig. 16.6: Sort1.java
2   // Collections method sort.
3   import java.util.List;
4   import java.util.Arrays;
5   import java.util.Collections;
6
7   public class Sort1
8   {
9      public static void main(String[] args)
10     {
11        String[] suits = {"Hearts", "Diamonds", "Clubs", "Spades"};
12
13        // Create and display a list containing the suits array elements
14        List<String> list = Arrays.asList(suits);
15        System.out.printf("Unsorted array elements: %s%n", list);
16
17        Collections.sort(list); // sort ArrayList
18        System.out.printf("Sorted array elements: %s%n", list);
19     }
20  } // end class Sort1
```

```
Unsorted array elements: [Hearts, Diamonds, Clubs, Spades]
Sorted array elements: [Clubs, Diamonds, Hearts, Spades]
```

Fig. 16.6 | Collections method sort.

Sorting in Descending Order

Figure 16.7 sorts the same list of strings used in Fig. 16.6 in *descending* order. The example introduces the Comparator interface, which is used for sorting a Collection's elements in a different order. Line 18 calls Collections's method sort to order the List in descending order. The static **Collections method reverseOrder** returns a Comparator object that orders the collection's elements in reverse order.

```
1   // Fig. 16.7: Sort2.java
2   // Using a Comparator object with method sort.
3   import java.util.List;
4   import java.util.Arrays;
5   import java.util.Collections;
6
7   public class Sort2
8   {
9      public static void main(String[] args)
10     {
11        String[] suits = {"Hearts", "Diamonds", "Clubs", "Spades"};
12
13        // Create and display a list containing the suits array elements
14        List<String> list = Arrays.asList(suits); // create List
15        System.out.printf("Unsorted array elements: %s%n", list);
16
17        // sort in descending order using a comparator
18        Collections.sort(list, Collections.reverseOrder());
19        System.out.printf("Sorted list elements: %s%n", list);
20     }
21  } // end class Sort2
```

```
Unsorted array elements: [Hearts, Diamonds, Clubs, Spades]
Sorted list elements: [Spades, Hearts, Diamonds, Clubs]
```

Fig. 16.7 | Collections method sort with a Comparator object.

Sorting with a *Comparator*

Figure 16.8 creates a custom Comparator class, named TimeComparator, that implements interface Comparator to compare two Time2 objects. Class Time2, declared in Fig. 8.5, represents times with hours, minutes and seconds.

```
1   // Fig. 16.8: TimeComparator.java
2   // Custom Comparator class that compares two Time2 objects.
3   import java.util.Comparator;
4
5   public class TimeComparator implements Comparator<Time2>
6   {
7      @Override
8      public int compare(Time2 time1, Time2 time2)
9      {
10        int hourDifference = time1.getHour() - time2.getHour();
11
12        if (hourDifference != 0) // test the hour first
13           return hourCompare;
```

Fig. 16.8 | Custom Comparator class that compares two Time2 objects. (Part 1 of 2.)

```
14
15          int minuteDifference = time1.getMinute() - time2.getMinute();
16
17          if (minuteDifference != 0) // then test the minute
18             return minuteDifference;
19
20          int secondDifference = time1.getSecond() - time2.getSecond();
21          return secondDifference;
22       }
23    } // end class TimeComparator
```

Fig. 16.8 | Custom `Comparator` class that compares two `Time2` objects. (Part 2 of 2.)

Class `TimeComparator` implements interface `Comparator`, a generic type that takes one type argument (in this case `Time2`). A class that implements `Comparator` must declare a `compare` method that receives two arguments and returns a *negative* integer if the first argument is *less than* the second, 0 if the arguments are *equal* or a *positive* integer if the first argument is *greater than* the second. Method `compare` (lines 7–22) performs comparisons between `Time2` objects. Line 10 calculates the difference between the hours of the two `Time2` objects. If the hours are different (line 12), then we return this value. If this value is *positive*, then the first hour is greater than the second and the first time is greater than the second. If this value is *negative*, then the first hour is less than the second and the first time is less than the second. If this value is zero, the hours are the same and we must test the minutes (and maybe the seconds) to determine which time is greater.

Figure 16.9 sorts a list using the custom `Comparator` class `TimeComparator`. Line 11 creates an `ArrayList` of `Time2` objects. Recall that both `ArrayList` and `List` are generic types and accept a type argument that specifies the element type of the collection. Lines 13–17 create five `Time2` objects and add them to this list. Line 23 calls method `sort`, passing it an object of our `TimeComparator` class (Fig. 16.8).

```
1    // Fig. 16.9: Sort3.java
2    // Collections method sort with a custom Comparator object.
3    import java.util.List;
4    import java.util.ArrayList;
5    import java.util.Collections;
6
7    public class Sort3
8    {
9       public static void main(String[] args)
10      {
11         List<Time2> list = new ArrayList<>(); // create List
12
13         list.add(new Time2(6, 24, 34));
14         list.add(new Time2(18, 14, 58));
15         list.add(new Time2(6, 05, 34));
16         list.add(new Time2(12, 14, 58));
17         list.add(new Time2(6, 24, 22));
18
```

Fig. 16.9 | Collections method `sort` with a custom `Comparator` object. (Part 1 of 2.)

```
19          // output List elements
20          System.out.printf("Unsorted array elements:%n%s%n", list);
21
22          // sort in order using a comparator
23          Collections.sort(list, new TimeComparator());
24
25          // output List elements
26          System.out.printf("Sorted list elements:%n%s%n", list);
27      }
28  } // end class Sort3
```

```
Unsorted array elements:
[6:24:34 AM, 6:14:58 PM, 6:05:34 AM, 12:14:58 PM, 6:24:22 AM]
Sorted list elements:
[6:05:34 AM, 6:24:22 AM, 6:24:34 AM, 12:14:58 PM, 6:14:58 PM]
```

Fig. 16.9 | Collections method sort with a custom Comparator object. (Part 2 of 2.)

16.7.2 Method shuffle

Method **shuffle** randomly orders a List's elements. Chapter 7 presented a card shuffling and dealing simulation that shuffled a deck of cards with a loop. Figure 16.10 uses method shuffle to shuffle a deck of Card objects that might be used in a card-game simulator.

```
1   // Fig. 16.10: DeckOfCards.java
2   // Card shuffling and dealing with Collections method shuffle.
3   import java.util.List;
4   import java.util.Arrays;
5   import java.util.Collections;
6
7   // class to represent a Card in a deck of cards
8   class Card
9   {
10     public static enum Face {Ace, Deuce, Three, Four, Five, Six,
11         Seven, Eight, Nine, Ten, Jack, Queen, King };
12     public static enum Suit {Clubs, Diamonds, Hearts, Spades};
13
14     private final Face face;
15     private final Suit suit;
16
17     // constructor
18     public Card(Face face, Suit suit)
19     {
20         this.face = face;
21         this.suit = suit;
22     }
23
24     // return face of the card
25     public Face getFace()
26     {
```

Fig. 16.10 | Card shuffling and dealing with Collections method shuffle. (Part 1 of 3.)

```
27          return face;
28       }
29
30       // return suit of Card
31       public Suit getSuit()
32       {
33          return suit;
34       }
35
36       // return String representation of Card
37       public String toString()
38       {
39          return String.format("%s of %s", face, suit);
40       }
41    } // end class Card
42
43    // class DeckOfCards declaration
44    public class DeckOfCards
45    {
46       private List<Card> list; // declare List that will store Cards
47
48       // set up deck of Cards and shuffle
49       public DeckOfCards()
50       {
51          Card[] deck = new Card[52];
52          int count = 0; // number of cards
53
54          // populate deck with Card objects
55          for (Card.Suit suit: Card.Suit.values())
56          {
57             for (Card.Face face: Card.Face.values())
58             {
59                deck[count] = new Card(face, suit);
60                ++count;
61             }
62          }
63
64          list = Arrays.asList(deck); // get List
65          Collections.shuffle(list);  // shuffle deck
66       } // end DeckOfCards constructor
67
68       // output deck
69       public void printCards()
70       {
71          // display 52 cards in two columns
72          for (int i = 0; i < list.size(); i++)
73             System.out.printf("%-19s%s", list.get(i),
74                ((i + 1) % 4 == 0) ? "%n" : "");
75       }
76
77       public static void main(String[] args)
78       {
```

Fig. 16.10 | Card shuffling and dealing with Collections method shuffle. (Part 2 of 3.)

```
79          DeckOfCards cards = new DeckOfCards();
80          cards.printCards();
81      }
82  } // end class DeckOfCards
```

Deuce of Clubs	Six of Spades	Nine of Diamonds	Ten of Hearts
Three of Diamonds	Five of Clubs	Deuce of Diamonds	Seven of Clubs
Three of Spades	Six of Diamonds	King of Clubs	Jack of Hearts
Ten of Spades	King of Diamonds	Eight of Spades	Six of Hearts
Nine of Clubs	Ten of Diamonds	Eight of Diamonds	Eight of Hearts
Ten of Clubs	Five of Hearts	Ace of Clubs	Deuce of Hearts
Queen of Diamonds	Ace of Diamonds	Four of Clubs	Nine of Hearts
Ace of Spades	Deuce of Spades	Ace of Hearts	Jack of Diamonds
Seven of Diamonds	Three of Hearts	Four of Spades	Four of Diamonds
Seven of Spades	King of Hearts	Seven of Hearts	Five of Diamonds
Eight of Clubs	Three of Clubs	Queen of Clubs	Queen of Spades
Six of Clubs	Nine of Spades	Four of Hearts	Jack of Clubs
Five of Spades	King of Spades	Jack of Spades	Queen of Hearts

Fig. 16.10 | Card shuffling and dealing with `Collections` method `shuffle`. (Part 3 of 3.)

Class `Card` (lines 8–41) represents a card in a deck of cards. Each `Card` has a face and a suit. Lines 10–12 declare two enum types—`Face` and `Suit`—which represent the face and the suit of the card, respectively. Method `toString` (lines 37–40) returns a `String` containing the face and suit of the `Card` separated by the string `" of "`. When an enum constant is converted to a `String`, the constant's identifier is used as the `String` representation. Normally we would use all uppercase letters for enum constants. In this example, we chose to use capital letters for only the first letter of each enum constant because we want the card to be displayed with initial capital letters for the face and the suit (e.g., `"Ace of Spades"`).

Lines 55–62 populate the deck array with cards that have unique face and suit combinations. Both `Face` and `Suit` are `public static` enum types of class `Card`. To use these enum types outside of class `Card`, you must qualify each enum's type name with the name of the class in which it resides (i.e., `Card`) and a dot (`.`) separator. Hence, lines 55 and 57 use `Card.Suit` and `Card.Face` to declare the control variables of the `for` statements. Recall that method `values` of an enum type returns an array that contains all the constants of the enum type. Lines 55–62 use enhanced `for` statements to construct 52 new `Cards`.

The shuffling occurs in line 65, which calls `static` method `shuffle` of class `Collections` to shuffle the elements of the array. Method `shuffle` requires a `List` argument, so we must obtain a `List` view of the array before we can shuffle it. Line 64 invokes `static` method `asList` of class `Arrays` to get a `List` view of the deck array.

Method `printCards` (lines 69–75) displays the deck of cards in four columns. In each iteration of the loop, lines 73–74 output a card left justified in a 19-character field followed by either a newline or an empty string based on the number of cards output so far. If the number of cards is divisible by 4, a newline is output; otherwise, the empty string is output.

16.7.3 Methods reverse, fill, copy, max and min

Class `Collections` provides methods for *reversing*, *filling* and *copying* Lists. **Collections method reverse** reverses the order of the elements in a `List`, and **method fill** *overwrites* elements in a List with a specified value. The fill operation is useful for reinitializing a List. **Method copy** takes two arguments—a destination List and a source List. Each source List element is copied to the destination List. The destination List must be at least as long as the source List; otherwise, an IndexOutOfBoundsException occurs. If the destination List is longer, the elements not overwritten are unchanged.

Each method we've seen so far operates on Lists. Methods **min** and **max** each operate on any Collection. Method min returns the smallest element in a Collection, and method max returns the largest element in a Collection. Both of these methods can be called with a Comparator object as a second argument to perform *custom comparisons* of objects, such as the TimeComparator in Fig. 16.9. Figure 16.11 demonstrates methods reverse, fill, copy, max and min.

```java
 1   // Fig. 16.11: Algorithms1.java
 2   // Collections methods reverse, fill, copy, max and min.
 3   import java.util.List;
 4   import java.util.Arrays;
 5   import java.util.Collections;
 6
 7   public class Algorithms1
 8   {
 9      public static void main(String[] args)
10      {
11         // create and display a List<Character>
12         Character[] letters = {'P', 'C', 'M'};
13         List<Character> list = Arrays.asList(letters); // get List
14         System.out.println("list contains: ");
15         output(list);
16
17         // reverse and display the List<Character>
18         Collections.reverse(list); // reverse order the elements
19         System.out.printf("%nAfter calling reverse, list contains:%n");
20         output(list);
21
22         // create copyList from an array of 3 Characters
23         Character[] lettersCopy = new Character[3];
24         List<Character> copyList = Arrays.asList(lettersCopy);
25
26         // copy the contents of list into copyList
27         Collections.copy(copyList, list);
28         System.out.printf("%nAfter copying, copyList contains:%n");
29         output(copyList);
30
31         // fill list with Rs
32         Collections.fill(list, 'R');
33         System.out.printf("%nAfter calling fill, list contains:%n");
34         output(list);
35      }
36
37      // output List information
38      private static void output(List<Character> listRef)
39      {
```

Fig. 16.11 | Collections methods reverse, fill, copy, max and min. (Part 1 of 2.)

```
40          System.out.print("The list is: ");
41
42          for (Character element : listRef)
43              System.out.printf("%s ", element);
44
45          System.out.printf("%nMax: %s", Collections.max(listRef));
46          System.out.printf("  Min: %s%n", Collections.min(listRef));
47      }
48  } // end class Algorithms1
```

```
list contains:
The list is: P C M
Max: P  Min: C

After calling reverse, list contains:
The list is: M C P
Max: P  Min: C

After copying, copyList contains:
The list is: M C P
Max: P  Min: C

After calling fill, list contains:
The list is: R R R
Max: R  Min: R
```

Fig. 16.11 | Collections methods reverse, fill, copy, max and min. (Part 2 of 2.)

Line 13 creates List<Character> variable list and initializes it with a List view of the Character array letters. Lines 14–15 output the current contents of the List. Line 18 calls Collections method reverse to reverse the order of list. Method reverse takes one List argument. Since list is a List view of array letters, the array's elements are now in reverse order. The reversed contents are output in lines 19–20. Line 27 uses Collections method copy to copy list's elements into copyList. Changes to copyList do not change letters, because copyList is a separate List that's not a List view of the array letters. Method copy requires two List arguments—the destination List and the source List. Line 32 calls Collections method fill to place the character 'R' in each list element. Because list is a List view of the array letters, this operation changes each element in letters to 'R'. Method fill requires a List for the first argument and an Object for the second argument—in this case, the Object is the *boxed* version of the character 'R'. Lines 45–46 call Collections methods max and min to find the largest and the smallest element of a Collection, respectively. Recall that interface List extends interface Collection, so a List *is a* Collection.

16.7.4 Method binarySearch

The high-speed binary search algorithm is built into the Java collections framework as a static **Collections method binarySearch**. This method locates an object in a List (e.g., a LinkedList or an ArrayList). If the object is found, its index is returned. If the object is not found, binarySearch returns a negative value. Method binarySearch determines this negative value by first calculating the insertion point and making its sign negative. Then, binarySearch subtracts 1 from the insertion point to obtain the return value, which guarantees that method binarySearch returns positive numbers (>= 0) if and only if the object is found. If multiple elements in the list match the search key, there's no guarantee which one will be located first. Figure 16.12 uses method binarySearch to search for a series of strings in an ArrayList.

```java
1   // Fig. 16.12: BinarySearchTest.java
2   // Collections method binarySearch.
3   import java.util.List;
4   import java.util.Arrays;
5   import java.util.Collections;
6   import java.util.ArrayList;
7
8   public class BinarySearchTest
9   {
10     public static void main(String[] args)
11     {
12        // create an ArrayList<String> from the contents of colors array
13        String[] colors = {"red", "white", "blue", "black", "yellow",
14           "purple", "tan", "pink"};
15        List<String> list =
16           new ArrayList<>(Arrays.asList(colors));
17
18        Collections.sort(list); // sort the ArrayList
19        System.out.printf("Sorted ArrayList: %s%n", list);
20
21        // search list for various values
22        printSearchResults(list, "black"); // first item
23        printSearchResults(list, "red"); // middle item
24        printSearchResults(list, "pink"); // last item
25        printSearchResults(list, "aqua"); // below lowest
26        printSearchResults(list, "gray"); // does not exist
27        printSearchResults(list, "teal"); // does not exist
28     }
29
30     // perform search and display result
31     private static void printSearchResults(
32        List<String> list, String key)
33     {
34        int result = 0;
35
36        System.out.printf("%nSearching for: %s%n", key);
37        result = Collections.binarySearch(list, key);
38
39        if (result >= 0)
40           System.out.printf("Found at index %d%n", result);
41        else
42           System.out.printf("Not Found (%d)%n",result);
43     }
44   } // end class BinarySearchTest
```

Fig. 16.12 | Collections method binarySearch. (Part 1 of 2.)

```
Sorted ArrayList: [black, blue, pink, purple, red, tan, white, yellow]

Searching for: black
Found at index 0

Searching for: red
Found at index 4

Searching for: pink
Found at index 2

Searching for: aqua
Not Found (-1)

Searching for: gray
Not Found (-3)

Searching for: teal
Not Found (-7)
```

Fig. 16.12 | Collections method binarySearch. (Part 2 of 2.)

Lines 15–16 initialize list with an ArrayList containing a copy of the elements in array colors. Collections method binarySearch expects its List argument's elements to be sorted in *ascending* order, so line 18 uses Collections method sort to sort the list. If the List argument's elements are *not* sorted, the result of using binarySearch is *undefined*. Line 19 outputs the sorted list. Lines 22–27 call method printSearchResults (lines 31–43) to perform searches and output the results. Line 37 calls Collections method binarySearch to search list for the specified key. Method binarySearch takes a List as the first argument and an Object as the second argument. Lines 39–42 output the results of the search. An overloaded version of binarySearch takes a Comparator object as its third argument, which specifies how binarySearch should compare the search key to the List's elements.

16.7.5 Methods addAll, frequency and disjoint

Class Collections also provides the methods addAll, frequency and disjoint. **Collections method addAll** takes two arguments—a Collection into which to *insert* the new element(s) and an array that provides elements to be inserted. **Collections method frequency** takes two arguments—a Collection to be searched and an Object to be searched for in the collection. Method frequency returns the number of times that the second argument appears in the collection. **Collections method disjoint** takes two Collections and returns true if they have *no elements in common*. Figure 16.13 demonstrates the use of methods addAll, frequency and disjoint.

```
1   // Fig. Fig. 16.13: Algorithms2.java
2   // Collections methods addAll, frequency and disjoint.
3   import java.util.ArrayList;
4   import java.util.List;
5   import java.util.Arrays;
6   import java.util.Collections;
```

Fig. 16.13 | Collections methods addAll, frequency and disjoint. (Part 1 of 2.)

```
 7
 8    public class Algorithms2
 9    {
10       public static void main(String[] args)
11       {
12          // initialize list1 and list2
13          String[] colors = {"red", "white", "yellow", "blue"};
14          List<String> list1 = Arrays.asList(colors);
15          ArrayList<String> list2 = new ArrayList<>();
16
17          list2.add("black"); // add "black" to the end of list2
18          list2.add("red"); // add "red" to the end of list2
19          list2.add("green"); // add "green" to the end of list2
20
21          System.out.print("Before addAll, list2 contains: ");
22
23          // display elements in list2
24          for (String s : list2)
25             System.out.printf("%s ", s);
26
27          Collections.addAll(list2, colors); // add colors Strings to list2
28
29          System.out.printf("%nAfter addAll, list2 contains: ");
30
31          // display elements in list2
32          for (String s : list2)
33             System.out.printf("%s ", s);
34
35          // get frequency of "red"
36          int frequency = Collections.frequency(list2, "red");
37          System.out.printf(
38             "%nFrequency of red in list2: %d%n", frequency);
39
40          // check whether list1 and list2 have elements in common
41          boolean disjoint = Collections.disjoint(list1, list2);
42
43          System.out.printf("list1 and list2 %s elements in common%n",
44             (disjoint ? "do not have" : "have"));
45       }
46    } // end class Algorithms2
```

```
Before addAll, list2 contains: black red green
After addAll, list2 contains: black red green red white yellow blue
Frequency of red in list2: 2
list1 and list2 have elements in common
```

Fig. 16.13 | Collections methods addAll, frequency and disjoint. (Part 2 of 2.)

Line 14 initializes list1 with elements in array colors, and lines 17–19 add Strings "black", "red" and "green" to list2. Line 27 invokes method addAll to add elements in array colors to list2. Line 36 gets the frequency of String "red" in list2 using method frequency. Line 41 invokes method disjoint to test whether Collections list1 and list2 have elements in common, which they do in this example.

16.8 Stack Class of Package java.util

In this section, we investigate class **Stack** in the Java utilities package (java.util). Class Stack extends class Vector to implement a stack data structure. Figure 16.14 demonstrates several Stack methods. For the details of class Stack, visit http://docs.oracle.com/javase/7/docs/api/java/util/Stack.html.

```java
1   // Fig. 16.14: StackTest.java
2   // Stack class of package java.util.
3   import java.util.Stack;
4   import java.util.EmptyStackException;
5
6   public class StackTest
7   {
8      public static void main(String[] args)
9      {
10        Stack<Number> stack = new Stack<>(); // create a Stack
11
12        // use push method
13        stack.push(12L); // push long value 12L
14        System.out.println("Pushed 12L");
15        printStack(stack);
16        stack.push(34567); // push int value 34567
17        System.out.println("Pushed 34567");
18        printStack(stack);
19        stack.push(1.0F); // push float value 1.0F
20        System.out.println("Pushed 1.0F");
21        printStack(stack);
22        stack.push(1234.5678); // push double value 1234.5678
23        System.out.println("Pushed 1234.5678 ");
24        printStack(stack);
25
26        // remove items from stack
27        try
28        {
29           Number removedObject = null;
30
31           // pop elements from stack
32           while (true)
33           {
34              removedObject = stack.pop(); // use pop method
35              System.out.printf("Popped %s%n", removedObject);
36              printStack(stack);
37           }
38        }
39        catch (EmptyStackException emptyStackException)
40        {
41           emptyStackException.printStackTrace();
42        }
43     }
44
```

Fig. 16.14 | Stack class of package java.util. (Part 1 of 2.)

```
45        // display Stack contents
46        private static void printStack(Stack<Number> stack)
47        {
48           if (stack.isEmpty())
49              System.out.printf("stack is empty%n%n"); // the stack is empty
50           else // stack is not empty
51              System.out.printf("stack contains: %s (top)%n", stack);
52        }
53     } // end class StackTest
```

```
Pushed 12L
stack contains: [12] (top)
Pushed 34567
stack contains: [12, 34567] (top)
Pushed 1.0F
stack contains: [12, 34567, 1.0] (top)
Pushed 1234.5678
stack contains: [12, 34567, 1.0, 1234.5678] (top)
Popped 1234.5678
stack contains: [12, 34567, 1.0] (top)
Popped 1.0
stack contains: [12, 34567] (top)
Popped 34567
stack contains: [12] (top)
Popped 12
stack is empty

java.util.EmptyStackException
        at java.util.Stack.peek(Unknown Source)
        at java.util.Stack.pop(Unknown Source)
        at StackTest.main(StackTest.java:34)
```

Fig. 16.14 | Stack class of package `java.util`. (Part 2 of 2.)

Error-Prevention Tip 16.1

Because Stack extends Vector, all public Vector methods can be called on Stack objects, even if the methods do not represent conventional stack operations. For example, Vector method add can be used to insert an element anywhere in a stack—an operation that could "corrupt" the stack. When manipulating a Stack, only methods push and pop should be used to add elements to and remove elements from the Stack, respectively.

Line 10 creates an empty Stack of Numbers. Class Number (in package java.lang) is the superclass of the type-wrapper classes for the primitive numeric types (e.g., Integer, Double). By creating a Stack of Numbers, objects of any class that extends Number can be pushed onto the Stack. Lines 13, 16, 19 and 22 each call Stack method **push** to add a Number object to the *top* of the stack. Note the literals 12L (line 13) and 1.0F (line 19). Any integer literal that has the **suffix L** is a long value. An integer literal without a suffix is an int value. Similarly, any floating-point literal that has the **suffix F** is a float value. A floating-point literal without a suffix is a double value. You can learn more about numeric literals in the *Java Language Specification* at http://docs.oracle.com/javase/specs/jls/se7/html/jls-15.html#jls-15.8.1.

An infinite loop (lines 32–37) calls **Stack method pop** to remove the *top* element of the stack. The method returns a Number reference to the removed element. If there are no elements in the Stack, method pop throws an **EmptyStackException**, which terminates the loop. Class Stack also declares **method peek**. This method returns the *top* element of the stack *without* popping the element off the stack.

Method printStack (lines 46–52) displays the stack's contents. The current *top* of the stack (the last value pushed onto the stack) is the *first* value printed. Line 48 calls **Stack method isEmpty** (inherited by Stack from class Vector) to determine whether the stack is empty. If it's empty, the method returns true; otherwise, false.

16.9 Class PriorityQueue and Interface Queue

Recall that a queue is a collection that represents a waiting line—typically, *insertions* are made at the back of a queue and *deletions* are made from the front. In this section, we investigate Java's **Queue** interface and **PriorityQueue** class from package java.util. Interface Queue extends interface Collection and provides additional operations for *inserting*, *removing* and *inspecting* elements in a queue. PriorityQueue, which implements the Queue interface, orders elements by their natural ordering as specified by Comparable elements' compareTo method or by a Comparator object that's supplied to the constructor.

Class PriorityQueue provides functionality that enables *insertions in sorted order* into the underlying data structure and *deletions* from the *front* of the underlying data structure. When adding elements to a PriorityQueue, the elements are inserted in priority order such that the *highest-priority element* (i.e., the largest value) will be the first element removed from the PriorityQueue.

The common PriorityQueue operations are **offer** to *insert* an element at the appropriate location based on priority order, **poll** to *remove* the highest-priority element of the priority queue (i.e., the head of the queue), **peek** to get a reference to the highest-priority element of the priority queue (without removing that element), **clear** to *remove all elements* in the priority queue and **size** to get the number of elements in the priority queue.

Figure 16.15 demonstrates the PriorityQueue class. Line 10 creates a PriorityQueue that stores Doubles with an *initial capacity* of 11 elements and orders the elements according to the object's natural ordering (the defaults for a PriorityQueue). PriorityQueue is a generic class. Line 10 instantiates a PriorityQueue with a type argument Double. Class PriorityQueue provides five additional constructors. One of these takes an int and a Comparator object to create a PriorityQueue with the *initial capacity* specified by the int and the *ordering* by the Comparator. Lines 13–15 use method offer to add elements to the priority queue. Method offer throws a NullPointerException if the program attempts to add a null object to the queue. The loop in lines 20–24 uses method size to determine whether the priority queue is *empty* (line 20). While there are more elements, line 22 uses PriorityQueue method peek to retrieve the *highest-priority element* in the queue for output (*without* actually removing it from the queue). Line 23 removes the highest-priority element in the queue with method poll, which returns the removed element.

```
 1   // Fig. 16.15: PriorityQueueTest.java
 2   // PriorityQueue test program.
 3   import java.util.PriorityQueue;
 4
 5   public class PriorityQueueTest
 6   {
 7      public static void main(String[] args)
 8      {
 9         // queue of capacity 11
10         PriorityQueue<Double> queue = new PriorityQueue<>();
11
12         // insert elements to queue
13         queue.offer(3.2);
14         queue.offer(9.8);
15         queue.offer(5.4);
16
17         System.out.print("Polling from queue: ");
18
19         // display elements in queue
20         while (queue.size() > 0)
21         {
22            System.out.printf("%.1f ", queue.peek()); // view top element
23            queue.poll(); // remove top element
24         }
25      }
26   } // end class PriorityQueueTest
```

```
Polling from queue: 3.2 5.4 9.8
```

Fig. 16.15 | PriorityQueue test program.

16.10 Sets

A **Set** is an *unordered* Collection of unique elements (i.e., *no duplicates*). The collections framework contains several Set implementations, including **HashSet** and **TreeSet**. HashSet stores its elements in a *hash table*, and TreeSet stores its elements in a *tree*. Hash tables are presented in Section 16.11.

Figure 16.16 uses a HashSet to *remove duplicate strings* from a List. Recall that both List and Collection are generic types, so line 16 creates a List that contains String objects, and line 20 passes a Collection of Strings to method printNonDuplicates. Method printNonDuplicates (lines 24–35) takes a Collection argument. Line 27 constructs a HashSet<String> from the Collection<String> argument. By definition, Sets do *not* contain duplicates, so when the HashSet is constructed, it *removes any duplicates* in the Collection. Lines 31–32 output elements in the Set.

```
 1   // Fig. 16.16: SetTest.java
 2   // HashSet used to remove duplicate values from array of strings.
 3   import java.util.List;
 4   import java.util.Arrays;
```

Fig. 16.16 | HashSet used to remove duplicate values from an array of strings. (Part 1 of 2.)

```
5   import java.util.HashSet;
6   import java.util.Set;
7   import java.util.Collection;
8
9   public class SetTest
10  {
11     public static void main(String[] args)
12     {
13        // create and display a List<String>
14        String[] colors = {"red", "white", "blue", "green", "gray",
15           "orange", "tan", "white", "cyan", "peach", "gray", "orange"};
16        List<String> list = Arrays.asList(colors);
17        System.out.printf("List: %s%n", list);
18
19        // eliminate duplicates then print the unique values
20        printNonDuplicates(list);
21     }
22
23     // create a Set from a Collection to eliminate duplicates
24     private static void printNonDuplicates(Collection<String> values)
25     {
26        // create a HashSet
27        Set<String> set = new HashSet<>(values);
28
29        System.out.printf("%nNonduplicates are: ");
30
31        for (String value : set)
32           System.out.printf("%s ", value);
33
34        System.out.println();
35     }
36  } // end class SetTest
```

```
List: [red, white, blue, green, gray, orange, tan, white, cyan, peach, gray,
orange]

Nonduplicates are: orange green white peach gray cyan red blue tan
```

Fig. 16.16 | HashSet used to remove duplicate values from an array of strings. (Part 2 of 2.)

Sorted Sets

The collections framework also includes the **SortedSet interface** (which extends Set) for sets that maintain their elements in *sorted* order—either the *elements' natural order* (e.g., numbers are in *ascending* order) or an order specified by a Comparator. Class TreeSet implements SortedSet. The program in Fig. 16.17 places Strings into a TreeSet. The Strings are sorted as they're added to the TreeSet. This example also demonstrates *range-view* methods, which enable a program to view a portion of a collection.

Line 14 creates a TreeSet<String> that contains the elements of array colors, then assigns the new TreeSet<String> to SortedSet<String> variable tree. Line 17 outputs the initial set of strings using method printSet (lines 33–39), which we discuss momentarily. Line 31 calls **TreeSet method headSet** to get a subset of the TreeSet in which every element is less than "orange". The view returned from headSet is then output with printSet. If any changes are made to the subset, they'll *also* be made to the original TreeSet, because the subset returned by headSet is a view of the TreeSet.

Line 25 calls **TreeSet method tailSet** to get a subset in which each element is greater than or equal to "orange", then outputs the result. Any changes made through the tailSet view are made to the original TreeSet. Lines 28–29 call **SortedSet methods first** and **last** to get the smallest and largest elements of the set, respectively.

Method printSet (lines 33–39) accepts a SortedSet as an argument and prints it. Lines 35–36 print each element of the SortedSet using the enhanced for statement.

```java
1   // Fig. 16.17: SortedSetTest.java
2   // Using SortedSets and TreeSets.
3   import java.util.Arrays;
4   import java.util.SortedSet;
5   import java.util.TreeSet;
6
7   public class SortedSetTest
8   {
9      public static void main(String[] args)
10     {
11        // create TreeSet from array colors
12        String[] colors = {"yellow", "green", "black", "tan", "grey",
13           "white", "orange", "red", "green"};
14        SortedSet<String> tree = new TreeSet<>(Arrays.asList(colors));
15
16        System.out.print("sorted set: ");
17        printSet(tree);
18
19        // get headSet based on "orange"
20        System.out.print("headSet (\"orange\"):  ");
21        printSet(tree.headSet("orange")  );
22
23        // get tailSet based upon "orange"
24        System.out.print("tailSet (\"orange\"):  ");
25        printSet(tree.tailSet("orange")  );
26
27        // get first and last elements
28        System.out.printf("first: %s%n", tree.first());
29        System.out.printf("last : %s%n", tree.last());
30     }
31
32     // output SortedSet using enhanced for statement
33     private static void printSet(SortedSet<String> set)
34     {
35        for (String s : set)
36           System.out.printf("%s ", s);
37
38        System.out.println();
39     }
40  } // end class SortedSetTest
```

Fig. 16.17 | Using SortedSets and TreeSets. (Part I of 2.)

```
sorted set: black green grey orange red tan white yellow
headSet ("orange"):  black green grey
tailSet ("orange"):  orange red tan white yellow
first: black
last : yellow
```

Fig. 16.17 | Using SortedSets and TreeSets. (Part 2 of 2.)

16.11 Maps

Maps associate *keys* to *values*. The keys in a Map must be *unique*, but the associated values need not be. If a Map contains both unique keys and unique values, it's said to implement a **one-to-one mapping**. If only the keys are unique, the Map is said to implement a **many-to-one mapping**—many keys can map to one value.

Maps differ from Sets in that Maps contain keys and values, whereas Sets contain only values. Three of the several classes that implement interface Map are **Hashtable**, **HashMap** and **TreeMap**. Hashtables and HashMaps store elements in hash tables, and TreeMaps store elements in trees. This section discusses hash tables and provides an example that uses a HashMap to store key–value pairs. **Interface SortedMap** extends Map and maintains its keys in *sorted* order—either the elements' *natural* order or an order specified by a Comparator. Class TreeMap implements SortedMap.

Map Implementation with Hash Tables

When a program creates objects, it may need to store and retrieve them efficiently. Storing and retrieving information with arrays is efficient if some aspect of your data directly matches a numerical key value and if the *keys are unique* and tightly packed. If you have 100 employees with nine-digit social security numbers and you want to store and retrieve employee data by using the social security number as a key, the task will require an array with over 800 million elements, because nine-digit Social Security numbers must begin with 001–899 (excluding 666) as per the Social Security Administration's website

http://www.socialsecurity.gov/employer/randomization.html

This is impractical for virtually all applications that use social security numbers as keys. A program having an array that large could achieve high performance for both storing and retrieving employee records by simply using the social security number as the array index.

Numerous applications have this problem—namely, that either the keys are of the wrong type (e.g., not positive integers that correspond to array subscripts) or they're of the right type, but *sparsely* spread over a *huge range*. What is needed is a high-speed scheme for converting keys such as social security numbers, inventory part numbers and the like into unique array indices. Then, when an application needs to store something, the scheme could convert the application's key rapidly into an index, and the record could be stored at that slot in the array. Retrieval is accomplished the same way: Once the application has a key for which it wants to retrieve a data record, the application simply applies the conversion to the key—this produces the array index where the data is stored and retrieved.

The scheme we describe here is the basis of a technique called **hashing**. Why the name? When we convert a key into an array index, we literally scramble the bits, forming a kind of "mishmashed," or hashed, number. The number actually has no real significance beyond its usefulness in storing and retrieving a particular data record.

A glitch in the scheme is called a **collision**—this occurs when two different keys "hash into" the same cell (or element) in the array. We cannot store two values in the same space, so we need to find an alternative home for all values beyond the first that hash to a particular array index. There are many schemes for doing this. One is to "hash again" (i.e., to apply another hashing transformation to the key to provide a next candidate cell in the array). The hashing process is designed to *distribute* the values throughout the table, so the assumption is that an available cell will be found with just a few hashes.

Another scheme uses one hash to locate the first candidate cell. If that cell is occupied, successive cells are searched in order until an available cell is found. Retrieval works the same way: The key is hashed once to determine the initial location and check whether it contains the desired data. If it does, the search is finished. If it does not, successive cells are searched linearly until the desired data is found.

The most popular solution to hash-table collisions is to have each cell of the table be a hash "bucket," typically a linked list of all the key–value pairs that hash to that cell. This is the solution that Java's Hashtable and HashMap classes (from package java.util) implement. Both Hashtable and HashMap implement the Map interface. The primary differences between them are that HashMap is *unsynchronized* (multiple threads should not modify a HashMap concurrently) and allows null keys and null values.

A hash table's **load factor** affects the performance of hashing schemes. The load factor is the ratio of the number of occupied cells in the hash table to the total number of cells in the hash table. The closer this ratio gets to 1.0, the greater the chance of collisions.

Performance Tip 16.2

The load factor in a hash table is a classic example of a memory-space/execution-time trade-off: By increasing the load factor, we get better memory utilization, but the program runs slower, due to increased hashing collisions. By decreasing the load factor, we get better program speed, because of reduced hashing collisions, but we get poorer memory utilization, because a larger portion of the hash table remains empty.

Classes Hashtable and HashMap enable you to use hashing without having to implement hash-table mechanisms—a classic example of reuse. This concept is profoundly important in our study of object-oriented programming. As discussed in earlier chapters, classes encapsulate and hide complexity (i.e., implementation details) and offer user-friendly interfaces. Properly crafting classes to exhibit such behavior is one of the most valued skills in the field of object-oriented programming. Figure 16.18 uses a HashMap to count the number of occurrences of each word in a string.

```
1   // Fig. 16.18: WordTypeCount.java
2   // Program counts the number of occurrences of each word in a String.
3   import java.util.Map;
4   import java.util.HashMap;
5   import java.util.Set;
6   import java.util.TreeSet;
```

Fig. 16.18 | Program counts the number of occurrences of each word in a String. (Part 1 of 3.)

```
 7    import java.util.Scanner;
 8
 9    public class WordTypeCount
10    {
11       public static void main(String[] args)
12       {
13          // create HashMap to store String keys and Integer values
14          Map<String, Integer> myMap = new HashMap<>();
15
16          createMap(myMap); // create map based on user input
17          displayMap(myMap); // display map content
18       }
19
20       // create map from user input
21       private static void createMap(Map<String, Integer> map)
22       {
23          Scanner scanner = new Scanner(System.in); // create scanner
24          System.out.println("Enter a string:"); // prompt for user input
25          String input = scanner.nextLine();
26
27          // tokenize the input
28          String[] tokens = input.split(" ");
29
30          // processing input text
31          for (String token : tokens)
32          {
33             String word = token.toLowerCase(); // get lowercase word
34
35             // if the map contains the word
36             if (map.containsKey(word)) // is word in map
37             {
38                int count = map.get(word); // get current count
39                map.put(word, count + 1); // increment count
40             }
41             else
42                map.put(word, 1); // add new word with a count of 1 to map
43          }
44       }
45
46       // display map content
47       private static void displayMap(Map<String, Integer> map)
48       {
49          Set<String> keys = map.keySet(); // get keys
50
51          // sort keys
52          TreeSet<String> sortedKeys = new TreeSet<>(keys);
53
54          System.out.printf("%nMap contains:%nKey\t\tValue%n");
55
56          // generate output for each key in map
57          for (String key : sortedKeys)
58             System.out.printf("%-10s%10s%n", key, map.get(key));
59
```

Fig. 16.18 | Program counts the number of occurrences of each word in a String. (Part 2 of 3.)

```
60          System.out.printf(
61              "%nsize: %d%nisEmpty: %b%n", map.size(), map.isEmpty());
62      }
63  } // end class WordTypeCount
```

```
Enter a string:
this is a sample sentence with several words this is another sample
sentence with several different words

Map contains:
Key            Value
a                1
another          1
different        1
is               2
sample           2
sentence         2
several          2
this             2
with             2
words            2

size: 10
isEmpty: false
```

Fig. 16.18 | Program counts the number of occurrences of each word in a String. (Part 3 of 3.)

Line 14 creates an empty HashMap with a *default initial capacity* (16 elements) and a default load factor (0.75)—these defaults are built into the implementation of HashMap. When the number of occupied slots in the HashMap becomes greater than the capacity times the load factor, the capacity is doubled automatically. HashMap is a generic class that takes two type arguments—the type of key (i.e., String) and the type of value (i.e., Integer). Recall that the type arguments passed to a generic class must be reference types, hence the second type argument is Integer, not int.

Line 16 calls method createMap (lines 21–44), which uses a Map to store the number of occurrences of each word in the sentence. Line 25 obtains the user input, and line 28 tokenizes it. Lines 31–43 convert the next token to lowercase letters (line 33), then call **Map method containsKey** (line 36) to determine whether the word is in the map (and thus has occurred previously in the string). If the Map does *not* contain the word, line 42 uses **Map method put** to create a new entry, with the word as the key and an Integer object containing 1 as the value. Autoboxing occurs when the program passes integer 1 to method put, because the map stores the number of occurrences as an Integer. If the word does exist in the map, line 38 uses **Map method get** to obtain the key's associated value (the count) in the map. Line 39 increments that value and uses put to replace the key's associated value. Method put returns the key's prior associated value, or null if the key was not in the map.

Error-Prevention Tip 16.2

Always use immutable keys with a Map. The key determines where the corresponding value is placed. If the key has changed since the insert operation, when you subsequently attempt to retrieve that value, it might not be found. In this chapter's examples, we use Strings as keys and Strings are immutable.

Method `displayMap` (lines 47–62) displays all the entries in the map. It uses **HashMap method keySet** (line 49) to get a set of the keys. The keys have type `String` in the map, so method `keySet` returns a generic type `Set` with type parameter specified to be `String`. Line 52 creates a `TreeSet` of the keys, in which the keys are sorted. The loop in lines 57–58 accesses each key and its value in the map. Line 58 displays each key and its value using format specifier %-10s to *left align* each key and format specifier %10s to *right align* each value. The keys are displayed in *ascending* order. Line 61 calls **Map method size** to get the number of key–value pairs in the `Map`. Line 61 also calls **Map method isEmpty**, which returns a `boolean` indicating whether the `Map` is empty.

16.12 Properties Class

A **Properties** object is a *persistent* `Hashtable` that stores *key–value pairs* of `Strings`—assuming that you use methods **setProperty** and **getProperty** to manipulate the table rather than inherited `Hashtable` methods `put` and `get`. By "persistent," we mean that the `Properties` object can be written to an output stream (possibly a file) and read back in through an input stream. A common use of `Properties` objects in prior versions of Java was to maintain application-configuration data or user preferences for applications. [*Note:* The **Preferences API** (package **java.util.prefs**) is meant to replace this particular use of class `Properties` but is beyond the scope of this book. To learn more, visit `http://bit.ly/JavaPreferences`.] Class `Properties` extends class `Hashtable<Object, Object>`. Figure 16.19 demonstrates several methods of class `Properties`.

Line 13 creates an empty `Properties` table with no default properties. Class `Properties` also provides an overloaded constructor that receives a reference to a `Properties` object containing default property values. Lines 16 and 17 each call `Properties` method `setProperty` to store a value for the specified key. If the key does not exist in the `table`, `setProperty` returns `null`; otherwise, it returns the previous value for that key.

```java
 1   // Fig. 16.19: PropertiesTest.java
 2   // Demonstrates class Properties of the java.util package.
 3   import java.io.FileOutputStream;
 4   import java.io.FileInputStream;
 5   import java.io.IOException;
 6   import java.util.Properties;
 7   import java.util.Set;
 8
 9   public class PropertiesTest
10   {
11      public static void main(String[] args)
12      {
13         Properties table = new Properties();
14
15         // set properties
16         table.setProperty("color", "blue");
17         table.setProperty("width", "200");
18
19         System.out.println("After setting properties");
20         listProperties(table);
```

Fig. 16.19 | `Properties` class of package `java.util`. (Part 1 of 3.)

```
21
22          // replace property value
23          table.setProperty("color", "red");
24
25          System.out.println("After replacing properties");
26          listProperties(table);
27
28          saveProperties(table);
29
30          table.clear(); // empty table
31
32          System.out.println("After clearing properties");
33          listProperties(table);
34
35          loadProperties(table);
36
37          // get value of property color
38          Object value = table.getProperty("color");
39
40          // check if value is in table
41          if (value != null)
42             System.out.printf("Property color's value is %s%n", value);
43          else
44             System.out.println("Property color is not in table");
45       }
46
47       // save properties to a file
48       private static void saveProperties(Properties props)
49       {
50          // save contents of table
51          try
52          {
53             FileOutputStream output = new FileOutputStream("props.dat");
54             props.store(output, "Sample Properties"); // save properties
55             output.close();
56             System.out.println("After saving properties");
57             listProperties(props);
58          }
59          catch (IOException ioException)
60          {
61             ioException.printStackTrace();
62          }
63       }
64
65       // load properties from a file
66       private static void loadProperties(Properties props)
67       {
68          // load contents of table
69          try
70          {
71             FileInputStream input = new FileInputStream("props.dat");
72             props.load(input); // load properties
73             input.close();
```

Fig. 16.19 | Properties class of package java.util. (Part 2 of 3.)

```
74              System.out.println("After loading properties");
75              listProperties(props);
76         }
77         catch (IOException ioException)
78         {
79              ioException.printStackTrace();
80         }
81     }
82
83     // output property values
84     private static void listProperties(Properties props)
85     {
86         Set<Object> keys = props.keySet(); // get property names
87
88         // output name/value pairs
89         for (Object key : keys)
90             System.out.printf(
91                 "%s\t%s%n", key, props.getProperty((String) key));
92
93         System.out.println();
94     }
95 } // end class PropertiesTest
```

```
After setting properties
color    blue
width    200

After replacing properties
color    red
width    200

After saving properties
color    red
width    200

After clearing properties

After loading properties
color    red
width    200

Property color's value is red
```

Fig. 16.19 | Properties class of package java.util. (Part 3 of 3.)

Line 38 calls Properties method getProperty to locate the value associated with the specified key. If the key is *not* found in this Properties object, getProperty returns null. An overloaded version of this method receives a second argument that specifies the default value to return if getProperty cannot locate the key.

Line 54 calls **Properties method store** to save the Properties object's contents to the OutputStream specified as the first argument (in this case, a FileOutputStream). The second argument, a String, is a description written into the file. **Properties method list**, which takes a PrintStream argument, is useful for displaying the list of properties.

Line 72 calls **Properties method load** to restore the contents of the Properties object from the InputStream specified as the first argument (in this case, a FileInput-Stream). Line 86 calls Properties method keySet to obtain a Set of the property names. Because class Properties stores its contents as Objects, a Set of Object references is returned. Line 91 obtains the value of a property by passing a key to method getProperty.

16.13 Synchronized Collections

In Chapter 20, we discuss *multithreading*. Except for Vector and Hashtable, the collections in the collections framework are *unsynchronized* by default, so they can operate efficiently when multithreading is not required. Because they're unsynchronized, however, concurrent access to a Collection by multiple threads could cause indeterminate results or fatal errors—as we demonstrate in Chapter 20. To prevent potential threading problems, **synchronization wrappers** are used for collections that might be accessed by multiple threads. A **wrapper** object receives method calls, adds thread synchronization (to prevent concurrent access to the collection) and *delegates* the calls to the wrapped collection object. The Collections API provides a set of static methods for wrapping collections as synchronized versions. Method headers for the synchronization wrappers are listed in Fig. 16.20. Details about these methods are available at http://docs.oracle.com/javase/7/docs/api/java/util/Collections.html. All these methods take a generic type and return a *synchronized view* of the generic type. For example, the following code creates a synchronized List (list2) that stores String objects:

```
List<String> list1 = new ArrayList<>();
List<String> list2 = Collections.synchronizedList(list1);
```

public static method headers
<T> Collection<T> synchronizedCollection(Collection<T> c)
<T> List<T> synchronizedList(List<T> aList)
<T> Set<T> synchronizedSet(Set<T> s)
<T> SortedSet<T> synchronizedSortedSet(SortedSet<T> s)
<K, V> Map<K, V> synchronizedMap(Map<K, V> m)
<K, V> SortedMap<K, V> synchronizedSortedMap(SortedMap<K, V> m)

Fig. 16.20 | Synchronization wrapper methods.

16.14 Unmodifiable Collections

The Collections class provides a set of static methods that create **unmodifiable wrappers** for collections. Unmodifiable wrappers throw UnsupportedOperationExceptions if attempts are made to modify the collection. In an unmodifiable collection, the references stored in the collection are not modifiable, but the objects they refer *are modifiable* unless they belong to an immutable class like String. Headers for these methods are listed in Fig. 16.21. Details about these methods are available at http://docs.oracle.com/javase/7/docs/api/java/util/Collections.html. All these methods take a generic type and return an unmodifiable view of the generic type. For example, the following code creates an unmodifiable List (list2) that stores String objects:

```
List<String> list1 = new ArrayList<>();
List<String> list2 = Collections.unmodifiableList(list1);
```

Software Engineering Observation 16.6

You can use an unmodifiable wrapper to create a collection that offers read-only access to others, while allowing read–write access to yourself. You do this simply by giving others a reference to the unmodifiable wrapper while retaining for yourself a reference to the original collection.

---

public static method headers

`<T> Collection<T> unmodifiableCollection(Collection<T> c)`

`<T> List<T> unmodifiableList(List<T> aList)`

`<T> Set<T> unmodifiableSet(Set<T> s)`

`<T> SortedSet<T> unmodifiableSortedSet(SortedSet<T> s)`

`<K, V> Map<K, V> unmodifiableMap(Map<K, V> m)`

`<K, V> SortedMap<K, V> unmodifiableSortedMap(SortedMap<K, V> m)`

Fig. 16.21 | Unmodifiable wrapper methods.

16.15 Abstract Implementations

The collections framework provides various abstract implementations of Collection interfaces from which you can quickly "flesh out" complete customized implementations. These abstract implementations include a thin Collection implementation called an **AbstractCollection**, a List implementation that allows *array-like access* to its elements called an **AbstractList**, a Map implementation called an **AbstractMap**, a List implementation that allows *sequential access* (from beginning to end) to its elements called an **AbstractSequentialList**, a Set implementation called an **AbstractSet** and a Queue implementation called **AbstractQueue**. You can learn more about these classes at http://docs.oracle.com/javase/7/docs/api/java/util/package-summary.html. To write a *custom* implementation, you can extend the abstract implementation that best meets your needs, implement each of the class's abstract methods and override the class's concrete methods as necessary.

16.16 Wrap-Up

This chapter introduced the Java collections framework. You learned the collection hierarchy and how to use the collections-framework interfaces to program with collections polymorphically. You used classes ArrayList and LinkedList, which both implement the List interface. We presented Java's built-in interfaces and classes for manipulating stacks and queues. You used several predefined methods for manipulating collections. You learned how to use the Set interface and class HashSet to manipulate an unordered collection of unique values. We continued our presentation of sets with the SortedSet interface and class TreeSet for manipulating a sorted collection of unique values. You then learned about Java's interfaces and classes for manipulating key–value pairs—Map, SortedMap, Hashtable, HashMap and TreeMap. We discussed the specialized Properties class for manipulating key–value pairs of Strings that can be stored to a file and retrieved from a file. Finally, we discussed the Collections class's static methods for obtaining unmodifiable and synchronized views of collections. For additional information on the collections framework, visit http://docs.oracle.com/javase/7/docs/technotes/guides/collections. In Chapter 17, Java SE 8 Lambdas and Streams, you'll use Java SE 8's new functional programming capabilities to simplify collection operations. In Chapter 20, Concurrency, you'll learn how to improve performance on multi-core systems using Java's concurrent collections and parallel stream operations.

17

Java SE 8 Lambdas and Streams

Objectives

In this chapter you'll:

- Learn what functional programming is and how it complements object-oriented programming.

- Use functional programming to simplify programming tasks you've performed with other techniques.

- Write lambda expressions that implement functional interfaces.

- Learn what streams are and how stream pipelines are formed from stream sources, intermediate operations and terminal operations.

- Perform operations on `IntStream`s, including `forEach`, `count`, `min`, `max`, `sum`, `average`, `reduce`, `filter` and `sorted`.

- Perform operations on `Stream`s, including `filter`, `map`, `sorted`, `collect`, `forEach`, `findFirst`, `distinct`, `mapToDouble` and `reduce`.

- Create streams representing ranges of `int` values and random `int` values.

17.1 Introduction

The way you think about Java programming is about to change profoundly. Prior to Java SE 8, Java supported three programming paradigms—*procedural programming*, *object-oriented programming* and *generic programming*. Java SE 8 adds *functional programming*. The new language and library capabilities that support this paradigm were added to Java as part of *Project Lambda:*

```
http://openjdk.java.net/projects/lambda
```

In this chapter, we'll define functional programming and show how to use it to write programs faster, more concisely and with fewer bugs than programs written with previous techniques. In Chapter 20, Concurrency, you'll see that functional programs are easier to *parallelize* (i.e., perform multiple operations simultaneously) so that your programs can take advantage of multi-core architectures to enhance performance. Before reading this chapter, you should review Section 10.10, which introduced Java SE 8's new interface features (the ability to include `default` and `static` methods) and discussed the concept of functional interfaces.

This chapter presents many examples of functional programming, often showing simpler ways to implement tasks that you programmed in earlier chapters (Fig. 17.1)

Pre-Java-SE-8 topics	Corresponding Java SE 8 discussions and examples
Chapter 7, Arrays and ArrayLists	Sections 17.3—17.4 introduce basic lambda and streams capabilities that process one-dimensional arrays.
Chapter 10, Object-Oriented Programming: Polymorphism and Interfaces	Section 10.10 introduced the new Java SE 8 interface features (default methods, static methods and the concept of functional interfaces) that support functional programming.
Chapter 12, Swing GUI Components: Part 1	Section 17.9 shows how to use a lambda to implement a Swing event-listener functional interface.
Chapter 14, Strings, Characters and Regular Expressions	Section 17.5 shows how to use lambdas and streams to process collections of String objects.
Chapter 15, Files, Streams and Object Serialization	Section 17.7 shows how to use lambdas and streams to process lines of text from a file.
Chapter 19, Swing GUI Components: Part 2	Discusses using lambdas to implement Swing event-listener functional interfaces.
Chapter 20, Concurrency	Shows that functional programs are easier to parallelize so that they can take advantage of multi-core architectures to enhance performance. Demonstrates parallel stream processing. Shows that Arrays method parallelSort improves performance on multi-core architectures when sorting large arrays.
Chapter 22, JavaFX GUI	Discusses using lambdas to implement JavaFX event-listener functional interfaces.

Fig. 17.1 | Java SE 8 lambdas and streams discussions and examples.

17.2 Functional Programming Technologies Overview

In the preceding chapters, you learned various procedural, object-oriented and generic programming techniques. Though you often used Java library classes and interfaces to perform various tasks, you typically determine *what* you want to accomplish in a task then specify precisely *how* to accomplish it. For example, let's assume that *what* you'd like to accomplish is to sum the elements of an array named values (the *data source*). You might use the following code:

```
int sum = 0;

for (int counter = 0; counter < values.length; counter++)
    sum += values[counter];
```

This loop specifies *how* we'd like to add each array element's value to the sum—with a for repetition statement that processes each element one at a time, adding each element's value to the sum. This iteration technique is known as **external iteration** (because you specify how to iterate, not the library) and requires you to access the elements sequentially from beginning to end in a single thread of execution. To perform the preceding task, you also create two variables (sum and counter) that are *mutated* repeatedly—that is, their values change—while the task is performed. You performed many similar array and collection tasks, such as displaying the elements of an array, summarizing the faces of a die that was rolled 6,000,000 times, calculating the average of an array's elements and more.

External Iteration Is Error Prone

Most Java programmers are comfortable with external iteration. However, there are several opportunities for error. For example, you could initialize variable sum incorrectly, initialize control variable counter incorrectly, use the wrong loop-continuation condition, increment control variable counter incorrectly or incorrectly add each value in the array to the sum.

Internal Iteration

In **functional programming**, you specify *what* you want to accomplish in a task, but *not how* to accomplish it. As you'll see in this chapter, to sum a numeric data source's elements (such as those in an array or collection), you can use new Java SE 8 library capabilities that allow you to say, "Here's a data source, give me the sum of its elements." You do *not* need to specify *how* to iterate through the elements or declare and use *any* mutable variables. This is known as **internal iteration**, because the *library* determines how to access all the elements to perform the task. With internal iteration, you can easily tell the library that you want to perform this task with *parallel processing* to take advantage of your computer's multi-core architecture—this can significantly improve the task's performance. As you'll learn in Chapter 20, it's hard to create parallel tasks that operate correctly if those tasks modify a program's state information (that is, its variable values). So the functional programming capabilities that you'll learn here focus on **immutability**—not modifying the data source being processed or any other program state.

17.2.1 Functional Interfaces

Section 10.10 introduced Java SE 8's new interface features—default methods and static methods—and discussed the concept of a *functional interface*—an interface that contains exactly one abstract method (and may also contain default and static methods). Such interfaces are also known as *single abstract method* (SAM) interfaces. Functional interfaces are used extensively in functional programming, because they act as an object-oriented model for a function.

Functional Interfaces in Package `java.util.function`

Package java.util.function contains several functional interfaces. Figure 17.2 shows the six basic generic functional interfaces. Throughout the table, T and R are generic type names that represent the type of the object on which the functional interface operates and the return type of a method, respectively. There are many other functional interfaces in package java.util.function that are specialized versions of those in Fig. 17.2. Most are for use with int, long and double primitive values, but there are also generic customizations of Consumer, Function and Predicate for binary operations—that is, methods that take two arguments.

Interface	Description
BinaryOperator<T>	Contains method apply that takes two T arguments, performs an operation on them (such as a calculation) and returns a value of type T. You'll see several examples of BinaryOperators starting in Section 17.3.
Consumer<T>	Contains method accept that takes a T argument and returns void. Performs a task with it's T argument, such as outputting the object, invoking a method of the object, etc. You'll see several examples of Consumers starting in Section 17.3.
Function<T,R>	Contains method apply that takes a T argument and returns a value of type R. Calls a method on the T argument and returns that method's result. You'll see several examples of Functions starting in Section 17.5.
Predicate<T>	Contains method test that takes a T argument and returns a boolean. Tests whether the T argument satisfies a condition. You'll see several examples of Predicates starting in Section 17.3.
Supplier<T>	Contains method get that takes no arguments and produces a value of type T. Often used to create a collection object in which a stream operation's results are placed. You'll see several examples of Suppliers starting in Section 17.7.
UnaryOperator<T>	Contains method get that takes no arguments and returns a value of type T. You'll see several examples of UnaryOperators starting in Section 17.3.

Fig. 17.2 | The six basic generic functional interfaces in package `java.util.function`.

17.2.2 Lambda Expressions

Functional programming is accomplished with lambda expressions. A **lambda expression** represents an *anonymous method*—a shorthand notation for implementing a functional interface, similar to an anonymous inner class (Section 12.11). The type of a lambda expression is the type of the functional interface that the lambda expression implements. Lambda expressions can be used anywhere functional interfaces are expected. From this point forward, we'll refer to lambda expressions simply as lambdas. We show basic lambda syntax in this section and discuss additional lambda features as we use them throughout this and later chapters.

Lambda Syntax
A lambda consists of a *parameter list* followed by the **arrow token** (->) and a body, as in:

```
(parameterList) -> {statements}
```

The following lambda receives two ints and returns their sum:

```
(int x, int y) -> {return x + y;}
```

In this case, the body is a *statement block* that may contain *one or more* statements enclosed in curly braces. There are several variations of this syntax. For example, the parameter types usually may be omitted, as in:

```
(x, y) -> {return x + y;}
```

in which case, the compiler determines the parameter and return types by the lambda's context—we'll say more about this later.

When the body contains only one expression, the return keyword and curly braces may be omitted, as in:

```
(x, y) -> x + y
```

in this case, the expression's value is *implicitly* returned. When the parameter list contains only one parameter, the parentheses may be omitted, as in:

```
value -> System.out.printf("%d ", value)
```

To define a lambda with an empty parameter list, specify the parameter list as empty parentheses to the left of the arrow token (->), as in:

```
() -> System.out.println("Welcome to lambdas!")
```

In addition, to the preceding lambda syntax, there are specialized shorthand forms of lambdas that are known as *method references*, which we introduce in Section 17.5.1.

17.2.3 Streams

Java SE 8 introduces the concept of **streams**, which are similar to the iterators you learned in Chapter 16. Streams are objects of classes that implement interface **Stream** (from the package java.util.stream) or one of the specialized stream interfacess for processing collections of int, long or double values (which we introduce in Section 17.3). Together with lambdas, streams enable you to perform tasks on collections of elements—often from an array or collection object.

Stream Pipelines

Streams move elements through a sequence of processing steps—known as a **stream pipeline**—that begins with a *data source* (such as an array or collection), performs various *intermediate operations* on the data source's elements and ends with a *terminal operation*. A stream pipeline is formed by *chaining* method calls. Unlike collections, streams do *not* have their own storage—once a stream is processed, it cannot be reused, because it does not maintain a copy of the original data source.

Intermediate and Terminal Operations

An **intermediate operation** specifies tasks to perform on the stream's elements and always results in a new stream. Intermediate operations are **lazy**—they aren't performed until a terminal operation is invoked. This allows library developers to optimize stream-processing performance. For example, if you have a collection of 1,000,000 Person objects and you're looking for the *first* one with the last name "Jones", stream processing can terminate as soon as the first such Person object is found.

A **terminal operation** initiates processing of a stream pipeline's intermediate operations and produces a result. Terminal operations are **eager**—they perform the requested operation when they are called. We say more about lazy and eager operations as we encounter them throughout the chapter and you'll see how lazy operations can improve performance. Figure 17.3 shows some common intermediate operations. Figure 17.4 shows some common terminal operations.

Intermediate `Stream` operations	
`filter`	Results in a stream containing only the elements that satisfy a condition.
`distinct`	Results in a stream containing only the unique elements.
`limit`	Results in a stream with the specified number of elements from the beginning of the original stream.
`map`	Results in a stream in which each element of the original stream is mapped to a new value (possibly of a different type)—e.g., mapping numeric values to the squares of the numeric values. The new stream has the same number of elements as the original stream.
`sorted`	Results in a stream in which the elements are in sorted order. The new stream has the same number of elements as the original stream.

Fig. 17.3 | Common intermediate `Stream` operations.

Terminal `Stream` operations	
`forEach`	Performs processing on every element in a stream (e.g., display each element).
Reduction operations—Take all values in the stream and return a single value	
`average`	Calculates the *average* of the elements in a numeric stream.
`count`	Returns the *number of elements* in the stream.
`max`	Locates the *largest* value in a numeric stream.
`min`	Locates the *smallest* value in a numeric stream.
`reduce`	Reduces the elements of a collection to a *single value* using an associative accumulation function (e.g., a lambda that adds two elements).
Mutable reduction operations—Create a container (such as a collection or `StringBuilder`)	
`collect`	Creates a *new collection* of elements containing the results of the stream's prior operations.
`toArray`	Creates an *array* containing the results of the stream's prior operations.
Search operations	
`findFirst`	Finds the *first* stream element based on the prior intermediate operations; immediately terminates processing of the stream pipeline once such an element is found.
`findAny`	Finds *any* stream element based on the prior intermediate operations; immediately terminates processing of the stream pipeline once such an element is found.
`anyMatch`	Determines whether *any* stream elements match a specified condition; immediately terminates processing of the stream pipeline if an element matches.
`allMatch`	Determines whether *all* of the elements in the stream match a specified condition.

Fig. 17.4 | Common terminal `Stream` operations.

Stream in File Processing vs. Stream in Functional Programming

Throughout this chapter, we use the term *stream* in the context of functional programming—this is not the same concept as the I/O streams we discussed in Chapter 15, Files,

Streams and Object Serialization, in which a program reads a stream of bytes from a file or outputs a stream of bytes to a file. As you'll see in Section 17.7, you also can use functional programming to manipulate the contents of a file.

17.3 IntStream Operations

[This section demonstrates how lambdas and streams can be used to simplify programming tasks that you learned in Chapter 7, Arrays and ArrayLists.]

Figure 17.5 demonstrates operations on an **IntStream** (package **java.util.stream**)—a specialized stream for manipulating int values. The techniques shown in this example also apply to **LongStreams** and **DoubleStreams** for long and double values, respectively.

```java
 1   // Fig. 17.5: IntStreamOperations.java
 2   // Demonstrating IntStream operations.
 3   import java.util.Arrays;
 4   import java.util.stream.IntStream;
 5
 6   public class IntStreamOperations
 7   {
 8      public static void main(String[] args)
 9      {
10         int[] values = {3, 10, 6, 1, 4, 8, 2, 5, 9, 7};
11
12         // display original values
13         System.out.print("Original values: ");
14         IntStream.of(values)
15               .forEach(value -> System.out.printf("%d ", value));
16         System.out.println();
17
18         // count, min, max, sum and average of the values
19         System.out.printf("%nCount: %d%n", IntStream.of(values).count());
20         System.out.printf("Min: %d%n",
21            IntStream.of(values).min().getAsInt());
22         System.out.printf("Max: %d%n",
23            IntStream.of(values).max().getAsInt());
24         System.out.printf("Sum: %d%n", IntStream.of(values).sum());
25         System.out.printf("Average: %.2f%n",
26            IntStream.of(values).average().getAsDouble());
27
28         // sum of values with reduce method
29         System.out.printf("%nSum via reduce method: %d%n",
30            IntStream.of(values)
31                  .reduce(0, (x, y) -> x + y));
32
33         // sum of squares of values with reduce method
34         System.out.printf("Sum of squares via reduce method: %d%n",
35            IntStream.of(values)
36                  .reduce(0, (x, y) -> x + y * y));
```

Fig. 17.5 | Demonstrating IntStream operations. (Part 1 of 2.)

```
37
38        // product of values with reduce method
39        System.out.printf("Product via reduce method: %d%n",
40           IntStream.of(values)
41                    .reduce(1, (x, y) -> x * y));
42
43        // even values displayed in sorted order
44        System.out.printf("%nEven values displayed in sorted order: ");
45        IntStream.of(values)
46                 .filter(value -> value % 2 == 0)
47                 .sorted()
48                 .forEach(value -> System.out.printf("%d ", value));
49        System.out.println();
50
51        // odd values multiplied by 10 and displayed in sorted order
52        System.out.printf(
53           "Odd values multiplied by 10 displayed in sorted order: ");
54        IntStream.of(values)
55                 .filter(value -> value % 2 != 0)
56                 .map(value -> value * 10)
57                 .sorted()
58                 .forEach(value -> System.out.printf("%d ", value));
59        System.out.println();
60
61        // sum range of integers from 1 to 10, exlusive
62        System.out.printf("%nSum of integers from 1 to 9: %d%n",
63           IntStream.range(1, 10).sum());
64
65        // sum range of integers from 1 to 10, inclusive
66        System.out.printf("Sum of integers from 1 to 10: %d%n",
67           IntStream.rangeClosed(1, 10).sum());
68     }
69  } // end class IntStreamOperations
```

```
Original values: 3 10 6 1 4 8 2 5 9 7

Count: 10
Min: 1
Max: 10
Sum: 55
Average: 5.50

Sum via reduce method: 55
Sum of squares via reduce method: 385
Product via reduce method: 3628800

Even values displayed in sorted order: 2 4 6 8 10
Odd values multiplied by 10 displayed in sorted order: 10 30 50 70 90

Sum of integers from 1 to 9: 45
Sum of integers from 1 to 10: 55
```

Fig. 17.5 | Demonstrating IntStream operations. (Part 2 of 2.)

17.3.1 Creating an `IntStream` and Displaying Its Values with the `forEach` Terminal Operation

`IntStream` static method **of** (line 14) receives an `int` array as an argument and returns an `IntStream` for processing the array's values. Once you create a stream, you can *chain* together multiple method calls to create a *stream pipeline*. The statement in lines 14–15 creates an `IntStream` for the `values` array, then uses `IntStream` method **forEach** (a terminal operation) to perform a task on each stream element. Method `forEach` receives as its argument an object that implements the **IntConsumer** functional interface (package **java.util.function**)—this is an `int`-specific version of the generic `Consumer` functional interface. This interface's **accept** method receives one `int` value and performs a task with it—in this case, displaying the value and a space. Prior to Java SE 8, you'd typically implement interface `IntConsumer` using an anonymous inner class like:

```
new IntConsumer()
{
   public void accept(int value)
   {
      System.out.printf("%d ", value);
   }
}
```

but in Java SE 8, you simply write the lambda

```
value -> System.out.printf("%d ", value)
```

The `accept` method's parameter name (`value`) becomes the lambda's parameter, and the `accept` method's body statement becomes the lambda expression's body. As you can see, the lambda syntax is clearer and more concise than the anonymous inner class.

Type Inference and a Lambda's Target Type

The Java compiler can usually *infer* the types of a lambda's parameters and the type returned by a lambda from the context in which the lambda is used. This is determined by the lambda's **target type**—the functional interface type that is expected where the lambda appears in the code. In line 15, the target type is `IntConsumer`. In this case, the lambda parameter's type is *inferred* to be `int`, because interface `IntConsumer`'s accept method expects to receive an `int`. You can *explicitly* declare the parameter's type, as in:

```
(int value) -> System.out.printf("%d ", value)
```

When doing so, the lambda's parameter list *must* be enclosed in parentheses. We generally let the compiler *infer* the lambda parameter's type in our examples.

final Local Variables, Effectively final Local Variables and Capturing Lambdas

Prior to Java SE 8, when implementing an anonymous inner class, you could use local variables from the enclosing method (known as the *lexical scope*), but you were required to declare those local variables `final`. Lambdas may also use `final` local variables. In Java SE 8, anonymous inner classes and lambdas can also use **effectively final local variables**—that is, local variables that are *not* modified after they're initially declared and initialized. A lambda that refers to a local variable in the enclosing lexical scope is known as a **capturing lambda**. The compiler captures the local variable's value and ensures that the value can be used when the lambda *eventually* executes, which may be *after* its lexical scope *no longer exists*.

*Using **this** in a Lambda That Appears in an Instance Method*

As in an anonymous inner class, a lambda can use the outer class's this reference. In an an anonymous inner class, you must use the syntax *OuterClassName*.this—otherwise, the this reference would refer to *the object of the anonymous inner class*. In a lambda, you refer to the object of the outer class, simply as this.

Parameter and Variable Names in a Lambda

The parameter names and variable names that you use in lambdas cannot be the same as as any other local variables in the lambda's lexical scope; otherwise, a compilation error occurs.

17.3.2 Terminal Operations count, min, max, sum and average

Class IntStream provides various terminal operations for common stream reductions on streams of int values. Terminal operations are *eager*—they immediately process the items in the stream. Common reduction operations for IntStreams include:

- **count** (line 19) returns the number of elements in the stream.
- **min** (line 21) returns the smallest int in the stream.
- **max** (line 23) returns the largest int in the stream.
- **sum** (line 24) returns the sum of all the ints in the stream.
- **average** (line 26) returns an **OptionalDouble** (package java.util) containing the average of the ints in the stream as a value of type double. For any stream, it's possible that there are *no elements* in the stream. Returning OptionalDouble enables method average to return the average if the stream contains *at least one element*. In this example, we know the stream has 10 elements, so we call class OptionalDouble's **getAsDouble** method to obtain the average. If there were no *elements*, the OptionalDouble would not contain the average and getAsDouble would throw a NoSuchElementException. To prevent this exception, you can instead call method **orElse**, which returns the OptionalDouble's value if there is one, or the value you pass to orElse, otherwise.

Class IntStream also provides method summaryStatistics that performs the count, min, max, sum and average operations *in one pass* of an IntStream's elements and returns the results as an IntSummaryStatistics object (package java.util). This provides a significant performance boost over reprocessing an IntStream repeatedly for each individual operation. This object has methods for obtaining each result and a toString method that summarizes all the results. For example, the statement:

```
System.out.println(IntStream.of(values).summaryStatistics());
```

produces:

```
IntSummaryStatistics{count=10, sum=55, min=1, average=5.500000,
max=10}
```

for the array values in Fig. 17.5.

17.3.3 Terminal Operation reduce

You can define your own reductions for an IntStream by calling its **reduce** method as shown in lines 29–31 of Fig. 17.5. Each of the terminal operations in Section 17.3.2 is a specialized implementation of reduce. For example, line 31 shows how to sum an Int-Steam's values using reduce, rather than sum. The first argument (0) is a value that helps you begin the reduction operation and the second argument is an object that implements the **IntBinaryOperator** functional interface (package java.util.function). The lambda:

```
(x, y) -> x + y
```

implements the interface's **applyAsInt** method, which receives two int values (representing the left and right operands of a binary operator) and performs a calculation with the values—in this case, adding the values. A lambda with two or more parameters *must* enclose them in parentheses. Evaluation of the reduction proceeds as follows:

- On the first call to reduce, lambda parameter x's value is the identity value (0) and lambda parameter y's value is the *first* int in the stream (3), producing the sum 3 (0 + 3).

- On the next call to reduce, lambda parameter x's value is the result of the first calculation (3) and lambda parameter y's value is the *second* int in the stream (10), producing the sum 13 (3 + 10).

- On the next call to reduce, lambda parameter x's value is the result of the previous calculation (13) and lambda parameter y's value is the *third* int in the stream (6), producing the sum 19 (13 + 6).

This process continues producing a running total of the IntSteam's values until they've all been used, at which point the final sum is returned.

Method *reduce's Identity Value Argument*
Method reduce's first argument is formally called an **identity value**—a value that, when combined with any stream element using the IntBinaryOperator produces that element's original value. For example, when summing the elements, the identity value is 0 (any int value added to 0 results in the original value) and when getting the product of the elements the identity value is 1 (any int value multiplied by 1 results in the original value).

Summing the Squares of the Values with Method *reduce*
Lines 34–36 of Fig. 17.5 use method reduce to calculate the sums of the squares of the IntSteam's values. The lambda in this case, adds the *square* of the current value to the running total. Evaluation of the reduction proceeds as follows:

- On the first call to reduce, lambda parameter x's value is the identity value (0) and lambda parameter y's value is the *first* int in the stream (3), producing the value 9 (0 + 3^2).

- On the next call to reduce, lambda parameter x's value is the result of the first calculation (9) and lambda parameter y's value is the *second* int in the stream (10), producing the sum 109 (9 + 10^2).

- On the next call to reduce, lambda parameter x's value is the result of the previous calculation (109) and lambda parameter y's value is the *third* int in the stream (6), producing the sum 145 (109 + 6^2).

This process continues producing a running total of the squares of the IntSteam's values until they've all been used, at which point the final sum is returned.

Calculating the Product of the Values with Method *reduce*

Lines 39–41 of Fig. 17.5 use method `reduce` to calculate the product of the `IntSteam`'s values. In this case, the lambda multiplies its two arguments. Because we're producing a product, we begin with the identity value 1 in this case. Evaluation of the reduction proceeds as follows:

- On the first call to `reduce`, lambda parameter x's value is the identity value (1) and lambda parameter y's value is the *first* `int` in the stream (3), producing the value 3 (1 * 3).

- On the next call to `reduce`, lambda parameter x's value is the result of the first calculation (3) and lambda parameter y's value is the *second* `int` in the stream (10), producing the sum 30 (3 * 10).

- On the next call to `reduce`, lambda parameter x's value is the result of the previous calculation (30) and lambda parameter y's value is the *third* `int` in the stream (6), producing the sum 180 (30 * 6).

This process continues producing a running product of the `IntSteam`'s values until they've all been used, at which point the final product is returned.

17.3.4 Intermediate Operations: Filtering and Sorting `IntStream` Values

Lines 45–48 of Fig. 17.5 create a stream pipeline that *locates* the even integers in an `IntStream`, *sorts* them in ascending order and *displays* each value followed by a space.

Intermediate Operation *filter*

You *filter* elements to produce a stream of intermediate results that match a condition—known as a *predicate*. `IntStream` method **filter** (line 46) receives an object that implements the **IntPredicate** functional interface (package `java.util.function`). The lambda in line 46:

```
value -> value % 2 == 0
```

implements the interface's **test** method, which receives an `int` and returns a `boolean` indicating whether the `int` satisfies the predicate—in this case, the `IntPredicate` returns `true` if the value it receives is divisible by 2. Calls to `filter` and other intermediate streams are *lazy*—they aren't evaluated until a *terminal operation* (which is *eager*) is performed—and produce new streams of elements. In lines 45–48, this occurs when `forEach` is called (line 48).

Intermediate Operation *sorted*

`IntStream` method **sorted** orders the elements of the stream into *ascending* order. Like `filter`, `sorted` is a *lazy* operation; however, when the sorting is eventually performed, all prior intermediate operations in the stream pipeline must be complete so that method `sorted` knows which elements to sort.

Processing the Stream Pipeline and Stateless vs. Stateful Intermediate Operations

When `forEach` is called, the stream pipeline is processed. Line 46 produces an intermediate `IntStream` containing only the even integers, then line 47 sorts them and line 48 displays each element.

Method `filter` is a **stateless intermediate operation**—it does not require any information about other elements in the stream in order to test whether the current element satisfies the predicate. Similarly method `map` (discussed shortly) is a stateless intermediate operation. Method `sorted` is a **stateful intermediate operation** that requires information about *all* of the other elements in the stream in order to sort them. Similarly method `distinct` is a stateful intermediate operation. The online documentation for each intermediate stream operation specifies whether it is a stateless or stateful operation.

Other Methods of the `IntPredicate` Functional Interface
Interface `IntPredicate` also contains three `default` methods:

- **and**—performs a *logical AND* with *short-circuit evaluation* (Section 5.9) between the `IntPredicate` on which it's called and the `IntPredicate` it receives as an argument.

- **negate**—*reverses* the `boolean` value of the `IntPredicate` on which it's called.

- **or**—performs a *logical OR* with *short-circuit evaluation* between the `IntPredicate` on which it's called and the `IntPredicate` it receives as an argument.

Composing Lambda Expressions
You can use these methods and `IntPredicate` objects to compose more complex conditions. For example, consider the following two `IntPredicate`s:

```
IntPredicate even = value -> value % 2 == 0;
IntPredicate greaterThan5 = value -> value > 5;
```

To locate all the even integers greater than 5, you could replace the lambda in line 46 with the `IntPredicate`

```
even.and(greaterThan5)
```

17.3.5 Intermediate Operation: Mapping
Lines 54–58 of Fig. 17.5 create a stream pipeline that *locates* the odd integers in an `IntStream`, *multiplies* each odd integer by 10, *sorts* the values in ascending order and *displays* each value followed by a space.

Intermediate Operation `map`
The new feature here is the *mapping* operation that takes each value and multiplies it by 10. Mapping is an *intermediate operation* that transforms a stream's elements to new values and produces a stream containing the resulting elements. Sometimes these are of different types from the original stream's elements.

`IntStream` method **map** (line 56) receives an object that implements the **IntUnaryOperator** functional interface (package `java.util.function`). The lambda in line 55:

```
value -> value * 10
```

implements the interface's **applyAsInt** method, which receives an `int` and maps it to a new `int` value. Calls to map are *lazy*. Method map is a *stateless* stream operation.

Processing the Stream Pipeline

When forEach is called (line 58), the stream pipeline is processed. First, line 55 produces an intermediate IntStream containing only the odd values. Next, line 56 multiplies each odd integer by 10. Then, line 57 sorts the values and line 58 displays each element.

17.3.6 Creating Streams of ints with IntStream Methods range and rangeClosed

If you need an *ordered sequence* of int values, you can create an IntStream containing such values with IntStream methods range (line 63 of Fig. 17.5) and rangeClosed (line 67). Both methods take two int arguments representing the range of values. Method **range** produces a sequence of values from its first argument up to, but *not* including its second argument. Method **rangeClosed** produces a sequence of values including *both* of its arguments. Lines 63 and 67 demonstrate these methods for producing sequences of int values from 1–9 and 1–10, respectively. For the complete list of IntStream methods, visit:

```
http://download.java.net/jdk8/docs/api/java/util/stream/
    IntStream.html
```

17.4 Stream<Integer> Manipulations

[This section demonstrates how lambdas and streams can be used to simplify programming tasks that you learned in Chapter 7, Arrays and ArrayLists.]

Just as class IntStream's method of can create an IntStream from an array of ints, class Array's **stream** method can be used to create a Stream from an array of objects. Figure 17.6 performs *filtering* and *sorting* on a Stream<Integer>, using the same techniques you learned in Section 17.3. The program also shows how to *collect* the results of a stream pipeline's operations into a new collection that you can process in subsequent statements. Throughout this example, we use the Integer array values (line 12) that's initialized with int values—the compiler *boxes* each int into an Integer object. Line 15 displays the contents of values before we perform any stream processing.

```java
1    // Fig. 17.6: ArraysAndStreams.java
2    // Demonstrating lambdas and streams with an array of Integers.
3    import java.util.Arrays;
4    import java.util.Comparator;
5    import java.util.List;
6    import java.util.stream.Collectors;
7
8    public class ArraysAndStreams
9    {
10       public static void main(String[] args)
11       {
12          Integer[] values = {2, 9, 5, 0, 3, 7, 1, 4, 8, 6};
13
14          // display original values
15          System.out.printf("Original values: %s%n", Arrays.asList(values));
```

Fig. 17.6 | Demonstrating lambdas and streams with an array of Integers. (Part 1 of 2.)

```
16
17        // sort values in ascending order with streams
18        System.out.printf("Sorted values: %s%n",
19           Arrays.stream(values)
20              .sorted()
21              .collect(Collectors.toList()));
22
23        // values greater than 4
24        List<Integer> greaterThan4 =
25           Arrays.stream(values)
26              .filter(value -> value > 4)
27              .collect(Collectors.toList());
28        System.out.printf("Values greater than 4: %s%n", greaterThan4);
29
30        // filter values greater than 4 then sort the results
31        System.out.printf("Sorted values greater than 4: %s%n",
32           Arrays.stream(values)
33              .filter(value -> value > 4)
34              .sorted()
35              .collect(Collectors.toList()));
36
37        // greaterThan4 List sorted with streams
38        System.out.printf(
39           "Values greater than 4 (ascending with streams): %s%n",
40           greaterThan4.stream()
41              .sorted()
42              .collect(Collectors.toList()));
43     }
44  } // end class ArraysAndStreams
```

```
Original values: [2, 9, 5, 0, 3, 7, 1, 4, 8, 6]
Sorted values: [0, 1, 2, 3, 4, 5, 6, 7, 8, 9]
Values greater than 4: [9, 5, 7, 8, 6]
Sorted values greater than 4: [5, 6, 7, 8, 9]
Values greater than 4 (ascending with streams): [5, 6, 7, 8, 9]
```

Fig. 17.6 | Demonstrating lambdas and streams with an array of Integers. (Part 2 of 2.)

17.4.1 Creating a Stream<Integer>

When you pass an array of objects to class Arrays's static method stream, the method returns a Stream of the appropriate type—e.g., line 19 produces a Stream<Integer> from an Integer array. Interface **Stream** (package java.util.stream) is a generic interface for performing stream operations on any *non-primitive* type. The types of objects that are processed are determined by the Stream's source.

Class Arrays also provides overloaded versions of method stream for creating Int-Streams, LongStreams and DoubleStreams from entire int, long and double arrays or from ranges of elements in the arrays. The specialized IntStream, LongStream and DoubleStream classes provide various methods for common operations on numerical streams, as you learned in Section 17.3.

17.4.2 Sorting a Stream and Collecting the Results

In Section 7.15, you learned how to sort arrays with the sort and parallelSort static methods of class Arrays. You'll often sort the results of stream operations, so in lines 18–21 we'll sort the values array using stream techniques and display the sorted values. First, line 19 creates a Stream<Integer> from values. Next, line 20 calls Stream method sorted which sort the elements—this results in an intermediate Stream<Integers> with the values in *ascending* order.

To display the sorted results, we could output each value using Stream terminal operation forEach (as in line 15 of Fig. 17.5). However, when processing streams, you often create *new* collections containing the results so that you can perform additional operations on them. To create a collection, you can use Stream method **collect** (Fig. 17.6, line 21), which is a *terminal operation*. As the stream pipeline is processed, method collect performs a **mutable reduction** operation that places the results into an object which subsequently *can be modified*—often a collection, such as a List, Map or Set. The version of method collect in line 21 receives as it's argument an object that implements interface **Collector** (package java.util.stream), which specifies how to perform the mutable reduction. Class **Collectors** (package java.util.stream) provides static methods that return predefined Collector implementations. For example, Collectors method **toList** (line 21) transforms the Stream<Integer> into a List<Integer> collection. In lines 18–21, the resulting List<Integer> is then displayed with an *implicit* call to its toString method.

We demonstrate another version of method collect in Section 17.6. For more details on class Collectors, visit:

```
http://download.java.net/jdk8/docs/api/java/util/stream/
    Collectors.html
```

17.4.3 Filtering a Stream and Storing the Results for Later Use

Lines 24–27 of Fig. 17.6 create a Stream<Integer>, call Stream method filter (which receives a Predicate) to locate all the values greater than 4 and collect the results into a List<Integer>. Like IntPredicate (Section 17.3.4), functional interface Predicate has a test method that returns a boolean indicating whether the argument satisfies a condition, as well as methods **and**, **negate** and **or**.

We assign the stream pipeline's resulting List<Integer> to variable greaterThan4, which is used in line 28 to display the values greater than 4 and used again in lines 40–42 to perform additional operations on only the values greater than 4.

17.4.4 Filtering and Sorting a Stream and Collecting the Results

Lines 31–35 display the values greater than 4 in sorted order. First, line 32 creates a Stream<Integer>. Then line 33 filters the elements to locate all the values greater than 4. Next, line 34 indicates that we'd like the results sorted. Finally, line 35 collects the results into a List<Integer>, which is then displayed as a String.

17.4.5 Sorting Previously Collected Results

Lines 40–42 use the greaterThan4 collection that was created in lines 24–27 to show additional processing on a collection containing the results of a prior stream pipeline. In this case, we use streams to sort the values in greaterThan4, collect the results into a new List<Integers> and display the sorted values.

17.5 Stream<String> Manipulations

[This section demonstrates how lambdas and streams can be used to simplify programming tasks that you learned in Chapter 14, Strings, Characters and Regular Expressions.]
Figure 17.7 performs some of the same stream operations you learned in Sections 17.3–17.4 but on a Stream<String>. In addition, we demonstrate *case-insensitive sorting* and sorting in *descending* order. Throughout this example, we use the String array strings (lines 11–12) that's initialized with color names—some with an initial uppercase letter. Line 15 displays the contents of strings *before* we perform any stream processing.

```java
 1   // Fig. 17.7: ArraysAndStreams2.java
 2   // Demonstrating lambdas and streams with an array of Strings.
 3   import java.util.Arrays;
 4   import java.util.Comparator;
 5   import java.util.stream.Collectors;
 6
 7   public class ArraysAndStreams2
 8   {
 9      public static void main(String[] args)
10      {
11         String[] strings =
12            {"Red", "orange", "Yellow", "green", "Blue", "indigo", "Violet"};
13
14         // display original strings
15         System.out.printf("Original strings: %s%n", Arrays.asList(strings));
16
17         // strings in uppercase
18         System.out.printf("strings in uppercase: %s%n",
19            Arrays.stream(strings)
20                  .map(String::toUpperCase)
21                  .collect(Collectors.toList()));
22
23         // strings less than "n" (case insensitive) sorted ascending
24         System.out.printf("strings greater than m sorted ascending: %s%n",
25            Arrays.stream(strings)
26                  .filter(s -> s.compareToIgnoreCase("n") < 0)
27                  .sorted(String.CASE_INSENSITIVE_ORDER)
28                  .collect(Collectors.toList()));
29
30         // strings less than "n" (case insensitive) sorted descending
31         System.out.printf("strings greater than m sorted descending: %s%n",
32            Arrays.stream(strings)
33                  .filter(s -> s.compareToIgnoreCase("n") < 0)
34                  .sorted(String.CASE_INSENSITIVE_ORDER.reversed())
35                  .collect(Collectors.toList()));
36      }
37   } // end class ArraysAndStreams2
```

Fig. 17.7 | Demonstrating lambdas and streams with an array of Strings. (Part 1 of 2.)

```
Original strings: [Red, orange, Yellow, green, Blue, indigo, Violet]
strings in uppercase: [RED, ORANGE, YELLOW, GREEN, BLUE, INDIGO, VIOLET]
strings greater than m sorted ascending: [orange, Red, Violet, Yellow]
strings greater than m sorted descending: [Yellow, Violet, Red, orange]
```

Fig. 17.7 | Demonstrating lambdas and streams with an array of Strings. (Part 2 of 2.)

17.5.1 Mapping Strings to Uppercase Using a Method Reference

Lines 18–21 display the Strings in uppercase letters. To do so, line 19 creates a Stream<String> from the array strings, then line 20 calls Stream method map to map each String to its uppercase version by calling String instance method toUpperCase. String::toUpperCase is known as a **method reference** and is a shorthand notation for a lambda expression—in this case, for a lambda expression like:

```
(String s) -> {return s.toUpperCase();}
```

or

```
s -> s.toUpperCase()
```

String::toUpperCase is a method reference for String instance method toUpperCase. Figure 17.8 shows the four method reference types.

Lambda	Description
String::toUpperCase	Method reference for an instance method of a class. Creates a one-parameter lambda that invokes the instance method on the lambda's argument and returns the method's result. Used in Fig. 17.7.
System.out::println	Method reference for an instance method that should be called on a specific object. Creates a one-parameter lambda that invokes the instance method on the specified object—passing the lambda's argument to the instance method—and returns the method's result. Used in Fig. 17.10.
Math::sqrt	Method reference for a static method of a class. Creates a one-parameter lambda in which the lambda's argument is passed to the specified a static method and the lambda returns the method's result.
TreeMap::new	Constructor reference. Creates a lambda that invokes the no-argument constructor of the specified class to create and initialize a new object of that class. Used in Fig. 17.17.

Fig. 17.8 | Types of method references.

Stream method map receives as an argument an object that implements the functional interface Function—the instance method reference String::toUpperCase is treated as a lambda that implements interface Function. This interface's **apply** method receives one parameter and returns a result—in this case, method apply receives a String and returns the uppercase version of the String. Line 21 *collects* the results into a List<String> that we output as a String.

17.5.2 Filtering Strings Then Sorting Them in Case-Insensitive Ascending Order

Lines 24–28 filter and sort the Strings. Line 25 creates a Stream<String> from the array strings, then line 26 calls Stream method filter to locate all the Strings that are greater than "m", using a *case-insensitive* comparison in the Predicate lambda. Line 27 sorts the results and line 28 collects them into a List<String> that we output as a String. In this case, line 27 invokes the version of Stream method sorted that receives a Comparator as an argument. As you learned in Section 16.7.1, a Comparator defines a compare method that returns a negative value if the first value being compared is less than the second, 0 if they're equal and a positive value if the first value is greater than the second. By default, method sorted uses the *natural order* for the type—for Strings, the natural order is case sensitive, which means that "Z" is less than "a". Passing the predefined Comparator String.CASE_INSENSITIVE_ORDER performs a *case-insensitive* sort.

17.5.3 Filtering Strings Then Sorting Them in Case-Insensitive Descending Order

Lines 31–35 perform the same tasks as lines 24–28, but sort the Strings in *descending* order. Functional interface Comparator contains default method **reversed**, which reverses an existing Comparator's ordering. When applied to String.CASE_INSENSITIVE_ORDER, the Strings are sorted in *descending* order.

17.6 Stream<Employee> Manipulations

The example in Figs. 17.9–17.16 demonstrates various lambda and stream capabilities using a Stream<Employee>. Class Employee (Fig. 17.9) represents an employee with a first name, last name, salary and department and provides methods for manipulating these values. In addition, the class provides a getName method (lines 69–72) that returns the combined first and last name as a String, and a toString method (lines 75–80) that returns a formatted String containing the employee's first name, last name, salary and department.

```java
1    // Fig. 17.9: Employee.java
2    // Employee class.
3    public class Employee
4    {
5        private String firstName;
6        private String lastName;
7        private double salary;
8        private String department;
9
10       // constructor
11       public Employee(String firstName, String lastName,
12          double salary, String department)
13       {
14          this.firstName = firstName;
15          this.lastName = lastName;
```

Fig. 17.9 | Employee class for use in Figs. 17.10–17.16. (Part 1 of 3.)

```
16          this.salary = salary;
17          this.department = department;
18      }
19
20      // set firstName
21      public void setFirstName(String firstName)
22      {
23          this.firstName = firstName;
24      }
25
26      // get firstName
27      public String getFirstName()
28      {
29          return firstName;
30      }
31
32      // set lastName
33      public void setLastName(String lastName)
34      {
35          this.lastName = lastName;
36      }
37
38      // get lastName
39      public String getLastName()
40      {
41          return lastName;
42      }
43
44      // set salary
45      public void setSalary(double salary)
46      {
47          this.salary = salary;
48      }
49
50      // get salary
51      public double getSalary()
52      {
53          return salary;
54      }
55
56      // set department
57      public void setDepartment(String department)
58      {
59          this.department = department;
60      }
61
62      // get department
63      public String getDepartment()
64      {
65          return department;
66      }
67
```

Fig. 17.9 | `Employee` class for use in Figs. 17.10–17.16. (Part 2 of 3.)

```
68      // return Employee's first and last name combined
69      public String getName()
70      {
71         return String.format("%s %s", getFirstName(), getLastName());
72      }
73
74      // return a String containing the Employee's information
75      @Override
76      public String toString()
77      {
78         return String.format("%-8s %-8s %8.2f   %s",
79            getFirstName(), getLastName(), getSalary(), getDepartment());
80      } // end method toString
81   } // end class Employee
```

Fig. 17.9 | Employee class for use in Figs. 17.10–17.16. (Part 3 of 3.)

17.6.1 Creating and Displaying a List<Employee>

Class ProcessingEmployees (Figs. 17.10–17.16) is split into several figures so we can show you the lambda and streams operations with their corresponding outputs. Figure 17.10 creates an array of Employees (lines 17–24) and gets its List view (line 27).

```
1    // Fig. 17.10: ProcessingEmployees.java
2    // Processing streams of Employee objects.
3    import java.util.Arrays;
4    import java.util.Comparator;
5    import java.util.List;
6    import java.util.Map;
7    import java.util.TreeMap;
8    import java.util.function.Function;
9    import java.util.function.Predicate;
10   import java.util.stream.Collectors;
11
12   public class ProcessingEmployees
13   {
14      public static void main(String[] args)
15      {
16         // initialize array of Employees
17         Employee[] employees = {
18            new Employee("Jason", "Red", 5000, "IT"),
19            new Employee("Ashley", "Green", 7600, "IT"),
20            new Employee("Matthew", "Indigo", 3587.5, "Sales"),
21            new Employee("James", "Indigo", 4700.77, "Marketing"),
22            new Employee("Luke", "Indigo", 6200, "IT"),
23            new Employee("Jason", "Blue", 3200, "Sales"),
24            new Employee("Wendy", "Brown", 4236.4, "Marketing")};
25
26         // get List view of the Employees
27         List<Employee> list = Arrays.asList(employees);
```

Fig. 17.10 | Creating an array of Employees, converting it to a List and displaying the List. (Part 1 of 2.)

```
28
29        // display all Employees
30        System.out.println("Complete Employee list:");
31        list.stream().forEach(System.out::println);
32
```

```
Complete Employee list:
Jason    Red      5000.00    IT
Ashley   Green    7600.00    IT
Matthew  Indigo   3587.50    Sales
James    Indigo   4700.77    Marketing
Luke     Indigo   6200.00    IT
Jason    Blue     3200.00    Sales
Wendy    Brown    4236.40    Marketing
```

Fig. 17.10 | Creating an array of Employees, converting it to a List and displaying the List. (Part 2 of 2.)

Line 31 creates a Stream<Employee>, then uses Stream method forEach to display each Employee's String representation. The instance method reference System.out::println is converted by the compiler into an object that implements the Consumer functional interface. This interface's **accept** method receives one argument and returns void. In this example, the accept method passes each Employee to the System.out object's println instance method, which implicitly calls class Employee's toString method to get the String representation. The output at the end of Fig. 17.10 shows the results of displaying all the Employees.

17.6.2 Filtering Employees with Salaries in a Specified Range

Figure 17.11 demonstrates filtering Employees with an object that implements the functional interface Predicate<Employee>, which is defined with a lambda in lines 34–35. Defining lambdas in this manner enables you to reuse them multiple times, as we do in lines 42 and 49. Lines 41–44 output the Employees with salaries in the range 4000–6000 sorted by salary as follows:

- Line 41 creates a Stream<Employee> from the List<Employee>.

- Line 42 filters the stream using the Predicate named fourToSixThousand.

- Line 43 sorts by salary the Employees that remain in the stream. To specify a Comparator for salaries, we use the Comparator interface's static method comparing. The method reference Employee::getSalary that's passed as an argument is converted by the compiler into an object that implements the Function interface. This Function is used to extract a value from an object in the stream for use in comparisons. Method comparing returns a Comparator object that calls getSalary on each of two Employee objects, then returns a negative value if the first Employee's salary is less than the second, 0 if they're equal and a positive value if the first Employee's salary is greater than the second.

- Finally, line 44 performs the terminal forEach operation that processes the stream pipeline and outputs the Employees sorted by salary.

```
33          // Predicate that returns true for salaries in the range $4000-$6000
34          Predicate<Employee> fourToSixThousand =
35             e -> (e.getSalary() >= 4000 && e.getSalary() <= 6000);
36
37          // Display Employees with salaries in the range $4000-$6000
38          // sorted into ascending order by salary
39          System.out.printf(
40             "%nEmployees earning $4000-$6000 per month sorted by salary:%n");
41          list.stream()
42             .filter(fourToSixThousand)
43             .sorted(Comparator.comparing(Employee::getSalary))
44             .forEach(System.out::println);
45
46          // Display first Employee with salary in the range $4000-$6000
47          System.out.printf("%nFirst employee who earns $4000-$6000:%n%s%n",
48             list.stream()
49                .filter(fourToSixThousand)
50                .findFirst()
51                .get());
52
```

```
Employees earning $4000-$6000 per month sorted by salary:
Wendy     Brown      4236.40     Marketing
James     Indigo     4700.77     Marketing
Jason     Red        5000.00     IT

First employee who earns $4000-$6000:
Jason     Red        5000.00     IT
```

Fig. 17.11 | Filtering Employees with salaries in the range $4000–$6000.

Short-Circuit Stream Pipeline Processing

In Section 5.9, you studied short-circuit evaluation with the logical AND (&&) and logical OR (||) operators. One of the nice performance features of lazy evaluation is the ability to perform *short circuit evaluation*—that is, to stop processing the stream pipeline as soon as the desired result is available. Line 50 demonstrates Stream method **findFirst**—a *short-circuiting terminal operation* that processes the stream pipeline and terminates processing as soon as the *first* object from the stream pipeline is found. Based on the original list of Employees, the processing of the stream in lines 48–51—which filters Employees with salaries in the range $4000–$6000—proceeds as follows: The Predicate fourTo-SixThousand is applied to the first Employee (Jason Red). His salary ($5000.00) is in the range $4000–$6000, so the Predicate returns true and processing of the stream terminates *immediately*, having processed only one of the eight objects in the stream. Method findFirst then returns an Optional (in this case, an Optional<Employee>) containing the object that was found, if any. The call to Optional method get (line 51) returns the matching Employee object in this example. Even if the stream contained millions of Employee objects, the filter operation would be performed only until a match is found.

17.6.3 Sorting Employees By Multiple Fields

Figure 17.12 shows how to use streams to sort objects by *multiple* fields. In this example, we sort Employees by last name, then, for Employees with the same last name, we also sort them by first name. To do so, we begin by creating two Functions that each receive an Employee and return a String:

- byFirstName (line 54) is assigned a method reference for Employee instance method getFirstName

- byLastName (line 55) is assigned a method reference for Employee instance method getLastName

Next, we use these Functions to create a Comparator (lastThenFirst; lines 58–59) that first compares two Employees by last name, then compares them by first name. We use Comparator method comparing to create a Comparator that calls Function byLastName on an Employee to get its last name. On the resulting Comparator, we call Comparator method **thenComparing** to create a Comparator that first compares Employees by last name and, *if the last names are equal*, then compares them by first name. Lines 64–65 use this new lastThenFirst Comparator to sort the Employees in *ascending* order, then display the results. We reuse the Comparator in lines 71–73, but call its reversed method to indicate that the Employees should be sorted in *descending* order by last name, then first name.

```
53          // Functions for getting first and last names from an Employee
54          Function<Employee, String> byFirstName = Employee::getFirstName;
55          Function<Employee, String> byLastName = Employee::getLastName;
56
57          // Comparator for comparing Employees by first name then last name
58          Comparator<Employee> lastThenFirst =
59             Comparator.comparing(byLastName).thenComparing(byFirstName);
60
61          // sort employees by last name, then first name
62          System.out.printf(
63             "%nEmployees in ascending order by last name then first:%n");
64          list.stream()
65             .sorted(lastThenFirst)
66             .forEach(System.out::println);
67
68          // sort employees in descending order by last name, then first name
69          System.out.printf(
70             "%nEmployees in descending order by last name then first:%n");
71          list.stream()
72             .sorted(lastThenFirst.reversed())
73             .forEach(System.out::println);
74
```

```
Employees in ascending order by last name then first:
Jason      Blue       3200.00    Sales
Wendy      Brown      4236.40    Marketing
Ashley     Green      7600.00    IT
James      Indigo     4700.77    Marketing
Luke       Indigo     6200.00    IT
Matthew    Indigo     3587.50    Sales
Jason      Red        5000.00    IT
```

Fig. 17.12 | Sorting Employees by last name then first name. (Part 1 of 2.)

```
Employees in descending order by last name then first:
Jason    Red      5000.00   IT
Matthew  Indigo   3587.50   Sales
Luke     Indigo   6200.00   IT
James    Indigo   4700.77   Marketing
Ashley   Green    7600.00   IT
Wendy    Brown    4236.40   Marketing
Jason    Blue     3200.00   Sales
```

Fig. 17.12 | Sorting Employees by last name then first name. (Part 2 of 2.)

17.6.4 Mapping Employees to Unique Last Name Strings

You previously used map operations to perform calculations on int values and to convert Strings to uppercase letters. In both cases, the resulting streams contained values of the same types as the original streams. Figure 17.13 shows how to map objects of one type (Employee) to objects of a different type (String). Lines 77–81 perform the following tasks:

- Line 77 creates a Stream<Employee>.

- Line 78 maps the Employees to their last names using the instance method reference Employee::getName as method map's Function argument. The result is a Stream<String>.

- Line 79 calls Stream method **distinct** on the Stream<String> to eliminate any duplicate String objects in a Stream<String>.

- Line 80 sorts the unique last names.

- Finally, line 81 performs a terminal forEach operation that processes the stream pipeline and outputs the unique last names in sorted order.

Lines 86–89 sort the Employees by last name then first name, then map the Employees to Strings with Employee instance method getName (line 88) and display the sorted names in a terminal forEach operation.

```
75      // display unique employee last names sorted
76      System.out.printf("%nUnique employee last names:%n");
77      list.stream()
78          .map(Employee::getLastName)
79          .distinct()
80          .sorted()
81          .forEach(System.out::println);
82
83      // display only first and last names
84      System.out.printf(
85          "%nEmployee names in order by last name then first name:%n");
86      list.stream()
87          .sorted(lastThenFirst)
88          .map(Employee::getName)
89          .forEach(System.out::println);
90
```

Fig. 17.13 | Mapping Employee objects to last names and whole names. (Part 1 of 2.)

```
Unique employee last names:
Blue
Brown
Green
Indigo
Red

Employee names in order by last name then first name:
Jason Blue
Wendy Brown
Ashley Green
James Indigo
Luke Indigo
Matthew Indigo
Jason Red
```

Fig. 17.13 | Mapping Employee objects to last names and whole names. (Part 2 of 2.)

17.6.5 Grouping Employees By Department

Figure 17.14 uses Stream method collect (line 95) to group Employees by department. Method collect's argument is a Collector that specifies how to summarize the data into a useful form. In this case, we use the Collector returned by Collectors static method **groupingBy**, which receives a Function that classifies the objects in the stream—the values returned by this function are used as the keys in a Map. The corresponding values, by default, are Lists containing the stream elements in a given category. When method collect is used with this Collector, the result is a Map<String, List<Employee>> in which each String key is a department and each List<Employee> contains the Employees in that department. We assign this Map to variable groupedByDepartment, which is used in lines 96–103 to display the Employees grouped by department. Map method **forEach** performs an operation on each of the Map's key–value pairs. The argument to the method is an object that implements functional interface **BiConsumer**. This interface's accept method has two parameters. For Maps, the first parameter represents the key and the second represents the corresponding value.

```
91      // group Employees by department
92      System.out.printf("%nEmployees by department:%n");
93      Map<String, List<Employee>> groupedByDepartment =
94         list.stream()
95            .collect(Collectors.groupingBy(Employee::getDepartment));
96      groupedByDepartment.forEach(
97         (department, employeesInDepartment) ->
98         {
99            System.out.println(department);
100           employeesInDepartment.forEach(
101              employee -> System.out.printf("   %s%n", employee));
102        }
103     );
104
```

Fig. 17.14 | Grouping Employees by department. (Part 1 of 2.)

```
Employees by department:
Sales
    Matthew   Indigo     3587.50    Sales
    Jason     Blue       3200.00    Sales
IT
    Jason     Red        5000.00    IT
    Ashley    Green      7600.00    IT
    Luke      Indigo     6200.00    IT
Marketing
    James     Indigo     4700.77    Marketing
    Wendy     Brown      4236.40    Marketing
```

Fig. 17.14 | Grouping Employees by department. (Part 2 of 2.)

17.6.6 Counting the Number of Employees in Each Department

Figure 17.15 once again demonstrates Stream method collect and Collectors static method groupingBy, but in this case we count the number of Employees in each department. Lines 107–110 produce a Map<String, Long> in which each String key is a department name and the corresponding Long value is the number of Employees in that department. In this case, we use a version of Collectors static method groupingBy that receives two arguments—the first is a Function that classifies the objects in the stream and the second is another Collector (known as the **downstream Collector**). In this case, we use a call to Collectors static method counting as the second argument. This method returns a Collector that counts the number of objects in a given classification, rather than collecting them into a List. Lines 111–113 then output the key–value pairs from the resulting Map<String, Long>.

```
105      // count number of Employees in each department
106      System.out.printf("%nCount of Employees by department:%n");
107      Map<String, Long> employeeCountByDepartment =
108         list.stream()
109            .collect(Collectors.groupingBy(Employee::getDepartment,
110               Collectors.counting()));
111      employeeCountByDepartment.forEach(
112         (department, count) -> System.out.printf(
113            "%s has %d employee(s)%n", department, count));
114
```

```
Count of Employees by department:
IT has 3 employee(s)
Marketing has 2 employee(s)
Sales has 2 employee(s)
```

Fig. 17.15 | Counting the number of Employees in each department.

17.6.7 Summing and Averaging Employee Salaries

Figure 17.16 demonstrates Stream method **mapToDouble** (lines 119, 126 and 132), which maps objects to double values and returns a DoubleStream. In this case, we map Employee objects to their salaries so that we can calculate the *sum* and *average*. Method mapToDouble receives an object that implements the functional interface **ToDoubleFunction** (package java.util.function). This interface's **applyAsDouble** method invokes an instance method on an object and returns a double value. Lines 119, 126 and 132 each pass to mapToDouble the Employee instance method reference Employee::getSalary, which returns the current Employee's salary as a double. The compiler converts this method reference into an object that implements the functional interface ToDoubleFunction.

```
115        // sum of Employee salaries with DoubleStream sum method
116        System.out.printf(
117           "%nSum of Employees' salaries (via sum method): %.2f%n",
118           list.stream()
119              .mapToDouble(Employee::getSalary)
120              .sum());
121
122        // calculate sum of Employee salaries with Stream reduce method
123        System.out.printf(
124           "Sum of Employees' salaries (via reduce method): %.2f%n",
125           list.stream()
126              .mapToDouble(Employee::getSalary)
127              .reduce(0, (value1, value2) -> value1 + value2));
128
129        // average of Employee salaries with DoubleStream average method
130        System.out.printf("Average of Employees' salaries: %.2f%n",
131           list.stream()
132              .mapToDouble(Employee::getSalary)
133              .average()
134              .getAsDouble());
135     } // end main
136  } // end class ProcessingEmployees
```

```
Sum of Employees' salaries (via sum method): 34524.67
Sum of Employees' salaries (via reduce method): 34525.67
Average of Employees' salaries: 4932.10
```

Fig. 17.16 | Summing and averaging Employee salaries.

Lines 118–120 create a Stream<Employee>, map it to a DoubleStream, then invoke DoubleStream method sum to calculate the sum of the Employees' salaries. Lines 125–127 also sum the Employees' salaries, but do so using DoubleStream method reduce rather than sum—we introduced method reduce in Section 17.3 with IntStreams. Finally, lines 131–134 calculate the average of the Employees' salaries using DoubleStream method average, which returns an OptionalDouble in case the DoubleStream does not contain any elements. In this case, we know the stream has elements, so we simply call method OptionalDouble method getAsDouble to get the result. Recall that you can also use method orElse to specify a value that should be used if the average method was called on an empty DoubleStream, and thus could not calculate the average.

17.7 Creating a `Stream<String>` from a File

Figure 17.17 uses lambdas and streams to summarize the number of occurrences of each word in a file then display a summary of the words in alphabetical order grouped by starting letter. This is commonly called a concordance (http://en.wikipedia.org/wiki/Concordance_(publishing)). Concordances are often used to analyze published works. For example, concordances of William Shakespeare's and Christopher Marlowe's works have been used to question whether they are the same person. Figure 17.18 shows the program's output. Line 16 of Fig. 17.17 creates a regular expression `Pattern` that we'll use to split lines of text into their individual words. This `Pattern` represents one or more consecutive white-space characters. (We introduced regular expressions in Section 14.7.)

```java
1  // Fig. 17.17: StreamOfLines.java
2  // Counting word occurrences in a text file.
3  import java.io.IOException;
4  import java.nio.file.Files;
5  import java.nio.file.Paths;
6  import java.util.Map;
7  import java.util.TreeMap;
8  import java.util.regex.Pattern;
9  import java.util.stream.Collectors;
10
11 public class StreamOfLines
12 {
13    public static void main(String[] args) throws IOException
14    {
15       // Regex that matches one or more consecutive whitespace characters
16       Pattern pattern = Pattern.compile("\\s+");
17
18       // count occurrences of each word in a Stream<String> sorted by word
19       Map<String, Long> wordCounts =
20          Files.lines(Paths.get("Chapter2Paragraph.txt"))
21             .map(line -> line.replaceAll("(?!')\\p{P}", ""))
22             .flatMap(line -> pattern.splitAsStream(line))
23             .collect(Collectors.groupingBy(String::toLowerCase,
24                TreeMap::new, Collectors.counting()));
25
26       // display the words grouped by starting letter
27       wordCounts.entrySet()
28          .stream()
29          .collect(
30             Collectors.groupingBy(entry -> entry.getKey().charAt(0),
31                TreeMap::new, Collectors.toList()))
32          .forEach((letter, wordList) ->
33             {
34                System.out.printf("%n%C%n", letter);
35                wordList.stream().forEach(word -> System.out.printf(
36                   "%13s: %d%n", word.getKey(), word.getValue()));
37             });
38    }
39 } // end class StreamOfLines
```

Fig. 17.17 | Counting word occurrences in a text file.

```
A                        I                        R
            a: 2                 inputs: 1                result: 1
          and: 3               instruct: 1               results: 2
  application: 2             introduces: 1                   run: 1
   arithmetic: 1
                         J                        S
B                                java: 1                  save: 1
        begin: 1                   jdk: 1                screen: 1
                                                           show: 1
C                        L                                  sum: 1
   calculates: 1                 last: 1
 calculations: 1                later: 1         T
      chapter: 1                 learn: 1                  that: 3
     chapters: 1                                           the: 7
  commandline: 1         M                              their: 2
     compares: 1                 make: 1                  then: 2
   comparison: 1             messages: 2                  this: 2
      compile: 1                                            to: 4
     computer: 1         N                              tools: 1
D                            numbers: 2                   two: 2
    decisions: 1
 demonstrates: 1         O                        U
      display: 1              obtains: 1                   use: 2
     displays: 2                  of: 1                   user: 1
                                  on: 1
E                             output: 1          W
      example: 1                                            we: 2
     examples: 1         P                               with: 1
                             perform: 1
F                            present: 1          Y
          for: 1             program: 1                you'll: 2
         from: 1         programming: 1
                            programs: 2
H
         how: 2
```

Fig. 17.18 | Output for the program of Fig. 17.17 arranged in three columns.

Summarizing the Occurrences of Each Word in the File

Lines 19–24 summarize contents of the text file "Chapter2Paragraph.txt" (which is located in the folder with the example) into a Map<String, Long> in which each String key is a word in the file and the corresponding Long value is the number of occurrences of that word. The statement performs the following tasks:

- Line 20 uses Files method **lines** to create a Stream<String> for reading the lines of text from a file. Class Files (package java.nio.file) is one of many classes throughout the Java APIs that have been enhanced to support Streams.

- Line 21 uses Stream method map to remove all the punctuation, except apostrophes, in the lines of text. The lambda argument represents a Function that invokes String method replaceAll on its String argument. This method receives two arguments—the first is a regular expression String to match and the second is a String with which every match is replaced. In the regular expression,

"(?!')" indicates that the rest of the regular expression should ignore apostrophes (such as in a contraction, like "you'll") and "\\p{P}" matches any punctuation character. For any match, the call to replaceAll removes the punctuation by replacing it with an empty String. The result of line 21 is an intermediate Stream<String> containing the lines without punctuation.

- Line 22 uses Stream method **flatMap** to break each line of text into its separate words. Method flatMap receives a Function that maps an object into a stream of elements. In this case, the object is a String containing words and the result is another intermediate Stream<String> for the individual words. The lambda in line 22 passes the String representing a line of text to Pattern method **split-AsStream** (new in Java SE 8), which uses the regular expression specified in the Pattern (line 16) to tokenize the String into its individual words.

- Lines 23–24 use Stream method collect to count the frequency of each word and place the words and their counts into the TreeMap<String, Long>. Here, we use a version of Collectors method groupingBy that receives three arguments— a classifier, a Map factory and a downstream Collector. The classifier is a Function that returns objects for use as keys in the resulting Map—the method reference String::toLowerCase converts each word in the Stream<String> to lowercase. The Map factory is an object that implements interface Supplier and returns a new Map collection—the *constructor reference* TreeMap::new returns a TreeMap that maintains its keys in sorted order. Collectors.counting() is the downstream Collector that determines the number of occurrences of each key in the stream.

Displaying the Summary Grouped by Starting Letter

Next, lines 27–37 group the key–value pairs in the Map wordCounts by the keys' first letter. This produces a new Map in which each key is a Character and the corresponding value is a List of the key–value pairs in wordCounts in which the key starts with the Character. The statement performs the following tasks:

- First we need to get a Stream for processing the key–value pairs in wordCounts. Interface Map does not contain any methods that return Streams. So, line 27 calls Map method entrySet on wordCounts to get a Set of **Map.Entry** objects that each contain one key–value pair from wordCounts. This produces an object of type Set<Map.Entry<String, Long>>.

- Line 28 calls Set method stream to get a Stream<Map.Entry<String, Long>>.

- Lines 29–31 call Stream method collect with three arguments—a classifier, a Map factory and a downstream Collector. The classifier Function in this case gets the key from the Map.Entry then uses String method charAt to get the key's first character—this becomes a Character key in the resulting Map. Once again, we use the constructor reference TreeMap::new as the Map factory to create a TreeMap that maintains its keys in sorted order. The downstream Collector (Collectors.toList()) places the Map.Entry objects into a List collection. The result of collect is a Map<Character, List<Map.Entry<String, Long>>>.

- Finally, to display the summary of the words and their counts by letter (i.e., the concordance), lines 32–37 pass a lambda to Map method forEach. The lambda (a BiConsumer) receives two parameters—letter and wordList represent the Character key and the List value, respectively, for each key–value pair in the Map produced by the preceding collect operation. The body of this lambda has two statements, so it *must* be enclosed in curly braces. The statement in line 34 displays the Character key on its own line. The statement in lines 35–36 gets a Stream<Map.Entry<String, Long>> from the wordList, then calls Stream method forEach to display the key and value from each Map.Entry object.

17.8 Generating Streams of Random Values

In Fig. 6.6, we demonstrated rolling a six-sided die 6,000,000 times and summarizing the frequencies of each face using *external iteration* (a for loop) and a switch statement that determined which counter to increment. We then displayed the results using separate statements that performed external iteration. In Fig. 7.7, we reimplemented Fig. 6.6, replacing the entire switch statement with a single statement that incremented counters in an array—that version of rolling the die still used external iteration to produce and summarize 6,000,000 random rolls and to display the final results. Both prior versions of this example, used mutable variables to control the external iteration and to summarize the results. Figure 17.19 reimplements those programs with a *single statement* that does it all, using lambdas, streams, internal iteration and no mutable variables to roll the die 6,000,000 times, calculate the frequencies and display the results.

```
1   // Fig. 17.19: RandomIntStream.java
2   // Rolling a die 6,000,000 times with streams
3   import java.security.SecureRandom;
4   import java.util.Map;
5   import java.util.function.Function;
6   import java.util.stream.IntStream;
7   import java.util.stream.Collectors;
8
9   public class RandomIntStream
10  {
11     public static void main(String[] args)
12     {
13        SecureRandom random = new SecureRandom();
14
15        // roll a die 6,000,000 times and summarize the results
16        System.out.printf("%-6s%s%n", "Face", "Frequency");
17        random.ints(6_000_000, 1, 7)
18           .boxed()
19           .collect(Collectors.groupingBy(Function.identity(),
20              Collectors.counting()))
21           .forEach((face, frequency) ->
22              System.out.printf("%-6d%d%n", face, frequency));
23     }
24  } // end class RandomIntStream
```

Fig. 17.19 | Rolling a die 6,000,000 times with streams. (Part 1 of 2.)

Face	Frequency
1	999339
2	999937
3	1000302
4	999323
5	1000183
6	1000916

Fig. 17.19 | Rolling a die 6,000,000 times with streams. (Part 2 of 2.)

Creating an *IntStream of Random Values*

In Java SE 8, class SecureRandom has overloaded methods **ints**, **longs** and **doubles**, which it inherits from class Random (package java.util). These methods return IntStream, Long-Stream and DoubleStream, respectively, that represent streams of random numbers. Each method has four overloads. We describe the ints overloads here—methods longs and doubles perform the same tasks for streams of long and double values, respectively:

- ints()—creates an IntStream for an *infinite stream* of random ints. An **infinite stream** has an *unknown* number of elements—you use a short-circuiting terminal operation to complete processing on an infinite stream. We'll use an infinite stream in Chapter 20 to find prime numbers with the Sieve of Eratosthenes.

- ints(long)—creates an IntStream with the specified number of random ints.

- ints(int, int)—creates an IntStream for an *infinite stream* of random int values in the range starting with the first argument and up to, but not including, the second argument.

- ints(long, int, int)—creates an IntStream with the specified number of random int values in the range starting with the first argument and up to, but not including, the second argument.

Line 17 uses the last overloaded version of ints to create an IntStream of 6,000,000 random integer values in the range 1–6.

Converting an *IntStream to a Stream<Integer>*

We summarize the roll frequencies in this example by collecting them into a Map<Integer, Long> in which each Integer key is a side of the die and each Long value is the frequency of that side. Unfortunately, Java does not allow primitive values in collections, so to summarize the results in a Map, we must first convert the IntStream to a Stream<Integer>. We do this by calling IntStream method **boxed**.

Summarizing the Die Frequencies

Lines 19–20 call Stream method collect to summarize the results into a Map<Integer, Long>. The first argument to Collectors method groupingBy (line 19) calls static method **identity** from interface Function, which creates a Function that simply returns its argument. This allows the actual random values to be used as the Map's keys. The second argument to method groupingBy counts the number of occurrences of each key.

Displaying the Results

Lines 21–22 call the resulting Map's forEach method to display the summary of the results. This method receives an object that implements the BiConsumer functional interface as an argument. Recall that for Maps, the first parameter represents the key and the second represents the corresponding value. The lambda in lines 21–22 uses parameter face as the key and frequency as the value, and displays the face and frequency.

17.9 Lambda Event Handlers

In Section 12.11, you learned how to implement an event handler using an anonymous inner class. Some event-listener interfaces—such as ActionListener and ItemListener—are functional interfaces. For such interfaces, you can implement event handlers with lambdas. For example, the following statement from Fig. 12.21:

```
imagesJComboBox.addItemListener(
    new ItemListener() // anonymous inner class
    {
        // handle JComboBox event
        @Override
        public void itemStateChanged(ItemEvent event)
        {
            // determine whether item selected
            if (event.getStateChange() == ItemEvent.SELECTED)
                label.setIcon(icons[
                    imagesJComboBox.getSelectedIndex()]);
        }
    } // end anonymous inner class
); // end call to addItemListener
```

which registers an event handler for a JComboBox can be implemented more concisely as

```
imagesJComboBox.addItemListener(event -> {
    if (event.getStateChange() == ItemEvent.SELECTED)
        label.setIcon(icons[imagesJComboBox.getSelectedIndex()]);
});
```

For a simple event handler like this one, a lambda significantly reduces the amount of code you need to write.

17.10 Additional Notes on Java SE 8 Interfaces

Java SE 8 Interfaces Allow Inheritance of Method Implementations
Functional interfaces *must* contain only one abstract method, but may also contain default methods and static methods that are fully implemented in the interface declarations. For example, the Function interface—which is used extensively in functional programming—has methods apply (abstract), compose (default), andThen (default) and identity (static).

When a class implements an interface with default methods and does *not* override them, the class inherits the default methods' implementations. An interface's designer can now evolve an interface by adding new default and static methods without breaking existing code that implements the interface. For example, interface Comparator (Section 16.7.1) now contains many default and static methods, but older classes that implement this interface will still compile and operate properly in Java SE 8.

If one class inherits the same default method from two unrelated interfaces, the class *must* override that method; otherwise, the compiler will not know which method to use, so it will generate a compilation error.

Java SE 8: @FunctionalInterface Annotation

You can create your own functional interfaces by ensuring that each contains only one abstract method and zero or more default or static methods. Though not required, you can declare that an interface is a functional interface by preceding it with the **@FunctionalInterface annotation**. The compiler will then ensure that the interface contains only one abstract method; otherwise, it'll generate a compilation error.

17.11 Java SE 8 and Functional Programming Resources

Check out the book's web page at

```
http://www.deitel.com/books/javafp3
```

for links to the online Deitel Resource Centers that we built as we were writing *Java SE 8 for Programmers, 3/e.*

17.12 Wrap-Up

In this chapter, you learned about Java SE 8's new functional programming capabilities. We presented many examples, often showing simpler ways to implement tasks that you programmed in earlier chapters.

We overviewed the key functional programming technologies—functional interfaces, lambdas and streams. You learned how to process elements in an IntStream—a stream of int values. You created an IntStream from an array of ints, then used intermediate and terminal stream operations to create and process a stream pipeline that produced a result. You used lambdas to create anonymous methods that implemented functional interfaces.

We showed how to use a forEach terminal operation to perform an operation on each stream element. We used reduction operations to count the number of stream elements, determine the minimum and maximum values, and sum and average the values. You also learned how to use method reduce to create your own reduction operations.

You used intermediate operations to filter elements that matched a predicate and map elements to new values—in each case, these operations produced intermediate streams on which you could perform additional processing. You also learned how to sort elements in ascending and descending order and how to sort objects by multiple fields.

We demonstrated how to store the results of a stream pipeline into a collection for later use. To do so, you took advantage of various predefined Collector implementations provided by class Collectors. You also learned how to use a Collector to group elements into categories.

You learned that various Java SE 8 classes have been enhanced to support functional programming. You then used Files method lines to get a Stream<String> that read lines of text from a file and used SecureRandom method ints to get an IntStream of random values. You also learned how to convert an IntStream into a Stream<Integer> (via method boxed) so that you could use Stream method collect to summarize the frequencies of the Integer values and store the results in a Map.

Next, you learned how to implement an event-handling functional interface using a lambda. Finally, we presented some additional information about Java SE 8 interfaces and streams. In the next chapter, we demonstrate how to use Java's generics capabilities to implement generic methods and classes.

18

Generic Classes and Methods

- Create generic methods that perform identical tasks on arguments of different types.

- Create a generic Stack class that can be used to store objects of any class or interface type.

- Undestand compile-time translation of generic methods and classes.

- Understand how to overload generic methods with nongeneric methods or other generic methods.

- Understand raw types.

- Use wildcards when precise type information about a parameter is not required in the method body.

18.1 Introduction

You've used existing generic methods and classes in Chapters 7 and 16. In this chapter, you'll learn how to write your own.

It would be nice if we could write a single sort method to sort the elements in an Integer array, a String array or an array of any type that supports ordering (i.e., its elements can be compared). It would also be nice if we could write a single Stack class that could be used as a Stack of integers, a Stack of floating-point numbers, a Stack of Strings or a Stack of any other type. It would be even nicer if we could detect type mismatches at *compile time*—known as **compile-time type safety**. For example, if a Stack should store only integers, an attempt to push a String onto that Stack should issue a *compilation* error. This chapter discusses **generics**—specifically **generic methods** and **generic classes**—which provide the means to create the type-safe general models mentioned above.

18.2 Motivation for Generic Methods

Overloaded methods are often used to perform *similar* operations on *different* types of data. To motivate generic methods, let's begin with an example (Fig. 18.1) containing overloaded printArray methods (lines 22–29, 32–39 and 42–49) that print the String representations of the elements of an Integer array, a Double array and a Character array, respectively. We could have used arrays of primitive types int, double and char. We're using arrays of the type-wrapper classes to set up our generic method example, because *only reference types can be used to specify generic types in generic methods and classes*.

```
1   // Fig. 18.1: OverloadedMethods.java
2   // Printing array elements using overloaded methods.
3
4   public class OverloadedMethods
5   {
6      public static void main(String[] args)
7      {
8         // create arrays of Integer, Double and Character
9         Integer[] integerArray = {1, 2, 3, 4, 5, 6};
10        Double[] doubleArray = {1.1, 2.2, 3.3, 4.4, 5.5, 6.6, 7.7};
11        Character[] characterArray = {'H', 'E', 'L', 'L', 'O'};
```

Fig. 18.1 | Printing array elements using overloaded methods. (Part 1 of 2.)

```
12
13          System.out.printf("Array integerArray contains:%n");
14          printArray(integerArray); // pass an Integer array
15          System.out.printf("%nArray doubleArray contains:%n");
16          printArray(doubleArray); // pass a Double array
17          System.out.printg("%nArray characterArray contains:%n");
18          printArray(characterArray); // pass a Character array
19      }
20
21      // method printArray to print Integer array
22      public static void printArray(Integer[] inputArray)
23      {
24          // display array elements
25          for (Integer element : inputArray)
26              System.out.printf("%s ", element);
27
28          System.out.println();
29      }
30
31      // method printArray to print Double array
32      public static void printArray(Double[] inputArray)
33      {
34          // display array elements
35          for (Double element : inputArray)
36              System.out.printf("%s ", element);
37
38          System.out.println();
39      }
40
41      // method printArray to print Character array
42      public static void printArray(Character[] inputArray)
43      {
44          // display array elements
45          for (Character element : inputArray)
46              System.out.printf("%s ", element);
47
48          System.out.println();
49      }
50  } // end class OverloadedMethods
```

```
Array integerArray contains:
1 2 3 4 5 6

Array doubleArray contains:
1.1 2.2 3.3 4.4 5.5 6.6 7.7

Array characterArray contains:
H E L L O
```

Fig. 18.1 | Printing array elements using overloaded methods. (Part 2 of 2.)

The program begins by declaring and initializing three arrays—six-element Integer array integerArray (line 9), seven-element Double array doubleArray (line 10) and five-element Character array characterArray (line 11). Then lines 13–18 display the contents of each array.

When the compiler encounters a method call, it attempts to locate a method declaration with the same name and with parameters that match the argument types in the call. In this example, each printArray call matches one of the printArray method declarations. For example, line 14 calls printArray with integerArray as its argument. The compiler determines the argument's type (i.e., Integer[]) and attempts to locate a printArray method that specifies an Integer[] parameter (lines 22–29), then sets up a call to that method. Similarly, when the compiler encounters the call at line 16, it determines the argument's type (i.e., Double[]), then attempts to locate a printArray method that specifies a Double[] parameter (lines 32–39), then sets up a call to that method. Finally, when the compiler encounters the call at line 18, it determines the argument's type (i.e., Character[]), then attempts to locate a printArray method that specifies a Character[] parameter (lines 42–49), then sets up a call to that method.

Common Features in the Overloaded printArray Methods
Study each printArray method. The array element type appears in each method's header (lines 22, 32 and 42) and for-statement header (lines 25, 35 and 45). If we were to replace the element types in each method with a generic name—T by convention—then all three methods would look like the one in Fig. 18.2. It appears that if we can replace the array element type in each of the three methods with a *single generic type*, then we should be able to declare *one* printArray method that can display the String representations of the elements of *any* array that contains objects. The method in Fig. 18.2 is similar to the generic printArray method declaration you'll see in Section 18.3. The one shown here *will not compile*—we use this simply to show that the three printArray methods of Fig. 18.1 are identical except for the types they process.

```
1   public static void printArray(T[] inputArray)
2   {
3      // display array elements
4      for (T element : inputArray)
5         System.out.printf("%s ", element);
6
7      System.out.println();
8   }
```

Fig. 18.2 | printArray method in which actual type names are replaced with a generic type name (in this case T).

18.3 Generic Methods: Implementation and Compile-Time Translation

If the operations performed by several overloaded methods are *identical* for each argument type, the overloaded methods can be more conveniently coded using a generic method. You can write a single generic method declaration that can be called with arguments of different types. Based on the types of the arguments passed to the generic method, the compiler handles each method call appropriately. At *compilation time*, the compiler ensures the *type safety* of your code, preventing many runtime errors.

Figure 18.3 reimplements Fig. 18.1 using a generic printArray method (lines 22–29 of Fig. 18.3). The printArray calls in lines 14, 16 and 18 are identical to those of

Fig. 18.1 (lines 14, 16 and 18) and the outputs of the two applications are identical. This demonstrates the expressive power of generics.

```
1   // Fig. 18.3: GenericMethodTest.java
2   // Printing array elements using generic method printArray.
3
4   public class GenericMethodTest
5   {
6      public static void main(String[] args)
7      {
8         // create arrays of Integer, Double and Character
9         Integer[] intArray = {1, 2, 3, 4, 5};
10        Double[] doubleArray = {1.1, 2.2, 3.3, 4.4, 5.5, 6.6, 7.7};
11        Character[] charArray = {'H', 'E', 'L', 'L', 'O'};
12
13        System.out.printf("Array integerArray contains:%n");
14        printArray(integerArray); // pass an Integer array
15        System.out.printf("%nArray doubleArray contains:%n");
16        printArray(doubleArray); // pass a Double array
17        System.out.printf("%nArray characterArray contains:%n");
18        printArray(characterArray); // pass a Character array
19     }
20
21     // generic method printArray
22     public static <T> void printArray(T[] inputArray)
23     {
24        // display array elements
25        for (T element : inputArray)
26           System.out.printf("%s ", element);
27
28        System.out.println();
29     }
30  } // end class GenericMethodTest
```

```
Array integerArray contains:
1 2 3 4 5 6

Array doubleArray contains:
1.1 2.2 3.3 4.4 5.5 6.6 7.7

Array characterArray contains:
H E L L O
```

Fig. 18.3 | Printing array elements using generic method printArray.

Type Parameter Section of a Generic Method
Line 22 begins method printArray's declaration. All generic method declarations have a **type-parameter section** (<T> in this example) delimited by **angle brackets** that precedes the method's return type. Each type-parameter section contains one or more **type parameters**, separated by commas. A type parameter, also known as a **type variable**, is an identifier that specifies a generic type name. The type parameters can be used to declare the return type, parameter types and local variable types in a generic method declaration, and

they act as placeholders for the types of the arguments passed to the generic method, which are known as **actual type arguments**. A generic method's body is declared like that of any other method. *Type parameters can represent only reference types*—not primitive types (like int, double and char). Note, too, that the type-parameter names throughout the method declaration must match those declared in the type-parameter section. For example, line 25 declares element as type T, which matches the type parameter (T) declared in line 22. Also, a type parameter can be declared only once in the type-parameter section but can appear more than once in the method's parameter list. For example, the type-parameter name T appears twice in the following method's parameter list:

```
public static <T> T maximum(T value1, T value2)
```

Type-parameter names need not be unique among different generic methods. In method printArray, T appears in the same two locations where the overloaded printArray methods of Fig. 18.1 specified Integer, Double or Character as the array element type. The remainder of printArray is identical to the versions presented in Fig. 18.1.

Good Programming Practice 18.1

The letters T (for "type"), E (for "element"), K (for "key") and V (for "value") are commonly used as type parameters. For other common ones, see http://docs.oracle.com/javase/ tutorial/java/generics/types.html.

Testing the Generic *printArray* Method

As in Fig. 18.1, the program in Fig. 18.3 begins by declaring and initializing six-element Integer array integerArray (line 9), seven-element Double array doubleArray (line 10) and five-element Character array characterArray (line 11). Then each array is output by calling printArray (lines 14, 16 and 18)—once with argument integerArray, once with argument doubleArray and once with argument characterArray.

When the compiler encounters line 14, it first determines argument integerArray's type (i.e., Integer[]) and attempts to locate a method named printArray that specifies a single Integer[] parameter. There's no such method in this example. Next, the compiler determines whether there's a generic method named printArray that specifies a single array parameter and uses a type parameter to represent the array element type. The compiler determines that printArray (lines 22–29) is a match and sets up a call to the method. The same process is repeated for the calls to method printArray at lines 16 and 18.

Common Programming Error 18.1

If the compiler cannot match a method call to a nongeneric or a generic method declaration, a compilation error occurs.

Common Programming Error 18.2

If the compiler doesn't find a method declaration that matches a method call exactly, but does find two or more methods that can satisfy the method call, a compilation error occurs. For the complete details of resolving calls to overloaded and generic methods, see http:// docs.oracle.com/javase/specs/jls/se7/html/jls-15.html#jls-15.12.

In addition to setting up the method calls, the compiler also determines whether the operations in the method body can be applied to elements of the type stored in the array argument. The only operation performed on the array elements in this example is to output their String representation. Line 26 performs an *implicit toString call* on every element. *To work with generics, every element of the array must be an object of a class or interface type.* Since all objects have a toString method, the compiler is satisfied that line 26 performs a *valid* operation for any object in printArray's array argument. The toString methods of classes Integer, Double and Character return the String representation of the underlying int, double or char value, respectively.

Erasure at Compilation Time

When the compiler translates generic method printArray into Java bytecodes, it removes the type-parameter section and *replaces the type parameters with actual types.* This process is known as **erasure**. By default all generic types are replaced with type Object. So the compiled version of method printArray appears as shown in Fig. 18.4—there's only *one* copy of this code, which is used for all printArray calls in the example. This is quite different from similar mechanisms in other programming languages, such as C++'s templates, in which a *separate copy of the source code* is generated and compiled for *every* type passed as an argument to the method. As you'll see in Section 18.4, the translation and compilation of generics is a bit more involved than what we've discussed in this section.

By declaring printArray as a generic method in Fig. 18.3, we eliminated the need for the overloaded methods of Fig. 18.1 and created a reusable method that can output the String representations of the elements in any array that contains objects. However, this particular example could have simply declared the printArray method as shown in Fig. 18.4, using an Object array as the parameter. This would have yielded the same results, because any Object can be output as a String. In a generic method, the benefits become more apparent when you place restrictions on the type parameters, as we demonstrate in the next section.

```java
1   public static void printArray(Object[] inputArray)
2   {
3      // display array elements
4      for (Object element : inputArray)
5         System.out.printf("%s ", element);
6
7      System.out.println();
8   }
```

Fig. 18.4 | Generic method printArray after the compiler performs erasure.

18.4 Additional Compile-Time Translation Issues: Methods That Use a Type Parameter as the Return Type

Let's consider a generic method in which type parameters are used in the return type and in the parameter list (Fig. 18.5). The application uses a generic method maximum to determine and return the largest of its three arguments of the same type. Unfortunately, *the relational operator > cannot be used with reference types.* However, it's possible to compare two objects of the same class if that class implements the generic **interface Comparable<T>** (from package java.lang). All the type-wrapper classes for primitive types implement this interface.

Generic interfaces enable you to specify, with a single interface declaration, a set of related types. Comparable<T> objects have a **compareTo method**. For example, if we have two Integer objects, integer1 and integer2, they can be compared with the expression:

```
integer1.compareTo(integer2)
```

When you declare a class that implements Comparable<T>, you must implement method compareTo such that it compares the contents of two objects of that class and returns the comparison results. As specified in interface Comparable<T>'s documentation, compareTo *must* return 0 if the objects are equal, a negative integer if object1 is less than object2 or a positive integer if object1 is greater than object2. For example, class Integer's compareTo method compares the int values stored in two Integer objects. A benefit of implementing interface Comparable<T> is that Comparable<T> objects can be used with the sorting and searching methods of class Collections (package java.util). We discussed those methods in Chapter 16. In this example, we'll use method compareTo in method maximum to help determine the largest value.

```java
 1   // Fig. 18.5: MaximumTest.java
 2   // Generic method maximum returns the largest of three objects.
 3
 4   public class MaximumTest
 5   {
 6      public static void main(String[] args)
 7      {
 8         System.out.printf("Maximum of %d, %d and %d is %d%n%n", 3, 4, 5,
 9            maximum(3, 4, 5));
10         System.out.printf("Maximum of %.1f, %.1f and %.1f is %.1f%n%n",
11            6.6, 8.8, 7.7, maximum(6.6, 8.8, 7.7));
12         System.out.printf("Maximum of %s, %s and %s is %s%n", "pear",
13            "apple", "orange", maximum("pear", "apple", "orange"));
14      }
15
16      // determines the largest of three Comparable objects
17      public static <T extends Comparable<T>> T maximum(T x, T y, T z)
18      {
19         T max = x; // assume x is initially the largest
20
21         if (y.compareTo(max) > 0)
22            max = y; // y is the largest so far
23
24         if (z.compareTo(max) > 0)
25            max = z; // z is the largest
26
27         return max; // returns the largest object
28      }
29   } // end class MaximumTest
```

```
Maximum of 3, 4 and 5 is 5
Maximum of 6.6, 8.8 and 7.7 is 8.8
Maximum of pear, apple and orange is pear
```

Fig. 18.5 | Generic method maximum with an upper bound on its type parameter.

*Generic Method **maximum** and Specifying a Type Parameter's Upper Bound*

Generic method maximum (lines 17–28) uses type parameter T as the return type of the method (line 17), as the type of method parameters x, y and z (line 17), and as the type of local variable max (line 19). The type-parameter section specifies that T extends Comparable<T>—only objects of classes that implement interface Comparable<T> can be used with this method. Comparable<T> is known as the type parameter's **upper bound**. By default, Object is the upper bound, meaning that an object of any type can be used. Type-parameter declarations that bound the parameter always use keyword extends regardless of whether the type parameter extends a class or implements an interface. The upper bound may be a comma-separated list that contains zero or one class and zero or more interfaces.

Method maximum's type parameter is more restrictive than the one specified for print-Array in Fig. 18.3, which was able to output arrays containing any type of object. The Comparable<T> restriction is important, because not all objects can be compared. However, Comparable<T> objects are guaranteed to have a compareTo method.

Method maximum uses the same algorithm that we used in Section 6.4 to determine the largest of its three arguments. The method assumes that its first argument (x) is the largest and assigns it to local variable max (line 19). Next, the if statement at lines 21–22 determines whether y is greater than max. The condition invokes y's compareTo method with the expression y.compareTo(max), which returns a negative integer, 0 or a positive integer, to determine y's relationship to max. If the return value of the compareTo is greater than 0, then y is greater and is assigned to variable max. Similarly, the if statement at lines 24–25 determines whether z is greater than max. If so, line 25 assigns z to max. Then line 27 returns max to the caller.

*Calling Method **maximum***

In main (lines 6–14), line 9 calls maximum with the integers 3, 4 and 5. When the compiler encounters this call, it first looks for a maximum method that takes three arguments of type int. There's no such method, so the compiler looks for a generic method that can be used and finds generic method maximum. However, recall that the arguments to a generic method must be of a *reference type*. So the compiler autoboxes the three int values as Integer objects and specifies that the three Integer objects will be passed to maximum. Class Integer (package java.lang) implements the Comparable<Integer> interface such that method compareTo compares the int values in two Integer objects. Therefore, Integers are valid arguments to method maximum. When the Integer representing the maximum is returned, we attempt to output it with the %d format specifier, which outputs an int primitive-type value. So maximum's return value is output as an int value.

A similar process occurs for the three double arguments passed to maximum in line 11. Each double is autoboxed as a Double object and passed to maximum. Again, this is allowed because class Double (package java.lang) implements the Comparable<Double> interface. The Double returned by maximum is output with the format specifier %.1f, which outputs a double primitive-type value. So maximum's return value is auto-unboxed and output as a double. The call to maximum in line 13 receives three Strings, which are also Comparable<String> objects. We intentionally placed the largest value in a different position in each method call (lines 9, 11 and 13) to show that the generic method always finds the maximum value, regardless of its position in the argument list.

Erasure and the Upper Bound of a Type Parameter

When the compiler translates method maximum into bytecodes, it uses erasure to replace the type parameters with actual types. In Fig. 18.3, all generic types were replaced with type Object. Actually, all type parameters are replaced with the *upper bound* of the type parameter, which is specified in the type-parameter section. Figure 18.6 simulates the erasure of method maximum's types by showing the method's source code after the type-parameter section is removed and type parameter T is replaced with the upper bound, Comparable, throughout the method declaration. The erasure of Comparable<T> is simply Comparable.

```
 1  public static Comparable maximum(Comparable x, Comparable y, Comparable z)
 2  {
 3     Comparable max = x; // assume x is initially the largest
 4
 5     if (y.compareTo(max) > 0)
 6        max = y; // y is the largest so far
 7
 8     if (z.compareTo(max) > 0)
 9        max = z; // z is the largest
10
11     return max; // returns the largest object
12  }
```

Fig. 18.6 | Generic method maximum after erasure is performed by the compiler.

After erasure, method maximum specifies that it returns type Comparable. However, the calling method does not expect to receive a Comparable. It expects to receive an object of the same type that was passed to maximum as an argument—Integer, Double or String in this example. When the compiler replaces the type-parameter information with the upper-bound type in the method declaration, it also inserts *explicit cast operations* in front of each method call to ensure that the returned value is of the type expected by the caller. Thus, the call to maximum in line 9 (Fig. 18.5) is preceded by an Integer cast, as in

```
(Integer) maximum(3, 4, 5)
```

the call to maximum in line 11 is preceded by a Double cast, as in

```
(Double) maximum(6.6, 8.8, 7.7)
```

and the call to maximum in line 13 is preceded by a String cast, as in

```
(String) maximum("pear", "apple", "orange")
```

In each case, the type of the cast for the return value is *inferred* from the types of the method arguments in the particular method call, because, according to the method declaration, the return type and the argument types match. Without generics, you'd be responsible for implementing the cast operation.

18.5 Overloading Generic Methods

A generic method may be overloaded like any other method. A class can provide two or more generic methods that specify the same method name but different method parameters. For example, generic method printArray of Fig. 18.3 could be overloaded with another printArray generic method with the additional parameters lowSubscript and highSubscript to specify the portion of the array to output.

A generic method can also be overloaded by nongeneric methods. When the compiler encounters a method call, it searches for the method declaration that best matches the method name and the argument types specified in the call—an error occurs if two or more overloaded methods both could be considered best matches. For example, generic method printArray of Fig. 18.3 could be overloaded with a version that's specific to Strings, which outputs the Strings in neat, tabular format.

18.6 Generic Classes

The concept of a data structure, such as a stack, can be understood *independently* of the element type it manipulates. Generic classes provide a means for describing the concept of a stack (or any other class) in a *type-independent* manner. We can then instantiate *type-specific* objects of the generic class. Generics provide a nice opportunity for software reusability.

Once you have a generic class, you can use a simple, concise notation to indicate the type(s) that should be used in place of the class's type parameter(s). At compilation time, the compiler ensures the *type safety* of your code and uses the *erasure* techniques described in Sections 18.3—18.4 to enable your client code to interact with the generic class.

One generic Stack class, for example, could be the basis for creating many logical Stack classes (e.g., "Stack of Double," "Stack of Integer," "Stack of Character," "Stack of Employee"). These classes are known as **parameterized classes** or **parameterized types** because they accept one or more type parameters. Recall that type parameters represent only *reference types*, which means the Stack generic class cannot be instantiated with primitive types. However, we can instantiate a Stack that stores objects of Java's type-wrapper classes and allow Java to use *autoboxing* to convert the primitive values into objects. Recall that autoboxing occurs when a value of a primitive type (e.g., int) is pushed onto a Stack that contains wrapper-class objects (e.g., Integer). *Auto-unboxing* occurs when an object of the wrapper class is popped off the Stack and assigned to a primitive-type variable.

*Implementing a Generic **Stack** Class*

Figure 18.7 declares a generic Stack class for demonstration purposes—the java.util package already contains a generic Stack class. A generic class declaration looks like a nongeneric one, but the class name is followed by *a type-parameter section* (line 5). In this case, type parameter T represents the element type the Stack will manipulate. As with generic methods, the type-parameter section of a generic class can have one or more type parameters separated by commas. Type parameter T is used throughout the Stack class declaration to represent the element type. This example implements a Stack as an ArrayList.

Class Stack declares variable elements as an ArrayList<T> (line 7). This ArrayList will store the Stack's elements. As you know, an ArrayList can grow dynamically, so objects of our Stack class can also grow dynamically. The Stack class's no-argument constructor (lines 10–13) invokes the one-argument constructor (lines 16–20) to create a Stack in which the underlying ArrayList has a capacity of 10 elements. The one-argument constructor can also be called directly to create a Stack with a specified initial capacity. Line 18 validates the constructor's argument. Line 19 creates the ArrayList of the specified capacity (or 10 if the capacity was invalid).

```
 1   // Fig. 18.7: Stack.java
 2   // Stack generic class declaration.
 3   import java.util.ArrayList;
 4
 5   public class Stack<T>
 6   {
 7      private final ArrayList<T> elements; // ArrayList stores stack elements
 8
 9      // no-argument constructor creates a stack of the default size
10      public Stack()
11      {
12         this(10); // default stack size
13      }
14
15      // constructor creates a stack of the specified number of elements
16      public Stack(int capacity)
17      {
18         int initCapacity = capacity > 0 ? capacity : 10; // validate
19         elements = new ArrayList<T>(initCapacity); // create ArrayList
20      }
21
22      // push element onto stack
23      public void push(T pushValue)
24      {
25         elements.add(pushValue); // place pushValue on Stack
26      }
27
28      // return the top element if not empty; else throw EmptyStackException
29      public T pop()
30      {
31         if (elements.isEmpty()) // if stack is empty
32            throw new EmptyStackException("Stack is empty, cannot pop");
33
34         // remove and return top element of Stack
35         return elements.remove(elements.size() - 1);
36      }
37   } // end class Stack<T>
```

Fig. 18.7 | Stack generic class declaration.

Method push (lines 23–26) uses ArrayList method add to append the pushed item to the end of the ArrayList elements. The last element in the ArrayList represents the *top* of the stack.

Method pop (lines 29–36) first determines whether an attempt is being made to pop an element from an empty Stack. If so, line 32 throws an EmptyStackException (declared in Fig. 18.8). Otherwise, line 35 in Fig. 18.7 returns the top element of the Stack by removing the last element in the underlying ArrayList.

Class EmptyStackException (Fig. 18.8) provides a no-argument constructor and a one-argument constructor. The no-argument constructor sets the default error message, and the one-argument constructor sets a custom error message.

As with generic methods, when a generic class is compiled, the compiler performs *erasure* on the class's type parameters and replaces them with their upper bounds. For class

Stack (Fig. 18.7), no upper bound is specified, so the default upper bound, Object, is used. The scope of a generic class's type parameter is the entire class. However, type parameters *cannot* be used in a class's static variable declarations.

```
1   // Fig. 18.8: EmptyStackException.java
2   // EmptyStackException class declaration.
3   public class EmptyStackException extends RuntimeException
4   {
5      // no-argument constructor
6      public EmptyStackException()
7      {
8         this("Stack is empty");
9      }
10
11     // one-argument constructor
12     public EmptyStackException(String message)
13     {
14        super(message);
15     }
16  } // end class EmptyStackException
```

Fig. 18.8 | EmptyStackException class declaration.

Testing the Generic **Stack** Class of Fig. 18.7

Now, let's consider the application (Fig. 18.9) that uses the Stack generic class (Fig. 18.7). Lines 12–13 in Fig. 18.9 create and initialize variables of type Stack<Double> (pronounced "Stack of Double") and Stack<Integer> (pronounced "Stack of Integer"). The types Double and Integer are known as the Stack's **type arguments**. The compiler uses them to replace the type parameters so that it can perform type checking and insert cast operations as necessary. We'll discuss the cast operations in more detail shortly. Lines 12–13 instantiate doubleStack with a capacity of 5 and integerStack with a capacity of 10 (the default). Lines 16–17 and 20–21 call methods testPushDouble (lines 25–36), testPopDouble (lines 39–59), testPushInteger (lines 62–73) and testPopInteger (lines 76–96), respectively, to demonstrate the two Stacks in this example.

```
1   // Fig. 18.9: StackTest.java
2   // Stack generic class test program.
3
4   public class StackTest
5   {
6      public static void main(String[] args)
7      {
8         double[] doubleElements = {1.1, 2.2, 3.3, 4.4, 5.5};
9         int[] integerElements = {1, 2, 3, 4, 5, 6, 7, 8, 9, 10};
10
11        // Create a Stack<Double> and a Stack<Integer>
12        Stack<Double> doubleStack = new Stack<>(5);
13        Stack<Integer> integerStack = new Stack<>();
14
```

Fig. 18.9 | Stack generic class test program. (Part 1 of 3.)

```
15          // push elements of doubleElements onto doubleStack
16          testPushDouble(doubleStack, doubleElements);
17          testPopDouble(doubleStack); // pop from doubleStack
18
19          // push elements of integerElements onto integerStack
20          testPushInteger(integerStack, integerElements);
21          testPopInteger(integerStack); // pop from integerStack
22       }
23
24       // test push method with double stack
25       private static void testPushDouble(
26          Stack<Double> stack, double[] values)
27       {
28          System.out.printf("%nPushing elements onto doubleStack%n");
29
30          // push elements to Stack
31          for (double value : values)
32          {
33             System.out.printf("%.1f ", value);
34             stack.push(value); // push onto doubleStack
35          }
36       }
37
38       // test pop method with double stack
39       private static void testPopDouble(Stack<Double> stack)
40       {
41          // pop elements from stack
42          try
43          {
44             System.out.printf("%nPopping elements from doubleStack%n");
45             double popValue; // store element removed from stack
46
47             // remove all elements from Stack
48             while (true)
49             {
50                popValue = stack.pop(); // pop from doubleStack
51                System.out.printf("%.1f ", popValue);
52             }
53          }
54          catch(EmptyStackException emptyStackException)
55          {
56             System.err.println();
57             emptyStackException.printStackTrace();
58          }
59       }
60
61       // test push method with integer stack
62       private static void testPushInteger(
63          Stack<Integer> stack, int[] values)
64       {
65          System.out.printf("%nPushing elements onto integerStack%n");
66
```

Fig. 18.9 | Stack generic class test program. (Part 2 of 3.)

```
67          // push elements to Stack
68          for (int value : values)
69          {
70              System.out.printf("%d ", value);
71              stack.push(value); // push onto integerStack
72          }
73      }
74
75      // test pop method with integer stack
76      private static void testPopInteger(Stack<Integer> stack)
77      {
78          // pop elements from stack
79          try
80          {
81              System.out.printf("%nPopping elements from integerStack%n");
82              int popValue; // store element removed from stack
83
84              // remove all elements from Stack
85              while (true)
86              {
87                  popValue = stack.pop(); // pop from intStack
88                  System.out.printf("%d ", popValue);
89              }
90          }
91          catch(EmptyStackException emptyStackException)
92          {
93              System.err.println();
94              emptyStackException.printStackTrace();
95          }
96      }
97  } // end class StackTest
```

```
Pushing elements onto doubleStack
1.1 2.2 3.3 4.4 5.5
Popping elements from doubleStack
5.5 4.4 3.3 2.2 1.1
EmptyStackException: Stack is empty, cannot pop
        at Stack.pop(Stack.java:32)
        at StackTest.testPopDouble(StackTest.java:50)
        at StackTest.main(StackTest.java:17)

Pushing elements onto integerStack
1 2 3 4 5 6 7 8 9 10
Popping elements from integerStack
10 9 8 7 6 5 4 3 2 1
EmptyStackException: Stack is empty, cannot pop
        at Stack.pop(Stack.java:32)
        at StackTest.testPopInteger(StackTest.java:87)
        at StackTest.main(StackTest.java:21)
```

Fig. 18.9 | Stack generic class test program. (Part 3 of 3.)

Methods **testPushDouble** *and* **testPopDouble**

Method testPushDouble (lines 25–36) invokes method push (line 34) to place the double values 1.1, 2.2, 3.3, 4.4 and 5.5 from array doubleElements onto doubleStack. *Autobox-*

ing occurs in line 34 when the program tries to push a primitive `double` value onto the doubleStack, which stores only references to `Double` objects.

Method `testPopDouble` (lines 39–59) invokes `Stack` method `pop` (line 50) in an infinite loop (lines 48–52) to remove all the values from the stack. The output shows that the values indeed pop off in last-in, first-out order (the defining characteristic of stacks). When the loop attempts to pop a sixth value, the doubleStack is empty, so pop throws an `EmptyStackException`, which causes the program to proceed to the `catch` block (lines 54–58). The stack trace indicates the exception that occurred and shows that method pop generated the exception at line 32 of the file `Stack.java` (Fig. 18.7). The trace also shows that pop was called by `StackTest` method `testPopDouble` at line 50 (Fig. 18.9) of `Stack-Test.java` and that method `testPopDouble` was called from method `main` at line 17 of `StackTest.java`. This information enables you to determine the methods that were on the method-call stack at the time that the exception occurred. Because the program catches the exception, the exception is considered to have been handled and the program can continue executing.

Auto-unboxing occurs in line 50 when the program assigns the `Double` object popped from the stack to a `double` primitive variable. Recall from Section 18.4 that the compiler inserts casts to ensure that the proper types are returned from generic methods. After erasure, `Stack` method pop returns type `Object`, but the client code in `testPopDouble` expects to receive a `double` when method pop returns. So the compiler inserts a `Double` cast, as in

```
popValue = (Double) stack.pop();
```

The value assigned to popValue will be *unboxed* from the `Double` object returned by pop.

Methods `testPushInteger` and `testPopInteger`

Method `testPushInteger` (lines 62–73) invokes `Stack` method push to place values onto integerStack until it's full. Method `testPopInteger` (lines 76–96) invokes `Stack` method pop to remove values from integerStack. Once again, the values are popped in last-in, first-out order. During *erasure*, the compiler recognizes that the client code in method testPopInteger expects to receive an `int` when method pop returns. So the compiler inserts an `Integer` cast, as in

```
popValue = (Integer) stack.pop();
```

The value assigned to popValue will be unboxed from the `Integer` object returned by pop.

Creating Generic Methods to Test Class `Stack<T>`

The code in methods `testPushDouble` and `testPushInteger` is *almost identical* for pushing values onto a Stack<Double> or a Stack<Integer>, respectively, and the code in methods `testPopDouble` and `testPopInteger` is almost identical for popping values from a Stack<Double> or a Stack<Integer>, respectively. This presents another opportunity to use generic methods. Figure 18.10 declares generic method `testPush` (lines 24–35) to perform the same tasks as testPushDouble and testPushInteger in Fig. 18.9—that is, push values onto a Stack<T>. Similarly, generic method `testPop` (Fig. 18.10, lines 38–58) performs the same tasks as testPopDouble and testPopInteger in Fig. 18.9—that is, pop values off a Stack<T>. The output of Fig. 18.10 precisely matches that of Fig. 18.9.

```
 1    // Fig. 18.10: StackTest2.java
 2    // Passing generic Stack objects to generic methods.
 3    public class StackTest2
 4    {
 5       public static void main(String[] args)
 6       {
 7          Double[] doubleElements = {1.1, 2.2, 3.3, 4.4, 5.5};
 8          Integer[] integerElements = {1, 2, 3, 4, 5, 6, 7, 8, 9, 10};
 9
10          // Create a Stack<Double> and a Stack<Integer>
11          Stack<Double> doubleStack = new Stack<>(5);
12          Stack<Integer> integerStack = new Stack<>();
13
14          // push elements of doubleElements onto doubleStack
15          testPush("doubleStack", doubleStack, doubleElements);
16          testPop("doubleStack", doubleStack); // pop from doubleStack
17
18          // push elements of integerElements onto integerStack
19          testPush("integerStack", integerStack, integerElements);
20          testPop("integerStack", integerStack); // pop from integerStack
21       }
22
23       // generic method testPush pushes elements onto a Stack
24       public static <T> void testPush(String name , Stack<T> stack,
25          T[] elements)
26       {
27          System.out.printf("%nPushing elements onto %s%n", name);
28
29          // push elements onto Stack
30          for (T element : elements)
31          {
32             System.out.printf("%s ", element);
33             stack.push(element); // push element onto stack
34          }
35       }
36
37       // generic method testPop pops elements from a Stack
38       public static <T> void testPop(String name, Stack<T> stack)
39       {
40          // pop elements from stack
41          try
42          {
43             System.out.printf("%nPopping elements from %s%n", name);
44             T popValue; // store element removed from stack
45
46             // remove all elements from Stack
47             while (true)
48             {
49                popValue = stack.pop();
50                System.out.printf("%s ", popValue);
51             }
52          }
```

Fig. 18.10 | Passing generic Stack objects to generic methods. (Part 1 of 2.)

```
53            catch(EmptyStackException emptyStackException)
54            {
55                System.out.println();
56                emptyStackException.printStackTrace();
57            }
58        }
59    } // end class StackTest2
```

```
Pushing elements onto doubleStack
1.1 2.2 3.3 4.4 5.5
Popping elements from doubleStack
5.5 4.4 3.3 2.2 1.1
EmptyStackException: Stack is empty, cannot pop
        at Stack.pop(Stack.java:32)
        at StackTest2.testPop(StackTest2.java:50)
        at StackTest2.main(StackTest2.java:17)

Pushing elements onto integerStack
1 2 3 4 5 6 7 8 9 10
Popping elements from integerStack
10 9 8 7 6 5 4 3 2 1
EmptyStackException: Stack is empty, cannot pop
        at Stack.pop(Stack.java:32)
        at StackTest2.testPop(StackTest2.java:50)
        at StackTest2.main(StackTest2.java:21
```

Fig. 18.10 | Passing generic Stack objects to generic methods. (Part 2 of 2.)

Lines 11–12 create the Stack<Double> and Stack<Integer> objects, respectively. Lines 15–16 and 19–20 invoke generic methods testPush and testPop to test the Stack objects. Because type parameters can represent only reference types, to be able to pass arrays doubleElements and integerElements to generic method testPush, the arrays declared in lines 7–8 must be declared with the wrapper types Double and Integer. When these arrays are initialized with primitive values, the compiler *autoboxes* each primitive value.

Generic method testPush (lines 24–35) uses type parameter T (specified at line 24) to represent the data type stored in the Stack<T>. The generic method takes three arguments—a String that represents the name of the Stack<T> object for output purposes, a reference to an object of type Stack<T> and an array of type T—the type of elements that will be pushed onto Stack<T>. The compiler enforces *consistency* between the type of the Stack and the elements that will be pushed onto the Stack when push is invoked, which is the real value of the generic method call. Generic method testPop (lines 38–58) takes two arguments—a String that represents the name of the Stack<T> object for output purposes and a reference to an object of type Stack<T>.

18.7 Raw Types

The test programs for generic class Stack in Section 18.6 instantiate Stacks with type arguments Double and Integer. It's also possible to instantiate generic class Stack without specifying a type argument, as follows:

```
Stack objectStack = new Stack(5); // no type argument specified
```

In this case, the objectStack has a **raw type**—the compiler implicitly uses type Object throughout the generic class for each type argument. Thus the preceding statement creates a Stack that can store objects of *any* type. This is important for *backward compatibility* with prior Java versions. For example, the data structures of the Java Collections Framework (Chapter 16) all stored references to Objects, but are now implemented as generic types.

A raw-type Stack variable can be assigned a Stack that specifies a type argument, such as a Stack<Double> object, as follows:

```
Stack rawTypeStack2 = new Stack<Double>(5);
```

because type Double is a subclass of Object. This assignment is allowed because the elements in a Stack<Double> (i.e., Double objects) are certainly objects—class Double is an indirect subclass of Object.

Similarly, a Stack variable that specifies a type argument in its declaration can be assigned a raw-type Stack object, as in:

```
Stack<Integer> integerStack = new Stack(10);
```

Although this assignment is permitted, it's *unsafe*, because a Stack of raw type might store types other than Integer. In this case, the compiler issues a warning message which indicates the unsafe assignment.

Using Raw Types with Generic Class Stack

The test program of Fig. 18.11 uses the notion of raw type. Line 11 instantiates generic class Stack with raw type, which indicates that rawTypeStack1 can hold objects of any type. Line 14 assigns a Stack<Double> to variable rawTypeStack2, which is declared as a Stack of raw type. Line 17 assigns a Stack of raw type to Stack<Integer> variable, which is legal but causes the compiler to issue a warning message (Fig. 18.12) indicating a *potentially unsafe assignment*—again, this occurs because a Stack of raw type might store types other than Integer. Also, the calls to generic methods testPush and testPop in lines 19–22 result in compiler warning messages (Fig. 18.12). These occur because rawTypeStack1 and rawTypeStack2 are declared as Stacks of raw type, but methods testPush and testPop each expect a second argument that is a Stack with a specific type argument. The warnings indicate that the compiler cannot guarantee the types manipulated by the stacks to be the correct types, since we did not supply a variable declared with a type argument. Methods testPush (Fig. 18.11, lines 28–39) and testPop (lines 42–62) are the same as in Fig. 18.10.

```
 1   // Fig. 18.11: RawTypeTest.java
 2   // Raw type test program.
 3   public class RawTypeTest
 4   {
 5      public static void main(String[] args)
 6      {
 7         Double[] doubleElements = {1.1, 2.2, 3.3, 4.4, 5.5};
 8         Integer[] integerElements = {1, 2, 3, 4, 5, 6, 7, 8, 9, 10};
 9
10         // Stack of raw types assigned to Stack of raw types variable
11         Stack rawTypeStack1 = new Stack(5);
```

Fig. 18.11 | Raw-type test program. (Part 1 of 3.)

```
12
13        // Stack<Double> assigned to Stack of raw types variable
14        Stack rawTypeStack2 = new Stack<Double>(5);
15
16        // Stack of raw types assigned to Stack<Integer> variable
17        Stack<Integer> integerStack = new Stack(10);
18
19        testPush("rawTypeStack1", rawTypeStack1, doubleElements);
20        testPop("rawTypeStack1", rawTypeStack1);
21        testPush("rawTypeStack2", rawTypeStack2, doubleElements);
22        testPop("rawTypeStack2", rawTypeStack2);
23        testPush("integerStack", integerStack, integerElements);
24        testPop("integerStack", integerStack);
25     }
26
27     // generic method pushes elements onto stack
28     public static <T> void testPush(String name, Stack<T> stack,
29        T[] elements)
30     {
31        System.out.printf("%nPushing elements onto %s%n", name);
32
33        // push elements onto Stack
34        for (T element : elements)
35        {
36           System.out.printf("%s ", element);
37           stack.push(element); // push element onto stack
38        }
39     }
40
41     // generic method testPop pops elements from stack
42     public static <T> void testPop(String name, Stack<T> stack)
43     {
44        // pop elements from stack
45        try
46        {
47           System.out.printf("%nPopping elements from %s%n", name);
48           T popValue; // store element removed from stack
49
50           // remove elements from Stack
51           while (true)
52           {
53              popValue = stack.pop(); // pop from stack
54              System.out.printf("%s ", popValue);
55           }
56        } // end try
57        catch(EmptyStackException emptyStackException)
58        {
59           System.out.println();
60           emptyStackException.printStackTrace();
61        }
62     }
63  } // end class RawTypeTest
```

Fig. 18.11 | Raw-type test program. (Part 2 of 3.)

```
Pushing elements onto rawTypeStack1
1.1 2.2 3.3 4.4 5.5
Popping elements from rawTypeStack1
5.5 4.4 3.3 2.2 1.1
EmptyStackException: Stack is empty, cannot pop
        at Stack.pop(Stack.java:32)
        at RawTypeTest.testPop(RawTypeTest.java:53)
        at RawTypeTest.main(RawTypeTest.java:20)

Pushing elements onto rawTypeStack2
1.1 2.2 3.3 4.4 5.5
Popping elements from rawTypeStack2
5.5 4.4 3.3 2.2 1.1
EmptyStackException: Stack is empty, cannot pop
        at Stack.pop(Stack.java:32)
        at RawTypeTest.testPop(RawTypeTest.java:53)
        at RawTypeTest.main(RawTypeTest.java:22)

Pushing elements onto integerStack
1 2 3 4 5 6 7 8 9 10
Popping elements from integerStack
10 9 8 7 6 5 4 3 2 1
EmptyStackException: Stack is empty, cannot pop
        at Stack.pop(Stack.java:32)
        at RawTypeTest.testPop(RawTypeTest.java:53)
        at RawTypeTest.main(RawTypeTest.java:24)
```

Fig. 18.11 | Raw-type test program. (Part 3 of 3.)

Compiler Warnings

Figure 18.12 shows the warning messages generated by the compiler when the file Raw-TypeTest.java (Fig. 18.11) is compiled with the -Xlint:unchecked option, which provides more information about potentially unsafe operations in code that uses generics. The first warning in Fig. 18.11 is generated for line 17, which assigned a raw-type Stack to a Stack<Integer> variable—the compiler cannot ensure that all objects in the Stack will be Integer objects. The next warning occurs at line 19. The compiler determines method testPush's type argument from the Double array passed as the third argument, because the second method argument is a raw-type Stack variable. In this case, Double is the type argument, so the compiler expects a Stack<Double> as the second argument. The warning occurs because the compiler cannot ensure that a raw-type Stack contains only Doubles. The warning at line 21 occurs for the same reason, even though the actual Stack that rawTypeStack2 references is a Stack<Double>. The compiler cannot guarantee that the variable will always refer to the same Stack object, so it must use the variable's declared type to perform all type checking. Lines 20 and 22 each generate warnings because method testPop expects as an argument a Stack for which a type argument has been specified. However, in each call to testPop, we pass a raw-type Stack variable. Thus, the compiler indicates a warning because it cannot check the types used in the body of the method. In general, you should avoid using raw types.

```
RawTypeTest.java:17: warning: [unchecked] unchecked conversion
found    : Stack
required: Stack<java.lang.Integer>
     Stack<Integer> integerStack = new Stack(10);
                                   ^
RawTypeTest.java:19: warning: [unchecked] unchecked conversion
found    : Stack
required: Stack<java.lang.Double>
     testPush("rawTypeStack1", rawTypeStack1, doubleElements);
                              ^
RawTypeTest.java:19: warning: [unchecked] unchecked method invocation:
<T>testPush(java.lang.String,Stack<T>,T[]) in RawTypeTest is applied to
(java.lang.String,Stack,java.lang.Double[])
     testPush("rawTypeStack1", rawTypeStack1, doubleElements);
         ^
RawTypeTest.java:20: warning: [unchecked] unchecked conversion
found    : Stack
required: Stack<T>
     testPop("rawTypeStack1", rawTypeStack1);
                             ^
RawTypeTest.java:20: warning: [unchecked] unchecked method invocation:
<T>testPop(java.lang.String,Stack<T>) in RawTypeTest is applied to
(java.lang.String,Stack)
     testPop("rawTypeStack1", rawTypeStack1);
         ^
RawTypeTest.java:21: warning: [unchecked] unchecked conversion
found    : Stack
required: Stack<java.lang.Double>
     testPush("rawTypeStack2", rawTypeStack2, doubleElements);
                              ^
RawTypeTest.java:21: warning: [unchecked] unchecked method invocation:
<T>testPush(java.lang.String,Stack<T>,T[]) in RawTypeTest is applied to
(java.lang.String,Stack,java.lang.Double[])
     testPush("rawTypeStack2", rawTypeStack2, doubleElements);
         ^
RawTypeTest.java:22: warning: [unchecked] unchecked conversion
found    : Stack
required: Stack<T>
     testPop("rawTypeStack2", rawTypeStack2);
                             ^
RawTypeTest.java:22: warning: [unchecked] unchecked method invocation:
<T>testPop(java.lang.String,Stack<T>) in RawTypeTest is applied to
(java.lang.String,Stack)
     testPop("rawTypeStack2", rawTypeStack2);
         ^
9 warnings
```

Fig. 18.12 | Warning messages from the compiler.

18.8 Wildcards in Methods That Accept Type Parameters

In this section, we introduce a powerful generics concept known as **wildcards**. Let's consider an example that motivates wildcards. Suppose that you'd like to implement a generic method sum that totals the numbers in a collection, such as an ArrayList. You'd begin by inserting the numbers in the collection. Because generic classes can be used only with class or interface types, the numbers would be *autoboxed* as objects of the type-wrapper classes. For example, any int value would be *autoboxed* as an Integer object, and any double value would be *autoboxed* as a Double object. We'd like to be able to total all the numbers in the ArrayList regardless of their type. For this reason, we'll declare the ArrayList with the type argument Number, which is the superclass of both Integer and Double. In addition, method sum will receive a parameter of type ArrayList<Number> and total its elements. Figure 18.13 demonstrates totaling the elements of an ArrayList of Numbers.

```java
1   // Fig. 18.13: TotalNumbers.java
2   // Totaling the numbers in an ArrayList<Number>.
3   import java.util.ArrayList;
4
5   public class TotalNumbers
6   {
7      public static void main(String[] args)
8      {
9         // create, initialize and output ArrayList of Numbers containing
10        // both Integers and Doubles, then display total of the elements
11        Number[] numbers = {1, 2.4, 3, 4.1}; // Integers and Doubles
12        ArrayList<Number> numberList = new ArrayList<>();
13
14        for (Number element : numbers)
15           numberList.add(element); // place each number in numberList
16
17        System.out.printf("numberList contains: %s%n", numberList);
18        System.out.printf("Total of the elements in numberList: %.1f%n",
19           sum(numberList));
20     }
21
22     // calculate total of ArrayList elements
23     public static double sum(ArrayList<Number> list)
24     {
25        double total = 0; // initialize total
26
27        // calculate sum
28        for (Number element : list)
29           total += element.doubleValue();
30
31        return total;
32     }
33  } // end class TotalNumbers
```

```
numberList contains: [1, 2.4, 3, 4.1]
Total of the elements in numberList: 10.5
```

Fig. 18.13 | Totaling the numbers in an ArrayList<Number>.

Line 11 declares and initializes an array of Numbers. Because the initializers are primitive values, Java *autoboxes* each primitive value as an object of its corresponding wrapper type. The int values 1 and 3 are *autoboxed* as Integer objects, and the double values 2.4

and 4.1 are *autoboxed* as Double objects. Line 12 declares and creates an ArrayList object that stores Numbers and assigns it to variable numberList.

Lines 14–15 traverse array numbers and place each element in numberList. Line 17 outputs the contents of the ArrayList as a String. This statement implicitly invokes the ArrayList's toString method, which returns a String of the form "[*elements*]" in which *elements* is a comma-separated list of the elements' String representations. Lines 18–19 display the sum of the elements that is returned by the call to method sum.

Method sum (lines 23–32) receives an ArrayList of Numbers and calculates the total of the Numbers in the collection. The method uses double values to perform the calculations and returns the result as a double. Lines 28–29 use the enhanced for statement, which is designed to work with both arrays and the collections of the Collections Framework, to total the elements of the ArrayList. The for statement assigns each Number in the ArrayList to variable element, then uses **Number method doubleValue** to obtain the Number's underlying primitive value as a double value. The result is added to total. When the loop terminates, the method returns the total.

Implementing Method **sum** *With a Wildcard Type Argument in Its Parameter*

Recall that the purpose of method sum in Fig. 18.13 was to total any type of Numbers stored in an ArrayList. We created an ArrayList of Numbers that contained both Integer and Double objects. The output of Fig. 18.13 demonstrates that method sum worked properly. Given that method sum can total the elements of an ArrayList of Numbers, you might expect that the method would also work for ArrayLists that contain elements of only one numeric type, such as ArrayList<Integer>. So we modified class TotalNumbers to create an ArrayList of Integers and pass it to method sum. When we compile the program, the compiler issues the following error message:

```
sum(java.util.ArrayList<java.lang.Number>) in TotalNumbersErrors
cannot be applied to (java.util.ArrayList<java.lang.Integer>)
```

Although Number is the superclass of Integer, the compiler doesn't consider the type Array-List<Number> to be a superclass of ArrayList<Integer>. If it were, then every operation we could perform on ArrayList<Number> would also work on an ArrayList<Integer>. Consider the fact that you can add a Double object to an ArrayList<Number> because a Double *is a* Number, but you cannot add a Double object to an ArrayList<Integer> because a Double *is not an* Integer. Thus, the subtype relationship does not hold.

How do we create a more flexible version of the sum method that can total the elements of any ArrayList containing elements of any subclass of Number? This is where **wildcard type arguments** are important. Wildcards enable you to specify method parameters, return values, variables or fields, and so on, that act as supertypes or subtypes of parameterized types. In Fig. 18.14, method sum's parameter is declared in line 50 with the type:

```
ArrayList<? extends Number>
```

A wildcard type argument is denoted by a question mark (**?**), which by itself represents an "unknown type." In this case, the wildcard extends class Number, which means that the wildcard has an upper bound of Number. Thus, the unknown-type argument must be either Number or a subclass of Number. With the parameter type shown here, method sum can receive an ArrayList argument that contains any type of Number, such as ArrayList<Integer> (line 20), ArrayList<Double> (line 33) or ArrayList<Number> (line 46).

```java
 1   // Fig. 18.14: WildcardTest.java
 2   // Wildcard test program.
 3   import java.util.ArrayList;
 4
 5   public class WildcardTest
 6   {
 7      public static void main(String[] args)
 8      {
 9         // create, initialize and output ArrayList of Integers, then
10         // display total of the elements
11         Integer[] integers = {1, 2, 3, 4, 5};
12         ArrayList<Integer> integerList = new ArrayList<>();
13
14         // insert elements in integerList
15         for (Integer element : integers)
16            integerList.add(element);
17
18         System.out.printf("integerList contains: %s%n", integerList);
19         System.out.printf("Total of the elements in integerList: %.0f%n%n",
20            sum(integerList));
21
22         // create, initialize and output ArrayList of Doubles, then
23         // display total of the elements
24         Double[] doubles = {1.1, 3.3, 5.5};
25         ArrayList<Double> doubleList = new ArrayList<>();
26
27         // insert elements in doubleList
28         for (Double element : doubles)
29            doubleList.add(element);
30
31         System.out.printf("doubleList contains: %s%n", doubleList);
32         System.out.printf("Total of the elements in doubleList: %.1f%n%n",
33            sum(doubleList));
34
35         // create, initialize and output ArrayList of Numbers containing
36         // both Integers and Doubles, then display total of the elements
37         Number[] numbers = {1, 2.4, 3, 4.1}; // Integers and Doubles
38         ArrayList<Number> numberList = new ArrayList<>();
39
40         // insert elements in numberList
41         for (Number element : numbers)
42            numberList.add(element);
43
44         System.out.printf("numberList contains: %s%n", numberList);
45         System.out.printf("Total of the elements in numberList: %.1f%n",
46            sum(numberList));
47      } // end main
48
49      // total the elements; using a wildcard in the ArrayList parameter
50      public static double sum(ArrayList<? extends Number> list)
51      {
52         double total = 0; // initialize total
53
```

Fig. 18.14 | Wildcard test program. (Part 1 of 2.)

```
54          // calculate sum
55          for (Number element : list)
56              total += element.doubleValue();
57
58          return total;
59      }
60  } // end class WildcardTest
```

```
integerList contains: [1, 2, 3, 4, 5]
Total of the elements in integerList: 15

doubleList contains: [1.1, 3.3, 5.5]
Total of the elements in doubleList: 9.9

numberList contains: [1, 2.4, 3, 4.1]
Total of the elements in numberList: 10.5
```

Fig. 18.14 | Wildcard test program. (Part 2 of 2.)

Lines 11–20 create and initialize an `ArrayList<Integer>`, output its elements and total them by calling method sum (line 20). Lines 24–33 perform the same operations for an `ArrayList<Double>`. Lines 37–46 perform the same operations for an `Array-List<Number>` that contains `Integer`s and `Double`s.

In method sum (lines 50–59), although the `ArrayList` argument's element types are not directly known by the method, they're known to be at least of type `Number`, because the wildcard was specified with the upper bound `Number`. For this reason line 56 is allowed, because all `Number` objects have a `doubleValue` method.

Although wildcards provide flexibility when passing parameterized types to a method, they also have some disadvantages. Because the wildcard (?) in the method's header (line 50) does not specify a type-parameter name, you cannot use it as a type name throughout the method's body (i.e., you cannot replace `Number` with ? in line 55). You could, however, declare method sum as follows:

public static <T **extends** Number> **double** sum(ArrayList<T> list)

which allows the method to receive an `ArrayList` that contains elements of any `Number` subclass. You could then use the type parameter `T` throughout the method body.

If the wildcard is specified without an upper bound, then only the methods of type `Object` can be invoked on values of the wildcard type. Also, methods that use wildcards in their parameter's type arguments cannot be used to add elements to a collection referenced by the parameter.

Common Programming Error 18.3

Using a wildcard in a method's type-parameter section or using a wildcard as an explicit type of a variable in the method body is a syntax error.

18.9 Wrap-Up

This chapter introduced generics. You learned how to declare generic methods and classes with type parameters specified in type-parameter sections. You also learned how to specify the upper bound for a type parameter and how the Java compiler uses erasure and casts to support multiple types with generic methods and classes. We discussed how backward compatibility is achieved via raw types. You also learned how to use wildcards in a generic method or a generic class.

In the next chapter, you'll continue your study of Swing GUI concepts, building on the techniques you learned in Chapter 12. In Chapter 22, we'll introduce JavaFX GUI.

Swing GUI Components: Part 2

Objectives

In this chapter you'll:

- Create and manipulate sliders, menus, pop-up menus and windows.
- Programatically change the look-and-feel of a GUI, using Swing's pluggable look-and-feel.
- Create a multiple-document interface with `JDesktopPane` and `JInternalFrame`.
- Use additional layout managers `BoxLayout` and `GridBagLayout`.

19.1 Introduction

In this chapter, we continue our study of Swing GUIs. We discuss additional components and layout managers and lay the groundwork for building more complex GUIs. We begin with sliders for selecting from a range of integer values, then discuss additional details of windows. Next, you'll use menus to organize an application's commands.

The look-and-feel of a Swing GUI can be uniform across all platforms on which a Java program executes, or the GUI can be customized by using Swing's **pluggable look-and-feel** (**PLAF**). We provide an example that illustrates how to change between Swing's default metal look-and-feel (which looks and behaves the same across platforms), the Nimbus look-and-feel (introduced in Chapter 12), a look-and-feel that simulates **Motif** (a UNIX look-and-feel) and one that simulates the Microsoft Windows look-and-feel.

Many of today's applications use a multiple-document interface (MDI)—a main window (often called the *parent window*) containing other windows (often called *child windows*) to manage several open documents in parallel. For example, many e-mail programs allow you to have several e-mail windows open at the same time so that you can compose or read multiple e-mail messages. We demonstrate Swing's classes for creating multiple-document interfaces. Finally, you'll learn about additional layout managers for organizing graphical user interfaces. We use several more Swing GUI components in later chapters as they're needed.

Swing is now considered a legacy technology. For GUIs, graphics and multimedia in new Java apps, you should use the features presented in this book's JavaFX chapters.

Java SE 8: Implementing Event Listeners with Lambdas
Throughout this chapter, we use anonymous inner classes and nested classes to implement event handlers so that the examples can compile and execute with both Java SE 7 and Java SE 8. In many of the examples, you could implement the functional event-listener interfaces with Java SE 8 lambdas (as demonstrated in Section 17.9).

19.2 `JSlider`

`JSlider`s enable a user to select from a range of integer values. Class `JSlider` inherits from `JComponent`. Figure 19.1 shows a horizontal `JSlider` with **tick marks** and the **thumb** that allows a user to select a value. `JSlider`s can be customized to display *major tick marks*, *minor tick marks* and labels for the tick marks. They also support **snap-to ticks**, which cause the *thumb*, when positioned between two tick marks, to snap to the closest one.

Thumb   Tick mark

Fig. 19.1 | JSlider component with horizontal orientation.

Most Swing GUI components support mouse and keyboard interactions—e.g., if a JSlider has the focus (i.e., it's the currently selected GUI component in the user interface), pressing the left arrow key or right arrow key causes the JSlider's thumb to decrease or increase by 1, respectively. The down arrow key and up arrow key also cause the thumb to decrease or increase by 1 tick, respectively. The *PgDn* (page down) *key* and *PgUp* (page up) *key* cause the thumb to decrease or increase by **block increments** of one-tenth of the range of values, respectively. The *Home key* moves the thumb to the minimum value of the JSlider, and the *End key* moves the thumb to the maximum value of the JSlider.

JSliders have either a horizontal or a vertical orientation. For a horizontal JSlider, the minimum value is at the left end and the maximum is at the right end. For a vertical JSlider, the minimum value is at the bottom and the maximum is at the top. The minimum and maximum value positions on a JSlider can be reversed by invoking JSlider method **setInverted** with boolean argument true. The relative position of the thumb indicates the current value of the JSlider.

The program in Figs. 19.2–19.4 allows the user to size a circle drawn on a subclass of JPanel called OvalPanel (Fig. 19.2). The user specifies the circle's diameter with a horizontal JSlider. Class OvalPanel knows how to draw a circle on itself, using its own instance variable diameter to determine the diameter of the circle—the diameter is used as the width and height of the bounding box in which the circle is displayed. The diameter value is set when the user interacts with the JSlider. The event handler calls method setDiameter in class OvalPanel to set the diameter and calls repaint to draw the new circle. The repaint call results in a call to OvalPanel's paintComponent method.

```java
1   // Fig. 19.2: OvalPanel.java
2   // A customized JPanel class.
3   import java.awt.Graphics;
4   import java.awt.Dimension;
5   import javax.swing.JPanel;
6
7   public class OvalPanel extends JPanel
8   {
9      private int diameter = 10; // default diameter
10
11     // draw an oval of the specified diameter
12     @Override
13     public void paintComponent(Graphics g)
14     {
15        super.paintComponent(g);
16        g.fillOval(10, 10, diameter, diameter);
17     }
18
```

Fig. 19.2 | JPanel subclass for drawing circles of a specified diameter. (Part 1 of 2.)

```
19      // validate and set diameter, then repaint
20      public void setDiameter(int newDiameter)
21      {
22         // if diameter invalid, default to 10
23         diameter = (newDiameter >= 0 ? newDiameter : 10);
24         repaint(); // repaint panel
25      }
26
27      // used by layout manager to determine preferred size
28      public Dimension getPreferredSize()
29      {
30         return new Dimension(200, 200);
31      }
32
33      // used by layout manager to determine minimum size
34      public Dimension getMinimumSize()
35      {
36         return getPreferredSize();
37      }
38   } // end class OvalPanel
```

Fig. 19.2 | JPanel subclass for drawing circles of a specified diameter. (Part 2 of 2.)

```
1   // Fig. 19.3: SliderFrame.java
2   // Using JSliders to size an oval.
3   import java.awt.BorderLayout;
4   import java.awt.Color;
5   import javax.swing.JFrame;
6   import javax.swing.JSlider;
7   import javax.swing.SwingConstants;
8   import javax.swing.event.ChangeListener;
9   import javax.swing.event.ChangeEvent;
10
11  public class SliderFrame extends JFrame
12  {
13     private final JSlider diameterJSlider; // slider to select diameter
14     private final OvalPanel myPanel; // panel to draw circle
15
16     // no-argument constructor
17     public SliderFrame()
18     {
19        super("Slider Demo");
20
21        myPanel = new OvalPanel(); // create panel to draw circle
22        myPanel.setBackground(Color.YELLOW);
23
24        // set up JSlider to control diameter value
25        diameterJSlider =
26           new JSlider(SwingConstants.HORIZONTAL, 0, 200, 10);
27        diameterJSlider.setMajorTickSpacing(10); // create tick every 10
28        diameterJSlider.setPaintTicks(true); // paint ticks on slider
29
```

Fig. 19.3 | JSlider value used to determine the diameter of a circle. (Part 1 of 2.)

```
30              // register JSlider event listener
31              diameterJSlider.addChangeListener(
32                 new ChangeListener() // anonymous inner class
33                 {
34                    // handle change in slider value
35                    @Override
36                    public void stateChanged(ChangeEvent e)
37                    {
38                       myPanel.setDiameter(diameterJSlider.getValue());
39                    }
40                 }
41              );
42
43              add(diameterJSlider, BorderLayout.SOUTH);
44              add(myPanel, BorderLayout.CENTER);
45           }
46        } // end class SliderFrame
```

Fig. 19.3 | JSlider value used to determine the diameter of a circle. (Part 2 of 2.)

```
1     // Fig. 19.4: SliderDemo.java
2     // Testing SliderFrame.
3     import javax.swing.JFrame;
4
5     public class SliderDemo
6     {
7        public static void main(String[] args)
8        {
9           SliderFrame sliderFrame = new SliderFrame();
10          sliderFrame.setDefaultCloseOperation(JFrame.EXIT_ON_CLOSE);
11          sliderFrame.setSize(220, 270);
12          sliderFrame.setVisible(true);
13       }
14    } // end class SliderDemo
```

a) Initial GUI with default circle

b) GUI after the user moves the JSlider's thumb to the right

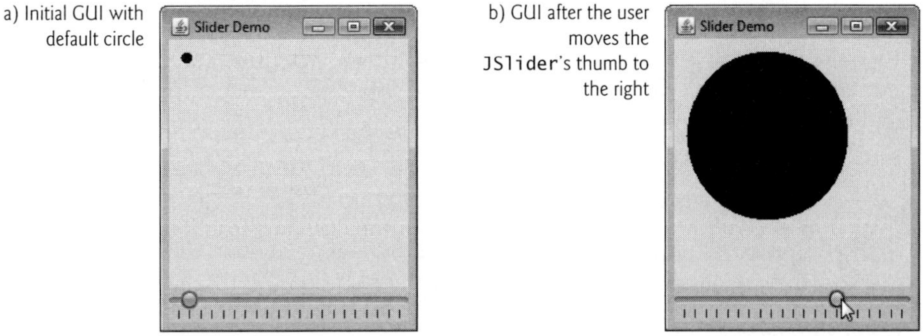

Fig. 19.4 | Test class for SliderFrame.

Class OvalPanel (Fig. 19.2) contains a paintComponent method (lines 12–17) that draws a filled oval (a circle in this example), a setDiameter method (lines 20–25) that changes the circle's diameter and repaints the OvalPanel, a getPreferredSize method (lines 28–31) that returns the preferred width and height of an OvalPanel and a getMinimumSize method (lines 34–37) that returns an OvalPanel's minimum width and height. Methods getPreferredSize and getMinimumSize are used by some layout managers to determine the size of a component.

Class SliderFrame (Fig. 19.3) creates the JSlider that controls the diameter of the circle. Class SliderFrame's constructor (lines 17–45) creates OvalPanel object myPanel (line 21) and sets its background color (line 22). Lines 25–26 create JSlider object diameterJSlider to control the diameter of the circle drawn on the OvalPanel. The JSlider constructor takes four arguments. The first specifies the orientation of diameterJSlider, which is HORIZONTAL (a constant in interface SwingConstants). The second and third arguments indicate the minimum and maximum integer values in the range of values for this JSlider. The last argument indicates that the initial value of the JSlider (i.e., where the thumb is displayed) should be 10.

Lines 27–28 customize the appearance of the JSlider. Method **setMajorTickSpacing** indicates that each major tick mark represents 10 values in the range of values supported by the JSlider. Method **setPaintTicks** with a true argument indicates that the tick marks should be displayed (they aren't displayed by default). For other methods that are used to customize a JSlider's appearance, see the JSlider online documentation (docs.oracle.com/javase/7/docs/api/javax/swing/JSlider.html).

JSliders generate **ChangeEvents** (package javax.swing.event) in response to user interactions. An object of a class that implements interface **ChangeListener** (package javax.swing.event) and declares method **stateChanged** can respond to ChangeEvents. Lines 31–41 register a ChangeListener to handle diameterJSlider's events. When method stateChanged (lines 35–39) is called in response to a user interaction, line 38 calls myPanel's setDiameter method and passes the current value of the JSlider as an argument. JSlider method **getValue** returns the current thumb position.

19.3 Understanding Windows in Java

A JFrame is a **window** with a **title bar** and a **border**. Class JFrame is a subclass of Frame (package java.awt), which is a subclass of Window (package java.awt). As such, JFrame is one of the *heavyweight* Swing GUI components. When you display a window from a Java program, the window is provided by the local platform's windowing toolkit, and therefore the window will look like every other window displayed on that platform. When a Java application executes on a Macintosh and displays a window, the window's title bar and borders will look like those of other Macintosh applications. When a Java application executes on a Microsoft Windows system and displays a window, the window's title bar and borders will look like those of other Microsoft Windows applications. And when a Java application executes on a UNIX platform and displays a window, the window's title bar and borders will look like those of other UNIX applications on that platform.

Returning Window Resources to the System
By default, when the user closes a JFrame window, it's hidden (i.e., removed from the screen), but you can control this with JFrame method **setDefaultCloseOperation**. Interface **WindowConstants** (package javax.swing), which class JFrame implements, declares three constants—DISPOSE_ON_CLOSE, DO_NOTHING_ON_CLOSE and HIDE_ON_CLOSE (the default)—for use with this method. Some platforms allow only a limited number of windows

to be displayed on the screen. Thus, a window is a valuable resource that should be given back to the system when it's no longer needed. Class Window (an indirect superclass of JFrame) declares method **dispose** for this purpose. When a Window is no longer needed in an application, you should explicitly dispose of it. This can be done by calling the Window's dispose method or by calling method setDefaultCloseOperation with the argument WindowConstants.DISPOSE_ON_CLOSE. Terminating an application also returns window resources to the system. Using DO_NOTHING_ON_CLOSE indicates that the program will determine what to do when the user attempts to close the window. For example, the program might want to ask whether to save a file's changes before closing a window.

Displaying and Positioning Windows
By default, a window is not displayed on the screen until the program invokes the window's setVisible method (inherited from class java.awt.Component) with a true argument. A window's size should be set with a call to method setSize (inherited from class java.awt.Component). The position of a window when it appears on the screen is specified with method **setLocation** (inherited from class java.awt.Component).

Window Events
When the user manipulates the window, this action generates **window events**. Event listeners are registered for window events with Window method **addWindowListener**. The **WindowListener** interface provides seven window-event-handling methods—**windowActivated** (called when the user makes a window the active window), **windowClosed** (called after the window is closed), **windowClosing** (called when the user initiates closing of the window), **windowDeactivated** (called when the user makes another window the active window), **windowDeiconified** (called when the user restores a minimized window), **windowIconified** (called when the user minimizes a window) and **windowOpened** (called when a program first displays a window on the screen).

19.4 Using Menus with Frames
Menus are an integral part of GUIs. They allow the user to perform actions without unnecessarily cluttering a GUI with extra components. In Swing GUIs, menus can be attached only to objects of the classes that provide method **setJMenuBar**. Two such classes are JFrame and JApplet. The classes used to declare menus are JMenuBar, JMenu, JMenuItem, JCheckBoxMenuItem and class JRadioButtonMenuItem.

Look-and-Feel Observation 19.1
Menus simplify GUIs because components can be hidden within them. These components will be visible only when the user looks for them by selecting the menu.

Overview of Several Menu-Related Components
Class **JMenuBar** (a subclass of JComponent) contains the methods necessary to manage a **menu bar**, which is a container for menus. Class **JMenu** (a subclass of javax.swing.JMenuItem) contains the methods necessary for managing menus. Menus contain menu items and are added to menu bars or to other menus as submenus. When a menu is clicked, it expands to show its list of menu items.

Class **JMenuItem** (a subclass of javax.swing.AbstractButton) contains the methods necessary to manage **menu items**. A menu item is a GUI component inside a menu that, when selected, causes an action event. A menu item can be used to initiate an action, or it can be a **submenu** that provides more menu items from which the user can select. Submenus are useful for grouping related menu items in a menu.

Class **JCheckBoxMenuItem** (a subclass of javax.swing.JMenuItem) contains the methods necessary to manage menu items that can be toggled on or off. When a JCheck-BoxMenuItem is selected, a check appears to the left of the menu item. When the JCheck-BoxMenuItem is selected again, the check is removed.

Class **JRadioButtonMenuItem** (a subclass of javax.swing.JMenuItem) contains the methods necessary to manage menu items that can be toggled on or off like JCheckBox-MenuItems. When multiple JRadioButtonMenuItems are maintained as part of a Button-Group, only one item in the group can be selected at a given time. When a JRadioButtonMenuItem is selected, a filled circle appears to the left of the menu item. When another JRadioButtonMenuItem is selected, the filled circle of the previously selected menu item is removed.

Using Menus in an Application

Figures 19.5–19.6 demonstrate various menu items and how to specify special characters called **mnemonics** that can provide quick access to a menu or menu item from the keyboard. Mnemonics can be used with all subclasses of javax.swing.AbstractButton. Class MenuFrame (Fig. 19.5) creates the GUI and handles the menu-item events. Most of the code in this application appears in the class's constructor (lines 34–151).

```
1   // Fig. 19.5: MenuFrame.java
2   // Demonstrating menus.
3   import java.awt.Color;
4   import java.awt.Font;
5   import java.awt.BorderLayout;
6   import java.awt.event.ActionListener;
7   import java.awt.event.ActionEvent;
8   import java.awt.event.ItemListener;
9   import java.awt.event.ItemEvent;
10  import javax.swing.JFrame;
11  import javax.swing.JRadioButtonMenuItem;
12  import javax.swing.JCheckBoxMenuItem;
13  import javax.swing.JOptionPane;
14  import javax.swing.JLabel;
15  import javax.swing.SwingConstants;
16  import javax.swing.ButtonGroup;
17  import javax.swing.JMenu;
18  import javax.swing.JMenuItem;
19  import javax.swing.JMenuBar;
20
21  public class MenuFrame extends JFrame
22  {
23     private final Color[] colorValues =
24        {Color.BLACK, Color.BLUE, Color.RED, Color.GREEN};
```

Fig. 19.5 | JMenus and mnemonics. (Part 1 of 5.)

```java
25    private final JRadioButtonMenuItem[] colorItems; // color menu items
26    private final JRadioButtonMenuItem[] fonts; // font menu items
27    private final JCheckBoxMenuItem[] styleItems; // font style menu items
28    private final JLabel displayJLabel; // displays sample text
29    private final ButtonGroup fontButtonGroup; // manages font menu items
30    private final ButtonGroup colorButtonGroup; // manages color menu items
31    private int style; // used to create style for font
32
33    // no-argument constructor set up GUI
34    public MenuFrame()
35    {
36       super("Using JMenus");
37
38       JMenu fileMenu = new JMenu("File"); // create file menu
39       fileMenu.setMnemonic('F'); // set mnemonic to F
40
41       // create About... menu item
42       JMenuItem aboutItem = new JMenuItem("About...");
43       aboutItem.setMnemonic('A'); // set mnemonic to A
44       fileMenu.add(aboutItem); // add about item to file menu
45       aboutItem.addActionListener(
46          new ActionListener() // anonymous inner class
47          {
48             // display message dialog when user selects About...
49             @Override
50             public void actionPerformed(ActionEvent event)
51             {
52                JOptionPane.showMessageDialog(MenuFrame.this,
53                   "This is an example\nof using menus",
54                   "About", JOptionPane.PLAIN_MESSAGE);
55             }
56          }
57       );
58
59       JMenuItem exitItem = new JMenuItem("Exit"); // create exit item
60       exitItem.setMnemonic('x'); // set mnemonic to x
61       fileMenu.add(exitItem); // add exit item to file menu
62       exitItem.addActionListener(
63          new ActionListener() // anonymous inner class
64          {
65             // terminate application when user clicks exitItem
66             @Override
67             public void actionPerformed(ActionEvent event)
68             {
69                System.exit(0); // exit application
70             }
71          }
72       );
73
74       JMenuBar bar = new JMenuBar(); // create menu bar
75       setJMenuBar(bar); // add menu bar to application
76       bar.add(fileMenu); // add file menu to menu bar
77
```

Fig. 19.5 | JMenus and mnemonics. (Part 2 of 5.)

```
78      JMenu formatMenu = new JMenu("Format"); // create format menu
79      formatMenu.setMnemonic('r'); // set mnemonic to r
80
81      // array listing string colors
82      String[] colors = { "Black", "Blue", "Red", "Green" };
83
84      JMenu colorMenu = new JMenu("Color"); // create color menu
85      colorMenu.setMnemonic('C'); // set mnemonic to C
86
87      // create radio button menu items for colors
88      colorItems = new JRadioButtonMenuItem[colors.length];
89      colorButtonGroup = new ButtonGroup(); // manages colors
90      ItemHandler itemHandler = new ItemHandler(); // handler for colors
91
92      // create color radio button menu items
93      for (int count = 0; count < colors.length; count++)
94      {
95         colorItems[count] =
96            new JRadioButtonMenuItem(colors[count]); // create item
97         colorMenu.add(colorItems[count]); // add item to color menu
98         colorButtonGroup.add(colorItems[count]); // add to group
99         colorItems[count].addActionListener(itemHandler);
100     }
101
102     colorItems[0].setSelected(true); // select first Color item
103
104     formatMenu.add(colorMenu); // add color menu to format menu
105     formatMenu.addSeparator(); // add separator in menu
106
107     // array listing font names
108     String[] fontNames = { "Serif", "Monospaced", "SansSerif" };
109     JMenu fontMenu = new JMenu("Font"); // create font menu
110     fontMenu.setMnemonic('n'); // set mnemonic to n
111
112     // create radio button menu items for font names
113     fonts = new JRadioButtonMenuItem[fontNames.length];
114     fontButtonGroup = new ButtonGroup(); // manages font names
115
116     // create Font radio button menu items
117     for (int count = 0; count < fonts.length; count++)
118     {
119        fonts[count] = new JRadioButtonMenuItem(fontNames[count]);
120        fontMenu.add(fonts[count]); // add font to font menu
121        fontButtonGroup.add(fonts[count]); // add to button group
122        fonts[count].addActionListener(itemHandler); // add handler
123     }
124
125     fonts[0].setSelected(true); // select first Font menu item
126     fontMenu.addSeparator(); // add separator bar to font menu
127
128     String[] styleNames = { "Bold", "Italic" }; // names of styles
129     styleItems = new JCheckBoxMenuItem[styleNames.length];
130     StyleHandler styleHandler = new StyleHandler(); // style handler
```

Fig. 19.5 | JMenus and mnemonics. (Part 3 of 5.)

```
131
132        // create style checkbox menu items
133        for (int count = 0; count < styleNames.length; count++)
134        {
135           styleItems[count] =
136              new JCheckBoxMenuItem(styleNames[count]); // for style
137           fontMenu.add(styleItems[count]); // add to font menu
138           styleItems[count].addItemListener(styleHandler); // handler
139        }
140
141        formatMenu.add(fontMenu); // add Font menu to Format menu
142        bar.add(formatMenu); // add Format menu to menu bar
143
144        // set up label to display text
145        displayJLabel = new JLabel("Sample Text", SwingConstants.CENTER);
146        displayJLabel.setForeground(colorValues[0]);
147        displayJLabel.setFont(new Font("Serif", Font.PLAIN, 72));
148
149        getContentPane().setBackground(Color.CYAN); // set background
150        add(displayJLabel, BorderLayout.CENTER); // add displayJLabel
151     } // end MenuFrame constructor
152
153     // inner class to handle action events from menu items
154     private class ItemHandler implements ActionListener
155     {
156        // process color and font selections
157        @Override
158        public void actionPerformed(ActionEvent event)
159        {
160           // process color selection
161           for (int count = 0; count < colorItems.length; count++)
162           {
163              if (colorItems[count].isSelected())
164              {
165                 displayJLabel.setForeground(colorValues[count]);
166                 break;
167              }
168           }
169
170           // process font selection
171           for (int count = 0; count < fonts.length; count++)
172           {
173              if (event.getSource() == fonts[count])
174              {
175                 displayJLabel.setFont(
176                    new Font(fonts[count].getText(), style, 72));
177              }
178           }
179
180           repaint(); // redraw application
181        }
182     } // end class ItemHandler
183
```

Fig. 19.5 | JMenus and mnemonics. (Part 4 of 5.)

```
184    // inner class to handle item events from checkbox menu items
185    private class StyleHandler implements ItemListener
186    {
187       // process font style selections
188       @Override
189       public void itemStateChanged(ItemEvent e)
190       {
191          String name = displayJLabel.getFont().getName(); // current Font
192          Font font; // new font based on user selections
193
194          // determine which items are checked and create Font
195          if (styleItems[0].isSelected() &&
196              styleItems[1].isSelected())
197             font = new Font(name, Font.BOLD + Font.ITALIC, 72);
198          else if (styleItems[0].isSelected())
199             font = new Font(name, Font.BOLD, 72);
200          else if (styleItems[1].isSelected())
201             font = new Font(name, Font.ITALIC, 72);
202          else
203             font = new Font(name, Font.PLAIN, 72);
204
205          displayJLabel.setFont(font);
206          repaint(); // redraw application
207       }
208    }
209 } // end class MenuFrame
```

Fig. 19.5 | JMenus and mnemonics. (Part 5 of 5.)

```
1   // Fig. 19.6: MenuTest.java
2   // Testing MenuFrame.
3   import javax.swing.JFrame;
4
5   public class MenuTest
6   {
7      public static void main(String[] args)
8      {
9         MenuFrame menuFrame = new MenuFrame();
10        menuFrame.setDefaultCloseOperation(JFrame.EXIT_ON_CLOSE);
11        menuFrame.setSize(500, 200);
12        menuFrame.setVisible(true);
13     }
14  } // end class MenuTest
```

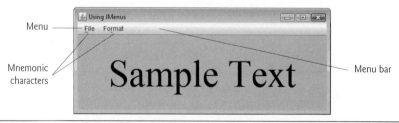

Fig. 19.6 | Test class for MenuFrame. (Part 1 of 2.)

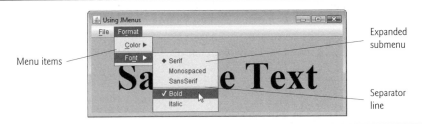

Fig. 19.6 | Test class for `MenuFrame`. (Part 2 of 2.)

Setting Up the File Menu

Lines 38–76 set up the **File** menu and attach it to the menu bar. The **File** menu contains an **About...** menu item that displays a message dialog when the menu item is selected and an **Exit** menu item that can be selected to terminate the application. Line 38 creates a JMenu and passes to the constructor the string `"File"` as the name of the menu. Line 39 uses JMenu method **setMnemonic** (inherited from class AbstractButton) to indicate that F is the mnemonic for this menu. Pressing the *Alt* key and the letter *F* opens the menu, just as clicking the menu name with the mouse would. In the GUI, the mnemonic character in the menu's name is displayed with an underline. (See the screen captures in Fig. 19.6.)

Look-and-Feel Observation 19.2

Mnemonics provide quick access to menu commands and button commands through the keyboard.

Look-and-Feel Observation 19.3

*Different mnemonics should be used for each button or menu item. Normally, the first letter in the label on the menu item or button is used as the mnemonic. If several buttons or menu items start with the same letter, choose the next most prominent letter in the name (e.g., x is commonly chosen for an **Exit** button or menu item). Mnemonics are case insensitive.*

Lines 42–43 create JMenuItem aboutItem with the text "About..." and set its mnemonic to the letter A. This menu item is added to fileMenu at line 44 with JMenu method **add**. To access the **About...** menu item through the keyboard, press the *Alt* key and letter *F* to open the **File** menu, then press *A* to select the **About...** menu item. Lines 46–56 create an ActionListener to process aboutItem's action event. Lines 52–54 display a message dialog box. In most prior uses of showMessageDialog, the first argument was null. The purpose of the first argument is to specify the **parent window** that helps determine where the dialog box will be displayed. If the parent window is specified as null, the dialog box appears in the center of the screen. Otherwise, it appears centered over the specified parent window. In this example, the program specifies the parent window with Menu-Frame.this—the this reference of the MenuFrame object. When using the this reference in an inner class, specifying this by itself refers to the inner-class object. To reference the outer-class object's this reference, qualify this with the outer-class name and a dot (.).

Recall that dialog boxes are typically modal. A modal dialog box does not allow any other window in the application to be accessed until the dialog box is dismissed. The dialogs displayed with class JOptionPane are modal dialogs. Class **JDialog** can be used to create your own modal or nonmodal dialogs.

Lines 59–72 create menu item exitItem, set its mnemonic to x, add it to fileMenu and register an ActionListener that terminates the program when the user selects exit-Item. Lines 74–76 create the JMenuBar, attach it to the window with JFrame method set-JMenuBar and use JMenuBar method **add** to attach the fileMenu to the JMenuBar.

Look-and-Feel Observation 19.4

Menus appear left to right in the order they're added to a JMenuBar.

Setting Up the Format Menu

Lines 78–79 create the formatMenu and set its mnemonic to r. F is not used because that's the **File** menu's mnemonic. Lines 84–85 create colorMenu (this will be a submenu in **Format**) and set its mnemonic to C. Line 88 creates JRadioButtonMenuItem array colorItems, which refers to the menu items in colorMenu. Line 89 creates ButtonGroup colorButtonGroup, which ensures that only one of the **Color** submenu items is selected at a time. Line 90 creates an instance of inner class ItemHandler (declared at lines 154–181) that responds to selections from the **Color** and **Font** submenus (discussed shortly). The loop at lines 93–100 creates each JRadioButtonMenuItem in array colorItems, adds each menu item to colorMenu and to colorButtonGroup and registers the ActionListener for each menu item.

Line 102 invokes AbstractButton method **setSelected** to select the first element in array colorItems. Line 104 adds colorMenu as a submenu of formatMenu. Line 105 invokes JMenu method **addSeparator** to add a horizontal **separator** line to the menu.

Look-and-Feel Observation 19.5

A submenu is created by adding a menu as a menu item in another menu.

Look-and-Feel Observation 19.6

Separators can be added to a menu to group menu items logically.

Look-and-Feel Observation 19.7

Any JComponent can be added to a JMenu or to a JMenuBar.

Lines 108–126 create the **Font** submenu and several JRadioButtonMenuItems and select the first element of JRadioButtonMenuItem array fonts. Line 129 creates a JCheckBoxMenu-Item array to represent the menu items for specifying bold and italic styles for the fonts. Line 130 creates an instance of inner class StyleHandler (declared at lines 185–208) to respond to the JCheckBoxMenuItem events. The for statement at lines 133–139 creates each JCheck-BoxMenuItem, adds it to fontMenu and registers its ItemListener. Line 141 adds fontMenu as a submenu of formatMenu. Line 142 adds the formatMenu to bar (the menu bar).

Creating the Rest of the GUI and Defining the Event Handlers

Lines 145–147 create a JLabel for which the **Format** menu items control the font, font color and font style. The initial foreground color is set to the first element of array color-Values (Color.BLACK) by invoking JComponent method **setForeground**. The initial font is set to Serif with PLAIN style and 72-point size. Line 149 sets the background color of the window's content pane to cyan, and line 150 attaches the JLabel to the CENTER of the content pane's BorderLayout.

ItemHandler method actionPerformed (lines 157–181) uses two for statements to determine which font or color menu item generated the event and sets the font or color of the JLabel displayLabel, respectively. The if condition at line 163 uses Abstract-Button method **isSelected** to determine the selected JRadioButtonMenuItem. The if condition at line 173 invokes the event object's getSource method to get a reference to the JRadioButtonMenuItem that generated the event. Line 176 invokes AbstractButton method getText to obtain the name of the font from the menu item.

StyleHandler method itemStateChanged (lines 188–207) is called if the user selects a JCheckBoxMenuItem in the fontMenu. Lines 195–203 determine which JCheckBoxMenu-Items are selected and use their combined state to determine the new font style.

19.5 JPopupMenu

Applications often provide **context-sensitive pop-up menus** for several reasons—they can be convenient, there might not be a menu bar and the options they display can be specific to individual on-screen components. In Swing, such menus are created with class **JPopup-Menu** (a subclass of JComponent). These menus provide options that are specific to the component for which the **popup trigger event** occurred—on most systems, when the user presses and releases the right mouse button.

Look-and-Feel Observation 19.8

The pop-up trigger event is platform specific. On most platforms that use a mouse with multiple buttons, the pop-up trigger event occurs when the user clicks the right mouse button on a component that supports a pop-up menu.

The application in Figs. 19.7–19.8 creates a JPopupMenu that allows the user to select one of three colors and change the background color of the window. When the user clicks the right mouse button on the PopupFrame window's background, a JPopupMenu containing colors appears. If the user clicks a JRadioButtonMenuItem for a color, ItemHandler method actionPerformed changes the background color of the window's content pane.

Line 25 of the PopupFrame constructor (Fig. 19.7, lines 21–70) creates an instance of class ItemHandler (declared in lines 73–89) that will process the item events from the menu items in the pop-up menu. Line 29 creates the JPopupMenu. The for statement (lines 33–39) creates a JRadioButtonMenuItem object (line 35), adds it to popupMenu (line 36), adds it to ButtonGroup colorGroup (line 37) to maintain one selected JRadioButtonMenuItem at a time and registers its ActionListener (line 38). Line 41 sets the initial background to white by invoking method setBackground.

```
1   // Fig. 19.7: PopupFrame.java
2   // Demonstrating JPopupMenus.
3   import java.awt.Color;
4   import java.awt.event.MouseAdapter;
5   import java.awt.event.MouseEvent;
6   import java.awt.event.ActionListener;
```

Fig. 19.7 | JPopupMenu for selecting colors. (Part 1 of 3.)

```
7    import java.awt.event.ActionEvent;
8    import javax.swing.JFrame;
9    import javax.swing.JRadioButtonMenuItem;
10   import javax.swing.JPopupMenu;
11   import javax.swing.ButtonGroup;
12
13   public class PopupFrame extends JFrame
14   {
15      private final JRadioButtonMenuItem[] items; // holds items for colors
16      private final Color[] colorValues =
17         { Color.BLUE, Color.YELLOW, Color.RED }; // colors to be used
18      private final JPopupMenu popupMenu; // allows user to select color
19
20      // no-argument constructor sets up GUI
21      public PopupFrame()
22      {
23         super("Using JPopupMenus");
24
25         ItemHandler handler = new ItemHandler(); // handler for menu items
26         String[] colors = { "Blue", "Yellow", "Red" };
27
28         ButtonGroup colorGroup = new ButtonGroup(); // manages color items
29         popupMenu = new JPopupMenu(); // create pop-up menu
30         items = new JRadioButtonMenuItem[colors.length];
31
32         // construct menu item, add to pop-up menu, enable event handling
33         for (int count = 0; count < items.length; count++)
34         {
35            items[count] = new JRadioButtonMenuItem(colors[count]);
36            popupMenu.add(items[count]); // add item to pop-up menu
37            colorGroup.add(items[count]); // add item to button group
38            items[count].addActionListener(handler); // add handler
39         }
40
41         setBackground(Color.WHITE);
42
43         // declare a MouseListener for the window to display pop-up menu
44         addMouseListener(
45            new MouseAdapter() // anonymous inner class
46            {
47               // handle mouse press event
48               @Override
49               public void mousePressed(MouseEvent event)
50               {
51                  checkForTriggerEvent(event);
52               }
53
54               // handle mouse release event
55               @Override
56               public void mouseReleased(MouseEvent event)
57               {
58                  checkForTriggerEvent(event);
59               }
```

Fig. 19.7 | JPopupMenu for selecting colors. (Part 2 of 3.)

```
60
61                     // determine whether event should trigger pop-up menu
62                     private void checkForTriggerEvent(MouseEvent event)
63                     {
64                        if (event.isPopupTrigger())
65                           popupMenu.show(
66                              event.getComponent(), event.getX(), event.getY());
67                     }
68                  }
69               );
70            } // end PopupFrame constructor
71
72            // private inner class to handle menu item events
73            private class ItemHandler implements ActionListener
74            {
75               // process menu item selections
76               @Override
77               public void actionPerformed(ActionEvent event)
78               {
79                  // determine which menu item was selected
80                  for (int i = 0; i < items.length; i++)
81                  {
82                     if (event.getSource() == items[i])
83                     {
84                        getContentPane().setBackground(colorValues[i]);
85                        return;
86                     }
87                  }
88               }
89            } // end private inner class ItemHandler
90         } // end class PopupFrame
```

Fig. 19.7 | JPopupMenu for selecting colors. (Part 3 of 3.)

```
1   // Fig. 19.8: PopupTest.java
2   // Testing PopupFrame.
3   import javax.swing.JFrame;
4
5   public class PopupTest
6   {
7      public static void main(String[] args)
8      {
9         PopupFrame popupFrame = new PopupFrame();
10        popupFrame.setDefaultCloseOperation(JFrame.EXIT_ON_CLOSE);
11        popupFrame.setSize(300, 200);
12        popupFrame.setVisible(true);
13     }
14  } // end class PopupTest
```

Fig. 19.8 | Test class for PopupFrame. (Part 1 of 2.)

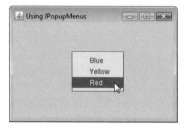

Fig. 19.8 | Test class for `PopupFrame`. (Part 2 of 2.)

Lines 44–69 register a `MouseListener` to handle the mouse events of the application window. Methods `mousePressed` (lines 48–52) and `mouseReleased` (lines 55–59) check for the pop-up trigger event. Each method calls private utility method `checkForTrigger-Event` (lines 62–67) to determine whether the pop-up trigger event occurred. If it did, `MouseEvent` method **isPopupTrigger** returns `true`, and `JPopupMenu` method **show** displays the `JPopupMenu`. The first argument to method `show` specifies the **origin component**, whose position helps determine where the `JPopupMenu` will appear on the screen. The last two arguments are the *x-y* coordinates (measured from the origin component's upper-left corner) at which the `JPopupMenu` is to appear.

 Look-and-Feel Observation 19.9
Displaying a `JPopupMenu` for the pop-up trigger event of multiple GUI components requires registering mouse-event handlers for each of those GUI components.

When the user selects a menu item from the pop-up menu, class `ItemHandler`'s method `actionPerformed` (lines 76–88) determines which `JRadioButtonMenuItem` the user selected and sets the background color of the window's content pane.

19.6 Pluggable Look-and-Feel

A program that uses Java's AWT GUI components (package `java.awt`) takes on the look-and-feel of the platform on which the program executes. A Java application running on a Mac OS X looks like other Mac OS X applications, one running on Microsoft Windows looks like other Windows applications, and one running on a Linux platform looks like other applications on that Linux platform. This is sometimes desirable, because it allows users of the application on each platform to use GUI components with which they're already familiar. However, it also introduces interesting portability issues.

 Portability Tip 19.1
GUI components often look different on different platforms (fonts, font sizes, component borders, etc.) and might require different amounts of space to display. This could change their layout and alignments.

 Portability Tip 19.2
GUI components on different platforms have might different default functionality—e.g., not all platforms allow a button with the focus to be "pressed" with the space bar.

Swing's lightweight GUI components eliminate many of these issues by providing uniform functionality across platforms and by defining a uniform cross-platform look-and-feel. Section 12.2 introduced the *Nimbus* look-and-feel. Earlier versions of Java used the **metal look-and-feel**, which is still the default. Swing also provides the flexibility to customize the look-and-feel to appear as a Microsoft Windows-style look-and-feel (only on Windows systems), a Motif-style (UNIX) look-and-feel (across all platforms) or a Macintosh look-and-feel (only on Mac systems).

Figures 19.9–19.10 demonstrate a way to change the look-and-feel of a Swing GUI. It creates several GUI components, so you can see the change in their look-and-feel at the same time. The output windows show the Metal, Nimbus, CDE/Motif, Windows and Windows Classic look-and-feels that are available on Windows systems. The installed look-and-feels will vary by platform.

We've covered the GUI components and event-handling concepts in this example previously, so we focus here on the mechanism for changing the look-and-feel. Class **UIManager** (package `javax.swing`) contains nested class **LookAndFeelInfo** (a public static class) that maintains information about a look-and-feel. Line 20 (Fig. 19.9) declares an array of type `UIManager.LookAndFeelInfo` (note the syntax used to identify the static inner class `LookAndFeelInfo`). Line 34 uses `UIManager` static method **get-InstalledLookAndFeels** to get the array of `UIManager.LookAndFeelInfo` objects that describe each look-and-feel available on your system.

Performance Tip 19.1

Each look-and-feel is represented by a Java class. `UIManager` method `getInstalled-LookAndFeels` does not load each class. Rather, it provides the names of the available look-and-feel classes so that a choice can be made (presumably once at program start-up). This reduces the overhead of having to load all the look-and-feel classes even if the program will not use some of them.

```java
1   // Fig. 19.9: LookAndFeelFrame.java
2   // Changing the look-and-feel.
3   import java.awt.GridLayout;
4   import java.awt.BorderLayout;
5   import java.awt.event.ItemListener;
6   import java.awt.event.ItemEvent;
7   import javax.swing.JFrame;
8   import javax.swing.UIManager;
9   import javax.swing.JRadioButton;
10  import javax.swing.ButtonGroup;
11  import javax.swing.JButton;
12  import javax.swing.JLabel;
13  import javax.swing.JComboBox;
14  import javax.swing.JPanel;
15  import javax.swing.SwingConstants;
16  import javax.swing.SwingUtilities;
17
18  public class LookAndFeelFrame extends JFrame
19  {
```

Fig. 19.9 | Look-and-feel of a Swing-based GUI. (Part 1 of 3.)

```
20    private final UIManager.LookAndFeelInfo[] looks;
21    private final String[] lookNames; // look-and-feel names
22    private final JRadioButton[] radio; // for selecting look-and-feel
23    private final ButtonGroup group; // group for radio buttons
24    private final JButton button; // displays look of button
25    private final JLabel label; // displays look of label
26    private final JComboBox<String> comboBox; // displays look of combo box
27
28    // set up GUI
29    public LookAndFeelFrame()
30    {
31       super("Look and Feel Demo");
32
33       // get installed look-and-feel information
34       looks = UIManager.getInstalledLookAndFeels();
35       lookNames = new String[looks.length];
36
37       // get names of installed look-and-feels
38       for (int i = 0; i < looks.length; i++)
39          lookNames[i] = looks[i].getName();
40
41       JPanel northPanel = new JPanel();
42       northPanel.setLayout(new GridLayout(3, 1, 0, 5));
43
44       label = new JLabel("This is a " + lookNames[0] + " look-and-feel",
45          SwingConstants.CENTER);
46       northPanel.add(label);
47
48       button = new JButton("JButton");
49       northPanel.add(button);
50
51       comboBox = new JComboBox<String>(lookNames);
52       northPanel.add(comboBox);
53
54       // create array for radio buttons
55       radio = new JRadioButton[looks.length];
56
57       JPanel southPanel = new JPanel();
58
59       // use a GridLayout with 3 buttons in each row
60       int rows = (int) Math.ceil(radio.length / 3.0);
61       southPanel.setLayout(new GridLayout(rows, 3));
62
63       group = new ButtonGroup(); // button group for look-and-feels
64       ItemHandler handler = new ItemHandler(); // look-and-feel handler
65
66       for (int count = 0; count < radio.length; count++)
67       {
68          radio[count] = new JRadioButton(lookNames[count]);
69          radio[count].addItemListener(handler); // add handler
70          group.add(radio[count]); // add radio button to group
71          southPanel.add(radio[count]); // add radio button to panel
72       }
```

Fig. 19.9 | Look-and-feel of a Swing-based GUI. (Part 2 of 3.)

```
73
74          add(northPanel, BorderLayout.NORTH); // add north panel
75          add(southPanel, BorderLayout.SOUTH); // add south panel
76
77          radio[0].setSelected(true); // set default selection
78      } // end LookAndFeelFrame constructor
79
80      // use UIManager to change look-and-feel of GUI
81      private void changeTheLookAndFeel(int value)
82      {
83          try // change look-and-feel
84          {
85              // set look-and-feel for this application
86              UIManager.setLookAndFeel(looks[value].getClassName());
87
88              // update components in this application
89              SwingUtilities.updateComponentTreeUI(this);
90          }
91          catch (Exception exception)
92          {
93              exception.printStackTrace();
94          }
95      }
96
97      // private inner class to handle radio button events
98      private class ItemHandler implements ItemListener
99      {
100         // process user's look-and-feel selection
101         @Override
102         public void itemStateChanged(ItemEvent event)
103         {
104             for (int count = 0; count < radio.length; count++)
105             {
106                 if (radio[count].isSelected())
107                 {
108                     label.setText(String.format(
109                         "This is a %s look-and-feel", lookNames[count]));
110                     comboBox.setSelectedIndex(count); // set combobox index
111                     changeTheLookAndFeel(count); // change look-and-feel
112                 }
113             }
114         }
115     } // end private inner class ItemHandler
116 } // end class LookAndFeelFrame
```

Fig. 19.9 | Look-and-feel of a Swing-based GUI. (Part 3 of 3.)

```
1   // Fig. 19.10: LookAndFeelDemo.java
2   // Changing the look-and-feel.
3   import javax.swing.JFrame;
4
```

Fig. 19.10 | Test class for LookAndFeelFrame. (Part 1 of 2.)

```
5    public class LookAndFeelDemo
6    {
7       public static void main(String[] args)
8       {
9          LookAndFeelFrame lookAndFeelFrame = new LookAndFeelFrame();
10         lookAndFeelFrame.setDefaultCloseOperation(JFrame.EXIT_ON_CLOSE);
11         lookAndFeelFrame.setSize(400, 220);
12         lookAndFeelFrame.setVisible(true);
13      }
14   } // end class LookAndFeelDemo
```

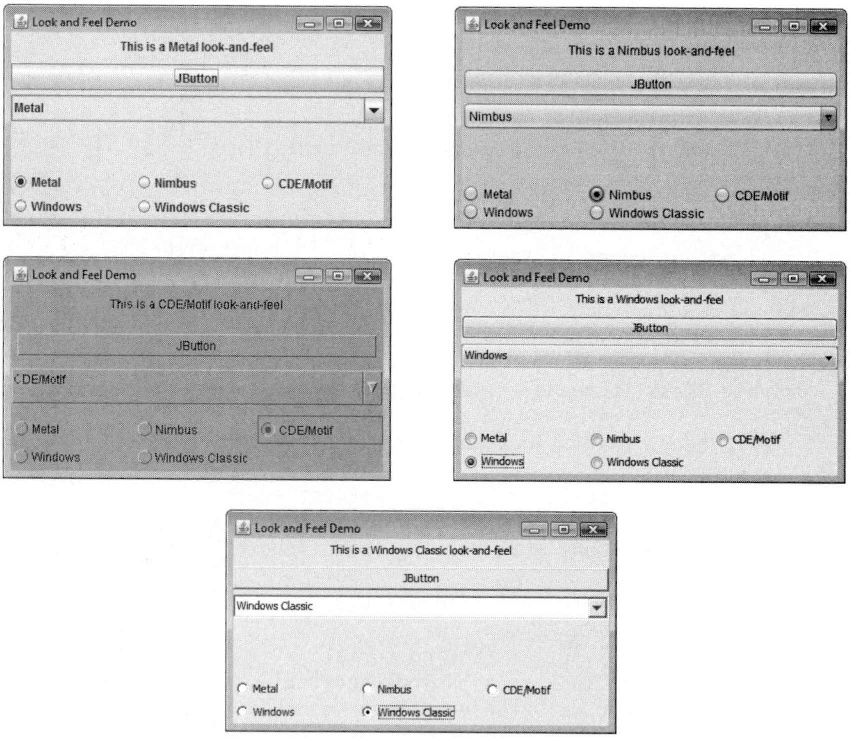

Fig. 19.10 | Test class for LookAndFeelFrame. (Part 2 of 2.)

Our utility method changeTheLookAndFeel (lines 81–95) is called by the event handler for the JRadioButtons at the bottom of the user interface. The event handler (declared in private inner class ItemHandler at lines 98–115) passes an integer representing the element in array looks that should be used to change the look-and-feel. Line 86 invokes static method **setLookAndFeel** of UIManager to change the look-and-feel. The **getClassName** method of class UIManager.LookAndFeelInfo determines the name of the look-and-feel class that corresponds to the UIManager.LookAndFeelInfo object. If the look-and-feel is not already loaded, it will be loaded as part of the call to setLookAndFeel. Line 89 invokes the static method **updateComponentTreeUI** of class **SwingUtilities** (package javax.swing) to change the look-and-feel of every GUI component attached to its argument (this instance of our application class LookAndFeelFrame) to the new look-and-feel.

19.7 JDesktopPane and JInternalFrame

A **multiple-document interface** (MDI) is a main window (called the **parent window**) containing other windows (called **child windows**) and is often used to manage several open documents. For example, many e-mail programs allow you to have several windows open at the same time, so you can compose or read multiple e-mail messages simultaneously. Similarly, many word processors allow the user to open multiple documents in separate windows within a main window, making it possible to switch between them without having to close one to open another. The application in Figs. 19.11–19.12 demonstrates Swing's **JDesktopPane** and **JInternalFrame** classes for implementing multiple-document interfaces.

```java
1   // Fig. 19.11: DesktopFrame.java
2   // Demonstrating JDesktopPane.
3   import java.awt.BorderLayout;
4   import java.awt.Dimension;
5   import java.awt.Graphics;
6   import java.awt.event.ActionListener;
7   import java.awt.event.ActionEvent;
8   import java.util.Random;
9   import javax.swing.JFrame;
10  import javax.swing.JDesktopPane;
11  import javax.swing.JMenuBar;
12  import javax.swing.JMenu;
13  import javax.swing.JMenuItem;
14  import javax.swing.JInternalFrame;
15  import javax.swing.JPanel;
16  import javax.swing.ImageIcon;
17
18  public class DesktopFrame extends JFrame
19  {
20     private final JDesktopPane theDesktop;
21
22     // set up GUI
23     public DesktopFrame()
24     {
25        super("Using a JDesktopPane");
26
27        JMenuBar bar = new JMenuBar();
28        JMenu addMenu = new JMenu("Add");
29        JMenuItem newFrame = new JMenuItem("Internal Frame");
30
31        addMenu.add(newFrame); // add new frame item to Add menu
32        bar.add(addMenu); // add Add menu to menu bar
33        setJMenuBar(bar); // set menu bar for this application
34
35        theDesktop = new JDesktopPane();
36        add(theDesktop); // add desktop pane to frame
37
38        // set up listener for newFrame menu item
39        newFrame.addActionListener(
```

Fig. 19.11 | Multiple-document interface. (Part 1 of 2.)

```
40                  new ActionListener() // anonymous inner class
41                  {
42                      // display new internal window
43                      @Override
44                      public void actionPerformed(ActionEvent event)
45                      {
46                          // create internal frame
47                          JInternalFrame frame = new JInternalFrame(
48                              "Internal Frame", true, true, true, true);
49
50                          MyJPanel panel = new MyJPanel();
51                          frame.add(panel, BorderLayout.CENTER);
52                          frame.pack(); // set internal frame to size of contents
53
54                          theDesktop.add(frame); // attach internal frame
55                          frame.setVisible(true); // show internal frame
56                      }
57                  }
58              );
59          } // end DesktopFrame constructor
60      } // end class DesktopFrame
61
62      // class to display an ImageIcon on a panel
63      class MyJPanel extends JPanel
64      {
65          private static final SecureRandom generator = new SecureRandom();
66          private final ImageIcon picture; // image to be displayed
67          private final static String[] images = { "yellowflowers.png",
68              "purpleflowers.png", "redflowers.png", "redflowers2.png",
69              "lavenderflowers.png" };
70
71          // load image
72          public MyJPanel()
73          {
74              int randomNumber = generator.nextInt(images.length);
75              picture = new ImageIcon(images[randomNumber]); // set icon
76          }
77
78          // display imageIcon on panel
79          @Override
80          public void paintComponent(Graphics g)
81          {
82              super.paintComponent(g);
83              picture.paintIcon(this, g, 0, 0); // display icon
84          }
85
86          // return image dimensions
87          public Dimension getPreferredSize()
88          {
89              return new Dimension(picture.getIconWidth(),
90                  picture.getIconHeight());
91          }
92      } // end class MyJPanel
```

Fig. 19.11 | Multiple-document interface. (Part 2 of 2.)

Lines 27–33 create a JMenuBar, a JMenu and a JMenuItem, add the JMenuItem to the JMenu, add the JMenu to the JMenuBar and set the JMenuBar for the application window. When the user selects the JMenuItem newFrame, the application creates and displays a new JInternalFrame object containing an image.

Line 35 assigns JDesktopPane (package javax.swing) variable theDesktop a new JDesktopPane object that will be used to manage the JInternalFrame child windows. Line 36 adds the JDesktopPane to the JFrame. By default, the JDesktopPane is added to the center of the content pane's BorderLayout, so the JDesktopPane expands to fill the entire application window.

```
1   // Fig. 19.12: DesktopTest.java
2   // Demonstrating JDesktopPane.
3   import javax.swing.JFrame;
4
5   public class DesktopTest
6   {
7      public static void main(String[] args)
8      {
9         DesktopFrame desktopFrame = new DesktopFrame();
10        desktopFrame.setDefaultCloseOperation(JFrame.EXIT_ON_CLOSE);
11        desktopFrame.setSize(600, 480);
12        desktopFrame.setVisible(true);
13     }
14  } // end class DesktopTest
```

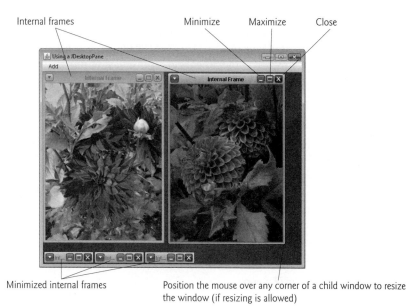

Internal frames   Minimize   Maximize   Close

Minimized internal frames   Position the mouse over any corner of a child window to resize the window (if resizing is allowed)

Fig. 19.12 | Test class for DeskTopFrame. (Part 1 of 2.)

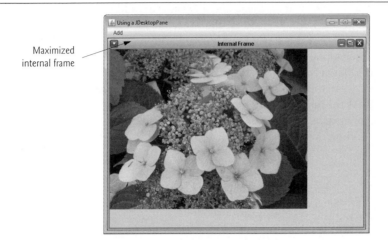

Maximized internal frame

Fig. 19.12 | Test class for `DeskTopFrame`. (Part 2 of 2.)

Lines 39–58 register an `ActionListener` to handle the event when the user selects the newFrame menu item. When the event occurs, method `actionPerformed` (lines 43–56) creates a `JInternalFrame` object in lines 47–48. The `JInternalFrame` constructor used here takes five arguments—a `String` for the title bar of the internal window, a `boolean` indicating whether the internal frame can be resized by the user, a `boolean` indicating whether the internal frame can be closed by the user, a `boolean` indicating whether the internal frame can be maximized by the user and a `boolean` indicating whether the internal frame can be minimized by the user. For each of the `boolean` arguments, a `true` value indicates that the operation should be allowed (as is the case here).

As with `JFrame`s and `JApplet`s, a `JInternalFrame` has a content pane to which GUI components can be attached. Line 50 creates an instance of our class `MyJPanel` (declared at lines 63–91) that is added to the `JInternalFrame` at line 51.

Line 52 uses `JInternalFrame` method **pack** to set the size of the child window. Method pack uses the preferred sizes of the components to determine the window's size. Class `MyJPanel` declares method `getPreferredSize` (lines 87–91) to specify the panel's preferred size for use by the pack method. Line 54 adds the `JInternalFrame` to the `JDesktopPane`, and line 55 displays the `JInternalFrame`.

Classes `JInternalFrame` and `JDesktopPane` provide many methods for managing child windows. See the `JInternalFrame` and `JDesktopPane` online API documentation for complete lists of these methods:

```
docs.oracle.com/javase/7/docs/api/javax/swing/JInternalFrame.html
docs.oracle.com/javase/7/docs/api/javax/swing/JDesktopPane.html
```

19.8 JTabbedPane

A **JTabbedPane** arranges GUI components into layers, of which only one is visible at a time. Users access each layer via a tab—similar to folders in a file cabinet. When the user clicks a tab, the appropriate layer is displayed. The tabs appear at the top by default but also can be positioned at the left, right or bottom of the `JTabbedPane`. Any component can be placed on a tab. If the component is a container, such as a panel, it can use any layout manager to lay out several components on the tab. Class JTabbedPane is a subclass of JComponent. The application in Figs. 19.13–19.14 creates one tabbed pane with three tabs. Each tab displays one of the JPanels—panel1, panel2 or panel3.

```java
 1   // Fig. 19.13: JTabbedPaneFrame.java
 2   // Demonstrating JTabbedPane.
 3   import java.awt.BorderLayout;
 4   import java.awt.Color;
 5   import javax.swing.JFrame;
 6   import javax.swing.JTabbedPane;
 7   import javax.swing.JLabel;
 8   import javax.swing.JPanel;
 9   import javax.swing.JButton;
10   import javax.swing.SwingConstants;
11
12   public class JTabbedPaneFrame extends JFrame
13   {
14      // set up GUI
15      public JTabbedPaneFrame()
16      {
17         super("JTabbedPane Demo ");
18
19         JTabbedPane tabbedPane = new JTabbedPane(); // create JTabbedPane
20
21         // set up panel1 and add it to JTabbedPane
22         JLabel label1 = new JLabel("panel one", SwingConstants.CENTER);
23         JPanel panel1 = new JPanel();
24         panel1.add(label1);
25         tabbedPane.addTab("Tab One", null, panel1, "First Panel");
26
27         // set up panel2 and add it to JTabbedPane
28         JLabel label2 = new JLabel("panel two", SwingConstants.CENTER);
29         JPanel panel2 = new JPanel();
30         panel2.setBackground(Color.YELLOW);
31         panel2.add(label2);
32         tabbedPane.addTab("Tab Two", null, panel2, "Second Panel");
33
34         // set up panel3 and add it to JTabbedPane
35         JLabel label3 = new JLabel("panel three");
36         JPanel panel3 = new JPanel();
37         panel3.setLayout(new BorderLayout());
38         panel3.add(new JButton("North"), BorderLayout.NORTH);
39         panel3.add(new JButton("West"), BorderLayout.WEST);
40         panel3.add(new JButton("East"), BorderLayout.EAST);
41         panel3.add(new JButton("South"), BorderLayout.SOUTH);
42         panel3.add(label3, BorderLayout.CENTER);
43         tabbedPane.addTab("Tab Three", null, panel3, "Third Panel");
44
45         add(tabbedPane); // add JTabbedPane to frame
46      }
47   } // end class JTabbedPaneFrame
```

Fig. 19.13 | JTabbedPane used to organize GUI components.

```
 1   // Fig. 19.14: JTabbedPaneDemo.java
 2   // Demonstrating JTabbedPane.
 3   import javax.swing.JFrame;
 4
 5   public class JTabbedPaneDemo
 6   {
 7      public static void main(String[] args)
 8      {
 9         JTabbedPaneFrame tabbedPaneFrame = new JTabbedPaneFrame();
10         tabbedPaneFrame.setDefaultCloseOperation(JFrame.EXIT_ON_CLOSE);
11         tabbedPaneFrame.setSize(250, 200);
12         tabbedPaneFrame.setVisible(true);
13      }
14   } // end class JTabbedPaneDemo
```

Fig. 19.14 | Test class for `JTabbedPaneFrame`.

The constructor (lines 15–46) builds the GUI. Line 19 creates an empty `JTabbedPane` with default settings—that is, tabs across the top. If the tabs do not fit on one line, they'll wrap to form additional lines of tabs. Next the constructor creates the `JPanels` `panel1`, `panel2` and `panel3` and their GUI components. As we set up each panel, we add it to `tabbedPane`, using `JTabbedPane` method **addTab** with four arguments. The first argument is a `String` that specifies the title of the tab. The second argument is an `Icon` reference that specifies an icon to display on the tab. If the `Icon` is a `null` reference, no image is displayed. The third argument is a `Component` reference that represents the GUI component to display when the user clicks the tab. The last argument is a `String` that specifies the tool tip for the tab. For example, line 25 adds `JPanel panel1` to `tabbedPane` with title `"Tab One"` and the tool tip `"First Panel"`. `JPanels` `panel2` and `panel3` are added to `tabbedPane` at lines 32 and 43. To view a tab, click it with the mouse or use the arrow keys to cycle through the tabs.

19.9 BoxLayout Layout Manager

In Chapter 12, we introduced three layout managers—`FlowLayout`, `BorderLayout` and `GridLayout`. This section and Section 19.10 present two additional layout managers (summarized in Fig. 19.15). We discuss them in the examples that follow.

Layout manager	Description
BoxLayout	Allows GUI components to be arranged left-to-right or top-to-bottom in a container. Class Box declares a container that uses BoxLayout and provides static methods to create a Box with a horizontal or vertical BoxLayout.
GridBagLayout	Similar to GridLayout, but the components can vary in size and can be added in any order.

Fig. 19.15 | Additional layout managers.

The BoxLayout layout manager (in package java.swing) arranges GUI components horizontally along a container's *x*-axis or vertically along its *y*-axis. The application in Figs. 19.16–19.17 demonstrate BoxLayout and the container class Box that uses Box-Layout as its default layout manager.

```java
 1   // Fig. 19.16: BoxLayoutFrame.java
 2   // Demonstrating BoxLayout.
 3   import java.awt.Dimension;
 4   import javax.swing.JFrame;
 5   import javax.swing.Box;
 6   import javax.swing.JButton;
 7   import javax.swing.BoxLayout;
 8   import javax.swing.JPanel;
 9   import javax.swing.JTabbedPane;
10
11   public class BoxLayoutFrame extends JFrame
12   {
13      // set up GUI
14      public BoxLayoutFrame()
15      {
16         super("Demonstrating BoxLayout");
17
18         // create Box containers with BoxLayout
19         Box horizontal1 = Box.createHorizontalBox();
20         Box vertical1 = Box.createVerticalBox();
21         Box horizontal2 = Box.createHorizontalBox();
22         Box vertical2 = Box.createVerticalBox();
23
24         final int SIZE = 3; // number of buttons on each Box
25
26         // add buttons to Box horizontal1
27         for (int count = 0; count < SIZE; count++)
28            horizontal1.add(new JButton("Button " + count));
29
30         // create strut and add buttons to Box vertical1
31         for (int count = 0; count < SIZE; count++)
32         {
33            vertical1.add(Box.createVerticalStrut(25));
34            vertical1.add(new JButton("Button " + count));
35         }
```

Fig. 19.16 | BoxLayout layout manager. (Part 1 of 2.)

```
36
37        // create horizontal glue and add buttons to Box horizontal2
38        for (int count = 0; count < SIZE; count++)
39        {
40            horizontal2.add(Box.createHorizontalGlue());
41            horizontal2.add(new JButton("Button " + count));
42        }
43
44        // create rigid area and add buttons to Box vertical2
45        for (int count = 0; count < SIZE; count++)
46        {
47            vertical2.add(Box.createRigidArea(new Dimension(12, 8)));
48            vertical2.add(new JButton("Button " + count));
49        }
50
51        // create vertical glue and add buttons to panel
52        JPanel panel = new JPanel();
53        panel.setLayout(new BoxLayout(panel, BoxLayout.Y_AXIS));
54
55        for (int count = 0; count < SIZE; count++)
56        {
57            panel.add(Box.createGlue());
58            panel.add(new JButton("Button " + count));
59        }
60
61        // create a JTabbedPane
62        JTabbedPane tabs = new JTabbedPane(
63            JTabbedPane.TOP, JTabbedPane.SCROLL_TAB_LAYOUT);
64
65        // place each container on tabbed pane
66        tabs.addTab("Horizontal Box", horizontal1);
67        tabs.addTab("Vertical Box with Struts", vertical1);
68        tabs.addTab("Horizontal Box with Glue", horizontal2);
69        tabs.addTab("Vertical Box with Rigid Areas", vertical2);
70        tabs.addTab("Vertical Box with Glue", panel);
71
72        add(tabs); // place tabbed pane on frame
73    } // end BoxLayoutFrame constructor
74 } // end class BoxLayoutFrame
```

Fig. 19.16 | BoxLayout layout manager. (Part 2 of 2.)

```
1  // Fig. 19.17: BoxLayoutDemo.java
2  // Demonstrating BoxLayout.
3  import javax.swing.JFrame;
4
5  public class BoxLayoutDemo
6  {
7     public static void main(String[] args)
8     {
9        BoxLayoutFrame boxLayoutFrame = new BoxLayoutFrame();
```

Fig. 19.17 | Test class for BoxLayoutFrame. (Part 1 of 2.)

```
10              boxLayoutFrame.setDefaultCloseOperation(JFrame.EXIT_ON_CLOSE);
11              boxLayoutFrame.setSize(400, 220);
12              boxLayoutFrame.setVisible(true);
13          }
14      } // end class BoxLayoutDemo
```

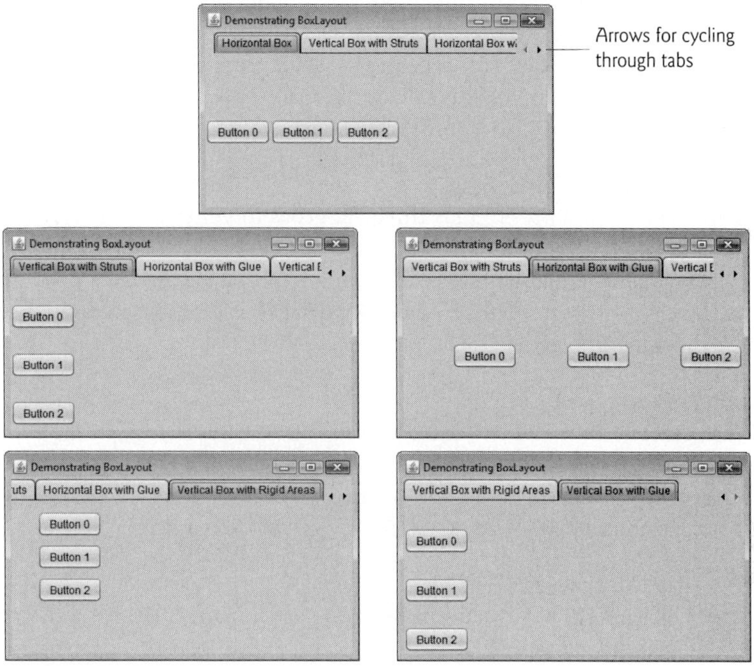

Fig. 19.17 | Test class for BoxLayoutFrame. (Part 2 of 2.)

Creating Box Containers

Lines 19–22 create Box containers. References horizontal1 and horizontal2 are initialized with static Box method createHorizontalBox, which returns a Box container with a horizontal BoxLayout in which GUI components are arranged left-to-right. Variables vertical1 and vertical2 are initialized with static Box method **createVerticalBox**, which returns references to Box containers with a vertical BoxLayout in which GUI components are arranged top-to-bottom.

Struts

The loop at lines 27–28 adds three JButtons to horizontal1. The for statement at lines 31–35 adds three JButtons to vertical1. Before adding each button, line 33 adds a **vertical strut** to the container with static Box method **createVerticalStrut**. A vertical strut is an invisible GUI component that has a fixed pixel height and is used to guarantee a fixed amount of space between GUI components. The int argument to method create-VerticalStrut determines the height of the strut in pixels. When the container is resized, the distance between GUI components separated by struts does not change. Class Box also declares method **createHorizontalStrut** for horizontal BoxLayouts.

Glue
The for statement at lines 38–42 adds three JButtons to horizontal2. Before adding each button, line 40 adds **horizontal glue** to the container with static Box method **createHorizontalGlue**. Horizontal glue is an invisible GUI component that can be used between fixed-size GUI components to occupy additional space. Normally, extra space appears to the right of the last horizontal GUI component or below the last vertical one in a BoxLayout. Glue allows the extra space to be placed between GUI components. When the container is resized, components separated by glue components remain the same size, but the glue stretches or contracts to occupy the space between them. Class Box also declares method **createVerticalGlue** for vertical BoxLayouts.

Rigid Areas
The for statement at lines 45–49 adds three JButtons to vertical2. Before each button is added, line 47 adds a **rigid area** to the container with static Box method **createRigidArea**. A rigid area is an invisible GUI component that always has a fixed pixel width and height. The argument to method createRigidArea is a Dimension object that specifies the area's width and height.

Setting a BoxLayout for a Container
Lines 52–53 create a JPanel object and set its layout to a BoxLayout in the conventional manner, using Container method setLayout. The BoxLayout constructor receives a reference to the container for which it controls the layout and a constant indicating whether the layout is horizontal (**BoxLayout.X_AXIS**) or vertical (**BoxLayout.Y_AXIS**).

Adding Glue and JButtons
The for statement at lines 55–59 adds three JButtons to panel. Before adding each button, line 57 adds a glue component to the container with static Box method **createGlue**. This component expands or contracts based on the size of the Box.

Creating the JTabbedPane
Lines 62–63 create a JTabbedPane to display the five containers in this program. The argument **JTabbedPane.TOP** sent to the constructor indicates that the tabs should appear at the top of the JTabbedPane. The argument **JTabbedPane.SCROLL_TAB_LAYOUT** specifies that the tabs should wrap to a new line if there are too many to fit on one line.

Attaching the Box Containers and JPanel to the JTabbedPane
The Box containers and the JPanel are attached to the JTabbedPane at lines 66–70. Try executing the application. When the window appears, resize the window to see how the glue components, strut components and rigid area affect the layout on each tab.

19.10 GridBagLayout Layout Manager

One of the most powerful predefined layout managers is **GridBagLayout** (in package java.awt). This layout is similar to GridLayout in that it arranges components in a grid, but it's more flexible. The components can vary in size (i.e., they can occupy multiple rows and columns) and can be added in any order.

The first step in using GridBagLayout is determining the appearance of the GUI. For this step you need only a piece of paper. Draw the GUI, then draw a grid over it, dividing the components into rows and columns. The initial row and column numbers should be 0, so that the GridBagLayout layout manager can use the row and column numbers to properly place the components in the grid. Figure 19.18 demonstrates drawing the lines for the rows and columns over a GUI.

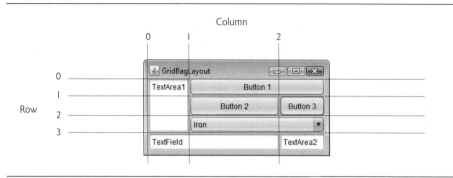

Fig. 19.18 | Designing a GUI that will use GridBagLayout.

GridBagConstraints

A **GridBagConstraints** object describes how a component is placed in a GridBagLayout. Several GridBagConstraints fields are summarized in Fig. 19.19.

Field	Description
anchor	Specifies the relative position (NORTH, NORTHEAST, EAST, SOUTHEAST, SOUTH, SOUTHWEST, WEST, NORTHWEST, CENTER) of the component in an area that it does not fill.
fill	Resizes the component in the specified direction (NONE, HORIZONTAL, VERTICAL, BOTH) when the display area is larger than the component.
gridx	The column in which the component will be placed.
gridy	The row in which the component will be placed.
gridwidth	The number of columns the component occupies.
gridheight	The number of rows the component occupies.
weightx	The amount of extra space to allocate horizontally. The grid slot can become wider when extra space is available.
weighty	The amount of extra space to allocate vertically. The grid slot can become taller when extra space is available.

Fig. 19.19 | GridBagConstraints fields.

GridBagConstraints Field anchor

GridBagConstraints field **anchor** specifies the relative position of the component in an area that it does not fill. The variable anchor is assigned one of the following GridBagConstraints constants: **NORTH, NORTHEAST, EAST, SOUTHEAST, SOUTH, SOUTHWEST, WEST, NORTHWEST** or **CENTER**. The default value is CENTER.

GridBagConstraints Field fill
GridBagConstraints field fill defines how the component grows if the area in which it can be displayed is larger than the component. The variable fill is assigned one of the following GridBagConstraints constants: **NONE**, **VERTICAL**, **HORIZONTAL** or **BOTH**. The default value is NONE, which indicates that the component will not grow in either direction. VERTICAL indicates that it will grow vertically. HORIZONTAL indicates that it will grow horizontally. BOTH indicates that it will grow in both directions.

GridBagConstraints Fields gridx *and* gridy
Variables **gridx** and **gridy** specify where the upper-left corner of the component is placed in the grid. Variable gridx corresponds to the column, and variable gridy corresponds to the row. In Fig. 19.18, the JComboBox (displaying "Iron") has a gridx value of 1 and a gridy value of 2.

GridBagConstraints Field gridwidth
Variable **gridwidth** specifies the number of columns a component occupies. The JComboBox occupies two columns. Variable **gridheight** specifies the number of rows a component occupies. The JTextArea on the left side of Fig. 19.18 occupies three rows.

GridBagConstraints Field weightx
Variable **weightx** specifies how to distribute extra horizontal space to grid slots in a GridBagLayout when the container is resized. A zero value indicates that the grid slot does not grow horizontally on its own. However, if the component spans a column containing a component with nonzero weightx value, the component with zero weightx value will grow horizontally in the same proportion as the other component(s) in that column. This is because each component must be maintained in the same row and column in which it was originally placed.

GridBagConstraints Field weighty
Variable **weighty** specifies how to distribute extra vertical space to grid slots in a GridBagLayout when the container is resized. A zero value indicates that the grid slot does not grow vertically on its own. However, if the component spans a row containing a component with nonzero weighty value, the component with zero weighty value grows vertically in the same proportion as the other component(s) in the same row.

Effects of weightx *and* weighty
In Fig. 19.18, the effects of weighty and weightx cannot easily be seen until the container is resized and additional space becomes available. Components with larger weight values occupy more of the additional space than those with smaller weight values.

Components should be given nonzero positive weight values—otherwise they'll "huddle" together in the middle of the container. Figure 19.20 shows the GUI of Fig. 19.18 with all weights set to zero.

Demonstrating GridBagLayout
The application in Figs. 19.21–19.22 uses the GridBagLayout layout manager to arrange the components of the GUI in Fig. 19.18. The application does nothing except demonstrate how to use GridBagLayout.

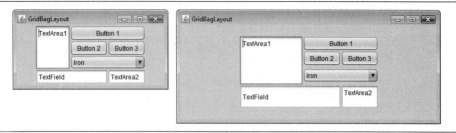

Fig. 19.20 | GridBagLayout with the weights set to zero.

```java
1   // Fig. 19.21: GridBagFrame.java
2   // Demonstrating GridBagLayout.
3   import java.awt.GridBagLayout;
4   import java.awt.GridBagConstraints;
5   import java.awt.Component;
6   import javax.swing.JFrame;
7   import javax.swing.JTextArea;
8   import javax.swing.JTextField;
9   import javax.swing.JButton;
10  import javax.swing.JComboBox;
11
12  public class GridBagFrame extends JFrame
13  {
14     private final GridBagLayout layout; // layout of this frame
15     private final GridBagConstraints constraints; // layout's constraints
16
17     // set up GUI
18     public GridBagFrame()
19     {
20        super("GridBagLayout");
21        layout = new GridBagLayout();
22        setLayout(layout); // set frame layout
23        constraints = new GridBagConstraints(); // instantiate constraints
24
25        // create GUI components
26        JTextArea textArea1 = new JTextArea("TextArea1", 5, 10);
27        JTextArea textArea2 = new JTextArea("TextArea2", 2, 2);
28
29        String[] names = { "Iron", "Steel", "Brass" };
30        JComboBox<String> comboBox = new JComboBox<String>(names);
31
32        JTextField textField = new JTextField("TextField");
33        JButton button1 = new JButton("Button 1");
34        JButton button2 = new JButton("Button 2");
35        JButton button3 = new JButton("Button 3");
36
37        // weightx and weighty for textArea1 are both 0: the default
38        // anchor for all components is CENTER: the default
39        constraints.fill = GridBagConstraints.BOTH;
40        addComponent(textArea1, 0, 0, 1, 3);
```

Fig. 19.21 | GridBagLayout layout manager. (Part 1 of 2.)

```
41
42        // weightx and weighty for button1 are both 0: the default
43        constraints.fill = GridBagConstraints.HORIZONTAL;
44        addComponent(button1, 0, 1, 2, 1);
45
46        // weightx and weighty for comboBox are both 0: the default
47        // fill is HORIZONTAL
48        addComponent(comboBox, 2, 1, 2, 1);
49
50        // button2
51        constraints.weightx = 1000;  // can grow wider
52        constraints.weighty = 1;     // can grow taller
53        constraints.fill = GridBagConstraints.BOTH;
54        addComponent(button2, 1, 1, 1, 1);
55
56        // fill is BOTH for button3
57        constraints.weightx = 0;
58        constraints.weighty = 0;
59        addComponent(button3, 1, 2, 1, 1);
60
61        // weightx and weighty for textField are both 0, fill is BOTH
62        addComponent(textField, 3, 0, 2, 1);
63
64        // weightx and weighty for textArea2 are both 0, fill is BOTH
65        addComponent(textArea2, 3, 2, 1, 1);
66     } // end GridBagFrame constructor
67
68     // method to set constraints on
69     private void addComponent(Component component,
70        int row, int column, int width, int height)
71     {
72        constraints.gridx = column;
73        constraints.gridy = row;
74        constraints.gridwidth = width;
75        constraints.gridheight = height;
76        layout.setConstraints(component, constraints); // set constraints
77        add(component); // add component
78     }
79  } // end class GridBagFrame
```

Fig. 19.21 | GridBagLayout layout manager. (Part 2 of 2.)

```
1   // Fig. 19.22: GridBagDemo.java
2   // Demonstrating GridBagLayout.
3   import javax.swing.JFrame;
4
5   public class GridBagDemo
6   {
7      public static void main(String[] args)
8      {
9         GridBagFrame gridBagFrame = new GridBagFrame();
```

Fig. 19.22 | Test class for GridBagFrame. (Part 1 of 2.)

```
10          gridBagFrame.setDefaultCloseOperation(JFrame.EXIT_ON_CLOSE);
11          gridBagFrame.setSize(300, 150);
12          gridBagFrame.setVisible(true);
13       }
14   } // end class GridBagDemo
```

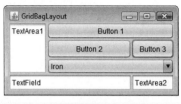

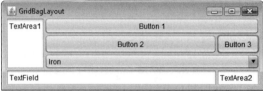

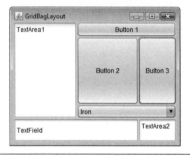

Fig. 19.22 | Test class for `GridBagFrame`. (Part 2 of 2.)

GUI Overview

The GUI contains three `JButton`s, two `JTextArea`s, a `JComboBox` and a `JTextField`. The layout manager is `GridBagLayout`. Lines 21–22 create the `GridBagLayout` object and set the layout manager for the `JFrame` to layout. Line 23 creates the `GridBagConstraints` object used to determine the location and size of each component in the grid. Lines 26–35 create each GUI component that will be added to the content pane.

JTextArea textArea1

Lines 39–40 configure `JTextArea` `textArea1` and add it to the content pane. The values for `weightx` and `weighty` values are not specified in `constraints`, so each has the value zero by default. Thus, the `JTextArea` will not resize itself even if space is available. However, it spans multiple rows, so the vertical size is subject to the `weighty` values of `JButton`s `button2` and `button3`. When either button is resized vertically based on its `weighty` value, the `JTextArea` is also resized.

Line 39 sets variable `fill` in `constraints` to `GridBagConstraints.BOTH`, causing the `JTextArea` to always fill its entire allocated area in the grid. An anchor value is not specified in `constraints`, so the default `CENTER` is used. We do not use variable anchor in this application, so all the components will use the default. Line 40 calls our utility method addComponent (declared at lines 69–78). The JTextArea object, the row, the column, the number of columns to span and the number of rows to span are passed as arguments.

JButton button1

JButton button1 is the next component added (lines 43–44). By default, the weightx and weighty values are still zero. The fill variable is set to HORIZONTAL—the component will always fill its area in the horizontal direction. The vertical direction is not filled. The weighty value is zero, so the button will become taller only if another component in the same row has a nonzero weighty value. JButton button1 is located at row 0, column 1. One row and two columns are occupied.

JComboBox comboBox

JComboBox comboBox is the next component added (line 48). By default, the weightx and weighty values are zero, and the fill variable is set to HORIZONTAL. The JComboBox button will grow only in the horizontal direction. The weightx, weighty and fill variables retain the values set in constraints until they're changed. The JComboBox button is placed at row 2, column 1. One row and two columns are occupied.

JButton button2

JButton button2 is the next component added (lines 51–54). It's given a weightx value of 1000 and a weighty value of 1. The area occupied by the button is capable of growing in the vertical and horizontal directions. The fill variable is set to BOTH, which specifies that the button will always fill the entire area. When the window is resized, button2 will grow. The button is placed at row 1, column 1. One row and one column are occupied.

JButton button3

JButton button3 is added next (lines 57–59). Both the weightx value and weighty value are set to zero, and the value of fill is BOTH. JButton button3 will grow if the window is resized—it's affected by the weight values of button2. The weightx value for button2 is much larger than that for button3. When resizing occurs, button2 will occupy a larger percentage of the new space. The button is placed at row 1, column 2. One row and one column are occupied.

JTextField textField *and* JTextArea textArea2

Both the JTextField textField (line 62) and JTextArea textArea2 (line 65) have a weightx value of 0 and a weighty value of 0. The value of fill is BOTH. The JTextField is placed at row 3, column 0, and the JTextArea at row 3, column 2. The JTextField occupies one row and two columns, the JTextArea one row and one column.

Method addComponent

Method addComponent's parameters are a Component reference component and integers row, column, width and height. Lines 72–73 set the GridBagConstraints variables gridx and gridy. The gridx variable is assigned the column in which the Component will be placed, and the gridy value is assigned the row in which the Component will be placed. Lines 74–75 set the GridBagConstraints variables gridwidth and gridheight. The gridwidth variable specifies the number of columns the Component will span in the grid, and the gridheight variable specifies the number of rows the Component will span in the grid. Line 76 sets the GridBagConstraints for a component in the GridBagLayout. Method **setConstraints** of class GridBagLayout takes a Component argument and a GridBagConstraints argument. Line 77 adds the component to the JFrame.

When you execute this application, try resizing the window to see how the constraints for each GUI component affect its position and size in the window.

GridBagConstraints Constants *RELATIVE* and *REMAINDER*

Instead of gridx and gridy, a variation of GridBagLayout uses GridBagConstraints constants **RELATIVE** and **REMAINDER**. RELATIVE specifies that the next-to-last component in a particular row should be placed to the right of the previous component in the row. REMAINDER specifies that a component is the last component in a row. Any component that is not the second-to-last or last component on a row must specify values for GridbagConstraints variables gridwidth and gridheight. The application in Figs. 19.23–19.24 arranges components in GridBagLayout, using these constants.

```java
1   // Fig. 19.23: GridBagFrame2.java
2   // Demonstrating GridBagLayout constants.
3   import java.awt.GridBagLayout;
4   import java.awt.GridBagConstraints;
5   import java.awt.Component;
6   import javax.swing.JFrame;
7   import javax.swing.JComboBox;
8   import javax.swing.JTextField;
9   import javax.swing.JList;
10  import javax.swing.JButton;
11
12  public class GridBagFrame2 extends JFrame
13  {
14     private final GridBagLayout layout; // layout of this frame
15     private final GridBagConstraints constraints; // layout's constraints
16
17     // set up GUI
18     public GridBagFrame2()
19     {
20        super("GridBagLayout");
21        layout = new GridBagLayout();
22        setLayout(layout); // set frame layout
23        constraints = new GridBagConstraints(); // instantiate constraints
24
25        // create GUI components
26        String[] metals = { "Copper", "Aluminum", "Silver" };
27        JComboBox comboBox = new JComboBox(metals);
28
29        JTextField textField = new JTextField("TextField");
30
31        String[] fonts = { "Serif", "Monospaced" };
32        JList list = new JList(fonts);
33
```

Fig. 19.23 | GridBagConstraints constants RELATIVE and REMAINDER. (Part I of 2.)

```
34          String[] names = { "zero", "one", "two", "three", "four" };
35          JButton[] buttons = new JButton[names.length];
36
37          for (int count = 0; count < buttons.length; count++)
38             buttons[count] = new JButton(names[count]);
39
40          // define GUI component constraints for textField
41          constraints.weightx = 1;
42          constraints.weighty = 1;
43          constraints.fill = GridBagConstraints.BOTH;
44          constraints.gridwidth = GridBagConstraints.REMAINDER;
45          addComponent(textField);
46
47          // buttons[0] -- weightx and weighty are 1: fill is BOTH
48          constraints.gridwidth = 1;
49          addComponent(buttons[0]);
50
51          // buttons[1] -- weightx and weighty are 1: fill is BOTH
52          constraints.gridwidth = GridBagConstraints.RELATIVE;
53          addComponent(buttons[1]);
54
55          // buttons[2] -- weightx and weighty are 1: fill is BOTH
56          constraints.gridwidth = GridBagConstraints.REMAINDER;
57          addComponent(buttons[2]);
58
59          // comboBox -- weightx is 1: fill is BOTH
60          constraints.weighty = 0;
61          constraints.gridwidth = GridBagConstraints.REMAINDER;
62          addComponent(comboBox);
63
64          // buttons[3] -- weightx is 1: fill is BOTH
65          constraints.weighty = 1;
66          constraints.gridwidth = GridBagConstraints.REMAINDER;
67          addComponent(buttons[3]);
68
69          // buttons[4] -- weightx and weighty are 1: fill is BOTH
70          constraints.gridwidth = GridBagConstraints.RELATIVE;
71          addComponent(buttons[4]);
72
73          // list -- weightx and weighty are 1: fill is BOTH
74          constraints.gridwidth = GridBagConstraints.REMAINDER;
75          addComponent(list);
76       } // end GridBagFrame2 constructor
77
78       // add a component to the container
79       private void addComponent(Component component)
80       {
81          layout.setConstraints(component, constraints);
82          add(component); // add component
83       }
84    } // end class GridBagFrame2
```

Fig. 19.23 | GridBagConstraints constants RELATIVE and REMAINDER. (Part 2 of 2.)

```
 1   // Fig. 19.24: GridBagDemo2.java
 2   // Demonstrating GridBagLayout constants.
 3   import javax.swing.JFrame;
 4
 5   public class GridBagDemo2
 6   {
 7      public static void main(String[] args)
 8      {
 9         GridBagFrame2 gridBagFrame = new GridBagFrame2();
10         gridBagFrame.setDefaultCloseOperation(JFrame.EXIT_ON_CLOSE);
11         gridBagFrame.setSize(300, 200);
12         gridBagFrame.setVisible(true);
13      }
14   } // end class GridBagDemo2
```

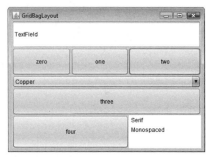

Fig. 19.24 | Test class for GridBagDemo2.

Setting the JFrame's Layout to a GridBagLayout

Lines 21–22 create a GridBagLayout and use it to set the JFrame's layout manager. The components that are placed in GridBagLayout are created in lines 27–38—they are a JComboBox, a JTextField, a JList and five JButtons.

Configuring the JTextField

The JTextField is added first (lines 41–45). The weightx and weighty values are set to 1. The fill variable is set to BOTH. Line 44 specifies that the JTextField is the last component on the line. The JTextField is added to the content pane with a call to our utility method addComponent (declared at lines 79–83). Method addComponent takes a Component argument and uses GridBagLayout method setConstraints to set the constraints for the Component. Method add attaches the component to the content pane.

Configuring JButton buttons[0]

JButton buttons[0] (lines 48–49) has weightx and weighty values of 1. The fill variable is BOTH. Because buttons[0] is not one of the last two components on the row, it's given a gridwidth of 1 and so will occupy one column. The JButton is added to the content pane with a call to utility method addComponent.

*Configuring **JButton buttons[1]***

JButton buttons[1] (lines 52–53) has weightx and weighty values of 1. The fill variable is BOTH. Line 52 specifies that the JButton is to be placed relative to the previous component. The Button is added to the JFrame with a call to addComponent.

*Configuring **JButton buttons[2]***

JButton buttons[2] (lines 56–57) has weightx and weighty values of 1. The fill variable is BOTH. This JButton is the last component on the line, so REMAINDER is used. The JButton is added to the content pane with a call to addComponent.

*Configuring **JComboBox***

The JComboBox (lines 60–62) has a weightx of 1 and a weighty of 0. The JComboBox will not grow vertically. The JComboBox is the only component on the line, so REMAINDER is used. The JComboBox is added to the content pane with a call to addComponent.

*Configuring **JButton buttons[3]***

JButton buttons[3] (lines 65–67) has weightx and weighty values of 1. The fill variable is BOTH. This JButton is the only component on the line, so REMAINDER is used. The JButton is added to the content pane with a call to addComponent.

*Configuring **JButton buttons[4]***

JButton buttons[4] (lines 70–71) has weightx and weighty values of 1. The fill variable is BOTH. This JButton is the next-to-last component on the line, so RELATIVE is used. The JButton is added to the content pane with a call to addComponent.

*Configuring **JList***

The JList (lines 74–75) has weightx and weighty values of 1. The fill variable is BOTH. The JList is added to the content pane with a call to addComponent.

19.11 Wrap-Up

This chapter completes our introduction to GUIs. In this chapter, we discussed additional GUI topics, such as menus, sliders, pop-up menus, multiple-document interfaces, tabbed panes and Java's pluggable look-and-feel. All these components can be added to existing applications to make them easier to use and understand. We also presented additional layout managers for organizing and sizing GUI components. In the next chapter, you'll learn about concurrency, which allows you to specify that an application should perform multiple tasks at once.

20

Concurrency

Objectives

In this chapter you'll:

- Understand concurrency, parallelism and multithreading.

- Learn the thread life cycle.

- Use `ExecutorService` to launch concurrent threads that execute `Runnable`s.

- Use `synchronized` methods to coordinate access to shared mutable data.

- Understand producer/consumer relationships.

- Use `SwingWorker` to update Swing GUIs in a thread-safe manner.

- Compare the performance of `Arrays` methods `sort` and `parallelSort` on a multi-core system.

- Use parallel streams for better performance on multi-core systems.

- Use `CompletableFuture`s to execute long calculations asynchronously and get the results in the future.

20.1 Introduction

[Note: Sections marked "Advanced" are intended for readers who wish a deeper treatment of concurrency and may be skipped by readers preferring only basic coverage.] It would be nice if we could focus our attention on performing only one task at a time and doing it well. That's usually difficult to do in a complex world in which there's so much going on at once. This chapter presents Java's capabilities for developing programs that create and manage multiple tasks. As we'll demonstrate, this can greatly improve program performance.

When we say that two tasks are operating **concurrently**, we mean that they're both *making progress* at once. Until recently, most computers had only a single processor. Operating systems on such computers execute tasks concurrently by rapidly switching between them, doing a small portion of each before moving on to the next, so that all tasks keep progressing. For example, it's common for personal computers to compile a program, send a file to a printer, receive electronic mail messages over a network and more, concurrently. Since its inception, Java has supported concurrency.

When we say that two tasks are operating **in parallel**, we mean that they're executing *simultaneously*. In this sense, parallelism is a subset of concurrency. The human body performs a great variety of operations in parallel. Respiration, blood circulation, digestion, thinking and walking, for example, can occur in parallel, as can all the senses—sight, hearing, touch, smell and taste. It's believed that this parallelism is possible because the human brain is thought to contain billions of "processors." Today's multi-core computers have multiple processors that can perform tasks in parallel.

Java Concurrency

Java makes concurrency available to you through the language and APIs. Java programs can have multiple **threads of execution**, where each thread has its own method-call stack and program counter, allowing it to execute concurrently with other threads while sharing with them application-wide resources such as memory and file handles. This capability is called **multithreading**.

Performance Tip 20.1

A problem with single-threaded applications that can lead to poor responsiveness is that lengthy activities must complete before others can begin. In a multithreaded application, threads can be distributed across multiple cores (if available) so that multiple tasks execute in parallel and the application can operate more efficiently. Multithreading can also increase performance on single-processor systems—when one thread cannot proceed (because, for example, it's waiting for the result of an I/O operation), another can use the processor.

Concurrent Programming Uses

We'll discuss many applications of **concurrent programming**. For example, when streaming an audio or video over the Internet, the user may not want to wait until the entire audio or video downloads before starting the playback. To solve this problem, multiple threads can be used—one to download the audio or video (later in the chapter we'll refer to this as a *producer*), and another to play it (later in the chapter we'll refer to this as a *consumer*). These activities proceed concurrently. To avoid choppy playback, the threads are **synchronized** (that is, their actions are coordinated) so that the player thread doesn't begin until there's a sufficient amount of the audio or video in memory to keep the player thread busy. Producer and consumer threads *share memory*—we'll show how to coordinate these threads to ensure correct execution. The Java Virtual Machine (JVM) creates threads to run programs and threads to perform housekeeping tasks such as garbage collection.

Concurrent Programming Is Difficult

Writing multithreaded programs can be tricky. Although the human mind can perform functions concurrently, people find it difficult to jump between parallel trains of thought. To see why multithreaded programs can be difficult to write and understand, try the following experiment: Open three books to page 1, and try reading the books concurrently. Read a few words from the first book, then a few from the second, then a few from the third, then loop back and read the next few words from the first book, and so on. After this experiment, you'll appreciate many of the challenges of multithreading—switching between the books, reading briefly, remembering your place in each book, moving the book you're reading closer so that you can see it and pushing the books you're not reading aside—and, amid all this chaos, trying to comprehend the content of the books!

Use the Prebuilt Classes of the Concurrency APIs Whenever Possible

Programming concurrent applications is difficult and error prone. If you must use synchronization in a program, follow these guidelines:

1. *The vast majority of programmers should use existing collection classes and interfaces from the concurrency APIs that manage synchronization for you—such as the* `Array-`

BlockingQueue class (an implementation of interface BlockingQueue) we discuss in Section 20.6. Two other concurrency API classes that you'll use frequently are LinkedBlockingQueue and ConcurrentHashMap (each summarized in Fig. 20.22). The concurrency API classes are written by experts, have been thoroughly tested and debugged, operate efficiently and help you avoid common traps and pitfalls. Section 20.10 overviews Java's pre-built concurrent collections.

2. For advanced programmers who want to control synchronization, use the synchronized keyword and Object methods wait, notify and notifyAll, which we discuss in the optional Section 20.7.

3. Only the most advanced programmers should use Locks and Conditions, which we introduce in the optional Section 20.9, and classes like LinkedTransferQueue—an implementation of interface TransferQueue—which we summarize in Fig. 20.22.

You might want to read our discussions of the more advanced features in items 2 and 3 above, even though you most likely will not use them. We explain these because:

- They provide a solid basis for understanding how concurrent applications synchronize access to shared memory.

- By showing you the complexity involved in using these low-level features, we hope to impress upon you the message: *Use the simpler prebuilt concurrency capabilities whenever possible.*

20.2 Thread States and Life Cycle

At any time, a thread is said to be in one of several **thread states**—illustrated in the UML state diagram in Fig. 20.1. Several of the terms in the diagram are defined in later sections. We include this discussion to help you understand what's going on "under the hood" in a Java multithreaded environment. Java hides most of this detail from you, greatly simplifying the task of developing multithreaded applications.

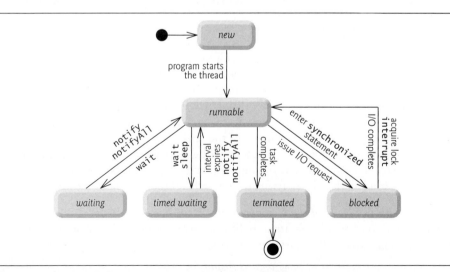

Fig. 20.1 | Thread life-cycle UML state diagram.

20.2.1 *New* and *Runnable* States

A new thread begins its life cycle in the ***new*** state. It remains in this state until the program starts the thread, which places it in the ***runnable*** state. A thread in the *runnable* state is considered to be executing its task.

20.2.2 *Waiting* State

Sometimes a *runnable* thread transitions to the ***waiting*** state while it waits for another thread to perform a task. A *waiting* thread transitions back to the *runnable* state only when another thread notifies it to continue executing.

20.2.3 *Timed Waiting* State

A *runnable* thread can enter the ***timed waiting*** state for a specified interval of time. It transitions back to the *runnable* state when that time interval expires or when the event it's waiting for occurs. *Timed waiting* threads and *waiting* threads cannot use a processor, even if one is available. A *runnable* thread can transition to the *timed waiting* state if it provides an optional wait interval when it's waiting for another thread to perform a task. Such a thread returns to the *runnable* state when it's notified by another thread or when the timed interval expires—whichever comes first. Another way to place a thread in the *timed waiting* state is to put a *runnable* thread to sleep—a **sleeping thread** remains in the *timed waiting* state for a designated period of time (called a **sleep interval**), after which it returns to the *runnable* state. Threads sleep when they momentarily do not have work to perform. For example, a word processor may contain a thread that periodically backs up (i.e., writes a copy of) the current document to disk for recovery purposes. If the thread did not sleep between successive backups, it would require a loop in which it continually tested whether it should write a copy of the document to disk. This loop would consume processor time without performing productive work, thus reducing system performance. In this case, it's more efficient for the thread to specify a sleep interval (equal to the period between successive backups) and enter the *timed waiting* state. This thread is returned to the *runnable* state when its sleep interval expires, at which point it writes a copy of the document to disk and reenters the *timed waiting* state.

20.2.4 *Blocked* State

A *runnable* thread transitions to the ***blocked*** state when it attempts to perform a task that cannot be completed immediately and it must temporarily wait until that task completes. For example, when a thread issues an input/output request, the operating system blocks the thread from executing until that I/O request completes—at that point, the *blocked* thread transitions to the *runnable* state, so it can resume execution. A *blocked* thread cannot use a processor, even if one is available.

20.2.5 *Terminated* State

A *runnable* thread enters the ***terminated*** state (sometimes called the ***dead*** state) when it successfully completes its task or otherwise terminates (perhaps due to an error). In the UML state diagram of Fig. 20.1, the *terminated* state is followed by the UML final state (the bull's-eye symbol) to indicate the end of the state transitions.

20.2.6 Operating-System View of the *Runnable* State

At the operating system level, Java's *runnable* state typically encompasses *two separate* states (Fig. 20.2). The operating system hides these states from the Java Virtual Machine (JVM), which sees only the *runnable* state. When a thread first transitions to the *runnable* state from the *new* state, it's in the *ready* state. A *ready* thread enters the *running* state (i.e., begins executing) when the operating system assigns it to a processor—also known as **dispatching the thread**. In most operating systems, each thread is given a small amount of processor time—called a **quantum** or **timeslice**—with which to perform its task. Deciding how large the quantum should be is a key topic in operating systems courses. When its quantum expires, the thread returns to the *ready* state, and the operating system assigns another thread to the processor. Transitions between the *ready* and *running* states are handled solely by the operating system. The JVM does not "see" the transitions—it simply views the thread as being *runnable* and leaves it up to the operating system to transition the thread between *ready* and *running*. The process that an operating system uses to determine which thread to dispatch is called **thread scheduling** and is dependent on thread priorities.

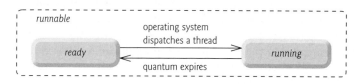

Fig. 20.2 | Operating system's internal view of Java's *runnable* state.

20.2.7 Thread Priorities and Thread Scheduling

Every Java thread has a **thread priority** that helps determine the order in which threads are scheduled. Each new thread inherits the priority of the thread that created it. Informally, higher-priority threads are more important to a program and should be allocated processor time before lower-priority threads. *Nevertheless, thread priorities cannot guarantee the order in which threads execute.*

It's recommended that you do not explicitly create and use `Thread` objects to implement concurrency, but rather use the `Executor` interface (which is described in Section 20.3). The `Thread` class does contain some useful `static` methods, which you *will* use later in the chapter.

Most operating systems support timeslicing, which enables threads of equal priority to share a processor. Without timeslicing, each thread in a set of equal-priority threads runs to completion (unless it leaves the *runnable* state and enters the *waiting* or *timed waiting* state, or gets interrupted by a higher-priority thread) before other threads of equal priority get a chance to execute. With timeslicing, even if a thread has *not* finished executing when its quantum expires, the processor is taken away from the thread and given to the next thread of equal priority, if one is available.

An *operating system's* **thread scheduler** determines which thread runs next. One simple thread-scheduler implementation keeps the highest-priority thread *running* at all times and, if there's more than one highest-priority thread, ensures that all such threads execute for a quantum each in **round-robin** fashion. This process continues until all threads run to completion.

Software Engineering Observation 20.1

Java provides higher-level concurrency utilities to hide much of this complexity and make multithreaded programming less error prone. Thread priorities are used behind the scenes to interact with the operating system, but most programmers who use Java multithreading will not be concerned with setting and adjusting thread priorities.

Portability Tip 20.1

Thread scheduling is platform dependent—the behavior of a multithreaded program could vary across different Java implementations.

20.2.8 Indefinite Postponement and Deadlock

When a higher-priority thread enters the *ready* state, the operating system generally preempts the currently *running* thread (an operation known as **preemptive scheduling**). Depending on the operating system, a steady influx of higher-priority threads could postpone—possibly indefinitely—the execution of lower-priority threads. Such **indefinite postponement** is sometimes referred to more colorfully as **starvation**. Operating systems employ a technique called *aging* to prevent starvation—as a thread waits in the *ready* state, the operating system gradually increases the thread's priority to ensure that the thread will eventually run.

Another problem related to indefinite postponement is called **deadlock**. This occurs when a waiting thread (let's call this thread1) cannot proceed because it's waiting (either directly or indirectly) for another thread (let's call this thread2) to proceed, while simultaneously thread2 cannot proceed because it's waiting (either directly or indirectly) for thread1 to proceed. The two threads are waiting for each other, so the actions that would enable each thread to continue execution can never occur.

20.3 Creating and Executing Threads with the Executor Framework

This section demonstrates how to perform concurrent tasks in an application by using Executors and Runnable objects.

Creating Concurrent Tasks with the *Runnable Interface*

You implement the **Runnable** interface (of package java.lang) to specify a task that can execute concurrently with other tasks. The Runnable interface declares the single method **run**, which contains the code that defines the task that a Runnable object should perform.

Executing *Runnable Objects with an Executor*

To allow a Runnable to perform its task, you must execute it. An **Executor** object executes Runnables. It does this by creating and managing a group of threads called a **thread pool**. When an Executor begins executing a Runnable, the Executor calls the Runnable object's run method, which executes in the new thread.

The Executor interface declares a single method named **execute** which accepts a Runnable as an argument. The Executor assigns every Runnable passed to its execute method to one of the available threads in the thread pool. If there are no available threads, the Executor creates a new thread or waits for a thread to become available and assigns that thread the Runnable that was passed to method execute.

Using an Executor has many advantages over creating threads yourself. Executors can *reuse existing threads* to eliminate the overhead of creating a new thread for each task and can improve performance by *optimizing the number of threads* to ensure that the processor stays busy, without creating so many threads that the application runs out of resources.

Software Engineering Observation 20.2

Though it's possible to create threads explicitly, it's recommended that you use the Executor interface to manage the execution of Runnable objects.

Using Class *Executors* to Obtain an *ExecutorService*

The **ExecutorService interface** (of package java.util.concurrent) *extends* Executor and declares various methods for managing the life cycle of an Executor. You obtain an ExecutorService object by calling one of the static methods declared in class **Executors** (of package java.util.concurrent). We use interface ExecutorService and a method of class Executors in our example, which executes three tasks.

Implementing the *Runnable* Interface

Class PrintTask (Fig. 20.3) implements Runnable (line 5), *so that multiple PrintTasks can execute concurrently.* Variable sleepTime (line 8) stores a random integer value from 0 to 5 seconds created in the PrintTask constructor (line 17). Each thread running a Print-Task sleeps for the amount of time specified by sleepTime, then outputs its task's name and a message indicating that it's done sleeping.

```
1   // Fig. 20.3: PrintTask.java
2   // PrintTask class sleeps for a random time from 0 to 5 seconds
3   import java.security.SecureRandom;
4
5   public class PrintTask implements Runnable
6   {
7      private static final SecureRandom generator = new SecureRandom();
8      private final int sleepTime; // random sleep time for thread
9      private final String taskName;
10
11     // constructor
12     public PrintTask(String taskName)
13     {
14        this.taskName = taskName;
15
16        // pick random sleep time between 0 and 5 seconds
17        sleepTime = generator.nextInt(5000); // milliseconds
18     }
19
20     // method run contains the code that a thread will execute
21     public void run()
22     {
23        try // put thread to sleep for sleepTime amount of time
24        {
25           System.out.printf("%s going to sleep for %d milliseconds.%n",
26              taskName, sleepTime);
```

Fig. 20.3 | PrintTask class sleeps for a random time from 0 to 5 seconds. (Part 1 of 2.)

```
27              Thread.sleep(sleepTime); // put thread to sleep
28          }
29          catch (InterruptedException exception)
30          {
31              exception.printStackTrace();
32              Thread.currentThread().interrupt(); // re-interrupt the thread
33          }
34
35          // print task name
36          System.out.printf("%s done sleeping%n", taskName);
37      }
38  } // end class PrintTask
```

Fig. 20.3 | PrintTask class sleeps for a random time from 0 to 5 seconds. (Part 2 of 2.)

A PrintTask executes when a thread calls the PrintTask's run method. Lines 25–26 display a message indicating the name of the currently executing task and that the task is going to sleep for sleepTime milliseconds. Line 27 invokes static method **sleep** of class Thread to place the thread in the *timed waiting* state for the specified amount of time. At this point, the thread loses the processor, and the system allows another thread to execute. When the thread awakens, it reenters the *runnable* state. When the PrintTask is assigned to a processor again, line 36 outputs a message indicating that the task is done sleeping, then method run terminates. The catch at lines 29–33 is required because method sleep might throw a *checked* exception of type **InterruptedException** if a sleeping thread's **interrupt** method is called.

Let the Thread Handle *InterruptedExceptions*
It's considered good practice to let the executing thread handle InterruptedExceptions. Normally, you'd do this by declaring that method run throws the exception, rather than catching the exception. However, recall from Chapter 11 that when you override a method, the throws may contain only the same exception types or a subset of the exception types declared in the original method's throws clause. Runnable method run does not have a throws clause in its original declaration, so we cannot provide one in line 21. To ensure that the executing thread receives the InterruptedException, line 32 first obtains a reference to the currently executing Thread by calling static method **currentThread**, then uses that Thread's interrupt method to deliver the InterruptedException to the current thread.[1]

Using the *ExecutorService* to Manage Threads that Execute *PrintTasks*
Figure 20.4 uses an ExecutorService object to manage threads that execute PrintTasks (as defined in Fig. 20.3). Lines 11–13 create and name three PrintTasks to execute. Line 18 uses Executors method **newCachedThreadPool** to obtain an ExecutorService that's capable of creating new threads as they're needed by the application. These threads are used by ExecutorService to execute the Runnables.

---

1. For detailed information on handling thread interruptions, see Chapter 7 of *Java Concurrency in Practice* by Brian Goetz, et al., Addison-Wesley Professional, 2006.

```
 1    // Fig. 20.4: TaskExecutor.java
 2    // Using an ExecutorService to execute Runnables.
 3    import java.util.concurrent.Executors;
 4    import java.util.concurrent.ExecutorService;
 5
 6    public class TaskExecutor
 7    {
 8       public static void main(String[] args)
 9       {
10          // create and name each runnable
11          PrintTask task1 = new PrintTask("task1");
12          PrintTask task2 = new PrintTask("task2");
13          PrintTask task3 = new PrintTask("task3");
14
15          System.out.println("Starting Executor");
16
17          // create ExecutorService to manage threads
18          ExecutorService executorService = Executors.newCachedThreadPool();
19
20          // start the three PrintTasks
21          executorService.execute(task1); // start task1
22          executorService.execute(task2); // start task2
23          executorService.execute(task3); // start task3
24
25          // shut down ExecutorService--it decides when to shut down threads
26          executorService.shutdown();
27
28          System.out.printf("Tasks started, main ends.%n%n");
29       }
30    } // end class TaskExecutor
```

```
Starting Executor
Tasks started, main ends

task1 going to sleep for 4806 milliseconds
task2 going to sleep for 2513 milliseconds
task3 going to sleep for 1132 milliseconds
task3 done sleeping
task2 done sleeping
task1 done sleeping
```

```
Starting Executor
task1 going to sleep for 3161 milliseconds.
task3 going to sleep for 532 milliseconds.
task2 going to sleep for 3440 milliseconds.
Tasks started, main ends.

task3 done sleeping
task1 done sleeping
task2 done sleeping
```

Fig. 20.4 | Using an ExecutorService to execute Runnables.

Lines 21–23 each invoke the ExecutorService's execute method, which executes its Runnable argument (in this case a PrintTask) some time in the future. The specified task may execute in one of the threads in the ExecutorService's thread pool, in a new thread created to execute it, or in the thread that called the execute method—the ExecutorService manages these details. Method execute returns immediately from each invocation—the program does *not* wait for each PrintTask to finish. Line 26 calls ExecutorService method **shutdown**, which notifies the ExecutorService to *stop accepting new tasks, but continues executing tasks that have already been submitted*. Once all of the previously submitted Runnables have completed, the ExecutorService terminates. Line 28 outputs a message indicating that the tasks were started and the main thread is finishing its execution.

Main Thread

The code in main executes in the **main thread**, which is created by the JVM. The code in the run method of PrintTask (lines 21–37 of Fig. 20.3) executes whenever the Executor starts each PrintTask—again, this is sometime after they're passed to the ExecutorService's execute method (Fig. 20.4, lines 21–23). When main terminates, the program itself continues running because there are still tasks that must finish executing. The program will not terminate until these tasks complete.

Sample Outputs

The sample outputs show each task's name and sleep time as the thread goes to sleep. The thread with the shortest sleep time *in most cases* awakens first, indicates that it's done sleeping and terminates. In Section 20.8, we discuss multithreading issues that could prevent the thread with the shortest sleep time from awakening first. In the first output, the main thread terminates *before* any of the PrintTasks output their names and sleep times. This shows that the main thread runs to completion before any of the PrintTasks gets a chance to run. In the second output, all of the PrintTasks output their names and sleep times *before* the main thread terminates. This shows that the PrintTasks started executing before the main thread terminated. Also, notice in the second example output, task3 goes to sleep before task2 last, even though we passed task2 to the ExecutorService's execute method before task3. This illustrates the fact that *we cannot predict the order in which the tasks will start executing, even if we know the order in which they were created and started.*

Waiting for Previously Scheduled Tasks to Terminate

After scheduling tasks to execute, you'll typically want to *wait for the tasks to complete*—for example, so that you can use the tasks' results. After calling method shutdown, you can call ExecutorService method awaitTermination to wait for scheduled tasks to complete. We demonstrate this in Fig. 20.7. We purposely did not call awaitTermination in Fig. 20.4 to demonstrate that a program can continue executing after the main thread terminates.

20.4 Thread Synchronization

When multiple threads share an object and it's *modified* by one or more of them, indeterminate results may occur (as we'll see in the examples) unless access to the shared object is managed properly. If one thread is in the process of updating a shared object and another thread also tries to update it, it's uncertain which thread's update takes effect. Similarly, if one thread is in the process of updating a shared object and another thread tries to read it, it's uncertain whether the reading thread will see the old value or the new one. In such cases, the program's behavior cannot be trusted—sometimes the program will produce the correct results, and sometimes it won't, and there won't be any indication that the shared object was manipulated incorrectly.

The problem can be solved by giving only one thread at a time *exclusive access* to code that accesses the shared object. During that time, other threads desiring to access the object are kept waiting. When the thread with exclusive access finishes accessing the object, one of the waiting threads is allowed to proceed. This process, called **thread synchronization**, coordinates access to shared data by multiple concurrent threads. By synchronizing threads in this manner, you can ensure that each thread accessing a shared object *excludes* all other threads from doing so simultaneously—this is called **mutual exclusion**.

20.4.1 Immutable Data

Actually, thread synchronization is necessary *only* for shared **mutable data**, i.e., data that may *change* during its lifetime. With shared **immutable data** that will *not* change, it's not possible for a thread to see old or incorrect values as a result of another thread's manipulation of that data.

When you share *immutable data* across threads, declare the corresponding data fields final to indicate that the values of the variables will *not* change after they're initialized. This prevents accidental modification of the shared data, which could compromise thread safety. *Labeling object references as* final *indicates that the reference will not change, but it does not guarantee that the referenced object is immutable—this depends entirely on the object's properties.* However, it's still good practice to mark references that will not change as final.

Software Engineering Observation 20.3

Always declare data fields that you do not expect to change as final. *Primitive variables that are declared as* final *can safely be shared across threads. An object reference that's declared as* final *ensures that the object it refers to will be fully constructed and initialized before it's used by the program, and prevents the reference from pointing to another object.*

20.4.2 Monitors

A common way to perform synchronization is to use Java's built-in **monitors**. Every object has a monitor and a **monitor lock** (or **intrinsic lock**). The monitor ensures that its object's monitor lock is held by a maximum of only one thread at any time. Monitors and monitor locks can thus be used to enforce mutual exclusion. If an operation requires the executing thread to *hold a lock* while the operation is performed, a thread must *acquire the lock* before proceeding with the operation. Other threads attempting to perform an operation that requires the same lock will be *blocked* until the first thread *releases the lock*, at which point the *blocked* threads may attempt to acquire the lock and proceed with the operation.

To specify that a thread must hold a monitor lock to execute a block of code, the code should be placed in a **synchronized statement**. Such code is said to be **guarded** by the monitor lock; a thread must **acquire the lock** to execute the guarded statements. The monitor allows only one thread at a time to execute statements within synchronized statements that lock on the same object, as only one thread at a time can hold the monitor lock. The synchronized statements are declared using the **synchronized keyword**:

```
synchronized (object)
{
    statements
}
```

where *object* is the object whose monitor lock will be acquired; *object* is normally `this` if it's the object in which the `synchronized` statement appears. If several `synchronized` statements in different threads are trying to execute on an object at the same time, only one of them may be active on the object—all the other threads attempting to enter a `synchronized` statement on the same object are placed in the *blocked* state.

When a `synchronized` statement finishes executing, the object's monitor lock is released and one of the *blocked* threads attempting to enter a `synchronized` statement can be allowed to acquire the lock to proceed. Java also allows **synchronized methods**. Before executing, a `synchronized` instance method must acquire the lock on the object that's used to call the method. Similarly, a `static` `synchronized` method must acquire the lock on the class that's used to call the method.

Software Engineering Observation 20.4

Using a synchronized *block to enforce mutual exclusion is an example of the design pattern known as the Java Monitor Pattern (see section 4.2.1 of* Java Concurrency in Practice *by Brian Goetz, et al., Addison-Wesley Professional, 2006).*

20.4.3 Unsynchronized Mutable Data Sharing

First, we illustrate the dangers of sharing an object across threads *without* proper synchronization. In this example (Figs. 20.5–20.7), two `Runnable`s maintain references to a single integer array. Each `Runnable` writes three values to the array, then terminates. This may seem harmless, but we'll see that it can result in errors if the array is manipulated without synchronization.

Class *SimpleArray*

A `SimpleArray` object (Fig. 20.5) will be *shared* across multiple threads. `SimpleArray` will enable those threads to place `int` values into `array` (declared at line 9). Line 10 initializes variable `writeIndex`, which will be used to determine the array element that should be written to next. The constructor (lines 13–16) creates an integer array of the desired size.

```
1   // Fig. 20.5: SimpleArray.java
2   // Class that manages an integer array to be shared by multiple threads.
3   import java.security.SecureRandom;
4   import java.util.Arrays;
5
6   public class SimpleArray // CAUTION: NOT THREAD SAFE!
7   {
8       private static final SecureRandom generator = new SecureRandom();
9       private final int[] array; // the shared integer array
10      private int writeIndex = 0; // shared index of next element to write
11
```

Fig. 20.5 | Class that manages an integer array to be shared by multiple threads. (*Caution:* The example of Figs. 20.5–20.7 is *not* thread safe.) (Part 1 of 2.)

```
12      // construct a SimpleArray of a given size
13      public SimpleArray(int size)
14      {
15          array = new int[size];
16      }
17
18      // add a value to the shared array
19      public void add(int value)
20      {
21          int position = writeIndex; // store the write index
22
23          try
24          {
25              // put thread to sleep for 0-499 milliseconds
26              Thread.sleep(generator.nextInt(500));
27          }
28          catch (InterruptedException ex)
29          {
30              Thread.currentThread().interrupt(); // re-interrupt the thread
31          }
32
33          // put value in the appropriate element
34          array[position] = value;
35          System.out.printf("%s wrote %2d to element %d.%n",
36              Thread.currentThread().getName(), value, position);
37
38          ++writeIndex; // increment index of element to be written next
39          System.out.printf("Next write index: %d%n", writeIndex);
40      }
41
42      // used for outputting the contents of the shared integer array
43      public String toString()
44      {
45          return Arrays.toString(array);
46      }
47  } // end class SimpleArray
```

Fig. 20.5 | Class that manages an integer array to be shared by multiple threads. (*Caution:* The example of Figs. 20.5–20.7 is *not* thread safe.) (Part 2 of 2.)

Method add (lines 19–40) allows new values to be inserted at the end of the array. Line 21 stores the current writeIndex value. Line 26 puts the thread that invokes add to sleep for a random interval from 0 to 499 milliseconds. This is done to make the problems associated with *unsynchronized access to shared mutable data* more obvious. After the thread is done sleeping, line 34 inserts the value passed to add into the array at the element specified by position. Lines 35–36 output a message indicating the executing thread's name, the value that was inserted in the array and where it was inserted. The expression Thread.currentThread().getName() (line 36) first obtains a reference to the currently executing Thread, then uses that Thread's getName method to obtain its name. Line 38 increments writeIndex so that the next call to add will insert a value in the array's next element. Lines 43–46 override method toString to create a String representation of the array's contents.

Class *ArrayWriter*

Class ArrayWriter (Fig. 20.6) implements the interface Runnable to define a task for inserting values in a SimpleArray object. The constructor (lines 10–14) takes two arguments—an integer value, which is the first value this task will insert in the SimpleArray object, and a reference to the SimpleArray object. Line 20 invokes method add on the SimpleArray object. The task completes after three consecutive integers beginning with startValue are inserted in the SimpleArray object.

```java
1   // Fig. 20.6: ArrayWriter.java
2   // Adds integers to an array shared with other Runnables
3   import java.lang.Runnable;
4
5   public class ArrayWriter implements Runnable
6   {
7       private final SimpleArray sharedSimpleArray;
8       private final int startValue;
9
10      public ArrayWriter(int value, SimpleArray array)
11      {
12          startValue = value;
13          sharedSimpleArray = array;
14      }
15
16      public void run()
17      {
18          for (int i = startValue; i < startValue + 3; i++)
19          {
20              sharedSimpleArray.add(i); // add an element to the shared array
21          }
22      }
23  } // end class ArrayWriter
```

Fig. 20.6 | Adds integers to an array shared with other Runnables. (*Caution:* The example of Figs. 20.5–20.7 is *not* thread safe.)

Class *SharedArrayTest*

Class SharedArrayTest (Fig. 20.7) executes two ArrayWriter tasks that add values to a single SimpleArray object. Line 12 constructs a six-element SimpleArray object. Lines 15–16 create two new ArrayWriter tasks, one that places the values 1–3 in the Simple-Array object, and one that places the values 11–13. Lines 19–21 create an ExecutorService and execute the two ArrayWriters. Line 23 invokes the ExecutorService's shutDown method to *prevent additional tasks from starting* and to enable the application to terminate when the currently executing tasks complete execution.

```java
1   // Fig. 20.7: SharedArrayTest.java
2   // Executing two Runnables to add elements to a shared SimpleArray.
3   import java.util.concurrent.Executors;
```

Fig. 20.7 | Executing two Runnables to add elements to a shared array. (*Caution:* The example of Figs. 20.5–20.7 is *not* thread safe.) (Part 1 of 3.)

```
 4   import java.util.concurrent.ExecutorService;
 5   import java.util.concurrent.TimeUnit;
 6
 7   public class SharedArrayTest
 8   {
 9      public static void main(String[] arg)
10      {
11         // construct the shared object
12         SimpleArray sharedSimpleArray = new SimpleArray(6);
13
14         // create two tasks to write to the shared SimpleArray
15         ArrayWriter writer1 = new ArrayWriter(1, sharedSimpleArray);
16         ArrayWriter writer2 = new ArrayWriter(11, sharedSimpleArray);
17
18         // execute the tasks with an ExecutorService
19         ExecutorService executorService = Executors.newCachedThreadPool();
20         executorService.execute(writer1);
21         executorService.execute(writer2);
22
23         executorService.shutdown();
24
25         try
26         {
27            // wait 1 minute for both writers to finish executing
28            boolean tasksEnded =
29               executorService.awaitTermination(1, TimeUnit.MINUTES);
30
31            if (tasksEnded)
32            {
33               System.out.printf("%nContents of SimpleArray:%n");
34               System.out.println(sharedSimpleArray); // print contents
35            }
36            else
37               System.out.println(
38                  "Timed out while waiting for tasks to finish.");
39         }
40         catch (InterruptedException ex)
41         {
42            ex.printStackTrace();
43         }
44      } // end main
45   } // end class SharedArrayTest
```

```
pool-1-thread-1 wrote  1 to element 0.
Next write index: 1
pool-1-thread-1 wrote  2 to element 1.
Next write index: 2
pool-1-thread-1 wrote  3 to element 2.
Next write index: 3
pool-1-thread-2 wrote 11 to element 0.
Next write index: 4
```

First pool-1-thread-1 wrote the value 1 to element 0. Later pool-1-thread-2 wrote the value 11 to element 0, thus *overwriting* the previously stored value.

Fig. 20.7 | Executing two Runnables to add elements to a shared array. (*Caution:* The example of Figs. 20.5–20.7 is *not* thread safe.) (Part 2 of 3.)

```
pool-1-thread-2 wrote 12 to element 4.
Next write index: 5
pool-1-thread-2 wrote 13 to element 5.
Next write index: 6

Contents of SimpleArray:
[11, 2, 3, 0, 12, 13]
```

Fig. 20.7 | Executing two Runnables to add elements to a shared array. (*Caution:* The example of Figs. 20.5–20.7 is *not* thread safe.) (Part 3 of 3.)

ExecutorService Method awaitTermination

Recall that ExecutorService method shutdown returns immediately. Thus any code that appears *after* the call to ExecutorService method shutdown in line 23 *will continue executing as long as the* main *thread is still assigned to a processor*. We'd like to output the SimpleArray object to show you the results *after* the threads complete their tasks. So, we need the program to wait for the threads to complete before main outputs the SimpleArray object's contents. Interface ExecutorService provides the **awaitTermination** method for this purpose. This method returns control to its caller either when all tasks executing in the ExecutorService complete or when the specified timeout elapses. If all tasks are completed before awaitTermination times out, this method returns true; otherwise it returns false. The two arguments to awaitTermination represent a timeout value and a unit of measure specified with a constant from class TimeUnit (in this case, TimeUnit.MINUTES).

Method awaitTermination throws an InterruptedException if the calling thread is interrupted while waiting for other threads to terminate. Because we catch this exception in the application's main method, there's no need to re-interrupt the main thread as this program will terminate as soon as main terminates.

In this example, if *both* tasks complete before awaitTermination times out, line 34 displays the SimpleArray object's contents. Otherwise, lines 37–38 display a message indicating that the tasks did not finish executing before awaitTermination timed out.

Sample Program Output

Figure 20.7's output shows the problems (highlighted in the output) that can be caused by *failure to synchronize access to shared mutable data*. The value 1 was written to element 0, then *overwritten* later by the value 11. Also, when writeIndex was incremented to 3, *nothing was written to that element*, as indicated by the 0 in that element of the printed array.

Recall that we added calls to Thread method sleep between operations on the shared mutable data to emphasize the *unpredictability of thread scheduling* and increase the likelihood of producing erroneous output. Even if these operations were allowed to proceed at their normal pace, you could still see errors in the program's output. However, modern processors can handle the simple operations of the SimpleArray method add so quickly that you might not see the errors caused by the two threads executing this method concurrently, even if you tested the program dozens of times. *One of the challenges of multithreaded programming is spotting the errors—they may occur so infrequently and unpredictably that a broken program does not produce incorrect results during testing, creating the illusion that the program is correct.* This is all the more reason to use predefined collections that handle the synchronization for you.

20.4.4 Synchronized Mutable Data Sharing—Making Operations Atomic

The output errors of Fig. 20.7 can be attributed to the fact that the shared object, Simple-Array, is not **thread safe**—SimpleArray is susceptible to errors if it's *accessed concurrently by multiple threads*. The problem lies in method add, which stores the value of writeIndex, places a new value in that element, then increments writeIndex. Such a method would present no problem in a single-threaded program. However, if one thread obtains the value of writeIndex, there's no guarantee that another thread cannot come along and increment writeIndex *before* the first thread has had a chance to place a value in the array. If this happens, the first thread will be writing to the array based on a **stale value** of writeIndex—a value that's no longer valid. Another possibility is that one thread might obtain the value of writeIndex *after* another thread adds an element to the array but *before* writeIndex is incremented. In this case, too, the first thread would write to the array based on an invalid value for writeIndex.

SimpleArray is *not thread safe because it allows any number of threads to read and modify shared mutable data concurrently*, which can cause errors. To make SimpleArray thread safe, we must ensure that no two threads can access its shared mutable data at the same time. While one thread is in the process of storing writeIndex, adding a value to the array, and incrementing writeIndex, *no other thread* may read or change the value of writeIndex or modify the contents of the array at any point during these three operations. In other words, we want these three operations—storing writeIndex, writing to the array, incrementing writeIndex—to be an **atomic operation**, which cannot be divided into smaller suboperations. (As you'll see in later examples, read operations on shared mutable data should also be atomic.) We can simulate atomicity by ensuring that only one thread carries out the three operations at a time. Any other threads that need to perform the operation must *wait* until the first thread has finished the add operation in its entirety.

Atomicity can be achieved using the synchronized keyword. By placing our three suboperations in a synchronized statement or synchronized method, we allow only one thread at a time to acquire the lock and perform the operations. When that thread has completed all of the operations in the synchronized block and releases the lock, another thread may acquire the lock and begin executing the operations. This ensures that a thread executing the operations will see the actual values of the shared mutable data and that *these values will not change unexpectedly in the middle of the operations as a result of another thread's modifying them.*

Software Engineering Observation 20.5

Place all accesses to mutable data that may be shared by multiple threads inside synchronized statements or synchronized methods that synchronize on the same lock. When performing multiple operations on shared mutable data, hold the lock for the entirety of the operation to ensure that the operation is effectively atomic.

Class *SimpleArray* with Synchronization

Figure 20.8 displays class SimpleArray with the proper synchronization. Notice that it's identical to the SimpleArray class of Fig. 20.5, except that add is now a synchronized method (line 20). So, only one thread at a time can execute this method. We reuse classes ArrayWriter (Fig. 20.6) and SharedArrayTest (Fig. 20.7) from the previous example.

```
 1    // Fig. 20.8: SimpleArray.java
 2    // Class that manages an integer array to be shared by multiple
 3    // threads with synchronization.
 4    import java.security.SecureRandom;
 5    import java.util.Arrays;
 6
 7    public class SimpleArray
 8    {
 9       private static final SecureRandom generator = new SecureRandom();
10       private final int[] array; // the shared integer array
11       private int writeIndex = 0; // index of next element to be written
12
13       // construct a SimpleArray of a given size
14       public SimpleArray(int size)
15       {
16          array = new int[size];
17       }
18
19       // add a value to the shared array
20       public synchronized void add(int value)
21       {
22          int position = writeIndex; // store the write index
23
24          try
25          {
26             // in real applications, you shouldn't sleep while holding a lock
27             Thread.sleep(generator.nextInt(500)); // for demo only
28          }
29          catch (InterruptedException ex)
30          {
31             Thread.currentThread().interrupt();
32          }
33
34          // put value in the appropriate element
35          array[position] = value;
36          System.out.printf("%s wrote %2d to element %d.%n",
37             Thread.currentThread().getName(), value, position);
38
39          ++writeIndex; // increment index of element to be written next
40          System.out.printf("Next write index: %d%n", writeIndex);
41       }
42
43       // used for outputting the contents of the shared integer array
44       public synchronized String toString()
45       {
46          return Arrays.toString(array);
47       }
48    } // end class SimpleArray
```

Fig. 20.8 | Class that manages an integer array to be shared by multiple threads with synchronization. (Part 1 of 2.)

```
pool-1-thread-1 wrote  1 to element 0.
Next write index: 1
pool-1-thread-2 wrote 11 to element 1.
Next write index: 2
pool-1-thread-2 wrote 12 to element 2.
Next write index: 3
pool-1-thread-2 wrote 13 to element 3.
Next write index: 4
pool-1-thread-1 wrote  2 to element 4.
Next write index: 5
pool-1-thread-1 wrote  3 to element 5.
Next write index: 6

Contents of SimpleArray:
[1, 11, 12, 13, 2, 3]
```

Fig. 20.8 | Class that manages an integer array to be shared by multiple threads with synchronization. (Part 2 of 2.)

Line 20 declares method add as synchronized, making all of the operations in this method behave as a single, atomic operation. Line 22 performs the first suboperation—storing the value of writeIndex. Line 35 defines the second suboperation, writing an element to the element at the index position. Line 39 increments writeIndex. When the method finishes executing at line 41, the executing thread implicitly *releases* the Simple-Array lock, making it possible for another thread to begin executing the add method.

In the synchronized add method, we print messages to the console indicating the progress of threads as they execute this method, in addition to performing the actual operations required to insert a value in the array. We do this so that the messages will be printed in the correct order, allowing us to see whether the method is properly synchronized by comparing these outputs with those of the previous, unsynchronized example. We continue to output messages from synchronized blocks in later examples for demonstration purposes only; typically, however, I/O *should not* be performed in synchronized blocks, because it's important to minimize the amount of time that an object is "locked." [*Note:* Line 27 in this example calls **Thread** method **sleep** (for demo purposes only) to emphasize the unpredictability of thread scheduling. You should never call **sleep** while holding a lock in a real application.]

Performance Tip 20.2

Keep the duration of synchronized statements as short as possible while maintaining the needed synchronization. This minimizes the wait time for blocked threads. Avoid performing I/O, lengthy calculations and operations that do not require synchronization while holding a lock.

20.5 Producer/Consumer Relationship without Synchronization

In a **producer/consumer relationship**, the **producer** portion of an application generates data and *stores it in a shared object*, and the **consumer** portion of the application *reads data* *from the shared object.* The producer/consumer relationship separates the task of identifying work to be done from the tasks involved in actually carrying out the work.

Examples of Producer/Consumer Relationship

One example of a common producer/consumer relationship is **print spooling**. Although a printer might not be available when you want to print from an application (i.e., the producer), you can still "complete" the print task, as the data is temporarily placed on disk until the printer becomes available. Similarly, when the printer (i.e., a consumer) is available, it doesn't have to wait until a current user wants to print. The spooled print jobs can be printed as soon as the printer becomes available. Another example of the producer/consumer relationship is an application that copies data onto DVDs by placing data in a fixed-size buffer, which is emptied as the DVD drive "burns" the data onto the DVD.

Synchronization and State Dependence

In a multithreaded producer/consumer relationship, a **producer thread** generates data and places it in a shared object called a **buffer**. A **consumer thread** reads data from the buffer. This relationship requires *synchronization* to ensure that values are produced and consumed properly. All operations on *mutable* data that's shared by multiple threads (e.g., the data in the buffer) must be guarded with a lock to prevent corruption, as discussed in Section 20.4. Operations on the buffer data shared by a producer and consumer thread are also **state dependent**—the operations should proceed only if the buffer is in the correct state. If the buffer is in a *not-full state*, the producer may produce; if the buffer is in a *not-empty state*, the consumer may consume. All operations that access the buffer must use synchronization to ensure that data is written to the buffer or read from the buffer only if the buffer is in the proper state. If the producer attempting to put the next data into the buffer determines that it's full, the producer thread must *wait* until there's space to write a new value. If a consumer thread finds the buffer empty or finds that the previous data has already been read, the consumer must also *wait* for new data to become available. Other examples of state dependence are that you can't drive your car if its gas tank is empty and you can't put more gas into the tank if it's already full.

Logic Errors from Lack of Synchronization

Consider how logic errors can arise if we do not synchronize access among multiple threads manipulating shared mutable data. Our next example (Figs. 20.9–20.13) implements a producer/consumer relationship *without the proper synchronization*. A producer thread writes the numbers 1 through 10 into a shared buffer—a single memory location shared between two threads (a single `int` variable called `buffer` in line 6 of Fig. 20.12 in this example). The consumer thread reads this data from the shared buffer and displays the data. The program's output shows the values that the producer writes (produces) into the shared buffer and the values that the consumer reads (consumes) from the shared buffer.

Each value the producer thread writes to the shared buffer must be consumed *exactly once* by the consumer thread. However, the threads in this example are not synchronized. Therefore, *data can be lost or garbled if the producer places new data into the shared buffer before the consumer reads the previous data.* Also, data can be incorrectly *duplicated* if the consumer consumes data again before the producer produces the next value. To show these possibilities, the consumer thread in the following example keeps a total of all the values it reads. The producer thread produces values from 1 through 10. If the consumer reads each value produced once and only once, the total will be 55. However, if you execute this program several times, you'll see that the total is not always 55 (as shown in the outputs in Fig. 20.13). To emphasize the point, the producer and consumer threads in the example each sleep for random intervals of up to three seconds between performing their tasks. Thus, we do not know when the producer thread will attempt to write a new value, or when the consumer thread will attempt to read a value.

*Interface **Buffer***

The program consists of interface Buffer (Fig. 20.9) and classes Producer (Fig. 20.10), Consumer (Fig. 20.11), UnsynchronizedBuffer (Fig. 20.12) and SharedBufferTest (Fig. 20.13). Interface Buffer (Fig. 20.9) declares methods blockingPut (line 6) and blockingGet (line 9) that a Buffer (such as UnsynchronizedBuffer) must implement to enable the Producer thread to place a value in the Buffer and the Consumer thread to retrieve a value from the Buffer, respectively. In subsequent examples, methods blockingPut and blockingGet will call methods that throw InterruptedExceptions—typically this indicates that a method temporarily could be blocked from performing a task. We declare each method with a throws clause here so that we don't have to modify this interface for the later examples.

```
 1   // Fig. 20.9: Buffer.java
 2   // Buffer interface specifies methods called by Producer and Consumer.
 3   public interface Buffer
 4   {
 5      // place int value into Buffer
 6      public void blockingPut(int value) throws InterruptedException;
 7
 8      // return int value from Buffer
 9      public int blockingGet() throws InterruptedException;
10   } // end interface Buffer
```

Fig. 20.9 | Buffer interface specifies methods called by Producer and Consumer. (*Caution:* The example of Figs. 20.9–20.13 is *not* thread safe.)

*Class **Producer***

Class Producer (Fig. 20.10) implements the Runnable interface, allowing it to be executed as a task in a separate thread. The constructor (lines 11–14) initializes the Buffer reference sharedLocation with an object created in main (line 15 of Fig. 20.13) and passed to the constructor. As we'll see, this is an UnsynchronizedBuffer object that implements interface Buffer *without synchronizing access to the shared object*. The Producer thread in this program executes the tasks specified in the method run (Fig. 20.10, lines 17–39). Each iteration of the loop (lines 21–35) invokes Thread method sleep (line 25) to place the Producer thread into the *timed waiting* state for a random time interval between 0 and 3 seconds. When the thread awakens, line 26 passes the value of control variable count to the Buffer object's blockingPut method to set the shared buffer's value. Lines 27–28 keep a total of all the values produced so far and output that value. When the loop completes, lines 36–37 display a message indicating that the Producer has finished producing data and is terminating. Next, method run terminates, which indicates that the Producer completed its task. Any method called from a Runnable's run method (e.g., Buffer method blockingPut) executes as part of that task's thread of execution. This fact becomes important in Sections 20.6—20.8 when we add synchronization to the producer/consumer relationship.

```java
1   // Fig. 20.10: Producer.java
2   // Producer with a run method that inserts the values 1 to 10 in buffer.
3   import java.security.SecureRandom;
4
5   public class Producer implements Runnable
6   {
7      private static final SecureRandom generator = new SecureRandom();
8      private final Buffer sharedLocation; // reference to shared object
9
10     // constructor
11     public Producer(Buffer sharedLocation)
12     {
13        this.sharedLocation = sharedLocation;
14     }
15
16     // store values from 1 to 10 in sharedLocation
17     public void run()
18     {
19        int sum = 0;
20
21        for (int count = 1; count <= 10; count++)
22        {
23           try // sleep 0 to 3 seconds, then place value in Buffer
24           {
25              Thread.sleep(generator.nextInt(3000)); // random sleep
26              sharedLocation.blockingPut(count); // set value in buffer
27              sum += count; // increment sum of values
28              System.out.printf("\t%2d%n", sum);
29           }
30           catch (InterruptedException exception)
31           {
32              Thread.currentThread().interrupt();
33           }
34        }
35
36        System.out.printf(
37           "Producer done producing%nTerminating Producer%n");
38     }
39  } // end class Producer
```

Fig. 20.10 | Producer with a run method that inserts the values 1 to 10 in buffer. (*Caution:* The example of Figs. 20.9–20.13 is *not* thread safe.)

Class Consumer

Class Consumer (Fig. 20.11) also implements interface Runnable, allowing the Consumer to execute concurrently with the Producer. Lines 11–14 initialize Buffer reference sharedLocation with an object that implements the Buffer interface (created in main, Fig. 20.13) and passed to the constructor as the parameter shared. As we'll see, this is the same UnsynchronizedBuffer object that's used to initialize the Producer object—thus, the two threads share the same object. The Consumer thread in this program performs the tasks specified in method run (lines 17–39). Lines 21–34 iterate 10 times. Each iteration invokes Thread method sleep (line 26) to put the Consumer thread into the *timed waiting* state for up to 3 seconds. Next, line 27 uses the Buffer's blockingGet method to retrieve the value in the shared buffer, then adds the value to variable sum. Line 28 displays the total of all the values consumed so far. When the loop completes, lines 36–37 display a line indicating the sum of the consumed values. Then method run terminates, which indicates that the Consumer completed its task. Once both threads enter the *terminated* state, the program ends.

```
1   // Fig. 20.11: Consumer.java
2   // Consumer with a run method that loops, reading 10 values from buffer.
3   import java.security.SecureRandom;
4
5   public class Consumer implements Runnable
6   {
7      private static final SecureRandom generator = new SecureRandom();
8      private final Buffer sharedLocation; // reference to shared object
9
10     // constructor
11     public Consumer(Buffer sharedLocation)
12     {
13        this.sharedLocation = sharedLocation;
14     }
15
16     // read sharedLocation's value 10 times and sum the values
17     public void run()
18     {
19        int sum = 0;
20
21        for (int count = 1; count <= 10; count++)
22        {
23           // sleep 0 to 3 seconds, read value from buffer and add to sum
24           try
25           {
26              Thread.sleep(generator.nextInt(3000));
27              sum += sharedLocation.blockingGet();
28              System.out.printf("\t\t\t%2d%n", sum);
29           }
30           catch (InterruptedException exception)
31           {
32              Thread.currentThread().interrupt();
33           }
34        }
35
36        System.out.printf("%n%s %d%n%s%n",
37           "Consumer read values totaling", sum, "Terminating Consumer");
38     }
39  } // end class Consumer
```

Fig. 20.11 | Consumer with a run method that loops, reading 10 values from buffer. (*Caution:* The example of Figs. 20.9–20.13 is *not* thread safe.)

*We Call **Thread** Method **sleep** Only for Demonstration Purposes*

We call method sleep in method run of the Producer and Consumer classes to emphasize the fact that, *in multithreaded applications, it's unpredictable when each thread will perform its task and for how long it will perform the task when it has a processor.* Normally, these thread scheduling issues are beyond the control of the Java developer. In this program, our thread's tasks are quite simple—the Producer writes the values 1 to 10 to the buffer, and the Consumer reads 10 values from the buffer and adds each value to variable sum. Without the sleep method call, and if the Producer executes first, given today's phenomenally fast processors, the Producer would likely complete its task before the Consumer got a chance to execute. If the Consumer executed first, it would likely consume garbage data ten times, then terminate before the Producer could produce the first real value.

*Class **UnsynchronizedBuffer** Does Not Synchronize Access to the Buffer*

Class UnsynchronizedBuffer (Fig. 20.12) implements interface Buffer (line 4), but does *not* synchronize access to the buffer's state—we purposely do this to demonstrate the problems that occur when multiple threads access *shared mutable data* in *without* synchronization. Line 6 declares instance variable buffer and initializes it to –1. This value is used to demonstrate the case in which the Consumer attempts to consume a value *before* the Producer ever places a value in buffer. Again, methods blockingPut (lines 9–13) and blockingGet (lines 16–20) do *not* synchronize access to the buffer instance variable. Method blockingPut simply assigns its argument to buffer (line 12), and method blockingGet simply returns the value of buffer (line 19). As you'll see in Fig. 20.13, Unsynchronized-Buffer object is shared between the Producer and the Consumer.

```
1   // Fig. 20.12: UnsynchronizedBuffer.java
2   // UnsynchronizedBuffer maintains the shared integer that is accessed by
3   // a producer thread and a consumer thread.
4   public class UnsynchronizedBuffer implements Buffer
5   {
6      private int buffer = -1; // shared by producer and consumer threads
7
8      // place value into buffer
9      public void blockingPut(int value) throws InterruptedException
10     {
11        System.out.printf("Producer writes\t%2d", value);
12        buffer = value;
13     }
14
15     // return value from buffer
16     public int blockingGet() throws InterruptedException
17     {
18        System.out.printf("Consumer reads\t%2d", buffer);
19        return buffer;
20     }
21  } // end class UnsynchronizedBuffer
```

Fig. 20.12 | UnsynchronizedBuffer maintains the shared integer that is accessed by a producer thread and a consumer thread. (*Caution:* The example of Fig. 20.9–Fig. 20.13 is *not* thread safe.)

Class SharedBufferTest

In class SharedBufferTest (Fig. 20.13), line 12 creates an ExecutorService to execute the Producer and Consumer Runnables. Line 15 creates an UnsynchronizedBuffer and assigns it to Buffer variable sharedLocation. This object stores the data that the Producer and Consumer threads will share. Lines 24–25 create and execute the Producer and Consumer. The Producer and Consumer constructors are each passed the same Buffer object (sharedLocation), so each object refers to the same Buffer. These lines also implicitly launch the threads and call each Runnable's run method. Finally, line 27 calls method shutdown so that the application can terminate when the threads executing the Producer and Consumer complete their tasks and line 28 waits for the scheduled tasks to complete. When main terminates (line 29), the main thread of execution enters the *terminated* state.

```
 1   // Fig. 20.13: SharedBufferTest.java
 2   // Application with two threads manipulating an unsynchronized buffer.
 3   import java.util.concurrent.ExecutorService;
 4   import java.util.concurrent.Executors;
 5   import java.util.concurrent.TimeUnit;
 6
 7   public class SharedBufferTest
 8   {
 9      public static void main(String[] args) throws InterruptedException
10      {
11         // create new thread pool with two threads
12         ExecutorService executorService = Executors.newCachedThreadPool();
13
14         // create UnsynchronizedBuffer to store ints
15         Buffer sharedLocation = new UnsynchronizedBuffer();
16
17         System.out.println(
18            "Action\t\tValue\tSum of Produced\tSum of Consumed");
19         System.out.printf(
20            "------\t\t-----\t---------------\t---------------%n%n");
21
22         // execute the Producer and Consumer, giving each
23         // access to the sharedLocation
24         executorService.execute(new Producer(sharedLocation));
25         executorService.execute(new Consumer(sharedLocation));
26
27         executorService.shutdown(); // terminate app when tasks complete
28         executorService.awaitTermination(1, TimeUnit.MINUTES);
29      }
30   } // end class SharedBufferTest
```

Action	Value	Sum of Produced	Sum of Consumed
Producer writes 1	1		
Producer writes 2	3		—— 1 is lost
Producer writes 3	6		—— 2 is lost

Fig. 20.13 | Application with two threads manipulating an unsynchronized buffer. (*Caution:* The example of Figs. 20.9–20.13 is *not* thread safe.) (Part 1 of 2.)

```
Consumer reads   3                      3
Producer writes  4      10
Consumer reads   4                      7
Producer writes  5      15
Producer writes  6      21              ——— 5 is lost
Producer writes  7      28              ——— 6 is lost
Consumer reads   7                      14
Consumer reads   7                      21 ——— 7 read again
Producer writes  8      36
Consumer reads   8                      29
Consumer reads   8                      37 ——— 8 read again
Producer writes  9      45
Producer writes 10      55              ——— 9 is lost

Producer done producing
Terminating Producer
Consumer reads  10                      47
Consumer reads  10                      57 ——— 10 read again
Consumer reads  10                      67 ——— 10 read again
Consumer reads  10                      77 ——— 10 read again

Consumer read values totaling 77
Terminating Consumer
```

```
Action           Value  Sum of Produced Sum of Consumed
------           -----  --------------- ---------------

Consumer reads  -1                      -1 ——— reads -1 bad data
Producer writes  1       1
Consumer reads   1                       0
Consumer reads   1                       1 ——— 1 read again
Consumer reads   1                       2 ——— 1 read again
Consumer reads   1                       3 ——— 1 read again
Consumer reads   1                       4 ——— 1 read again
Producer writes  2       3
Consumer reads   2                       6
Producer writes  3       6
Consumer reads   3                       9
Producer writes  4      10
Consumer reads   4                      13
Producer writes  5      15
Producer writes  6      21              ——— 5 is lost
Consumer reads   6                      19

Consumer read values totaling 19
Terminating Consumer
Producer writes  7      28              ——— 7 never read
Producer writes  8      36              ——— 8 never read
Producer writes  9      45              ——— 9 never read
Producer writes 10      55              ——— 10 never read

Producer done producing
Terminating Producer
```

Fig. 20.13 | Application with two threads manipulating an unsynchronized buffer. (*Caution:* The example of Figs. 20.9–20.13 is *not* thread safe.) (Part 2 of 2.)

Recall from this example's overview that the Producer should execute first and every value produced by the Producer should be consumed exactly once by the Consumer. However, when you study the first output of Fig. 20.13, notice that the Producer writes the values 1, 2 and 3 before the Consumer reads its first value (3). Therefore, the values 1 and 2 are *lost*. Later, the values 5, 6 and 9 are *lost*, while 7 and 8 are *read twice* and 10 is read four times. So the first output produces an incorrect total of 77, instead of the correct total of 55. In the second output, the Consumer reads the value -1 *before* the Producer ever writes a value. The Consumer reads the value 1 *five times* before the Producer writes the value 2. Meanwhile, the values 5, 7, 8, 9 and 10 are all *lost*—the last four because the Consumer terminates *before* the Producer. An incorrect consumer total of 19 is displayed. (Lines in the output where the Producer or Consumer has acted out of order are highlighted.)

Error-Prevention Tip 20.1

Access to a shared object by concurrent threads must be controlled carefully or a program may produce incorrect results.

To solve the problems of *lost* and *duplicated* data, Section 20.6 presents an example in which we use an ArrayBlockingQueue (from package java.util.concurrent) to synchronize access to the shared object, guaranteeing that each and every value will be processed once and only once.

20.6 Producer/Consumer Relationship: ArrayBlockingQueue

The best way to synchronize producer and consumer threads is to use classes from Java's java.util.concurrent package that *encapsulate the synchronization for you.* Java includes the class **ArrayBlockingQueue**—a fully implemented, *thread-safe buffer class* that implements interface **BlockingQueue**. This interface extends the Queue interface discussed in Chapter 16 and declares methods **put** and **take**, the blocking equivalents of Queue methods offer and poll, respectively. Method put places an element at the end of the BlockingQueue, waiting if the queue is full. Method take removes an element from the head of the BlockingQueue, waiting if the queue is empty. These methods make class ArrayBlockingQueue a good choice for implementing a shared buffer. Because method put blocks until there's room in the buffer to write data, and method take blocks until there's new data to read, the producer must produce a value first, the consumer correctly consumes only after the producer writes a value and the producer correctly produces the next value (after the first) only after the consumer reads the previous (or first) value. ArrayBlockingQueue stores the shared mutable data in an array, the size of which is specified as an ArrayBlockingQueue constructor argument. Once created, an ArrayBlockingQueue is fixed in size and will not expand to accommodate extra elements.

Class *BlockingBuffer*
Figures 20.14–20.15 demonstrate a Producer and a Consumer accessing an ArrayBlockingQueue. Class BlockingBuffer (Fig. 20.14) uses an ArrayBlockingQueue object that stores an Integer (line 7). Line 11 creates the ArrayBlockingQueue and passes 1 to the constructor so that the object holds a single value to mimic the UnsynchronizedBuffer example in Fig. 20.12. Lines 7 and 11 (Fig. 20.14) use generics, which we discussed in

Chapters 16–18. We discuss *multiple-element buffers* in Section 20.8. Because our Block-ingBuffer class uses the *thread-safe* ArrayBlockingQueue class to manage all of its shared state (the shared buffer in this case), BlockingBuffer is itself *thread safe*, even though we have not implemented the synchronization ourselves.

```
 1   // Fig. 20.14: BlockingBuffer.java
 2   // Creating a synchronized buffer using an ArrayBlockingQueue.
 3   import java.util.concurrent.ArrayBlockingQueue;
 4
 5   public class BlockingBuffer implements Buffer
 6   {
 7      private final ArrayBlockingQueue<Integer> buffer; // shared buffer
 8
 9      public BlockingBuffer()
10      {
11         buffer = new ArrayBlockingQueue<Integer>(1);
12      }
13
14      // place value into buffer
15      public void blockingPut(int value) throws InterruptedException
16      {
17         buffer.put(value); // place value in buffer
18         System.out.printf("%s%2d\t%s%d%n", "Producer writes ", value,
19            "Buffer cells occupied: ", buffer.size());
20      }
21
22      // return value from buffer
23      public int blockingGet() throws InterruptedException
24      {
25         int readValue = buffer.take(); // remove value from buffer
26         System.out.printf("%s %2d\t%s%d%n", "Consumer reads ",
27            readValue, "Buffer cells occupied: ", buffer.size());
28
29         return readValue;
30      }
31   } // end class BlockingBuffer
```

Fig. 20.14 | Creating a synchronized buffer using an `ArrayBlockingQueue`.

BlockingBuffer implements interface Buffer (Fig. 20.9) and uses classes Producer (Fig. 20.10 modified to remove line 28) and Consumer (Fig. 20.11 modified to remove line 28) from the example in Section 20.5. This approach demonstrates encapsulated syn-chronization—*the threads accessing the shared object are unaware that their buffer accesses are now synchronized.* The synchronization is handled entirely in the blockingPut and block-ingGet methods of BlockingBuffer by calling the synchronized ArrayBlockingQueue methods put and take, respectively. Thus, the Producer and Consumer Runnables are properly synchronized simply by calling the shared object's blockingPut and block-ingGet methods.

Line 17 in method blockingPut (Fig. 20.14, lines 15–20) calls the ArrayBlocking-Queue object's put method. This method call blocks if necessary until there's room in the buffer to place the value. Method blockingGet (lines 23–30) calls the ArrayBlocking-

Queue object's take method (line 25). This method call *blocks* if necessary until there's an element in the buffer to remove. Lines 18–19 and 26–27 use the ArrayBlockingQueue object's **size** method to display the total number of elements currently in the Array-BlockingQueue.

Class *BlockingBufferTest*

Class BlockingBufferTest (Fig. 20.15) contains the main method that launches the application. Line 13 creates an ExecutorService, and line 16 creates a BlockingBuffer object and assigns its reference to the Buffer variable sharedLocation. Lines 18–19 execute the Producer and Consumer Runnables. Line 21 calls method shutdown to end the application when the threads finish executing the Producer and Consumer tasks and line 22 waits for the scheduled tasks to complete.

```
1   // Fig. 20.15: BlockingBufferTest.java
2   // Two threads manipulating a blocking buffer that properly
3   // implements the producer/consumer relationship.
4   import java.util.concurrent.ExecutorService;
5   import java.util.concurrent.Executors;
6   import java.util.concurrent.TimeUnit;
7
8   public class BlockingBufferTest
9   {
10     public static void main(String[] args) throws InterruptedException
11     {
12        // create new thread pool with two threads
13        ExecutorService executorService = Executors.newCachedThreadPool();
14
15        // create BlockingBuffer to store ints
16        Buffer sharedLocation = new BlockingBuffer();
17
18        executorService.execute(new Producer(sharedLocation));
19        executorService.execute(new Consumer(sharedLocation));
20
21        executorService.shutdown();
22        executorService.awaitTermination(1, TimeUnit.MINUTES);
23     }
24  } // end class BlockingBufferTest
```

```
Producer writes   1     Buffer cells occupied: 1
Consumer reads    1     Buffer cells occupied: 0
Producer writes   2     Buffer cells occupied: 1
Consumer reads    2     Buffer cells occupied: 0
Producer writes   3     Buffer cells occupied: 1
Consumer reads    3     Buffer cells occupied: 0
Producer writes   4     Buffer cells occupied: 1
Consumer reads    4     Buffer cells occupied: 0
Producer writes   5     Buffer cells occupied: 1
Consumer reads    5     Buffer cells occupied: 0
Producer writes   6     Buffer cells occupied: 1
```

Fig. 20.15 | Two threads manipulating a blocking buffer that properly implements the producer/consumer relationship. (Part 1 of 2.)

```
Consumer reads   6      Buffer cells occupied: 0
Producer writes  7      Buffer cells occupied: 1
Consumer reads   7      Buffer cells occupied: 0
Producer writes  8      Buffer cells occupied: 1
Consumer reads   8      Buffer cells occupied: 0
Producer writes  9      Buffer cells occupied: 1
Consumer reads   9      Buffer cells occupied: 0
Producer writes 10      Buffer cells occupied: 1

Producer done producing
Terminating Producer
Consumer reads  10      Buffer cells occupied: 0

Consumer read values totaling 55
Terminating Consumer
```

Fig. 20.15 | Two threads manipulating a blocking buffer that properly implements the producer/consumer relationship. (Part 2 of 2.)

While methods put and take of ArrayBlockingQueue are properly synchronized, BlockingBuffer methods blockingPut and blockingGet (Fig. 20.14) are not declared to be synchronized. Thus, the statements performed in method blockingPut—the put operation (line 17) and the output (lines 18–19)—are *not atomic*; nor are the statements in method blockingGet—the take operation (line 25) and the output (lines 26–27). So there's no guarantee that each output will occur immediately after the corresponding put or take operation, and the outputs may appear out of order. Even if they do, the Array-BlockingQueue object is properly synchronizing access to the data, as evidenced by the fact that the sum of values read by the consumer is always correct.

20.7 (Advanced) Producer/Consumer Relationship with synchronized, wait, notify and notifyAll

[*Note:* This section is intended for *advanced* programmers who want to control synchronization.[2]] The previous example showed how multiple threads can share a single-element buffer in a thread-safe manner by using the ArrayBlockingQueue class that encapsulates the synchronization necessary to protect the shared mutable data. For educational purposes, we now explain how you can implement a shared buffer yourself using the synchronized keyword and methods of class Object. *Using an ArrayBlockingQueue generally results in more-maintainable, better-performing code.*

After identifying the shared mutable data and the *synchronization policy* (i.e., associating the data with a lock that guards it), the next step in synchronizing access to the buffer is to implement methods blockingGet and blockingPut as synchronized methods. This requires that a thread obtain the *monitor lock* on the Buffer object before attempting to access the buffer data, but it does not automatically ensure that threads proceed with an operation only if the buffer is in the proper state. We need a way to allow our threads to *wait*, depending on whether certain conditions are true. In the case of placing a new item in the buffer, the condition that allows the operation to proceed is that the *buffer is not full*.

---

2. For detailed information on wait, notify and notifyAll, see Chapter 14 of *Java Concurrency in Practice* by Brian Goetz, et al., Addison-Wesley Professional, 2006.

In the case of fetching an item from the buffer, the condition that allows the operation to proceed is that the *buffer is not empty*. If the condition in question is true, the operation may proceed; if it's false, the thread must *wait* until it becomes true. When a thread is waiting on a condition, it's removed from contention for the processor and placed into the *waiting* state and the lock it holds is released.

Methods `wait`, `notify` and `notifyAll`

`Object` methods `wait`, `notify` and `notifyAll` can be used with conditions to make threads *wait* when they cannot perform their tasks. If a thread obtains the *monitor lock* on an object, then determines that it cannot continue with its task on that object until some condition is satisfied, the thread can call `Object` method **wait** on the synchronized object; this *releases the monitor lock* on the object, and the thread waits in the *waiting* state while the other threads try to enter the object's synchronized statement(s) or method(s). When a thread executing a synchronized statement (or method) completes or satisfies the condition on which another thread may be waiting, it can call `Object` method **notify** on the synchronized object to allow a waiting thread to transition to the *runnable* state again. At this point, the thread that was transitioned from the *waiting* state to the *runnable* state can attempt to *reacquire the monitor lock* on the object. Even if the thread is able to reacquire the monitor lock, it still might not be able to perform its task at this time—in which case the thread will reenter the *waiting* state and implicitly *release the monitor lock*. If a thread calls **notifyAll** on the synchronized object, then *all* the threads waiting for the monitor lock become eligible to *reacquire the lock* (that is, they all transition to the *runnable* state).

Remember that only *one* thread at a time can obtain the monitor lock on the object—other threads that attempt to acquire the same monitor lock will be *blocked* until the monitor lock becomes available again (i.e., until no other thread is executing in a synchronized statement on that object).

Common Programming Error 20.1

It's an error if a thread issues a wait, a notify or a notifyAll on an object without having acquired a lock for it. This causes an **IllegalMonitorStateException**.

Error-Prevention Tip 20.2

It's a good practice to use notifyAll to notify waiting threads to become runnable. Doing so avoids the possibility that your program would forget about waiting threads, which would otherwise starve.

Figures 20.16 and 20.17 demonstrate a `Producer` and a `Consumer` accessing a shared buffer with synchronization. In this case, the `Producer` always produces a value *first*, the `Consumer` correctly consumes only *after* the `Producer` produces a value and the `Producer` correctly produces the next value only after the `Consumer` consumes the previous (or first) value. We reuse interface `Buffer` and classes `Producer` and `Consumer` from the example in Section 20.5, except that line 28 is removed from class `Producer` and class `Consumer`.

Class *SynchronizedBuffer*

The synchronization is handled in class `SynchronizedBuffer`'s `blockingPut` and `blocking-Get` methods (Fig. 20.16), which implements interface `Buffer` (line 4). Thus, the `Producer`'s and `Consumer`'s run methods simply call the shared object's synchronized `blockingPut` and blockingGet methods. Again, we output messages from this class's synchronized methods for demonstration purposes only—I/O *should not* be performed in synchronized blocks, because it's important to minimize the amount of time that an object is "locked."

```java
1    // Fig. 20.16: SynchronizedBuffer.java
2    // Synchronizing access to shared mutable data using Object
3    // methods wait and notifyAll.
4    public class SynchronizedBuffer implements Buffer
5    {
6       private int buffer = -1; // shared by producer and consumer threads
7       private boolean occupied = false;
8
9       // place value into buffer
10      public synchronized void blockingPut(int value)
11         throws InterruptedException
12      {
13         // while there are no empty locations, place thread in waiting state
14         while (occupied)
15         {
16            // output thread information and buffer information, then wait
17            System.out.println("Producer tries to write."); // for demo only
18            displayState("Buffer full. Producer waits."); // for demo only
19            wait();
20         }
21
22         buffer = value; // set new buffer value
23
24         // indicate producer cannot store another value
25         // until consumer retrieves current buffer value
26         occupied = true;
27
28         displayState("Producer writes " + buffer); // for demo only
29
30         notifyAll(); // tell waiting thread(s) to enter runnable state
31      } // end method blockingPut; releases lock on SynchronizedBuffer
32
33      // return value from buffer
34      public synchronized int blockingGet() throws InterruptedException
35      {
36         // while no data to read, place thread in waiting state
37         while (!occupied)
38         {
39            // output thread information and buffer information, then wait
40            System.out.println("Consumer tries to read."); // for demo only
41            displayState("Buffer empty. Consumer waits."); // for demo only
42            wait();
43         }
44
45         // indicate that producer can store another value
46         // because consumer just retrieved buffer value
47         occupied = false;
```

Fig. 20.16 | Synchronizing access to shared mutable data using Object methods wait and notifyAll. (Part 1 of 2.)

```
48
49          displayState("Consumer reads " + buffer); // for demo only
50
51          notifyAll(); // tell waiting thread(s) to enter runnable state
52
53          return buffer;
54       } // end method blockingGet; releases lock on SynchronizedBuffer
55
56       // display current operation and buffer state; for demo only
57       private synchronized void displayState(String operation)
58       {
59          System.out.printf("%-40s%d\t\t%b%n%n", operation, buffer,
60             occupied);
61       }
62    } // end class SynchronizedBuffer
```

Fig. 20.16 | Synchronizing access to shared mutable data using `Object` methods `wait` and `notifyAll`. (Part 2 of 2.)

Fields and Methods of Class *SynchronizedBuffer*

Class `SynchronizedBuffer` contains fields `buffer` (line 6) and `occupied` (line 7)—you must synchronize access to *both* fields to ensure that class `SynchronizedBuffer` is thread safe. Methods `blockingPut` (lines 10–31) and `blockingGet` (lines 34–54) are declared as synchronized—only *one* thread can call either of these methods at a time on a particular `SynchronizedBuffer` object. Field `occupied` is used to determine whether it's the Producer's or the Consumer's turn to perform a task. This field is used in conditional expressions in both the `blockingPut` and `blockingGet` methods. If `occupied` is `false`, then `buffer` is empty, so the Consumer cannot read the value of `buffer`, but the Producer can place a value into `buffer`. If `occupied` is `true`, the Consumer can read a value from `buffer`, but the Producer cannot place a value into `buffer`.

Method *blockingPut* and the *Producer* Thread

When the `Producer` thread's run method invokes synchronized method `blockingPut`, the thread implicitly attempts to acquire the `SynchronizedBuffer` object's monitor lock. If the monitor lock is available, the `Producer` thread *implicitly* acquires the lock. Then the loop at lines 14–20 first determines whether `occupied` is `true`. If so, `buffer` is *full* and we want to wait until the buffer is empty, so line 17 outputs a message indicating that the Producer thread is trying to write a value, and line 18 invokes method `displayState` (lines 57–61) to output another message indicating that `buffer` is *full* and that the Producer thread is *waiting* until there's space. Line 19 invokes method `wait` (inherited from `Object` by `SynchronizedBuffer`) to place the thread that called method `blockingPut` (i.e., the Producer thread) in the *waiting* state for the `SynchronizedBuffer` object. The call to `wait` causes the calling thread to *implicitly* release the lock on the `SynchronizedBuffer` object. This is important because the thread cannot currently perform its task and because other threads (in this case, the Consumer) should be allowed to access the object to allow the condition (`occupied`) to change. Now another thread can attempt to acquire the `SynchronizedBuffer` object's lock and invoke the object's `blockingPut` or `blockingGet` method.

The Producer thread remains in the *waiting* state until another thread *notifies* the Producer that it may proceed—at which point the Producer returns to the *runnable* state and attempts to implicitly reacquire the lock on the SynchronizedBuffer object. If the lock is available, the Producer thread reacquires it, and method blockingPut continues executing with the next statement after the wait call. Because wait is called in a loop, the loop-continuation condition is tested again to determine whether the thread can proceed. If not, then wait is invoked again—otherwise, method blockingPut continues with the next statement after the loop.

Line 22 in method blockingPut assigns the value to the buffer. Line 26 sets occupied to true to indicate that the buffer now contains a value (i.e., a consumer can read the value, but a Producer cannot yet put another value there). Line 28 invokes method displayState to output a message indicating that the Producer is writing a new value into the buffer. Line 30 invokes method notifyAll (inherited from Object). If any threads are *waiting* on the SynchronizedBuffer object's monitor lock, those threads enter the *runnable* state and can now attempt to *reacquire the lock*. Method notifyAll returns immediately, and method blockingPut then returns to the caller (i.e., the Producer's run method). When method blockingPut returns, it *implicitly releases the monitor lock* on the SynchronizedBuffer object.

Method blockingGet and the Consumer Thread
Methods blockingGet and blockingPut are implemented similarly. When the Consumer thread's run method invokes synchronized method blockingGet, the thread attempts to *acquire the monitor lock* on the SynchronizedBuffer object. If the lock is available, the Consumer thread acquires it. Then the while loop at lines 37–43 determines whether occupied is false. If so, the buffer is empty, so line 40 outputs a message indicating that the Consumer thread is trying to read a value, and line 41 invokes method displayState to output a message indicating that the buffer is *empty* and that the Consumer thread is *waiting*. Line 42 invokes method wait to place the thread that called method blockingGet (i.e., the Consumer) in the *waiting* state for the SynchronizedBuffer object. Again, the call to wait causes the calling thread to *implicitly release the lock* on the SynchronizedBuffer object, so another thread can attempt to acquire the SynchronizedBuffer object's lock and invoke the object's blockingPut or blockingGet method. If the lock on the SynchronizedBuffer is not available (e.g., if the Producer has not yet returned from method blockingPut), the Consumer is *blocked* until the lock becomes available.

The Consumer thread remains in the *waiting* state until it's *notified* by another thread that it may proceed—at which point the Consumer thread returns to the *runnable* state and attempts to *implicitly reacquire the lock* on the SynchronizedBuffer object. If the lock is available, the Consumer reacquires it, and method blockingGet continues executing with the next statement after wait. Because wait is called in a loop, the loop-continuation condition is tested again to determine whether the thread can proceed with its execution. If not, wait is invoked again—otherwise, method blockingGet continues with the next statement after the loop. Line 47 sets occupied to false to indicate that buffer is now empty (i.e., a Consumer cannot read the value, but a Producer can place another value in buffer), line 49 calls method displayState to indicate that the consumer is reading and line 51 invokes method notifyAll. If any threads are in the *waiting* state for the lock on this SynchronizedBuffer object, they enter the *runnable* state and can now attempt to *reacquire the lock.* Method `notifyAll` returns immediately, then method `blockingGet` returns the value of `buffer` to its caller. When method `blockingGet` returns, the lock on the `SynchronizedBuffer` object is *implicitly released.*

Error-Prevention Tip 20.3

Always invoke method `wait` in a loop that tests the condition the task is waiting on. It's possible that a thread will reenter the runnable *state (via a timed wait or another thread calling* `notifyAll`*) before the condition is satisfied. Testing the condition again ensures that the thread will not erroneously execute if it was notified early.*

Method `displayState` Is Also synchronized

Notice that method `displayState` is a synchronized method. This is important because it, too, reads the `SynchronizedBuffer`'s shared mutable data. Though only one thread at a time may acquire a given object's lock, one thread may acquire the same object's lock *multiple* times—this is known as a **reentrant lock** and enables one synchronized method to invoke another on the same object.

Testing Class *SynchronizedBuffer*

Class `SharedBufferTest2` (Fig. 20.17) is similar to class `SharedBufferTest` (Fig. 20.13). `SharedBufferTest2` contains method `main` (Fig. 20.17, lines 9–26), which launches the application. Line 12 creates an `ExecutorService` to run the `Producer` and `Consumer` tasks. Line 15 creates a `SynchronizedBuffer` object and assigns its reference to `Buffer` variable `sharedLocation`. This object stores the data that will be shared between the `Producer` and `Consumer`. Lines 17–18 display the column heads for the output. Lines 21–22 execute a `Producer` and a `Consumer`. Finally, line 24 calls method `shutdown` to end the application when the `Producer` and `Consumer` complete their tasks and line 25 waits for the scheduled tasks to complete. When method `main` ends (line 26), the main thread of execution terminates.

```
1   // Fig. 20.17: SharedBufferTest2.java
2   // Two threads correctly manipulating a synchronized buffer.
3   import java.util.concurrent.ExecutorService;
4   import java.util.concurrent.Executors;
5   import java.util.concurrent.TimeUnit;
6
7   public class SharedBufferTest2
8   {
9      public static void main(String[] args) throws InterruptedException
10     {
11        // create a newCachedThreadPool
12        ExecutorService executorService = Executors.newCachedThreadPool();
13
14        // create SynchronizedBuffer to store ints
15        Buffer sharedLocation = new SynchronizedBuffer();
16
17        System.out.printf("%-40s%s\t\t%s%n%-40s%s%n%n", "Operation",
18           "Buffer", "Occupied", "---------", "------\t\t--------");
19
```

Fig. 20.17 | Two threads correctly manipulating a synchronized buffer. (Part 1 of 3.)

```
20          // execute the Producer and Consumer tasks
21          executorService.execute(new Producer(sharedLocation));
22          executorService.execute(new Consumer(sharedLocation));
23
24          executorService.shutdown();
25          executorService.awaitTermination(1, TimeUnit.MINUTES);
26       }
27    } // end class SharedBufferTest2
```

Operation	Buffer	Occupied
Consumer tries to read. Buffer empty. Consumer waits.	-1	false
Producer writes 1	1	true
Consumer reads 1	1	false
Consumer tries to read. Buffer empty. Consumer waits.	1	false
Producer writes 2	2	true
Consumer reads 2	2	false
Producer writes 3	3	true
Consumer reads 3	3	false
Producer writes 4	4	true
Producer tries to write. Buffer full. Producer waits.	4	true
Consumer reads 4	4	false
Producer writes 5	5	true
Consumer reads 5	5	false
Producer writes 6	6	true
Producer tries to write. Buffer full. Producer waits.	6	true
Consumer reads 6	6	false
Producer writes 7	7	true
Producer tries to write. Buffer full. Producer waits.	7	true
Consumer reads 7	7	false
Producer writes 8	8	true
Consumer reads 8	8	false
Consumer tries to read. Buffer empty. Consumer waits.	8	false

Fig. 20.17 | Two threads correctly manipulating a synchronized buffer. (Part 2 of 3.)

```
Producer writes 9                     9              true

Consumer reads 9                      9              false

Consumer tries to read.
Buffer empty. Consumer waits.         9              false

Producer writes 10                    10             true

Consumer reads 10                     10             false


Producer done producing
Terminating Producer

Consumer read values totaling 55
Terminating Consumer
```

Fig. 20.17 | Two threads correctly manipulating a synchronized buffer. (Part 3 of 3.)

Study the outputs in Fig. 20.17. Observe that *every integer produced is consumed exactly once—no values are lost, and no values are consumed more than once.* The synchronization ensures that the Producer produces a value only when the buffer is *empty* and the Consumer consumes only when the buffer is *full*. The Producer always goes first, the Consumer *waits* if the Producer has not produced since the Consumer last consumed, and the Producer waits if the Consumer has not yet consumed the value that the Producer most recently produced. Execute this program several times to confirm that every integer produced is consumed exactly *once*. In the sample output, note the highlighted lines indicating when the Producer and Consumer must *wait* to perform their respective tasks.

20.8 (Advanced) Producer/Consumer Relationship: Bounded Buffers

The program in Section 20.7 uses thread synchronization to guarantee that two threads manipulate data in a shared buffer correctly. However, the application may not perform optimally. If the two threads operate at different speeds, one of them will spend more (or most) of its time waiting. For example, in the program in Section 20.7 we shared a single integer variable between the two threads. If the Producer thread produces values *faster* than the Consumer can consume them, then the Producer thread *waits* for the Consumer, because there are no other locations in the buffer in which to place the next value. Similarly, if the Consumer consumes values *faster* than the Producer produces them, the Consumer *waits* until the Producer places the next value in the shared buffer. Even when we have threads that operate at the *same* relative speeds, those threads may occasionally become "out of sync" over a period of time, causing one of them to *wait* for the other.

Performance Tip 20.3

We cannot make assumptions about the relative speeds of concurrent threads—*interactions that occur with the operating system, the network, the user and other components can cause the threads to operate at different and ever-changing speeds. When this happens, threads wait. When threads wait excessively, programs become less efficient, interactive programs become less responsive and applications suffer longer delays.*

Bounded Buffers

To minimize the amount of waiting time for threads that share resources and operate at the same average speeds, we can implement a **bounded buffer** that provides a fixed number of buffer cells into which the Producer can place values, and from which the Consumer can retrieve those values. (In fact, we've already done this with the ArrayBlockingQueue class in Section 20.6.) If the Producer temporarily produces values faster than the Consumer can consume them, the Producer can write additional values into the extra buffer cells, if any are available. This capability enables the Producer to perform its task even though the Consumer is not ready to retrieve the current value being produced. Similarly, if the Consumer consumes faster than the Producer produces new values, the Consumer can read additional values (if there are any) from the buffer. This enables the Consumer to keep busy even though the Producer is not ready to produce additional values. An example of the producer/consumer relationship that uses a bounded buffer is video streaming, which we discussed in Section 20.1.

Even a *bounded buffer* is inappropriate if the Producer and the Consumer operate consistently at different speeds. If the Consumer always executes faster than the Producer, then a buffer containing one location is enough. If the Producer always executes faster, only a buffer with an "infinite" number of locations would be able to absorb the extra production. However, if the Producer and Consumer execute at about the same average speed, a bounded buffer helps to smooth the effects of any occasional speeding up or slowing down in either thread's execution.

The key to using a *bounded buffer* with a Producer and Consumer that operate at about the same speed is to provide the buffer with enough locations to handle the anticipated "extra" production. If, over a period of time, we determine that the Producer often produces as many as three more values than the Consumer can consume, we can provide a buffer of at least three cells to handle the extra production. Making the buffer too small would cause threads to wait longer.

[*Note:* As we mention in Fig. 20.22, ArrayBlockingQueue can work with multiple producers and multiple consumers. For example, a factory that produces its product very fast will need to have many more delivery trucks (i.e., consumers) to remove those products quickly from the warehousing area (i.e., the bounded buffer) so that the factory can continue to produce products at full capacity.]

Performance Tip 20.4
Even when using a bounded buffer, it's possible that a producer thread could fill the buffer, which would force the producer to wait until a consumer consumed a value to free an element in the buffer. Similarly, if the buffer is empty at any given time, a consumer thread must wait until the producer produces another value. The key to using a bounded buffer is to optimize the buffer size to minimize the amount of thread wait time, while not wasting space.

Bounded Buffers Using `ArrayBlockingQueue`

The simplest way to implement a bounded buffer is to use an ArrayBlockingQueue for the buffer so that *all of the synchronization details are handled for you*. This can be done by modifying the example from Section 20.6 to pass the desired size for the bounded buffer into the ArrayBlockingQueue constructor. Rather than repeat our previous ArrayBlockingQueue example with a different size, we instead present an example that illustrates how you can build a bounded buffer yourself. Again, using an `ArrayBlockingQueue` will result in more-maintainable and better-performing code.

Implementing Your Own Bounded Buffer as a Circular Buffer

The program in Figs. 20.18 and 20.19 demonstrates a `Producer` and a `Consumer` accessing a *bounded buffer with synchronization*. Again, we reuse interface `Buffer` and classes `Producer` and `Consumer` from the example in Section 20.5, except that line 28 is removed from class `Producer` and class `Consumer`. We implement the bounded buffer in class `CircularBuffer` (Fig. 20.18) as a **circular buffer** that uses a shared array of three elements. A circular buffer writes into and reads from the array elements in order, beginning at the first cell and moving toward the last. When a `Producer` or `Consumer` reaches the last element, it returns to the first and begins writing or reading, respectively, from there. In this version of the producer/consumer relationship, the `Consumer` consumes a value only when the array is not empty and the `Producer` produces a value only when the array is not full. Once again, the output statements used in this class's `synchronized` methods are for *demonstration purposes only*.

```
 1   // Fig. 20.18: CircularBuffer.java
 2   // Synchronizing access to a shared three-element bounded buffer.
 3   public class CircularBuffer implements Buffer
 4   {
 5      private final int[] buffer = {-1, -1, -1}; // shared buffer
 6
 7      private int occupiedCells = 0; // count number of buffers used
 8      private int writeIndex = 0; // index of next element to write to
 9      private int readIndex = 0; // index of next element to read
10
11      // place value into buffer
12      public synchronized void blockingPut(int value)
13         throws InterruptedException
14      {
15         // wait until buffer has space available, then write value;
16         // while no empty locations, place thread in blocked state
17         while (occupiedCells == buffer.length)
18         {
19            System.out.printf("Buffer is full. Producer waits.%n");
20            wait(); // wait until a buffer cell is free
21         } // end while
22
23         buffer[writeIndex] = value; // set new buffer value
24
25         // update circular write index
26         writeIndex = (writeIndex + 1) % buffer.length;
27
28         ++occupiedCells; // one more buffer cell is full
29         displayState("Producer writes " + value);
30         notifyAll(); // notify threads waiting to read from buffer
31      }
```

Fig. 20.18 | Synchronizing access to a shared three-element bounded buffer. (Part 1 of 3.)

```
32
33      // return value from buffer
34      public synchronized int blockingGet() throws InterruptedException
35      {
36         // wait until buffer has data, then read value;
37         // while no data to read, place thread in waiting state
38         while (occupiedCells == 0)
39         {
40            System.out.printf("Buffer is empty. Consumer waits.%n");
41            wait(); // wait until a buffer cell is filled
42         } // end while
43
44         int readValue = buffer[readIndex]; // read value from buffer
45
46         // update circular read index
47         readIndex = (readIndex + 1) % buffer.length;
48
49         --occupiedCells; // one fewer buffer cells are occupied
50         displayState("Consumer reads " + readValue);
51         notifyAll(); // notify threads waiting to write to buffer
52
53         return readValue;
54      }
55
56      // display current operation and buffer state
57      public synchronized void displayState(String operation)
58      {
59         // output operation and number of occupied buffer cells
60         System.out.printf("%s%s%d)%n%s", operation,
61            " (buffer cells occupied: ", occupiedCells, "buffer cells:   ");
62
63         for (int value : buffer)
64            System.out.printf(" %2d  ", value); // output values in buffer
65
66         System.out.printf("%n                ");
67
68         for (int i = 0; i < buffer.length; i++)
69            System.out.print("---- ");
70
71         System.out.printf("%n                ");
72
73         for (int i = 0; i < buffer.length; i++)
74         {
75            if (i == writeIndex && i == readIndex)
76               System.out.print(" WR"); // both write and read index
77            else if (i == writeIndex)
78               System.out.print(" W  "); // just write index
79            else if (i == readIndex)
80               System.out.print(" R  "); // just read index
81            else
82               System.out.print("    "); // neither index
83         }
84
```

Fig. 20.18 | Synchronizing access to a shared three-element bounded buffer. (Part 2 of 3.)

```
85            System.out.printf("%n%n");
86      }
87   } // end class CircularBuffer
```

Fig. 20.18 | Synchronizing access to a shared three-element bounded buffer. (Part 3 of 3.)

Line 5 initializes array `buffer` as a three-element `int` array that represents the circular buffer. Variable `occupiedCells` (line 7) counts the number of elements in `buffer` that contain data to be read. When `occupiedBuffers` is 0, the circular buffer is *empty* and the Consumer must *wait*—when `occupiedCells` is 3 (the size of the circular buffer), the circular buffer is *full* and the Producer must *wait*. Variable `writeIndex` (line 8) indicates the next location in which a value can be placed by a Producer. Variable `readIndex` (line 9) indicates the position from which the next value can be read by a Consumer. CircularBuffer's instance variables are *all* part of the class's shared mutable data, thus access to all of these variables must be synchronized to ensure that a `CircularBuffer` is thread safe.

CircularBuffer *Method* blockingPut

CircularBuffer method `blockingPut` (lines 12–31) performs the same tasks as in Fig. 20.16, with a few modifications. The loop at lines 17–21 determines whether the Producer must *wait* (i.e., all buffer cells are *full*). If so, line 19 indicates that the Producer is *waiting* to perform its task. Then line 20 invokes method `wait`, causing the Producer thread to *release* the CircularBuffer's *lock* and *wait* until there's space for a new value to be written into the buffer. When execution continues at line 23 after the `while` loop, the value written by the Producer is placed in the circular buffer at location `writeIndex`. Then line 26 updates `writeIndex` for the next call to CircularBuffer method `blockingPut`. This line is the key to the buffer's *circularity*. When `writeIndex` is incremented *past the end of the buffer*, the line sets it to 0. Line 28 increments `occupiedCells`, because there's now one more value in the buffer that the Consumer can read. Next, line 29 invokes method `displayState` (lines 57–86) to update the output with the value produced, the number of occupied buffer cells, the contents of the buffer cells and the current `writeIndex` and `readIndex`. Line 30 invokes method `notifyAll` to transition *waiting* threads to the *runnable* state, so that a waiting Consumer thread (if there is one) can now try again to read a value from the buffer.

CircularBuffer *Method* blockingGet

CircularBuffer method `blockingGet` (lines 34–54) also performs the same tasks as it did in Fig. 20.16, with a few minor modifications. The loop at lines 38–42 (Fig. 20.18) determines whether the Consumer must wait (i.e., all buffer cells are *empty*). If the Consumer must *wait*, line 40 updates the output to indicate that the Consumer is *waiting* to perform its task. Then line 41 invokes method `wait`, causing the current thread to *release the lock* on the CircularBuffer and *wait* until data is available to read. When execution eventually continues at line 44 after a `notifyAll` call from the Producer, `readValue` is assigned the value at location `readIndex` in the circular buffer. Then line 47 updates `readIndex` for the next call to CircularBuffer method `blockingGet`. This line and line 26 implement the *circularity* of the buffer. Line 49 decrements `occupiedCells`, because there's now one more position in the buffer in which the Producer thread can place a value. Line 50 invokes method `displayState` to update the output with the consumed value, the number of occupied buffer cells, the contents of the buffer cells and the current `writeIndex` and `readIndex`. Line 51 invokes method `notifyAll` to allow any `Producer` threads *waiting to write* into the `CircularBuffer` object to attempt to write again. Then line 53 returns the consumed value to the caller.

CircularBuffer Method `displayState`
Method `displayState` (lines 57–86) outputs the application's state. Lines 63–64 output the values of the buffer cells. Line 64 uses method `printf` with a `"%2d"` format specifier to print the contents of each buffer with a leading space if it's a single digit. Lines 71–83 output the current `writeIndex` and `readIndex` with the letters `W` and `R`, respectively. Once again, `displayState` is a synchronized method because it accesses class `CircularBuffer`'s shared mutable data.

Testing Class `CircularBuffer`
Class `CircularBufferTest` (Fig. 20.19) contains the `main` method that launches the application. Line 12 creates the `ExecutorService`, and line 15 creates a `CircularBuffer` object and assigns its reference to `CircularBuffer` variable `sharedLocation`. Line 18 invokes the `CircularBuffer`'s `displayState` method to show the initial state of the buffer. Lines 21–22 execute the `Producer` and `Consumer` tasks. Line 24 calls method `shutdown` to end the application when the threads complete the `Producer` and `Consumer` tasks and line 25 waits for the tasks to complete.

```
1   // Fig. 20.19: CircularBufferTest.java
2   // Producer and Consumer threads correctly manipulating a circular buffer.
3   import java.util.concurrent.ExecutorService;
4   import java.util.concurrent.Executors;
5   import java.util.concurrent.TimeUnit;
6
7   public class CircularBufferTest
8   {
9      public static void main(String[] args) throws InterruptedException
10     {
11        // create new thread pool with two threads
12        ExecutorService executorService = Executors.newCachedThreadPool();
13
14        // create CircularBuffer to store ints
15        CircularBuffer sharedLocation = new CircularBuffer();
16
17        // display the initial state of the CircularBuffer
18        sharedLocation.displayState("Initial State");
19
20        // execute the Producer and Consumer tasks
21        executorService.execute(new Producer(sharedLocation));
22        executorService.execute(new Consumer(sharedLocation));
23
24        executorService.shutdown();
25        executorService.awaitTermination(1, TimeUnit.MINUTES);
26     }
27  } // end class CircularBufferTest
```

Fig. 20.19 | Producer and Consumer threads correctly manipulating a circular buffer. (Part 1 of 3.)

```
Initial State (buffer cells occupied: 0)
buffer cells:    -1   -1   -1
                ---- ---- ----
                 WR

Producer writes 1 (buffer cells occupied: 1)
buffer cells:     1   -1   -1
                ---- ---- ----
                 R    W

Consumer reads 1 (buffer cells occupied: 0)
buffer cells:     1   -1   -1
                ---- ---- ----
                      WR

Buffer is empty. Consumer waits.
Producer writes 2 (buffer cells occupied: 1)
buffer cells:     1    2   -1
                ---- ---- ----
                      R    W

Consumer reads 2 (buffer cells occupied: 0)
buffer cells:     1    2   -1
                ---- ---- ----
                           WR

Producer writes 3 (buffer cells occupied: 1)
buffer cells:     1    2    3
                ---- ---- ----
                 W         R

Consumer reads 3 (buffer cells occupied: 0)
buffer cells:     1    2    3
                ---- ---- ----
                 WR

Producer writes 4 (buffer cells occupied: 1)
buffer cells:     4    2    3
                ---- ---- ----
                 R    W

Producer writes 5 (buffer cells occupied: 2)
buffer cells:     4    5    3
                ---- ---- ----
                 R         W

Consumer reads 4 (buffer cells occupied: 1)
buffer cells:     4    5    3
                ---- ---- ----
                      R    W

Producer writes 6 (buffer cells occupied: 2)
buffer cells:     4    5    6
                ---- ---- ----
                 W    R
```

Fig. 20.19 | Producer and Consumer threads correctly manipulating a circular buffer. (Part 2 of 3.)

```
Producer writes 7 (buffer cells occupied: 3)
buffer cells:    7    5    6
                ---- ---- ----
                     WR

Consumer reads 5 (buffer cells occupied: 2)
buffer cells:    7    5    6
                ---- ---- ----
                 W    R

Producer writes 8 (buffer cells occupied: 3)
buffer cells:    7    8    6
                ---- ---- ----
                          WR

Consumer reads 6 (buffer cells occupied: 2)
buffer cells:    7    8    6
                ---- ---- ----
                 R         W

Consumer reads 7 (buffer cells occupied: 1)
buffer cells:    7    8    6
                ---- ---- ----
                 R    W

Producer writes 9 (buffer cells occupied: 2)
buffer cells:    7    8    9
                ---- ---- ----
                 W    R

Consumer reads 8 (buffer cells occupied: 1)
buffer cells:    7    8    9
                ---- ---- ----
                 W         R

Consumer reads 9 (buffer cells occupied: 0)
buffer cells:    7    8    9
                ---- ---- ----
                 WR

Producer writes 10 (buffer cells occupied: 1)
buffer cells:   10    8    9
                ---- ---- ----
                 R    W


Producer done producing
Terminating Producer
Consumer reads 10 (buffer cells occupied: 0)
buffer cells:   10    8    9
                ---- ---- ----
                      WR


Consumer read values totaling: 55
Terminating Consumer
```

Fig. 20.19 | Producer and Consumer threads correctly manipulating a circular buffer. (Part 3 of 3.)

Each time the Producer writes a value or the Consumer reads a value, the program outputs a message indicating the action performed (a read or a write), the contents of buffer, and the location of writeIndex and readIndex. In the output of Fig. 20.19, the Producer first writes the value 1. The buffer then contains the value 1 in the first cell and the value −1 (the default value that we use for output purposes) in the other two cells. The write index is updated to the second cell, while the read index stays at the first cell. Next, the Consumer reads 1. The buffer contains the same values, but the read index has been updated to the second cell. The Consumer then tries to read again, but the buffer is empty and the Consumer is forced to wait. Only once in this execution of the program was it necessary for either thread to wait.

20.9 (Advanced) Producer/Consumer Relationship: The Lock and Condition Interfaces

Though the synchronized keyword provides for most basic thread-synchronization needs, Java provides other tools to assist in developing concurrent programs. In this section, we discuss the Lock and Condition interfaces. These interfaces give you more precise control over thread synchronization, but are more complicated to use. *Only the most advanced programmers should use these interfaces.*

Interface *Lock* and Class *ReentrantLock*

Any object can contain a reference to an object that implements the **Lock** interface (of package java.util.concurrent.locks). A thread calls the Lock's **lock** method (analogous to entering a synchronized block) to acquire the lock. Once a Lock has been obtained by one thread, the Lock object will not allow another thread to obtain the Lock until the first thread releases the Lock (by calling the Lock's **unlock** method—analogous to exiting a synchronized block). If several threads are trying to call method lock on the same Lock object at the same time, only one of these threads can obtain the lock—all the others are placed in the *waiting* state for that lock. When a thread calls method unlock, the lock on the object is released and a waiting thread attempting to lock the object proceeds.

Error-Prevention Tip 20.4

Place calls to Lock method unlock in a finally block. If an exception is thrown, unlock must still be called or deadlock could occur.

Class **ReentrantLock** (of package java.util.concurrent.locks) is a basic implementation of the Lock interface. The constructor for a ReentrantLock takes a boolean argument that specifies whether the lock has a **fairness policy**. If the argument is true, the ReentrantLock's fairness policy is "the longest-waiting thread will acquire the lock when it's available." Such a fairness policy guarantees that *indefinite postponement* (also called *starvation*) cannot occur. If the fairness policy argument is set to false, there's no guarantee as to which waiting thread will acquire the lock when it's available.

Software Engineering Observation 20.6

Using a ReentrantLock with a fairness policy avoids indefinite postponement.

Performance Tip 20.5

In most cases, a non-fair lock is preferable, because using a fair lock can decrease program performance.

Condition Objects and Interface Condition

If a thread that owns a Lock determines that it cannot continue with its task until some condition is satisfied, the thread can wait on a **condition object**. Using Lock objects allows you to explicitly declare the condition objects on which a thread may need to wait. For example, in the producer/consumer relationship, producers can wait on *one* object and consumers can wait on *another*. This is not possible when using the synchronized keywords and an object's built-in monitor lock. Condition objects are associated with a specific Lock and are created by calling a Lock's **newCondition** method, which returns an object that implements the **Condition** interface (of package java.util.concurrent.locks). To wait on a condition object, the thread can call the Condition's **await** method (analogous to Object method wait). This immediately releases the associated Lock and places the thread in the *waiting* state for that Condition. Other threads can then try to obtain the Lock. When a *runnable* thread completes a task and determines that the *waiting* thread can now continue, the *runnable* thread can call Condition method **signal** (analogous to Object method notify) to allow a thread in that Condition's *waiting* state to return to the *runnable* state. At this point, the thread that transitioned from the *waiting* state to the *runnable* state can attempt to reacquire the Lock. Even if it's able to *reacquire* the Lock, the thread still might not be able to perform its task at this time—in which case the thread can call the Condition's await method to *release* the Lock and reenter the *waiting* state. If multiple threads are in a Condition's *waiting* state when signal is called, the default implementation of Condition signals the longest-waiting thread to transition to the *runnable* state. If a thread calls Condition method **signalAll** (analogous to Object method notifyAll), then all the threads waiting for that condition transition to the *runnable* state and become eligible to reacquire the Lock. Only one of those threads can obtain the Lock on the object—the others will wait until the Lock becomes available again. If the Lock has a *fairness policy*, the longest-waiting thread acquires the Lock. When a thread is finished with a shared object, it must call method unlock to release the Lock.

Error-Prevention Tip 20.5

When multiple threads manipulate a shared object using locks, ensure that if one thread calls method await *to enter the* waiting *state for a condition object, a separate thread eventually will call Condition method* signal *to transition the thread waiting on the condition object back to the* runnable *state. If multiple threads may be waiting on the condition object, a separate thread can call Condition method* signalAll *as a safeguard to ensure that all the waiting threads have another opportunity to perform their tasks. If this is not done, starvation might occur.*

Common Programming Error 20.2

An IllegalMonitorStateException *occurs if a thread issues an* await*, a* signal*, or a* signalAll *on a Condition object that was created from a* ReentrantLock *without having acquired the lock for that Condition object.*

Lock *and* Condition *vs. the* synchronized *Keyword*

In some applications, using Lock and Condition objects may be preferable to using the synchronized keyword. Locks allow you to *interrupt* waiting threads or to specify a *timeout* for waiting to acquire a lock, which is not possible using the synchronized keyword. Also, a Lock is *not* constrained to be acquired and released in the *same* block of code, which is the case with the synchronized keyword. Condition objects allow you to specify multiple conditions on which threads may *wait*. Thus, it's possible to indicate to waiting threads that a specific condition object is now true by calling signal or signallAll on that Condition object. With synchronized, there's no way to explicitly state the condition on which threads are waiting, and thus there's no way to notify threads waiting on one condition that they may proceed without also signaling threads waiting on any other conditions. There are other possible advantages to using Lock and Condition objects, but generally it's best to use the synchronized keyword unless your application requires advanced synchronization capabilities.

Software Engineering Observation 20.7

Think of Lock *and* Condition *as an advanced version of synchronized.* Lock *and* Condition *support timed waits, interruptible waits and multiple* Condition *queues per* Lock—*if you do not need one of these features, you do not need* Lock *and* Condition.

Error-Prevention Tip 20.6

Using interfaces Lock *and* Condition *is error prone—*unlock *is not guaranteed to be called, whereas the monitor in a synchronized statement will always be released when the statement completes execution. Of course, you can guarantee that* unlock *will be called if it's placed in a* finally *block, as we do in Fig. 20.20.*

Using Locks *and* Conditions *to Implement Synchronization*

We now implement the producer/consumer relationship using Lock and Condition objects to coordinate access to a shared single-element buffer (Figs. 20.20 and 20.21). In this case, each produced value is correctly consumed exactly once. Again, we reuse interface Buffer and classes Producer and Consumer from the example in Section 20.5, except that line 28 is removed from class Producer and class Consumer.

Class SynchronizedBuffer

Class SynchronizedBuffer (Fig. 20.20) contains five fields. Line 11 creates a new object of type ReentrantLock and assigns its reference to Lock variable accessLock. The ReentrantLock is created without the *fairness policy* because at any time only a single Producer or Consumer will be waiting to acquire the Lock in this example. Lines 14–15 create two Conditions using Lock method newCondition. Condition canWrite contains a queue for a Producer thread waiting while the buffer is *full* (i.e., there's data in the buffer that the Consumer has not read yet). If the buffer is *full*, the Producer calls method await on this Condition. When the Consumer reads data from a *full* buffer, it calls method signal on this Condition. Condition canRead contains a queue for a Consumer thread waiting while the buffer is *empty* (i.e., there's no data in the buffer for the Consumer to read). If the buffer is *empty*, the Consumer calls method await on this Condition. When the Producer writes to the *empty* buffer, it calls method signal on this Condition. The int variable buffer (line 17) holds the shared mutable data. The boolean variable occupied (line 18) keeps track of whether the buffer currently holds data (that the Consumer should read).

```
 I   // Fig. 20.20: SynchronizedBuffer.java
 2   // Synchronizing access to a shared integer using the Lock and Condition
 3   // interfaces
 4   import java.util.concurrent.locks.Lock;
 5   import java.util.concurrent.locks.ReentrantLock;
 6   import java.util.concurrent.locks.Condition;
 7
 8   public class SynchronizedBuffer implements Buffer
 9   {
10      // Lock to control synchronization with this buffer
11      private final Lock accessLock = new ReentrantLock();
12
13      // conditions to control reading and writing
14      private final Condition canWrite = accessLock.newCondition();
15      private final Condition canRead = accessLock.newCondition();
16
17      private int buffer = -1; // shared by producer and consumer threads
18      private boolean occupied = false; // whether buffer is occupied
19
20      // place int value into buffer
21      public void blockingPut(int value) throws InterruptedException
22      {
23         accessLock.lock(); // lock this object
24
25         // output thread information and buffer information, then wait
26         try
27         {
28            // while buffer is not empty, place thread in waiting state
29            while (occupied)
30            {
31               System.out.println("Producer tries to write.");
32               displayState("Buffer full. Producer waits.");
33               canWrite.await(); // wait until buffer is empty
34            }
35
36            buffer = value; // set new buffer value
37
38            // indicate producer cannot store another value
39            // until consumer retrieves current buffer value
40            occupied = true;
41
42            displayState("Producer writes " + buffer);
43
44            // signal any threads waiting to read from buffer
45            canRead.signalAll();
46         }
47         finally
48         {
49            accessLock.unlock(); // unlock this object
50         }
51      }
```

Fig. 20.20 | Synchronizing access to a shared integer using the Lock and Condition interfaces. (Part 1 of 2.)

```
52
53       // return value from buffer
54       public int blockingGet() throws InterruptedException
55       {
56          int readValue = 0; // initialize value read from buffer
57          accessLock.lock(); // lock this object
58
59          // output thread information and buffer information, then wait
60          try
61          {
62             // if there is no data to read, place thread in waiting state
63             while (!occupied)
64             {
65                System.out.println("Consumer tries to read.");
66                displayState("Buffer empty. Consumer waits.");
67                canRead.await(); // wait until buffer is full
68             }
69
70             // indicate that producer can store another value
71             // because consumer just retrieved buffer value
72             occupied = false;
73
74             readValue = buffer; // retrieve value from buffer
75             displayState("Consumer reads " + readValue);
76
77             // signal any threads waiting for buffer to be empty
78             canWrite.signalAll();
79          }
80          finally
81          {
82             accessLock.unlock(); // unlock this object
83          }
84
85          return readValue;
86       }
87
88       // display current operation and buffer state
89       private void displayState(String operation)
90       {
91          try
92          {
93             accessLock.lock(); // lock this object
94             System.out.printf("%-40s%d\t\t%b%n%n", operation, buffer,
95                occupied);
96          }
97          finally
98          {
99             accessLock.unlock(); // unlock this objects
100         }
101      }
102   } // end class SynchronizedBuffer
```

Fig. 20.20 | Synchronizing access to a shared integer using the Lock and Condition interfaces. (Part 2 of 2.)

Line 23 in method `blockingPut` calls method `lock` on the SynchronizedBuffer's `accessLock`. If the lock is *available* (i.e., no other thread has acquired it), this thread now owns the lock and the thread continues. If the lock is *unavailable* (i.e., it's held by another thread), method `lock` waits until the lock is released. After the lock is acquired, lines 26–46 execute. Line 29 tests `occupied` to determine whether `buffer` is full. If it is, lines 31–32 display a message indicating that the thread will *wait*. Line 33 calls Condition method `await` on the `canWrite` condition object, which temporarily releases the Synchronized-Buffer's Lock and *waits* for a signal from the Consumer that `buffer` is available for writing. When `buffer` is available, the method proceeds, writing to `buffer` (line 36), setting occupied to `true` (line 40) and displaying a message indicating that the producer wrote a value (line 42). Line 45 calls Condition method `signal` on condition object `canRead` to notify the waiting Consumer (if there is one) that the buffer has new data to be read. Line 49 calls method `unlock` from a `finally` block to *release* the lock and allow the Consumer to proceed.

Line 57 of method `blockingGet` (lines 54–86) calls method `lock` to *acquire* the Lock. This method *waits* until the Lock is *available*. Once the Lock is *acquired*, line 63 tests whether occupied is `false`, indicating that the buffer is *empty*. If so, line 67 calls method `await` on condition object `canRead`. Recall that method `signal` is called on variable can-Read in the `blockingPut` method (line 45). When the Condition object is *signaled*, the `blockingGet` method continues. Lines 72–74 set occupied to `false`, store the value of `buffer` in `readValue` and output the `readValue`. Then line 78 *signals* the condition object `canWrite`. This awakens the Producer if it's indeed *waiting* for the buffer to be *emptied*. Line 82 calls method `unlock` from a `finally` block to *release* the lock, and line 85 returns `readValue` to the caller.

Common Programming Error 20.3

Forgetting to `signal` a waiting thread is a logic error. The thread will remain in the waiting state, which will prevent it from proceeding. Such waiting can lead to indefinite postponement or deadlock.

Class *SharedBufferTest2*

Class SharedBufferTest2 (Fig. 20.21) is identical to that of Fig. 20.17. Study the outputs in Fig. 20.21. *Observe that every integer produced is consumed exactly once—no values are lost, and no values are consumed more than once.* The Lock and Condition objects ensure that the Producer and Consumer cannot perform their tasks unless it's their turn. The Producer *must* go first, the Consumer *must wait* if the Producer has not produced since the Consumer last consumed and the Producer *must wait* if the Consumer has not yet consumed the value that the Producer most recently produced. Execute this program several times to confirm that every integer produced is consumed exactly once. In the sample output, note the highlighted lines indicating when the Producer and Consumer must *wait* to perform their respective tasks.

```
1   // Fig. 20.21: SharedBufferTest2.java
2   // Two threads manipulating a synchronized buffer.
3   import java.util.concurrent.ExecutorService;
```

Fig. 20.21 | Two threads manipulating a synchronized buffer. (Part 1 of 3.)

```
4   import java.util.concurrent.Executors;
5   import java.util.concurrent.TimeUnit;
6
7   public class SharedBufferTest2
8   {
9      public static void main(String[] args) throws InterruptedException
10     {
11        // create new thread pool with two threads
12        ExecutorService executorService = Executors.newCachedThreadPool();
13
14        // create SynchronizedBuffer to store ints
15        Buffer sharedLocation = new SynchronizedBuffer();
16
17        System.out.printf("%-40s%s\t\t%s%n%-40s%s%n%n", "Operation",
18           "Buffer", "Occupied", "---------", "------\t\t--------");
19
20        // execute the Producer and Consumer tasks
21        executorService.execute(new Producer(sharedLocation));
22        executorService.execute(new Consumer(sharedLocation));
23
24        executorService.shutdown();
25        executorService.awaitTermination(1, TimeUnit.MINUTES);
26     }
27  } // end class SharedBufferTest2
```

Operation	Buffer	Occupied
Producer writes 1	1	true
Producer tries to write. Buffer full. Producer waits.	1	true
Consumer reads 1	1	false
Producer writes 2	2	true
Producer tries to write. Buffer full. Producer waits.	2	true
Consumer reads 2	2	false
Producer writes 3	3	true
Consumer reads 3	3	false
Producer writes 4	4	true
Consumer reads 4	4	false
Consumer tries to read. Buffer empty. Consumer waits.	4	false

Fig. 20.21 | Two threads manipulating a synchronized buffer. (Part 2 of 3.)

Producer writes 5	5	true
Consumer reads 5	5	false
Consumer tries to read. Buffer empty. Consumer waits.	5	false
Producer writes 6	6	true
Consumer reads 6	6	false
Producer writes 7	7	true
Consumer reads 7	7	false
Producer writes 8	8	true
Consumer reads 8	8	false
Producer writes 9	9	true
Consumer reads 9	9	false
Producer writes 10	10	true
Producer done producing Terminating Producer Consumer reads 10	10	false
Consumer read values totaling 55 Terminating Consumer		

Fig. 20.21 | Two threads manipulating a synchronized buffer. (Part 3 of 3.)

20.10 Concurrent Collections

In Chapter 16, we introduced various collections from the Java Collections API. We also mentioned that you can obtain *synchronized* versions of those collections to allow only one thread at a time to access a collection that might be shared among several threads. The collections from the java.util.concurrent package are specifically designed and optimized for sharing collections among multiple threads.

Figure 20.22 lists the many concurrent collections in package java.util.concurrent. The entries for ConcurrentHashMap and LinkedBlockingQueue are shown in bold because these are by far the most frequently used concurrent collections. Like the collections introduced in Chapter 16, the concurrent collections have been enhanced to support lambdas. However, rather than providing methods to support streams, the concurrent collections provide their own implementations of various stream-like operations—e.g., ConcurrentHashMap has methods forEach, reduce and search—that are designed and optimized for concurrent collections that are shared among threads. For more information on the concurrent collections, visit

Java SE 7:
http://docs.oracle.com/javase/7/docs/api/java/util/concurrent/
    package-summary.html

Java SE 8
http://download.java.net/jdk8/docs/api/java/util/concurrent/
    package-summary.html

Collection	Description
ArrayBlockingQueue	A fixed-size queue that supports the producer/consumer relationship—possibly with many producers and consumers.
ConcurrentHashMap	**A hash-based map (similar to the HashMap introduced in Chapter 16) that allows an arbitrary number of reader threads and a limited number of writer threads. This and the LinkedBlockingQueue are by far the most frequently used concurrent collections.**
ConcurrentLinkedDeque	A concurrent linked-list implementation of a double-ended queue.
ConcurrentLinkedQueue	A concurrent linked-list implementation of a queue that can grow dynamically.
ConcurrentSkipListMap	A concurrent map that is sorted by its keys.
ConcurrentSkipListSet	A sorted concurrent set.
CopyOnWriteArrayList	A thread-safe ArrayList. Each operation that modifies the collection first creates a new copy of the contents. Used when the collection is traversed much more frequently than the collection's contents are modified.
CopyOnWriteArraySet	A set that's implemented using CopyOnWriteArrayList.
DelayQueue	A variable-size queue containing Delayed objects. An object can be removed only after its delay has expired.
LinkedBlockingDeque	A double-ended blocking queue implemented as a linked list that can optionally be fixed in size.
LinkedBlockingQueue	**A blocking queue implemented as a linked list that can optionally be fixed in size. This and the ConcurrentHashMap are by far the most frequently used concurrent collections.**
LinkedTransferQueue	A linked-list implementation of interface TransferQueue. Each producer has the option of waiting for a consumer to take an element being inserted (via method transfer) or simply placing the element into the queue (via method put). Also provides overloaded method tryTransfer to immediately transfer an element to a waiting consumer or to do so within a specified timeout period. If the transfer cannot be completed, the element is not placed in the queue. Typically used in applications that pass messages between threads.
PriorityBlockingQueue	A variable-length priority-based blocking queue (like a PriorityQueue).
SynchronousQueue	[For experts.] A blocking queue implementation that does not have an internal capacity. Each insert operation by one thread must wait for a remove operation from another thread and vice versa.

Fig. 20.22 | Concurrent collections summary (package java.util.concurrent).

20.11 Multithreading with GUI: SwingWorker

Swing applications present a unique set of challenges for multithreaded programming. All Swing applications have a single thread, called the **event dispatch thread**, to handle interactions with the application's GUI components. Typical interactions include *updating GUI components* or *processing user actions* such as mouse clicks. All tasks that require interaction with an application's GUI are placed in an *event queue* and are executed sequentially by the event dispatch thread.

Swing GUI components are not thread safe—they cannot be manipulated by multiple threads without the risk of incorrect results that might corrupt the GUI. Unlike the other examples presented in this chapter, thread safety in GUI applications is achieved not by synchronizing thread actions, but by *ensuring that Swing components are accessed from only the event dispatch thread.* This technique is called **thread confinement**. Allowing just one thread to access non-thread-safe objects eliminates the possibility of corruption due to multiple threads accessing these objects concurrently.

It's acceptable to perform brief calculations on the event dispatch thread in sequence with GUI component manipulations. If an application must perform a lengthy computation in response to a user interaction, the event dispatch thread cannot attend to other tasks in the event queue while the thread is tied up in that computation. This causes the GUI components to become unresponsive. It's preferable to handle a long-running computation in a separate thread, freeing the event dispatch thread to continue managing other GUI interactions. Of course, you must update the GUI with the computation's results from the event dispatch thread, rather than from the worker thread that performed the computation.

Class SwingWorker

Class **SwingWorker** (in package java.swing) enables you to perform an asynchronous task in a worker thread (such as a long-running computation) then update Swing components from the event dispatch thread based on the task's results. SwingWorker implements the Runnable interface, meaning that *a SwingWorker object can be scheduled to execute in a separate thread.* The SwingWorker class provides several methods to simplify performing a task in a worker thread and making its results available for display in a GUI. Some common SwingWorker methods are described in Fig. 20.23.

Method	Description
doInBackground	Defines a long computation and is called in a worker thread.
done	Executes on the event dispatch thread when doInBackground returns.
execute	Schedules the SwingWorker object to be executed in a worker thread.
get	Waits for the computation to complete, then returns the result of the computation (i.e., the return value of doInBackground).
publish	Sends intermediate results from the doInBackground method to the process method for processing on the event dispatch thread.

Fig. 20.23 | Commonly used SwingWorker methods. (Part 1 of 2.)

Method	Description
process	Receives intermediate results from the publish method and processes these results on the event dispatch thread.
setProgress	Sets the progress property to notify any property change listeners on the event dispatch thread of progress bar updates.

Fig. 20.23 | Commonly used SwingWorker methods. (Part 2 of 2.)

20.11.1 Performing Computations in a Worker Thread: Fibonacci Numbers

In the next example, the user enters a number *n* and the program gets the *n*th Fibonacci number, which we calculate using a recursive algorithm, which is time consuming for large values. For this reason, we use a SwingWorker object to perform the calculation in a worker thread. The GUI also provides a separate set of components that get the next Fibonacci number in the sequence with each click of a button, beginning with fibonacci(1). This set of components performs its short computation directly in the event dispatch thread. This program is capable of producing up to the 92nd Fibonacci number—subsequent values are outside the range that can be represented by a long. Recall that you can use class BigInteger to represent arbitrarily large integer values.

Class BackgroundCalculator (Fig. 20.24) performs the recursive Fibonacci calculation in a *worker thread*. This class extends SwingWorker (line 8), overriding the methods doInBackground and done. Method doInBackground (lines 21–24) computes the *n*th Fibonacci number in a worker thread and returns the result. Method done (lines 27–43) displays the result in a JLabel.

```
 1   // Fig. 20.24: BackgroundCalculator.java
 2   // SwingWorker subclass for calculating Fibonacci numbers
 3   // in a background thread.
 4   import javax.swing.SwingWorker;
 5   import javax.swing.JLabel;
 6   import java.util.concurrent.ExecutionException;
 7
 8   public class BackgroundCalculator extends SwingWorker<Long, Object>
 9   {
10      private final int n; // Fibonacci number to calculate
11      private final JLabel resultJLabel; // JLabel to display the result
12
13      // constructor
14      public BackgroundCalculator(int n, JLabel resultJLabel)
15      {
16         this.n = n;
17         this.resultJLabel = resultJLabel;
18      }
```

Fig. 20.24 | SwingWorker subclass for calculating Fibonacci numbers in a background thread. (Part 1 of 2.)

```
19
20        // long-running code to be run in a worker thread
21        public Long doInBackground()
22        {
23            return nthFib = fibonacci(n);
24        }
25
26        // code to run on the event dispatch thread when doInBackground returns
27        protected void done()
28        {
29            try
30            {
31                // get the result of doInBackground and display it
32                resultJLabel.setText(get().toString());
33            }
34            catch (InterruptedException ex)
35            {
36                resultJLabel.setText("Interrupted while waiting for results.");
37            }
38            catch (ExecutionException ex)
39            {
40                resultJLabel.setText(
41                    "Error encountered while performing calculation.");
42            }
43        }
44
45        // recursive method fibonacci; calculates nth Fibonacci number
46        public long fibonacci(long number)
47        {
48            if (number == 0 || number == 1)
49                return number;
50            else
51                return fibonacci(number - 1) + fibonacci(number - 2);
52        }
53   } // end class BackgroundCalculator
```

Fig. 20.24 | SwingWorker subclass for calculating Fibonacci numbers in a background thread.
(Part 2 of 2.)

SwingWorker is a *generic class*. In line 8, the first type parameter is Long and the second
is Object. The first type parameter indicates the type returned by the doInBackground
method; the second indicates the type that's passed between the publish and process
methods to handle intermediate results. Since we do not use publish and process in this
example, we simply use Object as the second type parameter. We discuss publish and
process in Section 20.11.2.

A BackgroundCalculator object can be instantiated from a class that controls a GUI.
A BackgroundCalculator maintains instance variables for an integer that represents the
Fibonacci number to be calculated and a JLabel that displays the results of the calculation
(lines 10–11). The BackgroundCalculator constructor (lines 14–18) initializes these
instance variables with the arguments that are passed to the constructor.

Software Engineering Observation 20.8

Any GUI components that will be manipulated by SwingWorker methods, such as components that will be updated from methods process or done, should be passed to the SwingWorker subclass's constructor and stored in the subclass object. This gives these methods access to the GUI components they'll manipulate.

When method execute is called on a BackgroundCalculator object, the object is scheduled for execution in a worker thread. Method doInBackground is called from the worker thread and invokes the fibonacci method (lines 46–52), passing instance variable n as an argument (line 23). Method fibonacci uses recursion to compute the Fibonacci of n. When fibonacci returns, method doInBackground returns the result.

After doInBackground returns, method done is called from the event dispatch thread. This method attempts to set the result JLabel to the return value of doInBackground by calling method get to retrieve this return value (line 32). Method get *waits* for the result to be ready if necessary, but since we call it from method done, the computation will be complete *before* get is called. Lines 34–37 catch InterruptedException if the current thread is interrupted while waiting for get to return. This exception will not occur in this example since the calculation will have already completed by the time get is called. Lines 38–42 catch ExecutionException, which is thrown if an exception occurs during the computation.

Class FibonacciNumbers

Class FibonacciNumbers (Fig. 20.25) displays a window containing two sets of GUI components—one set to compute a Fibonacci number in a worker thread and another to get the next Fibonacci number in response to the user's clicking a JButton. The constructor (lines 38–109) places these components in separate titled JPanels. Lines 46–47 and 78–79 add two JLabels, a JTextField and a JButton to the workerJPanel to allow the user to enter an integer whose Fibonacci number will be calculated by the BackgroundWorker. Lines 84–85 and 103 add two JLabels and a JButton to the eventThreadJPanel to allow the user to get the next Fibonacci number in the sequence. Instance variables n1 and n2 contain the previous two Fibonacci numbers in the sequence and are initialized to 0 and 1, respectively (lines 29–30). Instance variable count stores the most recently computed sequence number and is initialized to 1 (line 31). The two JLabels display count and n2 initially, so that the user will see the text Fibonacci of 1: 1 in the eventThreadJPanel when the GUI starts.

```
1   // Fig. 20.25: FibonacciNumbers.java
2   // Using SwingWorker to perform a long calculation with
3   // results displayed in a GUI.
4   import java.awt.GridLayout;
5   import java.awt.event.ActionEvent;
6   import java.awt.event.ActionListener;
7   import javax.swing.JButton;
8   import javax.swing.JFrame;
9   import javax.swing.JPanel;
10  import javax.swing.JLabel;
```

Fig. 20.25 | Using SwingWorker to perform a long calculation with results displayed in a GUI. (Part 1 of 4.)

```java
11   import javax.swing.JTextField;
12   import javax.swing.border.TitledBorder;
13   import javax.swing.border.LineBorder;
14   import java.awt.Color;
15   import java.util.concurrent.ExecutionException;
16
17   public class FibonacciNumbers extends JFrame
18   {
19      // components for calculating the Fibonacci of a user-entered number
20      private final JPanel workerJPanel =
21         new JPanel(new GridLayout(2, 2, 5, 5));
22      private final JTextField numberJTextField = new JTextField();
23      private final JButton goJButton = new JButton("Go");
24      private final JLabel fibonacciJLabel = new JLabel();
25
26      // components and variables for getting the next Fibonacci number
27      private final JPanel eventThreadJPanel =
28         new JPanel(new GridLayout(2, 2, 5, 5));
29      private long n1 = 0; // initialize with first Fibonacci number
30      private long n2 = 1; // initialize with second Fibonacci number
31      private int count = 1; // current Fibonacci number to display
32      private final JLabel nJLabel = new JLabel("Fibonacci of 1: ");
33      private final JLabel nFibonacciJLabel =
34         new JLabel(String.valueOf(n2));
35      private final JButton nextNumberJButton = new JButton("Next Number");
36
37      // constructor
38      public FibonacciNumbers()
39      {
40         super("Fibonacci Numbers");
41         setLayout(new GridLayout(2, 1, 10, 10));
42
43         // add GUI components to the SwingWorker panel
44         workerJPanel.setBorder(new TitledBorder(
45            new LineBorder(Color.BLACK), "With SwingWorker"));
46         workerJPanel.add(new JLabel("Get Fibonacci of:"));
47         workerJPanel.add(numberJTextField);
48         goJButton.addActionListener(
49            new ActionListener()
50            {
51               public void actionPerformed(ActionEvent event)
52               {
53                  int n;
54
55                  try
56                  {
57                     // retrieve user's input as an integer
58                     n = Integer.parseInt(numberJTextField.getText());
59                  }
```

Fig. 20.25 | Using `SwingWorker` to perform a long calculation with results displayed in a GUI. (Part 2 of 4.)

```
60                      catch(NumberFormatException ex)
61                      {
62                          // display an error message if the user did not
63                          // enter an integer
64                          fibonacciJLabel.setText("Enter an integer.");
65                          return;
66                      }
67
68                      // indicate that the calculation has begun
69                      fibonacciJLabel.setText("Calculating...");
70
71                      // create a task to perform calculation in background
72                      BackgroundCalculator task =
73                          new BackgroundCalculator(n, fibonacciJLabel);
74                      task.execute(); // execute the task
75                  }
76          } // end anonymous inner class
77      ); // end call to addActionListener
78      workerJPanel.add(goJButton);
79      workerJPanel.add(fibonacciJLabel);
80
81      // add GUI components to the event-dispatching thread panel
82      eventThreadJPanel.setBorder(new TitledBorder(
83          new LineBorder(Color.BLACK), "Without SwingWorker"));
84      eventThreadJPanel.add(nJLabel);
85      eventThreadJPanel.add(nFibonacciJLabel);
86      nextNumberJButton.addActionListener(
87          new ActionListener()
88          {
89              public void actionPerformed(ActionEvent event)
90              {
91                  // calculate the Fibonacci number after n2
92                  long temp = n1 + n2;
93                  n1 = n2;
94                  n2 = temp;
95                  ++count;
96
97                  // display the next Fibonacci number
98                  nJLabel.setText("Fibonacci of " + count + ": ");
99                  nFibonacciJLabel.setText(String.valueOf(n2));
100             }
101         } // end anonymous inner class
102     ); // end call to addActionListener
103     eventThreadJPanel.add(nextNumberJButton);
104
105     add(workerJPanel);
106     add(eventThreadJPanel);
107     setSize(275, 200);
108     setVisible(true);
109 } // end constructor
```

Fig. 20.25 | Using SwingWorker to perform a long calculation with results displayed in a GUI. (Part 3 of 4.)

```
110
111     // main method begins program execution
112     public static void main(String[] args)
113     {
114         FibonacciNumbers application = new FibonacciNumbers();
115         application.setDefaultCloseOperation(EXIT_ON_CLOSE);
116     }
117  } // end class FibonacciNumbers
```

a) Begin calculating Fibonacci of 40 in the background

b) Calculating other Fibonacci values while Fibonacci of 40 continues calculating

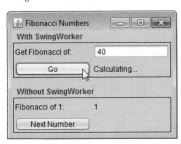

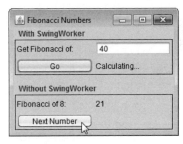

c) Fibonacci of 40 calculation finishes

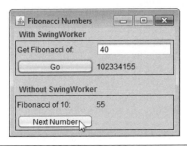

Fig. 20.25 | Using SwingWorker to perform a long calculation with results displayed in a GUI. (Part 4 of 4.)

Lines 48–77 register the event handler for the goJButton. If the user clicks this JButton, line 58 gets the value entered in the numberJTextField and attempts to parse it as an integer. Lines 72–73 create a new BackgroundCalculator object, passing in the user-entered value and the fibonacciJLabel that's used to display the calculation's results. Line 74 calls method execute on the BackgroundCalculator, scheduling it for execution in a separate worker thread. Method execute does not wait for the BackgroundCalculator to finish executing. It returns immediately, allowing the GUI to continue processing other events while the computation is performed.

If the user clicks the nextNumberJButton in the eventThreadJPanel, the event handler registered in lines 86–102 executes. Lines 92–95 add the previous two Fibonacci numbers stored in n1 and n2 to determine the next number in the sequence, update n1 and n2 to their new values and increment count. Then lines 98–99 update the GUI to display the next number. The code for these calculations is in method actionPerformed, so they're performed on the *event dispatch thread*. Handling such short computations in the event dispatch thread does not cause the GUI to become unresponsive, as with the recursive algorithm for calculating the Fibonacci of a large number. Because the longer Fibonacci computation is performed in a separate worker thread using the SwingWorker, it's possible to get the next Fibonacci number while the recursive computation is still in progress.

20.11.2 Processing Intermediate Results: Sieve of Eratosthenes

We've presented an example that uses the SwingWorker class to execute a long process in a *background thread* and update the GUI when the process is finished. We now present an example of updating the GUI with intermediate results before the long process completes. Figure 20.26 presents class PrimeCalculator, which extends SwingWorker to compute the first *n* prime numbers in a *worker thread*. In addition to the doInBackground and done methods used in the previous example, this class uses SwingWorker methods publish, process and setProgress. In this example, method publish sends prime numbers to method process as they're found, method process displays these primes in a GUI component and method setProgress updates the progress property. We later show how to use this property to update a JProgressBar.

```java
 1   // Fig. 20.26: PrimeCalculator.java
 2   // Calculates the first n primes, displaying them as they are found.
 3   import javax.swing.JTextArea;
 4   import javax.swing.JLabel;
 5   import javax.swing.JButton;
 6   import javax.swing.SwingWorker;
 7   import java.security.SecureRandom;
 8   import java.util.Arrays;
 9   import java.util.List;
10   import java.util.concurrent.CancellationException;
11   import java.util.concurrent.ExecutionException;
12
13   public class PrimeCalculator extends SwingWorker<Integer, Integer>
14   {
15      private static final SecureRandom generator = new SecureRandom();
16      private final JTextArea intermediateJTextArea; // displays found primes
17      private final JButton getPrimesJButton;
18      private final JButton cancelJButton;
19      private final JLabel statusJLabel; // displays status of calculation
20      private final boolean[] primes; // boolean array for finding primes
21
22      // constructor
23      public PrimeCalculator(int max, JTextArea intermediateJTextArea,
24         JLabel statusJLabel, JButton getPrimesJButton,
25         JButton cancelJButton)
26      {
27         this.intermediateJTextArea = intermediateJTextArea;
28         this.statusJLabel = statusJLabel;
29         this.getPrimesJButton = getPrimesJButton;
30         this.cancelJButton = cancelJButton;
31         primes = new boolean[max];
32
```

Fig. 20.26 | Calculates the first *n* primes, displaying them as they are found. (Part 1 of 3.)

```
33          Arrays.fill(primes, true); // initialize all primes elements to true
34       }
35
36       // finds all primes up to max using the Sieve of Eratosthenes
37       public Integer doInBackground()
38       {
39          int count = 0; // the number of primes found
40
41          // starting at the third value, cycle through the array and put
42          // false as the value of any greater number that is a multiple
43          for (int i = 2; i < primes.length; i++)
44          {
45             if (isCancelled()) // if calculation has been canceled
46                return count;
47             else
48             {
49                setProgress(100 * (i + 1) / primes.length);
50
51                try
52                {
53                   Thread.sleep(generator.nextInt(5));
54                }
55                catch (InterruptedException ex)
56                {
57                   statusJLabel.setText("Worker thread interrupted");
58                   return count;
59                }
60
61                if (primes[i]) // i is prime
62                {
63                   publish(i); // make i available for display in prime list
64                   ++count;
65
66                   for (int j = i + i; j < primes.length; j += i)
67                      primes[j] = false; // i is not prime
68                }
69             }
70          }
71
72          return count;
73       }
74
75       // displays published values in primes list
76       protected void process(List<Integer> publishedVals)
77       {
78          for (int i = 0; i < publishedVals.size(); i++)
79             intermediateJTextArea.append(publishedVals.get(i) + "\n");
80       }
81
82       // code to execute when doInBackground completes
83       protected void done()
84       {
85          getPrimesJButton.setEnabled(true); // enable Get Primes button
```

Fig. 20.26 | Calculates the first *n* primes, displaying them as they are found. (Part 2 of 3.)

```
86            cancelJButton.setEnabled(false); // disable Cancel button
87
88         try
89         {
90            // retrieve and display doInBackground return value
91            statusJLabel.setText("Found " + get() + " primes.");
92         }
93         catch (InterruptedException | ExecutionException |
94            CancellationException ex)
95         {
96            statusJLabel.setText(ex.getMessage());
97         }
98      }
99   } // end class PrimeCalculator
```

Fig. 20.26 | Calculates the first *n* primes, displaying them as they are found. (Part 3 of 3.)

Class `PrimeCalculator` extends `SwingWorker` (line 13), with the first type parameter indicating the return type of method `doInBackground` and the second indicating the type of intermediate results passed between methods `publish` and `process`. In this case, both type parameters are `Integers`. The constructor (lines 23–34) takes as arguments an integer that indicates the upper limit of the prime numbers to locate, a `JTextArea` used to display primes in the GUI, one `JButton` for initiating a calculation and one for canceling it, and a `JLabel` used to display the status of the calculation.

Sieve of Eratosthenes

Line 33 initializes the elements of the `boolean` array `primes` to `true` with `Arrays` method `fill`. `PrimeCalculator` uses this array and the **Sieve of Eratosthenes** algorithm to find all primes less than `max`. The Sieve of Eratosthenes takes a list of integers and, beginning with the first prime number, filters out all multiples of that prime. It then moves to the next prime, which will be the next number that's not yet filtered out, and eliminates all of its multiples. It continues until the end of the list is reached and all nonprimes have been filtered out. Algorithmically, we begin with element 2 of the `boolean` array and set the cells corresponding to all values that are multiples of 2 to `false` to indicate that they're divisible by 2 and thus not prime. We then move to the next array element, check whether it's `true`, and if so set all of its multiples to `false` to indicate that they're divisible by the current index. When the whole array has been traversed in this way, all indices that contain `true` are prime, as they have no divisors.

Method *doInBackground*

In method `doInBackground` (lines 37–73), the control variable `i` for the loop (lines 43–70) controls the current index for implementing the Sieve of Eratosthenes. Line 45 calls the inherited `SwingWorker` method **`isCancelled`** to determine whether the user has clicked the **Cancel** button. If `isCancelled` returns `true`, method `doInBackground` returns the number of primes found so far (line 46) without finishing the computation.

If the calculation isn't canceled, line 49 calls `setProgress` to update the percentage of the array that's been traversed so far. Line 53 puts the currently executing thread to sleep for up to 4 milliseconds. We discuss the reason for this shortly. Line 61 tests whether the element of array `primes` at the current index is `true` (and thus prime). If so, line 63 passes the index to method publish so that it can be displayed as an *intermediate result* in the GUI and line 64 increments the number of primes found. Lines 66–67 set all multiples of the current index to false to indicate that they're not prime. When the entire array has been traversed, line 72 returns the number of primes found.

Method *process*

Lines 76–80 declare method process, which executes in the event dispatch thread and receives its argument publishedVals from method publish. The passing of values between publish in the worker thread and process in the event dispatch thread is asynchronous; process might not be invoked for every call to publish. All Integers published since the last call to process are received as a List by method process. Lines 78–79 iterate through this list and display the published values in a JTextArea. Because the computation in method doInBackground progresses quickly, publishing values often, updates to the JTextArea can pile up on the event dispatch thread, causing the GUI to become sluggish. In fact, when searching for a large number of primes, the *event dispatch thread* may receive so many requests in quick succession to update the JTextArea that it *runs out of memory in its event queue*. This is why we put the worker thread to *sleep* for a few milliseconds between calls to publish. The calculation is slowed just enough to allow the event dispatch thread to keep up with requests to update the JTextArea with new primes, enabling the GUI to update smoothly and remain responsive.

Method *done*

Lines 83–98 define method done. When the calculation is finished or canceled, method done enables the **Get Primes** button and disables the **Cancel** button (lines 85–86). Line 91 gets and displays the return value—the number of primes found—from method doInBackground. Lines 93–97 catch the exceptions thrown by method get and display an appropriate message in the statusJLabel.

Class *FindPrimes*

Class FindPrimes (Fig. 20.27) displays a JTextField that allows the user to enter a number, a JButton to begin finding all primes less than that number and a JTextArea to display the primes. A JButton allows the user to cancel the calculation, and a JProgressBar shows the calculation's progress. The constructor (lines 32–125) sets up the GUI.

```
1   // Fig. 20.27: FindPrimes.java
2   // Using a SwingWorker to display prime numbers and update a JProgressBar
3   // while the prime numbers are being calculated.
4   import javax.swing.JFrame;
5   import javax.swing.JTextField;
6   import javax.swing.JTextArea;
7   import javax.swing.JButton;
8   import javax.swing.JProgressBar;
9   import javax.swing.JLabel;
10  import javax.swing.JPanel;
11  import javax.swing.JScrollPane;
12  import javax.swing.ScrollPaneConstants;
```

Fig. 20.27 | Using a SwingWorker to display prime numbers and update a JProgressBar while the prime numbers are being calculated. (Part 1 of 4.)

```
13   import java.awt.BorderLayout;
14   import java.awt.GridLayout;
15   import java.awt.event.ActionListener;
16   import java.awt.event.ActionEvent;
17   import java.util.concurrent.ExecutionException;
18   import java.beans.PropertyChangeListener;
19   import java.beans.PropertyChangeEvent;
20
21   public class FindPrimes extends JFrame
22   {
23      private final JTextField highestPrimeJTextField = new JTextField();
24      private final JButton getPrimesJButton = new JButton("Get Primes");
25      private final JTextArea displayPrimesJTextArea = new JTextArea();
26      private final JButton cancelJButton = new JButton("Cancel");
27      private final JProgressBar progressJProgressBar = new JProgressBar();
28      private final JLabel statusJLabel = new JLabel();
29      private PrimeCalculator calculator;
30
31      // constructor
32      public FindPrimes()
33      {
34         super("Finding Primes with SwingWorker");
35         setLayout(new BorderLayout());
36
37         // initialize panel to get a number from the user
38         JPanel northJPanel = new JPanel();
39         northJPanel.add(new JLabel("Find primes less than: "));
40         highestPrimeJTextField.setColumns(5);
41         northJPanel.add(highestPrimeJTextField);
42         getPrimesJButton.addActionListener(
43            new ActionListener()
44            {
45               public void actionPerformed(ActionEvent e)
46               {
47                  progressJProgressBar.setValue(0); // reset JProgressBar
48                  displayPrimesJTextArea.setText(""); // clear JTextArea
49                  statusJLabel.setText(""); // clear JLabel
50
51                  int number; // search for primes up through this value
52
53                  try
54                  {
55                     // get user input
56                     number = Integer.parseInt(
57                        highestPrimeJTextField.getText());
58                  }
59                  catch (NumberFormatException ex)
60                  {
61                     statusJLabel.setText("Enter an integer.");
62                     return;
63                  }
64
```

Fig. 20.27 | Using a SwingWorker to display prime numbers and update a JProgressBar while the prime numbers are being calculated. (Part 2 of 4.)

```
65                    // construct a new PrimeCalculator object
66                    calculator = new PrimeCalculator(number,
67                        displayPrimesJTextArea, statusJLabel, getPrimesJButton,
68                        cancelJButton);
69
70                    // listen for progress bar property changes
71                    calculator.addPropertyChangeListener(
72                        new PropertyChangeListener()
73                        {
74                            public void propertyChange(PropertyChangeEvent e)
75                            {
76                                // if the changed property is progress,
77                                // update the progress bar
78                                if (e.getPropertyName().equals("progress"))
79                                {
80                                    int newValue = (Integer) e.getNewValue();
81                                    progressJProgressBar.setValue(newValue);
82                                }
83                            }
84                        } // end anonymous inner class
85                    ); // end call to addPropertyChangeListener
86
87                    // disable Get Primes button and enable Cancel button
88                    getPrimesJButton.setEnabled(false);
89                    cancelJButton.setEnabled(true);
90
91                    calculator.execute(); // execute the PrimeCalculator object
92                }
93            } // end anonymous inner class
94        ); // end call to addActionListener
95        northJPanel.add(getPrimesJButton);
96
97        // add a scrollable JList to display results of calculation
98        displayPrimesJTextArea.setEditable(false);
99        add(new JScrollPane(displayPrimesJTextArea,
100           ScrollPaneConstants.VERTICAL_SCROLLBAR_ALWAYS,
101           ScrollPaneConstants.HORIZONTAL_SCROLLBAR_NEVER));
102
103       // initialize a panel to display cancelJButton,
104       // progressJProgressBar, and statusJLabel
105       JPanel southJPanel = new JPanel(new GridLayout(1, 3, 10, 10));
106       cancelJButton.setEnabled(false);
107       cancelJButton.addActionListener(
108           new ActionListener()
109           {
110               public void actionPerformed(ActionEvent e)
111               {
112                   calculator.cancel(true); // cancel the calculation
113               }
114           } // end anonymous inner class
115       ); // end call to addActionListener
```

Fig. 20.27 | Using a SwingWorker to display prime numbers and update a JProgressBar while the prime numbers are being calculated. (Part 3 of 4.)

```
116            southJPanel.add(cancelJButton);
117            progressJProgressBar.setStringPainted(true);
118            southJPanel.add(progressJProgressBar);
119            southJPanel.add(statusJLabel);
120
121            add(northJPanel, BorderLayout.NORTH);
122            add(southJPanel, BorderLayout.SOUTH);
123            setSize(350, 300);
124            setVisible(true);
125        } // end constructor
126
127        // main method begins program execution
128        public static void main(String[] args)
129        {
130            FindPrimes application = new FindPrimes();
131            application.setDefaultCloseOperation(EXIT_ON_CLOSE);
132        } // end main
133   } // end class FindPrimes
```

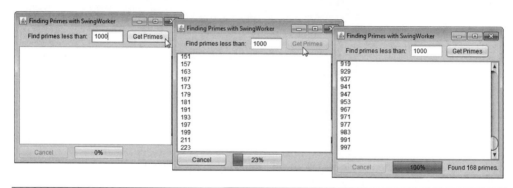

Fig. 20.27 | Using a SwingWorker to display prime numbers and update a JProgressBar while the prime numbers are being calculated. (Part 4 of 4.)

Lines 42–94 register the event handler for the getPrimesJButton. When the user clicks this JButton, lines 47–49 reset the JProgressBar and clear the displayPrimes-JTextArea and the statusJLabel. Lines 53–63 parse the value in the JTextField and display an error message if the value is not an integer. Lines 66–68 construct a new PrimeCalculator object, passing as arguments the integer the user entered, the display-PrimesJTextArea for displaying the primes, the statusJLabel and the two JButtons.

Lines 71–85 register a PropertyChangeListener for the PrimeCalculator object. **PropertyChangeListener** is an interface from package java.beans that defines a single method, propertyChange. Every time method setProgress is invoked on a PrimeCalculator, the PrimeCalculator generates a PropertyChangeEvent to indicate that the progress property has changed. Method propertyChange listens for these events. Line 78 tests whether a given PropertyChangeEvent indicates a change to the progress property. If so, line 80 gets the new value of the property and line 81 updates the JProgressBar with the new progress property value.

The **Get Primes** JButton is disabled (line 88) so only one calculation that updates the GUI can execute at a time, and the **Cancel** JButton is enabled (line 89) to allow the user to stop the computation before it completes. Line 91 executes the PrimeCalculator to begin finding primes. If the user clicks the cancelJButton, the event handler registered at lines 107–115 calls PrimeCalculator's method **cancel** (line 112), which is inherited from class SwingWorker, and the calculation returns early. The argument true to method cancel indicates that the thread performing the task should be interrupted in an attempt to cancel the task.

20.12 sort/parallelSort Timings with the Java SE 8 Date/Time API

In Section 7.15, we used class Arrays's static method sort to sort an array and we introduced static method parallelSort for sorting large arrays more efficiently on multi-core systems. Figure 20.28 uses both methods to sort 15,000,000 element arrays of random int values so that we can demonstrate parallelSort's performance improvement of over sort on a multi-core system (we ran this on a dual-core system).

```
1   // SortComparison.java
2   // Comparing performance of Arrays methods sort and parallelSort.
3   import java.time.Duration;
4   import java.time.Instant;
5   import java.text.NumberFormat;
6   import java.util.Arrays;
7   import java.security.SecureRandom;
8
9   public class SortComparison
10  {
11     public static void main(String[] args)
12     {
13        SecureRandom random = new SecureRandom();
14
15        // create array of random ints, then copy it
16        int[] array1 = random.ints(15_000_000).toArray();
17        int[] array2 = new int[array1.length];
18        System.arraycopy(array1, 0, array2, 0, array1.length);
19
20        // time the sorting of array1 with Arrays method sort
21        System.out.println("Starting sort");
22        Instant sortStart = Instant.now();
23        Arrays.sort(array1);
24        Instant sortEnd = Instant.now();
25
26        // display timing results
27        long sortTime = Duration.between(sortStart, sortEnd).toMillis();
28        System.out.printf("Total time in milliseconds: %d%n%n", sortTime);
29
30        // time the sorting of array2 with Arrays method parallelSort
31        System.out.println("Starting parallelSort");
32        Instant parallelSortStart = Instant.now();
```

Fig. 20.28 | Comparing performance of Arrays methods sort and parallelSort. (Part 1 of 2.)

```
33          Arrays.parallelSort(array2);
34          Instant parallelSortEnd = Instant.now();
35
36          // display timing results
37          long parallelSortTime =
38              Duration.between(parallelSortStart, parallelSortEnd).toMillis();
39          System.out.printf("Total time in milliseconds: %d%n%n",
40              parallelSortTime);
41
42          // display time difference as a percentage
43          String percentage = NumberFormat.getPercentInstance().format(
44              (double) sortTime / parallelSortTime);
45          System.out.printf("%nsort took %s more time than parallelSort%n",
46              percentage);
47      }
48  } // end class SortComparison
```

```
Starting sort
Total time in milliseconds: 1319

Starting parallelSort
Total time in milliseconds: 323

sort took 408% more time than parallelSort
```

Fig. 20.28 | Comparing performance of Arrays methods sort and parallelSort. (Part 2 of 2.)

Creating the Arrays
Line 16 uses SecureRandom method ints to create an IntStream of 15,000,000 random int values, then calls IntStream method toArray to place the values into an array. Lines 17 and 18 copy the array so that the calls to both sort and parallelSort work with the same set of values.

*Timing **Arrays** Method **sort** with Date/Time API Classes **Instant** and **Duration***
Lines 22 and 24 each call class Instant's static method **now** to get the current time before and after the call to sort. To determine the difference between two Instants, line 27 uses class Duration's static method **between**, which returns a Duration object containing the time difference. Next, we call Duration method **toMillis** to get the difference in milliseconds.

*Timing **Arrays** Method **parallelSort** with Date/Time API Classes **Instant** and **Duration***
Lines 32–34 time the call to Arrays method parallelSort. Then, lines 37–38 calculate the difference between the Instants.

Displaying the Percentage Difference Between the Sorting Times
Lines 43–44 use a NumberFormat (package java.text) to format the ratio of the sort times as a percentage. NumberFormat static method **getPercentInstance** returns a Number-Format that's used to format a number as a percentage. NumberFormat method format performs the formatting. As you can see in the sample output, the sort method took over *400% more time* to sort the 15,000,000 random int values.

Other Parallel Array Operations

In addition to method parallelSort, class Arrays now contains methods parallelSetAll and parallelPrefix, which perform the following tasks:

- **parallelSetAll**—Fills an array with values produced by a generator function that receives an int and returns a value of type int, long or double. Depending on which overload of method parallelSetAll is used, the generator function is an object of a class that implements IntToDoubleFunction (for double arrays), IntUnaryOperator (for int arrays), IntToLongFunction (for long arrays) or IntFunction (for arrays of any non-primitive type).

- **parallelPrefix**—Applies a BinaryOperator to the current and previous array elements and stores the result in the current element. For example, consider:

```
int[] values = {1, 2, 3, 4, 5};
Arrays.parallelPrefix(values, (x, y) -> x + y);
```

This call to parallelPrefix uses a BinaryOperator that *adds* two values. After the call completes, the array contains 1, 3, 6, 10 and 15. Similarly, the following call to parallelPrefix, uses a BinaryOperator that *multiplies* two values. After the call completes, the array contains 1, 2, 6, 24 and 120:

```
int[] values = {1, 2, 3, 4, 5};
Arrays.parallelPrefix(values, (x, y) -> x * y);
```

20.13 Java SE 8: Sequential vs. Parallel Streams

In Chapter 17, you learned about Java SE 8 lambdas and streams. We mentioned that streams are easy to *parallelize*, enabling programs to benefit from enhanced performance on multi-core systems. Using the timing capabilities introduced in Section 20.12, Fig. 20.29 demonstrates both *sequential* and *parallel* stream operations on a 10,000,000-element array of random long values (created at line 17) to compare the performance.

```
1   // StreamStatisticsComparison.java
2   // Comparing performance of sequential and parallel stream operations.
3   import java.time.Duration;
4   import java.time.Instant;
5   import java.util.Arrays;
6   import java.util.LongSummaryStatistics;
7   import java.util.stream.LongStream;
8   import java.security.SecureRandom;
9
10  public class StreamStatisticsComparison
11  {
12     public static void main(String[] args)
13     {
14        SecureRandom random = new SecureRandom();
15
16        // create array of random long values
17        long[] values = random.longs(10_000_000, 1, 1001).toArray();
```

Fig. 20.29 | Comparing performance of sequential and parallel stream operations. (Part 1 of 3.)

```
18
19       // perform calculcations separately
20       Instant separateStart = Instant.now();
21       long count = Arrays.stream(values).count();
22       long sum = Arrays.stream(values).sum();
23       long min = Arrays.stream(values).min().getAsLong();
24       long max = Arrays.stream(values).max().getAsLong();
25       double average = Arrays.stream(values).average().getAsDouble();
26       Instant separateEnd = Instant.now();
27
28       // display results
29       System.out.println("Calculations performed separately");
30       System.out.printf("    count: %,d%n", count);
31       System.out.printf("      sum: %,d%n", sum);
32       System.out.printf("      min: %,d%n", min);
33       System.out.printf("      max: %,d%n", max);
34       System.out.printf("  average: %f%n", average);
35       System.out.printf("Total time in milliseconds: %d%n%n",
36          Duration.between(separateStart, separateEnd).toMillis());
37
38       // time sum operation with sequential stream
39       LongStream stream1 = Arrays.stream(values);
40       System.out.println("Calculating statistics on sequential stream");
41       Instant sequentialStart = Instant.now();
42       LongSummaryStatistics results1 = stream1.summaryStatistics();
43       Instant sequentialEnd = Instant.now();
44
45       // display results
46       displayStatistics(results1);
47       System.out.printf("Total time in milliseconds: %d%n%n",
48          Duration.between(sequentialStart, sequentialEnd).toMillis());
49
50       // time sum operation with parallel stream
51       LongStream stream2 = Arrays.stream(values).parallel();
52       System.out.println("Calculating statistics on parallel stream");
53       Instant parallelStart = Instant.now();
54       LongSummaryStatistics results2 = stream2.summaryStatistics();
55       Instant parallelEnd = Instant.now();
56
57       // display results
58       displayStatistics(results1);
59       System.out.printf("Total time in milliseconds: %d%n%n",
60          Duration.between(parallelStart, parallelEnd).toMillis());
61    }
62
63    // display's LongSummaryStatistics values
64    private static void displayStatistics(LongSummaryStatistics stats)
65    {
66       System.out.println("Statistics");
67       System.out.printf("    count: %,d%n", stats.getCount());
68       System.out.printf("      sum: %,d%n", stats.getSum());
69       System.out.printf("      min: %,d%n", stats.getMin());
70       System.out.printf("      max: %,d%n", stats.getMax());
```

Fig. 20.29 | Comparing performance of sequential and parallel stream operations. (Part 2 of 3.)

```
71          System.out.printf("   average: %f%n", stats.getAverage());
72      }
73  } // end class StreamStatisticsComparison
```

```
Calculations performed separately
    count: 10,000,000
      sum: 5,003,695,285
      min: 1
      max: 1,000
  average: 500.369529
Total time in milliseconds: 173

Calculating statistics on sequential stream
Statistics
    count: 10,000,000
      sum: 5,003,695,285
      min: 1
      max: 1,000
  average: 500.369529
Total time in milliseconds: 69

Calculating statistics on parallel stream
Statistics
    count: 10,000,000
      sum: 5,003,695,285
      min: 1
      max: 1,000
  average: 500.369529
Total time in milliseconds: 38
```

Fig. 20.29 | Comparing performance of sequential and parallel stream operations. (Part 3 of 3.)

Performing Stream Operations with Separate Passes of a Sequential Stream
Section 17.3 demonstrated various numerical operations on IntStreams. Lines 20–26 perform and time the count, sum, min, max and average stream operations each performed individually on a LongStream returned by Arrays method stream. Lines 29–36 then display the results and the total time required to perform all five operations.

Performing Stream Operations with a Single Pass of a Sequential Stream
Lines 39–48 demonstrate the performance improvement you get by using LongStream method summaryStatistics to determine the count, sum, minimum value, maximum value and average in one pass of a *sequential* LongStream—all streams are sequential by default. This operation took approximately 40% of the time required to perform the five operations separately.

Performing Stream Operations with a Single Pass of a Parallel Stream
Lines 51–60 demonstrate the performance improvement you get by using LongStream method summaryStatistics on a *parallel* LongStream. To obtain a parallel stream that can take advantage of multi-core processors, simply invoke method parallel on an existing stream. As you can see from the sample output, performing the operations on a parallel stream decreased the total time required even further—taking approximately 55% of the

calculation time for the sequential LongStream and just 22% of the time required to perform the five operations separately.

20.14 (Advanced) Interfaces Callable and Future

Interface Runnable provides only the most basic functionality for multithreaded programming. In fact, this interface has limitations. Suppose a Runnable is performing a long calculation and the application wants to retrieve the result of that calculation. The run method cannot return a value, so *shared mutable data* would be required to pass the value back to the calling thread. As you now know, this would require thread synchronization. The **Callable** interface (of package java.util.concurrent) fixes this limitation. The interface declares a single method named **call** which returns a value representing the result of the Callable's task—such as the result of a long running calculation.

An application that creates a Callable likely wants to run it concurrently with other Runnables and Callables. ExecutorService method **submit** executes its Callable argument and returns an object of type **Future** (of package java.util.concurrent), which represents the Callable's future result. The Future interface **get** method *blocks* the calling thread, and waits for the Callable to complete and return its result. The interface also provides methods that enable you to cancel a Callable's execution, determine whether the Callable was cancelled and determine whether the Callable completed its task.

Executing Aysnchronous Tasks with CompletableFuture
Java SE 8 introduces class **CompletableFuture** (package java.util.concurrent), which implements the Future interface and enables you to *asynchronously* execute Runnables that perform tasks or Suppliers that return values. Interface **Supplier**, like interface Callable, is a functional interface with a single method (in this case, get) that receives no arguments and returns a result. Class CompletableFuture provides many additional capabilities that for advanced programmers, such as creating CompletableFutures without executing them immediately, composing one or more CompletableFutures so that you can wait for any or all of them to complete, executing code after a CompletableFuture completes and more.

Figure 20.30 performs two long-running calculations sequentially, then performs them again asynchronously using CompletableFutures to demonstrate the performance improvement from asynchronous execution on a multi-core system. For demonstration purposes, our long-running calculation is performed by a recursive fibonacci method (lines 73–79). For larger Fibonacci values, the recursive implementation can require *significant* computation time—in practice, it's much faster to calculate Fibonacci values using a loop.

```
1   // FibonacciDemo.java
2   // Fibonacci calculations performed synchronously and asynchronously
3   import java.time.Duration;
4   import java.text.NumberFormat;
5   import java.time.Instant;
6   import java.util.concurrent.CompletableFuture;
7   import java.util.concurrent.ExecutionException;
8
```

Fig. 20.30 | Fibonacci calculations performed synchronously and asynchronously. (Part 1 of 4.)

```
 9    // class that stores two Instants in time
10    class TimeData
11    {
12        public Instant start;
13        public Instant end;
14
15        // return total time in seconds
16        public double timeInSeconds()
17        {
18            return Duration.between(start, end).toMillis() / 1000.0;
19        }
20    } // end class TimeData
21
22    public class FibonacciDemo
23    {
24        public static void main(String[] args)
25            throws InterruptedException, ExecutionException
26        {
27            // perform synchronous fibonacci(45) and fibonacci(44) calculations
28            System.out.println("Synchronous Long Running Calculations");
29            TimeData synchronousResult1 = startFibonacci(45);
30            TimeData synchronousResult2 = startFibonacci(44);
31            double synchronousTime =
32                calculateTime(synchronousResult1, synchronousResult2);
33            System.out.printf(
34                "  Total calculation time = %.3f seconds%n", synchronousTime);
35
36            // perform asynchronous fibonacci(45) and fibonacci(44) calculations
37            System.out.printf("%nAsynchronous Long Running Calculations%n");
38            CompletableFuture<TimeData> futureResult1 =
39                CompletableFuture.supplyAsync(() -> startFibonacci(45));
40            CompletableFuture<TimeData> futureResult2 =
41                CompletableFuture.supplyAsync(() -> startFibonacci(44));
42
43            // wait for results from the asynchronous operations
44            TimeData asynchronousResult1 = futureResult1.get();
45            TimeData asynchronousResult2 = futureResult2.get();
46            double asynchronousTime =
47                calculateTime(asynchronousResult1, asynchronousResult2);
48            System.out.printf(
49                "  Total calculation time = %.3f seconds%n", asynchronousTime);
50
51            // display time difference as a percentage
52            String percentage = NumberFormat.getPercentInstance().format(
53                synchronousTime / asynchronousTime);
54            System.out.printf("%nSynchronous calculations took %s" +
55                " more time than the asynchronous calculations%n", percentage);
56        }
57
58        // executes function fibonacci asynchronously
59        private static TimeData startFibonacci(int n)
60        {
```

Fig. 20.30 | Fibonacci calculations performed synchronously and asynchronously. (Part 2 of 4.)

```
61        // create a TimeData object to store times
62        TimeData timeData = new TimeData();
63
64        System.out.printf("  Calculating fibonacci(%d)%n", n);
65        timeData.start = Instant.now();
66        long fibonacciValue = fibonacci(n);
67        timeData.end = Instant.now();
68        displayResult(n, fibonacciValue, timeData);
69        return timeData;
70     }
71
72     // recursive method fibonacci; calculates nth Fibonacci number
73     private static long fibonacci(long n)
74     {
75        if (n == 0 || n == 1)
76           return n;
77        else
78           return fibonacci(n - 1) + fibonacci(n - 2);
79     }
80
81     // display fibonacci calculation result and total calculation time
82     private static void displayResult(int n, long value, TimeData timeData)
83     {
84        System.out.printf("  fibonacci(%d) = %d%n", n, value);
85        System.out.printf(
86           "  Calculation time for fibonacci(%d) = %.3f seconds%n",
87           n, timeData.timeInSeconds());
88     }
89
90     // display fibonacci calculation result and total calculation time
91     private static double calculateTime(TimeData result1, TimeData result2)
92     {
93        TimeData bothThreads = new TimeData();
94
95        // determine earlier start time
96        bothThreads.start = result1.start.compareTo(result2.start) < 0 ?
97           result1.start : result2.start;
98
99        // determine later end time
100       bothThreads.end = result1.end.compareTo(result2.end) > 0 ?
101          result1.end : result2.end;
102
103       return bothThreads.timeInSeconds();
104    }
105 } // end class FibonacciDemo
```

```
Synchronous Long Running Calculations
  Calculating fibonacci(45)
  fibonacci(45) = 1134903170
  Calculation time for fibonacci(45) = 5.884 seconds
  Calculating fibonacci(44)
  fibonacci(44) = 701408733
```

Fig. 20.30 | Fibonacci calculations performed synchronously and asynchronously. (Part 3 of 4.)

```
 Calculation time for fibonacci(44) = 3.605 seconds
 Total calculation time = 9.506 seconds

Asynchronous Long Running Calculations
 Calculating fibonacci(45)
 Calculating fibonacci(44)
 fibonacci(44) = 701408733
 Calculation time for fibonacci(44) = 3.650 seconds
 fibonacci(45) = 1134903170
 Calculation time for fibonacci(45) = 5.911 seconds
 Total calculation time = 5.911 seconds

Synchronous calculations took 161% more time than the asynchronous ones
```

Fig. 20.30 | Fibonacci calculations performed synchronously and asynchronously. (Part 4 of 4.)

Class *TimeData*

Class TimeData (lines 10–20) stores two Instants representing the start and end time of a task, and provides method timeInSeconds to calculate the total time between them. We use TimeData objects throughout this example to calculate the time required to perform Fibonacci calculations.

Method *startFibonacci* for Performing and Timing Fibonacci Calculations

Method startFibonacci (lines 59–70) is called several times in main (lines 29, 30, 39 and 41) to initiate Fibonacci calculations and to calculate the time each calculation requires. The method receives the Fibonacci number to calculate and performs the following tasks:

- Line 62 creates a TimeData object to store the calculation's start and end times.
- Line 64 displays the Fibonacci number to be calculated.
- Line 65 stores the current time before method fibonacci is called.
- Line 66 calls method fibonacci to perform the calculation.
- Line 67 stores the current time after the call to fibonacci completes.
- Line 68 displays the result and the total time required for the calculation.
- Line 69 returns the TimeData object for use in method main.

Performing Fibonacci Calculations Synchronously

Method main (lines 24–56) first demonstrates synchronous Fibonacci calculations. Line 29 calls startFibonacci(45) to initiate the fibonacci(45) calculation and store the TimeData object containing the calculation's start and end times. When this call completes, line 30 calls startFibonacci(44) to initiate the fibonacci(44) calculation and store its TimeData. Next, lines 31–32 pass both TimeData objects to method calculateTime (lines 91–104), which returns the total calculation time in seconds. Lines 33–34 display the total calculation time for the synchronous Fibonacci calculations.

Performing Fibonacci Calculations Asynchronously

Lines 38–41 in main launch the asynchronous Fibonacci calculations in separate threads. CompletableFuture static method **supplyAsync** executes an asynchronous task that returns a value. The method receives as its argument an object that implements interface Supplier—in this case, we use a lambdas with empty parameter lists to invoke `startFibonacci(45)` (line 39) and `startFibonacci(44)` (line 41). The compiler infers that `supplyAsync` returns a `CompletableFuture<TimeData>` because method `startFibonacci` returns type `TimeData`. Class `CompletableFuture` also provides static method **runAsync** to execute an asynchronous task that does not return a result—this method receives a `Runnable`.

Getting the Asynchronous Calculations' Results
Class `CompletableFuture` implements interface `Future`, so we can obtain the asynchronous tasks' results by calling `Future` method `get` (lines 44–45). These are *blocking* calls—they cause the `main` thread to *wait* until the asynchronous tasks complete and return their results. In our case, the results are `TimeData` objects. Once both tasks return, lines 46–47 pass both `TimeData` objects to method `calculateTime` (lines 91–104) to get the total calculation time in seconds. Then, lines 48–49 display the total calculation time for the asynchronous Fibonacci calculations. Finally, lines 52–55 calculate and display the percentage difference in execution time for the synchronous and asynchronous calculations.

Program Outputs
On our dual-core computer, the synchronous calculations took a total of 9.506 seconds. Though the individual asynchronous calculations took approximately the same amount of time as the corresponding synchronous calculations, the total time for the asynchronous calculations was only 5.911 seconds, because the two calculations were actually performed *in parallel*. As you can see in the output, the synchronous calculations took 161% more time to complete, so asynchronous execution provided a significant performance improvement.

20.15 (Advanced) Fork/Join Framework
Java's concurrency APIs include the fork/join framework, which helps programmers parallelize algorithms. The framework is beyond the scope of this book. Experts tell us that most Java programmers will nevertheless benefit by the fork/join framework's use "behind the scenes" in the Java API and other third party libraries. For example, the parallel capabilities of Java SE 8 streams are implemented using this framework.

The fork/join framework is particularly well suited to divide-and-conquer-style algorithms, such as a merge sort. The recursive merge-sort algorithm sorts an array by *splitting* it into two equal-sized subarrays, *sorting* each subarray, then *merging* them into one larger array. Each subarray is sorted by performing the same algorithm on the subarray. For algorithms like merge sort, the fork/join framework can be used to create concurrent tasks so that they can be distributed across multiple processors and be truly performed in parallel— the details of assigning the tasks to different processors are handled for you by the framework.

20.16 Wrap-Up
In this chapter, we presented Java's concurrency capabilities for enhancing application performance on multi-core systems. You learned the differences between concurrent and parallel execution. We discussed that Java makes concurrency available to you through multithreading. You also learned that the JVM itself creates threads to run a program, and that it also can create threads to perform housekeeping tasks such as garbage collection.

We discussed the life cycle of a thread and the states that a thread may occupy during its lifetime. Next, we presented the interface `Runnable`, which is used to specify a task that can execute concurrently with other tasks. This interface's `run` method is invoked by the thread executing the task. We showed how to execute a `Runnable` object by associating it with an object of class `Thread`. Then we showed how to use the `Executor` interface to manage the execution of `Runnable` objects via thread pools, which can reuse existing threads to eliminate the overhead of creating a new thread for each task and can improve performance by optimizing the number of threads to ensure that the processor stays busy.

You learned that when multiple threads share an object and one or more of them modify that object, indeterminate results may occur unless access to the shared object is managed properly. We showed you how to solve this problem via thread synchronization, which coordinates access to shared mutable data by multiple concurrent threads. You learned several techniques for performing synchronization—first with the built-in class `ArrayBlockingQueue` (which handles *all* the synchronization details for you), then with Java's built-in monitors and the `synchronized` keyword, and finally with interfaces `Lock` and `Condition`.

We discussed the fact that Swing GUIs are not thread safe, so all interactions with and modifications to the GUI must be performed in the event dispatch thread. We also discussed the problems associated with performing long-running calculations in the event dispatch thread. Then we showed how you can use the `SwingWorker` class to perform long-running calculations in worker threads. You learned how to display the results of a `Swing-Worker` in a GUI when the calculation completed and how to display intermediate results while the calculation was still in process.

We revisited the `Arrays` class's `sort` and `parallelSort` methods to demonstrate the benefit of using a parallel sorting algorithm on a multi-core processor. We used the Java SE 8 Date/Time API's `Instant` and `Duration` classes to time the sort operations.

You learned that Java SE 8 streams are easy to parallelize, enabling programs to benefit from enhanced performance on multi-core systems, and that to obtain a parallel stream, you simply invoke method `parallel` on an existing stream.

We discussed the `Callable` and `Future` interfaces, which enable you to execute tasks that return results and to obtain those results, respectively. We then presented an example of performing long-running tasks synchronously and asynchronously using Java SE 8's new `CompletableFuture` class. In the next chapter, we introduce database-application development with Java's JDBC API.

21

Accessing Databases with JDBC

Objectives

In this chapter you'll:

- Relational database concepts.

- To use Structured Query Language (SQL) to retrieve data from and manipulate data in a database.

- To use the JDBC™ API to access databases.

- To use the RowSet interface from package `javax.sql` to manipulate databases.

- To use JDBC 4's automatic JDBC driver discovery.

- To create precompiled SQL statements with parameters via `PreparedStatement`s.

- How transaction processing makes database applications more robust.

21.1 Introduction

A **database** is an organized collection of data. There are many different strategies for organizing data to facilitate easy access and manipulation. A **database management system (DBMS)** provides mechanisms for storing, organizing, retrieving and modifying data for many users. Database management systems allow for the access and storage of data without concern for the internal representation of data.

Structured Query Language
Today's most popular database systems are *relational databases* (Section 21.2). A language called **SQL**—pronounced "sequel," or as its individual letters—is the international standard language used almost universally with relational databases to perform **queries** (i.e., to request information that satisfies given criteria) and to manipulate data. [*Note:* As you learn about SQL, you'll see some authors writing "a SQL statement" (which assumes the pronunciation "sequel") and others writing "an SQL statement" (which assumes that the individual letters are pronounced). In this book we pronounce SQL as "sequel."]

Popular Relational Database Management Systems
Some popular **relational database management systems (RDBMSs)** are Microsoft SQL Server®, Oracle®, Sybase®, IBM DB2®, Informix®, PostgreSQL and MySQL™. The JDK comes with a pure-Java RDBMS called Java DB—the Oracle-branded version of Apache Derby™.

JDBC
Java programs interact with databases using the **Java Database Connectivity (JDBC™) API**. A **JDBC driver** enables Java applications to connect to a database in a particular DBMS and allows you to manipulate that database using the JDBC API.

Software Engineering Observation 21.1

The JDBC API is portable—the same code can manipulate databases in various RDBMSs.

Most popular database management systems provide JDBC drivers. In this chapter, we introduce JDBC and use it to manipulate Java DB databases. The techniques we demonstrate here can be used to manipulate other databases that have JDBC drivers. If not, third-party vendors provide JDBC drivers for many DBMSs. This chapter's examples were tested with Java DB using both the Java SE 7 and Java SE 8 JDKs.

21.2 Relational Databases

A **relational database** is a logical representation of data that allows the data to be accessed without consideration of its physical structure. A relational database stores data in **tables**. Figure 21.1 illustrates a sample table that might be used in a personnel system. The table name is Employee, and its primary purpose is to store the attributes of employees. Tables are composed of **rows**, each describing a single entity—in Fig. 21.1, an employee. Rows are composed of **columns** in which values are stored. This table consists of six rows. The Number column of each row is the table's **primary key**—a column (or group of columns) with a value that is *unique* for each row. This guarantees that each row can be identified by its primary key. Good examples of primary-key columns are a social security number, an employee ID number and a part number in an inventory system, as values in each of these columns are guaranteed to be unique. The rows in Fig. 21.1 are displayed in order by primary key. In this case, the rows are listed in ascending order by primary key, but they could be listed in descending order or in no particular order at all.

	Number	Name	Department	Salary	Location
	23603	Jones	413	1100	New Jersey
	24568	Kerwin	413	2000	New Jersey
Row	34589	Larson	642	1800	Los Angeles
	35761	Myers	611	1400	Orlando
	47132	Neumann	413	9000	New Jersey
	78321	Stephens	611	8500	Orlando
	Primary key		Column		

Fig. 21.1 | Employee table sample data.

Each column represents a different data attribute. Rows are unique (by primary key) within a table, but particular column values may be duplicated between rows. For example, three different rows in the Employee table's Department column contain number 413.

Selecting Data Subsets

Different users of a database are often interested in different data and different relationships among the data. Most users require only subsets of the rows and columns. Queries specify which subsets of the data to select from a table. You use SQL to define queries. For example, you might select data from the Employee table to create a result that shows where each department is located, presenting the data sorted in increasing order by department number. This result is shown in Fig. 21.2. SQL is discussed in Section 21.4.

Department	Location
413	New Jersey
611	Orlando
642	Los Angeles

Fig. 21.2 | Distinct Department and Location data from the Employees table.

21.3 A books Database

We introduce relational databases in the context of this chapter's books database, which you'll use in several examples. Before we discuss SQL, we discuss the *tables* of the books database. We use this database to introduce various database concepts, including how to use SQL to obtain information from the database and to manipulate the data. We provide a script to create the database. You can find the script in the examples directory for this chapter. Section 21.5 explains how to use this script.

Authors *Table*

The database consists of three tables: Authors, AuthorISBN and Titles. The Authors table (described in Fig. 21.3) consists of three columns that maintain each author's unique ID number, first name and last name. Figure 21.4 contains sample data from the Authors table.

Column	Description
AuthorID	Author's ID number in the database. In the books database, this integer column is defined as **autoincremented**—for each row inserted in this table, the AuthorID value is increased by 1 automatically to ensure that each row has a unique AuthorID. This column represents the table's primary key. Autoincremented columns are so-called identity columns. The SQL script we provide for this database uses the SQL **IDENTITY** keyword to mark the AuthorID column as an identity column. For more information on using the IDENTITY keyword and creating databases, see the Java DB Developer's Guide at http://docs.oracle.com/javadb/10.10.1.1/devguide/derbydev.pdf.
FirstName	Author's first name (a string).
LastName	Author's last name (a string).

Fig. 21.3 | Authors table from the books database.

AuthorID	FirstName	LastName
1	Paul	Deitel
2	Harvey	Deitel
3	Abbey	Deitel
4	Dan	Quirk
5	Michael	Morgano

Fig. 21.4 | Sample data from the Authors table.

Titles *Table*

The Titles table described in Fig. 21.5 consists of four columns that maintain information about each book in the database, including its ISBN, title, edition number and copyright year. Figure 21.8 contains the data from the Titles table.

Column	Description
ISBN	ISBN of the book (a string). The table's primary key. ISBN is an abbreviation for "International Standard Book Number"—a numbering scheme that publishers use to give every book a unique identification number.
Title	Title of the book (a string).
EditionNumber	Edition number of the book (an integer).
Copyright	Copyright year of the book (a string).

Fig. 21.5 | Titles table from the books database.

ISBN	Title	EditionNumber	Copyright
0132151006	Internet & World Wide Web How to Program	5	2012
0133807800	Java How to Program	10	2015
0132575655	Java How to Program, Late Objects Version	10	2015
013299044X	C How to Program	7	2013
0132990601	Simply Visual Basic 2010	4	2013
0133406954	Visual Basic 2012 How to Program	6	2014
0133379337	Visual C# 2012 How to Program	5	2014
0136151574	Visual C++ 2008 How to Program	2	2008
0133378713	C++ How to Program	9	2014
0133570924	Android How to Program	2	2015
0133570924	Android for Programmers: An App-Driven Approach, Volume 1	2	2014
0132121360	Android for Programmers: An App-Driven Approach	1	2012

Fig. 21.6 | Sample data from the Titles table of the books database .

AuthorISBN *Table*

The AuthorISBN table (described in Fig. 21.7) consists of two columns that maintain ISBNs for each book and their corresponding authors' ID numbers. This table associates authors with their books. The AuthorID column is a **foreign key**—a column in this table that matches the primary-key column in another table (that is, AuthorID in the Authors table). The ISBN column is also a foreign key—it matches the primary-key column (that is, ISBN) in the Titles table. A database might consist of many tables. A goal when designing a database is to *minimize* the amount of *duplicated* data among the database's tables. Foreign keys, which are specified when a database table is created in the database, link the data in *multiple* tables. Together the AuthorID and ISBN columns in this table form a *composite primary key*. Every row in this table *uniquely* matches *one* author to *one* book's ISBN. Figure 21.8 contains the data from the AuthorISBN table of the books database.

Column	Description
AuthorID	The author's ID number, a foreign key to the Authors table.
ISBN	The ISBN for a book, a foreign key to the Titles table.

Fig. 21.7 | AuthorISBN table from the books database.

AuthorID	ISBN	AuthorID	ISBN
1	0132151006	2	0133379337
2	0132151006	1	0136151574
3	0132151006	2	0136151574
1	0133807800	4	0136151574
2	0133807800	1	0133378713
1	0132575655	2	0133378713
2	0132575655	1	0133764036
1	013299044X	2	0133764036
2	013299044X	3	0133764036
1	0132990601	1	0133570924
2	0132990601	2	0133570924
3	0132990601	3	0133570924
1	0133406954	1	0132121360
2	0133406954	2	0132121360
3	0133406954	3	0132121360
1	0133379337	5	0132121360

Fig. 21.8 | Sample data from the AuthorISBN table of books.

Every foreign-key value must appear as another table's primary-key value so the DBMS can ensure that the foreign key value is valid—this is known as the **Rule of Referential Integrity**. For example, the DBMS ensures that the AuthorID value for a particular row of the AuthorISBN table is valid by checking that there is a row in the Authors table with that AuthorID as the primary key.

Foreign keys also allow *related* data in *multiple* tables to be *selected* from those tables—this is known as **joining** the data. There is a **one-to-many relationship** between a primary key and a corresponding foreign key (for example, one author can write many books and one book can be written by many authors). This means that a foreign key can appear *many* times in its own table but only *once* (as the primary key) in another table. For example, the ISBN 0132151006 can appear in several rows of AuthorISBN (because this book has several authors) but only once in Titles, where ISBN is the primary key.

Entity-Relationship (ER) Diagram

There's a one-to-many relationship between a primary key and a corresponding foreign key (e.g., one author can write many books). A foreign key can appear many times in its own table, but only once (as the primary key) in another table. Figure 21.9 is an **entity-relationship (ER) diagram** for the books database. This diagram shows the *database tables* and the *relationships* among them. The first compartment in each box contains the table's name and the remaining compartments contain the table's columns. The names in italic are primary keys. *A table's primary key uniquely identifies each row in the table.* Every row must have a primary-key value, and that value must be unique in the table. This is known as the **Rule of Entity Integrity**. Again, for the AuthorISBN table, the primary key is the combination of both columns—this is known as a composite primary key.

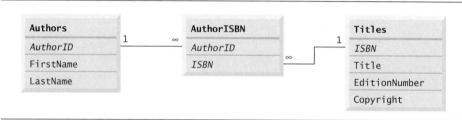

Fig. 21.9 | Table relationships in the books database.

The lines connecting the tables in Fig. 21.9 represent the *relationships* among the tables. Consider the line between the Authors and AuthorISBN tables. On the Authors end of the line, there's a 1, and on the AuthorISBN end, an infinity symbol (∞). This indicates a *one-to-many relationship*—for *each* author in the Authors table, there can be an *arbitrary number* of ISBNs for books written by that author in the AuthorISBN table (that is, an author can write *any* number of books). Note that the relationship line links the AuthorID column in the Authors table (where AuthorID is the primary key) to the AuthorID column in the AuthorISBN table (where AuthorID is a foreign key)—the line between the tables links the primary key to the matching foreign key.

The line between the Titles and AuthorISBN tables illustrates a *one-to-many relationship*—one book can be written by many authors. Note that the line between the tables links the primary key ISBN in table Titles to the corresponding foreign key in table AuthorISBN. The relationships in Fig. 21.9 illustrate that the sole purpose of the AuthorISBN table is to provide a **many-to-many relationship** between the Authors and Titles tables—an author can write *many* books, and a book can have *many* authors.

21.4 SQL

We now discuss SQL in the context of our books database. You'll be able to use the SQL discussed here in the examples later in the chapter. The next several subsections demonstrate SQL queries and statements using the SQL keywords in Fig. 21.10. Other SQL keywords are beyond this text's scope.

SQL keyword	Description
SELECT	Retrieves data from one or more tables.
FROM	Tables involved in the query. Required in every SELECT.
WHERE	Criteria for selection that determine the rows to be retrieved, deleted or updated. Optional in a SQL query or a SQL statement.
GROUP BY	Criteria for grouping rows. Optional in a SELECT query.
ORDER BY	Criteria for ordering rows. Optional in a SELECT query.
INNER JOIN	Merge rows from multiple tables.
INSERT	Insert rows into a specified table.
UPDATE	Update rows in a specified table.
DELETE	Delete rows from a specified table.

Fig. 21.10 | SQL query keywords.

21.4.1 Basic SELECT Query

Let's consider several SQL queries that extract information from database books. A SQL query "selects" rows and columns from one or more tables in a database. Such selections are performed by queries with the **SELECT** keyword. The basic form of a SELECT query is

> **SELECT** * **FROM** *tableName*

in which the **asterisk** (*) *wildcard character* indicates that all columns from the *tableName* table should be retrieved. For example, to retrieve all the data in the Authors table, use

> **SELECT** * **FROM** Authors

Most programs do not require all the data in a table. To retrieve only specific columns, replace the * with a comma-separated list of column names. For example, to retrieve only the columns AuthorID and LastName for all rows in the Authors table, use the query

> **SELECT** AuthorID, LastName **FROM** Authors

This query returns the data listed in Fig. 21.11.

AuthorID	LastName	AuthorID	LastName
1	Deitel	4	Quirk
2	Deitel	5	Morgano
3	Deitel		

Fig. 21.11 | Sample AuthorID and LastName data from the Authors table.

Software Engineering Observation 21.2

In general, you process results by knowing in advance the order of the columns in the result—for example, selecting AuthorID *and* LastName *from table* Authors *ensures that the columns will appear in the result with* AuthorID *as the first column and* LastName *as the second column. Programs typically process result columns by specifying the column number in the result (starting from number 1 for the first column). Selecting columns by name avoids returning unneeded columns and protects against changes in the actual order of the columns in the table(s) by returning the columns in the exact order specified.*

Common Programming Error 21.1

If you assume that the columns are always returned in the same order from a query that uses the asterisk (*), the program may process the results incorrectly. If the column order in the table(s) changes or if additional columns are added at a later time, the order of the columns in the result will change accordingly.

21.4.2 WHERE Clause

In most cases, it's necessary to locate rows in a database that satisfy certain **selection criteria**. Only rows that satisfy the selection criteria (formally called **predicates**) are selected. SQL uses the optional **WHERE clause** in a query to specify the selection criteria for the query. The basic form of a query with selection criteria is

> **SELECT** *columnName1*, *columnName2*, … **FROM** *tableName* **WHERE** *criteria*

For example, to select the Title, EditionNumber and Copyright columns from table Titles for which the Copyright date is greater than 2013, use the query

```
SELECT Title, EditionNumber, Copyright
    FROM Titles
    WHERE Copyright > '2013'
```

Strings in SQL are delimited by single (') rather than double (") quotes. Figure 21.12 shows the result of the preceding query.

Title	EditionNumber	Copyright
Java How to Program	10	2015
Java How to Program, Late Objects Version	10	2015
Visual Basic 2012 How to Program	6	2014
Visual C# 2012 How to Program	5	2014
C++ How to Program	9	2014
Android How to Program	2	2015
Android for Programmers: An App-Driven Approach, Volume 1	2	2014

Fig. 21.12 | Sampling of titles with copyrights after 2005 from table Titles.

Pattern Matching: Zero or More Characters
The WHERE clause criteria can contain the operators <, >, <=, >=, =, <> and LIKE. Operator **LIKE** is used for **pattern matching** with wildcard characters **percent (%)** and **underscore** (_). Pattern matching allows SQL to search for strings that match a given pattern.

A pattern that contains a percent character (%) searches for strings that have zero or more characters at the percent character's position in the pattern. For example, the next query locates the rows of all the authors whose last name starts with the letter D:

```
SELECT AuthorID, FirstName, LastName
    FROM Authors
    WHERE LastName LIKE 'D%'
```

This query selects the two rows shown in Fig. 21.13—three of the five authors have a last name starting with the letter D (followed by zero or more characters). The % symbol in the WHERE clause's LIKE pattern indicates that any number of characters can appear after the letter D in the LastName. The pattern string is surrounded by single-quote characters.

AuthorID	FirstName	LastName
1	Paul	Deitel
2	Harvey	Deitel
3	Abbey	Deitel

Fig. 21.13 | Authors whose last name starts with D from the Authors table.

Portability Tip 21.1
See the documentation for your database system to determine whether SQL is case sensitive on your system and to determine the syntax for SQL keywords.

Portability Tip 21.2
Read your database system's documentation carefully to determine whether it supports the LIKE operator as discussed here.

Pattern Matching: Any Character
An underscore (_) in the pattern string indicates a single wildcard character at that position in the pattern. For example, the following query locates the rows of all the authors whose last names start with any character (specified by _), followed by the letter o, followed by any number of additional characters (specified by %):

```
SELECT AuthorID, FirstName, LastName
    FROM Authors
    WHERE LastName LIKE '_o%'
```

The preceding query produces the row shown in Fig. 21.14, because only one author in our database has a last name that contains the letter o as its second letter.

AuthorID	FirstName	LastName
5	Michael	Morgano

Fig. 21.14 | The only author from the Authors table whose last name contains o as the second letter.

21.4.3 ORDER BY Clause

The rows in the result of a query can be sorted into ascending or descending order by using the optional **ORDER BY clause**. The basic form of a query with an ORDER BY clause is

> **SELECT** *columnName1*, *columnName2*, … **FROM** *tableName* **ORDER BY** *column* **ASC**
> **SELECT** *columnName1*, *columnName2*, … **FROM** *tableName* **ORDER BY** *column* **DESC**

where ASC specifies ascending order (lowest to highest), DESC specifies descending order (highest to lowest) and *column* specifies the column on which the sort is based. For example, to obtain the list of authors in ascending order by last name (Fig. 21.15), use the query

```
SELECT AuthorID, FirstName, LastName
   FROM Authors
   ORDER BY LastName ASC
```

AuthorID	FirstName	LastName
1	Paul	Deitel
2	Harvey	Deitel
3	Abbey	Deitel
5	Michael	Morgano
4	Dan	Quirk

Fig. 21.15 | Sample data from table Authors in ascending order by LastName.

Sorting in Descending Order

The default sorting order is ascending, so ASC is optional. To obtain the same list of authors in descending order by last name (Fig. 21.16), use the query

```
SELECT AuthorID, FirstName, LastName
   FROM Authors
   ORDER BY LastName DESC
```

AuthorID	FirstName	LastName
4	Dan	Quirk
5	Michael	Morgano
1	Paul	Deitel
2	Harvey	Deitel
3	Abbey	Deitel

Fig. 21.16 | Sample data from table Authors in descending order by LastName.

Sorting By Multiple Columns

Multiple columns can be used for sorting with an ORDER BY clause of the form

> **ORDER BY** *column1 sortingOrder*, *column2 sortingOrder*, …

where *sortingOrder* is either ASC or DESC. The *sortingOrder* does not have to be identical for each column. The query

```
SELECT AuthorID, FirstName, LastName
    FROM Authors
    ORDER BY LastName, FirstName
```

sorts all the rows in ascending order by last name, then by first name. If any rows have the same last-name value, they're returned sorted by first name (Fig. 21.17).

AuthorID	FirstName	LastName
3	Abbey	Deitel
2	Harvey	Deitel
1	Paul	Deitel
5	Michael	Morgano
4	Dan	Quirk

Fig. 21.17 | Sample data from `Authors` in ascending order by `LastName` and `FirstName`.

Combining the *WHERE* and *ORDER BY* Clauses
The WHERE and ORDER BY clauses can be combined in one query, as in

```
SELECT ISBN, Title, EditionNumber, Copyright
    FROM Titles
    WHERE Title LIKE '%How to Program'
    ORDER BY Title ASC
```

which returns the ISBN, Title, EditionNumber and Copyright of each book in the Titles table that has a Title ending with "How to Program" and sorts them in ascending order by Title. The query results are shown in Fig. 21.18.

ISBN	Title	EditionNumber	Copyright
0133764036	Android How to Program	2	2015
013299044X	C How to Program	7	2013
0133378713	C++ How to Program	9	2014
0132151006	Internet & World Wide Web How to Program	5	2012
0133807800	Java How to Program	10	2015
0133406954	Visual Basic 2012 How to Program	6	2014
0133379337	Visual C# 2012 How to Program	5	2014
0136151574	Visual C++ 2008 How to Program	2	2008

Fig. 21.18 | Sampling of books from table `Titles` whose titles end with `How to Program` in ascending order by `Title`.

21.4.4 Merging Data from Multiple Tables: INNER JOIN

Database designers often split related data into separate tables to ensure that a database does not store data redundantly. For example, in the books database, we use an AuthorISBN table to store the relationship data between authors and their corresponding titles. If we did not separate this information into individual tables, we'd need to include author information with each entry in the Titles table. This would result in the database's storing *duplicate* author information for authors who wrote multiple books. Often, it's necessary to merge data from multiple tables into a single result. Referred to as joining the tables, this is specified by an **INNER JOIN** operator, which merges rows from two tables by matching values in columns that are common to the tables. The basic form of an INNER JOIN is:

```
SELECT columnName1, columnName2, ...
FROM table1
INNER JOIN table2
    ON table1.columnName = table2.columnName
```

The **ON clause** of the INNER JOIN specifies the columns from each table that are compared to determine which rows are merged—these fields almost always correspond to the foreign-key fields in the tables being joined. For example, the following query produces a list of authors accompanied by the ISBNs for books written by each author:

```
SELECT FirstName, LastName, ISBN
FROM Authors
INNER JOIN AuthorISBN
    ON Authors.AuthorID = AuthorISBN.AuthorID
ORDER BY LastName, FirstName
```

The query merges the FirstName and LastName columns from table Authors with the ISBN column from table AuthorISBN, sorting the results in ascending order by LastName and FirstName. Note the use of the syntax *tableName.columnName* in the ON clause. This syntax, called a **qualified name**, specifies the columns from each table that should be compared to join the tables. The "*tableName.*" syntax is required if the columns have the same name in both tables. The same syntax can be used in any SQL statement to distinguish columns in different tables that have the same name. In some systems, table names qualified with the database name can be used to perform cross-database queries. As always, the query can contain an ORDER BY clause. Figure 21.19 shows the results of the preceding query, ordered by LastName and FirstName. [*Note:* To save space, we split the result of the query into two columns, each containing the FirstName, LastName and ISBN columns.]

 Common Programming Error 21.2

Failure to qualify names for columns that have the same name in two or more tables is an error. In such cases, the statement must precede those column names with their table names and a dot (e.g., Authors.AuthorID).

FirstName	LastName	ISBN	FirstName	LastName	ISBN
Abbey	Deitel	0132121360	Harvey	Deitel	0133764036
Abbey	Deitel	0133570924	Harvey	Deitel	0133378713
Abbey	Deitel	0133764036	Harvey	Deitel	0136151574
Abbey	Deitel	0133406954	Harvey	Deitel	0133379337
Abbey	Deitel	0132990601	Harvey	Deitel	0133406954
Abbey	Deitel	0132151006	Harvey	Deitel	0132990601
Harvey	Deitel	0132121360	Harvey	Deitel	013299044X
Harvey	Deitel	0133570924	Harvey	Deitel	0132575655

Fig. 21.19 | Sampling of authors and ISBNs for the books they have written in ascending order by LastName and FirstName. (Part 1 of 2.)

FirstName	LastName	ISBN	FirstName	LastName	ISBN
Harvey	Deitel	0133807800	Paul	Deitel	0133406954
Harvey	Deitel	0132151006	Paul	Deitel	0132990601
Paul	Deitel	0132121360	Paul	Deitel	013299044X
Paul	Deitel	0133570924	Paul	Deitel	0132575655
Paul	Deitel	0133764036	Paul	Deitel	0133807800
Paul	Deitel	0133378713	Paul	Deitel	0132151006
Paul	Deitel	0136151574	Michael	Morgano	0132121360
Paul	Deitel	0133379337	Dan	Quirk	0136151574

Fig. 21.19 | Sampling of authors and ISBNs for the books they have written in ascending order by LastName and FirstName. (Part 2 of 2.)

21.4.5 INSERT Statement

The **INSERT** statement inserts a row into a table. The basic form of this statement is

> **INSERT INTO** *tableName* (*columnName1*, *columnName2*, ..., *columnNameN*)
>   **VALUES** (*value1*, *value2*, ..., *valueN*)

where *tableName* is the table in which to insert the row. The *tableName* is followed by a comma-separated list of column names in parentheses (this list is not required if the INSERT operation specifies a value for every column of the table in the correct order). The list of column names is followed by the SQL keyword **VALUES** and a comma-separated list of values in parentheses. The values specified here must match the columns specified after the table name in both order and type (e.g., if *columnName1* is supposed to be the FirstName column, then *value1* should be a string in single quotes representing the first name). Always explicitly list the columns when inserting rows. If the table's column order changes or a new column is added, using only VALUES may cause an error. The INSERT statement

> **INSERT INTO** Authors (FirstName, LastName)
>   **VALUES** ('Sue', 'Red')

inserts a row into the Authors table. The statement indicates that values are provided for the FirstName and LastName columns. The corresponding values are 'Sue' and 'Smith'. We do not specify an AuthorID in this example because AuthorID is an autoincremented column in the Authors table. For every row added to this table, the DBMS assigns a unique AuthorID value that is the next value in the autoincremented sequence (i.e., 1, 2, 3 and so on). In this case, Sue Red would be assigned AuthorID number 6. Figure 21.20 shows the Authors table after the INSERT operation. [*Note:* Not every database management system supports autoincremented columns. Check the documentation for your DBMS for alternatives to autoincremented columns.]

Common Programming Error 21.3

SQL delimits strings with single quotes ('). A string containing a single quote (e.g., O'Malley) must have two single quotes in the position where the single quote appears (e.g., 'O''Malley'). The first acts as an escape character for the second. Not escaping single-quote characters in a string that's part of a SQL statement is a SQL syntax error.

Common Programming Error 21.4
It's normally an error to specify a value for an autoincrement column.

AuthorID	FirstName	LastName
1	Paul	Deitel
2	Harvey	Deitel
3	Abbey	Deitel
4	Dan	Quirk
5	Michael	Morgano
6	Sue	Red

Fig. 21.20 | Sample data from table `Authors` after an `INSERT` operation.

21.4.6 UPDATE Statement

An **UPDATE** statement modifies data in a table. Its basic form is

```
UPDATE tableName
    SET columnName1 = value1, columnName2 = value2, ..., columnNameN = valueN
    WHERE criteria
```

where *tableName* is the table to update. The *tableName* is followed by keyword **SET** and a comma-separated list of *columnName = value* pairs. The optional WHERE clause provides criteria that determine which rows to update. Though not required, the WHERE clause is typically used, unless a change is to be made to every row. The UPDATE statement

```
UPDATE Authors
    SET LastName = 'Black'
    WHERE LastName = 'Red' AND FirstName = 'Sue'
```

updates a row in the Authors table. The statement indicates that LastName will be assigned the value Black for the row where LastName is Red and FirstName is Sue. [*Note:* If there are multiple matching rows, this statement will modify *all* such rows to have the last name "Black."] If we know the AuthorID in advance of the UPDATE operation (possibly because we searched for it previously), the WHERE clause can be simplified as follows:

```
WHERE AuthorID = 6
```

Figure 21.21 shows the Authors table after the UPDATE operation has taken place.

AuthorID	FirstName	LastName
1	Paul	Deitel
2	Harvey	Deitel
3	Abbey	Deitel
4	Dan	Quirk
5	Michael	Morgano
6	Sue	Black

Fig. 21.21 | Sample data from table `Authors` after an `UPDATE` operation.

21.4.7 DELETE Statement

A SQL **DELETE** statement removes rows from a table. Its basic form is

> **DELETE FROM** *tableName* **WHERE** *criteria*

where *tableName* is the table from which to delete. The optional WHERE clause specifies the criteria used to determine which rows to delete. If this clause is omitted, all the table's rows are deleted. The DELETE statement

```
DELETE FROM Authors
    WHERE LastName = 'Black' AND FirstName = 'Sue'
```

deletes the row for Sue Black in the Authors table. If we know the AuthorID in advance of the DELETE operation, the WHERE clause can be simplified as follows:

```
WHERE AuthorID = 5
```

Figure 21.22 shows the Authors table after the DELETE operation has taken place.

AuthorID	FirstName	LastName
1	Paul	Deitel
2	Harvey	Deitel
3	Abbey	Deitel
4	Dan	Quirk
5	Michael	Morgano

Fig. 21.22 | Sample data from table Authors after a DELETE operation.

21.5 Setting up a Java DB Database

This chapter's examples use Oracle's pure Java database **Java DB**, which is installed with Oracle's JDK on Windows, Mac OS X and Linux. Before you can execute this chapter's applications, you must set up in Java DB the books database that's used in Sections 21.6––21.7 and the addressbook database that's used in Section 21.8.

For this chapter, you'll be using the embedded version of Java DB. This means that the database you manipulate in each example must be located in that example's folder. This chapter's examples are located in two subfolders of the ch24 examples folder—books_examples and addressbook_example. Java DB may also act as a server that can receive database requests over a network, but that is beyond this chapter's scope.

JDK Installation Folders
The Java DB software is located in the db subdirectory of your JDK's installation directory. The directories listed below are for Oracle's JDK 7 update 51:

- 32-bit JDK on Windows:
  ```
  C:\Program Files (x86)\Java\jdk1.7.0_51
  ```

- 64-bit JDK on Windows:
  ```
  C:\Program Files\Java\jdk1.7.0_51
  ```

- Mac OS X:
  `/Library/Java/JavaVirtualMachines/jdk1.7.0_51.jdk/Contents/Home`
- Ubuntu Linux:
  `/usr/lib/jvm/java-7-oracle`

For Linux, the install location depends on the installer you use and possibly the version of Linux that you use. We used Ubuntu Linux for testing purposes.

Depending on your platform, the JDK installation folder's name might differ if you're using a different update of JDK 7 or using JDK 8. In the following instructions, you should update the JDK installation folder's name based on the JDK version you're using.

Java DB Configuration

Java DB comes with several files that enable you to configure and run it. Before executing these files from a command window, you must set the environment variable `JAVA_HOME` to refer to the JDK's exact installation directory listed above (or the location where you installed the JDK if it differs from those listed above). See the Before You Begin section of this book for information on setting environment variables.

21.5.1 Creating the Chapter's Databases on Windows

After setting the `JAVA_HOME` environment variable, perform the following steps:

1. Run Notepad as an administrator. To do this on Windows 7, select **Start > All Programs > Accessories**, right click Notepad and select **Run as administrator**. On Windows 8, search for Notepad, right click it in the search results and select **Advanced** in the app bar, then select **Run as administrator**.

2. From Notepad, open the batch file `setEmbeddedCP.bat` that is located in the JDK installation folder's `db\bin` folder.

3. Locate the line

   ```
   @rem set DERBY_INSTALL=
   ```

   and change it to

   ```
   @set DERBY_INSTALL=%JAVA_HOME%\db
   ```

   Save your changes and close this file.

4. Open a Command Prompt window and change directories to the JDK installation folder's `db\bin` folder. Then, type `setEmbeddedCP.bat` and press *Enter* to set the environment variables required by Java DB.

5. Use the `cd` command to change to this chapter's `books_examples` directory. This directory contains a SQL script `books.sql` that builds the `books` database.

6. Execute the following command (with the quotation marks):

   ```
   "%JAVA_HOME%\db\bin\ij"
   ```

   to start the command-line tool for interacting with Java DB. The double quotes are necessary because the path that the environment variable `%JAVA_HOME%` represents contains a space. This will display the `ij>` prompt.

7. At the ij> prompt type

```
connect 'jdbc:derby:books;create=true;user=deitel;
    password=deitel';
```

and press *Enter* to create the books database in the current directory and to create the user deitel with the password deitel for accessing the database.

8. To create the database table and insert sample data in it, we've provided the file address.sql in this example's directory. To execute this SQL script, type

```
run 'books.sql';
```

Once you create the database, you can execute the SQL statements presented in Section 21.4 to confirm their execution. Each command you enter at the ij> prompt must be terminated with a semicolon (;).

9. To terminate the Java DB command-line tool, type

```
exit;
```

10. Change directories to the addressbook_example subfolder of the ch24 examples folder, which contains the SQL script addressbook.sql that builds the address-book database. Repeat Steps 6–9. In each step, replace books with addressbook.

You're now ready to execute this chapter's examples.

21.5.2 Creating the Chapter's Databases on Mac OS X

After setting the JAVA_HOME environment variable, perform the following steps:

1. Open a Terminal, then type:

```
DERBY_HOME=/Library/Java/JavaVirtualMachines/jdk1.7.0_51.jdk/
    Contents/Home/db
```

and press *Enter*. Then type

```
export DERBY_HOME
```

and press *Enter*. This specifies where Java DB is located on your Mac.

2. In the Terminal window, change directories to the JDK installation folder's db/bin folder. Then, type ./setEmbeddedCP and press *Enter* to set the environment variables required by Java DB.

3. In the Terminal window, use the cd command to change to the books_examples directory. This directory contains a SQL script books.sql that builds the books database.

4. Execute the following command (with the quotation marks):

```
$JAVA_HOME/db/bin/ij
```

to start the command-line tool for interacting with Java DB. This will display the ij> prompt.

5. Perform Steps 7–9 of Section 21.5.1 to create the books database.

6. Use the cd command to change to the addressbook_example directory. This directory contains a SQL script addressbook.sql that builds the addressbook database.

7. Perform Steps 7–9 of Section 21.5.1 to create the addressbook database. In each step, replace books with addressbook.

You're now ready to execute this chapter's examples.

21.5.3 Creating the Chapter's Databases on Linux

After setting the JAVA_HOME environment variable, perform the following steps:

1. Open a shell window.

2. Perform the steps in Section 21.5.2, but in Step 1, set DERBY_HOME to

> DERBY_HOME=*YourLinuxJDKInstallationFolder*/db

On our Ubuntu Linux system, this was:

> DERBY_HOME=/usr/lib/jvm/java-7-oracle/db

You're now ready to execute this chapter's examples.

21.6 Manipulating Databases with JDBC

This section presents two examples. The first introduces how to connect to a database and query it. The second demonstrates how to display the result of the query in a JTable.

21.6.1 Connecting to and Querying a Database

The example of Fig. 21.23 performs a simple query on the books database that retrieves the entire Authors table and displays the data. The program illustrates connecting to the database, querying the database and processing the result. The discussion that follows presents the key JDBC aspects of the program.

Lines 3–8 import the JDBC interfaces and classes from package java.sql used in this program. Method main (lines 12–48) connects to the books database, queries the database, displays the query result and closes the database connection. Line 14 declares a String constant for the database URL. This identifies the name of the database to connect to, as well as information about the protocol used by the JDBC driver (discussed shortly). Lines 15–16 declare a String constant representing the SQL query that will select the authorID, firstName and lastName columns in the database's authors table.

```
1   // Fig. 21.23: DisplayAuthors.java
2   // Displaying the contents of the Authors table.
3   import java.sql.Connection;
4   import java.sql.Statement;
5   import java.sql.DriverManager;
6   import java.sql.ResultSet;
7   import java.sql.ResultSetMetaData;
8   import java.sql.SQLException;
9
10  public class DisplayAuthors
11  {
```

Fig. 21.23 | Displaying the contents of the Authors table. (Part 1 of 2.)

```
12      public static void main(String args[])
13      {
14          final String DATABASE_URL = "jdbc:derby:books";
15          final String SELECT_QUERY =
16             "SELECT authorID, firstName, lastName FROM authors";
17
18          // use try-with-resources to connect to and query the database
19          try (
20             Connection connection = DriverManager.getConnection(
21                DATABASE_URL, "deitel", "deitel");
22             Statement statement = connection.createStatement();
23             ResultSet resultSet = statement.executeQuery(SELECT_QUERY))
24          {
25             // get ResultSet's meta data
26             ResultSetMetaData metaData = resultSet.getMetaData();
27             int numberOfColumns = metaData.getColumnCount();
28
29             System.out.printf("Authors Table of Books Database:%n%n");
30
31             // display the names of the columns in the ResultSet
32             for (int i = 1; i <= numberOfColumns; i++)
33                System.out.printf("%-8s\t", metaData.getColumnName(i));
34             System.out.println();
35
36             // display query results
37             while (resultSet.next())
38             {
39                for (int i = 1; i <= numberOfColumns; i++)
40                   System.out.printf("%-8s\t", resultSet.getObject(i));
41                System.out.println();
42             }
43          } // AutoCloseable objects' close methods are called now
44          catch (SQLException sqlException)
45          {
46             sqlException.printStackTrace();
47          }
48       }
49    } // end class DisplayAuthors
```

```
Authors Table of Books Database:

AUTHORID        FIRSTNAME       LASTNAME
1               Paul            Deitel
2               Harvey          Deitel
3               Abbey           Deitel
4               Dan             Quirk
5               Michael         Morgano
```

Fig. 21.23 | Displaying the contents of the Authors table. (Part 2 of 2.)

JDBC supports **automatic driver discovery**—it loads the database driver into memory for you. To ensure that the program can locate the driver class, you must include the class's location in the program's classpath when you execute the program. You did this for Java DB in Section 21.5 when you executed the setEmbeddedCP.bat or setEmbeddedCP file on your system—that step configured a CLASSPATH environment variable in the command window for your platform. After doing so, you can run this application simply using the command

```
java DisplayAuthors
```

Connecting to the Database

The JDBC interfaces we use in this example each extend the AutoCloseable interface, so you can use objects that implement these interfaces with the try-with-resources statement (introduced in Section 11.12). Lines 19–23 create this example's AutoCloseable objects in the parentheses following keyword try—such objects are automatically closed when the try block terminates (line 43) or if an exception occurs during the try block's execution. Each object created in the parentheses following keyword try must be separated from the next by a semicolon (;).

Lines 20–21 create a **Connection** object (package java.sql) referenced by connection. An object that implements interface Connection manages the connection between the Java program and the database. Connection objects enable programs to create SQL statements that manipulate databases. The program initializes connection with the result of a call to static method **getConnection** of class **DriverManager** (package java.sql), which attempts to connect to the database specified by its URL.

Method getConnection takes three arguments

- a String that specifies the database URL,
- a String that specifies the username and
- a String that specifies the password.

The username and password for the books database were set in Section 21.5. If you used a different username and password there, you'll need to replace the username (second argument) and password (third argument) passed to method getConnection in line 21.

The URL locates the database (possibly on a network or in the local file system of the computer). The URL jdbc:derby:books specifies the protocol for communication (jdbc), the **subprotocol** for communication (derby) and the location of the database (books). The subprotocol derby indicates that the program uses a Java DB/Apache Derby-specific subprotocol to connect to the database—recall that Java DB is simply the Oracle branded version of Apache Derby. If the DriverManager cannot connect to the database, method getConnection throws a **SQLException** (package java.sql). Figure 21.24 lists the JDBC driver names and database URL formats of several popular RDBMSs.

RDBMS	Database URL format
MySQL	jdbc:mysql://*hostname*:*portNumber*/*databaseName*
ORACLE	jdbc:oracle:thin:@*hostname*:*portNumber*:*databaseName*
DB2	jdbc:db2:*hostname*:*portNumber*/*databaseName*
PostgreSQL	jdbc:postgresql://*hostname*:*portNumber*/*databaseName*
Java DB/Apache Derby	jdbc:derby:*dataBaseName* (embedded)
	jdbc:derby://*hostname*:*portNumber*/*databaseName* (network)

Fig. 21.24 | Popular JDBC database URL formats. (Part 1 of 2.)

RDBMS	Database URL format
Microsoft SQL Server	jdbc:sqlserver://*hostname*:*portNumber*;databaseName=*dataBaseName*
Sybase	jdbc:sybase:Tds:*hostname*:*portNumber*/*databaseName*

Fig. 21.24 | Popular JDBC database URL formats. (Part 2 of 2.)

Software Engineering Observation 21.3

Most database management systems require the user to log in before accessing the database contents. DriverManager method getConnection is overloaded with versions that enable the program to supply the username and password to gain access.

*Creating a **Statement** for Executing Queries*

Line 22 of Fig. 21.23 invokes Connection method **createStatement** to obtain an object that implements interface Statement (package java.sql). The program uses the **Statement** object to submit SQL statements to the database.

Executing a Query

Line 23 use the Statement object's **executeQuery** method to submit a query that selects all the author information from table Authors. This method returns an object that implements interface **ResultSet** and contains the query results. The ResultSet methods enable the program to manipulate the query result.

*Processing a Query's **ResultSet***

Lines 26–42 process the ResultSet. Line 26 obtains the ResultSet's **ResultSetMetaData** (package java.sql) object. The **metadata** describes the ResultSet's contents. Programs can use metadata programmatically to obtain information about the ResultSet's column names and types. Line 27 uses ResultSetMetaData method **getColumnCount** to retrieve the number of columns in the ResultSet. Lines 32–33 display the column names.

Software Engineering Observation 21.4

Metadata enables programs to process ResultSet contents dynamically when detailed information about the ResultSet is not known in advance.

Lines 37–42 display the data in each ResultSet row. First, the program positions the ResultSet cursor (which points to the row being processed) to the first row in the ResultSet with method **next** (line 37). Method next returns boolean value true if it's able to position to the next row; otherwise, the method returns false.

Common Programming Error 21.5

Initially, a ResultSet cursor is positioned before the first row. A SQLException occurs if you attempt to access a ResultSet's contents before positioning the ResultSet cursor to the first row with method next.

If there are rows in the ResultSet, lines 39–40 extract and display the contents of each column in the current row. When a ResultSet is processed, each column can be extracted as a specific Java type—ResultSetMetaData method **getColumnType** returns a constant integer from class **Types** (package java.sql) indicating the type of a specified column. Programs can use these values in a switch statement to invoke ResultSet methods that return the column values as appropriate Java types. For example, if the type of a column is Types.INTEGER, ResultSet method **getInt** can be used to get the column value as an int. For simplicity, this example treats each value as an Object. We retrieve each column value with ResultSet method **getObject** (line 40), then print the Object's String representation. ResultSet *get* methods typically receive as an argument either a column number (as an int) or a column name (as a String) indicating which column's value to obtain. Unlike array indices, ResultSet *column numbers start at 1.*

Performance Tip 21.1
If a query specifies the exact columns to select from the database, the ResultSet contains the columns in the specified order. In this case, using the column number to obtain the column's value is more efficient than using the column name. The column number provides direct access to the specified column. Using the column name requires a search of the column names to locate the appropriate column.

Error-Prevention Tip 21.1
Using column names to obtain values from a ResultSet produces code that is less error prone than obtaining values by column number—you don't need to remember the column order. Also, if the column order changes, your code does not have to change.

Common Programming Error 21.6
Specifying column index 0 when obtaining values from a ResultSet causes a SQL-Exception—the first column index in a ResultSet is always 1.

When the end of the try block is reached (line 43), the close method is called on the ResultSet, Statement and Connection that were obtained by the try-with-resources statement.

Common Programming Error 21.7
A SQLException occurs if you attempt to manipulate a ResultSet after closing the Statement that created it. The ResultSet is discarded when the Statement is closed.

Software Engineering Observation 21.5
Each Statement object can open only one ResultSet object at a time. When a Statement returns a new ResultSet, the Statement closes the prior ResultSet. To use multiple ResultSets in parallel, separate Statement objects must return the ResultSets.

21.6.2 Querying the books Database

The next example (Figs. 21.25 and 21.28) allows the user to enter any query into the program. The example displays the result of a query in a **JTable**, using a **TableModel** object to provide the ResultSet data to the JTable. A JTable is a swing GUI component that can be bound to a database to display the results of a query. Class ResultSetTableModel (Fig. 21.25) performs the connection to the database via a TableModel and maintains the ResultSet. Class DisplayQueryResults (Fig. 21.28) creates the GUI and specifies an instance of class ResultSetTableModel to provide data for the JTable.

ResultSetTableModel Class

Class ResultSetTableModel (Fig. 21.25) extends class **AbstractTableModel** (package javax.swing.table), which implements interface TableModel. ResultSetTableModel overrides TableModel methods **getColumnClass**, **getColumnCount**, **getColumnName**, **get-RowCount** and **getValueAt**. The default implementations of TableModel methods is-CellEditable and setValueAt (provided by AbstractTableModel) are not overridden, because this example does not support editing the JTable cells. The default implementations of TableModel methods **addTableModelListener** and **removeTableModelListener** (provided by AbstractTableModel) are not overridden, because the implementations of these methods in AbstractTableModel properly add and remove event listeners.

```
1   // Fig. 21.25: ResultSetTableModel.java
2   // A TableModel that supplies ResultSet data to a JTable.
3   import java.sql.Connection;
4   import java.sql.Statement;
5   import java.sql.DriverManager;
6   import java.sql.ResultSet;
7   import java.sql.ResultSetMetaData;
8   import java.sql.SQLException;
9   import javax.swing.table.AbstractTableModel;
10
11  // ResultSet rows and columns are counted from 1 and JTable
12  // rows and columns are counted from 0. When processing
13  // ResultSet rows or columns for use in a JTable, it is
14  // necessary to add 1 to the row or column number to manipulate
15  // the appropriate ResultSet column (i.e., JTable column 0 is
16  // ResultSet column 1 and JTable row 0 is ResultSet row 1).
17  public class ResultSetTableModel extends AbstractTableModel
18  {
19     private final Connection connection;
20     private final Statement statement;
21     private ResultSet resultSet;
22     private ResultSetMetaData metaData;
23     private int numberOfRows;
24
25     // keep track of database connection status
26     private boolean connectedToDatabase = false;
27
28     // constructor initializes resultSet and obtains its metadata object;
29     // determines number of rows
30     public ResultSetTableModel(String url, String username,
31        String password, String query) throws SQLException
32     {
33        // connect to database
34        connection = DriverManager.getConnection(url, username, password);
35
36        // create Statement to query database
37        statement = connection.createStatement(
38           ResultSet.TYPE_SCROLL_INSENSITIVE,
39           ResultSet.CONCUR_READ_ONLY);
```

Fig. 21.25 | A TableModel that supplies ResultSet data to a JTable. (Part 1 of 4.)

```
40
41        // update database connection status
42        connectedToDatabase = true;
43
44        // set query and execute it
45        setQuery(query);
46     }
47
48     // get class that represents column type
49     public Class getColumnClass(int column) throws IllegalStateException
50     {
51        // ensure database connection is available
52        if (!connectedToDatabase)
53           throw new IllegalStateException("Not Connected to Database");
54
55        // determine Java class of column
56        try
57        {
58           String className = metaData.getColumnClassName(column + 1);
59
60           // return Class object that represents className
61           return Class.forName(className);
62        }
63        catch (Exception exception)
64        {
65           exception.printStackTrace();
66        }
67
68        return Object.class; // if problems occur above, assume type Object
69     }
70
71     // get number of columns in ResultSet
72     public int getColumnCount() throws IllegalStateException
73     {
74        // ensure database connection is available
75        if (!connectedToDatabase)
76           throw new IllegalStateException("Not Connected to Database");
77
78        // determine number of columns
79        try
80        {
81           return metaData.getColumnCount();
82        }
83        catch (SQLException sqlException)
84        {
85           sqlException.printStackTrace();
86        }
87
88        return 0; // if problems occur above, return 0 for number of columns
89     }
90
```

Fig. 21.25 | A TableModel that supplies ResultSet data to a JTable. (Part 2 of 4.)

```
91      // get name of a particular column in ResultSet
92      public String getColumnName(int column) throws IllegalStateException
93      {
94          // ensure database connection is available
95          if (!connectedToDatabase)
96              throw new IllegalStateException("Not Connected to Database");
97
98          // determine column name
99          try
100         {
101             return metaData.getColumnName(column + 1);
102         }
103         catch (SQLException sqlException)
104         {
105             sqlException.printStackTrace();
106         }
107
108         return ""; // if problems, return empty string for column name
109     }
110
111     // return number of rows in ResultSet
112     public int getRowCount() throws IllegalStateException
113     {
114         // ensure database connection is available
115         if (!connectedToDatabase)
116             throw new IllegalStateException("Not Connected to Database");
117
118         return numberOfRows;
119     }
120
121     // obtain value in particular row and column
122     public Object getValueAt(int row, int column)
123         throws IllegalStateException
124     {
125         // ensure database connection is available
126         if (!connectedToDatabase)
127             throw new IllegalStateException("Not Connected to Database");
128
129         // obtain a value at specified ResultSet row and column
130         try
131         {
132             resultSet.absolute(row + 1);
133             return resultSet.getObject(column + 1);
134         }
135         catch (SQLException sqlException)
136         {
137             sqlException.printStackTrace();
138         }
139
140         return ""; // if problems, return empty string object
141     }
```

Fig. 21.25 | A TableModel that supplies ResultSet data to a JTable. (Part 3 of 4.)

```
142
143        // set new database query string
144        public void setQuery(String query)
145           throws SQLException, IllegalStateException
146        {
147           // ensure database connection is available
148           if (!connectedToDatabase)
149              throw new IllegalStateException("Not Connected to Database");
150
151           // specify query and execute it
152           resultSet = statement.executeQuery(query);
153
154           // obtain metadata for ResultSet
155           metaData = resultSet.getMetaData();
156
157           // determine number of rows in ResultSet
158           resultSet.last(); // move to last row
159           numberOfRows = resultSet.getRow(); // get row number
160
161           // notify JTable that model has changed
162           fireTableStructureChanged();
163        }
164
165        // close Statement and Connection
166        public void disconnectFromDatabase()
167        {
168           if (connectedToDatabase)
169           {
170              // close Statement and Connection
171              try
172              {
173                 resultSet.close();
174                 statement.close();
175                 connection.close();
176              }
177              catch (SQLException sqlException)
178              {
179                 sqlException.printStackTrace();
180              }
181              finally  // update database connection status
182              {
183                 connectedToDatabase = false;
184              }
185           }
186        }
187     } // end class ResultSetTableModel
```

Fig. 21.25 | A TableModel that supplies ResultSet data to a JTable. (Part 4 of 4.)

ResultSetTableModel *Constructor*

The ResultSetTableModel constructor (lines 30–46) accepts four String arguments—
the URL of the database, the username, the password and the default query to perform.
The constructor throws any exceptions that occur in its body back to the application that
created the ResultSetTableModel object, so that the application can determine how to

handle the exception (e.g., report an error and terminate the application). Line 34 establishes a connection to the database. Lines 37–39 invoke Connection method createStatement to create a Statement object. This example uses a version of method createStatement that takes two arguments—the result set type and the result set concurrency. The **result set type** (Fig. 21.26) specifies whether the ResultSet's cursor is able to scroll in both directions or forward only and whether the ResultSet is sensitive to changes made to the underlying data.

ResultSet constant	Description
TYPE_FORWARD_ONLY	Specifies that a ResultSet's cursor can move only in the forward direction (i.e., from the first to the last row in the ResultSet).
TYPE_SCROLL_INSENSITIVE	Specifies that a ResultSet's cursor can scroll in either direction and that the changes made to the underlying data during ResultSet processing are not reflected in the ResultSet unless the program queries the database again.
TYPE_SCROLL_SENSITIVE	Specifies that a ResultSet's cursor can scroll in either direction and that the changes made to the underlying data during ResultSet processing are reflected immediately in the ResultSet.

Fig. 21.26 | ResultSet constants for specifying ResultSet type.

Portability Tip 21.3

Some JDBC drivers do not support scrollable ResultSets. In such cases, the driver typically returns a ResultSet in which the cursor can move only forward. For more information, see your database driver documentation.

Common Programming Error 21.8

Attempting to move the cursor backward through a ResultSet when the database driver does not support backward scrolling causes a SQLFeatureNotSupportedException.

ResultSets that are sensitive to changes reflect those changes immediately after they're made with methods of interface ResultSet. If a ResultSet is insensitive to changes, the query that produced the ResultSet must be executed again to reflect any changes made. The **result set concurrency** (Fig. 21.27) specifies whether the ResultSet can be updated with ResultSet's update methods.

ResultSet static concurrency constant	Description
CONCUR_READ_ONLY	Specifies that a ResultSet can't be updated—changes to the ResultSet contents cannot be reflected in the database with ResultSet's update methods.
CONCUR_UPDATABLE	Specifies that a ResultSet can be updated (i.e., changes to its contents can be reflected in the database with ResultSet's update methods).

Fig. 21.27 | ResultSet constants for specifying result properties.

Portability Tip 21.4

Some JDBC drivers do not support updatable ResultSets. *In such cases, the driver typically returns a read-only* ResultSet. *For more information, see your database driver documentation.*

Common Programming Error 21.9

Attempting to update a ResultSet *when the database driver does not support updatable* ResultSets *causes* SQLFeatureNotSupportedExceptions.

This example uses a ResultSet that is scrollable, insensitive to changes and read only. Line 45 (Fig. 21.25) invokes method setQuery (lines 144–163) to perform the default query.

ResultSetTableModel Method getColumnClass

Method getColumnClass (lines 49–69) returns a Class object that represents the superclass of all objects in a particular column. The JTable uses this information to configure the default cell renderer and cell editor for that column in the JTable. Line 58 uses ResultSet-MetaData method **getColumnClassName** to obtain the fully qualified class name for the specified column. Line 61 loads the class and returns the corresponding Class object. If an exception occurs, the catch in lines 63–66 prints a stack trace and line 68 returns Object.class—the Class instance that represents class Object—as the default type. [*Note:* Line 58 uses the argument column + 1. Like arrays, JTable row and column numbers are counted from 0. However, ResultSet row and column numbers are counted from 1. Thus, when processing ResultSet rows or columns for use in a JTable, it's necessary to add 1 to the row or column number to manipulate the appropriate ResultSet row or column.]

ResultSetTableModel Method getColumnCount

Method getColumnCount (lines 72–89) returns the number of columns in the model's underlying ResultSet. Line 81 uses ResultSetMetaData method **getColumnCount** to obtain the number of columns in the ResultSet. If an exception occurs, the catch in lines 83–86 prints a stack trace and line 88 returns 0 as the default number of columns.

ResultSetTableModel Method getColumnName

Method getColumnName (lines 92–109) returns the name of the column in the model's underlying ResultSet. Line 101 uses ResultSetMetaData method **getColumnName** to obtain the column name from the ResultSet. If an exception occurs, the catch in lines 103–106 prints a stack trace and line 108 returns the empty string as the default column name.

ResultSetTableModel Method getRowCount

Method getRowCount (lines 112–119) returns the number of rows in the model's underlying ResultSet. When method setQuery (lines 144–163) performs a query, it stores the number of rows in variable numberOfRows.

ResultSetTableModel Method getValueAt

Method getValueAt (lines 122–141) returns the Object in a particular row and column of the model's underlying ResultSet. Line 132 uses ResultSet method **absolute** to position the ResultSet cursor at a specific row. Line 133 uses ResultSet method getObject to obtain the Object in a specific column of the current row. If an exception occurs, the catch in lines 135–138 prints a stack trace and line 140 returns an empty string as the default value.

ResultSetTableModel *Method* setQuery

Method setQuery (lines 144–163) executes the query it receives as an argument to obtain a new ResultSet (line 152). Line 155 gets the ResultSetMetaData for the new Result-Set. Line 158 uses ResultSet method **last** to position the ResultSet cursor at the last row in the ResultSet. [*Note:* This can be slow if the table contains many rows.] Line 159 uses ResultSet method **getRow** to obtain the row number for the current row in the ResultSet. Line 162 invokes method **fireTableStructureChanged** (inherited from class AbstractTableModel) to notify any JTable using this ResultSetTableModel object as its model that the structure of the model has changed. This causes the JTable to repopulate its rows and columns with the new ResultSet data. Method setQuery throws any exceptions that occur in its body back to the application that invoked setQuery.

ResultSetTableModel *Method* disconnectFromDatabase

Method disconnectFromDatabase (lines 166–186) implements an appropriate termination method for class ResultSetTableModel. A class designer should provide a public method that clients of the class must invoke explicitly to free resources that an object has used. In this case, method disconnectFromDatabase closes the ResultSet, Statement and Connection (lines 173–175), which are considered limited resources. Clients of the ResultSetTableModel class should always invoke this method when the instance of this class is no longer needed. Before releasing resources, line 168 verifies whether the connection is already terminated. If not, the method proceeds. The other methods in class ResultSetTableModel each throw an IllegalStateException if connectedToDatabase is false. Method disconnectFromDatabase sets connectedToDatabase to false (line 183) to ensure that clients do not use an instance of ResultSetTableModel after that instance has already been terminated. IllegalStateException is an exception from the Java libraries that is appropriate for indicating this error condition.

DisplayQueryResults *Class*

Class DisplayQueryResults (Fig. 21.28) implements the application's GUI and interacts with the ResultSetTableModel via a JTable object. This application also demonstrates the JTable sorting and filtering capabilities.

```
 1    // Fig. 21.28: DisplayQueryResults.java
 2    // Display the contents of the Authors table in the books database.
 3    import java.awt.BorderLayout;
 4    import java.awt.event.ActionListener;
 5    import java.awt.event.ActionEvent;
 6    import java.awt.event.WindowAdapter;
 7    import java.awt.event.WindowEvent;
 8    import java.sql.SQLException;
 9    import java.util.regex.PatternSyntaxException;
10    import javax.swing.JFrame;
11    import javax.swing.JTextArea;
12    import javax.swing.JScrollPane;
13    import javax.swing.ScrollPaneConstants;
14    import javax.swing.JTable;
15    import javax.swing.JOptionPane;
```

Fig. 21.28 | Display the contents of the Authors table in the books database. (Part 1 of 5.)

```
16  import javax.swing.JButton;
17  import javax.swing.Box;
18  import javax.swing.JLabel;
19  import javax.swing.JTextField;
20  import javax.swing.RowFilter;
21  import javax.swing.table.TableRowSorter;
22  import javax.swing.table.TableModel;
23
24  public class DisplayQueryResults extends JFrame
25  {
26     // database URL, username and password
27     private static final String DATABASE_URL = "jdbc:derby:books";
28     private static final String USERNAME = "deitel";
29     private static final String PASSWORD = "deitel";
30
31     // default query retrieves all data from Authors table
32     private static final String DEFAULT_QUERY = "SELECT * FROM Authors";
33
34     private static ResultSetTableModel tableModel;
35
36     public static void main(String args[])
37     {
38        // create ResultSetTableModel and display database table
39        try
40        {
41           // create TableModel for results of query SELECT * FROM Authors
42           tableModel = new ResultSetTableModel(DATABASE_URL,
43              USERNAME, PASSWORD, DEFAULT_QUERY);
44
45           // set up JTextArea in which user types queries
46           final JTextArea queryArea = new JTextArea(DEFAULT_QUERY, 3, 100);
47           queryArea.setWrapStyleWord(true);
48           queryArea.setLineWrap(true);
49
50           JScrollPane scrollPane = new JScrollPane(queryArea,
51              ScrollPaneConstants.VERTICAL_SCROLLBAR_AS_NEEDED,
52              ScrollPaneConstants.HORIZONTAL_SCROLLBAR_NEVER);
53
54           // set up JButton for submitting queries
55           JButton submitButton = new JButton("Submit Query");
56
57           // create Box to manage placement of queryArea and
58           // submitButton in GUI
59           Box boxNorth = Box.createHorizontalBox();
60           boxNorth.add(scrollPane);
61           boxNorth.add(submitButton);
62
63           // create JTable based on the tableModel
64           JTable resultTable = new JTable(tableModel);
65
66           JLabel filterLabel = new JLabel("Filter:");
67           final JTextField filterText = new JTextField();
68           JButton filterButton = new JButton("Apply Filter");
```

Fig. 21.28 | Display the contents of the Authors table in the books database. (Part 2 of 5.)

```
69                Box boxSouth = Box.createHorizontalBox();
70
71                boxSouth.add(filterLabel);
72                boxSouth.add(filterText);
73                boxSouth.add(filterButton);
74
75                // place GUI components on JFrame's content pane
76                JFrame window = new JFrame("Displaying Query Results");
77                add(boxNorth, BorderLayout.NORTH);
78                add(new JScrollPane(resultTable), BorderLayout.CENTER);
79                add(boxSouth, BorderLayout.SOUTH);
80
81                // create event listener for submitButton
82                submitButton.addActionListener(
83                   new ActionListener()
84                   {
85                      public void actionPerformed(ActionEvent event)
86                      {
87                         // perform a new query
88                         try
89                         {
90                            tableModel.setQuery(queryArea.getText());
91                         }
92                         catch (SQLException sqlException)
93                         {
94                            JOptionPane.showMessageDialog(null,
95                               sqlException.getMessage(), "Database error",
96                               JOptionPane.ERROR_MESSAGE);
97
98                            // try to recover from invalid user query
99                            // by executing default query
100                           try
101                           {
102                              tableModel.setQuery(DEFAULT_QUERY);
103                              queryArea.setText(DEFAULT_QUERY);
104                           }
105                           catch (SQLException sqlException2)
106                           {
107                              JOptionPane.showMessageDialog(null,
108                                 sqlException2.getMessage(), "Database error",
109                                 JOptionPane.ERROR_MESSAGE);
110
111                              // ensure database connection is closed
112                              tableModel.disconnectFromDatabase();
113
114                              System.exit(1); // terminate application
115                           }
116                        }
117                     }
118                  }
119               );
120
```

Fig. 21.28 | Display the contents of the Authors table in the books database. (Part 3 of 5.)

```
121            final TableRowSorter<TableModel> sorter =
122               new TableRowSorter<TableModel>(tableModel);
123            resultTable.setRowSorter(sorter);
124
125            // create listener for filterButton
126            filterButton.addActionListener(
127               new ActionListener()
128               {
129                  // pass filter text to listener
130                  public void actionPerformed(ActionEvent e)
131                  {
132                     String text = filterText.getText();
133
134                     if (text.length() == 0)
135                        sorter.setRowFilter(null);
136                     else
137                     {
138                        try
139                        {
140                           sorter.setRowFilter(
141                              RowFilter.regexFilter(text));
142                        }
143                        catch (PatternSyntaxException pse)
144                        {
145                           JOptionPane.showMessageDialog(null,
146                              "Bad regex pattern", "Bad regex pattern",
147                              JOptionPane.ERROR_MESSAGE);
148                        }
149                     }
150                  }
151               }
152            );
153            // dispose of window when user quits application (this overrides
154            // the default of HIDE_ON_CLOSE)
155            window.setDefaultCloseOperation(DISPOSE_ON_CLOSE);
156            window.setSize(500, 250);
157            window.setVisible(true);
158
159            // ensure database is closed when user quits application
160            addWindowListener(
161               new WindowAdapter()
162               {
163                  // disconnect from database and exit when window has closed
164                  public void windowClosed(WindowEvent event)
165                  {
166                     tableModel.disconnectFromDatabase();
167                     System.exit(0);
168                  }
169               }
170            );
171         }
172         catch (SQLException sqlException)
173         {
```

Fig. 21.28 | Display the contents of the Authors table in the books database. (Part 4 of 5.)

```
174            JOptionPane.showMessageDialog(null, sqlException.getMessage(),
175               "Database error", JOptionPane.ERROR_MESSAGE);
176            tableModel.disconnectFromDatabase();
177            System.exit(1); // terminate application
178         }
179      }
180   } // end class DisplayQueryResults
```

a) Displaying all authors from
the Authors table

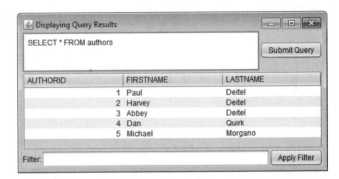

b) Displaying the the authors'
first and last names joined with
the titles and edition numbers
of the books they've authored

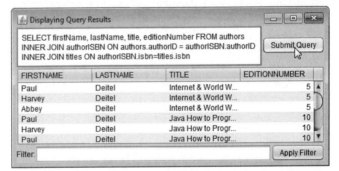

c) Filtering the results of the
previous query to show only the
books with Java in the title

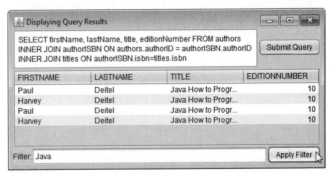

Fig. 21.28 | Display the contents of the Authors table in the books database. (Part 5 of 5.)

Lines 27–29 and 32 declare the URL, username, password and default query that are passed to the ResultSetTableModel constructor to make the initial connection to the database and perform the default query. The main method (lines 36–179) creates a

ResultSetTableModel object and the GUI for the application and displays the GUI in a
JFrame. Line 64 creates the JTable object and passes a ResultSetTableModel object (created at lines 42–43) to the JTable constructor, which then registers the JTable as a listener
for TableModelEvents generated by the ResultSetTableModel.

The local variables queryArea (line 46), filterText (line 67) and sorter (lines 121–
122) are declared final because they're used from anonymous inner classes. Recall that
any local variable that will be used in an anonymous inner class must be declared final;
otherwise, a compilation error occurs. (In Java SE 8, this program would compile without
declaring these variables final because these variables would be effectively final, as discussed in Chapter 17.)

Lines 82–119 register an event handler for the submitButton that the user clicks to
submit a query to the database. When the user clicks the button, method actionPerformed (lines 85–117) invokes method setQuery from the class ResultSetTableModel to
execute the new query (line 90). If the user's query fails (e.g., because of a syntax error in
the user's input), lines 102–103 execute the default query. If the default query also fails,
there could be a more serious error, so line 112 ensures that the database connection is
closed and line 114 exits the program. The screen captures in Fig. 21.28 show the results
of two queries. The first screen capture shows the default query that retrieves all the data
from table Authors of database books. The second screen capture shows a query that
selects each author's first name and last name from the Authors table and combines that
information with the title and edition number from the Titles table. Try entering your
own queries in the text area and clicking the **Submit Query** button to execute the query.

Lines 161–170 register a **WindowListener** for the **windowClosed** event, which occurs
when the user closes the window. Since WindowListeners can handle several window
events, we extend class **WindowAdapter** and override only the windowClosed event handler.

Sorting Rows in a JTable
JTables allow users to sort rows by the data in a specific column. Lines 121–122 use the
TableRowSorter class (from package **javax.swing.table**) to create an object that uses our
ResultSetTableModel to sort rows in the JTable that displays query results. When the
user clicks the title of a particular JTable column, the TableRowSorter interacts with the
underlying TableModel to reorder the rows based on the data in that column. Line 123
uses JTable method **setRowSorter** to specify the TableRowSorter for resultTable.

Filtering Rows in a JTable
JTables can now show subsets of the data from the underlying TableModel. This is known
as filtering the data. Lines 126–152 register an event handler for the filterButton that
the user clicks to filter the data. In method actionPerformed (lines 130–150), line 132
obtains the filter text. If the user did not specify filter text, line 135 uses JTable method
setRowFilter to remove any prior filter by setting the filter to null. Otherwise, lines 140–
141 use setRowFilter to specify a **RowFilter** (from package javax.swing) based on the
user's input. Class RowFilter provides several methods for creating filters. The static
method **regexFilter** receives a String containing a regular expression pattern as its argument and an optional set of indices that specify which columns to filter. If no indices are
specified, then all the columns are searched. In this example, the regular expression pattern
is the text the user typed. Once the filter is set, the data displayed in the JTable is updated
based on the filtered TableModel.

21.7 RowSet Interface

In the preceding examples, you learned how to query a database by explicitly establishing a Connection to the database, preparing a Statement for querying the database and executing the query. In this section, we demonstrate the **RowSet interface**, which configures the database connection and prepares query statements automatically. The interface RowSet provides several *set* methods that allow you to specify the properties needed to establish a connection (such as the database URL, username and password of the database) and create a Statement (such as a query). RowSet also provides several *get* methods that return these properties.

Connected and Disconnected RowSets
There are two types of RowSet objects—connected and disconnected. A **connected RowSet** object connects to the database once and remains connected while the object is in use. A **disconnected RowSet** object connects to the database, executes a query to retrieve the data from the database and then closes the connection. A program may change the data in a disconnected RowSet while it's disconnected. Modified data can be updated in the database after a disconnected RowSet reestablishes the connection with the database.

Package **javax.sql.rowset** contains two subinterfaces of RowSet—JdbcRowSet and CachedRowSet. **JdbcRowSet**, a connected RowSet, acts as a wrapper around a ResultSet object and allows you to scroll through and update the rows in the ResultSet. Recall that by default, a ResultSet object is nonscrollable and read only—you must explicitly set the result-set type constant to TYPE_SCROLL_INSENSITIVE and set the result-set concurrency constant to CONCUR_UPDATABLE to make a ResultSet object scrollable and updatable. A JdbcRowSet object is scrollable and updatable by default. **CachedRowSet**, a disconnected RowSet, caches the data of a ResultSet in memory and disconnects from the database. Like JdbcRowSet, a CachedRowSet object is scrollable and updatable by default. A CachedRowSet object is also *serializable*, so it can be passed between Java applications through a network, such as the Internet. However, CachedRowSet has a limitation—the amount of data that can be stored in memory is limited. Package javax.sql.rowset contains three other subinterfaces of RowSet.

> **Portability Tip 21.5**
> *A RowSet can provide scrolling capability for drivers that do not support scrollable ResultSets.*

Using a RowSet
Figure 21.29 reimplements the example of Fig. 21.23 using a RowSet. Rather than establish the connection and create a Statement explicitly, Fig. 21.29 uses a JdbcRowSet object to create a Connection and a Statement automatically.

Class **RowSetProvider** (package javax.sql.rowset) provides static method **newFactory** which returns a an object that implements interface **RowSetFactory** (package javax.sql.rowset) that can be used to create various types of RowSets. Lines 18–19 in the try-with-resources statement use RowSetFactory method **createJdbcRowSet** to obtain a JdbcRowSet object.

Lines 22–24 set the RowSet properties that the DriverManager uses to establish a database connection. Line 22 invokes JdbcRowSet method **setUrl** to specify the database

```java
 1   // Fig. 21.29: JdbcRowSetTest.java
 2   // Displaying the contents of the Authors table using JdbcRowSet.
 3   import java.sql.ResultSetMetaData;
 4   import java.sql.SQLException;
 5   import javax.sql.rowset.JdbcRowSet;
 6   import javax.sql.rowset.RowSetProvider;
 7
 8   public class JdbcRowSetTest
 9   {
10      // JDBC driver name and database URL
11      private static final String DATABASE_URL = "jdbc:derby:books";
12      private static final String USERNAME = "deitel";
13      private static final String PASSWORD = "deitel";
14
15      public static void main(String args[])
16      {
17         // connect to database books and query database
18         try (JdbcRowSet rowSet =
19            RowSetProvider.newFactory().createJdbcRowSet())
20         {
21            // specify JdbcRowSet properties
22            rowSet.setUrl(DATABASE_URL);
23            rowSet.setUsername(USERNAME);
24            rowSet.setPassword(PASSWORD);
25            rowSet.setCommand("SELECT * FROM Authors"); // set query
26            rowSet.execute(); // execute query
27
28            // process query results
29            ResultSetMetaData metaData = rowSet.getMetaData();
30            int numberOfColumns = metaData.getColumnCount();
31            System.out.printf("Authors Table of Books Database:%n%n");
32
33            // display rowset header
34            for (int i = 1; i <= numberOfColumns; i++)
35               System.out.printf("%-8s\t", metaData.getColumnName(i));
36            System.out.println();
37
38            // display each row
39            while (rowSet.next())
40            {
41               for (int i = 1; i <= numberOfColumns; i++)
42                  System.out.printf("%-8s\t", rowSet.getObject(i));
43               System.out.println();
44            }
45         }
46         catch (SQLException sqlException)
47         {
48            sqlException.printStackTrace();
49            System.exit(1);
50         }
51      }
52   } // end class JdbcRowSetTest
```

Fig. 21.29 | Displaying the contents of the Authors table using JdbcRowSet. (Part 1 of 2.)

```
Authors Table of Books Database:

AUTHORID        FIRSTNAME       LASTNAME
1               Paul            Deitel
2               Harvey          Deitel
3               Abbey           Deitel
4               Dan             Quirk
5               Michael         Morgano
```

Fig. 21.29 | Displaying the contents of the Authors table using JdbcRowSet. (Part 2 of 2.)

URL. Line 23 invokes JdbcRowSet method **setUsername** to specify the username. Line 24 invokes JdbcRowSet method **setPassword** to specify the password. Line 25 invokes Jdbc-RowSet method **setCommand** to specify the SQL query that will be used to populate the RowSet. Line 26 invokes JdbcRowSet method **execute** to execute the SQL query. Method execute performs four actions—it establishes a Connection to the database, prepares the query Statement, executes the query and stores the ResultSet returned by query. The Connection, Statement and ResultSet are encapsulated in the JdbcRowSet object.

The remaining code is almost identical to Fig. 21.23, except that line 29 (Fig. 21.29) obtains a ResultSetMetaData object from the JdbcRowSet, line 39 uses the JdbcRowSet's next method to get the next row of the result and line 42 uses the JdbcRowSet's getObject method to obtain a column's value. When the end of the try block is reached, the try-with-resources statement invokes JdbcRowSet method **close**, which closes the RowSet's encapsulated ResultSet, Statement and Connection. In a CachedRowSet, invoking close also releases the resources held by that RowSet. The output of this application is the same as that of Fig. 21.23.

21.8 PreparedStatements

A **PreparedStatement** enables you to create compiled SQL statements that execute more efficiently than Statements. PreparedStatements can also specify parameters, making them more flexible than Statements—you can execute the same query repeatedly with different parameter values. For example, in the books database, you might want to locate all book titles for an author with a specific last and first name, and you might want to execute that query for several authors. With a PreparedStatement, that query is defined as follows:

```
PreparedStatement authorBooks = connection.prepareStatement(
   "SELECT LastName, FirstName, Title " +
   "FROM Authors INNER JOIN AuthorISBN " +
      "ON Authors.AuthorID=AuthorISBN.AuthorID " +
   "INNER JOIN Titles " +
      "ON AuthorISBN.ISBN=Titles.ISBN " +
   "WHERE LastName = ? AND FirstName = ?");
```

The two question marks (?) in the the preceding SQL statement's last line are placeholders for values that will be passed as part of the query to the database. Before executing a PreparedStatement, the program must specify the parameter values by using the PreparedStatement interface's *set* methods.

For the preceding query, both parameters are strings that can be set with PreparedStatement method **setString** as follows:

```
authorBooks.setString(1, "Deitel");
authorBooks.setString(2, "Paul");
```

Method `setString`'s first argument represents the parameter number being set, and the second argument is that parameter's value. Parameter numbers are *counted from 1*, starting with the first question mark (?). When the program executes the preceding `Prepared-Statement` with the parameter values set above, the SQL passed to the database is

```
SELECT LastName, FirstName, Title
FROM Authors INNER JOIN AuthorISBN
   ON Authors.AuthorID=AuthorISBN.AuthorID
INNER JOIN Titles
   ON AuthorISBN.ISBN=Titles.ISBN
WHERE LastName = 'Deitel' AND FirstName = 'Paul'
```

Method `setString` automatically escapes `String` parameter values as necessary. For example, if the last name is O'Brien, the statement

```
authorBooks.setString(1, "O'Brien");
```

escapes the ' character in O'Brien by replacing it with two single-quote characters, so that the ' appears correctly in the database.

Performance Tip 21.2

PreparedStatements are more efficient than Statements when executing SQL statements multiple times and with different parameter values.

Error-Prevention Tip 21.2

Use PreparedStatements with parameters for queries that receive String values as arguments to ensure that the Strings are quoted properly in the SQL statement.

Error-Prevention Tip 21.3

PreparedStatements help prevent SQL injection attacks, which typically occur in SQL statements that include user input improperly. To avoid this security issue, use Prepared-Statements in which user input can be supplied only via parameters—indicated with ? when creating a PreparedStatement. Once you've created such a PreparedStatement, you can use its set methods to specify the user input as arguments for those parameters.

Interface `PreparedStatement` provides *set* methods for each supported SQL type. It's important to use the *set* method that is appropriate for the parameter's SQL type in the database—`SQLExceptions` occur when a program attempts to convert a parameter value to an incorrect type.

Address Book Application that Uses *PreparedStatements*
We now present an address book app that enables you to browse existing entries, add new entries and search for entries with a specific last name. Our `AddressBook` Java DB database contains an `Addresses` table with the columns `addressID`, `FirstName`, `LastName`, `Email` and `PhoneNumber`. The column `addressID` is an identity column in the `Addresses` table.

Class *Person*
Our address book application consists of three classes—`Person` (Fig. 21.30), `PersonQueries` (Fig. 21.31) and `AddressBookDisplay` (Fig. 21.32). Class `Person` is a simple class

that represents one person in the address book. The class contains fields for the address ID, first name, last name, email address and phone number, as well as *set* and *get* methods for manipulating these fields.

```java
1   // Fig. 21.30: Person.java
2   // Person class that represents an entry in an address book.
3   public class Person
4   {
5      private int addressID;
6      private String firstName;
7      private String lastName;
8      private String email;
9      private String phoneNumber;
10
11     // constructor
12     public Person()
13     {
14     }
15
16     // constructor
17     public Person(int addressID, String firstName, String lastName,
18        String email, String phoneNumber)
19     {
20        setAddressID(addressID);
21        setFirstName(firstName);
22        setLastName(lastName);
23        setEmail(email);
24        setPhoneNumber(phoneNumber);
25     }
26
27     // sets the addressID
28     public void setAddressID(int addressID)
29     {
30        this.addressID = addressID;
31     }
32
33     // returns the addressID
34     public int getAddressID()
35     {
36        return addressID;
37     }
38
39     // sets the firstName
40     public void setFirstName(String firstName)
41     {
42        this.firstName = firstName;
43     }
44
45     // returns the first name
46     public String getFirstName()
47     {
```

Fig. 21.30 | Person class that represents an entry in an AddressBook. (Part 1 of 2.)

```
48          return firstName;
49      }
50
51      // sets the lastName
52      public void setLastName(String lastName)
53      {
54          this.lastName = lastName;
55      }
56
57      // returns the last name
58      public String getLastName()
59      {
60          return lastName;
61      }
62
63      // sets the email address
64      public void setEmail(String email)
65      {
66          this.email = email;
67      }
68
69      // returns the email address
70      public String getEmail()
71      {
72          return email;
73      }
74
75      // sets the phone number
76      public void setPhoneNumber(String phone)
77      {
78          this.phoneNumber = phone;
79      }
80
81      // returns the phone number
82      public String getPhoneNumber()
83      {
84          return phoneNumber;
85      }
86  } // end class Person
```

Fig. 21.30 | Person class that represents an entry in an AddressBook. (Part 2 of 2.)

Class PersonQueries

Class PersonQueries (Fig. 21.31) manages the address book application's database connection and creates the PreparedStatements that the application uses to interact with the database. Lines 18–20 declare three PreparedStatement variables. The constructor (lines 23–49) connects to the database at lines 27–28.

```
1   // Fig. 21.31: PersonQueries.java
2   // PreparedStatements used by the Address Book application.
3   import java.sql.Connection;
```

Fig. 21.31 | PreparedStatements used by the Address Book application. (Part 1 of 5.)

```
4   import java.sql.DriverManager;
5   import java.sql.PreparedStatement;
6   import java.sql.ResultSet;
7   import java.sql.SQLException;
8   import java.util.List;
9   import java.util.ArrayList;
10
11  public class PersonQueries
12  {
13     private static final String URL = "jdbc:derby:AddressBook";
14     private static final String USERNAME = "deitel";
15     private static final String PASSWORD = "deitel";
16
17     private Connection connection; // manages connection
18     private PreparedStatement selectAllPeople;
19     private PreparedStatement selectPeopleByLastName;
20     private PreparedStatement insertNewPerson;
21
22     // constructor
23     public PersonQueries()
24     {
25        try
26        {
27           connection =
28              DriverManager.getConnection(URL, USERNAME, PASSWORD);
29
30           // create query that selects all entries in the AddressBook
31           selectAllPeople =
32              connection.prepareStatement("SELECT * FROM Addresses");
33
34           // create query that selects entries with a specific last name
35           selectPeopleByLastName = connection.prepareStatement(
36              "SELECT * FROM Addresses WHERE LastName = ?");
37
38           // create insert that adds a new entry into the database
39           insertNewPerson = connection.prepareStatement(
40              "INSERT INTO Addresses " +
41              "(FirstName, LastName, Email, PhoneNumber) " +
42              "VALUES (?, ?, ?, ?)");
43        }
44        catch (SQLException sqlException)
45        {
46           sqlException.printStackTrace();
47           System.exit(1);
48        }
49     }
50
51     // select all of the addresses in the database
52     public List< Person > getAllPeople()
53     {
54        List< Person > results = null;
55        ResultSet resultSet = null;
56
```

Fig. 21.31 | PreparedStatements used by the Address Book application. (Part 2 of 5.)

```
57      try
58      {
59         // executeQuery returns ResultSet containing matching entries
60         resultSet = selectAllPeople.executeQuery();
61         results = new ArrayList< Person >();
62
63         while (resultSet.next())
64         {
65            results.add(new Person(
66               resultSet.getInt("addressID"),
67               resultSet.getString("FirstName"),
68               resultSet.getString("LastName"),
69               resultSet.getString("Email"),
70               resultSet.getString("PhoneNumber")));
71         }
72      }
73      catch (SQLException sqlException)
74      {
75         sqlException.printStackTrace();
76      }
77      finally
78      {
79         try
80         {
81            resultSet.close();
82         }
83         catch (SQLException sqlException)
84         {
85            sqlException.printStackTrace();
86            close();
87         }
88      }
89
90      return results;
91   }
92
93   // select person by last name
94   public List< Person > getPeopleByLastName(String name)
95   {
96      List< Person > results = null;
97      ResultSet resultSet = null;
98
99      try
100     {
101        selectPeopleByLastName.setString(1, name); // specify last name
102
103        // executeQuery returns ResultSet containing matching entries
104        resultSet = selectPeopleByLastName.executeQuery();
105
106        results = new ArrayList< Person >();
107
108        while (resultSet.next())
109        {
```

Fig. 21.31 | PreparedStatements used by the Address Book application. (Part 3 of 5.)

```
110              results.add(new Person(resultSet.getInt("addressID"),
111                  resultSet.getString("FirstName"),
112                  resultSet.getString("LastName"),
113                  resultSet.getString("Email"),
114                  resultSet.getString("PhoneNumber")));
115          }
116      }
117      catch (SQLException sqlException)
118      {
119          sqlException.printStackTrace();
120      }
121      finally
122      {
123          try
124          {
125              resultSet.close();
126          }
127          catch (SQLException sqlException)
128          {
129              sqlException.printStackTrace();
130              close();
131          }
132      }
133
134      return results;
135  }
136
137  // add an entry
138  public int addPerson(
139      String fname, String lname, String email, String num)
140  {
141      int result = 0;
142
143      // set parameters, then execute insertNewPerson
144      try
145      {
146          insertNewPerson.setString(1, fname);
147          insertNewPerson.setString(2, lname);
148          insertNewPerson.setString(3, email);
149          insertNewPerson.setString(4, num);
150
151          // insert the new entry; returns # of rows updated
152          result = insertNewPerson.executeUpdate();
153      }
154      catch (SQLException sqlException)
155      {
156          sqlException.printStackTrace();
157          close();
158      }
159
160      return result;
161  }
162
```

Fig. 21.31 | PreparedStatements used by the Address Book application. (Part 4 of 5.)

```
163    // close the database connection
164    public void close()
165    {
166       try
167       {
168          connection.close();
169       }
170       catch (SQLException sqlException)
171       {
172          sqlException.printStackTrace();
173       }
174    }
175 } // end class PersonQueries
```

Fig. 21.31 | PreparedStatements used by the Address Book application. (Part 5 of 5.)

Creating *PreparedStatements*
Lines 31–32 invoke Connection method **prepareStatement** to create the Prepared-Statement named selectAllPeople that selects all the rows in the Addresses table. Lines 35–36 create the PreparedStatement named selectPeopleByLastName with a parameter. This statement selects all the rows in the Addresses table that match a particular last name. Notice the ? character that's used to specify the last-name parameter. Lines 39–42 create the PreparedStatement named insertNewPerson with four parameters that represent the first name, last name, email address and phone number for a new entry. Again, notice the ? characters used to represent these parameters.

PersonQueries *Method* getAllPeople
Method getAllPeople (lines 52–91) executes PreparedStatement selectAllPeople (line 60) by calling method **executeQuery**, which returns a ResultSet containing the rows that match the query (in this case, all the rows in the Addresses table). Lines 61–71 place the query results in an ArrayList of Person objects, which is returned to the caller at line 90. Method getPeopleByLastName (lines 94–135) uses PreparedStatement method setString to set the parameter to selectPeopleByLastName (line 101). Then, line 104 executes the query and lines 106–115 place the query results in an ArrayList of Person objects. Line 134 returns the ArrayList to the caller.

PersonQueries *Methods* addPerson *and* Close
Method addPerson (lines 138–161) uses PreparedStatement method setString (lines 146–149) to set the parameters for the insertNewPerson PreparedStatement. Line 152 uses PreparedStatement method **executeUpdate** to insert the new record. This method returns an integer indicating the number of rows that were updated (or inserted) in the database. Method close (lines 164–174) simply closes the database connection.

Class *AddressBookDisplay*
The AddressBookDisplay (Fig. 21.32) application uses a PersonQueries object to interact with the database. Line 59 creates the PersonQueries object. When the user presses the **Browse All Entries** JButton, the browseButtonActionPerformed handler (lines 309–335) is called. Line 313 calls the method getAllPeople on the PersonQueries object to obtain all the entries in the database. The user can then scroll through the entries using the

Previous and **Next** JButtons. When the user presses the **Find** JButton, the queryButtonAc-tionPerformed handler (lines 265–287) is called. Lines 267–268 call method getPeo-pleByLastName on the PersonQueries object to obtain the entries in the database that match the specified last name. If there are several such entries, the user can then scroll through them using the **Previous** and **Next** JButtons.

```java
1   // Fig. 21.32: AddressBookDisplay.java
2   // A simple address book
3   import java.awt.event.ActionEvent;
4   import java.awt.event.ActionListener;
5   import java.awt.event.WindowAdapter;
6   import java.awt.event.WindowEvent;
7   import java.awt.FlowLayout;
8   import java.awt.GridLayout;
9   import java.util.List;
10  import javax.swing.JButton;
11  import javax.swing.Box;
12  import javax.swing.JFrame;
13  import javax.swing.JLabel;
14  import javax.swing.JPanel;
15  import javax.swing.JTextField;
16  import javax.swing.WindowConstants;
17  import javax.swing.BoxLayout;
18  import javax.swing.BorderFactory;
19  import javax.swing.JOptionPane;
20
21  public class AddressBookDisplay extends JFrame
22  {
23     private Person currentEntry;
24     private PersonQueries personQueries;
25     private List<Person> results;
26     private int numberOfEntries = 0;
27     private int currentEntryIndex;
28
29     private JButton browseButton;
30     private JLabel emailLabel;
31     private JTextField emailTextField;
32     private JLabel firstNameLabel;
33     private JTextField firstNameTextField;
34     private JLabel idLabel;
35     private JTextField idTextField;
36     private JTextField indexTextField;
37     private JLabel lastNameLabel;
38     private JTextField lastNameTextField;
39     private JTextField maxTextField;
40     private JButton nextButton;
41     private JLabel ofLabel;
42     private JLabel phoneLabel;
43     private JTextField phoneTextField;
44     private JButton previousButton;
45     private JButton queryButton;
46     private JLabel queryLabel;
```

Fig. 21.32 | A simple address book. (Part 1 of 8.)

```
47    private JPanel queryPanel;
48    private JPanel navigatePanel;
49    private JPanel displayPanel;
50    private JTextField queryTextField;
51    private JButton insertButton;
52
53    // constructor
54    public AddressBookDisplay()
55    {
56        super("Address Book");
57
58        // establish database connection and set up PreparedStatements
59        personQueries = new PersonQueries();
60
61        // create GUI
62        navigatePanel = new JPanel();
63        previousButton = new JButton();
64        indexTextField = new JTextField(2);
65        ofLabel = new JLabel();
66        maxTextField = new JTextField(2);
67        nextButton = new JButton();
68        displayPanel = new JPanel();
69        idLabel = new JLabel();
70        idTextField = new JTextField(10);
71        firstNameLabel = new JLabel();
72        firstNameTextField = new JTextField(10);
73        lastNameLabel = new JLabel();
74        lastNameTextField = new JTextField(10);
75        emailLabel = new JLabel();
76        emailTextField = new JTextField(10);
77        phoneLabel = new JLabel();
78        phoneTextField = new JTextField(10);
79        queryPanel = new JPanel();
80        queryLabel = new JLabel();
81        queryTextField = new JTextField(10);
82        queryButton = new JButton();
83        browseButton = new JButton();
84        insertButton = new JButton();
85
86        setLayout(new FlowLayout(FlowLayout.CENTER, 10, 10));
87        setSize(400, 300);
88        setResizable(false);
89
90        navigatePanel.setLayout(
91            new BoxLayout(navigatePanel, BoxLayout.X_AXIS));
92
93        previousButton.setText("Previous");
94        previousButton.setEnabled(false);
95        previousButton.addActionListener(
96            new ActionListener()
97            {
98                public void actionPerformed(ActionEvent evt)
99                {
```

Fig. 21.32 | A simple address book. (Part 2 of 8.)

```
100                    previousButtonActionPerformed(evt);
101               }
102          }
103     );
104
105     navigatePanel.add(previousButton);
106     navigatePanel.add(Box.createHorizontalStrut(10));
107
108     indexTextField.setHorizontalAlignment(
109        JTextField.CENTER);
110     indexTextField.addActionListener(
111        new ActionListener()
112        {
113           public void actionPerformed(ActionEvent evt)
114           {
115              indexTextFieldActionPerformed(evt);
116           }
117        }
118     );
119
120     navigatePanel.add(indexTextField);
121     navigatePanel.add(Box.createHorizontalStrut(10));
122
123     ofLabel.setText("of");
124     navigatePanel.add(ofLabel);
125     navigatePanel.add(Box.createHorizontalStrut(10));
126
127     maxTextField.setHorizontalAlignment(
128        JTextField.CENTER);
129     maxTextField.setEditable(false);
130     navigatePanel.add(maxTextField);
131     navigatePanel.add(Box.createHorizontalStrut(10));
132
133     nextButton.setText("Next");
134     nextButton.setEnabled(false);
135     nextButton.addActionListener(
136        new ActionListener()
137        {
138           public void actionPerformed(ActionEvent evt)
139           {
140              nextButtonActionPerformed(evt);
141           }
142        }
143     );
144
145     navigatePanel.add(nextButton);
146     add(navigatePanel);
147
148     displayPanel.setLayout(new GridLayout(5, 2, 4, 4));
149
150     idLabel.setText("Address ID:");
151     displayPanel.add(idLabel);
152
```

Fig. 21.32 | A simple address book. (Part 3 of 8.)

```
153         idTextField.setEditable(false);
154         displayPanel.add(idTextField);
155
156         firstNameLabel.setText("First Name:");
157         displayPanel.add(firstNameLabel);
158         displayPanel.add(firstNameTextField);
159
160         lastNameLabel.setText("Last Name:");
161         displayPanel.add(lastNameLabel);
162         displayPanel.add(lastNameTextField);
163
164         emailLabel.setText("Email:");
165         displayPanel.add(emailLabel);
166         displayPanel.add(emailTextField);
167
168         phoneLabel.setText("Phone Number:");
169         displayPanel.add(phoneLabel);
170         displayPanel.add(phoneTextField);
171         add(displayPanel);
172
173         queryPanel.setLayout(
174            new BoxLayout(queryPanel, BoxLayout.X_AXIS));
175
176         queryPanel.setBorder(BorderFactory.createTitledBorder(
177            "Find an entry by last name"));
178         queryLabel.setText("Last Name:");
179         queryPanel.add(Box.createHorizontalStrut(5));
180         queryPanel.add(queryLabel);
181         queryPanel.add(Box.createHorizontalStrut(10));
182         queryPanel.add(queryTextField);
183         queryPanel.add(Box.createHorizontalStrut(10));
184
185         queryButton.setText("Find");
186         queryButton.addActionListener(
187            new ActionListener()
188            {
189               public void actionPerformed(ActionEvent evt)
190               {
191                  queryButtonActionPerformed(evt);
192               }
193            }
194         );
195
196         queryPanel.add(queryButton);
197         queryPanel.add(Box.createHorizontalStrut(5));
198         add(queryPanel);
199
200         browseButton.setText("Browse All Entries");
201         browseButton.addActionListener(
202            new ActionListener()
203            {
204               public void actionPerformed(ActionEvent evt)
205               {
```

Fig. 21.32 | A simple address book. (Part 4 of 8.)

```
206                       browseButtonActionPerformed(evt);
207                    }
208                 }
209              );
210
211           add(browseButton);
212
213           insertButton.setText("Insert New Entry");
214           insertButton.addActionListener(
215              new ActionListener()
216              {
217                 public void actionPerformed(ActionEvent evt)
218                 {
219                    insertButtonActionPerformed(evt);
220                 }
221              }
222           );
223
224           add(insertButton);
225
226           addWindowListener(
227              new WindowAdapter()
228              {
229                 public void windowClosing(WindowEvent evt)
230                 {
231                    personQueries.close(); // close database connection
232                    System.exit(0);
233                 }
234              }
235           );
236
237           setVisible(true);
238        } // end constructor
239
240        // handles call when previousButton is clicked
241        private void previousButtonActionPerformed(ActionEvent evt)
242        {
243           currentEntryIndex--;
244
245           if (currentEntryIndex < 0)
246              currentEntryIndex = numberOfEntries - 1;
247
248           indexTextField.setText("" + (currentEntryIndex + 1));
249           indexTextFieldActionPerformed(evt);
250        }
251
252        // handles call when nextButton is clicked
253        private void nextButtonActionPerformed(ActionEvent evt)
254        {
255           currentEntryIndex++;
256
257           if (currentEntryIndex >= numberOfEntries)
258              currentEntryIndex = 0;
```

Fig. 21.32 | A simple address book. (Part 5 of 8.)

```
259
260          indexTextField.setText("" + (currentEntryIndex + 1));
261          indexTextFieldActionPerformed(evt);
262       }
263
264       // handles call when queryButton is clicked
265       private void queryButtonActionPerformed(ActionEvent evt)
266       {
267          results =
268             personQueries.getPeopleByLastName(queryTextField.getText());
269          numberOfEntries = results.size();
270
271          if (numberOfEntries != 0)
272          {
273             currentEntryIndex = 0;
274             currentEntry = results.get(currentEntryIndex);
275             idTextField.setText("" + currentEntry.getAddressID());
276             firstNameTextField.setText(currentEntry.getFirstName());
277             lastNameTextField.setText(currentEntry.getLastName());
278             emailTextField.setText(currentEntry.getEmail());
279             phoneTextField.setText(currentEntry.getPhoneNumber());
280             maxTextField.setText("" + numberOfEntries);
281             indexTextField.setText("" + (currentEntryIndex + 1));
282             nextButton.setEnabled(true);
283             previousButton.setEnabled(true);
284          }
285          else
286             browseButtonActionPerformed(evt);
287       }
288
289       // handles call when a new value is entered in indexTextField
290       private void indexTextFieldActionPerformed(ActionEvent evt)
291       {
292          currentEntryIndex =
293             (Integer.parseInt(indexTextField.getText()) - 1);
294
295          if (numberOfEntries != 0 && currentEntryIndex < numberOfEntries)
296          {
297             currentEntry = results.get(currentEntryIndex);
298             idTextField.setText("" + currentEntry.getAddressID());
299             firstNameTextField.setText(currentEntry.getFirstName());
300             lastNameTextField.setText(currentEntry.getLastName());
301             emailTextField.setText(currentEntry.getEmail());
302             phoneTextField.setText(currentEntry.getPhoneNumber());
303             maxTextField.setText("" + numberOfEntries);
304             indexTextField.setText("" + (currentEntryIndex + 1));
305          }
306       }
307
308       // handles call when browseButton is clicked
309       private void browseButtonActionPerformed(ActionEvent evt)
310       {
```

Fig. 21.32 | A simple address book. (Part 6 of 8.)

```
311        try
312        {
313            results = personQueries.getAllPeople();
314            numberOfEntries = results.size();
315
316            if (numberOfEntries != 0)
317            {
318                currentEntryIndex = 0;
319                currentEntry = results.get(currentEntryIndex);
320                idTextField.setText("" + currentEntry.getAddressID());
321                firstNameTextField.setText(currentEntry.getFirstName());
322                lastNameTextField.setText(currentEntry.getLastName());
323                emailTextField.setText(currentEntry.getEmail());
324                phoneTextField.setText(currentEntry.getPhoneNumber());
325                maxTextField.setText("" + numberOfEntries);
326                indexTextField.setText("" + (currentEntryIndex + 1));
327                nextButton.setEnabled(true);
328                previousButton.setEnabled(true);
329            }
330        }
331        catch (Exception e)
332        {
333            e.printStackTrace();
334        }
335    }
336
337    // handles call when insertButton is clicked
338    private void insertButtonActionPerformed(ActionEvent evt)
339    {
340        int result = personQueries.addPerson(firstNameTextField.getText(),
341            lastNameTextField.getText(), emailTextField.getText(),
342            phoneTextField.getText());
343
344        if (result == 1)
345            JOptionPane.showMessageDialog(this, "Person added!",
346                "Person added", JOptionPane.PLAIN_MESSAGE);
347        else
348            JOptionPane.showMessageDialog(this, "Person not added!",
349                "Error", JOptionPane.PLAIN_MESSAGE);
350
351        browseButtonActionPerformed(evt);
352    }
353
354    // main method
355    public static void main(String args[])
356    {
357        new AddressBookDisplay();
358    }
359 } // end class AddressBookDisplay
```

Fig. 21.32 | A simple address book. (Part 7 of 8.)

a) Initial **Address Book** screen.

b) Results of clicking **Browse All Entries**.

c) Browsing to the next entry.

d) Finding entries with the last name **Green**.

e) After adding a new entry and browsing to it.

Fig. 21.32 | A simple address book. (Part 8 of 8.)

To add a new entry into the AddressBook database, the user can enter the first name, last name, email and phone number (the AddressID will *autoincrement*) in the JTextFields and press the **Insert New Entry** JButton. The insertButtonActionPerformed handler (lines 338–352) is called. Lines 340–342 call the method addPerson on the PersonQueries object to add a new entry to the database. Line 351 calls browseButtonActionPerformed to obtain the updated set of people in the address book and update the GUI accordingly.

The user can then view different entries by pressing the **Previous** JButton or **Next** JButton, which results in calls to methods previousButtonActionPerformed (lines 241–250) or nextButtonActionPerformed (lines 253–262), respectively. Alternatively, the user can enter a number in the indexTextField and press *Enter* to view a particular entry. This results in a call to method indexTextFieldActionPerformed (lines 290–306) to display the specified record.

21.9 Stored Procedures

Many database management systems can store individual or sets of SQL statements in a database, so that programs accessing that database can invoke them. Such named collections of SQL statements are called **stored procedures**. JDBC enables programs to invoke stored procedures using objects that implement the interface **CallableStatement**. CallableStatements can receive arguments specified with the methods inherited from interface PreparedStatement. In addition, CallableStatements can specify **output parameters** in which a stored procedure can place return values. Interface CallableStatement includes methods to specify which parameters in a stored procedure are output parameters. The interface also includes methods to obtain the values of output parameters returned from a stored procedure.

Portability Tip 21.6

Although the syntax for creating stored procedures differs across database management systems, the interface CallableStatement provides a uniform interface for specifying input and output parameters for stored procedures and for invoking stored procedures.

Portability Tip 21.7

According to the Java API documentation for interface CallableStatement, for maximum portability between database systems, programs should process the update counts (which indicate how many rows were updated) or ResultSets returned from a CallableStatement before obtaining the values of any output parameters.

21.10 Transaction Processing

Many database applications require guarantees that a series of database insertions, updates and deletions executes properly before the application continues processing the next database operation. For example, when you transfer money electronically between bank accounts, several factors determine if the transaction is successful. You begin by specifying the source account and the amount you wish to transfer from that account to a destination account. Next, you specify the destination account. The bank checks the source account to determine whether its funds are sufficient to complete the transfer. If so, the bank withdraws the specified amount and, if all goes well, deposits it into the destination account to complete the transfer. What happens if the transfer fails after the bank withdraws the money from the source account? In a proper banking system, the bank redeposits the money in the source account. How would you feel if the money was subtracted from your source account and the bank *did not* deposit the money in the destination account?

Transaction processing enables a program that interacts with a database to *treat a database operation (or set of operations) as a single operation*. Such an operation also is known as an **atomic operation** or a **transaction**. At the end of a transaction, a decision can be made either to **commit the transaction** or **roll back the transaction**. Committing the transaction finalizes the database operation(s); all insertions, updates and deletions performed as part of the transaction cannot be reversed without performing a new database operation. Rolling back the transaction leaves the database in its state prior to the database operation. This is useful when a portion of a transaction fails to complete properly. In our bank-account-transfer discussion, the transaction would be rolled back if the deposit could not be made into the destination account.

Java provides transaction processing via methods of interface `Connection`. Method `setAutoCommit` specifies whether each SQL statement commits after it completes (a `true` argument) or whether several SQL statements should be grouped as a transaction (a `false` argument). If the argument to `setAutoCommit` is `false`, the program must follow the last SQL statement in the transaction with a call to `Connection` method **commit** (to commit the changes to the database) or `Connection` method **rollback** (to return the database to its state prior to the transaction). Interface `Connection` also provides method **getAutoCommit** to determine the autocommit state for the `Connection`.

21.11 Wrap-Up

In this chapter, you learned basic database concepts, how to query and manipulate data in a database using SQL and how to use JDBC to allow Java applications to interact with Java DB databases. You learned about the SQL commands SELECT, INSERT, UPDATE and DE-LETE, as well as clauses such as WHERE, ORDER BY and INNER JOIN. You created and configured databases in Java DB by using predefined SQL scripts. You learned the steps for obtaining a `Connection` to the database, creating a `Statement` to interact with the database's data, executing the statement and processing the results. Then you used a `RowSet` to simplify the process of connecting to a database and creating statements. You used `PreparedStatements` to create precompiled SQL statements. We also provided overviews of `CallableStatements` and transaction processing. In the next chapter, you'll build graphical user interfaces using JavaFX—Java's GUI technology of the future.

JavaFX GUI

Outline

22.1 Introduction

[*Note:* The prerequisites for this chapter are Chapters 1–11. This chapter does not require that you've read Chapter 12, Swing GUI Components: Part 1.]

A **graphical user interface** (**GUI**) presents a user-friendly mechanism for interacting with an app. A GUI (pronounced "GOO-ee") gives an app a distinctive "look-and-feel." GUIs are built from **GUI components**. These are sometimes called *controls* or *widgets*—short for window gadgets. A GUI component is an object with which the user interacts via the mouse, the keyboard or another form of input, such as voice recognition.

Look-and-Feel Observation 22.1

Providing different apps with consistent, intuitive user-interface components gives users a sense of familiarity with a new app, so that they can learn it more quickly and use it more productively.

History of GUI in Java

Java's original GUI library was the Abstract Window Toolkit (AWT). Swing (Chapters 12 and 19) was added to the platform in Java SE 1.2. Since then, Swing has remained the primary Java GUI technology. Swing is now in maintenance mode—Oracle has stopped development and will provide only bug fixes going forward; however, it will remain part of Java and is still widely used.

Java's GUI, graphics and multimedia API of the future is **JavaFX**. Sun Microsystems (acquired by Oracle in 2010) announced JavaFX in 2007 as a competitor to Adobe Flash and Microsoft Silverlight. JavaFX 1.0 was released in 2008. Prior to version 2.0, developers used JavaFX Script—which was similar to JavaScript—to write JavaFX apps. The JavaFX Script source code compiled to Java bytecode, allowing JavaFX apps to run on the Java Virtual Machine. Starting with version 2.0 in 2011, JavaFX was reimplemented as a set of Java libraries that could be used directly in Java apps. Some of the benefits of JavaFX vs. Swing include:

- JavaFX is easier to use—it provides one API for GUI, graphics and multimedia (images, animation, audio and video), whereas Swing is only for GUIs, so you need to use other APIs for graphics and multimedia apps.

- With Swing, many IDEs provided GUI design tools for dragging and dropping components onto a layout; however, each IDE produced different code. JavaFX Scene Builder (Section 22.2) can be used standalone or integrated with many IDEs and it produces the same code regardless of the IDE.

- Though Swing components could be customized, JavaFX gives you complete control over a JavaFX GUI's look-and-feel via Cascading Style Sheets (CSS).

- JavaFX was designed for improved thread safety, which is important for today's multi-core systems.

- JavaFX supports transformations for repositioning and reorienting JavaFX components, and animations for changing the properties of JavaFX components over time. These can be used to make apps more intuitive and easier to use.

JavaFX Version Used in This Chapter

In this chapter, we use JavaFX 2.2 (released in late 2012) with Java SE 7. We tested the chapter's apps on Windows, Mac OS X and Linux. At the time of this writing, Oracle was about to release JavaFX 8 and Java SE 8.

22.2 JavaFX Scene Builder and the NetBeans IDE

Most Java textbooks that introduce GUI programming provide hand-coded GUIs—that is, the authors build the GUIs from scratch in Java code, rather than using a visual GUI design tool. This is due to the fractured Java IDE market—there are many Java IDEs, so authors can't depend on any one IDE being used.

JavaFX is organized differently. The **JavaFX Scene Builder** tool is a standalone JavaFX GUI visual layout tool that can also be used with various IDEs, including the most popular ones—NetBeans, Eclipse and IntelliJ IDEA. JavaFX Scene Builder is most tightly integrated with NetBeans,[1] which is why we use it in our JavaFX presentation.

JavaFX Scene Builder enables you to create GUIs by dragging and dropping GUI components from Scene Builder's library onto a design area, then modifying and styling the GUI—all without writing any code. JavaFX Scene Builder's live editing and preview features allow you to view your GUI as you create and modify it, without compiling and running the app. You can use **Cascading Style Sheets (CSS)** to change the entire look-and-feel of your GUI—a concept sometimes called **skinning**.

In this chapter, we use JavaFX Scene Builder version 1.1 and NetBeans 7.4 to create two complete introductory JavaFX apps.

What is FXML?

As you create and modify a GUI, JavaFX Scene Builder generates **FXML (FX Markup Language)**—an XML vocabulary for defining and arranging JavaFX GUI controls without writing any Java code. You do not need to know FXML or XML to study this chapter.

---

1. http://www.oracle.com/technetwork/java/javafx/tools/index.html.

As you'll see in Section 22.4, JavaFX Scene Builder hides the FXML details from you, so you can focus on defining *what* the GUI should contain without specifying *how* to generate it—this is another example of declarative programming, which we used with Java SE lambdas in Chapter 17.

Software Engineering Observation 22.1

The FXML code is separate from the program logic that's defined in Java source code—this separation of the interface (the GUI) from the implementation (the Java code) makes it easier to debug, modify and maintain JavaFX GUI apps.

22.3 JavaFX App Window Structure

A JavaFX app window consists of several parts (Fig. 22.1) that you'll use in Sections 22.4––22.5:

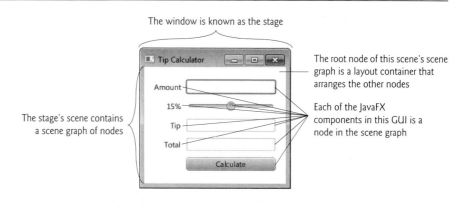

Fig. 22.1 | JavaFX app window parts.

- The window in which a JavaFX app's GUI is displayed is known as the **stage** and is an instance of class **Stage** (package javafx.stage).

- The stage contains one active **scene** that defines the GUI as a **scene graph**—a tree data structure of an app's visual elements, such as GUI controls, shapes, images, video, text and more. The scene is an instance of class **Scene** (package javafx.scene).

- Each visual element in the scene graph is a **node**—an instance of a subclass of **Node** (package javafx.scene), which defines common attributes and behaviors for all nodes in the scene graph. With the exception of the first node in the scene graph—known as the **root node**—each node has one parent. Nodes can have transforms (e.g., moving, rotating, scaling and skewing), opacity (which controls whether a node is transparent, partially transparent or opaque), effects (e.g., drop shadows, blurs, reflection and lighting) and more.

- Nodes that have children are typically **layout containers** that arrange their child nodes in the scene. You'll use two layout containers (VBox and GridPane) in this chapter.

- The nodes arranged in a layout container are a combination of controls and, in more complex GUIs, possibly other layout containers. **Controls** are GUI components, such as Labels that display text, TextFields that enable a program to receive text typed by the user, Buttons that initiate actions and more. When the user interacts with a control, such as clicking a Button, the control generates an event. Programs can respond to these events—known as event handling—to specify what should happen when each user interaction occurs.

- An event handler is a method that responds to a user interaction. An FXML GUI's event handlers are defined in a so-called **controller class** (as you'll see in Section 22.5.5).

22.4 Welcome App—Displaying Text and an Image

In this section, *without writing any code* you'll build a JavaFX **Welcome** app that displays text in a **Label** and an image in an **ImageView** (Fig. 22.2). First, you'll create a JavaFX app project in the *NetBeans IDE*. Then, you'll use visual-programming techniques and JavaFX Scene Builder to *drag-and-drop* JavaFX components onto the design area. Next, you'll use JavaFX Scene Builder's **Inspector** window to configure options, such as the Label's text and font size, and the ImageView's image. Finally, you'll execute the app from NetBeans. This section assumes that you've read the Before You Begin section, and installed NetBeans and Scene Builder. We used NetBeans 7.4, Scene Builder 1.1 and Java SE 7 for this chapter's examples.

Fig. 22.2 | Final **Welcome** app running on Windows 7.

22.4.1 Creating the App's Project

You'll now use NetBeans to create a **JavaFX FXML App**. Open NetBeans on your system. Initially, the **Start Page** (Fig. 22.3) is displayed—this page gives you links to the NetBeans documentation and displays a list of your recent projects, if any.

Fig. 22.3 | NetBeans IDE showing the **Start Page**.

Creating a New Project

To create an app, you must first create a **project**—a group of related files, such as code files and images that make up an app. Click the **New Project...** ( ) button on the toolbar or select **File > New Project...** to display the **New Project dialog** (Fig. 22.4). Under **Categories**, select **JavaFX** and under **Projects** select **JavaFX FXML Application**, then click **Next >**.

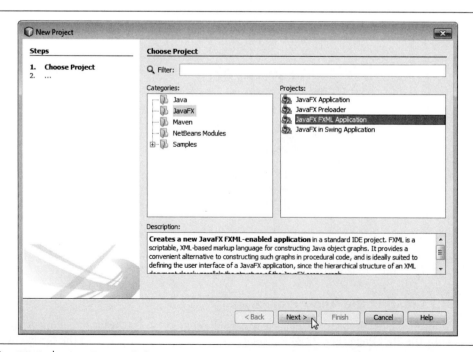

Fig. 22.4 | **New Project** dialog.

New JavaFX Application Dialog
In the **New JavaFX Application** dialog (Fig. 22.5), specify the following information:

1. **Project Name:** field—This is your app's name. Enter Welcome in this field.

2. **Project Location:** field—The project's location on your system. NetBeans places new projects in a subdirectory of NetBeansProjects within your user account's Documents folder. You can click the **Browse...** button to specify a different location. Your project's name is used as the subdirectory name.

3. **FXML name:** field—The name of the FXML filename that will contain the app's GUI. Enter Welcome here—the IDE creates the file Welcome.fxml in the project.

4. **Create Application Class:** checkbox—When this is checked, NetBeans creates a class with the specified name. This class contains the app's main method. Enter Welcome in this field. If you precede the class name with a package name, Net-Beans creates the class in that package; otherwise, NetBeans will place the class in the default package.

Click **Finish** to create the project.

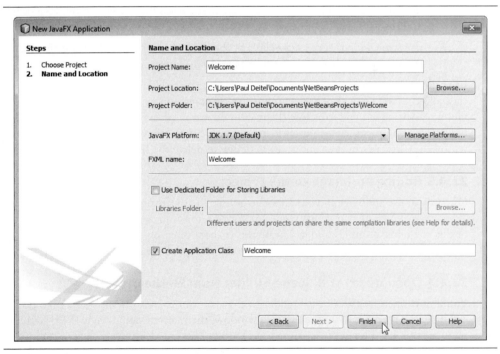

Fig. 22.5 | New JavaFX Application dialog.

22.4.2 NetBeans Projects Window—Viewing the Project Contents

The NetBeans **Projects** window provides access to all of your projects. The **Welcome** node represents this app's project. You can have many projects open at once—each will have its own top-level node. Within a project's node, the contents are organized into folders and files. You can view the Welcome project's contents by expanding the **Welcome > Source**

Packages > <default package> node (Fig. 22.6). If you specified a package name for the app class in Fig. 22.5, then that package's name will appear rather than **<default package>**.

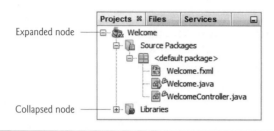

Fig. 22.6 | NetBeans **Projects** window.

NetBeans creates and opens three files for a **JavaFX FXML Application** project:

- `Welcome.fxml`—This file contains the FXML markup for the GUI. By default, the IDE creates a GUI containing a `Button` and a `Label`.

- `Welcome.java`—This is the main class that creates the GUI from the FXML file and displays the GUI in a window.

- `WelcomeController.java`—This is the class in which you'd define the GUI's event handlers that allow the app to respond to user interactions with the GUI.

In Section 22.5, when we present an app with event handlers, we'll discuss the main app class and the controller class in detail. For the **Welcome** app, you will not edit any of these files in NetBeans, so you can close them. You do not need the `WelcomeController.java` file in this app, so you can right click the file in the **Projects** window and select **Delete** to remove it. Click **Yes** in the confirmation dialog to delete the file.

22.4.3 Adding an Image to the Project

One way to use an image in your app is to add its file to the project, then display it on an `ImageView`. The `bug.png` image you'll use for this app is located in the `images` subfolder of this chapter's examples folder. Locate the `images` folder on your file system, then drag `bug.png` onto the project's **<default package>** node to add the file to the project.

22.4.4 Opening JavaFX Scene Builder from NetBeans

You'll now open JavaFX Scene Builder so that you can create this app's GUI. To do so, right click `Welcome.fxml` in the **Projects** window, then select **Open** to view the FXML file in Scene Builder (Fig. 22.7).

Deleting the Default Controls

The FXML file provided by NetBeans contains a default GUI consisting of a `Button` control and a `Label` control. The **Welcome** app will not use these default controls, so you can delete them. To do so, click each in the content panel (or in the **Hierarchy** window at the bottom-left of Scene Builder's window), then press the *Backspace* or *Delete* key. In each case, Scene Builder displays the warning "**Some components have an fx:id. Do you really want to delete them?**". This means that there could be Java code in the project that refers

The **Library** contains JavaFX **Containers**, **Controls** and other items that can be dragged and dropped on the canvas

You use the content panel to design the GUI

You use the **Inspector** window to configure the currently selected item in the content panel

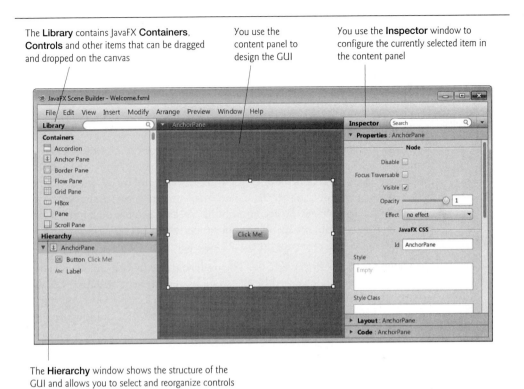

The **Hierarchy** window shows the structure of the GUI and allows you to select and reorganize controls

Fig. 22.7 | JavaFX Scene Builder displaying the default GUI in `Welcome.fxml`.

to these controls—for this app, there will not be any such code, so you can click **Delete** to remove these controls.

Deleting the Reference to the *WelcomeController* Class

As you'll learn in Section 22.5, in Scene Builder, you can specify the name of the controller class that contains methods for responding to the user's interactions with the GUI. The **Welcome** app does not need to respond to any user interactions, so you'll remove the reference in the FXML file to class `WelcomeController`. To do so, select the `AnchorPane` node in the **Hierarchy** window, then click the **Inspector** window's **Code** section to expand it and delete the value specified in the **Controller class** field. You're now ready to create the **Welcome** app's GUI.

22.4.5 Changing to a VBox Layout Container

For this app, you'll place a `Label` and an `ImageView` in a **VBox layout container** (package `javafx.scene.layout`), which will be the scene graph's root node. Layout containers help you arrange and size GUI components. A `VBox` arranges its nodes *vertically* from top to bottom. `VBox` is one of several JavaFX layout containers for arranging controls in a GUI. We discuss the `GridPane` layout container in Section 22.5. By default, NetBeans provides an `AnchorPane` as the root layout. To change from the default `AnchorPane` to a `VBox`:

1. *Adding a VBox to the Default Layout.* Drag a VBox from the **Library** window's **Containers** section onto the default AnchorPane in Scene Builder's content panel.

2. *Making the VBox the Root Layout.* Select **Edit > Trim Document to Selection** to make the VBox the root layout and remove the AnchorPane.

22.4.6 Configuring the VBox Layout Container

You'll now specify the VBox's alignment, initial size and padding:

1. *Specifying the VBox's Alignment.* A VBox's **alignment** determines the layout positioning of the VBox's children. In this app, we'd like each child node (the Label and the ImageView) to be centered horizontally in the scene, and we'd like both children to be centered vertically, so that there is an equal amount of space above the Label and below the ImageView. To accomplish this, select the VBox, then in the **Inspector**'s **Properties** section, set the **Alignment** property to CENTER. When you set the **Alignment**, notice the variety of potential alignment values you can use.

2. *Specifying the VBox's Preferred Size.* The **preferred size** (width and height) of the scene graph's root node is used by the scene to determine its window size when the app begins executing. To set the preferred size, select the VBox, then in the **Inspector**'s **Layout** section, set the **Pref Width** property to 450 and the **Pref Height** property to 300.

22.4.7 Adding and Configuring a Label

Next, you'll create the Label that displays "Welcome to JavaFX!":

1. *Adding a Label to the VBox.* Drag a Label from the **Library** window's **Controls** section onto the VBox. The Label is automatically centered in the VBox because you set the VBox's alignment to CENTER in Section 22.4.6.

2. *Changing the Label's text.* You can set a Label's text either by double clicking it and typing the text, or by selecting the Label and setting its **Text** property in the **Inspector**'s **Properties** section. Set the Label's text to "Welcome to JavaFX!".

3. *Changing the Label's font.* For this app, we set the Label to display in a large bold font. To do so, select the Label, then in the **Inspector**'s **Preferences** section, click the value to the right of the **Font** property. In the window that appears, set the **style** property to Bold and the **size** property to 30.

22.4.8 Adding and Configuring an ImageView

Finally, you'll add the ImageView that displays bug.png:

1. *Adding an ImageView to the VBox.* Drag an ImageView from the **Library** window's **Controls** section onto the VBox. The ImageView is automatically placed below the Label. Each new control you add to a VBox is placed below the VBox's other children, though you can change the order by dragging the children in Scene Builder's **Hierarchy** window. Like the Label, the ImageView is also automatically centered in the VBox.

2. *Setting the ImageViews's image.* To set the image to display, select the ImageView and click the ellipsis (...) button to the right of the **Image** property in the **Inspec-**

tor's **Properties** section. By default, Scene Builder opens a dialog showing the project's source-code folder, which is where you placed the image file bug.png in Section 22.4.3. Select the image file, then click **Open**. Scene Builder displays the image and resizes the ImageView to match the image's aspect ratio—the ratio of the image's width to its height—by setting the ImageView's **Fit Width** and **Fit Height** properties.

3. *Changing the ImageView's size.* We'd like to display the image in its original size. To do so, you must delete the default values for the ImageView's **Fit Width** and **Fit Height** properties, which are located in the **Inspector's Layout** section. Once you delete these values, Scene Builder resizes the ImageView to the image's exact dimensions. Save the FXML file.

You've now completed the GUI. Scene Builder's content panel should now appear as shown in Fig. 22.8.

Fig. 22.8 | Completed design of the **Welcome** app's GUI in Scene Builder.

22.4.9 Running the **Welcome** App

You can run the app from NetBeans in one of three ways:

- Select the project's root node in the NetBeans **Projects** window, then click the **Run Project** (▷) button on the toolbar.
- Select the project's root node in the NetBeans **Projects** window, then press F6.
- Right click the project's root node in the NetBeans **Projects** window, then select **Run**.

In each case, the IDE will compile the app (if it isn't already compiled), then run the app. The **Welcome** app should now appear as shown in Fig. 22.2.

22.5 Tip Calculator App—Introduction to Event Handling

The **Tip Calculator** app (Fig. 22.9(a)) calculates and displays a restaurant bill tip and total. By default, the app calculates the total with a 15% tip. You can specify a tip percentage from 0% to 30% by moving the Slider *thumb*—this updates the tip percentage (Fig. 22.9(b) and (c)). In this section, you'll build a **Tip Calculator** app using several JavaFX components and learn how to respond to user interactions with the GUI.

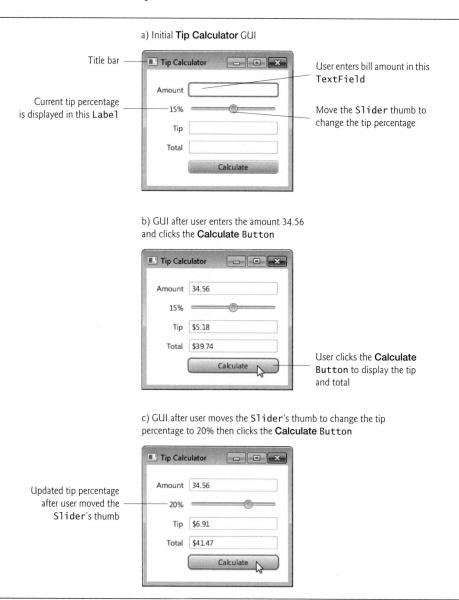

a) Initial **Tip Calculator** GUI

Title bar — User enters bill amount in this TextField

Current tip percentage is displayed in this Label — Move the Slider thumb to change the tip percentage

b) GUI after user enters the amount 34.56 and clicks the **Calculate** Button

User clicks the **Calculate** Button to display the tip and total

c) GUI after user moves the Slider's thumb to change the tip percentage to 20% then clicks the **Calculate** Button

Updated tip percentage after user moved the Slider's thumb

Fig. 22.9 | Entering the bill amount and calculating the tip.

You'll begin by test-driving the app, using it to calculate 15% and 10% tips. Then we'll overview the technologies you'll use to create the app. You'll build the app's GUI using the NetBeans and JavaFX SceneBuilder. Finally, we'll present the complete Java code for the app and do a detailed code walkthrough.

22.5.1 Test-Driving the Tip Calculator App

Opening and Running the App

Open the NetBeans IDE, then perform the following steps to open the **Tip Calculator** app's project and run it:

1. *Opening the Tip Calculator app's project.* Select **File > Open Project...** or click the **Open Project...** ( ) button on the toolbar to display the **Open Project** dialog. Navigate to this chapter's examples folder, select TipCalculator and click the **Open Project** button. A TipCalculator node now appears in the **Projects** window.

2. *Running the Tip Calculator app.* Right click the TipCalculator project in the **Projects** window, then click the **Run Project** ( ) button on the toolbar.

Entering a Bill Total

Using your keyboard, enter 34.56, then press the **Calculate** Button. The **Tip** and **Total** TextFields show the tip amount and the total bill for a 15% tip (Fig. 22.9(b)).

Selecting a Custom Tip Percentage

Use the Slider to specify a *custom* tip percentage. Drag the Slider's *thumb* until the percentage reads **20%** (Fig. 22.9(c)), then press the **Calculate** Button to display the updated tip and total. As you drag the thumb, the tip percentage in the Label to the Slider's left updates continuously. By default, the Slider allows you to select values from 0.0 to 100.0, but in this app we'll restrict the Slider to selecting whole numbers from 0 to 30.

22.5.2 Technologies Overview

This section introduces the technologies you'll use to build the **Tip Calculator** app.

Class Application

The main class in a JavaFX app is a subclass of **Application** (package **javafx.application.Application**). The app's main method calls class Application's static **launch** method to begin executing a JavaFX app. This method, in turn, causes the JavaFX runtime to create an object of the Application subclass and call its **start** method, which creates the GUI, attaches it to a Scene and places it on the Stage that method start receives as an argument.

Arranging JavaFX Components with a GridPane

Recall that layout containers arrange JavaFX components in a Scene. A **GridPane** (package **javafx.scene.layout**) arranges JavaFX components into *columns* and *rows* in a rectangular grid.

This app uses a GridPane (Fig. 22.10) to arrange views into two columns and five rows. Each cell in a GridPane can be empty or can hold one or more JavaFX components, including layout containers that arrange other controls. Each component in a GridPane can span *multiple* columns or rows, though we did not use that capability in this GUI.

When you drag a GridPane onto Scene Builder's content panel, Scene Builder creates the GridPane with two columns and three rows by default. You can add and remove columns and rows as necessary. We'll discuss other GridPane features as we present the GUI-building steps. To learn more about class GridPane, visit:

```
http://docs.oracle.com/javafx/2/api/javafx/scene/layout/GridPane.html
```

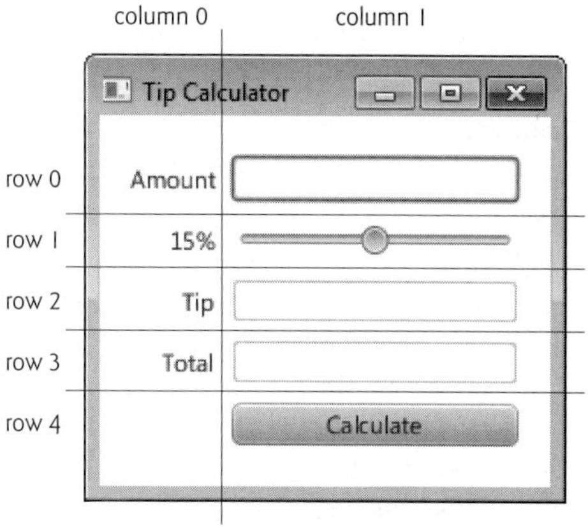

Fig. 22.10 | Tip Calculator GUI's GridPane labeled by its rows and columns.

Creating and Customizing the GUI with Scene Builder

You'll create Labels, TextFields, a Slider and a Button by dragging them onto the content panel in Scene Builder, then customize them using the **Inspector** window.

- A **TextField** (package javafx.scene.control) can accept text input from the user or display text. You'll use one editable TextField to input the bill amount from the user and two *uneditable* TextFields to display the tip and total amounts.

- A **Slider** (package javafx.scene.control) represents a value in the range 0.0–100.0 by default and allows the user to select a number in that range by moving the Slider's thumb. You'll customize the Slider so the user can choose a custom tip percentage *only* from the more limited range 0 to 30.

- A **Button** (package javafx.scene.control) allows the user to initiate an action—in this app, pressing the **Calculate** Button calculates and displays the tip and total amounts.

Formatting Numbers as Locale-Specific Currency and Percentage Strings

You'll use class **NumberFormat** (package **java.text**) to create *locale-specific* currency and percentage strings—an important part of *internationalization*.

Event Handling

Normally, a user interacts with an app's GUI to indicate the tasks that the app should perform. For example, when you write an e-mail in an e-mail app, clicking the **Send** button tells the app to send the e-mail to the specified e-mail addresses. GUIs are **event driven**. When the user interacts with a GUI component, the interaction—known as an **event**—

drives the program to perform a task. Some common user interactions that cause an app to perform a task include *clicking* a button, *typing* in a text field, *selecting* an item from a menu, *closing* a window and *moving* the mouse. The code that performs a task in response to an event is called an **event handler**, and the process of responding to events is known as **event handling**.

Before an app can respond to an event for a particular control, you must:

1. Create a class that represents the event handler and implements an appropriate interface—known as an **event-listener interface**.

2. Indicate that an object of that class should be notified when the event occurs—known as **registering the event handler**.

In this app, you'll respond to two events—when the user moves the Slider's thumb, the app will update the Label that displays the current tip percentage, and when the user clicks the **Calculate** Button, the app will calculate and display the tip and total bill amount.

You'll see that for certain events—such as when the user clicks a Button—you can link a control to its event-handling method by using the **Code** section of Scene Builder's **Inspector** window. In this case, the class that implements the event-listener interface will be created for you and will call the method you specify. For events that occur when the value of control's property changes—such as when the user moves a Slider's thumb to change the Slider's value—you'll see that you must create the event handler entirely in code.

Implementing Interface ChangeListener for Handling Slider Thumb Position Changes

You'll implement the **ChangeListener** interface (from package javafx.beans.value) to respond to the user moving the Slider's thumb. In particular, you'll use method changed to display the user-selected tip percentage as the user moves the Slider's thumb.

Model-View-Controller (MVC) Architecture

JavaFX applications in which the GUI is implemented as FXML adhere to the **Model-View-Controller (MVC) design pattern**, which separates an app's data (contained in the **model**) from the app's GUI (the **view**) and the app's processing logic (the **controller**).

The controller implements logic for processing user inputs. The model contains application data, and the view presents the data stored in the model. When a user provides some input, the controller modifies the model with the given input. In the **Tip Calculator**, the model is the bill amount, the tip and the total. When the model changes, the controller updates the view to present the changed data.

In a JavaFX FXML app, you define the app's event handlers in a **controller class**. The controller class defines instance variables for interacting with controls programmatically, as well as event-handling methods. The controller class may also declare additional instance variables, static variables and methods that support the app's operation. In a simple app like the **Tip Calculator**, the model and controller are often combined into a single class, as we'll do in this example.

FXMLLoader Class

When a JavaFX FXML app begins executing, class **FXMLLoader**'s static method **load** is used to load the FXML file that represents the app's GUI. This method:

- Creates the GUI's scene graph and returns a **Parent** (package javafx.scene) reference to the scene graph's root node.

- Initializes the controller's instance variables for the components that are manipulated programmatically.

- Creates and registers the event handlers for any events specified in the FXML.

We'll discuss these steps in more detail in Sections 22.5.4—22.5.5.

22.5.3 Building the App's GUI

In this section, we'll show the precise steps for using Scene Builder to create the **Tip Calculator**'s GUI. The GUI will not look like the one shown in Fig. 22.9 until you've completed the steps.

fx:id Property Values for This App's Controls

If a control or layout will be manipulated programmatically in the controller class (as we'll do with one of the Labels, all of the TextFields and the Slider in this app), you must provide a name for that control or layout. In Section 22.5.4, you'll learn how to declare variables in your source code for each such component in the FXML, and we'll discuss how those variables are initialized for you. Each object's name is specified via its **fx:id** property. You can set this property's value by selecting a component in your scene, then expanding the **Inspector** window's **Code** section—the **fx:id** property appears at the top of the **Code** section. Figure 22.11 shows the **fx:id** properties of the **Tip Calculator**'s programmatically manipulated controls. For clarity, our naming convention is to use the control's class name in the **fx:id** property.

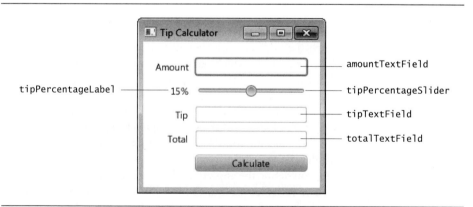

Fig. 22.11 | **Tip Calculator**'s programmatically manipulated controls labeled with their **fx:id**s.

Creating the TipCalculator Project

Click the **New Project...** (🗔) button on the toolbar or select **File > New Project....** In the **New Project** dialog. Under **Categories**, select **JavaFX** and under **Projects** select **JavaFX FXML Application**, then click **Next >** and specify TipCalculator in the **Project Name**, **FXML name** and **Create Application Class** fields. Click **Finish** to create the project.

*Step 1: Changing the Root Layout from an **AnchorPane** to a **GridPane***
Open TipCalculator.fxml in Scene Builder so that you can build the GUI and delete the default controls, then change from the default AnchorPane to a GridPane:

   1. *Adding a **GridPane** to the Default Layout.* Drag a GridPane from the **Library** window's **Containers** section onto the default AnchorPane in Scene Builder's content panel.

   2. *Making the **GridPane** the Root Layout.* Select **Edit > Trim Document to Selection** to make the GridPane the root layout and remove the AnchorPane.

*Step 2: Adding Rows to the **GridPane***
By default, the GridPane contains two columns and three rows. Recall that the GUI in Fig. 22.10 consists of five rows. You can add a row above or below an existing row by right clicking a row and selecting **Grid Pane > Add Row Above** or **Grid Pane > Add Row Below**. After adding two rows, the GridPane should appear as shown in Fig. 22.12. You can use similar steps to add columns. You can delete a row or column by right clicking the tab containing its row or column number and selecting **Delete**.

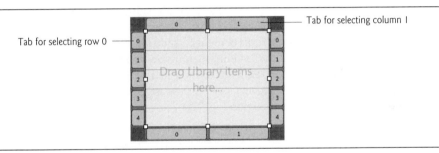

Fig. 22.12 | GridPane with five rows.

*Step 3: Adding the Controls to the **GridPane***
You'll now add the controls in Fig. 22.10 to the GridPane. For those that have **fx:ids** (see Fig. 22.11), while the control is selected, set its **fx:id** property in the **Inspector** window's **Code** section. Perform the following steps:

   1. *Adding the **Labels**.* Drag Labels from the **Library** window's **Controls** section into the first four rows of the GridPane's left column (i.e., column 0). As you add each Label, set its text as shown Fig. 22.10.

   2. *Adding the **TextFields**.* Drag TextFields from the **Library** window's **Controls** section into rows 0, 2 and 3 of the GridPane's right column (i.e., column 1).

   3. *Adding a **Slider**.* Drag a horizontal Slider from the **Library** window's **Controls** section into row 1 of the GridPane's right column.

   4. *Adding a **Button**.* Drag a Button from the **Library** window's **Controls** section into row 4 of the GridPane's right column. You can set the Button's text by double clicking it, or by selecting the Button, then setting its **Text** property in the **Inspector** window's **Properties** section.

The GridPane should appear as shown in Fig. 22.13.

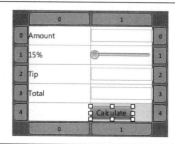

Fig. 22.13 | GridPane filled with the **Tip Calculator**'s controls.

Step 4: Right-Aligning *GridPane Column 0's Contents*
A GridPane column's contents are left-aligned by default. To right-align the contents of column 0, select it by clicking the tab at the top or bottom of the column, then in the **Inspector**'s **Layout** section, set the **Halignment** (horizontal alignment) property to RIGHT.

Step 5: Sizing the *GridPane Columns to Fit Their Contents*
By default, Scene Builder sets each GridPane column's width to 100 pixels and each row's height to 30 pixels to ensure that you can easily drag controls into the GridPane's cells. In this app, we sized each column to fit its contents. To do so, select the column 0 by clicking the tab at the top or bottom of the column, then in the **Inspector**'s **Layout** section, set the **Pref Width** property to USE_COMPUTED_SIZE to indicate that the column's width should be based on the widest child—the **Amount** Label in this case. Repeat this process for column 1. The GridPane should appear as shown in Fig. 22.14.

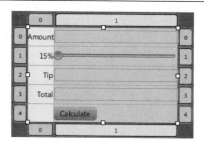

Fig. 22.14 | GridPane with columns sized to fit their contents.

Step 6: Sizing the *TextFields*
Scene Builder sets each TextField's width to 200 pixels by default. You may size controls as appropriate for each GUI you create. In this app, we do not need the TextFields to be so wide, so we used the preferred width for each TextField, which is somewhat narrower. When setting a property to the same value for several controls, you can select all of them and specify the value once. To select all three TextFields, hold the *Ctrl* (or *Command*) key and click each TextField. Then in the **Inspector**'s **Layout** section, set the **Pref Width** property to USE_COMPUTED_SIZE. This indicates that each TextField should use its preferred width (as defined by JavaFX). Notice that the GridPane's right column resizes to the TextFields' preferred widths.

Step 7: Sizing the **Button**

By default, Scene Builder sets a Button's width based on its text. For this app, we chose to make the Button the same width as the other controls in the GridPane's right column. To do so, select the Button, then in the **Inspector**'s **Layout** section, set the **Max Width** property to MAX_VALUE. This causes the Button's width to grow to fill the column's width.

Previewing the GUI

As you design your GUI, you can preview it by selecting **Preview > Show Preview in Window**. As you can see in Fig. 22.15, there's no space between the Labels in the left column and the controls in the right column. In addition, there's no space around the GridPane, because the Stage is sized to fit the Scene's content. Thus, many of the controls touch or come close to the window's borders. You'll fix these issues in the next step.

Fig. 22.15 | GridPane with the TextFields and Button resized.

Step 8: Configuring the **GridPane**'s Padding and Horizontal Gap Between Its Columns

The space between a node's contents and its top, right, bottom and left edges is known as the **padding**, which separates the contents from the node's edges. Since the GridPane's size determines the size of the Stage's window, the padding in this example also separates the GridPane's children from the window's edges. To set the padding, select the GridPane, then in the **Inspector**'s **Layout** section, set the **Padding** property's four values (**TOP**, **RIGHT**, **BOTTOM** and **LEFT**) to 14—the JavaFX recommended distance between the edge of a control and the edge of a Scene.

You can specify the default amount of space between a GridPane's columns and rows with its **Hgap** (horizontal gap) and **Vgap** (vertical gap) properties, respectively. Because Scene Builder sets each GridPane row's height to 30 pixels—which is greater than the heights of this app's controls—there's already some vertical space between the components. To specify the horizontal gap between the columns, select the GridPane in the **Hierarchy** window, then in the **Inspector**'s **Layout** section, set the **Hgap** property to 8. If you'd like to precisely control the vertical space between components, you can set each row's **Pref Height** property to USE_COMPUTED_SIZE (as we did for the columns' **Pref Width** property in Step 5), then set the GridPane's **Vgap** property.

Step 9: Making the **tipTextField** and **totalTextField** Uneditable and Not Focusable

The tipTextField and totalTextField are used in this app only to display results, not receive text input. For this reason, they should not be interactive. You can type in a TextField only if it's "in **focus**"—that is, it's the control that the user is interacting with. When you click an interactive control, it receives the focus. Similarly, when you press the *Tab* key, the focus transfers from the current focusable control to the next one—this occurs in the order the controls were added to the GUI. Interactive controls—such as `TextFields`, `Sliders` and `Buttons`—are focusable by default. Non-interactive controls—like `Labels`—are not focusable.

In this app, the `tipTextField` and `totalTextField` are neither editable nor focusable. To make these changes, select both `TextFields`, then in the **Inspector**'s **Properties** section, uncheck the **Editable** and **Focus Traversable** properties.

Step 10: Setting the `Slider`'s Properties

To complete the GUI, you'll now configure the **Tip Calculator**'s `Slider`. By default, a `Slider`'s range is 0.0 to 100.0 and its initial value is 0.0. This app allows tip percentages from 0 to 30 with a default of 15. To make these changes, select the `Slider`, then in the **Inspector**'s **Properties** section, set the `Slider`'s **Max** property to 30 and the **Value** property to 15. We also set the **Block Increment** property to 5—this is the amount by which the **Value** property increases or decreases when the user clicks between an end of the `Slider` and the `Slider`'s thumb. Save the FXML file by selecting **File > Save**.

Previewing the Final Layout

Select **Preview > Show Preview in Window** to view the final GUI (Fig. 22.16). When we discuss the `TipCalculatorController` class in Section 22.5.5, we'll show how to specify the **Calculate** `Button`'s event handler in the FXML file.

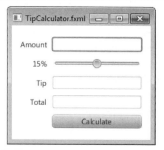

Fig. 22.16 | Final GUI design previewed in Scene Builder.

22.5.4 `TipCalculator` Class

When you created the **Tip Calculator** app's project, NetBeans created two Java source-code files for you:

- `TipCalculator.java`—This file contains the `TipCalculator` class, in which the `main` method (discussed in this section) loads the FXML file to create the GUI and attaches the GUI to a `Scene` that's displayed on the app's `Stage`.

- `TipCalculatorController.java`—This file contains the `TipCalculatorController` class (discussed in Section 22.5.5), which is where you'll specify the `Slider` and `Button` controls' event handlers.

Figure 22.17 presents class `TipCalculator`. We reformatted the code to meet our conventions. With the exception of line 18, all of the code in this class was generated by Net-

Beans. As we discussed in Section 22.5.2, the `Application` subclass is the starting point for a JavaFX app. The `main` method calls class `Application`'s `static launch` method (line 26) to begin executing the app. This method, in turn, causes the JavaFX runtime to create an object of the `TipCalculator` class and calls its `start` method.

```java
1   // Fig. 22.17: TipCalculator.java
2   // Main app class that loads and displays the Tip Calculator's GUI
3   import javafx.application.Application;
4   import javafx.fxml.FXMLLoader;
5   import javafx.scene.Parent;
6   import javafx.scene.Scene;
7   import javafx.stage.Stage;
8
9   public class TipCalculator extends Application
10  {
11     @Override
12     public void start(Stage stage) throws Exception
13     {
14        Parent root =
15           FXMLLoader.load(getClass().getResource("TipCalculator.fxml"));
16
17        Scene scene = new Scene(root); // attach scene graph to scene
18        stage.setTitle("Tip Calculator"); // displayed in window's title bar
19        stage.setScene(scene); // attach scene to stage
20        stage.show(); // display the stage
21     }
22
23     public static void main(String[] args)
24     {
25        // create a TipCalculator object and call its start method
26        launch(args);
27     }
28  }
```

Fig. 22.17 | Main app class that loads and displays the **Tip Calculator**'s GUI.

Overridden *Application* Method *start*

Method `start` (lines 11–21) creates the GUI, attaches it to a `Scene` and places it on the `Stage` that method `start` receives as an argument. Lines 14–15 use class `FXMLLoader`'s `static` method `load` to create the GUI's scene graph. This method:

- Returns a `Parent` (package `javafx.scene`) reference to the scene graph's root node (the `GridPane` in this example).

- Creates an object of the controller class.

- Initializes the controller's instance variables for the components that are manipulated programmatically.

- Registers the event handlers for any events specified in the FXML.

We discuss the initialization of the controller's instance variables and the registration of the event handlers in Section 22.5.5.

Creating the **Scene**

To display the GUI, you must attach it to a Scene, then attach the Scene to the Stage that's passed into method start. Line 17 creates a Scene, passing root (the scene graph's root node) as an argument to the constructor. By default, the Scene's size is determined by the size of the scene graph's root node. Overloaded versions of the Scene constructor allow you to specify the Scene's size and fill (a color, gradient or image), which appears in the Scene's background. Line 18 uses Scene method setTitle to specify the text that appears in the Stage window's title bar. Line 19 places Stage method setScene to place the Scene onto the Stage. Finally, line 20 calls Stage method show to display the Stage window.

22.5.5 TipCalculatorController Class

Figures 22.18–22.21 present the TipCalculatorController class that responds to user interactions with the app's Button and Slider. Replace the code that NetBeans generated in TipCalculatorController.java with the code in Figs. 22.18–22.21.

Class **TipCalculatorController's** *import Statements*

Figure 22.18 shows class TipCalculatorController's import statements.

```
 1   // TipCalculatorController.jav
 2   // Controller that handles calculateButton and tipPercentageSlider events
 3   import java.math.BigDecimal;
 4   import java.math.RoundingMode;
 5   import java.text.NumberFormat;
 6   import javafx.beans.value.ChangeListener;
 7   import javafx.beans.value.ObservableValue;
 8   import javafx.event.ActionEvent;
 9   import javafx.fxml.FXML;
10   import javafx.scene.control.Label;
11   import javafx.scene.control.Slider;
12   import javafx.scene.control.TextField;
13
```

Fig. 22.18 | TipCalculatorController's import declarations.

Lines 3–12 import the classes and interfaces used by class TipCalculatorController:

- Class BigDecimal of package java.math (line 3) is used to perform precise monetary calculations. The RoundingMode enum of package java.math (line 4) is used to specify how BigDecimal values are rounded during calculations or when formatting floating-point numbers as Strings.

- Class NumberFormat of package java.text (line 5) provides numeric formatting capabilities, such as locale-specific currency and percentage formats. For example, in the U.S. locale, the monetary value 34.56 is formatted as $34.95 and the percentage 15 is formatted as 15%. Class NumberFormat determines the locale of the system on which your app runs, then formats currency amounts and percentages accordingly.

- You implement interface ChangeListener of package javafx.beans.value (line 6) to respond to the user moving the Slider's thumb. This interface's changed method receives an object that implements interface `ObservableValue` (line 7)—that is, a value that generates an event when it changes.

- A `Button`'s event handler receives an `ActionEvent` (line 8; package `javafx.event`), which indicates that the `Button` was clicked. Many JavaFX controls support `ActionEvents`.

- The annotation `FXML` (line 9; package `javafx.fxml`) is used in a JavaFX controller class's code to mark instance variables that should refer to JavaFX components in the GUI's FXML file and methods that can respond to the events of JavaFX components in the GUI's FXML file.

- Package `javafx.scene.control` (lines 10–12) contains many JavaFX control classes, including `Label`, `Slider` and `TextField`.

As you write code with various classes and interfaces, you can use the the NetBeans IDE's **Source > Organize Imports** command to let the IDE insert the `import` statements for you. If the same class or interface name appears in more than one package, the IDE will display a dialog in which you can select the appropriate `import` statement.

TipCalculatorController's static Variables and Instance Variables
Lines 17–38 of Fig. 22.19 present class `TipCalculatorController`'s `static` and instance variables. The `NumberFormat` objects (lines 17–20) are used to format currency values and percentages, respectively. Method `getCurrencyInstance` returns a `NumberFormat` object that formats values as currency using the default locale for the system on which the app is running. Similarly, method `getPercentInstance` returns a `NumberFormat` object that formats values as percentages using the system's default locale. The `BigDecimal` object `tipPercentage` (line 22) stores the current tip percentage and is used in the tip calculation (Fig. 22.20) when the user clicks the app's **Calculate** `Button`.

```
14   public class TipCalculatorController
15   {
16       // formatters for currency and percentages
17       private static final NumberFormat currency =
18           NumberFormat.getCurrencyInstance();
19       private static final NumberFormat percent =
20           NumberFormat.getPercentInstance();
21
22       private BigDecimal tipPercentage = new BigDecimal(0.15); // 15% default
23
24       // GUI controls defined in FXML and used by the controller's code
25       @FXML
26       private TextField amountTextField;
27
28       @FXML
29       private Label tipPercentageLabel;
30
31       @FXML
32       private Slider tipPercentageSlider;
33
```

Fig. 22.19 | `TipCalculatorController`'s `static` variables and instance variables. (Part 1 of 2.)

```
34        @FXML
35        private TextField tipTextField;
36
37        @FXML
38        private TextField totalTextField;
39
```

Fig. 22.19 | TipCalculatorController's static variables and instance variables. (Part 2 of 2.)

@FXML Annotation

Recall from Section 22.5.3 that each control that this app manipulates in its Java source code needs an **fx:id**. Lines 25–38 (Fig. 22.19) declare the controller class's corresponding instance variables. The **@FXML annotation** that precedes each declaration (lines 25, 28, 31, 34 and 37) indicates that the variable name can be used in the FXML file that describes the app's GUI. The variable names that you specify in the controller class must precisely match the **fx:id** values you specified when building the GUI. When the FXMLLoader loads TipCalculator.fxml to create the GUI, it also initializes each of the controller's instance variables that are declared with @FXML to ensure that they refer to the corresponding GUI components in the FXML file.

TipCalculatorController's calculateButtonPressed Event Handler

Figure 22.20 presents class TipCalculatorController's calculateButtonPressed method, which is called with the user clicks the **Calculate** Button. The @FXML annotation (line 41) preceding the method indicates that this method can be used to specify a control's event handler in the FXML file that describes the app's GUI. For a control that generates an ActionEvent (as is the case for many JavaFX controls), the event-handling method must return void and receive one ActionEvent parameter (line 42).

```
40        // calculates and displays the tip and total amounts
41        @FXML
42        private void calculateButtonPressed(ActionEvent event)
43        {
44           try
45           {
46              BigDecimal amount = new BigDecimal(amountTextField.getText());
47              BigDecimal tip = amount.multiply(tipPercentage);
48              BigDecimal total = amount.add(tip);
49
50              tipTextField.setText(currency.format(tip));
51              totalTextField.setText(currency.format(total));
52           }
53           catch (NumberFormatException ex)
54           {
55              amountTextField.setText("Enter amount");
56              amountTextField.selectAll();
57              amountTextField.requestFocus();
58           }
59        }
60
```

Fig. 22.20 | TipCalculatorController's calculateButtonPressed event handler.

Specifying the Calculate Button's Event Handler in Scene Builder

When you created the TipCalculator project with NetBeans, it preconfigured the class TipCalculatorController as the controller for the GUI in TipCalculator.fxml. You can see this in Scene Builder by selecting the scene's root node (i.e., the GridPane), then expanding the **Inspector** window's **Code** section. The controller class's name is specified in the **Controller class** field. If you declare the method calculateButtonPressed in the controller class before specifying the **Calculate** Button's event handler in the FXML, when you open Scene Builder it scans the controller class for methods prefixed with @FXML and allows you to select from those methods to configure event handlers.

To indicate that calculateButtonPressed should be called when the user clicks the **Calculate** Button, open TipCalculator.fxml in Scene Builder, then:

1. Select the **Calculate** Button.

2. In the **Inspector** window, expand the **Code** section.

3. Under **On Action**, select #calculateButtonPressed from the drop-down list and save the FXML file.

When the FXMLLoader loads TipCalculator.fxml to create the GUI, it creates and registers an event handler for the **Calculate** Button's ActionEvent. An ActionEvent's handler is an object of a class that implements the **EventHandler<ActionEvent>** interface, which contains a handle method that returns void and receives an ActionEvent parameter. This method, in turn, calls method calculateButtonPressed when the user clicks the **Calculate** Button. The FXMLLoader performs similar tasks for every event listener you specified via the **Inspector** window's **Code** section.

Calculating and Displaying the Tip and Total Amounts

Lines 46–51 calculate and display the tip and total amounts. Line 46 calls method getText to get from the amountTextField the bill amount typed by the user. This String is passed to the BigDecimal constructor, which throws a NumberFormatException if its argument is not a number. In that case, line 55 calls amountTextField's setText method to display the message "Enter amount" in the TextField. Line 56 then calls method selectAll to select the TextField's text and line 57 calls requestFocus, which gives the TextField the focus. This allows the user to immediately type a new value in the amountTextField without having to first select its text. Methods getText, setText and selectAll are inherited into class TextField from class TextInputControl (package javafx.scene.control), and method requestFocus is inherited into class TextField from class Node (package javafx.scene).

If line 46 does not throw an exception, line 47 calculates the tip by calling method multiply to multiply the amount by the tipPercentage, and line 48 calculates the total by calling method add to add the tip to the bill amount. Next lines 50 and 51 use the currency object's format method to create currency-formatted Strings representing the tip and total amounts—these are displayed in tipTextField and totalTextField, respectively.

TipCalculatorController's initalize Method

Figure 22.21 presents class TipCalculatorController's initialize method. When the FXMLLoader creates an object of class TipCalculatorController, it determines whether the class contains an initialize method with no parameters and, if so, calls that method to initialize the controller. This method can be used to configure the controller before the GUI is displayed. Line 65 calls the currency object's setRoundingMode method to specify how currency values should be rounded. The value RoundingMode.HALF_UP indicates that values greater than or equal to .5 should round up—for example, 34.567 would be formatted as 34.57 and 34.564 would be formatted as 34.56.

```
61      // called by FXMLLoader to initialize the controller
62      public void initialize()
63      {
64          // 0-4 rounds down, 5-9 rounds up
65          currency.setRoundingMode(RoundingMode.HALF_UP);
66
67          // listener for changes to tipPercentageSlider's value
68          tipPercentageSlider.valueProperty().addListener(
69              new ChangeListener<Number>()
70              {
71                  @Override
72                  public void changed(ObservableValue<? extends Number> ov,
73                      Number oldValue, Number newValue)
74                  {
75                      tipPercentage =
76                          BigDecimal.valueOf(newValue.intValue() / 100.0);
77                      tipPercentageLabel.setText(percent.format(tipPercentage));
78                  }
79              }
80          );
81      }
82  }
```

Fig. 22.21 | TipCalculatorController's initalize method.

Using an Anonymous Inner Class for Event Handling
Each JavaFX control has various properties, some of which—such as a Slider's value—can notify an event listener when they change. For such properties, you must manually register as the event handler an object of a class that implements the ChangeListener interface from package javafx.beans.value. If such an event handler is not reused, you'd typically define it as an instance of an **anonymous inner class**—a class that's declared without a name and typically appears inside a method declaration. Lines 68–80 are one statement that declares the event listener's class, creates an object of that class and registers it as the listener for changes to the tipPercentageSlider's value.

The call to method valueProperty (line 68) returns an object of class DoubleProperty (package javax.beans.property) that represents the Slider's value. A DoubleProperty is an ObservableValue that can notify listeners when the value changes. Each class that implements interface ObservableValue provides method addListener (called on line 68) for registering a ChangeListener. In the case of a Slider's value, addListener's argument is an object that implements ChangeListener<Number>, because the Slider's value is a numeric value.

Since an anonymous inner class has no name, one object of the class must be created at the point where the class is declared (starting at line 69). Method addListener's argument is defined in lines 69–79 as a class-instance creation expression that declares an anonymous inner class and creates one object of that class. A reference to that object is then passed to addListener. After the new keyword, the syntax ChangeListener<Number>() (line 69) begins the declaration of an anonymous inner class that implements interface ChangeListener<Number>. This is similar to beginning a class declaration with

```
public class MyHandler implements ChangeListener<Number>
```

The opening left brace at 70 and the closing right brace at line 79 delimit the body of the anonymous inner class. Lines 71–78 declare the ChangeListener<Number>'s changed method, which receives a reference to the ObservableValue that changed, a Number containing the Slider's old value before the event occurred and a Number containing the Slider's new value. When the user moves the Slider's thumb, lines 75–76 store the new tip percentage and line 77 updates the tipPercentageLabel.

An anonymous inner class can access its top-level class's instance variables, static variables and methods—in this case, the anonymous inner class uses instance variables tipPercentage and tipPercentageLabel, and static variable percent. However, an anonymous inner class has limited access to the local variables of the method in which it's declared—it can access only the final local variables declared in the enclosing method's body. (As of Java SE 8, an anonymous inner class may also access a class's effectively final local variables—see Section 17.3.1 for more information.)

Java SE 8: Using a Lambda to Implement the *ChangeListener*
Recall from Section 10.10 that in Java SE 8 an interface containing one method is a functional interface and recall from Chapter 17 that such interfaces may be implemented with lambdas. Section 17.9 showed how to implement an event-handling functional interface using a lambda. The event handler in Fig. 22.21 can be implemented with a lambda as follows:

```
tipPercentageSlider.valueProperty().addListener(
   (ov, oldValue, newValue) ->
   {
      tipPercentage =
         BigDecimal.valueOf(newValue.intValue() / 100.0);
      tipPercentageLabel.setText(percent.format(tipPercentage));
   });
```

22.6 Wrap-Up

In this chapter, we introduced JavaFX. We presented the structure of a JavaFX stage (the application window). You learned that the stage displays a scene's scene graph, that the scene graph is composed of nodes and that nodes consist of layouts and controls.

You designed GUIs using visual programming techniques in JavaFX Scene Builder, which enabled you to create GUIs without writing any Java code. You arranged Label, ImageView, TextField, Slider and Button controls using the VBox and GridPane layout containers. You learned how class FXMLLoader uses the FXML created in Scene Builder to create the GUI.

You implemented a controller class to respond to user interactions with Button and Slider controls. We showed that certain event handlers can be specified directly in FXML from Scene Builder, but event handlers for changes to a control's property values must be implemented directly in the controllers code. You also learned that the FXMLLoader creates and initializes an instance of an application's controller class, initializes the controller's instance variables that are declared with the @FXML annotation, and creates and registers event handlers for any events specified in the FXML. In the next chapter, we begin our two-chapter, case study on object-oriented design with the UML.

23

ATM Case Study, Part 1: Object-Oriented Design with the UML

Objectives

In this chapter you'll:

- A simple object-oriented design methodology.
- What a requirements document is.
- To identify classes and class attributes from a requirements document.
- To identify objects' states, activities and operations from a requirements document.
- To determine the collaborations among objects in a system.
- To work with the UML's use case, class, state, activity, communication and sequence diagrams to graphically model an object-oriented system.

23.1 Case Study Introduction

Now we begin the *optional* portion of our object-oriented design and implementation case study. In this chapter and Chapter 24, you'll design and implement an object-oriented automated teller machine (ATM) software system. The case study provides you with a concise, carefully paced, complete design and implementation experience. In Sections 23.2–23.7 and 24.2–24.3, you'll perform the steps of an object-oriented design (OOD) process using the UML while relating these steps to the object-oriented concepts discussed in Chapters 2–10. In this chapter, you'll work with six popular types of UML diagrams to graphically represent the design. In Chapter 24, you'll tune the design with inheritance, then fully implement the ATM in a 673-line Java application (Section 24.4).

This is not an exercise; rather, it's an end-to-end learning experience that concludes with a detailed walkthrough of the complete Java code that implements our design. It will begin to acquaint you with the kinds of substantial problems encountered in industry.

These chapters can be studied as a continuous unit after you've completed the introduction to object-oriented programming in Chapters 8–11. Or, you can pace the sections one at a time after Chapters 2–8 and 10. Each section of the case study begins with a note telling you the chapter after which it can be covered.

23.2 Examining the Requirements Document

We begin our design process by presenting a **requirements document** that specifies the purpose of the ATM system and *what* it must do. Throughout the case study, we refer often to this requirements document.

Requirements Document

A local bank intends to install a new automated teller machine (ATM) to allow users (i.e., bank customers) to perform basic financial transactions (Fig. 23.1). Each user can have only one account at the bank. ATM users should be able to view their account balance, withdraw cash (i.e., take money out of an account) and deposit funds (i.e., place money into an account). The user interface of the automated teller machine contains:

- a screen that displays messages to the user
- a keypad that receives numeric input from the user
- a cash dispenser that dispenses cash to the user and
- a deposit slot that receives deposit envelopes from the user.

The cash dispenser begins each day loaded with 500 $20 bills. [*Note:* Owing to the limited scope of this case study, certain elements of the ATM described here do not accurately mimic those of a real ATM. For example, a real ATM typically contains a device that reads a user's account number from an ATM card, whereas this ATM asks the user to type the account number on the keypad. A real ATM also usually prints a receipt at the end of a session, but all output from this ATM appears on the screen.]

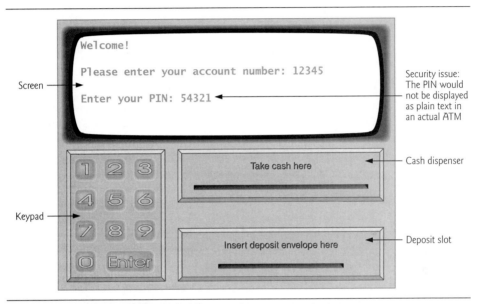

Fig. 23.1 | Automated teller machine user interface.

The bank wants you to develop software to perform the financial transactions initiated by bank customers through the ATM. The bank will integrate the software with the ATM's hardware at a later time. The software should encapsulate the functionality of the hardware devices (e.g., cash dispenser, deposit slot) within software components, but it need not concern itself with how these devices perform their duties. The ATM hardware has not been developed yet, so instead of writing your software to run on the ATM, you should develop a first version to run on a personal computer. This version should use the computer's monitor to simulate the ATM's screen, and the computer's keyboard to simulate the ATM's keypad.

An ATM session consists of authenticating a user (i.e., proving the user's identity) based on an account number and personal identification number (PIN), followed by creating and executing financial transactions. To authenticate a user and perform transactions, the ATM must interact with the bank's account information database (database access was presented in Chapter 21, but we do not use it in this case study). For each bank account, the database stores an account number, a PIN and a balance indicating the amount of money in the account. [*Note:* We assume that the bank plans to build only one ATM, so we need not worry about multiple ATMs accessing this database at the same time. Furthermore, we assume that the bank does not make any changes to the information in the database while a user is accessing the ATM. Also, any business system like an

ATM faces complex and challenging security issues that are beyond the scope of a first or second programming course. We make the simplifying assumption, however, that the bank trusts the ATM to access and manipulate the information in the database without significant security measures.]

Upon first approaching the ATM (assuming no one is currently using it), the user should experience the following sequence of events (shown in Fig. 23.1):

1. The screen displays Welcome! and prompts the user to enter an account number.

2. The user enters a five-digit account number using the keypad.

3. The screen prompts the user to enter the PIN (personal identification number) associated with the specified account number.

4. The user enters a five-digit PIN using the keypad.[1]

5. If the user enters a valid account number and the correct PIN for that account, the screen displays the main menu (Fig. 23.2). If the user enters an invalid account number or an incorrect PIN, the screen displays an appropriate message, then the ATM returns to *Step 1* to restart the authentication process.

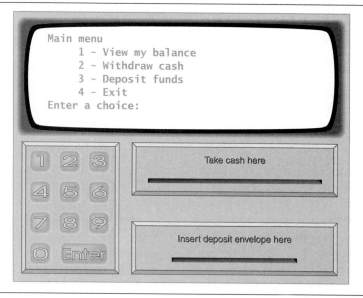

Fig. 23.2 | ATM main menu.

After the ATM authenticates the user, the main menu (Fig. 23.2) should contain a numbered option for each of the three types of transactions: balance inquiry (option 1), withdrawal (option 2) and deposit (option 3). It also should contain an option to allow

---

1. In this simple, command-line, text-based ATM, as you type the PIN, it appears on the screen. This is an obvious security breach—you would not want someone looking over your shoulder at an ATM and seeing your PIN displayed on the screen. In Chapter 12, we introduce the JPasswordField GUI component, which displays asterisks as the user types—making it more appropriate for entering PIN numbers and passwords.

the user to exit the system (option 4). The user then chooses either to perform a transaction (by entering 1, 2 or 3) or to exit the system (by entering 4).

If the user enters 1 to make a balance inquiry, the screen displays the user's account balance. To do so, the ATM must retrieve the balance from the bank's database. The following steps describe what occurs when the user enters 2 to make a withdrawal:

1. The screen displays a menu (Fig. 23.3) containing standard withdrawal amounts: $20 (option 1), $40 (option 2), $60 (option 3), $100 (option 4) and $200 (option 5). The menu also contains an option to allow the user to cancel the transaction (option 6).

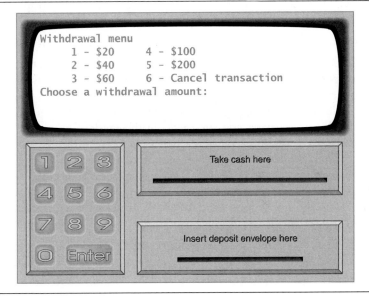

Fig. 23.3 | ATM withdrawal menu.

2. The user enters a menu selection using the keypad.

3. If the withdrawal amount chosen is greater than the user's account balance, the screen displays a message stating this and telling the user to choose a smaller amount. The ATM then returns to *Step 1*. If the withdrawal amount chosen is less than or equal to the user's account balance (i.e., an acceptable amount), the ATM proceeds to *Step 4*. If the user chooses to cancel the transaction (option 6), the ATM displays the main menu and waits for user input.

4. If the cash dispenser contains enough cash, the ATM proceeds to *Step 5*. Otherwise, the screen displays a message indicating the problem and telling the user to choose a smaller withdrawal amount. The ATM then returns to *Step 1*.

5. The ATM debits the withdrawal amount from the user's account in the bank's database (i.e., subtracts the withdrawal amount from the user's account balance).

6. The cash dispenser dispenses the desired amount of money to the user.

7. The screen displays a message reminding the user to take the money.

The following steps describe the actions that occur when the user enters 3 (when viewing the main menu of Fig. 23.2) to make a deposit:

1. The screen prompts the user to enter a deposit amount or type 0 (zero) to cancel.

2. The user enters a deposit amount or 0 using the keypad. [*Note:* The keypad does not contain a decimal point or a dollar sign, so the user cannot type a real dollar amount (e.g., $27.25). Instead, the user must enter a deposit amount as a number of cents (e.g., 2725). The ATM then divides this number by 100 to obtain a number representing a dollar amount (e.g., 2725 ÷ 100 = 27.25).]

3. If the user specifies a deposit amount, the ATM proceeds to *Step 4*. If the user chooses to cancel the transaction (by entering 0), the ATM displays the main menu and waits for user input.

4. The screen displays a message telling the user to insert a deposit envelope.

5. If the deposit slot receives a deposit envelope within two minutes, the ATM credits the deposit amount to the user's account in the bank's database (i.e., adds the deposit amount to the user's account balance). [*Note:* This money is *not* immediately available for withdrawal. The bank first must physically verify the amount of cash in the deposit envelope, and any checks in the envelope must clear (i.e., money must be transferred from the check writer's account to the check recipient's account). When either of these events occurs, the bank appropriately updates the user's balance stored in its database. This occurs independently of the ATM system.] If the deposit slot does not receive a deposit envelope within this time period, the screen displays a message that the system has canceled the transaction due to inactivity. The ATM then displays the main menu and waits for user input.

After the system successfully executes a transaction, it should return to the main menu so that the user can perform additional transactions. If the user exits the system, the screen should display a thank you message, then display the welcome message for the next user.

Analyzing the ATM System

The preceding statement is a simplified example of a requirements document. Typically, such a document is the result of a detailed process of **requirements gathering**, which might include interviews with possible users of the system and specialists in fields related to the system. For example, a systems analyst who is hired to prepare a requirements document for banking software (e.g., the ATM system described here) might interview banking experts to gain a better understanding of what the software must do. The analyst would use the information gained to compile a list of **system requirements** to guide systems designers as they design the system.

The process of requirements gathering is a key task of the first stage of the software life cycle. The **software life cycle** specifies the stages through which software goes from the time it's first conceived to the time it's retired from use. These stages typically include: analysis, design, implementation, testing and debugging, deployment, maintenance and retirement. Several software life-cycle models exist, each with its own preferences and specifications for when and how often software engineers should perform each of these stages. **Waterfall models** perform each stage once in succession, whereas **iterative models** may *repeat* one or more stages several times throughout a product's life cycle.

The analysis stage focuses on defining the problem to be solved. When designing any system, one must *solve the problem right*, but of equal importance, one must *solve the right problem*. Systems analysts collect the requirements that indicate the specific problem to solve. Our requirements document describes the requirements of our ATM system in sufficient detail that you need not go through an extensive analysis stage—it's been done for you.

To capture what a proposed system should do, developers often employ a technique known as **use case modeling**. This process identifies the **use cases** of the system, each representing a different capability that the system provides to its clients. For example, ATMs typically have several use cases, such as "View Account Balance," "Withdraw Cash," "Deposit Funds," "Transfer Funds Between Accounts" and "Buy Postage Stamps." The simplified ATM system we build in this case study allows only the first three.

Each use case describes a typical scenario for which the user uses the system. You've already read descriptions of the ATM system's use cases in the requirements document; the lists of steps required to perform each transaction type (i.e., balance inquiry, withdrawal and deposit) actually described the three use cases of our ATM—"View Account Balance," "Withdraw Cash" and "Deposit Funds," respectively.

Use Case Diagrams

We now introduce the first of several UML diagrams in the case study. We create a **use case diagram** to model the interactions between a system's clients (in this case study, bank customers) and its use cases. The goal is to show the kinds of interactions users have with a system without providing the details—these are provided in other UML diagrams (which we present throughout this case study). Use case diagrams are often accompanied by informal text that gives more detail—like the text that appears in the requirements document. Use case diagrams are produced during the analysis stage of the software life cycle. In larger systems, use case diagrams are indispensable tools that help system designers remain focused on satisfying the users' needs.

Figure 23.4 shows the use case diagram for our ATM system. The stick figure represents an **actor**, which defines the roles that an external entity—such as a person or another system—plays when interacting with the system. For our automated teller machine, the actor is a User who can view an account balance, withdraw cash and deposit funds from

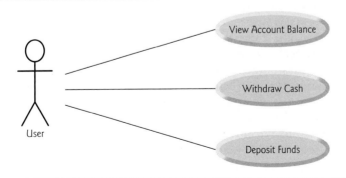

Fig. 23.4 | Use case diagram for the ATM system from the User's perspective.

the ATM. The User is not an actual person, but instead comprises the roles that a real person—when playing the part of a User—can play while interacting with the ATM. A use case diagram can include multiple actors. For example, the use case diagram for a real bank's ATM system might also include an actor named Administrator who refills the cash dispenser each day.

Our requirements document supplies the actors—"ATM users should be able to view their account balance, withdraw cash and deposit funds." Therefore, the actor in each of the three use cases is the user who interacts with the ATM. An external entity—a real person—plays the part of the user to perform financial transactions. Figure 23.4 shows one actor, whose name, User, appears below the actor in the diagram. The UML models each use case as an oval connected to an actor with a solid line.

Software engineers (more precisely, systems designers) must analyze the requirements document or a set of use cases and design the system before programmers implement it in a particular programming language. During the analysis stage, systems designers focus on understanding the requirements document to produce a high-level specification that describes *what* the system is supposed to do. The output of the design stage—a **design specification**—should specify clearly *how* the system should be constructed to satisfy these requirements. In the next several sections, we perform the steps of a simple object-oriented design (OOD) process on the ATM system to produce a design specification containing a collection of UML diagrams and supporting text.

The UML is designed for use with any OOD process. Many such processes exist, the best known of which is the Rational Unified Process™ (RUP) developed by Rational Software Corporation, now part of IBM. RUP is a rich process intended for designing "industrial strength" applications. For this case study, we present our own simplified design process.

Designing the ATM System

We now begin the design stage of our ATM system. A **system** is a set of components that interact to solve a problem. For example, to perform the ATM system's designated tasks, our ATM system has a user interface (Fig. 23.1), and contains software that executes financial transactions and interacts with a database of bank account information. **System structure** describes the system's objects and their interrelationships. **System behavior** describes how the system changes as its objects interact with one another.

Every system has both structure and behavior—designers must specify both. There are several types of system structures and behaviors. For example, the interactions among objects in the system differ from those between the user and the system, yet both constitute a portion of the system behavior.

The UML 2 standard specifies 13 diagram types for documenting the system models. Each models a distinct characteristic of a system's structure or behavior—six diagrams relate to system structure, the remaining seven to system behavior. We list here only the six diagram types used in our case study—one models system structure; the other five model system behavior. We provide an overview of the remaining seven UML diagram types in Appendix M, UML 2: Additional Diagram Types.

1. **Use case diagrams**, such as the one in Fig. 23.4, model the interactions between a system and its external entities (actors) in terms of use cases (system capabilities, such as "View Account Balance," "Withdraw Cash" and "Deposit Funds").

2. **Class diagrams**, which you'll study in Section 23.3, model the classes, or "building blocks," used in a system. Each noun or "thing" described in the requirements document is a candidate to be a class in the system (e.g., Account, Keypad). Class diagrams help us specify the *structural relationships* between parts of the system. For example, the ATM system class diagram will specify that the ATM is physically *composed of* a screen, a keypad, a cash dispenser and a deposit slot.

3. **State machine diagrams**, which you'll study in Section 23.5, model the ways in which an object changes state. An object's **state** is indicated by the values of all its attributes at a given time. When an object changes state, it may behave differently in the system. For example, after validating a user's PIN, the ATM transitions from the "user not authenticated" state to the "user authenticated" state, at which point it allows the user to perform financial transactions (e.g., view account balance, withdraw cash, deposit funds).

4. **Activity diagrams**, which you'll also study in Section 23.5, model an object's **activity**—is workflow (sequence of events) during program execution. An activity diagram models the *actions* the object performs and specifies the *order* in which it performs them. For example, an activity diagram shows that the ATM must obtain the balance of the user's account (from the bank's account information database) *before* the screen can display the balance to the user.

5. **Communication diagrams** (called **collaboration diagrams** in earlier versions of the UML) model the interactions among objects in a system, with an emphasis on *what* interactions occur. You'll learn in Section 23.7 that these diagrams show which objects must interact to perform an ATM transaction. For example, the ATM must communicate with the bank's account information database to retrieve an account balance.

6. **Sequence diagrams** also model the interactions among the objects in a system, but unlike communication diagrams, they emphasize *when* interactions occur. You'll learn in Section 23.7 that these diagrams help show the order in which interactions occur in executing a financial transaction. For example, the screen prompts the user to enter a withdrawal amount before cash is dispensed.

In Section 23.3, we continue designing our ATM system by identifying the classes from the requirements document. We accomplish this by extracting key *nouns and noun phrases* from the requirements document. Using these classes, we develop our first draft of the class diagram that models the structure of our ATM system.

Web Resource
We've created an extensive UML Resource Center that contains many links to additional information, including introductions, tutorials, blogs, books, certification, conferences, developer tools, documentation, e-books, FAQs, forums, groups, UML in Java, podcasts, security, tools, downloads, training courses, videos and more. Browse our UML Resource Center at www.deitel.com/UML/.

Self-Review Exercises for Section 23.2

23.1 Suppose we enabled a user of our ATM system to transfer money between two bank accounts. Modify the use case diagram of Fig. 23.4 to reflect this change.

23.2 _____ model the interactions among objects in a system with an emphasis on *when* these interactions occur.

    a) Class diagrams
    b) Sequence diagrams
    c) Communication diagrams
    d) Activity diagrams

23.3 Which of the following choices lists stages of a typical software life cycle in sequential order?

    a) design, analysis, implementation, testing
    b) design, analysis, testing, implementation
    c) analysis, design, testing, implementation
    d) analysis, design, implementation, testing

23.3 Identifying the Classes in a Requirements Document

Now we begin designing the ATM system. In this section, we identify the classes that are needed to build the system by analyzing the *nouns* and *noun phrases* that appear in the requirements document. We introduce UML class diagrams to model these classes. This is an important first step in defining the system's structure.

Identifying the Classes in a System

We begin our OOD process by identifying the classes required to build the ATM system. We'll eventually describe these classes using UML class diagrams and implement these classes in Java. First, we review the requirements document of Section 23.2 and identify key nouns and noun phrases to help us identify classes that comprise the ATM system. We may decide that some of these are actually attributes of other classes in the system. We may also conclude that some of the nouns do not correspond to parts of the system and thus should not be modeled at all. Additional classes may become apparent to us as we proceed through the design process.

Figure 23.5 lists the nouns and noun phrases found in the requirements document. We list them from left to right in the order in which we first encounter them. We list only the singular form of each.

Nouns and noun phrases in the ATM requirements document			
bank	money / funds	account number	ATM
screen	PIN	user	keypad
bank database	customer	cash dispenser	balance inquiry
transaction	$20 bill / cash	withdrawal	account
deposit slot	deposit	balance	deposit envelope

Fig. 23.5 | Nouns and noun phrases in the ATM requirements document.

We create classes only for the nouns and noun phrases that have significance in the ATM system. We don't model "bank" as a class, because the bank is not a part of the ATM system—the bank simply wants us to build the ATM. "Customer" and "user" also represent outside entities—they're important because they *interact* with our ATM system, but we do not need to model them as classes in the ATM software. Recall that we modeled an ATM user (i.e., a bank customer) as the actor in the use case diagram of Fig. 23.4.

We do not model "$20 bill" or "deposit envelope" as classes. These are physical objects in the real world, but they're not part of what is being automated. We can adequately represent the presence of bills in the system using an attribute of the class that models the cash dispenser. (We assign attributes to the ATM system's classes in Section 23.4.) For example, the cash dispenser maintains a count of the number of bills it contains. The requirements document does not say anything about what the system should do with deposit envelopes after it receives them. We can assume that simply acknowledging the receipt of an envelope—an operation performed by the class that models the deposit slot—is sufficient to represent the presence of an envelope in the system. We assign operations to the ATM system's classes in Section 23.6.

In our simplified ATM system, representing various amounts of "money," including an account's "balance," as attributes of classes seems most appropriate. Likewise, the nouns "account number" and "PIN" represent significant pieces of information in the ATM system. They're important attributes of a bank account. They do not, however, exhibit behaviors. Thus, we can most appropriately model them as attributes of an account class.

Though the requirements document frequently describes a "transaction" in a general sense, we do not model the broad notion of a financial transaction at this time. Instead, we model the three types of transactions (i.e., "balance inquiry," "withdrawal" and "deposit") as individual classes. These classes possess specific attributes needed for executing the transactions they represent. For example, a withdrawal needs to know the amount of the withdrawal. A balance inquiry, however, does not require any additional data other than the account number. Furthermore, the three transaction classes exhibit unique behaviors. A withdrawal includes dispensing cash to the user, whereas a deposit involves receiving deposit envelopes from the user. In Section 24.3, we "factor out" common features of all transactions into a general "transaction" class using the object-oriented concept of inheritance.

We determine the classes for our system based on the remaining nouns and noun phrases from Fig. 23.5. Each of these refers to one or more of the following:

- ATM
- screen
- keypad
- cash dispenser
- deposit slot
- account
- bank database
- balance inquiry
- withdrawal
- deposit

The elements of this list are likely to be classes that we'll need to implement our system.

We can now model the classes in our system based on the list we've created. We capitalize class names in the design process—a UML convention—as we'll do when we write the actual Java code that implements our design. If the name of a class contains more than one word, we run the words together and capitalize each word (e.g., `MultipleWordName`). Using this convention, we create classes `ATM`, `Screen`, `Keypad`, `CashDispenser`, `DepositSlot`, `Account`, `BankDatabase`, `BalanceInquiry`, `Withdrawal` and `Deposit`. We construct our system using these classes as building blocks. Before we begin building the system, however, we must gain a better understanding of how the classes relate to one another.

Modeling Classes
The UML enables us to model, via **class diagrams**, the classes in the ATM system and their interrelationships. Figure 23.6 represents class `ATM`. Each class is modeled as a rectangle with three compartments. The top one contains the name of the class centered horizontally in boldface. The middle compartment contains the class's attributes. (We discuss attributes in Sections 23.4—12.5.) The bottom compartment contains the class's operations (discussed in Section 23.6). In Fig. 23.6, the middle and bottom compartments are empty because we've not yet determined this class's attributes and operations.

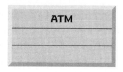

Fig. 23.6 | Representing a class in the UML using a class diagram.

Class diagrams also show the relationships between the classes of the system. Figure 23.7 shows how our classes `ATM` and `Withdrawal` relate to one another. For the moment, for simplicity, we choose to model only this subset of classes. We present a more complete class diagram later in this section. Notice that the rectangles representing classes in this diagram are not subdivided into compartments. The UML allows the suppression of class attributes and operations in this manner to create more readable diagrams, when appropriate. Such a diagram is said to be an **elided diagram**—one in which some information, such as the contents of the second and third compartments, is *not* modeled. We'll place information in these compartments in Sections 23.4—12.6.

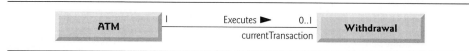

Fig. 23.7 | Class diagram showing an association among classes.

In Fig. 23.7, the solid line that connects the two classes represents an **association**—a relationship between classes. The numbers near each end of the line are **multiplicity** values, which indicate how many objects of each class participate in the association. In this case, following the line from left to right reveals that, at any given moment, one `ATM` object participates in an association with either zero or one `Withdrawal` objects—zero if the current user is not currently performing a transaction or has requested a different type of transaction, and one if the user has requested a withdrawal. The UML can model many types of multiplicity. Figure 23.8 lists and explains the multiplicity types.

Symbol	Meaning
0	None
1	One
m	An integer value
0..1	Zero or one
m, n	m or n
$m..n$	At least m, but not more than n
*	Any nonnegative integer (zero or more)
0..*	Zero or more (identical to *)
1..*	One or more

Fig. 23.8 | Multiplicity types.

An association can be named. For example, the word Executes above the line connecting classes ATM and Withdrawal in Fig. 23.7 indicates the name of that association. This part of the diagram reads "one object of class ATM executes zero or one objects of class Withdrawal." Association names are *directional*, as indicated by the filled arrowhead—so it would be improper, for example, to read the preceding association from right to left as "zero or one objects of class Withdrawal execute one object of class ATM."

The word currentTransaction at the Withdrawal end of the association line in Fig. 23.7 is a **role name**, identifying the role the Withdrawal object plays in its relationship with the ATM. A role name adds meaning to an association between classes by identifying the role a class plays in the context of an association. A class can play several roles in the same system. For example, in a school personnel system, a person may play the role of "professor" when relating to students. The same person may take on the role of "colleague" when participating in an association with another professor, and "coach" when coaching student athletes. In Fig. 23.7, the role name currentTransaction indicates that the Withdrawal object participating in the Executes association with an object of class ATM represents the transaction currently being processed by the ATM. In other contexts, a Withdrawal object may take on other roles (e.g., the "previous transaction"). Notice that we do not specify a role name for the ATM end of the Executes association. Role names in class diagrams are often omitted when the meaning of an association is clear without them.

In addition to indicating simple relationships, associations can specify more complex relationships, such as objects of one class being *composed of* objects of other classes. Consider a real-world automated teller machine. What "pieces" does a manufacturer put together to build a working ATM? Our requirements document tells us that the ATM is composed of a screen, a keypad, a cash dispenser and a deposit slot.

In Fig. 23.9, the **solid diamonds** attached to the ATM class's association lines indicate that ATM has a **composition** relationship with classes Screen, Keypad, CashDispenser and DepositSlot. Composition implies a *whole/part relationship*. The class that has the composition symbol (the solid diamond) on its end of the association line is the *whole* (in this case, ATM), and the classes on the other end of the association lines are the *parts*—in this case, Screen, Keypad, CashDispenser and DepositSlot. The compositions in Fig. 23.9 indicate that an object of class ATM is formed from one object of class Screen, one object of class CashDispenser, one object of class Keypad and one object of class DepositSlot. The ATM *has a* screen, a keypad, a cash dispenser and a deposit slot. (As we saw in Chapter 9, the *is-a* relationship defines inheritance. We'll see in Section 24.3 that there's a nice opportunity to use inheritance in the ATM system design.)

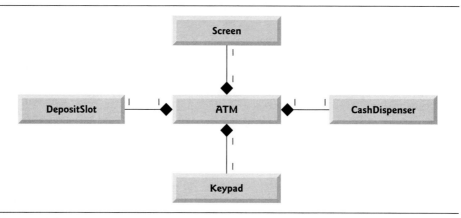

Fig. 23.9 | Class diagram showing composition relationships.

According to the UML specification (www.omg.org/technology/documents/formal/uml.htm), composition relationships have the following properties:

1. Only one class in the relationship can represent the *whole* (i.e., the diamond can be placed on only *one* end of the association line). For example, either the screen is part of the ATM or the ATM is part of the screen, but the screen and the ATM cannot both represent the whole in the relationship.

2. The *parts* in the composition relationship exist only as long as the whole does, and the whole is responsible for the creation and destruction of its parts. For example, the act of constructing an ATM includes manufacturing its parts. Also, if the ATM is destroyed, its screen, keypad, cash dispenser and deposit slot are also destroyed.

3. A *part* may belong to only one *whole* at a time, although it may be removed and attached to another whole, which then assumes responsibility for the part.

The solid diamonds in our class diagrams indicate composition relationships that fulfill these properties. If a *has-a* relationship does not satisfy one or more of these criteria, the UML specifies that **hollow diamonds** be attached to the ends of association lines to indicate **aggregation**—a weaker form of composition. For example, a personal computer and a computer monitor participate in an aggregation relationship—the computer *has a* monitor, but the two parts can exist independently, and the same monitor can be attached to multiple computers at once, thus violating composition's second and third properties.

Figure 23.10 shows a class diagram for the ATM system. This diagram models most of the classes that we've identified, as well as the associations between them that we can infer from the requirements document. Classes `BalanceInquiry` and `Deposit` participate in associations similar to those of class `Withdrawal`, so we've chosen to omit them from this diagram to keep it simple. In Section 24.3, we expand our class diagram to include all the classes in the ATM system.

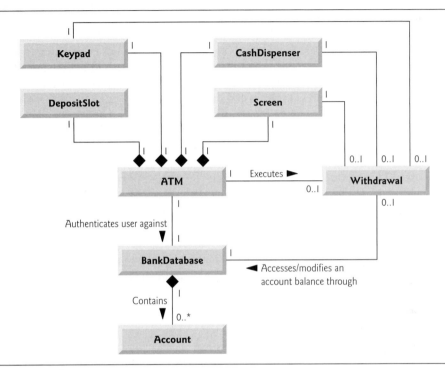

Fig. 23.10 | Class diagram for the ATM system model.

Figure 23.10 presents a graphical model of ATM system's structure. It includes classes `BankDatabase` and `Account`, and several associations that were not present in either Fig. 23.7 or Fig. 23.9. It shows that class `ATM` has a **one-to-one relationship** with class `BankDatabase`—one `ATM` object *authenticates users against* one `BankDatabase` object. In Fig. 23.10, we also model the fact that the bank's database contains information about many accounts—one `BankDatabase` object participates in a *composition* relationship with zero or more `Account` objects. The multiplicity value 0..* at the `Account` end of the association between class `BankDatabase` and class `Account` indicates that zero or more objects of class `Account` take part in the association. Class `BankDatabase` has a **one-to-many relationship** with class `Account`—the `BankDatabase` can contain many `Accounts`. Similarly, class `Account` has a **many-to-one relationship** with class `BankDatabase`—there can be many `Accounts` stored in the `BankDatabase`. Recall from Fig. 23.8 that the multiplicity value * is identical to 0..*. We include 0..* in our class diagrams for clarity.

Figure 23.10 also indicates that at any given time 0 or 1 `Withdrawal` objects can exist. If the user is performing a withdrawal, "one object of class `Withdrawal` accesses/modifies an account balance through one object of class `BankDatabase`." We could have created an association directly between class `Withdrawal` and class `Account`. The requirements document, however, states that the "ATM must interact with the bank's account information database" to perform transactions. A bank account contains sensitive information, and systems engineers must always consider the security of personal data when designing a system. Thus, only the BankDatabase can access and manipulate an account directly. All other parts of the system must interact with the database to retrieve or update account information (e.g., an account balance).

The class diagram in Fig. 23.10 also models associations between class Withdrawal and classes Screen, CashDispenser and Keypad. A withdrawal transaction includes prompting the user to choose a withdrawal amount, and receiving numeric input. These actions require the use of the screen and the keypad, respectively. Furthermore, dispensing cash to the user requires access to the cash dispenser.

Classes BalanceInquiry and Deposit, though not shown in Fig. 23.10, take part in several associations with the other classes of the ATM system. Like class Withdrawal, each of these classes associates with classes ATM and BankDatabase. An object of class Balance-Inquiry also associates with an object of class Screen to display the balance of an account to the user. Class Deposit associates with classes Screen, Keypad and DepositSlot. Like withdrawals, deposit transactions require use of the screen and the keypad to display prompts and receive input, respectively. To receive deposit envelopes, an object of class Deposit accesses the deposit slot.

We've now identified the initial classes in our ATM system—we may discover others as we proceed with the design and implementation. In Section 23.4 we determine the attributes for each of these classes, and in Section 23.5 we use these attributes to examine how the system changes over time.

Self-Review Exercises for Section 23.3

23.4   Suppose we have a class Car that represents a car. Think of some of the different pieces that a manufacturer would put together to produce a whole car. Create a class diagram (similar to Fig. 23.9) that models some of the composition relationships of class Car.

23.5   Suppose we have a class File that represents an electronic document in a standalone, non-networked computer represented by class Computer. What sort of association exists between class Computer and class File?
    a) Class Computer has a one-to-one relationship with class File.
    b) Class Computer has a many-to-one relationship with class File.
    c) Class Computer has a one-to-many relationship with class File.
    d) Class Computer has a many-to-many relationship with class File.

23.6   State whether the following statement is *true* or *false*, and if *false*, explain why: A UML diagram in which a class's second and third compartments are not modeled is said to be an elided diagram.

23.7   Modify the class diagram of Fig. 23.10 to include class Deposit instead of class Withdrawal.

23.4 Identifying Class Attributes

Classes have attributes (data) and operations (behaviors). Class attributes are implemented as fields, and class operations are implemented as methods. In this section, we determine many of the attributes needed in the ATM system. In Section 23.5 we examine how these attributes represent an object's state. In Section 23.6 we determine class operations.

Identifying Attributes

Consider the attributes of some real-world objects: A person's attributes include height, weight and whether the person is left-handed, right-handed or ambidextrous. A radio's attributes include its station, volume and AM or FM settings. A car's attributes include its speedometer and odometer readings, the amount of gas in its tank and what gear it's in. A personal computer's attributes include its manufacturer (e.g., Dell, Sun, Apple or IBM), type of screen (e.g., LCD or CRT), main memory size and hard disk size.

We can identify many attributes of the classes in our system by looking for descriptive words and phrases in the requirements document. For each such word and phrase we find that plays a significant role in the ATM system, we create an attribute and assign it to one or more of the classes identified in Section 23.3. We also create attributes to represent any additional data that a class may need, as such needs become clear throughout the design process.

Figure 23.11 lists the words or phrases from the requirements document that describe each class. We formed this list by reading the requirements document and identifying any words or phrases that refer to characteristics of the classes in the system. For example, the requirements document describes the steps taken to obtain a "withdrawal amount," so we list "amount" next to class `Withdrawal`.

Class	Descriptive words and phrases
ATM	user is authenticated
BalanceInquiry	account number
Withdrawal	account number
	amount
Deposit	account number
	amount
BankDatabase	*[no descriptive words or phrases]*
Account	account number
	PIN
	balance
Screen	*[no descriptive words or phrases]*
Keypad	*[no descriptive words or phrases]*
CashDispenser	begins each day loaded with 500 $20 bills
DepositSlot	*[no descriptive words or phrases]*

Fig. 23.11 | Descriptive words and phrases from the ATM requirements document.

Figure 23.11 leads us to create one attribute of class `ATM`. Class `ATM` maintains information about the state of the ATM. The phrase "user is authenticated" describes a state of the ATM (we introduce states in Section 23.5), so we include `userAuthenticated` as a **Boolean attribute** (i.e., an attribute that has a value of either `true` or `false`) in class `ATM`. The `Boolean` attribute type in the UML is equivalent to the `boolean` type in Java. This attribute indicates whether the ATM has successfully authenticated the current user—`userAuthenticated` must be `true` for the system to allow the user to perform transactions and access account information. This attribute helps ensure the security of the data in the system.

Classes BalanceInquiry, Withdrawal and Deposit share one attribute. Each transaction involves an "account number" that corresponds to the account of the user making the transaction. We assign an integer attribute accountNumber to each transaction class to identify the account to which an object of the class applies.

Descriptive words and phrases in the requirements document also suggest some differences in the attributes required by each transaction class. The requirements document indicates that to withdraw cash or deposit funds, users must input a specific "amount" of money to be withdrawn or deposited, respectively. Thus, we assign to classes Withdrawal and Deposit an attribute amount to store the value supplied by the user. The amounts of money related to a withdrawal and a deposit are defining characteristics of these transactions that the system requires for these transactions to take place. Class BalanceInquiry, however, needs no additional data to perform its task—it requires only an account number to indicate the account whose balance should be retrieved.

Class Account has several attributes. The requirements document states that each bank account has an "account number" and "PIN," which the system uses for identifying accounts and authenticating users. We assign to class Account two integer attributes: accountNumber and pin. The requirements document also specifies that an account maintains a "balance" of the amount of money in the account and that money the user deposits does not become available for a withdrawal until the bank verifies the amount of cash in the deposit envelope, and any checks in the envelope clear. An account must still record the amount of money that a user deposits, however. Therefore, we decide that an account should represent a balance using two attributes: availableBalance and totalBalance. Attribute availableBalance tracks the amount of money that a user can withdraw from the account. Attribute totalBalance refers to the total amount of money that the user has "on deposit" (i.e., the amount of money available, plus the amount waiting to be verified or cleared). For example, suppose an ATM user deposits $50.00 into an empty account. The totalBalance attribute would increase to $50.00 to record the deposit, but the availableBalance would remain at $0. [*Note:* We assume that the bank updates the availableBalance attribute of an Account some length of time after the ATM transaction occurs, in response to confirming that $50 worth of cash or checks was found in the deposit envelope. We assume that this update occurs through a transaction that a bank employee performs using some piece of bank software other than the ATM. Thus, we do not discuss this transaction in our case study.]

Class CashDispenser has one attribute. The requirements document states that the cash dispenser "begins each day loaded with 500 $20 bills." The cash dispenser must keep track of the number of bills it contains to determine whether enough cash is on hand to satisfy withdrawal requests. We assign to class CashDispenser an integer attribute count, which is initially set to 500.

For real problems in industry, there's no guarantee that requirements documents will be precise enough for the object-oriented systems designer to determine all the attributes or even all the classes. The need for additional classes, attributes and behaviors may become clear as the design process proceeds. As we progress through this case study, we will continue to add, modify and delete information about the classes in our system.

Modeling Attributes

The class diagram in Fig. 23.12 lists some of the attributes for the classes in our system—the descriptive words and phrases in Fig. 23.11 lead us to identify these attributes. For simplicity, Fig. 23.12 does not show the associations among classes—we showed these in Fig. 23.10. This is a common practice of systems designers when designs are being developed. Recall from Section 23.3 that in the UML, a class's attributes are placed in the middle compartment of the class's rectangle. We list each attribute's name and type separated by a colon (:), followed in some cases by an equal sign (=) and an initial value.

Consider the userAuthenticated attribute of class ATM:

```
userAuthenticated : Boolean = false
```

This attribute declaration contains three pieces of information about the attribute. The **attribute name** is userAuthenticated. The **attribute type** is Boolean. In Java, an attribute can be represented by a primitive type, such as boolean, int or double, or a reference type like a class. We've chosen to model only primitive-type attributes in Fig. 23.12—we discuss the reasoning behind this decision shortly. The attribute types in Fig. 23.12 are in UML notation. We'll associate the types Boolean, Integer and Double in the UML diagram with the primitive types boolean, int and double in Java, respectively.

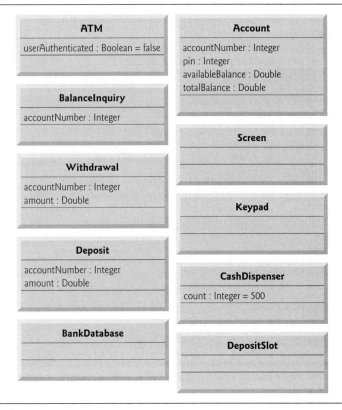

Fig. 23.12 | Classes with attributes.

We can also indicate an initial value for an attribute. The userAuthenticated attribute in class ATM has an initial value of false. This indicates that the system initially does not consider the user to be authenticated. If an attribute has no initial value specified, only its name and type (separated by a colon) are shown. For example, the accountNumber attribute of class BalanceInquiry is an integer. Here we show no initial value, because the value of this attribute is a number that we do not yet know. This number will be determined at execution time based on the account number entered by the current ATM user.

Figure 23.12 does not include attributes for classes Screen, Keypad and DepositSlot. These are important components of our system, for which our design process has not yet revealed any attributes. We may discover some, however, in the remaining phases of design or when we implement these classes in Java. This is perfectly normal.

Software Engineering Observation 23.1

At early stages in the design process, classes often lack attributes (and operations). Such classes should not be eliminated, however, because attributes (and operations) may become evident in the later phases of design and implementation.

Figure 23.12 also does not include attributes for class BankDatabase. Recall that attributes in Java can be represented by either primitive types or reference types. We've chosen to include only primitive-type attributes in the class diagram in Fig. 23.12 (and in similar class diagrams throughout the case study). A reference-type attribute is modeled more clearly as an association between the class holding the reference and the class of the object to which the reference points. For example, the class diagram in Fig. 23.10 indicates that class BankDatabase participates in a composition relationship with zero or more Account objects. From this composition, we can determine that when we implement the ATM system in Java, we'll be required to create an attribute of class BankDatabase to hold references to zero or more Account objects. Similarly, we can determine reference-type attributes of class ATM that correspond to its composition relationships with classes Screen, Keypad, CashDispenser and DepositSlot. These composition-based attributes would be redundant if modeled in Fig. 23.12, because the compositions modeled in Fig. 23.10 already convey the fact that the database contains information about zero or more accounts and that an ATM is composed of a screen, keypad, cash dispenser and deposit slot. Software developers typically model these whole/part relationships as compositions rather than as attributes required to implement the relationships.

The class diagram in Fig. 23.12 provides a solid basis for the structure of our model, but the diagram is not complete. In Section 23.5 we identify the states and activities of the objects in the model, and in Section 23.6 we identify the operations that the objects perform. As we present more of the UML and object-oriented design, we'll continue to strengthen the structure of our model.

Self-Review Exercises for Section 23.4

23.8 We typically identify the attributes of the classes in our system by analyzing the _____ in the requirements document.
    a) nouns and noun phrases
    b) descriptive words and phrases
    c) verbs and verb phrases
    d) All of the above.

23.9 Which of the following is *not* an attribute of an airplane?
    a) length
    b) wingspan

c) fly

d) number of seats

23.10 Describe the meaning of the following attribute declaration of class CashDispenser in the class diagram in Fig. 23.12:

```
count : Integer = 500
```

23.5 Identifying Objects' States and Activities

In Section 23.4, we identified many of the class attributes needed to implement the ATM system and added them to the class diagram in Fig. 23.12. We now show how these attributes represent an object's state. We identify some key states that our objects may occupy and discuss how objects *change state* in response to various events occurring in the system. We also discuss the workflow, or **activities**, that objects perform in the ATM system, and we present the activities of BalanceInquiry and Withdrawal transaction objects.

State Machine Diagrams
Each object in a system goes through a series of states. An object's state is indicated by the values of its attributes at a given time. **State machine diagrams** (commonly called **state diagrams**) model several states of an object and show under what circumstances the object changes state. Unlike the class diagrams presented in earlier case study sections, which focused primarily on the system's *structure*, state diagrams model some of the system's *behavior*.

Figure 23.13 is a simple state diagram that models some of the states of an object of class ATM. The UML represents each state in a state diagram as a **rounded rectangle** with the name of the state placed inside it. A **solid circle** with an attached stick (→) arrowhead designates the **initial state**. Recall that we modeled this state information as the Boolean attribute userAuthenticated in the class diagram of Fig. 23.12. This attribute is initialized to false, or the "User not authenticated" state, according to the state diagram.

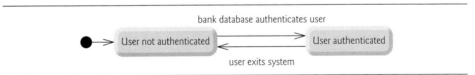

Fig. 23.13 | State diagram for the ATM object.

The arrows with stick (→) arrowhead indicate **transitions** between states. An object can transition from one state to another in response to various *events* that occur in the system. The name or description of the event that causes a transition is written near the line that corresponds to the transition. For example, the ATM object changes from the "User not authenticated" to the "User authenticated" state after the database authenticates the user. Recall from the requirements document that the database authenticates a user by comparing the account number and PIN entered by the user with those of an account in the database. If the user has entered a valid account number and the correct PIN, the ATM object transitions to the "User authenticated" state and changes its userAuthenticated attribute to a value of true. When the user exits the system by choosing the "exit" option from the main menu, the ATM object returns to the "User not authenticated" state.

Software Engineering Observation 23.2

Software designers do not generally create state diagrams showing every possible state and state transition for all attributes—there are simply too many of them. State diagrams typically show only key states and state transitions.

Activity Diagrams

Like a state diagram, an activity diagram models aspects of system behavior. Unlike a state diagram, an activity diagram models an object's **workflow** (sequence of events) during program execution. An activity diagram models the **actions** the object will perform and in what *order*. The activity diagram in Fig. 23.14 models the actions involved in executing a balance-inquiry transaction. We assume that a `BalanceInquiry` object has already been initialized and assigned a valid account number (that of the current user), so the object knows which balance to retrieve. The diagram includes the actions that occur after the user selects a balance inquiry from the main menu and before the ATM returns the user to the main menu—a `BalanceInquiry` object does not perform or initiate these actions, so we do not model them here. The diagram begins with retrieving the balance of the account from the database. Next, the `BalanceInquiry` displays the balance on the screen. This action completes the execution of the transaction. Recall that we've chosen to represent an account balance as both the `availableBalance` and `totalBalance` attributes of class `Account`, so the actions modeled in Fig. 23.14 refer to the retrieval and display of *both* balance attributes.

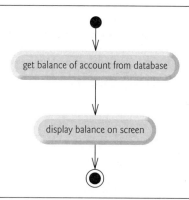

Fig. 23.14 | Activity diagram for a `BalanceInquiry` object.

The UML represents an action in an activity diagram as an action state modeled by a rectangle with its left and right sides replaced by arcs curving outward. Each action state contains an *action expression*—for example, "get balance of account from database"—that specifies an action to be performed. An arrow with a stick (⟶) arrowhead connects two action states, indicating the order in which the actions represented by the action states occur. The solid circle (at the top of Fig. 23.14) represents the activity's *initial state*—the beginning of the workflow before the object performs the modeled actions. In this case, the transaction first executes the "get balance of account from database" action expression. The transaction then displays *both* balances on the screen. The solid circle enclosed in an open circle (at the bottom of Fig. 23.14) represents the *final state*—the end of the workflow after the object performs the modeled actions. We used UML activity diagrams to illustrate the flow of control for the control statements presented in Chapters 4–5.

Figure 23.15 shows an activity diagram for a withdrawal transaction. We assume that a `Withdrawal` object has been assigned a valid account number. We do not model the user

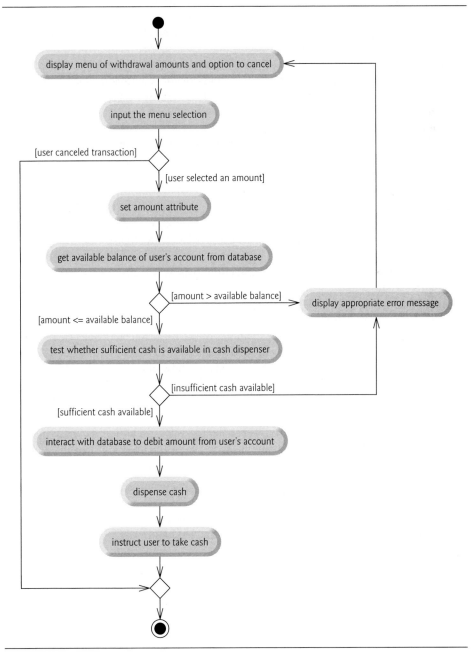

Fig. 23.15 | Activity diagram for a withdrawal transaction.

selecting a withdrawal from the main menu or the ATM returning the user to the main menu because these are not actions performed by a Withdrawal object. The transaction first displays a menu of standard withdrawal amounts (shown in Fig. 23.3) and an option to cancel the transaction. The transaction then receives a menu selection from the user. The activity flow now arrives at a decision (a fork indicated by the small diamond symbol). This point determines the next action based on the associated guard condition (in square brackets next to the transition), which states that the transition occurs if this guard condition is met. If the user cancels the transaction by choosing the "cancel" option from the menu, the activity flow immediately skips to the final state. Note the merge (indicated by the small diamond symbol) where the cancellation flow of activity joins the main flow of activity before reaching the activity's final state. If the user selects a withdrawal amount from the menu, Withdrawal sets amount (an attribute originally modeled in Fig. 23.12) to the value chosen by the user.

After setting the withdrawal amount, the transaction retrieves the available balance of the user's account (i.e., the availableBalance attribute of the user's Account object) from the database. The activity flow then arrives at another decision. If the requested withdrawal amount exceeds the user's available balance, the system displays an appropriate error message informing the user of the problem, then returns to the beginning of the activity diagram and prompts the user to input a new amount. If the requested withdrawal amount is less than or equal to the user's available balance, the transaction proceeds. The transaction next tests whether the cash dispenser has enough cash remaining to satisfy the withdrawal request. If it does not, the transaction displays an appropriate error message, then returns to the beginning of the activity diagram and prompts the user to choose a new amount. If sufficient cash is available, the transaction interacts with the database to debit the withdrawal amount from the user's account (i.e., subtract the amount from *both* the availableBalance and totalBalance attributes of the user's Account object). The transaction then dispenses the desired amount of cash and instructs the user to take it. Finally, the main flow of activity merges with the cancellation flow of activity before reaching the final state.

We've taken the first steps in modeling the ATM software system's behavior and have shown how an object's attributes participate in performing the object's activities. In Section 23.6, we investigate the behaviors for all classes to give a more accurate interpretation of the system behavior by filling in the third compartments of the classes in our class diagram.

Self-Review Exercises for Section 23.5

23.11 State whether the following statement is *true* or *false*, and if *false*, explain why: State diagrams model structural aspects of a system.

23.12 An activity diagram models the _____ that an object performs and the order in which it performs them.
   a) actions
   b) attributes
   c) states
   d) state transitions

23.13 Based on the requirements document, create an activity diagram for a deposit transaction.

23.6 Identifying Class Operations

In this section, we determine some of the class operations (or behaviors) needed to implement the ATM system. An operation is a service that objects of a class provide to clients (users) of the class. Consider the operations of some real-world objects. A radio's operations include setting its station and volume (typically invoked by a person's adjusting the radio's controls). A car's operations include accelerating (invoked by the driver's pressing the accelerator pedal), decelerating (invoked by the driver's pressing the brake pedal or releasing the gas pedal), turning and shifting gears. Software objects can offer operations as well—for example, a software graphics object might offer operations for drawing a circle, drawing a line, drawing a square and the like. A spreadsheet software object might offer operations like printing the spreadsheet, totaling the elements in a row or column and graphing information in the spreadsheet as a bar chart or pie chart.

We can derive many of the class operations by examining the key *verbs and verb phrases* in the requirements document. We then relate these verbs and verb phrases to classes in our system (Fig. 23.16). The verb phrases in Fig. 23.16 help us determine the operations of each class.

Class	Verbs and verb phrases
ATM	executes financial transactions
BalanceInquiry	*[none in the requirements document]*
Withdrawal	*[none in the requirements document]*
Deposit	*[none in the requirements document]*
BankDatabase	authenticates a user, retrieves an account balance, credits a deposit amount to an account, debits a withdrawal amount from an account
Account	retrieves an account balance, credits a deposit amount to an account, debits a withdrawal amount from an account
Screen	displays a message to the user
Keypad	receives numeric input from the user
CashDispenser	dispenses cash, indicates whether it contains enough cash to satisfy a withdrawal request
DepositSlot	receives a deposit envelope

Fig. 23.16 | Verbs and verb phrases for each class in the ATM system.

Modeling Operations

To identify operations, we examine the verb phrases listed for each class in Fig. 23.16. The "executes financial transactions" phrase associated with class ATM implies that class ATM instructs transactions to execute. Therefore, classes BalanceInquiry, Withdrawal and Deposit each need an operation to provide this service to the ATM. We place this operation (which we've named execute) in the third compartment of the three transaction classes in the updated class diagram of Fig. 23.17. During an ATM session, the ATM object will invoke these transaction operations as necessary.

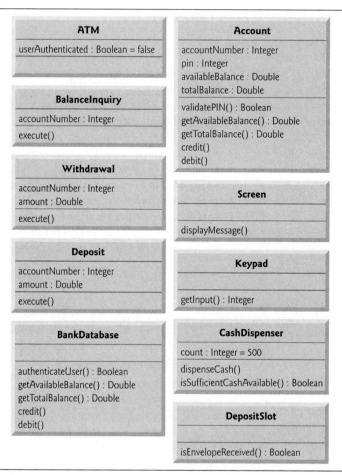

Fig. 23.17 | Classes in the ATM system with attributes and operations.

The UML represents operations (that is, methods) by listing the operation name, followed by a comma-separated list of parameters in parentheses, a colon and the return type:

operationName(parameter1, parameter2, …, parameterN) : return type

Each parameter in the comma-separated parameter list consists of a parameter name, followed by a colon and the parameter type:

parameterName : parameterType

For the moment, we do not list the parameters of our operations—we'll identify and model some of them shortly. For some of the operations, we do not yet know the return types, so we also omit them from the diagram. These omissions are perfectly normal at this point. As our design and implementation proceed, we'll add the remaining return types.

Authenticating a User
Figure 23.16 lists the phrase "authenticates a user" next to class BankDatabase—the database is the object that contains the account information necessary to determine whether

the account number and PIN entered by a user match those of an account held at the bank. Therefore, class BankDatabase needs an operation that provides an authentication service to the ATM. We place the operation authenticateUser in the third compartment of class BankDatabase (Fig. 23.17). However, an object of class Account, not class Bank-Database, stores the account number and PIN that must be accessed to authenticate a user, so class Account must provide a service to validate a PIN obtained through user input against a PIN stored in an Account object. Therefore, we add a validatePIN operation to class Account. We specify a return type of Boolean for the authenticateUser and validatePIN operations. Each operation returns a value indicating either that the operation was successful in performing its task (i.e., a return value of true) or that it was not (i.e., a return value of false).

Other BankDatabase and Account Operations
Figure 23.16 lists several additional verb phrases for class BankDatabase: "retrieves an account balance," "credits a deposit amount to an account" and "debits a withdrawal amount from an account." Like "authenticates a user," these remaining phrases refer to services that the database must provide to the ATM, because the database holds all the account data used to authenticate a user and perform ATM transactions. However, objects of class Account actually perform the operations to which these phrases refer. Thus, we assign an operation to both class BankDatabase and class Account to correspond to each of these phrases. Recall from Section 23.3 that, because a bank account contains sensitive information, we do not allow the ATM to access accounts directly. The database acts as an intermediary between the ATM and the account data, thus preventing unauthorized access. As we'll see in Section 23.7, class ATM invokes the operations of class BankDatabase, each of which in turn invokes the operation with the same name in class Account.

Getting the Balances
The phrase "retrieves an account balance" suggests that classes BankDatabase and Account each need a getBalance operation. However, recall that we created *two* attributes in class Account to represent a balance—availableBalance and totalBalance. A balance inquiry requires access to *both* balance attributes so that it can display them to the user, but a withdrawal needs to check *only* the value of availableBalance. To allow objects in the system to obtain each balance attribute individually, we add operations getAvailable-Balance and getTotalBalance to the third compartment of classes BankDatabase and Account (Fig. 23.17). We specify a return type of Double for these operations because the balance attributes they retrieve are of type Double.

Crediting and Debiting an Account
The phrases "credits a deposit amount to an account" and "debits a withdrawal amount from an account" indicate that classes BankDatabase and Account must perform operations to update an account during a deposit and withdrawal, respectively. We therefore assign credit and debit operations to classes BankDatabase and Account. You may recall that crediting an account (as in a deposit) adds an amount only to the totalBalance attribute. Debiting an account (as in a withdrawal), on the other hand, subtracts the amount from *both* balance attributes. We hide these implementation details inside class Account. This is a good example of encapsulation and information hiding.

Deposit Confirmations Performed by Another Banking System

If this were a real ATM system, classes BankDatabase and Account would also provide a set of operations to allow another banking system to update a user's account balance after either confirming or rejecting all or part of a deposit. Operation confirmDepositAmount, for example, would add an amount to the availableBalance attribute, thus making deposited funds available for withdrawal. Operation rejectDepositAmount would subtract an amount from the totalBalance attribute to indicate that a specified amount, which had recently been deposited through the ATM and added to the totalBalance, was not found in the deposit envelope. The bank would invoke this operation after determining either that the user failed to include the correct amount of cash or that any checks did not clear (i.e., they "bounced"). While adding these operations would make our system more complete, we do *not* include them in our class diagrams or our implementation because they're beyond the scope of the case study.

Displaying Messages

Class Screen "displays a message to the user" at various times in an ATM session. All visual output occurs through the screen of the ATM. The requirements document describes many types of messages (e.g., a welcome message, an error message, a thank you message) that the screen displays to the user. The requirements document also indicates that the screen displays prompts and menus to the user. However, a prompt is really just a message describing what the user should input next, and a menu is essentially a type of prompt consisting of a series of messages (i.e., menu options) displayed consecutively. Therefore, rather than assign class Screen an individual operation to display each type of message, prompt and menu, we simply create one operation that can display any message specified by a parameter. We place this operation (displayMessage) in the third compartment of class Screen in our class diagram (Fig. 23.17). We do not worry about the parameter of this operation at this time—we model it later in this section.

Keyboard Input

From the phrase "receives numeric input from the user" listed by class Keypad in Fig. 23.16, we conclude that class Keypad should perform a getInput operation. Because the ATM's keypad, unlike a computer keyboard, contains only the numbers 0–9, we specify that this operation returns an integer value. Recall from the requirements document that in different situations the user may be required to enter a different type of number (e.g., an account number, a PIN, the number of a menu option, a deposit amount as a number of cents). Class Keypad simply obtains a numeric value for a client of the class—it does not determine whether the value meets any specific criteria. Any class that uses this operation must verify that the user entered an appropriate number in a given situation, then respond accordingly (i.e., display an error message via class Screen). [*Note:* When we implement the system, we simulate the ATM's keypad with a computer keyboard, and for simplicity we assume that the user does not enter nonnumeric input using keys on the computer keyboard that do not appear on the ATM's keypad.]

Dispensing Cash

Figure 23.16 lists "dispenses cash" for class CashDispenser. Therefore, we create operation dispenseCash and list it under class CashDispenser in Fig. 23.17. Class CashDispenser also "indicates whether it contains enough cash to satisfy a withdrawal request."

Thus, we include `isSufficientCashAvailable`, an operation that returns a value of UML type `Boolean`, in class `CashDispenser`.

Figure 23.16 also lists "receives a deposit envelope" for class `DepositSlot`. The deposit slot must indicate whether it received an envelope, so we place an operation `isEnvelopeReceived`, which returns a `Boolean` value, in the third compartment of class `DepositSlot`. [*Note:* A real hardware deposit slot would most likely send the ATM a signal to indicate that an envelope was received. We simulate this behavior, however, with an operation in class `DepositSlot` that class ATM can invoke to find out whether the deposit slot received an envelope.]

Class *ATM*

We do not list any operations for class ATM at this time. We're not yet aware of any services that class ATM provides to other classes in the system. When we implement the system with Java code, however, operations of this class, and additional operations of the other classes in the system, may emerge.

Identifying and Modeling Operation Parameters for Class *BankDatabase*

So far, we've not been concerned with the *parameters* of our operations—we've attempted to gain only a basic understanding of the operations of each class. Let's now take a closer look at some operation parameters. We identify an operation's parameters by examining what data the operation requires to perform its assigned task.

Consider `BankDatabase`'s `authenticateUser` operation. To authenticate a user, this operation must know the account number and PIN supplied by the user. So we specify that `authenticateUser` takes integer parameters `userAccountNumber` and `userPIN`, which the operation must compare to an `Account` object's account number and PIN in the database. We prefix these parameter names with "user" to avoid confusion between the operation's parameter names and class `Account`'s attribute names. We list these parameters in the class diagram in Fig. 23.18 that models only class `BankDatabase`. [*Note:* It's perfectly normal to model only one class. In this case, we're examining the parameters of this one class, so we omit the other classes. In class diagrams later in the case study, in which parameters are no longer the focus of our attention, we omit these parameters to save space. Remember, however, that the operations listed in these diagrams still have parameters.]

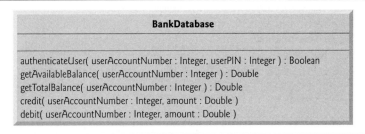

BankDatabase

authenticateUser(userAccountNumber : Integer, userPIN : Integer) : Boolean
getAvailableBalance(userAccountNumber : Integer) : Double
getTotalBalance(userAccountNumber : Integer) : Double
credit(userAccountNumber : Integer, amount : Double)
debit(userAccountNumber : Integer, amount : Double)

Fig. 23.18 | Class `BankDatabase` with operation parameters.

Recall that the UML models each parameter in an operation's comma-separated parameter list by listing the parameter name, followed by a colon and the parameter type (in UML notation). Figure 23.18 thus specifies that operation `authenticateUser` takes two parameters—userAccountNumber and userPIN, both of type Integer. When we implement the system in Java, we'll represent these parameters with int values.

Class BankDatabase operations getAvailableBalance, getTotalBalance, credit and debit also each require a userAccountNumber parameter to identify the account to which the database must apply the operations, so we include these parameters in the class diagram of Fig. 23.18. In addition, operations credit and debit each require a Double parameter amount to specify the amount of money to be credited or debited, respectively.

Identifying and Modeling Operation Parameters for Class *Account*

Figure 23.19 models class Account's operation parameters. Operation validatePIN requires only a userPIN parameter, which contains the user-specified PIN to be compared with the account's PIN. Like their BankDatabase counterparts, operations credit and debit in class Account each require a Double parameter amount that indicates the amount of money involved in the operation. Operations getAvailableBalance and getTotalBalance in class Account require no additional data to perform their tasks. Class Account's operations do *not* require an account-number parameter to distinguish between Accounts, because these operations can be invoked only on a specific Account object.

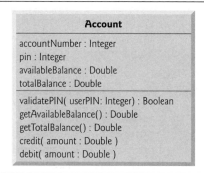

Fig. 23.19 | Class Account with operation parameters.

Identifying and Modeling Operation Parameters for Class *Screen*

Figure 23.20 models class Screen with a parameter specified for operation displayMessage. This operation requires only a String parameter message that indicates the text to be displayed. Recall that the parameter types listed in our class diagrams are in UML notation, so the String type listed in Fig. 23.20 refers to the UML type. When we implement the system in Java, we'll use the Java class String to represent this parameter.

Screen
displayMessage(message : String)

Fig. 23.20 | Class Screen with operation parameters.

Identifying and Modeling Operation Parameters for Class **CashDispenser**

Figure 23.21 specifies that operation dispenseCash of class CashDispenser takes a Double parameter amount to indicate the amount of cash (in dollars) to be dispensed. Operation isSufficientCashAvailable also takes a Double parameter amount to indicate the amount of cash in question.

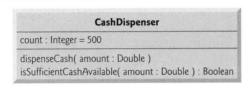

Fig. 23.21 | Class CashDispenser with operation parameters.

Identifying and Modeling Operation Parameters for Other Classes

We do not discuss parameters for operation execute of classes BalanceInquiry, Withdrawal and Deposit, operation getInput of class Keypad and operation isEnvelope-Received of class DepositSlot. At this point in our design process, we cannot determine whether these operations require additional data, so we leave their parameter lists empty. Later, we may decide to add parameters.

In this section, we've determined many of the operations performed by the classes in the ATM system. We've identified the parameters and return types of some of the operations. As we continue our design process, the number of operations belonging to each class may vary—we might find that new operations are needed or that some current operations are unnecessary. We also might determine that some of our class operations need additional parameters and different return types, or that some parameters are unnecessary or require different types.

Self-Review Exercises for Section 23.6

23.14 Which of the following is *not* a behavior?
   a) reading data from a file
   b) printing output
   c) text output
   d) obtaining input from the user

23.15 If you were to add to the ATM system an operation that returns the amount attribute of class Withdrawal, how and where would you specify this operation in the class diagram of Fig. 23.17?

23.16 Describe the meaning of the following operation listing that might appear in a class diagram for an object-oriented design of a calculator:

```
add(x : Integer, y : Integer) : Integer
```

23.7 Indicating Collaboration Among Objects

Next, we focus on the collaborations (interactions) among objects. When two objects communicate with each other to accomplish a task, they're said to **collaborate**—objects do this by invoking one another's operations. A **collaboration** consists of an object of one class sending a **message** to an object of another class. Messages are sent in Java via method calls.

In Section 23.6, we determined many of the operations of the system's classes. Now, we concentrate on the messages that invoke these operations. To identify the collaborations in the system, we return to the requirements document in Section 23.2. Recall that this document specifies the range of activities that occur during an ATM session (e.g., authenticating a user, performing transactions). The steps used to describe how the system must perform each of these tasks are our first indication of the collaborations in our system. As we proceed through this section and Chapter 24, we may discover additional collaborations.

Identifying the Collaborations in a System

We identify the collaborations in the system by carefully reading the sections of the requirements document that specify what the ATM should do to authenticate a user and to perform each transaction type. For each action or step described, we decide which objects in our system must interact to achieve the desired result. We identify one object as the sending object and another as the receiving object. We then select one of the receiving object's operations (identified in Section 23.6) that must be invoked by the sending object to produce the proper behavior. For example, the ATM displays a welcome message when idle. We know that an object of class Screen displays a message to the user via its displayMessage operation. Thus, we decide that the system can display a welcome message by employing a collaboration between the ATM and the Screen in which the ATM sends a displayMessage message to the Screen by invoking the displayMessage operation of class Screen. [*Note:* To avoid repeating the phrase "an object of class...," we refer to an object by using its class name preceded by an article (e.g., "a," "an" or "the")—for example, "the ATM" refers to an object of class ATM.]

Figure 23.22 lists the collaborations that can be derived from the requirements document. For each sending object, we list the collaborations in the order in which they first occur during an ATM session (i.e., the order in which they're discussed in the requirements document). We list each collaboration involving a unique sender, message and recipient only once, even though the collaborations may occur at several different times throughout an ATM session. For example, the first row in Fig. 23.22 indicates that the ATM collaborates with the Screen whenever the ATM needs to display a message to the user.

Let's consider the collaborations in Fig. 23.22. Before allowing a user to perform any transactions, the ATM must prompt the user to enter an account number, then to enter a PIN. It accomplishes these tasks by sending a displayMessage message to the Screen. Both actions refer to the same collaboration between the ATM and the Screen, which is already listed in Fig. 23.22. The ATM obtains input in response to a prompt by sending a getInput message to the Keypad. Next, the ATM must determine whether the user-specified account number and PIN match those of an account in the database. It does so by sending an authenticateUser message to the BankDatabase. Recall that the BankDatabase cannot authenticate a user directly—only the user's Account (i.e., the Account that contains the account number specified by the user) can access the user's PIN on record to authenticate the user. Figure 23.22 therefore lists a collaboration in which the BankDatabase sends a validatePIN message to an Account.

After the user is authenticated, the ATM displays the main menu by sending a series of displayMessage messages to the Screen and obtains input containing a menu selection by sending a getInput message to the Keypad. We've already accounted for these collaborations, so we do not add anything to Fig. 23.22. After the user chooses a type of transaction to perform, the ATM executes the transaction by sending an execute message to an object of the appropriate transaction class (i.e., a BalanceInquiry, a Withdrawal or a Deposit). For example, if the user chooses to perform a balance inquiry, the ATM sends an execute message to a BalanceInquiry.

An object of class...	sends the message...	to an object of class...
ATM	displayMessage	Screen
	getInput	Keypad
	authenticateUser	BankDatabase
	execute	BalanceInquiry
	execute	Withdrawal
	execute	Deposit
BalanceInquiry	getAvailableBalance	BankDatabase
	getTotalBalance	BankDatabase
	displayMessage	Screen
Withdrawal	displayMessage	Screen
	getInput	Keypad
	getAvailableBalance	BankDatabase
	isSufficientCashAvailable	CashDispenser
	debit	BankDatabase
	dispenseCash	CashDispenser
Deposit	displayMessage	Screen
	getInput	Keypad
	isEnvelopeReceived	DepositSlot
	credit	BankDatabase
BankDatabase	validatePIN	Account
	getAvailableBalance	Account
	getTotalBalance	Account
	debit	Account
	credit	Account

Fig. 23.22 | Collaborations in the ATM system.

Further examination of the requirements document reveals the collaborations involved in executing each transaction type. A BalanceInquiry retrieves the amount of money available in the user's account by sending a getAvailableBalance message to the BankDatabase, which responds by sending a getAvailableBalance message to the user's Account. Similarly, the BalanceInquiry retrieves the amount of money on deposit by sending a getTotalBalance message to the BankDatabase, which sends the same message to the user's Account. To display both parts of the user's account balance at the same time, the BalanceInquiry sends a displayMessage message to the Screen.

A Withdrawal responds to an execute message by sending displayMessage messages to the Screen to display a menu of standard withdrawal amounts (i.e., $20, $40, $60, $100, $200). The Withdrawal sends a getInput message to the Keypad to obtain the user's selection. Next, the Withdrawal determines whether the requested amount is less than or equal to the user's account balance. The Withdrawal can obtain the amount of money available by sending a getAvailableBalance message to the BankDatabase. The Withdrawal then tests whether the cash dispenser contains enough cash by sending an isSufficientCash-Available message to the CashDispenser. A Withdrawal sends a debit message to the BankDatabase to decrease the user's account balance. The BankDatabase in turn sends the same message to the appropriate Account, which decreases both the totalBalance and the availableBalance. To dispense the requested amount of cash, the Withdrawal sends a dispenseCash message to the CashDispenser. Finally, the Withdrawal sends a display-Message message to the Screen, instructing the user to take the cash.

A Deposit responds to an execute message first by sending a displayMessage message to the Screen to prompt the user for a deposit amount. The Deposit sends a get-Input message to the Keypad to obtain the user's input. The Deposit then sends a displayMessage message to the Screen to tell the user to insert a deposit envelope. To determine whether the deposit slot received an incoming deposit envelope, the Deposit sends an isEnvelopeReceived message to the DepositSlot. The Deposit updates the user's account by sending a credit message to the BankDatabase, which subsequently sends a credit message to the user's Account. Recall that crediting funds to an Account increases the totalBalance but not the availableBalance.

Interaction Diagrams

Now that we've identified possible collaborations between our ATM system's objects, let's graphically model these interactions using the UML. The UML provides several types of **interaction diagrams** that model the behavior of a system by modeling how objects interact. The **communication diagram** emphasizes *which objects* participate in collaborations. Like the communication diagram, the **sequence diagram** shows collaborations among objects, but it emphasizes *when* messages are sent between objects *over time*.

Communication Diagrams

Figure 23.23 shows a communication diagram that models the ATM executing a Balance-Inquiry. Objects are modeled in the UML as rectangles containing names in the form objectName : ClassName. In this example, which involves only one object of each type, we disregard the object name and list only a colon followed by the class name. [*Note:* Specifying each object's name in a communication diagram is recommended when modeling multiple objects of the same type.] Communicating objects are connected with solid lines, and messages are passed between objects along these lines in the direction shown by arrows. The name of the message, which appears next to the arrow, is the name of an operation (i.e., a method in Java) belonging to the receiving object—think of the name as a "service" that the receiving object provides to sending objects (its clients).

Fig. 23.23 | Communication diagram of the ATM executing a balance inquiry.

The solid filled arrow represents a message—or **synchronous call**—in the UML and a method call in Java. This arrow indicates that the flow of control is from the sending object (the ATM) to the receiving object (a BalanceInquiry). Since this is a synchronous call, the sending object can't send another message, or do anything at all, until the receiving object processes the message and returns control to the sending object. The sender just waits. In Fig. 23.23, the ATM calls BalanceInquiry method execute and can't send another message until execute has finished and returns control to the ATM. [*Note:* If this were an **asynchronous call**, represented by a stick ($\twoheadrightarrow$) arrowhead, the sending object would not have to wait for the receiving object to return control—it would continue sending additional messages immediately following the asynchronous call. Asynchronous calls are implemented in Java using multithreading, which we discussed in Chapter 20.]

Sequence of Messages in a Communication Diagram

Figure 23.24 shows a communication diagram that models the interactions among system objects when an object of class BalanceInquiry executes. We assume that the object's accountNumber attribute contains the account number of the current user. The collaborations in Fig. 23.24 begin after the ATM sends an execute message to a BalanceInquiry (i.e., the interaction modeled in Fig. 23.23). The number to the left of a message name indicates the order in which the message is passed. The **sequence of messages** in a communication diagram progresses in numerical order from least to greatest. In this diagram, the numbering starts with message 1 and ends with message 3. The BalanceInquiry first sends a getAvailableBalance message to the BankDatabase (message 1), then sends a getTotalBalance message to the BankDatabase (message 2). Within the parentheses following a message name, we can specify a comma-separated list of the names of the parameters sent with the message (i.e., arguments in a Java method call)—the BalanceInquiry passes attribute accountNumber with its messages to the BankDatabase to indicate which Account's balance information to retrieve. Recall from Fig. 23.18 that operations getAvailableBalance and getTotalBalance of class BankDatabase each require a parameter to identify an account. The BalanceInquiry next displays the availableBalance and the totalBalance to the user by passing a displayMessage message to the Screen (message 3) that includes a parameter indicating the message to be displayed.

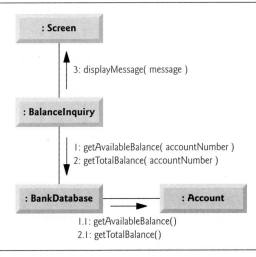

Fig. 23.24 | Communication diagram for executing a balance inquiry.

Figure 23.24 models two additional messages passing from the BankDatabase to an Account (message 1.1 and message 2.1). To provide the ATM with the *two* balances of the user's Account (as requested by messages 1 and 2), the BankDatabase must pass a getAvailableBalance and a getTotalBalance message to the user's Account. Such messages passed within the handling of another message are called **nested messages**. The UML recommends using a decimal numbering scheme to indicate nested messages. For example, message 1.1 is the first message nested in message 1—the BankDatabase passes a getAvailableBalance message during BankDatabase's processing of a message by the same name. [*Note:* If the BankDatabase needed to pass a second nested message while processing message 1, the second message would be numbered 1.2.] A message may be passed only when *all* the nested messages from the previous message have been passed. For example, the BalanceInquiry passes message 3 only after messages 2 and 2.1 have been passed, in that order.

The nested numbering scheme used in communication diagrams helps clarify precisely when and in what context each message is passed. For example, if we numbered the messages in Fig. 23.24 using a flat numbering scheme (i.e., 1, 2, 3, 4, 5), someone looking at the diagram might not be able to determine that BankDatabase passes the getAvailableBalance message (message 1.1) to an Account *during* the BankDatabase's processing of message 1, as opposed to *after* completing the processing of message 1. The nested decimal numbers make it clear that the second getAvailableBalance message (message 1.1) is passed to an Account within the handling of the first getAvailableBalance message (message 1) by the BankDatabase.

Sequence Diagrams

Communication diagrams emphasize the participants in collaborations, but model their timing a bit awkwardly. A sequence diagram helps model the timing of collaborations more clearly. Figure 23.25 shows a sequence diagram modeling the sequence of interactions that occur when a Withdrawal executes. The dotted line extending down from an object's rectangle is that object's **lifeline**, which represents the progression of time. Actions occur along an object's lifeline in chronological order from top to bottom—an action near the top happens before one near the bottom.

Message passing in sequence diagrams is similar to message passing in communication diagrams. A solid arrow with a filled arrowhead extending from the sending object to the receiving object represents a message between two objects. The arrowhead points to an activation on the receiving object's lifeline. An **activation**, shown as a thin vertical rectangle, indicates that an object is executing. When an object returns control, a return message, represented as a dashed line with a stick ($\rightarrow$) arrowhead, extends from the activation of the object returning control to the activation of the object that initially sent the message. To eliminate clutter, we omit the return-message arrows—the UML allows this practice to make diagrams more readable. Like communication diagrams, sequence diagrams can indicate message parameters between the parentheses following a message name.

The sequence of messages in Fig. 23.25 begins when a Withdrawal prompts the user to choose a withdrawal amount by sending a displayMessage message to the Screen. The Withdrawal then sends a getInput message to the Keypad, which obtains input from the user. We've already modeled the control logic involved in a Withdrawal in the activity diagram of Fig. 23.15, so we do not show this logic in the sequence diagram of Fig. 23.25. Instead, we model the best-case scenario in which the balance of the user's account is greater than or equal to the chosen withdrawal amount, and the cash dispenser contains a sufficient amount of cash to satisfy the request. You can model control logic in a sequence diagram with UML frames (which are not covered in this case study). For a quick overview of UML frames, visit www.agilemodeling.com/style/frame.htm.

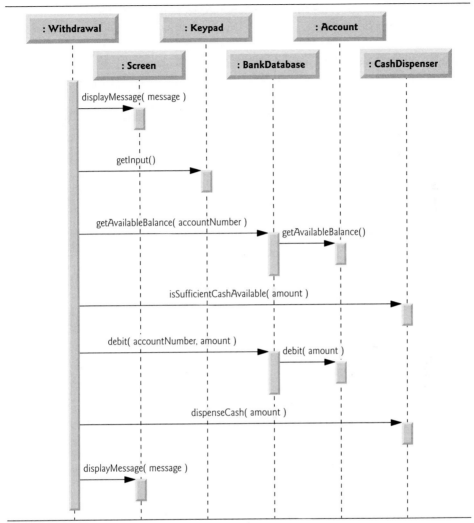

Fig. 23.25 | Sequence diagram that models a Withdrawal executing.

After obtaining a withdrawal amount, the Withdrawal sends a getAvailableBalance message to the BankDatabase, which in turn sends a getAvailableBalance message to the user's Account. Assuming that the user's account has enough money available to permit the transaction, the Withdrawal next sends an isSufficientCashAvailable message to the CashDispenser. Assuming that there's enough cash available, the Withdrawal decreases the balance of the user's account (i.e., both the totalBalance and the availableBalance) by sending a debit message to the BankDatabase. The BankDatabase responds by sending a debit message to the user's Account. Finally, the Withdrawal sends a dispenseCash message to the CashDispenser and a displayMessage message to the Screen, telling the user to remove the cash from the machine.

We've identified the collaborations among objects in the ATM system and modeled some of them using UML interaction diagrams—both communication diagrams and sequence diagrams. In Section 24.2, we enhance the structure of our model to complete a preliminary object-oriented design, then we begin implementing the ATM system in Java.

Self-Review Exercises for Section 23.7

23.17 A(n) _____ consists of an object of one class sending a message to an object of another class.

    a) association   b) aggregation
    c) collaboration   d) composition

23.18 Which form of interaction diagram emphasizes *what* collaborations occur? Which form emphasizes *when* collaborations occur?

23.19 Create a sequence diagram that models the interactions among objects in the ATM system that occur when a Deposit executes successfully, and explain the sequence of messages modeled by the diagram.

23.8 Wrap-Up

In this chapter, you learned how to work from a detailed requirements document to develop an object-oriented design. You worked with six popular types of UML diagrams to graphically model an object-oriented automated teller machine software system. In Chapter 24, we tune the design using inheritance, then completely implement the design as a Java application.

Answers to Self-Review Exercises

23.1 Figure 23.26 contains a use case diagram for a modified version of our ATM system that also allows users to transfer money between accounts.

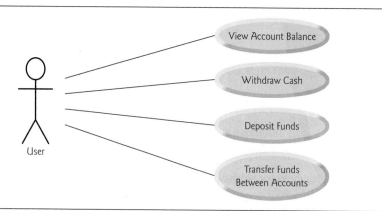

Fig. 23.26 | Use case diagram for a modified version of our ATM system that also allows users to transfer money between accounts.

23.2 b.

23.3 d.

23.4 [*Note:* Answers may vary.] Figure 23.27 presents a class diagram that shows some of the composition relationships of a class Car.

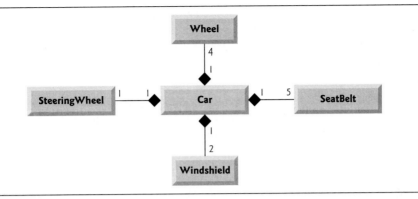

Fig. 23.27 | Class diagram showing composition relationships of a class Car.

23.5 c. [*Note:* In a computer network, this relationship could be many-to-many.]

23.6 True.

23.7 Figure 23.28 presents a class diagram for the ATM including class Deposit instead of class Withdrawal (as in Fig. 23.10). Deposit does not access CashDispenser, but does access DepositSlot.

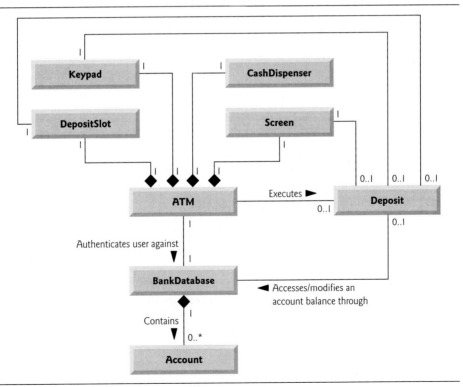

Fig. 23.28 | Class diagram for the ATM system model including class Deposit.

23.8 b.

23.9   c. Fly is an operation or behavior of an airplane, not an attribute.

23.10   This indicates that count is an Integer with an initial value of 500. This attribute keeps track of the number of bills available in the CashDispenser at any given time.

23.11   False. State diagrams model some of the behavior of a system.

23.12   a.

23.13   Figure 23.29 models the actions that occur after the user chooses the deposit option from the main menu and before the ATM returns the user to the main menu. Recall that part of receiving a deposit amount from the user involves converting an integer number of cents to a dollar amount. Also recall that crediting a deposit amount to an account increases only the totalBalance attribute of the user's Account object. The bank updates the availableBalance attribute of the user's Account object only after confirming the amount of cash in the deposit envelope and after the enclosed checks clear—this occurs independently of the ATM system.

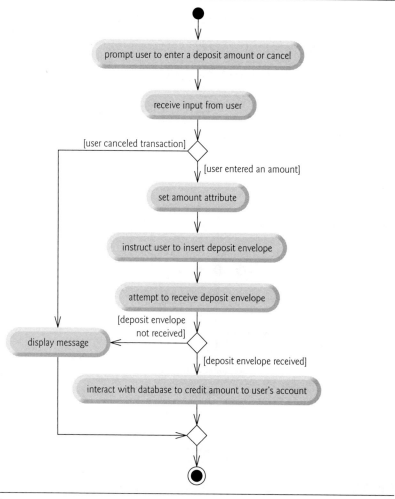

Fig. 23.29 | Activity diagram for a deposit transaction.

23.14 c.

23.15 To specify an operation that retrieves the amount attribute of class Withdrawal, the following operation listing would be placed in the operation (i.e., third) compartment of class Withdrawal:

        getAmount() : Double

23.16 This operation listing indicates an operation named add that takes integers x and y as parameters and returns an integer value.

23.17 c.

23.18 Communication diagrams emphasize *what* collaborations occur. Sequence diagrams emphasize *when* collaborations occur.

23.19 Figure 23.30 presents a sequence diagram that models the interactions between objects in the ATM system that occur when a Deposit executes successfully. A Deposit first sends a displayMessage message to the Screen to ask the user to enter a deposit amount. Next the Deposit sends a getInput message to the Keypad to receive input from the user. The Deposit then instructs the user to enter a deposit envelope by sending a displayMessage message to the Screen. The Deposit next sends an isEnvelopeReceived message to the DepositSlot to confirm that the deposit envelope has been received by the ATM. Finally, the Deposit increases the totalBalance attribute (but not the availableBalance attribute) of the user's Account by sending a credit message to the BankDatabase. The BankDatabase responds by sending the same message to the user's Account.

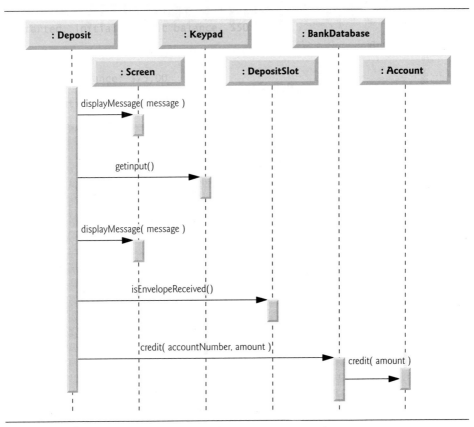

Fig. 23.30 | Sequence diagram that models a Deposit executing.

24

ATM Case Study Part 2: Implementing an Object-Oriented Design

Objectives

In this chapter you'll:

- Incorporate inheritance into the design of the ATM.
- Incorporate polymorphism into the design of the ATM.
- Fully implement in Java the UML-based object-oriented design of the ATM software.
- Study a detailed code walkthrough of the ATM software system that explains the implementation issues.

24.1 Introduction

In Chapter 23, we developed an object-oriented design for our ATM system. We now implement our object-oriented design in Java. In Section 24.2, we show how to convert class diagrams to Java code. In Section 24.3, we tune the design with inheritance and polymorphism. Then we present a full Java code implementation of the ATM software in Section 24.4. The code is carefully commented and the discussions of the implementation are thorough and precise. Studying this application provides the opportunity for you to see a more substantial application of the kind you're likely to encounter in industry.

24.2 Starting to Program the Classes of the ATM System

Visibility

We now apply access modifiers to the members of our classes. We've introduced access modifiers public and private. Access modifiers determine the **visibility** or accessibility of an object's attributes and methods to other objects. Before we can begin implementing our design, we must consider which attributes and methods of our classes should be public and which should be private.

We've observed that attributes normally should be private and that methods invoked by clients of a given class should be public. Methods that are called as "utility methods" only by other methods of the same class normally should be private. The UML employs **visibility markers** for modeling the visibility of attributes and operations. Public visibility is indicated by placing a plus sign (+) before an operation or an attribute, whereas a minus sign (–) indicates private visibility. Figure 24.1 shows our updated class diagram with visibility markers included. [*Note:* We do not include any operation parameters in Fig. 24.1—this is perfectly normal. Adding visibility markers does not affect the parameters already modeled in the class diagrams of Figs. 23.17–23.21.]

Navigability

Before we begin implementing our design in Java, we introduce an additional UML notation. The class diagram in Fig. 24.2 further refines the relationships among classes in the ATM system by adding navigability arrows to the association lines. **Navigability arrows** (represented as arrows with stick ($\rightarrow$) arrowheads in the class diagram) indicate in the direction which an association can be traversed. When implementing a system designed

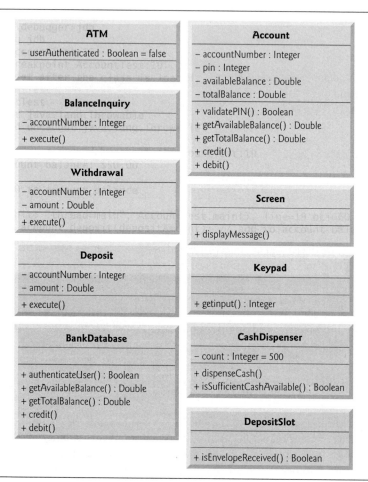

Fig. 24.1 | Class diagram with visibility markers.

using the UML, you use navigability arrows to determine which objects need references to other objects. For example, the navigability arrow pointing from class ATM to class Bank-Database indicates that we can navigate from the former to the latter, thereby enabling the ATM to invoke the BankDatabase's operations. However, since Fig. 24.2 does *not* contain a navigability arrow pointing from class BankDatabase to class ATM, the BankDatabase cannot access the ATM's operations. Associations in a class diagram that have navigability arrows at both ends or have none at all indicate **bidirectional navigability**—navigation can proceed in either direction across the association.

Like the class diagram of Fig. 23.10, that of Fig. 24.2 omits classes BalanceInquiry and Deposit for simplicity. The navigability of the associations in which these classes participate closely parallels that of class Withdrawal. Recall from Section 23.3 that BalanceInquiry has an association with class Screen. We can navigate from class BalanceInquiry to class Screen along this association, but we cannot navigate from class Screen to class BalanceInquiry. Thus, if we were to model class BalanceInquiry in Fig. 24.2, we would place a navigability arrow at class Screen's end of this association. Also recall that class Deposit associates with

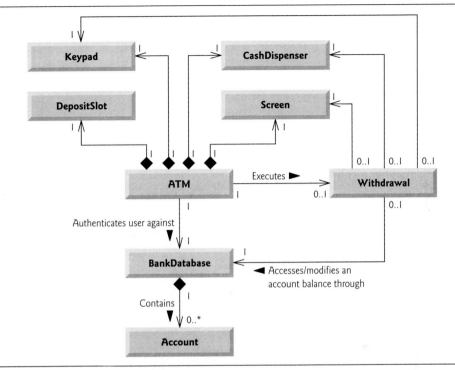

Fig. 24.2 | Class diagram with navigability arrows.

classes Screen, Keypad and DepositSlot. We can navigate from class Deposit to each of these classes, but *not* vice versa. We therefore would place navigability arrows at the Screen, Keypad and DepositSlot ends of these associations. [*Note:* We model these additional classes and associations in our final class diagram in Section 24.3, after we've simplified the structure of our system by incorporating the object-oriented concept of inheritance.]

Implementing the ATM System from Its UML Design
We're now ready to begin implementing the ATM system. We first convert the classes in the diagrams of Fig. 24.1 and Fig. 24.2 into Java code. The code will represent the "skeleton" of the system. In Section 24.3, we modify the code to incorporate inheritance. In Section 24.4, we present the complete working Java code for our model.

As an example, we develop the code from our design of class Withdrawal in Fig. 24.1. We use this figure to determine the attributes and operations of the class. We use the UML model in Fig. 24.2 to determine the associations among classes. We follow the following four guidelines for each class:

1. Use the name located in the first compartment to declare the class as a public class with an empty no-argument constructor. We include this constructor simply as a placeholder to remind us that *most classes will indeed need custom constructors*. In Section 24.4, when we complete a working version of this class, we'll add arguments and code the body of the constructor as needed. For example, class Withdrawal yields the code in Fig. 24.3. If we find that the class's instance vari-

ables require only default initialization, then we'll remove the empty no-argument constructor because it's unnecessary.

```
1   // Class Withdrawal represents an ATM withdrawal transaction
2   public class Withdrawal
3   {
4      // no-argument constructor
5      public Withdrawal()
6      {
7      } // end no-argument Withdrawal constructor
8   } // end class Withdrawal
```

Fig. 24.3 | Java code for class `Withdrawal` based on Figs. 24.1–24.2.

2. Use the attributes located in the second compartment to declare the instance variables. For example, the private attributes accountNumber and amount of class Withdrawal yield the code in Fig. 24.4. [*Note:* The constructor of the complete working version of this class will assign values to these attributes.]

```
1   // Class Withdrawal represents an ATM withdrawal transaction
2   public class Withdrawal
3   {
4      // attributes
5      private int accountNumber; // account to withdraw funds from
6      private double amount; // amount to withdraw
7
8      // no-argument constructor
9      public Withdrawal()
10     {
11     } // end no-argument Withdrawal constructor
12  } // end class Withdrawal
```

Fig. 24.4 | Java code for class `Withdrawal` based on Figs. 24.1–24.2.

3. Use the associations described in the class diagram to declare the references to other objects. For example, according to Fig. 24.2, Withdrawal can access one object of class Screen, one object of class Keypad, one object of class CashDispenser and one object of class BankDatabase. This yields the code in Fig. 24.5. [*Note:* The constructor of the complete working version of this class will initialize these instance variables with references to actual objects.]

4. Use the operations located in the third compartment of Fig. 24.1 to declare the shells of the methods. If we have not yet specified a return type for an operation, we declare the method with return type void. Refer to the class diagrams of Figs. 23.17–23.21 to declare any necessary parameters. For example, adding the public operation execute in class Withdrawal, which has an empty parameter list, yields the code in Fig. 24.6. [*Note:* We code the bodies of methods when we implement the complete system in Section 24.4.]

This concludes our discussion of the basics of generating classes from UML diagrams.

```
 1    // Class Withdrawal represents an ATM withdrawal transaction
 2    public class Withdrawal
 3    {
 4       // attributes
 5       private int accountNumber; // account to withdraw funds from
 6       private double amount; // amount to withdraw
 7
 8       // references to associated objects
 9       private Screen screen; // ATM's screen
10       private Keypad keypad; // ATM's keypad
11       private CashDispenser cashDispenser; // ATM's cash dispenser
12       private BankDatabase bankDatabase; // account info database
13
14       // no-argument constructor
15       public Withdrawal()
16       {
17       } // end no-argument Withdrawal constructor
18    } // end class Withdrawal
```

Fig. 24.5 | Java code for class Withdrawal based on Figs. 24.1–24.2.

```
 1    // Class Withdrawal represents an ATM withdrawal transaction
 2    public class Withdrawal
 3    {
 4       // attributes
 5       private int accountNumber; // account to withdraw funds from
 6       private double amount; // amount to withdraw
 7
 8       // references to associated objects
 9       private Screen screen; // ATM's screen
10       private Keypad keypad; // ATM's keypad
11       private CashDispenser cashDispenser; // ATM's cash dispenser
12       private BankDatabase bankDatabase; // account info database
13
14       // no-argument constructor
15       public Withdrawal()
16       {
17       } // end no-argument Withdrawal constructor
18
19       // operations
20       public void execute()
21       {
22       } // end method execute
23    } // end class Withdrawal
```

Fig. 24.6 | Java code for class Withdrawal based on Figs. 24.1–24.2.

Self-Review Exercises for Section 24.2

24.1   State whether the following statement is *true* or *false*, and if *false*, explain why: If an attribute of a class is marked with a minus sign (-) in a class diagram, the attribute is not directly accessible outside the class.

24.2   In Fig. 24.2, the association between the ATM and the Screen indicates that:

a) we can navigate from the Screen to the ATM
b) we can navigate from the ATM to the Screen
c) Both (a) and (b); the association is bidirectional
d) None of the above

24.3 Write Java code to begin implementing the design for class Keypad.

24.3 Incorporating Inheritance and Polymorphism into the ATM System

We now revisit our ATM system design to see how it might benefit from inheritance. To apply inheritance, we first look for *commonality among classes* in the system. We create an inheritance hierarchy to model similar (yet not identical) classes in a more elegant and efficient manner. We then modify our class diagram to incorporate the new inheritance relationships. Finally, we demonstrate how our updated design is translated into Java code.

In Section 23.3, we encountered the problem of representing a financial transaction in the system. Rather than create one class to represent all transaction types, we decided to create three individual transaction classes—BalanceInquiry, Withdrawal and Deposit—to represent the transactions that the ATM system can perform. Figure 24.7 shows the attributes and operations of classes BalanceInquiry, Withdrawal and Deposit. These classes have one attribute (accountNumber) and one operation (execute) in common. Each class requires attribute accountNumber to specify the account to which the transaction applies. Each class contains operation execute, which the ATM invokes to perform the transaction. Clearly, BalanceInquiry, Withdrawal and Deposit represent *types of* transactions. Figure 24.7 reveals commonality among the transaction classes, so using inheritance to factor out the common features seems appropriate for designing classes BalanceInquiry, Withdrawal and Deposit. We place the common functionality in a superclass, Transaction, that classes BalanceInquiry, Withdrawal and Deposit extend.

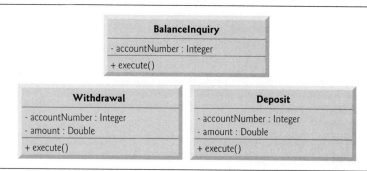

Fig. 24.7 | Attributes and operations of BalanceInquiry, Withdrawal and Deposit.

Generalization

The UML specifies a relationship called a **generalization** to model inheritance. Figure 24.8 is the class diagram that models the generalization of superclass Transaction and subclasses BalanceInquiry, Withdrawal and Deposit. The arrows with triangular hollow arrowheads indicate that classes BalanceInquiry, Withdrawal and Deposit extend class Transaction. Class Transaction is said to be a generalization of classes BalanceInquiry, Withdrawal and Deposit. Class BalanceInquiry, Withdrawal and Deposit are said to be **specializations** of class Transaction.

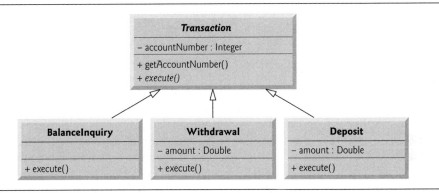

Fig. 24.8 | Class diagram modeling generalization of superclass Transaction and subclasses BalanceInquiry, Withdrawal and Deposit. Abstract class names (e.g., Transaction) and method names (e.g., execute in class Transaction) appear in italics.

Classes BalanceInquiry, Withdrawal and Deposit share integer attribute account-Number, so we *factor out* this *common attribute* and place it in superclass Transaction. We no longer list accountNumber in the second compartment of each subclass, because the three subclasses *inherit* this attribute from Transaction. Recall, however, that subclasses cannot directly access private attributes of a superclass. We therefore include public method getAccountNumber in class Transaction. Each subclass will inherit this method, enabling the subclass to access its accountNumber as needed to execute a transaction.

According to Fig. 24.7, classes BalanceInquiry, Withdrawal and Deposit also share operation execute, so we placed public method execute in superclass Transaction. However, it does *not* make sense to implement execute in class Transaction, because the functionality that this method provides *depends on the type of the actual transaction*. We therefore declare method execute as abstract in superclass Transaction. Any class that contains at least one abstract method must also be declared abstract. This forces any subclass of Transaction that must be a *concrete* class (i.e., BalanceInquiry, Withdrawal and Deposit) to implement method execute. The UML requires that we place abstract class names (and abstract methods) in italics, so Transaction and its method execute appear in italics in Fig. 24.8. Method execute is *not* italicized in subclasses BalanceInquiry, Withdrawal and Deposit. Each subclass overrides superclass Transaction's execute method with a concrete implementation that performs the steps appropriate for completing that type of transaction. Figure 24.8 includes operation execute in the third compartment of classes BalanceInquiry, Withdrawal and Deposit, because each class has a different concrete implementation of the overridden method.

Processing Transactions Polymorphically
Polymorphism provides the ATM with an elegant way to execute all transactions "in the general." For example, suppose a user chooses to perform a balance inquiry. The ATM sets a

`Transaction` reference to a new `BalanceInquiry` object. When the ATM uses its `Transaction` reference to invoke method `execute`, `BalanceInquiry`'s version of `execute` is called.

This *polymorphic* approach also makes the system easily *extensible*. Should we wish to create a new transaction type (e.g., funds transfer or bill payment), we would just create an additional `Transaction` subclass that overrides the `execute` method with a version of the method appropriate for executing the new transaction type. We would need to make only minimal changes to the system code to allow users to choose the new transaction type from the main menu and for the ATM to instantiate and execute objects of the new subclass. The ATM could execute transactions of the new type using the current code, because it executes all transactions *polymorphically* using a general `Transaction` reference.

Recall that an abstract class like `Transaction` is one for which you never intend to instantiate objects. An abstract class simply declares common attributes and behaviors of its subclasses in an inheritance hierarchy. Class `Transaction` defines the concept of what it means to be a transaction that has an account number and executes. You may wonder why we bother to include `abstract` method `execute` in class `Transaction` if it lacks a concrete implementation. Conceptually, we include it because it corresponds to the defining behavior of *all* transactions—executing. Technically, we must include method `execute` in superclass `Transaction` so that the ATM (or any other class) can polymorphically invoke each subclass's *overridden* version of this method through a `Transaction` reference. Also, from a software engineering perspective, including an abstract method in a superclass forces the implementor of the subclasses to override that method with concrete implementations in the subclasses, or else the subclasses, too, will be abstract, preventing objects of those subclasses from being instantiated.

Additional Attribute of Classes **Withdrawal** *and* **Deposit**
Subclasses `BalanceInquiry`, `Withdrawal` and `Deposit` inherit attribute `accountNumber` from superclass `Transaction`, but classes `Withdrawal` and `Deposit` contain the additional attribute `amount` that distinguishes them from class `BalanceInquiry`. Classes `Withdrawal` and `Deposit` require this additional attribute to store the amount of money that the user wishes to withdraw or deposit. Class `BalanceInquiry` has no need for such an attribute and requires only an account number to execute. Even though two of the three `Transaction` subclasses share this attribute, we do *not* place it in superclass `Transaction`—we place only features *common* to all the subclasses in the superclass, otherwise subclasses could inherit attributes (and methods) that they do not need and should not have.

Class Diagram with **Transaction** *Hierarchy Incorporated*
Figure 24.9 presents an updated class diagram of our model that incorporates inheritance and introduces class `Transaction`. We model an association between class ATM and class `Transaction` to show that the ATM, at any given moment, either is executing a transaction or is not (i.e., zero or one objects of type `Transaction` exist in the system at a time). Because a `Withdrawal` is a type of `Transaction`, we no longer draw an association line directly between class ATM and class `Withdrawal`. Subclass `Withdrawal` inherits superclass `Transaction`'s association with class ATM. Subclasses `BalanceInquiry` and `Deposit` inherit this association, too, so the previously omitted associations between ATM and classes `BalanceInquiry` and `Deposit` no longer exist either.

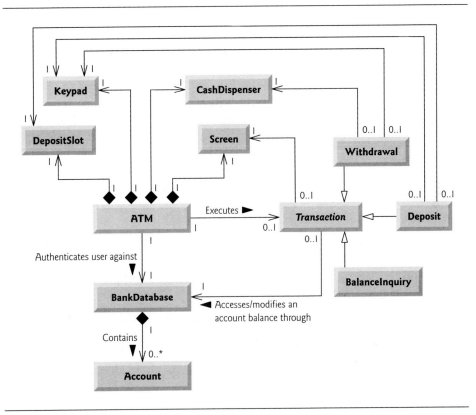

Fig. 24.9 | Class diagram of the ATM system (incorporating inheritance). The abstract class name Transaction appears in italics.

We also add an association between class Transaction and the BankDatabase (Fig. 24.9). All Transactions require a reference to the BankDatabase so they can access and modify account information. Because each Transaction subclass inherits this reference, we no longer model the association between class Withdrawal and the BankDatabase. Similarly, the previously omitted associations between the BankDatabase and classes BalanceInquiry and Deposit no longer exist.

We show an association between class Transaction and the Screen. All Transactions display output to the user via the Screen. Thus, we no longer include the association previously modeled between Withdrawal and the Screen, although Withdrawal still participates in associations with the CashDispenser and the Keypad. Our class diagram incorporating inheritance also models Deposit and BalanceInquiry. We show associations between Deposit and both the DepositSlot and the Keypad. Class BalanceInquiry takes part in no associations other than those inherited from class Transaction—a BalanceInquiry needs to interact only with the BankDatabase and with the Screen.

Figure 24.1 showed attributes and operations with visibility markers. Now in Fig. 24.10 we present a modified class diagram that incorporates inheritance. This abbreviated diagram does not show inheritance relationships, but instead shows the attributes and methods after we've employed inheritance in our system. To save space, as we did in Fig. 23.12, we do not include those attributes shown by associations in Fig. 24.9—we do, however, include them in the Java implementation in Section 24.4. We also omit all operation parameters, as we did in Fig. 24.1—incorporating inheritance does not affect the parameters already modeled in Figs. 23.17–23.21.

Software Engineering Observation 24.1

A complete class diagram shows all the associations among classes and all the attributes and operations for each class. When the number of class attributes, methods and associations is substantial (as in Figs. 24.9 and 24.10), a good practice that promotes readability is to divide this information between two class diagrams—one focusing on associations and the other on attributes and methods.

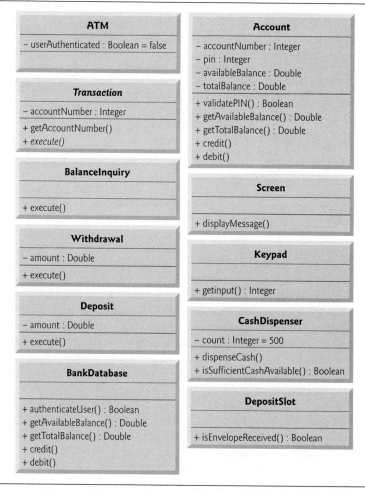

Fig. 24.10 │ Class diagram with attributes and operations (incorporating inheritance). The abstract class name Transaction and the abstract method name execute in class Transaction appear in italics.

Implementing the ATM System Design (Incorporating Inheritance)

In Section 24.2, we began implementing the ATM system design in Java code. We now modify our implementation to incorporate inheritance, using class Withdrawal as an example.

1. If a class A is a generalization of class B, then class B extends class A in the class declaration. For example, abstract superclass Transaction is a generalization of class Withdrawal. Figure 24.11 shows the declaration of class Withdrawal.

```
1   // Class Withdrawal represents an ATM withdrawal transaction
2   public class Withdrawal extends Transaction
3   {
4   } // end class Withdrawal
```

Fig. 24.11 | Java code for shell of class Withdrawal.

2. If class A is an abstract class and class B is a subclass of class A, then class B must implement the *abstract* methods of class A if class B is to be a *concrete* class. For example, class Transaction contains abstract method execute, so class Withdrawal must implement this method if we want to instantiate a Withdrawal object. Figure 24.12 is the Java code for class Withdrawal from Fig. 24.9 and Fig. 24.10. Class Withdrawal inherits field accountNumber from superclass Transaction, so Withdrawal does not need to declare this field. Class Withdrawal also inherits references to the Screen and the BankDatabase from its superclass Transaction, so we do not include these references in our code. Figure 24.10 specifies attribute amount and operation execute for class Withdrawal. Line 6 of Fig. 24.12 declares a field for attribute amount. Lines 16–19 declare the shell of a method for operation execute. Recall that subclass Withdrawal must provide a concrete implementation of the abstract method execute in superclass Transaction. The keypad and cashDispenser references (lines 7–8) are fields derived from Withdrawal's associations in Fig. 24.9. The constructor in the complete working version of this class will initialize these references to actual objects.

```
1   // Withdrawal.java
2   // Generated using the class diagrams in Fig. 24.9 and Fig. 24.10
3   public class Withdrawal extends Transaction
4   {
5      // attributes
6      private double amount; // amount to withdraw
7      private Keypad keypad; // reference to keypad
8      private CashDispenser cashDispenser; // reference to cash dispenser
9
10     // no-argument constructor
11     public Withdrawal()
12     {
13     } // end no-argument Withdrawal constructor
14
```

Fig. 24.12 | Java code for class Withdrawal based on Figs. 24.9 and 24.10. (Part 1 of 2.)

```
15        // method overriding execute
16        @Override
17        public void execute()
18        {
19        } // end method execute
20   } // end class Withdrawal
```

Fig. 24.12 | Java code for class `Withdrawal` based on Figs. 24.9 and 24.10. (Part 2 of 2.)

Software Engineering Observation 24.2

Several UML modeling tools can convert UML-based designs into Java code, speeding the implementation process considerably. For more information on these tools, visit our UML Resource Center at www.deitel.com/UML/.

Congratulations on completing the case study's design portion! We implement the ATM system in Java code in Section 24.4. We recommend that you carefully read the code and its description. The code is abundantly commented and precisely follows the design with which you're now familiar. The accompanying description is carefully written to guide your understanding of the implementation based on the UML design. Mastering this code is a wonderful culminating accomplishment after studying Sections 23.2—23.7 and 24.2–24.3.

Self-Review Exercises for Section 24.3

24.4   The UML uses an arrow with a _____ to indicate a generalization relationship.
a)   solid filled arrowhead
b)   triangular hollow arrowhead
c)   diamond-shaped hollow arrowhead
d)   stick arrowhead

24.5   State whether the following statement is *true* or *false*, and if *false*, explain why: The UML requires that we underline abstract class names and method names.

24.6   Write Java code to begin implementing the design for class `Transaction` specified in Figs. 24.9 and 24.10. Be sure to include `private` reference-type attributes based on class `Transaction`'s associations. Also be sure to include `public` *get* methods that provide access to any of these `private` attributes that the subclasses require to perform their tasks.

24.4 ATM Case Study Implementation

This section contains the complete working 673-line implementation of the ATM system. We consider the classes in the order in which we identified them in Section 23.3—ATM, Screen, Keypad, CashDispenser, DepositSlot, Account, BankDatabase, Transaction, BalanceInquiry, Withdrawal and Deposit.

We apply the guidelines discussed in Sections 24.2—13.3 to code these classes based on how we modeled them in the UML class diagrams of Figs. 24.9 and 24.10. To develop the bodies of class methods, we refer to the activity diagrams in Section 23.5 and the communication and sequence diagrams presented in Section 23.7. Our ATM design does *not* specify all the program logic and may not specify all the attributes and operations required to complete the ATM implementation. This is a *normal* part of the object-oriented design process. As we implement the system, we complete the program logic and add attributes and behaviors as necessary to construct the ATM system specified by the requirements document in Section 23.2.

We conclude the discussion by presenting a Java application (ATMCaseStudy) that starts the ATM and puts the other classes in the system in use. Recall that we're developing a first version of the ATM system that runs on a personal computer and uses the computer's keyboard and monitor to approximate the ATM's keypad and screen. We also simulate only the actions of the ATM's cash dispenser and deposit slot. We attempt to implement the system, however, so that real hardware versions of these devices could be integrated without significant changes in the code.

24.4.1 Class ATM

Class ATM (Fig. 24.13) represents the ATM as a whole. Lines 6–12 implement the class's attributes. We determine all but one of these attributes from the UML class diagrams of Figs. 24.9 and 24.10. We implement the UML Boolean attribute userAuthenticated in Fig. 24.10 as a boolean in Java (line 6). Line 7 declares an attribute not found in our UML design—an int attribute currentAccountNumber that keeps track of the account number of the current authenticated user. We'll soon see how the class uses this attribute. Lines 8–12 declare reference-type attributes corresponding to the ATM class's associations modeled in the class diagram of Fig. 24.9. These attributes allow the ATM to access its parts (i.e., its Screen, Keypad, CashDispenser and DepositSlot) and interact with the bank's account-information database (i.e., a BankDatabase object).

```java
1   // ATM.java
2   // Represents an automated teller machine
3
4   public class ATM
5   {
6      private boolean userAuthenticated; // whether user is authenticated
7      private int currentAccountNumber; // current user's account number
8      private Screen screen; // ATM's screen
9      private Keypad keypad; // ATM's keypad
10     private CashDispenser cashDispenser; // ATM's cash dispenser
11     private DepositSlot depositSlot; // ATM's deposit slot
12     private BankDatabase bankDatabase; // account information database
13
14     // constants corresponding to main menu options
15     private static final int BALANCE_INQUIRY = 1;
16     private static final int WITHDRAWAL = 2;
17     private static final int DEPOSIT = 3;
18     private static final int EXIT = 4;
19
20     // no-argument ATM constructor initializes instance variables
21     public ATM()
22     {
23        userAuthenticated = false; // user is not authenticated to start
24        currentAccountNumber = 0; // no current account number to start
25        screen = new Screen(); // create screen
```

Fig. 24.13 | Class ATM represents the ATM. (Part 1 of 4.)

```
26          keypad = new Keypad(); // create keypad
27          cashDispenser = new CashDispenser(); // create cash dispenser
28          depositSlot = new DepositSlot(); // create deposit slot
29          bankDatabase = new BankDatabase(); // create acct info database
30       } // end no-argument ATM constructor
31
32       // start ATM
33       public void run()
34       {
35          // welcome and authenticate user; perform transactions
36          while (true)
37          {
38             // loop while user is not yet authenticated
39             while (!userAuthenticated)
40             {
41                screen.displayMessageLine("\nWelcome!");
42                authenticateUser(); // authenticate user
43             } // end while
44
45             performTransactions(); // user is now authenticated
46             userAuthenticated = false; // reset before next ATM session
47             currentAccountNumber = 0; // reset before next ATM session
48             screen.displayMessageLine("\nThank you! Goodbye!");
49          } // end while
50       } // end method run
51
52       // attempts to authenticate user against database
53       private void authenticateUser()
54       {
55          screen.displayMessage("\nPlease enter your account number: ");
56          int accountNumber = keypad.getInput(); // input account number
57          screen.displayMessage("\nEnter your PIN: "); // prompt for PIN
58          int pin = keypad.getInput(); // input PIN
59
60          // set userAuthenticated to boolean value returned by database
61          userAuthenticated =
62             bankDatabase.authenticateUser(accountNumber, pin);
63
64          // check whether authentication succeeded
65          if (userAuthenticated)
66          {
67             currentAccountNumber = accountNumber; // save user's account #
68          } // end if
69          else
70             screen.displayMessageLine(
71                "Invalid account number or PIN. Please try again.");
72       } // end method authenticateUser
73
74       // display the main menu and perform transactions
75       private void performTransactions()
76       {
77          // local variable to store transaction currently being processed
78          Transaction currentTransaction = null;
```

Fig. 24.13 | Class ATM represents the ATM. (Part 2 of 4.)

```
79
80          boolean userExited = false; // user has not chosen to exit
81
82          // loop while user has not chosen option to exit system
83          while (!userExited)
84          {
85              // show main menu and get user selection
86              int mainMenuSelection = displayMainMenu();
87
88              // decide how to proceed based on user's menu selection
89              switch (mainMenuSelection)
90              {
91                  // user chose to perform one of three transaction types
92                  case BALANCE_INQUIRY:
93                  case WITHDRAWAL:
94                  case DEPOSIT:
95
96                      // initialize as new object of chosen type
97                      currentTransaction =
98                          createTransaction(mainMenuSelection);
99
100                     currentTransaction.execute(); // execute transaction
101                     break;
102                 case EXIT: // user chose to terminate session
103                     screen.displayMessageLine("\nExiting the system...");
104                     userExited = true; // this ATM session should end
105                     break;
106                 default: // user did not enter an integer from 1-4
107                     screen.displayMessageLine(
108                         "\nYou did not enter a valid selection. Try again.");
109                     break;
110             } // end switch
111         } // end while
112     } // end method performTransactions
113
114     // display the main menu and return an input selection
115     private int displayMainMenu()
116     {
117         screen.displayMessageLine("\nMain menu:");
118         screen.displayMessageLine("1 - View my balance");
119         screen.displayMessageLine("2 - Withdraw cash");
120         screen.displayMessageLine("3 - Deposit funds");
121         screen.displayMessageLine("4 - Exit\n");
122         screen.displayMessage("Enter a choice: ");
123         return keypad.getInput(); // return user's selection
124     } // end method displayMainMenu
125
126     // return object of specified Transaction subclass
127     private Transaction createTransaction(int type)
128     {
129         Transaction temp = null; // temporary Transaction variable
130
```

Fig. 24.13 | Class ATM represents the ATM. (Part 3 of 4.)

```
131          // determine which type of Transaction to create
132          switch (type)
133          {
134             case BALANCE_INQUIRY: // create new BalanceInquiry transaction
135                temp = new BalanceInquiry(
136                   currentAccountNumber, screen, bankDatabase);
137                break;
138             case WITHDRAWAL: // create new Withdrawal transaction
139                temp = new Withdrawal(currentAccountNumber, screen,
140                   bankDatabase, keypad, cashDispenser);
141                break;
142             case DEPOSIT: // create new Deposit transaction
143                temp = new Deposit(currentAccountNumber, screen,
144                   bankDatabase, keypad, depositSlot);
145                break;
146          } // end switch
147
148          return temp; // return the newly created object
149       } // end method createTransaction
150    } // end class ATM
```

Fig. 24.13 | Class ATM represents the ATM. (Part 4 of 4.)

Lines 15–18 declare integer constants that correspond to the four options in the ATM's main menu (i.e., balance inquiry, withdrawal, deposit and exit). Lines 21–30 declare the constructor, which initializes the class's attributes. When an ATM object is first created, no user is authenticated, so line 23 initializes userAuthenticated to false. Likewise, line 24 initializes currentAccountNumber to 0 because there's no current user yet. Lines 25–28 instantiate new objects to represent the ATM's parts. Recall that class ATM has composition relationships with classes Screen, Keypad, CashDispenser and DepositSlot, so class ATM is responsible for their creation. Line 29 creates a new BankDatabase. [*Note:* If this were a real ATM system, the ATM class would receive a reference to an existing database object created by the bank. However, in this implementation we're only simulating the bank's database, so class ATM creates the BankDatabase object with which it interacts.]

ATM *Method* run
The class diagram of Fig. 24.10 does not list any operations for class ATM. We now implement one operation (i.e., public method) in class ATM that allows an external client of the class (i.e., class ATMCaseStudy) to tell the ATM to run. ATM method run (lines 33–50) uses an infinite loop (lines 36–49) to repeatedly welcome a user, attempt to authenticate the user and, if authentication succeeds, allow the user to perform transactions. After an authenticated user performs the desired transactions and chooses to exit, the ATM resets itself, displays a goodbye message to the user and restarts the process. We use an infinite loop here to simulate the fact that an ATM appears to run continuously until the bank turns it off (an action beyond the user's control). An ATM user has the option to exit the system but not the ability to turn off the ATM completely.

Authenticating a User
In method run's infinite loop, lines 39–43 cause the ATM to repeatedly welcome and attempt to authenticate the user as long as the user has not been authenticated (i.e., !user-

Authenticated is true). Line 41 invokes method displayMessageLine of the ATM's screen to display a welcome message. Like Screen method displayMessage designed in the case study, method displayMessageLine (declared in lines 13–16 of Fig. 24.14) displays a message to the user, but this method also outputs a newline after the message. We've added this method during implementation to give class Screen's clients more control over the placement of displayed messages. Line 42 invokes class ATM's private utility method authenticateUser (declared in lines 53–72) to attempt to authenticate the user.

We refer to the requirements document to determine the steps necessary to authenticate the user before allowing transactions to occur. Line 55 of method authenticateUser invokes method displayMessage of the screen to prompt the user to enter an account number. Line 56 invokes method getInput of the keypad to obtain the user's input, then stores the integer value entered by the user in a local variable accountNumber. Method authenticateUser next prompts the user to enter a PIN (line 57), and stores the PIN input by the user in a local variable pin (line 58). Next, lines 61–62 attempt to authenticate the user by passing the accountNumber and pin entered by the user to the bankData-base's authenticateUser method. Class ATM sets its userAuthenticated attribute to the boolean value returned by this method—userAuthenticated becomes true if authentication succeeds (i.e., accountNumber and pin match those of an existing Account in bank-Database) and remains false otherwise. If userAuthenticated is true, line 67 saves the account number entered by the user (i.e., accountNumber) in the ATM attribute current-AccountNumber. The other ATM methods use this variable whenever an ATM session requires access to the user's account number. If userAuthenticated is false, lines 70–71 use the screen's displayMessageLine method to indicate that an invalid account number and/or PIN was entered and the user must try again. We set currentAccountNumber only after authenticating the user's account number and the associated PIN—if the database could not authenticate the user, currentAccountNumber remains 0.

After method run attempts to authenticate the user (line 42), if userAuthenticated is still false, the while loop in lines 39–43 executes again. If userAuthenticated is now true, the loop terminates and control continues with line 45, which calls class ATM's utility method performTransactions.

Performing Transactions

Method performTransactions (lines 75–112) carries out an ATM session for an authenticated user. Line 78 declares a local Transaction variable to which we'll assign a BalanceInquiry, Withdrawal or Deposit object representing the ATM transaction the user selected. We use a Transaction variable here to allow us to take advantage of polymorphism. Also, we name this variable after the *role name* included in the class diagram of Fig. 23.7—currentTransaction. Line 80 declares another local variable—a boolean called userExited that keeps track of whether the user has chosen to exit. This variable controls a while loop (lines 83–111) that allows the user to execute an unlimited number of transactions before choosing to exit. Within this loop, line 86 displays the main menu and obtains the user's menu selection by calling an ATM utility method displayMainMenu (declared in lines 115–124). This method displays the main menu by invoking methods of the ATM's screen and returns a menu selection obtained from the user through the ATM's keypad. Line 86 stores the user's selection returned by displayMainMenu in local variable mainMenuSelection.

After obtaining a main menu selection, method performTransactions uses a switch statement (lines 89–110) to respond to the selection appropriately. If mainMenuSelection is equal to any of the three integer constants representing transaction types (i.e., if the user chose to perform a transaction), lines 97–98 call utility method createTransaction (declared in lines 127–149) to return a newly instantiated object of the type that corresponds to the selected transaction. Variable currentTransaction is assigned the reference returned by createTransaction, then line 100 invokes method execute of this transaction to execute it. We'll discuss Transaction method execute and the three Transaction subclasses shortly. We assign the Transaction variable currentTransaction an object of one of the three Transaction subclasses so that we can execute transactions *polymorphically*. For example, if the user chooses to perform a balance inquiry, mainMenuSelection equals BALANCE_INQUIRY, leading createTransaction to return a BalanceInquiry object. Thus, currentTransaction refers to a BalanceInquiry, and invoking currentTransaction.execute() results in BalanceInquiry's version of execute being called.

Creating a Transaction
Method createTransaction (lines 127–149) uses a switch statement (lines 132–146) to instantiate a new Transaction subclass object of the type indicated by the parameter type. Recall that method performTransactions passes mainMenuSelection to this method only when mainMenuSelection contains a value corresponding to one of the three transaction types. Therefore type is BALANCE_INQUIRY, WITHDRAWAL or DEPOSIT. Each case in the switch statement instantiates a new object by calling the appropriate Transaction subclass constructor. Each constructor has a unique parameter list, based on the specific data required to initialize the subclass object. A BalanceInquiry requires only the account number of the current user and references to the ATM's screen and the bankDatabase. In addition to these parameters, a Withdrawal requires references to the ATM's keypad and cashDispenser, and a Deposit requires references to the ATM's keypad and depositSlot. We discuss the transaction classes in more detail in Sections 24.4.8—13.4.11.

Exiting the Main Menu and Processing Invalid Selections
After executing a transaction (line 100 in performTransactions), userExited remains false and lines 83–111 repeat, returning the user to the main menu. However, if a user does not perform a transaction and instead selects the main menu option to exit, line 104 sets userExited to true, causing the condition of the while loop (!userExited) to become false. This while is the final statement of method performTransactions, so control returns to the calling method run. If the user enters an invalid main menu selection (i.e., not an integer from 1–4), lines 107–108 display an appropriate error message, userExited remains false and the user returns to the main menu to try again.

Awaiting the Next ATM User
When performTransactions returns control to method run, the user has chosen to exit the system, so lines 46–47 reset the ATM's attributes userAuthenticated and currentAccountNumber to prepare for the next ATM user. Line 48 displays a goodbye message before the ATM starts over and welcomes the next user.

24.4.2 Class Screen

Class Screen (Fig. 24.14) represents the screen of the ATM and encapsulates all aspects of displaying output to the user. Class Screen approximates a real ATM's screen with a computer monitor and outputs text messages using standard console output methods

System.out.print, System.out.println and System.out.printf. In this case study, we designed class Screen to have one operation—displayMessage. For greater flexibility in displaying messages to the Screen, we now declare three Screen methods—displayMessage, displayMessageLine and displayDollarAmount.

```
1   // Screen.java
2   // Represents the screen of the ATM
3
4   public class Screen
5   {
6      // display a message without a carriage return
7      public void displayMessage(String message)
8      {
9         System.out.print(message);
10     } // end method displayMessage
11
12     // display a message with a carriage return
13     public void displayMessageLine(String message)
14     {
15        System.out.println(message);
16     } // end method displayMessageLine
17
18     // displays a dollar amount
19     public void displayDollarAmount(double amount)
20     {
21        System.out.printf("$%,.2f", amount);
22     } // end method displayDollarAmount
23  } // end class Screen
```

Fig. 24.14 | Class Screen represents the screen of the ATM.

Method displayMessage (lines 7–10) takes a String argument and prints it to the console. The cursor stays on the same line, making this method appropriate for displaying prompts to the user. Method displayMessageLine (lines 13–16) does the same using System.out.println, which outputs a newline to move the cursor to the next line. Finally, method displayDollarAmount (lines 19–22) outputs a properly formatted dollar amount (e.g., $1,234.56). Line 21 uses System.out.printf to output a double value formatted with commas to increase readability and two decimal places.

24.4.3 Class Keypad

Class Keypad (Fig. 24.15) represents the keypad of the ATM and is responsible for receiving all user input. Recall that we're simulating this hardware, so we use the computer's keyboard to approximate the keypad. We use class Scanner to obtain console input from the user. A computer keyboard contains many keys not found on the ATM's keypad. However, we assume that the user presses only the keys on the computer keyboard that also appear on the keypad—the keys numbered 0–9 and the *Enter* key.

Line 3 of class Keypad imports class Scanner for use in class Keypad. Line 7 declares Scanner variable input as an instance variable. Line 12 in the constructor creates a new Scanner object that reads input from the standard input stream (System.in) and assigns the object's reference to variable input. Method getInput (lines 16–19) invokes Scanner

```
1   // Keypad.java
2   // Represents the keypad of the ATM
3   import java.util.Scanner; // program uses Scanner to obtain user input
4
5   public class Keypad
6   {
7      private Scanner input; // reads data from the command line
8
9      // no-argument constructor initializes the Scanner
10     public Keypad()
11     {
12        input = new Scanner(System.in);
13     } // end no-argument Keypad constructor
14
15     // return an integer value entered by user
16     public int getInput()
17     {
18        return input.nextInt(); // we assume that user enters an integer
19     } // end method getInput
20  } // end class Keypad
```

Fig. 24.15 | Class Keypad represents the ATM's keypad.

method nextInt (line 18) to return the next integer input by the user. [*Note:* Method nextInt can throw an InputMismatchException if the user enters non-integer input. Because the real ATM's keypad permits only integer input, we assume that no exception will occur and do not attempt to fix this problem. See Chapter 11, Exception Handling: A Deeper Look, for information on catching exceptions.] Recall that nextInt obtains all the input used by the ATM. Keypad's getInput method simply returns the integer input by the user. If a client of class Keypad requires input that satisfies some criteria (i.e., a number corresponding to a valid menu option), the client must perform the error checking.

24.4.4 Class CashDispenser

Class CashDispenser (Fig. 24.16) represents the cash dispenser of the ATM. Line 7 declares constant INITIAL_COUNT, which indicates the initial count of bills in the cash dispenser when the ATM starts (i.e., 500). Line 8 implements attribute count (modeled in Fig. 24.10), which keeps track of the number of bills remaining in the CashDispenser at any time. The constructor (lines 11–14) sets count to the initial count. CashDispenser has two public methods—dispenseCash (lines 17–21) and isSufficientCashAvailable (lines 24–32). The class trusts that a client (i.e., Withdrawal) calls dispenseCash only after establishing that sufficient cash is available by calling isSufficientCashAvailable. Thus, dispenseCash simply simulates dispensing the requested amount without checking whether sufficient cash is available.

```
1   // CashDispenser.java
2   // Represents the cash dispenser of the ATM
3
```

Fig. 24.16 | Class CashDispenser represents the ATM's cash dispenser. (Part 1 of 2.)

```
4   public class CashDispenser
5   {
6      // the default initial number of bills in the cash dispenser
7      private final static int INITIAL_COUNT = 500;
8      private int count; // number of $20 bills remaining
9
10     // no-argument CashDispenser constructor initializes count to default
11     public CashDispenser()
12     {
13        count = INITIAL_COUNT; // set count attribute to default
14     } // end CashDispenser constructor
15
16     // simulates dispensing of specified amount of cash
17     public void dispenseCash(int amount)
18     {
19        int billsRequired = amount / 20; // number of $20 bills required
20        count -= billsRequired; // update the count of bills
21     } // end method dispenseCash
22
23     // indicates whether cash dispenser can dispense desired amount
24     public boolean isSufficientCashAvailable(int amount)
25     {
26        int billsRequired = amount / 20; // number of $20 bills required
27
28        if (count >= billsRequired)
29           return true; // enough bills available
30        else
31           return false; // not enough bills available
32     } // end method isSufficientCashAvailable
33  } // end class CashDispenser
```

Fig. 24.16 | Class CashDispenser represents the ATM's cash dispenser. (Part 2 of 2.)

Method isSufficientCashAvailable (lines 24–32) has a parameter amount that specifies the amount of cash in question. Line 26 calculates the number of $20 bills required to dispense the specified amount. The ATM allows the user to choose only withdrawal amounts that are multiples of $20, so we divide amount by 20 to obtain the number of billsRequired. Lines 28–31 return true if the CashDispenser's count is greater than or equal to billsRequired (i.e., enough bills are available) and false otherwise (i.e., not enough bills). For example, if a user wishes to withdraw $80 (i.e., billsRequired is 4), but only three bills remain (i.e., count is 3), the method returns false.

Method dispenseCash (lines 17–21) simulates cash dispensing. If our system were hooked up to a real hardware cash dispenser, this method would interact with the device to physically dispense cash. Our version of the method simply decreases the count of bills remaining by the number required to dispense the specified amount (line 20). It's the responsibility of the client of the class (i.e., Withdrawal) to inform the user that cash has been dispensed—CashDispenser cannot interact directly with Screen.

24.4.5 Class DepositSlot

Class DepositSlot (Fig. 24.17) represents the ATM's deposit slot. Like class CashDispenser, class DepositSlot merely simulates the functionality of a real hardware deposit slot. DepositSlot has no attributes and only one method—isEnvelopeReceived (lines 8–11)—which indicates whether a deposit envelope was received.

```
1   // DepositSlot.java
2   // Represents the deposit slot of the ATM
3
4   public class DepositSlot
5   {
6      // indicates whether envelope was received (always returns true,
7      // because this is only a software simulation of a real deposit slot)
8      public boolean isEnvelopeReceived()
9      {
10        return true; // deposit envelope was received
11     } // end method isEnvelopeReceived
12  } // end class DepositSlot
```

Fig. 24.17 | Class DepositSlot represents the ATM's deposit slot.

Recall from the requirements document that the ATM allows the user up to two minutes to insert an envelope. The current version of method isEnvelopeReceived simply returns true immediately (line 10), because this is only a software simulation, and we assume that the user has inserted an envelope within the required time frame. If an actual hardware deposit slot were connected to our system, method isEnvelopeReceived might be implemented to wait for a maximum of two minutes to receive a signal from the hardware deposit slot indicating that the user has indeed inserted a deposit envelope. If isEnvelopeReceived were to receive such a signal within two minutes, the method would return true. If two minutes elapsed and the method still had not received a signal, then the method would return false.

24.4.6 Class Account

Class Account (Fig. 24.18) represents a bank account. Each Account has four attributes (modeled in Fig. 24.10)—accountNumber, pin, availableBalance and totalBalance. Lines 6–9 implement these attributes as private fields. Variable availableBalance represents the amount of funds available for withdrawal. Variable totalBalance represents the amount of funds available, plus the amount of deposited funds still pending confirmation or clearance.

```
1   // Account.java
2   // Represents a bank account
3
4   public class Account
5   {
6      private int accountNumber; // account number
7      private int pin; // PIN for authentication
8      private double availableBalance; // funds available for withdrawal
9      private double totalBalance; // funds available + pending deposits
```

Fig. 24.18 | Class Account represents a bank account. (Part 1 of 2.)

```
10
11      // Account constructor initializes attributes
12      public Account(int theAccountNumber, int thePIN,
13         double theAvailableBalance, double theTotalBalance)
14      {
15         accountNumber = theAccountNumber;
16         pin = thePIN;
17         availableBalance = theAvailableBalance;
18         totalBalance = theTotalBalance;
19      } // end Account constructor
20
21      // determines whether a user-specified PIN matches PIN in Account
22      public boolean validatePIN(int userPIN)
23      {
24         if (userPIN == pin)
25            return true;
26         else
27            return false;
28      } // end method validatePIN
29
30      // returns available balance
31      public double getAvailableBalance()
32      {
33         return availableBalance;
34      } // end getAvailableBalance
35
36      // returns the total balance
37      public double getTotalBalance()
38      {
39         return totalBalance;
40      } // end method getTotalBalance
41
42      // credits an amount to the account
43      public void credit(double amount)
44      {
45         totalBalance += amount; // add to total balance
46      } // end method credit
47
48      // debits an amount from the account
49      public void debit(double amount)
50      {
51         availableBalance -= amount; // subtract from available balance
52         totalBalance -= amount; // subtract from total balance
53      } // end method debit
54
55      // returns account number
56      public int getAccountNumber()
57      {
58         return accountNumber;
59      } // end method getAccountNumber
60   } // end class Account
```

Fig. 24.18 | Class Account represents a bank account. (Part 2 of 2.)

The Account class has a constructor (lines 12–19) that takes an account number, the PIN established for the account, the account's initial available balance and the account's initial total balance as arguments. Lines 15–18 assign these values to the class's attributes (i.e., fields).

Method validatePIN (lines 22–28) determines whether a user-specified PIN (i.e., parameter userPIN) matches the PIN associated with the account (i.e., attribute pin). Recall that we modeled this method's parameter userPIN in Fig. 23.19. If the two PINs match, the method returns true (line 25); otherwise, it returns false (line 27).

Methods getAvailableBalance (lines 31–34) and getTotalBalance (lines 37–40) return the values of double attributes availableBalance and totalBalance, respectively.

Method credit (lines 43–46) adds an amount of money (i.e., parameter amount) to an Account as part of a deposit transaction. This method adds the amount only to attribute totalBalance (line 45). The money credited to an account during a deposit does *not* become available immediately, so we modify only the total balance. We assume that the bank updates the available balance appropriately at a later time. Our implementation of class Account includes only methods required for carrying out ATM transactions. Therefore, we omit the methods that some other bank system would invoke to add to attribute availableBalance (to confirm a deposit) or subtract from attribute totalBalance (to reject a deposit).

Method debit (lines 49–53) subtracts an amount of money (i.e., parameter amount) from an Account as part of a withdrawal transaction. This method subtracts the amount from *both* attribute availableBalance (line 51) and attribute totalBalance (line 52), because a withdrawal affects *both* measures of an account balance.

Method getAccountNumber (lines 56–59) provides access to an Account's account-Number. We include this method in our implementation so that a client of the class (i.e., BankDatabase) can identify a particular Account. For example, BankDatabase contains many Account objects, and it can invoke this method on each of its Account objects to locate the one with a specific account number.

24.4.7 Class BankDatabase

Class BankDatabase (Fig. 24.19) models the bank's database with which the ATM interacts to access and modify a user's account information. For this example, we model the database as an array, but you could use the techniques you learned in Chapter 21 to store account information in an actual database.

```
1   // BankDatabase.java
2   // Represents the bank account information database
3
4   public class BankDatabase
5   {
6      private Account[] accounts; // array of Accounts
7
8      // no-argument BankDatabase constructor initializes accounts
9      public BankDatabase()
10     {
```

Fig. 24.19 | Class BankDatabase represents the bank's account information database. (Part 1 of 3.)

```
11          accounts = new Account[2]; // just 2 accounts for testing
12          accounts[0] = new Account(12345, 54321, 1000.0, 1200.0);
13          accounts[1] = new Account(98765, 56789, 200.0, 200.0);
14       } // end no-argument BankDatabase constructor
15
16       // retrieve Account object containing specified account number
17       private Account getAccount(int accountNumber)
18       {
19          // loop through accounts searching for matching account number
20          for (Account currentAccount : accounts)
21          {
22             // return current account if match found
23             if (currentAccount.getAccountNumber() == accountNumber)
24                return currentAccount;
25          } // end for
26
27          return null; // if no matching account was found, return null
28       } // end method getAccount
29
30       // determine whether user-specified account number and PIN match
31       // those of an account in the database
32       public boolean authenticateUser(int userAccountNumber, int userPIN)
33       {
34          // attempt to retrieve the account with the account number
35          Account userAccount = getAccount(userAccountNumber);
36
37          // if account exists, return result of Account method validatePIN
38          if (userAccount != null)
39             return userAccount.validatePIN(userPIN);
40          else
41             return false; // account number not found, so return false
42       } // end method authenticateUser
43
44       // return available balance of Account with specified account number
45       public double getAvailableBalance(int userAccountNumber)
46       {
47          return getAccount(userAccountNumber).getAvailableBalance();
48       } // end method getAvailableBalance
49
50       // return total balance of Account with specified account number
51       public double getTotalBalance(int userAccountNumber)
52       {
53          return getAccount(userAccountNumber).getTotalBalance();
54       } // end method getTotalBalance
55
56       // credit an amount to Account with specified account number
57       public void credit(int userAccountNumber, double amount)
58       {
59          getAccount(userAccountNumber).credit(amount);
60       } // end method credit
61
```

Fig. 24.19 | Class BankDatabase represents the bank's account information database. (Part 2 of 3.)

```
62        // debit an amount from Account with specified account number
63        public void debit(int userAccountNumber, double amount)
64        {
65           getAccount(userAccountNumber).debit(amount);
66        } // end method debit
67     } // end class BankDatabase
```

Fig. 24.19 | Class `BankDatabase` represents the bank's account information database. (Part 3 of 3.)

We determine one reference-type attribute for class `BankDatabase` based on its composition relationship with class `Account`. Recall from Fig. 24.9 that a `BankDatabase` is composed of zero or more objects of class `Account`. Line 6 implements attribute accounts—an array of `Account` objects—to implement this composition relationship. Class `BankDatabase` has a no-argument constructor (lines 9–14) that initializes accounts to contain a set of new `Account` objects. For the sake of testing the system, we declare accounts to hold just two array elements (line 11), which we instantiate as new `Account` objects with test data (lines 12–13). The `Account` constructor has four parameters—the account number, the PIN assigned to the account, the initial available balance and the initial total balance. Recall that class `BankDatabase` serves as an intermediary between class `ATM` and the actual `Account` objects that contain a user's account information. Thus, the methods of class `BankDatabase` do nothing more than invoke the corresponding methods of the `Account` object belonging to the current ATM user.

We include `private` utility method `getAccount` (lines 17–28) to allow the `BankDatabase` to obtain a reference to a particular `Account` within array accounts. To locate the user's `Account`, the `BankDatabase` compares the value returned by method `getAccountNumber` for each element of accounts to a specified account number until it finds a match. Lines 20–25 traverse the accounts array. If the account number of currentAccount equals the value of parameter accountNumber, the method immediately returns the currentAccount. If no account has the given account number, then line 27 returns `null`.

Method `authenticateUser` (lines 32–42) proves or disproves the identity of an ATM user. This method takes a user-specified account number and PIN as arguments and indicates whether they match the account number and PIN of an `Account` in the database. Line 35 calls method `getAccount`, which returns either an `Account` with userAccountNumber as its account number or `null` to indicate that userAccountNumber is invalid. If getAccount returns an `Account` object, line 39 returns the `boolean` value returned by that object's `validatePIN` method. `BankDatabase`'s `authenticateUser` method does not perform the PIN comparison itself—rather, it forwards userPIN to the `Account` object's `validatePIN` method to do so. The value returned by `Account` method `validatePIN` indicates whether the user-specified PIN matches the PIN of the user's `Account`, so method `authenticateUser` simply returns this value to the class's client (i.e., ATM).

`BankDatabase` trusts the ATM to invoke method `authenticateUser` and receive a return value of `true` before allowing the user to perform transactions. `BankDatabase` also trusts that each `Transaction` object created by the ATM contains the valid account number of the current authenticated user and that this is the account number passed to the remaining `BankDatabase` methods as argument userAccountNumber. Methods getAvailableBalance (lines 45–48), getTotalBalance (lines 51–54), credit (lines 57–60) and debit (lines 63–66) therefore simply retrieve the user's Account object with utility method getAccount, then invoke the appropriate Account method on that object. We know that the calls to getAccount from these methods will never return null, because userAccountNumber must refer to an existing Account. Methods getAvailableBalance and getTotalBalance return the values returned by the corresponding Account methods. Also, credit and debit simply redirect parameter amount to the Account methods they invoke.

24.4.8 Class Transaction

Class Transaction (Fig. 24.20) is an abstract superclass that represents the notion of an ATM transaction. It contains the common features of subclasses BalanceInquiry, Withdrawal and Deposit. This class expands upon the "skeleton" code first developed in Section 24.3. Line 4 declares this class to be abstract. Lines 6–8 declare the class's private attributes. Recall from the class diagram of Fig. 24.10 that class Transaction contains an attribute accountNumber (line 6) that indicates the account involved in the Transaction. We derive attributes screen (line 7) and bankDatabase (line 8) from class Transaction's associations modeled in Fig. 24.9—all transactions require access to the ATM's screen and the bank's database.

```java
1   // Transaction.java
2   // Abstract superclass Transaction represents an ATM transaction
3
4   public abstract class Transaction
5   {
6      private int accountNumber; // indicates account involved
7      private Screen screen; // ATM's screen
8      private BankDatabase bankDatabase; // account info database
9
10     // Transaction constructor invoked by subclasses using super()
11     public Transaction(int userAccountNumber, Screen atmScreen,
12        BankDatabase atmBankDatabase)
13     {
14        accountNumber = userAccountNumber;
15        screen = atmScreen;
16        bankDatabase = atmBankDatabase;
17     } // end Transaction constructor
18
19     // return account number
20     public int getAccountNumber()
21     {
22        return accountNumber;
23     } // end method getAccountNumber
24
25     // return reference to screen
26     public Screen getScreen()
27     {
28        return screen;
29     } // end method getScreen
30
```

Fig. 24.20 | Abstract superclass Transaction represents an ATM transaction. (Part 1 of 2.)

```
31       // return reference to bank database
32       public BankDatabase getBankDatabase()
33       {
34          return bankDatabase;
35       } // end method getBankDatabase
36
37       // perform the transaction (overridden by each subclass)
38       abstract public void execute();
39    } // end class Transaction
```

Fig. 24.20 | Abstract superclass Transaction represents an ATM transaction. (Part 2 of 2.)

Class Transaction has a constructor (lines 11–17) that takes as arguments the current user's account number and references to the ATM's screen and the bank's database. Because Transaction is an *abstract* class, this constructor will be called only by the constructors of the Transaction subclasses.

The class has three public *get* methods—getAccountNumber (lines 20–23), getScreen (lines 26–29) and getBankDatabase (lines 32–35). These are inherited by Transaction subclasses and used to gain access to class Transaction's private attributes.

Class Transaction also declares abstract method execute (line 38). It does not make sense to provide this method's implementation, because a generic transaction cannot be executed. So, we declare this method abstract and force each Transaction subclass to provide a concrete implementation that executes that particular type of transaction.

24.4.9 Class BalanceInquiry

Class BalanceInquiry (Fig. 24.21) extends Transaction and represents a balance-inquiry ATM transaction. BalanceInquiry does not have any attributes of its own, but it inherits Transaction attributes accountNumber, screen and bankDatabase, which are accessible through Transaction's public *get* methods. The BalanceInquiry constructor takes arguments corresponding to these attributes and simply forwards them to Transaction's constructor using super (line 10).

```
 1    // BalanceInquiry.java
 2    // Represents a balance inquiry ATM transaction
 3
 4    public class BalanceInquiry extends Transaction
 5    {
 6       // BalanceInquiry constructor
 7       public BalanceInquiry(int userAccountNumber, Screen atmScreen,
 8          BankDatabase atmBankDatabase)
 9       {
10          super(userAccountNumber, atmScreen, atmBankDatabase);
11       } // end BalanceInquiry constructor
12
13       // performs the transaction
14       @Override
15       public void execute()
16       {
```

Fig. 24.21 | Class BalanceInquiry represents a balance-inquiry ATM transaction. (Part 1 of 2.)

```
17        // get references to bank database and screen
18        BankDatabase bankDatabase = getBankDatabase();
19        Screen screen = getScreen();
20
21        // get the available balance for the account involved
22        double availableBalance =
23           bankDatabase.getAvailableBalance(getAccountNumber());
24
25        // get the total balance for the account involved
26        double totalBalance =
27           bankDatabase.getTotalBalance(getAccountNumber());
28
29        // display the balance information on the screen
30        screen.displayMessageLine("\nBalance Information:");
31        screen.displayMessage(" - Available balance: ");
32        screen.displayDollarAmount(availableBalance);
33        screen.displayMessage("\n - Total balance:    ");
34        screen.displayDollarAmount(totalBalance);
35        screen.displayMessageLine("");
36     } // end method execute
37  } // end class BalanceInquiry
```

Fig. 24.21 | Class BalanceInquiry represents a balance-inquiry ATM transaction. (Part 2 of 2.)

Class BalanceInquiry overrides Transaction's abstract method execute to provide a concrete implementation (lines 14–36) that performs the steps involved in a balance inquiry. Lines 18–19 get references to the bank database and the ATM's screen by invoking methods inherited from superclass Transaction. Lines 22–23 retrieve the available balance of the account involved by invoking method getAvailableBalance of bankDatabase. Line 23 uses inherited method getAccountNumber to get the account number of the current user, which it then passes to getAvailableBalance. Lines 26–27 retrieve the total balance of the current user's account. Lines 30–35 display the balance information on the ATM's screen. Recall that displayDollarAmount takes a double argument and outputs it to the screen formatted as a dollar amount. For example, if a user's availableBalance is 1000.5, line 32 outputs $1,000.50. Line 35 inserts a blank line of output to separate the balance information from subsequent output (i.e., the main menu repeated by class ATM after executing the BalanceInquiry).

24.4.10 Class Withdrawal

Class Withdrawal (Fig. 24.22) extends Transaction and represents a withdrawal ATM transaction. This class expands upon the "skeleton" code for this class developed in Fig. 24.12. Recall from the class diagram of Fig. 24.10 that class Withdrawal has one attribute, amount, which line 6 implements as an int field. Figure 24.9 models associations between class Withdrawal and classes Keypad and CashDispenser, for which lines 7–8 implement reference-type attributes keypad and cashDispenser, respectively. Line 11 declares a constant corresponding to the cancel menu option. We'll soon discuss how the class uses this constant.

```java
1    // Withdrawal.java
2    // Represents a withdrawal ATM transaction
3
4    public class Withdrawal extends Transaction
5    {
6       private int amount; // amount to withdraw
7       private Keypad keypad; // reference to keypad
8       private CashDispenser cashDispenser; // reference to cash dispenser
9
10      // constant corresponding to menu option to cancel
11      private final static int CANCELED = 6;
12
13      // Withdrawal constructor
14      public Withdrawal(int userAccountNumber, Screen atmScreen,
15         BankDatabase atmBankDatabase, Keypad atmKeypad,
16         CashDispenser atmCashDispenser)
17      {
18         // initialize superclass variables
19         super(userAccountNumber, atmScreen, atmBankDatabase);
20
21         // initialize references to keypad and cash dispenser
22         keypad = atmKeypad;
23         cashDispenser = atmCashDispenser;
24      } // end Withdrawal constructor
25
26      // perform transaction
27      @Override
28      public void execute()
29      {
30         boolean cashDispensed = false; // cash was not dispensed yet
31         double availableBalance; // amount available for withdrawal
32
33         // get references to bank database and screen
34         BankDatabase bankDatabase = getBankDatabase();
35         Screen screen = getScreen();
36
37         // loop until cash is dispensed or the user cancels
38         do
39         {
40            // obtain a chosen withdrawal amount from the user
41            amount = displayMenuOfAmounts();
42
43            // check whether user chose a withdrawal amount or canceled
44            if (amount != CANCELED)
45            {
46               // get available balance of account involved
47               availableBalance =
48                  bankDatabase.getAvailableBalance(getAccountNumber());
49
50               // check whether the user has enough money in the account
51               if (amount <= availableBalance)
52               {
```

Fig. 24.22 | Class Withdrawal represents a withdrawal ATM transaction. (Part 1 of 3.)

```
53              // check whether the cash dispenser has enough money
54              if (cashDispenser.isSufficientCashAvailable(amount))
55              {
56                 // update the account involved to reflect the withdrawal
57                 bankDatabase.debit(getAccountNumber(), amount);
58
59                 cashDispenser.dispenseCash(amount); // dispense cash
60                 cashDispensed = true; // cash was dispensed
61
62                 // instruct user to take cash
63                 screen.displayMessageLine("\nYour cash has been" +
64                    " dispensed. Please take your cash now.");
65              } // end if
66              else // cash dispenser does not have enough cash
67                 screen.displayMessageLine(
68                    "\nInsufficient cash available in the ATM." +
69                    "\n\nPlease choose a smaller amount.");
70           } // end if
71           else // not enough money available in user's account
72           {
73              screen.displayMessageLine(
74                 "\nInsufficient funds in your account." +
75                 "\n\nPlease choose a smaller amount.");
76           } // end else
77        } // end if
78        else // user chose cancel menu option
79        {
80           screen.displayMessageLine("\nCanceling transaction...");
81           return; // return to main menu because user canceled
82        } // end else
83     } while (!cashDispensed);
84
85  } // end method execute
86
87  // display a menu of withdrawal amounts and the option to cancel;
88  // return the chosen amount or 0 if the user chooses to cancel
89  private int displayMenuOfAmounts()
90  {
91     int userChoice = 0; // local variable to store return value
92
93     Screen screen = getScreen(); // get screen reference
94
95     // array of amounts to correspond to menu numbers
96     int[] amounts = { 0, 20, 40, 60, 100, 200 };
97
98     // loop while no valid choice has been made
99     while (userChoice == 0)
100    {
101       // display the withdrawal menu
102       screen.displayMessageLine("\nWithdrawal Menu:");
103       screen.displayMessageLine("1 - $20");
104       screen.displayMessageLine("2 - $40");
105       screen.displayMessageLine("3 - $60");
```

Fig. 24.22 | Class Withdrawal represents a withdrawal ATM transaction. (Part 2 of 3.)

```
106              screen.displayMessageLine("4 - $100");
107              screen.displayMessageLine("5 - $200");
108              screen.displayMessageLine("6 - Cancel transaction");
109              screen.displayMessage("\nChoose a withdrawal amount: ");
110
111              int input = keypad.getInput(); // get user input through keypad
112
113              // determine how to proceed based on the input value
114              switch (input)
115              {
116                 case 1: // if the user chose a withdrawal amount
117                 case 2: // (i.e., chose option 1, 2, 3, 4 or 5), return the
118                 case 3: // corresponding amount from amounts array
119                 case 4:
120                 case 5:
121                    userChoice = amounts[input]; // save user's choice
122                    break;
123                 case CANCELED: // the user chose to cancel
124                    userChoice = CANCELED; // save user's choice
125                    break;
126                 default: // the user did not enter a value from 1-6
127                    screen.displayMessageLine(
128                       "\nInvalid selection. Try again.");
129              } // end switch
130           } // end while
131
132           return userChoice; // return withdrawal amount or CANCELED
133        } // end method displayMenuOfAmounts
134     } // end class Withdrawal
```

Fig. 24.22 | Class `Withdrawal` represents a withdrawal ATM transaction. (Part 3 of 3.)

Class `Withdrawal`'s constructor (lines 14–24) has five parameters. It uses `super` to pass parameters `userAccountNumber`, `atmScreen` and `atmBankDatabase` to superclass `Transaction`'s constructor to set the attributes that `Withdrawal` inherits from `Transaction`. The constructor also takes references `atmKeypad` and `atmCashDispenser` as parameters and assigns them to reference-type attributes `keypad` and `cashDispenser`.

Class `Withdrawal` overrides `Transaction` method `execute` with a concrete implementation (lines 27–85) that performs the steps of a withdrawal. Line 30 declares and initializes a local `boolean` variable `cashDispensed`, which indicates whether cash has been dispensed (i.e., whether the transaction has completed successfully) and is initially `false`. Line 31 declares local `double` variable `availableBalance`, which will store the user's available balance during a withdrawal transaction. Lines 34–35 get references to the bank database and the ATM's screen by invoking methods inherited from superclass `Transaction`.

Lines 38–83 contain a do...while that executes its body until cash is dispensed (i.e., until `cashDispensed` becomes `true`) or until the user chooses to cancel (in which case, the loop terminates). We use this loop to continuously return the user to the start of the transaction if an error occurs (i.e., the requested withdrawal amount is greater than the user's available balance or greater than the amount of cash in the cash dispenser). Line 41 displays a menu of withdrawal amounts and obtains a user selection by calling `private` utility method `displayMenuOfAmounts` (declared in lines 89–133). This method displays the menu of amounts and returns either an `int` withdrawal amount or an `int` constant `CANCELED` to indicate that the user has chosen to cancel the transaction.

Method `displayMenuOfAmounts` (lines 89–133) first declares local variable user-Choice (initially 0) to store the value that the method will return (line 91). Line 93 gets a reference to the screen by calling method `getScreen` inherited from superclass Transaction. Line 96 declares an integer array of withdrawal amounts that correspond to the amounts displayed in the withdrawal menu. We ignore the first element in the array (index 0) because the menu has no option 0. The `while` statement at lines 99–130 repeats until userChoice takes on a value other than 0. We'll see shortly that this occurs when the user makes a valid selection from the menu. Lines 102–109 display the withdrawal menu on the screen and prompt the user to enter a choice. Line 111 obtains integer input through the keypad. The `switch` statement at lines 114–129 determines how to proceed based on the user's input. If the user selects a number between 1 and 5, line 121 sets userChoice to the value of the element in amounts at index input. For example, if the user enters 3 to withdraw $60, line 121 sets userChoice to the value of amounts[3] (i.e., 60). Line 122 terminates the `switch`. Variable userChoice no longer equals 0, so the `while` at lines 99–130 terminates and line 132 returns userChoice. If the user selects the cancel menu option, lines 124–125 execute, setting userChoice to CANCELED and causing the method to return this value. If the user does not enter a valid menu selection, lines 127–128 display an error message and the user is returned to the withdrawal menu.

Line 44 in method `execute` determines whether the user has selected a withdrawal amount or chosen to cancel. If the user cancels, lines 80–81 execute and display an appropriate message to the user before returning control to the calling method (i.e., ATM method performTransactions). If the user has chosen a withdrawal amount, lines 47–48 retrieve the available balance of the current user's Account and store it in variable availableBalance. Next, line 51 determines whether the selected amount is less than or equal to the user's available balance. If it's not, lines 73–75 display an appropriate error message. Control then continues to the end of the do...while, and the loop repeats because cashDispensed is still `false`. If the user's balance is high enough, the `if` statement at line 54 determines whether the cash dispenser has enough money to satisfy the withdrawal request by invoking the cashDispenser's isSufficientCashAvailable method. If this method returns `false`, lines 67–69 display an appropriate error message and the do...while repeats. If sufficient cash is available, then the requirements for the withdrawal are satisfied, and line 57 debits amount from the user's account in the database. Lines 59–60 then instruct the cash dispenser to dispense the cash to the user and set cashDispensed to `true`. Finally, lines 63–64 display a message to the user that cash has been dispensed. Because cashDispensed is now `true`, control continues after the do...while. No additional statements appear below the loop, so the method returns.

24.4.11 Class `Deposit`

Class `Deposit` (Fig. 24.23) extends `Transaction` and represents a deposit transaction. Recall from Fig. 24.10 that class `Deposit` has one attribute amount, which line 6 implements as an `int` field. Lines 7–8 create reference attributes keypad and depositSlot that implement the associations between class `Deposit` and classes `Keypad` and `DepositSlot` modeled in Fig. 24.9. Line 9 declares a constant `CANCELED` that corresponds to the value a user enters to cancel. We'll soon discuss how the class uses this constant.

```java
 1  // Deposit.java
 2  // Represents a deposit ATM transaction
 3
 4  public class Deposit extends Transaction
 5  {
 6     private double amount; // amount to deposit
 7     private Keypad keypad; // reference to keypad
 8     private DepositSlot depositSlot; // reference to deposit slot
 9     private final static int CANCELED = 0; // constant for cancel option
10
11     // Deposit constructor
12     public Deposit(int userAccountNumber, Screen atmScreen,
13        BankDatabase atmBankDatabase, Keypad atmKeypad,
14        DepositSlot atmDepositSlot)
15     {
16        // initialize superclass variables
17        super(userAccountNumber, atmScreen, atmBankDatabase);
18
19        // initialize references to keypad and deposit slot
20        keypad = atmKeypad;
21        depositSlot = atmDepositSlot;
22     } // end Deposit constructor
23
24     // perform transaction
25     @Override
26     public void execute()
27     {
28        BankDatabase bankDatabase = getBankDatabase(); // get reference
29        Screen screen = getScreen(); // get reference
30
31        amount = promptForDepositAmount(); // get deposit amount from user
32
33        // check whether user entered a deposit amount or canceled
34        if (amount != CANCELED)
35        {
36           // request deposit envelope containing specified amount
37           screen.displayMessage(
38              "\nPlease insert a deposit envelope containing ");
39           screen.displayDollarAmount(amount);
40           screen.displayMessageLine(".");
41
42           // receive deposit envelope
43           boolean envelopeReceived = depositSlot.isEnvelopeReceived();
44
45           // check whether deposit envelope was received
46           if (envelopeReceived)
47           {
48              screen.displayMessageLine("\nYour envelope has been " +
49                 "received.\nNOTE: The money just deposited will not " +
50                 "be available until we verify the amount of any " +
51                 "enclosed cash and your checks clear.");
52
```

Fig. 24.23 | Class Deposit represents a deposit ATM transaction. (Part 1 of 2.)

```
53                  // credit account to reflect the deposit
54                  bankDatabase.credit(getAccountNumber(), amount);
55              } // end if
56              else // deposit envelope not received
57              {
58                  screen.displayMessageLine("\nYou did not insert an " +
59                      "envelope, so the ATM has canceled your transaction.");
60              } // end else
61          } // end if
62          else // user canceled instead of entering amount
63          {
64              screen.displayMessageLine("\nCanceling transaction...");
65          } // end else
66      } // end method execute
67
68      // prompt user to enter a deposit amount in cents
69      private double promptForDepositAmount()
70      {
71          Screen screen = getScreen(); // get reference to screen
72
73          // display the prompt
74          screen.displayMessage("\nPlease enter a deposit amount in " +
75              "CENTS (or 0 to cancel): ");
76          int input = keypad.getInput(); // receive input of deposit amount
77
78          // check whether the user canceled or entered a valid amount
79          if (input == CANCELED)
80              return CANCELED;
81          else
82          {
83              return (double) input / 100; // return dollar amount
84          } // end else
85      } // end method promptForDepositAmount
86  } // end class Deposit
```

Fig. 24.23 | Class Deposit represents a deposit ATM transaction. (Part 2 of 2.)

Like Withdrawal, class Deposit contains a constructor (lines 12–22) that passes three parameters to superclass Transaction's constructor. The constructor also has parameters atmKeypad and atmDepositSlot, which it assigns to corresponding attributes (lines 20–21).

Method execute (lines 25–66) overrides the abstract version in superclass Transaction with a concrete implementation that performs the steps required in a deposit transaction. Lines 28–29 get references to the database and the screen. Line 31 prompts the user to enter a deposit amount by invoking private utility method promptForDepositAmount (declared in lines 69–85) and sets attribute amount to the value returned. Method promptForDepositAmount asks the user to enter a deposit amount as an integer number of cents (because the ATM's keypad does not contain a decimal point; this is consistent with many real ATMs) and returns the double value representing the dollar amount to be deposited.

Line 71 in method promptForDepositAmount gets a reference to the ATM's screen. Lines 74–75 display a message asking the user to input a deposit amount as a number of cents or "0" to cancel the transaction. Line 76 receives the user's input from the keypad. Lines 79–84 determine whether the user has entered a real deposit amount or chosen to cancel. If the latter, line 80 returns the constant CANCELED. Otherwise, line 83 returns the deposit amount after converting from the number of cents to a dollar amount by casting input to a double, then dividing by 100. For example, if the user enters 125 as the number of cents, line 83 returns 125.0 divided by 100, or 1.25—125 cents is $1.25.

Lines 34–65 in method execute determine whether the user has chosen to cancel the transaction instead of entering a deposit amount. If the user cancels, line 64 displays an appropriate message, and the method returns. If the user enters a deposit amount, lines 37–40 instruct the user to insert a deposit envelope with the correct amount. Recall that Screen method displayDollarAmount outputs a double formatted as a dollar amount.

Line 43 sets a local boolean variable to the value returned by depositSlot's isEnvelopeReceived method, indicating whether a deposit envelope has been received. Recall that we coded method isEnvelopeReceived (lines 8–11 of Fig. 24.17) to always return true, because we're simulating the functionality of the deposit slot and assume that the user always inserts an envelope. However, we code method execute of class Deposit to test for the possibility that the user does not insert an envelope—good software engineering demands that programs account for *all* possible return values. Thus, class Deposit is prepared for future versions of isEnvelopeReceived that could return false. Lines 48–54 execute if the deposit slot receives an envelope. Lines 48–51 display an appropriate message to the user. Line 54 then credits the deposit amount to the user's account in the database. Lines 58–59 will execute if the deposit slot does not receive a deposit envelope. In this case, we display a message to the user stating that the ATM has canceled the transaction. The method then returns without modifying the user's account.

24.4.12 Class ATMCaseStudy

Class ATMCaseStudy (Fig. 24.24) is a simple class that allows us to start, or "turn on," the ATM and test the implementation of our ATM system model. Class ATMCaseStudy's main method (lines 7–11) does nothing more than instantiate a new ATM object named theATM (line 9) and invoke its run method (line 10) to start the ATM.

```
1   // ATMCaseStudy.java
2   // Driver program for the ATM case study
3
4   public class ATMCaseStudy
5   {
6      // main method creates and runs the ATM
7      public static void main(String[] args)
8      {
9         ATM theATM = new ATM();
10        theATM.run();
11     } // end main
12  } // end class ATMCaseStudy
```

Fig. 24.24 | ATMCaseStudy.java starts the ATM.

24.5 Wrap-Up

In this chapter, you used inheritance to tune the design of the ATM software system, and you fully implemented the ATM in Java. Congratulations on completing the entire ATM case study! We hope you found this experience to be valuable and that it reinforced many of the object-oriented programming concepts that you've learned. In the next chapter, we take a deeper look at graphical user interfaces (GUIs).

Answers to Self-Review Exercises

24.1   True. The minus sign (–) indicates private visibility.

24.2   b.

24.3   The design for class Keypad yields the code in Fig. 24.25. Recall that class Keypad has no attributes for the moment, but attributes may become apparent as we continue the implementation. Also, if we were designing a real ATM, method getInput would need to interact with the ATM's keypad hardware. We'll actually read input from the keyboard of a personal computer when we write the complete Java code in Section 24.4.

```
1   // Class Keypad represents an ATM's keypad
2   public class Keypad
3   {
4      // no attributes have been specified yet
5
6      // no-argument constructor
7      public Keypad()
8      {
9      } // end no-argument Keypad constructor
10
11     // operations
12     public int getInput()
13     {
14     } // end method getInput
15  } // end class Keypad
```

Fig. 24.25 | Java code for class Keypad based on Figs. 24.1–24.2.

24.4   b.

24.5   False. The UML requires that we italicize abstract class names and method names.

24.6   The design for class Transaction yields the code in Fig. 24.26. The bodies of the class constructor and methods are completed in Section 24.4. When fully implemented, methods getScreen and getBankDatabase will return superclass Transaction's private reference attributes screen and bankDatabase, respectively. These methods allow the Transaction subclasses to access the ATM's screen and interact with the bank's database.

```
1   // Abstract class Transaction represents an ATM transaction
2   public abstract class Transaction
3   {
```

Fig. 24.26 | Java code for class Transaction based on Figs. 24.9 and 24.10. (Part 1 of 2.)

```
4      // attributes
5      private int accountNumber; // indicates account involved
6      private Screen screen; // ATM's screen
7      private BankDatabase bankDatabase; // account info database
8
9      // no-argument constructor invoked by subclasses using super()
10     public Transaction()
11     {
12     } // end no-argument Transaction constructor
13
14     // return account number
15     public int getAccountNumber()
16     {
17     } // end method getAccountNumber
18
19     // return reference to screen
20     public Screen getScreen()
21     {
22     } // end method getScreen
23
24     // return reference to bank database
25     public BankDatabase getBankDatabase()
26     {
27     } // end method getBankDatabase
28
29     // abstract method overridden by subclasses
30     public abstract void execute();
31  } // end class Transaction
```

Fig. 24.26 | Java code for class `Transaction` based on Figs. 24.9 and 24.10. (Part 2 of 2.)

Operator Precedence Chart

Operators are shown in decreasing order of precedence from top to bottom (Fig. A.1).

Operator	Description	Associativity
++ --	unary postfix increment unary postfix decrement	right to left
++ -- + - ! ~ (*type*)	unary prefix increment unary prefix decrement unary plus unary minus unary logical negation unary bitwise complement unary cast	right to left
* / %	multiplication division remainder	left to right
+ -	addition or string concatenation subtraction	left to right
<< >> >>>	left shift signed right shift unsigned right shift	left to right
< <= > >= instanceof	less than less than or equal to greater than greater than or equal to type comparison	left to right

Fig. A.1 | Operator precedence chart. (Part 1 of 2.)

Operator	Description	Associativity
== !=	is equal to is not equal to	left to right
&	bitwise AND boolean logical AND	left to right
^	bitwise exclusive OR boolean logical exclusive OR	left to right
|	bitwise inclusive OR boolean logical inclusive OR	left to right
&&	conditional AND	left to right
||	conditional OR	left to right
?:	conditional	right to left
= += -= *= /= %= &= ^= |= <<= >>= >>>=	assignment addition assignment subtraction assignment multiplication assignment division assignment remainder assignment bitwise AND assignment bitwise exclusive OR assignment bitwise inclusive OR assignment bitwise left-shift assignment bitwise signed-right-shift assignment bitwise unsigned-right-shift assignment	right to left

Fig. A.1 | Operator precedence chart. (Part 2 of 2.)

B

ASCII Character Set

Fig. B.1 | ASCII character set.

	0	1	2	3	4	5	6	7	8	9
0	nul	soh	stx	etx	eot	enq	ack	bel	bs	ht
1	nl	vt	ff	cr	so	si	dle	dc1	dc2	dc3
2	dc4	nak	syn	etb	can	em	sub	esc	fs	gs
3	rs	us	sp	!	"	#	$	%	&	'
4	(	)	*	+	,	-	.	/	0	1
5	2	3	4	5	6	7	8	9	:	;
6	<	=	>	?	@	A	B	C	D	E
7	F	G	H	I	J	K	L	M	N	O
8	P	Q	R	S	T	U	V	W	X	Y
9	Z	[	\	]	^	_	'	a	b	c
10	d	e	f	g	h	i	j	k	l	m
11	n	o	p	q	r	s	t	u	v	w
12	x	y	z	{	|	}	~	del		

The digits at the left of the table are the left digits of the decimal equivalents (0–127) of the character codes, and the digits at the top of the table are the right digits of the character codes. For example, the character code for "F" is 70, and the character code for "&" is 38.

Most users of this book are interested in the ASCII character set used to represent English characters on many computers. The ASCII character set is a subset of the Unicode character set used by Java to represent characters from most of the world's languages. For more information on the Unicode character set, see the web bonus Appendix H.

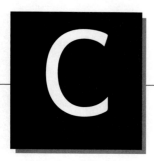

Keywords and Reserved Words

Java Keywords				
abstract	assert	boolean	break	byte
case	catch	char	class	continue
default	do	double	else	enum
extends	final	finally	float	for
if	implements	import	instanceof	int
interface	long	native	new	package
private	protected	public	return	short
static	strictfp	super	switch	synchronized
this	throw	throws	transient	try
void	volatile	while		

Keywords that are not currently used

const	goto

Fig. C.1 | Java keywords.

Java also contains the reserved words true and false, which are boolean literals, and null, which is the literal that represents a reference to nothing. Like keywords, these reserved words cannot be used as identifiers.

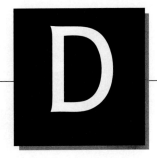

Primitive Types

Type	Size in bits	Values	Standard
boolean		true or false	
[*Note:* A boolean's representation is specific to the Java Virtual Machine on each platform.]			
char	16	'\u0000' to '\uFFFF' (0 to 65535)	(ISO Unicode character set)
byte	8	-128 to $+127$ (-2^7 to $2^7 - 1$)	
short	16	$-32,768$ to $+32,767$ (-2^{15} to $2^{15} - 1$)	
int	32	$-2,147,483,648$ to $+2,147,483,647$ (-2^{31} to $2^{31} - 1$)	
long	64	$-9,223,372,036,854,775,808$ to $+9,223,372,036,854,775,807$ (-2^{63} to $2^{63} - 1$)	
float	32	*Negative range:* $-3.4028234663852886E+38$ to $-1.40129846432481707e-45$ *Positive range:* $1.40129846432481707e-45$ to $3.4028234663852886E+38$	(IEEE 754 floating point)
double	64	*Negative range:* $-1.7976931348623157E+308$ to $-4.94065645841246544e-324$ *Positive range:* $4.94065645841246544e-324$ to $1.7976931348623157E+308$	(IEEE 754 floating point)

Fig. D.1 | Java primitive types.

You can use underscores to make numeric literal values more readable. For example, 1_000_000 is equivalent to 1000000.

For more information on IEEE 754 visit http://grouper.ieee.org/groups/754/. For more information on Unicode, see Appendix H.

E

Using the Debugger

Objectives

In this appendix you'll:

- Set breakpoints to debug applications.

- Use the **run** command to run an application through the debugger.

- Use the **stop** command to set a breakpoint.

- Use the **cont** command to continue execution.

- Use the **print** command to evaluate expressions.

- Use the **set** command to change variable values during program execution.

- Use the **step**, **step up** and **next** commands to control execution.

- Use the **watch** command to see how a field is modified during program execution.

- Use the **clear** command to list breakpoints or remove a breakpoint.

E.1 Introduction

In Chapter 2, you learned that there are two types of errors—syntax errors and logic errors—and you learned how to eliminate syntax errors from your code. Logic errors do not prevent the application from compiling successfully, but they do cause an application to produce erroneous results when it runs. The JDK includes software called a **debugger** that allows you to monitor the execution of your applications so you can locate and remove logic errors. The debugger will be one of your most important application development tools. Many IDEs provide their own debuggers similar to the one included in the JDK or provide a graphical user interface to the JDK's debugger.

This appendix demonstrates key features of the JDK's debugger using command-line applications that receive no input from the user. The same debugger features discussed here can be used to debug applications that take user input, but debugging such applications requires a slightly more complex setup. To focus on the debugger features, we've opted to demonstrate the debugger with simple command-line applications involving no user input. For more information on the Java debugger visit http://docs.oracle.com/javase/7/docs/technotes/tools/windows/jdb.html.

E.2 Breakpoints and the run, stop, cont and print Commands

We begin our study of the debugger by investigating **breakpoints**, which are markers that can be set at any executable line of code. When application execution reaches a breakpoint, execution pauses, allowing you to examine the values of variables to help determine whether logic errors exist. For example, you can examine the value of a variable that stores the result of a calculation to determine whether the calculation was performed correctly. Setting a breakpoint at a line of code that is not executable (such as a comment) causes the debugger to display an error message.

To illustrate the features of the debugger, we use application AccountTest (Fig. E.1), which creates and manipulates an object of class Account (Fig. 3.8). Execution of AccountTest begins in main (lines 7–24). Line 9 creates an Account object with an initial balance of $50.00. Recall that Account's constructor accepts one argument, which specifies the Account's initial balance. Lines 12–13 output the initial account balance using Account method getBalance. Line 15 declares and initializes a local variable depositAmount. Lines 17–19 then print depositAmount and add it to the Account's balance using its credit method. Finally, lines 22–23 display the new balance. [*Note:* The Appendix E examples directory contains a copy of Account.java identical to the one in Fig. 3.8.]

```
 1   // Fig. E.1: AccountTest.java
 2   // Create and manipulate an Account object.
 3
 4   public class AccountTest
 5   {
 6      // main method begins execution
 7      public static void main(String[] args)
 8      {
 9         Account account = new Account("Jane Green", 50.00);
10
11         // display initial balance of Account object
12         System.out.printf("initial account balance: $%.2f%n",
13            account.getBalance());
14
15         double depositAmount = 25.0; // deposit amount
16
17         System.out.printf("%nadding %.2f to account balance%n%n",
18            depositAmount);
19         account.deposit(depositAmount); // add to account balance
20
21         // display new balance
22         System.out.printf("new account balance: $%.2f%n",
23            account.getBalance());
24      }
25   } // end class AccountTest
```

```
initial account balance: $50.00

adding 25.00 to account balance

new account balance: $75.00
```

Fig. E.1 | Create and manipulate an Account object.

In the following steps, you'll use breakpoints and various debugger commands to examine the value of the variable depositAmount declared in AccountTest (Fig. E.1).

1. *Opening the Command Prompt window and changing directories.* Open the **Command Prompt** window by selecting **Start > Programs > Accessories > Command Prompt**. Change to the directory containing the Appendix E examples by typing cd C:\examples\debugger [*Note:* If your examples are in a different directory, use that directory here.]

2. *Compiling the application for debugging.* The Java debugger works only with .class files that were compiled with the -g compiler option, which generates information that is used by the debugger to help you debug your applications. Compile the application with the -g command-line option by typing javac -g AccountTest.java Account.java. Recall from Chapter 3 that this command compiles both AccountTest.java and Account.java. The command java -g *.java compiles all of the working directory's .java files for debugging.

3. *Starting the debugger.* In the **Command Prompt**, type **jdb** (Fig. E.2). This command will start the Java debugger and enable you to use its features. [*Note:* We modified the colors of our **Command Prompt** window for readability.]

```
C:\examples\debugger>javac -g AccountTest.java Account.java

C:\examples\debugger>jdb
Initializing jdb ...
>
```

Fig. E.2 | Starting the Java debugger.

4. *Running an application in the debugger.* Run the AccountTest application through the debugger by typing **run** AccountTest (Fig. E.3). If you do not set any breakpoints before running your application in the debugger, the application will run just as it would using the java command.

```
C:\examples\debugger>jdb
Initializing jdb ...
> run AccountTest
run  AccountTest
Set uncaught java.lang.Throwable
Set deferred uncaught java.lang.Throwable
>
VM Started: initial account balance: $50.00

adding 25.00 to account balance

new account balance: $75.00

The application exited
```

Fig. E.3 | Running the AccountTest application through the debugger.

5. *Restarting the debugger.* To make proper use of the debugger, you must set at least one breakpoint before running the application. Restart the debugger by typing jdb.

6. *Inserting breakpoints in Java.* You set a breakpoint at a specific line of code in your application. The line numbers used in these steps are from the source code in Fig. E.1. Set a breakpoint at line 12 in the source code by typing stop at AccountTest:12 (Fig. E.4). The **stop command** inserts a breakpoint at the line number specified after the command. You can set as many breakpoints as necessary. Set another breakpoint at line 19 by typing stop at AccountTest:19 (Fig. E.4). When the application runs, it suspends execution at any line that contains a breakpoint. The application is said to be in **break mode** when the debugger pauses the application's execution. Breakpoints can be set even after the debugging process has begun. The debugger command stop in, followed by a class name, a period and a method name (e.g., stop in Account.credit) instructs the debugger to set a breakpoint at the first executable statement in the specified method. The debugger pauses execution when program control enters the method.

```
C:\examples\debugger>jdb
Initializing jdb ...
> stop at AccountTest:12
Deferring breakpoint AccountTest:12.
It will be set after the class is loaded.
> stop at AccountTest:19
Deferring breakpoint AccountTest:19.
It will be set after the class is loaded.
>
```

Fig. E.4 | Setting breakpoints at lines 12 and 19.

7. *Running the application and beginning the debugging process.* Type run AccountTest to execute the application and begin the debugging process (Fig. E.5). The debugger prints text indicating that breakpoints were set at lines 12 and 19. It calls each breakpoint a "deferred breakpoint" because each was set before the application began running in the debugger. The application pauses when execution reaches the breakpoint on line 12. At this point, the debugger notifies you that a breakpoint has been reached and it displays the source code at that line (12). That line of code is the next statement that will execute.

```
It will be set after the class is loaded.
>run AccountTest
run  AccountTest
Set uncaught java.lang.Throwable
Set deferred uncaught java.lang.Throwable
>
VM Started: Set deferred breakpoint AccountTest:19
Set deferred breakpoint AccountTest:12

Breakpoint hit: "thread=main", AccountTest.main(), line=12 bci=13
12          System.out.printf("initial account balance: $%.2f%n",

main[1]
```

Fig. E.5 | Restarting the AccountTest application.

8. *Using the cont command to resume execution.* Type cont. The **cont command** causes the application to continue running until the next breakpoint is reached (line 19), at which point the debugger notifies you (Fig. E.6). AccountTest's normal output appears between messages from the debugger.

```
main[1] cont
> initial account balance: $50.00

adding 25.00 to account balance

Breakpoint hit: "thread=main", AccountTest.main(), line=19 bci=60
19          account.deposit(depositAmount); // add to account balance

main[1]
```

Fig. E.6 | Execution reaches the second breakpoint.

9. *Examining a variable's value.* Type print depositAmount to display the current value stored in the depositAmount variable (Fig. E.7). The **print command** allows you to peek inside the computer at the value of one of your variables. This command will help you find and eliminate logic errors in your code. The value displayed is 25.0—the value assigned to depositAmount in line 15 of Fig. E.1.

```
main[1] print depositAmount
 depositAmount = 25.0
main[1]
```

Fig. E.7 | Examining the value of variable depositAmount.

10. *Continuing application execution.* Type cont to continue the application's execution. There are no more breakpoints, so the application is no longer in break mode. The application continues executing and eventually terminates (Fig. E.8). The debugger will stop when the application ends.

```
main[1] cont
> new account balance: $75.00

The application exited
```

Fig. E.8 | Continuing application execution and exiting the debugger.

E.3 The print and set Commands

In the preceding section, you learned how to use the debugger's print command to examine the value of a variable during program execution. In this section, you'll learn how to use the print command to examine the value of more complex expressions. You'll also learn the **set command**, which allows the programmer to assign new values to variables.

For this section, we assume that you've followed *Step 1* and *Step 2* in Section E.2 to open the **Command Prompt** window, change to the directory containing the Appendix E examples (e.g., C:\examples\debugger) and compile the AccountTest application (and class Account) for debugging.

1. *Starting debugging.* In the **Command Prompt**, type jdb to start the Java debugger.

2. *Inserting a breakpoint.* Set a breakpoint at line 19 in the source code by typing stop at AccountTest:19.

3. *Running the application and reaching a breakpoint.* Type run AccountTest to begin the debugging process (Fig. E.9). This will cause AccountTest's main to execute until the breakpoint at line 19 is reached. This suspends application execution and switches the application into break mode. At this point, the statements in lines 9–13 created an Account object and printed the initial balance of the Account obtained by calling its getBalance method. The statement in line 15 (Fig. E.1) declared and initialized local variable depositAmount to 25.0. The statement in line 19 is the next statement that will execute.

```
C:\examples\debugger>jdb
Initializing jdb ...
> stop at AccountTest:19
Deferring breakpoint AccountTest:19.
It will be set after the class is loaded.
> run AccountTest
run  AccountTest
Set uncaught java.lang.Throwable
Set deferred uncaught java.lang.Throwable
>
VM Started: Set deferred breakpoint AccountTest:19
initial account balance: $50.00

adding 25.00 to account balance

Breakpoint hit: "thread=main", AccountTest.main(), line=19 bci=60
19              account.deposit(depositAmount); // add to account balance

main[1]
```

Fig. E.9 | Application execution suspended when debugger reaches the breakpoint at line 19.

4. *Evaluating arithmetic and boolean expressions.* Recall from Section E.2 that once the application has entered break mode, you can explore the values of the application's variables using the debugger's print command. You can also use the print command to evaluate arithmetic and boolean expressions. In the **Command Prompt** window, type print depositAmount - 2.0. The print command returns the value 23.0 (Fig. E.10). However, this command does not actually change the value of depositAmount. In the **Command Prompt** window, type print depositAmount == 23.0. Expressions containing the == symbol are treated as boolean expressions. The value returned is false (Fig. E.10) because depositAmount does not currently contain the value 23.0—depositAmount is still 25.0.

```
main[1] print depositAmount - 2.0
 depositAmount - 2.0 = 23.0
main[1] print depositAmount == 23.0
 depositAmount == 23.0 = false
main[1]
```

Fig. E.10 | Examining the values of an arithmetic and boolean expression.

5. *Modifying values.* The debugger allows you to change the values of variables during the application's execution. This can be valuable for experimenting with different values and for locating logic errors in applications. You can use the debugger's set command to change the value of a variable. Type set depositAmount = 75.0. The debugger changes the value of depositAmount and displays its new value (Fig. E.11).

```
main[1] set depositAmount = 75.0
 depositAmount = 75.0 = 75.0
main[1]
```

Fig. E.11 | Modifying values.

6. *Viewing the application result.* Type cont to continue application execution. Line 19 of AccountTest (Fig. E.1) executes, passing depositAmount to Account method credit. Method main then displays the new balance. The result is $125.00 (Fig. E.12). This shows that the preceding step changed the value of depositAmount from its initial value (25.0) to 75.0.

```
main[1] cont
> new account balance: $125.00

The application exited

C:\examples\debugger>
```

Fig. E.12 | Output showing new account balance based on altered value of depositAmount.

E.4 Controlling Execution Using the step, step up and next Commands

Sometimes you'll need to execute an application line by line to find and fix errors. Walking through a portion of your application this way can help you verify that a method's code executes correctly. In this section, you'll learn how to use the debugger for this task. The commands you learn in this section allow you to execute a method line by line, execute all the statements of a method at once or execute only the remaining statements of a method (if you've already executed some statements within the method).

Once again, we assume you're working in the directory containing the Appendix E examples and have compiled for debugging with the -g compiler option.

1. *Starting the debugger.* Start the debugger by typing jdb.

2. *Setting a breakpoint.* Type stop at AccountTest:19 to set a breakpoint at line 19.

3. *Running the application.* Run the application by typing run AccountTest. After the application displays its two output messages, the debugger indicates that the breakpoint has been reached and displays the code at line 19. The debugger and application then pause and wait for the next command to be entered.

4. *Using the step command.* The **step command** executes the next statement in the application. If the next statement to execute is a method call, control transfers to the called method. The step command enables you to enter a method and study the individual statements of that method. For instance, you can use the print and set commands to view and modify the variables within the method. You'll now use the step command to enter the credit method of class Account (Fig. 3.8) by typing step (Fig. E.13). The debugger indicates that the step has

been completed and displays the next executable statement—in this case, line 21 of class `Account` (Fig. 3.8).

```
main[1] step
>
Step completed: "thread=main", Account.deposit(), line=24 bci=0
24              if (depositAmount > 0.0) // if the depositAmount is valid

main[1]
```

Fig. E.13 | Stepping into the `credit` method.

5. *Using the step up command.* After you've stepped into the `credit` method, type **step up**. This command executes the remaining statements in the method and returns control to the place where the method was called. The `credit` method contains only one statement to add the method's parameter `amount` to instance variable `balance`. The `step up` command executes this statement, then pauses before line 22 in `AccountTest`. Thus, the next action to occur will be to print the new account balance (Fig. E.14). In lengthy methods, you may want to look at a few key lines of code, then continue debugging the caller's code. The `step up` command is useful for situations in which you do not want to continue stepping through the entire method line by line.

```
main[1] step up
>
Step completed: "thread=main", AccountTest.main(), line=22 bci=65
22              System.out.printf("new account balance: $%.2f%n",

main[1]
```

Fig. E.14 | Stepping out of a method.

6. *Using the cont command to continue execution.* Enter the `cont` command (Fig. E.15) to continue execution. The statement at lines 22–23 executes, displaying the new balance, then the application and the debugger terminate.

```
main[1] cont
> new account balance: $75.00

The application exited

C:\examples\debugger>
```

Fig. E.15 | Continuing execution of the `AccountTest` application.

7. *Restarting the debugger.* Restart the debugger by typing `jdb`.

8. *Setting a breakpoint.* Breakpoints persist only until the end of the debugging session in which they're set—once the debugger exits, all breakpoints are removed.

(In Section E.6, you'll learn how to manually clear a breakpoint before the end of the debugging session.) Thus, the breakpoint set for line 19 in *Step 2* no longer exists upon restarting the debugger in *Step 7*. To reset the breakpoint at line 19, once again type `stop at AccountTest:19`.

9. *Running the application.* Type `run AccountTest` to run the application. As in *Step 3*, `AccountTest` runs until the breakpoint at line 19 is reached, then the debugger pauses and waits for the next command.

10. *Using the next command.* Type **next**. This command behaves like the `step` command, except when the next statement to execute contains a method call. In that case, the called method executes in its entirety and the application advances to the next executable line after the method call (Fig. E.16). Recall from *Step 4* that the `step` command would enter the called method. In this example, the `next` command causes `Account` method `credit` to execute, then the debugger pauses at line 22 in `AccountTest`.

```
main[1] next
>
Step completed: "thread=main", AccountTest.main(), line=22 bci=65
22            System.out.printf("new account balance: $%.2f%n",

main[1]
```

Fig. E.16 | Stepping over a method call.

11. *Using the exit command.* Use the **exit command** to end the debugging session (Fig. E.17). This command causes the `AccountTest` application to immediately terminate rather than execute the remaining statements in `main`. When debugging some types of applications (e.g., GUI applications), the application continues to execute even after the debugging session ends.

```
main[1] exit

C:\examples\debugger>
```

Fig. E.17 | Exiting the debugger.

E.5 The watch Command

In this section, we present the **watch command**, which tells the debugger to watch a field. When that field is about to change, the debugger will notify you. In this section, you'll learn how to use the `watch` command to see how the `Account` object's field `balance` is modified during the execution of the `AccountTest` application.

As in the preceding two sections, we assume that you've followed *Step 1* and *Step 2* in Section E.2 to open the **Command Prompt**, change to the correct examples directory and compile classes `AccountTest` and `Account` for debugging (i.e., with the `-g` compiler option).

1. *Starting the debugger.* Start the debugger by typing jdb.

2. *Watching a class's field.* Set a watch on Account's balance field by typing watch Account.balance (Fig. E.18). You can set a watch on any field during execution of the debugger. Whenever the value in a field is about to change, the debugger enters break mode and notifies you that the value will change. Watches can be placed only on fields, not on local variables.

```
C:\examples\debugger>jdb
Initializing jdb ...
> watch Account.balance
Deferring watch modification of Account.balance.
It will be set after the class is loaded.
>
```

Fig. E.18 | Setting a watch on Account's balance field.

3. *Running the application.* Run the application with the command run Account-Test. The debugger will now notify you that field balance's value will change (Fig. E.19). When the application begins, an instance of Account is created with an initial balance of $50.00 and a reference to the Account object is assigned to the local variable account (line 9, Fig. E.1). Recall from Fig. 3.8 that when the constructor for this object runs, if parameter initialBalance is greater than 0.0, instance variable balance is assigned the value of parameter initialBalance. The debugger notifies you that the value of balance will be set to 50.0.

4. *Adding money to the account.* Type cont to continue executing the application. The application executes normally before reaching the code on line 19 of Fig. E.1 that calls Account method credit to raise the Account object's balance by a specified amount. The debugger notifies you that instance variable balance will change (Fig. E.20). Although line 19 of class AccountTest calls method deposit, line 25 in Account's method deposit actually changes the value of balance.

```
> run AccountTest
run  AccountTest
Set uncaught java.lang.Throwable
Set deferred uncaught java.lang.Throwable
>
VM Started: Set deferred watch modification of Account.balance

Field (Account.balance) is 0.0, will be 50.0: "thread=main", Acount.<init>(),
line=18 bci=17
18                this.balance = balance; // assign to instance variable balance

main[1]
```

Fig. E.19 | AccountTest application stops when account is created and its balance field will be modified.

```
main[1] cont
> initial account balance: $50.00

adding 25.00 to account balance
Field (Account.balance) is 50.0, will be 75.0: "thread=main",
Account.deposit(), line=25 bci=13

25                balance = balance + depositAmount; // add it to the balance

main[1]
```

Fig. E.20 | Changing the value of `balance` by calling `Account` method `credit`.

5. *Continuing execution.* Type cont—the application will finish executing because the application does not attempt any additional changes to `balance` (Fig. E.21).

```
main[1] cont
> new account balance: $75.00

The application exited

C:\examples\debugger>
```

Fig. E.21 | Continuing execution of `AccountTest`.

6. *Restarting the debugger and resetting the watch on the variable.* Type jdb to restart the debugger. Once again, set a watch on the `Account` instance variable `balance` by typing the watch `Account.balance`, then type run `AccountTest` to run the application.

7. *Removing the watch on the field.* Suppose you want to watch a field for only part of a program's execution. You can remove the debugger's watch on variable `balance` by typing **unwatch** `Account.balance` (Fig. E.22). Type cont—the application will finish executing without reentering break mode.

```
main[1] unwatch Account.balance
Removed: watch modification of Account.balance
main[1] cont
> initial account balance: $50.00

adding 25.00 to account balance

new account balance: $75.00

The application exited

C:\examples\debugger>
```

Fig. E.22 | Removing the watch on variable `balance`.

E.6 The clear Command

In the preceding section, you learned to use the unwatch command to remove a watch on a field. The debugger also provides the clear command to remove a breakpoint from an application. You'll often need to debug applications containing repetitive actions, such as a loop. You may want to examine the values of variables during several, but possibly not all, of the loop's iterations. If you set a breakpoint in the body of a loop, the debugger will pause before each execution of the line containing a breakpoint. After determining that the loop is working properly, you may want to remove the breakpoint and allow the remaining iterations to proceed normally. In this section, we use the compound interest application in Fig. 5.6 to demonstrate how the debugger behaves when you set a breakpoint in the body of a for statement and how to remove a breakpoint in the middle of a debugging session.

1. *Opening the* Command Prompt *window, changing directories and compiling the application for debugging.* Open the **Command Prompt** window, then change to the directory containing the Appendix E examples. For your convenience, we've provided a copy of the Interest.java file in this directory. Compile the application for debugging by typing javac -g Interest.java.

2. *Starting the debugger and setting breakpoints.* Start the debugger by typing jdb. Set breakpoints at lines 13 and 22 of class Interest by typing stop at Interest:13, then stop at Interest:22.

3. *Running the application.* Run the application by typing run Interest. The application executes until reaching the breakpoint at line 13 (Fig. E.23).

4. *Continuing execution.* Type cont to continue—the application executes line 13, printing the column headings "Year" and "Amount on deposit". Line 13 appears before the for statement at lines 16–23 in Interest (Fig. 5.6) and thus executes only once. Execution continues past line 13 until the breakpoint at line 22 is reached during the first iteration of the for statement (Fig. E.24).

5. *Examining variable values.* Type print year to examine the current value of variable year (i.e., the for's control variable). Print the value of variable amount too (Fig. E.25).

```
It will be set after the class is loaded.
> run Interest
run  Interest
Set uncaught java.lang.Throwable
Set deferred uncaught java.lang.Throwable
>
VM Started: Set deferred breakpoint Interest:22
Set deferred breakpoint Interest:13

Breakpoint hit: "thread=main", Interest.main(), line=13 bci=9
13           System.out.printf("%s%20s%n", "Year", "Amount on deposit");

main[1]
```

Fig. E.23 | Reaching the breakpoint at line 13 in the Interest application.

```
main[1] cont
> Year    Amount on deposit
Breakpoint hit: "thread=main", Interest.main(), line=22 bci=55
22              System.out.printf("%4d%,20.2f%n", year, amount);

main[1]
```

Fig. E.24 | Reaching the breakpoint at line 22 in the `Interest` application.

```
main[1] print year
 year = 1
main[1] print amount
 amount = 1050.0
main[1]
```

Fig. E.25 | Printing year and amount during the first iteration of `Interest`'s for.

6. *Continuing execution.* Type cont to continue execution. Line 22 executes and prints the current values of year and amount. After the for enters its second iteration, the debugger notifies you that the breakpoint at line 22 has been reached a second time. The debugger pauses each time a line where a breakpoint has been set is about to execute—when the breakpoint appears in a loop, the debugger pauses during each iteration. Print the values of variables year and amount again to see how the values have changed since the first iteration of the for (Fig. E.26).

```
main[1] cont
>    1             1,050.00
Breakpoint hit: "thread=main", Interest.main(), line=22 bci=55
22              System.out.printf("%4d%,20.2f%n", year, amount);

main[1] print amount
 amount = 1102.5
main[1] print year
 year = 2
main[1]
```

Fig. E.26 | Printing year and amount during the second iteration of `Interest`'s for.

7. *Removing a breakpoint.* You can display a list of all of the breakpoints in the application by typing **clear** (Fig. E.27). Suppose you're satisfied that the Interest application's for statement is working properly, so you want to remove the breakpoint at line 22 and allow the remaining iterations of the loop to proceed normally. You can remove the breakpoint at line 22 by typing clear Interest:22. Now type clear to list the remaining breakpoints in the application. The debugger should indicate that only the breakpoint at line 13 remains (Fig. E.27). This breakpoint has already been reached and thus will no longer affect execution.

```
main[1] clear
Breakpoints set:
        breakpoint Interest:13
        breakpoint Interest:22
main[1] clear Interest:22
Removed: breakpoint Interest:22
main[1] clear
Breakpoints set:
        breakpoint Interest:13
main[1]
```

Fig. E.27 | Removing the breakpoint at line 22.

8. *Continuing execution after removing a breakpoint.* Type cont to continue execution. Recall that execution last paused before the printf statement in line 22. If the breakpoint at line 22 was removed successfully, continuing the application will produce the correct output for the current and remaining iterations of the for statement without the application halting (Fig. E.28).

```
main[1] cont
>    2            1,102.50
     3            1,157.63
     4            1,215.51
     5            1,276.28
     6            1,340.10
     7            1,407.10
     8            1,477.46
     9            1,551.33
    10            1,628.89

The application exited

C:\examples\debugger>
```

Fig. E.28 | Application executes without a breakpoint set at line 22.

E.7 Wrap-Up

In this appendix, you learned how to insert and remove breakpoints in the debugger. Breakpoints allow you to pause application execution so you can examine variable values with the debugger's print command. This capability will help you locate and fix logic errors in your applications. You saw how to use the print command to examine the value of an expression and how to use the set command to change the value of a variable. You also learned debugger commands (including the step, step up and next commands) that can be used to determine whether a method is executing correctly. You learned how to use the watch command to keep track of a field throughout the life of an application. Finally, you learned how to use the clear command to list all the breakpoints set for an application or remove individual breakpoints to continue execution without breakpoints.

Using the Java API Documentation

F.1 Introduction

The Java class library contains thousands of predefined classes and interfaces that programmers can use to write their own applications. These classes are grouped into packages based on their functionality. For example, the classes and interfaces used for file processing are grouped into the `java.io` package, and the classes and interfaces for Java FX GUI, graphics and multimedia are grouped into packages that begin with `javafx`. The **Java API documentation** lists the `public` and `protected` members of each class and the `public` members of each interface in the Java class library. The documentation overviews all the classes and interfaces, summarizes their members (i.e., the fields, constructors and methods of classes, and the fields and methods of interfaces) and provides detailed descriptions of each member. Most Java programmers rely on this documentation when writing programs. Normally, programmers would search the API to find the following:

1. The package that contains a particular class or interface.

2. Relationships between a particular class or interface and other classes and interfaces.

3. Class or interface constants—normally declared as `public static final` fields.

4. Constructors to determine how an object of the class can be initialized.

5. The methods of a class to determine whether they're `static` or instance methods, the number and types of the arguments you need to pass, the return types and any exceptions that might be thrown from the method.

In addition, programmers often rely on the documentation to discover classes and interfaces that they have not used before. For this reason, we demonstrate the documentation with classes you know and classes you may not have studied yet. We show how to use the documentation to locate the information you need to use a class or interface effectively.

F.2 Navigating the Java API

To view the API documentation online, go to `http://docs.oracle.com/javase/7/docs/api/` (Fig. F.1).

Upper-left frame lists all packages in alphabetical order

Tree link displays the hierarchy of all packages and classes

Deprecated link lists portions of the API that should no longer be used

Index link lists fields, methods, classes and interfaces

Help link describes how the API is organized

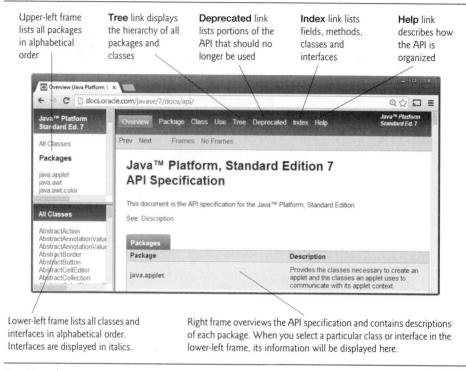

Lower-left frame lists all classes and interfaces in alphabetical order. Interfaces are displayed in italics.

Right frame overviews the API specification and contains descriptions of each package. When you select a particular class or interface in the lower-left frame, its information will be displayed here.

Fig. F.1 | Java API overview. (Courtesy of Oracle Corporation)

Frames in the API Documentation's `index.html` Page

The API documentation is divided into three frames (see Fig. F.1). The upper-left frame lists all of the Java API's packages in alphabetical order. The lower-left frame initially lists the Java API's classes and interfaces in alphabetical order. Interface names are displayed in italic. When you click a specific package in the upper-left frame, the lower-left frame lists the classes and interfaces of the selected package. The right frame initially provides a brief description of each package of the Java API specification—read this overview to become familiar wth the general capabilities of the Java APIs. If you select a class or interface in the lower-left frame, the right frame displays information about that class or interface.

Important Links in the `index.html` Page

At the top of the right frame (Fig. F.1), there are four links—**Tree**, **Deprecated**, **Index** and **Help**. The **Tree** link displays the hierarchy of all packages, classes and interfaces in a tree structure. The **Deprecated** link displays interfaces, classes, exceptions, fields, constructors and methods that should no longer be used. The **Index** link displays classes, interfaces, fields, constructors and methods in alphabetical order. The **Help** link describes how the API documentation is organized. You should probably begin by reading the **Help** page.

Viewing the Index Page

If you do not know the name of the class you're looking for, but you do know the name of a method or field, you can use the documentation's index to locate the class. The **Index** link is located near the upper-right corner of the right frame. The index page (Fig. F.2) displays fields, constructors, methods, interfaces and classes in alphabetical order. For example, if you're looking for Scanner method hasNextInt, but do not know the class name, you can click the **H** link to go to the alphabetical listing of all items in the Java API that begin with "h". Scroll to method hasNextInt (Fig. F.3). Once there, each method named hasNextInt is listed with the package name and class to which the method belongs. From there, you can click the class name to view the class's complete details, or you can click the method name to view the method's details.

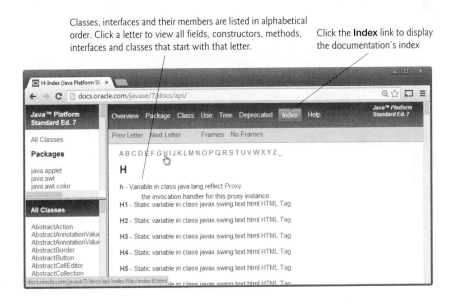

Fig. F.2 | Viewing the **Index** page. (Courtesy of Oracle Corporation.)

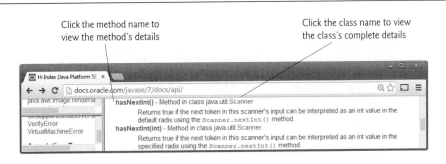

Fig. F.3 | Scroll to method hasNextInt. (Courtesy of Oracle Corporation)

Viewing a Specific Package

When you click the package name in the upper-left frame, all classes and interfaces from that package are displayed in the lower-left frame and are divided into five subsections—**Interfaces, Classes, Enums, Exceptions, Errors** and **Annotation Types**—each listed alphabetically. For example, the contents of package javax.swing are displayed in the lower-left frame (Fig. F.4) when you click javax.swing in the upper-left frame. You can click the package name in the lower-left frame to get an overview of the package. If you think that a package contains several classes that could be useful in your application, the package overview can be especially helpful.

Click a package name in the upper-left frame to view all classes and interfaces defined in the package

Click the package name in the lower-left frame to display a summary of that package in the right frame

Contents of package javax.swing are displayed in the lower-left frame

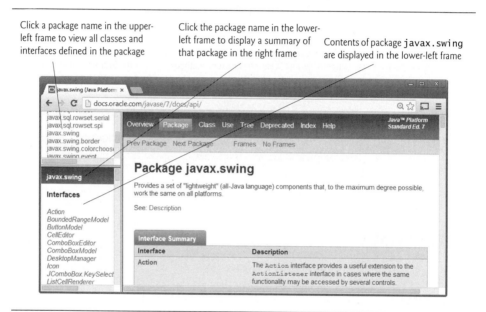

Fig. F.4 | Clicking a package name in the upper-left frame to view all classes and interfaces declared in this package. (Courtesy of Oracle Corporation)

Viewing the Details of a Class

When you click a class name or interface name in the lower-left frame, the right frame displays the details of that class or interface. First you'll see the class's package name followed by a hierarchy that shows the class's relationship to other classes. You'll also see a list of the interfaces implemented by the class and the class's known subclasses. Figure F.5 shows the beginning of the documentation page for class JButton from the javax.swing package. The page first shows the package name in which the class appears. This is followed by the class hierarchy that leads to class JButton, the interfaces class JButton implements and the subclasses of class JButton. The bottom of the right frame shows the beginning of class JButton's description. When you look at the documentation for an interface, the right frame does not display a hierarchy for that interface. Instead, the right frame lists the interface's superinterfaces, known subinterfaces and known implementing classes.

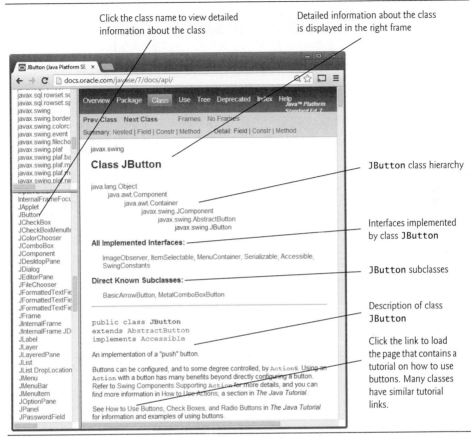

Click the class name to view detailed information about the class

Detailed information about the class is displayed in the right frame

JButton class hierarchy

Interfaces implemented by class JButton

JButton subclasses

Description of class JButton

Click the link to load the page that contains a tutorial on how to use buttons. Many classes have similar tutorial links.

Fig. F.5 | Clicking a class name to view detailed information about the class. (Courtesy of Oracle Corporation)

Summary Sections in a Class's Documentation Page

Other parts of each API page are listed below. Each part is presented only if the class contains or inherits the items specified. Class members shown in the summary sections are public unless they're explicitly marked as protected. A class's private members are not shown in the documentation, because they cannot be used directly in your programs.

1. The **Nested Class Summary** section summarizes the class's public and protected nested classes—i.e., classes that are defined inside the class. Unless explicitly specified, these classes are public and non-static.

2. The **Field Summary** section summarizes the class's public and protected fields. Unless explicitly specified, these fields are public and non-static. Figure F.6 shows the **Field Summary** section of class Color.

3. The **Constructor Summary** section summarizes the class's constructors. Constructors are not inherited, so this section appears in the documentation for a class only if the class declares one or more constructors. Figure F.7 shows the **Constructor Summary** section of class JButton.

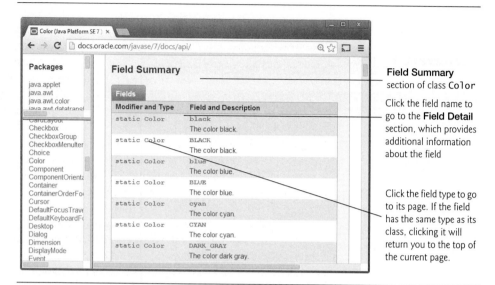

Fig. F.6 | **Field Summary** section of class Color. (Courtesy of Oracle Corporation)

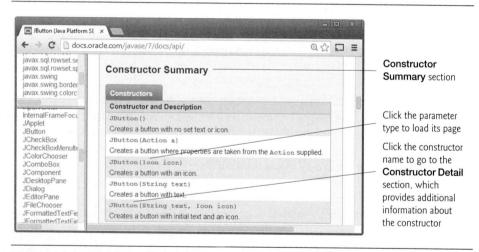

Fig. F.7 | **Constructor Summary** section of class JButton. (Courtesy of Oracle Corporation)

4. The **Method Summary** section summarizes the class's public and protected methods. Unless explicitly specified, these methods are public and non-static. Figure F.8 shows the **Method Summary** section of class Files.

The summary sections typically provide only a one-sentence description of a class member. Additional details are presented in the detail sections discussed next.

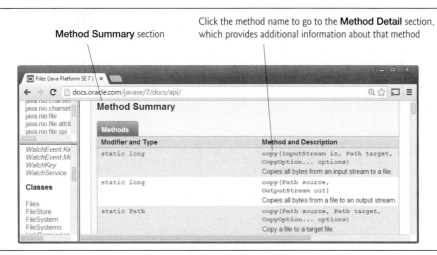

Fig. F.8 | **Method Summary** section of class `Files`. (Courtesy of Oracle Corporation)

Detail Sections in a Class's Documentation Page

After the summary sections are detail sections that normally provide more discussion of particular class members. There isn't a detail section for nested classes. When you click the link in the **Nested Class Summary** for a particular nested class, a documentation page describing that nested class is displayed. The detail sections are described below.

1. The **Field Detail** section provides the declaration of each field. It also discusses each field, including the field's modifiers and meaning. Figure F.9 shows the Field Detail section of class `Color`.

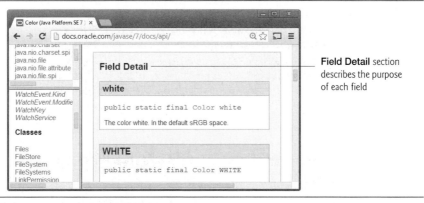

Fig. F.9 | Field Detail section of class `Color`. (Courtesy of Oracle Corporation)

2. The **Constructor Detail** section provides the first line of each constructor's declaration and discusses the constructors. The discussion includes the modifiers of each constructor, a description of each constructor, each constructor's parameters and any exceptions thrown by each constructor. Figure F.10 shows the **Constructor Detail** section of class `JButton`.

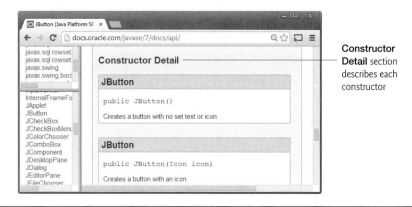

Fig. F.10 | **Constructor Detail** section of class `JButton`. (Courtesy of Oracle Corporation)

3. The **Method Detail** section provides the first line of each method. The discussion of each method includes its modifiers, a more complete method description, the method's parameters, the method's return type and any exceptions thrown by the method. Figure F.11 shows class `ObjectInputStream`'s **Method Detail** section for the `read` method. The method details show you other methods that might be of interest (labeled as **See Also**). If the method overrides a method of the superclass, the name of the superclass method and the name of the superclass are provided so you can link to the method or superclass for more information.

Method **read** throws **IOException**. Click **IOException** to load the **IOException** class information page and learn more about the exception type (e.g., why such an exception might be thrown)

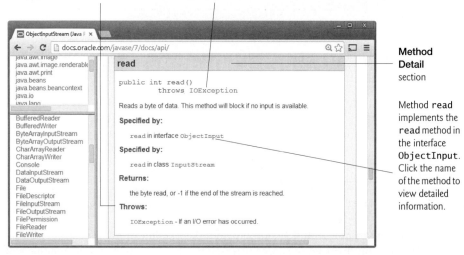

Fig. F.11 | **Method Detail** section of class `ObjectInputStream`. (Courtesy of Oracle Corporation)

As you look through the documentation, you'll notice that there are often links to other fields, methods, nested-classes and top-level classes. These links enable you to jump from the class you're looking at to another relevant portion of the documentation.

Creating Documentation with **javadoc**

G.1 Introduction

In this appendix, we provide an introduction to **javadoc**—a tool used to create HTML files that document Java code. This tool is used by Sun to create the Java API documentation (Fig. G.1). We discuss the special Java comments and tags required by javadoc to create documentation based on your source code and how to execute the javadoc tool. For detailed information on javadoc, visit the javadoc home page at

```
http://docs.oracle.com/javase/7/docs/technotes/guides/javadoc/
   index.html
```

G.2 Documentation Comments

Before HTML files can be generated with the javadoc tool, programmers must insert special comments—called **documentation comments**—into their source files. Documentation comments are the only comments recognized by javadoc. Documentation comments begin with /** and end with */. Like traditional comments, documentation comments can span multiple lines. An example of a simple documentation comment is

```
/** Sorts integer array using MySort algorithm */
```

Like other comments, documentation comments are not translated into bytecodes. Because javadoc is used to create HTML files, documentation comments can contain HTML tags. For example, the documentation comment

```
/** Sorts integer array using <strong>MySort</strong> algorithm */
```

contains the HTML bold tags <strong> and </strong>. In the generated HTML files, MySort will appear in bold. As we'll see, **javadoc tags** can also be inserted into the documentation comments to help javadoc document your source code. These tags—which begin with an @ symbol—are not HTML tags.

G.3 Documenting Java Source Code

In this section, we document a modified version of the Time2 class from Fig. 8.5 using documentation comments. In the text that follows the example, we thoroughly discuss each of the javadoc tags used in the documentation comments. In the next section, we discuss how to use the javadoc tool to generate HTML documentation from this file.

```java
 1   // Fig. G.1: Time.java
 2   // Time class declaration with overloaded constructors.
 3   package com.deitel; // place Time in a package
 4
 5   /**
 6    * This class maintains the time in 24-hour format.
 7    * @see java.lang.Object
 8    * @author Deitel & Associates, Inc.
 9    */
10   public class Time
11   {
12      private int hour;   // 0 - 23
13      private int minute; // 0 - 59
14      private int second; // 0 - 59
15
16      /**
17       *  Time no-argument constructor initializes each instance variable
18       *  to zero. This ensures that Time objects start in a consistent state
19       *  @throws IllegalArgumentException In the case of an invalid time
20       */
21      public Time()
22      {
23         this(0, 0, 0); // invoke constructor with three arguments
24      }
25
26      /**
27       *  Time constructor
28       *  @param hour the hour
29       *  @throws Exception In the case of an invalid time
30       */
31      public Time(int hour)
32      {
33         this(hour, 0, 0); // invoke constructor with three arguments
34      }
35
36      /**
37       *  Time constructor
38       *  @param hour the hour
39       *  @param minute the minute
40       *  @throws IllegalArgumentException In the case of an invalid time
41       */
42      public Time(int hour, int minute)
43      {
44         this(hour, minute, 0); // invoke constructor with three arguments
45      }
```

Fig. G.1 | Java source code file containing documentation comments. (Part 1 of 4.)

```
46
47      /**
48       *  Time constructor
49       * @param hour the hour
50       * @param minute the minute
51       * @param second the second
52       * @throws IllegalArgumentException In the case of an invalid time
53       */
54      public Time(int hour, int minute, int second)
55      {
56         if (hour < 0 || hour >= 24)
57            throw new IllegalArgumentException("hour must be 0-23");
58
59         if (minute < 0 || minute >= 60)
60            throw new IllegalArgumentException("minute must be 0-59");
61
62         if (second < 0 || second >= 60)
63            throw new IllegalArgumentException("second must be 0-59");
64
65         this.hour = hour;
66         this.minute = minute;
67         this.second = second;
68      }
69
70      /**
71       *  Time constructor
72       *  @param time A Time object with which to initialize
73       *  @throws IllegalArgumentException In the case of an invalid time
74       */
75      public Time(Time time)
76      {
77         // invoke constructor with three arguments
78         this(time.getHour(), time.getMinute(), time.getSecond());
79      }
80
81      /**
82       *  Set a new time value using universal time. Perform
83       *  validity checks on the data. Set invalid values to zero.
84       *  @param hour the hour
85       *  @param minute the minute
86       *  @param second the second
87       *  @see com.deitel.Time#setHour
88       *  @see Time#setMinute
89       *  @see #setSecond
90       *  @throws Exception In the case of an invalid time
91       */
92      public void setTime(int hour, int minute, int second)
93      {
94         if (hour < 0 || hour >= 24)
95            throw new IllegalArgumentException("hour must be 0-23");
96
97         if (minute < 0 || minute >= 60)
98            throw new IllegalArgumentException("minute must be 0-59");
```

Fig. G.1 | Java source code file containing documentation comments. (Part 2 of 4.)

```
 99
100          if (second < 0 || second >= 60)
101             throw new IllegalArgumentException("second must be 0-59");
102
103          this.hour = hour;
104          this.minute = minute;
105          this.second = second;
106       }
107
108       /**
109        *   Sets the hour.
110        *   @param hour the hour
111        *   @throws IllegalArgumentException In the case of an invalid hour
112        */
113       public void setHour(int hour)
114       {
115          if (hour < 0 || hour >= 24)
116             throw new IllegalArgumentException("hour must be 0-23");
117
118          this.hour = hour;
119       }
120
121       /**
122        *   Sets the minute.
123        *   @param minute the minute
124        *   @throws IllegalArgumentException In the case of an invalid minute
125        */
126       public void setMinute(int minute)
127       {
128          if (minute < 0 && minute >= 60)
129             throw new IllegalArgumentException("minute must be 0-59");
130
131          this.minute = minute;
132       }
133
134       /**
135        *   Sets the second.
136        *   @param second the second.
137        *   @throws Exception In the case of an invalid second
138        */
139       public void setSecond(int second)
140       {
141          if (second >= 0 && second < 60)
142             throw new IllegalArgumentException("second must be 0-59");
143
144          this.second = second;
145       }
146
147       /**
148        *   Gets the hour.
149        *   @return an <code>integer</code> specifying the hour.
150        */
```

Fig. G.1 | Java source code file containing documentation comments. (Part 3 of 4.)

```
151      public int getHour()
152      {
153         return hour;
154      }
155
156      /**
157       *  Gets the minute.
158       *  @return an <code>integer</code> specifying the minute.
159       */
160      public int getMinute()
161      {
162         return minute;
163      }
164
165      /**
166       *  Gets the second.
167       *  @return an <code>integer</code> specifying the second.
168       */
169      public int getSecond()
170      {
171         return second;
172      }
173
174      /**
175       *  Convert to String in universal-time format
176       *  @return a <code>String</code> representation
177       *  of the time in universal-time format
178       */
179      public String toUniversalString()
180      {
181         return String.format(
182            "%02d:%02d:%02d", getHour(), getMinute(), getSecond());
183      }
184
185      /**
186       *  Convert to String in standard-time format
187       *  @return a <code>String</code> representation
188       *  of the time in standard-time format
189       */
190      public String toString()
191      {
192         return String.format("%d:%02d:%02d %s",
193            ((getHour() == 0 || getHour() == 12) ? 12 : getHour() % 12),
194            getMinute(), getSecond(), (getHour() < 12 ? "AM" : "PM"));
195      }
196   } // end class Time
```

Fig. G.1 | Java source code file containing documentation comments. (Part 4 of 4.)

Documentation comments are placed on the line before a class declaration, an interface declaration, a constructor, a method and a field (i.e., an instance variable or a reference). The first documentation comment (lines 5–9) introduces class Time. Line 6 is a description of class Time provided by the programmer. The description can contain as many lines as necessary to provide a description of the class to any programmer who may use it. Tags **@see** and **@author** are used to specify a **See Also:** note and an **Author:** note, respectively in the HTML documentation. The **See Also:** note (Fig. G.2) specifies other related classes that may be of interest to a programmer using this class. The @author tag specifies the author of the class. More than one @author tag can be used to document multiple authors. [*Note:* The asterisks (*) on each line between /** and */ are not required. However, this is the recommended convention for aligning descriptions and javadoc tags. When parsing a documentation comment, javadoc discards all white-space characters up to the first non-white-space character in each line. If the first non-white-space character encountered is an asterisk, it's also discarded.]

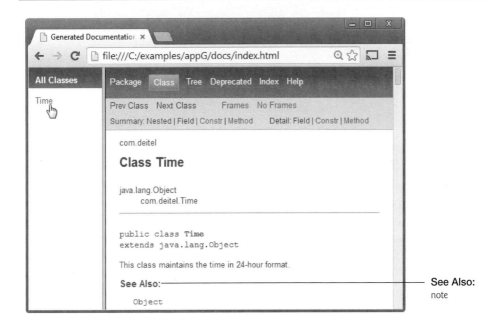

Fig. G.2 | **See Also:** note generated by javadoc.

This documentation comment immediately precedes the class declaration—any code placed between the documentation comment and the class declaration causes javadoc to ignore the documentation comment. This is also true of other code structures (e.g., constructors, methods, instance variables.).

Common Programming Error G.1

Placing an import statement between the class comment and the class declaration is a logic error. This causes the class comment to be ignored by javadoc.

Software Engineering Observation G.1

Defining several fields in one comma-separated statement with a single comment above that statement will result in javadoc using that comment for all of the fields.

> **Software Engineering Observation G.2**
>
> *To produce proper* `javadoc` *documentation, you must declare every instance variable on a separate line.*

The documentation comment on lines 26–30 describes one of the `Time` constructors. Tag **@param** describes a parameter to the constructor. Parameters appear in the HTML document in a **Parameters:** note (Fig. G.3) that is followed by a list of all parameters specified with the @param tag. For this constructor, the parameter's name is hour and its description is "`the hour`". Tag @param can be used only with methods and constructors.

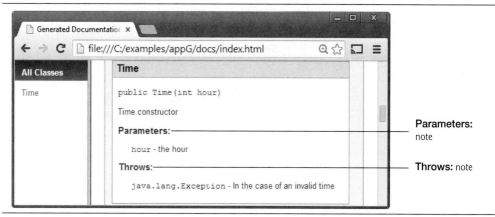

Fig. G.3 | Parameters: and Throws: notes generated by `javadoc`.

The **@throws** tag specifies the exceptions thrown by this constructor. Like @param tags, @throws tags are only used with methods and constructors. One @throws should be supplied for each type of exception thrown by the method.

Documentation comments can contain multiple @param and @see tags. The documentation comment on lines 81–91 describes method setTime. The HTML generated for this method is shown in Fig. G.4. Three @param tags describe the method's parameters. This results in one **Parameters:** note which lists the three parameters. Methods setHour, setMinute and setSecond are tagged with @see to create hyperlinks to their descriptions in the HTML document. A **#** character is used instead of a dot when tagging a method or a field. This creates a link to the field or method name that follows the **#** character. We demonstrate three different ways (i.e., the fully qualified name, the class name qualification and no qualification) to tag methods using @see on lines 87–89. Line 87 uses the fully qualified name to tag the setHour method. If the fully qualified name is not given (lines 88 and 89), `javadoc` looks for the specified method or field in the following order: current class, superclasses, package and imported files.

The only other tag used in this file is **@return**, which specifies a **Returns:** note in the HTML documentation (Fig. G.5). The comment on lines 147–150 documents method getHour. Tag @return describes a method's return type to help the programmer understand how to use the return value of the method. By `javadoc` convention, programmers typeset source code (i.e., keywords, identifiers and expressions) with the HTML tags <code> and </code>. Several other `javadoc` tags are briefly summarized in Fig. G.7.

Good Programming Practice G.1

Changing source code fonts in javadoc tags helps code names stand out from the rest of the description.

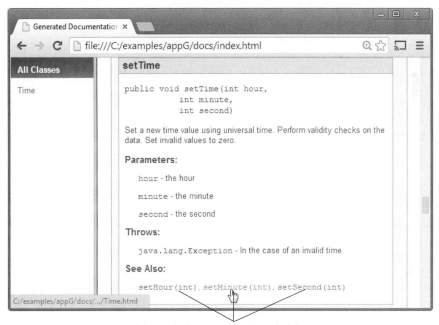

Click a method name to view the method description.

Fig. G.4 | HTML documentation for method setTime.

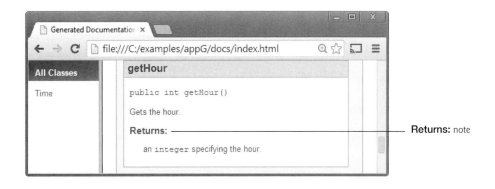

Fig. G.5 | HTML documentation for method getHour.

javadoc tag	Description
`@deprecated`	Adds a **Deprecated** note. These are notes to programmers indicating that they should not use the specified features of the class. **Deprecated** notes normally appear when a class has been enhanced with new and improved features, but older features are maintained for backwards compatibility.
`{@link}`	This allows the programmer to insert an explicit hyperlink to another HTML document.
`@since`	Adds a **Since:** note. These notes are used for new versions of a class to indicate when a feature was first introduced. For example, the Java API documentation uses this to indicate features that were introduced in Java 1.5.
`@version`	Adds a **Version** note. These notes help maintain version number of the software containing the class or method.

Fig. G.6 | Some additional `javadoc` tags—the complete list is located at `docs.oracle.com/javase/7/docs/technotes/tools/windows/javadoc.html#javadoctags`.

G.4 javadoc

In this section, we discuss how to execute the `javadoc` tool on a Java source file to create HTML documentation for the class in the file.

Downloading the Java Documentation

When you generate documentation with `javadoc`, you can link your documentation to the Java API documentation. This is useful when your classes use features of the Java API, such as extending an exiting class. The `javadoc` tool will create links to the existing classes. To link to the Java API documentation, you should first download and extract the documentation from

```
http://www.oracle.com/technetwork/java/javase/downloads/index.html
```

You can find the documentation download under additional resources. Normally, you'd extract the documentation into your JDK's installation folder.

Executing javadoc from the Command Line

Like other tools, `javadoc` is executed from the command line. The general form of the `javadoc` command is

```
javadoc options packages sources @files
```

where *options* is a list of command-line options, *packages* is a list of packages the user would like to document, *sources* is a list of java source files to document and *@files* is a list of text files containing the `javadoc` options, the names of packages and/or source files to send to the `javadoc` utility. [*Note:* All items are separated by spaces and *@files* is one word.] Figure G.7 shows a **Command Prompt** window containing the `javadoc` command we typed to generate the HTML documentation. For detailed information on the `javadoc` command, visit the `javadoc` reference guide and examples at `http://docs.oracle.com/javase/7/docs/technotes/guides/javadoc/index.html`.

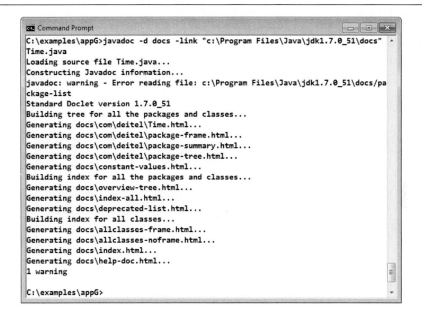

Fig. G.7 | Using the `javadoc` tool.

In Fig. G.7, the **-d** option specifies the directory (e.g., docs within the current folder) where the HTML files will be stored on disk. We use the **-link** option so that our documentation links to Sun's documentation (installed in the docs directory within the JDK's installation directory). If the Sun documentation located in a different directory, specify that directory here; otherwise, you'll receive an error from the `javadoc` tool. This creates a hyperlink between our documentation and Sun's documentation (see Fig. G.4, where Java class Exception from package java.lang is hyperlinked). Without the -link argument, Exception appears as text in the HTML document—not a hyperlink to the Java API documentation for class Exception. The **-author** option instructs `javadoc` to process the @author tag (it ignores this tag by default).

G.5 Files Produced by `javadoc`

In the last section, we executed the `javadoc` tool on the Time.java file. When `javadoc` executes, it displays the name of each HTML file it creates (see Fig. G.7). From the source file, `javadoc` created an HTML document for the class named Time.html. If the source file contains multiple classes or interfaces, a separate HTML document is created for each class. Because class Time belongs to a package, the page will be created in the directory

```
docs
    com
        deitel
```

The docs directory was specified with the -d command line option of `javadoc`, and the remaining directories were created based on the package statement.

The `javadoc` tool also creates **index.html**—the starting HTML page in the documentation. To view the documentation you generate with `javadoc`, load `index.html` from the docs directory into your web browser. In Fig. G.8, the right frame contains the page `index.html` and the left frame contains the page **allclasses-frame.html** which contains links to the source code's classes. [*Note:* Our example does not contain multiple packages, so there's no frame listing the packages. Normally this frame would appear above the left frame (containing "All Classes"), as in Fig. G.2.]

Fig. G.8 | Index page.

Figure G.9 shows class `Time`'s `index.html`. Click **Time** in the left frame to load the `Time` class description. The navigation bar (at the top of the right frame) indicates which HTML page is currently loaded by highlighting the page's link (e.g., the **Class** link).

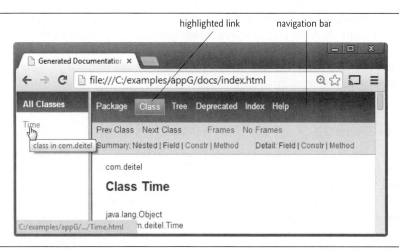

Fig. G.9 | Class page.

Clicking the **Tree** link (Fig. G.10) displays a class hierarchy for all the classes displayed in the left frame. In our example, we documented only class `Time`—which extends `Object`.

Clicking the **Deprecated** link loads **deprecated-list.html** into the right frame. This page contains a list of all deprecated names. Because we did not use the @deprecated tag in this example, this page does not contain any information.

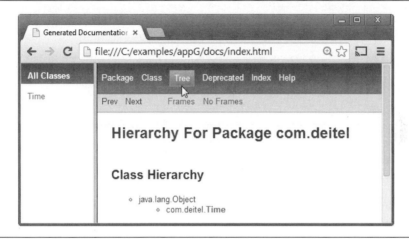

Fig. G.10 | Tree page.

Clicking the **Index** link loads the **index-all.html** page (Fig. G.11), which contains an alphabetical list of all classes, interfaces, methods and fields. Clicking the **Help** link loads **helpdoc.html** (Fig. G.12). This is a help file for navigating the documentation. A default help file is provided, but the programmer can specify other help files.

Fig. G.11 | Index page.

Among the other files generated by `javadoc` are **serialized-form.html** which documents `Serializable` and `Externalizable` classes and **package-list**, a text file rather than an HTML file, which lists package names and is not actually part of the documentation. The package-list file is used by the -link command-line argument to resolve the external cross references, i.e., allows other documentations to link to this documentation.

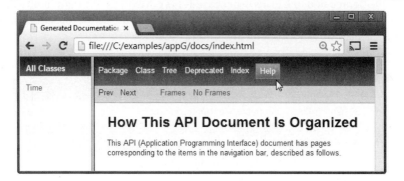

Fig. G.12 | Help page.

Unicode®

H.1 Introduction

The use of inconsistent **character encodings** (i.e., numeric values associated with characters) when developing global software products causes serious problems because computers process information using numbers. For example, the character "a" is converted to a numeric value so that a computer can manipulate that piece of data. Many countries and corporations have developed encoding systems that are incompatible with the encoding systems of other countries and corporations. For example, the Microsoft Windows operating system assigns the value 0xC0 to the character "A with a grave accent," while the Apple Macintosh operating system assigns the same value to an upside-down question mark. This results in the misrepresentation and possible corruption of data.

In the absence of a universal character encoding standard, global software developers had to localize their products extensively before distribution. **Localization** includes the language translation and cultural adaptation of content. The process of localization usually includes significant modifications to the source code (e.g., the conversion of numeric values and the underlying assumptions made by programmers), which results in increased costs and delays in releasing the software. For example, an English-speaking programmer might design a global software product assuming that a single character can be represented by one byte. However, when those products are localized in Asian markets, the programmer's assumptions are no longer valid because there are many more Asian characters, and therefore most, if not all, of the code needs to be rewritten. Localization is necessary with each release of a version. By the time a software product is localized for a particular market, a newer version, which needs to be localized as well, can be ready for distribution. As a result, it's cumbersome and costly to produce and distribute global software products in a market where there's no universal character encoding standard.

In response to this situation, the **Unicode Standard**, an encoding standard that facilitates the production and distribution of software, was created. The Unicode Standard outlines a specification to produce consistent encoding of the world's characters and symbols. Software products which handle text encoded in the Unicode Standard need to be localized, but the localization process is simpler and more efficient because the numeric values need not be converted and the assumptions made by programmers about the character encoding are universal. The Unicode Standard is maintained by a non-profit organization called the **Unicode Consortium**, whose members include Apple, IBM, Microsoft, Oracle, Sun Microsystems, Sybase and many others.

When the Consortium envisioned and developed the Unicode Standard, it wanted an encoding system that was **universal**, **efficient**, **uniform** and **unambiguous**. A universal encoding system encompasses all commonly used characters. An efficient encoding system allows text files to be parsed quickly. A uniform encoding system assigns fixed values to all characters. An unambiguous encoding system represents a given character in a consistent manner. These four terms are referred to as the Unicode Standard design basis.

H.2 Unicode Transformation Formats

Although Unicode incorporates the limited ASCII character set (i.e., a collection of characters), it encompasses a more comprehensive character set. In ASCII each character is represented by a byte containing 0s and 1s. One byte is capable of storing the binary numbers from 0 to 255. Each character is assigned a number between 0 and 255, thus ASCII-based systems can support only 256 characters, a tiny fraction of the world's characters. Unicode extends the ASCII character set by encoding the vast majority of the world's characters. The Unicode Standard encodes characters in a uniform numerical space from 0 to 10FFFF hexadecimal. An implementation will express these numbers in one of several transformation formats, choosing the one that best fits the particular application at hand.

Three such formats are in use, called **UTF-8**, **UTF-16** and **UTF-32**. UTF-8, a variable-width encoding form, requires one to four bytes to express each Unicode character. UTF-8 data consists of 8-bit bytes (sequences of one, two, three or four bytes depending on the character being encoded) and is well suited for ASCII-based systems when there's a predominance of one-byte characters (ASCII represents characters as one-byte). Currently, UTF-8 is widely implemented in UNIX systems and in databases.

The variable-width UTF-16 encoding form expresses Unicode characters in units of 16-bits (i.e., as two adjacent bytes, or a short integer in many machines). Most characters of Unicode are expressed in a single 16-bit unit. However, characters with values above FFFF hexadecimal are expressed with an ordered pair of 16-bit units called **surrogates**. Surrogates are 16-bit integers in the range D800 through DFFF, which are used solely for the purpose of "escaping" into higher numbered characters. Approximately one million characters can be expressed in this manner. Although a surrogate pair requires 32 bits to represent characters, it's space-efficient to use these 16-bit units. Surrogates are rare characters in current implementations. Many string-handling implementations are written in terms of UTF-16. [*Note:* Details and sample-code for UTF-16 handling are available on the Unicode Consortium website at `www.unicode.org`.]

Implementations that require significant use of rare characters or entire scripts encoded above FFFF hexadecimal, should use UTF-32, a 32-bit fixed-width encoding form that usually requires twice as much memory as UTF-16 encoded characters. The major advantage of the fixed-width UTF-32 encoding form is that it expresses all characters uniformly, so it's easy to handle in arrays.

There are few guidelines that state when to use a particular encoding form. The best encoding form to use depends on the computer system and business protocol, not on the data itself. Typically, the UTF-8 encoding form should be used where computer systems and business protocols require data to be handled in 8-bit units, particularly in legacy systems being upgraded, because it often simplifies changes to existing programs. For this reason, UTF-8 has become the encoding form of choice on the Internet. Likewise, UTF-16 is the encoding form of choice on Microsoft Windows applications. UTF-32 is likely to become more widely used in the future as more characters are encoded with values above FFFF hexadecimal. UTF-32 requires less sophisticated handling than UTF-16 in the presence of surrogate pairs. Figure H.1 shows the different ways in which the three encoding forms handle character encoding.

Character	UTF-8	UTF-16	UTF-32
LATIN CAPITAL LETTER A	0x41	0x0041	0x00000041
GREEK CAPITAL LETTER ALPHA	0xCD 0x91	0x0391	0x00000391
CJK UNIFIED IDEOGRAPH-4E95	0xE4 0xBA 0x95	0x4E95	0x00004E95
OLD ITALIC LETTER A	0xF0 0x80 0x83 0x80	0xDC00 0xDF00	0x00010300

Fig. H.1 | Correlation between the three encoding forms.

H.3 Characters and Glyphs

The Unicode Standard consists of characters—written components (i.e., alphabets, numbers, punctuation marks, accent marks, etc.) that can be represented by numeric values. An example of such a character is U+0041 LATIN CAPITAL LETTER A. In the first character representation, **U+**_yyyy_ is a **code value**, in which U+ refers to Unicode code values, as opposed to other hexadecimal values. The _yyyy_ represents a four-digit hexadecimal number of an encoded character. Code values are bit combinations that represent encoded characters. Characters are represented using **glyphs**—various shapes, fonts and sizes for displaying characters. There are no code values for glyphs in the Unicode Standard. Examples of glyphs are shown in Fig. H.2.

The Unicode Standard encompasses the alphabets, ideographs, syllabaries, punctuation marks, **diacritics**, mathematical operators and other features that comprise the written languages and scripts of the world. A diacritic is a special mark added to a character to distinguish it from another letter or to indicate an accent (e.g., in Spanish, the tilde "~" above the character "n"). Currently, Unicode provides code values for 96,382 character representations, with more than 878,000 code values reserved for future expansion.

Fig. H.2 | Various glyphs of the character A.

H.4 Advantages/Disadvantages of Unicode

The Unicode Standard has several significant advantages that promote its use. One is the impact it has on the performance of the international economy. Unicode standardizes the characters for the world's writing systems to a uniform model that promotes transferring and sharing data. Programs developed using such a schema maintain their accuracy because each character has a single definition (i.e., *a* is always U+0061, % is always U+0025). This enables corporations to manage the high demands of international markets by processing different writing systems at the same time. All characters can be managed in an identical manner, thus avoiding any confusion caused by different character-code architectures. Moreover, managing data in a consistent manner eliminates data corruption, because data can be sorted, searched and manipulated using a consistent process.

Another advantage of the Unicode Standard is portability (i.e., software that can execute on disparate computers or with disparate operating systems). Most operating systems, databases, programming languages (including Java and Microsoft's .NET languages) and web browsers currently support, or are planning to support, Unicode.

A disadvantage of the Unicode Standard is the amount of memory required by UTF-16 and UTF-32. ASCII character sets are 8-bits in length, so they require less storage than the default 16-bit Unicode character set. The **double-byte character set** (**DBCS**) encodes Asian characters with one or two bytes per character. The **multibyte character set** (**MBCS**) encodes characters with a variable number of bytes per character. In such instances, the UTF-16 or UTF-32 encoding forms may be used with little hindrance on memory and performance.

Another disadvantage of Unicode is that although it includes more characters than any other character set in common use, it does not yet encode all of the world's written characters. Also, UTF-8 and UTF-16 are variable-width encoding forms, so characters occupy different amounts of memory.

H.5 Using Unicode

Numerous programming languages (e.g., C, Java, JavaScript, Perl, Visual Basic) provide some level of support for the Unicode Standard. The application shown in Fig. H.3–Fig. H.4 prints the text "Welcome to Unicode!" in eight different languages: English, Russian, French, German, Japanese, Portuguese, Spanish and Traditional Chinese.

```
1   // Fig. L.3: UnicodeJFrame.java
2   // Demonstrating how to use Unicode in Java programs.
3   import java.awt.GridLayout;
4   import javax.swing.JFrame;
5   import javax.swing.JLabel;
6
7   public class UnicodeJFrame extends JFrame
8   {
9      // constructor creates JLabels to display Unicode
10     public UnicodeJFrame()
11     {
```

Fig. H.3 | Java application that uses Unicode encoding (Part 1 of 2.).

```
12          super("Demonstrating Unicode");
13
14          setLayout(new GridLayout(8, 1)); // set frame layout
15
16          // create JLabels using Unicode
17          JLabel englishJLabel = new JLabel("\u0057\u0065\u006C\u0063" +
18             "\u006F\u006D\u0065\u0020\u0074\u006F\u0020Unicode\u0021");
19          englishJLabel.setToolTipText("This is English");
20          add(englishJLabel);
21
22          JLabel chineseJLabel = new JLabel("\u6B22\u8FCE\u4F7F\u7528" +
23             "\u0020\u0020Unicode\u0021");
24          chineseJLabel.setToolTipText("This is Traditional Chinese");
25          add(chineseJLabel);
26
27          JLabel cyrillicJLabel = new JLabel("\u0414\u043E\u0431\u0440" +
28             "\u043E\u0020\u043F\u043E\u0436\u0430\u043B\u043E\u0432" +
29             "\u0430\u0442\u044A\u0020\u0432\u0020Unicode\u0021");
30          cyrillicJLabel.setToolTipText("This is Russian");
31          add(cyrillicJLabel);
32
33          JLabel frenchJLabel = new JLabel("\u0042\u0069\u0065\u006E\u0076" +
34             "\u0065\u006E\u0075\u0065\u0020\u0061\u0075\u0020Unicode\u0021");
35          frenchJLabel.setToolTipText("This is French");
36          add(frenchJLabel);
37
38          JLabel germanJLabel = new JLabel("\u0057\u0069\u006C\u006B\u006F" +
39             "\u006D\u006D\u0065\u006E\u0020\u007A\u0075\u0020Unicode\u0021");
40          germanJLabel.setToolTipText("This is German");
41          add(germanJLabel);
42
43          JLabel japaneseJLabel = new JLabel("Unicode\u3078\u3087\u3045" +
44             "\u3053\u305D\u0021");
45          japaneseJLabel.setToolTipText("This is Japanese");
46          add(japaneseJLabel);
47
48          JLabel portugueseJLabel = new JLabel("\u0053\u00E9\u006A\u0061" +
49             "\u0020\u0042\u0065\u006D\u0076\u0069\u006E\u0064\u006F\u0020" +
50             "Unicode\u0021");
51          portugueseJLabel.setToolTipText("This is Portuguese");
52          add(portugueseJLabel);
53
54          JLabel spanishJLabel = new JLabel("\u0042\u0069\u0065\u006E" +
55             "\u0076\u0065\u006E\u0069\u0064\u0061\u0020\u0061\u0020" +
56             "Unicode\u0021");
57          spanishJLabel.setToolTipText("This is Spanish");
58          add(spanishJLabel);
59       } // end UnicodeJFrame constructor
60    } // end class UnicodeJFrame
```

Fig. H.3 | Java application that uses Unicode encoding (Part 2 of 2.).

```
 I   // Fig. L.4: Unicode.java
 2   // Displaying Unicode.
 3   import javax.swing.JFrame;
 4
 5   public class Unicode
 6   {
 7      public static void main(String[] args)
 8      {
 9         UnicodeJFrame unicodeJFrame = new UnicodeJFrame();
10         unicodeJFrame.setDefaultCloseOperation(JFrame.EXIT_ON_CLOSE);
11         unicodeJFrame.setSize(350, 250);
12         unicodeJFrame.setVisible(true);
13      } // end method main
14   } // end class Unicode
```

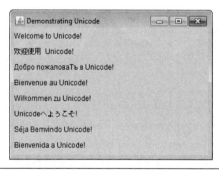

Fig. H.4 | Displaying Unicode.

Class UnicodeJFrame (Fig. H.3) uses escape sequences to represent characters. An escape sequence is in the form \u*yyyy*, where *yyyy* represents the four-digit hexadecimal code value. Lines 17–18 contain the series of escape sequences necessary to display "Welcome to Unicode!" in English. The first escape sequence (\u0057) equates to the character "W," the second escape sequence (\u0065) equates to the character "e," and so on. The \u0020 escape sequence (line 18) is the encoding for the space character. The \u0074 and \u006F escape sequences equate to the word "to." "Unicode" is not encoded because it's a registered trademark and has no equivalent translation in most languages. Line 18 also contains the \u0021 escape sequence for the exclamation point (!).

Lines 22–56 contain the escape sequences for the other seven languages. The Unicode Consortium's website contains a link to code charts that lists the 16-bit Unicode code values. The English, French, German, Portuguese and Spanish characters are located in the **Basic Latin** block, the Japanese characters are located in the **Hiragana** block, the Russian characters are located in the **Cyrillic** block and the Traditional Chinese characters are located in the **CJK Unified Ideographs** block. The next section discusses these blocks.

H.6 Character Ranges

The Unicode Standard assigns code values, which range from 0000 (**Basic Latin**) to E007F (**Tags**), to the written characters of the world. Currently, there are code values for 96,382 characters. To simplify the search for a character and its associated code value, the Unicode

Standard generally groups code values by **script** and function (i.e., Latin characters are grouped in a block, mathematical operators are grouped in another block, etc.). As a rule, a script is a single writing system that is used for multiple languages (e.g., the Latin script is used for English, French, Spanish, etc.). The **Code Charts** page on the Unicode Consortium website lists all the defined blocks and their respective code values. Figure H.5 lists some blocks (scripts) from the website and their range of code values.

Script	Range of code values
Arabic	U+0600–U+06FF
Basic Latin	U+0000–U+007F
Bengali (India)	U+0980–U+09FF
Cherokee (Native America)	U+13A0–U+13FF
CJK Unified Ideographs (East Asia)	U+4E00–U+9FFF
Cyrillic (Russia and Eastern Europe)	U+0400–U+04FF
Ethiopic	U+1200–U+137F
Greek	U+0370–U+03FF
Hangul Jamo (Korea)	U+1100–U+11FF
Hebrew	U+0590–U+05FF
Hiragana (Japan)	U+3040–U+309F
Khmer (Cambodia)	U+1780–U+17FF
Lao (Laos)	U+0E80–U+0EFF
Mongolian	U+1800–U+18AF
Myanmar	U+1000–U+109F
Ogham (Ireland)	U+1680–U+169F
Runic (Germany and Scandinavia)	U+16A0–U+16FF
Sinhala (Sri Lanka)	U+0D80–U+0DFF
Telugu (India)	U+0C00–U+0C7F
Thai	U+0E00–U+0E7F

Fig. H.5 | Some character ranges.

Formatted Output

Objectives

In this appendix you'll:

- Use **printf** formatting.
- Print with field widths and precisions.
- Use formatting flags in the **printf** format string.
- Print with an argument index.
- Output literals and escape sequences.
- Format output with class **Formatter**.

I.1 Introduction

In this appendix, we discuss the formatting features of method `printf` and class `Formatter` (package `java.util`). Class **Formatter** formats and outputs data to a specified destination, such as a string or a file output stream. Many features of `printf` were discussed earlier in the text. This appendix summarizes those features and introduces others, such as displaying date and time data in various formats, reordering output based on the index of the argument and displaying numbers and strings with various flags.

I.2 Streams

Input and output are usually performed with streams, which are sequences of bytes. In input operations, the bytes flow from a device (e.g., a keyboard, a disk drive, a network connection) to main memory. In output operations, bytes flow from main memory to a device (e.g., a display screen, a printer, a disk drive, a network connection).

When program execution begins, three streams are created. The standard input stream typically reads bytes from the keyboard, and the standard output stream typically outputs characters to a command window. A third stream, the **standard error stream** (`System.err`), typically outputs characters to a command window and is used to output error messages so they can be viewed immediately. Operating systems typically allow these streams to be redirected to other devices. Streams are discussed in detail in Chapter 15, Files, Streams and Object Serialization.

I.3 Formatting Output with `printf`

Precise output formatting is accomplished with `printf`. Java borrowed (and enhanced) this feature from the C programming language. Method `printf` can perform the following formatting capabilities, each of which is discussed in this appendix:

1. Rounding floating-point values to an indicated number of decimal places.

2. Aligning a column of numbers with decimal points appearing one above the other.

3. Right justification and left justification of outputs.

4. Inserting literal characters at precise locations in a line of output.

5. Representing floating-point numbers in exponential format.

6. Representing integers in octal and hexadecimal format.

7. Displaying all types of data with fixed-size field widths and precisions.

8. Displaying dates and times in various formats.

Every call to printf supplies as the first argument a **format string** that describes the output format. The format string may consist of **fixed text** and **format specifiers**. Fixed text is output by printf just as it would be output by System.out methods print or println. Each format specifier is a placeholder for a value and specifies the type of data to output. Format specifiers also may include optional formatting information.

In the simplest form, each format specifier begins with a percent sign (%) and is followed by a **conversion character** that represents the data type of the value to output. For example, the format specifier %s is a placeholder for a string, and the format specifier %d is a placeholder for an int value. The optional formatting information, such as an argument index, flags, field width and precision, is specified between the percent sign and the conversion character. We demonstrate each of these capabilities.

I.4 Printing Integers

Figure I.1 describes the **integer conversion characters**. (See Appendix J for an overview of the binary, octal, decimal and hexadecimal number systems.) Figure I.2 uses each to print an integer. In lines 9–10, the plus sign is not displayed by default, but the minus sign is. Later in this appendix (Fig. I.14) we'll see how to force plus signs to print.

Conversion character	Description
d	Display a decimal (base 10) integer.
o	Display an octal (base 8) integer.
x or X	Display a hexadecimal (base 16) integer. X uses uppercase letters.

Fig. I.1 | Integer conversion characters.

```
 1   // Fig. I.2: IntegerConversionTest.java
 2   // Using the integer conversion characters.
 3
 4   public class IntegerConversionTest
 5   {
 6      public static void main(String[] args)
 7      {
 8         System.out.printf("%d\n", 26);
 9         System.out.printf("%d\n", +26);
10         System.out.printf("%d\n", -26);
11         System.out.printf("%o\n", 26);
12         System.out.printf("%x\n", 26);
```

Fig. I.2 | Using the integer conversion characters. (Part I of 2.)

```
13          System.out.printf("%X\n", 26);
14      } // end main
15  } // end class IntegerConversionTest
```

```
26
26
-26
32
1a
1A
```

Fig. I.2 | Using the integer conversion characters. (Part 2 of 2.)

The printf method has the form

```
printf(format-string, argument-list);
```

where *format-string* describes the output format, and the optional *argument-list* contains the values that correspond to each format specifier in *format-string*. There can be many format specifiers in one format string.

Each format string in lines 8–10 specifies that printf should output a decimal integer (%d) followed by a newline character. At the format specifier's position, printf substitutes the value of the first argument after the format string. If the format string contains multiple format specifiers, at each subsequent format specifier's position printf substitutes the value of the next argument in the argument list. The %o format specifier in line 11 outputs the integer in octal format. The %x format specifier in line 12 outputs the integer in hexadecimal format. The %X format specifier in line 13 outputs the integer in hexadecimal format with capital letters.

I.5 Printing Floating-Point Numbers

Figure I.3 describes the floating-point conversions. The **conversion characters e** and **E** display floating-point values in **computerized scientific notation** (also called **exponential notation**). Exponential notation is the computer equivalent of the scientific notation used in mathematics. For example, the value 150.4582 is represented in scientific notation in mathematics as

$$1.504582 \times 10^2$$

and is represented in exponential notation as

```
1.504582e+02
```

in Java. This notation indicates that 1.504582 is multiplied by 10 raised to the second power (e+02). The e stands for "exponent."

Values printed with the conversion characters e, E and f are output with six digits of precision to the right of the decimal point by default (e.g., 1.045921)—other precisions must be specified explicitly. For values printed with the conversion character g, the precision represents the total number of digits displayed, excluding the exponent. The default is six digits (e.g., 12345678.9 is displayed as 1.23457e+07). **Conversion character f** always prints at least one digit to the left of the decimal point. Conversion characters e and E print

Conversion character	Description
e or E	Display a floating-point value in exponential notation. Conversion character E displays the output in uppercase letters.
f	Display a floating-point value in decimal format.
g or G	Display a floating-point value in either the floating-point format f or the exponential format e based on the magnitude of the value. If the magnitude is less than 10^{-3}, or greater than or equal to 10^7, the floating-point value is printed with e (or E). Otherwise, the value is printed in format f. When conversion character G is used, the output is displayed in uppercase letters.
a or A	Display a floating-point number in hexadecimal format. Conversion character A displays the output in uppercase letters.

Fig. I.3 | Floating-point conversion characters.

lowercase e and uppercase E preceding the exponent and always print exactly one digit to the left of the decimal point. Rounding occurs if the value being formatted has more significant digits than the precision.

Conversion character **g** (or **G**) prints in either e (E) or f format, depending on the floating-point value. For example, the values 0.0000875, 87500000.0, 8.75, 87.50 and 875.0 are printed as 8.750000e-05, 8.750000e+07, 8.750000, 87.500000 and 875.000000 with the conversion character g. The value 0.0000875 uses e notation because the magnitude is less than 10-3. The value 87500000.0 uses e notation because the magnitude is greater than 10⁷. Figure I.4 demonstrates the floating-point conversion characters.

```
1   // Fig. I.4: FloatingNumberTest.java
2   // Using floating-point conversion characters.
3
4   public class FloatingNumberTest
5   {
6      public static void main(String[] args)
7      {
8         System.out.printf("%e\n", 12345678.9);
9         System.out.printf("%e\n", +12345678.9 );
10        System.out.printf("%e\n", -12345678.9);
11        System.out.printf("%E\n", 12345678.9);
12        System.out.printf("%f\n", 12345678.9);
13        System.out.printf("%g\n", 12345678.9);
14        System.out.printf("%G\n", 12345678.9);
15     } // end main
16  } // end class FloatingNumberTest
```

```
1.234568e+07
1.234568e+07
-1.234568e+07
```

Fig. I.4 | Using floating-point conversion characters. (Part I of 2.)

```
1.234568E+07
12345678.900000
1.23457e+07
1.23457E+07
```

Fig. I.4 | Using floating-point conversion characters. (Part 2 of 2.)

I.6 Printing Strings and Characters

The c and s conversion characters print individual characters and strings, respectively. **Conversion characters c and C** require a char argument. **Conversion characters s and S** can take a String or any Object as an argument. When conversion characters C and S are used, the output is displayed in uppercase letters. Figure I.5 displays characters, strings and objects with conversion characters c and s. Autoboxing occurs at line 9 when an int constant is assigned to an Integer object. Line 15 outputs an Integer argument with the conversion character s, which implicitly invokes the toString method to get the integer value. You can also output an Integer object using the %d format specifier. In this case, the int value in the Integer object will be unboxed and output.

> **Common Programming Error I.1**
>
> *Using %c to print a String causes an IllegalFormatConversionException—a String cannot be converted to a character.*

```
1    // Fig. I.5: CharStringConversion.java
2    // Using character and string conversion characters.
3    public class CharStringConversion
4    {
5       public static void main(String[] args)
6       {
7          char character = 'A';  // initialize char
8          String string = "This is also a string";  // String object
9          Integer integer = 1234;  // initialize integer (autoboxing)
10
11         System.out.printf("%c\n", character);
12         System.out.printf("%s\n", "This is a string");
13         System.out.printf("%s\n", string);
14         System.out.printf("%S\n", string);
15         System.out.printf("%s\n", integer); // implicit call to toString
16      } // end main
17   } // end class CharStringConversion
```

```
A
This is a string
This is also a string
THIS IS ALSO A STRING
1234
```

Fig. I.5 | Using character and string conversion characters.

I.7 Printing Dates and Times

The **conversion character t** (or **T**) is used to print dates and times in various formats. It's always followed by a **conversion suffix character** that specifies the date and/or time format. When conversion character T is used, the output is displayed in uppercase letters. Figure I.6 lists the common conversion suffix characters for formatting **date and time compositions** that display both the date and the time. Figure I.7 lists the common conversion suffix characters for formatting dates. Figure I.8 lists the common conversion suffix characters for formatting times. For the complete list of conversion suffix characters, visit http://docs.oracle.com/javase/7/docs/api/java/util/Formatter.html.

Conversion suffix character	Description
c	Display date and time formatted as day month date hour:minute:second time-zone year with three characters for day and month, two digits for date, hour, minute and second and four digits for year—for example, Wed Mar 03 16:30:25 GMT-05:00 2004. The 24-hour clock is used. GMT-05:00 is the time zone.
F	Display date formatted as year-month-date with four digits for the year and two digits each for the month and date (e.g., 2004-05-04).
D	Display date formatted as month/day/year with two digits each for the month, day and year (e.g., 03/03/04).
r	Display time in 12-hour format as hour:minute:second AM|PM with two digits each for the hour, minute and second (e.g., 04:30:25 PM).
R	Display time formatted as hour:minute with two digits each for the hour and minute (e.g., 16:30). The 24-hour clock is used.
T	Display time as hour:minute:second with two digits for the hour, minute and second (e.g., 16:30:25). The 24-hour clock is used.

Fig. I.6 | Date and time composition conversion suffix characters.

Conversion suffix character	Description
A	Display full name of the day of the week (e.g., Wednesday).
a	Display the three-character name of the day of the week (e.g., Wed).
B	Display full name of the month (e.g., March).
b	Display the three-character short name of the month (e.g., Mar).
d	Display the day of the month with two digits, padding with leading zeros as necessary (e.g., 03).
m	Display the month with two digits, padding with leading zeros as necessary (e.g., 07).

Fig. I.7 | Date formatting conversion suffix characters. (Part 1 of 2.)

Conversion suffix character	Description
e	Display the day of month without leading zeros (e.g., 3).
Y	Display the year with four digits (e.g., 2004).
y	Display the last two digits of the year with leading zeros (e.g., 04).
j	Display the day of the year with three digits, padding with leading zeros as necessary (e.g., 016).

Fig. I.7 | Date formatting conversion suffix characters. (Part 2 of 2.)

Conversion suffix character	Description
H	Display hour in 24-hour clock with a leading zero as necessary (e.g., 16).
I	Display hour in 12-hour clock with a leading zero as necessary (e.g., 04).
k	Display hour in 24-hour clock without leading zeros (e.g., 16).
l	Display hour in 12-hour clock without leading zeros (e.g., 4).
M	Display minute with a leading zero as necessary (e.g., 06).
S	Display second with a leading zero as necessary (e.g., 05).
Z	Display the abbreviation for the time zone (e.g., EST, stands for Eastern Standard Time, which is 5 hours behind Greenwich Mean Time).
p	Display morning or afternoon marker in lowercase (e.g., pm).
P	Display morning or afternoon marker in uppercase (e.g., PM).

Fig. I.8 | Time formatting conversion suffix characters.

Figure I.9 uses the conversion characters t and T with the conversion suffix characters to display dates and times in various formats. Conversion character t requires the corresponding argument to be a date or time of type long, Long, **Calendar** (package java.util) or **Date** (package java.util)—objects of each of these classes can represent dates and times. Class Calendar is preferred for this purpose because some constructors and

```
1   // Fig. I.9: DateTimeTest.java
2   // Formatting dates and times with conversion characters t and T.
3   import java.util.Calendar;
4
5   public class DateTimeTest
6   {
7      public static void main(String[] args)
8      {
9         // get current date and time
10        Calendar dateTime = Calendar.getInstance();
```

Fig. I.9 | Formatting dates and times with conversion characters t and T. (Part 1 of 2.)

```
11
12          // printing with conversion characters for date/time compositions
13          System.out.printf("%tc\n", dateTime);
14          System.out.printf("%tF\n", dateTime);
15          System.out.printf("%tD\n", dateTime);
16          System.out.printf("%tr\n", dateTime);
17          System.out.printf("%tT\n", dateTime);
18
19          // printing with conversion characters for date
20          System.out.printf("%1$tA, %1$tB %1$td, %1$tY\n", dateTime);
21          System.out.printf("%1$TA, %1$TB %1$Td, %1$TY\n", dateTime);
22          System.out.printf("%1$ta, %1$tb %1$te, %1$ty\n", dateTime);
23
24          // printing with conversion characters for time
25          System.out.printf("%1$tH:%1$tM:%1$tS\n", dateTime);
26          System.out.printf("%1$tZ %1$tI:%1$tM:%1$tS %tP", dateTime);
27      } // end main
28  } // end class DateTimeTest
```

```
Wed Feb 25 15:00:22 EST 2009
2009-02-25
02/25/09
03:00:22 PM
15:00:22
Wednesday, February 25, 2009
WEDNESDAY, FEBRUARY 25, 2009
Wed, Feb 25, 09
15:00:22
EST 03:00:22 PM
```

Fig. I.9 | Formatting dates and times with conversion characters t and T. (Part 2 of 2.)

methods in class Date are replaced by those in class Calendar. Line 10 invokes static method **getInstance** of Calendar to obtain a calendar with the current date and time. Lines 13–17, 20–22 and 25–26 use this Calendar object in printf statements as the value to be formatted with conversion character t. Lines 20–22 and 25–26 use the optional **argument index** ("1$") to indicate that all format specifiers in the format string use the first argument after the format string in the argument list. You'll learn more about argument indices in Section I.11. Using the argument index eliminates the need to repeatedly list the same argument.

I.8 Other Conversion Characters

The remaining conversion characters are **b**, **B**, **h**, **H**, **%** and **n**. These are described in Fig. I.10. Lines 9–10 of Fig. I.11 use %b to print the value of boolean (or Boolean) values false and true. Line 11 associates a String to %b, which returns true because it's not null. Line 12 associates a null object to %B, which displays FALSE because test is null. Lines 13–14 use %h to print the string representations of the hash-code values for strings "hello" and "Hello". These values could be used to store or locate the strings in a Hashtable or HashMap (both discussed in Chapter 16, Generic Collections). The hash-code values for these two strings differ, because one string starts with a lowercase letter and the other with an uppercase letter. Line 15 uses %H to print null in uppercase letters. The last two printf statements (lines 16–17) use %% to print the % character in a string and %n to print a platform-specific line separator.

Conversion character	Description
b or B	Print "true" or "false" for the value of a boolean or Boolean. These conversion characters can also format the value of any reference. If the reference is non-null, "true" is output; otherwise, "false". When conversion character B is used, the output is displayed in uppercase letters.
h or H	Print the string representation of an object's hash-code value in hexadecimal format. If the corresponding argument is null, "null" is printed. When conversion character H is used, the output is displayed in uppercase letters.
%	Print the percent character.
n	Print the platform-specific line separator (e.g., \r\n on Windows or \n on UNIX/LINUX).

Fig. I.10 | Other conversion characters.

```java
1   // Fig. I.11: OtherConversion.java
2   // Using the b, B, h, H, % and n conversion characters.
3
4   public class OtherConversion
5   {
6      public static void main(String[] args)
7      {
8         Object test = null;
9         System.out.printf("%b\n", false);
10        System.out.printf("%b\n", true);
11        System.out.printf("%b\n", "Test");
12        System.out.printf("%B\n", test);
13        System.out.printf("Hashcode of \"hello\" is %h\n", "hello");
14        System.out.printf("Hashcode of \"Hello\" is %h\n", "Hello");
15        System.out.printf("Hashcode of null is %H\n", test);
16        System.out.printf("Printing a %% in a format string\n");
17        System.out.printf("Printing a new line %nnext line starts here");
18     } // end main
19  } // end class OtherConversion
```

```
false
true
true
FALSE
Hashcode of "hello" is 5e918d2
```

Fig. I.11 | Using the b, B, h, H, % and n conversion characters. (Part 1 of 2.)

```
Hashcode of "Hello" is 42628b2
Hashcode of null is NULL
Printing a % in a format string
Printing a new line
next line starts here
```

Fig. I.11 | Using the b, B, h, H, % and n conversion characters. (Part 2 of 2.)

Common Programming Error I.2

Trying to print a literal percent character using % rather than %% in the format string might cause a difficult-to-detect logic error. When % appears in a format string, it must be followed by a conversion character in the string. The single percent could accidentally be followed by a legitimate conversion character, thus causing a logic error.

I.9 Printing with Field Widths and Precisions

The size of a field in which data is printed is specified by a **field width**. If the field width is larger than the data being printed, the data is right justified in that field by default. We discuss left justification in Section I.10. You insert an integer representing the field width between the % and the conversion character (e.g., %4d) in the format specifier. Figure I.12 prints two groups of five numbers each, right justifying those numbers that contain fewer digits than the field width. The field width is increased to print values wider than the field and that the minus sign for a negative value uses one character position in the field. Also, if no field width is specified, the data prints in exactly as many positions as it needs. Field widths can be used with all format specifiers except the line separator (%n).

```
1   // Fig. I.12: FieldWidthTest.java
2   // Right justifying integers in fields.
3
4   public class FieldWidthTest
5   {
6      public static void main(String[] args)
7      {
8         System.out.printf("%4d\n", 1);
9         System.out.printf("%4d\n", 12);
10        System.out.printf("%4d\n", 123);
11        System.out.printf("%4d\n", 1234);
12        System.out.printf("%4d\n\n", 12345); // data too large
13
14        System.out.printf("%4d\n", -1);
15        System.out.printf("%4d\n", -12);
16        System.out.printf("%4d\n", -123);
17        System.out.printf("%4d\n", -1234); // data too large
18        System.out.printf("%4d\n", -12345); // data too large
19     } // end main
20  } // end class RightJustifyTest
```

Fig. I.12 | Right justifying integers in fields. (Part 1 of 2.)

```
    1
   12
  123
 1234
12345

   -1
  -12
 -123
-1234
-12345
```

Fig. I.12 | Right justifying integers in fields. (Part 2 of 2.)

Common Programming Error I.3

Not providing a sufficiently large field width to handle a value to be printed can offset other data being printed and produce confusing outputs. Know your data!

Method `printf` also provides the ability to specify the precision with which data is printed. Precision has different meanings for different types. When used with floating-point conversion characters e and f, the precision is the number of digits that appear after the decimal point. When used with conversion characters g, a or A, the precision is the maximum number of significant digits to be printed. When used with conversion character s, the precision is the maximum number of characters to be written from the string. To use precision, place between the percent sign and the conversion specifier a decimal point (.) followed by an integer representing the precision. Figure I.13 demonstrates the use of precision in format strings. When a floating-point value is printed with a precision smaller than the original number of decimal places in the value, the value is rounded. Also, the format specifier %.3g indicates that the total number of digits used to display the floating-point value is 3. Because the value has three digits to the left of the decimal point, the value is rounded to the ones position.

The field width and the precision can be combined by placing the field width, followed by a decimal point, followed by a precision between the percent sign and the conversion character, as in the statement

```
printf("%9.3f", 123.456789);
```

which displays 123.457 with three digits to the right of the decimal point right justified in a nine-digit field—this number will be preceded in its field by two blanks.

```
1   // Fig. I.13: PrecisionTest.java
2   // Using precision for floating-point numbers and strings.
3   public class PrecisionTest
4   {
5      public static void main(String[] args)
6      {
7         double f = 123.94536;
8         String s = "Happy Birthday";
```

Fig. I.13 | Using precision for floating-point numbers and strings. (Part I of 2.)

```
 9
10          System.out.printf("Using precision for floating-point numbers\n");
11          System.out.printf("\t%.3f\n\t%.3e\n\t%.3g\n\n", f, f, f);
12
13          System.out.printf("Using precision for strings\n");
14          System.out.printf("\t%.11s\n", s);
15      } // end main
16   } // end class PrecisionTest
```

```
Using precision for floating-point numbers
        123.945
        1.239e+02
        124

Using precision for strings
        Happy Birth
```

Fig. I.13 | Using precision for floating-point numbers and strings. (Part 2 of 2.)

I.10 Using Flags in the `printf` Format String

Various flags may be used with method `printf` to supplement its output formatting capabilities. Seven flags are available for use in format strings (Fig. I.14).

Flag	Description
– (minus sign)	Left justify the output within the specified field.
+ (plus sign)	Display a plus sign preceding positive values and a minus sign preceding negative values.
space	Print a space before a positive value not printed with the + flag.
#	Prefix 0 to the output value when used with the octal conversion character o. Prefix 0x to the output value when used with the hexadecimal conversion character x.
0 (zero)	Pad a field with leading zeros.
, (comma)	Use the locale-specific thousands separator (i.e., ',' for U.S. locale) to display decimal and floating-point numbers.
(	Enclose negative numbers in parentheses.

Fig. I.14 | Format string flags.

To use a flag in a format string, place it immediately to the right of the percent sign. Several flags may be used in the same format specifier. Figure I.15 demonstrates right justification and left justification of a string, an integer, a character and a floating-point number. Line 9 serves as a counting mechanism for the screen output.

Figure I.16 prints a positive number and a negative number, each with and without the **+ flag**. The minus sign is displayed in both cases, the plus sign only when the + flag is used.

```
 1   // Fig. I.15: MinusFlagTest.java
 2   // Right justifying and left justifying values.
 3
 4   public class MinusFlagTest
 5   {
 6      public static void main(String[] args)
 7      {
 8         System.out.println("Columns:");
 9         System.out.println("012345678901234567890123456789\n");
10         System.out.printf("%10s%10d%10c%10f\n\n", "hello", 7, 'a', 1.23);
11         System.out.printf(
12            "%-10s%-10d%-10c%-10f\n", "hello", 7, 'a', 1.23);
13      } // end main
14   } // end class MinusFlagTest
```

```
Columns:
012345678901234567890123456789

     hello         7         a  1.230000

hello     7         a         1.230000
```

Fig. I.15 | Right justifying and left justifying values.

```
 1   // Fig. I.16: PlusFlagTest.java
 2   // Printing numbers with and without the + flag.
 3
 4   public class PlusFlagTest
 5   {
 6      public static void main(String[] args)
 7      {
 8         System.out.printf("%d\t%d\n", 786, -786);
 9         System.out.printf("%+d\t%+d\n", 786, -786);
10      } // end main
11   } // end class PlusFlagTest
```

```
786      -786
+786     -786
```

Fig. I.16 | Printing numbers with and without the + flag.

Figure I.17 prefixes a space to the positive number with the **space flag**. This is useful for aligning positive and negative numbers with the same number of digits. The value -547 is not preceded by a space in the output because of its minus sign. Figure I.18 uses the **# flag** to prefix 0 to the octal value and 0x to the hexadecimal value.

```
 1   // Fig. I.17: SpaceFlagTest.java
 2   // Printing a space before non-negative values.
 3
```

Fig. I.17 | Printing a space before nonnegative values. (Part I of 2.)

```
 4    public class SpaceFlagTest
 5    {
 6       public static void main(String[] args)
 7       {
 8          System.out.printf("% d\n% d\n", 547, -547);
 9       } // end main
10    } // end class SpaceFlagTest
```

```
 547
-547
```

Fig. I.17 | Printing a space before nonnegative values. (Part 2 of 2.)

```
 1    // Fig. I.18: PoundFlagTest.java
 2    // Using the # flag with conversion characters o and x.
 3
 4    public class PoundFlagTest
 5    {
 6       public static void main(String[] args)
 7       {
 8          int c = 31;        // initialize c
 9
10          System.out.printf("%#o\n", c);
11          System.out.printf("%#x\n", c);
12       } // end main
13    } // end class PoundFlagTest
```

```
037
0x1f
```

Fig. I.18 | Using the # flag with conversion characters o and x.

Figure I.19 combines the + flag the **0 flag** and the space flag to print 452 in a field of width 9 with a + sign and leading zeros, next prints 452 in a field of width 9 using only the 0 flag, then prints 452 in a field of width 9 using only the space flag.

```
 1    // Fig. I.19: ZeroFlagTest.java
 2    // Printing with the 0 (zero) flag fills in leading zeros.
 3
 4    public class ZeroFlagTest
 5    {
 6       public static void main(String[] args)
 7       {
 8          System.out.printf("%+09d\n", 452);
 9          System.out.printf("%09d\n", 452);
10          System.out.printf("% 9d\n", 452);
11       } // end main
12    } // end class ZeroFlagTest
```

Fig. I.19 | Printing with the 0 (zero) flag fills in leading zeros. (Part 1 of 2.)

```
+00000452
000000452
      452
```

Fig. I.19 | Printing with the 0 (zero) flag fills in leading zeros. (Part 2 of 2.)

Figure I.20 uses the comma (,) flag to display a decimal and a floating-point number with the thousands separator. Figure I.21 encloses negative numbers in parentheses using the (flag. The value 50 is not enclosed in parentheses in the output because it's a positive number.

```
 1   // Fig. I.20: CommaFlagTest.java
 2   // Using the comma (,) flag to display numbers with thousands separator.
 3
 4   public class CommaFlagTest
 5   {
 6      public static void main(String[] args)
 7      {
 8         System.out.printf("%,d\n", 58625);
 9         System.out.printf("%,.2f", 58625.21);
10         System.out.printf("%,.2f", 12345678.9);
11      } // end main
12   } // end class CommaFlagTest
```

```
58,625
58,625.21
12,345,678.90
```

Fig. I.20 | Using the comma (,) flag to display numbers with the thousands separator.

```
 1   // Fig. I.21: ParenthesesFlagTest.java
 2   // Using the (flag to place parentheses around negative numbers.
 3
 4   public class ParenthesesFlagTest
 5   {
 6      public static void main(String[] args)
 7      {
 8         System.out.printf("%(d\n", 50);
 9         System.out.printf("%(d\n", -50);
10         System.out.printf("%(.1e\n", -50.0);
11      } // end main
12   } // end class ParenthesesFlagTest
```

```
50
(50)
(5.0e+01)
```

Fig. I.21 | Using the (flag to place parentheses around negative numbers.

I.11 Printing with Argument Indices

An **argument index** is an optional integer followed by a $ sign that indicates the argument's position in the argument list. For example, lines 20–22 and 25–26 in Fig. I.9 use argument index "1$" to indicate that all format specifiers use the first argument in the argument list. Argument indices enable programmers to reorder the output so that the arguments in the argument list are not necessarily in the order of their corresponding format specifiers. Argument indices also help avoid duplicating arguments. Figure I.22 prints arguments in the argument list in reverse order using the argument index.

```
1   // Fig. I.22: ArgumentIndexTest
2   // Reordering output with argument indices.
3
4   public class ArgumentIndexTest
5   {
6      public static void main(String[] args)
7      {
8         System.out.printf(
9            "Parameter list without reordering: %s %s %s %s\n",
10           "first", "second", "third", "fourth");
11        System.out.printf(
12           "Parameter list after reordering: %4$s %3$s %2$s %1$s\n",
13           "first", "second", "third", "fourth");
14     } // end main
15  } // end class ArgumentIndexTest
```

```
Parameter list without reordering: first second third fourth
Parameter list after reordering: fourth third second first
```

Fig. I.22 | Reordering output with argument indices.

I.12 Printing Literals and Escape Sequences

Most literal characters to be printed in a `printf` statement can simply be included in the format string. However, there are several "problem" characters, such as the quotation mark (") that delimits the format string itself. Various control characters, such as newline and tab, must be represented by escape sequences. An escape sequence is represented by a backslash (\), followed by an escape character. Figure I.23 lists the escape sequences and the actions they cause.

Escape sequence	Description
\' (single quote)	Output the single quote (') character.
\" (double quote)	Output the double quote (") character.
\\ (backslash)	Output the backslash (\) character.
\b (backspace)	Move the cursor back one position on the current line.

Fig. I.23 | Escape sequences. (Part 1 of 2.)

Escape sequence	Description
\f (new page or form feed)	Move the cursor to the start of the next logical page.
\n (newline)	Move the cursor to the beginning of the next line.
\r (carriage return)	Move the cursor to the beginning of the current line.
\t (horizontal tab)	Move the cursor to the next horizontal tab position.

Fig. I.23 | Escape sequences. (Part 2 of 2.)

 Common Programming Error I.4
Attempting to print as literal data in a printf statement a double quote or backslash character without preceding that character with a backslash to form a proper escape sequence might result in a syntax error.

I.13 Formatting Output with Class `Formatter`

So far, we've discussed displaying formatted output to the standard output stream. What should we do if we want to send formatted outputs to other output streams or devices, such as a JTextArea or a file? The solution relies on class Formatter (in package java.util), which provides the same formatting capabilities as printf. Formatter is a utility class that enables programmers to output formatted data to a specified destination, such as a file on disk. By default, a Formatter creates a string in memory. Figure I.24 demonstrates how to use a Formatter to build a formatted string, which is then displayed in a message dialog.

Line 11 creates a Formatter object using the default constructor, so this object will build a string in memory. Other constructors are provided to allow you to specify the destination to which the formatted data should be output. For details, see http://docs.oracle.com/javase/7/docs/api/java/util/Formatter.html.

```java
// Fig. Fig. I.24: FormatterTest.java
// Formatting output with class Formatter.
import java.util.Formatter;
import javax.swing.JOptionPane;

public class FormatterTest
{
   public static void main(String[] args)
   {
      // create Formatter and format output
      Formatter formatter = new Formatter();
      formatter.format("%d = %#o = %#X", 10, 10, 10);

      // display output in JOptionPane
      JOptionPane.showMessageDialog(null, formatter.toString());
   } // end main
} // end class FormatterTest
```

Fig. I.24 | Formatting output with class Formatter. (Part 1 of 2.)

Fig. I.24 | Formatting output with class `Formatter`. (Part 2 of 2.)

Line 12 invokes method **format** to format the output. Like `printf`, method `format` takes a format string and an argument list. The difference is that `printf` sends the formatted output directly to the standard output stream, while `format` sends the formatted output to the destination specified by its constructor (a string in memory in this program). Line 15 invokes the `Formatter`'s `toString` method to get the formatted data as a string, which is then displayed in a message dialog.

Class `String` also provides a `static` convenience method named `format` that enables you to create a string in memory without the need to first create a `Formatter` object. Lines 11–12 and line 15 in Fig. I.24 could have been replaced by

```
String s = String.format("%d = %#o = %#x", 10, 10, 10);
JOptionPane.showMessageDialog(null, s);
```

I.14 Wrap-Up

This appendix summarized how to display formatted output with various format characters and flags. We displayed decimal numbers using format characters d, o, x and X; floating-point numbers using format characters e, E, f, g and G; and dates and times in various format using format characters t and T and their conversion suffix characters. You learned how to display output with field widths and precisions. We introduced the flags +, -, space, #, 0, comma and (that are used together with the format characters to produce output. We also demonstrated how to format output with class `Formatter`.

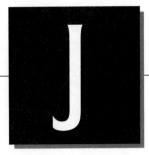

Number Systems

Objectives

In this appendix you'll:

- Learn basic number systems concepts, such as base, positional value and symbol value.

- Learn how to work with numbers represented in the binary, octal and hexadecimal number systems.

- Abbreviate binary numbers as octal numbers or hexadecimal numbers.

- Convert octal numbers and hexadecimal numbers to binary numbers.

- Convert back and forth between decimal numbers and their binary, octal and hexadecimal equivalents.

- Learn binary arithmetic and how negative binary numbers are represented using two's complement notation.

J.1 Introduction

In this appendix, we introduce the key number systems that Java programmers use, especially when they're working on software projects that require close interaction with machine-level hardware. Projects like this include operating systems, computer networking software, compilers, database systems and applications requiring high performance.

When we write an integer such as 227 or –63 in a Java program, the number is assumed to be in the decimal (base 10) number system. The digits in the decimal number system are 0, 1, 2, 3, 4, 5, 6, 7, 8 and 9. The lowest digit is 0 and the highest digit is 9—one less than the base of 10. Internally, computers use the binary (base 2) number system. The binary number system has only two digits, namely 0 and 1. Its lowest digit is 0 and its highest digit is 1—one less than the base of 2.

As we'll see, binary numbers tend to be much longer than their decimal equivalents. Programmers who work in assembly languages and in high-level languages like Java that enable programmers to reach down to the machine level find it cumbersome to work with binary numbers. So two other number systems—the octal number system (base 8) and the hexadecimal number system (base 16)—are popular primarily because they make it convenient to abbreviate binary numbers.

In the octal number system, the digits range from 0 to 7. Because both the binary number system and the octal number system have fewer digits than the decimal number system, their digits are the same as the corresponding digits in decimal.

The hexadecimal number system poses a problem because it requires 16 digits—a lowest digit of 0 and a highest digit with a value equivalent to decimal 15 (one less than the base of 16). By convention, we use the letters A through F to represent the hexadecimal digits corresponding to decimal values 10 through 15. Thus in hexadecimal we can have numbers like 876 consisting solely of decimal-like digits, numbers like 8A55F consisting of digits and letters and numbers like FFE consisting solely of letters. Occasionally, a hexadecimal number spells a common word such as FACE or FEED—this can appear strange to programmers accustomed to working with numbers. The digits of the binary, octal, decimal and hexadecimal number systems are summarized in Fig. J.1 and Fig. J.2.

Each of these number systems uses positional notation—each position in which a digit is written has a different positional value. For example, in the decimal number 937 (the 9, the 3 and the 7 are referred to as symbol values), we say that the 7 is written in the ones position, the 3 is written in the tens position and the 9 is written in the hundreds position. Each of these positions is a power of the base (base 10) and that these powers begin at 0 and increase by 1 as we move left in the number (Fig. J.3).

Binary digit	Octal digit	Decimal digit	Hexadecimal digit
0	0	0	0
1	1	1	1
	2	2	2
	3	3	3
	4	4	4
	5	5	5
	6	6	6
	7	7	7
		8	8
		9	9
			A (decimal value of 10)
			B (decimal value of 11)
			C (decimal value of 12)
			D (decimal value of 13)
			E (decimal value of 14)
			F (decimal value of 15)

Fig. J.1 | Digits of the binary, octal, decimal and hexadecimal number systems.

Attribute	Binary	Octal	Decimal	Hexadecimal
Base	2	8	10	16
Lowest digit	0	0	0	0
Highest digit	1	7	9	F

Fig. J.2 | Comparing the binary, octal, decimal and hexadecimal number systems.

Positional values in the decimal number system			
Decimal digit	9	3	7
Position name	Hundreds	Tens	Ones
Positional value	100	10	1
Positional value as a power of the base (10)	10^2	10^1	10^0

Fig. J.3 | Positional values in the decimal number system.

For longer decimal numbers, the next positions to the left would be the thousands position (10 to the 3rd power), the ten-thousands position (10 to the 4th power), the hundred-thousands position (10 to the 5th power), the millions position (10 to the 6th power), the ten-millions position (10 to the 7th power) and so on.

In the binary number 101, the rightmost 1 is written in the ones position, the 0 is written in the twos position and the leftmost 1 is written in the fours position. Each position is a power of the base (base 2) and that these powers begin at 0 and increase by 1 as we move left in the number (Fig. J.4). So, $101 = 2^2 + 2^0 = 4 + 1 = 5$.

Positional values in the binary number system			
Binary digit	1	0	1
Position name	Fours	Twos	Ones
Positional value	4	2	1
Positional value as a power of the base (2)	2^2	2^1	2^0

Fig. J.4 | Positional values in the binary number system.

For longer binary numbers, the next positions to the left would be the eights position (2 to the 3rd power), the sixteens position (2 to the 4th power), the thirty-twos position (2 to the 5th power), the sixty-fours position (2 to the 6th power) and so on.

In the octal number 425, we say that the 5 is written in the ones position, the 2 is written in the eights position and the 4 is written in the sixty-fours position. Each of these positions is a power of the base (base 8) and that these powers begin at 0 and increase by 1 as we move left in the number (Fig. J.5).

Positional values in the octal number system			
Decimal digit	4	2	5
Position name	Sixty-fours	Eights	Ones
Positional value	64	8	1
Positional value as a power of the base (8)	8^2	8^1	8^0

Fig. J.5 | Positional values in the octal number system.

For longer octal numbers, the next positions to the left would be the five-hundred-and-twelves position (8 to the 3rd power), the four-thousand-and-ninety-sixes position (8 to the 4th power), the thirty-two-thousand-seven-hundred-and-sixty-eights position (8 to the 5th power) and so on.

In the hexadecimal number 3DA, we say that the A is written in the ones position, the D is written in the sixteens position and the 3 is written in the two-hundred-and-fifty-sixes position. Each of these positions is a power of the base (base 16) and that these powers begin at 0 and increase by 1 as we move left in the number (Fig. J.6).

For longer hexadecimal numbers, the next positions to the left would be the four-thousand-and-ninety-sixes position (16 to the 3rd power), the sixty-five-thousand-five-hundred-and-thirty-sixes position (16 to the 4th power) and so on.

Positional values in the hexadecimal number system			
Decimal digit	3	D	A
Position name	Two-hundred-and-fifty-sixes	Sixteens	Ones
Positional value	256	16	1
Positional value as a power of the base (16)	16^2	16^1	16^0

Fig. J.6 | Positional values in the hexadecimal number system.

J.2 Abbreviating Binary Numbers as Octal and Hexadecimal Numbers

The main use for octal and hexadecimal numbers in computing is for abbreviating lengthy binary representations. Figure J.7 highlights the fact that lengthy binary numbers can be expressed concisely in number systems with higher bases than the binary number system.

Decimal number	Binary representation	Octal representation	Hexadecimal representation
0	0	0	0
1	1	1	1
2	10	2	2
3	11	3	3
4	100	4	4
5	101	5	5
6	110	6	6
7	111	7	7
8	1000	10	8
9	1001	11	9
10	1010	12	A
11	1011	13	B
12	1100	14	C
13	1101	15	D
14	1110	16	E
15	1111	17	F
16	10000	20	10

Fig. J.7 | Decimal, binary, octal and hexadecimal equivalents.

A particularly important relationship that both the octal number system and the hexadecimal number system have to the binary system is that the bases of octal and hexadecimal (8 and 16 respectively) are powers of the base of the binary number system (base 2). Consider the following 12-digit binary number and its octal and hexadecimal equivalents. See if you can determine how this relationship makes it convenient to abbreviate binary numbers in octal or hexadecimal. The answer follows the numbers.

Binary number	Octal equivalent	Hexadecimal equivalent
100011010001	4321	8D1

To see how the binary number converts easily to octal, simply break the 12-digit binary number into groups of three consecutive bits each and write those groups over the corresponding digits of the octal number as follows:

100	011	010	001
4	3	2	1

The octal digit you've written under each group of three bits corresponds precisely to the octal equivalent of that 3-digit binary number, as shown in Fig. J.7.

The same kind of relationship can be observed in converting from binary to hexadecimal. Break the 12-digit binary number into groups of four consecutive bits each and write those groups over the corresponding digits of the hexadecimal number as follows:

1000	1101	0001
8	D	1

Notice that the hexadecimal digit you wrote under each group of four bits corresponds precisely to the hexadecimal equivalent of that 4-digit binary number as shown in Fig. J.7.

J.3 Converting Octal and Hexadecimal Numbers to Binary Numbers

In the previous section, we saw how to convert binary numbers to their octal and hexadecimal equivalents by forming groups of binary digits and simply rewriting them as their equivalent octal digit values or hexadecimal digit values. This process may be used in reverse to produce the binary equivalent of a given octal or hexadecimal number.

For example, the octal number 653 is converted to binary simply by writing the 6 as its 3-digit binary equivalent 110, the 5 as its 3-digit binary equivalent 101 and the 3 as its 3-digit binary equivalent 011 to form the 9-digit binary number 110101011.

The hexadecimal number FAD5 is converted to binary simply by writing the F as its 4-digit binary equivalent 1111, the A as its 4-digit binary equivalent 1010, the D as its 4-digit binary equivalent 1101 and the 5 as its 4-digit binary equivalent 0101 to form the 16-digit 1111101011010101.

J.4 Converting from Binary, Octal or Hexadecimal to Decimal

We're accustomed to working in decimal, and therefore it's often convenient to convert a binary, octal, or hexadecimal number to decimal to get a sense of what the number is "really" worth. Our diagrams in Section J.1 express the positional values in decimal. To convert a number to decimal from another base, multiply the decimal equivalent of each digit by its positional value and sum these products. For example, the binary number 110101 is converted to decimal 53, as shown in Fig. J.8.

Converting a binary number to decimal					
Postional values:	32	16	8	4	2	1
Symbol values:	1	1	0	1	0	1
Products:	1*32=32	1*16=16	0*8=0	1*4=4	0*2=0	1*1=1
Sum:	= 32 + 16 + 0 + 4 + 0s + 1 = 53					

Fig. J.8 | Converting a binary number to decimal.

To convert octal 7614 to decimal 3980, we use the same technique, this time using appropriate octal positional values, as shown in Fig. J.9.

Converting an octal number to decimal			
Positional values:	512	64	8	1
Symbol values:	7	6	1	4
Products	7*512=3584	6*64=384	1*8=8	4*1=4
Sum:	= 3584 + 384 + 8 + 4 = 3980			

Fig. J.9 | Converting an octal number to decimal.

To convert hexadecimal AD3B to decimal 44347, we use the same technique, this time using appropriate hexadecimal positional values, as shown in Fig. J.10.

Converting a hexadecimal number to decimal			
Postional values:	4096	256	16	1
Symbol values:	A	D	3	B
Products	A*4096=40960	D*256=3328	3*16=48	B*1=11
Sum:	= 40960 + 3328 + 48 + 11 = 44347			

Fig. J.10 | Converting a hexadecimal number to decimal.

J.5 Converting from Decimal to Binary, Octal or Hexadecimal

The conversions in Section J.4 follow naturally from the positional notation conventions. Converting from decimal to binary, octal, or hexadecimal also follows these conventions.

Suppose we wish to convert decimal 57 to binary. We begin by writing the positional values of the columns right to left until we reach a column whose positional value is greater than the decimal number. We don't need that column, so we discard it. Thus, we first write:

Positional values: 64   32   16   8   4   2   1

Then we discard the column with positional value 64, leaving:

Positional values:	32	16	8	4	2	1

Next we work from the leftmost column to the right. We divide 32 into 57 and observe that there's one 32 in 57 with a remainder of 25, so we write 1 in the 32 column. We divide 16 into 25 and observe that there's one 16 in 25 with a remainder of 9 and write 1 in the 16 column. We divide 8 into 9 and observe that there's one 8 in 9 with a remainder of 1. The next two columns each produce quotients of 0 when their positional values are divided into 1, so we write 0s in the 4 and 2 columns. Finally, 1 into 1 is 1, so we write 1 in the 1 column. This yields:

Positional values:	32	16	8	4	2	1
Symbol values:	1	1	1	0	0	1

and thus decimal 57 is equivalent to binary 111001.

To convert decimal 103 to octal, we begin by writing the positional values of the columns until we reach a column whose positional value is greater than the decimal number. We do not need that column, so we discard it. Thus, we first write:

Positional values:	512	64	8	1

Then we discard the column with positional value 512, yielding:

Positional values:	64	8	1

Next we work from the leftmost column to the right. We divide 64 into 103 and observe that there's one 64 in 103 with a remainder of 39, so we write 1 in the 64 column. We divide 8 into 39 and observe that there are four 8s in 39 with a remainder of 7 and write 4 in the 8 column. Finally, we divide 1 into 7 and observe that there are seven 1s in 7 with no remainder, so we write 7 in the 1 column. This yields:

Positional values:	64	8	1
Symbol values:	1	4	7

and thus decimal 103 is equivalent to octal 147.

To convert decimal 375 to hexadecimal, we begin by writing the positional values of the columns until we reach a column whose positional value is greater than the decimal number. We do not need that column, so we discard it. Thus, we first write:

Positional values:	4096	256	16	1

Then we discard the column with positional value 4096, yielding:

Positional values:	256	16	1

Next we work from the leftmost column to the right. We divide 256 into 375 and observe that there's one 256 in 375 with a remainder of 119, so we write 1 in the 256 column. We divide 16 into 119 and observe that there are seven 16s in 119 with a remainder of 7 and write 7 in the 16 column. Finally, we divide 1 into 7 and observe that there are seven 1s in 7 with no remainder, so we write 7 in the 1 column. This yields:

Positional values:	256	16	1
Symbol values:	1	7	7

and thus decimal 375 is equivalent to hexadecimal 177.

J.6 Negative Binary Numbers: Two's Complement Notation

The discussion so far in this appendix has focused on positive numbers. In this section, we explain how computers represent negative numbers using *two's complement notation*. First we explain how the two's complement of a binary number is formed, then we show why it represents the negative value of the given binary number.

Consider a machine with 32-bit integers. Suppose

```
int value = 13;
```

The 32-bit representation of value is

```
00000000 00000000 00000000 00001101
```

To form the negative of value we first form its *one's complement* by applying Java's bitwise complement operator (~):

```
onesComplementOfValue = ~value;
```

Internally, ~value is now value with each of its bits reversed—ones become zeros and zeros become ones, as follows:

```
value:
00000000 00000000 00000000 00001101

~value (i.e., value's ones complement):
11111111 11111111 11111111 11110010
```

To form the two's complement of value, we simply add 1 to value's one's complement. Thus

```
Two's complement of value:
11111111 11111111 11111111 11110011
```

Now if this is in fact equal to –13, we should be able to add it to binary 13 and obtain a result of 0. Let's try this:

```
 00000000 00000000 00000000 00001101
+11111111 11111111 11111111 11110011
-------------------------------------
 00000000 00000000 00000000 00000000
```

The carry bit coming out of the leftmost column is discarded and we indeed get 0 as a result. If we add the one's complement of a number to the number, the result would be all 1s. The key to getting a result of all zeros is that the two's complement is one more than the one's complement. The addition of 1 causes each column to add to 0 with a carry of 1. The carry keeps moving leftward until it's discarded from the leftmost bit, and thus the resulting number is all zeros.

Computers actually perform a subtraction, such as

```
x = a - value;
```

by adding the two's complement of value to a, as follows:

```
x = a + (~value + 1);
```

Suppose a is 27 and value is 13 as before. If the two's complement of value is actually the negative of value, then adding the two's complement of value to a should produce the result 14. Let's try this:

```
a (i.e., 27)        00000000 00000000 00000000 00011011
+(~value + 1)      +11111111 11111111 11111111 11110011
                   -------------------------------------
                    00000000 00000000 00000000 00001110
```

which is indeed equal to 14.

Bit Manipulation

K.1 Introduction

This appendix presents an extensive discussion of bit-manipulation operators, followed by a discussion of class **BitSet**, which enables the creation of bit-array-like objects for setting and getting individual bit values. Java provides extensive bit-manipulation capabilities for programmers who need to get down to the "bits-and-bytes" level. Operating systems, test equipment software, networking software and many other kinds of software require that the programmer communicate "directly with the hardware." We now discuss Java's bit-manipulation capabilities and bitwise operators.

K.2 Bit Manipulation and the Bitwise Operators

Computers represent all data internally as sequences of bits. Each bit can assume the value 0 or the value 1. On most systems, a sequence of eight bits forms a byte—the standard storage unit for a variable of type byte. Other types are stored in larger numbers of bytes. The bitwise operators can manipulate the bits of integral operands (i.e., operations of type byte, char, short, int and long), but not floating-point operands.

The discussions of bitwise operators in this section show the binary representations of the integer operands. For a detailed explanation of the binary (also called base 2) number system, see Appendix J, Number Systems.

The bitwise operators are **bitwise AND (&)**, **bitwise inclusive OR (|)**, **bitwise exclusive OR (^)**, **left shift (<<)**, **signed right shift (>>)**, **unsigned right shift (>>>)** and **bitwise complement (~)**. The bitwise AND, bitwise inclusive OR and bitwise exclusive OR operators compare their two operands bit by bit. The bitwise AND operator sets each bit in the result to 1 if and only if the corresponding bit in both operands is 1. The bitwise inclusive OR operator sets each bit in the result to 1 if the corresponding bit in either (or both) operand(s) is 1. The bitwise exclusive OR operator sets each bit in the result to 1 if the corresponding bit in exactly one operand is 1. The left-shift operator shifts the bits of its left operand to the left by the number of bits specified in its right operand. The signed right shift operator shifts the bits in its left operand to the right by the number of bits specified in its right operand—if the left operand is negative, 1s are shifted in from the left; otherwise, 0s are shifted in from the left. The unsigned right shift operator shifts the bits in its left operand to the right by the number of bits specified in its right operand—0s are shifted in from the left. The bitwise complement operator sets all 0 bits in its operand to 1 in the result and sets all 1 bits in its operand to 0 in the result. The bitwise operators are summarized in Fig. K.1.

Operator	Name	Description
&	bitwise AND	The bits in the result are set to 1 if the corresponding bits in the two operands are both 1.
|	bitwise inclusive OR	The bits in the result are set to 1 if at least one of the corresponding bits in the two operands is 1.
^	bitwise exclusive OR	The bits in the result are set to 1 if exactly one of the corresponding bits in the two operands is 1.
<<	left shift	Shifts the bits of the left operand left by the number of bits specified by the right operand; fill from the right with 0.
>>	signed right shift	Shifts the bits of the left operand right by the number of bits specified by the right operand. If the left operand is negative, 1s are filled in from the left; otherwise, 0s are filled in from the left.
>>>	unsigned right shift	Shifts the bits of the left operand right by the number of bits specified by the second operand; 0s are filled in from the left.
~	bitwise complement	All 0 bits are set to 1, and all 1 bits are set to 0.

Fig. K.1 | Bitwise operators.

When using the bitwise operators, it's useful to display values in their binary representation to illustrate the effects of these operators. The application of Fig. K.2 allows the user to enter an integer from the standard input. Lines 10–12 read the integer from the standard input. The integer is displayed in its binary representation in groups of eight bits each. Often, the bitwise AND operator is used with an operand called a **mask**—an integer value with specific bits set to 1. Masks are used to hide some bits in a value while selecting other bits. In line 18, mask variable displayMask is assigned the value 1 << 31, or

```
10000000 00000000 00000000 00000000
```

Lines 21–30 obtains a string representation of the integer, in bits. Line 24 uses the bitwise AND operator to combine variable input with variable displayMask. The left-shift operator shifts the value 1 from the low-order (rightmost) bit to the high-order (leftmost) bit in displayMask and fills in 0 from the right.

```
1   // Fig. K.2: PrintBits.java
2   // Printing an unsigned integer in bits.
3   import java.util.Scanner;
```

Fig. K.2 | Printing the bits in an integer. (Part 1 of 2.)

```
4
5   public class PrintBits
6   {
7       public static void main(String[] args)
8       {
9           // get input integer
10          Scanner scanner = new Scanner(System.in);
11          System.out.println("Please enter an integer:");
12          int input = scanner.nextInt();
13
14          // display bit representation of an integer
15          System.out.println("\nThe integer in bits is:");
16
17          // create int value with 1 in leftmost bit and 0s elsewhere
18          int displayMask = 1 << 31;
19
20          // for each bit display 0 or 1
21          for (int bit = 1; bit <= 32; bit++)
22          {
23              // use displayMask to isolate bit
24              System.out.print((input & displayMask) == 0 ? '0' : '1' );
25
26              input <<= 1; // shift value one position to left
27
28              if (bit % 8 == 0)
29                  System.out.print(' '); // display space every 8 bits
30          } // end for
31      } // end main
32  } // end class PrintBits
```

```
Please enter an integer:
0

The integer in bits is:
00000000 00000000 00000000 00000000
```

```
Please enter an integer:
-1

The integer in bits is:
11111111 11111111 11111111 11111111
```

```
Please enter an integer:
65535

The integer in bits is:
00000000 00000000 11111111 11111111
```

Fig. K.2 | Printing the bits in an integer. (Part 2 of 2.)

Line 24 determines whether the current leftmost bit of variable value is a 1 or 0 and displays '1' or '0', respectively, to the standard output. Assume that input contains 2000000000 (01110111 00110101 10010100 00000000). When input and displayMask are combined using &, all the bits except the high-order (leftmost) bit in variable input are "masked off" (hidden), because any bit "ANDed" with 0 yields 0. If the leftmost bit is 1, the expression input & displayMask evaluates to 1 and line 24 displays '1'; otherwise, line 24 displays '0'. Then line 26 left shifts variable input to the left by one bit with the expression input <<= 1. (This expression is equivalent to input = input << 1.) These steps are repeated for each bit in variable input. [*Note:* Class Integer provides method **toBinaryString**, which returns a string containing the binary representation of an integer.] Figure K.3 summarizes the results of combining two bits with the bitwise AND (&) operator.

Common Programming Error K.1

Using the conditional AND operator (&&) instead of the bitwise AND operator (&) is a compilation error.

Bit 1	Bit 2	Bit 1 & Bit 2
0	0	0
1	0	0
0	1	0
1	1	1

Fig. K.3 | Bitwise AND operator (&) combining two bits.

Figure K.4 demonstrates the bitwise AND operator, the bitwise inclusive OR operator, the bitwise exclusive OR operator and the bitwise complement operator. The program uses the display method (lines 7–25) of the utility class BitRepresentation (Fig. K.5) to get a string representation of the integer values. Notice that method display performs the same task as lines 17–30 in Fig. K.2. Declaring display as a static method of class BitRepresentation allows display to be reused by later applications. The application of Fig. K.4 asks users to choose the operation they would like to test, gets input integer(s), performs the operation and displays the result of each operation in both integer and bitwise representations.

```
 1   // Fig. K.4: MiscBitOps.java
 2   // Using the bitwise operators.
 3   import java.util.Scanner;
 4
 5   public class MiscBitOps
 6   {
 7      public static void main(String[] args)
 8      {
 9         int choice = 0; // store operation type
```

Fig. K.4 | Bitwise AND, bitwise inclusive OR, bitwise exclusive OR and bitwise complement operators. (Part 1 of 4.)

```
10          int first = 0; // store first input integer
11          int second = 0; // store second input integer
12          int result = 0; // store operation result
13          Scanner scanner = new Scanner(System.in); // create Scanner
14
15          // continue execution until user exit
16          while (true)
17          {
18             // get selected operation
19             System.out.println("\n\nPlease choose the operation:");
20             System.out.printf("%s%s", "1--AND\n2--Inclusive OR\n",
21                "3--Exclusive OR\n4--Complement\n5--Exit\n");
22             choice = scanner.nextInt();
23
24             // perform bitwise operation
25             switch (choice)
26             {
27                case 1: // AND
28                   System.out.print("Please enter two integers:");
29                   first = scanner.nextInt(); // get first input integer
30                   BitRepresentation.display(first);
31                   second = scanner.nextInt(); // get second input integer
32                   BitRepresentation.display(second);
33                   result = first & second; // perform bitwise AND
34                   System.out.printf(
35                      "\n\n%d & %d = %d", first, second, result);
36                   BitRepresentation.display(result);
37                   break;
38                case 2: // Inclusive OR
39                   System.out.print("Please enter two integers:");
40                   first = scanner.nextInt(); // get first input integer
41                   BitRepresentation.display(first);
42                   second = scanner.nextInt(); // get second input integer
43                   BitRepresentation.display(second);
44                   result = first | second; // perform bitwise inclusive OR
45                   System.out.printf(
46                      "\n\n%d | %d = %d", first, second, result);
47                   BitRepresentation.display(result);
48                   break;
49                case 3: // Exclusive OR
50                   System.out.print("Please enter two integers:");
51                   first = scanner.nextInt(); // get first input integer
52                   BitRepresentation.display(first);
53                   second = scanner.nextInt(); // get second input integer
54                   BitRepresentation.display(second);
55                   result = first ^ second; // perform bitwise exclusive OR
56                   System.out.printf(
57                      "\n\n%d ^ %d = %d", first, second, result);
58                   BitRepresentation.display(result);
59                   break;
60                case 4: // Complement
61                   System.out.print("Please enter one integer:");
```

Fig. K.4 | Bitwise AND, bitwise inclusive OR, bitwise exclusive OR and bitwise complement operators. (Part 2 of 4.)

```
62              first = scanner.nextInt(); // get input integer
63              BitRepresentation.display(first);
64              result = ~first; // perform bitwise complement on first
65              System.out.printf("\n\n~%d = %d", first, result);
66              BitRepresentation.display(result);
67              break;
68          case 5: default:
69              System.exit(0); // exit application
70          } // end switch
71      } // end while
72   } // end main
73 } // end class MiscBitOps
```

```
Please choose the operation:
1--AND
2--Inclusive OR
3--Exclusive OR
4--Complement
5--Exit
1
Please enter two integers:65535 1

Bit representation of 65535 is:
00000000 00000000 11111111 11111111
Bit representation of 1 is:
00000000 00000000 00000000 00000001

65535 & 1 = 1
Bit representation of 1 is:
00000000 00000000 00000000 00000001

Please choose the operation:
1--AND
2--Inclusive OR
3--Exclusive OR
4--Complement
5--Exit
2
Please enter two integers:15 241

Bit representation of 15 is:
00000000 00000000 00000000 00001111
Bit representation of 241 is:
00000000 00000000 00000000 11110001

15 | 241 = 255
Bit representation of 255 is:
00000000 00000000 00000000 11111111

Please choose the operation:
1--AND
2--Inclusive OR
3--Exclusive OR
4--Complement
5--Exit
3
```

Fig. K.4 | Bitwise AND, bitwise inclusive OR, bitwise exclusive OR and bitwise complement operators. (Part 3 of 4.)

```
Please enter two integers:139 199

Bit representation of 139 is:
00000000 00000000 00000000 10001011
Bit representation of 199 is:
00000000 00000000 00000000 11000111

139 ^ 199 = 76
Bit representation of 76 is:
00000000 00000000 00000000 01001100

Please choose the operation:
1--AND
2--Inclusive OR
3--Exclusive OR
4--Complement
5--Exit
4
Please enter one integer:21845

Bit representation of 21845 is:
00000000 00000000 01010101 01010101

~21845 = -21846
Bit representation of -21846 is:
11111111 11111111 10101010 10101010
```

Fig. K.4 | Bitwise AND, bitwise inclusive OR, bitwise exclusive OR and bitwise complement operators. (Part 4 of 4.)

```
1   // Fig K.5: BitRepresentation.java
2   // Utility class that displays bit representation of an integer.
3
4   public class BitRepresentation
5   {
6      // display bit representation of specified int value
7      public static void display(int value)
8      {
9         System.out.printf("\nBit representation of %d is: \n", value);
10
11        // create int value with 1 in leftmost bit and 0s elsewhere
12        int displayMask = 1 << 31;
13
14        // for each bit display 0 or 1
15        for (int bit = 1; bit <= 32; bit++)
16        {
17           // use displayMask to isolate bit
18           System.out.print((value & displayMask) == 0 ? '0' : '1');
19
20           value <<= 1; // shift value one position to left
21
```

Fig. K.5 | Utility class that displays bit representation of an integer.

```
22                if (bit % 8 == 0)
23                   System.out.print(' '); // display space every 8 bits
24             } // end for
25          } // end method display
26       } // end class BitRepresentation
```

Fig. K.5 | Utility class that displays bit representation of an integer.

The first output window in Fig. K.4 shows the results of combining the value 65535 and the value 1 with the bitwise AND operator (&; line 33). All the bits except the low-order bit in the value 65535 are "masked off" (hidden) by "ANDing" with the value 1.

The bitwise inclusive OR operator (|) sets each bit in the result to 1 if the corresponding bit in either (or both) operand(s) is 1. The second output window in Fig. K.4 shows the results of combining the value 15 and the value 241 by using the bitwise OR operator (line 44)—the result is 255. Figure K.6 summarizes the results of combining two bits with the bitwise inclusive OR operator.

Bit 1	Bit 2	Bit 1 | Bit 2
0	0	0
1	0	1
0	1	1
1	1	1

Fig. K.6 | Bitwise inclusive OR operator (|) combining two bits.

The bitwise exclusive OR operator (^) sets each bit in the result to 1 if *exactly* one of the corresponding bits in its two operands is 1. The third output window in Fig. K.4 shows the results of combining the value 139 and the value 199 by using the exclusive OR operator (line 55)—the result is 76. Figure K.7 summarizes the results of combining two bits with the bitwise exclusive OR operator.

Bit 1	Bit 2	Bit 1 ^ Bit 2
0	0	0
1	0	1
0	1	1
1	1	0

Fig. K.7 | Bitwise exclusive OR operator (^) combining two bits.

The bitwise complement operator (~) sets all 1 bits in its operand to 0 in the result and sets all 0 bits in its operand to 1 in the result—otherwise referred to as "taking the one's complement of the value." The fourth output window in Fig. K.4 shows the results of taking the one's complement of the value 21845 (line 64). The result is -21846.

The application of Fig. K.8 demonstrates the left-shift operator (<<), the signed right-shift operator (>>) and the unsigned right-shift operator (>>>). The application asks the user to enter an integer and choose the operation, then performs a one-bit shift and displays the results of the shift in both integer and bitwise representation. We use the utility class BitRepresentation (Fig. K.5) to display the bit representation of an integer.

The left-shift operator (<<) shifts the bits of its left operand to the left by the number of bits specified in its right operand (performed at line 31 in Fig. K.8). Bits vacated to the right are replaced with 0s; 1s shifted off the left are lost. The first output window in Fig. K.8 demonstrates the left-shift operator. Starting with the value 1, the left shift operation was chosen, resulting in the value 2.

```java
 1   // Fig. K.8: BitShift.java
 2   // Using the bitwise shift operators.
 3   import java.util.Scanner;
 4
 5   public class BitShift
 6   {
 7      public static void main(String[] args)
 8      {
 9         int choice = 0; // store operation type
10         int input = 0; // store input integer
11         int result = 0; // store operation result
12         Scanner scanner = new Scanner(System.in); // create Scanner
13
14         // continue execution until user exit
15         while (true)
16         {
17            // get shift operation
18            System.out.println("\n\nPlease choose the shift operation:");
19            System.out.println("1--Left Shift (<<)");
20            System.out.println("2--Signed Right Shift (>>)");
21            System.out.println("3--Unsigned Right Shift (>>>)");
22            System.out.println("4--Exit");
23            choice = scanner.nextInt();
24
25            // perform shift operation
26            switch (choice)
27            {
28               case 1: // <<
29                  System.out.println("Please enter an integer to shift:");
30                  input = scanner.nextInt(); // get input integer
31                  result = input << 1; // left shift one position
32                  System.out.printf("\n%d << 1 = %d", input, result);
33                  break;
34               case 2: // >>
35                  System.out.println("Please enter an integer to shift:");
36                  input = scanner.nextInt(); // get input integer
37                  result = input >> 1; // signed right shift one position
38                  System.out.printf("\n%d >> 1 = %d", input, result);
39                  break;
40               case 3: // >>>
41                  System.out.println("Please enter an integer to shift:");
42                  input = scanner.nextInt(); // get input integer
```

Fig. K.8 | Bitwise shift operations. (Part 1 of 3.)

```
43                    result = input >>> 1; // unsigned right shift one position
44                    System.out.printf("\n%d >>> 1 = %d", input, result);
45                    break;
46                case 4: default: // default operation is <<
47                    System.exit(0); // exit application
48            } // end switch
49
50            // display input integer and result in bits
51            BitRepresentation.display(input);
52            BitRepresentation.display(result);
53        } // end while
54    } // end main
55 } // end class BitShift
```

```
Please choose the shift operation:
1--Left Shift (<<)
2--Signed Right Shift (>>)
3--Unsigned Right Shift (>>>)
4--Exit
1
Please enter an integer to shift:
1

1 << 1 = 2
Bit representation of 1 is:
00000000 00000000 00000000 00000001
Bit representation of 2 is:
00000000 00000000 00000000 00000010

Please choose the shift operation:
1--Left Shift (<<)
2--Signed Right Shift (>>)
3--Unsigned Right Shift (>>>)
4--Exit
2
Please enter an integer to shift:
-2147483648

-2147483648 >> 1 = -1073741824
Bit representation of -2147483648 is:
10000000 00000000 00000000 00000000
Bit representation of -1073741824 is:
11000000 00000000 00000000 00000000

Please choose the shift operation:
1--Left Shift (<<)
2--Signed Right Shift (>>)
3--Unsigned Right Shift (>>>)
4--Exit
3
Please enter an integer to shift:
-2147483648
```

Fig. K.8 | Bitwise shift operations. (Part 2 of 3.)

```
-2147483648 >>> 1 = 1073741824
Bit representation of -2147483648 is:
10000000 00000000 00000000 00000000
Bit representation of 1073741824 is:
01000000 00000000 00000000 00000000
```

Fig. K.8 | Bitwise shift operations. (Part 3 of 3.)

The signed right-shift operator (>>) shifts the bits of its left operand to the right by the number of bits specified in its right operand (performed at line 37 in Fig. K.8). Performing a right shift causes the vacated bits at the left to be replaced by 0s if the number is positive or by 1s if the number is negative. Any 1s shifted off the right are lost. Next, the output window the results of signed right shifting the value -2147483648, which is the value 1 being left shifted 31 times. Notice that the leftmost bit is replaced by 1 because the number is negative.

The unsigned right-shift operator (>>>) shifts the bits of its left operand to the right by the number of bits specified in its right operand (performed at line 43 Fig. K.8). Performing an unsigned right shift causes the vacated bits at the left to be replaced by 0s. Any 1s shifted off the right are lost. The third output window of Fig. K.8 shows the results of unsigned right shifting the value -2147483648. Notice that the leftmost bit is replaced by 0. Each bitwise operator (except the bitwise complement operator) has a corresponding assignment operator. These **bitwise assignment operators** are shown in Fig. K.9.

Bitwise assignment operators	
&=	Bitwise AND assignment operator.
|=	Bitwise inclusive OR assignment operator.
^=	Bitwise exclusive OR assignment operator.
<<=	Left-shift assignment operator.
>>=	Signed right-shift assignment operator.
>>>=	Unsigned right-shift assignment operator.

Fig. K.9 | Bitwise assignment operators.

K.3 BitSet Class

Class BitSet makes it easy to create and manipulate **bit sets**, which are useful for representing sets of boolean flags. BitSets are dynamically resizable—more bits can be added as needed, and a BitSet will grow to accommodate the additional bits. Class BitSet provides two constructors—a no-argument constructor that creates an empty BitSet and a constructor that receives an integer representing the number of bits in the BitSet. By default, each bit in a BitSet has a false value—the underlying bit has the value 0. A bit is set to true (also called "on") with a call to BitSet method **set**, which receives the index of the bit to set as an argument. This makes the underlying value of that bit 1. Bit indices are zero based, like arrays. A bit is set to false (also called "off") by calling BitSet method

clear. This makes the underlying value of that bit 0. To obtain the value of a bit, use Bit-Set method **get**, which receives the index of the bit to get and returns a boolean value representing whether the bit at that index is on (true) or off (false).

Class BitSet also provides methods for combining the bits in two BitSets, using bitwise logical AND (**and**), bitwise logical inclusive OR (**or**), and bitwise logical exclusive OR (**xor**). Assuming that b1 and b2 are BitSets, the statement

```
b1.and(b2);
```

performs a bit-by-bit logical AND operation between BitSets b1 and b2. The result is stored in b1. When b2 has more bits than b1, the extra bits of b2 are ignored. Hence, the size of b1 remain unchanged. Bitwise logical inclusive OR and bitwise logical exclusive OR are performed by the statements

```
b1.or(b2);
b1.xor(b2);
```

When b2 has more bits than b1, the extra bits of b2 are ignored. Hence the size of b1 remains unchanged.

BitSet method **size** returns the number of bits in a BitSet. BitSet method **equals** compares two BitSets for equality. Two BitSets are equal if and only if each BitSet has identical values in corresponding bits. BitSet method **toString** creates a string representation of a BitSet's contents.

Figure K.10 implements the Sieve of Eratosthenes (for finding prime numbers). We use a BitSet to implement the algorithm. The application asks the user to enter an integer between 2 and 1023, displays all the prime numbers from 2 to 1023 and determines whether that number is prime.

```java
1   // Fig. K.10: BitSetTest.java
2   // Using a BitSet to demonstrate the Sieve of Eratosthenes.
3   import java.util.BitSet;
4   import java.util.Scanner;
5
6   public class BitSetTest
7   {
8      public static void main(String[] args)
9      {
10        // get input integer
11        Scanner scanner = new Scanner(System.in);
12        System.out.println("Please enter an integer from 2 to 1023");
13        int input = scanner.nextInt();
14
15        // perform Sieve of Eratosthenes
16        BitSet sieve = new BitSet(1024);
17        int size = sieve.size();
18
19        // set all bits from 2 to 1023
20        for (int i = 2; i < size; i++)
21           sieve.set(i);
22
```

Fig. K.10 | Sieve of Eratosthenes, using a BitSet. (Part 1 of 3.)

```
23          // perform Sieve of Eratosthenes
24          int finalBit = (int) Math.sqrt(size);
25
26          for (int i = 2; i < finalBit; i++)
27          {
28             if (sieve.get(i)  )
29             {
30                for (int j = 2 * i; j < size; j += i)
31                   sieve.clear(j);
32             } // end if
33          } // end for
34
35          int counter = 0;
36
37          // display prime numbers from 2 to 1023
38          for (int i = 2; i < size; i++)
39          {
40             if (sieve.get(i)  )
41             {
42                System.out.print(String.valueOf(i));
43                System.out.print(++counter % 7 == 0 ? "\n" : "\t");
44             } // end if
45          } // end for
46
47          // display result
48          if (sieve.get(input)  )
49             System.out.printf("\n%d is a prime number", input);
50          else
51             System.out.printf("\n%d is not a prime number", input);
52       } // end main
53    } // end class BitSetTest
```

```
Please enter an integer from 2 to 1023
773
2       3       5       7       11      13      17
19      23      29      31      37      41      43
47      53      59      61      67      71      73
79      83      89      97      101     103     107
109     113     127     131     137     139     149
151     157     163     167     173     179     181
191     193     197     199     211     223     227
229     233     239     241     251     257     263
269     271     277     281     283     293     307
311     313     317     331     337     347     349
353     359     367     373     379     383     389
397     401     409     419     421     431     433
439     443     449     457     461     463     467
479     487     491     499     503     509     521
523     541     547     557     563     569     571
577     587     593     599     601     607     613
617     619     631     641     643     647     653
659     661     673     677     683     691     701
709     719     727     733     739     743     751
```

Fig. K.10 | Sieve of Eratosthenes, using a BitSet. (Part 2 of 3.)

```
757      761      769      773      787      797      809
811      821      823      827      829      839      853
857      859      863      877      881      883      887
907      911      919      929      937      941      947
953      967      971      977      983      991      997
1009     1013     1019     1021
773 is a prime number
```

Fig. K.10 | Sieve of Eratosthenes, using a BitSet. (Part 3 of 3.)

Line 16 creates a BitSet of 1024 bits. We ignore the bits at indices zero and one in this application. Lines 20–21 set all the bits in the BitSet to "on" with BitSet method set. Lines 24–33 determine all the prime numbers from 2 to 1023. The integer finalBit specifies when the algorithm is complete. The basic algorithm is that a number is prime if it has no divisors other than 1 and itself. Starting with the number 2, once we know that a number is prime, we can eliminate all multiples of that number. The number 2 is divisible only by 1 and itself, so it's prime. Therefore, we can eliminate 4, 6, 8 and so on. Elimination of a value consists of setting its bit to "off" with BitSet method clear (line 31). The number 3 is divisible by 1 and itself. Therefore, we can eliminate all multiples of 3. (Keep in mind that all even numbers have already been eliminated.) After the list of primes is displayed, lines 48–51 uses BitSet method get (line 48) to determine whether the bit for the number the user entered is set. If so, line 49 displays a message indicating that the number is prime. Otherwise, line 51 displays a message indicating that the number is not prime.

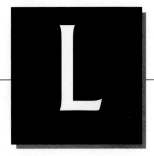

Labeled **break** and **continue** Statements

L.1 Introduction

In Chapter 5, we discussed Java's break and continue statements, which enable programmers to alter the flow of control in control statements. Java also provides the labeled break and continue statements for cases in which a programmer needs to conveniently alter the flow of control in nested control statements. This appendix demonstrates the labeled break and continue statements with examples using nested for statements.

L.2 Labeled **break** Statement

The break statement presented in Section 5.8 enables a program to break out of the while, for, do...while or switch in which the break statement appears. Sometimes these control statements are nested in other repetition statements. A program might need to exit the entire nested control statement in one operation, rather than wait for it to complete execution normally. To break out of such nested control statements, you can use the **labeled break statement**. This statement, when executed in a while, for, do...while or switch, causes immediate exit from that control statement and any number of enclosing statements. Program execution resumes with the first statement after the enclosing **labeled statement**. The statement that follows the label can be either a repetition statement or a block in which a repetition statement appears. Figure L.1 demonstrates the labeled break statement in a nested for statement.

```
1   // Fig. L.1: BreakLabelTest.java
2   // Labeled break statement exiting a nested for statement.
3   public class BreakLabelTest
4   {
5      public static void main(String[] args)
6      {
```

Fig. L.1 | Labeled break statement exiting a nested for statement. (Part 1 of 2.)

```
 7              stop: // labeled block
 8              {
 9                  // count 10 rows
10                  for (int row = 1; row <= 10; row++)
11                  {
12                      // count 5 columns
13                      for (int column = 1; column <= 5 ; column++)
14                      {
15                          if (row == 5) // if row is 5,
16                              break stop;   // jump to end of stop block
17
18                          System.out.print("* ");
19                      } // end inner for
20
21                      System.out.println(); // outputs a newline
22                  } // end outer for
23
24                  // following line is skipped
25                  System.out.println("\nLoops terminated normally");
26              } // end labeled block
27          } // end main
28      } // end class BreakLabelTest
```

```
* * * * *
* * * * *
* * * * *
* * * * *
```

Fig. L.1 | Labeled **break** statement exiting a nested **for** statement. (Part 2 of 2.)

The block (lines 7–26 in Fig. L.1) begins with a **label** (an identifier followed by a colon) at line 7; here we use the stop: label. The block is enclosed in braces (lines 8 and 26) and includes the nested for (lines 10–22) and the output statement at line 25. When the if at line 15 detects that row is equal to 5, the break statement at line 16 executes. This statement terminates both the for at lines 13–19 and its enclosing for at lines 10–22. Then the program proceeds immediately to the first statement after the labeled block—in this case, the end of main is reached and the program terminates. The outer for fully executes its body only four times. The output statement at line 25 never executes, because it's in the labeled block's body, and the outer for never completes.

Good Programming Practice L.1

Too many levels of nested control statements can make a program difficult to read. As a general rule, try to avoid using more than three levels of nesting.

L.3 Labeled **continue** Statement

The continue statement presented in Section 5.8 proceeds with the next iteration (repetition) of the immediately enclosing while, for or do...while. The **labeled continue statement** skips the remaining statements in that statement's body and any number of enclosing repetition statements and proceeds with the next iteration of the enclosing **labeled**

repetition statement (i.e., a for, while or do...while preceded by a label). In labeled while and do...while statements, the program evaluates the loop-continuation test of the labeled loop immediately after the continue statement executes. In a labeled for, the increment expression is executed and the loop-continuation test is evaluated. Figure L.2 uses a labeled continue statement in a nested for to enable execution to continue with the next iteration of the outer for.

```java
1   // Fig. L.2: ContinueLabelTest.java
2   // Labeled continue statement terminating a nested for statement.
3   public class ContinueLabelTest
4   {
5      public static void main(String[] args)
6      {
7         nextRow: // target label of continue statement
8
9            // count 5 rows
10           for (int row = 1; row <= 5; row++)
11           {
12              System.out.println(); // outputs a newline
13
14              // count 10 columns per row
15              for (int column = 1; column <= 10; column++)
16              {
17                 // if column greater than row, start next row
18                 if (column > row)
19                    continue nextRow; // next iteration of labeled loop
20
21                 System.out.print("* ");
22              } // end inner for
23           } // end outer for
24
25         System.out.println(); // outputs a newline
26      } // end main
27   } // end class ContinueLabelTest
```

```
*
* *
* * *
* * * *
* * * * *
```

Fig. L.2 | Labeled continue statement terminating a nested for statement.

The labeled for (lines 7–23) actually starts at the nextRow label. When the if at line 18 in the inner for (lines 15–22) detects that column is greater than row, the continue statement at line 19 executes, and program control continues with the increment of the control variable row of the outer for loop. Even though the inner for counts from 1 to 10, the number of * characters output on a row never exceeds the value of row, creating an interesting triangle pattern.

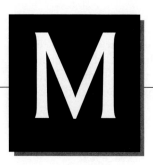

UML 2: Additional Diagram Types

M.1 Introduction

If you read the optional Software Engineering Case Study in Chapters 23–24, you should now have a comfortable grasp on the UML diagram types that we use to model our ATM system. The case study is intended for use in first- or second-semester courses, so we limit our discussion to a concise, subset of the UML. The UML 2 provides a total of 13 diagram types. The end of Section 23.2 summarizes the six diagram types that we use in the case study. This appendix lists and briefly defines the seven remaining diagram types.

M.2 Additional Diagram Types

The following are the seven diagram types that we chose not to use in our Software Engineering Case Study.

- **Object diagrams** model a "snapshot" of the system by modeling a system's objects and their relationships at a specific point in time. Each object represents an instance of a class from a class diagram, and there may be several objects created from one class. For our ATM system, an object diagram could show several distinct Account objects side by side, illustrating that they're all part of the bank's account database.

- **Component diagrams** model the **artifacts** and **components**—resources (which include source files)—that make up the system.

- **Deployment diagrams** model the runtime requirements of the system (such as the computer or computers on which the system will reside), memory requirements for the system, or other devices the system requires during execution.

- **Package diagrams** model the hierarchical structure of **packages** (which are groups of classes) in the system at compile-time and the relationships that exist between the packages.

- **Composite structure diagrams** model the internal structure of a complex object at runtime. Composite structure diagrams are new in UML 2 and allow system designers to hierarchically decompose a complex object into smaller parts. Composite structure diagrams are beyond the scope of our case study. Composite structure diagrams are more appropriate for larger industrial applications, which exhibit complex groupings of objects at execution time.

- **Interaction overview diagrams**, which are new in UML 2, provide a summary of control flow in the system by combining elements of several types of behavioral diagrams (e.g., activity diagrams, sequence diagrams).

- **Timing diagrams**, also new in UML 2, model the timing constraints imposed on stage changes and interactions between objects in a system.

If you're interested in learning more about these diagrams and advanced UML topics, please visit our UML Resource Center at `www.deitel.com/UML/`.

Design Patterns

N.1 Introduction

Most of the examples provided in this book are relatively small. These examples do not require an extensive design process, because they use only a few classes and illustrate introductory programming concepts. However, some programs are more complex—they can require thousands of lines of code or even more, contain many interactions among objects and involve many user interactions. Larger systems, such as air-traffic control systems or the systems that control a major bank's thousands of automated teller machines, could contain millions of lines of code. Effective design is crucial to the proper construction of such complex systems.

Over the past decade, the software-engineering industry has made significant progress in the field of **design patterns**—proven architectures for constructing flexible and maintainable object-oriented software. Using design patterns can substantially reduce the complexity of the design process. Designing an air-traffic control system will be a somewhat less formidable task if developers use design patterns. Design patterns benefit system developers by

- helping to construct reliable software using proven architectures and accumulated industry expertise.

- promoting design reuse in future systems.

- helping identify common mistakes and pitfalls that occur when building systems.

- helping to design systems independently of the language in which they'll ultimately be implemented.

- establishing a common design vocabulary among developers.

- shortening the design phase in a software-development process.

The notion of using design patterns to construct software systems originated in the field of architecture. Architects use a set of established architectural design elements, such as arches and columns, when designing buildings. Designing with arches and columns is a proven strategy for constructing sound buildings—these elements may be viewed as architectural design patterns.

In software, design patterns are neither classes nor objects. Rather, designers use design patterns to construct sets of classes and objects. To use design patterns effectively, designers must familiarize themselves with the most popular and effective patterns used in the software-engineering industry. In this appendix, we discuss fundamental object-oriented design patterns and architectures, as well as their importance in constructing well-engineered software.

This appendix presents several design patterns in Java, but these can be implemented in any object-oriented language, such as C++ or Visual Basic. We describe several design patterns used by Sun Microsystems in the Java API. We use design patterns in many programs in this book, which we'll identify throughout our discussion. These programs provide examples of the use of design patterns to construct reliable, robust object-oriented software.

History of Object-Oriented Design Patterns

During 1991–1994, Erich Gamma, Richard Helm, Ralph Johnson, and John Vlissides—collectively known as the "Gang of Four"—used their combined expertise to write the book *Design Patterns: Elements of Reusable Object-Oriented Software*. This book describes 23 design patterns, each providing a solution to a common software design problem in industry. The book groups design patterns into three categories—**creational design patterns**, **structural design patterns** and **behavioral design patterns**. Creational design patterns describe techniques to instantiate objects (or groups of objects). Structural design patterns allow designers to organize classes and objects into larger structures. Behavioral design patterns assign responsibilities to classes and objects.

The Gang-of-Four book showed that design patterns evolved naturally through years of industry experience. In his article "Seven Habits of Successful Pattern Writers,"[1] John Vlissides states that "the single most important activity in pattern writing is reflection." This statement implies that, to create patterns, developers must reflect on, and document, their successes (and mistakes). Developers use design patterns to capture and employ this collective industry experience, which ultimately helps them avoid repeating the same mistakes. New design patterns are being created all the time and are introduced rapidly to designers worldwide via the Internet.

Design patterns are a somewhat advanced topic that might not appear in most introductory course sequences. As you proceed in your Java studies, design patterns will surely increase in value.

N.2 Creational, Structural and Behavioral Design Patterns

In Section N.1, we mentioned that the "Gang of Four" described 23 design patterns using three categories—creational, structural and behavioral. In this and the remaining sections of this appendix, we discuss design patterns in each category and their importance, and how each pattern relates to the Java material in the book. For example, several Java Swing

---

1.   Vlissides, J. *Pattern Hatching: Design Patterns Applied.* Reading, MA: Addison-Wesley, 1998.

components that we introduce in Chapters 12 and 19 use the Composite design pattern. Figure N.1 identifies the 18 Gang of Four design patterns discussed in this appendix.

Section	Creational design patterns	Structural design patterns	Behavioral design patterns
Section N.2	Singleton	Proxy	Memento, State
Section N.3	Factory Method	Adapter, Bridge, Composite	Chain of Responsibility, Command, Observer, Strategy, Template Method
Section N.5	Abstract Factory	Decorator, Facade	
Section N.6	Prototype		Iterator

Fig. N.1 | 18 Gang-of-Four design patterns discussed in this appendix.

Many popular patterns have been documented since the Gang-of-Four book—these include the **concurrency design patterns**, which are especially helpful in the design of multithreaded systems. Section N.4 discusses some of these patterns used in industry. Architectural patterns, as we discuss in Section N.5, specify how subsystems interact with each other. Figure N.2 lists the concurrency patterns and architectural patterns that we discuss in this appendix.

Section	Concurrency design patterns	Architectural patterns
Section N.4	Single-Threaded Execution, Guarded Suspension, Balking, Read/Write Lock, Two-Phase Termination	
Section N.5		Model-View-Controller, Layers

Fig. N.2 | Concurrency design patterns and architectural patterns discussed in this appendix.

N.2.1 Creational Design Patterns

Creational design patterns address issues related to the creation of objects, such as preventing a system from creating more than one object of a class (the Singleton creational design pattern) or deferring until execution time the decision as to what types of objects are going to be created (the purpose of the other creational design patterns discussed here). For example, suppose we're designing a 3-D drawing program, in which the user can create several 3-D geometric objects, such as cylinders, spheres, cubes, tetrahedrons, etc. Further suppose that each shape in the drawing program is represented by an object. At compile time, the program does not know what shapes the user will choose to draw. Based on user input, this program should be able to determine the class from which to instantiate an appropriate object for the shape the user selected. If the user creates a cylinder in the GUI, our program should "know" to instantiate an object of class `Cylinder`. When the user decides what geometric object to draw, the program should determine the specific subclass from which to instantiate that object.

The Gang-of-Four book describes five creational patterns (four of which we discuss in this appendix):

- Abstract Factory (Section N.5)
- Builder (not discussed)
- Factory Method (Section N.3)
- Prototype (Section N.6)
- Singleton (Section N.2)

Singleton

Occasionally, a system should contain exactly one object of a class—that is, once the program instantiates that object, the program should not be allowed to create additional objects of that class. For example, some systems connect to a database using only one object that manages database connections, which ensures that other objects cannot initialize unnecessary connections that would slow the system. The **Singleton design pattern** guarantees that a system instantiates a maximum of one object of a class.

Figure N.3 demonstrates Java code using the Singleton design pattern. Line 4 declares class Singleton as final, so subclasses cannot be created that could provide multiple instantiations. Lines 10–13 declare a private constructor—only class Singleton can instantiate a Singleton object using this constructor. Line 7 declares a static reference to a Singleton object and invokes the private constructor. This creates the one instance of class Singleton that will be provided to clients. When invoked, static method getSingletonInstance (lines 16–19) simply returns a copy of this reference.

```java
1   // Singleton.java
2   // Demonstrates Singleton design pattern
3
4   public final class Singleton
5   {
6      // Singleton object to be returned by getSingletonInstance
7      private static final Singleton singleton = new Singleton();
8
9      // private constructor prevents instantiation by clients
10     private Singleton()
11     {
12        System.err.println("Singleton object created.");
13     } // end Singleton constructor
14
15     // return static Singleton object
16     public static Singleton getInstance()
17     {
18        return singleton;
19     } // end method getInstance
20  } // end class Singleton
```

Fig. N.3 | Class Singleton ensures that only one object of its class is created.

Lines 9–10 of class SingletonTest (Fig. N.4) declare two references to Singleton objects—firstSingleton and secondSingleton. Lines 13–14 call method getSingletonInstance and assign Singleton references to firstSingleton and secondSingleton, respectively. Line 17 tests whether these references both refer to the same Singleton object. Figure N.4 shows that firstSingleton and secondSingleton indeed are both references to the same Singleton object, because each time method getSingletonInstance is called, it returns a reference to the same Singleton object.

```java
 1   // SingletonTest.java
 2   // Attempt to create two Singleton objects
 3
 4   public class SingletonTest
 5   {
 6      // run SingletonExample
 7      public static void main(String[] args)
 8      {
 9         Singleton firstSingleton;
10         Singleton secondSingleton;
11
12         // create Singleton objects
13         firstSingleton = Singleton.getInstance();
14         secondSingleton = Singleton.getInstance();
15
16         // the "two" Singletons should refer to same Singleton
17         if (firstSingleton == secondSingleton)
18            System.err.println("firstSingleton and secondSingleton " +
19               "refer to the same Singleton object");
20      } // end main
21   } // end class SingletonTest
```

```
Singleton object created.
firstSingleton and secondSingleton refer to the same Singleton object
```

Fig. N.4 | Class SingletonTest creates a Singleton object more than once.

N.2.2 Structural Design Patterns

Structural design patterns describe common ways to organize classes and objects in a system. The Gang-of-Four book describes seven structural design patterns (six of which we discuss in this appendix):

- Adapter (Section N.3)
- Bridge (Section N.3)
- Composite (Section N.3)
- Decorator (Section N.5)
- Facade (Section N.5)
- Flyweight (not discussed)
- Proxy (Section N.2)

Proxy

An applet should always display something while images load to provide positive feedback to users, so they know the applet is working. Whether that "something" is a smaller image or a string of text informing the user that the images are loading, the **Proxy design pattern** can be applied to achieve this effect. Consider loading several large images (several megabytes) in a Java applet. Ideally, we would like to see these images instantaneously—however, loading large images into memory can take time to complete (especially across a network). The Proxy design pattern allows the system to use one object—called a **proxy object**—in place of another. In our example, the proxy object could be a gauge that shows the user what percentage of a large image has been loaded. When this image finishes loading, the proxy object is no longer needed—the applet can then display an image instead of the proxy. Class `javax.swing.JProgressBar` can be used to create such proxy objects.

N.2.3 Behavioral Design Patterns

Behavioral design patterns provide proven strategies to model how objects collaborate with one another in a system and offer special behaviors appropriate for a wide variety of applications. Let's consider the Observer behavioral design pattern—a classic example illustrating collaborations between objects. For example, GUI components collaborate with their listeners to respond to user interactions. GUI components use this pattern to process user interface events. A listener observes state changes in a particular GUI component by registering to handle its events. When the user interacts with that GUI component, the component notifies its listeners (also known as its observers) that its state has changed (e.g., a button has been pressed).

We also consider the Memento behavioral design pattern—an example of offering special behavior for many applications. The Memento pattern enables a system to save an object's state, so that state can be restored at a later time. For example, many applications provide an "undo" capability that allows users to revert to previous versions of their work.

The Gang-of-Four book describes 11 behavioral design patterns (eight of which we discuss in this appendix):

- Chain of Responsibility (Section N.3)
- Command (Section N.3)
- Interpreter (not discussed)
- Iterator (Section N.6)
- Mediator (not discussed)
- Memento (Section N.2)
- Observer (Section N.3)
- State (Section N.2)
- Strategy (Section N.3)
- Template Method (Section N.3)
- Visitor (not discussed)

Memento

Consider a painting program, which allows a user to create graphics. Occasionally the user may position a graphic improperly in the drawing area. Painting programs offer an "undo" feature that allows the user to unwind such an error. Specifically, the program restores the drawing area to its state before the user placed the graphic. More sophisticated painting programs offer a history, which stores several states in a list, allowing the user to restore the program to any state in the history.The **Memento design pattern** allows an object to save its state, so that—if necessary—the object can be restored to its former state.

The Memento design pattern requires three types of objects. The **originator object** occupies some state—the set of attribute values at a specific time in program execution. In our painting-program example, the drawing area acts as the originator, because it contains attribute information describing its state—when the program first executes, the area contains no elements. The **memento object** stores a copy of necessary attributes associated with the originator's state (i.e., the memento saves the drawing area's state). The memento is stored as the first item in the history list, which acts as the **caretaker object**—the object that contains references to all memento objects associated with the originator. Now, suppose that the user draws a circle in the drawing area. The area contains different information describing its state—a circle object centered at specified *x-y* coordinates. The drawing area then uses another memento to store this information. This memento becomes the second item in the history list. The history list displays all mementos on screen, so the user can select which state to restore. Suppose that the user wishes to remove the circle—if the user selects the first memento, the drawing area uses it to restore the blank drawing area.

State

In certain designs, we must convey an object's state information or represent the various states that an object can occupy. The **State design pattern** uses an abstract superclass—called the **State class**—which contains methods that describe behaviors for states that an object (called the **context object**) can occupy. A **State subclass**, which extends the State class, represents an individual state that the context can occupy. Each State subclass contains methods that implement the State class's abstract methods. The context contains exactly one reference to an object of the State class—this object is called the **state object**. When the context changes state, the state object references the State subclass object associated with that new state.

N.2.4 Conclusion

In this section, we listed the three types of design patterns introduced in the Gang-of-Four book, we identified 18 of these design patterns that we discuss in this appendix and we discussed specific design patterns: Singleton, Proxy, Memento and State. In the next section, we introduce some design patterns associated with AWT and Swing GUI components.

N.3 Design Patterns in Packages `java.awt` and `javax.swing`

This section introduces those design patterns associated with Java GUI components. It will help you understand better how these components take advantage of design patterns and how developers integrate design patterns with Java GUI applications.

N.3.1 Creational Design Patterns

Now, we continue our treatment of creational design patterns, which provide ways to instantiate objects in a system.

Factory Method

Suppose that we're designing a system that opens an image from a specified file. Several different image formats exist, such as GIF and JPEG. We can use method `createImage` of class `java.awt.Component` to create an `Image` object. For example, to create a JPEG and GIF image in an object of a `Component` subclass—such as a `JPanel` object—we pass the name of the image file to method `createImage`, which returns an `Image` object that stores the image data. We can create two `Image` objects, each containing data for two images having entirely different structures. For example, a JPEG image can hold up to 16.7 million colors, a GIF image up to only 256. Also, a GIF image can contain transparent pixels that are not rendered on screen, whereas a JPEG image cannot.

Class `Image` is an abstract class that represents an image we can display on screen. Using the parameter passed by the programmer, method `createImage` determines the specific `Image` subclass from which to instantiate the `Image` object. We can design systems to allow the user to specify which image to create, and method `createImage` will determine the subclass from which to instantiate the `Image`. If the parameter passed to method `createImage` references a JPEG file, method `createImage` instantiates and returns an object of an `Image` subclass suitable for JPEG images. If the parameter references a GIF file, `createImage` instantiates and returns an object of an `Image` subclass suitable for GIF images.

Method `createImage` is an example of the **Factory Method design pattern**. The sole purpose of this **factory method** is to create objects by allowing the system to determine which class to instantiate at runtime. We can design a system that allows a user to specify what type of image to create at runtime. Class `Component` might not be able to determine which `Image` subclass to instantiate until the user specifies the image to load. For more information on method `createImage`, visit

```
http://docs.oracle.com/javase/7/docs/api/java/awt/Component.html
```

N.3.2 Structural Design Patterns

We now discuss three more structural design patterns. The Adapter design pattern helps objects with incompatible interfaces collaborate with one another. The Bridge design pattern helps designers enhance platform independence in their systems. The Composite design pattern provides a way for designers to organize and manipulate objects.

Adapter

The **Adapter design pattern** provides an object with a new interface that *adapts* to another object's interface, allowing both objects to collaborate with one another. We might liken the adapter in this pattern to an adapter for a plug on an electrical device—electrical sockets in Europe are shaped differently from those in the United States, so an adapter is needed to plug an American device into a European socket and vice versa.

Java provides several classes that use the Adapter design pattern. Objects of the concrete subclasses of these classes act as adapters between objects that generate certain events and objects that handle the events. For example, a `MouseAdapter` (Section 12.15), adapts an object that generates `MouseEvents` to an object that handles `MouseEvents`.

Bridge

Suppose that we're designing class `Button` for both the Windows and Macintosh operating systems. Class `Button` contains specific button information such as an `ActionListener` and a label. We design classes `Win32Button` and `MacButton` to extend class `Button`. Class `Win32Button` contains look-and-feel information on how to display a `Button` on the Windows operating system, and class `MacButton` contains look-and-feel information on how to display a `Button` on the Macintosh operating system.

Two problems arise here. First, if we create new `Button` subclasses, we must create corresponding `Win32Button` and `MacButton` subclasses. For example, if we create class `Image-Button` (a `Button` with an overlapping `Image`) that extends class `Button`, we must create additional subclasses `Win32ImageButton` and `MacImageButton`. In fact, we must create `Button` subclasses for every operating system we wish to support, which increases development time. Second, when a new operating system enters the market, we must create additional `Button` subclasses specific to it.

The **Bridge design pattern** avoids these problems by dividing an abstraction (e.g., a `Button`) and its implementations (e.g., `Win32Button`, `MacButton`, etc.) into separate class hierarchies. For example, the Java AWT classes use the Bridge design pattern to enable designers to create AWT `Button` subclasses without needing to create additional operating-system specific subclasses. Each AWT `Button` maintains a reference to a `Button-Peer`, which is the superclass for platform-specific implementations, such as `Win32ButtonPeer`, `MacButtonPeer`, etc. When a programmer creates a `Button` object, class `Button` calls factory method `createButton` of class `Toolkit` to create the platform-specific `ButtonPeer` object. The `Button` object stores a reference to its `ButtonPeer`—this reference is the "bridge" in the Bridge design pattern. When the programmer invokes methods on the `Button` object, the `Button` object delegates the work to the appropriate lower-level method on its `ButtonPeer` to fulfill the request. A designer who creates a `Button` subclass called, e.g., `ImageButton`, does not need to create a corresponding `Win32ImageButton` or `MacImageButton` with platform-specific image-drawing capabilities. An `ImageButton` *is a* `Button`. Therefore, when an `ImageButton` needs to display its image, the `ImageButton` uses its `ButtonPeer`'s `Graphics` object to render the image on each platform. This design pattern enables designers to create new cross-platform GUI components using a "bridge" to hide platform-specific details.

Portability Tip N.1

Designers often use the Bridge design pattern to enhance the platform independence of their systems. This design pattern enables designers to create new cross-platform components using a "bridge" to hide platform-specific details.

Composite

Designers often organize components into hierarchical structures (e.g., a hierarchy of directories and files in a file system)—each node in the structure represents a component (e.g., a file or directory). Each node can contain references to one or more other nodes, and if it does so, it's called a **branch** (e.g., a directory containing files); otherwise, it's called a **leaf** (e.g., a file). Occasionally, a structure contains objects from several different classes (e.g., a directory can contain files and directories). An object—called a **client**—that wants to traverse the structure must determine the particular class for each node. Making this determination can be time consuming, and the structure can become hard to maintain.

In the **Composite design pattern**, each component in a hierarchical structure implements the same interface or extends a common superclass. This polymorphism (introduced in Chapter 10) ensures that clients can traverse all elements—branch or leaf—uniformly in the structure and do not have to determine each component type, because all components implement the same interface or extend the same superclass.

Java GUI components use the Composite design pattern. Consider the Swing component class JPanel, which extends class JComponent. Class JComponent extends class `java.awt.Container`, which extends class `java.awt.Component` (Fig. N.5). Class Container provides method add, which appends a Component object (or Component subclass object) to that Container object. Therefore, a JPanel object may be added to any object of a Component subclass, and any object from a Component subclass may be added to that JPanel object. A JPanel object can contain any GUI component while remaining unaware of its specific type. Nearly all GUI classes are both containers and components, enabling arbitrarily complex nesting and structuring of GUIs.

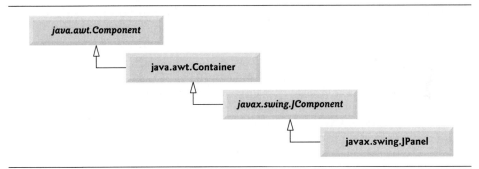

Fig. N.5 | Inheritance hierarchy for class JPanel.

A client, such as a JPanel object, can traverse all components uniformly in the hierarchy. For example, if the JPanel object calls method repaint of superclass Container, method repaint displays the JPanel object and all components added to the JPanel object. Method repaint does not have to determine each component's type, because all components inherit from superclass Container, which contains method repaint.

N.3.3 Behavioral Design Patterns

This section continues our discussion on behavioral design patterns. We discuss the Chain of Responsibility, Command, Observer, Strategy and Template Method design patterns.

Chain of Responsibility

In object-oriented systems, objects interact by sending messages to one another. Often, a system needs to determine at runtime the object that will handle a particular message. For example, consider the design of a three-line office phone system. When a person calls the office, the first line handles the call—if the first line is busy, the second line handles the call, and if the second line is busy, the third line handles the call. If all lines in the system are busy, an automated speaker instructs the caller to wait for the next available line. When a line becomes available, that line handles the call.

The **Chain of Responsibility design pattern** enables a system to determine at run time the object that will handle a message. This pattern allows an object to send a message to several objects in a **chain**. Each object in the chain either may handle the message or pass it to the next object. For instance, the first line in the phone system is the first object in the chain of responsibility, the second line is the second object, the third line is the third object and the automated speaker is the fourth object. The final object in the chain is the next available line that handles the message. The chain is created dynamically in response to the presence or absence of specific message handlers.

Several Java AWT GUI components use the Chain of Responsibility design pattern to handle certain events. For example, class `java.awt.Button` overrides method `process-Event` of class `java.awt.Component` to process `AWTEvent` objects. Method `processEvent` attempts to handle the `AWTEvent` upon receiving it as an argument. If method `process-Event` determines that the `AWTEvent` is an `ActionEvent` (i.e., the `Button` has been pressed), it handles the event by invoking method `processActionEvent`, which informs any `ActionListener` registered with the `Button` that the `Button` has been pressed. If method `processEvent` determines that the `AWTEvent` is not an `ActionEvent`, the method is unable to handle it and passes it to method `processEvent` of superclass `Component` (the next listener in the chain).

Command

Applications often provide users with several ways to perform a given task. For example, in a word processor there might be an **Edit** menu with menu items for cutting, copying and pasting text. A toolbar or a popup menu could also offer the same items. The functionality the application provides is the same in each case—the different interface components for invoking the functionality are provided for the user's convenience. However, the same GUI component instance (e.g., `JButton`) cannot be used for menus, toolbars and popup menus, so the developer must code the same functionality three times. If there were many such interface items, repeating this functionality would become tedious and error prone.

The **Command design pattern** solves this problem by enabling developers to encapsulate the desired functionality (e.g., copying text) once in a reusable object; that functionality can then be added to a menu, toolbar, popup menu or other mechanism. This design pattern is called Command because it defines a command, or instruction, to be executed. It allows a designer to encapsulate a command, so that it may be used among several objects.

Observer

Suppose that we want to design a program for viewing bank account information. This system includes class `BankStatementData` to store data pertaining to bank statements and classes `TextDisplay`, `BarGraphDisplay` and `PieChartDisplay` to display the data. [*Note:* This approach is the basis for the Model-View-Controller architecture pattern, discussed in Section N.5.3.] Figure N.6 shows the design for our system. The data is displayed by class `TextDisplay` in text format, by class `BarGraphDisplay` in bar-graph format and by class `PieChartDisplay` as a pie chart. We want to design the system so that the `BankStatementData` object notifies the objects displaying the data of a change in the data. We also want to design the system to loosen **coupling**—the degree to which classes depend on each other in a system.

Software Engineering Observation N.1

Loosely coupled classes are easier to reuse and modify than are tightly coupled classes, which depend heavily on each other. A modification in a class in a tightly coupled system usually results in modifying other classes in that system. A modification to one of a group of loosely coupled classes would require little or no modification to the other classes.

The **Observer design pattern** is appropriate for systems like that of Fig. N.6. This pattern promotes loose coupling between a **subject object** and **observer objects**—a subject notifies the observers when the subject changes state. When notified by the subject, the observers change in response. In our example, the BankStatementData object is the subject, and the objects displaying the data are the observers. A subject can notify several observers; therefore, the subject has a one-to-many relationship with the observers.

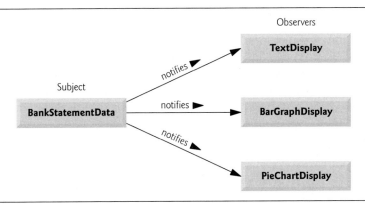

Fig. N.6 | Basis for the Observer design pattern.

The Java API contains classes that use the Observer design pattern. Class **java.util.Observable** represents a subject. Class Observable provides method addObserver, which takes a **java.util.Observer** argument. Interface Observer allows the Observable object to notify the Observer when the Observable object changes state. The Observer can be an instance of any class that implements interface Observer; because the Observable object invokes methods declared in interface Observer, the objects remain loosely coupled. If a developer changes the way in which a particular Observer responds to changes in the Observable object, the developer does not need to change the object. The Observable object interacts with its Observers only through interface Observer, which enables the loose coupling.

The Swing GUI components use the Observer design pattern. GUI components collaborate with their listeners to respond to user interactions. For example, an ActionListener observes state changes in a JButton (the subject) by registering to handle that JButton's events. When pressed by the user, the JButton notifies its ActionListener objects (the observers) that the JButton's state has changed (i.e., the JButton has been pressed).

Strategy

The **Strategy design pattern** is similar to the State design pattern (discussed in Section N.2.3). We mentioned that the State design pattern contains a state object, which encapsulates the state of a context object. The Strategy design pattern contains a **strategy object**, which is analogous to the State design pattern's state object. The key difference is that the strategy object encapsulates an algorithm rather than state information.

For example, `java.awt.Container` components implement the Strategy design pattern using `LayoutManagers` (discussed in Section 12.18) as strategy objects. In package `java.awt`, classes `FlowLayout`, `BorderLayout` and `GridLayout` implement interface `LayoutManager`. Each class uses method `addLayoutComponent` to add GUI components to a `Container` object. However, each method uses a different algorithm to display these GUI components: A `FlowLayout` displays them in a left-to-right sequence, a `BorderLayout` displays them in five regions and a `GridLayout` displays them in row-column format.

Class `Container` contains a reference to a `LayoutManager` object (the strategy object). An interface reference (i.e., the reference to the `LayoutManager` object) can hold references to objects of classes that implement that interface (i.e., the `FlowLayout`, `BorderLayout` or `GridLayout` objects), so the `LayoutManager` object can reference a `FlowLayout`, `BorderLayout` or `GridLayout` at any time. Class `Container` can change this reference through method `setLayout` to select different layouts at runtime.

Class `FlowLayoutFrame` (Fig. 12.39) demonstrates the application of the Strategy pattern—line 23 declares a new `FlowLayout` object and line 25 invokes the `Container` object's method `setLayout` to assign the `FlowLayout` object to the `Container` object. In this example, the `FlowLayout` provides the strategy for laying out the components.

Template Method

The **Template Method design pattern** also deals with algorithms. The Strategy design pattern allows several objects to contain distinct algorithms. However, the Template Method design pattern requires all objects to share a single algorithm defined by a superclass.

For example, consider the design of Fig. N.6, which we presented in the Observer design pattern discussion earlier in this section. Objects of classes `TextDisplay`, `BarGraphDisplay` and `PieChartDisplay` use the same basic algorithm for acquiring and displaying the data—get all statements from the `BankStatementData` object, parse the statements, then display the statements. The Template Method design pattern allows us to create an abstract superclass called `BankStatementDisplay` that provides the common algorithm for displaying the data. In this example, the algorithm invokes abstract methods `getData`, `parseData` and `displayData`. Classes `TextDisplay`, `BarGraphDisplay` and `PieChartDisplay` extend class `BankStatementDisplay` to inherit the algorithm, so each object can use the same algorithm. Each `BankStatementDisplay` subclass then overrides each method in a way specific to that subclass, because each class implements the algorithm differently. For example, classes `TextDisplay`, `BarGraphDisplay` and `PieChartDisplay` might get and parse the data identically, but each displays that data differently.

The Template Method design pattern allows us to extend the algorithm to other `BankStatementDisplay` subclasses—e.g., we could create classes, such as `LineGraphDisplay` or class `3DimensionalDisplay`, that use the same algorithm inherited from class `BankStatementDisplay` and provide different implementations of the abstract methods the algorithm calls.

N.3.4 Conclusion

In this section, we discussed how Swing components take advantage of design patterns and how developers can integrate design patterns with GUI applications in Java. In the next section, we discuss concurrency design patterns, which are particularly useful for developing multithreaded systems.

N.4 Concurrency Design Patterns

Many additional design patterns have been discovered since the publication of the Gang of Four book, which introduced patterns involving object-oriented systems. Some of these new patterns involve specific types of object-oriented systems, such as concurrent, distributed or parallel systems. In this section, we discuss concurrency patterns to complement our discussion of concurrent programming in Chapter 20.

Concurrency Design Patterns
Multithreaded programming languages such as Java allow designers to specify concurrent activities—that is, those that operate in parallel with one another. Designing concurrent systems improperly can introduce concurrency problems. For example, two objects attempting to alter shared data at the same time could corrupt that data. In addition, if two objects wait for one another to finish tasks, and if neither can complete their task, these objects could potentially wait forever—a situation called **deadlock**. Using Java, Doug Lea[2] and Mark Grand[3] documented **concurrency patterns** for multithreaded design architectures to prevent various problems associated with multithreading. We provide a partial list of these design patterns:

- The **Single-Threaded Execution design pattern** (Grand, 2002) prevents several threads from executing the same method of another object concurrently. Chapter 20 discusses various techniques that can be used to apply this pattern.

- The **Guarded Suspension design pattern** (Lea, 2000) suspends a thread's activity and resumes that thread's activity when some condition is satisfied.

- The **Balking design pattern** (Lea, 2000) ensures that a method will **balk**—that is, return without performing any actions—if an object occupies a state that cannot execute that method. A variation of this pattern is that the method throws an exception describing why that method is unable to execute—for example, a method throwing an exception when accessing a data structure that does not exist.

- The **Read/Write Lock design pattern** (Lea, 2000) allows multiple threads to obtain concurrent read access on an object but prevents multiple threads from obtaining concurrent write access on that object. Only one thread at a time may obtain write access to an object—when that thread obtains write access, the object is **locked** to all other threads.

2.   Lea, D. *Concurrent Programming in Java, Second Edition: Design Principles and Patterns.* Boston: Addison-Wesley, 2000.
3.   Grand, M. *Patterns in Java; A Catalog of Reusable Design Patterns Illustrated with UML, Second Edition, Volume I.* New York: John Wiley and Sons, 2002.

- The **Two-Phase Termination design pattern** (Grand, 2002) uses a two-phase termination process for a thread to ensure that a thread has the opportunity to free resources—such as other spawned threads—in memory (phase one) before termination (phase two). In Java, a `Runnable` object can use this pattern in method run. For instance, method run can contain an infinite loop that is terminated by some state change—upon termination, method `run` can invoke a `private` method responsible for stopping any other spawned threads (phase one). The thread then terminates after method run terminates (phase two).

In the next section, we return to the Gang of Four design patterns. Using the material introduced in Chapter 15, we identify those classes in package `java.io` and `java.net` that use design patterns.

N.5 Design Patterns Used in Packages `java.io` and `java.net`

This section introduces those design patterns associated with the Java file, streams and networking packages.

N.5.1 Creational Design Patterns

We now continue our discussion of creational design patterns.

Abstract Factory

Like the Factory Method design pattern, the **Abstract Factory design pattern** allows a system to determine the subclass from which to instantiate an object at runtime. Often, this subclass is unknown during development. However, Abstract Factory uses an object known as a **factory** that uses an interface to instantiate objects. A factory creates a product, which in this case is an object of a subclass determined at runtime.

The Java socket library in package `java.net` uses the Abstract Factory design pattern. A socket describes a connection, or a stream of data, between two processes. Class `Socket` references an object of a `SocketImpl` subclass. Class `Socket` also contains a `static` reference to an object implementing interface `SocketImplFactory`. The Socket constructor invokes method `createSocketImpl` of interface `SocketImplFactory` to create the `Socket-Impl` object. The object that implements interface `SocketImplFactory` is the factory, and an object of a `SocketImpl` subclass is the product of that factory. The system cannot specify the `SocketImpl` subclass from which to instantiate until runtime, because the system has no knowledge of what type of `Socket` implementation is required (e.g., a socket configured to the local network's security requirements). Method `createSocketImpl` decides the `SocketImpl` subclass from which to instantiate the object at runtime.

N.5.2 Structural Design Patterns

This section concludes our discussion of structural design patterns.

Decorator

Let's reexamine class `CreateSequentialFile` (Fig. 15.10). Lines 20–21 of this class allow a `FileOutputStream` object, which writes bytes to a file, to gain the functionality of an ObjectOutputStream, which provides methods for writing entire objects to an Output-Stream. Class CreateSequentialFile appears to "wrap" an ObjectOutputStream object around a FileOutputStream object. The fact that we can dynamically add the behavior of an ObjectOutputStream to a FileOutputStream obviates the need for a separate class called ObjectFileOutputStream, which would implement the behaviors of both classes.

Lines 20–21 of class CreateSequentialFile show an example of the **Decorator design pattern**, which allows an object to gain additional functionality dynamically. Using this pattern, designers do not have to create separate, unnecessary classes to add responsibilities to objects of a given class.

Let's consider a more complex example to discover how the Decorator design pattern can simplify a system's structure. Suppose that we wanted to enhance the I/O performance of the previous example by using a BufferedOutputStream. Using the Decorator design pattern, we would write

```
output = new ObjectOutputStream(
    new BufferedOutputStream(
        new FileOutputStream(fileName)));
```

We can combine objects in this manner, because ObjectOutputStream, Buffered-OutputStream and FileOutputStream extend abstract superclass OutputStream, and each subclass constructor takes an OutputStream object as a parameter. If the stream objects in package java.io did not use the Decorator pattern (i.e., did not satisfy these two requirements), package java.io would have to provide classes BufferedFileOutputStream, ObjectBufferedOutputStream, ObjectBufferedFileOutputStream and ObjectFile-OutputStream. Consider how many classes we would have to create if we combined even more stream objects without applying the Decorator pattern.

Facade

When driving, you know that pressing the gas pedal accelerates your car, but you're unaware of exactly how it does so. This principle is the foundation of the **Facade design pattern**, which allows an object—called a **facade object**—to provide a simple interface for the behaviors of a **subsystem** (an aggregate of objects that comprise collectively a major system responsibility). The gas pedal, for example, is the facade object for the car's acceleration subsystem, the steering wheel is the facade object for the car's steering subsystem and the brake is the facade object for the car's deceleration subsystem. A **client object** uses the facade object to access the objects behind the facade. The client remains unaware of how the objects behind the facade fulfill responsibilities, so the subsystem complexity is hidden from the client. When you press the gas pedal, you act as a client object. The Facade design pattern reduces system complexity, because a client interacts with only one object (the facade) to access the behaviors of the subsystem the facade represents. This pattern shields applications developers from subsystem complexities. Developers need to be familiar with only the operations of the facade object, rather than with the more detailed operations of the entire subsystem. The implementation behind the facade may be changed without changes to the clients.

In package java.net, an object of class URL is a facade object. This object contains a reference to an InetAddress object that specifies the host computer's IP address. The URL facade object also references an object from class URLStreamHandler, which opens the URL connection. The client object that uses the URL facade object accesses the Inet-

Address object and the URLStreamHandler object through the facade object. However, the client object does not know how the objects behind the URL facade object accomplish their responsibilities.

N.5.3 Architectural Patterns

Design patterns allow developers to design specific parts of systems, such as abstracting object instantiations or aggregating classes into larger structures. Design patterns also promote loose coupling among objects. **Architectural patterns** promote loose coupling among subsystems. These patterns specify how subsystems interact with one another.[4] We introduce the popular Model-View-Controller and Layers architectural patterns.

MVC

Consider the design of a simple text editor. In this program, the user enters text from the keyboard and formats it using the mouse. Our program stores this text and format information into a series of data structures, then displays this information on screen for the user to read what has been inputted.

This program adheres to the **Model-View-Controller (MVC) architectural pattern**, which separates application data (contained in the **model**) from graphical presentation components (the **view**) and input-processing logic (the **controller**). Figure N.7 shows the relationships between components in MVC.

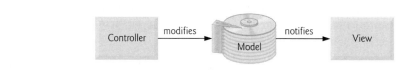

Fig. N.7 | Model-View-Controller Architecture.

The controller implements logic for processing user inputs. The model contains application data, and the view presents the data stored in the model. When a user provides some input, the controller modifies the model with the given input. With regard to the text-editor example, the model might contain only the characters that make up the document. When the model changes, it notifies the view of the change so that it can update its presentation with the changed data. The view in a word processor might display characters using a particular font, with a particular size, etc.

MVC does not restrict an application to a single view and a single controller. In a more sophisticated program (such as a word processor), there might be two views of a document model. One view might display an outline of the document and the other might display the complete document. The word processor also might implement multiple controllers—one for handling keyboard input and another for handling mouse selections. If either controller makes a change in the model, both the outline view and the print-preview window will show the change immediately when the model notifies all views of changes.

---

4.   R. Hartman. "Building on Patterns." *Application Development Trends,* May 2001: 19–26.

Another key benefit to the MVC architectural pattern is that developers can modify each component individually without having to modify the others. For example, developers could modify the view that displays the document outline without having to modify either the model or other views or controllers.

Layers
Consider the design in Fig. N.8, which presents the basic structure of a **three-tier application**, in which each tier contains a unique system component.

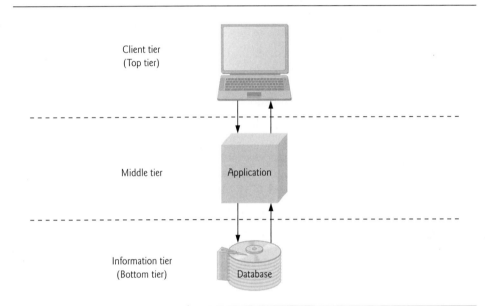

Fig. N.8 | Three-tier application model.

The **information tier** (also called the bottom tier) maintains data for the application, typically storing it in a database. The information tier for an online store may contain product information, such as descriptions, prices and quantities in stock, and customer information, such as user names, billing addresses and credit-card numbers.

The **middle tier** acts as an intermediary between the information tier and the client tier. The middle tier processes client-tier requests, and reads data from and writes data to the database. It then processes data from the information tier and presents the content to the client tier. This processing is the application's **business logic**, which handles such tasks as retrieving data from the information tier, ensuring that data is reliable before updating the database and presenting data to the client tier. For example, the business logic associated with the middle tier for the online store can verify a customer's credit card with the credit-card issuer before the warehouse ships the customer's order. This business logic could then store (or retrieve) the credit information in the database and notify the client tier that the verification was successful.

The **client tier** (also called the top tier) is the application's user interface, such as a standard web browser. Users interact directly with the application through the user interface. The client tier interacts with the middle tier to make requests and retrieve data from the information tier. The client tier then displays data retrieved from the middle tier.

Figure N.8 is an implementation of the **Layers architectural pattern**, which divides functionality into separate **layers**. Each layer contains a set of system responsibilities and depends on the services of only the next lower layer. In Fig. N.8, each tier corresponds to a layer. This architectural pattern is useful, because a designer can modify one layer without having to modify the others. For example, a designer could modify the information tier in Fig. N.8 to accommodate a particular database product but would not have to modify either the client tier or the middle tier.

N.5.4 Conclusion

In this section, we discussed how packages `java.io` and `java.net` take advantage of specific design patterns and how developers can integrate design patterns with networking/file-processing applications in Java. We also introduced the MVC and Layers architectural patterns, which both assign system functionality to separate subsystems. These patterns make designing a system easier for developers. In the next section, we conclude our presentation of design patterns by discussing those patterns used in package `java.util`.

N.6 Design Patterns Used in Package `java.util`

In this section, we use the material on data structures and collections discussed in Chapter 16 to identify classes from package `java.util` that use design patterns.

N.6.1 Creational Design Patterns

We conclude our discussion of creational design patterns by presenting the Prototype design pattern.

Prototype

Sometimes a system must make a copy of an object but will not "know" that object's class until execution time. The **Prototype design pattern** allows an object—called a **prototype**—to return a copy of that prototype to a requesting object—called a **client**. Every prototype must belong to a class that implements a common interface that allows the prototype to clone itself. For example, the Java API provides method `clone` from class `java.lang.Object` and interface `java.lang.Cloneable`—any object from a class implementing `Cloneable` can use method `clone` to copy itself. Specifically, method `clone` creates a copy of an object, then returns a reference to that object. To copy a preexisting object, we clone that object. Method `clone` also is useful in methods that return a reference to an object, but the developer does not want that object to be altered through that reference—method `clone` returns a reference to the copy of the object instead of returning that object's reference. For more information on interface `Cloneable`, visit

```
http://docs.oracle.com/javase/7/docs/api/java/lang/Cloneable.html
```

N.6.2 Behavioral Design Patterns

We conclude our discussion of behavioral design patterns by discussing the Iterator design pattern.

Iterator

Designers use data structures such as arrays, linked lists and hash tables to organize data in a program. The **Iterator design pattern** allows objects to access individual objects from any data structure without "knowing" the data structure's behavior (such as traversing the structure or removing an element from that structure) or how that data structure stores objects. Instructions for traversing the data structure and accessing its elements are stored in a separate object called an **iterator**. Each data structure can create an iterator—each iterator implements methods of a common interface to traverse the data structure and access its data. A client can traverse two differently structured data structures—such as a linked list and a hash table—in the same manner, because both data structures provide an iterator object that belongs to a class implementing a common interface. Java provides interface Iterator from package `java.util`, which we used in Fig. 16.2.

N.7 Wrap-Up

In this appendix, we've introduced the importance, usefulness and prevalence of design patterns. In their book *Design Patterns, Elements of Reusable Object-Oriented Software*, the Gang of Four described 23 design patterns that provide proven strategies for building systems. Each pattern belongs to one of three pattern categories—creational patterns address issues related to object creation; structural patterns provide ways to organize classes and objects in a system; and behavioral patterns offer strategies for modeling how objects collaborate with one another in a system.

Of the 23 design patterns, we discussed 18 of the more popular ones used by the Java community. The discussion was divided according to how certain packages of the Java API—such as package `java.awt`, `javax.swing`, `java.io`, `java.net` and `java.util`—use these design patterns. Also discussed were patterns not described by the Gang of Four, such as concurrency patterns, which are useful in multithreaded systems, and architectural patterns, which help designers assign functionality to various subsystems in a system. We motivated each pattern—explained why it's important and explained how it may be used. When appropriate, we supplied several examples in the form of real-world analogies (e.g., the adapter in the Adapter design pattern is similar to an adapter for a plug on an electrical device). You learned also how Java API packages take advantage of design patterns (e.g., Swing GUI components use the Observer design pattern to collaborate with their listeners to respond to user interactions). We provided examples of how certain programs in this book used design patterns.

We hope that you view this appendix as a beginning to further study of design patterns. Design patterns are used most prevalently in the J2EE (Java 2 Platform, Enterprise Edition) community, where systems tend to be exceedingly large and complex, and where robustness, portability and performance are critical. However, even beginner programmers can benefit from early exposure to design patterns. We recommend that you visit our Java Design Patterns Resource Center (`http://www.deitel.com/JavaDesignPatterns/`), and that you read the Gang-of-Four book. This information will help you build better systems using the collective wisdom of the object-technology industry.

Index

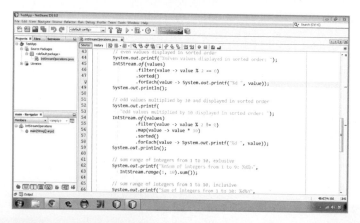

DEITEL DEVELOPER SERIES
THIRD EDITION

Use with
Java™ SE 7
or Java™ SE 8

Java™ SE 8
for Programmers

PAUL DEITEL · HARVEY DEITEL

Safari
Books Online

45-day
FREE access
to Online Edition

Your purchase of *Java™ SE 8 for Programmers, Third Edition,* includes access to a free online edition for 45 days through the **Safari Books Online** subscription service. Nearly every Prentice Hall book is available online through **Safari Books Online**, along with thousands of books and videos from publishers such as Addison-Wesley Professional, Cisco Press, Exam Cram, IBM Press, O'Reilly Media, Que, Sams, and VMware Press.

Safari Books Online is a digital library providing searchable, on-demand access to thousands of technology, digital media, and professional development books and videos from leading publishers. With one monthly or yearly subscription price, you get unlimited access to learning tools and information on topics including mobile app and software development, tips and tricks on using your favorite gadgets, networking, project management, graphic design, and much more.

Activate your 45-day FREE access to Online Edition at
informit.com/safarifree

STEP 1: Enter the coupon code: BGBWXFA.

STEP 2: New Safari users, complete the brief registration form.
Safari subscribers, just log in.

If you have difficulty registering on Safari or accessing the online edition,
please e-mail customer-service@safaribooksonline.com

Addison Wesley · AdobePress · ALPHA · Cisco Press · FT Press · IBM Press · Microsoft Press · New Riders · O'REILLY

Peachpit Press · PRENTICE HALL · que · Redbooks · SAMS · SAS Publishing · vmware PRESS · WILEY · wrox

━━ COMMENTS FROM RECENT EDITIONS REVIEWERS *(Continued From Back Cover)* ━━

"Comprehensive treatment of Java programming, covering both the latest version of the language and Java SE APIs."
—Dr. Danny Coward, Oracle Corporation

"A nice illustration of how to use Java to generate impressive graphics."**—Amr Sabry, Indiana University**

"The OOD ATM case study puts many concepts from previous chapters together in a plan for a large program, showing the object-oriented design process—the discussion of inheritance and polymorphism is especially good as the authors integrate these into the design."**—Susan Rodger, Duke University**

"The transition from design to implementation is explained powerfully—the reader can easily understand the design issues and how to implement them in Java."**—S. Sivakumar, Astro Infotech Private Limited**

"If you think a 3rd edition is just going to be a repeat then you would not do this book justice. It has the breadth and depth to get a beginning Java programmer started, but at the same time it is a good companion for a more seasoned programmer who wants to get updated to the latest version of Java. Perfect introduction to strings. Good explanation of static vs. non-static methods and variables. Best introduction to Java 2D I've seen! The collections framework is well explained. A nice introduction to JavaFX."
—Manfred Riem, Java Champion

"Clearly describes the use cases for different parts of the Java APIs. The tips and observations are very useful. Clearly explains opportunities and pitfalls in Java. Rather than telling the reader what to do and not do, the rationale behind these opportunities and pitfalls is explained. The new features introduced in Java 8 are well mixed with older functionality."
—Johan Vos, LodgON and Java Champion

"Really good, clear explanation of object-oriented programming fundamentals. Excellent polymorphism chapter. Covers all the essentials of strings. Good to see things like try-with-resources and DirectoryStream being used. Excellent generic collections chapter. Covering lambdas and streams in one chapter is a tough challenge; you've done well. Concurrency chapter gives good coverage of numerous aspects."**—Simon Ritter, Oracle Corporation**

"GUI examples are very good. Graphics examples are easy to follow. The JavaFX GUI chapter provides a solid introduction to using the JavaFX Scene Builder, demonstrating how easy it is to create Java-based GUI applications."
—Lance Andersen, Oracle Corporation

"Nice breadth of coverage of traditional core Java and programming topics as well as newer areas such as lambda expressions and areas becoming more critical such as concurrent programming. Very nice coverage of files, streams, object serialization and generics."
—Evan Golub, University of Maryland

"The real-world examples can be used with Java SE 7 or 8; great case studies. The inheritance chapter is excellent; examples are gender neutral which is perfect."**—Khallai Taylor, Triton College and Lonestar College-Kingwood**

"Good approach to important concepts like static, accessors and private fields and their validation. [Classes and Objects: A Deeper Look] coverage is very interesting—I like how the book flows. Excellent explanations of Java SE 8 interfaces and exceptions."**—Jorge Vargas, Yumbling and a Java Champion**

45 DAYS FREE
ACCESS TO ONLINE EDITION
with purchase of this book
❮•• Details on Last Pages

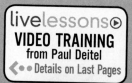
livelessons⊙
VIDEO TRAINING
from Paul Deitel
❮•• Details on Last Pages